DEBT

by
Nicholas Grier
Writer to the Signet
Lecturer in Law, Napier University

EDINBURGH
W. GREEN / Sweet & Maxwell
1998

First published, 1998

Published in 1998 by W. Green & Son Limited of
21 Alva Street,
Edinburgh, EH2 4PS

Computerset by LBJ Typesetting Ltd
Kingsclere

Printed in Great Britain by Redwood Books
Trowbridge, Wiltshire

No natural forests were destroyed to make this product; only
farmed timber was used and replanted

A CIP catalogue record of this book is available from the British
Library

ISBN 0 414 01238 0

PREFACE

This book is designed to serve as an overview of and general introduction to the law of debt in Scotland. I have deliberately tried to avoid providing too much detail in order to keep the main issues clear and intelligible.

I should like to record my thanks to my colleagues at Napier University, and in particular to Josephine Bisacre, whose advice I have often sought. My thanks are also extended to Anne Bryce of the Institute of Chartered Accountants of Scotland and Elanor Bower of Greens for their unfailing encouragement. Finally I should like to thank my wife, Jean, for her forbearance as I laboured long into the night writing this book.

Nicholas Grier
Napier University
Edinburgh
January 1998

CONTENTS

TABLE OF CASES

ix

TABLE OF STATUTES

TABLE OF STATUTORY INSTRUMENTS

CHAPTER 1

INTRODUCTION

ORIGINS

Barter is probably the oldest form of trade: goods of equal **1.1**
value were exchanged. Sometimes, however, the exchanged
goods were not of equal value or one of the parties had
insufficient goods to make a full exchange. Out of such
deficiency debt arose. When a purchaser could not make a
full exchange for all the goods he wanted, he would ask
the seller for time to produce the difference. Depending on
the degree of suspicion of the seller, he would allow the
purchaser to make good the difference on the next occasion they met, or to make good the difference on some
specified date together with a little extra to compensate the
seller for his inconvenience. Equally, the seller might tell
the buyer to obtain funds or goods from some other source
(eventually known as a bank) in order to be able to acquire
his goods there and then from the seller.

Little has changed since those early days of commerce, **1.2**
save that instead of always having to exchange one set of
goods or services for another, currency, formerly in the
tangible shape of gold or silver, has developed as a
method of assessing the value of the goods transferred, of
recording what was transferred or due to be transferred,
and of preserving funds for a later occasion. Subsequently,
paper money took the place of precious metals, but the
commercial principles remained the same. Throughout
history, the essential issues which confront sellers and
purchasers, borrowers and lenders have scarcely changed
at all, though the speed at which decisions on credit can be
made has increased immensely within this century.

Lenders have traditionally always wanted security, some method of ensuring that they have a hold over the borrower so that they can get their money back; while borrowers have always wanted their money in a hurry in order to make the most of some opportunity. Lenders often were craftier, more numerate and better at keeping records than borrowers, and many banking families, such as the Barings, the Medici, and the Rothschilds, rose to great wealth and eminence as a result of the skilful use of these attributes. Indeed it is said that the traditional sign of the pawnbroker, the three golden balls, is derived from the escutcheon of the Medici family, of seven golden balls against a blue background. Equally, moneylenders were reviled, as can be seen in plays such as *The Merchant of Venice*, where Shylock extracts a hard bargain by insisting on a pound of flesh in exchange for his loan. Historically, part of the contempt shown for lenders arose from the fact that in some countries a debtor could be imprisoned for his debt, leading to opprobrium directed to the moneylender. While imprisonment for debt may have had the social effect of discouraging people from getting into debt in the first place, it also had the effect of discouraging commerce, since a failed enterprise could result in incarceration. To compound the indignity of being imprisoned, the debtor was expected to pay for his imprisonment while unable, by virtue of being in gaol, to earn anything. The position in Britain was not perhaps as bad as in some other cultures: in India, until recently, a child could be born into debt incurred by his grandparents, and in Japan, such is the price of domestic property that mortgages can endure for a hundred years or more. Other cultures forbade the lending of money at interest to members of their own creed (although non-members could be charged interest) but a way was often found round such restrictions by the use of arrangement fees and termination fees.

SOCIAL AND ECONOMIC CONSIDERATIONS

1.3   Society has to strike a balance between permitting debtors to borrow money if they want to, and preventing creditors from extracting every possible advantage from their position as lenders to those who need money urgently. Society has to find a middle path between allowing creditors the right to make sure that debtors fulfil their proper obligation to repay their loans, if necessary by having their possessions taken from them and sold for the creditors' benefit, while preventing creditors from abusing that right in an oppressive manner. Equally, society does not wish to deter the promotion of commerce, with its opportunities for wealth creation (out of which taxes can be paid for the common good) and employment. Entrepreneurs who promote commerce must be encouraged. One way of doing this is to ensure that if their businesses fail entrepreneurs will not be dealt with unjustly or harshly while securing that their creditors are not prejudiced. From this standpoint stem the bankruptcy laws, which try to be fair to both the entrepreneur and his creditors. Another way of encouraging entrepreneurs is to let them use the medium of the limited company through which they may be able to avoid personal liability for their businesses' debts.

The lending of money or, to put it another way, the **1.4** financing of debt, is one of the United Kingdom's major areas of expertise. Most of the world's important banks are represented in the U.K., and banking and the provision of finance for industry generally are huge sources of employment and wealth creation throughout the country. On a more domestic level, few homes in the U.K. are bought nowadays without a loan from a building society or a bank, and few people do not at some stage in their lives borrow from a bank or a credit card company. Few businesses operate without borrowing to some extent, not least because, in the U.K. at any rate, it is possible to obtain tax relief on business borrowing.

It was once said that a large number of court cases relating **1.5** to debt involve people purchasing things they don't need, using money they don't have, borrowed from people who shouldn't have lent it to them. It is a sad fact that, despite the best efforts of legislators, consumer welfare advisers and other philanthropic agencies, there are many people who find that coping with the extent of their borrowings is quite beyond them. This is partly attributable to the

reduction of state benefits to the unemployed, who therefore have to borrow to pay for the necessities of life, and
partly to the fact that many consumers are not very
numerate, and often neither read nor understand the
"small print" attached to any loan documentation.

CHAPTER 2

THE DEBTOR AND HIS OBLIGATIONS

THE DEBTOR

When raising an action of debt, it is important to establish **2.1** that the apparent debtor is the true debtor. Sometimes the apparent debtor will not be liable for the debt, as he is acting on another's behalf. On other occasions, the law provides that no liability attaches to the apparent debtor.

The agent as debtor

An agent who acts for a named principal within the proper **2.2** terms of his authority is not liable for his principal's debts.[1] The principal will be liable for debts incurred on his behalf, and even if the principal has forbidden the agent to carry out certain acts, if the agent continues to do those acts and they are within the ostensible or implied authority of similar agents in that line of business, or of that particular agent, the principal will be liable.[2] The principal will also be liable if he ratifies his agent's unauthorised act. Where the agent acts for an *undisclosed* principal in a contract, the agent is, however, liable for the debts arising out of that contract, except where the other party discovers who the principal is, in which case he can elect to sue either the agent or the principal, but not both[3]; and once the election is made it cannot be changed.

If the agent does not have the authority to act at all, the **2.3** other party can sue the agent, not for debt, but for

---

[1] Bell, *Comm.*, i, 540.
[2] *Watteau v. Fenwick* [1893] 1 Q.B. 346.
[3] *David Logan & Sons Ltd v. Schuldt* (1903) 10 S.L.T. 598.

damages for breach of warranty of authority, as in *Anderson v. Croall & Sons*[4] where an auctioneer sold at auction a horse which should not have been sold.

The trustee as debtor

2.4   Similar rules apply to trustees and executors under a will (hereafter referred to as "trustees"). When trustees contract any obligation on behalf of the trust of which they are trustees, they should make it very clear that they do so as trustees and not in their personal capacity. Then if the trust fails to pay a creditor what it should, it will be clear that it is the trust which is the debtor, not the trustees. However, on some occasions, the trustees will be contracting in their personal capacity too, as in the case of a partnership acquiring heritage (*i.e.* land and buildings) when the partners contract both as trustees for their partnership and personally as the partners of the partnership.

The company director as debtor

2.5   A company director is not usually liable for the debts of his company, so if a company is sued for payment of a debt, it will not be the duty of the directors personally to pay the debt, except where their liability arises out of an ancillary obligation, such as a guarantee for the company's liabilities. A company director may be due to pay money to his company, as when, for example, there has been a breach of the fiduciary duty of a director to his company, such as the retention of a secret commission which should have been disclosed to and approved by the company's directors, in which case he may be required to account to the company for his illicit gains[5] unless he can persuade the court under section 727 of the Companies Act 1985 that he should not be found liable as his actions were reasonable under the circumstances. While, as far as the director is concerned, he has a debt payable to the company, strictly speaking the claim against him will be for damages

---

[4] (1903) 6F. 153.
[5] *Boston Deep Sea Fishing Co. Ltd v. Ansell* (1888) 39 Ch. D. 339.

for breach of his fiduciary duty. There are also the, in practice fairly rare, occasions when directors have to contribute to an insolvent company's funds, as when a director is required to compensate the company for its losses where he had caused the company to trade wrongfully[6] or fraudulently.[7] Only once the courts have stated that the compensation must be paid does the amount due by the director become a debt due to the company in liquidation.

The shareholder or company member as debtor

A shareholder usually has no liability to the company of **2.6** which he is a shareholder provided that he has paid in full the nominal value for each share which he owns, together with any premium on that share which he may have contracted to pay. Once he has paid that, he is not required to contribute any further to the company's funds. If, however, each share is partly paid, he will be required to pay the outstanding balance on the nominal value of the share when called upon to do so by the directors or by the liquidator. A company can neither (a) insist that the shareholder acquire more shares[8] nor (b) increase the nominal value of the shares and force him to pay the outstanding amount on each share[9] unless he agrees in writing to do so.[10] On certain occasions, such as when a company purchases its own shares out of capital and becomes insolvent within a year of the redemption, the members whose shares were repurchased may have to make good any loss to the company occasioned by the repurchase.[11] Members of guarantee companies will be liable for the debts of the company up to the full extent of the guarantee stated in the memorandum of association plus, if applicable, any outstanding liability of any shares in the company.[12] Members of unlimited companies are

---

[6] Insolvency Act 1986, s.214.
[7] *ibid.* s.213.
[8] Companies Act 1985, s.16(1)(a).
[9] *ibid.* s.16(1)(b).
[10] *ibid.* s.16(2).
[11] Insolvency Act 1986, s.76(1)(a).
[12] *ibid.* s.74(3).

jointly and severally liable for their company's debts. Members who knowingly receive an improperly declared dividend will be required to repay the company.[13] If a member of a company is unwise enough to grant a personal guarantee for the company's debts, he will be liable to the extent of the guarantee.

The company as debtor

2.7 Formerly it was the case that a company could avoid responsibility for its debts by asserting that the activity which occasioned the debt was *ultra vires* (beyond the powers of the objects clause in the company's memorandum of association).[14] While this was very convenient for companies trying to avoid their responsibilities, it was not entirely fair on innocent consumers. Now because of section 35 of the Companies Act 1985, as far as parties to a contract with a company are concerned, nothing is *ultra vires* the company unless the other party is a director of the company itself, in which case the company can refuse to honour a debt arising out of an *ultra vires* contract.[15] However, if the company in question is a charitable company, the former *ultra vires* rule continues to apply, except where the person contracting with the charitable company is unaware that that company is charitable or the contract itself imposes a liability upon the charitable company which that company tries to evade on the ground that the contract is *ultra vires*.[16]

The employee as debtor

2.8 Being an employee does not usually make a person liable for his employer's debts, even if his actions caused those debts. However, in an employee's contract of employment there may be an obligation on him to reimburse the employer for any loss which the employee might cause the employer. Such an admittedly rare clause in an

---

[13] Companies Act 1985, s.277.
[14] *Ashbury Railway Carriage and Iron Co. Ltd v. Riche* (1875) L.R. 7 H.L. 653.
[15] Companies Act 1985, s.322A.
[16] Companies Act 1989, s.112(3).

employment contract would be worth having only if the employee was sufficiently wealthy to be worth suing.

The child as debtor

The contractual capacity of young persons in Scotland is divided into two age groups, those aged 15 and under, and those aged between 16 and 18. Children in the first group, strictly speaking, have no contractual capacity and only their guardians can contract on their behalf.[17] However, this does not prevent such children entering into contracts which children of that age would normally make.[18] If a child attempts to enter into a contract which would not be appropriate for its age, the contract would be void and it would be impossible to sue the child for the unpaid amount on the contract.

2.9

For children aged between 16 and 18, there is no bar to full contractual capacity[19] but a contract made in that period may be set aside by the courts at any time until the child's 21st birthday[20] if it is established that it is a "prejudicial transaction".[21] A prejudicial transaction is a contract (including a promise) which a reasonable and prudent adult would not have made if he had been in the child's position and which either causes, or is likely to cause, prejudice or hardship to the child.[22] However, if a child is in business and the contract is connected with that business,[23] or if he pretends that he is older than he is and thus persuades the other party to the contract to proceed with the contract,[24] or if, after his 18th birthday, he subsequently ratifies the contract while aware that he could challenge it,[25] the contract will not be set aside by the courts, and if necessary an action of debt arising out of the contract could be raised against the child.

2.10

---

[17] Age of Legal Capacity (Scotland) Act 1991, s.5(1).
[18] *ibid.* s.2(1).
[19] *ibid.* s.1(1)(b).
[20] *ibid.* s.3(1).
[21] *ibid.*
[22] *ibid.* s.3(2).
[23] *ibid.* s.3(3)(f).
[24] *ibid.* s.3(3)(g).
[25] *ibid.* s.3(3)(h).

2.11 Since these rules could leave those purportedly contracting with young persons in doubt as to the enforceability of their contracts, it is possible to make a joint application to a sheriff for him to approve the terms of the contract.[26] Once so approved, the contract cannot be challenged by the child.[27]

2.12 It is still possible for children to have their affairs looked after by a *curator bonis* should that be deemed suitable.[28]

Insane persons and bankrupts as debtors

2.13 Insane persons have no contractual capacity once they are insane[29] but if they acquire "necessaries" (such as food and drink) they must pay a proper price for them.[30] Some insane persons have a *curator bonis* to oversee their affairs, and the *curator* will be treated as a trustee as stated in paragraph 2.4. Similarly, debtors who have been sequestrated have no contractual capacity in respect of the assets which have been vested in the trustee in sequestration. Bankrupts can, however, enter into normal contracts for necessaries, but they are prohibited from obtaining credit for anything in excess of £250 in value.[31] In an ideal world a bankrupt's affairs would be dealt with by his trustee in sequestration, without whose approval no contract with the bankrupt would endure. It is, however, a sad fact that due to the practice of many bankrupts of having a variety of aliases, and the fact that a bankrupt sequestrated in one sheriff court might not immediately be recognised as a bankrupt in another, quite apart from their propensity to flee the jurisdiction, bankrupts do often try to acquire assets for which they have no hope or sometimes intention of paying. It is not usually worth suing such people because they have no funds anyway. The true extent of the contractual capacity of a bankrupt in a practical sense appears to be an area

---

[26] Age of Legal Capacity (Scotland) Act 1991, s.4(1) and (3).
[27] *ibid.* s.3(3)(j).
[28] *ibid.* s.1(3)(f).
[29] Stair, I, x, 3.
[30] Sale of Goods Act 1979, s.3.
[31] Bankruptcy (Scotland) Act 1985, s.67.

of uncertainty, since he can enter into a contract of employment and can acquire certain assets; but (a) any substantial acquisition would require the consent of the trustee were it to be secure, and (b) the bankrupt would not generally be worth suing if he defaulted on his obligation. Equally, a person buying goods from a bankrupt should, as a matter of good business practice, insist where possible that the trustee's consent to the sale is obtained, lest the sale be to the prejudice of the bankrupt's creditors. Limited protection is, however, given to a third party dealing with a bankrupt but unaware of the bankrupt's sequestration.[31a]

THE DEBTOR'S OBLIGATIONS

A debt is a sum of money owed by one person, the debtor, to another person, the creditor. When a creditor allows a debtor to create a debt, there are five issues which the creditor must address: **2.14**

- (i) How much is the debt?
- (ii) When will the debt be repaid?
- (iii) On what terms, including the rate of interest, will the debt be repaid?
- (iv) What is the risk of non-payment?
- (v) What sanctions are there for non-payment?

These are all matters which a creditor will need to consider before the debt is actually incurred by the debtor. However, on the whole, the creditor is in a better position than the debtor because the creditor is not usually obliged to let the debt arise, whereas the debtor generally very much wants the debt to exist. There are occasions when the debtor is in a stronger position than the creditor as, for example, when a supermarket purchases vegetables from a farmer, and the supermarket can impose its terms of postponed payment upon the farmer/creditor, or when the debtor has borrowed so heavily from the creditor that the creditor's own financial position is dependent upon the debtor's continuing viability. But usually, particularly in the context of loans, the creditor is in a strong position and a desperate debtor has to accept the terms the creditor offers.

Consequently, a debtor must consider the following: **2.15**

[31a] Bankruptcy (Scotland) Act 1985, s.32(8) and (9).

   (i) How great is the debt he is incurring?

   (ii) When must the debt be repaid?

   (iii) Is it feasible to repay the debt on the terms proposed—inclusive of interest?

   (iv) What type of debt is he incurring?

   (v) What will happen to the debtor if he fails to pay?

These will now be examined in turn.

(i) How great is the debt he is incurring?

2.16   Generally, there is no limit to the amount of debt that a debtor can incur, provided that a creditor is willing to give him credit. However, under consumer credit legislation, dealt with in Chapter 5, extensive rules apply to the provision of credit of less than £15,000 in terms of consumer credit agreements, regulated agreements and running account credit facilities. As the name indicates, these provisions apply mainly in the context of provision of finance to consumers: loans to incorporated businesses are not caught by them.

(ii) When must the debt be repaid?

2.17   Usually a debt should be repaid on the date specified in the contract between the creditor and the debtor. If a debt is repaid late usually the creditor is entitled to extra interest at a pre-specified rate (permitted as long as it is not penal in nature), or at the judicial rate specified in any decree from the courts in an action of debt. Such a rate will typically be slightly higher than the current rate in order to force the debtor to pay quickly. If a debt is repaid early the lender may lose some of the interest he might otherwise have expected to have received, and may insist that the debtor pay an early termination fee or pay some or all of the interest the creditor would otherwise have expected to receive.

2.18   There are special rules for pawnbroking, discussed in Chapter 5, whereby, depending on their value, pawned goods are usually redeemable within a period of six months, after which the pawnbroker can dispose of the pawned goods as he sees fit—subject to any agreement to the contrary.

(iii) Is it feasible to repay the debt on the terms specified—inclusive of interest?

With the exception of agreements governed by the Consumer Credit Act 1974 and extortionate credit transactions caught by the Bankruptcy (Scotland) Act 1985, s.61(2) and the Insolvency Act 1986, s.244, most agreements for the provision of debt are entirely contractual and it is up to the parties concerned to agree terms between themselves. Accordingly, the usual rules of contract apply, in that both parties must have full contractual capacity, be agreed on the principal terms of the contract, intend to contract with each other and have the same item in mind as the subject of the contract. In addition, in the context of loans by banks to businesses, banks will generally adhere to a statement of principles drawn up by the British Banking Association which sets out a code of best practice suitable for both banks and their customers. The statement of principles emphasises the need for banks to express their terms in clear, jargon-free English, to make clear the extent of any security required, what circumstances will trigger a review of any loan and what information the customer must regularly give the bank. Banks must also indicate the need for independent advice wherever appropriate. There is a right of appeal to an ombudsman should the customer feel unfairly treated. The rationale behind the statement of principles is that responsible banks will ultimately gain market share, maintain their business relationships and obtain better quality business in the long term if they are seen to deal fairly and honestly with their customers. **2.19**

(iv) What type of debt is the creditor incurring?

A debt is a requirement to make payment of money at a certain date. This is not the same as an obligation to account, which is only a requirement to calculate what may be due. The amount of money need not be certain but there will be practical difficulties in enforcing any payment of the debt unless it is ascertainable. The debt need not be in pounds sterling, but if in a contract there is a requirement to pay in a particular currency, that currency must be used. Usually a debt arises out of a contract. In most **2.20** contracts, one person undertakes to do something, such as supply goods or services, and the other to pay for it. If the debtor pays the money, but the goods or services turn out to be unsatisfactory, he is then entitled to sue for damages but in so doing he must (a) take steps to minimise his loss and (b) if there is a liquidated damages clause in the contract (such as a clause which says that in the event of the supplier failing to supply his goods on time, an agreed sum will be paid by the supplier to the purchaser each day until the goods are supplied), ensure that that clause is not penal in nature, in other words, unreasonable and oppressive. If it is penal, the courts will disregard it. However, if the supplier supplies his goods or services and is not paid, he does not sue for damages: he raises an action of debt under the terms of the contract of supply. In that case there is no requirement to minimise the supplier's loss, nor to take account of liquidated damages clauses.

(v)   What will happen to the debtor if he fails to pay?

2.21   This issue will be examined in greater issue in Chapter 9 but, broadly speaking, if a debtor fails to pay what he owes, the creditor, assuming he is not exercising any other rights he may have, such as lien or retention, will raise an action in the appropriate court (sheriff court or Court of Session) where, if he wins, he will obtain a decree in his favour. Decree is the Scots legal term for the decision of the court in England, known as a judgment. The decree will state what the debtor has to pay, the judicial rate of interest on the unpaid debt, and the date by which it must be paid. After that date, the creditor is entitled to send court officials known as sheriff officers (for the sheriff courts) and messengers-at-arms (for the Court of Session) to take steps to seize the debtor's assets, either from the debtor's own premises or in the hands of third parties. This is similar to the procedure in England with sheriff's officers and bailiffs. Ultimately, this can lead to a sale of the debtor's goods other than those necessary for him to ply his trade and to maintain his family. All these methods of enforcing payment are known collectively as "diligence". In the case of failure to pay the sums due under a standard security, the heritable creditor (usually a bank or building society) is entitled, after due warning and proper procedure, to evict the owners and to sell the property. In the case of a tenant, the tenant can also be removed and his goods, other than those vital to his trade and family obligations, sold to pay his outstanding rent. In the case of a limited company which has granted a bond and floating charge, the charge holder can appoint a receiver who will proceed to gather in the assets caught by the crystallised floating charge (see Chapter 12).

Ultimately, if the debtor is insolvent, he can be forced into **2.22** bankruptcy or apply to be declared bankrupt. "Bankruptcy" is not really a term of Scots law, except as used in the titles of the Bankruptcy (Scotland) Acts 1985 and 1993. The proper term is "sequestration", and the debtor, whether sequestrated by a creditor or at his own wish, has his affairs looked after by a trustee in sequestration. However, as the term "bankrupt" is well recognised, it will be used generally hereafter except where inappropriate. Once a person is bankrupt, he cannot be a company director[32] nor, among other professions, can he become or remain a solicitor, accountant or banker. It can often be a condition of employment that bankruptcy will trigger dismissal. In Scotland, a bankrupt can remain undischarged for up to five years, though the common period is three years.[33] In exceptional circumstances, bankrupts may be publicly examined by a sheriff and, ultimately, sent to prison.[34] The above rules apply to partnerships as well as to private individuals. Personal insolvency is dealt with in Chapters 10 and 11.

Limited companies cannot be sequestrated: they are **2.23** "wound up", and the assets of the company divided up between the creditors. The company may continue in existence under new control or may be dissolved. This is dealt with in Chapter 13.

MISCELLANEOUS SOURCES OF DEBT

On occasion, debt arises from causes other than contract. **2.24** *Repetition* is where a sum of money is mistakenly paid to

---

[32] Company Directors Disqualification Act 1986, s.11.
[33] Bankruptcy (Scotland) Act 1993, s.54.
[34] *ibid.* ss.45, 67.

someone who should not receive it. The recipient is obliged to pay the money to the true owner. *Recompense* is where someone confers a benefit on someone else when he did not need to, when he did not intend to give the benefit as a gift, and when he did not expect to gain from the provision of the benefit. For example, a manufacturer might, through oversight, repair some equipment free of charge under the misapprehension that it was obliged to do so under a guarantee which, unbeknown to the manufacturer, had expired. In such a case the manufacturer could claim for the cost of the repairs. Both repetition and recompense are examples of unjust enrichment, whereby one person has to repay a benefit which he should not have received.

2.25   Under the law of agency, an agent of necessity (*negotiorum gestio*) who acts without express instruction on behalf of an absent or unreachable principal, is entitled to claim his expenses.

2.26   In marine matters, a salvagor who rescues a ship which would otherwise have been destroyed or hijacked is entitled to payment for his trouble even in the absence of a contract. Nowadays, however, it is unlikely that a salvagor would start any salvage operation without the comfort of a properly drawn-up contract.

2.27   Various different types of debt arise out of the ownership of land. These include feu duty, formerly a considerable burden on a property owner but now rarely worth collecting, payments under standard securities (known colloquially as mortgage payments), and payments due for the maintenance of property held in common with other proprietors, such as roof burdens and garden upkeep payments. Although from the point of view of the debtor a debt is a sum due to be paid, from a legal point of view the important issue is that the obligation to pay arises from owning the property: the moment the debtor relinquishes the property, or the standard security is discharged, the liability ceases. However as a matter of practice building societies and banks generally have a clause in their loan documentation in connection with standard securities stating that notwithstanding the discharge of the standard security, perhaps by a forced sale, there will be a continuing personal obligation to pay any arrears due to the lender.

CHAPTER 3

LOANS AND BONDS

BANK LENDING

This chapter is concerned with uncomplicated loans to **3.1** which the consumer credit legislation does not apply either because of a specific exemption, such as overdrafts, or because of the more general exemption where a loan is a business loan rather than a consumer loan. Consumer credit is dealt with in Chapter 5.

Overdrafts

The commonest type of loan from a bank is the overdraft. **3.2** The principal feature of an overdraft is that it is repayable on demand by the bank. The rate of interest chargeable by the bank on the sums overdrawn will depend on various factors, among them being the prevailing base rate charged (the minimum rate at which the bank will lend money), the extent to which the overdraft has been authorised, and the extent of any security the borrower may have granted the bank. When a customer opens an account with a bank he is advised of the terms on which it will do business: these will specify the dates from which interest will run on overdrawn accounts, the cost of intimation to the customer of the overdrawn account and what rights the bank may have against the borrower on the occasion of the borrower's default. Overdrawn accounts are specifically exempted from the consumer credit legislation.[1]

Term loans

The next most common type of loan is the term loan. From **3.3** the point of view of the debtor the term loan is

---

[1] Consumer Credit Act 1974, s.74(1).

advantageous, because he knows when the duration of the loan will expire and by when he must repay it. This allows him the opportunity to refinance with another lender or renegotiate terms with the existing lender. It is not so satisfactory for the lender, for he cannot demand instant repayment. Equally, he would not offer a term loan if he did not think that the borrower was a reasonably sensible one who was relatively secure.

3.4 A term loan, and indeed an overdraft, will usually be constituted by an initial exchange of letters, followed by a contract, known as a loan agreement, which supersedes the exchange of letters. This will, among other things, specify the amount of the loan, the rate of interest, the method of calculation of interest relative to base rate or the London inter-bank offered rate ("LIBOR"), any agreed restrictions on the interest rate above which (known as a "cap") or below which (known as a "collar") the interest rate may not move, the dates or occasions on which funds can be drawn from the lender, the extent of the security to be provided by the borrower (see Chapter 7) and any guarantors (see Chapter 6), the requirement to produce regular audited accounts showing the borrower's expenditure and income, confirmation of the satisfactory completion of work which entitles the borrower to draw funds from the lender, the assignation of any insurance policies both over the subjects for which the loan is granted and, if appropriate, over the lives of the directors of any corporate borrowers, and such other terms as may be appropriate to the circumstances. There are various methods of dealing with the repayment of the capital and interest, varying from the "balloon", which is when the capital and all the accumulated interest is repaid in one lump sum at the end of the project, to "bullets", which are regular large repayments of capital and interest.

3.5 Common conditions within a term loan may also include the following:

Arrangement or commitment fee

This may be a percentage of the capital sum lent. Some- **3.6**
times there is commitment commission on the undrawn
amount of the loan. This is a fee payable to the lender for
keeping the line of credit open to the borrower.

Termination fee

This too may be a percentage of the capital sum lent. **3.7**
Depending on circumstances, it may be waived if the loan
is renegotiated, or may apply only if the borrower
attempts to terminate the loan early on the occasion of the
early completion of the project for which the loan was
granted or the refinancing of the loan with another lender.

Drawdown fee

This is a fee payable on each occasion on which the **3.8**
borrower draws funds from the lender. Sometimes a
drawdown is permitted by the bank only on completion of
a part of the project for which the loan has been granted,
as certified by an appropriate independent expert. Alternatively a drawdown is only permitted for certain items
once the borrower requires to pay for them.

Revolving credit

This is where the borrower borrows money, repays it and **3.9**
having repaid it is entitled to borrow it again. Such an
arrangement prevents the borrowing becoming too
extended.

Negative pledges

These are clauses which prevent the borrower either **3.10**
refinancing the loan with another lender or, more commonly, trying to grant another lender another security over
the borrower's assets which would rank in priority to the
first lender's security.

Compliance with pre-determined financial ratios

The lender may require that the borrower always maintain **3.11**
a certain level of asset-to-liability cover, so that if the
borrower's assets had to be liquidated there would be a

surplus of assets out of which to repay the lender. These may be tied into restrictions on the amount of salary the borrower (if a company) can pay its directors.

Guarantees

3.12 Commonly, directors of a company will be required to give personal guarantees for any loans to it. Sometimes holding companies will be obliged to provide guarantees for their subsidiaries as a condition of a loan to the subsidiaries.

Debentures

3.13 A debenture is the written acknowledgment of a loan and commonly arises in the context of lending to companies. It is also more usually associated with English law since the Scottish, and indeed American, term for the same thing was and is respectively a bond. A debenture states the amount of the loan, the rate of interest payable on the loan (sometimes known as the coupon) and the date or dates upon which the loan is repayable or, more properly, to be redeemed. Sometimes the debenture will state one date upon which it is to be redeemed and sometimes two possible dates, at the choice of the lender or the borrowing company, depending on the terms of the loan. A debenture can be the term for one loan made by one person to a company but, equally, it is possible for many lenders each to lend a certain amount of money to a company and for their individual loans to be amalgamated within one large loan, also known as a debenture, made to the company. The large loan, and the interests of the individual lenders, known variously as debenture holders, or more accurately as debenture-stock holders, will be under the management of a debenture trustee, operating under the terms of a debenture trust deed which regulates the position of the debenture trustee, the debenture-stock holders and the company. The trustee, commonly a professional registrar, bank or insurance company, keeps a register of the individual debenture-stock holders. When they buy and sell their units of debenture stock, he records their individual holdings and convenes meetings from time to time to report on the continued viability of the loan. He also ensures on their behalf that the company honours its obligations under the debenture. It is common for a debenture to be backed up by a security over the company's assets, by either a fixed charge or a floating charge or indeed both (see Chapter 7). The debenture trustee ensures that the subjects of the security are properly insured and that the company is taking proper care of the security subjects. In the event of the company's failure to adhere to the terms of the debenture, the trustee would exercise his rights under any standard security or in the case of a floating charge appoint a receiver (see Chapter 12). The interest payable on a debenture is usually allowable against the pre-tax profits of a company, and so from the point of view of a lender a debenture can be a relatively safe form of investment since there is a high likelihood of the interest always being paid, even if shareholders fail to obtain a dividend. In addition, a secured debenture will have the comfort of being able to realise any secured assets out of which to repay the loan. The less advantageous aspect of a debenture is that the rate of interest may be low compared to the dividends shareholders are receiving, though it is possible to devise convertible debentures which will change into shares on the fulfilment of a certain event. Debentures are marketable in the same manner as shares, and their value will depend on the rate of interest being offered relative to prevailing interest rates generally, the date of redemption of the debenture and the likelihood of the company being able to redeem the debenture when it says it will.

Eurobonds

Commercially traded debentures are usually expressed in pounds sterling but there may be occasions when a company wishes to borrow money not only in pounds sterling but in another currency which it happens to believe will be better for it. Equally, there may be investors who wish to lend across borders where they believe that currency movements may be advantageous to them. A Eurobond satisfies this need and is a form of debenture, usually issued by a large multinational company in one of the European currencies, but unlike a normal debenture it

3.14

does not contain the name of the debenture holder. A Eurobond is a bearer instrument, in other words, he who holds it legitimately has good title to it. They are, however, numbered, so despite various attempts to steal and subsequently sell misappropriated Eurobonds, it is fairly easy to prevent fraudsters dealing with them.

CHAPTER 4

NEGOTIABLE INSTRUMENTS

BILLS OF EXCHANGE

4.1 Bills of exchange are often little understood because consumers, in general, are unaware of their use. They are still used in international trade but increasingly less so in domestic trade, mainly because most businesses now have bank accounts. A cheque is a bill of exchange drawn on a banker, payable on demand. Cheques are discussed in the later part of this chapter, as are promissory notes.

4.2 A bill of exchange arose out of the medieval *lex mercatoria*, the rules which formerly governed commercial transactions throughout Europe. If merchant A bought goods from merchant B but merchant C owed money to merchant A, A could instruct C to pay B the sum of money which C owed A. This would settle A's debt to B. The letter of instruction by A to C to pay B ultimately became the bill of exchange. The simplicity of the basic concept is lost in the technical terms used to describe the three merchants above. A is known as the "drawer" of the bill. His letter of instruction is known as an "order", and the process of ordering the payment in this manner is known as "drawing a bill" on C. The person whom he instructs to pay the money, in this case, C, is known as the "drawee". The recipient of the money, in this case, B, is the "payee". The payee can be someone specific such as B, whose name is clearly indicated on the bill of exchange; it can be the drawer himself, so that in the above case A could, if he wished, instruct C to pay A; or the payee need not be specified, but be designated "bearer", which means the person who happens to be bearing (*i.e.* having in his possession) the bill of exchange at the time. When the bill is payable to bearer, it means that if the bill falls into the wrong hands, an unintended recipient may obtain the money, which is why it is generally unwise to designate the payee as "bearer".

Presentation to and acceptance by the drawee

4.3   The drawee's duty is to "honour" the bill, in other words to pay it when he is supposed to do so. Although the drawer of a bill can be liable on the bill from the moment he creates it, the drawee is liable only from the moment that it is presented to him or, as the case may be, accepted by him. The bill may say that it is to be paid at sight or on demand, in which case it must be paid there and then by the drawee or it will be "dishonoured". Dishonour will entitle the payee to claim against the drawer. More commonly, the bill is presented to the drawee by the payee for "acceptance". This means that the drawee accepts his responsibility to pay the bill at a date specified on the bill, that date being known as its "maturity date". The maturity date can be whichever date the parties to the bill agree, though it is quite common to have a maturity date of 90 days from presentment. Usually a drawer will have a preexisting arrangement with the drawee that bills of exchange will be presented for acceptance by the drawee. Acceptance is usually indicated by the drawee writing his name across the bill together with the word "accepted". Acceptance changes the designation of the drawee to "acceptor". The maturity allows the drawee credit, which can be very useful if the drawee is also the purchaser from a seller who has drawn a bill on the purchaser. It is also useful for the seller, for once he has the bill back in his hands, with the drawee's acceptance written on it, and provided there are no restrictions on transfer, he has a "negotiable instrument", in other words a document entitling him to payment on representation to the drawee/acceptor for payment, but which can in the meantime be transferred to someone else ("negotiated"). The seller can sell the bill to someone else who then becomes entitled to the payment from the drawee. Commonly, a bill will be sold to a discount house or merchant bank specialising in the acquisition of bills of exchange. When a discount house buys a bill of exchange, it pays the seller less than the full expected sum that the drawee would have paid the seller, the amount of the reduction being known as the discount. The discount arises because there is always a risk that the drawee may not pay, and because the money the discount house pays to the seller could have been earning interest elsewhere in the period between the sale to the discount house and the maturity date. The discount house itself may sell the bill or wait for payment of the full amount from the drawee. The advantage to the seller of the sale to the discount house is that the seller has his money now, which is more useful to him than money in 90 days' time. A further option for a seller holding an accepted bill of exchange is that he can borrow against the value of the accepted bill of exchange: he can provide it as security for a loan.

The bill of exchange as an independent obligation

As can be seen from the above, a bill of exchange is not exactly the same as cash, but it is almost as liquid as cash. Furthermore, a bill of exchange is an obligation in its own right which is nothing to do with the underlying transaction. So if a seller draws a bill on a buyer, and the bill is accepted by the buyer, the buyer has no grounds for refusing payment under the bill, even if the seller's goods are entirely unsatisfactory. The defective goods are not a relevant issue as far as the payment of the bill is concerned. The bill must be paid first, and then the buyer must raise a claim for damages for the unsatisfactory goods. Bills of exchange accordingly favour the seller in these circumstances.

4.4

The definition of a bill of exchange

The definition of a bill of exchange is given in the Bills of Exchange Act 1882, s.3:

4.5

> "A bill of exchange is an unconditional order in writing, addressed by one person to another, signed by the person giving it, requiring the person to whom

it is addressed to pay on demand or at a fixed or
determinable future time a sum certain in money to
or to the order of a specified person, or to bearer."

4.6 The wording of this section means entirely what it says.
Unconditional means that no terms or conditions can be
attached to the bill: if there are any it is not a bill[1]—which
is why in paragraph 4.4 the underlying transaction is
irrelevant as far as the bill is concerned . The bill must be a
clear order. There must be a clearly identified drawee or
drawees,[2] but if there is more than one drawee, one cannot
elect to have one drawee rather than the other, and one
drawee cannot be in succession to the other.[3] If the drawee
does not exist or is *incapax* (*i.e.* has no legal capacity to
contract) the holder (the person entitled to payment under
the bill) can opt to treat the bill as either a bill or a
promissory note, according to which may give him a more
advantageous right against the drawer.[4] The payee or
payees must be named or indicated with reasonable certainty[5] and payees may be alternatives or in succession to
each other. If the payee does not exist the bill may be
treated as payable to bearer.[6] The sum to be paid must be
certain, or at least ascertainable, and if there is a discrepancy between the words and figures the words prevail.[7] If
a bill is stated to be payable on demand, then it must be so
paid within a reasonable time after its issue.[8] A bill cannot
be paid on the occurrence of some uncertain event as that
would make the bill conditional—and hence not a bill of
exchange. A bill is not required to have a date,[9] to have
consideration given for it[10] or indicate a place for payment.[11] Bills must be paid on business days, and if the

---

[1] Bills of Exchange Act 1882, s.3(2).
[2] *ibid.* s.6(1).
[3] *ibid.* s.6(2).
[4] *ibid.* s.5(2).
[5] *ibid.* s.7(1).
[6] *ibid.* s.7(3).
[7] *ibid.* s.9.
[8] *ibid.* s.45(2).
[9] *ibid.* s.3(a).
[10] *ibid.* s.3(b).
[11] *ibid.* s.3(c).

maturity date falls on a holiday, the bill must be paid on the next succeeding business day.[12]

Negotiation

Negotiation of a bill is permissible provided: **4.7**

- (a) the bill states that it is payable "to order" . This means that the payee has the right to order that the bill be paid to someone else;
- (b) it is payable to a designated payee and there is nothing on the bill forbidding the transfer of the bill, such as the words "not negotiable" or "non-transferable"; or
- (c) the bill is payable to bearer.

For (a) and (b) above the bill is negotiated by the payee's **4.8** endorsement of the bill. He writes his signature on the bill and delivers it to the endorsee.[13] The payee can specify the endorsee, in which case the endorsement must say "Pay X" (or "Pay X or to order") followed by the payee's signature. This is known as a "special" endorsement.[14] If no endorsee is specified, the bill becomes payable to bearer. This is known as endorsement "in blank".[15] A bill payable to bearer needs no endorsement and is merely delivered.[16] It is not possible to have conditions attached to any endorsement[17] though it is possible to have restrictions, such as "Pay X only" which in theory ought to prevent X further endorsing the bill. A payee or an endorsee, or the endorsee's endorsee, or any subsequent endorsee, is known as a *holder*, as is anyone holding a bill made out to bearer.[18] It is possible to have a bill that is stated to be "not negotiable" in which case it should be neither endorsed nor negotiated, or if it is, the holder takes it at his own risk.

[12] Bills of Exchange Act 1882, s.14(1).
[13] *ibid.* s.31(1).
[14] *ibid.* s.34(2).
[15] *ibid.* s.34(1).
[16] *ibid.* s.31(2).
[17] *ibid.* s.33.
[18] *ibid.* s.2.

4.9 A payee on a bill not payable to bearer would endorse it when he sells his bill. It is possible to become an endorsee of an unaccepted bill, though any endorsee would probably insist on a substantial discount unless the drawee were of good standing.

4.10 If the drawee refuses to accept a bill, the holder can immediately claim against the drawer and the other endorsers.[19] If the bill has been accepted, but the acceptor cannot pay the holder, the holder can again claim against the drawer and the endorsers[20] and the acceptor. Where a bill is dishonoured by non-payment or non-acceptance, the holder must intimate the dishonour (known as "giving notice of dishonour") to the drawer and to each endorser. Any drawer or endorser who is not told of the dishonour is relieved of his liability.[21] In the event of dishonour, the holder will normally claim against the most recent endorser, or any other endorser or the drawer, and any endorser who is compelled to relieve the holder may then in turn claim against any other endorser or the drawer provided that he has given notice of dishonour to each of them.[22] If a drawer has to pay the bill he claims against the acceptor.[23] If the bill is made out to bearer and is transferred by delivery without endorsement, the holder cannot be liable under the bill to any transferee[24]: the acceptor is liable instead, and if he cannot pay, the holder can claim against the drawer[25] or subsequent endorsees.[26]

Holder in due course

4.11 In order to establish certainty in commercial dealings, there has to be a rule to establish who should be protected if a bill turns out to be tainted for some reason. Put simply, the rule is that a person who takes a bill which on the face of it is:

---

[19] Bills of Exchange Act 1882, s.43(2).
[20] *ibid*. s.47.
[21] *ibid*. s.48.
[22] *ibid*. s.55.
[23] *ibid*. s.59(2)(a).
[24] *ibid*. s.58.
[25] *ibid*. s.55(1)(a) .
[26] *ibid*. s.55(2)(a).

(a) drawn up in a regular manner;

(b) not overdue;

and for which he had

(c) given some consideration (usually the payment of money);

(d) in good faith; and

(e) without notice at the time of any defect in the title of the person who had negotiated the bill to him;

is entitled to rely on the bill, and holds the bill free from any defect in title. Such a person is known as a "holder in due course".[27] He is able to obtain payment from the drawee or any endorsee or even the drawer even if at some stage the bill passed through the hands of someone who was not entitled to it. Such a person would be someone who had obtained the bill or its acceptance through fraud, duress, force and fear, or other unlawful means, or for an illegal consideration, or if he negotiated the bill in breach of faith or in such circumstances as amounted to a fraud.[28] A holder in due course is also able to give good title to the bill if he negotiates the bill to someone else. Furthermore there is a general presumption that a holder of a bill is a holder in due course until the contrary is proved.[29] The exception to this is that under limited circumstances a forged endorsement conveys no entitlement to payment.[30]

The presumption that the holder is a holder in due course **4.12** until the contrary is proved may be negated when it is admitted or proved that the acceptance, issue or negotiation of the bill involved fraud, force or fear, duress or illegality in which case the holder has to prove that despite these factors he gave value (*i.e.* paid a proper price) in good faith for the bill.[31]

---

[27] Bills of Exchange Act 1882, s.29(1).

[28] *ibid.* s.29(2).

[29] *ibid.* s.30(1),(2).

[30] *ibid.* s.24.

[31] *ibid.* s.30(2).

4.13   It is possible to be a holder without being a holder in due course. This occurs when someone acquires an overdue or dishonoured bill. A holder of an overdue bill can neither give nor obtain a better title than the previous holder had.[32] What is meant by "overdue" in the context of a bill payable on demand is that it has been in circulation for an unreasonable length of time.[33] A holder of a dishonoured bill who is aware of the dishonour acquires it subject to the dishonour but a holder in due course is not caught by this rule[34] since in order to be a holder in due course the holder must be unaware of the dishonour.

Protest

4.14   When a bill is dishonoured, the holder will wish to claim against those liable. In addition to giving notice as indicated in paragraph 4.10, the holder may need to "protest" the bill.[35] Protest is necessary in order to preserve the holder's rights in the case of a foreign bill[36] but not necessary in the case of an inland bill.[37] However, if the holder wishes to enforce an inland bill by summary diligence, he will need to protest it. Protest is a method of noting formally, in front of a notary public, that the bill has been dishonoured.[38] Summary diligence is a method of enforcing the payment of a debt without the requirement to go to court first. Once the protest has been completed, the relevant documents can be handed to sheriff officers or messengers-at-arms who will proceed to carry out one or more of the appropriate forms of diligence outlined in Chapter 9. Summary diligence is available for the amount of the bill only and not for any ancillary matters such as expenses or damages[39] for which a separate action must be raised, and is available only against someone who is subject to the jurisdiction of the Scottish courts.[40] Summary

---

[32] Bills of Exchange Act 1882, s.36(2).
[33] *ibid.* s.36(3).
[34] *ibid.* s.36(5).
[35] *ibid.* s.51.
[36] *ibid.* s.51(2).
[37] *ibid.* s.51(1).
[38] *ibid.* s.51(6),(7).
[39] Erskine, III, ii, 36.
[40] *Charteris v. Clydesdale Bank* (1882) 19 S.L.R. 602.

diligence following protest has the benefit of swiftness but it may be advantageous in the longer term to raise an action of damages under section 57 of the Bills of Exchange Act 1882 since the claimant can claim all sums due to him, such as expenses of the action, as well as being able to obtain an extract decree which could be registered for enforcement in another jurisdiction should the person liable have left Scotland.

Discharge

A bill is discharged by payment in due course, which means: **4.15**

(a) payment by or on behalf of the drawee or acceptor[41]
(b) at or after the maturity of the bill to the holder in good faith and without notice that his title is defective.[42]

If the drawer pays the bill, it is not discharged, since the drawer still has a right against the acceptor.[43] If an endorsee pays the bill, again it is not discharged, since the endorsee may have rights against some antecedent holder.[44] A bill can also be discharged by renunciation in writing[45] and when an acceptor becomes the holder of a bill after it matures, the bill is discharged.[46] **4.16**

Alteration and forgeries

A bill which is materially altered without the consent of all the parties liable on it is void against all those parties except the person who was responsible for the alteration or, if not responsible, knowingly took no steps to prevent the alteration.[47] However, if the alteration is material but **4.17**

---

[41] Bills of Exchange Act 1882, s.59(1).
[42] *ibid.*
[43] *ibid.* s.59(2)(a).
[44] *ibid.* s.59(2)(b).
[45] *ibid.* s.63(1).
[46] *ibid.* s.61.
[47] *ibid.* s.64.

not apparent, a holder in due course can rely on the bill as if it had not been altered.[48]

4.18 A person whose signature on a bill is forged, or whose signature was inserted on the bill without his authority, incurs no liability under the bill.[49] Although this is a general rule, there are exceptions to the rule, these being:

> (a) when a bank pays a cheque on a forged endorsement[50];
> (b) when the payee is fictitious or non-existent, in which case the bill is treated as payable to bearer[51];
> (c) when there is doubt about the genuineness of the drawer's signature, the acceptor cannot deny to a holder in due course the authenticity of the drawer's signature[52];
> (d) likewise, an endorser cannot deny to a holder in due course the genuineness of the drawer's signature or prior endorser's signature[53]; and
> (e) an endorser cannot deny to his subsequent endorsee that the bill was a valid bill to which he had good title.[54]

Prescription

4.19 Any unasserted claim under a bill of exchange expires after five years[55] and any claim is then extinguished.

CHEQUES

4.20 A cheque is a specialised bill of exchange and the law relating to cheques is to be found in the Bills of Exchange Act 1882, the Cheques Act 1957 and the Cheques Act 1992.

---

[48] Bills of Exchange Act 1882, s.64.
[49] *ibid.* s.24.
[50] Cheques Act 1957, s.1.
[51] Bills of Exchange Act 1882, s.7(3).
[52] *ibid.* s.54(2)(a).
[53] *ibid.* s.55(2)(b).
[54] *ibid.* s.55(2)(c).
[55] Prescription and Limitation (Scotland) Act 1973, s.6.

A cheque is defined as "a bill of exchange drawn on a **4.21** banker payable on demand".[56] Another way of putting this is that the account holder who writes a cheque is the drawer, the bank is the drawee and the recipient of the cheque is the payee who expects, on presentment of the cheque at the drawer's bank, to be paid cash there and then. The drawer and the payee may be the same person, and indeed the drawee and the payee may be the same. A cheque is payable on demand and does not require acceptance. By convention, a cheque becomes stale after six months and cannot be presented but must be reissued. A banker is not liable if he pays on a forged or unauthorised endorsement.[57] Cheques must be in writing and in practice must be typed or in ink on paper. Usually a customer will be barred by his contract with the bank from using any type of cheque other than the bank's usual cheques.

Cheque guarantee cards

When a customer opens an account with a bank, he signs a **4.22** contract with the bank outlining the terms and conditions on which he and the bank will do business. One of these conditions is that the bank will pay cheques drawn on it while it has funds in the customer's account to do so. But since a payee cannot always be assured that there will be funds in a drawer's account with which to pay a cheque, payees may be suspicious of cheques, since there is no guarantee that they will be paid. Cheque guarantee cards are therefore provided to customers on a contractual basis in order to reassure payees that following the noting of the guarantee card number on the back of the cheque, and providing the amount of the cheque is within the limit of the guarantee, the cheque will be paid by the bank to the payee irrespective of the lack of funds in the customer's account. Under the terms of the contract for use of a cheque guarantee card, it is not possible to countermand a cheque backed by a guarantee card. If the amount of the cheque is in excess of the guarantee card, the payee, on

[56] Bills of Exchange Act 1882, s.73.
[57] Cheques Act 1957, s.1.

receiving a cheque from a drawer, takes the risk that the bank may not pay. If this happens the payee must claim against the drawer, which is why the payee often asks for the drawer's name and address. Alternatively a payee may insist on a banker's draft or certified cheque, these being respectively a cheque issued by the bank and payable by the bank to the payee, and a cheque drawn on the drawer's account but certified by the bank that it will be paid. On a contractual basis a bank may agree to honour cheques up to the level of an agreed overdraft but is under no obligation to pay cheques beyond that level unless the cheques have been accompanied by a cheque guarantee card.

Payment of a cheque

4.23 Nowadays it is rare for a payee to go to the drawer's bank and ask for payment from the bank there and then, though that would not be impossible. The common practice is for a payee to pay the cheque made out to him into his own bank account. His bank then contacts the drawer's bank, or if the payee's bank and the drawer's bank are the same, the appropriate branch of the drawer's bank. Assuming funds are available, the drawer's bank account is debited with the amount of the cheque and the payee's bank account is credited with the same amount less any charges if exigible. This process is known as clearing the cheque and can take two or three days unless special clearance is requested. When a cheque is dishonoured by the bank on which it is drawn, it is either re-presented in the hope that on a second occasion it will be honoured or it is returned to the payee for him to take such steps as may be necessary against the drawer.

Dishonoured cheques

4.24 If a cheque is returned to the payee the amount which had formerly been credited to the payee is debited to the payee's account if there are any funds or if he has an overdraft facility. If this is not possible, the bank can instead retain the cheque, debit a suspense account and claim against the drawer as a holder for value. If it is claiming as a holder for value it must have either paid out funds on the strength of the moneys believed to be in the cheque or reduced the payee's overdraft.[58]

If the reason that the cheque apparently in favour of the **4.25** customer was dishonoured was that the cheque was stolen or the customer had no title to the cheque, the bank cannot claim as a holder for value.[59] However if the bank can prove that it was a holder in due course under section 29 of the Bills of Exchange Act 1882 it will be protected.[60]

If a stolen or fraudulently obtained cheque is presented by **4.26** a customer and the bank receives payment from the drawee's bank account, it is unclear whether or not the true owner can claim against the bank which collected the money as well as against the thief or fraudster. In England such a practice would be caught by the tort of conversion applicable to negotiable instruments, but the law in Scotland is less certain.[61] However, where a stolen or fraudulently obtained cheque is paid into a customer's account, and that customer is not the true owner, the bank will be free from liability if it has collected the funds from the cheque in good faith and without negligence and for the account of the customer.[62] This is true even when the funds are credited to the customer's account and then taken by the bank to settle sums due to the bank from the customer.[63]

Endorsement

Just as with a bill of exchange, unless the contrary is **4.27** indicated, a cheque may be negotiated by endorsement, in which case the endorsee is a holder in due course. It is possible to make out a cheque to bearer, in which case no endorsement is necessary for negotiation. Endorsement is effected by putting the endorser's signature on the back of

---

[58] Bills of Exchange Act 1882, s.27(1).
[59] *ibid.* s.38(2).
[60] See para. 4.11.
[61] Wallace and McNeil's *Banking Law* (10th ed., 1991) at p.127.
[62] Cheques Act 1957, s.4(1)(a).
[63] *ibid.* s.4(1)(b).

the cheque (unless the cheque is payable to bearer, in which case endorsement is not an issue). The rules which apply to bills of exchange with regard to special endorsement and endorsement in blank, apply to cheques.[64] Formerly a cheque drawn on a bank had to be endorsed before it could be paid to the payee. Since the advent of section 1 of the Cheques Act 1957 this is no longer necessary, and the bank will not be liable where it pays an endorsed cheque in good faith in the ordinary course of business. However, if there has been a material alteration in the cheque, the banker pays it at his own risk. Where a forger endorses a cheque, the person whose forged name appears as the endorser incurs no liability.[65] The forgery cannot be founded on even by a holder for value. So if A, to pay B, writes B a cheque which is stolen by C, who forges B's signature and by means of the forgery induces D to take the cheque in good faith, for value and without notice of the forgery, and if A stops the cheque, D is unable to claim against A or the bank.[66] D's remedy is to claim against C, if he can find him. Had D instead in good faith endorsed the cheque to E, E could have claimed against D and D would have claimed against C.

Crossed cheques

4.28 Following the Cheques Act 1992, which introduced section 81A of the Bills of Exchange Act 1882, all cheques issued by banks are usually issued pre-crossed with the words "a/c payee" between the parallel lines. The purpose of crossing is to ensure that cheques can be paid only into a bank account. This makes it impossible for a holder of a cheque to go to the drawer's bank and ask for cash from the drawer's account on presentation of the cheque. Formerly, when few people had bank accounts, such requests were common. Nowadays, with crossed cheques and many more bank account holders, in theory the cheque should be paid only into the payee's bank account, and if the payee wishes to obtain cash, he must then draw on his own account.

---

[64] See para. 4.7.
[65] Bills of Exchange Act 1882, s.24.
[66] *ibid.*

The significance of the words "account payee" or "a/c **4.29** payee" is that they are an instruction to the bank collecting the money for the payee that the money is to be credited to the payee's bank account alone and must not be transferred to any other account.[67] However, if the cheque is made out to bearer or to order (*i.e.* the order of the payee) the cheque will inherently be transferable, though as a matter of practice nowadays (unless one instructs the bank otherwise) the words "or bearer" or "or order" are no longer printed on cheques. It is arguable that the absence of "or bearer" or "or order" does not prohibit the negotiation of a cheque, because section 8 of the Bills of Exchange Act 1882 states that for a bill of exchange (and therefore a cheque) to be non-transferable, there must be wording on the bill prohibiting the transfer. The deletion or absence of the words "or bearer" or "or order" does not amount to the insertion of prohibitory wording. So if one wishes to be reasonably certain that a cheque should not be paid at any stage to anyone other than the intended payee, the cheque should be crossed, with the words "a/c payee only" or "a/c payee" within the crossing—as indeed cheque nowadays are usually printed.

In theory, negotiation of such a crossed cheque ought to be **4.30** impossible—as was the intention of the Cheques Act 1992. The intention of the Act was to make cheques non-transferable[68] in order to limit the opportunities for thieves to steal cheques, apparently endorse them and obtain funds thereby. This was to protect the rights of the true owner of the cheque, who might not otherwise have received his money, and of the drawer, who could rely on his bank to pay only the true owner.

However, what has happened in practice is that it is still **4.31** possible to endorse cheques, even though they say "not negotiable" or are crossed "a/c payee only", at specialist cheque encashment agencies. A payee, who may not have a bank account for whatever reason, or who perhaps does

---

[67] Bills of Exchange Act 1882, s.81A(1), as inserted by the Cheques Act 1992, s.1.
[68] White Paper, Cm.1026, Annex 5, s.5.6.

not wish to present a cheque to his usual bank because he is already overdrawn and therefore will not be able to get funds, endorses the cheque and presents it to the agency. The agency pays the payee the figure on the cheque less the agency's fee. The agency runs the risk that the cheque is stolen or that the drawee bank will not honour the cheque. The drawee bank generally does honour the cheque provided the drawer has funds. It would not be negligent of a drawee bank to pay on an endorsement because of the protective effect of section 81A(2) which safeguards the bank in the event of paying an endorsed cheque. The agency obtains no better title than the endorser, and inevitably some of the cheques the agency cashes are void. This is compensated for by the large fees they usually charge their customers.

4.32 If a drawer deliberately wishes to make a cheque negotiable, the crossing must be "opened", *i.e.* crossed out by the drawer, and the words "pay cash" inserted instead. Alternatively, the cheque must be made out to bearer and the wording inside the crossing deleted and initialed.

4.33 If a bank does pay a crossed cheque to someone other than the true owner, the bank will have to compensate the true owner[69] unless (a) the cheque did not at the time of presentment appear to have been crossed, or to have had an apparently obliterated crossing or to have been added to or otherwise altered, and (b) the bank paid in good faith and without negligence.[70] However the occasions where the drawer does suffer loss as a result of payment to someone else will be rare (save perhaps where a cheque has been stolen) since the victim of the theft will usually ask the drawer to stop the cheque. In any event it is not usually the drawer who suffers loss as a result of the theft but the payee, who is expected to take care of his own interests by alerting the drawer to the theft. Even if the drawer does suffer loss, a bank paying a cheque in good faith and without negligence (within the restrictions on a bank's liability for negligence under section 81A(2)) can avoid liability.[71]

[69] Bills of Exchange Act 1882, s.79(2).
[70] *ibid.* s.79(2).
[71] *ibid.* s.80.

The apparent endorsement of a cheque when one pays it **4.34** into a bank or building society is not an endorsement by way of negotiation but a receipt to prove that the apparent payee lodged the cheque with the bank. It is arguable that such endorsement is unnecessary, and not all banks insist on the practice of signing on the back of paid-in cheques.

If a cheque is marked "not negotiable" then the transferee **4.35** who accepts the cheque from the payee takes it at his risk. The payee cannot give title and the transferee can give no better title than he received if he attempts to negotiate the cheque to another transferee.[72]

It is usually permissible to write a post-dated cheque and it **4.36** should be lodged for presentment when the appropriate date arrives.

PROMISSORY NOTES

A promissory note is   **4.37**

> "an unconditional promise in writing made by one person to another signed by the maker, engaging to pay, on demand, or at a fixed or determinable future time, a sum certain in money to, or to the order of, a specified person or bearer".[73]

Delivery of the note to the payee or bearer is necessary[74] **4.38** and a promissory note can be negotiated and endorsed in the same manner as a bill of exchange. If it is endorsed, the note must be presented for payment in order to make the endorser liable.[75] Broadly speaking, the requirements of the Bills of Exchange Act 1882 apply to promissory notes save that the rules applicable to acceptance are irrelevant. A promissory note can be protested and summary diligence can follow thereon.

---

[72] Bills of Exchange Act 1882, s.81.

[73] *ibid.* s.83(1).

[74] *ibid.* s.84.

[75] *ibid.* s.87(2)

CHAPTER 5

CONSUMER CREDIT

Consumer credit is a large and highly technical subject. **5.1**
This chapter does not attempt to provide more than an
overview of the major areas as space precludes a detailed
examination of the topic.

The Consumer Credit Act 1974 ("CCA") was introduced in **5.2**
order to rationalise various Acts regulating the provision
of credit. In particular, it introduced a requirement under
section 21 that only licensed traders, lenders or credit
brokers could carry on such businesses as consumer credit
and consumer hire, while under section 147 the business of
credit brokerage, debt adjustment, debt counselling, debt
collecting or the operation of credit reference agencies
(known collectively as "ancillary credit business") also
requires a licence. Occasional or "one-off" loans, which do
not form part of a business, do not normally require the
credit provider or arranger to be licensed,[1] and certain
bodies, such as local authorities, are exempt from the
licence requirement.[2] There are two types of licence, these
being a "standard" licence (the more usual) and a group
licence.[3] Group licences are only given to such bodies as
the Law Society of Scotland (thereby covering all its
members) and local enterprise agencies. All other businesses carrying on licensable credit business must obtain a
standard licence, and each company within a group, as
with a bank and its subsidiaries, must obtain a separate
licence. Licences will be issued only if the Director General

[1] CCA, s.189(2).
[2] *ibid.* s.21(2).
[3] *ibid.* s.22(1).

of Fair Trading, who supervises the operation of CCA, is satisfied that the licensee is fit to hold a licence, taking into account not only the licensee's business name (lest there be any confusion with any other business of a similar name and nature) but also its compliance, and its employees' compliance, with the requirements of the Act.[4] There is a public register of licensees and penalties for carrying on a licensable credit business without a suitable licence.[5]

THE APPLICATION OF CCA

In the context of CCA, what is meant by a "consumer"?

5.3   The emphasis of CCA is on *consumer* credit which, broadly speaking, covers credit or hire arrangements of less than £15,000 offered or provided to individuals.[6] "Individuals" in this context means private persons, partnerships of private persons (partnerships where both parties are limited companies are excluded), unincorporated clubs, charities and societies.[7] Except in the context of a joint hire to an individual and a limited company under section 185(5) incorporated bodies (such as limited companies) are not counted as "individuals". The rationale for this generally is that an individual who wishes to borrow more than £15,000 should be sufficiently responsible to take care of his own arrangements, while incorporated bodies, many of which will have limited liability, should not in principle need the same degree of protection as a private individual. Equally, when CCA was designed, it was intended to protect the unwary or financially bewildered borrower or hirer who might otherwise be lured into taking on onerous or unreasonable commitments.

What is meant by "credit"?

5.4   Under section 9(1), credit is a cash loan and any other form of financial accommodation, "cash" here meaning money

---

[4] CCA, s.25.
[5] *ibid.* ss.39, 147.
[6] *ibid.* s.8(2).
[7] *ibid.* s.189(1).

in any form. The deliberately widely framed wording is designed to give latitude to the meaning, and thereby ensure that most forms of credit will be caught by the legislation—in the interests of the consumer.

What is meant by "hire"?

A hire is different from a hire-purchase agreement (as defined later). Generally, hire (in England called "bail-ment") is the transfer to and use by the hirer for a limited period of goods belonging to the owner in exchange for payment, followed by a retransfer to the owner at the expiry of the hire. Hire-purchase agreements are regulated by CCA under sections 9(3), 15(1)(a) and 189(1) where they are dealt with as consumer credit agreements for fixed-sum credit. But for the purposes of CCA a hire is any hire which is not a hire-purchase agreement, which will last for more than three months and does not require the hirer to make payment in excess of £15,000.[8]

5.5

Regulated Agreements

Definitions

A *consumer credit agreement* is one whereby the creditor provides the debtor, who must be an individual as defined above, with credit of no more than £15,000.

5.6

A *hire-purchase agreement* is one for the provision to an individual of a fixed sum of credit with which to finance the acquisition of goods. The amount lent is the purchase price of the goods less any deposit plus the total interest for the period of the credit. The goods are hired by the individual from the finance provider in exchange for a series of periodical payments followed usually by one final payment on which occasion the individual will exercise an option to purchase the goods from the finance provider.[9] Assuming that all the conditions of the agreement are

5.7

---

[8] CCA, s.15.
[9] *ibid.* s.189(1).

fulfilled, the finance provider transfers the ownership of the property to the individual. In a typical hire-purchase agreement of, say, a motor car, the car dealer will act as an agent for a finance company which will then buy the car. The finance company then hires the car to the customer, who makes regular payments to the agent or the finance company as the case may be. Following the final payment the ownership of the car is transferred to the customer. In the meantime the customer is responsible for the maintenance, insurance and registration of the vehicle. A *conditional sale agreement* is very similar to a hire-purchase agreement save that the property in the goods is not transferred until all the conditions are fulfilled. With both hire-purchase agreements and conditional sale agreements there are extensive provisions designed to ensure that consumers do not have their goods removed from them without due notice, and that if the goods are removed, the consumer is treated fairly with regard to the sums he has already paid the finance company for the goods.

5.8 A *running-account credit* is a facility whereby the borrower can borrow up to £15,000. He can make repayments into the account and then borrow again from it providing that at no stage is the total amount borrowed greater than £15,000. This is a more flexible arrangement than a fixed-sum credit where a sum of money is borrowed in one amount or in instalments.

5.9 A *restricted-use agreement* is one where the credit can be used for only one purpose, as opposed to an *unrestricted-use agreement*. A restricted-use agreement enables the creditor to monitor the debtor's use of the credit more closely, and may be appropriate in the acquisition of one particular item by the debtor.

5.10 A *debtor-creditor-supplier agreement* is an agreement between a debtor (usually a customer), a creditor (usually a finance company) and a supplier (the retailer). A common example of this is an agreement for use of a credit card such as Barclaycard or Mastercard. If a customer buys a holiday from a travel company using his Barclaycard, he pays for the holiday with the credit facility offered by

Barclaycard. Barclaycard pays the travel company, and the customer will find the cost of the holiday on his next statement from Barclaycard. He has to pay the amount due on his statement plus any interest if due. The advantage to the travel company is that it knows it will be paid, whereas a cheque from the customer might not clear; the advantage to the customer is that he can book the holiday quickly and if the travel company defaults, the customer has a claim against both the travel company and the credit card company, which is jointly and severally liable with the supplier, albeit that the credit card company can then be indemnified by the travel company.[10] This is known as "connected lender liability".

What sort of credit or hire is excluded from the terms of CCA?

All agreements regulated by CCA have to follow certain specified forms and procedures, one of which is a "cooling-off" period during which time the debtor can change his mind. However section 74 excludes four types of agreement, these being: **5.11**

- (a) non-commercial agreements (*i.e* one-off non-business loans);
- (b) current account overdrafts;
- (c) loans in connection with debts due after a death (such as a loan by a bank to pay inheritance tax due by the deceased's estate); and
- (d) small agreements for restricted-use credit, for the provision of credit of less than £50.

Paragraph 5.11 refers to agreements which are excluded from the requirements to provide specific wording for the terms to the credit arrangements and cooling-off periods, though in other respects the legislation applies to the arrangements. However there are also various agreements which are specifically exempt from the consumer credit legislation. These are: **5.12**

[10] CCA, s.75.

(a) normal trade credit agreements for a fixed sum repayable in no more than four payments within a period of a year[11] and for a running-account credit repayable in one lump sum within a designated period[12]—as in a Gold Card or Diners' Club card;

(b) land transactions repayable in no more than four repayments[13];

(c) mortgage lending[14] for the acquisition of land or the securing of a loan upon land;

(d) low-cost credit, where the cost of the loan is not greater than base rate plus 1 per cent, or 13 per cent, whichever is the higher[15];

(e) loans for certain insurance policies,[16] usually to pay the premiums on property insurance or mortgage protection policies;

(f) credit agreements for the financing of exports from or imports into the U.K.[17]

5.13   In addition, the hiring of gas, electricity or water meters is exempt from the legislation.[18] All other agreements covered by CCA and not exempt are "regulated agreements".

5.14   CCA operates to ensure that any advertising carried out by consumer credit businesses are accurate and intelligible, complete with "health warnings" alerting the borrower or hirer to the risk of non-fulfilment of his obligations. The annual percentage charge for credit ("APR") must be clearly visible and include most hidden charges. Quotations are similarly closely regulated. The APR was designed as a benchmark so that debtors could compare the cost of one loan with the cost of another. However, while to some extent this purpose has been achieved, it is

[11] Consumer Credit (Exempt Agreements) Order 1989 (S.I. 1989 No. 869), art. 3(1)(a)(i).

[12] *ibid*. art. 3(1)(a)(ii).

[13] *ibid*. art. 3(1)(b).

[14] CCA, s.16(1), (2) and S.I. 1989 No. 869, art. 2.

[15] S.I. 1989 No. 869, art. 4.

[16] *ibid*. art. 3.

[17] *ibid*. art. 5.

[18] *ibid*. art. 6.

well known that whereas most consumers know what the APR is, they have no idea how it is calculated and are unable to work out if the credit provider has overcharged them.

With all the above regulated agreements, the creditor cannot enforce his rights unless he has notified the debtor of his intention to do so on the appropriate form. In the process of enforcing his rights, or should the debtor choose to object to the enforcement, the matter may come before the courts, which may grant a time order. This will usually be a method of allowing the debtor time to pay off his debt by instalments or to remedy any breach.[19] Any lapse by the creditor in the provision of all the necessary forms and documentation for the agreement may make the creditor's application for enforcement invalid. For this reason it is very important for creditors to comply strictly with the standard wording and procedures in their credit or hire documentation. Anybody granting security as part of any credit transaction must also be given the appropriate documentation to ensure that he is aware of the implication of his grant of security.   **5.15**

Pawnbroking

Pawnbrokers must also be scrupulous in their documentation with regard to the pawning of goods. Anybody pawning his goods should receive from the pawnbroker a copy of the pawn agreement, a notice of his cancellation rights and a receipt.[20] The pawn will be redeemable within a period of six months or such longer period as may be agreed.[21] Thereafter the goods pass to the pawnbroker who may sell the goods after intimation to the pawnor[22] (the person who has pawned his goods). If after the sale of the goods there is a surplus following repayment of the loan, interest and expenses, that surplus is repayable to the pawnor.[23] Equally, where the sale proceeds are less than   **5.16**

[19] CCA, s.129.
[20] *ibid.* s.115.
[21] *ibid.* s.116.
[22] *ibid.* s.121.
[23] *ibid.* s.121(3).

the sum due, the balance remains outstanding from the pawnor to the pawnbroker.[24]

Extortionate credit transactions

5.17 An extortionate credit transaction is one which the court decides is extortionate. Effectively, it is open to the court to rewrite the transaction so that a fairer contract subsists. The factors which the court would look at would include unreasonable rates of interests, the financial pressure the borrower was under and any salient facts about the borrower. The legislation works in favour of the borrower, in that if he alleges that the transaction is extortionate, it is for the creditor to prove that it is not.[25]

5.18 It will be seen that CCA is designed to protect borrowers borrowing less than £15,000. Over the years there have been various revisions to CCA and there are criticisms of its operation, some saying that it should be extended to include all business customers (including limited companies) and not just consumers, others saying that business customers do not require the nanny-like hand of the Government to help them borrow money. It is generally agreed that the carefully designed forms and copy documentation, while no doubt worthily intended, are widely ignored or, if read, sadly often fail to be understood by those whom CCA was intended to protect.

---

[24] CCA, s.121(4).
[25] *ibid.* s.171(7).

CHAPTER 6

CAUTIONARY OBLIGATIONS

CAUTION

Caution, pronounced "cay-shun", is the old Scots legal **6.1**
term for the guaranteeing of the payment of a sum of
money, or the performance of an obligation. It arose out of
the concept of a surety for good behaviour, rather as in the
manner of bail for a criminal offence, save within a civil
context. The major use of the word "caution" nowadays is
in court procedure, where a pursuer who wishes to raise
an action may be required to "lodge caution" against the
expenses of the action lest the decision of the court be
against him. This means that the pursuer has to pay a sum
of money into the court to cover his opponent's and the
court's expenses. Sometimes, instead of a sum of money
the pursuer may lodge a bond (an insurance policy) which
will pay out in the event of the action being decided
against him. The rationale behind a defendant's application to the court to make the pursuer lodge caution is to
deter wild and speculative actions which stand little
chance of success but which would involve the defender in
needless and possibly unrecoverable expense. As a wily
defender could use this as a means of putting pressure on
a genuine but impoverished pursuer, the defender's application to make the pursuer lodge caution will succeed only
where the court thinks it appropriate.

Nowadays, the term "caution" is rarely used outwith this **6.2**
context, the more common term being "guarantee" or
"indemnity". The term "guarantee" is not without its
difficulties, since a guarantee in many people's minds is an
undertaking by a manufacturer that he will replace, with-

out charge, a faulty product provided there is intimation of the defect within a specified period of time. Such a guarantee is also known as a warranty. In the context of this chapter, however, a guarantee or a cautionary obligation requires that there be:

(i) a guarantor or cautioner who undertakes the obligation to pay money to or perform some act for

(ii) a creditor in the event of the failure by

(iii) the principal debtor to pay the sum due or perform the act for the creditor.

6.3 There can be no guarantee without a principal debt; and the guarantee is ancillary to the principal debt. If the principal debt is extinguished, the guarantee is discharged.

Common uses of a guarantee

6.4 Nowadays guarantees arise most commonly in the context of bank loans or the opening of bank accounts. For example, a holding company operating a new business through a newly-formed subsidiary may be asked to provide a guarantee on any loans to the subsidiary; a student opening a bank account may find that his parents are required to guarantee any indebtedness in the account; or a director of a newly-formed company may be asked to provide a personal guarantee, perhaps backed up by a standard security over his own home, to cover any debts incurred by the new company. Most banks have tightly-worded standard form guarantees which they are very reluctant to alter, and guarantors should read the terms of such guarantees very carefully before signing them.

Constitution of the guarantee

6.5 Although technically a guarantee does not always have to be in writing, the proof of its existence is difficult in the absence of writing. Where the guarantee is gratuitous and is not given in the course of business, it must be in writing.[1] Where the guarantee is not gratuitous, is in the

---

[1] Requirements of Writing (Scotland) Act 1995, s.1(2)(ii).

course of business or is part of a reciprocal agreement with another person, it need not be in writing and may be established by the actings of the parties or by parole evidence. The guarantor should execute any written guarantee.

Common terms under a guarantee

A guarantee cannot exceed the amount owed by the debtor **6.6** to the creditor. However most guarantees will be worded to allow the creditor to recover not just the principal sum or the performance of the obligation, but also any outstanding interest, judicial fees and agents' expenses. Guarantors may be able to negotiate limits to their liability, in terms of either the amount for which they are liable or the period for which the guarantee endures. If there are other co-guarantors, the guarantor would be well advised to ensure that his own liability is capped and that he is not jointly and severally liable for the guaranteed sum: in the event of the co-guarantors being jointly and severally liable, he may find that while he is able to claim against his co-guarantors if he has had to honour the guarantee on behalf of them all, it may take time and effort to recover funds from them. A guarantor should insist that if he pays the guarantee he obtains an assignation of the debtor's debt to the creditor, together with an assignation of any security the debtor may have granted the creditor. This may enable the guarantor to claim against the debtor at a later date when the debtor is either present, having perhaps been absent earlier, or solvent. Formerly there was a rule under common law that where a creditor had given a debtor time to pay, he effectively discharged the guarantor, since if the creditor delayed in payment, the guarantor, who was entitled to have the creditor's claim assigned to him, was thus unable to press the debtor for payment.[2] While this rule is still technically extant, no creditor would be likely to permit it to apply and there will generally be a clause in the guarantee contract permitting the creditor to give the debtor as much time to pay as the creditor

[2] Bell, *Principles*, s.262.

chooses, while still being able to enforce the rights under the guarantee. If a creditor validly calls upon a guarantor to pay what he is owing under the guarantee but takes no steps to enforce that payment, five years after the call the guarantee will prescribe and the creditor will be unable to enforce it.[3]

Guarantees and fraud

6.7   Historically, the courts used to look kindly upon guarantors, believing them to be gullible and in need of judicial protection if they were unwise enough to sign guarantees. Guarantees were construed *contra proferentem*, in other words, against the interests of the creditor, should the wording be ambiguous. Furthermore, the courts were keen to ensure that the good nature of guarantors should not be imposed upon by unscrupulous creditors. Consequently if a creditor fraudulently misrepresents to the guarantor what his liabilities are, the guarantee is invalid. However if a debtor fraudulently misrepresents to the guarantor what the debtor's own position is, and thereby induces the guarantor to become surety for the debtor's debt to the creditor, the creditor is still entitled to claim under the guarantee. The guarantor is then entitled to claim against the debtor, for what it may be worth, for the debtor's misrepresentation. Furthermore, a creditor is not obliged to reveal all the facts it knows about a debtor to the guarantor before the guarantor supplies the creditor with the guarantee.[4] However, in the context of a spouse providing a guarantee to a lender for the other spouse's debts, and in particular business debts, following the recent House of Lords decision in *Smith v. Bank of Scotland*[5] and the current banking codes of practice, it is probably the case that a lender would not be able to enforce such a guarantee unless the spouse had taken independent advice, or had received specific information from the lender (without the other spouse being present) detailing the extent of the potential liability under the guarantee.

---

[3] Prescription and Limitation (Scotland) Act 1973, s.6.
[4] *Royal Bank v. Greenshields*, 1914 S.C. 259.
[5] 1997 G.W.D. 7.

The discharge of guarantees

In addition to prescription, a guarantee is discharged upon **6.8** the extinction of the principal obligation and, subject to any agreement to the contrary, by the death of the debtor (though not the death of the creditor or the guarantor), by variation of the terms of the underlying obligation between the debtor and the creditor, by the discharge of one co-guarantor without the consent of any others,[6] and by the alteration of a partnership receiving the benefit of the guarantee,[7] as, for example, when a partnership adopts new partners or incorporates itself as a limited company. However, as a matter of practice, a well-worded guarantee may take account of most of these methods of extinction, or may provide that the guarantor be required to execute a new guarantee in favour of the creditor in the case of the incorporation of a former partnership.

---

[6] Mercantile Law Amendment (Scotland) Act 1856, s.9.
[7] Partnership Act 1890, s.18.

CHAPTER 7

SECURITY FOR DEBT

SECURITY FOR PERSONAL BORROWING

When a lender lends a borrower money, the lender expects **7.1**
that the loan, and any interest and expenses arising therefrom, will be repaid within the timescale of the loan. If
there is any danger that this requirement will not be met,
the lender may wish to have rights over some asset
belonging to the borrower, both to encourage the borrower
to fulfil his part of the bargain and also so that the lender
can if necessary sell the asset in order to recoup any loss—
as happens, for example, when someone borrows money
from a pawnbroker. When the loan and interest are repaid,
but not until then, the pawnbroker returns the asset and
until it is returned the borrower is clearly unable to use it.
If the loan and interest are not fully paid, the pawnbroker
is entitled to sell the asset to recoup his loss, though once
his loss is recouped, the pawnbroker must hand back any
surplus to the customer. The asset while in the possession
of the pawnbroker acts as *security* for the loan; it can also
be said that there is a *charge* over the asset in favour of the
pawnbroker. The significance of the existence of a security
or a charge over an asset is considerable: the security
holder or charge holder has a prior right to the asset, or the
proceeds of sale of that asset, which overrides any other
interest in the asset itself. Without this assurance, the
security holder might not lend to the borrower or, if
he did, he would charge a higher rate of interest. If the
security holder has the prior right, he is not obliged to
consider any interest other than prior ranking securities,[1]

---

[1] See para. 7.8.

although in respect of companies, a lesser type of security known as a floating charge (discussed in paras. 7–13 *et seq.*) is also usually postponed to certain other claims known as the preferential debts. The prior right, known generally as a fixed charge, prevents the borrower selling the secured asset without the consent of the security holder, either because the security holder has it in his possession, or because the borrower cannot give clear title to a purchaser until the security is discharged.

The need for delivery

7.2   Scots law, echoing its Roman law origins, formerly insisted that security was impossible without physical delivery to the security holder of the secured item.[2] This was for the practical reason that unless the item was handed over to the security holder, the borrower could then sell it or charge it in favour of somebody else. Then there would be a dispute about the true ownership of the item. In addition, if the borrower still had the item in his hands there was less incentive for him to fulfil his side of the bargain. Delivery of the item to the security holder dispenses with these problems. While it is an easy matter to hand over, say, a gold watch to a pawnbroker, the Roman law origins of Scots law find it more difficult to cope with the delivery to a lender of items of security which are large and bulky or intangible. Scots law also finds it difficult to cope with the idea of using as security an item which the borrower actually needs in order to be able to generate the income to repay his loan. These problems will be looked at in turn.

Pledge

7.3   If a person wished to raise a loan against the value of her jewels, she could deposit the jewels with a bank and sign a contract permitting the bank to sell the jewels to pay for the loan in the event of her default. There are few difficulties with physically small items such as these. However, if the secured asset is bulky the law recognises an equivalent to

---

[2] Bell, *Comm.*, ii, 21.

delivery. If a fuel manufacturer wished a bank to lend him money on the security of the fuel in his barrels, it would be unrealistic to roll the barrels into the bank vaults. What used to happen in practice was that the barrels were marked as being secured to the bank; they were placed in a designated locked area in a warehouse; and the bank was given the key.[3] These are examples of *pledge,* and are still valid methods of obtaining security over tangible, or to use the Scottish term, corporeal items today. On the repayment of the loan, the items are returned to the owner.

Ships and aircraft

Ships and aircraft are security subjects which also cannot 7.4 always be kept easily by a creditor. Accordingly there are registers of ship mortgages, fishing vessel mortgages and aircraft mortgages. It is not obligatory to register such mortgages, though absence of registration means that an unregistered mortgage is postponed to a registered one. The owner of the craft is still able to use it, but he may not sell it until the mortgagee (the creditor) has released the ship or aircraft from its charge—which will not usually take place until the mortgage has been repaid.

Assignation of life policies and rental income

With intangible or incorporeal items, such as the entitle- 7.5 ment to the proceeds of a life policy, or to rental income arising from a lease, it is less possible physically to deliver the asset. In Scotland, if a life assurance policyholder wishes to use the proceeds of a life policy as security for a loan, the policyholder must hand the policy documents to the lender and sign a document known as an assignation of life policy.[4] This transfers the right to the proceeds from the policyholder to the lender. This must be intimated to the insurance company which wrote the policy,[5] partly so that it knows to whom to pay the proceeds, and also to

---

[3] *Liquidator of West Lothian Oil Co. Ltd v. Mair* (1892) 20 R. 64.
[4] Transmission of Moveable Property (Scotland) Act 1862, Scheds. A and B.
[5] *ibid.* s.2.

alert it to check that there is no restriction on the assignation. At the end of the period of the loan for which the life assurance policy is being offered as security, and unless the assignation is *ex facie* absolute (*i.e.* the assignation does not specify the debt for which the policy is being assigned, and therefore allows the lender to use the policy as security for any debt due to the lender) the policy must be retrocessed—in other words, transferred back to the policyholder, and the insurance company is informed that the lender no longer has an interest in the proceeds of the policy. The same principle, broadly speaking, is followed when rental income is assigned to a bank. The assignation is intimated to the tenant by recorded delivery together with a mandate that the rent should be paid to the bank. This course of action is not without its difficulties because not all tenants will understand that they are being asked to redirect their rental payments to somewhere other than the landlord and may refuse or delay to do so. At the end of the period of the loan the rental income must be redirected to the landlord. The requirement of intimation for the transfer of incorporeal rights is not obligatory in England though as a matter of practice it is often carried out anyway. In England assignation is known as assignment.

Security over shares

7.6   If someone wishes to grant a security over his shares, he must transfer them to the lender and receive an undertaking, usually by a back letter, from the lender that it will retransfer the shares on the expiry of the loan. The undertaking should specify what is to be done with the dividends arising on the shares and the voting decisions. In order to avoid any conceivable difficulties under the Companies Act 1985, s.143, when a bank accepts its own shares as security for a customer's loan it should arrange to have the shares transferred into the name of one of the bank's subsidiaries. It is arguable that this method of taking security over shares is not a true form of security, merely a back-to-back arrangement which has the virtue of efficiency. Nonetheless it remains a common practice, so far unchallenged. Occasionally banks in Scotland have been known to take a deposit of a customer's shares,

without transfer into the bank's name or into the name of a
nominee for the bank, as security for a loan. This is not a
true security, and would not stand up in court: it is merely
a method of inconveniencing the borrower should he
attempt to sell his shares, since he would be required to
produce the original share certificates to sell them. In
England such a method of granting security is perfectly
acceptable and is a form of equitable mortgage. The issue
of granting security over listed company shares held in
electronic registers under CREST is still being addressed at
the time of writing.

Security over heritage

Land and buildings, and the rights attaching to them, **7.7**
known in Scotland as heritage and in England as real
estate, are probably the most common form of security
there is, not least because land is a commodity which in
the long term generally holds its value and because it is
relatively easy to identify through the land registers. Land
is difficult to steal so there are relatively few disputes
about ownership. A security over land and buildings in
England is commonly known as a (land) mortgage, and the
term has crept into Scotland. The term in Scotland for a
mortgage is a *standard security*, though the concept is the
same. There is a standard form of wording for a standard
security, set down in the Conveyancing and Feudal
Reform (Scotland) Act 1970, Sched. 2, Forms A and B.
There are standard conditions set out in Sched. 3 to the Act
and these are adopted unless varied. The form specifies the
secured property and the obligations of the person granting the security. Not everyone who grants a standard
security is a borrower from the standard security holder
(sometimes also known as the heritable creditor). Someone
who wishes to have the first option to buy a property may
protect his option by obtaining a standard security. The
standard security, as with all documents relating to the
title to land in Scotland, is recorded in the Register of
Sasines for those counties in Scotland still using this
method, or registered in the Land Register for the remaining counties in Scotland.

Ranking of standard securities

7.8   It is quite common for a property to have more than one
standard security over it, each standard security being in
favour of a different heritable creditor. In the absence of
any ranking agreement to the contrary, the first recorded
or registered standard security has priority as regards the
proceeds of sale of the property over any subsequent
standard security. If there is no such agreement the first
heritable creditor will, on being notified of the second
standard security, find that his priority is restricted to
security for the loan which he has already made, together
with any further loans that he has contracted to provide,
along with interest, outlays and expenses.[6] This means that
any hitherto uncontracted-for loans, not covered by the
obligations under the first standard security, will be
postponed to the security covered by the second standard
security. Usually in commercial matters there is a ranking
agreement to regulate the order of priority of standard
securities, but in relation to domestic property it is sometimes the case that borrowers have granted second or third
securities over their properties without really being aware
that they have done so. The first heritable creditor commonly retains the titles of the property (*i.e.* the actual
property deeds) with the exception of the other heritable
creditors' standard securities, which will usually be
retained by those heritable creditors. When the property
owner comes to sell his property, he may direct his
solicitor to obtain the titles from the first heritable creditor
without informing the solicitor of the other standard
securities. Their presence will be revealed only by a search
of the property registers, and may cause difficulties in the
sale of the property, not to mention difficulties in providing enough free proceeds for the property owner to buy
his next property.

Discharge of standard security

7.9   A standard security is discharged by a deed known as a
discharge of standard security, which also must be
recorded or registered in the appropriate register. The

[6] Conveyancing and Feudal Reform (Scotland) Act 1970, s.13.

heritable creditor will only execute the discharge once he has the sums which he is due.

Calling up a standard security

Where a borrower fails to honour the obligations required **7.10** under the standard security, these generally being to pay the interest on the loan on time and in full, the heritable creditor may serve a "notice of default" requiring the borrower to make good any deficiencies. If this fails to achieve the desired result, under the Act the heritable creditor has a number of remedies, of which the principal one is the serving of a calling-up notice. The correct procedure having been followed, the heritable creditor is entitled to enter into possession of the property and to sell it.[7] There is also a number of alternative remedies including occupying the property and receiving the rent therefrom, enforcing the personal obligation against the borrower, or foreclosure. Foreclosure is where the heritable creditor is unable to sell the property at a price greater than the debt due to the heritable creditor, and title to the property is passed directly to the heritable creditor.

Security over leases

It is possible to obtain a security over a lease of heritage. If **7.11** the lease is for, or could be extended up to, a period of 20 years or more, it is registrable in the appropriate land register, and the security must be in the form of a standard security and properly recorded or registered as appropriate. For a lesser period of lease, which will not be registrable, it is possible to have a security, but this can be done only by assignation of the lease followed by possession— and the assignation itself might not be permissible by the landlord, depending on the terms of the lease. It is not unknown for non-registrable leases to be registered in the Books of Council and Session and a security granted over the leasehold interest; the personal obligation under the

---

[7] Conveyancing and Feudal Reform (Scotland) Act 1970, ss.19–25.

security may well be valid as between the lessee and the security holder, but a purchaser of the lease is not bound to consider the security holder's interest on acquisition of the lease.

SECURITY FOR CORPORATE BORROWING

Companies and their charges

7.12 Companies can grant securities over their assets in identical ways to private persons or partnerships, but there are additional rules applicable to security granted by companies because of the requirement that the granting of securities be disclosed at the Register of Companies. This is because anyone dealing with a company, as either an investor or a creditor, will wish to know how much remains of the company's assets after satisfaction of the secured creditors. Accordingly, certain charges (as securities are generally known in the context of companies) must be registered with the Registrar of Companies within 21 days of their creation. In the absence of registration the charge is void against a liquidator, administrator or creditor of the company.[8] This will be discussed shortly. The registered details of each registered charge for a company should, in theory, provide enough information to assist the potential investor or creditor. In practice, the information contained at the Register of Companies is usually fairly superficial. More information about its charges can be obtained from the company's registered office which is required to hold copies of each charge.[9] These copies may be inspected by any member or creditor (but not any potential member or creditor) at a cost of not more than 5 pence per charge.[10]

Floating charges

7.13 The additional feature concerning companies is that they can grant floating charges, which private individuals and

---

[8] Companies Act 1985, s.410(2).
[9] *ibid.* s.421.
[10] *ibid.* s.423.

partnerships cannot. A floating charge is a concept from English law and was introduced when it became apparent that Scottish commerce was unable to borrow on the security of all its moveable assets as effectively as English businesses could. This was because of the previously mentioned requirement that security could be granted only with delivery. A Scottish company which had heritage could grant standard securities over its land and buildings and raise a loan on their value, but could not grant a security over its equally valuable but non-deliverable moveable stock, intellectual property and other incorporeal property without a formal assignation. Assignations were clumsy and time-consuming and in any case the company often needed the moveable assets in order to work and trade. The floating charge was eventually introduced, and now a company can grant a security over all its assets (except where specifically excluded or where subject to a prior-ranking security), while continuing to use and trade with those assets. Provided that the borrowing company continues to fulfil its obligations to the floating charge holder the latter will let the company continue to use and trade with all its assets. Lest there be any likelihood that the floating charge holder might crystallise the charge (as described shortly), in practice it is common for a company whose assets are secured by a floating charge to arrange to provide a purchaser of any of its substantial assets with a "letter of non-crystallisation" from the floating charge holder, confirming that within a specified number of days the floating charge holder will not put the company into receivership, and that consequently the purchase may proceed. On the occasion of default by the company, the floating charge holder is entitled to make the floating charge "attach" to the company's assets. In addition, on the winding-up of the company the floating charge automatically attaches to the company's assets.[11] This process is more often known by the English term of "crystallisation". A metaphorical way of describing this is to imagine a spread net suspended over the company's assets, the centre of the net being held up by the hand of the floating

[11] Companies Act 1985, s.463(1).

charge holder. Provided that the company fulfils its obligations, the net remains suspended; on default the net is dropped onto the company, trapping its assets, and thereby preventing the company having any further dealing with them. Certain untrapped items escape through the net, amongst these being assets with a prior security over them (to the extent of the prior security) and funds which will be required to be used to pay preferential debts. On the crystallisation of the floating charge, the charge holder appoints an official known as a receiver[12] who gathers in the trapped assets and realises them in as advantageous a manner as possible in order to repay the floating charge holder. The process of crystallisation in effect converts the floating charge into a fixed charge, in that from the moment of crystallisation the trapped assets are no longer at the unfettered disposal of the company owning them. It is worth observing that the English concept of the "fixed and floating charge", being a floating charge which converts to a fixed charge at the whim of the charge holder without other creditors necessarily being aware of when this might take place or even that it has taken place, is alien to Scots law.

Ranking of floating charges

7.14 The usual rule concerning the ranking of multiple floating charges is that they rank in date order unless there is any agreement to the contrary[13]; floating charges arriving in the same post rank equally,[14] but fixed securities rank in priority to floating charges[15] unless, again, there is any agreement to the contrary. The principal type of fixed security in this context is a standard security, the methods of registration of which will be narrated shortly. Fixed securities arising by operation of law rank in priority to floating charges, so, for example, a landlord's hypothec for unpaid rent takes precedence over a floating charge.[16]

---

[12] See Chap.12.
[13] Companies Act 1985, s.464(4)(b).
[14] *ibid.* s.464(4)(c).
[15] *ibid.* s.464(4)(a).
[16] *Grampian Regional Council v. Drill Stem (Inspection Services) Ltd (in receivership)*, 1994 S.C.L.R. 36.

When a first floating charge holder is given notice of a subsequent floating charge, the security for which the first floating charge is granted is restricted[17] in the same manner and to the same effect as with standard securities as narrated in paragraph 7.8.

The security assets comprised in a floating charge

Floating charges usually cover "the entire assets and undertaking" of the company, but it is possible, albeit rare, to have selective floating charges. Floating charges are usually described as being in security of "all sums due and that become due, together with interest and expenses", though it is possible to have specific figures mentioned in them.

7.15

Negative pledges

In Scotland, although not in England, the Form 410 on which the floating charge is registered with the Registrar of Companies has space on which to state whether or not the terms of the floating charge contain a clause which prohibits the creation of any other charge ranking in priority or *pari passu* (*i.e.* having equal priority) with the current floating charge.[18] Such a clause is known as a negative pledge clause. Any attempt by a subsequent charge holder to make his charge rank in priority to the existing floating charge, without the consent of the prior floating charge holder, will not succeed.[19] This issue arose in *AIB Finance Ltd v. Bank of Scotland*[20] where a company granted a floating charge to the Bank of Scotland and a standard security to AIB. It had been intended that the standard security, which usually would be registered first by the method to be subsequently described, would be in place before the floating charge was registered. By some oversight, the floating charge, which contained a negative pledge clause, was registered first. This meant that, contrary to expectation, the

7.16

[17] Companies Act 1985, s.464(5).
[18] *ibid.* s.464(1)(a).
[19] *ibid.* s.464(1A).
[20] [1994] B.C.C. 184.

standard security was postponed to the floating charge, and that the receiver appointed by the Bank of Scotland was able to take precedence over the claims of AIB with its standard security. A particular benefit for the Bank of Scotland receiver was that he was able to treat the floating charge over the company's heritage as an effective standard security, notwithstanding the fact that there was no standard security recorded in favour of the Bank of Scotland. Although it is usually the case that a heritable security must be recorded or registered in the appropriate land register, where a company has unsecured heritage and has granted a floating charge, the floating charge attaches to that heritage in the absence of a standard security, and the receiver can legitimately transfer such heritage. If a floating charge is altered, the alteration must be registered.[21]

The effect of non-registration of charges

7.17   Although not all charges which a company can grant are registrable, most of the common charges are registrable and are void against a liquidator, administrator or creditor unless they are properly registered within 21 days of the creation of the charge.[22] This means that if, say, a company received a loan from a bank with which to buy a patent from its inventor, duly bought the patent, failed to register the charge in favour of the bank over the patent within 21 days and then went into liquidation, the liquidator would be able to take all the company assets, including the newly-acquired patent, and sell them to pay all the creditors including the bank. The bank, had it had its charge registered, would have expected to have been a secured creditor and to be able to exercise its prior rights over the patent; but if the charge had not been registered, the bank would be a mere unsecured creditor and consequently unlikely to get its money back. If, for some reason, the 21-day period in which to register the charges is missed, it is possible, at great expense and embarrassment, to petition the court for late registration. This will generally be permitted, providing that no creditor has been prejudiced

[21] Companies Act 1985, s.466(4).
[22] *ibid.* s.410(2).

in the meantime.[23] If, during the 21-day period, the company does go into liquidation or administration or a creditor attempts to exercise his rights against the charged assets, the charge is treated as valid, though it must still be registered within the 21-day period.

Registrable charges

The charges which a company must register are the **7.18** following[24]:

(a) charges on land (effectual standard securities, land mortgages and their equivalents from other jurisdictions);
(b) charges over uncalled share capital of the company;
(c) charges over the following items of incorporeal moveable property of the company:

    (i) book debts;
    (ii) calls (on shares) made but not paid;
    (iii) goodwill;
    (iv) a patent or licence under a patent;
    (v) a trademark;
    (vi) a copyright or licence under a copyright;

(d) a security over a ship, share of a ship or an aircraft; and
(e) a floating charge.

All these charges must be registered within 21 days of **7.19** their creation, which in nearly all cases effectively means the date of execution by the company of the charging document. However, in the case of standard securities, the charge is said to be created when the standard security is recorded or registered in the appropriate land register, because on that occasion the charge holder obtains a real right in the property, and the creation of the security is deemed to run from that date, and not the date

---

[23] Companies Act 1985, s.420.
[24] *ibid.* s.410(4).

of execution of the standard security. Provided that the particulars of the charges are correct and in time, the Registrar of Companies will issue a certificate of registration of charge, which is conclusive evidence of the registration of the charge[25]—though no assertion is made about the validity of the underlying transaction. Mortgages over land abroad are given an extension to the 21-day period to allow for delays in the post.[26] Ships, aircraft and land have to be doubly registered, once in the appropriate shipping or aircraft registers, and once with the Registrar of Companies.

Non-registrable charges

7.20   Non-registrable charges are those arising by operation of law, such as repairer's lien (*i.e.* a right of retention by a repairer pending payment) or a landlord's hypothec. There are some charges which do not appear to be registrable, for no very good reason: for example a fixed charge over government stocks is non-registrable, though such stock could be covered by a floating charge.

Discharges of charges

7.21   It is not obligatory, but generally considered prudent, to provide a discharge for each registered charge in order to prove that the creditor under the charge has no further interest in a charge.[27] Such discharges are technically known as entries of satisfaction; if the charge is only partially discharged, it is an entry of relief.

Enforcement of right under a charge

7.22   The rights of a receiver under a floating charge will be discussed in detail in Chapter 12. The rights of a standard security holder are discussed in paragraph 7.10. The rights of the charge holders in all other circumstances will be as specified in the charging documents, but in principle, the

---

[25] Companies Act 1985, s.418(2).
[26] *ibid.* s.411.
[27] *ibid.* s.419.

charge holder will have a fixed right over the asset, and can therefore sell it (or keep it) to recoup any debt due to him. Should there be a surplus on sale after repayment of any loan and any interest and expenses thereon, the balance would be returned to the company.

CHAPTER 8

COMPENSATION AND RETENTION

COMPENSATION

Compensation is more commonly known as set-off, and is **8.1** the right to set a debt owed by A to B against a separate debt owed by B to A. It can be distinguished from a counterclaim, which is a term of court procedure, whereby when a pursuer raises any action against a defender, the defender can raise a claim by return against the pursuer provided that the subject-matter of the counterclaim is also the subject-matter of the pursuer's original action.

The law relating to compensation is derived from the **8.2** Compensation Act 1592 (c.143), and provided that the following rules are followed it is possible to allow set-off to take place:

(a) the debts must be of the same type;
(b) the debts must both be liquid (*i.e.* a requirement that cash be paid, as opposed to, say, the performance of services);
(c) there must be *concursus debiti et crediti*;
(d) it must be pleaded before decree: once decree has been given, the claim under the decree must be met and a separate action started for a counterclaim.

The effect of these rules is that the use of set-off where one **8.3** claim is for a present debt and the other a contingent debt is barred, as would also be set-off where one claim is for damages for breach of contract and the other for, say, damages for defamation. *Concursus debiti et crediti* means

that the set-off must be against a person in the same
capacity: so, for example, a debt due to a single-member
private limited company could not be set off against a debt
due by the same individual in his personal, as opposed to
his corporate, capacity, and a debt incurred by a bankrupt
cannot be set off against a credit due to him after his
bankruptcy.[1] A bank cannot set off the sums held to the
credit of a solicitor's client account against the solicitor's
own drawings.[2] Set-off is also impossible where the terms
of the contract forbid it, or where funds are deposited for a
specific purpose and no other.

8.4   Under the Crown Proceedings Act 1947, s.50, any claims
by or against a government department by way of set-off
are effective only as regards that department. So, for
example, if a company owed money to the Ministry of
Defence, but was due money by way of a tax repayment
from the Inland Revenue, the company could not reduce
its payment to the Ministry of Defence by the amount due
from the Inland Revenue.

8.5   Given these restrictions on set-off, it is not surprising that
banks and other financial institutions when offering a loan
or banking facilities always try to include among the terms
of their contracts of business a clause permitting them to
combine accounts or to exercise unrestricted rights of set-
off. There is further discusion of set-off in the chapters on
receivership[3] and liquidation.[4]

RETENTION

8.6   Retention arises in disputes where the defender alleges
that he is not due to carry out some obligation (such as to
pay an account) because of the failure of the pursuer to
carry out his side of the contract. So, for example, a storage

---

[1] Despite this, a future, contingent or illiquid claim payable by a bankrupt
can be set off against a debt due to the bankrupt (*Hannay and Sons' Tr. v.
Armstrong & Co.* (1875) 4 R. (H.L.) 43).
[2] *Greenwood Teale v. William, Williams Brown & Co.* (1894) 11 T.L.R. 56).
[3] Chap. 12.
[4] Chap. 13.

warehouse seeking payment of its warehousing bill might be met with a claim for the cost of repairing items which had been inadequately stored by it. Because of the effectiveness of such potential claims, it is not uncommon to see in certain contracts a provision specifically excluding one party from exercising any right of retention.[5]

[5] *Redpath Dorman Long Ltd v. Cummins Engine Co. Ltd*, 1981 S.C. 370.

CHAPTER 9

RECOVERY OF DEBT AND DILIGENCE

RECOVERY OF DEBT

An action of debt can be raised in the Court of Session, the **9.1**
sheriff court or the small claims court. It would be unusual
to raise an action in the Court of Session for recovery of a
debt on account of the high court expenses payable there.
The usual place for raising such an action is the sheriff
court, and there is no upper limit on the size of the claim
which may be entertained in that forum. However, where
the sums involved are £1,500 or less, the claim may not be
heard initially in the Court of Session.[1] Claims of more
than £1,500 are heard in the ordinary court, and claims of
£1,500 or less (excluding interest and expenses) are heard
in the summary cause court.[2] A summary court has
simplified procedure and is cheaper than the ordinary
court. For claims of £750 or less there is the small claims
court, in which the normal rules of admissibility of evidence are considerably relaxed. Only limited expenses are
recoverable.

The great majority of actions of debt are unopposed and **9.2**
decree is granted for the sums sued for, together with
interest and expenses. Interest is at the judicial rate for the
time being, which is generally more than base rate. The
court expenses are those laid down in the sheriff court
rules and bear little proportion to the actual cost of raising
an action, so that even for a successful litigant the expenses

---

[1] Sheriff Courts (Scotland) Act 1907, s.7 (as amended).
[2] Sheriff Courts (Scotland) Act 1971.

he may recover from the other party will be only a proportion of the true cost of employing solicitors. The expenses will be greater for opposed actions as there are set fees for each time the action comes before the court.

DILIGENCE

9.3 The court's decision is known as a "decree", and may be enforced by various forms of "diligence". This use of the word "diligence" is unconnected with other uses of that word in the context of obtaining information from witnesses or checking the accounts and business of an undertaking about to be acquired.

9.4 The main forms of diligence are arrestment, diligence against earnings, poinding and inhibition. There are other forms, virtually unused but still extant, being adjudication, maills and duties, poinding of the ground and civil imprisonment. Historically, there were such exciting forms of diligence as being "put to the horn" (as happened to Rob Roy) whereby following three blasts of a horn in the market square, a debtor was declared an outlaw and all his belongings forfeit to his creditors—if they dared fetch them. It is possible to use arrestment and inhibition in an anticipatory manner. This is known as diligence "on the dependence" and may be used where there is a danger that the debtor will abscond, will remove all his belongings or is about to become insolvent. Diligence is carried out by messengers-at-arms, in respect of decrees from the Court of Session, and by sheriff officers, in respect of decrees from the sheriff court. Messengers-at-arms and sheriff officers perform much the same function as bailiffs and sheriff's officers in England. They frequently also act as enquiry agents and a large number of them are ex-policemen. They usually work in pairs so that one can be a witness for the other's actions, and their fees and outlays are recoverable in the same manner as court expenses. They are under the supervision of the Lord Lyon King of Arms. For the sake of convenience the following paragraphs will refer to both messengers-at-arms and sheriff officers as "sheriff officers".

Arrestment

Arrestment is the term for the attachment of debtor's **9.5** moveable assets in the hands of a third party. If the assets are in the debtor's own hands, poinding, not arrestment, is required, except in the case of ships which, on being arrested, are effectively unable to leave harbour. Arrestment prevents the third party (the "arrestee") handing the arrested assets to the debtor, and if the arrestee passes the debtor's assets to the debtor in defiance of the arrestment he is in contempt of court and the matter can be reported to the police. The arrested goods stay in the hands of the arrestee until such time as the debtor signs a mandate allowing the arrestee to hand over the goods to the creditor, or the creditor raises an "action of furthcoming" which is an additional action in which decree entitles the creditor to take the arrested assets. Arrestment is not without its practical difficulties: arrestment in one sheriff court is not automatically acceptable in another,[3] and arresting a bank account can be a hit-or-miss affair until the sheriff officers find the right bank (or building society) where the debtor keeps his money. Crafty Scottish debtors keep their money in English banks or in little-known building societies.

Arrestment on the dependence

Arrestment on the dependence of an action is a method of **9.6** arresting assets in the hands of an arrestee before the action has been heard in the courts. It is usually available for only a current as opposed to a future debt, but it is permissible for a future debt if there is a danger that the debtor is *vergens ad inopiam* (about to become insolvent) or *in meditatione fugae* (considering absconding). It is not possible to arrest wages or a pension by means of an arrestment on the dependence.[4] Arrestment on the dependence of an action needs to be sought specifically from the appropriate court and is not granted automatically. It usually brings quick results, especially when

[3] Debtors (Scotland) Act 1987, s.91.
[4] Law Reform (Miscellaneous Provisions) (Scotland) Act 1966, s.1.

the debtor finds that he cannot operate a bank account or retrieve his goods from the arrestee's hands.

Arrestment in execution

9.7 A decree will automatically entitle the creditor to proceed to arrestment, but arrestment is also possible where a bond, lease or any contract specifically states that the bond, etc. is to be registered in the Books of Council and Session (or sheriff court books) for preservation *and execution*. This means that on presentation of an extract (a form of certified copy) the creditor can instruct that arrestment follow without any further process.[5] Likewise a bill of exchange, duly protested in front of a notary public,[6] can permit arrestment to take place without further process. Arrestment without a prior decree is also available for the recovery of rates and taxes, provided that the appropriate application has been made to the sheriff beforehand.[7]

Actions of furthcoming

9.8 The arrested items are said to be "litigious" and neither the arrestee nor the debtor may transfer them to anyone. Arrestment is not completed until the creditor has obtained from the court a decree of furthcoming. The creditor will specify in his crave to the court what he wishes to do with the arrested assets. Generally, the creditor will want the arrested assets, if they are corporeal or incorporeal moveable property other than cash, to be sold and the net proceeds plus interest paid to him. The sheriff officers who carried out the arrestment will be entitled to their expenses out of the sale proceeds. The method of sale of a debtor's assets is discussed later in the context of poinding. If there are several arrestments in respect of the same assets, usually the first in date order has priority, but in complicated cases an action of multiple-poinding may be necessary. This is an action designed to ascertain how much each creditor may receive.

---

[5] Writs Execution (Scotland) Act 1877.
[6] See para. 4.14.
[7] Debtors (Scotland) Act 1987 (see Gloag and Henderson, p. 1005).

Arrestable assets

Most corporeal moveable property and most incorporeal   **9.9**
moveable property is arrestable, though bills of exchange
cannot be arrested[8] and assets in the hands of the debtor
himself cannot be arrested since poinding is thereby necessary. The proceeds of life assurance policies, shares, funds
held in bank accounts, furniture in warehouses, interests in
trust estates, etc. are all arrestable. It is not permissible to
arrest funds which are said to be alimentary,[9] in other
words those made available expressly to feed and clothe
the debtor, unless the creditor is a person who has been
supplying the debtor with such food and clothing.[10]
Equally, it is not possible to arrest items necessary for the
wellbeing of the debtors and his family, such as his tools of
trade and various other items specified in the Debtors
(Scotland) Act 1987, s.16.[11] Ships can be arrested within
limited circumstances, provided that the appropriate
requirements of the Administration of Justice Act 1956,
s.47, are followed. It is possible to defeat an arrestment if it
can be proved that the subjects arrested do not belong to
the debtor[12] or if the property is owned jointly by the
debtor and another person.[13] Arrestments prescribe within
three years unless the debt is a future or contingent debt in
which case the three-year period runs from the date the
debt becomes due.[14]

Diligence against earnings

This is similar to an arrestment, and was introduced by the   **9.10**
Debtors (Scotland) Act 1987 to solve the difficulties and
expense arising from repeated arrestments of the earnings
of employees and to facilitate the payment of court fines
and periodical payments for maintenance for a debtor's

---

[8] Bell, *Comm.*, ii, 68.
[9] *Cuthbert v. Cuthbert's Trs.*, 1908 S.C. 967.
[10] *Lord Ruthven v. Pulford*, 1909 S.C. 951.
[11] See para. 9.14.
[12] *Sir James Laing & Sons Ltd v. Barclay Curle & Co. Ltd*, 1908 S.C. 82.
[13] *Byng v. Campbell* (1893) 1 S.L.T. 371.
[14] Debtors (Scotland) Act 1838, s.22.

spouse and children. It has also been used extensively to facilitate the collection of sums due first by the "poll tax" and later by council tax. The Child Support Agency has powers to deduct sums from earnings on a similar basis[15] by means of deductions from earnings orders.

Earnings arrestment and maintenance arrestment

9.11 An earnings arrestment is the appropriate type of diligence against earnings for ordinary debts and court fines, whereas a maintenance arrestment is appropriate for payments required in connection with divorce and the maintenance of children. A debtor can suffer an earnings arrestment and a maintenance arrestment against his earnings at the same time, but cannot suffer any more than one of each.[16] The employer pays a specified and statutorily laid down proportion of the earnings[17] to each creditor. As this may prejudice further creditors, such a creditor must apply to the court to have the arrestments conjoined and a global payment directed to the sheriff clerk who will then pay the various creditors.[18] Either or both types of arrestment continue in force until the debt is paid, the debtor ceases to work for the employer, the arrestment is recalled or the debtor is sequestrated.[19] The employer, for whom these arrangements may well be a considerable inconvenience, is liable to the creditor if he fails to pay the arrested sums. The employer is entitled to charge the debtor a fee of 50p per payment of the arrested amount.[20] Some employers, notably in the defence and financial services industries, often put a clause in their employees' contracts to the effect that an earnings arrestment or current maintenance arrestment will entitle the employer to terminate the employment. This is on the ground that an employee who is feckless with his own funds is clearly not a responsible person to be looking after important matters potentially relating to the nation's security or other people's money.

[15] Child Support Act 1991, s.38.
[16] Debtors (Scotland) Act 1987, s.58(1).
[17] *ibid*. Sched. 2.
[18] *ibid*. s.60.
[19] *ibid*. s.72.
[20] *ibid*. s.71.

Poinding

Poinding (pronounced "pin-ding") is the attachment by **9.12**
the creditor of personal property in the hands of the
debtor. Following attachment, the creditor is entitled to sell
the poinded assets and the proceeds therefrom are used to
satisfy the debtor's debt to the creditor. Like arrestment,
poinding can proceed from an extract decree, from a deed
registered in the Books of Council and Session or sheriff
court books (provided that the deed has been registered
for preservation and execution), from a protested bill and
summarily for recovery of rates and taxes, provided that
authority has been received from the sheriff. However, it is
not possible to use a poinding on the dependence of an
action.

Poinding procedure

The extract decree or other document permitting poinding **9.13**
to proceed having been handed to sheriff officers, the
sheriff officers serve a charge (a formal request for payment) at the debtor's home or business either by recorded
delivery or in person. If the debtor's address is unknown
or he is abroad, recorded delivery must be attempted
together with advertisement in his last known area of
residence. After the charge is served the debtor has 14
days in which to pay the debt, the court fees, the interest
and sheriff officers' fees. These 14 days are known as the
induciae of the charge. If payment is still not made, the
sheriff officers are then entitled to carry out a poinding.
The sheriff officers attend the debtor's home or place of
business, as the case may be, show the debtor the warrant
to poind and a certificate of execution and ask for payment
from the debtor or his representative. If payment is still not
forthcoming, the sheriff officers then poind goods, which
means that they prepare a schedule of the debtor's goods,
together with their estimated value, which should cover
the debt and the other expenses. Although the goods are
left in the debtor's hands at this stage, removal of them is
technically a contempt of court.[21] There is then a further

---

[21] Debtors (Scotland) Act 1987, s.29.

period of 14 days during which the goods can be redeemed by the debtor, failing which, after a further application to the sheriff, authority for a warrant sale is given to the sheriff officers. The sale can be by public roup or auction and may take place in the debtor's own home but is more usually conducted in an auction room. The poinded goods are then sold and the proceeds used to pay the debt and the other expenses. If the poinded goods are not sold the creditor can keep them though he must pay for them.[22]

Poindable goods

9.14   Not all goods in the possession of the debtor are poindable. Broadly speaking, the necessities of life including basic furniture and the tools for earning a living are not poindable. Likewise medical equipment, toys, educational books and other items for the welfare of the debtor's family are not poindable. It is unclear how poindable televisions are. In practice there are three major impediments to the efficacy of poinding: the first is that when the sheriff officers arrive at a home where the goods are to be poinded the debtor will usually claim that all the goods belong to a third party—which may or may not be true but is certainly difficult to establish. The second, as was discovered when local authorities attempted to carry out poindings for recovery of the poll tax, was that sheriff officers were often physically unable to carry out their task of serving demands on debtors, make schedules of poindable goods or conduct warrant sales because of the crowds which would intimidate them on their arrival in some of Scotland's less easily controlled areas. Thirdly, the amount of notice required under statute ensured that some debtors had had time to take all their belongings away, hide them with friends and then leave the neighbourhood. In practice warrant sales, at least as far as the sale of non-business assets are concerned, do not generate very much by way of funds for the creditor since the goods are often tatty and elderly. At warrant sales there are usually many sets of

[22] Debtors (Scotland) Act 1987, s.37(6), (9).

golf clubs, musical instruments, cameras, computers and typewriters available. Warrant sales of businesses' assets are less common because any limited company which is in such financial straits that its assets are being poinded usually rapidly goes into receivership or liquidation anyway. Warrant sales are generally agreed to be a somewhat unsatisfactory and sometimes inhumane ultimate deterrent for a debtor who will not pay his creditors, but they do at least allow creditors a limited opportunity to recoup their losses.

Inhibition

Inhibition is an extremely effective remedy whereby a **9.15** creditor is able to prevent a debtor from selling or raising a security over his heritable property without payment to the creditor. Anyone who tries to buy property or receive a standard security from an inhibited debtor will find that the transaction is voidable at the instance of the creditor. Consequently no purchaser will complete the transaction until he knows that the inhibition has been discharged. Although an inhibition affects the disposal of heritable property, it is in fact a personal diligence, and prevents the debtor disposing of any of his heritable property in Scotland. An inhibition may be obtained by virtue of an extract decree, registered bond or protested bill of exchange (as with arrestments and poindings) and may also be available on the dependence of an action (*i.e.* the creditor, on raising a court action against the debtor, can ask in the summons for a pre-emptive inhibition to prevent the debtor immediately trying to sell his property once he knows that court action is being taken against him). It is usually possible to obtain an inhibition on the dependence only if the debtor is *vergens ad inopiam* (about to become insolvent) or *in meditatione fugae* (considering absconding).

Competition between heritable creditors and inhibiting creditors

The usual rule with inhibitions is that where a debtor has **9.16** been inhibited by more than one creditor, the first creditor is entitled to his debt, while a later creditor will have to take his debt from what is left over. If there is a heritable security in place over the heritable property, or in the case of a company a floating charge, registered prior to the inhibition, the heritable creditor or the receiver, as the case may be, is entitled to sell the heritable assets in question. In these cases, the heritable creditor or receiver will repay himself out of the free proceeds and the inhibiting creditor will be entitled to the balance, if any, of the free proceeds in priority to other ordinary creditors whose debts were contracted after the registration of the inhibition. It is unlikely that a heritable creditor would obtain a standard security over a property owned by a person who had been inhibited, since, as already indicated, the grant of the standard security would be voidable. It is possible that a company might grant a floating charge over its assets and undertaking while at the same time being inhibited. In that event, the receiver's claim to the heritable property would be postponed to the inhibiting creditor's claim.[23]

Landlord's hypothec

9.17 A landlord's hypothec is a right in security available to a landlord. It covers certain moveable items brought on to the leased property, even if they are leased from a hire-purchase company or goods on sale or return. It does not cover any of the items which are non-poindable.[24] The hypothec is in security for up to one year's rent only. If the landlord wants to realise his security, he must do so by means of an action known as "sequestration for rent" which must take place within three months of the last date for payment. Following decree in such an action, the landlord is entitled to send in sheriff officers to prepare an inventory of specific goods and subsequently to sell them. A landlord's hypothec is nowadays available only for town properties or agricultural land not greater than two acres in size.[25] Where a debtor has been sequestrated but his assets are subject to a landlord's hypothec, the landlord has a right to the assets in priority to the trustee in sequestration.[26]

---

[23] Insolvency Act 1986, s.53(3)(a).
[24] See para. 9.14.
[25] Hypothec (Abolition) (Scotland) Act 1880, s.1.
[26] Bankruptcy (Scotland) Act 1985, s.33(2).

Adjudication

This is a still valid but extremely rare form of diligence **9.18** whereby a creditor attaches (generally) heritable property by means of a registered adjudication obtained much as in the manner of an inhibition. Anyone acquiring the adjudicated property then becomes liable for the debt—thus effectively ensuring that the property is unlikely to be sold. Following certain procedures, the creditor is entitled to hold the adjudicated property for a period of 10 years, known as the "legal", during which time the debtor is still able to redeem the property. On the expiry of the legal, the creditor can obtain from the courts a declarator of expiry of the legal, which has the effect of precluding redemption and the creditor can take the title to the property himself.

Poinding of the ground

This is a form of diligence, again virtually obsolete, avail- **9.19** able to feudal superiors, heritable creditors and certain other persons who may have rights over heritage. The creditor, having followed the appropriate procedure, is able to poind the moveable assets of the debtor and his tenants up to the extent of the tenants' rent due and unpaid to the debtor. The reason for the obsolescence of this remedy is that feudal superiors' rights are now much curtailed, to the extent that feuduty is generally scarcely worth obtaining, and alternative remedies are more easily available under the usual terms of standard securities.

Maills and duties

This is a further virtually obsolete form of diligence **9.20** entitling a heritable creditor to attach the rents due to the debtor. In many respects its effect is to put the heritable creditor into the shoes of the debtor until the debt is repaid. Its objects are nowadays more easily achieved through the use of a standard security.

Civil imprisonment

It is still possible to be imprisoned for non-payment of **9.21** fines for contempt of court[27] or for wilful refusal to pay

---

[27] Debtors (Scotland) Act 1880, s.4.

aliment (maintenance and upkeep for one's spouse and children) when the debtor is in a position to do so.[28] It is sometimes threatened against obstinate individuals who refuse to recognise a court decree or recalcitrant debtors unwilling to provide for their families. Imprisonment does not cancel the fine or the debt.[29] In respect of aliment, the Child Support Act 1995 nowadays is much more likely to be used to ensure payment of such sums as are due.

DILIGENCE AND SEQUESTRATION

9.22 In countries where respect for the law is slender, when a debtor fails to pay his debt a creditor is likely to force entry to the debtor's place of business and remove an asset equivalent in value to the debt. Consequently the most fiercesome and the quickest creditors tend to be repaid in priority to other equally deserving creditors who may have been more gentle in their approach, discovering in the meantime that the debtor has gone bankrupt. In order to prevent this form of prejudice to creditors, the Bankruptcy (Scotland) Act 1985 has devised methods of ensuring that creditors are treated fairly in the context of bankruptcy. In particular, it states that any diligence carried out before or after the date of sequestration is treated as completed diligence.[30] So, for example, an arresting creditor who had arrested funds would not need to proceed to an action of furthcoming: the sequestration is equivalent to that action of furthcoming.

The "cutting down" of sequestration

9.23 Once a debtor has been sequestrated (*i.e.* adjudged bankrupt) his estate is vested in his trustee in sequestration.[31] No diligence may take place after the date of sequestration, even if the creditor was unaware of the sequestration. Any assets removed by or on behalf of the creditor must be returned to the trustee.[32] However, the position is more

---

[28] Civil Imprisonment (Scotland) Act 1882, s.4.
[29] *Glenday v. Johnston* (1905) 8 F. 24.
[30] Bankruptcy (Scotland) Act 1985, s.37(1).
[31] See Chaps. 10 and 11.
[32] Bankruptcy (Scotland) Act 1985, s.37(4).

complicated when diligence takes place before sequestration.

Arrestment and poinding

Where arrestment or poinding of the debtor's assets takes place within a period of 60 days prior to sequestration, or on or after the date of sequestration, the arrestment or poinding will not serve to create a preference in favour of the arresting or poinding creditor.[33]

9.24

Inhibition

No inhibition within a period of 60 days before the date of inhibition will serve to create a preference for the inhibiting creditor.[34]

9.25

Date of sequestration

The date of sequestration, in both cases, is the date on which the court makes an award of sequestration.[35] During this period, although the above methods of diligence may take place, the creditor effecting diligence is no better off than if he had been any other creditor. The diligence is thus sometimes said to be "cut down". All the creditor may obtain, in respect of arrestment and poinding only, is his expenses as a preference.[36]

9.26

Diligence prior to the 60-day period not cut down

If an arrestment or poinding took place before the 60-day period commenced, but the action of furthcoming or the warrant sale had not taken place, the assets arrested or poinded pass from the arrestee or the debtor to the permanent trustee in sequestration because all the debtor's assets or funds which have not been transferred outwith the 60-day period pass to the trustee.[37] However, the

9.27

---

[33] Bankruptcy (Scotland) Act 1985, s.37(4)(a), (b).
[34] *ibid.* s.37(2).
[35] *ibid.* s.12(4).
[36] *ibid.* s.37(5).
[37] *ibid.* s.31(1)(a).

arresting or poinding creditor is treated as a secured creditor, and the assets or funds (to the extent of the sums due) are then handed to the creditor. With inhibition the position is a little different. The inhibiting creditor is entitled to a preference over those who contracted debts after the inhibition but not over those who contracted debts prior to the inhibition.[38] The trustee in sequestration is still entitled to sell the debtor's property even though the debtor is inhibited: what the trustee must do is ensure that funds realised thereby are applied to the inhibiting creditor subject to the claims of prior creditors as stated above.

Equalisation of diligence and apparent insolvency

9.28 A further complication is that in addition to the 60-day rule narrated above, a second rule pertains to diligence. It is designed to deal with the fact that the 60-day rule only applies to the 60 days prior to sequestration.[39] It is often the case that diligence takes place more than 60 days before sequestration. Where arrestment or poinding has taken place within 60 days of apparent insolvency, or within a period of four months after apparent insolvency (a total of six months), it is open to the trustee in sequestration to cut down such arrestment or insolvency with the effect that all such arrestments and poindings are treated as ranking *pari passu* under Schedule 7, paragraph 24 of the Bankruptcy (Scotland) Act 1985. The significance of this is that although when a person is sequestrated he is apparently insolvent in terms of section 7(1)(a) of the Bankruptcy (Scotland) Act 1985, it is possible to be apparently insolvent without being sequestrated. This is because apparent insolvency can cover a number of other definitions, among them being written notice of the debtor's inability to pay his debts,[40] the granting of a trust deed for creditors,[41] the expiry of a charge without payment,[42] the poinding of the debtor's assets for rates or taxes[43] and the

---

[38] *Baird and Brown v. Stirrat's Tr.* (1872) 10 M. 414.

[39] Bankruptcy (Scotland) Act 1985, s.37(2), (4).

[40] *ibid.* s.7(1)(b).

[41] *ibid.* s.7(c)(i).

[42] *ibid.* s.7(c)(ii).

[43] *ibid.* s.7(c)(iii).

failure to pay a sum of £1,500 or more to a creditor or creditors following a demand in the appropriate form.[44] Under some of these the debtor could remain apparently insolvent without actually being sequestrated, perhaps because no creditor might think it worthwhile petitioning for the debtor's sequestration, perhaps because the debtor himself might be so bewildered by his debts that he would not even consider granting a trust deed or trying to obtain an award of sequestration. While he is thus apparently insolvent, creditors could be effecting diligence against him. But if they did so within the six-month period the trustee in sequestration, when finally appointed, could equalise all the diligence. As indicated earlier, sequestration has the effect of completing all diligence in favour of the various creditors,[45] and making them all rank *pari passu*. Schedule 7, paragraph 24 effectively broadens the net of diligence which can be cut down, and in theory means that creditors who have, say, arrested funds in the belief that the debtor has not been sequestrated may find that the sums arrested for their benefit have in fact to be shared out amongst other creditors notwithstanding the lack of sequestration at the time of the arrestment.[46] This rule extends the period during which diligence may be equalised and in principle is fairer to the general body of creditors, albeit at the expense of those creditors who were swiftest to carry out diligence against the debtor.

---

[44] Bankruptcy (Scotland) Act 1985, s.7(d).
[45] *ibid.* s.37(1)(b).
[46] *Stewart v. Jarvie*, 1938 S.C. 309.

CHAPTER 10

BANKRUPTCY I

INSOLVENCY

The process of bankruptcy in Scotland is known as **10.1** *sequestration*. The bankrupt is known as the *debtor*, and once sequestrated his affairs are looked after by a *trustee in sequestration*. *Practical insolvency* is the inability to pay debts as they fall due, though the debtor may in fact have plenty of capital—as in a cash flow problem. *Absolute insolvency* is when total liabilities exceed total assets. *Apparent insolvency*, which is a term several times encountered in this area of law, is defined at section 7 of the Bankruptcy (Scotland) Act 1985 ("the Act").

Apparent insolvency

Apparent insolvency is triggered by: **10.2**

    (a) sequestration[1];
    (b) bankruptcy elsewhere in England, Wales or Northern Ireland[2];
    (c) written notice by the debtor that he is unable to pay his debts in the ordinary course of business[3];
    (d) the granting of a trust deed for creditors (see Chapter 11)[4];
    (e) the expiry of the *induciae* of a charge (14 days) without payment (irrespective of the size of the

---

[1] Bankruptcy (Scotland) Act 1985, s.7(1)(a).
[2] *ibid*.
[3] Bankruptcy (Scotland) Act 1985, s.7(1)(b).
[4] *ibid*. s.7(1)(c)(i).

debt) arising out of either a decree, a registered bond or a protested bill of exchange[5];

(f) the poinding or seizing of the debtor's assets in pursuance of a summary warrant for rates or taxes followed by a period of 14 days during which payment is not received[6];

(g) adjudication of the debtor's estate[7];

(h) the debtor's assets are sold following a sequestration for rent under a landlord's hypothec[8];

(i) the making of a receiving order in England and Wales[9];

(j) the failure to pay a debt or debts amounting to more than £1,500 within three weeks following a requirement to do so by notice in the prescribed form—unless the claim out of which the debt arises is disputed.[10]

10.3 Apparent insolvency remains in place until either the debtor is discharged[11] or he becomes able to pay his debts and does so.[12] It is possible to be apparently insolvent several times in succession, perhaps by the expiry of several charges without payment.

SEQUESTRATION

Petitions for sequestration

10.4 Those who can petition for sequestration are the debtor himself, a creditor, an executor of a deceased debtor and a trustee under a trust deed. The debtor can petition for his own sequestration provided that he does so with a concurring creditor, who is due £1,500 or more[13]; or, in the absence of a concurring creditor, provided that the

---

[5] Bankruptcy (Scotland) Act 1985, s.7(1)(c)(ii).
[6] *ibid.* s.7(1)(c)(iii).
[7] *ibid.* s.7(1)(c)(iv).
[8] *ibid.* s.7(1)(c)(v).
[9] *ibid.* s.7(1)(c)(vi).
[10] *ibid.* s.7(1)(d).
[11] *ibid.* s.7(2)(a).
[12] *ibid.* s.7(2)(b).
[13] *ibid.* s.5(2A).

debtor's debts are greater than £1,500, there has been no previous award of sequestration within the previous five years, and the debtor is apparently insolvent or has granted a trust deed which was unable to become a protected trust deed because of a creditor's objections.[14] A creditor can petition for the debtor's sequestration, provided that the debtor has been apparently insolvent within the previous four months,[15] and the creditor is qualified (*i.e.* the debt is for over £1,500) though he may join up with other creditors so that the total sum due is over £1,500.[16] An executor can petition for the sequestration of the deceased's debtor's estate at any time.[17] The trustee under a trust deed can petition for the debtor's sequestration provided that the debtor has unreasonably failed to comply with any term of the trust deed, or any order arising therefrom,[18] or the trustee states in the petition that it would be in the best interests of the creditors that an award of sequestration should be made.[19] Trust deeds are explained more fully in the next chapter. A further type of sequestration, known as summary administration, and which applies to debtor's estates of less than £20,000, is also discussed in the next chapter.

Who or what may be sequestrated?

Under section 6 of the 1985 Act, the following can be sequestrated: **10.5**

   (a) private individuals;
   (b) the estate of a deceased debtor;
   (c) trust estates;
   (d) partnerships and limited partnerships;
   (e) bodies corporate and unincorporated (*e.g.* associations, clubs, etc.)

but not companies incorporated under the Companies Act.[20]

---

[14] Bankruptcy (Scotland) Act 1985, s.5(2B).
[15] *ibid.* s.8(1)(b).
[16] *ibid.* s.5(2)(b).
[17] *ibid.* s.8(3)(a).
[18] *ibid.* s.5(2C)(a).
[19] *ibid.* s.5(2C)(b).
[20] *ibid.* s.6(2)(a).

The trustee in sequestration

10.6 Only a nominated insolvency practitioner or the Accountant in Bankruptcy may be appointed a trustee in sequestration. Insolvency practitioners are specially qualified accountants and lawyers who are well versed in all aspects of the law of insolvency.

The Accountant in Bankruptcy

10.7 The Accountant in Bankruptcy is a designated official whose principal task is to oversee bankruptcies and the practice of sequestration in Scotland. He can, if necessary, also act as the interim trustee and/or permanent trustee in any sequestration. The Accountant maintains a list of insolvency practitioners who will carry out work on his behalf and he maintains a register of bankruptcies from which he is required to make an annual report to the Court of Session and the Secretary of State. If he believes that either debtors or trustees have committed any offence in connection with bankruptcy, he is required to inform the Lord Advocate who may institute criminal proceedings. These offences, particularly as they relate to debtors, are dealt with more fully in the next chapter.

The date of sequestration

10.8 It is competent to seek an award of sequestration from the Court of Session, but as a matter of practice it is generally obtained from the sheriff court where the expenses are less. Following the lodging of the requisite papers with the sheriff clerk, the petition is presented to the sheriff in chambers who will grant the "first order". Where a debtor seeks his own sequestration under section 12(4)(a) of the 1985 Act the first order will be the award of sequestration, and this will then be the date of sequestration. Where a debtor presents his own petition, it is generally granted swiftly.[21] Where a creditor or a trustee under a trust deed seeks an award, the first order will be a warrant of citation

---

[21] Bankruptcy (Scotland) Act 1985, s.12(1).

under section 12(2) for the debtor to appear before the court to explain why he should not be sequestrated.[22] The date of sequestration under section 12(2) is the date of warrant of citation to the debtor.[23] The significance of the date of sequestration is that from that date run the various time periods within which, among other things, creditors can challenge the debtor's antecedent transactions, the debtor can seek a recall of sequestration, and the debtor will remain sequestrated. The court will grant an award of sequestration only where it is satisfied that the requirements of section 12 of the Act have been fulfilled.[24]

Intimation of the award of sequestration

Following the date of sequestration, the sheriff clerk informs the Register of Inhibitions and Adjudications in Meadowbank House of the debtor's sequestration.[25] This means that the debtor is effectively inhibited from selling any heritage he may own with effect from the date of sequestration. The interim trustee, on appointment, will also intimate the award of sequestration in the *Edinburgh Gazette*, thus officially informing the world of the debtor's sequestration. He also invites creditors to submit their claims to him.[26] **10.9**

The debtor relinquishes control of his assets

If the award is granted, all the debtor's estate at the time of the award until his discharge belongs to his creditors, but the estate is placed in the hands of the duly appointed interim trustee[27] whose duty is to safeguard the estate. **10.10**

Recall of sequestration

It is possible for the debtor, a creditor, the interim trustee, the permanent trustee or the Accountant in Bankruptcy[28] **10.11**

[22] Bankruptcy (Scotland) Act 1985, s.12(1).
[23] *ibid.* s.12(4)(b).
[24] See para.10.4.
[25] Bankruptcy (Scotland) Act 1985, s.14.
[26] *ibid.* s.15(6).
[27] *ibid.* s.2.
[28] *ibid.* s.16(1).

to recall an award of sequestration within 10 weeks of the date of sequestration,[29] except where the debtor has paid all his debts in full or given sufficient security for them[30]; where a majority of the creditors live outside Scotland, so that it would be more suitable for the debtor's estate to be dealt with elsewhere[31]; or where there are awards of sequestration or other bankruptcy proceedings taking place elsewhere.[32] It should be pointed out that recall of the award is different from an appeal against sequestration. Recall is a wider term and allows those who were not party to the original petition to ask for it to be revoked, and a recall deals not only with the circumstances of the original petition but the circumstances at the time of the recall. Recall is available only through the Court of Session.[33] The court can recall the award if it is satisfied that in all the circumstances of the case it is appropriate to do so.[34] The recall places the debtor and anyone else involved in the position they would have been in had sequestration not been awarded.[35] The sheriff clerk intimates to the Register of Inhibitions and Adjudications that the award of sequestration is recalled.[36]

The interim trustee's duties

10.12 An interim trustee is appointed to look after the debtor's assets. If there is no nominated interim trustee, the Accountant in Bankruptcy will be the interim trustee.[37] The interim trustee then meets with the debtor, demands a list of his assets and liabilities within seven days,[38] and warns him of the dangers of continuing to obtain credit in excess of £250 without warning any lender first.[39] Likewise the

[29] Bankruptcy (Scotland) Act 1985, s.16(4).
[30] ibid. s.17(1)(a).
[31] ibid. s.17(1)(b).
[32] ibid. s.17(1)(c).
[33] ibid. s.16(1).
[34] ibid. s.17(1).
[35] ibid. s.17(4).
[36] ibid. s.17(8).
[37] ibid. s.13.
[38] ibid. s.19.
[39] ibid. s.67(9).

debtor is instructed not to pay any bills, nor let people remove his assets. The interim trustee can require the debtor to complete certain transactions or can close down the debtor's business.[40] The interim trustee posts a notice of the award of sequestration in the *Edinburgh Gazette*, thus alerting credit reference agencies and banks to the debtor's sequestration. The interim trustee can also decide whether or not to continue the debtor's business in the hope that when the permanent trustee is appointed he may be able to sell the business as a going concern.

First statutory meeting of creditors

The interim trustee *must* convene a first statutory meeting of creditors within 60 days of the date of sequestration.[41] The Accountant in Bankruptcy *may* convene one if to do so would be worthwhile.[42] At the meeting the interim trustee or Accountant in Bankruptcy, as the case may be, will table a statement of the debtor's affairs, and the creditors, under the eye of the chairman (usually the interim trustee, the Accountant in Bankruptcy or a creditor[43]) will have their claims examined. Each creditor must have submitted his claim, without which he will be unable to vote at the meeting.[44] The interim trustee or Accountant in Bankruptcy will then consider what the chances of repayment are.[45] Then the meeting will elect a permanent trustee who quite often is the interim trustee.[46] Once the permanent trustee has been elected, his election is reported to the sheriff and in due course confirmed.[47] The permanent trustee then receives an "act and warrant" which gives the permanent trustee the authority to carry out his tasks.[48]

10.13

---

[40] Bankruptcy (Scotland) Act 1985, s.18(2).
[41] *ibid.* s.21.
[42] *ibid.* s.21A.
[43] *ibid.* s.23(1)(b).
[44] *ibid.* s.22.
[45] *ibid.* s.23(3)(c).
[46] *ibid.* s.24(1).
[47] *ibid.* s.25(2).
[48] *ibid.*

Commissioners

10.14 Commissioners may also be elected from the body of creditors, to advise the permanent trustee.[49] Commissioners must not be associated with the debtor in a personal, domestic or business capacity.[50] They are used in a number of situations, such as interrogating the debtor, seeking replacements for the trustee if necessary, and approving or being consulted on various arrangements. Commissioners cannot benefit from their office and do not even receive their expenses. It is consequently sometimes difficult to recruit commissioners, though there is no obligation to have them. From the permanent trustee's point of view, he protects his position if he has discussed matters with the commissioners: he cannot then be accused of having acted arbitrarily.

Vesting of the estate in the permanent trustee

10.15 To have something vested in oneself means to be legally empowered to grant good title to it. The act and warrant states that the debtor's assets are vested in the permanent trustee as at the date of sequestration.[51] This means that he can sell them—unlike the interim trustee who has no such power except in respect of perishable goods.[52]

Powers of the permanent trustee

10.16 Under section 31 of the Act, the permanent trustee may dispose of the debtor's assets, including selling any heritage the debtor may have owned, may complete title to partly completed transactions and may dispose of the debtor's business. He may adopt any contract entered into by the bankrupt except where the terms of the contract forbid it. He has to take account of any interest of an entitled spouse in the debtor's heritage.[53] He has extensive powers under

---

[49] Bankruptcy (Scotland) Act 1985, s.30(1).
[50] *ibid.* s.30(2).
[51] *ibid.* s.31.
[52] *ibid.* s.18(2)(c).
[53] *ibid.* s.41.

section 3 to do whatever may be necessary for him to fulfil his role as permanent trustee, and in addition he has a policing role in that he must report any suspected criminal activity in connection with the debtor's insolvency to the Accountant in Bankruptcy, who may in turn pass the matter on to the Lord Advocate. In order to ensure the probity of the permanent trustee's intromissions with regard to the debtor's estate, the permanent trustee's accounts are checked by the commissioners or the Accountant in Bankruptcy where there are no commissioners.

The position of *acquirenda*

Although the permanent trustee can uplift sums due to the debtor by way of pensions and proceeds of insurance policies, receive damages or debts arising out of court actions undertaken on behalf of the debtor, and sell heritable and moveable estate, all of which were in the debtor's hands, or to which he was entitled, before the award of sequestration, the matter is more complicated with assets and income which come into the debtor's hands after sequestration.   **10.17**

Post-sequestration assets received by the debtor are known as *acquirenda*. If the asset in question would have come into the debtor's estate at the date of sequestration or during the time of his sequestration, then the permanent trustee is entitled to it,[54] as happened in *Alliance and Leicester Building Society v. Murray's Trustee*.[55] In this case, a disposition in favour of Murray, the debtor, and a standard security granted by the debtor in favour of the building society, were recorded about six weeks after the warrant the debtor for sequestration, the date of warrant being the relevant date of sequestration.[56] The effect of the warrant was to inhibit Murray from granting the standard security, even though he did in fact sign it and had it recorded. The consequence was that not only was the house that Murray bought deemed to be *acquirenda*, in that it came into the debtor's   **10.18**

[54] Bankruptcy (Scotland) Act 1985, s.32(6).
[55] 1995 S.L.T. (Sh.Ct.) 77.
[56] Bankruptcy (Scotland) Act 1985, s.12(4), and see para. 10.8.

possession after the date of sequestration, but also the funds advanced by the building society for the house-purchase were also *acquirenda* and could be used by the trustee for the general body of creditors. The building society was of the view that the sums advanced by them for the house purchase were secured and therefore protected from the trustee. It was held that the building society did not have a security as Murray had been effectively inhibited from granting securities. The building society merely had a claim as an unsecured creditor against the estate. As a matter of practice, in so far as the building society suffered loss, it should have been able to claim against the debtor's solicitors who allowed the transaction to proceed notwithstanding the fact that the debtor was in no position to grant a standard security.

10.19 The debtor is obliged to inform the permanent trustee as soon as he receives any *acquirenda*, such as lottery winnings or legacies. Failure on the debtor's part to inform the permanent trustee of any such *acquirenda* is a criminal offence.[57]

Income received after the date of sequestration

10.20 The position regarding income is different. Income received after the date of sequestration remains with the debtor,[58] although the permanent trustee is entitled to ask for contributions therefrom, provided sufficient remains for the debtor's aliment and any other relevant obligations (such as maintenance for an ex-spouse). If agreement cannot be reached on the level of contributions the matter can go to the sheriff.[59] In *Brown's Trustee v. Brown*[60] it was decided by the sheriff principal that the balance to be found between the conflicting demands of the need to provide for the debtor's family and the need to repay creditors should not be assessed on the basis of the extent to which someone might be able to repay a personal loan,

[57] Bankruptcy (Scotland) Act 1985, s.32(7).
[58] *ibid.* s.32(1).
[59] *ibid.* s.32(2).
[60] 1994 S.L.T. 470.

but should be assessed on a fairly restrictive basis that ensured a proper diversion of a substantial portion of the debtor's income to the trustee. The sheriff principal in this case may have taken note of the fact that a substantial portion of the debtor's income was being dedicated to the premiums on a life policy in his daughter's life. In turn the policy was being used as security for the purchase of a house by the debtor's daughter where the debtor was residing.

Assets held in trust by the debtor

The permanent trustee has no rights in assets owned by **10.21** someone other than the debtor albeit in the debtor's hands. In addition there is a large list of items which cannot be vested in the permanent trustee, these being items necessary for the upkeep of the debtor's family and unpoindable assets in terms of the Debtors (Scotland) Act 1987, s.16. The permanent trustee may not dispose of assets covered by the landlord's hypothec[61] provided that the landlord enforces his rights by means of sequestration for rent.

The permanent trustee and the debtor's heritage

The permanent trustee can, however, sell heritable prop- **10.22** erty, subject to the rights of any entitled spouse or the needs of any children of the debtor.[62] If there is a standard security over the debtor's heritage, he can still sell the heritage[63] provided that the proceeds will cover the security holder's debt.[64] The standard security holder in most cases would want to sell anyway, if it could. As a practical matter in domestic situations where the debtor's property is jointly owned with the debtor's spouse it is quite common for the debtor's spouse to arrange to acquire the debtor's share of the property from the trustee.

"Swelling the estate"

A further task of the permanent trustee is to maximise the **10.23** available assets, the proceeds of which will be used to

---

[61] Bankruptcy (Scotland) Act 1985, s.33(2).
[62] *ibid.* s.40.
[63] *ibid.* s.31.
[64] *ibid.* s.39(4).

repay the creditors. This is known as "swelling the estate". To do this he is able to look at certain antecedent transactions, these being:

(i) gratuitous alienations[65];
(ii) the recalling of a capital sum paid on divorce[66];
(iii) unfair preferences[67];
(iv) certain forms of diligence carried out within certain time-periods relative to the date of apparent insolvency[68];
(v) extortionate credit transactions[69] which can be varied or set aside by the courts.

(i) Gratuitous alienations

10.24 A gratuitous alienation is one whereby the debtor has transferred an asset, or renounced a right or discharged a claim, for less than full value.[70] Transfer may be to friends or family in order to frustrate creditors, or with a view to return at some future point. A gratuitous alienation can be challenged under statute or at common law, though the latter course is rare nowadays.

Challenge under statute

10.25 A gratuitous alienation can be challenged under section 34(1) of the 1985 Act by:

- a pre-sequestration creditor;
- the permanent trustee;
- the trustee under a protected trust deed; or
- a judicial factor

where, under s.34(2)(b):

- the debtor has been sequestrated;

---

[65] Bankruptcy (Scotland) Act 1985, s.34.
[66] *ibid.* s.35.
[67] *ibid.* s.36.
[68] *ibid.* s.37 and Sched. 7, para. 24.
[69] *ibid.* s.61.
[70] *ibid.* s.34(2)(a).

- the debtor has granted a trust deed which is subsequently protected; or
- the debtor has died and within 12 months his estate has been sequestrated or a judicial factor appointed over it

and the alienation took place on a *relevant day*. A relevant day means the day the alienation became completely effectual (such as, depending on the type of asset and the terms of the disposal of the alienated asset, the date of delivery, the date of recording or registration, or the date of payment) but this depends on who the recipient of the alienated asset is.

The status of the recipient

If the recipient is an associate[71] of the debtor, the relevant day is a day not earlier than five years before the date of sequestration, the granting of the trust deed or the debtor's death[72]; for anyone else it is a day not earlier than two years before the above date.[73] **10.26**

If the alienation took place within those time-limits, the court can reduce the alienation, thereby transferring the property (or sometimes, instead, getting the value of the property) back to the debtor's estate for ultimate division between the creditors. **10.27**

Grounds for exemption from reduction

The gratuitous alienation will not be reduced if the person seeking to uphold the alienation (*i.e.* the debtor or the recipient) can prove that: **10.28**

- at the time of the alienation, the debtor's assets were greater than his liabilities (*i.e.* that he was solvent)[74]; or

---

[71] An associate is effectively a business partner, a close relative, an employee or employer, or a company with which the debtor has a strong connection or over which he has substantial control (s.74). Curiously, the term "associate" does not cover such persons as fiancé(e)s, girlfriends or lovers, godchildren, cousins or even close friends.

[72] Bankruptcy (Scotland) Act 1985, s.34(3)(a).

[73] *ibid.* s.34(3)(b).

[74] *ibid.* s.34(4)(a).

- the alienation was for a proper price[75];
- the alienation was a gift for a special occasion such as Christmas or was a gift given to a non-associate for a charitable purpose and under the circumstances reasonable for the debtor to make[76];

though the rights of innocent third parties who subsequently obtain the donated items in good faith and for value are protected.[77]

10.29 The above requirements may be difficult for the recipient or debtor to prove, and five years after the event it may be difficult to establish whether or not the debtor was solvent. Accordingly, cases involving gratuitous alienations come before the courts fairly regularly, as in *Short's Trustee v. Chung*,[78] where, within two years of Short's sequestration, where property had been sold at conspicuously less than full value by Short to Chung, who had then transferred the flats to his wife for "love, favour and affection"—in other words, at no cost. The sales and the subsequent transfers were reduced and the flats were restored to Short's estate. This was beneficial for Short's trustee as the value of the flats had increased. Mrs Chung argued that she should be allowed to pay the difference in value between the price her husband had paid for the flats and the market value as at the time of the court case, but it was held that where reduction or restoration could take place, it should do so: only where reduction or restoration was unavailable should other redress be permitted.[79] Strict adherence to the wording of section 34 can result in unfairness to the donee, as the statute, as presently interpreted, does not readily allow an equitable remedy.[79a] Where a donee is required to return the property he received at an undervalue, he is

---

[75] Bankruptcy (Scotland) Act 1985, s.34(4)(b).

[76] *ibid.* s.34(c).

[77] *ibid.* s.34.

[78] 1991 S.L.T. 472.

[79] Bankruptcy (Scotland) Act 1985, s.34(4).

[79a] See also P. Eager, "*Shorts' Trustee v. Chung* Revisited", 1996 Prop. L.B. 22–2.

entitled to claim as a deferred creditor against the debtor's estate to the extent of the consideration paid to the debtor for the property. In practice, he would be fortunate to have his claim met in full, and could lose both the property and his money.

At common law

At common law there are no time-limits, and so a chal- **10.30** lenge to a gratuitous alienation may be made much earlier than under statute. If a creditor is suspicious of the debtor's actions, he can challenge the alienation. If he is successful the alienated asset is transferred back to the debtor (as opposed to the trustee) whereupon it would be open to any creditor to carry out diligence against it. This could be frustrating for the challenging creditor, since he could go to the trouble of having the asset restored to the debtor's estate only to find that some other creditor has carried out diligence against the asset before he does.

The problem with the common law is that to challenge an **10.31** alienation the creditor must prove:

- that the alienation was for less than full consideration;
- that it was to the prejudice of the general body of creditors;
- that the debtor was absolutely insolvent at the time of the alienation or became so as a result of the alienation; and
- that the debtor has remained absolutely insolvent since the alienation.

All this can be difficult to prove unless the challenging **10.32** creditor knows the debtor's affairs very well. In addition, it is a good defence to say that the alienation was entered into before the debtor's bankruptcy, as in *Pringle's Trustee v. Wright*,[80] where a deed was validly granted by a person who was solvent at the time he entered into an

---

[80] (1903) 5 F. 522.

undertaking, even though he was bankrupt by the time he executed the deed. It is not necessary to prove intent to defraud, though the issue of fraud arose in the case of *Dobie v. Mitchell*,[81] where McFarlane collected various moneys which were due to him, and gave the funds to his sister, Mitchell, to look after for him. She put them in a deposit account in her name, this being evidenced by a deposit receipt in her name. McFarlane then disappeared, having failed to pay Dobie what he owed him. It was held that if it were true that McFarlane and his sister had entered into a fraudulent scheme to avoid paying creditors such as Dobie, Dobie was entitled to have the deposit receipt reduced, so that the funds in the deposit account might be made available to McFarlane's creditors. In *Main v. Fleming's Trustees*,[82] Fleming spent much of his own money improving an estate which was held in trust for his children. Even when he became insolvent he continued to spend money on the estate when he should have been repaying his creditors. It was held that Main and the other creditors were entitled to claim from the trustees the amount which had been directed to the trust estate but which should have been used for Fleming's creditors. Likewise in *Boyle's Trustee v. Boyle*[83] the trustee was able successfully to claim that the need for the debtor's wife to have a house to live in was not a "true, just and necessary cause" which would allow the debtor to make payments to his wife for the house purchase instead of paying funds to the trustee for the benefit of the debtor's creditors. Under common law the rights of third parties, acquiring assets in good faith and for value from recipients of gratuitous alienations, are protected.

(ii) Recalling a capital sum paid on divorce

10.33   If, following a court order on divorce, a debtor pays a capital sum on divorce, and at the time he was absolutely insolvent or became so as a result of the payment, and within five years he:

---

[81] (1854) 17 D. 97.
[82] (1881) 8 R. 880.
[83] 1988 S.L.T. 581.

- is sequestrated; or
- grants a trust deed which becomes protected; or
- dies and within 12 months his estate is sequestrated; or
- dies and within 12 months a judicial factor has been appointed to manage his estate,

the court can make an order recalling the order for the payment of the capital sum.[84]

(iii)   Unfair preferences

Unfair preferences are transactions whereby one creditor is **10.34** preferred to other creditors, usually so that he is in a better position than the others when the debtor ceases trading. Unfair preferences often arise in the context of the repayment of loans from members of the debtor's family or where a debtor wishes to ensure the retention of a creditor's future goodwill should the debtor ever set up in business again.

Under statute

Under section 36 of the 1985 Act a transaction which is an **10.35** unfair preference is challengeable by:

- a pre-sequestration creditor;
- the permanent trustee;
- the trustee acting under a protected trust deed; or
- a judicial factor,

and section 36(1) applies to any such transaction taking place not more than six months before:

- the debtor's sequestration;
- the granting of a trust deed which becomes protected;
- the debtor's death where within 12 months his estate is sequestrated or a judicial factor is appointed over it.

---

[84] Bankruptcy (Scotland) Act 1985, s.35.

Exempt transactions

10.36 However, under section 36(2) the following do not count as unfair preferences:

- a payment in the ordinary course of business;
- a payment in cash, unless it was collusive in order to prejudice the general body of creditors;
- a transaction whereby there are reciprocal obligations (sometimes known as *nova debita*), unless collusive as above;
- the granting of a mandate authorising an arrestee to pay over arrested funds to an arresting creditor.

10.37 Where it is established that there is an unfair preference, the court can reduce the transaction and have the funds or the asset restored to the sequestrated estate. This is subject to the usual rights of protection for innocent third parties as stated above in the context of gratuitous alienations.[85] Note the advantage to the challenger that he only has to prove that the transaction took place within the six-month period.

10.38 For a modern example, see *Balcraig House's Trustee v. Roosevelt Property Services Ltd*,[86] where a partnership which ran the Balcraig House Hotel arranged to transfer some of the hotel's assets to Roosevelt Property Services Ltd as a means of repaying a debt of £20,000 lent by Roosevelt to Balcraig four years prior to the date of the partnership's sequestration. The transferred goods remained in the hotel. It was held that not only was this an attempt to create a security without delivery, which is not possible for partnerships in Scotland, but that the transaction was not in the ordinary course of business. The transfer of the assets was an unfair preference as it was an attempt to benefit Roosevelt at the expense of the other creditors. The transfer could not be said to have been in exchange for a fair price: it was in fulfilment of a debt, and consequently the court reduced it.

---

[85] Bankruptcy (Scotland) Act 1985, s.26(5).
[86] 1994 S.L.T. 1133.

As to the meaning of "collusion", it is suggested that there **10.39** must be a positive intention on both the debtor's and the creditor's parts to defraud other creditors or to benefit the particular creditor who has his loan repaid early or is given security over the debtor's assets, to the disadvantage of the other creditors. In *Nordic Travel Ltd v. Scotprint Ltd*,[87] a case decided before the 1995 Act, it was held that the creditor's knowledge of a debtor's insolvency did not of itself make an apparent preference objectionable, provided that the payment was in the ordinary course of business and notwithstanding that it was made in cash rather than by some other method.

Nova debita means "new debts" and in principle it is **10.40** acceptable for a debtor to enter into a new obligation for which he expects both to receive something and to give something in return. Commonly a debtor will obtain a new loan and in consideration of it will simultaneously grant a security over his heritable property. Provided that the two operations are reasonably close in time, the granting of security by the debtor will be unobjectionable. In *Nicoll v. Steelpress (Supplies) Ltd*,[88] a case decided under the similar provisions of the Insolvency Act 1986, s.243, Steelpress arranged that it would only supply goods to the company for which Nicoll was ultimately appointed liquidator if it knew that it was going to be paid. The company's account with Steelpress was in debit and unless it reduced the debit balance it would have attracted penalties. Accordingly, when the company was paid cheques for work it had done for other businesses, it endorsed those cheques in favour of Steelpress. It was established that these payments to Steelpress were entirely valid, as they had been in the ordinary course of business, and there was an exact element of reciprocity between the value of the goods supplied and the amounts of the endorsed cheques. The company's assets had not been diminished by the transactions and accordingly the transactions were valid and not reducible as unfair preferences.

---

[87] 1980 S.C. 1.
[88] 1992 S.C.L.R. 332.

At common law

10.41   At common law unfair preferences are known as fraudulent preferences. The significant issues at common law are
that in order to render the preference reducible it must be
voluntary and the debtor must know that he is insolvent.
In *Wylie, Stewart and Marshall v. Jervis*[89] an insolvent debtor
transferred his house to his father (who had lent him the
money for the house purchase) in the vain hope that he
could place the house out of the reach of his creditors. The
disposition in favour of the father was reduced. Unlike
under statute, there are no time-limits on a challenge at
common law. Those who can challenge gratuitous alienations at common law can also challenge fraudulent preferences. There are exemptions similar to the statutory ones:
non-collusive payments in cash in the ordinary course of
business in settlement of outstanding obligations are
acceptable, as in *Whatmough's Trustee v. British Linen Bank,*[90]
where the debtor, who knew he was insolvent, sold his
business and paid the proceeds to the bank in settlement of
his overdrawn account, and *nova debita*, as in *Thomas
Montgomery & Sons v. Gallacher,*[91] where a debtor granted a
standard security to a creditor who was concerned about
the debtor's creditworthiness. The security was valid in so
far as it covered goods supplied to the debtor in the period
between the grant of the standard security and the date of
the debtor's sequestration. Despite its name, it is unneces-
ary to prove fraud in a fraudulent preference, though it is
necessary for the challenger to prove:

- that the debtor was absolutely insolvent at the
  time of the preference or became so as a result of
  the preference;
- that he remained insolvent up to the time of the
  challenge; and
- that the debtor was aware of his insolvency.

There may be practical difficulties in establishing these
points, because the challenger may not know the extent of

[89] 1913 1 S.L.T. 465.
[90] 1934 S.C. (H.L.) 51.
[91] 1982 S.L.T. 138.

the debtor's awareness of his own insolvency. The creditor's knowledge of the debtor's insolvency is irrelevant, as was established in *Nordic Travel Ltd v. Scotprint Ltd.*[92]

(iv) Equalisation of diligence[93]

Simple equalisation of diligence within 60 days prior to the date of sequestration

One of the advantages of being sequestrated is that once **10.42** sequestration has taken place, no further diligence can take place against the debtor,[94] since all his assets are vested in the trustee. On sequestration, there is a deemed completion by the trustee of any incomplete diligence in favour of the respective creditors (with the exception of sequestration for rent[95]) though this does not necessarily mean that the creditors receive their funds: it just means that their claims are established and treated as all taking place on the same day. This process means that the creditors effecting diligence are treated as being equal with each other. Without this, the most pressing creditor, or the one who proceeds most swiftly to carry out any diligence, would be favoured at the expense of all the others. Creditors who had been less aggressive in obtaining redress for the non-payment of their bills might find that the more demanding creditors had taken all the debtor's assets already.

For the diligence to be cut down in this way by the trustee **10.43** it must come within certain time-limits. Furthermore this rule applies only to certain types of diligence.[96] Any arrestment or poinding within 60 days prior to the date of sequestration fails to create a preference for the creditor concerned[97] though he may get his expenses.[98] Likewise

---

[92] 1980 S.C. 1.
[93] See Chap. 9.
[94] Bankruptcy (Scotland) Act 1985, s.37(4).
[95] *ibid.* s.37(1).
[96] Technically, the rules relating to equalisation of diligence also apply to adjudication, poinding of the ground and maills and duties, though it is very unlikely that such types of diligence would be used nowadays.
[97] Bankruptcy (Scotland) Act 1985, s.37(4).
[98] *ibid.* s.37(5).

any inhibition in the 60-day period before the date of sequestration is ineffective to create a preference for that creditor.[99]

Arrestment, poinding and inhibition more than 60 days before the date of sequestration

10.44   If there is an arrestment more than 60 days before the date of sequestration, which is not followed up by an action of furthcoming, the arrested funds have to be paid over by the arrestee to the trustee, who then makes them over to the arresting creditor. The same is true of poindings: if poindings do not proceed to a warrant sale, the poinded assets still have to be passed to the trustee who then can make them or their value over to the poinding creditor. But with inhibitions, the trustee is able to sell the debtor's heritage, even though the debtor is inhibited, but the monetary effect of the inhibition is retained so that the inhibitor cannot stop the sale but can obtain the proceeds to the extent of his debt[1] at the expense of other later creditors. Earnings arrestments stop on sequestration.[2] A deductions from earnings order under the Child Support Act 1991 also ceases to have effect on sequestration.

Complicated equalisation of diligence

10.45   If the above diligences take place more than 60 days before the date of sequestration in terms of section 37(2) and (4), the diligence is not effectively taken over by the trustee. But under Schedule 7, paragraph 24 to the Act, any arrestments or poindings within a period of 60 days before or four months after the constitution of apparent insolvency[3] can also be equalised. So even if a debtor is not sequestrated a creditor might find that his diligence was taken out of his hands and added to sums ingathered by the trustee for distribution to all creditors. The equalised creditors then rank *pari passu*. This particular rule is not in

---

[99] Bankruptcy (Scotland) Act 1985, s.37(2).

[1] *ibid.* s.31(2).

[2] Debtors (Scotland) Act 1987, s.72.

[3] For the definition of apparent insolvency, see para. 10.2.

practice followed much, mainly because of the uncertainty which surrounds the precise date or dates of the debtor's apparent insolvency, and also because it is not widely known to be available. Nonetheless it is still a further sword in the hands of the trustee to ensure a fair division of the assets among all the creditors.

(v) Extortionate credit transactions

An extortionate credit transaction is, in broad terms, a loan **10.46** made on terms which are beyond the "ordinary principles of fair dealing",[4] and which require grossly exorbitant payments to be made by the debtor to a creditor. If the trustee discovers that the debtor has within the three years before the date of sequestration entered into such a transaction, he can apply to the court to have the transaction set aside.[5] The onus is on the creditor to prove that the terms of an apparently extortionate transaction are in fact acceptable.[6] The court can set aside the transaction in full or in part, vary the terms of the transaction or require the creditor to make over to the trustee any sums paid or any property transferred to the creditor by the debtor.[7] The sums or assets thus passed to the debtor's estate thereupon become vested in the permanent trustee.[8] This section of the Act was designed to strike at "back-street loans". It is not entirely clear how successful this provision has been. This is partly because there is similar legislation under the Consumer Credit Act 1974, ss.137–139 and partly because back-street loan creditors often have non-legal methods of enforcing payment.[9]

Further realisation of the debtor's estate

There are other methods the trustee can use to manage, **10.47** realise and swell the debtor's estate, such as completing

---

[4] Bankruptcy (Scotland) Act 1985, s.61(3).
[5] *ibid.* s.61(2).
[6] *ibid.* s.61(3)(b).
[7] *ibid.* s.61(4).
[8] *ibid.* s.61(5).
[9] See para. 5.17.

contracts, pursuing law suits, etc.[10] He can even renounce contracts[11] though to do so may cause the other party to the contract to raise an action for breach of contract—if it is worthwhile doing so. The trustee can have the debtor publicly or privately examined by the sheriff to find out any further relevant information.[12] Once all the assets are in the hands of the trustee, he must divide them up between the creditors. The creditors are required to submit their vouched claims under section 48 and the trustee can then accept or reject them.

Division of the debtor's estate

10.48 Once the trustee has collected as much of the debtor's estate as he can, the estate is divided up in the following order[13]:

- interim trustee's fees and outlays;
- permanent trustee's fees and outlays;
- funeral expenses of the debtor (where appropriate);
- petitioning creditor's expenses (where a creditor has petitioned for the debtor's sequestration);
- preferred debts;
- ordinary debts;
- interest on preferred debts and ordinary debts;
- postponed debts.

Explanation of the various debts

10.49 The trustees receive their money first as without it they would not carry out their work. Should the debtor die during the sequestration, or the sequestration be of his estate shortly after his death, his funeral expenses are deducted from the overall sum due to the creditors. The petitioning creditor is allowed his expenses, for otherwise he might find that although he had the satisfaction of

[10] Bankruptcy (Scotland) Act 1985, s.39.
[11] *ibid.* s.42.
[12] *ibid.* ss.44, 45.
[13] *ibid.* s.51.

bankrupting the debtor, he had had to pay for the privilege of doing so. This would serve as a disincentive to creditors to petition for debtors' sequestration. Preferred debts are those in Schedule 3, Part 1 to the Act, being mostly DSS contributions, debts to the Inland Revenue for the last 12 months in respect of PAYE for the debtor personally and for his employees, value added tax arising within the last six months, car tax within the last 12 months, betting, gaming or bingo duty arising within the last 12 months, contributions to occupational pension schemes, employees' wages up to the sum of £800 arising within the last four months, employees' holiday pay, any sums borrowed by the debtor to fund the wages up to £800 and holiday pay due to the debtor's employees, and any payments due by the debtor to any employees who are in such reserve forces as the Territorial Army or the Royal Naval Volunteer Reserve. Postponed debts are loans by the debtor or his spouse to his business, and a creditor's right to anything vesting in the trustee because it was taken back by the trustee following a challenge to a gratuitous alienation under section 34.[14] If there are insufficient funds to pay all the preferred creditors all they are due, the preferred creditors are treated as ranking equally and each is entitled to, say, 10 pence for every pound each is due.

The position of the ordinary creditors

Often the total value of the debtor's assets is insufficient to meet the claims of all the creditors, especially once the trustees' fees and the preferred creditors have been paid, thus leaving little left over for the ordinary creditors whose dividends may consequently only be a percentage of their claims. Occasionally there are sufficient funds to enable everyone to be paid, in which case there will be a surplus repayable to the debtor.[15] **10.50**

Discharge of the debtor

After three years the debtor is automatically discharged[16] unless, having regard to the debtor's assets and liabilities, **10.51**

---

[14] Bankruptcy (Scotland) Act 1985, s.51(3).
[15] *ibid.* s.51(5).
[16] *ibid.* s.54(1).

his financial and business affairs and his conduct throughout the period of sequestration, there are good grounds for having the period of sequestration extended for a further period of two years.[17] Once the debtor is discharged, he is free to start a new business in the role of a company director, stand for certain public offices and resume his normal business life. As a matter of practice he may have trouble obtaining credit because he will have been "blacklisted" by credit reference agencies.

Discharge of the trustee

10.52 Following the discharge of the debtor, the trustee sends to the Accountant in Bankruptcy his sederunt book, his audited accounts and a receipt for any unclaimed dividends. The trustee applies to the Accountant in Bankruptcy for a discharge of his permanent trusteeship[18] and the debtor and the creditors are invited to write to the Accountant in Bankruptcy if they have any reason to consider that the discharge should not be granted.[19] If the discharge is duly granted the trustee is discharged from any liability to the creditors or the debtor arising out of his trusteeship except where fraud has taken place.[20] There are similar rules for the discharge of the Accountant in Bankruptcy where he has acted as the permanent trustee.[21]

---

[17] Bankruptcy (Scotland) Act 1985, s.54(6).
[18] *ibid*. s.57(1)(c).
[19] *ibid*. s.57(2)(a).
[20] *ibid*. s.57(5).
[21] *ibid*. s.58A

CHAPTER 11

BANKRUPTCY II

TRUST DEEDS FOR CREDITORS, ETC.

The previous chapter narrated the main aspects of insol- **11.1**
vency as it relates to individual persons, partnerships and
unincorporated associations. However there are other
routes which a bankrupt person can follow, depending on
the size of the estate and the degree of co-operation
available from his creditors.

The trust deed for creditors

One of the problems with the procedure outlined in the **11.2**
previous chapter is that it is highly regulated, with strict
time-limits. This may not always be appropriate for the
circumstances of the bankrupt and indeed his creditors. It
is possible instead to use a trust deed, which is a unilateral
undertaking by a debtor to convey all or some of his assets
and all or some of his future income to a trustee, who will
then disburse any sums arising therefrom to the debtor's
creditors in satisfaction of their debts. The trustee then
takes over the debtor's business and acts in many respects
like a permanent trustee in sequestration, except that the
trustee has none of the permanent trustee's power to
reduce antecedent transactions and equalise diligence.
Once he has gathered in such of the debtor's estate as is
covered by the trust deed, he pays dividends to the
creditors in the usual manner, and ultimately he is discharged. However, as a trust deed is a unilateral undertaking, it is binding on the debtor but not on the creditors.
Creditors will be willing to agree to a trust deed only if
they believe it is worthwhile in their greater long-term

interest. If they do agree they are subsequently barred from objecting to its terms. However there is often little incentive for creditors to accede to a trust deed, since to do so would bar them from sequestrating the debtor if they subsequently believed that that might be more advantageous to them.

The former abuse of the trust deed procedure

11.3 Until the introduction of the Bankruptcy (Scotland) Act 1993 it was possible for debtors to arrange their own sequestration. This was a convenient way of allowing debtors to avoid paying their debts, often without the creditors being aware of the debtor's sequestration. In addition the Government paid the fees for the trustee in sequestration where there were insufficient assets in the debtor's estate. This was an unforeseen consequence of the Bankruptcy (Scotland) Act 1985. One of the methods particularly favoured by debtors and their trustees was the "trust deed route". A trustee acting under a trust deed could petition for the debtor's sequestration, thereby relieving the debtor from any further diligence and responsibility for his debts, while ensuring that the taxpayer paid the trustee's fees. Since the coming into force of the 1993 Act, a trustee under a trust deed can petition for the debtor's sequestration only where the trust deed has not become protected[1] or where the debtor has refused to comply with (a) any obligation under the terms of the trust deed with which he reasonably could have complied[2] or (b) any reasonable instruction to the debtor from the trustee.[3] Once a trust deed is protected, a debtor is precluded from petitioning for his own sequestration.[4]

The protected trust deed

11.4 In order to deal with precisely this problem, the Act set up a new mechanism known as the protected trust deed. Where:

[1] Bankruptcy (Scotland) Act 1993, s.5(2B)(c)(ii).
[2] *ibid*. s.5(2C)(a)(i).
[3] *ibid*. s.5(2C)(a)(ii).
[4] *ibid*. Sched. 5, para. 6(b).

(i) a trust deed has been granted by a debtor;

(ii) the entire estate of the debtor, with the exception of those assets which would not be poindable under the terms of the Debtors (Scotland) Act 1987, s.33 (these being assets held in trust by the debtor for another person and assets necessary for the maintenance of the debtor and his family), is conveyed to the trust by the debtor[5];

(iii) the trustee thereof is an insolvency practitioner and not an associate of the debtor[6];

(iv) within one week of the grant of the trust deed, the existence of the trust deed has been published in the *Gazette*,[7] and within one week of publication, the trustee has sent a copy of the trust deed to all known creditors[8] inviting them to raise any objections to the trust deed within a period of five weeks from the date of publication of the requisite notice,

and where:

(v) within that period a majority in number and not less than one-third in value of the creditors have not intimated that they object to the trust deed and do not wish to accede to it,[9] and

(vi) no objecting creditor or creditor who has not been informed of the trust deed has presented a petition for sequestration of the debtor's estate within a period of six weeks from the date of the publication of the notice in (iv) above,[10]

the deed will become a protected trust deed.[11] This is, however, subject to:

(vii) the right of an objecting creditor or a creditor who has not been informed of the trust deed at

---

[5] Bankruptcy (Scotland) Act 1993, s.5(4A).
[6] *ibid*. Sched. 5, para. 5(a).
[7] *ibid*. para. 5(b).
[8] *ibid*. para. 5(c).
[9] *ibid*. para. 5(d).
[10] *ibid*. para. 7(a).
[11] *ibid*. para. 8.

any time to petition for the debtor's sequestration
if he is of the view that the terms of the trust
deed relating to the division of the debtor's estate
are or might be unduly prejudicial to a creditor
or a class of creditors,[12] and subject to

(viii) the requirement that the trust deed is registered
in the Register of Insolvencies held by the
Accountant in Bankruptcy.[13]

11.5 The onus is on creditors to object within the time-limits if
they wish to prevent the trust deed being protected, and
failure to object is treated, on an "inertia" basis, as
accession. It is well recognised that two problems with
the above procedure are that the rules do not explain
what is needed for a "valid" objection nor cover the
position of the overlooked creditor, who is known to the
trustee, who for one reason or another never receives
intimation of the existence of the trust deed. Such a
creditor could find that the debtor is subject to the terms
of a protected trust deed and that there is nothing the
creditor can do about it.

*Position of creditors after the trust deed has become protected,
and discharge of the trustee*

11.6 Once the trust deed is protected, the creditors who
approved the deed's terms and those who objected or did
nothing are all treated alike by the trustee.[14] The trustee
then proceeds to ingather as much of the debtor's estate as
he can. He will then disburse it in the manner outlined in
the previous chapter, and within 28 days of the final
distribution will intimate the fact to the Accountant in
Bankruptcy.[15] He will then seek a discharge from the
acceding creditors which will also be intimated to and
registered by the Accountant in Bankruptcy.[16] This effec-

---

[12] Bankruptcy (Scotland) Act 1993, Sched. 5, para. 7(1)(a).
[13] *ibid.* para. 5(e).
[14] *ibid.* para. 6(a).
[15] *ibid.* para. 9.
[16] *ibid.* para. 10.

tively also acts as a discharge of the debtor's liability to the acceding creditors. However there are limited rights available to a non-acceding creditor to object to the intromissions of the trustee and therefore not to be bound by the terms of the trustee's discharge, thus permitting the non-acceding creditor not to give a discharge to the debtor.[17] One of the advantages of a protected trust deed is that there is a formal mechanism for drawing the trust deed to a close, thus effectively allowing the debtor to start his business life again. With an unprotected trust deed, it may still be open for the debtor himself to petition for his own sequestration, or for a creditor to do so instead.

Advantages of a protected trust deed

A protected trust deed has various advantages, these being:

11.7

- simplicity, informality and relative cheapness;
- there are no humiliating public examinations of the debtor;
- a debtor could still hold some public offices and might (depending on a company's articles) still be able to hold office as a company director;
- a trustee can challenge antecedent transactions (gratuitous alienations, unfair preferences, capital payments on divorce, diligence within certain time-periods), thus swelling the assets for the benefit of the creditors;
- once a trust deed is protected, no more diligence can take place against the debtor.

Advantages and disadvantages of an unprotected trust deed

There are few advantages to unprotected trust deeds. In order for an unprotected trust deed to be worth considering, the affairs of the debtor would need to be uncomplicated and all parties involved would have to be co-operative and reasonable. A non-protected trust deed

11.8

---

[17] Bankruptcy (Scotland) Act 1993, Sched. 5, para. 12.

might, however, be cheap to carry out. There are many more disadvantages. These include:

- the fact that a non-acceding creditor could still sequestrate the debtor during or after the period of the trust deed;
- non-acceding creditors could still exercise diligence against the debtor;
- the trustee cannot challenge antecedent transactions and prior diligence;
- there may be difficulties in persuading inhibiting creditors to discharge their inhibitions against the debtor when the trustee tries to sell heritage—and indeed there may be difficulty in giving good title to heritage anyway;
- an unco-operative debtor cannot be forced by the courts to co-operate in the way that a sequestrated debtor can.

Comparison with sequestration

11.9 Sequestration may be expensive, formal and require the intervention of the court. However because of this, standards of scrutiny are high, creditors will stand a better chance of getting some distribution of the debtor's estate, and the trustee has wide-ranging powers to swell the estate. The debtor can also be publicly examined and if offences have been committed, he may be convicted in a criminal court.

Composition for creditors

11.10 This is a little-used device available to debtors and creditors where the creditors agree to make a settlement with the debtor. The rules relating to composition are to be found in Schedule 4 to the Act. Its principal advantage is that unlike a normal period of sequestration which endures for three (or occasionally five) years a composition allows a debtor to be discharged from his debt before the three-year period is over. It is likely to arise where the debtor comes into sufficient funds, perhaps through inheritance or good fortune, or where the family and friends of the debtor decide to "bail the debtor out" such that his estate is able to pay at least 25p in the pound to the ordinary creditors (after the trustee and the secured and preferred creditors have received what they are due). If the debtor wishes to do this, he makes an offer to the permanent trustee who prepares a report on it and submits it to his commissioners, if any, or to the Accountant in Bankruptcy. If they are satisfied with its terms, a notice to that effect is published in the *Gazette*, all the creditors are informed and two-thirds of them must approve it. An application to approve the composition is placed before the sheriff who will, if satisfied with its terms, grant approval thereof. The composition will then take place and, following payment to all the creditors as directed, the debtor and the trustee are both discharged.

Summary procedure

This is a method of sequestration where the debtor's non-heritable assets are worth less than £2,000 and his unsecured liabilities are less than £20,000, and the chances of repayments to creditors are slender. This procedure is designed to be quick, cheap and easy. If a debtor comes within the above parameters, the interim trustee can apply for a certificate of summary administration ("COSA") at the same time as he applies for the act and warrant (to cite the debtor to explain why he should not be sequestrated). There is an exception to this general rule: if a debtor petitions for his own sequestration, the Accountant in Bankruptcy can apply for a COSA within seven days of the date of sequestration. The court will then appoint the Accountant as the permanent trustee, even though there has been no creditors' meeting (although in practice the Accountant does inform the creditors). It is open to the Accountant in Bankruptcy or other interim trustee to apply at a later stage too. Once appointed, the Accountant, or trustee as the case may be, is directed to proceed to realise the estate having regard to the financial benefit to the estate and its creditors of doing so. This means that where it would be uneconomic for the Accountant or trustee to investigate all the debtor's prior transactions or to trace all his assets, there is no requirement for him to do

11.11

so. While it is recognised that this may cause some unscrupulous activity by some debtors to avoid detection, it takes account of the fact that many small estates are not worth investigating. Once the Accountant or trustee has gathered in what he can and distributed the estate in so far as there is anything to distribute, the debtor and the accountant or trustee will be discharged.

CHAPTER 12

RECEIVERSHIP

PURPOSE OF RECEIVERSHIP

Receivership was introduced in Chapter 7 in the context of **12.1** floating charges. Receivers are creatures of English law, introduced in Scotland some 11 years after floating charges were established.[1] Formerly, if a company defaulted under the terms of a floating charge, the floating charge holder's only remedy was the particularly drastic one of liquidation. However under the Companies (Floating Charges and Receivers) (Scotland) Act 1972 receivers were admitted to the law of Scotland, thus bringing Scotland into line with the law in the rest of the United Kingdom. Consequently, when a company defaults under the terms of a debenture or bond and floating charge, the floating charge holder will now arrange for the appointment of a receiver. Once the appointed receiver has complied with the formalities of the appointment under the Insolvency Act 1986, s.53, the floating charge is deemed to attach to the assets secured by the floating charge (a process nowadays more commonly known by the English term "crystallisation") and the floating charge is treated thereafter as a fixed charge. This means that the company's directors can no longer deal with the assets secured by the fixed charge as all such assets are under the control and management of the receiver.[2]

Disadvantages of floating charges and receivers

While it is true that the use of a floating charge allows a **12.2** company to borrow more money in a hurry in order to

[1] Companies (Floating Charges and Receivers) (Scotland) Act 1972.
[2] Insolvency Act 1986, s.53(7).

take advantage of a commercial opportunity, it is from time to time suggested that the ease of granting a floating charge encourages "bad" lending, in other words, lending which is not perhaps commercially justified or prudent. On occasion it might actually be better for the financial health of a company if it learned to live without borrowing, or financed its undertakings from internally generated funds, rather than relying on a bank. A second objection to floating charges and receivers is that the advantageous position which a floating charge enjoys, and consequently which a receiver enjoys in relation to other creditors, means that unsecured creditors, who are probably less able to cope with their debtors' defaults, are placed in a weak position compared to floating charge-holding banks which, generally speaking, can afford to cope with default. A third objection is that as receivership is relatively easy to operate from a floating charge holder's point of view, some holders are said to be keener to safeguard their own loans by appointing a receiver rather than to provide a helping hand to a company in financial difficulties. One final objection, seen from the floating charge holder's perspective, is that increasingly the receiver's privileged position is being eroded by the use of retention of title clauses. This will be discussed in paragraph 12.15.

The task of the receiver

12.3   A receiver is appointed by the floating charge holder for one principal purpose, which is to recover the funds advanced by and obtain the sums due to the floating charge holder. He does this, as narrated in Chapter 7, by gathering in the assets secured by the crystallised floating charge which usually traps most assets owned by the company, although certain assets may be reserved to other parties, such as creditors with a prior-ranking security, or preferential creditors, etc. Such creditors will be discussed later in this chapter. The receiver is not necessarily interested in the greater good of the company, though he cannot act in a cavalier manner with regard to the company's assets. His main concern is to satisfy the floating charge holder.

The difference between an English receiver and a Scottish receiver

In England, the word "receiver" usually means a property **12.4**
manager who is appointed by a creditor to receive the
rents from a large block of offices or flats. A common term
of the English equivalent of a standard security (a land
mortgage) is that if the borrower defaults, one of the
lender's rights is to appoint a receiver to collect the rents
from the secured property in satisfaction of the debt due to
the lender. Such a receiver is different from the insolvency
practitioner who is appointed under an English floating
charge, under English law, over an English company's
assets, in order to obtain the sums due to the floating
charge holder. Such an insolvency practitioner is known as
an "administrative receiver", though confusingly, as a
matter of common speech, he is known as a receiver. A
Scottish receiver is therefore equivalent to an English
administrative receiver. The Official Receiver is a creation
of English law and is (loosely speaking) an administrative
receiver of last resort, available when no other receiver will
carry out the necessary work, through either incompetence
in the drafting of a debenture or absence of funds with
which to pay an administrative receiver. Scotland has no
Official Receiver.

The difference between a receiver and a liquidator

The essential difference between a receiver and a liqui- **12.5**
dator is that a receiver is interested primarily only in
looking after the interests of the floating charge holder.
Once the floating charge holder has been paid all sums
due to him out of the assets secured by the crystallised
floating charge, the receiver is discharged and in theory
the company may continue in business. Although this does
not happen very often in practice, there is no reason in law
why it should not. The reality is that once the sums due to
the floating charge holder have been paid there are commonly no assets left in the company with which it can
trade. In addition, having been put into receivership once,
it will generally be perceived as a credit risk and so will be
unable to attract further funding to continue in business.

Unlike the receiver, who only has to satisfy the one secured creditor, a liquidator has to act to safeguard the interests of the company and its creditors as a whole. A liquidator, once appointed, will usually turn into cash all the company's assets which he can lawfully take. However, in so doing, his rights in the company's assets are postponed to any creditor holding a fixed security (such as a building subject to a standard security, except to the extent that the value of the building is in excess of the sums lent in respect of that building) or a floating charge (except to the extent that the value of the assets caught by the crystallised floating charge are in excess of the sums due to the receiver). In a sense, the liquidator gets what is left over once the secured creditors and any others with a prior-ranking claim (such as suppliers with valid retention of title clauses) have taken what they are due. The liquidator divides up the remaining company assets among the unsecured creditors, and if anything is left over, the residue is divided up among the shareholders in accordance with the terms of the company's articles.

Difference between a receiver and an administrator

12.6   An administrator is an insolvency practitioner appointed by the court where the court has been satisfied that it would be in the best interests of the company and/or its creditors to be in administration rather than receivership or liquidation.[3] An administration order can be granted only where floating charge holders, if present, agree to it, or where, if there already is a receiver in office, the floating charge holder instructs the receiver to demit office. Receivership and administration are mutually incompatible. Administration effectively temporarily insulates a company from its creditors, during which period a receiver cannot be appointed. The relatively small number of administration orders granted each year suggests that floating charge holders generally prefer to exercise their right of receivership and obtain their money quickly rather than suffer the delay and expense of an administration order.

---

[3] Insolvency Act 1986, s.9.

Appointment of a Receiver

The appointment of a receiver in Scotland

The appointment of a receiver in Scotland is entirely 12.7
governed by statute, there being no tradition of common
law as there is in England on this matter. The appointed
receiver must be an individual qualified insolvency practitioner[4] and cannot be a partnership.[5] The grounds of
appointment are any specific grounds expressly stated in
the debenture or the bond and floating charge[6] and/or any
of the following:

(i) the expiry of a period of 21 days after a demand
for payment of the whole or part of the principal
sum secured by the charge, without payment
having been made[7];

(ii) the expiry of a period of two months during
which interest has been unpaid and in arrears[8];

(iii) the making of an order or the passing of a
resolution to wind up the company[9];

(iv) the appointment of a receiver by virtue of any
other floating charge created by the company[10];

(v) the making of an order by the court to appoint a
receiver[11] (this would be extremely unusual and
would be likely to arise only where there was
uncertainty about the wording of the floating
charge or doubt as to the validity or wisdom of
appointing a receiver).

Of these methods, the most common are the failure to 12.8
repay the full sum due within 21 days—21 days being little
time within which to refinance a loan for a company
probably already in difficulty—or failure to pay interest for

---

[4] Insolvency Act 1986, ss. 388–398.
[5] *ibid.* s.51(3).
[6] *ibid.* s.52(1).
[7] *ibid.* s.52(1)(a).
[8] *ibid.* s.52(1)(b).
[9] *ibid.* s.52(1)(c).
[10] *ibid.* s.52(1)(d).
[11] *ibid.* ss.51(2), 52(2) and 54.

two months or more. It is customary, but by no means obligatory, for a floating charge holder to warn the company that it is considering putting the company into receivership. When a company goes into liquidation, the floating charge automatically crystallises, thus preserving the receiver's rights in the assets secured by the floating charge. The crystallisation of any other floating charge, whether prior-ranking, postponed or *pari passu*, also automatically triggers the crystallisation of an existing floating charge.

The mechanics of appointment

12.9 Once the company has defaulted as above, the floating charge holder formally notifies the expectant insolvency practitioner that he has been appointed. The receivership starts at the date and time when the receiver receives the notification.[12] He must then accept the appointment by the following day if using the standard form known as the instrument of appointment.[13] The instrument of appointment, or a copy thereof, must be forwarded to the Registrar of Companies within seven days for registration within the company's register of charges.[14] There may be more than one receiver appointed[15] if the company's affairs are very complicated. There are separate, similar and probably so far unused provisions for the appointment of a receiver by the court.[16] The newly-appointed receiver must within 28 days tell the company of his appointment and publish it, usually in the local newspapers and the *Edinburgh Gazette*.[17]

PRACTICE OF RECEIVERSHIP

12.10 The receiver has a large number of powers granted to him under statute[18] and contractually under the terms of the

---

[12] Insolvency Act 1986, s.54(6)(b).
[13] *ibid*. s.53(6)(a).
[14] *ibid*. s.53(1), (6).
[15] *ibid*. s.56(3).
[16] *ibid*. s.54.
[17] *ibid*. s.65(1).
[18] *ibid*. s.55(2), and Sched. 2.

floating charge[19] to enable him to carry out his principal task of ingathering funds to repay the floating charge holder. If there is any doubt about whether or how he may exercise any of these powers, he may go to court to seek a declarator or decision on the matter. Commonly the receiver will dispose of as much of the company as he can, sometimes selling off whole subsidiaries or alternatively transferring profitable or marketable parts of a business off to a new "hived-down" company which he can then sell. He is able to sell heritage subject to the rights of the standard security holder and a liquidator must hand over to the receiver any assets which he has ingathered but which are in fact caught by the crystallised floating charge.[20] Out of the sums realised from the crystallised floating charge the receiver must pay any fixed charge holders what they are due and also the preferential debts. The receiver is the agent of the company[21] which means that in the absence of the directors[22] he has the authority to dispose of the company's assets in so far as they form part of the assets secured by the floating charge. He acts as an agent for a disclosed principal, the company, notwithstanding the fact that the ultimate beneficiary of his acts will be the floating charge holder. Under the normal rules of agency he has a fiduciary duty towards the company and accordingly is not allowed to take personal advantage from his position. He is personally liable when he makes the company enter into a new contract in the course of his duties as a receiver unless the terms of the contract provide otherwise.[23] The rationale for the personal liability was that no contracting party would wish to deal with the receiver as agent for a probably insolvent company. Making the receiver personally liable ought, in theory, to give reassurance to the contracting party. However, as personal liability serves as a disincentive to the receiver to make the company embark on any contract, as a matter of practice a receiver will invariably

---

[19] Insolvency Act 1986, s.55(1).

[20] *Manley, Petr.*, 1985 S.L.T. 42, and see also the Insolvency Act 1986, s.55(2) and Sched. 2.

[21] Insolvency Act 1986, s.57(1).

[22] See para. 12.12.

[23] Insolvency Act 1986, s.57(2).

have a clause in any contract with a contracting party stating that he is not personally liable and that he is acting as receiver only, not as principal. If the contracting party wants the business badly enough, he will accept such a clause. If the contracting party refuses to accept such a clause and the contract still takes place, the receiver is personally liable but entitled to be indemnified out of the company's assets[24] if there are any left after the preferential creditors have received payments of the sums due to them. A receiver will not be personally liable for contracts entered into prior to the receivership and which the receiver continues or adopts.[25]

The receiver and employment contracts

12.11 Following the decision in *Paramount Airways* (*No. 2*),[26] the Insolvency Act 1986 was amended to clarify the position of receivers with regard to employment contracts adopted by the receiver after March 15, 1994.[27] Where the receiver adopts an employment contract, he becomes personally liable for the payment to the employee of wages and pension contributions arising out of services performed after the adoption of the contract by the receiver[28] though he is entitled to be indemnified out of the assets of the company.[29] He cannot contract out of this liability to an employee whose contract he has adopted. A receiver is not deemed to have adopted an employee's contract because of anything he does (or fails to do) in connection with that employee within 14 days of his appointment.[30] This allows the receiver time to make up his mind as to whether or not to adopt an employee's contract of employment. However after the 14-day period has elapsed the receiver will be deemed to have adopted contracts of employment unless he has already formally intimated to those employees whom he does not wish to retain that their contracts are not being adopted.

---

[24] Insolvency Act 1986, s.57(3).
[25] *ibid*. s.57(4).
[26] [1994] B.C.C. 172.
[27] Insolvency Act 1986, s.57(2B).
[28] *ibid*. s.57(2) and (2B).
[29] *ibid*. s.57(3).
[30] *ibid*. s.57(5).

The existing directors and the receiver

The usual rule is that once a company is in receivership, **12.12** the directors have little further right to manage the company,[31] except:

- where not all the company's assets are secured by the floating charge, so that the directors could still manage what is left;
- where the directors resolve to wind up the company;
- where the company is solvent after the completion and discharge of the receivership, so that the company can continue trading.

There have been occasions where the directors have proved **12.13** successfully to the courts that the receiver was not carrying out an act which he should have done (as in the case of *Newhart Development Ltd v. Co-operative Commercial Bank Ltd*,[32] where the receiver failed to raise an action against the bank which had appointed him) in which case the directors were allowed to assert their residual directorial rights. The Scottish case of *Shanks v. Central Regional Council*[33] broadly followed this rule, but there has been a subsequent English case doubting it.[34] A recent Scottish case[35] on this issue was decided in favour of the receiver. It was held that directors could usurp the receiver's powers only where there was a conflict of interest or where the receiver had clearly abandoned some claim or entitlement which he should have retained. Where directors are able to assert their right to make the company carry out an act which the receiver would not carry, such as recovering a debt, the sums recovered are then added to the sums out of which the receiver will repay the floating charge holder. Although it

---

[31] It should be noted that despite receivership directors are still obliged to prepare and return the company's accounts and other statutorily required documentation to the Registrar of Companies.

[32] [1978] 1 Q.B. 814.

[33] 1987 S.L.T. 410.

[34] *Tudor Grange Holdings Ltd v. Citibank N.A.* [1991] B.C.L.C. 1009.

[35] *Independent Pension Trustee Ltd v. Law Construction Co. Ltd*, 1996 G.W.D. 33–1956.

may seem ironic that the directors' labours should merely reward the floating charge holder, it should be remembered that the more money the company pays to the floating charge holder, the less may have to be paid by directors who have personally guaranteed the company's debts.

What assets are caught by the crystallised floating charge?

12.14 The crystallised floating charge traps all the assets to which the terms of the charge relate. Usually the wording of a floating charge states that the charge is over "the entire assets and undertaking" of a company. What this means is the assets and undertaking of the company as at the time of crystallisation. This can mean all the stock, all the intellectual property, all the equipment and anything which is unequivocally owned by the company, including heritage not already subject to a security—even though there will be no mention of the floating charge in the Scottish land registers—and which is not in the process of being sold to a third party. In addition, where there is a standard security over heritage and either the standard security holder exercises his right under the standard security to sell the secured property or, more commonly, the receiver sells the property with an undertaking to remit the sums due to the standard security holder, the receiver will be entitled to any balance arising out of the sale of the property after satisfaction of all sums due to the standard security holder and to any preferential creditors.

Assets not caught by the floating charge

12.15 What a receivership does not cover is assets being used by the company, but not owned by it, such as goods supplied under valid retention of title clauses,[36] goods subject to hire-purchase agreements, leased goods or premises, goods and assets subject to effectually executed diligence[37] and goods or funds clearly and identifiably held in trust for another.[38] There is extensive legal literature devoted

---

[36] *Armour v. Thyssen Edelstahlwerke AG*, 1986 S.L.T. 452.
[37] See para. 12.17.
[38] *Smith v. Liquidator of James Birrell Ltd*, 1968 S.L.T. 174; *Tay Valley Joinery Ltd v. C.F. Financial Services Ltd*, 1987 S.L.T. 207.

to the question of retention of title and the question of how far title can be retained if the company, acting as a supplier, (a) sells the asset on to a purchaser buying in good faith without notice of defect in title (in which case the purchaser is protected by the Sale of Goods Act 1979, s.25(1)), (b) alters the goods sufficiently so that the goods cannot be altered back to their original state,[39] or (c) devises a method whereby the supplier retains a degree of ownership of any new product which the purchaser makes out of the supplier's goods and a degree of ownership of any funds resulting from the sale of the new product. This is a vexed and unresolved area of law, with much depending on the precise wording of the retention of title clause in each case. The issue of retention of title applies to receivership (and to liquidation too) in two ways. Where a company which supplies goods goes into receivership, the receiver will wish to be able to recover goods which are in the hands of third parties if the company still has title to them, because in so doing he increases the sum due to the floating charge holder. The receiver may then attempt to trace the funds due to the company. Equally, where a purchasing company goes into receivership, the suppliers will wish to retrieve their goods from the receiver, thus diminishing the sums available to the floating charge holder. It must not be forgotten that although the receiver catches all the above assets covered by the floating charge, he may not necessarily be able to pay the entire value of those assets to the floating charge holder because of the requirement that he pay the preferential creditors first[40] before remitting the balance to the floating charge holder.

To what extent is heritage caught by a floating charge?

The most difficult issue at present regarding the assets **12.16** which a receiver can take relates to heritage. Until the case

---

[39] Known technically as *specificatio*, the rule being that altered goods belong to the workman, and goods which can be restored to their original position belong to the supplier (Bell, *Principles* (10th ed.), p. 1298(1)).

[40] Insolvency Act 1986, s.59(1).

of *Sharp v. Thomson*[41] it was believed that any heritage a company owned, right up to the moment that a purchaser of the heritage recorded a disposition of that heritage, could be seized by a receiver appointed by that company's floating charge holder, subject to the rights of any prior-ranking security. As this placed a purchaser from a company at some risk, the company's solicitor would provide a purchaser's solicitor with a letter, known as a letter of non-crystallisation, from the company's floating charge holder, confirming that the floating charge holder consented to the sale provided that the disposition in favour of the purchaser was recorded within seven or 14 days (as the case might be) and that during that time the floating charge holder would not put the company into receivership. This was because the floating charge holder usually would be receiving the proceeds of sale anyway. However, in the case of *Sharp v. Thomson* the purchaser's solicitors did not obtain such a letter. The solicitors concluded missives (the first stage in a Scottish property transaction) with a building company, the purchase price was paid and the purchasers expected to be living in their new house—all before the recording of the disposition. The company was put into receivership and the receiver proposed to keep not only the purchase price but also the house itself, in effect obtaining a double benefit, and thus leaving the unfortunate purchasers both homeless and penniless. It was confidently expected that, regrettable as this might be, the purchasers' remedy was ultimately against their solicitors. However, the House of Lords held that notwithstanding the absence of the recording of the disposition, the purchasers were entitled to retain their house, as they had, after all, paid for it already. This decision was well received by consumer groups, who saw no reason why the innocent consumers (the purchasers) should have to suffer from something completely beyond their control, but less well received by lawyers, who have now lost their faith in the long-standing precept that a purchaser has good title to heritage only once the disposition of the heritage is recorded (or registered) in the appropriate land register.

[41] 1997 S.C.L.R. 328 (HL).

This begs the question of when exactly title to heritage passes. There has been much academic discussion of the above decision and it remains to be seen what the long-term implications of this decision are: it is possible that new legislation will be needed in order to revise this uncertain area of law. Notwithstanding the problems raised by *Sharp v. Thomson*, however, it is still the case that heritage which is not in the process of being sold to another party and which is not subject to a prior-ranking security can be seized by the receiver; or if the property is subject to such a security, the receiver is entitled to the balance after satisfaction of the sums due under the prior ranking security.

Receivership and effectually executed diligence

As narrated in Chapter 9, diligence is the term for the **12.17** enforcement of a court decree. Usually a receiver's right to an asset of the company is subject to effectually executed diligence, that is, diligence which has completed all the procedural steps necessary to take the asset into the hands of the creditor effecting the diligence. Some forms of diligence, in particular arrestment, have more than one stage, and for the diligence to be "effectually executed" the arrestment must have been followed up by an action of furthcoming.[42] Similarly, in the case of a poinding, a warrant sale must have taken place. In respect of inhibitions, a creditor who inhibits a company which has already granted a floating charge may find that the inhibition does not secure him priority over all other creditors. In *Armour & Mycroft, Petitioners*[43] the joint receivers of a company applied to the court under the then equivalent of the Insolvency Act 1986, s.61, for authority to sell the company's property free of any encumbrance. The court held that the petitioners could indeed override the inhibition, that the receiver's claims should first be satisfied out of the funds generated by the sale of the company's property, but that the inhibiting creditors should be entitled to the remaining proceeds of sale in priority to the other ordinary

---

[42] *Lord Advocate v. Royal Bank of Scotland*, 1978 S.L.T. 38.
[43] 1983 S.L.T. 453.

creditors. Section 61 confers upon the court discretion to permit receivers to sell charged or encumbered property on such terms and conditions as it sees fit.[44]

The receiver and prior-ranking securities arising by operation of law

12.18 A receiver's rights may also be postponed to a prior-ranking security arising by operation of law, such as a landlord's hypothec followed by a sequestration for rent.[45]

Invalidity of appointment of a receiver

12.19 A receiver might find that his appointment was invalid if:

    (i) the floating charge was in itself invalid, perhaps because it had not been registered within the required 21-day period[46];

    (ii) in the event of the company being in insolvent liquidation, the floating charge had been granted within six months of the date of insolvent liquidation and came within the ambit of the rules relating to unfair preferences in terms of the Insolvency Act 1986, s.243(1)[47];

    (iii) the floating charge was granted within either two years of winding-up in favour of a person connected with the company, or one year of winding-up in favour of anyone else, at a time when the company was insolvent, and the floating charge was a gratuitous alienation in terms of the Insolvency Act 1986, s.245[48];

    (iv) the floating charge was granted between the presentation of a petition for the granting of an

---

[44] Insolvency Act 1986, s.61(2).
[45] *Grampian Regional Council v. Drill Stem (Inspection Services) Ltd (in receivership) and Smith International (North Sea) Ltd as minuters*, 1994 S.C.L.R. 36.
[46] Companies Act 1985, s.410.
[47] See Chap. 13.
[48] See Chap. 13.

administration order and the actual granting of
the order[49];

(v) an administration order was already in place[50];

(vi) the floating charge was part of an extortionate
credit transaction which could be struck down by
the courts[51];

(vii) the precise grounds for appointment in term of
the floating charge had not occurred, or the
procedure for appointment had not been properly followed.

Where the receiver is invalidly appointed because of a
defect in the floating charge, there may be a personal
action against the receiver.[52]

PAYMENT BY THE RECEIVER

Receivership and set-off (compensation)

The position of set-off in receivership is not entirely clear, **12.20**
and probably needs to be resolved by statute as suggested
by the Scottish Law Commission.[53] The problem arises out
of the fact that although receivership often involves the
insolvency of a company, it is possible to put a company
into receivership without the company actually being
insolvent. The grounds for receivership could be the
failure to perform a certain task specified in the floating
charge, such as maintaining a certain assets-to-liabilities
ratio. If a particular receivership is not caused by insolvency, it is illogical to apply the usual rules of insolvency
to it. These allow for set-off, so that a debtor who is also a
creditor of an insolvent company may set off his liability
against his claim. It would appear that where receivership
is connected with insolvency set-off is available, at least as
regards debts incurred prior to receivership.[54] The Scottish

---

[49] Insolvency Act 1986, s.245(3)(c).

[50] *ibid.* s.11(3)(b),(c).

[51] *ibid.* s.244.

[52] *Windsor Refrigerator Co. Ltd v. Branch Nominees Ltd* [1961] Ch. 375.

[53] Consultative Memorandum No. 72.

[54] *Forth and Clyde Construction Co. Ltd v. Trinity Timber and Plywood Co.
Ltd,* 1984 S.L.T. 94.

Law Commission has recommended that this approach should be followed, and should be extended to receivership generally, even where there is no insolvency. This, however, has not yet been enacted and the position remains uncertain.

12.21   If a company raises proceedings against a government department, the Crown is not allowed, without leave of the court, to set off the claim in the proceedings against other sums due by the company to another government department.[55] This issue was touched on in *Turner v. Inland Revenue Commissioners*,[56] where the Inland Revenue was due money from a company in receivership but the company was due money from the Customs and Excise. The receiver was due to pay preferential debts to the Inland Revenue and the company was due to pay a further non-preferential and unsecured debt to the Inland Revenue. From the Exchequer's point of view, it was advantageous to set off the Customs and Excise repayment against the non-preferential debt, thus ensuring that at least some of the non-preferential debt was paid (which it might not otherwise have been) and allowing the Inland Revenue to make a full claim as a preferential creditor—thus diminishing the sums available to the receiver for the benefit of the floating charge holder. The receiver, hopeful of obtaining the funds from Customs and Excise, sought directions on the validity of this course of action. It was held that it was acceptable for any creditor entitled to both a preferential debt and a non-preferential debt to elect to set off sums it was already holding against the non-preferential debt; and that in this case in terms of the Crown Proceedings Act 1947, s. 35(2)(d), leave to offset the sums due by Customs and Excise against an Inland Revenue debt could be given, if applied for (though it was not sought at the actual proceedings).

The order of payment by the receiver

12.22   Once the receiver has ingathered and sold the assets secured by the floating charge, his first task is to pay any

[55] Crown Proceedings Act 1947, s.35(2)(d).
[56] 1994 S.L.T. 811.

fixed security holders (such as standard security holders)
what they are due if they have not already obtained what
they are due by their own actions; any unpaid creditors
whom the receiver instructed to carry out work for the
receiver[57]; followed by the receiver's own fees, expenses,
etc.[58]; and the preferential creditors, out of the secured
assets. The preferential creditors are those creditors who
have responded to newspaper advertisements and a
Gazette notice by the receiver requesting preferential claimants to intimate their claims to him within six months after
the advertisement or the notice.[59] They are specified in the
Insolvency Act 1986, s.386, further details of which are
given in Schedule 6 to the Act. Briefly, the preferential
creditors are the Inland Revenue in respect of (i) PAYE on
employees' and others' wages for the preceding six
months; (ii) money due to the Inland Revenue or Customs
and Excise in respect of insurance premium tax, car tax,
betting tax, gaming duties, beer duty, lottery duty, air
passenger duty, social security and pension scheme contributions, levies on coal and steel production, and value
added tax, for varying periods of six or 12 months prior to
the receivership; (iii) wages due to employees up to £800
arising over the preceding four months, inclusive of holiday pay and of any monies borrowed from banks to fund
employees' wages to the above amount. If there are
insufficient funds for each creditor to be paid in full, their
claims are abated proportionally. Only after all these have
been paid is any balance remitted to the floating charge
holder. If, after satisfaction of the sums due to him, there
are still some funds left over, they should be passed to any
other postponed receiver, any lower-ranking fixed security
holder, the company (if it is still solvent) or the liquidator
(if it is not).[60]

Further tasks of the receiver

Before the receiver demits office having carried out his   **12.23**
task for the floating charge holder, it is his duty to report

---

[57] Insolvency Act 1986, s.60(1)(d).
[58] *ibid.*
[59] Insolvency Act 1986, s.59(2).
[60] *ibid.* s.60(2).

to the Secretary of State if he considers that there is anything that should be reported concerning the behaviour of any directors of a company which has gone into receivership. This is to enable the Secretary of State to commence proceedings to have the directors banned from being directors under the Company Directors Disqualification Act 1986. Unlike a liquidator, however, a receiver cannot apply to the court for an order requiring an errant director to compensate the company (and indirectly the floating charge holder) where he has caused the company to trade fraudulently[61] or wrongfully,[62] to trade as a phoenix company,[63] or where the director has breached his fiduciary or other duties to the company.[64] As only a liquidator (or an administrator) can do this, it may be necessary for the liquidator to obtain compensation in this manner. Ironically, the compensation payments could probably then be seized by the receiver.[65] Regrettably, the Insolvency Act 1986 omitted to state what should be done with sums recovered by way of compensation under sections 212–214 and under sections 238–244 other than passing them to the liquidator. The receiver must also send the statements of his accounts from time to time to the Registrar of Companies, together with his notice of vacation of office on the termination of the receivership.[66]

Problems with cross-border receiverships

12.24   A receiver appointed in Scotland is able to exercise his powers outside Scotland and elsewhere within Great Britain provided that this is not contrary to any rule of law operating in that other part of Great Britain.[67] Likewise any non-Scottish receiver can exercise his powers in Scotland save where his powers are contrary to Scots law. This

---

[61] Insolvency Act 1986, s.213.
[62] *ibid.* s.214.
[63] *ibid.* s.216.
[64] *ibid.* s.212.
[65] Following on the principle of *Ross v. Taylor*, 1985 S.L.T. 387 where assets which came into the company after the receivership were held to be available to the receiver.
[66] Insolvency (Scotland) Rules 1986, Pt. 4, Chap. 4.
[67] Administration of Justice Act 1977, s.7, and Insolvency Act 1986, s.72.

could possibly cause problems where there is no true receivership as understood by Scots law. For example, an English fixed and floating charge would impact in Scotland in respect of the crystallisation of the floating charge and the subsequent appointment of an administrative receiver only. The conversion into a fixed charge (over heritage) without the appointment of a receiver could not be governed by the Insolvency Act 1986, s.72, and the newly converted fixed charge would not be recognised, since it is alien to the law of Scotland. In *Norfolk House plc (in receivership) v. Repsol Petroleum Ltd*[68] a fixed and floating charge could not be converted into a fixed charge over heritage in Scotland; but the appointment of a receiver under the terms of the floating charge was acceptable, and was sufficient to give title to the receiver to dispose of heritage. The aim of the legislation is to allow parity, consistency and ease of cross-border operations and in the above case the courts tried to follow that general policy.

---

[68] 1992 S.L.T. 235.

CHAPTER 13

LIQUIDATION

PURPOSE OF LIQUIDATION

Winding-up is a huge and complex subject and this **13.1** chapter does not pretend to do more than present an overview of the subject. For detailed points of the law reference should be made to specialist publications on this area.

Winding-up or liquidation?

Winding-up and liquidation are not exactly synonymous, **13.2** since any business could wind itself up by paying all its debts and returning its capital to the members without using a liquidator. But in common speech and practice the two terms are the same, the essential point of liquidation being that a company's assets are turned by a liquidator, who must be a qualified insolvency practitioner, into cash (or money's worth), and thereafter made available to those who are entitled to it.

The effect of liquidation

Once a company is in insolvent liquidation the liquidator **13.3** usually takes control of the company's assets. Shares may no longer be transferred.[1] Existing court actions will be stayed by the court.[2] The company usually stops trading though the liquidator may keep all or some parts of it

---

[1] Insolvency Act 1986, ss.88 and 127.
[2] *ibid*. ss.130(2) and 147.

trading in order that the winding-up may proceed more effectively or advantageously.[3] The liquidator will generally sell the company's assets for cash, and has extensive powers to help him do this. He is able to maximise the extent of the assets of the liquidated company by means of challenging antecedent transactions,[4] requiring directors under certain circumstances to compensate the company[5] and equalising diligence within certain defined time-limits,[6] all in much the same way as a trustee in bankruptcy can with a sequestrated debtor. After satisfaction of the secured creditors and the preferential creditors he divides what is left rateably among the unsecured creditors; and if there are still funds left, he divides those funds rateably among the shareholders in accordance with the terms of the articles.

The benefit of liquidation

13.4 The benefit of liquidation is that as a procedure it is open to judicial and creditor scrutiny, minimising the opportunities for fraud. Liquidators must be insolvency practitioners,[7] specialists in their field. Liquidators must procure an indemnity (known as "caution") for their actings, so that if they defalcate with the company's money, funds will be available to make good the loss. Creditors stand a reasonable chance of getting some money back if there is a fair system for dividing up the company's assets. In the absence of a system of liquidation the most aggressive creditors would receive payment at the expense of the others. Through the process of liquidation, entrepreneurs whose companies have been wound up are given the chance to set up new businesses unless their behaviour has been sufficiently heinous for there to be criminal or disqualificatory action taken against them.

Types of winding-up

13.5 There are three types of winding-up. These are:

---

[3] Insolvency Act 1986, s.87.
[4] *ibid*. ss.242–247.
[5] *ibid*. ss.212–217.
[6] *ibid*. s.185.
[7] *ibid*. s.230(3).

    (i) compulsory winding-up;
    (ii) members' voluntary winding-up;
  (iii) creditors' voluntary winding-up.

A compulsory winding-up is one ordered by the courts.[8] A members' voluntary winding-up is one voted on and approved by the members in the expectation that the company is solvent and that after payment in full of the creditors there will be funds left over to repay the members all or at least some of their capital. A creditors' voluntary winding-up is one voted on and approved by the members in the knowledge that there will be insufficient funds to repay anything to the members or that there will be insufficient to repay the creditors in full. In a members' voluntary winding-up the members have the greater say in the procedure of winding-up because they know that the creditors will be paid in full and therefore have no grounds for complaint. In a creditors' voluntary winding-up the creditors have the greater say in the procedure since it is their interests at stake. A members' voluntary winding-up sometimes turns into a creditors' voluntary winding-up when it transpires that the value of the company's net assets is less than initially estimated. A members' or creditors' voluntary winding-up is generally cheaper than a compulsory winding-up, mainly because the courts are not involved.

COMPULSORY WINDING-UP

Jurisdiction and grounds for compulsory winding-up

The Court of Session can wind up any company registered **13.6** in Scotland[9] but the sheriff court can wind up any company with a paid-up share capital of £120,000 provided the company's registered office has been in its sheriffdom for at least six months prior to the winding-up.[10] The grounds for the compulsory winding-up of a company are as follows:

---

[8] See para. 13.6.
[9] Insolvency Act 1986, s.120(1).
[10] *ibid*. s.120(3).

(a) where the members have by special resolution resolved that the company be wound up by the court[11];

(b) where a public company, registered as such on initial incorporation, has not been issued with a section 117 trading certificate and more than a year has elapsed since the company's registration[12];

(c) it is an old public company within the meaning of the Companies Consolidation (Consequential Provisions) Act 1985[13];

(d) the company has not commenced its business within a year of incorporation or has suspended its business for a whole year[14];

(e) being a public limited company, there is only one shareholder[15];

(f) the company is unable to pay its debts[16];

(g) the court is of the opinion that it is just and equitable that the company should be wound up.[17]

On a practical basis, it is almost unheard of for (a) to (e) ever to be used. Technically there is one further ground, available in Scotland only, being the winding-up of a Scottish company where a floating charge holder is concerned that his security may be threatened.[18] This is a relic from the time when receivers were not known in Scots law. The important grounds for winding-up in practice are the company's inability to pay its debts and the "just and equitable" grounds.

The inability to pay debts

13.7 A company is unable to pay its debts in terms of the Insolvency Act 1986, s.123(1), where:

[11] Insolvency Act 1986, s.122(1)(a).
[12] *ibid.* s.122(1)(b).
[13] *ibid.* s.122(1)(c).
[14] *ibid.* s.122(1)(d).
[15] *ibid.* s.122(1)(e).
[16] *ibid.* s.122(1)(f).
[17] *ibid.* s.122(1)(g).
[18] *ibid.* s.122(2).

(a) a creditor (or group of creditors) has served a written demand, in the appropriate form, on the company at its registered office, demanding either payment of the sum of £750 or more, compounding for the sum of £750 (which could be done by the debtor company making over to the creditor assets worth £750 or more) or granting security to the satisfaction of the creditor or creditors for the sum of £750 or more within three weeks after the date of service of the demand[19]; or

(b) in England and Wales, execution or other process issued on a judgment, decree or order of any court in favour of any creditor of the company is returned unsatisfied in whole or in part[20]; or

(c) in Scotland, the *induciae* of a charge for payment on an extract decree, extract registered bond or extract registered process on a bill of exchange have expired without payment having been made[21]; or

(d) in Northern Ireland, a certificate of enforceability has been granted in respect of a judgment against the company[22]; or

(e) it is proved to the satisfaction of the court that the company cannot pay its debts as they fall due.[23]

The demand for £750

To pay £750 within three weeks is in some respects a surprisingly small amount of money for which to put a company into liquidation, and the Secretary of State has power to increase the sum due. The equivalent bankruptcy legislation refers to £1,500[24] and it is likely that the liquidation figure will in due course be increased to that amount. However, before attempting to put a company into   **13.8**

---

[19] Insolvency Act 1986, s.123(1)(a).
[20] *ibid.* s.123(1)(b).
[21] *ibid.* s.123(1)(c).
[22] *ibid.* s.123(1)(d).
[23] *ibid.* s.123(1)(e).
[24] Bankruptcy (Scotland) Act 1985, s.5(2A).

liquidation for the sum of £750, the creditor must be sure that the debt is indeed due.[25] If the debt is disputed, perhaps because there is a dispute about the quality of the goods out of which the claim arises, or the terms of the contract out of which the debt arises provide for payment to be deferred for, say, 90 days and those 90 days have not expired, the courts will not grant the petition for winding-up.

Executions of judgments, expiry of induciae *and certificates of unenforceability*

13.9 The above are all methods of enforcing payment out of creditors following a court decree or procedure equivalent to a court decree. Where the court officials (sheriff officers, bailiffs, etc.) are unable to effect payment, the absence of payment can trigger liquidation.

The inability to pay debts as they fall due

13.10 The inability to pay debts as they fall due is a particularly useful ground for petitioning for winding-up because there is no requirement to wait 21 days while the debtor company tries to find enough money to pay the petitioning creditor. During the 21-day period an unscrupulous company might try to dispose of its assets beyond the reach of any liquidator. The inability to pay debts as they fall due does not necessarily mean that the company is insolvent: it could mean that it is either dilatory about paying its bills or that it has a cash flow problem. Alternatively, under the Insolvency Act 1986, s.123(2), this phrase can also mean that the court is satisfied that the company's assets are less than its liabilities, taking into account its contingent and prospective liabilities, these being expected but not necessarily definite liabilities which are dependent on some other uncertain matter, such as the result of a claim for damages against the company. In order to bring a successful petition for winding-up on this particular ground it is necessary to

---

[25] *Re Lympne Investments Ltd* [1972] 1 W.L.R. 524.

have a good knowledge of the company's accounts. Such knowledge is likely to be available only to those closely connected with the company such as its directors, bankers, lawyers, etc.

The just and equitable grounds for winding-up

These grounds are a general category where winding-up **13.11** would be the most sensible or the fairest action under the circumstances. Historically, these grounds have been used:

(a) where the company failed to adhere to its object clause in its memorandum of association,[26] though following the decline in the importance of objects clauses since the introduction of the Companies Act, s.35(1), it is unlikely that the courts would nowadays wind up a company on that particular ground;

(b) where a company was founded for an illegal purpose[27];

(c) where there is deadlock in the management of the company,[28] although nowadays such an issue would be more likely to be dealt with by an arbitration clause in the articles;

(d) where prior to the company's incorporation or to a shareholder subscribing for shares certain understandings had been accepted which were subsequently ignored by the majority of the shareholders (the cases being decided on this ground being sometimes known as "quasi-partnership" cases)[29];

(e) where there has been oppressive conduct by the majority shareholders and/or directors[30];

[26] *Re German Date Coffee Co.* (1882) 20 Ch. D. 169.
[27] *Re Thomas Brinsmead & Sons Ltd* [1987] 1 Ch. 45.
[28] *Re Yenidje Tobacco Co. Ltd* [1935] Ch. 693.
[29] *Ebrahimi v. Westbourne Galleries Ltd* [1973] A.C. 360; *Virdi v. Abbey Leisure Ltd* [1990] B.C.L.C. 342.
[30] *Loch v. John Blackwood Ltd* [1924] A.C. 783.

(f) where the directors by their actings collectively have lost the confidence of all or some of the members.[31]

13.12 In winding up the company on the just and equitable grounds, the court must be satisfied that no other remedy would be more suitable for the problem afflicting the company[32] and that the company is solvent, since it would be unreasonable to wind it up on these grounds if there were no funds available to the members anyway. The exception to the solvency rule is where the majority shareholders' or directors' actings make it impossible to establish the true financial position of the company.[33]

Who may petition to wind up the company?

13.13 The following may petition to wind up the company:

- the company[34];
- the directors[35];
- any creditor or creditors (including contingent or prospective creditors)[36];
- a contributory[37];
- the Secretary of State, under various grounds, of which the most used and useful is where he believes it would be in the public interest to do so following a DTI investigators' report[38];
- an administrator[39];
- a receiver in Scotland[40];

---

[31] *Handyman, Petr.*, 1989 S.C.L.R. 294; *Jesner v. Jarrad Properties Ltd*, 1994 S.L.T. 83.
[32] Insolvency Act 1986, s. 125(2). It is worth noting that many of the cases which relate to unfair treatment of shareholders, as in *Ebrahimi*, nowadays would be more likely to be resolved by the use of a minority prejudice petition under the Companies Act 1985, s.459.
[33] *Loch v. John Blackwood Ltd* [1924] AC 783.
[34] Insolvency Act 1986, s.124(1).
[35] *ibid.*
[36] *ibid.*
[37] Insolvency Act 1986, s.124(2).
[38] *ibid.* s.124A.
[39] *ibid.* s.14(1).
[40] *ibid.* s.55(2).

- the Bank of England if the company is a deposit-taking institution[41];
- the DTI if the company is an insurance company[42];
- the Lord Advocate if the company is a Scottish charity.[43]

Of all the above, by far the commonest is the creditor as petitioner. Assuming that the creditor's grounds for his petition are valid, the court will usually grant the creditor his petition for winding-up, even if by doing so he prejudices the position of employees of the company or other creditors. However, there is a residual role for judicial discretion in the Insolvency Act 1986, s.195, where all creditors' and contributories' views in all matters relating to the winding-up may be judicially considered. A contributory is someone liable to contribute to the assets of a company on winding-up, commonly:

- a shareholder whose shares are partly paid at the time of winding-up;
- a guarantor in a guarantee company;
- a former member who within the previous year has had his shares redeemed or purchased from him by the company out of its capital[44] or a director who has approved such redemption of purchase[45];
- a past member who transferred his partly-paid shares to another person within the previous 12 months[46] and the other person has failed to pay the outstanding balance on the shares,[47] but only in respect of debts arising while he was still a member[48] and only to the extent of the unpaid balance.[49]

---

[41] Banking Act 1987, s.92(1).
[42] Insurance Companies Act 1982, s.54(1).
[43] Law Reform (Miscellaneous Provisions) (Scotland) Act 1990, s.14.
[44] Insolvency Act 1986, s.76(3).
[45] *ibid.* s.76(2).
[46] *ibid.* s. 74(2)(a).
[47] *ibid.* s.74(2)(c).
[48] *ibid.* s.74(2)(b).
[49] *ibid.* s.74(2)(d).

In order for a contributory to petition for winding-up the contributory must be the one remaining member of a public limited company,[50] and was either allotted the shares or had the shares registered in his name for at least six out of the preceding 18 months[51] or had inherited the shares.[52] The Secretary of State regularly winds up companies in the public interest or where it would be just and equitable to do so.

The procedure for compulsory winding-up

13.14 Any petition to wind up a company must be intimated to the company in question at its registered office and to any others who may have an interest in the company such as any administrator or receiver. The company may, if there are grounds to do so, oppose the petition, and in response the court can grant the petition, dismiss it or adjourn for investigation. Prior to the actual winding-up order being granted a provisional liquidator may be appointed if the company's assets are perishable or likely to be removed.[53] Any provisional liquidator (or indeed any other liquidator) must find "caution" (*i.e.* provide the court with a financial guarantee or indemnity for his actions). Unless the winding-up order is granted on first application, there may be a gap between the presentation of the petition and the actual grant of the petition. During that period any creditor or contributory may prevent further actions against the company taking place[54] and any transfer of the company's property or its shares are void.[55] Once the petition has been granted and the winding-up order made, no further actions can be raised against the company without permission from the court[56] and there must be notices inserted in the Register of Companies,[57] the *Edinburgh Gazette* and local newspapers intimating the company's liquidation.[58]

---

[50] Insolvency Act 1986, s.124(2)(a).
[51] *ibid*. s.124(2)(b).
[52] *ibid*. s.124(2)(b).
[53] *ibid*. s.135.
[54] *ibid*. s.126.
[55] *ibid*. s.127.
[56] *ibid*. s.130(2).
[57] *ibid*. s.130(1).
[58] *ibid*. s.138(6).

The Registrar of Companies must be informed too. The liquidator appointed at the stage of granting the petition for winding-up is known as the interim liquidator, and he acts as liquidator until the first creditors' meeting at which he as interim liquidator demits office and a "full" liquidator is appointed. Quite often the interim liquidator becomes the full liquidator. During the interim liquidation, the interim liquidator may dispose of any perishable assets, investigate the reasons for the collapse of the company and obtain statements about the company's assets and liabilities from the company's officers and employees.[59] If the directors are fleeing the country, he can arrange for their arrest and have any company assets in their hands seized.[60] The interim liquidator must issue within 28 days a notice to convene a creditors' meeting[61] and the meeting itself must be held within 42 days of the notice.[62] If the company is being wound up on the grounds of the inability of the company to pay its debts, it is permissible to restrict the meetings to the creditors alone without contributories being present.[63]

The subsequent conduct of the liquidation will be dealt with after discussion of the procedure for appointing a liquidator in members' or creditors' voluntary winding-up.   **13.15**

VOLUNTARY WINDING-UP

Grounds for voluntary winding-up

A company can be voluntarily wound up, by way of either a members' voluntary winding-up or a creditors' voluntary winding-up, on the following grounds: **13.16**

    (a) when the time-limit for the duration of the company in terms of the articles expires, or when any event specified in the articles has occurred on the

---

[59] Insolvency Act 1986, s.131.
[60] *ibid.* s.134.
[61] *ibid.* s.138(3).
[62] Insolvency (Scotland) Rules 1986, r.4.12(2A).
[63] Insolvency Act 1986, s.138(4).

occasion of which the company is to be dissolved, in either case to be followed by an ordinary resolution[64];

(b) if the company by special resolution resolves to be wound up voluntarily[65];

(c) if the company by extraordinary resolution resolves that it cannot by reason of its liabilities continue its business, and that it is advisable to wind up.[66]

Of the above (a) might arise where a company was set up for a particular event, such as a festival or other commemorative event, which, once completed, would cause the company to have no further reason for existence, and (c) is useful because an extraordinary resolution requires less notice than a special resolution (14 days rather than 21 days) although where a company is able to obtain short notice of a meeting this may make little difference. Once the appropriate resolution has been passed, the Registrar of Companies must be informed[67] and the notice of the resolution printed in the *Edinburgh Gazette*.[68] Once the company has been put into liquidation, the company may no longer continue its business except for the better purpose of its winding-up[69] and its shares may no longer be transferred.[70]

Directors' statutory declaration of solvency

13.17   A directors' declaration of solvency is a statement made by the directors within five weeks prior to the resolution for winding-up (or indeed on the same day as but prior to the passing of the resolution)[71] stating that they have investigated the company's financial affairs and that they are of the view that the company will be able to pay its debts, plus any exigible interest, in full, within the succeeding 12

[64] Insolvency Act 1986, s.84(1)(a).
[65] *ibid.* s.84(1)(b).
[66] *ibid.* s.84(1)(c).
[67] *ibid.* s.84(3).
[68] *ibid.* s.85(1).
[69] *ibid.* s.87(1).
[70] *ibid.* s.88.
[71] *ibid.* s.89(2)(a).

months (or such lesser period as may be stated in the declaration).[72] The declaration must be accompanied by a statement of the company's assets and liabilities as at the date just before the declaration.[73] The declaration must be forwarded to the Registrar of Companies within 15 days of the passing of the resolution to wind up the company.[74] If a director makes the declaration without having reasonable grounds for his assertion that the company can pay off its debts in full within the time specified, he is liable to be imprisoned or fined. There is a rebuttable presumption that where the company fails to make full payment of its debts within the time specified the director did not have reasonable grounds for his assertion of the company's solvency. This accordingly lays a considerable duty on a director to ensure that he truly is well informed of the company's financial affairs and solvency before he makes his declaration.

Significance of the directors' statutory declaration

The directors' statutory declaration is designed to prevent **13.18** the cavalier passing of a resolution to wind up the company on a members' voluntary basis where in fact the company is insolvent and should be wound up on a creditors' voluntary basis. It is also meant to encourage directors to treat the winding-up seriously. A directors' statutory declaration is obligatory for a members' voluntary winding-up but not required for a creditors' voluntary winding-up.[75]

MEMBERS' VOLUNTARY WINDING-UP

Procedure for members' voluntary winding-up

Assuming that the directors' statutory declaration has **13.19** taken place, the members may resolve to wind up the company and appoint one or more liquidators.[76] The

---

[72] Insolvency Act 1986, s.89(1).
[73] *ibid.* s.89(2)(b).
[74] *ibid.* s.89(3).
[75] *ibid.* s.90.
[76] *ibid.* s.91(1).

directors' powers cease at this point.[77] The liquidator then carries on with the liquidation in the manner outlined in paragraphs 13.25 to 13.44 hereafter until such time as all the assets have been converted into cash, the creditors all repaid and the balance distributed according to their rights in the articles to the members. From time to time the liquidator will have to hold meetings of the members to keep them informed of progress and to let them see his accounts. Finally, there will be an advertised final meeting[78] and after the accounts have been presented and subsequently lodged with the Registrar of Companies, the liquidation will be over.

13.20 It may be asked why a company would wish to go into members' voluntary winding-up. In practice it is indeed not very common, but it can arise where a business has reached its natural end: the resource which it was using or exploiting has all been used up or there is no further call for the product which the company makes, and it is best to stop trading before there are any difficulties. Alternatively the members may take the view that the business, while solvent, is not sufficiently attractive to be worth selling as a going concern and the members would rather have the cash. Other reasons include the retiral or demise of the founders of the business with no one to continue it, or, more cynically, the directors' secret awareness of longer-term problems, such as anticipated environmental damage caused by the company's products for which the directors do not want to be held accountable in years to come.

The problem of the insolvent company

13.21 Although the directors, having made their declaration, may be of the view that the company is solvent, this view may be ill-founded. In that case the liquidator will convert the members' voluntary winding-up into a creditors' voluntary winding-up,[79] and organise creditors' meetings within

---

[77] Insolvency Act 1986, s.91(2).
[78] *ibid*. s.94(1).
[79] *ibid*. ss.95, 96.

certain time-limits[80] all in the manner of a creditors' voluntary winding-up.

Procedure for a creditors' voluntary winding-up

Following the members' resolution to wind up the com- **13.22** pany when they will appoint an insolvency practitioner to act as a temporary liquidator, the company will within 14 days arrange a meeting of the creditors. The meeting must be advertised in the *Edinburgh Gazette* and in two local newspapers.[81] The notice of the meeting will indicate the name and address of the temporary liquidator from whom creditors can obtain information about the company and the name and addresses of all the creditors. At the creditors' meeting (not to be confused with the aforementioned members' meeting), the directors will table and speak about a prepared financial statement of the company's affairs.[82] The statement should contain details of the entire assets and liabilities of the company, creditors' names and addresses, and details of any securities held by the creditors.[83] The statement must be supported by directors' affidavits,[84] the absence of which will be a criminal matter.[85] The creditors also can make their own appointment of a liquidator in place of the temporary liquidator. Often both the members' choice of liquidator and the creditors' choice of liquidator will be the same, but in the event of dispute the creditors' choice of liquidator will prevail[86] unless no choice has been made[87] or the courts decide otherwise.[88] Historically, some liquidators were sometimes a little too director-friendly at the expense of the creditors: the current procedure is designed to minimise such opportunities for inappropriate conduct.

---

[80] Insolvency Act 1986, s.95(2).
[81] *ibid.* s.98(1)(c).
[82] *ibid.* s.99(2).
[83] *ibid.*
[84] *ibid.*
[85] Insolvency Act 1986, s.99(3).
[86] *ibid.* s.100(2).
[87] *ibid.*
[88] Insolvency Act 1986, s.100(3).

13.23   Once the liquidator has been appointed, he exercises his functions in the manner outlined in paras. 13.25 to 13.44 hereafter. From time to time he will need to prepare and exhibit accounts and explain his actions to the members and creditors. Once the entire business of the liquidated company has been wound up, the liquidator calls a final meeting to explain his final distribution of the liquidated company's assets to the creditors, and intimates the end of the liquidation to the Registrar of Companies.[89]

Creditors' committees

13.24   There is no obligation to appoint a committee to advise the liquidator, but it is common to do so, as a way of ensuring that the liquidator bears the interests of the creditors and members in mind, and indeed to protect the position of the liquidator should he be called to account for unpopular decisions. The creditors have the greater say in the membership of the committee, subject to any contrary direction from the courts.[90] Generally speaking, creditors will not wish to have the former directors on the committee, since it is probably the conduct of the directors that caused the company to be in liquidation in the first place.

CONDUCT OF THE WINDING-UP

The practice of the winding-up

13.25   As stated earlier, the principal task of the liquidator is to raise as much money as possible to repay the creditors and, if possible, the members. This process, analogous to that of the trustee in bankruptcy, is sometimes known as "getting in" the company's assets. The liquidator is given substantial powers to enable him to do this. He is able to raise court actions to recover sums due to the company and he will ask all debtors to pay what they owe to the company. In addition the liquidator can do the following:

---

[89] Insolvency Act 1986, s.106.
[90] *ibid.* s.101(3).

(a) he can ask the contributories to contribute what they are due to pay[91];

(b) he can equalise diligence within certain time-limits[92];

(c) he can have certain antecedent charges and transactions set aside[93];

(d) he can set aside any extortionate credit transactions[94];

(e) he can have certain floating charges reduced[95];

(f) he can obtain compensation from directors and others in respect of misfeasance and breaches of fiduciary or other duties,[96] fraudulent trading[97] or wrongful trading[98];

(g) in the case of the winding-up of a phoenix company he can require any person involved in its management to pay its debts.[99]

In addition the liquidator has a large number of ancillary **13.26** powers to help him carry out his task. These are specified in Schedule 4 to the Insolvency Act 1986. If there is doubt as to whether or not he has the appropriate power for a certain action, he can always go to court for approval of his proposed action.

Payment by contributories

Contributories have already been explained in paragraph **13.27** 13.13. If they are due to pay funds to the company, the liquidator will call upon them to do so.

Equalisation of diligence

Diligence is the method of enforcement of a decree or **13.28** certain instruments of debt such as a protested bill of

---

[91] Insolvency Act 1986, Sched. 3.
[92] *ibid*. s.185.
[93] *ibid*. ss.242 and 243.
[94] *ibid*. s.244.
[95] *ibid*. s.245.
[96] *ibid*. s.212.
[97] *ibid*. s.213.
[98] *ibid*. s.214.
[99] *ibid*. s.216.

exchange or registered bond.[1] If a creditor carries out
diligence within a period of 60 days prior to the commencement of the liquidation, or within a period of four
months after the commencement of diligence, the diligence
is treated as taking place on the date of the commencement
of liquidation.[2] This has the effect of treating equally all
creditors effecting diligence within that time span. Without
this rule the company could be subject to repeated poindings or other diligence, or one creditor would unfairly seize
the entire assets of the company at the expense of other
gentler and slower creditors. The working of the rules of
diligence is taken entirely from the Bankruptcy (Scotland)
Act 1985, ss. 37 and 39, and reference to the discussion of
those sections in Chapter 10 of this book is recommended,[3]
with substitution of the word "company" for the word
"debtor", the word "liquidator" for the words "permanent
trustee", and the words "date of commencement of liquidation" for the words "date of sequestration".[4]

Setting aside certain antecedent charges and transactions

13.29 This too is broadly similar to the equivalent sections of the
Bankruptcy (Scotland) Act 1985[5] and reference should
accordingly be made to Chapter 10.[6] The two main types of
antecedent transaction are gratuitous alienations and
unfair preferences. A gratuitous alienation is a disposal of,
or granting a security over, an asset of the company for no
value or for less than full value or, to put it more
colloquially, a gift or a partial gift of the company's
property. Such gifts are commonly made by unscrupulous
company directors, anxious to keep the company's assets
out of the hands of its creditors. A liquidator (or indeed
any creditor or administrator[7]) may be able to challenge
any disposition of the company's property which took place

[1] See Chap. 9.
[2] Bankruptcy (Scotland) Act 1985, s.185.
[3] See paras. 10.42–45.
[4] Bankruptcy (Scotland) Act 1985, s.185(2).
[5] See *ibid*. ss.34 and 36.
[6] See paras. 10.24–30, and 10.34–41.
[7] Insolvency Act 1986, s.9(3)(b)(iii).

up to five years[8] before the commencement of liquidation where the recipient was an associate[9] or for up to two years prior to the commencement of liquidation where the recipient was any other person.[10] These periods are considerably longer than the equivalent periods in English law.[11] A successful challenge is possible where the person seeking to uphold the transaction (*i.e.* either the company or the recipient of the gift) is unable to prove that:

(a) at or after the time of the alienation the company's assets were greater than its liabilities[12]; or
(b) the alienation was made for adequate consideration[13]; or
(c) the alienation was a Christmas or festive present or a charitable donation to someone not associated with the company and it was reasonable for the company to have given the present or donation anyway.[14]

The second type of transaction which can be set aside is the unfair preference. This is the repayment of a creditor to the prejudice of other creditors. This might occur where a company has borrowed money from a director's family. The director would be likely to want to repay his family's loans even if no one else's loans were repaid, and where such a loan is repaid before it need be, there is often a suspicion that this was done to protect the lender. Sometimes rather than repaying a loan early, a company will grant a security over its assets in favour of one particular favoured creditor, so that in the event of the company's insolvency that creditor is unfairly preferred to the other creditors. The following are not unfair preferences:

(a) transactions in the ordinary course of business[15];

13.30

---

[8] Insolvency Act 1986, s.242(3)(a).
[9] An associate is, broadly speaking, any close relative, partner, associated company or partnership, employee or employer. See the Bankruptcy (Scotland) Act 1985, s.74.
[10] Insolvency Act 1986, s.242(3)(b).
[11] *ibid.* s.240(1)(a) and (b).
[12] *ibid.* s.242(4)(a).
[13] *ibid.* s.242(4)(b).
[14] *ibid.* s.242(4)(c).
[15] *ibid.* s.243(2)(a).

(b) payments in cash when a debt was due and payable, unless the transaction was part of a covert plan to reduce other creditors' rights to the sums paid[16];

(c) a transaction whereby the parties to it undertake reciprocal obligations to each other, either at the time or over a period of time, unless the transaction was collusive as in (b) above[17];

(d) the granting of a mandate authorising an arrestee to pay over arrested funds to an arresting creditor acting on a decree or warrant.[18]

13.31 If a gratuitous alienation or unfair preference is successfully challenged, the court can order the alienation or preference to be reduced, the funds or assets returned to the company and thence passed to the liquidator for disbursement to the creditors, and any associated charge can be set aside.[19] In each case, from the point of view of the recipient of the gratuitous alienation or the unfair preference, the recipient loses not only the asset or funds, but whatever he may have originally paid or lent to the company, and he ranks as a postponed creditor for his entire loss. In England, it is possible to keep the alienated asset by making good the loss to the company or paying the balance which ought to be due. Such an option is available in Scotland only if the courts permit it.[20] The rights of third parties acquiring former company assets from the recipients of gratuitous alienations or unfair preferences are protected, provided that the third parties are acting in good faith and paid a proper price for the assets.[21]

Extortionate credit transactions

13.32 Under the Insolvency Act 1986, s.244, where a company has entered into a loan or other obligation whereby

---

[16] Insolvency Act 1986, s.243(2)(b).

[17] *ibid.* s.243(2)(c).

[18] *ibid.* s.243(2)(d).

[19] This procedure is also available to administrators—Insolvency Act 1986, s.9(3)(b)(iii).

[20] Insolvency Act 1986, s.242(4). See the discussion on this issue in para. 18.15.

[21] *ibid.* and 243(5).

"grossly exorbitant payments" require to be made, the liquidator can apply to the courts to have the loan or obligations set aside and/or any other remedy the court sees appropriate. This will usually mean that further funds are returned to the company for ultimate disbursement among the creditors by the liquidator.

Reduction of floating charges

Under certain circumstances a liquidator can have a floating charge invalidated.[22]   **13.33**

These are as follows:

(a) the failure to have a floating charge properly registered within 21 days of its creation[23];

(b) the company grants a floating charge at a relevant time (as explained later) except to the extent of any money paid or goods or services provided at the time of or after the granting of the charge[24] or to the extent of the reduction or discharge of any debt of the company carried out at the time of or after the creation of the charge.[25] The point of this rule is to ensure that if, say, a lender lends money to a company, secured by a floating charge, he should obtain the floating charge on the occasion of the loan. What he should not do is lend the money first and then attempt to backdate his security by taking out a floating charge at a later date. This would be unfair on other creditors who might not otherwise have lent money to the company had they known that a creditor either had some security or was attempting to backdate his security. This is because obtaining a charge puts the secured lender in a better position to get his money back than the unsecured lenders. The "relevant time" depends

---

[22] See para. 12.19.
[23] Companies Act 1985, s.410.
[24] Insolvency Act 1986, s.245(2)(a).
[25] *ibid*. s.245(2)(b).

on who the floating charge holder is. If he is a connected person[26] *any* floating charge granted in his favour within a period of two years prior to the commencement of the winding-up of the company is rendered invalid.[27] By contrast, where the floating charge holder is not a connected person, a floating charge granted by the company within a period of 12 months prior to the commencement of the winding-up is invalid[28] *only if* the company was at the time of the creation of the charge unable to pay its debts as they fell due in terms of the Insolvency Act 1986, s.123[29] *or* became unable to pay its debts as they fell due because of the transaction for which the floating charge was granted,[30] *except* to the extent that the floating charge was in respect of new sums lent or obligations undertaken at the time of the creation of the floating charge or the reduction or discharge of any debt of the company.

13.34 The rationale for the different rules applicable to connected persons and unconnected persons is that the connected persons are more likely to know that the company is in financial difficulties and will therefore be keen to protect their own positions at the expense of other creditors.

The effect of the reduction of the floating charge will be to set aside the apparent floating charge and, where a receiver has already taken office under the terms of the floating charge, to set aside the receivership and to have the charged assets or their value returned to the company for distribution to the creditors generally. This practice is also available to administrators.[31]

---

[26] Similar to an associate—see n. 104 and the Insolvency Act 1986, s.249.
[27] Insolvency Act 1986, s.245(3)(a).
[28] *ibid*. s.245(3)(b).
[29] See para 13.10.
[30] Insolvency Act 1986, s.245(4)(b).
[31] *ibid*. s.9(3)(b)(ii).

Compensation from directors and others

On liquidation (not necessarily insolvent), directors and **13.35**
others may find themselves required to compensate the
company for any losses occasioned by their own conduct. A
liquidator (or creditor or contributory) can apply under the
Insolvency Act 1986, s.212(3), to make a director repay,
restore or account for any money or property belonging to
the company which he may have abstracted from it, and in
addition to compensate the company for any breach of his
fiduciary or other duties towards it. This section applies not
only to directors, but to officers of the company generally,
and to any liquidator, administrator, receiver or promoter of
the company.[32] This is commonly known as the "misfeasance" provision, and acts as a catch-all for errant directors
who, by virtue of their proximity to the company, are
sometimes tempted to remove its assets for their own
benefit, particularly when they know that the company is
financially troubled. A well-known example of failure to
adhere to a director's fiduciary duty involved Ian Maxwell's
signature on the improper transfer of shares in the Mirror
Group employees' pension fund company to other private
Maxwell interests.[33]

Compensation in the event of fraudulent trading

Fraudulent trading is, as a matter of practice, difficult to **13.36**
establish since there is a requirement that the company's
business has been carried out with an intent to defraud
creditors.[34] While this does happen very occasionally, and
as such often leads to criminal prosecution,[35] it is much
more common that the directors of a company have no
deliberate and concerted intention to defraud creditors, but
inadvertently make the company drift, through a mixture
of muddle and incompetence, into insolvency. As intent is
difficult to prove, there are few cases on this matter,

---

[32] Insolvency Act 1986, s.212(1).
[33] *Bishopsgate Investment Management Ltd (in liquidation) v. Maxwell* [1993]
B.C.L.C. 1282.
[34] Insolvency Act 1986, s.213(1).
[35] *R v. Grantham* [1984] B.C.L.C. 270.

although in *Re A Company (No. 001418 of 1988)*[36] not only was fraudulent trading successfully established but the courts, in making an award for compensation to cover the company's debts, added an extra punitive element to take account of the fact that the director deliberately kept the company trading when he knew it would never meet its debts. This section is applicable to anyone involved in the company's fraudulent activities, and therefore covers shareholders as well as directors or other officers of the company.

Wrongful trading by the directors

13.37 Where a company has gone into insolvent liquidation[37] and at some time before the commencement of the winding-up of the company, a director at that time[38] knew, or ought to have concluded, that there was no reasonable prospect that the company would avoid going into insolvent liquidation,[39] and where the court is satisfied that in the above circumstances that director did not take every step with a view to minimising the potential loss to the company's creditors as he ought to have done,[40] the court will grant an order requiring the director to make such a contribution to the company's assets as the court sees proper.[41] This section is rightly feared by directors because of the difficulty of establishing that they had taken every step to minimise the potential loss to the company's creditors. One way of dealing with this particular issue is for the directors to be seen to take independent advice from bankers, lawyers and accountants before the financial situation of the company becomes too dangerous. In any case such advisers might well recommend winding-up sooner rather than later which, done effectively and swiftly in its own

---

[36] [1991] B.C.L.C. 197.
[37] Insolvency Act 1986, s.214(2)(a).
[38] *ibid*. s.214(2)(c).
[39] *ibid*. s.214(2)(b).
[40] *ibid*. s.214(3).
[41] *ibid*. s.214(1).

right, would minimise the loss to creditors.[42] There is an ever-increasing number of cases under this provision and it is having a salutary effect upon directors who are keeping a company trading when it has no or little prospect of being able to pay its creditors, and upon directors who are awarding themselves unjustified sums by way of salary and expenses at a time when the company is having trouble meeting its debts.[43] The standard of skill expected of the director in assessing what he ought to have done is judged against an objective standard for directors generally of reasonable competence expected of any director carrying out his functions within the company in question, plus, if appropriate, any higher standard relative to the experience a particular director has.[44] What this means is that a technical director of, say, a tweed-making factory might be expected to have a good knowledge of wool but would not be expected to be an expert on financial matters and would not therefore be held accountable for them; but another director of the same factory who was the company's finance director could be expected to have the requisite financial skills and to be accountable for them; and if he happened to be a chartered accountant too, a yet higher standard would be expected of him because of his additional qualification.

Phoenix companies

A phoenix company, so called because it rises out of the ashes of a recently liquidated company, is not allowed to use the name of the liquidated company or a name so similar as to suggest an association with the liquidated company[45] unless the court grants leave otherwise.[46] If the

13.38

---

[42] In *Re Purpoint Ltd* [1991] B.C.L.C. 491, the director had the benefit of an accountant's advice and warnings as to his potential personal liability. Such advice was apparently ignored, since he failed to keep proper financial accounts for the company. He was held liable for the company's debts from the date when he should have realised that the company could not avoid going into insolvent liquidation.

[43] *Re DKG Contractors Ltd* [1990] B.C.C. 903.

[44] Insolvency Act 1986, s.214.

[45] *ibid*. s.216(2).

[46] *ibid*. s.217(3). Such permission was given, with conditions, in *Re Bonus Breaks Ltd* [1991] B.C.C. 546.

new phoenix company, bearing the prohibited name, becomes insolvent, any director who was also a director of the liquidated company and who is a director of the phoenix company will become jointly and severally liable for the debts of the phoenix company along with any other directors so involved and the company itself.[47] This rule serves to increase the funds available to the liquidator of the phoenix company.

Creditors' entitlement to funds obtained from the directors

13.39   It is one of the ironies of liquidation that all the above methods of "swelling the assets" carried out by the liquidator in the company's name may serve only to benefit the receiver under a floating charge. From time to time there will inevitably be occasions where the extra funds so generated are available to benefit the unsecured creditors, but commonly the only beneficiaries of the liquidator's efforts are the preferential creditors and the receiver.

The distribution of the company's assets

13.40   Assuming that the liquidator has been able to gather in all the sums due to the company, including such sums as have been obtained from directors, he will have to distribute them in the required order of priority. Each unsecured creditor must have vouched his claim, the amount of which will reflect the extent to which he is able to vote at meetings of the creditors.[48] Secured creditors are also entitled to be treated as unsecured creditors to the extent of the difference between the sums for which the security was granted and the lesser value of the assets secured in their favour.

In the case of a company which is solvent and which has granted no charges, the order of priority of payment by the liquidator is as follows, in so far as each category is applicable[49]:

[47] Insolvency Act 1986, s.217(2).
[48] Insolvency (Scotland) Rules 1986, r. 4.15.
[49] *ibid.* r. 4.66(1).

(a) the expenses of the liquidation (explained below);
(b) the expenses of any winding-up order in connection with a voluntary arrangement[50];
(c) any preferential debts[51] exclusive of any interest thereon (explained below);
(d) ordinary debts from unsecured creditors;
(e) interest at the official rate on:
    (i) the preferential debts;
    (ii) the ordinary debts;
    between the date of the commencement of the winding-up and the date of payment of the debt;
(f) postponed debts (explained below);
(g) the members in accordance with the terms of the articles.

Where funds are insufficient for payment of all of the above, the rule is that the priority of categories of payment in full in turn is maintained until there are insufficient funds to allow for full payment to the claimants in the next appropriate category. At that stage the claimants within the category which will not be paid in full because of insufficient funds will have to abate their claims in rateable proportions, and the categories postponed to that category will naturally receive nothing. **13.41**

The expenses of the liquidation are as follows[52] in so far as they are applicable: **13.42**

(a) outlays incurred by or chargeable by the provisional liquidator or liquidator, except as subsequently mentioned;
(b) the cost of any caution (guarantee) required by any provisional liquidator, the liquidator or special manager (a specialist with expertise in the business of the company in liquidation);
(c) the remuneration of the provisional liquidator;
(d) the expenses of any petitioner for compulsory liquidation;

---

[50] See Chap. 14.
[51] As defined in the Insolvency Act 1986, s.386 and Sched. 6.
[52] Insolvency (Scotland) Rules 1986, r.67(1).

(e) the remuneration of any special manager;

(f) any allowances permitted by the liquidator by way of assistance to the directors in preparing their financial statements for the creditors;

(g) the fees of anyone carrying out work for the company under the direction of the liquidator;

(h) the liquidator's fees;

(i) any corporation tax on chargeable gains accruing on the realisation of any asset of the company.

13.43 The preferential debts are the same as those in receivership, and they rank equally among themselves, so that if there are insufficient funds to pay them, they abate in equal proportions.[53] Where there is no receivership, the liquidator must pay the preferential debts; but where there is a receivership, the receiver must pay the preferential debts out of the sums caught by his crystallised floating charge.[54]

Postponed debts include the right of repayment of a creditor who had an asset removed from him and restored to the company in terms of the reduction of gratuitous alienation provisions.[55]

The interaction of secured charges and the order of priority

13.44 Where there is a fixed charge over heritage, the liquidator will usually sell the secured asset (unless there are good reasons why the heritable creditor should do so) but must account to the heritable creditor for the sums due to him out of the sale proceeds up to the level of the debt payable to the heritable creditor. Where there is a floating charge, liquidation will automatically trigger receivership. The receiver is entitled to all the assets secured by his floating charge in priority to unsecured creditors, and anything mistakenly in the hands of the liquidator but which should be caught by the floating charge must be handed to the receiver. This includes such things as compensation payable

[53] Insolvency Act 1986, s.175(2).
[54] *ibid.* s.175(2)(b).
[55] Insolvency (Scotland) Rules 1986, r.4.66(2)(a), and see para. 13.31.

by the directors under the Insolvency Act 1986, ss.212–216, and the sums returned to the company following the reduction of diligence. The receiver must pay the preferential debts.[56] Where there is an excess in the hands of the receiver after deduction of the sums due to the floating charge holder, the receiver's fees and outlays and the preferential debts, the excess is handed to the liquidator.

MISCELLANEOUS ISSUES IN LIQUIDATION

Compensation (set-off) in liquidation

The central issue of compensation or set-off is that one debt cancels out another, either wholly or partially. So an insolvent company's creditor, such as a bank, which has simultaneously lent money to the company and holds company funds on an interest-bearing deposit account, is entitled to set off its claim for repayment of the loan against the funds which it already holds in the deposit account. In the context of solvency, set-off is more restricted than in the context of insolvency.[57] In insolvency and insolvent liquidation, a liquid claim can be set off against an illiquid claim[58]; the claims need not be of the same type, so that a claim for debt could be set off against a claim for the delivery of supplies[59]; and debts do not have to be due at the same time, so that a future, a contingent or a disputed claim could be set off against an established claim.[60] However the *concursus debiti et crediti* rule still applies, so that a sum due to a company from a private individual cannot be set off against a repayment to that individual in his capacity as a trustee for another. **13.45**

Dissolution of the company

In a liquidation it is quite common for the liquidator to sell the assets of the company, or to sell subsidiaries which are **13.46**

---

[56] Insolvency Act 1986, s.185.
[57] See Chap. 8.
[58] *Scott's Tr. v. Scott* (1887) 14 R. 1043 at 1051.
[59] Bell, *Comm.*, ii, 122.
[60] *Smith v. Lord Advocate (No. 2)*, 1981 S.L.T. 19.

still profitable. Where there finally is a company with no assets left and all distributions made, the company will be an empty shell. The liquidator can then write to the Registrar of Companies to have it struck from the register.[61] If, however, it turns out that there are overlooked assets which were unknown at the time of the liquidation, within two years of the striking-off it is possible to petition the court to resurrect the company to enable the asset to be sold and the proceeds divided among those entitled to them.[62]

Problems with retentions of title

13.47 As with receivership, assets not owned by the company cannot be seized by the liquidator. So assets in the hands of the company but subject to a valid retention of title agreement can be taken back by the supplier, assets on hire-purchase are restored to the hirer and assets held in trust for another person are returned to their true owner. This may reduce the overall value of the assets realisable by the liquidator.

Problems in cross-border winding-up

13.48 When the Insolvency Act 1986 was enacted, certain anomalies between the two jurisdictions were overlooked or ignored. For example, in Scotland, there is no power for a liquidator to disclaim onerous obligations as there is in England under the Insolvency Act 1986, s.178. There is no equivalent in Scotland to the Official Receiver. The English equivalents of gratuitous alienations have shorter time-periods than the Scottish version. Caution should therefore always be exercised in dealing with cross-border matters.[63] The overall policy under the Insolvency Act, s.426, is that the different parts of the U.K. are supposed to recognise the powers of liquidators wherever they may be

---

[61] Insolvency Act 1986, ss.201, 204 and 205.
[62] Companies Act 1985, s.651.
[63] For a thoughtful discussion of the inconsistencies of the insolvency legislation, see David P. Sellar, "The Insolvency Act 1986 and Cross-Border Winding-up", 1995 J.L.S.S. 102.

appointed. Rules were supposed to have been drawn up by the Secretary of State to enable the better operation of this policy but, to date, no such rules have been produced.

CHAPTER 14

ADMINISTRATION ORDERS AND OTHER FORMS OF ARRANGEMENT WITH CREDITORS

PURPOSE OF ADMINISTRATION

Receiticevership benefits floating charge holders, although it often does so at the expense of the unsecured creditors. Winding-up gives creditors a fair opportunity of getting all or some of their money back, but is effectively the end of the company. However, until the invention of the administration order there was no straightforward method of dealing with or rescuing an insolvent or nearly insolvent company in a manner which benefited the company and indirectly its employees or even its suppliers. **14.1**

The advent of administration

Administration, which was designed to fill the above omission, was the result of the deliberations of the Cork Committee,[1] as were company voluntary arrangements, dealt with later in this chapter.[2] The Insolvency Act 1986 implemented both these new methods of dealing with troubled companies. Neither method has been particularly successful, for reasons to be outlined shortly, but each has its uses. **14.2**

The grounds under which an administration order can be made

If the court is satisfied: **14.3**

---

[1] "The Cork Report" (*Insolvency Law and Practice: Report of the Review Committee*, 1982, cmnd. 8898).
[2] See paras. 14.15–14.18.

    (a) that a company is or is likely to become unable to pay its debts within the meaning given in the Insolvency Act 1986, s.123,[3] and

    (b) that the making of the order would be likely to achieve one or more of the purposes specified in the Insolvency Act 1986, s.8(3),

the court may grant an administration order in relation to that company.[4]

14.4 The purposes specified in the Insolvency Act 1986, s.8(3), are as follows:

    (a) the survival of the company and the whole or any part of its undertaking as a going concern;

    (b) the approval of a company voluntary arrangement;

    (c) the sanctioning under the Companies Act 1985, s.425, of a scheme of arrangement;

    (d) a more advantageous realisation of the company's assets than would be effected on a winding-up.

14.5 Of these four purposes, (a) and (d) are predominantly the purposes for which an administration order is granted. It is not obligatory for a company voluntary arrangement that an administration order be granted, and a section 425 scheme of arrangement, which, broadly speaking, is a court-sanctioned rearrangement of a company's debt and equity, does not always need an administration order for its implementation anyway. Provided that all or most of those involved want an administration order to take place, such an order is generally granted by the courts and, indeed, given that the point of an administration order is either to keep the company going or to ensure better terms for its creditors, it would be surprising if the courts refused to entertain such an order. Equally, in one case[5] all the creditors wanted a company to be wound up, mainly

---

[3] See para. 13.7.

[4] Insolvency Act 1986, s.8(1).

[5] *Re Arrows Ltd (No. 3)* [1992] B.C.C. 131.

because the company's former activities required investigation, but a sole director and shareholder sought administration instead. The petition for administration was
refused on the grounds that the creditors would be better
served by a winding-up whereby a proper investigation
could take place.

EFFECT OF ADMINISTRATION

Once a company is in administration, creditors may not **14.6**
effect diligence or any other rights against the company[6]
and charges and liens may not be enforced without the
consent of the administrator or leave of the court.[7] The
lessors in hire-purchase agreements may not repossess
their goods being used by the company.[8] During administration the company may not be wound up. The company becomes effectively temporarily insulated from its
creditors. The directors have only a residual management
role in the company. Subject to certain directions from the
court and creditors, an insolvency practitioner is free to
manage the company in the best way he sees fit to achieve
the stated purpose of the administration order, free (unlike
a liquidator) of the restriction of being able to deal only
with assets not secured by the crystallised floating charge,
and to continue trading with such assets as the company
has in its possession at the time of the grant of the
administration order. His extensive powers, identical to an
English administrative receiver, are stated in the Insolvency Act 1986, Sched. 1. Once the administrator's purposes have been fulfilled, the administrator will generally
apply for the discharge of the administration order under
the Insolvency Act 1986, s.18(1). This will be commonly
followed by a petition for liquidation on which occasion
the administrator may be appointed the liquidator[9] and he
will then proceed to distribute the assets of the company

[6] Insolvency Act 1986, s.11(3)(d).
[7] *ibid.* s.11(3)(c).
[8] *ibid.* It should be noted that in this context the term "lessor" also
includes conditional sale sellers and others using retention of title
agreements (s.10(4)).
[9] Insolvency Act 1986, s.140.

and pay such creditors as have not already settled with the company. As liquidator he will be able to do certain things which as administrator he could not do, such as investigate the dealings of the directors to see if they could be liable to compensate the company for misfeasance, wrongful trading or other breach of duty to the company.

Prohibitions on the grant of administration orders

14.7 Notwithstanding the above, the courts cannot grant an administration order if:

    (a) the company already is in liquidation[10]; or
    (b) if the company in question is an insurance company[11]; or
    (c) if the company in question is a money-lending institution[12]; or
    (d) subject to the following, a receiver is in place.[13]

14.8 Receivership and administration are mutually incompatible. If a receiver is in place, an administration order can be made only where the floating charge holder consents to the administration order being granted[14]; or where the receivership is in itself invalid, through being open to a successful challenge under the Insolvency Act 1986, s.245 (the avoidance of floating charges[15]), s.242 (the reduction of gratuitous alienations) or s.243 (the reduction of unfair preferences[16]). Given the above, those who wish the company to go into administration must convince any existing floating charge holder that his needs would be better served by an administration order than by his existing

---

[10] Insolvency Act 1986, s.8(4).
[11] Within the terms of the Insurance Companies Act 1982; Insolvency Act 1986, s.8(4)(a).
[12] Within the terms of the Banking Act 1987; Insolvency Act 1986, s.8(4)(b).
[13] Insolvency Act 1986, s.9(3).
[14] *ibid.* s.9(3)(a).
[15] See para.13.33.
[16] For the reduction of both gratuitous alienations and unfair preferences: see para. 13.29.

receivership. Reasons which might be used to convince a floating charge holder of this include the fact that an administrator, unlike a receiver, can set aside certain antecedent transactions in the same manner as a liquidator.[17] Furthermore, even though a receiver is not appointed, the floating charge holder's priority in terms of payment is still preserved—even if he loses the advantage of speed in realising the company's assets and the chance of unfettered control of the realisation process. An additional matter for the floating charge holder's consideration is that receivership is not always recognised abroad in the way that a court-approved administration order is, so that an administration order might ultimately generate more funds for the floating charge holder. On the other hand, a receiver with a secured charge is already in a good position with regard to the company's assets and generally will be reluctant to forgo this without good cause.

PROCEDURE

Permissible petitioners for an administration order

Under the Insolvency Act 1986, s.9(1), the following are permitted to petition for an administration order: **14.9**

   (a) the company itself;
   (b) the directors;
   (c) a creditor or creditors;
   (d) all or any of the above, together or separately.

Of the above, it should be noted that neither a shareholder (unless he has a majority of the voting right in the company) nor one director on his own may petition the company for the grant of an administration order. Only all the directors together may petition for an administration order.[18] Unsecured creditors are more likely to succeed in   **14.10**

---

[17] Such as the reduction of gratuitous alienations and unfair preferences under ss.242 and 243, the reduction of extortionate credit transactions under s.244, and the setting aside of floating charges under s.245. See paras. 13.29–33.
[18] *Re Equitcorp International plc* [1989] 5 B.C.C. 599; *Re Instrumentation Electrical Services Ltd* [1988] B.C.C. 301.

obtaining an administration order than secured creditors since unsecured creditors have more to lose in a liquidation and consequently more to gain by an administration.[19]

The procedure for petitioning for an administration order

14.11 Once a petition is presented to the court, there must be intimation of it to any floating charge holder, existing receiver, petitioner for liquidation, provisional liquidator, the proposed administrator, the company itself (but only in the context of a creditors' petition for administration) and anyone else to whom the court orders the petition to be intimated.[20] Having heard the petition, the court can dismiss, adjourn or grant the order, on either an interim or full basis. The court has discretion to grant such order as it sees fit.[21] There may be an interval between the presentation of the petition and the grant or dismissal of the order. In that interval, the company can neither resolve to wind itself up nor be wound up compulsorily,[22] no creditor can enforce any security over the company's property without leave of the court,[23] no lessor in a hire-purchase agreement can repossess his goods without leave of the court[24] and no diligence or other legal proceedings can be brought against the company without leave of the court.[25] During this interval any attempted winding up proceedings will lie in abeyance pending the decision of the courts[26] although the company can still be put into receivership[27] and no administration order can be granted unless and until the floating charge holder consents to the grant of the administration order.[28] Assuming the order is granted, the position of the

---

[19] *Consumer and Industrial Press Ltd* [1988] 4 B.C.C. 68; *Re Imperial Motors (U.K.) Ltd* [1989] 5 B.C.C. 214.
[20] Insolvency (Scotland) Rules 1986, r. 2.(1)(2).
[21] Insolvency Act 1986, s.9(4).
[22] *ibid.* s.10(1)(a).
[23] *ibid.* s.10(1)(b).
[24] *ibid.* s.10(1)(b).
[25] *ibid.* s.10(1)(c).
[26] *ibid.* s.10(2)(a).
[27] *ibid.* s.10(2)(b).
[28] *ibid.* s.10(2)(c).

company in administration is as stated in paragraph 14.6. Not surprisingly, the inability of certain creditors to retrieve either their money or their goods from the administrator's hands has occasioned applications to the court for leave to set aside the administrator's powers for certain items. This issue was discussed in *Re Atlantic Computer Systems plc*[29] where broad guidelines were given on this matter. For a creditor to obtain leave from the court for the retrieval of goods or the seizure of other charged assets the creditor would need to show that it would cause him hardship if leave were refused, that the return of the goods or the seizure of the assets would not cause difficulties for other creditors, and that overall it would not hinder the fulfilment of the purpose of the administration order. From time to time an administrator may wish to sell a charged asset or an asset subject to a hire-purchase agreement, conditional sale agreement or retention of title agreement.[30] Although he would usually seek to obtain the consent of the creditor, if such consent is unavailable the administrator may obtain permission from the court if he can demonstrate that by doing so there will be better promotion of the purpose for which the administration order was granted.[31] The creditor concerned is still entitled to his right of priority in payment[32] and the person to whom any of the company's goods are sold (where they had been subject to a charge or any other encumbrance as stated above) has good title to the goods.[33]

The duties and powers of the administrator

The administrator has extensive powers to carry out his duties,[34] and in so doing he may choose to remove the directors from their posts.[35] He is deemed to be the agent of the company and thus able to execute documents on the   **14.12**

---

[29] [1992] 2 W.L.R. 367.
[30] Insolvency Act 1986, s.15(1).
[31] *ibid.* s.15(2).
[32] *ibid.* s.15(4).
[33] *ibid.* s.16.
[34] *ibid.* s.14(1) and see also Sched. 1.
[35] *ibid.* s.14(2)(a).

company's behalf,[36] although (unlike a receiver) he does not incur any personal liability on contracts he enters into on behalf of the company. Those who deal with the administrator in good faith and having paid a fair price for items within the administrator's control need not concern themselves to establish whether or not the administrator is acting within the powers granted to him.[37] The administrator must make it clear on any company documentation that the company is in administration.[38] The administrator is entitled to his fees and expenses out of the company's assets and in priority to the claims of other creditors, secured or unsecured.[39] Likewise liabilities incurred by the administrator in the course of his administration, such as paying contractors to complete a particular task, are allowable against the company in priority to other creditors' claims.[40] Costs due under employment contracts adopted by the administrator are also payable out of the company's assets in priority to other claims (unlike those due under contracts adopted by a receiver, who is personally liable unless the contracts indicate otherwise), but only to the extent of services provided wholly or partly after the adoption of the contracts of employment by the administrator. The administrator has a period of 14 days during which he must make up his mind whether or not he is to adopt any employee's contract.[41] During that period he is not to be taken to have adopted any employment contracts, even if his actions, or indeed inaction, might have suggested that he has adopted any contracts of employment.[42] But once the 14-day period is over he is deemed to have adopted the employment contract of any employee still under his control. The administrator is not responsible for the payment of any wages other than those arising after the appointment of the administrator.

---

[36] Insolvency Act 1986, s.14(5).
[37] *ibid.* s.14(6).
[38] *ibid.* s.12(1).
[39] *ibid.* s.19(4).
[40] *ibid.* s.19(5).
[41] *ibid.* s.19(6).
[42] *ibid.*

The administrators and creditors

Creditors generally will have been informed of the administration order because of the posting of a note to that effect in the *Gazette*[43] but they are also separately informed of the order by the administrator.[44] The administrator must obtain a statement of affairs from those who have been involved with the company in their positions as officer of the company, employees or even consultants.[45] The statement should indicate the company's assets and liabilities, and all information about any securities granted by the company.[46] The statement of affairs is made available to all the creditors.[47] With the benefit of this information, the administrator must within three months of the granting of the order frame proposals[48] which are intimated to all creditors and to the Registrar of Companies.[49] The proposals are the administrator's plans for the fulfilment of the purpose for which the administration order was granted. The proposals are presented to a creditors' meeting for their consideration and approval.[50] The creditors can suggest modification, but the administrator is not bound to follow their advice[51] and at that stage either creditors or administrator may if necessary go to court to have the administration order discharged.[52] The proposals may need to be revised, in which case the creditors must be advised of the changes[53] and approval sought as before. The creditors may form a committee to advise the administrator.[54] If during the management of the administration any member or creditor can prove that the administrator is prejudicing the interests of any creditor or member, he is

14.13

[43] Insolvency (Scotland) Rules 1986, r. 2.3(2).
[44] Insolvency Act 1986, s.21(1).
[45] *ibid*. s.22(3).
[46] *ibid*. s.22(2).
[47] *ibid*. s.23(2).
[48] *ibid*. s.23(1).
[49] *ibid*. s.23(1).
[50] *ibid*. s.24(1).
[51] *ibid*. s.24(2).
[52] *ibid*. s.24(5).
[53] *ibid*. s.25.
[54] *ibid*. s.26.

entitled to go to court to seek such remedy as the court sees fit to deal with the prejudice the administrator's actions are causing.[55]

However, assuming the administrator's proposals are acceptable and are achieved, ultimately the administrator will sell such parts of the company as he can. What remains of the company commonly goes into liquidation, with the liquidator dividing the sums realised by the administrator among the creditors in the normal manner. The administrator will obtain his discharge under the Insolvency Act 1986, s.18. If the administrator is unable to achieve the result sought by the administration order, he must state as much in his application for discharge. It is also possible to have the administration order varied if that would prove more effective.[56]

Problems with Administration

14.14 It is often said that there is little incentive for a floating charge holder to appoint an administrator when he could get his money back with less effort and possibly more cheaply with a receivership. Receivership does not involve going to court and is quicker than an administration order. For small companies administration does not appear to be a realistic option, though it has its uses where the company has an underlying valuable business which is worth preserving and which an administrator might be able to sell on more effectively than a receiver. Equally, it is sometimes said that the establishment of the administrator is the first step towards beating back the power of banks eager to put companies into receivership. Whether or not banks are keen to put companies into receivership, which is unlikely, it must be remembered that anything which makes life more difficult for banks to get their money back will only increase the cost of borrowed funds or result in an increased use of guarantees. A further criticism of administration is the requirement for all directors to decide together to seek an administration order. One dissentient

---

[55] Insolvency Act 1986, s.27.
[56] *ibid.* s.18(3).

director could block this, or equally he could find that the company was put into liquidation when administration might have been a better idea. The Government is reviewing insolvency legislation generally and it remains to be seen what its new proposals will be.

COMPANY VOLUNTARY ARRANGEMENTS

These are very little used and have not been a successful **14.15** feature of insolvency legislation. In a fashion similar to the voluntary arrangements discussed in Chapter 10, a company agrees terms with its creditors instead of being wound up. Creditors will have to be convinced that the effective new management of an insolvency practitioner on an interim basis will result in a better return than that available on a winding-up.

Procedure

The directors of the company apply to the courts for **14.16** preliminary approval of a proposal for either a compromise with creditors or a scheme of arrangement of its affairs, in either case known as a "voluntary arrangement".[57] The proposal must contain all such information about the company's assets and liabilities and other relevant information as may be necessary. The arrangement requires an insolvency practitioner, acting in the capacity of trustee and known as the "nominee", to supervise the arrangement.[58] Within 28 days, the nominee must submit a report to the court stating whether or not in his view the members of the company and the creditors should be invited to meetings to consider the proposal and, if so, when those meetings should be held.[59] Alternatively, where the company is already in liquidation or administration, the liquidator or administrator makes his own proposal and acts as nominee.[60] He too must summon meetings of the members and creditors to consider his

[57] Insolvency Act 1986, s.1(1).
[58] *ibid.* s.1(2).
[59] *ibid.* s.2(2).
[60] Insolvency (Scotland) Rules 1986, r. 1.10.

proposal.[61] At the meetings the terms of the proposal are considered. The rights of preferential creditors[62] and secured creditors[63] are maintained and the proposal can vary those rights only with the consent of the relevant creditor.[64] If the proposal is approved by both members and creditors it beomes the voluntary arrangement. To secure members' approval a majority of votes must be cast in its favour[65] and to secure creditors' approval three-quarters in value of the creditors must approve.[66] Once approval at both meetings is obtained, the voluntary arrangement binds the members, the creditors and the company,[67] including those who voted against the proposal. There is then a delay of 28 days during which any objections to the voluntary arrangement may be entertained by the court.[68] Such objections will succeed only where the objector can demonstrate that the voluntary arrangement prejudices a member, a contributory or a creditor of the company,[69] or where there has been some material irregularity in the meetings.[70] The court can revoke or suspend the voluntary arrangement, or require further meetings to be held, if it establishes that the objection is well-founded.[71] In the event of there being no successful objection, and the company already being in liquidation or administration, the court can sist (defer for the time being) the liquidation or discharge the administration order.[72]

Implementation

14.17   Once the voluntary arrangement is in place, the nominee becomes known as the "supervisor". He implements the

---

[61] Insolvency (Scotland) Act 1986, s.3(2).

[62] Insolvency Act 1986, s.4(4).

[63] *ibid.* s.4(3).

[64] This is in contrast to a s.425 scheme of arrangement, where preferential creditors and secured creditors are not given such rights, although the court in considering whether or not to give its approval to such a scheme of arrangement may take account of the views of the preferential and secured creditors.

[65] Insolvency (Scotland) Rules 1986, r. 7.12(1).

[66] *ibid.* r. 7.12(2).

[67] Insolvency Act 1986, s.5.

[68] *ibid.* s.5(4)(a).

[69] *ibid.* s.6(1)(a).

[70] *ibid.* s.6(1)(b).

[71] *ibid.* s.6(4).

[72] *ibid.* s.5(3).

voluntary arrangement, subject to the right of any creditor or anyone else to return to court for redress if the creditor or other person is dissatisfied with the supervisor's actions.[73] Likewise the supervisor can return to court for directions on any contentious matter.[74] Assuming that the arrangement is to everyone's satisfaction, the supervisor than carries out the voluntary arrangement as planned.

Problems with voluntary arrangements

There are several reasons why company voluntary **14.18** arrangements are little used. The main reason is that a voluntary arrangement which turns out not to be well carried out or inherently unsatisfactory is no better than a winding-up. Furthermore, secured and preferential creditors can prevent the voluntary arrangement ever taking place. In addition, it is slow-moving and requires an application to the court. There have been moves to improve company voluntary arrangements but it remains to be seen what proposals will ultimately be adopted. It should be noted that there are other forms of arrangement with creditors (and sometimes shareholders as well) such as schemes of arrangement under the Companies Act 1985, s.425, and compromises with creditors. These are beyond the scope of this book and reference should be made to technical books on these matters such as St Clair and Drummond Young, *The Law of Corporate Insolvency in Scotland*.[75]

---

[73] Insolvency Act 1986, s.7(3).
[74] *ibid.* s.7(4).
[75] Butterworths (Edinburgh, 1992).

CHAPTER 15

ASSIGNATION OF DEBT

Assignation of debt takes place when a person who is **15.1** entitled to receive payment of a debt transfers his right to another, usually in exchange for payment of a sum slightly less than the debt. An example of this is factoring, where a creditor, in order to receive immediate payment of outstanding debts due to him, sells the debts at a discount to a factor (or debt collector) who then takes on the burden of collecting the debts and chasing the debtors through the courts. Debt is not the only thing that is assignable: a right to inherit an asset (known as a *spes successionis*), the right to damages for breach of contract or for injury, a right of repayment of and interest arising from a bond or debenture, a floating charge, the proceeds of an insurance policy and the rights to rental income may all be assigned.

Reasons for assignation

Assignation is used for two main purposes. The first is to **15.2** enable the person entitled to the payment to use the entitlement as security for some other transaction. So someone who knew he was going to benefit under his father's will could borrow today against the expectation that he would receive a large sum from his father's estate in years to come. To do so, he would need to assign his interest in his father's estate to the lender. Another version of the same principle is when a property owner arranges for the rental income arising from leases he has granted to be paid to the bank which has lent him the money to develop the property. The rents are thus assigned to the bank. If the property owner is a company it will need to register a charge over the rental income in favour of the bank.[1] The second use is to obtain funds now from a person to whom the debts are assigned, such as in the example of factoring or debt collecting in paragraph 15.1.

Non-assignable debts

15.3 Certain debts cannot be assigned, among these being the sums payable from guarantees granted by members of a guarantee company[2] and social security benefits.[3] It is not uncommon to see a clause in a contract stating that the right to payment of a debt is non-assignable, but it is not known how effective this prohibition would be. Commonly the prohibition is tempered by the words "without the consent of the debtor which must not be unreasonably withheld" or similar wording.

Method of assignation

15.4 There is no special wording or deed which is required for a valid assignation,[4] but without a written form of assignation it would be extremely difficult to prove that the assignation had taken place. Provided that the wording gives an unequivocal transfer by the assignor to the assignee of the right to payment from the debtor, the assignation will usually be valid. The Transmission of Moveable Property (Scotland) Act 1862 provides a form of assignation which may be used for bonds and any other type of personal property, and the Schedule to the Policies of Assurance Act 1867 provides a style for the assignation of insurance policies. It is not enough merely to hand the document of debt to the transferee,[5] since not only is there no intimation to the debtor, but also there is no proof that the transferee is holding the document of debt legitimately. A mandate signed by the assignor instructing the debtor to pay the assignee whatever would otherwise have been paid to the assignor is also deemed to be an assignation:

[1] Companies Act 1985, s.410 (4)(c)(i).
[2] *Robertson v. British Linen Co.* (1891) 2 Ch. 28.
[3] Social Security Act 1975, s.87(1).
[4] *Brownlee v. Robb*, 1907 S.C. 1302.
[5] *Strachan v. McDougle* (1835) 13 S. 954.

this procedure is common in the case of payments of rent. If the assignor owes the assignee money then the mandate will almost certainly have been drawn up by the assignee and will contain a clause preventing the transferor from revoking the mandate. The reversion of an assigned right to its original owner is known as retrocession, and in the context of an assurance policy assigned in favour of a building society as additional security for a loan, retrocession would take place on the repayment of the loan.

Intimation

Intimation is vital for a valid assignation in Scotland[6] and is usually carried out by the assignee but may be carried out for him by the assignor. Under the Transmission of Moveable Property (Scotland) Act 1862, s.2, intimation can be effected either by a notary public sending the debtor a duly notarised certified copy of the assignation, or by the more common method of sending a certified copy of the assignation to the debtor, with a requirement that it be acknowledged. This practice is commonly followed when obtaining a mortgage for domestic house purchases: as part of the security for a loan a building society usually insists on receiving the life assurance policy which forms the security for the loan, the deed of assignation, a copy of the intimation of the deed of assignation and the acknowledgment by the insurance company that it has noted the building society's interest in the policy. This means that should the house-purchaser/borrower die during the period of his mortgage, the building society will obtain the benefit of the proceeds of the life policy. Some English building societies are extremely reluctant to deal with intimation and prefer to hold the life policy documentation on its own, despite the best efforts of Scottish solicitors to persuade them that this may be prejudicial to the building society's interests. This is because, without intimation, the funds arising from the life policy could be arrested and the arresting creditor might be found to have a higher priority to the building society. In addition the Policies of

15.5

---

[6] *Grigor Allan v. Urquhart* (1887) 15 R. 56.

Assurance Act 1867, s.3, states that the assignee cannot claim the sums due from the policy unless there is written intimation to the assurance company of the assignation, together with acknowledgment of receipt. The receipt provides comfort to the assignee that he now has the highest claim to the proceeds of the policy. If the debtor is sequestrated prior to intimation the trustee in sequestration will obtain the proceeds rather than the assignee.[7]

The assignor's right

15.6   The assignor can only assign such rights as he holds at the time (*assignatus utitor jure auctoris*) and equally the assignee takes the assignor's rights subject to such qualifications as may be in existence at the time. In *Scottish Widows' Fund and Life Assurance Society v. Buist*[8] the assignor assigned a life policy to Buist as security for a loan. When the insured assignor died, Buist claimed the sums he believed were due to him from Scottish Widows. Scottish Widows refused to pay out the policy on the grounds that the assignor had fraudulently misrepresented the state of his health and had therefore breached the terms of his warranty. Buist had to take his title as assignee as he found it, and was unable to claim against Scottish Widows.

---

[7] *Tod's Tr. v. Wilson* (1869) 7 M. 1100.
[8] (1876) 3 R. 1078.

CHAPTER 16

JOINT AND SEVERAL LIABILITY

MEANING OF JOINT AND SEVERAL LIABILITY

Joint and several liability arises in the context of liability **16.1** for a debt being spread between two or more persons. *Joint liability* means that all the debtors are liable collectively for the total sum due, but each debtor is not required to pay more than his share. This means that where there is a debt due jointly by various debtors, any one debtor can be required to pay the entire amount and in so doing can discharge the entire debt. One who pays is able to recover the others' shares from them in order to reimburse himself for what he has laid out on their behalf. *Liability pro rata* means liability for an equal share of the debt, but if one of the other obligants becomes bankrupt, one is not required to pay his share for him. Naturally it is in a creditor's interest to ensure that debtors are bound jointly and severally rather than *pro rata* since the burden of extracting any sums not paid then falls upon the body of debtors generally rather than the creditor having to accept that one or more debtors may never pay. There is an assumption that liability is usually *pro rata*[1] unless the words "jointly and severally" or, less commonly, "conjunctly and severally" are used.[2] The assumption that a liability is *pro rata* is also reversed in certain circumstances, among these being partnership.[3] Co-drawers and co-acceptors of bills of exchange,[4] and

---

[1] Stair I, xvii, 20.
[2] Bell, *Comm.*, i, 361.
[3] Partnership Act 1890, s.9.
[4] Bell, *Comm.*, i, 363.

co-makers of a promissory note,[5] will each find themselves jointly and severally liable unless there is some
agreement to the contrary. The point about *joint and
several liability* is that a creditor may proceed against any
one or more debts for the entire sum due although in
practice he is likely to start with either the most accessible
or the wealthiest debtors. It is not the creditor's responsibility to sue each debtor in turn: it is up to that debtor
or those debtors who have paid the sum due to claim his
or their right of relief from the remaining debtors.[6] To do
this any such debtor paying the whole debt due by other,
non-paying debtors is entitled to an assignation of the
debt in respect of the non-paying debtors from the
creditor and to any securities held by the creditor[7] from
the non-paying debtors.

16.2   As the advantage to the creditor of joint and several
liability is so great it is not surprising that creditors in
their standard documentation for bonds of caution, guarantees or any other contracts involving more than one
debtor will insist on joint and several liability. Indeed
there are few occasions where the law states that the
liability cannot be joint and several, except perhaps
where a creditor has elected to take a *pro rata* share from
one debtor.[8] If the creditor discharges one debtor who has
paid his share, he effectively permits the other creditors
to pay *pro rata*. However, if the creditor merely chooses to
permit (as opposed to discharge) one debtor to make a
payment of whatever amount, the creditor should do so
on the understanding that he reserves all his rights
against the other debtors. The other debtors will then
remain liable for the full amount and are permitted to
claim a *pro rata* share from the debtor who has paid.[9]
Some creditors make a practice of not making debtors

---

[5] Bills of Exchange Act 1882, s.9.
[6] Bell, *Prin.*, S. 62.
[7] Bell, *Prin.*, S. 255.
[8] *Muir v. Crawford* (1875) 2 R. (H.L.) 148.
[9] *Secretary of State for Scotland v. Coltness Industries Ltd*, 1979 S.L.T. (Sh. Ct.)
56.

jointly and severally liable: in common repair schemes to tenement blocks which are undertaken by civic bodies such as local authorities, each proprietor will be liable for his own share but not for any of his neighbours'. On the other hand, the council will have effectively indemnified itself against the cost of attempting to recover the sums due from the individual proprietors by making a 10 per cent or more surcharge over the actual cost of the repairs.

Effective joint and several liability in consumer credit transactions

Under the Consumer Credit Act 1974, s.75, where there is a   **16.3** debtor-creditor-supplier agreement, as when a consumer (the debtor) buys a car from a car dealer (the supplier) using funds supplied by a finance company (the creditor), and where the debtor makes a claim against the supplier for breach of contract or misrepresentation, the debtor can make that claim against either the supplier or the creditor, thus effectively making them jointly and severally liable. The same principle applies with credit cards, so that a consumer buying unsatisfactory goods from a supplier using a credit card is able to claim against either the supplier or the credit card company. There will be a further arrangement between the supplier and the credit card company that in the event of a successful claim against the credit card company, the latter can claim against the supplier for any loss it has suffered.

PARTNERSHIPS AND JOINT AND SEVERAL LIABILITY

The liability of partnerships generally

The Partnership Act 1890 ("the Act") provides a standard   **16.4** set of rules for the management of a partnership, though a partnership can choose to substitute its own set of rules wherever permitted to do so by the Act. The Act also lays down rules for the liabilities attaching to the partnership as regards outsiders and the liabilities of the partners among themselves, the latter being of no concern to outsiders. A partnership will usually be responsible to outsiders for its own debts arising in the ordinary course of business.[10] It will also be liable where one partner acting within his apparent authority as a partner wrongfully receives assets from a third party and uses them personally, or hands the assets to the partnership[11-12] for its use. A partnership will not, however, be liable where someone, without the partnership's knowledge, represents himself as an agent of a partnership or as a partner for the partnership (known as "holding out") though that person may instead himself become liable for the partnership's debts. A partnership will not be liable for the actions of a partner obviously acting in his own interests alone[13] or beyond his authority to such an exceptional extent that the other party ought to have realised that he was not acting in the ordinary course of business.[14] For such acts, the partner himself will be personally liable.[15] A partner cannot make the partnership liable for an injury caused by one partner to another even in the course of partnership business.[16]

The liability of retired, deceased and new partners

16.5 Partners are liable jointly and severally for the debts of the partnership.[17] Such liability is extended to past members of the partnership (at least as far as the liability relates to a liability incurred while the past member was still a partner[18]) and to the estates of dead partners.[19] While both a retired partner and the estate of a dead partner can be liable as far as outsiders are concerned, it is common either for retiring partners to negotiate terms with the existing partnership to cover any liabilities arising after they have ceased to be partners, or for a well-drafted partnership agreement to deal with the liabilities of retiring or

---

[10] Partnership Act 1890, s.6.
[11-12] *ibid.* s.11.
[13] *Walker v. Smith* (1906) 8 F. 619.
[14] *Paterson Bros v. Gladstone* (1891) 18 R. 403.
[15] *Fortune v. Young*, 1918, S.C. 1.
[16] *Mair v. Wood*, 1948 S.C. 83.
[17] Partnership Act 1890, s.9.
[18] *ibid.* s.17(2).
[19] *ibid.* s.9.

deceased partners generally. A retired partner who gives the impression that he is still connected with his former partnership may become liable for any debts arising out of any transaction in which the partnership apparently has an interest.[20] The other party to the contract is entitled to treat the apparent members of the partnership (including the retired partner) as continuing members until he is specifically told otherwise.[21] The usual method of intimation of the retiral of a partner as far as people who have had no previous dealings with the partnership are concerned is publication of the notice of retiral in the *Edinburgh Gazette*.[22] As far as existing clients of the partnership are concerned, strictly speaking, intimation to the client by a notice or by a change of name of the partnership is required.[23] Despite this apparent requirement this procedure does not happen very much in practice, the partners of accountancy and legal firms often rapidly changing without such intimation.[24] This is because such firms are well aware that few of their clients read the *Gazette* and because the cost of individual notification to clients of a change is high. Furthermore a reputable firm would wish to give the impression that it can bear the liabilities arising out of any failure to intimate the retiral of a partner. Nonetheless the fact remains that proper notification of retiral is, properly speaking, what is required, and where there is any possible doubt as to the continued solvency of a partnership with which the retiring partner no longer wishes to be associated, it would be prudent to insert the relevant notice in the *Gazette* and to be seen to tell all the partnership's existing clients of the retiral.

[20] Partnership Act 1890, s.36(1).

[21] *ibid.*

[22] Partnership Act 1890, s.36(2).

[23] Bell, *Comm.*, ii, 530.

[24] The retiral of a partner may, however, be evident from the absence of the partner's name from the firm's headed notepaper, or, where there are too many partners to insert their names on the headed notepaper, there will be a direction as to an address where a full list of partners is held. It is possible that these two methods may be tantamount to intimation: the point has not been decided in the courts or clarified by statute.

16.6   A bankrupt partner is not liable for the debts of his
partnership arising after his bankruptcy.[25] A new partner is
not liable for the debts of a partnership arising from the
time prior to his joining the partnership.[26] When a new
partnership is constituted out of the whole assets of a
former partnership the assumption is that any liabilities
are transferred along with the assets, but this assumption
may be set aside if one or more of the new partners pays in
a great deal of capital and the other partners only transferred their shares of their former partnership. In such an
event there is sufficient difference between the old partnership and the new that the old liabilities are not transferred to the new partnership.[27] The same assumption may
be set aside where the new partnership specifically does
not collect the debts of the old partnership.

The property of a partnership

16.7   When a partnership owns heritable property, the title to
the property must be taken in the names of the partners of
the partnership as trustees for the partnership,[28] notwithstanding the fact that in Scotland a partnership has a
separate legal personality. Each partner is entitled to a *pro
indiviso* right to the assets of the partnership—in other
words, they have only a right to their share of the proceeds
of the property after division and sale, but until then they
cannot insist on their physical actual share of the partnership's assets (or its value) being handed over to them,
unless there is some agreement to the contrary. Partnership assets are owned primarily by the partnership,
with the partners having only a reversionary right, and
accordingly a creditor effecting diligence against a partner
in his personal capacity cannot actually arrest or poind
partnership assets: what he should do is to arrest the
partner's interest (such as, say, his right to his share of the
partnership capital) in the hands of the partnership.[29]

---

[25] Partnership Act 1890, s.36(3).
[26] *ibid.* s.17(1).
[27] *Miller v. Macleod*, 1973 S.C. 172.
[28] Bell, *Prin.*, S. 357.
[29] Erskine, III, iii, 24.

Enforcement of decrees, etc. against a partnership: sequestration

Even though a decree may have been taken against a **16.8** partnership as a whole, the enforcement of a decree (or registered bond or protested bill) can be against one partner alone[30] though he will be entitled to repayment *pro rata* from the firm itself and from the other partners. If a partnership is sequestrated, the grounds for sequestration and the subsequent procedure are generally as specified in Chapter 10,[31] subject to the point that the trustee in sequestration of a partnership can realise the partnership's assets and pay off the partnership's debts only to the extent of the assets contained within the partnership. Should there still remain a balance due to the creditors, the creditors may then claim jointly and severally against each partner, but only to the overall extent of the outstanding balance.[32] At that stage the creditor may find himself competing for his outstanding balance with any other personal (*i.e.* non-partnership) creditors that each partner in his personal capacity may have. Any creditor raising an action against a partnership, or proposing to sequestrate a partnership, would be well advised to raise the relevant action against both the partnership and the individual partners just in case the partnership assets are insufficient to meet the creditor's claim. If the spouse of a partner lends money to his or her spouse's partnership, the loan is not postponed to other creditors' claims.[33]

MISCELLANEOUS INSTANCES OF JOINT AND SEVERAL LIABILITY

European Economic Interest Groupings ("EEIG")

EIGGs are corporate bodies (*i.e.* with a legal personality, **16.9** similar to a registered company or a Scottish partnership)

---

[30] Partnership Act 1890, s.4(2).
[31] There are technical differences, such as the fact that a partnership can petition for its own sequestration only where creditors support it, and a qualified creditor can sequestrate the partnership only if it is apparently insolvent (Bankruptcy (Scotland) Act 1985, s.6(4)).
[32] Bankruptcy (Scotland) Act 1985, Sched. 1, para. 6.
[33] *Lumsden v. Sym* (1912) 28 Sh.Ct. Rep. 168.

set up under the aegis of the European Community.[34] They exist to act as co-ordinating bodies for the promotion of particular types of businesses throughout Europe and in particular to enable the companies, firms and persons practising such businesses to be able to co-operate and overcome the various bureaucratic obstacles to doing business together in Europe. So, for example, an EEIG for the haulage industry, with members drawn from leading haulage companies throughout Europe, would attempt to lobby the European Parliament for a harmonised transportation policy. The members of an EEIG are jointly and severally liable for the liability of the EEIG on an unlimited basis.[35]

Joint and several liability for clubs and associations

16.10 This is dealt with in Chapter 17.

Liability of parents for their children

16.11 Parents are required to aliment (provide for) their children if they are in a position to do so, and refuse or delay to do so. This issue has recently arisen in the context of university students raising actions of aliment against their own parents. Although it might be thought that parents are jointly and severally liable to aliment their children, under the Family Law (Scotland) Act 1985, ss.1 and 4, the courts assess how much each parent should or could pay, taking account of each parent's individual circumstances, rather than imposing a global sum which the child can extract from either parent as the child pleases. Accordingly joint and several liability, perhaps unexpectedly, does not apply in these circumstances.

Trusts

16.12 Where trustees all breach the duty of trust which they owe to their beneficiary, they are jointly and severally liable to

---

[34] Reg. No. 2137/85, supplemented by the European Economic Interest Grouping Regulations 1989 (S.I. 1989 No. 638).
[35] Art. 24.1 of Reg. 2137/85.

him.[36] However under the Trusts (Scotland) Act 1921, s.3, unless a trust deed says otherwise, a trustee will usually be liable for his own acts and omissions only, not those of his fellow trustees, but may become liable for their acts and omissions if he was aware of their deficiencies or of their breaches of trust and did nothing about them.

Company law

Under company law, there are various defined occasions **16.13** when directors or others may be jointly and severally liable with each other, and sometimes the company, for the debts of their company. Such occasions are liability for the debts of a phoenix company[37]; the liability of directors of a newly-created public limited company if trading without the benefit of a section 117 trading certificate and failing to pay the company's debts[38]; the liability of directors and former members of a subsequently insolvent company which had redeemed its shares out of capital[39]; and many other occasions.

Limited partnerships

Limited partnerships are a cross between companies and **16.14** partnerships. They are much used by farmers as a result of ill-considered legislation introduced to give security of tenure to tenant farmers and their families. As the new legislation, in landlords' eyes, considerably favoured tenants and the tenants' descendants, landlords in many cases terminated the tenants' leases and instead let their former tenants have the benefit of a limited partnership, whereby the tenant is the general partner, responsible on an unlimited basis for the limited partnership's liabilities,[40] and the landlord is the limited partner, obtaining a fixed

---

[36] *Allan v. McCombie's Trs.*, 1909 S.C. 710.
[37] Insolvency Act 1986, s.217(2).
[38] Companies Act 1985, s.117(8).
[39] Insolvency Act 1986, s.76(3).
[40] Limited Partnerships Act 1907, s. 4(2).

return on capital equivalent to rent but allowed no powers of management.[41] If the limited partner does become involved in any way with the management, or attempt to take back his capital, he ceases to have the benefit of limited liability[42] though he can in practice limit his liability anyway by being a limited company.[43] A limited partnership can be wound up by the general partner,[44] or sequestrated in the manner outlined in the Bankruptcy (Scotland) Act. [45]

THE FUTURE OF JOINT AND SEVERAL LIABILITY?

16.15 Joint and several liability is not without merit in that it ensures professional standards, with pressure on each partner not to make his fellow partners liable for his own misdeeds. However, in the USA, where there are such penalties as triple damages in negligence claims, the major accountancy firms are increasingly concerned that major claims against them could drain the firms of their entire insurance cover and indeed their partnerships' capital. The area that accountants are most concerned about is auditing, and there are fears that one day similar claims will arise in the United Kingdom too. Accordingly some auditing in the United Kingdom is being carried out by limited companies wholly owned by accountancy firms. The auditing companies' accounts are published (and indeed audited) in the same manner as any other company. The benefit to the firm of accountants is that their liability, should any of their audits be negligently carried out, is limited; the benefit to the company which is having its accounts audited is that because the auditing company's liability is limited, the cost of the audit ought to be less than it might be because of the reduced insurance cover needed by the auditing company.

16.16 This small step may be a precursor of the demise of joint and several liability for partnerships such as accountants

---

[41] Limited Partnerships Act 1907, s.6(1).
[42] *ibid.* and s.5.
[43] Limited Partnerships Act 1907, s.4(4).
[44] *ibid.* s.6(3).
[45] Bankruptcy (Scotland) Act 1985, s.6(1)(d).

and lawyers. It is possible that unless limited liability is permitted, or a form of restricted joint and several liability is introduced, the major accountancy firms may decline to do any contentious accounting work at all, in favour of less risky pursuits. A major argument in favour of restricted joint and several liability is that it is not sensible to make a partner in an accountancy firm who is, say, involved in corporate finance, responsible for paying the debts incurred by his fellow accountant who audits, when the two persons have no connection with each other except that they are in the partnership together and there is no control of the auditing partner by the corporate finance partner. These matters are still being discussed at the time of writing and may take some time to be resolved.

CHAPTER 17

LIABILITY FOR DEBTS OF UNINCORPORATED ASSOCIATIONS AND CHARITIES

THE UNINCORPORATED ASSOCIATION

The law is never entirely happy dealing with unincorpo- **17.1** rated associations, such as voluntary bodies, societies, social clubs, churches other than the Church of Scotland, playgroups and the like. The law does not know whether to treat such associations as something approaching a contractual association or as a trust. In order to overcome their anomalous status, some unincorporated associations have been given legal recognition, among these being trades unions, employers' associations, friendly societies, industrial and provident societies and building societies. These are all beyond the scope of this book.

The difficulty for the law with regard to unincorporated **17.2** associations is that if too great a responsibility is placed on office-holders, who may not necessarily be well qualified for their posts, especially in the smaller groups, it will become rapidly apparent that no sensible person should even stand for office lest he be saddled with unwelcome administrative and possibly financial burdens. Equally, where there is any money involved it is right that it should be properly accounted for. In addition many small associations are not very well organised, have limited funds and cannot afford to go to court in the event of a dispute. There are further complications: it is not always clear who should raise an action on behalf of an association, and equally it is not always clear who may be liable for its debts. It is therefore wise for well-funded associations to regularise their affairs by adopting some form of corporate structure. Many bowling clubs, for example, are in the form of guarantee companies or non-profit-making private limited companies limited by shares, precisely because the corporate structure imposes some order upon the association's activities. However, many associations have neither the means nor the inclination to embark upon the relatively bureaucratic procedures of incorporation, and often no one will want to take the responsibility of preparing the annual return or registering the accounts. A body of more than 20 persons intending to carry out business with a view to profit (which would usually be a partnership) must incorporate anyway[1]: for an association to avoid incorporation, it must be seen not to be set up with the intention to trade nor to make a profit.

The voluntary association as contractual association

17.3 Where a group of persons agree to set up an association, on a non-profit-making basis, but with a common purpose, it is at least arguable that the members have formed a contract with each other to promote that purpose through the medium of the association. If the members choose to elect office-bearers, there is at the least an expectation that the office-bearers will represent the members, and that in exchange for being nominated as such, the office-bearers oblige themselves to exercise fiduciary duties toward the association. The members contract that they will pay their subscriptions to the association[2] in return for the promotion of the purpose of the association through the office-bearers. If in the members' eyes the contract is not fulfilled they can always dismiss the office-bearers or fail to renew their subscription.

Litigation, liability and voluntary associations

17.4 Where there is no corporate structure, if a contractual association wishes to raise an action in the Court of

---

[1] Companies Act 1985, s.715.
[2] *Re New University Club (Duty on Estate)* [1887] 18 Q.B.D. 720.

Session, it should do so in the name of the association followed by the names of all the members or the office-bearers.[3] In the sheriff court an association can sue or be sued under its usual name alone[4] and there is no requirement that the office-bearers' names be included, though any creditor raising an action against an association would be well advised to raise it against not just the association but also the office-bearers or all the members so that if necessary he can effect diligence against them personally after carrying out diligence against the association. The difficulty of taking a decree against an association alone is that if the association's funds are insufficient to pay the sum for which decree was obtained, a decree against the association would not necessarily automatically entitle the creditor to effect diligence against the office-bearers or the members unless he had actually sought that in his court proceedings. The question of who can have diligence effected against them is a matter of legal procedure and the wording of the writ and is a different issue from the general liability of a member. Ordinary members may be liable for their association's debts provided that they authorised the obligation from which the debt arose. But where some did not authorise the contract, but a majority of the members did, it would appear that in the absence of a constitution or evidence supplied by minutes of meetings, specifying otherwise, the authorising members are liable and the non-authorising members are not.[5] This could lead to considerable practical difficulties for the creditor as he tries to ascertain who is liable to him and who is not. If there are office-bearers, they can act as agents for the entire association and will not themselves be liable for the association's debts provided that they act within the authority delegated to them by the association or the ostensible authority expected of people in their position. With a small association with clear lines of communication the delegation of authority to office-bearers is not likely to cause much difficulty: with a large association all members may find themselves liable for the

---

[3] *Bridge v. South Portland Street Synagogue* (1906) 14 S.L.T. 466.
[4] Ordinary Cause Rules 1993, r. 5.7.
[5] *Thomson and Gillespie v. Victoria Eighty Club* (1905) 13 S.L.T. 399.

apparently authorised actions of a committee even though those members may have very little knowledge of what the office-bearers were doing. Yet at the same time it would clearly be unwise on a public policy level to let such uninformed members have no liability or limited liability. Though it may be unjust to make them liable for actions taken without their knowledge or approval, it would seem more unjust if, say, a creditor supplying goods in good faith for a proper price were not to be paid. As can be seen, the law in relation to liability in this area is by no means certain, and is not helped by the fact that few associations have the funds to go to court to get a modern ruling on the liability attaching to members in small unincorporated voluntary associations formed on a contractual basis.

The association's right of ownership of its assets

17.5 In the absence of a constitution, where a contractual association owns an asset, it is owned jointly by all the members, although they may delegate their right of management of the asset to the office-bearers who will usually hold it as trustees for the association and the members thereof. The position is complicated when the purpose of the association is to benefit some sector of the public such as, say, disadvantaged children. In such an event the office-bearers hold the association's assets in trust not just for the association itself but also for the purposes of the trust and/or the beneficiaries of the trust, namely that section of the public which the trust was set up to benefit, or indeed both the purposes and beneficiaries. Such trusts are known as quasi-public trusts, and as such are subject to the terms of the Trusts (Scotland) Act 1921 and to the regulations introduced by Part 1 of the Law Reform (Miscellaneous Provisions)(Scotland) Act 1990. The dividing line between a contractual association and a quasi-public trust association is by no means clear but, as an example, a group of people who meet regularly to go hillwalking for their own pleasure, hire transport and organise regular social functions could be said to be a contractual association, whereas a group of people who meet regularly to promote a desirable end, such as better architectural design in Scotland's cities, are a quasi-public trust association. In the case of the latter, what starts off as a loose association frequently grows into a properly registered charitable trust or registered company in which case there ought to be no doubt as to who or what is liable for its debts.

Entitlement to the assets of a contractual association

Although each member is entitled to a right of common **17.6** property in the asset, unless the association's constitution (if there is one) says otherwise he is not thereby entitled to demand the sale of the asset. He would need to have approval from all the other members to do so, unless there is a provision in the association's constitution permitting majority decision-making on such matters as the sale of association assets. When a member resigns or leaves, his interest in the asset ceases. If the association finds that it cannot continue its existence, in its winding-up its assets are divided among the current members after payment of all liabilities unless there is some term to the contrary in the association's constitution. Since this could play into the hands of unscrupulous members who may be more interested in their personal acquisition of the association's assets than in the promotion of the causes for which the association was originally set up, it is common to find a clause in the association's constitution requiring that any assets remaining after payment of all debts must be transferred to a similar and compatible association. In the case of a church which was founded with an insufficiently flexible constitution, a split among the attenders resulted in the courts having to ascertain who maintained the original principles under which the church was set up and who therefore was entitled to its assets.[6] It cannot be stressed too strongly that however boring or inconvenient it may be to draw up a constitution for any association, a well-drafted constitution saves a great deal of trouble in the long run when it comes to such matters as decisionmaking, acceptance of liability, variation of the purposes of

---

[6] *Free Church of Scotland v. Lord Overtoun* (1904) 7 F. (H.L.) 1.

the association and the transfer of assets on dissolution of the association.

Entitlement to the assets of a quasi-public trust association

17.7 In this situation, unless the constitution says otherwise, the members are not entitled to the assets because the assets are not held ultimately for the members' benefit. A well-drafted constitution will specify what is to be done with the association's assets should the original purpose for which the association was set up be unable any longer to be achieved and the association is to be wound up. Commonly, as with a contractual association, there will be a direction that the assets are to be transferred to a similar association. In the absence of that, or in the absence of a method of altering the constitution (as sometimes happens in older, less well-drafted constitutions) the association has to apply to court for approval of a scheme under the *cyprès* jurisdiction at common law or a court-approved reorganisation or one approved by the Lord Advocate in terms of the Law Reform (Miscellaneous Provisions) (Scotland) Act 1990, ss.9, 10 and 11. These methods allow for the reorganisation of such associations subject to judicial scrutiny. Many such associations are charities, in which case readers are referred to the publication *Charity Law in Scotland*[7] produced by the Charity Law Research Unit at Dundee University. Where a charity is a registered company, it must comply with the requirements of the Companies Act 1985 and the ancillary subordinate legislation applicable to charities.

---

[7] Barker, Ford, Moody and Elliot ed. (W.Green, Edinburgh, 1996).

CHAPTER 18

THE ENGLISH LAW OF DEBT

DEBT RECOVERY IN ENGLAND

This chapter provides a very brief and selective summary of some of the considerations which apply to the English process of debt recovery. As in Scotland, many debt actions are undefended and judgment is granted by default; where there is a defence it is often dropped or struck out by the courts as being unjustified. In many cases the parties come to an agreed settlement. This chapter does not concern itself with the procedural mechanics of English court procedure, instead concentrating on the remedies available to a creditor in attempting to obtain payment of the money owed to him. **18.1**

The equivalent to the Scottish sheriff court is the county court, which will generally hear proceedings relating to claims of £25,000 or less. Claims of between £25,000 and £50,000 can be heard in either the county court or the High Court (the equivalent to the Outer House of the Court of Session) and claims of over £50,000 are usually heard in the High Court. *Anton Piller* orders (of which more later) can be made only in the High Court, and *Mareva* injunctions (of which more later), with certain exceptions, are generally heard only in the High Court also. Claims of less than £1,000 are dealt with by means of a small claims procedure within the county court. **18.2**

Prescription

For most ordinary debt issues, the period of prescription is six years,[1] as opposed to five years in Scotland. In relation **18.3**

---

[1] Limitation Act 1980, ss.2 and 5.

to agreements made under seal, these usually being more significant contracts, especially those relating to land, the period of prescription is 12 years.[2]

Privity of contract

18.4 English law finds the concept of a third party benefiting from or being burdened by a contract involving two other parties difficult to accept. This is because a person may not wish to receive a benefit and should not therefore be forced to receive it, since he might, for example, find that he was liable to tax upon it or have to pay for its upkeep. Equally, as regards being burdened by a contract made by others, if he was not party to that particular contract, why should he be liable for something in which he was not involved or in respect of which he did not give his consent? The doctrine of privity of contract, while not without its merits, has occasioned a number of exceptions, among them being garnishee orders (the English equivalent to arrestment), attachment of earnings orders, sureties and guarantees.

Anton Piller orders

18.5 Strictly speaking, *Anton Piller* orders do not arise much in the context of debt recovery, but they still are extremely useful in the context of civil wrongdoing. An *Anton Piller* order allows a plaintiff to seize evidence which the defendant might be tempted to destroy lest it incriminate him, and might be useful to prevent a company director shredding evidence which might point to his responsibility for, say, wrongful trading. Such orders are often used in the areas of dishonest appropriation of intellectual property or misuse of trade secrets by former employees.

Mareva injunctions

18.6 A *Mareva* injunction is similar to arrestment on the dependence of an action, and freezes the defendant's assets before

[2] Limitation Act 1980, s.8.

he has time to transport them out of the country or telex his funds abroad. The freezing of the assets also acts as an effective security to prevent the debtor absconding without at least some effort to defend the action raised against him in order to get his funds released.

Bayer v. Winter orders

This is an order commonly used in conjunction with *Anton Piller* and *Mareva* orders. The effect of this order is to compel a defendant to surrender his passport to prevent him fleeing the country. It is not particularly effective against the well-organised fraudster with a number of passports.   **18.7**

Court officials

Where a court has pronounced a judgment (the English term for a decree), the officials designated to carry out enforcement are known as under-sheriffs (usually referred to as sheriff's officers) in respect of High Court judgments and bailiffs for county court judgments.   **18.8**

ENFORCEMENT OF JUDGMENTS

Fieri facias

This writ lasts for 12 months, and empowers a sheriff's officer or bailiff (henceforth referred to as the sheriff) to seize goods belonging to a debtor and to sell them after a public auction. The sheriff may not seize the tools of the debtor's trade nor his necessities of life and is not supposed to sell goods which do not belong to the debtor, though it is up to the true owner to substantiate any claim that the sheriff unlawfully sold the true owner's goods. This process is similar to poinding in Scotland.   **18.9**

Garnishee order

A garnishee order is where a debtor of the judgment debtor can be required by court order to pay the creditor.   **18.10**

As the debtor to the judgment debtor would have had to pay the debt anyway he is no worse off, and once he has paid the creditor he is not required to pay the judgment debtor the sums he has already paid the creditor. It is similar to an arrestment of goods in the hands of a third party in Scotland.

Attachment of earnings

18.11 This is a method of attaching earnings from employment (though not self-employment). The employer is required to deduct sums from the debtor's wages and pay them direct to the creditor.

Charging order

18.12 This is a method of imposing a security over land, securities or funds in court[3] and prevents the disposal by the debtor of the asset in question without payment to the debtor. There is a second stage to the order which must be completed before the creditor can realise the asset and obtain his funds. With regard to securities, a charging order can lead to a stop notice which prevents a company from transferring the debtor's securities.

Administration order

18.13 This is a method whereby, in the county court, the court will take over the supervision and administration of the payment of "proved debts".[4] This can be at the instance of the creditor, the debtor or the court itself. It gives priority to the creditors of the proved debts, and usually endures for a period of three years.

Equitable receivership[5]

18.14 This is a method of obtaining funds not easily accessible by other methods. It is common in property, where if a debtor

---

[3] Charging Orders Act 1979, s.2.
[4] County Courts Act 1984, s.112.
[5] Supreme Court Act 1981, s.37.

fails to pay to a creditor sums due, the creditor can appoint a receiver to collect the rents and apply them to the creditor. It is an expensive process.

The English law of bankruptcy is governed by the Insolvency Act 1986, ss.264–385. In many respects it is similar to the Scottish law of bankruptcy, though there are certain differences: for example the rules on the renunciation of onerous contracts are more complicated in England[6]; and there is no equivalent to the Scottish rules on equalisation of diligence, so that the toughest and swiftest creditor fares best. Incomplete enforcement of a judgment remains incomplete at the time of bankruptcy,[7] and there is no question of all creditors being treated *pari passu* as at the date of bankruptcy. Landlords can levy distress for rent at the time of the debtor's bankruptcy but only for up to six months' outstanding rent.[8] Curiously, in the context of transactions at an undervalue (the English equivalent of gratuitous alienations) the personal bankruptcy rules in England and Scotland are not the same: the five-year rule applies to all recipients of transactions at an undervalue in England[9] irrespective of the degree of association, whereas in Scotland the rule is five years for associates and two years for others[10]; but in terms of corporate insolvency, companies in England enjoy a lighter regime than in Scotland. In England transactions at an undervalue do not draw any distinction between associates and others,[11] and the period referred to is one of two years in all circumstances. In Scotland the corporate rules are the same as the personal bankruptcy rules.[12] It is hard to see what is gained by the anomaly.

18.15

---

[6] Insolvency Act 1986, ss.315–321.
[7] *ibid.* s.346.
[8] *ibid.* s.347.
[9] *ibid.* ss339, 341.
[10] Bankruptcy (Scotland) Act 1985, s.34.
[11] Insolvency Act 1986, ss.238, 240.
[12] *ibid.* s.242.

CHAPTER 19

MISCELLANEOUS DEBT-RELATED ISSUES

CLAIMS FROM OUTSIDE SCOTLAND

If a creditor has a claim against a company or a person **19.1** domiciled in Scotland, it is usually the case that he must sue that company or person in Scotland in the sheriff court applicable to the area where the debtor is domiciled, or in the Court of Session.[1] This is partly so as to permit the defender a fairer chance to resist the claim than he would have if he had to cope with the pursuer's legal system. It is also because it is easier to enforce the decree where the debtor's assets are situated than in some other place where he has no assets worth seizing in satisfaction of the debt. The question of domicile varies from country to country, and to establish whether a person is domiciled in any particular country it is necessary to apply the rules of that country. As far as the United Kingdom is concerned, a person is said to be domiciled in the U.K. if he is resident and has a substantial connection with the U.K., "substantial connection" being three months' residence in the U.K.[2] It is possible to be domiciled in more than one country. Companies are usually sued in the country of their registration, though in the case of consumer contracts, a person raising an action against a business can sue the business in either the country of the business's registration or any country where it has a branch or agency.[3] Insurers can be

[1] Civil Jurisdiction and Judgments Act 1982, Sched. 8, para. 1.
[2] *ibid.* s.41(2).
[3] Art. 13 of "the Conventions", these being the Brussels and the Parallel Conventions which form the underlying treaties on which the Civil Jurisdiction and Judgments Act 1982 is based.

sued in the policyholder's own domicile, the insurer's own country of registration, or any country where it has a branch, office or agency.[4] Insurers can also be sued in the place of the event occasioning the policy. Although this might appear to inconvenience the insurer, an insurer wishing to attract business has little option but to comply with this rule. Sometimes even when a party to a dispute is not obliged to accept the jurisdiction of a particular court it will do so in order to resolve an issue or to demonstrate confidence in its own products. Commonly, commercial contracts will contain a prorogation clause specifying which law is to apply, and which courts can hear the dispute. Unless these are well drafted, it can lead to timewasting exercises, where, at its worst, a Scottish court has to have English or some other foreign law proved and, if necessary, used. A party can sometimes legitimately claim that the court in which a dispute is being heard is *forum non conveniens* (not the correct court to deal with the action) or that another court elsewhere is already dealing with it (the plea known as *lis alibi pendens*).

19.2   International disputes are notoriously difficult and expensive, so it is also common to have an arbitration clause, satisfactory to both parties, which will avoid the inconvenience of conflicting evidential, procedural and jurisdictional rules.

JUDGMENTS FROM OUTSIDE SCOTLAND

Acceptance of judgments from outside Scotland

19.3   This matter is governed by the Rules of the Court of Session 1994, Chapter 62, which, among other things, enforces Part 2 of the Administration of Justice Act 1920 and the Foreign Judgments (Reciprocal Enforcement) Act 1933.

Judgments from England, Wales and Northern Ireland

19.4   In respect of money claims, the usual procedure is to send the Keeper of the Registers of Scotland the principal

---

[4] Art. 10 of the Conventions.

judgment from the English court, requiring him to register it in the Register of Judgments of the Books of Council and Session. Once registered, the Keeper will issue a certificate to that effect, together with a warrant for execution, and the certificate can then be handed to sheriff officers for them to carry out diligence against the debtor.[5]

Registration of judgments from Commonwealth and certain former Commonwealth countries

In this case, the creditor must petition the Outer House of **19.5** the Court of Session for warrant to register the foreign judgment in the Register of Judgments referred to above. If the court entertains the petition, it will grant warrant to cite the defender and to present the judgment to the Keeper, as referred to above. If the debtor does not respond to the citation or, having contested the authority to grant warrant to cite, the court decides that the debtor's objections are ill-founded, the court will pronounce an interlocutor authorising the Keeper to register the judgment in the Register of judgments and to grant warrant for execution as above.[6]

Registration of judgments from E.C. countries

The procedure is broadly similar to that described in **19.6** paragraph 19.5, though there are opportunities for legal aid to be extended to those who need it. The court has greater discretion to waive some of the procedural requirements, though a solicitor must provide an affidavit showing the sum due, the extent of any interest, a service address for the creditor, and the debtor's last known address.[7] Assuming that the petition is granted, the court will grant a warrant for registration of the judgment by the Keeper, and for execution to follow thereafter.

No investigation of the merits of the case

In each of the above issues, it is not the function of the **19.7** court to look behind the judgment issued by a foreign

---

[5] Rules of the Court of Session 1994, r. 62.2.
[6] *ibid*. rr. 62.5–62.11.
[7] *ibid*. r. 62.18.

Debt

court unless it is contrary to public policy or where the judgment is obtained by fraud. If there is something untoward about the original judgment, the problem must be resolved in the country whose courts issued the judgment. In addition, certain foreign judgments are not entertained by the courts here, these being maintenance orders and insolvency orders.

Registration of judgments from elsewhere

19.8 Any judgment not coming within the above three categories must proceed through the courts as an ordinary action for debt, using the judgment of the foreign court as the instrument of debt.

THE MAN OF STRAW

19.9 The "man of straw" is a fictional term for someone who turns out not to be worth suing because he has no assets. Such a person may not even be officially bankrupt because it is not worth anyone's while sequestrating him, but he exists to incur expense and to waste time as far as creditors are concerned. When a creditor is considering suing a debtor for non-payment of sums due, it is often worth considering from a commercial point of view whether the effort involved will justify the expense of litigation. A decree against a man of straw is pointless if the debtor's assets are minimal. There will be no virtue in proceeding to a poinding since if there are insufficient assets to make a poinding worthwhile, the sheriff officer's fees will have to be borne by the creditor. Some finance companies do carry on with poindings even when they know it may not be advantageous to do so just because they do not wish to be seen by unscrupulous debtors as a soft touch. In many cases it may be commercially more sensible to write off the debt and claim VAT bad debt relief where necessary. It is a sad fact that there will always be debtors who "play the system", whose assets always turn out to be owned by Channel Island-registered companies, whose properties are always in their spouses' names, whose bank accounts are kept offshore and who always promise more than they can deliver. Sometimes checks with credit reference agencies and with the registers of bankruptcies may provide some information on such people, but dedicated fraudsters change their names and addresses sufficiently frequently to render continual detection pretty well impossible.

SECURITISATION OF SECURITIES

When a customer obtains a loan from a bank to purchase his home, he will in due course be providing a regular income stream to the bank. The bank itself can use that income stream, along with the income stream from many other mortgages, as security for any loan from a secondary bank, so that in effect the secondary bank has a security over securities. This is unexceptionable until the day when the customers fail to pay their regular mortgage payments: this will have a knock-on effect to the secondary bank. The secondary bank may then iself run into difficulties and may call up its security over the first bank—which may find itself, in order to meet its liabilities, forced to realise the securities which have been granted in its favour by its customers. While this may not affect the customers who are already in difficulties and have had to renounce their homes already, it may have a serious effect on those customers who have so far been paying their mortgage payments satisfactorily. They may find that their interest rates creep up through no fault of their own or that the bank pressurises them to sell their homes. While this is not generally a problem with reputable banks or building societies, some borrowers who find themselves unable to obtain a loan from the high street banks or building societies may be forced to borrow from more specialised lenders whose terms of loan may allow such draconian action to be taken. Any agent for such a borrower would therefore be well advised to inspect the terms of any such loan very carefully. **19.10**

AUTHORISED USE OF BANK ACCOUNTS

A popular fraud, common some years ago, was for reputable persons, such as solicitors or accountants, to be approached by people from certain central African countries or elsewhere with an application to use their firm's **19.11** bank accounts as a temporary resting place for the deposit of certain funds which needed to be kept offshore. Absolute discretion was assured, and all the accountant or solicitor had to do was to provide the applicant with details of the firm's bank account. In return for the "parking" of the funds on a temporary basis, the applicant would pay the bank account holder a commission. Sadly, some persons responded to these implausible requests and found their accounts cleared out by the applicant. A variation of the same technique was for the applicant to ask for an advance to secure the parking of the funds in the bank account; and naturally the advance was never seen again. Where the accountant or solicitor allowed this to happen with the clients' account, serious professional penalties arose in addition to the requirement to repay the sums lost to the clients out of the clients' account.

LETTERS OF CREDIT

19.12 Letters of credit are a common method of financing payment for exported goods. An exporter may agree to give an importer credit for the goods as part of the terms of trade, and so when the goods are delivered to the importer, the importer gives the exporter a letter of credit which is in effect a promissory note granted by a bank or other institution, or a bill of exchange, which ensure the payment by the bank or other payer at the end of the credit period of three, six or 12 months as the case may be. In addition, depending on the terms of the letter of credit, there may be a right to interest in the meantime plus a premium on maturity. The letter of credit can be sold by the exporter who can then receive a discounted sum. The purchaser will be a specialist purchaser of letters of credit who will assess the risk of non-payment, the prevailing interest rates, the maturity figure and the amount of discount before he pays the exporter. Brokers may be involved to put the exporter in touch with the purchaser. The purchaser in turn may sell the letter of credit on, and so on until the ultimate holder receives funds from the original payer.

19.13 A fraud which still surfaces from time to time is for a fraudster to pretend that he has such a letter of credit (or similar instruments, known as standby letters of credit, prime bank guarantees, trade letters of credit or prime bank notes) which he does not actually have and to try to sell it to a purchaser. As part of convincing the purchaser that he has the letter of credit he will try to get banks to confirm that the letter of credit does exist. The fraudster also will try to persuade the bank issuing the letter of credit (or the current holder of it) that he will buy it from the bank or the current holder. Naturally the selling bank or holder will not release the letter of credit until it knows that the fraudster has the funds; and the purchasing bank will not release the funds until it knows the fraudster has the letter of credit. The seller will want a guarantee or some form of collateral in case the fraudster does not come up with the money. The purchaser will also want some form of collateral in case, having handed over the money, there is no letter of credit. It is at this stage that accountants and solicitors have occasionally become involved in what, were a fraudster not involved, is not in itself an objectionable transaction, being in reality nothing more than a back-to-back transaction with an individual making a perfectly legitimate profit from buying and selling the letter of credit. Because of the large sums of money involved, and the potential risk, certain fraudsters are keen to use lawyers and accountants, both backed by their professional indemnity insurance, to legitimise any transaction. In order to encourage the accountant or solicitor to become involved the fraudster may promise a commission, or if he prevails upon the greed of the accountant or solicitor, he can even involve the accountant or solicitor personally, and in doing so may require the accountant or solicitor to make an advance payment as earnest of his goodwill. Needless to say, the advance payment is never seen again. While there are some transactions involving the above letters of credit which are not necessarily fraudulent, some financial transactions involving letters of credit above are transacted on an international basis often to limit any tax exposure or indeed any possibility for unwelcome scrutiny. Unfortunately, in so doing this practice also allows for the introduction of funds from dubious sources and indeed substantially increases the opportunities for fraud. It makes it very difficult to sue for any losses in the event of fraud and any debt incurred might well be unrecoverable. Both accountants' and solicitors' professional bodies strongly recommend having nothing to do with such schemes.

MONEY LAUNDERING

19.14 Money laundering is the transformation of funds obtained illegally into apparently legitimate funds. It arises particularly in the context of drug money and illicit arms sales.[8] A problem for drug dealers making a great quantity of money is that it is physically dangerous to keep a lot of cash on their persons, but to invest it and to generate income from it may excite the attention of banks, who may wonder where a sudden surge of funds comes from, and the Inland Revenue and Customs and Excise both of whom will be interested in the profits generated by any businesses funded by illicit money. Equally, from the point of view of solicitors and accountants, clients appearing with briefcases full of cash pose a security risk, leaving aside the question of the provenance of the funds. Formerly certain banks had a reputation for deviant behaviour (the Bank of Commerce and Credit International being particularly favoured) and funds could be safely deposited there before entering the international banking system. The courts now have powers to seize the proceeds of drug-related crime and do from time to time exercise their powers to realise drug dealers' assets, close bank accounts and sell property, and they may have the power to retrieve assets nominally in the hands of third parties but truly in the ownership of such criminals. A problem for major drug dealers is that there is often more money available than they can find legitimate uses for, but when the law does catch up with such persons, it is in a position to remove it all from them.

---

[8] The Drug Trafficking Offences Act 1986, the Prevention of Terrorism (Temporary Provisions) Act 1989 and the Proceeds of Crime Act 1995 both require banks to report suspicious movements of money, or of their clients' financial behaviour, which might be connected with these two issues.

INDEX

229

HUMAN DEVELOPMENT

SELECTED READINGS

SECOND EDITION

EDITED BY
MORRIS L. HAIMOWITZ
Director, Human Relations, Chicago Public Schools

AND
NATALIE READER HAIMOWITZ
Consulting Psychologist

THOMAS Y. CROWELL COMPANY
New York   Established 1834

TO OUR PARENTS AND TO OUR CHILDREN

L.C. CARD 66-10924
ISBN: 0-690-42419-1

DESIGNED BY JUDITH WORACEK BARRY

FIRST PRINTING, MAY, 1966
SECOND PRINTING, SEPTEMBER, 1966
THIRD PRINTING, APRIL, 1967
FOURTH PRINTING, JANUARY, 1968
FIFTH PRINTING, JULY, 1968
SIXTH PRINTING, JULY, 1969
SEVENTH PRINTING, AUGUST, 1970
EIGHTH PRINTING, JUNE, 1971

MANUFACTURED IN THE UNITED STATES OF AMERICA

PREFACE

The articles in this book have been selected because they were important and because they were clear; important to us, the editors, and written clearly enough to be understood by college students and interested adults.

Observations made of children around the world show that a wide variety of personalities is possible. Do we want our children to grow up to be friendly and generous, tough or industrious, frugal or creative? To help determine the kinds of personalities we want for them, the selections in the first part of the book explore the rich variety of possible values and personality characteristics, some of them conflicting with others.

Once we have decided what kind of adults we would like our children to become, then what must we know and what steps might we take to help them develop as we wish? Presumably, scientific knowledge tells us about children, about how they grow and mature as unique persons. Perhaps science can help us achieve the desired ends. The major portion of this volume is composed of scientific studies, descriptive and theoretical, dealing with the psychological, physical, and social behavior of infants and children. Once we know what we want and we understand the nature of the human being we are working with, then we still have the problem of applying our knowledge to achieve the desired outcomes. We might call this the art of applied psychology. The part entitled "Planned Intervention" describes some of the approaches in current use.

In selecting materials, we were guided by the outline just described, namely:

What kind of children do we want? What are the values cherished by human beings throughout the ages? Which are inconsistent with one another and rarely achieved together?

What readings in science, philosophy, or fiction eloquently describe the nature of infants and children?

How can this knowledge and understanding be applied to help children grow?

If there is an attitude of manipulation here, so be it. Most of the studies of creativity show that creative children come from homes with a permissive atmosphere. Studies of disturbed children show that most come from homes with a punitive or over-controlled atmosphere. If we are to manipulate, then let us do so with knowledge of the consequences. After a child has become disturbed, manipulative techniques are sometimes required and prove therapeutic, and a wide and ever-growing variety of correctional approaches are coming to the fore to be used in correcting a variety of disturbances. Some of these new and creative appoaches to treatment are presented.

We found many exciting readings and often could not place them in our outline, so we often revised the outline and remained uncertain. Some were dropped; others were included because they could not be ignored in any significant review of the current scene. A good many issues are controversial. Outstanding studies sometimes contradict studies equally outstanding. Much of what we believe to be true today may be found inadequate tomorrow. Since we have faith in the scientific method, we present many kinds of scientific studies. Great psychological insights by artists and writers, which often precede the studies that affirm them to be scientific truths, have also been included.

Because one may be led to believe that juvenile delinquency is a modern urban invention, we have included selections from the Holy Bible so that the reader may see in perspective how ancient and perhaps universal are some of the human problems between young and old, and how local and transitory are others.

Recent investigations of maternal deprivation have begun to clarify the nature of maternal love; moreover, important new developments such as transactional analysis and reality therapy provide such stimulating new approaches to understanding how the infant becomes a person that articles introducing these concepts were written for this book.

We are grateful to the authors and publishers who so graciously permitted us to use their materials, and to Herman Makler for his indispensable suggestions in editing. We are also grateful to our many colleagues for the generous and valuable recommendations as to materials to include. Especially helpful has been the advice of Jerome L. Schulman and Jack Tanzman, who led us to new and greener pastures. We wish to thank Mary Ainsworth and Kurt Glaser for their considerable contributions in selecting from the diversity of material available dealing with maternal deprivation, as well as to the following colleagues for their helpful suggestions, advice or inspiration: Theron Alexander, Sister Mary Amatora, O.S.F., Bernard Aronov, Edyth Barry, Bruno Bettelheim, Sidney W. Bijou, Charlotte Buhler, Ruth C. Bussey, Hy Chausow, James M. Dunlap, Horace English, Clifford G. Erickson, Jacob W. Getzels, Jacob L. Gewirtz, Jack Gibb, Joseph Harney, Sara S. Hawk, Majorie P. Honzik, Philip W. Jackson, Barney Katz, Stanley Lipkin, Gordon L. Lippitt, Ner Litner, Boyd McCandless, Willis H. McCann, Carson McGuire, Frieda and Ralph Merry, Elizabeth H. Morris, Norman L. Munn, Hugh V. Perkins, Edward Reinfranck, Reuben Segal, Oscar Shabat, Beatrice G. Shuttleworth, Marvin Steinberg, Ruth Strang, Florence M. Teagarden, George G. Thompson, Regina H. Westcott, and Ben Wright.

M.L.H.
N.R.H.

Evanston, Ill.
March, 1966

CONTENTS

PART TWO

INFANCY   115

SATISFYING FUNDAMENTAL NEEDS:
SOME DIMENSIONS OF LOVE

PART ONE
GOALS
WHAT KIND OF PEOPLE DO WE WANT?

It is one thing to investigate the values of exotic cultures—commenting on
how strange, primitive, or vulgar they are—and quite another to examine
one's own standards critically in order to select carefully. Men at all
times have sought truth, beauty, and justice, but they have rarely
agreed on what these are. Each generation inherits the values of
its fathers and adds some of its own. In one generation, firm
discipline is advocated, but in the next, a thousand reasons for sparing
the rod are manufactured. Should we be governed by fashion in
such matters? Or should we study and reevaluate our own cultural
heritage?

What do we want in life? What do we want for our children?
If it is pleasure we seek, why do we work so hard? If "freedom,"
then, specifically, freedom from what and to do what? Wealth might be
the goal, but it often appears that the rich are slaves to their
riches. Courage—to thumb our noses at the law, or at our
neighbors? Or perhaps we desire to love our neighbors as ourselves;
child sacrifice is not advocated in our families, but we manage—in a
land overflowing with milk and honey—to sacrifice many of our
neighbor's children to poverty, ignorance, and disease. Do we believe
that the meek shall inherit the earth? Or do we believe that might
makes right? If we believe in democracy, why are we ruled by
bureaucracy?

The articles in this part display our rich heritage of values; they
discuss, advocate, or condemn many different standards of behavior
and attitudes. Cultural values in France, Israel, India, Ireland, and
the U.S.S.R. are described. Watson and Foote and Cottrell state their
more general points of view in wider scientific terms.

The articles here might be compared with standards and statements
from other and previous cultures. For example, Machiavelli contended
during the Italian Renaissance that the Prince must do anything—
lie, cheat, steal, murder—in order to remain in power. Rousseau, in the
eighteenth century, believed that man needed freedom to express himself,
to do as *he* pleased, not as society demanded. Or Mussolini, in our
time, felt that people are not born equal and should be treated
accordingly. To him some were born wise and forceful; others were
born as sheep to be ruled. For himself, he declared, "Better one hour as a
lion than a thousand years as a sheep!"; the contrast with the point
of view expressed in, "The Lord is my shepherd," is obvious.

By comparing some of the articles in this part with those in later
sections, the reader may notice the essential differences between methods
that exort, moralize, or philosophize and those that are descriptive,
analytical, experimental or therapeutic.

1 | WHAT PRICE VIRTUE?

MORRIS L. HAIMOWITZ

"Virtue" conveys many different meanings to different people.
For one individual, to be "virtuous" he must be a saint; for
another, it may mean being a civil rights leader, businessman,
artist, or good mother. Each of these roles requires the cultivation
of different and sometimes contradictory "virtues." No man can
serve two masters; he is forced to choose the particular "virtues"
appropriate to his way of life.

This article points out that many social and psychological
troubles stem from the fact that one greatly desired pattern
of values may conflict with another that is desired as much.
If one is to be free and independent, he cannot also be
dutiful and obedient. A gentle and kindly individual
cannot also be cold and uncompromising. The parent who
wants his little boy to develop "masculine" self-confidence
must permit the child to win some family arguments. Aristotle's
Golden Mean, unfortunately, does not seem to provide an easy
solution to this problem.

Two thousand years ago Pericles declared the secret of happiness to be freedom, and the secret of freedom, a brave heart. Many parents today believe this, for when asked, "What kind of children do you want?" they replied, "bold and courageous." We wonder if parents wish for their children what the parents do not themselves have. Thus, parents who are fearful would wish for their children boldness and courage. Can the child be bold when his parents are afraid? Doesn't the child identify with his parents, become as they are rather than what they would like him to be? If the child really were bold, and the parents afraid, won't the parent envy his child, compete with him, and because of his greater strength, subdue the child—so that he could not be bold?

We assume that children grow up this

way and that; no two are the same, but in one society there is more docility; in another society, more independence; in another, hunger and misery; in another, tyranny and sadism. The Nazis developed sado-masochistic characters, people who loved to obey orders and to give orders to their underlings. Medieval Jews developed pious and scholarly characters, who loved learning and who felt nothing was so important as to study the Bible. The ancient Greeks and Romans developed men of courage, who loved to prove their bravery in battle. Some Americans want children who are free, independent, honest, and courageous. But such a child might be expected to talk back to his parents, to disagree with his teachers. How much of this freedom, independence, honesty, and courage can adults take? The most common question persons having trouble with their children bring to us is, "How can I get my child to behave, to do what I tell him to do?" This indicates that the parents want the child to be obedient, submissive. We suppose that a child can be both submissive and bold, but it would be

Revised from "What Kind of Children Do We Want?" in *Teleclass Study Guide in Child Psychology,* (1958), 22–29, by permission of the Chicago Board of Education. The author thanks Kenneth Telford and Jerry Cohen for their help in preparing this article.

impossible for him to be both at the same time.

Perhaps the parents want their children to be submissive to teachers, policemen, the clergy, and to other adults; but to be bold with children their own age and size—submissive in some situations, bold in others.

In children's literature one often finds the following theme: a few boys make a pledge to each other to perform some great obligation, which they carry out at considerable danger and pain to themselves and others. Such a pledge might be to keep their gang name a secret; or to save some prisoner, as in *Huckleberry Finn*; or to guard a make-believe warehouse in a public park, as in *Word of Honor* (a short story in a first grade 1957 Russian textbook, *Rodnaya Rech*, translated into English by Olga M. Beeks). In *Word of Honor* the little hero will not leave his guard post because he has given his word, even though it is getting dark and he is very hungry. In *Huckleberry Finn* the boys strenuously risk death in a dozen ways to fool the adults and to test themselves.

We showed *Word of Honor* to some parents. Here are their comments.

"You can really admire the courage of this little boy, bravely standing alone in the dark. His word means something to him." But Mrs. Smith said, "How foolish can a kid be! Standing alone in the dark! He doesn't know the difference between a game and the real thing! Is this courage that keeps him there? Or fear? Is he brave or submissive?"

Mrs. Gudensky felt very differently: "I think you are both wrong. He is just a cute kid. I admire his will; just as cute as he can be." This made Mrs. Smith angry. "Do you want children growing up like that, stubborn, foolish? Do we want kids cute, who will entertain us with their whimseys; or do we want them to be able to know the difference between what is important and what is just a game!" Mrs.

Gudensky was offended at this. "This little boy was learning something I wish we could teach to our kids and that is *obedience*." Mr. F. (we did not get his name) was quiet all this time, but when he heard the word *obedience*, his ears turned red and he could not wait to shout, "We don't want slaves; we don't want passive obedience to stupid authority. This is America! We want our children to be independent, to think for themselves, to judge for themselves, not to stand in the dark and cry for some childish phantasy." Mrs. Smith agreed, saying, "The ancient Greeks used to say a *liberal* education is one befitting a free man. A free man must know how to make wise decisions in ruling himself and his government. It is a slave who does only what he is told."

Whenever we hear a discussion on freedom, we think of Kant's *Foundations of the Metaphysics of Morals* and John Stuart Mill's essay *On Liberty*. If we were to imagine a conversation between Kant and Mill on the meaning of freedom, with those two gentlemen sitting before the fireplace, Kant knocking the ashes out of his pipe, it might go like this:

MILL: Freedom is the ability to do what you please. If you have to do something someone else wants you to do, then you are not free.

KANT: You are absolutely wrong. Freedom is the ability to do what is *right* for you to do. A man is not free who must follow every fancy, who is a slave to his impulse. A free man is a moral man.

MILL: That's what Buddha and Socrates said. A man must be free of his body if his soul is to soar. But to me body and soul are one. The man is a man, an individual. He must do what a man must do, not what a soul must do. I agree freedom is not license. There could be no freedom to anyone if there was license for one. If one man had license to go out and kill, there could be no freedom for anyone else. A man finds that some things are most pleasant; those are the things most truly befitting a man. He is most free who expresses his peculiar individuality, according to his own nature.

KANT: When I knock the ashes out of my pipe, I am careful not to get them on your floor. I do this of my own free will, feeling it is the best thing for me to do.

MILL: Of course, that would be obnoxious, and you are a gentleman.

We heard a more up-to-date conversation on the meanings of freedom recently in a corner drug store. Four ivy-leaguers were sitting around the table. One dropped his cigarette butt on the floor and squashed it with his toe.

I.L. 1: That's what I like about this country. Freedom [*and he downed his soda*].

I.L. 2: Yep, I drink to freedom, gentlemen.

I.L. 3: You guys don't even know what freedom means.

I.L. 2: You have a monopoly of knowledge, my friend? I know very well. It means the state of single blessedness. It means . . .

I.L. 3: See, I told you, you don't know. A single man is not free. He is the slave of a constant longing. As a hungry man is free to do nothing except seek food.

I.L. 4: Who has freedom? Are you free to be born or to die? You say you have freedom to think. What do you think about? Every thought you have, every action you take is determined by social or biological forces. Some of these forces were poured into you with your mother's milk. It used to be mother's; the social forces today make it cow's. You are conditioned in a thousand ways. Everything you feel, everything you want, everything you believe has been determined. You have no free will.

I.L. 2: You mean the good Lord did not give us a brain to choose between good and evil?

I.L. 3: Of course not. The only people who believe that use it as an excuse for cruelty. They say, "Johnny was a bad boy. He could have been a good boy like the rest of us. Let Johnny be punished." They don't wait for the good Lord to punish Johnny. They do it themselves, for they are full of hate. They were hated as children and grow up to be hateful. Their hate is as much determined as my pity for them. I have no freedom to love them or to kill them. I have been trained to believe I should understand them, and really try.

I.L. 1: You, my friend, are a supercilious fool and I will pray for you.

I.L. 3: You must pray. I must not. Neither of us has freedom or free will.

I.L. 2: Freedom means, nobody telling you what to do. Nobody pushing you around. We have a free country, we put in a government and if we don't like it, we can throw it out. The government doesn't push anybody around in this country.

I.L. 3: See. You just don't know. Look over the counter there. Six government licenses, to sell cigarettes, liquor, drugs, and what-not. Look over there by the cash register. While you have been yapping, I have been watching an interesting conversation. That man talking to the druggist works for the government. Just listen.

DRUGGIST: You government people! Boy, every week it's somebody. Last week the man from the pure food and drug administration; the week before it was the man from the jewelry tax, examining my books, testing my bottles, getting everything all mixed up! Now you want to look at my books for 1965. If you find something wrong, you fine me $1,000 or $10,000. If you don't find anything wrong it costs me a day's wages —two days' wages to look after you instead of after my own business. In addition, I and other taxpayers have to pay your salary whether you find anything wrong or not. 1965! That's ancient history!

GOVERNMENT MAN [*wiping his glasses*]: You need a central government stronger than any business; otherwise the people of this country would be fleeced by business men who suddenly turn into crooks. Before the pure food laws, people were getting poisoned; even with inspectors, half the people falsify their tax returns. Show me your books.

DRUGGIST: Maybe you are right, but every time I turn around, there are two government men (living off my taxes) telling me what to do.

I.L. 2: A government man should not talk like that to a private citizen. We don't get pushed around by our servants, our employees.

I.L. 1: A government man represents the common will, the conscience of the people. The big policeman. He represents our duty. We have a strong sense of duty. I used to be a Boy Scout: "On my honor, I will do my best to do my *duty* to God and my country, to obey the Scout laws at all times, to keep myself physically strong, mentally alert, and morally straight."

I.L. 3: There is a lot about duty and obedience in that oath, very little about courage or independent thinking. *Poor Richard's Almanac* was also full of duty and obedience. John Quincy Adams, one of the greatest presidents, the son of the second president, had a powerful sense of duty. Here are two letters he wrote at the age of 10 and 11, showing characteristics not too different from the story of honor above:

John Q. Adams,
Aged 10, to His Father[1]

Braintree, June the 2nd, 1777

DEAR SIR, I love to receive letters very well; much better than I love to write them. I make

a poor figure at composition, my head is much too fickle, my thoughts are running after birds eggs play and trifles, till I get vexed with myself. Mamma has a troublesome task to keep me steady, and I own I am ashamed of myself. I have but just entered the 3d volume of Smollet tho' I had designed to have got it half through by this time. I have determined this week to be more diligent, as Mr. Thaxter will be absent at Court, & I cannot persue my other studies. I have Set myself a Stent & determine to read the 3d volume Half out. If I can but keep my resolution, I will write again at the end of the week and give a better account of myself. I wish, Sir, you would give me some instructions, with regard to my time, & advise me how to proportion my Studies & my Play, in writing, & I will keep them by me, & endeavor to follow them. I am, dear Sir, with a present determination of growing better, yours.

P.S. if you will be so good as to favour me with a Blank Book, I will transcribe the most remarkable occurances I met with in my reading, which will serve to fix them upon my mind.

Aged 11, to His Mother[2]

Passy, September the 27th, 1778

(He was in Paris with his father who was representing the Continental Congress at the French court during the Revolutionary War.)

HONOURED MAMMA, My Pappa enjoins it upon me to keep a journal, or a diary of the Events that happen to me, and of objects that I see, and of Characters that I converse with from day to day; and altho. I am convinced of the utility, importance & necessity of this Exercise, yet I have no patience and perseverance enough to do it so Constantly as I ought. My Pappa, who takes a great deal of Pains to put me in the right way, has also advised me to Preserve copies of all my letters, & has given me a Convenient Blank Book for this end; and altho I shall have the mortification a few years hence to read a great deal of my Childish nonsense, yet I shall have the Pleasure and advantage of Remarking the several steps by which I shall have advanced in taste judgment and knowledge. A journal Book & a letter Book of a Lad of Eleven years old Can

---

[1] C. F. Adams, *Memoirs of John Quincy Adams* (J. B. Lippincott, 1874), Vol. 1, pp. 7–9.

[2] *Ibid.*

not be expected to contain much of Science, Literature, arts, wisdom, or wit, yet it may serve to perpetuate many observations that I may make, & may hereafter help me to reco-lect both persons & things that would other ways escape my memory. I have been to see the Palace & gardens of Versailles, the Mili-tary scholl at Paris, the hospital of Invalids, the hospital of Foundling Children, the Church of Notre Dame, the Heights of Cal-vare, of Montmartre, of Minemontan & other scenes of Magnificence in & about Paris, which, if I had written down in a diary or a letter Book, would give me at this time much pleasure to revise and would enable me hereafter to entertain my friends, but I have neglected it. & therefore can now only resolve to be more thoughtful and Industrious for the Future. & to encourage me in this resolution & enable me to keep it with more ease & advantage, my father has given me hopes of a Pencil and Pencil Book in which I can make notes upon the spot to be transfered after-wards in my Diary & my letters this will give me great pleasure both because it will be a sure means of improvement to myself & enable me to be more entertaining to you. I am my honoured and revered Mamma your Dutiful & affectionate Son.

John Quincy Adams

I.L. 2: Johnny Adams sure got around a lot. Here he is eleven years old writing home letters from Paris.

I.L. 3: There is another angle about free-dom. It means footloose and fancy free to move from place to place, from coun-try to country.

I.L. 2: When we read the *Journal of a Soul*[3] by the late Pope John XXIII we find much more concern for duty than for freedom. [*He reads*] "Who am I? Where do I come from? Where am I going? I am nothing. All I have, my being, my life, my understanding, were given me by God, so all belong to Him. . . . And You, O God, with a wonderful gesture of love, You drew me forth from nothingness, You gave me being, You created me. So You are my Master and

I am your creature, I am nothing with-out You. . . . If at every moment You did not support me I should slip back whence I came, into nothingness. And Yet I am boastful and display with pride before the eyes of God all the bless-ings He has showered on me, as if they were my own. Oh what a fool I am! What am I but an ant or a grain of sand? God is my supreme Master be-cause He created me and so I am His slave. My whole life must be conse-crated to Him, to carry out His wishes at all times. So when I do not think of God, when I attend to my own com-forts, I neglect my most compelling duty, I become a disobedient servant. And what will God do with me then? O Lord, do not strike me with the thunderbolts of Your justice. . . . Serve God, and then? What is the prize? Heaven, paradise, yes paradise, that is my goal, there is my peace and my joy. Paradise, where I shall see my God, 'face to face,' O Lord I thank You for this reward. . . ."

"God is my great Master, who with unheard-of-condescension has brought me out of nothing that I may praise Him, love Him, serve Him. I belong wholly to God and can and must do only what God wills, what serves His glory. To this end only must my every action, every thought and every breath be directed."

I.L. 3: "The old order changeth, giving place to new," and what God willed yesterday requires new solutions today.

I.L. 1: People move, up the ladder, away from guilt, away from constraint. That's why people move; some move down the ladder, into constraint.

I.L. 2: Jefferson was against that. He said good citizens were farmers, bound to the land, not rootless wanderers.

I.L. 3: He is out of date. He wrote a Con-stitution for farmers. We need a new Constitution for a country where every-thing is new.

---

[3] New York: McGraw-Hill Book Co., 1965.

I.L. 1: Boy, are you a radical!

I.L. 3: We need a Constitution based on today's realities. People are not tied to the family, to the church, to the community. City people won't repair their homes and schools, because they are afraid the government will come tear them down for a new highway or project, or because they want to move away.

I.L. 2: But if people don't feel attached to anything, they won't feel any past or any future, and they will have a wishy-washy present, wavering between alcoholism and nothing at all. If they are not attached to their family and neighborhood, their children will get run over in unkept streets, their schools will fall down in decay or go up in smoke. . . . That's what's happening every day.

I.L. 3: People are destined to move because of new inventions, floods, and wars, so we need a bigger sense of community. Maybe people can't feel tied to their neighborhood because they just moved in last week and may be moving out again next week. That's why neighborhoods run down. Freedom to move runs down neighborhoods.

I.L. 1. It isn't freedom that runs down neighborhoods; it's ignorance. People are ignorant of how to live, how to organize for today's civilization.

We had finished our business in the drug store and were filled with notions of freedom and duty. We know that duty to one person means something quite different from what it means to another but that in all duty there is a general idea of responsibility to others.

In Plutarch's *Lives* the conception of duty that stands out is the desire for greatness. This might be achieved in a number of ways, but among the most prominent was by courage in battle. For medieval and even some modern Jews

the conception of duty was different: to achieve by learning, by knowledge. To show how the Jewish child developed such a conception we looked through the Jewish lore. Their prayer books, textbooks, songs and poetry ring with the importance of learning. Here are two prayers illustrating this: "Make pleasant, therefore, we beseech thee, O Lord, the words of thy Torah (The Holy Bible and commentaries about it) in our mouth and in the mouth of thy people, so that we with our children and the children of thy people may all know thy name and thy Torah." This is a prayer which the children recited before going to school in the morning. Another daily prayer emphasized learning: ". . . and thou shalt teach them diligently unto thy children. . . ." Learning was not merely a duty; it was also a pleasure. To symbolize this pleasure the child's first day at school included an important ceremony:

On Pentecost, the feast commemorative of the giving of the Torah, the boy of five began his career at school. Neatly attired, he was put in the care of a member of the community distinguished for piety and scholarship, with whom he went to the synagogue at the break of day. There he was met by the teacher, who took him in his charge and began to instruct him. He was handed a slate on which the Hebrew alphabet was written forward and backward. The first lesson consisted in asking the pupil to repeat the names of the letters after the teacher. The slate was smeared with honey which the child licked from the letters, to taste the sweetness of Torah. Then the boy was given a cake on which several verses from the Prophets and Psalms were traced. . . .[4]

From early infancy the Jewish woman soothed her child with the lullaby that expressed the wish for the child to learn the Torah.

What is the best reward?
My baby will learn Torah.

[4] L. Ginsberg, *Students, Scholars, and Saints,* pp. 19–20.

Sforim (Books) he will write for me.
And a pious Jew—he'll always be.

Bialic, the Hebrew poet, expressed the pleasure and comfort in the Torah when he wrote:

In my worn, moth eaten Talmud leaves,
Dwell ancient legends, captivating tales,
In you my soul finds soothing from its woes,
To you I come whenever grief assails.[5]

Rabban Yochanan used to say, "If thou has learned much Torah, ascribe not any merit to thyself, for there unto wast thou created."[6]

To sum up, one may characterize this Jewish ideal as one who is scholarly and pious, both being part of a unified whole.

We in America have a problem primitive people did not have. Primitive people, living in an isolated area, out of communication with other peoples, never had to choose between rearing their children this way or that. They knew only one way; they had no choice. In this sense they had less freedom than we. But along with our freedom of choice comes responsibility. We have no real freedom to choose from the thousand and one varieties of cultures of which we are composed unless we understand what we are choosing. The problem of what we should do with our children leaves us in a quandary, or in a conflict with our neighbors.

One hundred and fifty years ago Jefferson and Madison brought forth a plan for a new kind of agrarian community. It was a remarkable plan, but today the United States is no longer agrarian; it is an industrial power where people live in megalopolitan aggregates facing space and time and TV. Today we are in the process of making a new plan. What kind of world do we want in the next 150 years? Before we can decide whether there is

too much or too little pap in our curriculum, too much science or not enough math, we must decide what kind of people we want. The decisions on these questions will be made by the minds and acts of men. Whether we deal with these issues or not, whether we know what we are doing or not, we are making the decisions. Our decisions must begin to flow from a rational control of the situation we desire, not from the crises of the immediate circumstance we find ourselves in. Ernest J. Seeton once stated "Manhood, not scholarship, is the first aim of education." It is now time to begin to think about the type of manhood that is desirable and needed in our world. It would be wise to study this for our own benefit and for the good of our children, and to keep in mind that the way we behave today will influence how our children will behave when they are our age.

SOME VIRTUES WE ADMIRE

Every parent wants a good child. The problem arises when we try to make more specific what we mean by "good."

Probably agreement on health, as meaning freedom from disease, would be unanimous. But sometimes we hear the expression, "it's not healthy to let the child practice music too much, or to let him swim so much," and then the meaning of "healthy" becomes controversial too. What is "good"? Does it mean active, even boisterous? Some people like children to be quiet, so that they grow up quiet, with spontaneous outbursts of curiosity, friendship, hostility curbed.

Does "good" mean working hard? Among some groups, working hard seems to be more important than producing, and to be overwhelming is more important than being equal.

Is a good child a popular child, that is, do other children like him? For early Americans, popularity was not an essential

---

[5] N. Bialic, "To the Aggadah," translated from Hebrew by Israel Efios in *Complete Works of H. N. Bialic.*

[6] *Sayings of the Fathers*, Chapter 2.

trait. The conception of freedom was much more important; men were free to disagree with one another, free to be unpopular, to do what their conscience told them was right. Current research of adolescents shows a majority agree with such statements as these: "Want people to like me more." "Want to gain (or lose) weight." "I try very hard to do everything that will please my friends."[7] They feel a need to be popular, which often involves giving up one's own taste, judgment, intelligence, and wisdom for the whimsicalities of the mob.

Is a good child an "average" child, that is, does he have the abilities, tastes, interests, and talents of the average person, with some people better, some less good, no matter how these may be measured? This means to many that if he is not average he is a "screwball." The men who developed immunization against small pox and polio, who developed TV and wrote symphonies and *The Grapes of Wrath* were not average; nor are the peacemakers, that special breed who mediate disputes between labor and management, between nations, or who have learned effective ways of minimizing friction at home, at work, or in school.

Well, then, is a good child a "great" child, one who hides in an ordinary body and behind an ordinary face a mysterious power of creativity, so that we might say a good child is a "creative" child? "Creativity" is again an elusive word. The creation of a fine meal is creativity, but it is not the same as the creation of a cure for syphilis. Nor is it the same as the special kind of creativity of the mother or teacher who creates an atmosphere in which children can grow.

Is the good child, then, the one who grows, that is, who learns, who is studious? The scholar was held in high esteem in China and among Jews of re-

cent centuries, yet what he learned and his mode of learning could not be considered creative. He did not use the scientific method. The Chinese scholar was meek, tremendously learned in the proper books, endowed with a great memory and had little or no effect in changing Chinese civilization. The Jewish scholar was not meek; a young man of ten might argue boldly with his teacher of sixty, and might even win the argument. And yet a basic precept among the Jews has been "To do justly, to love mercy and to walk humbly before God." (We should point out that to "do justice" may be opposed to "love mercy.")

Is a good child musical? or especially talented in chemistry or in persuading and leading others? or in tearing apart old clocks? so that he misses other activities, perhaps misses school, perhaps misses a neighbor's birthday party or his grandmother's funeral? This seems to have been true for a number of inventors, musicians, great scientists. We don't know for certain whether Mozart or Irving Berlin if faced with the same hectic schedule a middle-class child faces today would ever have written a note. Edison had trouble in school.

A good child is clean, neat, orderly. A child who is too meticulous will be a miserable adult. The Nazis had a great love for order. Every person and every thing was arranged in one grand order. Of course, no one had much freedom.

Then should the child be "free"? Free to do what? Anything he likes, to eat anything he likes, to hurt anybody he likes? In this sense one has freedom to do only what is good for society. If he were to hurt others, they would be free to hurt him. There could be no health, no society in such chaos. Freedom involves understanding. One is free who can make an intelligent choice. The truth alone will not make one free. Persons are not free unless they are free to be different.

---

[7] H. H. Remmers and D. H. Radler, "Teenage Attitudes," *Scientific American*, June, 1958.

A good child is an honest child. It is clear for some people what honesty involves. There is a rule that one should be courteous, and this often conflicts with the need for honesty. The tattletale is honest; he carries a message of doom, but he is disloyal to his peers. A good child is loyal. To what, to whom? Is he loyal to his own aspirations, to those of his parents, teachers, or friends? Loyalty to one's country in some countries means supporting the administration; we enjoy a broader definition. Loyalty to our country means supporting the principles of liberty to all (except to criminals, idiots, children, the insane, Communists) and means freedom and justice to all (except Negroes, American Indians, Mexican-Americans, Japanese-Americans, Jews, Italians, Greeks, Catholics, and Protestants). We believe in liberty and justice for all but sometimes fail to practice it because of the problems of political or economic power. Then should the child seek power, wealth? The meek shall inherit the earth, but did you ever see a meek politician, industrialist, or person of wealth or position?

The good child is happy, well adjusted. He sings, dances, plays, has fun, bubbles with good humor, and is a joy to all who behold him. Is the child well adjusted to poverty, to prejudice, to ignorance, to starvation, to atomic fallout, to murder on the highways, to one million juvenile delinquents, to the imminence of hydrogen death, to millions suffering of alcoholism, drug addiction, mental disease, and urban renewal? What does "well adjusted" mean?

The good child is sincere. Sincere means honest, genuine, saying what one thinks. For Germany, Hitler was sincere. He said what he thought.

The good child is one who makes his parents happy. He does all the things the parents wish they might have done for themselves.

The good child loves beauty, hates dirt and ugliness. Some are so preoccupied with dirt that they spend all their lives looking for it, cleaning up things. Others are so squeamish that they can't stand cleaning their own dish or their own mess after they have made it. Many a lover of beauty in the abstract lives in filth in reality.

A good child is full of love, of compassion for his fellow man, helping unselfishly the poor and the sick. In order to help the crippled, the insane, the ex-convict, one must identify with such people. To help those who suffer one must identify with the suffering. It follows that the saint would suffer most of all. He appears to be completely preoccupied with the suffering of others, as if he personally were responsible. And if he could devote himself to others, he could undo the harm he feels he has done them. Actually he has done others no harm, he may have helped many people, but his suffering is part of a grandiose delusion that he is responsible for all men. Some people feel we must be our brother's keepers, but others say that the most one can do is to realize his own potential growth. If we want our child to be a saint, let us keep in mind the cost to him. Pope John XXIII, a saintly man, had his moments of despair. How else could he write, "If in this life I feel myself blushing with shame and hardly dare to go into the presence of a superior who is dissatisfied with me, what terror shall I not feel when I think of entering into the presence of my angry God. . . ."[8] Or is the saint the happiest, the ideal?

A good child will be a great athlete, or a musician, or businessman, surgeon, or actress. These are the highest-paid occupations in our land for a very few, and the lowest paid for the majority. Such occupations involve tremendous drive, as well as talent and opportunity for train-

---

[8] Op. cit.

ing, usually from an early age, though there is no guaranteed formula for success.

A good child knows the great cultural heritage from Plato to Plutonium. He will spend his life trying to understand our past. But if he concentrates on the past he will never see the present and will be of no value in helping form the future. Even Einstein never heard of Sputnik. Some problems of today are the same old problems man has always had, and studying the past can illuminate our times; but many of today's problems are brand new, and require new thinking and new solutions.

We have heard it reported that the good child is independent, he gets ahead on his own. All great men have achieved on their own. Others say this is sheer nonsense. Most children (and adults, too) could not live a week on their own. Every man who achieved did so with the help, encouragement, food, and support of others. Inventions don't come fully blown from a dream. They come from people working together, using the information in our cultural legacy; many minds, many hands, many people are involved in every invention, novel, play, or business.

Here is a quotation from Laird Bell taking a position that people should be independent:

It seems to me no proper frame of mind for youth, to accept a world where not his own energy and talent but the plans that somebody else makes for him determine his life. I recognize that one should not be too censorious about people who accept the managed economy, security and planning as ideals. . . . A very great development of civilization took place under a relatively unplanned society in the last two centuries.

I find it hard to be reconciled to the thought that the young should turn away from an exciting world of risk and big stakes for a tame one planned, however expertly, for someone else. Our achievements at the University of Chicago have been possible not because we had economic security but rather

because we had ambitions. I trust you will go forth, not in search of security, but looking for high adventure.[9]

And here is a reply by Lloyd Lewis:

For every Daniel Boone who wanted to go it alone, there were 100,000 settlers hunting security from poverty, from landlessness, from unemployment. They didn't say to Uncle Sam, "Stand back! We'll handle our competitors!" Instead they yelled for him to send federal troops to eliminate the Indians. They made the trails resound with their howling for free land, internal improvements, canals, harbors, locks, roads, and high protective tariff. Advertisements in Europe told them that they could step off the boat and shoot a gun in any direction, day or night, and bring down at least three turkeys, four deer and a goose. This sounded like security to peasants who had never had enough meat in their lives and whose brothers had been hanged for poaching. The truth of the matter is that these peasants had spent so much of their lives dodging or fighting the constables who wanted to jail them for debt, or gibbet them for praying to the wrong dominie, or draft them for the stirring perils of professional soldiery, that it could hardly be said that they came to America seeking adventure.

If that was what they wanted, they'd have stayed at home.[10]

How is security related to adventure? Can one go forth to joyful adventure if his heart is heavy, his stomach empty, and if he has a wooden leg?

A good child is wise. Perhaps it is too much to expect of a child to be wise, when this gift occurs so infrequently even among adults. "Wisdom" would mean knowing how to temper the virtues enumerated above when they became obnoxious: how to combine honesty with courtesy; freedom with order; popularity with conscience; discretion with

---

[9] "Insecurity for Graduates," *English 3: Selected Readings* (Chicago: University of Chicago Bookstore, October, 1946), I, 301.

[10] "Security," Chicago *Sun Book Week*, June 24, 1945.

valor; creativity with humility; justice with mercy.

It is one of the requirements of wisdom to know what one wants. A very wise Yale professor, Harold Lasswell, once made a list of the eight values in life—he called them "social values"—that everyone wants. His list includes "power," or the ability to participate in decisons involving oneself; "respect," which means that one is given attention for the good things he does—people listen when he speaks, say good morning to him; "affection," which is distinguished from respect by the fact that we love some people, our children or our parents, for example, whether they do something good or bad; "enlightenment," which reminds us that human beings are curious animals, always seeking information; "skill" in speaking, writing, playing an instrument, dancing, or flying a kite; "security," which was described in the preceding paragraphs; "well-being," meaning good health and a feeling of safety; and, finally, Lasswell says, everyone wants a sense of "rectitude," the feeling that "I try to get these good things for others just as I try to get them for myself." Wisdom also includes the ability to assess oneself in these matters: "How much power do I want? How much do I have? How can I get more? Will I have to give up some security or other value to get more power?"

How does one feel when he loses some of these values? "How do I feel when someone steals my money or damages my car or steps on my roses or hurts my child? When the boss denies me his respect by speaking to me in a humiliating way, do I try to get respect from my family by speaking to them in a humiliating way?" The social values are like money in the bank: You can give them to someone if you have them yourself. Thus, a penniless tramp may not be able to give one money or security, but he may be able to give knowledge, skill, respect, affection, and rectitude. If he stops you on the street and asks for a dime, you must give it to him, for you have taken some of his time.

We are in the business of making children how we want them, but it too often appears we do not know how we want them, or what is involved. When we go to a tailor and say make me a coat of such and such a size, he can make it to our order. Can we make a child to specifications? If we could, what would be the specifications? In America we have been enriched by the thoughts, ideas, inventions, values of a thousand societies. With such a rich assortment of values from which to choose, it takes a heap of knowing to choose well.

Mr. Robert M. Hutchins of the Fund for the Republic gives his views on this. He says that there are three urgent problems facing the world. The first is making democracy work. He means making it work better. The second urgent problem is survival, for which we need draw no pictures. And the third question, the one we ask in more detail in this paper: If we should survive, what should we do with our lives?

2 | LIFE: THE IMPORTANT VALUE

GENESIS 22

In hundreds of places and among hundreds of peoples, the practice of infanticide—and sacrificial killing—has occurred. Even today newspapers frequently report incidents in which angry parents have beaten their children to death.

Although beating is often recommended (see selection 3), killing is condemned. What motives would a parent have for killing his own child?

The following passage from the biblical Book of Genesis relates a very important incident in which child sacrifice is rejected as improper. In this powerful story, God Himself indicates that the sacrifice of Isaac, the only son of Abraham, who at this time is a very old man, is no longer acceptable.

And it came to pass after these things, that God did tempt Abraham, and said unto him, Abraham; and he said, Behold, here I am. And he said, Take now thy son, thine only son Isaac, whom thou lovest, and get thee into the land of Moriah; and offer him there for a burnt offering upon one of the mountains which I will tell thee of.

And Abraham rose up early in the morning, and saddled his ass, and took two of his young men with him, and Isaac his son, and clave the wood for the burnt offering, and rose up, and went unto the place of which God had told him. Then on the third day Abraham lifted up his eyes, and saw the place afar off. And Abraham said unto his young men, Abide ye here with the ass; and I and the lad will go yonder and worship, and come again to you. And Abraham took the wood of the burnt offering, and laid it upon Isaac his son; and he took the fire in his hand, and a knife; and they went both of them together. And Isaac spake unto Abraham his father, and said, My father: and he said, Here am I, my son. And he said, Behold the fire and the wood: but where is the lamb for a burnt offering? And Abraham said, My son, God will provide himself a lamb for a burnt offering: so they went both of them together. And they came to the place which God had told him of; and Abraham built an altar there, and laid the wood in order, and bound Isaac his son, and laid him on the altar upon the wood. And Abraham stretched forth his hand, and took the knife to slay his son. And the angel of the Lord called unto him out of heaven, and said, Abraham, Abraham: and he said, Here am I. And he said, Lay not thine hand upon the lad, neither do thou any thing unto him: for now I know that thou fearest God, seeing thou has not withheld thy son, thine only son from me. And Abraham lifted up his eyes, and looked, and behold behind him a ram caught in a thicket by his horns: and Abraham went and took the ram and offered him up for a burnt offering in the stead of his son.

3 | THE TEN COMMANDMENTS AND OTHER BIBLICAL PRECEPTS

Like all peoples, the wandering tribes of Israel gave much thought to defining the nature of good and evil. Many of their observations were written down in what came to be called the Holy Scriptures.

The fact that the beautifully worded passages from the Old Testament reprinted here sometimes appear to contradict one another should in itself make them exciting and thought-provoking.

DEUTERONOMY 5

I am the Lord thy God, which brought thee out of the land of Egypt, out of the house of bondage.

Thou shalt have no other gods before me.

Thou shalt not make thee any graven image, or any likeness of any thing that is in heaven above, or that is in the earth beneath, or that is in the waters beneath the earth.

Thou shalt not bow down thyself unto them, nor serve them: for I the Lord thy God am a jealous God, visiting the iniquity of the fathers upon the children unto the third and fourth generation of them that hate me.

And showing mercy unto thousands of them that love me and keep my commandments.

Thou shalt not take the name of the Lord thy God in vain.

Keep the sabbath day to sanctify it. Six days shalt thou labor and do all thy work, but the seventh day is the sabbath. In it thou shalt not do any work, thou, nor thy son, nor thy daughter, nor thy manservant, nor thy maidservant, nor thine ox, nor thine ass, nor any of thy cattle, nor the stranger that is within thy gates.

Honour thy father and thy mother.

Thou shalt not kill.

Neither shalt thou commit adultery.

Neither shalt thou steal.

Neither shalt thou bear false witness against thy neighbor.

Neither shalt thou desire thy neighbor's wife; nor covet thy neighbor's house, his field or his servant, his ox, or his ass or any thing that is thy neighbor's.

LEVITICUS 26

If ye walk in my statutes, and keep my commandments, and do them:

Then I will give you rain in due season, and the land shall yield her increase, and the trees of the field shall yield their fruit.

And your threshings shall reach unto the vintage, and the vintage shall reach unto the sowing time: and ye shall eat your bread to the full, and dwell in your land safely, and ye shall lie down, and none shall make you afraid. And ye shall chase your enemies, and they shall fall before you by the sword. And five of you shall chase an hundred. And I will be your God, and ye shall be my people.

But if you will not hearken unto me, and will not do all these commandments: I will appoint over you terror, consumption and the burning ague that shall consume the eyes and cause sorrow of heart: and ye shall sow your seed in vain for your enemy will eat it, and ye shall be slain before your enemies; and ye shall flee when none pursueth you; ten women shall bake bread in one oven; ye shall eat and not be satisfied, and I will make your cities waste.

PROVERBS

Ch 1. The proverbs of Solomon the son of David, king of Israel; to know wisdom and instruction; to perceive the words of understanding. A wise man will hear, and will increase learning; and a man of understanding shall attain unto wise counsels; to understand a proverb, and the interpretation; the words of the wise, and their dark sayings.

Ch 3. Happy is the man that findeth wisdom which is better than the merchandise of silver, more precious than rubies, and all her paths are peace.

Ch 6. Go to the ant, thou sluggard; consider her ways and be wise: which having no guide, overseer or ruler, provideth her meat in the summer, and gathereth her food in the harvest. How long will thou sleep, Oh sluggard?

These six things doth the Lord hate: yea, seven are an abomination unto him: A proud look, a lying tongue, and hands that shed innocent blood. An heart that deviseth wicked imaginations, feet that be swift in running to mischief. A false witness that speaketh lies, and he that soweth discord among brethren.

Ch 14. Even in laughter the heart is sorrowful; and the end of that mirth is heaviness. A good man shall be satisfied from himself. A wise man feareth and departeth from evil, but the fool rageth, and is confident. The poor is hated even of his own neighbors, but the rich hath many friends. He that despiseth his neighbor sinneth; but he that hath mercy on the poor, happy is he.

Ch 15. A soft answer turneth away wrath; but grievous words stir up anger. Better is a dinner of herbs where love is, than a stalled ox and hatred therewith.

Ch 16. By mercy and truth iniquity is purged: and by the fear of the Lord men depart from evil. Pride goeth before destruction, and an haughty spirit before a fall. Pleasant words are as an honeycomb, sweet to the soul, and health to the bones. A whisperer separateth friends. He that is slow to anger is better than the mighty; and he that ruleth his spirit than he that taketh a city. A merry heart doeth good like a medicine: but a broken spirit drieth the bones.

Ch 18. Whoso findeth a wife findeth a good thing.

Ch 19. Better is the poor that walketh in his integrity, than he that is perverse in his lips and is a fool. Wealth maketh many friends, but the poor is separated from his neighbor. Every man is a friend to him that giveth gifts.

Chasten thy son while there is hope, and let not thy soul spare for his crying.

Ch 22. Foolishness is bound in the heart of a child; but the rod of correction shall drive it far from him. Train up a child in the way he should go; and when he is old he will not depart from it.

Ch 23. Withhold not correction from the child: for if thou beatest him with the rod, he shall not die. Thou shalt beat him with the rod and shalt deliver his soul from hell. Hearken unto thy father that begat thee, and despise not thy mother when she is old. Who hath woe? who hath sorrow? who hath contentions? who hath babbling? who hath wounds without cause? who hath redness of eyes? They that tarry long at the wine: they that go to seek mixed wine. Yea, thou shalt be as he that lieth down in the midst of the sea, or as he that lieth upon top of the mast. They have stricken me, shalt thou say and I was not sick; they have beaten me and I felt it not: when shall I awake? I will seek it yet again.

Ch 24. Be not thou envious against evil men, neither desire to be with them. For their heart studieth destruction, and their lips talk of mischief. Through wisdom is an house builded; and by understanding it is established, and by knowledge shall the chambers be filled with all precious and pleasant riches. My son, eat thou honey, because it is good; and the honeycomb which is sweet to the taste. So shall the knowledge of wisdom be unto the soul. Eat not the bread of him that hath an evil eye. Neither desire thou his dainty meats.

4 | THE SERMON ON THE MOUNT

MATTHEW 5–7

Although the ideals of The Sermon on the Mount are professed by hundreds of millions of people, they are as revolutionary now as they were 2,000 years ago. If one were to practice

what these stirring words preach, he would probably be
tagged as a "radical," if not imprisoned.
In any study of ethical values, Chapters 5, 6, and 7 of the
Gospel According to St. Matthew deserve most careful study.

And seeing the multitiudes, he went up into a mountain: and when he was set, his disciples came unto him: And he opened his mouth, and taught them, saying, Blessed are the poor in spirit: for theirs is the kingdom of heaven. Blessed are they that mourn: for they shall be comforted. Blessed are the meek: for they shall inherit the earth. Blessed are they which do hunger and thirst after righteousness: for they shall be filled. Blessed are the merciful: for they shall obtain mercy. Blessed are the pure in heart: for they shall see God. Blessed are the peacemakers: for they shall be called the children of God. Blessed are they which are persecuted for righteousness' sake: for theirs is the kingdom of heaven. Blessed are ye, when men shall revile you, and persecute you, and shall say all manner of evil against you falsely, for my sake. Rejoice, and be exceeding glad: for great is your reward in heaven: for so persecuted they the prophets which were before you.

Ye are the salt of the earth: but if the salt have lost his savour, wherewith shall it be salted? It is thenceforth good for nothing, but to be cast out, and to be trodden under foot of men. Ye are the light of the world. A city that is set on an hill cannot be hid. Neither do men light a candle, and put it under a bushel, but on a candlestick; and it giveth light unto all that are in the house. Let your light so shine before men, that they may see your good works, and glorify your Father which is in heaven.

Think not that I am come to destroy the law, or the prophets: I am not come to destroy, but to fulfil. For verily I say unto you, Till heaven and earth pass, one jot or one tittle shall in no wise pass from the law, till all be fulfilled. Who-

soever therefore shall break one of these commandments, and shall teach men so, he shall be called the least in the kingdom of heaven: but whosoever shall do and teach them, the same shall be called great in the kingdom of heaven. For I say unto you, That except your righteousness shall exceed the righteousness of the scribes and Pharisees, ye shall in no case enter into the kingdom of heaven.

Ye have heard that it was said by them of old time, Thou shalt not kill; and whosoever shall kill shall be in danger of the judgment: But I say unto you, That whosoever is angry with his brother without a cause shall be in danger of the judgment: and whosoever shall say to his brother, Raca, shall be in danger of the council: but whosoever shall say, Thou fool, shall be in danger of hell fire. Therefore if thou bring thy gift to the altar, and there rememberest that thy brother hath ought against thee; Leave there thy gift before the altar, and go thy way; first be reconciled to thy brother, and then come and offer thy gift. Agree with thine adversary quickly, whiles thou art in the way with him; lest at any time the adversary deliver thee to the judge, and the judge deliver thee to the officer, and thou be cast into prison. Verily I say unto thee, Thou shalt by no means come out thence, till thou hast paid the uttermost farthing.

Ye have heard that it was said by them of old time, Thou shalt not commit adultery: But I say unto you, That whosoever looketh on a woman to lust after her hath committed adultery with her already in his heart. And if thy right eye offend thee, pluck it out, and cast it from thee: for it is profitable for thee that one of thy members should perish, and not that thy whole body should be cast into hell. And if thy right hand offend thee, cut it off, and cast it from thee: for it is profitable for thee that one of thy members should perish, and not that thy whole body should be cast into hell. It hath been said, Whosoever shall put away his wife, let him give her a writing of divorcement: But I say unto you, That whosoever shall put away his wife, saving for the cause of fornication, causeth her to commit adultery: and whosoever shall marry her that is divorced committeth adultery.

Again, ye have heard that it hath been said by them of old time, Thou shalt not forswear thyself, but shalt perform unto the Lord thine oaths: But I say unto you, Swear not at all; neither by heaven; for it is God's throne: Nor by earth; for it is his footstool: neither by Jerusalem; for it is the city of the great King. Neither shalt thou swear by thy head, because thou canst not make one hair white or black. But let your communication be, Yea, yea; Nay, nay: for whatsoever is more than these cometh of evil.

Ye have heard that it hath been said, An eye for an eye, and a tooth for a tooth: But I say unto you, That ye resist not evil: but whosoever shall smite thee on thy right cheek, turn to him the other also. And if any man will sue thee at the law, and take away thy coat, let him have thy cloke also. And whosoever shall compel thee to go a mile, go with him twain. Give to him that asketh thee, and from him that would borrow of thee turn not thou away.

Ye have heard that it hath been said, Thou shalt love thy neighbour, and hate thine enemy. But I say unto you, Love your enemies, bless them that curse you, do good to them that hate you, and pray for them which despitefully use you, and persecute you; That ye may be the children of your Father which is in heaven: for he maketh his sun to rise on the evil and on the good, and sendeth rain on the just and on the unjust. For if ye love them which love you, what reward have ye? do not even the publicans the same? And if ye salute your brethren only, what do ye more than others? do not even the publicans so? Be ye therefore perfect, even as your Father which is in heaven is perfect.

Take heed that ye do not your alms before men, to be seen of them: otherwise ye have no reward of your Father which is in heaven. Therefore when thou doest thine alms, do not sound a trumpet before thee, as the hypocrites do in the synagogues and in the streets, that they may have glory of men. Verily I say unto you, They have their reward. But when thou doest alms, let not thy left hand know what thy right hand doeth: That thine alms may be in secret: and thy Father which seeth in secret himself shall reward thee openly.

And when thou prayest, thou shalt not be as the hypocrites are: for they love to pray standing in the synagogues and in the corners of the streets, that they may be seen of men. Verily I say unto you, They have their reward. But thou, when thou prayest, enter into thy closet, and when thou hast shut thy door, pray to thy Father which is in secret; and thy Father which seeth in secret shall reward thee openly. But when we pray, use not vain repetitions, as the heathen do: for they think that they shall be heard for their much speaking. Be not ye therefore like unto them: for your Father knoweth what things ye have need of, before ye ask him. After this manner therefore pray ye: Our Father which art in heaven, Hallowed be thy name. Thy kingdom come. Thy will be done in earth, as it is in heaven. Give us this day our daily bread. And forgive us our debts, as we forgive our debtors. And lead us not into temptation, but deliver us from evil: For thine is the kingdom, and the power, and the glory, for ever. Amen. For if ye forgive men their trespasses, your heavenly Father will also forgive you: but if ye forgive not men their trespasses, neither will your Father forgive your trespasses.

Moreover when ye fast, be not, as the hypocrites, of a sad countenance: for they disfigure their faces, that they may appear unto men to fast. Verily I say unto you, They have their reward. But thou, when thou fastest, anoint thine head, and wash thy face; That thou appear not unto men to fast, but unto thy Father which is in secret: and thy Father, which seeth in secret, shall reward thee openly.

Lay not up for yourselves treasures upon earth, where moth and rust doth corrupt, and where thieves break through and steal: But lay up for yourselves treasures in heaven, where neither moth nor rust doth corrupt, and where thieves do not break through nor steal: For where your treasure is, there will your heart be also. The light of the body is the eye: if therefore thine eye be single, thy whole body shall be full of light. But if thine eye be evil, thy whole body shall be full of darkness. If therefore the light that is in thee be darkness, how great is that darkness!

No man can serve two masters; for either he will hate the one, and love the other; or else he will hold to the one, and despise the other. Ye cannot serve God and mammon. Therefore I say unto you, Take no thought for your life, what ye shall eat, or what ye shall drink; nor yet for your body, what ye shall put on. Is not the life more than meat, and the body than raiment? Behold the fowls of the air: for they sow not, neither do they reap, nor gather into barns; yet your heavenly Father feedeth them. Are ye not much better than they? Which of you by taking thought can add one cubit unto his stature? And why take ye thought for

raiment? Consider the lilies of the field, how they grow; they toil not, neither do they spin: And yet I say unto you, That even Solomon in all his glory was not arrayed like one of these. Wherefore, if God so clothe the grass of the field, which today is, and tomorrow is cast into the oven, shall he not much more clothe you, O ye of little faith? Therefore take no thought, saying, What shall we eat? or, What shall we drink? or, Wherewithal shall we be clothed? (For after all these things do the Gentiles seek:) for your heavenly Father knoweth that ye have need of all these things. But seek ye first the kingdom of God, and his righteousness; and all these things shall be added unto you. Take therefore no thought for the morrow: for the morrow shall take thought for the things of itself. Sufficient unto the day is the evil thereof.

Judge not, that ye be not judged. For with what judgment ye judge, ye shall be judged: and with what measure ye mete, it shall be measured to you again. And why beholdest thou the mote that is in thy brother's eye, but considerest not the beam that is in thine own eye? Or how wilt thou say to thy brother, Let me pull out the mote out of thine eye; and, behold, a beam is in thine own eye? Thou hypocrite, first cast out the beam out of thine own eye; and then shalt thou see clearly to cast out the mote out of thy brother's eye.

Give not that which is holy unto the dogs, neither cast ye your pearls before swine, lest they trample them under their feet, and turn again and rend you.

Ask, and it shall be given you; seek, and ye shall find; knock, and it shall be opened unto you: For every one that asketh receiveth; and he that seeketh findeth; and to him that knocketh it shall be opened. Or what man is there of you, whom if his son ask bread, will he give him a stone? Or if he ask a fish, will he give him a serpent? If ye then, being evil, know how to give good gifts unto your children, how much more shall your Father which is in heaven give good things to them that ask him? Therefore all things whatsoever ye would that men should do to you, do ye even so to them: for this is the law and the prophets.

Enter ye in at the strait gate: for wide is the gate, and broad is the way, that leadeth to destruction, and many there be which go in thereat: Because strait is the gate, and narrow is the way, which leadeth unto life, and few there be that find it.

Beware of false prophets, which come to you in sheep's clothing, but inwardly they are ravening wolves. Ye shall know them by their fruits. Do men gather grapes of thorns, or figs of thistles? Even so every good tree bringeth forth good fruit; but a corrupt tree bringeth forth evil fruit. A good tree cannot bring forth evil fruit, neither can a corrupt tree bring forth good fruit. Every tree that bringeth not forth good fruit is hewn down, and cast into the fire. Wherefore by their fruits ye shall know them.

Not every one that saith unto me, Lord, Lord, shall enter into the kingdom of heaven; but he that doeth the will of my Father which is in heaven. Many will say to me in that day, Lord, Lord, have we not prophesied in thy name? and in thy name have cast our devils? and in thy name done many wonderful works? And then will I profess unto them, I never knew you: depart from me, ye that work iniquity.

Therefore whosoever heareth these sayings of mine, and doeth them, I will liken him unto a wise man, which built his house upon a rock: And the rain descended, and the floods came, and the winds blew, and beat upon that house; and it fell not: for it was founded upon a rock. And every one that heareth these sayings of mine, and doeth them not, shall be likened unto a foolish man, which built his house upon the sand: And the rain descended, and the floods came, and the winds blew, and beat upon that house; and it fell: and great was the fall of it. And it came to pass, when Jesus had ended these sayings, the people were astonished at his doctrine: For he taught them as one having authority, and not as the scribes.

5 | SOME PERSONALITY DIFFERENCES IN CHILDREN RELATED TO STRICT OR PERMISSIVE PARENTAL DISCIPLINE

GOODWIN WATSON

Determining the proper procedure for the socialization of children is difficult. Should the child be allowed to do as he pleases, his parents quietly hoping he will make the correct decisions? Or should the parents make the child do as he is told?

This important article, comparing 44 children from strict homes with 34 from permissive family groups, indicates that those from permissive backgrounds tend toward more independent, cooperative, and creative behavior than those with strict upbringings. Because of this and similar studies, psychologists have advocated permissiveness for two decades. In many ways, however, the groups are similar, and Watson reports that permissiveness is very rare.

A. INTRODUCTION

In controversies over parental discipline of children, few of the arguments advanced for more permissiveness or for more strict adult control have yet been empirically tested. Does early indulgence "spoil" children or does it give them a foundation of "security" to meet life's stress and strain? Does firm and consistent discipline by the parents create in children inner hostilities, anxieties, and self-rejection or does it relieve anxiety and foster more successful self-discipline? Psychologists, psychoanalysts, teachers, parents, grandparents have often spoken with strong conviction on one or the other side of these issues, but the evidence has usually come from personal experience, clinical cases, plausible theories, or unconscious bias.

A generation ago this writer made a first effort at empirical study of this problem, comparing the self-reports of 230 graduate students who rated their home discipline during childhood along a continuum from the most strict to the most lenient. Those who came from the strictest quartile of homes reported: (a) more hatred for and constraint in relation to parents; (b) more rejection of teachers; (c) poorer relations with classmates, more quarrels, and shyness; (d) more broken engagements and unsatisfactory love affairs; (e) more worry, anxiety, and guilt feeling; (f) more unhappiness and crying; (g) more dependence on parents; but (h) better school grades and stronger ambition. Two cogent criticisms should be made of this study. First, the "strict" category included homes where there was

Excerpts reprinted from *Journal of Psychology*, XLIV (1957), 227–49, by permission of the author and The Journal Press. (Seven tables have been omitted.)

severe punishment and quite possible rejection. The "lax" category included possible indifference and neglect along with genuine concern for freedom. Second, since all data came from the students' self-reports, a generally negative or optimistic outlook may have permeated both the reports on home discipline and the present self-evaluation.

A few years later (1938) Carpenter and Eisenberg (4) reported findings leading to similar conclusions. Among 500 college women, the 50 rated as most "dominant" reported a childhood in which their own "freedom" and "individuality" had been stressed. The more "submissive," like the shy, dependent, anxious students in our 1929 study, came almost entirely from adult-dominated homes. Those who "had to have parents' permission to do practically everything" turned out at college age to be "submissives" (21%) rather than "dominants" (2%).

Studies attempting to relate specific early child-rearing practices (e.g., breast feeding, self-demand feeding, method of toilet training, etc.) to child personality seem to have been inconclusive [Cf. Sewell (11) and review by Orlansky (9)]. Those which center upon the general social climate in the home, on the other hand, reveal marked and generally consistent differences. One exception is Myers (8) who, in 1935, reported that a pupil adjustment questionnaire and high school teacher ratings on quality of personality adjustment were unrelated to strictness of home discipline.

Hattwick (5) in 1936 found that "over-attentive" homes which "favor" the child or "revolve around" the child were positively correlated (.2 to .4) with tendencies of nursery school pupils to be babyish in such matters as "cries easily," "asks unnecessary help," and "avoids risk."

On the other hand, these same over-indulged children were less likely to take the property of others or to mistreat animals.

Ayer and Bernreuter (2) in 1937 reported on another study of the personality traits of nursery school children in relation to their home discipline. Significant correlations appeared between physical punishment at home and a tendency of children not to face reality ($r=.35$) and between permissiveness of parents (letting children learn from the natural consequences of their acts) and a more "attractive" personality in the child ($r=.33$).

Symonds (13) matched 28 parents who "dominated" their children in an authoritative way with 28 who permitted the child much freedom and who usually acceded to child wishes. He found the children from stricter homes more courteous, obedient, and neat, but also more shy, timid, withdrawing, docile, and troubled. The more permissive parents brought up children who were more aggressive, more disobedient, and who had more eating problems, but who also were more self-confident, better at self-expression, freer, and more independent.

Anderson (1) identified a group of junior high school pupils who had been brought up with warm affection but little adult dominance. He found these children marked by a high degree of maturity, poise, cheerfulness, coöperation, obedience, and responsibility.

Lafore (7), using techniques of direct, on-the-scene observation, made two half-hour visits in the homes of 21 nursery school children, and reported that:

Parents who presented the largest number of instances of dictating (to) and interfering with their children, received the largest number of expressions of hostility from their children. . . .

Parents who showed large numbers of instances of blaming, hurrying, punishing, threatening and interfering had children who presented large numbers of crying. . . .

Children who were frequently threatened scored high on fearfulness. . . .

Children who were cautioned most often scored low on resourcefulness.

Raelke's study (10) is in some ways closest to the one to be reported here. She studied 43 children of nursery school or kindergarten age, giving the parents a questionnaire and observing the children in free-play and picture-interpretation test situations. Children from more restrictive and autocratic home discipline showed less aggressiveness, less rivalry, were more passive, more colorless, and less popular. They did not get along so well with other children. The children from homes with freer discipline were more active, showed more rivalry, and were more popular. Raelke found that parents who were "democratic" in their disciplinary methods, giving more respect to the youngsters, fostered children who themselves showed more consideration for others.

Baldwin (3) in 1948, reported on a study of 64 four-year-olds, showing that parents who were strict and undemocratic in their methods of control were likely to have children who were quiet, well-behaved, unaggressive, but restricted in curiosity, originality, and imagination.

Shoben (12) found that when parents of "problem children" (defined as: referred for clinical help, or brought into custody of juvenile authorities at least twice) were given an attitude scale they were more apt than were parents of non-problem children to agree with statements approving strict discipline and demand for obedience. Bi-serial correlation was .80 on the original group and .62 on a validating group for this variable which Shoben called "Dominating."

There is considerable convergence among the findings of these studies. There seems to be reason to suppose that firm, strict adult domination will produce the conforming, obedient child but will handicap him in initiative and probably burden him with shyness and a sense of inadequacy. More permissive treatment seems, in these studies, to result in more independence and aggressiveness on the part of the child. These children are less docile but in some studies appear to be more popular and more considerate of others. Shoben's results challenge a popular belief that juvenile delinquency is associated with lack of punishment by parents.

B. SELECTION OF SUBJECTS—
DEFINING "STRICT"
AND "PERMISSIVE"

This study was conducted under the auspices of The Guidance Center, a child-guidance clinic in New Rochelle. Associated with the Guidance Center was a positive program of education in mental health and of community service, reaching hundreds of parents of "normal" children in the eastern part of Westchester County. Subjects for this study were limited to normal children in school from kindergarten through sixth grade. Only "good" homes where children were wanted, loved, and well cared for were included. Any children who had ever been referred for psychological or psychiatric treatment were excluded. Nominations were sought from parents, teachers, and social workers, to find good homes that were known to be clearly "strict" or "permissive."

During a preliminary period, social workers visited the recommended homes and talked with these parents about their practices in child-raising. On the basis of the interviews a multiple-answer questionnaire was constructed and printed under the title, *How I am Bringing Up My Child.* The instrument asked about parental reaction to each of 35 fairly common situations, such as children's eating, sleeping, toilet training, dressing, keeping clean, caring for toys, quarreling, anger at parents, sex curiosity, attendance at school and church, choice of television programs,

friends, etc. Each situation was followed by three kinds of possible response: (*a*) a clearly permissive reaction, (*b*) a middle-of-the-road or "'sometimes this and sometimes that" answer, and (*c*) a reply characteristic of the parent who sets standards and enforces strict obedience. The responses were assigned weights of 5 for the most permissive, 3 for the neutral, and 1 for the strict reaction. There was opportunity for parents to write in a response to each situation in their own words if none of the proposed answers seemed to fit well enough. If a parent's qualified answer fell between "strict" and "middle-of-the-road" it was given 2 points; if it fell between "middle-of-the-road" and "permissive" it was given 4 points. Consistent choice of the "strict" responses would result in a score of 35; consistent "middle-of-the-road" responses would give a total of 105; consistent "permissiveness" would bring a total score of 175. The actual range was from 55 to 158.

A range of 20 points on either side of the neutral point of 105 was arbitrarily set as representing the area of common practice—strict about some things at some times and more lenient on other matters or at other times. Although we had made special efforts to reach the more extreme groups—the permissive parents with scores of 125 or over, and the strict parents with scores of 85 or less—more than half (53%) of our responses fell in the 40 point middle range and were not used in this study.

The home discipline for 34 of the children was rated by fathers independently of the mother's rating. Fathers usually reported a less permissive attitude than did mothers. For these cases, fathers averaged a score of 105 and mothers 115. In only seven instances did the mother's report indicate a stricter attitude than that of the father. Correlation between mother's rating and father's was .61. For the sake of consistency, since mother's rating was available in all cases and since in suburban communities today the mother is more directly and more frequently responsible for discipline in the type of situation listed, our classification into strict or permissive is based only on the mother's report. In no instance would a child's classification have moved from one extreme category to the other if the father's questionnaire had been used instead of the mother's.

Responses of children to questions on home discipline as they saw it, usually confirmed the answers of the parents. Interviews and questionnaires, independently administered by Dr. Norris E. Fliegel, indicated that children from strict homes concurred with their mothers on 86 per cent of the items. It is interesting also that the children almost invariably approved the form of discipline they were receiving. Those from permissive homes believed it was best to give children freedom to make their own decisions; those from strict homes felt that parents knew best and should exercise firm control.

C. PROCEDURE

Parents whose questionnaire score was extreme, falling under 86 (strict) or over 124 (permissive), were visited by a trained social worker who conducted an interview designed to check both directly and indirectly on the reported attitudes and practices, to evaluate the general climate of the home, and to obtain the parents' perception of their child's strength and weaknesses. The social workers were not informed as to whether the home to be visited had been reported as permissive or as strict but the differences were so marked that this was seldom in doubt. In the few (3) instances in which the social worker felt that the questionnaire classification was questionable because the home really belonged in the middle-of-the-road category rather than at the extreme, the case was not included in our comparative study. Thus every case which

was included met both the criteria: extreme score on the questionnaire, and confirming judgment of a social worker who had independently observed parent and child in the home.

Children included in our study were voluntarily brought to the Guidance Center by their parents for an hour or two of psychological testing which included a free play period, a Rorschach test, selected pictures from the *TAT*, a figure-drawing test, and a performance test (Alexander Passalong) which gradually became too difficult and so gave opportunity to study reaction to stress or frustration. Some of the children returned for a second appointment in which they were given a vocabulary test and a questionnaire on their perception of the home discipline. Results from this latter instrument are being analyzed and reported by Norris Fliegel.

We endeavored to get school behavior ratings for all the children, but this proved impossible in some cases. Wherever they coöperated, teachers or school guidance officers rated the children on a scale which provided intervals from 1 to 5 on: (*a*) level of activity; (*b*) initiative; (*c*) independence, spontaneity, self-reliance; (*d*) confidence, good adjustment; (*e*) friendliness and popularity; (*f*) coöperation; (*g*) self-control; and (*h*) persistence. In the case of 16 of 36 children rated by teachers a trained worker from the Guidance Center made an independent appraisal using the same scale. Agreement of the teacher and the outside observer is represented by a correlation of .77. Of 121 parallel judgments, 59 per cent agreed exactly; 31 per cent differed by only one scale step; and 10 per cent were two steps apart. Thus 90 per cent assigned the same or an adjoining category.

D. RESULTS

1. Permissiveness Is Rare

The first surprise of the study was our difficulty in finding parents who were fairly consistently permissive. Perhaps this should have been anticipated.

Whiting and Child (15) have estimated the over-all indulgence or severity of child training in 47 societies studied by competent anthropological observers. The aspects of discipline which they included in their index were: (a) earliness and severity of weaning; (b) toilet training; (c) repression of sexual activity; (d) repression of aggression; and (e) effort toward child's independence. They found only two of the 47 cultures as severe on the younger child as is the typical American middle-class white family described by Davis and Havighurst. No culture in the records is less permissive with children than we are. The short-shift given to "progressive education" in this country might further have warned us.

We have been led to believe, however, that in certain sub-cultures of the United States the ideal of respecting the child and of permitting him great freedom to mature in his own way and at his own good time had taken root. We knew that psychoanalytic concepts were commonly heard in upper-middle class Westchester child-study groups and that "mental hygiene" was looked upon as favorably as Divine Grace once had been. Some teachers complained that children were being given too much freedom at home and

writers in popular journals freely listed lack of firm parental discipline as a major cause of juvenile delinquency. It was easy to find citizens who thought that some of their neighbors were overly-permissive parents.

We set the modest goal of 50 cases—25 boys and 25 girls—from child-centered, permissive homes. After strenuous search, with the cooperation of the Guidance Center, the Child Study Association, the Mental Hygiene Association, social workers, clergymen, teachers, pediatricians and P.T.A.'s; and after extending our quest for an extra year and modifying our qualifying scores a step or two downward toward the middle; we eventually located 38 permissively brought-up children—21 boys and 17 girls. (Four of these could not be included in the later testing.) The distribution of our questionnaire returns is shown in Table 1. We emphasize again that this is not a normal cross-section. We were not interested in "middle-of-the-road" cases for this particular comparison. The point of the table is that with much less effort, we found three times as many "strict" as "permissive" homes in the most "liberal" section of an upper-middle class suburban community. The obtained median score of 101 is below (i.e., more strict than) the arbitrary neutral score of 105.

TABLE 1.

DISTRIBUTION OF SCORES ON "HOW I AM BRINGING UP MY CHILD"

Score	No. of boys	No. of girls	Both	Per cent of total
"Permissive" Extreme				(12%)
145 and over	3	5	8	
135–144	5	4	9	
125–134	13	8	21	
"Middle-of-the-Road"				(53%)
115–124	13	14	27	
105–114	30	39	69	
95–104	31	48	79	
"Strict" Extreme				(35%)
85–94	33	41	74	
75–84	20	8	28	
74 and below	9	4	13	
TOTAL	157	171	328	(100%)

2. Age, Sex, and Discipline

Demands for conformity to adult standards become stronger as a child grows older. Babies are not expected, except by pathological parents, to "behave" themselves. Many cultures treat young children very indulgently, only later expecting them to exercise mature levels of self-control. Pearl Buck reports that in the China she knew, children were usually treated very permissively until about the age of seven. Their demands were gratified whenever possible. But after seven, they were expected to behave like proper adults, and they did so.

. . . . .

Our data from 328 children in Eastern Westchester County show no clear and consistent age trend. The anticipated transition from infant indulgence to mature demands does not appear in this cross-sectional survey. Longitudinal studies of qualitative changes in the same child-parent relationship might reveal that tolerance for some kinds of childish misbehavior is decreasing, but that with advancing age children are treated with increased freedom which offsets these restrictions.

Some might have expected that girls —sometimes reputed to be "less trouble" than boys—would be treated more permissively. Others would have expected that boys would be granted more license than girls. Our data do not give support to either interpretation as a general pattern. In some families, no doubt, girls are treated more indulgently but in others they are more restricted; on balance no difference is found between the discipline of sons and that of daughters, aged 5 to 12.

3. The Two Groups Compared

. . . Although our two groups of children, one from exceptionally "permissive" and the other from very "strict" homes, are far apart on Home Discipline score, they are not significantly different in proportion of boys (57 per cent and 62 per cent), or in age. The distributions of intelligence, as estimated from Rorschach or quite independently from a vocabulary test, show relatively a few more top-level IQ's from the permissive homes, but this difference is not large enough to be statistically significant. It is noteworthy that all children in this study have IQ's of 110 or higher as estimated from their vocabulary.

. . . . .

4. Plan of Personality Study

Children who are strictly brought up will be compared with children who are treated much more permissively, on each of nine dimensions of personality as follows:

Overt Behavior

1. Independence—dependence.
2. Socialization—ego-centrism.
3. Persistence—easy discouragement.
4. Self-control—disintegration.
5. Energy—passivity.
6. Creativity—stereotyping.

Inner Feelings

7. Friendliness—hostility.
8. Security—anxiety.
9. Happiness—sadness.

In each instance the null hypothesis— that there is no significant difference between the two groups—will be statistically tested.

a. Independence—Dependence: Hypothesis 1. Is there no difference between children from strict and those from permissive homes in the personality dimension of independence—dependence? Five measures bearing upon this hypothesis have been combined to give an index of independence. One is a rating by the psychologist of the child's behavior as he was brought into the playroom, shown the toys, games, puzzles, craft materials, etc., and told he might play with them in any way he chose. A rating of "5" is assigned to those children who promptly sized up the situation and went to work on their own responsibility with no further demands on the adult. The low extreme of the scale, a rating of "1," is assigned to those children who were unable to get going despite repeated instruction and reassurance. This rating correlates .70 with the composite index.

The second measure is a rating of the child's evident need for adult attention during the later activities of the testing period. Those children who independently judged their own performance with little reference to cues from the psychologist are at the high (5) end of the scale; those who were so dependent on adult approval that without definite reassurance their behavior was disrupted are given a rating of 1. This measure correlates .71 with the composite.

The third rating is based on a period of free play with doll figures representing a family. If the examiner was asked to make decisions for the child, the rating is low; high ratings represent independent, self-reliant structuring of the interpersonal play. This measure has the highest correlation (.76) with the composite index.

The fourth measure is based on the story interpretations which the child assigned to several TAT and CAT pictures. If the figures with whom the child seemed to identify most were self-reliant, acting on their own responsibility, the rating is 5. The lowest rating, 1, means that the identification figures were generally pas-sive, helpless, or dependent. This correlates only .51 with the composite.

Our fifth rating is derived from Rorschach responses. Whether M (movement responses were active and extensor or passive and flexor, or absent; whether the balance of C, CF, and FC tended toward or away from control, and the content of food and adult-child relationships were all taken into account. The Rorschach estimate correlates .67 with the composite.

The reliability of the total index is estimated (Spearman-Brown) at .80. Theoretically scores might range from 5 to 25; the actual range is from 9 (very dependent) to 23 (highly independent). Distributions shown in Table 2 find some children from each type of home at every level of independence but the null hypothesis—that no real difference will be found—must be rejected. Differences (based on X^2 with Yates' correction) are significant at better than the .01 level. The highly independent children include 29 per cent of our permissive sample, but only 5 per cent of the strictly disciplined children. The very dependent children represent 6 per cent of those from permissive homes and 21 per cent of those from strict homes. We find, therefore, a *marked tendency for greater freedom in the home to show itself in greater independence in the child's behavior outside the home.*

b. Socialization—Ego-centrism: Hypothesis 2. Is there no difference between children from strict and those from per-

TABLE 2.		BOYS		GIRLS		ALL	
DIFFERENCES IN			Per-		Per-		Per-
INDEPENDENCE—		Strict	missive	Strict	missive	Strict	missive
DEPENDENCE	High independ-						
	ence (20–23)	1	7	1	3	2	10
	Above average (17–19)	9	6	6	4	15	10
	Below average (13–16)	10	7	8	5	18	12
	Very dependent (9–12)	5	1	4	1	9	2
	TOTAL	25	21	19	13	44	34

$X^2 = 20.95$. P $<$ .01.

missive homes in the personality dimension of socialization—ego-centrism? Our index combines four separate ratings: (a) verbal negativism (or over-compliance) versus coöperative consideration of the child's own wishes and the adult requests; (b) behavioral negativism (or over-compliance) versus "positive but differentiated cooperation"; (c) stories told in response to several *TAT* and *CAT* pictures, rated for quality of parent-child relations from resistance to friendly interaction; and (d) responses to Card IV of Rorschach. Average intercorrelation of these ratings on socially integrative responses is .52, yielding a predicted reliability, for the four combined, of .81.

Differences . . . show markedly better coöperation by children from permissive homes. Differences are statistically significant, being large enough to have a probability of chance occurrence, less than .01. The highest level of mature coöperation is found among 32 per cent of the children from permissive homes but only 9 per cent of the children strictly disciplined. The null hypothesis must be rejected and so also must the "spoiled child" or "little monster" tradition. *Exceptionally permissive discipline seems on the whole to be associated with better socialization and more effective coöperation with others.* At the same time, it should be remembered that children from each type of home can be found at every step of the socialization scale.

This study does not demonstrate that the higher average level of independence reported earlier, or of coöperation reported here, is produced by the permissive discipline. It may be true—and the data on freedom from hostility to be reported later make this plausible—that the more relaxed home atmosphere is responsible for the observed differences in personality. Alternative explanations cannot, however, be excluded. Perhaps the kind of parents who choose the permissive role transmit, via heredity or via associated cultural influences, a different temperament or pattern of living. It should not be assumed that if parents who have heretofore practiced strict discipline were simply to change over to great permissiveness, their children would thereby become more independent or coöperative. They might, or might not. A correlational study cannot satisfactorily answer questions of causation. . . .

c. Persistence—Easy-discouragement: Hypothesis 3. Is there no difference between children from strict and those from permissive homes in the personality dimension of persistence versus being easily discouraged? All subjects were given the Alexander Passalong test which begins with easy problems in block movement and arrangement but proceeds to those which, although they seem workable, are impossibly difficult. The psychologist noted how long the child persisted at the task and also the effect of increasing difficulty and frustration upon personality organization and ability to make intelligent use of experience.

Table 3 is in accord with the null hypothesis, since the two groups cannot confidently be regarded as from different statistical distributions. The null hypothesis is likewise supported by teacher ratings (for 38 cases) on persistence at school tasks which showed similar distributions for children from strict and from permissive homes.

. . . . .

If our hypothesis were revised to state that permissive discipline is associated with a moderate degree of persistence, while strict discipline is associated with either unusually persistent or easily discouraged behavior, this *post hoc* revised hypothesis would be supported by the psychological test data of Table 3 at better than the .01 level of significance. The revised hypothesis makes good psychological sense. Since we already know that the children from permissive homes are more

TABLE 3.
DIFFERENCES IN
PERSISTENCE—EASY
DISCOURAGEMENT*

| | BOYS | | GIRLS | | ALL | |
RATING	Strict	Per-missive	Strict	Per-missive	Strict	Per-missive
4 Very persistent	13	6	8	3	21	9
3 Moderate	3	7	4	9	7	16
1–2 Evade, give up	9	7	7	1	16	8
TOTAL	25	20	19	13	44	33

* Distributions not statistically significant, but association of permissive discipline with moderate rather than high or low persistence is significant ($X^2 = 12.49$) at better than the .01 level of confidence.

TABLE 4.
DIFFERENCES IN
EFFECT OF
FRUSTRATION ON
LEARNING

| | BOYS | | GIRLS | | ALL | |
RATING	Strict	Per-missive	Strict	Per-missive	Strict	Per-missive
3 = Improves despite frustration	8	11	6	9	14	20
2 = No marked effect	7	8	7	3	14	11
1 = Deterioration from frustration	7	1	6	1	13	2
TOTAL	22	20	19	13	41	33

$X^2 = 6.73$. Differences significant at .02 to .05 level.

inclined to act independently and on their own initiative, we might expect them to make a try at a very difficult problem, but to use their own judgment in giving it up when no progress is made. In contrast, the children accustomed to firm adult control might more readily feel helpless, or, if instructed to keep on trying, persist in their vain efforts. The data on intellectual quality of the continued effort will be helpful in assessing this expectation.

As the task grew more difficult, some children became frustrated and deteriorated in their learning process. Others continued to study the problem, did not repeat errors, and evidenced growing insight into the difficulty. Type of home discipline does seem to be related to quality of behavior under difficulties, as reported in Table 4. Serious deterioration in intellectual quality of response was found in 13 (32 per cent) of the children with strict up-bringing, but in only 2 (6 per cent) of the children given greater freedom.

The hypothesis that home discipline is unrelated to persistence-discouragement should probably be rejected. The observed differences certainly do not sustain the popular fear that children who are allowed their own way much of the time at home will collapse when faced by difficult tasks. Apparently—with due allowance, again, for the fact that some children from each type of home can be found at every level—there is some tendency for *permissive discipline to foster the type of personality which makes a reasonable effort, continues effective intellectual attack upon problems, but is unlikely to persist indefinitely against odds.* Differences in school work are not significant.

d. Self-Control—Emotional Disintegration: Hypothesis 4. Is there no difference between children from strict and those from permissive homes in the personality dimension of self-control versus emotional disintegration? Closely related to the quality of intellectual attack upon a difficult problem is the emotional response during frustration. The data in Table 5 come from the psychologist's rating of the child's emotional reactions as the Passalong test became too difficult for him. The null hypothesis is acceptable; observed differences are not statistically significant. A further test of the hypothesis may be made, using teacher's ratings for 37 of the children.

Again, as shown in Table 6, differences fall within what might well be expected by chance.

Our data do not support the view that children given firm control at home are better able to withstand frustration; neither do they support those who argue that strict parental control interferes with the development of the child's self-control.

e. Energy—Passivity: Hypothesis 5. Is there no difference between children from strict and those from permissive homes in the dimension of energetic versus passive personality? Three ratings are applicable to testing of this hypothesis. One is a rating by the psychologist of the apparent energy level of the child. Scores range from 1 for "inert, uninvolved" manner during play and testing, through 2 for subdued activity, to 5 for lively participation. This variable refers to focused personality energy, not to merely physical, muscular activity.

The second rating is derived wholly from the Rorschach performance, taking account of total number of responses, number of content categories, number of wholes, and amount of movement.

The third estimate is based on an exercise in which the child drew a man, a woman, and himself.

Average intercorrelation of the three ratings is .46; predicted reliability for the three combined is .72.

As shown in Table 7, the differences between groups are not significant and the null hypothesis is acceptable.

Neither the data from the psychological test nor those from the classroom would support the view that strict home discipline typically represses impulses to such an extent as to make children inactive. In the test situation no difference is apparent, at school the well-disciplined children ap-

TABLE 5. DIFFERENCES IN SELF-CONTROL DURING FRUSTRATION TEST

	BOYS		GIRLS		ALL	
	Strict	Per-missive	Strict	Per-missive	Strict	Per-missive
Undisturbed	10	12	8	6	18	18
Moderate impatience	10	7	9	5	19	12
Extremely upset	4	1	2	2	6	3
TOTAL	24	20	19	13	43	33

Differences not statistically significant.

TABLE 6. TEACHER RATING ON SELF-CONTROL

	BOYS		GIRLS		ALL	
	Strict	Per-missive	Strict	Per-missive	Strict	Per-missive
Well balanced; not easily upset	5	2	6	6	11	8
About average	3	2	2	0	5	2
Loses temper, cries, easily upset	7	3	1	0	8	3
TOTAL	15	7	9	6	24	13

Differences not statistically significant.

TABLE 7.
DIFFERENCES IN
ENERGY—
PASSIVITY

	BOYS		GIRLS		ALL	
	Strict	Per-missive	Strict	Per-missive	Strict	Per-missive
Energetic, active productive (13–15)	3	4	3	4	6	8
Above Average (11–12)	10	4	8	5	18	9
Average (9–10)	10	3	3	4	13	7
Inert, passive (5–8)	2	9	5	0	7	9
TOTAL	25	20	19	13	44	33

Differences not statistically significant.

TABLE 8.
DIFFERENCES IN
CREATIVITY—
CONFORMITY

	BOYS		GIRLS		ALL	
	Strict	Per-missive	Strict	Per-missive	Strict	Per-missive
Highly creative, imaginative, spontaneous, original	1	6	1	5	2	11
Above average	12	5	6	1	18	6
Below average	8	4	8	7	16	11
Stereotyped, conventional, restricted	4	6	4	0	8	6
TOTAL	25	21	19	13	44	34

$X^2 = 29.35. P < .01.$

pear, on the whole, more active along approved lines.

f. *Creativity—Conformity: Hypothesis 6. Is there no difference between children from strict and those from permissive homes in the personality dimension of creativity versus conformity?* Five measures of this variable are available. One is based on the child's behavior, ranging from free and imaginative to stereotyped and monotonous, during a free play period. A second has been similarly observed during a period of play with a full family of dolls. The third estimates originality and imagination in stories composed as responses to *CAT* and *TAT* pictures. The fourth comes from Rorschach responses and the fifth from human figure-drawing. The average intercorrelation of these measures is .53 and the predicted reliability for the combined rating is .85.

The differences shown in Table 8 are the most impressive of any in our com-

parisons, and compel rejection of the null hypothesis. *High creativity characterizes 11 (33 per cent) of the children brought up with unusual freedom, but only 2 (5 per cent) of those from strict homes.* The more disciplined children are most apt to be found near the middle of the range in this variable.

The first six variables—independence, socialization, persistence, self-control, energy, and creativity—have focused on more overt, and directly observable behavior. The remaining three turn attention to the inner life of the child.

g. *Friendliness—Hostility: Hypothesis 7. Is there no difference between children from strict and those from permissive homes along the dimension of friendly versus hostile feelings toward others?* Our psychological testing yields four projective indications of inner hostility. One is based on observation of free play with dolls. Hostile contacts or avoidance of con-

TABLE 9. DIFFERENCES IN FRIENDLINESS— HOSTILITY	BOYS		GIRLS		ALL	
	Strict	*Per-missive*	*Strict*	*Per-missive*	*Strict*	*Per-missive*
High friendliness, little hostility (16 and over)	1	2	0	4	1	6
Above average friendliness; below average hostility (Scores 13–15)	5	8	8	6	13	14
Above average hostility (Scores 10–12)	12	8	10	1	22	9
High degree of aggressive hostility (Scores 9 and lower)	7	4	1	1	8	5
TOTAL	25	22	19	12	44	34

$X^2 = 10.64$ (Yates correction). $P < .02$.

tacts is rated 1; friendly interaction is rated 5.

The second is based on the *TAT* and *CAT* stories. The low end of scale (rating 1) is assigned to stories of violent conflict, death, and destruction. High scores represent stories of friendly interaction.

The third rating is based on such Rorschach signs as content items interpreted as aggressive weapons, mutilated human or animal bodies, and aggressive or hostile M or FM.

The fourth has been drawn from analysis of the figure-drawing test and responses during the drawing.

Intercorrelations among these tests range from .50 to .74, averaging .60; the predicted reliability for the four combined is .87—the highest of any of our measures.

Hostility versus friendliness scores of the two groups are compared in Table 9. The null hypothesis should be rejected. *More hostility is evident in those children who have been strictly disciplined; more positive feelings toward others are expressed by children whose parents have been permissive*; these differences are consistent through the distribution and are statistically significant. At the same time, it should be remembered that neither group has a complete monopoly on positive, friendly feelings toward others or on inner hostility.

Reactions to frustration on the Passalong test make possible another rating which has in it a high component of hostility for some children. Half of the TAT story-completion test was administered before the frustrating experience of failure on the too-difficult block test. The other half was given immediately after the somewhat annoying defeat. For a few children, the consequence was that the stories in the latter part of the test were briefer, the child was less coöperative and gave more evidence of hostility. This behavior characterized six (15 per cent) of the 41 children from strict homes; but only one (3 per cent) of the 32 children from permissive homes. This difference is not statistically significant, but its direction is in accord with the evidence from Table 9 indicating that strict discipline does leave a residue of inner hostility.

Supplementary research by Dr. Norris E. Fliegel, in which the Blacky Test was administered to 47 of our subjects, showed only one significant difference in the emotional life of the 24 adult-dominated as distinguished from that of the 23 self-regulating children. *"Children from strict homes did not feel free to express their* hostility, but had to inhibit it." As reported earlier, the children from strict homes did not openly resent adult control; indeed, they indorsed it. But on projective tests it was clear that they fancied that even a little puppy should submit to what is expected of him and never get angry at those who push him around.

h. Security—Anxiety: Hypothesis 8. Is there no difference between children from strict and those from permissive homes in the personality dimension security—anxiety? Five different ratings compose our measure of anxiety. One is the psychologist's general impression of the overtly confident or insecure behavior of the child. Three are based on projective tests: one on Card 9 of the CAT, one on the Rorschach, and one on the figure drawing test. The fifth measure is the anxiety evident during failure on the Passalong test. These five measures would have an average intercorrelation of .33; the combined index would have a predicted reliability of .71 which is not high but would suffice if the groups turn out to be markedly different.

As shown in Table 10 the two groups are not clearly distinguished. The null hypothesis is acceptable. Half a dozen children from each type of discipline show marked evidence of anxiety—another half-dozen from each category behave in an easy, secure manner. What makes for anxiety in a child must be something other than unusually strict or unusually lax parental control.

i. Happiness—Sadness: Hypothesis 9. Is there no difference between children from strict and those from permissive homes in the personality dimension of happiness versus sadness? Three measures are related to general level of happiness. One is a rating of the overt manner and apparent mood of the child during his play and testing periods. Scores range from 5 for the most euphoric to 1 for the most depressed. A second measure is derived by analysis of the imaginative stories given in response to CAT and TAT pictures. Predominantly optimistic and enjoyable events result in high ratings; stories in which distress, sadness, and unhappiness come to the leading figures result in a low score. The third measure is based upon Rorschach test responses. Predominant use of black, and perception of figures as torn and broken, are used as indicators of depression.

Intercorrelations among the several indices (except for overt behavior and the Rorschach which correlate .54) are low, averaging .28 and giving a combined predictive reliability of .54.

Results conform to the null hypothesis. While our data show a slightly larger proportion of permissive discipline subjects in both the "happy" and the "unhappy" categories, the differences are unreliable.

E. SUMMARY

Forty-four children brought up in good, loving, but strictly disciplined homes are

TABLE 10. DIFFERENCES IN SECURITY— ANXIETY		BOYS		GIRLS		ALL	
		Strict	*Permissive*	*Strict*	*Permissive*	*Strict*	*Permissive*
Secure, relaxed (16–19)		1	4	4	3	5	7
Less than average anxiety (14–15)		10	6	5	7	15	13
More than average anxiety (12–13)		8	7	7	1	15	8
Anxious, tense (7–11)		6	4	3	2	9	6
TOTAL		25	21	19	13	44	34

$X^2 = 1.81$. Differences not significant.

compared with 34 children from the same community and also brought up in good, loving homes but with an extraordinary degree of permissiveness. Two periods of psychological testing, supplemented (in 38 cases) by teacher ratings, have yielded measures of nine dimensions of personality. On three of the nine, no statistically significant difference is found: these are the dimensions of self-control, inner security, and happiness. Factors making for anxiety, emotional disorganization, and unhappiness are found about equally often under either type of home discipline. No difference in activity and energy level was observed during the psychological testing, but teacher ratings indicate higher activity level of an approved sort, at school for the children accustomed to stricter discipline.

On persistence, teachers observe no differences, but on a psychological test children from strict homes are more apt to fall in extreme categories, being either unusually persistent or very easily discouraged. A moderate persistence is more characteristic of the children from permissive homes. These children maintain a better quality of intellectual activity under difficulty than do the children from strict homes.

On the four remaining variables (which are also those most reliably measured, with predicted r's from .80 to .87) significant differences in each instance are in favor of the children from permissive homes. Greater freedom for the child is clearly associated with: (a) more initiative and independence (except, perhaps, at school tasks); (b) better socialization and coöperation; (c) less inner hostility and more friendly feelings toward others; and (d) a higher level of spontaneity, originality, and creativity.

None of the personality differences applies to all cases; some children from strict and some from permissive homes may be found at every level on every characteristic tested. It is impressive, however, to find no clear personality advantages associated in general with strict discipline in a good home. Where differences do emerge, these are consistently to the credit of the more permissive upbringing. This study cannot distinguish the extent to which the advantages associated with permissiveness are due to that procedure alone and the extent to which more permissive parents may convey hereditary or cultural assets with which the permissive attitudes happen to be correlated.

REFERENCES

1. ANDERSON, J. P. The Relationships between Certain Aspects of Parental Behavior and Attitudes of Junior High School Pupils. New York: Teachers College, Columbia University, 1940.

2. AYER, M. E., & BERNREUTER, R. A study of the relationship between discipline and personality traits in young children. J. Genet. Psychol., 1937, 50, 165–170.

3. BALDWIN, A. L. Socialization and the parent-child relationship. Child Devel., 1948, 19, 127–136.

4. CARPENTER, J., & EISENBERG, P. Some relationships between family background and personality. J. of Psychol., 1938, 6, 115–136.

5. HATTWICK, B. W. Interrelations between the preschool child's behavior and certain factors in the home. Child Devel., 1936, 7, 200–226.

6. HATTWICK, B. W., & STOWELL, M. The relation of parental over-attentiveness to children's work habits and social adjustment in kindergarten and the first six grades of school. J. Ed. Res., 1936, 30, 162–176.

7. LAFORE, G. Practices of parents in dealing with preschool children. Child Devel. Monog., 1945, 31, 3–150.

8. MYERS, T. R. Intrafamily Relationships and Pupil Adjustment. New York: Teachers College, Columbia University, 1935.

9. ORLANSKY, H. Infant care and personality. Psychol. Bull., 1949, 46, 1–48.

10. RAELKE, M. J. The Relation of Parental Authority to Children's Behavior and Attitudes. Minneapolis: Univ. Minnesota Press, 1946.

11. SEWELL, W. H. Infant training and the personality of the child. Am. J. Sociol., 1952, 58, 150–157.

12. SHOBEN, E. J., JR. The assessment of parental attitudes in relation to child adjustment. *Genet. Psychol. Monog.*, 1949, 39, 101–148.

13. SYMONDS, P. M. Psychology of Parent-Child Relationships. New York: Appleton-Century-Crofts, 1939.

14. WATSON, G. A comparison of the effects of lax versus strict home discipline. *J. Soc. Psychol.*, 1934, 5, 102–105.

15. WHITING, J. W. M., & CHILD, I. L. Child Training and Personality. New Haven: Yale Univ. Press, 1953.

6 | WHAT MAKES THEM CREATIVE?

NATALIE READER HAIMOWITZ

AND MORRIS L. HAIMOWITZ

What exactly is "creativity" and what factors in the child's background encourage its development?

Selection 5 suggested that a permissive home had some relation to creativity in children. This study, which differentiates between intelligence and creativity, identifies other factors.

Today the world is seeking creative men and women to invent better solutions to problems and to help us live together more peacefully in a rapidly changing and increasingly complex world.

Creativity, often regarded as a magical, inborn quality, sometimes equated with intelligence and talent, is neither of these. Many people, though possessed of high intelligence and able to grasp and use established methods, cannot innovate or invent. Similarly, many are born with a congenital "facility" known as talent, a physiological predisposition for certain skills and abilities, but are nevertheless unable to create or invent, even in the areas in which they demonstrate talent.

Creativity has been defined as the capacity to innovate, to invent, to place elements in a way in which they have never before been placed, such that their value or beauty is enhanced. Contrasted with conformity, it is the capacity to transcend the usual ways of dealing with problems or objects with new, more useful, and more effective patterns. MacKinnon, whose study of creativity of architects is summarized in the next selection, has defined creativity as "a process, ex-tended in time and characterized by orig-inality, adaptiveness and realization." "It may be brief," he observes, "as in a musical improvisation, or it may involve a considerable span of years, as was required for Darwin's creation of the theory of evolution." It will be the proposition of this paper that this ability is not inborn, but is a product of experience, that certain geographical, social, and cultural milieus favor or hamper creativity. We will explore some of the psychological and sociological phenomena that appear to be related to the emergence of creative adults.

WHAT IS CREATIVITY?

In problem solving, we may observe two different methods of approach, both of which have value in a complex culture. On the one hand there is "convergent" thinking, which integrates what is already known, unifying or harmonizing existing facts in a logical well-organized, orderly manner; it is thinking which conforms to existing knowledge and exacting methods. "Divergent" thinking, on the other hand, reaches into the unknown. Its essence is not its orderliness but its orginal-ity. Guilford (8), having elaborated on these qualitatively dissimilar kinds of thinking, demonstrates that existing intelligence tests rest heavily on skills which are convergent, reflecting cultural values which reward and esteem existing knowledge more highly than they reward innovation and invention.

Obviously, both convergent and divergent thinking are important in the development of a science. A report of the Foundation for Research on Human Behavior at Ann Arbor, Michigan (5), which defines creativity as "looking at things in a new and different way," points out that this kind of thinking occurs at the discovery phase, the insight phase, the intuitive phase of problem solving, and concludes that it is to be contrasted with the kind of restrained thinking concerned with validation of insights and testing of hypotheses. It is the former kinds of abilities, however, that are creative.

As in the world of physical objects and physical forces, creativity is often demonstrated in the interpersonal sphere by finding new ways to resolve interpersonal problems, by discovering new and more satisfying ways to interact with others. Foote and Cottrell in their book *Identity and Interpersonal Competence* (4) (see also selection 8) see creativity as "the actor's capacity to free himself from established routines of perception and action, and to redefine situations and act in the new roles called for by the situations." Anyone who has observed sensitive and insightful handling of an interpersonal problem can testify that there is such a thing as inventiveness in social relationships. In marked contrast are formal, traditional relationships, in which everyone's behavior is prearranged, where everyone knows what is to be done and who will do it.

COMPONENTS OF CREATIVITY

The following components of creativity have been suggested in the literature: basic security, intelligence, flexibility, spontaneity, humor, originality, ability to perceive a variety of essential features of an object or situation, playfulness, radicalness, eccentricity; we would add freedom, marginality, and secularity to this list. Conversely, characteristics which would hypothetically correlate negatively with creativity would be neatness, rigidity, control, thoroughness, reason, logic, respect for tradition and authority, and a tendency to routinize and organize tasks.

DISCOVERING CREATIVE PERSONS

One type of test wherein creative people function differently from equally "intelligent" but less creative persons is the word association test; the more creative person associates a larger number of categories with each word. Another is a hidden-shapes test which requires that the subject find a given geometrical form in a complex pattern in which it is "hidden." Another presents the beginning of a story and asks the subjects to compose first a funny, then a sad, and finally a moralistic ending.

An interesting, simple test asks the subject to draw two parallel lines and to use these lines in making a design. If he makes a design inside the lines, he is restricting himself more than if his design goes outside the two lines:

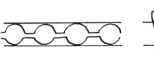

less creative stays
in bounds

more creative
transcends bounds
but holds close

still more creative
adds lines, invents
a melody

Another test gives the subject a problem. "You are newly married. About a month after the wedding your parents come to visit you for Sunday dinner. Your mother starts cleaning your house. You are angry about this. Let's act it out for 3 or 4 minutes. Now let's act it out again, you taking the part of your mother." The creative person finds new solutions to this stress situation.

Another test asks for a written story: "Here is a picture. Write a story about it." The creative person writes stories or endings to half-completed stories that few others imagine.

Still another test says: "Here is a newspaper. How many uses can you find for it?" The more creative can think of more and better uses than the less creative.

The Rorschach Test uses standardized ink blots. The subject is asked, "Tell me what you see." The creative person perceives objects, forms, and relationships others don't see.

In all these tests, it is assumed that the person who offers creative solutions in the test situation will be more creative in solving real life problems. This is a bold assumption, since many creative persons, being nonconformists, may not be willing to invest motivation and energy in the rather arbitrary test situation; they may not care at all about what a newspaper can be used for, nor will they necessarily find pleasure or even interest in making up stories about pictures or ink blots.

CREATIVITY AND OBSESSION

For some persons the act of creating is analogous to pains of labor for those women who can relax and enjoy it as a most exhilarating experience, the grandest, most exciting event of their lives. Others seem to be driven obsessively, without rest or diversion, until completing the task they had set for themselves. Einstein spoke of being driven by an obsession; the Curies worked without reward for many years before they discovered radium. Edison, the Wright brothers, and Louis Daguerre, who worked for six years to discover a way to make photographs —all seemed to have a clear purpose in mind. Andrew Carnegie said the key to success was first a clear, concise mental picture of the thing one seeks, "A Definite Major Purpose grown or forced into the proportions of an obsession. . . . I knew I wanted to go into the making of steel. I whipped up that desire until it became a driving obsession with me . . . my desire drove me day and night." His second step was the development of "a Mastermind principle," which meant that he involved others in the obsession, others who possessed the qualities he lacked and needed. Carnegie said, "Jesus understood the principle of the Mastermind and made effective use of it in His alliance with His Disciples. That is where I got my first clue. . . ."

Some of these highly creative persons could hardly be called well rounded. Mozart, for example, was busy writing music at a younger age than boys today can join the Boy Scouts, or even the Cub Scouts. Carnegie felt very strongly that anyone could accomplish just about anything he really tried to accomplish. His biographer Napoleon Hill said to him, "I take it that most of the men who work for you have no Definite Major Purpose in life, for if they had, they, too, would be as rich as you. Is this correct?" To this, Carnegie replied, "You will find that the highest aim of a majority of the men working for me is to hold the jobs they have. They are where they are and they are drawing the wages they receive solely because of the limitations they have set up in their own minds. Nothing I can do will change it. Only the men themselves can change it. . . ." He felt that the major requirement of persons in the Mastermind group was that they must have a single definite purpose, to work together in harmony, to feel and act positively toward others, and, most important of all, to WORK.

When Carnegie developed an idea, he used it conscientiously in all areas of his life. Thus, in his home his wife became the partner to the Mastermind: "There are but few marriages which do not need a new and improved plan of relationship at frequent intervals. . . . The time would be well spent if married people set aside a regular hour for a confidential Mastermind meeting at least once every week during which they would come to an understanding concerning every vital factor in their relationship. . . . Keep the fire of romance burning. Let it become a part of the Mastermind ceremony and your marital relationship will yield priceless returns. . . . The force that is born of a combination of love and sex is the very elixir of life through which nature expresses all creative effort. . . ." (9)

CREATIVITY AND BASIC SECURITY

There are two conflicting views concerning the relationship between inner security and creativity. The reluctance of some talented people to seek psychological help for their emotional problems is supported by the belief that if the individual becomes more comfortable, he may become less creative. We hear this view also from individuals who are associated with minority political or religious movements. The belief is held that with increased security one becomes more satisfied, more conforming, and one loses his need for and interest in unpopular, deviant opinions and activities. According to this view, creativity emerges from dissatisfaction and neurosis.

The other view regards creativity as emerging only when the organism has solved its basic problems of biological and social survival. Maslow, for instance, holds that only when the individual has achieved some sense of basic security—being fed, clothed, safe from harm, achieving sexual satisfaction, being loved by others, esteeming himself—can he spare the energy for the more whimsical, relaxed capacity to innovate and improvise. Similarly Erikson, with his concepts of "autonomy" and "initiative," suggests that only when the individual has solved his more primitive, elemental problems in relating to his world, only when he feels secure enough to initiate, and realistic enough to build a stable sense of personal identity, do "higher" kinds of human activity emerge. In this view, frustration blocks creativity. Both theorists postulate that while the individual is experiencing insecurity in the gratification of the "lower level" of needs, he cannot really be creative.

Carefully conducted, longitudinal studies of creative and not-so-creative individuals and societies might help to clarify the conflicting evidence. Scattered evidence from biographies of famous creative individuals in the arts and sciences (evidence obtained and presented by students of literature rather than by social scientists) fails to support the notion that creativity can only emerge under conditions wherein the individual's basic needs have been satisfied and his life prospects are for continued satisfaction. The childhood of such eminent innovators as Darwin, Schubert, Sarah Bernhardt, Brahms, Van Gogh, the Brontës, Gauguin do not stand out as models of security, love, and the satisfaction of basic needs. Darwin was shy, afraid of his successful father. Schubert lived in unbelievable poverty, loving music which his father denied him. Sarah Bernhardt was an illegitimate daughter of a milliner-courtesan with no home and no person to call her own. Alfred Nobel was a hunchback and Schiller reportedly an epileptic.

Of course, doting biographers often play up the Horatio Alger struggles of the impoverished, crippled child who by hard work and courage overcomes impossible obstacles and achieves greatness and immortality. When we attempt, as social scientists, to recreate the lives of those who are no longer living from biography, we must wonder whether what we read is factual or partly the inventiveness of the biographer.

When we study highly creative persons, we often find poverty or physical defects for which the individual must certainly have been striving to compensate. We find broken homes suggesting that the individuals must certainly have experienced loss of parental love through death, rejection, or desertion, and we often notice minority group status in political, religious, or racial groups such that the individual must have experienced some sense of insecurity in his "belongingness" to the larger society. If biography is enough rooted in fact, then we know that factors other than basic security are equally crucial. Some of these worthy of explanation are intelligence, freedom, marginality, and secular values.

CREATIVITY AND INTELLIGENCE

The observation has been made that the more creative are not necessarily the more intelligent. Creativity appears to be in some way associated with intelligence, but the two do not refer to the same dimensions of behavior. Just as creativity is measured operationally, that is, is defined as being what the creativity test measures, so is intelligence measured operationally, as what the intelligence test measures. We assume that the person who shows intelligence in an intelligence test will also show intelligence in other aspects of his life. Yet the intelligence test may fail to tap the devices used by a general planning campaign, or those of a young lady seeking a husband, or the behavior of an architect planning a new school. The kinds of intelligence valued on intelligence tests are verbal, memory, or convergent—organizing, logical *skills*— rather than divergent, original kinds of

talents. Creative talents may be penalized or missed in typical intelligence tests. While those who seem to innovate successfully are apparently those also with high intelligence, it is quite possible to discover highly intelligent persons who do not innovate and discover, and to find highly creative persons who do not show superiority on intelligence tests.

Getzels and Jackson (6) did just that. They gave both intelligence tests and tests of creativity to 449 adolescents. As might be expected, many scored high in both intelligence and creativity tests, others low in both kinds of tests. From the 449 subjects, two special groups were selected out: one of 24 individuals who scored in the highest 20 per cent in intelligence, but not highest in creativity; and the second group of 28 who scored in the top 20 per cent in creativity but did not excell in intelligence.

Comparing these two groups showed that "despite striking differences in mean IQ the creative and intelligent groups were equally superior to the total population in school performance as measured by the standardized achievement tests." Yet, from teachers' ratings, they found that teachers preferred the intelligent group rather than the creative. They also found that the need for achievement was no different in either group from the total population. Most striking differences were found when comparing the fantasy materials of the two groups. Judges, working blindly, could with high accuracy place authors of fantasy productions in the correct group—either "high intelligence" or "highly creative." The creative subjects consistently used more stimulus-free, humorous, and playful themes. Intelligent subjects' fantasy productions were orderly, logical, but "bound."

Other studies indicate that original people prefer certain types of intellectual tasks, prefer the complex to the simple problem or solution—they delay coming to conclusions until most of the pieces can be fitted together—and that creative people have more energy and are more impulsive and responsive to emotion, even when solving problems.

In *The Creative Process*, a study of 38 geniuses, including the introspective reports of such men as Einstein, Henry James, D. H. Lawrence, and Van Gogh, Ghiselin (7) suggests that those who are creative have passion and skill for their work and, when concerned with major problems which they cannot solve, appear to "forget" the problem for a time. But they would suddenly, while asleep, taking a walk, reading a book, or talking about something else, be struck with the solution as by lightning. The idea would appear to be coming from their own unconscious, which had been working on the problem all the time. Ghiselin's study suggests that in addition to intelligence there is a freedom of thought such that unconscious forces may be available in creative individuals for productive, constructive activity, assisting the more conscious intellectual processes.

CREATIVITY AND FREEDOM

Indeed, the creative person must be able to remain free from certain restraints. The very act of creating something new and different involves the courage to go beyond cultural limits. When we study the childhood biographies of creative artists, scientists, inventors, such as the Brontës, Fermi, Thomas Jefferson, Shaw, Whitney, Edison, Robert Burns, we are impressed with the apparent freedom they experienced in their early lives, even though it may have been associated with parental neglect, death, or desertion. They seemed to live in the midst of broad areas in which to roam, with freedom to explore, with privacy to contemplate. In many biographies, we find the absence of the parent of the same sex. Perhaps the trauma of the loss had its compensations in freedom, absence of parental coercion,

and less oedipal competition, and an absence of "a mold into which to fit oneself and with which to identify."

Such hypotheses arise as we recognize the fact that so many renowned persons have come from broken homes: Washington, Jefferson, Lincoln, Herbert Hoover, Bach, Beethoven, Schubert, Schumann, Stalin, Hitler, Stonewall Jackson, the Brontës, Robert Burns, Robert Fulton, Sibelius, Debussy, Andrew Johnson, Tchaikowsky, Gauguin, Leonardo da Vinci, James Garfield, Joseph Conrad, Andrew Jackson, and hundreds of others.

No statistical study has been made to determine whether such a hypothesis as this would be true: the fathers of eminent men died before the child reached puberty in greater proportions than the fathers of the noneminent. If this hypothesis is valid, precisely what in the experience of parental loss liberates creativity in some, imposes constraint in others?

Certainly the death of a parent in the child's infancy may so shatter basic security as to make creativity impossible. However, losing a parent in middle or late childhood may give the child more freedom and more responsibility. A number of studies by Watson, Baldwin, Lafore, Hattwick, Symonds, and Carpenter indicate that children from permissive homes, homes where considerable personal freedom is permitted, are much more likely to be creative than children from restrictive homes (see selection 5).

Imagine the courage it takes to tackle the proposition that the world is composed of atoms and that these atoms are made up of neutrons and electrons. One cannot see an atom, or an electron or neutron; one cannot even demonstrate them easily, as one can the invisible forces of gravity or electricity. The same is true for concepts in psychology. One cannot see motivation or the superego, and they are very difficult to demonstrate. If it takes courage to try to understand these concepts, think how much more courage would be required to imagine the concept, to create it. When developing new concepts, one is leaving the culture, leaving the traditional, taking off for a new world, in the manner of Columbus, and as with Columbus this requires courage, the courage to be different, not as a small religious sect is different, because here at least the members are all similar, but to be different from everyone else in the world, and the courage to test out one's ideas in the midst of disbelief, disapproval, and often ridicule.

Creativity thus appears to be associated with freedom in the self which arises from freedom in the family, in the committee, the club, the social gathering, or any small group. By "freedom" here is meant the absence of a domineering group member or leader and the absence of felt status differences. In our experiments with small groups we have noted more willingness of members to explore, to suggest wild ideas, to joke about the purposes or methods of the group when the designated leader is quietly receptive to such behavior. Very often a leader may superficially try to encourage group participation, but his domineering ways block participation and creativity. For example, he may ask the group to make suggestions but, instead of waiting patiently for them, would go ahead and make his own. Later he may report, "I tried to get them to open up, but they wouldn't. They just don't have ideas." The leader who tries to impose standards against the wishes of the group will evoke more apathy or rebellion than creativity.

Jack Gibbs' experiments show that more creative suggestions come from groups when the leader speaks, acts, and dresses informally than when his manner is formal. Studies in the classroom show similar results. We are not suggesting absence of leadership; we are suggesting absence of smothering leaders. The famous study of Lewin, Lippitt, and White (10) points out some differences between a no-leader (laissez-faire) situation and a democratic leadership situation (see selection 39).

Studies in group dynamics suggest leadership is essential for a creative atmosphere. Leadership may be defined as any act of any member which helps the progress of the group. Thus, if two members are blocking each other's actions and dividing the group into two anxious and opposing camps, progress may be blocked. An act of leadership might be to point this situation out to the group, or it might be a suggestion for a five-minute break, or a suggestion that the collection of some data would settle the differences, or a joke about how much we all hate each other. Every classroom needs creative ideas for the optimum advancement of the class. Thus, the best teacher is not only one skilled in the content of the subject matter, but also one skilled in group leadership.

Thelan in his exciting research tells us that some children learn better working alone; others work better in pairs or in small groups; still others do best in large groups. Some children are aware of their peculiar needs in this respect, but others are not. In our own classes we have often asked for volunteers for a committee job. When the job calls for six persons on one committee, different people will respond than when the task calls for three committees of two each. When we ask the students about this, some say, "I like to work with only one other person," or "I like to work in a larger group." Recognition, acceptance, and use of individual differences in such matters greatly benefits the teacher as well as the students; and leadership in the home, school, church, camp, or factory is a major factor in creativity. Leland Bradford and Gordon Lippitt of the National Training Laboratory are in the forefront of those developing creativity in group leadership.

CREATIVITY AND MARGINALITY

Some students of civilization, such as Hume, Teggart, Bucher, William James, and Robert Park, have described a catastrophic theory of progress. Park (13) in his book *Race and Culture* points out that races are the product of isolation and inbreeding, while civilization is a consequence of contact and communication. The decisive events in man's history have been those which brought men together through the catastrophes of mass migration. The collisions, conflicts, and fusions of peoples and cultures incidental to these migrations cause both tragedy and creativity. Bucher writes that every advance in culture commences with a new period of wandering.

Somewhere in his own wanderings over the earth, Robert Park invented the term "marginal man" to indicate what Simmel had called "the stranger." The stranger is one who stays but is a potential wanderer; he is thus not bound, as others are, by the local proprieties and customs. He is the freer man. He is less involved with others, and he can be more objective in his judgment since he is not confined by one set of customs, pieties, or precedents. The stranger is the man of the cities, where division of labor and increased production have emancipated him from the age-old struggle against starvation and have given him freedom from ancient customs as well as leisure to create.

The marginal man is a man who is part of a culture but not of it. In his autobiography *Up Stream*, Ludwig Lewisohn (11) wavers between the warm security of the ghetto which he has left and the cold freedom of the outer world where he is a stranger. Heine had the same problem, struggling to be a German and also a Jew. He was both, and being both he was not fully either. He was a marginal man, and he was creative.

The marginal man is the Okie in California, the Puerto Rican in New York, the southern white migrant in Chicago, the European in America and the American in Europe, the mulatto who mingles with whites, the white man in Africa, the Irishman in England, the Catholic in Asia or in the Protestant South.

The point is that marginality, while personally costly, also sets a man free, makes it possible for him to be creative, to see aspects of a culture in a new light because he comes from another culture. When we study the highly esteemed creative men of our culture, it seems that marginality is far more the rule than the exception.

George Bernard Shaw, for example, was born a Protestant in Catholic Ireland. Economically and socially on the fringes of the middle class, his social position was continually threatened by the economic embarrassment and alcoholism of his father. He was personally neglected by parents who found neither time for him nor interest in him. Shaw departed from the home of his childhood to live and work as an Irishman in London, clearly an outgroup position. His circumstances can be easily said to have led to his cynicism. And his cynicism about his father, his religion, his economic and social order, and most of the institutions of his day is the essence of his creativity.

In similar fashion, we note that Freud was a Jew in a non-Jewish society, as was Karl Marx; that Joseph Conrad was the orphaned child of Polish nationals exiled in Russia, that Sarah Bernhardt was the child of unmarried parents of different religions. Mme. Curie was Polish, living in France; Gershwin was the son of immigrants. Stalin was a Georgian; Hitler an Austrian; Napoleon a Corsican; and Churchill, half-American. Their marginality may lead to creativity or to other intense effort—the pursuit of political power. It may be that the outcast position of marginality enables the individual to get diverse, multidimensional views of values and customs that those thoroughly "in" any society or class fail to achieve or do not need. It may be this very multi-dimensionality, and perhaps the insecurity and defensiveness that goes with marginality, which prevents the individual from "swallowing" wholeheartedly the traditional values, practices, and beliefs of the dominant society. This very lack of acceptance of one set standard and one set tradition appears to free the individual to innovate. The marginal man can innovate partly because he does not accept the cultures as he sees them (his isolation creates resistance) and partly because he sees two or more divergent possibilities where "belongers" see only one way, the way to which they are accustomed.

The group most responsible for emotionalized attitudes is the primary group. If the individual is fairly secure in his early family relationships and if the values of the family place great emphasis on the family traditions, we would expect the individual to carry on the family traditions. If, however, he is marginal in his family (feels "left-out" emotionally, physically, or psychologically), we expect originality to emerge. It may also emerge when a person is thoroughly entrenched in a family which honors innovation and change as important values.

Although marginality may be a precondition of creativity, it is not always so. It may produce the reverse. No one can be so uncreative, so rigid as the marginal man. The new convert, for example, is typically the most conforming. The 100 per cent American is often a European who just got here, or one of his children. The *nouveau riche* are the most careful about their clothes, carpets, and coiffures. What makes the creative marginal man different from the marginal man who is an extreme conformist? We suggest that one major difference is the former's sense of humor, which involves an acceptance of one's own playful, childish, spontaneous, loving, hating, stingy, and

generous impulses. (Aristotle, St. Augustine, Newton, Galileo, and Freud are striking exceptions.) Watson (selection 5) suggests that a permissive home atmosphere is most important in the development of creativity, while MacKinnon, in the following article, finds that an openness to one's experience, a freedom to be aware of one's feelings, a preference for the complex and asymmetrical are essential qualities. Else Frenkel-Brunswik and Carl Rogers describe some of these characteristics in more detail in selections 47 and 55 respectively.

SACRED AND SECULAR VALUES

In a sacred or folk society, creativity is discouraged. The late Robert Redfield (14) defined a folk society as a relatively stable, small, homogeneous, isolated community, where unchanging traditions guide behavior. This kind of society does not seek change and tends to reject innovations. Most traditions have religious meaning. To alter them is sacrilegious.

Redfield contrasted the folk society with the secular society, which is rapidly changing, large, heterogeneous, in communication with distant lands; its values favor the new, the different, where nothing is more worthless than yesterday's newspaper or last season's styles, and nothing so valuable as a new cloth for men's shirts or a new spray for mosquitoes. A child reared in such a society, assimilating his culture, learns to value the novel, to adopt new fads, with pleasurable expectations, and perhaps he begins to look forward to setting the pace himself. If his innovations or inventions should strike the popular fancy, he is a great man, for a moment at least.

Thus, if the group has a favorable attitude toward change, a milieu is created in which creativity is favored. In interviews with 200 scientists and artists, we asked "Were you ever seriously encouraged by a teacher?" Nearly all said, "Yes."

In an analysis of the childhood of 1,400 great men and women, we repeatedly found the overwhelming importance of an outstanding teacher. We believe the single most crucial step in increasing creativity in our society would be to recruit and hold the best teachers.

SUMMARY

In exploring some of the environmental and experiential factors in creativity, the following have been considered: enough feeling of security to risk venturing beyond social norms; intelligence involving divergent rather than convergent thinking, which seems to be related to a highly developed sense of humor; freedom to explore, to think, to feel, to roam; enough pressure from marginality to push the person outside his family or social group; and a secular social climate which favors innovation. Such a social climate is fostered by good teachers, informality, freedom for all to participate, skilled but not domineering leadership, opportunity to rotate roles, and a feeling of trust and equality among group members.

BIBLIOGRAPHY

1. BARRON, F., "Originality in Relation to Personality and Intellect," *Journal of Psychology*, 25 (1957), 730–742.

2. BECK, S. J., *Rorschach's Test* (New York: Grune and Stratton, 1946), Vols. I and II.

3. CARTWRIGHT, D., AND A. ZANDER, *Group Dynamics: Research and Theory* (Evanston, Ill.: Row Peterson and Company, 1953).

4. FOOTE, NELSON N., AND L. S. COTTRELL, *Identity and Interpersonal Competence: A New Direction in Family Research* (Chicago: The University of Chicago Press, 1955).

5. FOUNDATION FOR RESEARCH ON HUMAN BEHAVIOR, "Creativity and Conformity" (Ann Arbor, Mich.: The Foundation, 1958). (Includes an excellent short bibliography.)

6. GETZELS, J. W., AND P. W. JACKSON. "The Highly Creative and the Highly Intelligent Adolescent: An Attempt at Differentiation." A paper presented at the American Psychological Association Convention, Washington, D.C., August, 1958.

7. GHISELIN, BREWSTER, *The Creative Process* (Berkeley: University of California Press, 1952).

8. GUILFORD, J. P., *et al.*, "A Factor-Analytic Study of Creative Thinking," report from Psychological Laboratory, University of Southern California, 1951–1952.

9. HILL, NAPOLEON, *How to Raise Your Salary* (Chicago: Combined Registry Co.).

10. LEWIN, K., R., LIPPITT, AND R. WHITE, "An Experimental Study of Leadership in Group Life." Selection 40 in the present volume.

11. LEWISOHN, L., *Upstream* (New York: Boni & Liveright, 1922).

12. MAIER, N. R. F., AND A. R. SOLEM, "The Contributions of a Discussion Leader to the Quality of Group Thinking: the Effective Use of Minority Opinions," *Human Relations*, 5 (1952), 277–288.

13. PARK, R. E., *Race and Culture* (Glencoe, Ill.: The Free Press, 1950).

14. REDFIELD, ROBERT, *The Folk Culture of Yucatan* (Chicago: University of Chicago Press, 1941).

15. SIMMEL, GEORG, *Soziologie* (Leipzig: Duncker und Humblot, 1908).

16. STANTON, H. R., AND E. LITWAK, "Toward the Development of a Short Form Test of Interpersonal Competence," *American Sociological Review*, 20, No. 6 (December, 1955), 668–674.

7 | THE NATURE AND NURTURE OF CREATIVE TALENT

DONALD W. MACKINNON

Let us look now at some specific research findings about a carefully selected group of contemporary creative persons: MacKinnon's study of exceptional architects, describing their remembrance of attitudes and values and early lives. From his findings, MacKinnon suggests how society may foster creative talent in future generations.

. . . Architecture, as a field of creative endeavor, requires that the successful practitioner be both artist and ·scientist— artist in that his designs must fulfill the demands of "Delight," and scientist in that they must meet the demands of "Firmnesse" and "Commodity," to use the words of Sir Henry Wotton (1624). But surely, one can hardly think that the requirements of effective architecture are limited to these three demands. The successful and effective architect must, with the skill of a juggler, combine, reconcile, and exercise the diverse skills of businessman, lawyer, artist, engineer, and advertising man, as well as those of author and journalist, psychiatrist, educator, and psychologist. In what other profession can one expect better to observe the multifarious expressions of creativity?

It should be clear that any attempt to discover the distinguishing traits of creative persons can succeed only in so far as some group of qualified experts can agree upon who are the more and who are the less creative workers in a given field of endeavor. In our study of architects we began by asking a panel of experts—five professors of architecture, each working independently—to nominate the 40 most creative architects in the United States. All told they supplied us with 86

Excerpts reprinted from *American Psychologist,* XVII (July, 1962), 484-94, by permission of the author and the American Psychological Association.

names instead of the 40 they would have mentioned had there been perfect agreement among them. While 13 of the 86 architects were nominated by all five panel members, and 9 nominated by four, 11 by three, and 13 by two, 40 were individual nominations each proposed by a single panel member.

The agreement among experts is not perfect, yet far greater than one might have expected. Later we asked 11 editors of the major American architectural journals, *Architectural Forum, Architectural Record*, the *Journal of the American Institute of Architects*, and *Progressive Architecture*, to rate the creativity of the 64 of the nominated architects whom we invited to participate in the study. Still later we asked the 40 nominated creative architects who actually accepted our invitation to be studied to rate the creativity of the invited 64 architects, themselves included. Since the editors' ratings of the creativity of the architects correlated +.88 with the architects' own ratings, it is clear that under certain conditions and for certain groups it is possible to obtain remarkable agreement about the relative creativeness of individual members of a profession and thus meet the first requirement for an effective study of creative persons.

A second requirement for the successful establishment of the traits of creative individuals is their willingness to make themselves available for study. Our hope was to win the cooperation of each person whom we invited to participate in the research, but as I have already indicated in the case of the architects, to obtain 40 acceptances, 64 invitations had to be sent out.

The invitation to this group, as to all the creative groups which we have studied, was to come to Berkeley for a weekend of intensive study in the Institute of Personality Assessment and Research. There, in groups of ten, they have been studied by the variety of means which constitute the assessment method—by problem solving experiments; by tests designed to discover what a person does not know or is unable or unwilling to reveal about himself; by tests and questionnaires that permit a person to manifest various aspects of his personality and to express his attitudes, interests, and values; by searching interviews that cover the life history and reveal the present structure of the person; and by specially contrived social situations of a stressful character which call for the subject's best behavior in a socially defined role.

The response of creative persons to the invitation to reveal themselves under such trying circumstances has varied considerably. At the one extreme there have been those who replied in anger at what they perceived to be the audacity of psychologists in presuming to study so ineffable and mysterious a thing as the creative process and so sensitive a being as a creative person. At the other extreme were those who replied courteously and warmheartedly, welcoming the invitation to be studied, and manifesting even an eagerness to contribute to a better understanding of the creative person and the creative process.

. . . . .

Certainly we cannot claim to have assessed the 40 most creative architects in the country, or the most creative of any of the groups we have studied; but it is clear that we have studied a highly cre-

ative group of architects indistinguishable in their creativity from the group of 24 who declined to be studied . . . .

A third requirement for the successful determination of the traits of highly creative persons in any field of endeavor is that the profession be widely sampled beyond those nominated as most creative, for the distinguishing characteristics of the restricted sample might well have nothing to do with their creativeness. Instead they might be traits characterizing all members of the profession whether creative or not, distinguishing the professional group as a whole but in no sense limited or peculiar to its highly creative members. In the case of the architects, to use them once again as an example, two additional samples were recruited for study, both of which matched the highly creative sample (whom I shall now call Architects I) with respect to age and geographic location of practice. The first supplementary sample (Architects II) had had at least two years of work experience and association with one of the originally nominated creative architects. The second additional sample (Architects III) was composed of architects who had never worked with any of the nominated creatives.

By selecting three samples in this manner, we hoped to tap a range of talent sufficiently wide to be fairly representative of the profession as a whole; and we appear to have succeeded. The mean rating of creativity for each of the three groups—the ratings having been made on a seven point scale by six groups of architects and experts on architecture—was for Architects I, 5.46; for Architects II, 4.25; and for Architects III, 3.54, the differences in mean ratings between each group being statistically highly significant.

. . . . .

Persons who are highly creative are inclined to have a good opinion of themselves, as evidenced by the large number of favorable adjectives which they use in self-description and by the relatively high scores they earn on a scale which measures basic acceptance of the self. Indeed, there is here a paradox, for in addition to their favorable self-perceptions the very basic self-acceptance of the more creative persons often permits them to speak more frankly and thus more critically and in unusual ways about themselves. It is clear, too, that the self-images of the more creative differ from the self-images of the less creative. For example, Architects I, in contrast to Architects II and III, more often describe themselves as inventive, determined, independent, individualistic, enthusiastic, and industrious. In striking contrast Architects II and III more often than Architects I describe themselves as responsible, sincere, reliable, dependable, clear thinking, tolerant, and understanding. In short, where creative architects more often stress their inventiveness, independence, and individuality, their enthusiasm, determination, and industry, less creative members of the profession are impressed by their virtue and good character and by their rationality and sympathetic concern for others.

The discrepancies between their descriptions of themselves as they are and as they would ideally be are remarkably alike for all architects regardless of their level of creativeness. All three groups reveal themselves as desiring more personal attractiveness, self-confidence, maturity, and intellectual competence, a higher level of energy, and better social relations. As for differences, however, Architects I would ideally be more sensitive, while both Architects II and III wish for opposites if not incompatibles; they would ideally be more original but at the same time more self-controlled and disciplined.

As for the relation between intelligence and creativity, save for the mathematicians where there is a low positive correlation between intelligence and the level of creativeness, we have found within our creative samples essentially

zero relationship between the two variables, and this is not due to a narrow restriction in range of intelligence. Among creative architects who have a mean score of 113 on the Terman Concept Mastery Test, individual scores range widely from 39 to 179, yet scores on this measure of intelligence correlate −.08 with rated creativity. Over the whole range of intelligence and creativity there is, of course, a positive relationship between the two variables. No feebleminded subjects have shown up in any of our creative groups. It is clear, however, that above a certain required minimum level of intelligence which varies from field to field and in some instances may be surprisingly low, being more intelligent does not guarantee a corresponding increase in creativeness. It just is not true that the more intelligent person is necessarily the more creative one.

In view of the often asserted close association of genius with insanity it is also of some interest to inquire into the psychological health of our creative subjects. To this end we can look at their profiles on the Minnesota Multiphasic Personality Inventory (MMPI), a test originally developed to measure tendencies toward the major psychiatric disturbances that man is heir to: depression, hysteria, paranoia, schizophrenia, and the like. On the eight scales which measure the strength of these dispositions in the person, our creative subjects earn scores which, on the average, are some 5 to 10 points above the general population's average score of 50. It must be noted, however, that elevated scores of this degree on these scales do not have the same meaning for the personality functioning of persons who, like our subjects, are getting along well in their personal lives and professional careers, that they have for hospitalized patients. The manner in which creative subjects describe themselves on this test as well as in the life history psychiatric interview is less suggestive of psychopathology than it is of good intellect, complexity and richness of personality, general lack of defensiveness, and candor in self-description —in other words, an openness to experience and especially to experience of one's inner life. It must also be noted, however, that in the self-reports and in the MMPI profiles of many of our creative subjects, one can find rather clear evidence of psychopathology, but also evidence of adequate control mechanisms, as the success with which they live their productive and creative lives testifies.

However, the most striking aspect of the MMPI profiles of all our male creative groups is an extremely high peak on the *Mf* (femininity) scale. This tendency for creative males to score relatively high on femininity is also demonstrated on the Fe (femininity) scale of the California Psychological Inventory (CPI) and on the masculinity-femininity scale of the Strong Vocational Interest Blank. Scores on the latter scale (where high score indicates more masculinity) correlate -4.9 with rated creativity.

The evidence is clear: The more creative a person is the more he reveals an openness to his own feelings and emotions, a sensitive intellect and understanding self-awareness, and wide-ranging interests including many which in the American culture are thought of as feminine. In the realm of sexual identification and interests, our creative subjects appear to give more expression to the feminine side of their nature than do less creative persons. In the language of the Swiss psychologist, Carl G. Jung, creative persons are not so completely identified with their masculine *persona* roles as to blind themselves to or to deny expression to the more feminine traits of the *anima*. For some, to be sure, the balance between masculine and feminine traits, interests, and identification, is a precarious one, and for several of our subjects it would appear that their presently achieved reconciliation of these opposites of their

nature has been barely effected and only after considerable psychic stress and turmoil.

The perceptiveness of the creative and his openness to richness and complexity of experience is strikingly revealed on the Barron-Welsh Art Scale of the Welsh Figure Preference Test, which presents to the subject a set of 62 abstract line drawings which range from simple and symmetrical figures to complex and asymmetrical ones. In the original study which standardized this scale, some 80 painters from New York, San Francisco, New Orleans, Chicago, and Minneapolis showed a marked preference for the complex and asymmetrical, or, as they often referred to them, the vital and dynamic figures. A contrasting sample of nonartists revealed a marked preference for the simple and symmetrical drawings.

All creative groups we have studied have shown a clear preference for the complex and asymmetrical, and in general the more creative a person is the stronger is this preference. Similarly, in our several samples, scores on an Institute scale which measures the preference for perceptual complexity are significantly correlated with creativity. In the sample of architects the correlation is $+.48$.

Presented with a large selection of one-inch squares of varicolored posterboard and asked to construct within a 30-minute period a pleasing, completely filled-in $8'' \times 10''$ mosaic, some subjects select the fewest colors possible (one used only one color, all white) while others seek to make order out of the largest possible number, using all of the 22 available colors. And, again citing results from the architects, there is a significant though low positive correlation of $+.38$ between the number of colors a subject chooses and his creativity as rated by the experts.

If one considers for a moment the meaning of these preferences on the art scale, on the mosaic test, and on the scale that measures preference for perceptual complexity, it is clear that creative persons are especially disposed to admit complexity and even disorder into their perceptions without being made anxious by the resulting chaos. It is not so much that they like disorder per se, but that they prefer the richness of the disordered to the stark barrenness of the simple. They appear to be challenged by disordered multiplicity which arouses in them a strong need which in them is serviced by a superior capacity to achieve the most difficult and far-reaching ordering of the richness they are willing to experience.

The creative person's openness to experience is further revealed on the Myers-Briggs Type Indicator, a test based largely upon Carl G. Jung's theory of psychological functions and types.

Employing the language of the test, though in doing so I oversimplify both it and the theory upon which it is based, one might say that whenever a person uses his mind for any purpose, he performs either an act of perception (he becomes aware of something) or an act of judgment (he comes to a conclusion about something). And most persons tend to show a rather consistent preference for and greater pleasure in one or the other of these, preferring either to perceive or to judge, though every one both perceives and judges.

An habitual preference for the judging attitude may lead to some prejudging and at the very least to the living of a life that is orderly, controlled, and carefully planned. A preference for the perceptive attitude results in a life that is more open to experience both from within and from without, and characterized by flexibility and spontaneity. A judging type places more emphasis upon the control and regulation of experience, while a perceptive type is inclined to be more open and receptive to all experience.

The majority of our creative writers, mathematicians, and architects are perceptive types. Only among research scientists do we find the majority to be judging types, and even in this group it is interesting to note that there is a positive correlation ($+.25$) between a scientist's preference for perception and his rated creativity as a scientific researcher. For architects, preference for perception correlates $+.41$ with rated creativity.

The second preference measured by the Type Indicator is for one of two types of perception: sense perception or sensation, which is a direct becoming aware of things by way of the senses versus intuitive perception or intuition, which is an indirect perception of the deeper meanings and possibilities inherent in things and situations. Again, everyone senses and intuits, but preliminary norms for the test suggest that in the United States three out of four persons show a preference for sense perception, concentrating upon immediate sensory experience and centering their attention upon existing facts. The one out of every four who shows a preference for intuitive perception, on the other hand, looks expectantly for a bridge or link between that which is given and present and that which is not yet thought of, focusing habitually upon possibilities.

One would expect creative persons not to be bound to the stimulus and the object but to be ever alert to the as-yet-not-realized. And that is precisely the way they show themselves to be on the Type Indicator. In contrast to an estimated 25% of the general population who are intuitive, 90% of the creative writers, 92% of the mathematicians, 93% of the research scientists, and 100% of the architects are intuitive as measured by this test.

In judging or evaluating experience, according to the underlying Jungian theory of the test, one makes use of thought or of feeling; thinking being a logical process aimed at an impersonal fact-weighing analysis, while feeling is a process of appreciation and evaluation of things that gives them a personal and subjective value. A preference for thinking or for feeling appears to be less related to one's creativity as such than to the type of materials or concepts with which one deals. Of our creative groups, writers prefer feeling, mathematicians, research scientists, and engineers prefer thinking, while architects split fifty-fifty in their preference for one or the other of the two functions.

The final preference in Jungian typology and on the test is the well-known one between introversion and extraversion. Approximately two-thirds of all our creative groups score as introverts, though there is no evidence that introverts as such are more creative than extraverts.

Turning to preferences among interests and values, one would expect the highly creative to be rather different from less creative people, and there is clear evidence that they are.

On the Strong Vocational Interest Blank, which measures the similarity of a person's expressed interests with the known interests of individuals successful in a number of occupations and professions, all of our creative subjects have shown, with only slight variation from group to group, interests similar to those of the psychologist, author-journalist, lawyer, architect, artist, and musician, and interests unlike those of the purchasing agent, office man, banker, farmer, carpenter, veterinarian, and interestingly enough, too, policeman and mortician. Leaving aside any consideration of the specific interests thus revealed we may focus our attention on the inferences that may be drawn from this pattern of scores which suggest that creative persons are relatively uninterested in small details, or in facts for their own sake, and more concerned with their meanings and implications, possessed of considerable cognitive flexibility, verbally skillful, interested in communicating with others and accurate

in so doing, intellectually curious, and relatively disinterested in policing either their own impulses and images or those of others.

On the Allport-Vernon-Lindzey Study of Values, a test designed to measure in the individual the relative strength of the six values of men as these values have been conceptualized and described by the German psychologist and educator, Eduard Spranger, namely, the theoretical, economic, esthetic, social, political, and religious values, all of our creative groups have as their highest values the theoretical and the esthetic.

For creative research scientists the theoretical value is the highest, closely followed by the esthetic. For creative architects the highest value is the esthetic, with the theoretical value almost as high. For creative mathematicians, the two values are both high and approximately equally strong.

If, as the authors of the test believe, there is some incompatibility and conflict between the theoretical value with its cognitive and rational concern with truth and the esthetic value with its emotional concern with form and beauty, it would appear that the creative person has the capacity to tolerate the tension that strong opposing values create in him, and in his creative striving he effects some reconciliation of them. For the truly creative person it is not sufficient that problems be solved, there is the further demand that the solutions be elegant. He seeks both truth and beauty.

A summary description of the creative person—especially of the creative architect—as he reveals himself in his profile on the California Psychological Inventory reads as follows:

He is dominant (Do scale); possessed of those qualities and attributes which underlie and lead to the achievement of social status (Cs); poised, spontaneous, and self-confident in personal and social interaction (Sp); though not an especially sociable or participative temperament (low Sy); intelligent, outspoken, sharp-witted, demanding, aggressive, and self-centered; persuasive and verbally fluent, self-confident and self-assured (Sa); and relatively uninhibited in expressing his worries and complaints (low Wb).

He is relatively free from conventional restraints and inhibitions (low So and Sc), not preoccupied with the impression which he makes on others and thus perhaps capable of great independence and autonomy (low Gi), and relatively ready to recognize and admit self-views that are unusual and unconventional (low Cm).

He is strongly motivated to achieve in situations in which independence in thought and action are called for (Ai). But, unlike his less creative colleagues, he is less inclined to strive for achievement in settings where conforming behavior is expected or required (Ac). In efficiency and steadiness of intellectual effort (Ie), however, he does not differ from his fellow workers.

Finally, he is definitely more psychologically minded (Py), more flexible (Fx), and possessed of more femininity of interests (Fe) than architects in general.

There is one last finding that I wish to present, one that was foreshadowed by a discovery of Dr. Bingham in one of his attempts to study creativity. The subject of his study was Amy Lowell, a close friend of his and Mrs. Bingham's, with whom he discussed at length the birth and growth of her poems, seeking insight into the creative processes of her mind. He also administered to her a word association test and "found that she gave a higher proportion of unique responses than those of any one outside a mental institution." We, too, administered a word association test to our subjects and found the unusualness of mental associations one of the best predictors of creativity, and especially so when associations given by no more than 1% to 10% of the population, using the Minnesota norms, are weighted more heavily than those given by less than 1% of the population. Among architects, for example, this weighted score is for Architects I, 204;

Architects II, 128; and Architects III, 114; while for the total sample this measure of unusualness of mental associations correlates +.50 with rated creativity.

And Dr. Bingham, like us, found that there are certain hazards in attempting to study a creative poet. His searchings were rewarded by a poem Amy Lowell later wrote which was first entitled "To the Impudent Psychologist" and published posthumously with the title "To a Gentleman who wanted to see the first drafts of my poems in the interest of psychological research into the workings of the creative mind." We, I must confess, were treated somewhat less kindly by one of our poets who, after assessment, published an article entitled "My Head Gets Tooken Apart" (Kenneth Rexroth, 1959).

Having described the overall design of our studies, and having presented a selection of our findings which reveal at least some aspects of the nature of creative talent, I turn now, but with considerably less confidence, to the question as to how we can early identify and best encourage the development of creative potential. Our findings concerning the characteristics of highly creative persons are by now reasonably well established, but their implications for the nurture of creative talent are far from clear.

It is one thing to discover the distinguishing characteristics of mature, creative, productive individuals. It is quite another matter to conclude that the traits of creative persons observed several years after school and college characterized these same individuals when they were students. Nor can we be certain that finding these same traits in youngsters today will identify those with creative potential. Only empirical, longitudinal research, which we do not yet have, can settle such issues. Considering, however, the nature of the traits which discriminate creative adults from their non-creative peers, I would venture to guess that most students with creative potential have personality structures congruent with, though possibly less sharply delineated than, those of mature creatives.

Our problem is further complicated by the fact that though our creative subjects have told us about their experiences at home, in school, and in college, and about the forces and persons and situations which, as they see it, nurtured their creativeness, these are, after all, self-reports subject to the misperceptions and self-deceptions of all self-reports. Even if we were to assume that their testimony is essentially accurate we would still have no assurance that the conditions in the home, in school, and society, the qualities of interpersonal relations between instructor and student, and the aspects of the teaching-learning process which would appear to have contributed to creative development a generation ago would facilitate rather than inhibit creativity if these same factors were created in today's quite different world and far different educational climate.

In reporting upon events and situations in the life histories of our subjects which appear to have fostered their creative potential and independent spirit, I shall again restrict myself to architects. One finds in their histories a number of circumstances which, in the early years, could well have provided an opportunity as well as the necessity for developing the secure sense of personal autonomy and zestful commitment to their profession which so markedly characterize them.

What appears most often to have characterized the parents of these future creative architects was an extraordinary respect for the child and confidence in his ability to do what was appropriate. Thus they did not hesitate to grant him rather unusual freedom in exploring his universe and in making decisions for himself—and this early as well as late. The expectation of the parent that the child would act independently but reasonably and respon-sibly appears to have contributed immensely to the latter's sense of personal autonomy which was to develop to such a marked degree.

The obverse side of this was that there was often a lack of intense closeness with one or both of the parents. Most often this appeared in relation to the father rather than to the mother, but often it characterized the relationship with both parents. There were not strong emotional ties of either a positive or a negative sort between parent and child, but neither was there the type of relationship that fosters overdependency nor the type that results in severe rejection. Thus, if there was a certain distance in the relationship between child and parent, it had a liberating effect so far as the child was concerned. If he lacked something of the emotional closeness which some children experience with their parents, he was also spared that type of psychological exploitation that is so frequently seen in the life histories of clinical patients.

Closely related to this factor of some distance between parent and child were ambiguities in identification with the parents. In place of the more unusual clear identification with one parent, there was a tendency for the architects to have identified either with both parents or with neither. It was not that the child's early milieu was a deprived one so far as models for identification and the promotion of ego ideals were concerned. It was rather that the larger familial sphere presented the child with a plentiful supply of diverse and effective models—in addition to the mother and father, grandfathers, uncles, and others who occupied prominent and responsible positions within their community—with whom important identifications could be made. Whatever the emotional interaction between father and son, whether distant, harmonious, or turbulent, the father presented a model of effective and resourceful behavior in an exceptionally demanding career. What is perhaps more significant, though, is the high incidence of distinctly autonomous mothers among families of the creative architects, who led active lives with interests and sometimes careers of their own apart from their husbands'.

Still other factors which would appear to have contributed to the development of the marked personal autonomy of our subjects were the types of discipline and religious training which they received, which suggest that within the family there existed clear standards of conduct and ideas to what was right and wrong but at the same time an expectation if not requirement of active expiration and internalization of a framework of personal conduct. Discipline was almost always consistent and predictable. In most cases there were rules, family standards, and parental injunctions which were known explicitly by the children and seldom infringed. In nearly half the cases, corporal punishment was not employed and in only a few instances was the punishment harsh or cruel.

As for religious practices, the families of the creative architects showed considerable diversity, but what was most widely emphasized was the development of personal ethical codes rather than formal religious practices. For one-third of the families formal religion was important for one parent or for both, but in two-thirds of the families formal religion was either unimportant or practiced only perfunctorily. For the majority of the families, in which emphasis was placed upon the development of one's own ethical code, it is of interest to inquire into the values that were most stressed. They were most often values related to integrity (e.g., forthrightness, honesty, respect for others), quality (e.g., pride, diligence, joy in work, development of talent), intellectual and cultural endeavor, success and ambition, and being respectable and doing the right thing.

The families of the more creative archi-

tects tended to move more frequently, whether within a single community, or from community to community, or even from country to country. This, combined with the fact that the more creative architects as youngsters were given very much more freedom to roam and to explore widely, provided for them an enrichment of experience both cultural and personal which their less creative peers did not have.

But the frequent moving appears also to have resulted frequently in some estrangement of the family from its immediate neighborhood. And it is of interest that in almost every case in which the architect reported that his family differed in its behavior and values from those in the neighborhood, the family was different in showing greater cultural, artistic, and intellectual interests and pursuits.

To what extent this sort of cultural dislocation contributed to the frequently reported experiences of aloneness, shyness, isolation, and solitariness during childhood and adolescence, with little or no dating during adolescence, or to what extent these experiences stemmed from a natural introversion of interests and unusual sensitivity, we cannot say. They were doubtless mutually reinforcing factors in stimulating the young architect's awareness of his own inner life and his growing interest in his artistic skills and his ideational, imaginal, and symbolic processes.

Almost without exception, the creative architects manifested very early considerable interest and skill in drawing and painting. And also, with almost no exception, one or both of the parents were of artistic temperament and considerable skill. Often it was the mother who in the architect's early years fostered his artistic potentialities by her example as well as by her instruction. It is especially interesting to note, however, that while the visual and artistic abilities and interests of the child were encouraged and rewarded, these interests and abilities were, by and large, allowed to develop at their own speed, and this pace varied considerably among the architects. There was not an anxious concern on the part of the parents about the skills and abilities of the child. What is perhaps most significant was the wide-spread definite lack of strong pressures from the parents toward a particular career. And this was true both for pressures away from architecture as well as for pressures toward architecture by parents who were themselves architects.

The several aspects of the life history which I have described were first noted by Kenneth Craik in the protocols for the highly creative Architects I. Subsequently, in reading the protocols for Architects II and III as well as Architects I, a credit of one point for the presence of each of the factors was assigned and the total for each person taken as a score. The correlation of these life history scores with rated creativity of the architects is $+.36$, significant beyond the .005 level of confidence.

And now I turn finally to a consideration of the implications of the nature of creative talent for the nurturing of it in school and college through the processes of education.

Our findings concerning the relations of intelligence to creativity suggest that we may have overestimated in our educational system the role of intelligence in creative achievement. If our expectation is that a child of a given intelligence will not respond creatively to a task which confronts him, and especially if we make this expectation known to the child, the probability that he will respond creatively is very much reduced. And later on, such a child, now grown older, may find doors closed to him so that he is definitely excluded from certain domains of learning. There is increasing reason to believe

that in selecting students for special training of their talent we may have over-weighted the role of intelligence either by setting the cutting point for selection on the intellective dimension too high or by assuming that regardless of other factors the student with the higher IQ is the more promising one and should consequently be chosen. Our data suggest, rather, that if a person has the minimum of intelligence required for mastery of a field of knowledge, whether he performs creatively or banally in that field will be crucially determined by nonintellective factors. We would do well then to pay more attention in the future than we have in the past to the nurturing of those nonintellective traits which in our studies have been shown to be intimately associated with creative talent.

There is the openness of the creative person to experience both from within and from without which suggests that whether we be parent or teacher we should use caution in setting limits upon what those whom we are nurturing experience and express.

Discipline and self-control are necessary. They must be learned if one is ever to be truly creative, but it is important that they not be overlearned. Furthermore, there is a time and place for their learning, and having been learned they should be used flexibly, not rigidly or compulsively.

If we consider this specifically with reference to the attitudes of perceiving and judging, everyone must judge as well as perceive. It is not a matter of using one to the exclusion of the other, but a question of how each is used and which is preferred. The danger for one's creative potential is not the judging or evaluating of one's experience but that one prejudges, thus excluding from perception large areas of experience. The danger in all parental instruction, as in all academic instruction, is that new ideas and new possibilities of action are criticized too soon and too often. Training in criticism is obviously important and so widely recognized that I need not plead its case. Rather I would urge that, if we wish to nurture creative potential, an equal emphasis be placed on perceptiveness, discussing with our students as well as with our children, at least upon occasion, the most fantastic of ideas and possibilities. It is the duty of parents to communicate and of professors to profess what they judge to be true, but it is no less their duty by example to encourage in their children and in their students an openness to all ideas and especially to those which most challenge and threaten their own judgments.

The creative person, as we have seen, is not only open to experience, but intuitive about it. We can train students to be accurate in their perceptions, and this, too, is a characteristic of the creative. But can we train them to be intuitive, and if so, how?

I would suggest that rote learning, learning of facts for their own sake, repeated drill of material, too much emphasis upon facts unrelated to other facts, and excessive concern with memorizing, can all strengthen and reinforce sense perception. On the other hand, emphasis upon the transfer of training from one subject to another, the searching for common principles in terms of which facts from quite different domains of knowledge can be related, the stressing of analogies, and similes, and metaphors, a seeking for symbolic equivalents of experience in the widest possible number of sensory and imaginal modalities, exercises in imaginative play, training in retreating from the facts in order to see them in larger perspective and in relation to more aspects of the larger context thus achieved—these and still other emphases in learning would, I believe, strengthen the disposition to intuitive perception as well as intuitive thinking.

If the widest possible relationships among facts are to be established, if the structure of knowledge is to be grasped, it is necessary that the student have a large body of facts which he has learned as well as a large array of reasoning skills which he has mastered. You will see, then, that what I am proposing is not that in teaching one disdain acute and accurate sense perception, but that one use it to build upon, leading the student always to an intuitive understanding of that which he experiences.

The independence of thought and action which our subjects reveal in the assessment setting appears to have long characterized them. It was already manifest in high school, though, according to their reports, tending to increase in college and thereafter.

In college our creative architects earned about a B average. In work and courses which caught their interest they could turn in an A performance, but in courses that failed to strike their imagination, they were quite willing to do no work at all. In general, their attitude in college appears to have been one of profound skepticism. They were unwilling to accept anything on the mere say-so of their instructors. Nothing was to be accepted on faith or because it had behind it the voice of authority. Such matters might be accepted, but only after the student on his own had demonstrated their validity to himself. In a sense, they were rebellious, but they did not run counter to the standards out of sheer rebelliousness. Rather, they were spirited in their disagreement and one gets the impression that they learned most from those who were not easy with them. But clearly many of them were not easy to take. One of the most rebellious, but, as it turned out, one of the most creative, was advised by the Dean of his School to quit because he had no talent; and another, having been failed in his design dissertation which attacked the stylism of the faculty, took his degree in the art department.

These and other data should remind all of us who teach that creative students will not always be to our liking. This will be due not only to their independence in situations in which nonconformity may be seriously disruptive of the work of others, but because, as we have seen, more than most they will be experiencing large quantities of tension produced in them by the richness of their experience and the strong opposites of their nature. In struggling to reconcile these opposites and in striving to achieve creative solutions to the difficult problems which they have set themselves they will often show that psychic turbulence which is so characteristic of the creative person. If, however, we can only recognize the sources of their disturbance, which often enough will result in behavior disturbing to us, we may be in a better position to support and encourage them in their creative striving.

8 | IDENTITY AND INTERPERSONAL COMPETENCE

NELSON N. FOOTE AND LEONARD S. COTTRELL, JR.

This selection answers the general question, "What kind of children do we want?" by replying, "Competent ones." But what is "competence" in operational terms and how can children acquire it?

The hypotheses presented here in reply to the last question are probably as representative of the current thinking of the behavioral scientists as any that could be found. Each of them almost immediately raises two related questions: "Is this really true?" and "How can it be proved to be true or false?"

INTERPERSONAL COMPETENCE

Competence is a synonym for ability. It means a satisfactory degree of ability for performing certain implied kinds of tasks. Each of the abilities described below as components of interpersonal competence is found to some degree in any normal person, regardless of his previous experience. Nevertheless, as with virtually all human abilities, by practice and purposeful training wide differences result. In this sense, interpersonal competence although based upon inherited potentialities, and directly contributing to self-conceptions, may be compared to acquired skills. To conceive of interpersonal relations as governed by relative degrees of skill in controlling the outcome of episodes of interaction is to diverge greatly from some other explanations of characteristic differences in behavior.

. . . . .

Some writers have attempted to define analytically the characteristics of mental health. At the 1953 National Conference on Social Work, for example, Dr. Marie Jahoda grappled with this quite metaphorical concept before an interdisciplinary symposium on the family. She first criticized previous conceptions which confused psychological health with (1) the absence of disease, (2) statistical normality, (3) psychological well-being (happiness), or (4) successful survival. These criteria were inappropriate, she asserted, because they neglected the social matrix of human behavior:

It follows that we must not conceive of psychological health as the final state in which the individual finds himself, for this state is dependent upon external events over which he has no control. Rather we should think of it as a style of behavior or a behavior tendency which would add to his happiness, satisfaction, and so on, if things in the external world were all right. Psychological health, then, manifests itself in behavior that has a promise of success under favorable conditions.

. . . . .

The Components of Competence

Each of the component aspects of competence in interpersonal relations can be considerably elaborated and investigated. The decision as to how far to go in any particular instance depends on the particular project in mind and the amount of resources available. Here it is deemed suitable only to outline roughly a recognizable conceptual definition of each component, and not to attempt operational definition or the construction of any measures. We can then go on to consider some hypotheses about the purposeful development of each of the six components of competence.

1. HEALTH | In this component we include much more than mere absence of disease. Rather it signifies the progressive maximization—within organic limits—of the ability of the organism to exercise all of its physiological functions, and to achieve its maximum of sensory acuity, strength, energy, co-ordination, dexterity, endurance, recuperative power, and immunity. A popular synonym is "good physical condition." In some medical research circles, there is, in this positive sense

considerable discussion of the better operational criteria of health to take the place of such crude indices as, for example, gain in weight among children. Research in psychiatry and psychosomatic medicine has been finding not only that sexual competence and fertility depend on psychosocial development, but also physical health in general. But the relationship runs in both directions.

Without good health, interpersonal episodes often diverge in outcome from wanted ends. Fatigue is a common example of this. While it can be and often is a symptom of complications in living, with certain other people it may also originate new difficulties. The overworked mother will lose her patience unless her reserve of energy, her ruggedness of physique, can carry her through the critical periods. The ailing person of either sex may find his dependence is not only a burden to others but means that he cannot complete the tasks that he formerly could. Endurance of strain makes physical demands, but the capacity to bear strain is not a constant; it can be cultivated in advance of its use. A striking example is the frequent recovery from despair and breakdown of interpersonal relations through vacation and rest, hygiene and recreation. On the positive, nontherapeutics side—in terms of optimal development—a benevolent spiral seems to extend from radiant health to a cheerful mien, from a cheerful mien to a friendly response, and back again to competence. . . .

. . . . .

2. INTELLIGENCE | Since this component has been studied continuously and widely for over two generations, it would be presumptuous to elaborate upon it here. Scope of perception of relationships among events; the capacity to abstract and symbolize experience, to manipulate the symbols into meaningful generalizations, and to be articulate in

communication; skill in mobilizing the resources of environment and experience in the services of a variety of goals; these are the kinds of capacities included in this category. It is significant that the construction of measures of intelligence is as controversial as ever, and that in any particular research project, the appropriateness and validity of the measure adopted is always a question of judgment.

. . . . .

3. EMPATHY | People appear to differ in their ability correctly to interpret the attitudes and intentions of others, in the accuracy with which they can perceive situations from others' standpoint, and thus anticipate and predict their behavior. This type of social sensitivity rests on what we call the empathic responses. Empathic responses are basic to "taking the role of the other" and hence to social interaction and the communicative processes upon which rests social integration. They are central in the development of the social self and the capacity for self-conscious behavior. No human association, and least of all democratic society, is possible without the processes indicated by this term. For this reason we must include empathic capacity as one of the essential components of interpersonal competence. The sign of its absence is misunderstanding; to measure its presence in the positive sense is a task now being attempted by a few investigators.

The kind of interaction experienced in the family as well as in other groups appears to depend heavily upon the degree to which emphatic capacity develops, but experimental research on fluctuations in this element of competence has hardly begun. This lack in research is paralleled by a lack of explicit programs in action agencies aimed at the development of this type of skill. Yet it is so fundamental to social life of every kind that some social psychologists have come close to defining their field as the study of empathy.

4. AUTONOMY | In the conception of the competent personality which we are defining in terms of its components, one essential element is perhaps best denoted by the word "autonomy," though the ordinary usage of the term does not include all the significance we shall assign to it here. Our present referents, expressed as aspects, are: the clarity of the individual's conception of self (identity); the extent to which he maintains a stable set of internal standards by which he acts; the degree to which he is self-directed and self-controlled in his actions; his confidence in and reliance upon himself; the degree of self-respect he maintains; and the capacity for recognizing real threats to self and of mobilizing realistic defenses when so threatened. That is, autonomy is taken to be genuine self-government, construed as an ability, not a state of affairs. A narrower definition, close to operational, is ease in giving and receiving evaluations of self and others.

Commencing with Piaget in the 1920's, the number of writers who have attempted to deal with autonomy has been growing steadily, but the process of making clearer what is meant by this term (or its near-equivalents like ego-strength and integrity) has as yet produced no satisfactory agreement upon its referents. Some writers treat it as a trait, some as a value, some as a set of rules for behavior, and some as a highly subjective, desired state of affairs. We believe that progress in definition and measurement of this obviously very important though subtle complex will come most rapidly if definition is sought in terms of an acquired ability for handling those kinds of problematic interpersonal situations where self-esteem is threatened or challenged.

5. JUDGMENT | While critical judgment

has long been understood to be acquired slowly with experience, more or less according to age, its operational definition and measurement is still a difficult task. Certain of the educational psychologists have perhaps gone furthest in differentiating this ability from intelligence, and in analyzing the conditions by which an educational or other agency may cultivate judgment among its pupils.

Judgment refers here to the ability which develops slowly in human beings to estimate and evaluate the meaning and consequences to one's self of alternative lines of conduct. It means the ability to adjudicate among values, or to make correct decisions; the index of lack of judgment (bad judgment) is mistakes, but these are the products of an antecedent process, in which skill is the important variable. Obviously neither small children nor incapacitated adults can make sound decisions in the sense indicated; and it is equally obvious that among normal adults there is wide variation in this ability. Some persons acquire reputations for unusually good judgment, and some others become conspicuous for the opposite. It is therefore highly proper to conceive of judgment as an acquired critical ability differing in degree among individuals.

. . . . .

. . . A thoroughly interpersonal concept of judgment, appropriate for studying its development, probably therefore must include the skill involved in getting others to be reasonable in discussion, and to handle criticism in a way that utilizes its value.

6. CREATIVITY | This component is perhaps the least amenable to precise definition and division into manageable variables which can be measured. It is ironical that the so-called tough-minded scientists and hard-headed practical people are inclined to look askance at this category as a proper object of scientific study, and

yet all of these people demand appraisals of this quality in prospective associates on whom heavy responsibility for leadership and initiative will fall.

The idea of creativity is commonly associated with artistic and intellectual activities. We define it here as any demonstrated capacity for innovations in behavior or real reconstruction of any aspect of the social environment. It involves the ability to develop fresh perspectives from which to view all accepted routines and to make novel combinations of ideas and objects and so define new goals, endowing old ones with fresh meaning, and inventing means for their realization. In interpersonal relations, it is the ability to invent or improvise new roles or alternative lines of action in problematic situations, and to evoke such behavior in others. Among other things it seems to involve curiosity, self-confidence, something of the venturesomeness and risk-taking tendencies of the explorer, a flexible mind with the kind of freedom which permits the orientation of spontaneous play. . . .

. . . . .

Why Six Components of Competence?

This brief outline of our conception of the essential components of interpersonal competence is offered with no illusions as to its adequacy or finality. If we have succeeded in giving to the reader at least a rough working idea of the content and meaning the term has for us, and have stimulated critical thinking on its contemporary relevance or implications, our purpose for the moment has been served. Perhaps such reflection will result in the discovery of other skills and qualities which should be added to this list. For the present we are unable to offer additions or corrections, and have some reasons for assuming its completeness.

Readers of George Herbert Mead will recall his distinction between the "me" and "I" phases of the self in personality development and social interaction. Looking at the elements of competence, three correspond roughly to the "me" phase and three to the "I" phase:

> Me: Intelligence   I: Health
>   Empathy   Autonomy
>   Judgment   Creativity

The former refer to the vested and organized experience of the community as incorporated within personal conduct; the latter, to the active, assertive, and emergent features of human behavior, not reducible to standard roles in conventional situations.

. . . . .

HYPOTHESES FOR EXPERIMENTATION | Within our focal interest of developing new research on the family, we are primarily concerned with research that has practical relevance for the planned development of interpersonal competence. For this reason we prefer to treat each component as a variable dependent on definable antecedent conditions. As a way of visualizing the task of proposing hypotheses of this kind, we suggest the reader keep the following table in mind. That the grouping of the relevant antecedent conditions is not entirely arbitrary may be visible upon inspection.

The hypotheses, now listed serially, would if the table were large enough be contained in the various cells. In addition, the table would have depth in the sense that each cell would contain hypotheses for different developmental periods—infancy, childhood, preadolescence, adolescence, adulthood, and later maturity —for successive phases of the family cycle—courtship, marriage, parenthood, and grandparenthood.

The table suggests that only relatively simple relations can be hypothesized. While this limitation does not necessarily follow, the testing of simpler relations is logically the place to start; the more complex interrelationships among antecedent conditions will suggest themselves soon enough.

The rest of this chapter will present some illustrative hypotheses affecting the development of competent personalities. They are arranged so as to fall into various cells of the table. We are not able to fill all the cells with promising hypotheses of the experimental, or even the descriptive, variety. To do so would require the collaboration of many investigators, but the scheme suggested may help to stimulate others to make additions.

. . . . .

TABLE 1. SCHEME FOR ARRAYING HYPOTHESES	CONSEQUENT VARIABLES— COMPONENTS OF COMPETENCE	ANTECEDENT CONDITIONS					
		1 Biological	2 Economic	3 Social-Legal	4 Inter-personal	5 Educa-tional	6 Recrea-tional
	1. Health	Infancy to later maturity					
	2. Intelligence	ditto					
	3. Empathy						
	4. Autonomy						
	5. Judgment						
	6. Creativity						

Some Conditions for Development of Health

BIOLOGICAL CONDITIONS DURING:

Infancy: The planned child is more likely to be born under favorable conditions of maternal health.[1]

Childhood: The health of the parents affects the child, and improvement of their health may often be more effective than direct approach to the child.

Preadolescence: Food fears run a course and abate if left alone; if alternate diets are kept at hand meanwhile, the range of taste will freely expand.

Adolescence: Developing rhythms of sleeping and eating, work and play, if disrupted arbitrarily, lead to stress reactions, but if respected, facilitate regular autonomic functioning.

ECONOMIC CONDITIONS DURING:

Infancy: The chances of life for each child increase with its family's rising level of living, and approach a point where chances are even.

Childhood: Since the health of each school child largely depends on the health of the other school children, where the school explicitly functions to bring community medical resources to bear in cases of need, the health of all improves.

Preadolescence: Progressive involvement in productive manual work which mobilizes energies for tasks of extended duration is conducive to good physical condition, and particularly to control of satiation.

Adolescence: Health is favorably affected by the development of clear-cut vocational identity through ideal models and confirming groups.

Adulthood: Security of employment fosters health; assurance of permanent

---

[1] *Ceteris paribus* [other things being equal] is a qualification that applies to all the following hypotheses.

---

worth to the employment unit fosters it even more.

Later maturity: Availability of rewarding work, regardless of age, prolongs the retention of vigor and faculties.

SOCIAL-LEGAL CONDITIONS DURING:

Infancy: To minimize the traditional penalties to minority status—crowding, deprivation, neglect—is to increase the chances of life for children in these restricted groups.

Childhood: If a family lives in a residential community designed for family living and for children's safety and play, then the children's health will thrive more than in an area oriented mainly to adult males.

Preadolescence: Dramatization of the public interest in the welfare of children —particularly its concern and intervention in cases of ill-treatment—causes parents to give children better protection than where the public seems indifferent.

Adolescence: Legal and moral emphasis on responsibility toward others creates an atmosphere more favorable to the growth of sexual competence than emphasis upon restraint of sexual interests.

Adulthood: As women feel accorded equal status at large, they gain in capacity for sexual response.

Later maturity: Health of the aged is directly a function of whether as a class they experience tangible evidence of respect or rejection.

INTERPERSONAL CONDITIONS DURING:

Infancy: If parents are accepted as adults by parental figures, they can in turn more readily give parental care. (The famous studies of Anna Freud, Rene Spitz *et al.*—summarized by Bowlby,— well cover the bearing of continuous affection upon physical and mental health, but they do not show how love might be enhanced for the unloved and the unloving.)

Childhood: The cared-for child learns to value and care for himself, by avoiding risks and following rules, when these rules are conceived as protection and not as restraint.

Preadolescence: An optimum alternation between isolation and stimulation is directly related to patterns of energy-use that fall between apathy and overstimulation.

Adolescence: Clear-cut models for sex identification improve the chances of sexual competence and reduce frigidity and impotency.

Adulthood: Control of fertility is a function of full communication and common intent between husband and wife.

Later maturity: Retaining an audience or finding new audiences, before whom one wishes to do well, is conducive to continuous health.

EDUCATIONAL CONDITIONS DURING:

Infancy: Recognition by parents and others of each gain made in the child's physical development builds up assurance and appetite for further ventures.

Childhood: Sympathetic responses of others to signs of the child's physical state help the child to recognize their meaning and importance: teaching him to report them explicitly is the basis for ultimate self-regulation.

Preadolescence: The responsibility of looking after pet animals provides a dramatic basis for learning hygiene.

Adolescence: Understanding of physiology reduces anxiety over rapid development and makes the emergence of sexual functioning a welcome attainment and thus contributes to sexual competence.

. . . . .

RECREATIONAL CONDITIONS DURING:

Infancy: Space and objects for exploration induce the growth of coordination.

Childhood: Full and free expression of evening bursts of energy in play, with adult consent or participation, do more for health than their suppression.

Preadolescence: If the physical demands of sports are adjusted to slightly exceed the margin of proven competence, their effect upon growth of physical competence is maximal.

Adolescence: The rhythm and phrasing of play episodes—if the demands increase in a graded series—affect the span of potential involvement, and thereby the capacity for flexible mobilization of energy.

. . . . .

Some Conditions of Intelligence

BIOLOGICAL CONDITIONS DURING:

Infancy: Physical stimulation through handling and caressing stimulates perceptive responsiveness to the environment.

Childhood: Having other children to play with fosters intelligence; having none retards it.

Preadolescence: Regular and thorough examination and correction of deficiencies in hearing and seeing improve intelligence in children; hearing difficulties particularly lead to attributions of lack of intelligence, and to self-conceptions as unintelligent.

Adolescence: The span of involvement in episodes of learning behavior can be steadily lengthened by progressively adjusting new tasks to the margin of ability.

. . . . .

Later maturity: Energy reluctantly expended is pathogenic, but energy expended willingly in response to stimulation, even in large amounts, is generally hygienic. Not quantity but quality of work is the gauge.

ECONOMIC CONDITIONS DURING:

Infancy: Objects that can be manipulated, and which disclose their principles by being disassembled and assembled, foster intelligence.

Childhood: Use of adult objects—despite cost and waste—improve the child's comprehension of its environment.

Preadolescence: If both father and mother can spend much time with their children, being responsive to their initiative, rather than doing things for them, the children's intelligence improves.

Adolescence: The opportunity to explore and experiment before being committed to a vocation makes more probable a choice which will utilize potentialities fully, thus fostering their growth.

. . . . .

SOCIAL-LEGAL CONDITIONS DURING:

Infancy: A general atmosphere of neighborhood interest in births and babies stimulates response and development.

Childhood: Subcultural emphasis on the values of learning and professionalism encourages the development of intelligence; anti-intellectualism discourages it.

Preadolescence: Cultural emphasis on the values of personal performance rather than on those of birth, race, and family connection, lifts the ceilings of motivation imposed by inherited status.

Adolescence: The complementarity of receptive and assertive approaches to knowledge and control of reality is best appreciated and employed in co-educational institutions. Thus all types of intelligence are cultivated best by coeducation.

INTERPERSONAL CONDITIONS DURING:

Infancy: Maternal responsiveness fosters alertness to novel elements in experience; her enjoyment in the child's discoveries intensifies his own.

Childhood: To involve the child in the pursuit of knowledge through discussion between parents, especially where there is dialectic and reasonable resolution, cultivates his intelligence.

Preadolescence: A chum with whom one can assimilate new intellectual challenges, by kindly mutual criticisms and by confiding fears, is a great help in forming strategies for mastering fears.

Adolescence: Reciprocal, frank discussion of the standards of adolescent peers versus the parent-teacher generation reduces ambiguity in the self-evaluation of progress, and makes criticism bear clearly on the sources of mistakes.

. . . . .

EDUCATIONAL CONDITIONS DURING:

Infancy: Abundant talking with the infant before he learns to talk stimulates the growth of intelligence.

Childhood: When teachers proceed explicitly, not on the notion of an original self that has to be trained, curbed, expressed, or molded, but by construing education as a joint process of discovery and mastery, they reduce resistance to learning and encourage the appetite for it.

Preadolescence: As the child is exposed to sympathetic adults of richer vocabulary, his intelligence develops more rapidly and fully.

Adolescence: Practice in group methods of problem-solving, e.g., through admission to family councils, furnishes an overt, dramatic model of careful thinking, which can be assumed individually by identification.

Adulthood: Children's questions—if welcomed and used—provide the parent with a review of his own intellectual biography and stimulate self-analysis of his resistances to learning, and so may reduce them.

. . . . .

Some Conditions for Development of Empathy

. . . . .

. . . In general it is widely suspected that underdevelopment or impairment of emphatic capacity plays a major role in many kinds of behavior disorders, particularly in schizophrenia.

Under biological conditions also belong hypotheses concerning the effects on emphatic capacity of various bodily states of extreme hunger, anger, pain, fear, excitement, intoxication, pleasure-anticipation, pain-anticipation, and similar conditions which restrict attention or reduce perception.

Additional types of hypotheses about the social psychological consequents of certain biological conditions and their effects in turn upon emphatic capacity are suggested here. For example:

1. Prolonged illness increases habituation to a relationship of dependency and thus depresses empathic capacity on both sides of the relationship, but especially in the dependent member.

2. Empathic capacity is negatively correlated with repression of biological functions. (a) There is a negative correlation between the degree of repression of sexual functions and empathic capacity. (b) Thus economic, social, and educational provision for minimizing the gap between organic sexual maturity and sexual functioning will have a positive effect on empathic capacity.

3. Unwanted children are lower in empathic development than children who are desired and planned for. (a) Instruction in how to safely and efficiently control the number of children born, and means to exercise this control, will result in a lower proportion of rejected people in the population. (b) By spreading the economic burden of having and rearing children over the whole population, the probability of children being born to people who want them will be increased, with a consequent increase in average empathic capacity.

4. There is a critical point beyond which closer contact with another person will no longer lead to an increase in empathy. (a) Up to a certain point, inti-

mate interaction with others increases the capacity to empathize with them. But when others are too constantly present, the organism appears to develop a protective resistance to responding to them. . . .

. . . . .

ECONOMIC CONDITIONS | Economic conditions (job stability, income, conditions of work, and leisure time) become factors in the development and exercise of empathic capacity when they affect the amount of unhurried and anxiety-free time, and the facilities for stimulating activities, that parents can give to their children. Their influence is also important to empathic development to the extent that they affect contact and participation in the life of the community. In less obvious ways they influence attitudes and values, and these in turn affect emphatic skill:

1. There is a negative correlation between the degree to which parents emphasize material possessions and other evidences of buying power in their evaluations of themselves and others, and their own and their children's emphatic capacity.

2. To the extent that criteria of wealth predominate in the selection of associates, social life becomes restricted and unstimulating and empathic capacity atrophies.

. . . . .

4. The assumption by children of appropriately graded responsibilities for the economic welfare of the family (as for example, regular duties and special jobs in the home, or limited jobs outside) increases empathic capacity. (Note: This is of course no argument for child labor in the old sense. But a revision of our economic, educational, and family institutional arrangements so as to make it a regular thing for all children, beginning at junior high school age, to have a limited and safe-guarded opportunity for

genuine participation in the world of business, industry, and government, would probably be a desirable thing in terms of their optimal development.)

SOCIAL-LEGAL CONDITIONS | 1. Members of an authoritarian, hierarchic social system will tend to develop higher empathic responsiveness to situations of superordinate-subordinate structure and lower empathic capacity for understanding other types of relations. (a) If the system is relatively stable and rigid, then those nearer the top exhibit the greatest empathy with persons in superior positions and the least with those in subordinate roles.

2. Family structure in such systems will tend to reflect social structure, and families are hence rendered less likely to provide the inter-personal conditions for maximizing empathic capacity.

3. In authoritarian families, the mother becomes the pivotal, mediating person, who is more able to understand both authoritarian father and subordinate children. (This may be why such characteristics as intuitiveness, sympathetic understanding, adaptability, and interest and skill in literary and artistic production have become identified as "feminine" in cultures characterized by patriarchal-authoritarian family systems.)

Age, sex, ethnic, religious, and socioeconomic differences tend to operate to inhibit the development of empathic capacity, and reduce its utilization where possessed, when these rankings serve as barriers to participation and communication.

· · · · ·

INTERPERSONAL CONDITIONS | 1. There is a positive linear relation between the emphatic capacity of a person at any point in his developmental career line and the extent to which his previous development has been characterized by stable, intimate communicative relations

of relative equality and reciprocity with the members of his family. (a) For the ideal type, middle-class American family, to the relative importance of the specific relationships are mother, father, siblings, in that order. (b) Affection is a highly important positive factor but its relative effectiveness is a function of the amount of communication sustained in the relationship. (c) Friction and conflict produce a negative effect to the extent that they impair communication. (d) The range of empathic capacity is a function of the number of different kinds of functional positions which the person has occupied in the family interaction. (By functional position of a person we mean the part played by him in a given social act, e.g., a giver or a receiver in an act of giving and receiving; leader or follower.) (e) Unilateral acts of parental subordination to the child's demands, or of administering rewards and punishment, minimize reciprocity and inhibit the development of empathic response. Striking the child in anger at something he has done and in other ways reacting to his acts so that he discovers that "parents too are human," is more in the direction of reciprocity and communication than the detached and impersonal application of rules of punishment and reward. The positive effect of "acting natural" is enhanced if the parent explains his reactions to the child and encourages him to consider how he would feel under similar circumstances, and then follows this by working out with the child some new line of action as an experimental solution to the problem.

2. Empathic capacity in children is positively related to the facility with which their parents learn to communicate and understand each other (though high empathic capacity does not insure marital harmony).

EDUCATIONAL CONDITIONS | Schools, secular and religious, are in a favorable situation to experiment with various ways of supplementing and facilitating the family in the development of emphatic capacity. Experimental and control groups could be used without detriment to the children used as subjects, indeed, with the conscious participation of the children and parents in the experiment. Hypotheses such as the following illustrate some of the possibilities.

1. Groups of children who are given the following experiences will show more empathic capacity than comparable groups who are not given such experiences: (a) Taught courses in fiction, biography, and drama in which the child is instructed and is given assistance in putting himself in the roles of the various characters studied. (b) Taught by teachers who themselves are high in empathic capacity. (c) Taught by a number of teachers who represent different subcultural backgrounds. (d) Given explicit instruction, training, and practice in accurate portrayal of others who represent different roles in his own life situations and different subcultural identities. (e) Taught in situations in which the emphasis on individualistic striving for grades is replaced by emphasis on collaborative responsibility for maximizing the skill and the mastery of the subject matter by each member of the collaborating group. (f) Participation in group activity which involves responsibility for cooperation in planning of significant programs, resolution of real problems, and genuine discipline of members.

. . . . .

RECREATIONAL CONDITIONS | 1. Unilateral giving of toys with no opportunity for the child to reciprocate and to occupy the role of giver inhibits his empathic development.

2. Toys which confine the child to role of spectator limit his empathic development.

3. Abundance of mimetic and dramatic play is positively correlated with empathic development. The genuine and full participation of the parents in this play greatly enhances its effect on empathic development.

4. Reading and films, radio and television programs, which provide rich opportunity for identification with a variety of characters, increase the empathic capacity of the child.

5. Forms of play which involve discussion, planning, teamwork, and resolution of differences are productive of empathic capacity.

Some Conditions for Development of Autonomy

Autonomy has been provisionally defined as the ability to be one's self. Analytically considered, it involves and requires knowing one's self; having or finding an unambiguous identity to refer to in each situation; and being able to govern one's self in the sense of being able to choose among alternatives. The development of autonomy is not synonymous with the development of a self, though emergence of a self is indispensable. The growth of autonomy is taken as measurable and as varying within and among individuals over time. . . .

. . . . .

BIOLOGICAL CONDITIONS | 1. Health which itself is one of the components of competence, significantly conditions all the other components including autonomy. The conditions of health—nutrition, rest, hygiene—are therefore indirectly biological conditions of autonomy. But there are a few biological conditions which more directly affect autonomy than through their influence upon physical health. In marriage and family living, these concern sexual adequacy and fertility, where these enter into self-respect and sense of worth, in the estimation of self and others. To the extent that sexual adequacy and skill can be improved by knowledge, practice, or medical treatment, a contribution is made to autonomy, i.e., the person becomes more able to handle interpersonal situations making demands upon his sexual competence. The fact that there is a circular relationship here, in which autonomy significantly affects sexual functioning, implies the reverse proposition as a corollary hypothesis worthy of investigation.

2. Fatigue as a biological variable distinguishable from health significantly conditions autonomy, and is also often the product of absence of autonomy. If practices are followed by which energy is fostered and fatigue diminished, at those times when the severest demands are made upon autonomy, autonomous capacity is itself increased.

3. Association in play exclusively with those with whom one is at a physical disadvantage, especially in the same family, leads to recurrent experiences of failure and submission which inhibit the development of autonomy. The optimal distribution of successes and failures occurs when physical opponents are evenly matched in competition.

4. The more adequate sexual satisfaction is in marriage, the less frequent is extra-marital sexual experience and consequent threats to mutually supported self-esteem.

5. Cultivation of physical appearance—complexion, weight, grace, posture, grooming—contributes to the growth of autonomy.

6. Space for physical privacy and quiet—reduction of stimulation—facilitates the integration of new conceptions of self, especially during adolescence, and thus contributes to the development of autonomy.

ECONOMIC CONDITIONS | 1. Autonomy is positively correlated with children's opportunity progressively to earn money for performance of economically significant work and to gain practice in the management of their own economic affairs. (Safeguards against exploitation are assumed.)

2. Economic independence develops autonomy, while (a) chronic dependence undermines autonomy, (b) unemployment undermines autonomy.

3. Work which continually challenges the capacities of the person without taxing them beyond their limits enhances autonomy. (a) Continuous employment at work far below one's level of capacity reduces autonomy. (b) Continuous employment at work which exceeds one's capacities and causes a chronic judgment of failure by others and self reduces autonomy.

4. Continual exposure to marked differences of reward for comparable efforts reduces autonomy, whereas recognition of differences of effort by differences of reward enhances autonomy.

. . . . .

9. There is an optimal balance of work and leisure which maximizes autonomy.

SOCIAL-LEGAL CONDITIONS | 1. Nonthreatening exposure to a wide range of cultural and subcultural alternatives for handling interpersonal situations enhances autonomy.

2. Repeated categorical discrimination without regard to performance damages autonomy, whereas equivalence of opportunity facilitates development of autonomy.

3. Customary community respect for individual differences enhances autonomy.

4. Persistent involvement or proffering of the opportunity for involvement in group activity, without forcing it, cultivates autonomy; persistent exclusion, ostracism, or forced participation reduces it.

5. Exclusive domination by others reduces autonomy; progressive increments of initiative and responsibility enhance it.

6. Procedures of assignment of duties and periodic reporting are more condu-

cive to autonomy than procedures of direct supervision.

7. Community enforcement of voluntary agreements and nullification of agreements obtained by duress encourage autonomy.

8. Marriage between persons regarding each other as social unequals reduces autonomy of both mates and children; social equality in marriage facilitates the development of autonomy in mates and children.

INTERPERSONAL CONDITIONS | 1. The strength and persistence of autonomy are positively correlated with the number of respect responses received by the self from significant others in the person's life situations.

2. Possession of a family name respected by others encourages autonomy.

3. Intimate presence of adequate models which enable the growing child to form correct sex identification is indispensable for the development of autonomy.

4. Exposure to other highly autonomous persons who can serve as models for identification facilities autonomy.

5. Recognition by significant others of progressive accomplishment encourages autonomy.

6. Correspondence between the level of performance expected by others and the capacity of the person to equal or exceed it is optimal for development of autonomy.

7. Autonomy increases as failure is met by assistance and encouragement for the next attempt rather than with derogatory personal condemnation.

8. Wherever accomplishment is competitive, matching of competitors is optimal for the development of autonomy.

9. Generally speaking, emphasis upon surpassing previous performance is more conducive to development of autonomy than is stress upon competitive standards of performance.

10. The growth of autonomy is assisted by the customary use of rituals for honoring the defeated party in situations of conflict.

11. Practice in the performance of roles conveying respect to others increases the autonomy of the self.

12. Autonomy is cultivated by participation in groups where one receives open and direct but nonaggressive evaluation of one's self by the others.

13. Autonomy is increased as appraisals of one's self by others come from a range of perspectives, thus giving one alternative evaluations to choose from.

14. When parents praise their children individually for characteristics that differentiate them noncompetitively from their siblings, so that each can feel uniquely appreciated, autonomy is cultivated.

15. When parents permit their children to compare them objectively with other parents they cultivate the autonomy both of their children and of themselves.

EDUCATIONAL CONDITIONS | 1. Rewards for expressions of curiosity and critical comparisons encourage autonomy; punishment for these reduces it.

2. Full and consistent recognition of the limitations of human knowledge, the debatability of issues, the disagreement of authorities, and the legitimacy of dissent encourage autonomy.

3. Given a broad grasp and perspective on world history, geography, and culture, one is less likely to be oppressed by the superiority or inferiority of any provincial culture or subculture.

4. Instruction and practice in scientific method foster autonomy.

5. Since teachers frequently are models for identification, they affect the autonomy of pupils favorably if they can serve as autonomous models of unambiguous sex identity.

6. If the curriculum recognizes the de-

velopment of diverse skills as an objective of education this will encourage autonomy, whereas approval solely for intelligence and intellectual achievement reduces it.

7. When questions by pupils are encouraged and welcomed, the autonomy of teachers and pupils is enhanced.

8. A programming of educational experience which affords intervals of solitude for the assimilation and integration of new knowledge increases autonomy more than programs which maintain a steady barrage of work and participation.

9. Participation in the pursuit of knowledge is more productive of autonomy than mere passive receipt of knowledge.

10. Recognition and facilitation of individual intellectual interests, as they arise, encourage autonomy; enforcement of conformity reduces its development.

11. Open reciprocal criticism by fellow-students of each other's work stimulates autonomy, provided personal aggression is minimized and objectivity of standards maintained.

12. Access by parents to objective and thorough appraisal of their children's performance, if done in a way to invoke their role as audience and not their anxiety as performers themselves, aids in the growth of parental autonomy.

RECREATIONAL CONDITIONS | 1. Positive encouragement and provision for play encourages autonomy; scorn, discouragement, or subordination of play to serve extrinsic interests, reduces its contribution to autonomy.

2. Games which, without threat, convey to a person appraisals of himself by others contribute to the development of autonomy.

3. Games which provide recognition of improvement on previous performance increase autonomy.

. . . . .

Some Conditions for Development of Judgment

. . . . .

1. If sufficient time is allowed for the completion of each sequence of decision-making, each experience can be assimilated with previous experience, and learning can occur in the sense of greater integration and efficiency in the process of judgment.

Conversely, pressure of time which forbids completion of the process is disruptive of particular instances of decision-making and inhibitory of the progressive improvement of judgment. (Generous allotments of time for making up one's mind may seem easier to obtain than the patience to utilize the time in careful weighing of alternatives, where in the past patience has been punished by parental figures.)

2. The greater one's experience as a decision-maker, the better judgment becomes. . . . Experience in decision-making is not only to run the risk of mistakes with costly consequences, but to make the mistakes and bear the consequences.

3. If the exercise of judgment is practiced in a playful and symbolic manner, competence in the judgment of real-life situations increases.

Judgment can be practiced in such forms of play as team debating, rhetoric, mock trials, window and catalogue shopping, and academic discussions. Symbolic practice in judgment can be obtained through vicarious participation in the solution of real or prototype problems by leaders or other representatives. Explicit training furnishes concentrated practice. Practice is increased by systematically taking the roles of others, e.g., changing sides in debate.

4. Judgment improves if responsibilities widen with the growth of judgment. Withdrawal of—or from—responsibility inhibits the growth of judgment.

. . . . .

7. As provocations to diffuse anxiety are lessened, judgment improves.

. . . . .

9. Exposure to highly competent decision-makers facilitates identification with them, and thereby the acquistion of their skills, and confidence in the exercise of judgment.

. . . . .

10. The greater the quantity and reliability of relevant knowledge available to participants in problematic interpersonal situations, the more likely is improvement in their judgment.

. . . . .

Without some rules, situations become wholly arbitrary, fluid, and chaotic. Yet if rules are applied to situations mechanically without deviation or change, there is no room for judgment, which cannot develop without exercise. The optimal function of rules is thus analogous to that of grammar in language—they limit and facilitate, without dictating what statements will be composed by users. . . .

Some Conditions for Development of Creativity

. . . . .

1. Participation in social relations which are permissive rather than repressive, equalitarian rather than hierarchical and authoritarian, mutual and reciprocal rather than unilateral, is favorable to creativity.

2. Rotation of functional positions among participants in a social relationship is a source of new experience, providing a broadening base for creativity and increasing the probability of its development. Role-reversal in role-playing is an almost universally usable substitute device when more extended rotation of roles is not feasible, as with children and parents.

3. Participation in social relations where diversity and individuality are val-

ued above uniformity and conformity increases the probability of creativity.

4. Extensive and obligatory routine is unfavorable to creativity. Routine in a particular activity may be favorable to creativity insofar as it frees the individual's attention, energy, and other resources for creative activity in another area. . . .

5. Situations which provide challenges that exceed the individual's previous achievement without exceeding his ability are favorable to the occurrence of creativity. . . .

6. Experiences increasing self-esteem will increase the probability of creativity. A distinction between self-esteem and self-satisfaction (a seeking for stability, permanence, perpetuation of the status quo of the self) is necessary. Self-esteem is conceived as a positive self-valuation operating independently from changes in other areas of the self-system. Involved in self-esteem is a kind of detachment which permits a person's appraisal of his general worth to stand independent from particular success and failure events; critical appraisal of products is thus not seen as directed against the performer.

7. If experiences are provided affecting the individual's self-organization and symbolic processes, so that his "threshold of stimulation" is lowered and he becomes able to be more fully responsive to the stimulation of other people and interpersonal events, the probability of creativity is increased. A playful and sociable atmosphere—as created by the capable host—is the best example.

8. Practice in make-believe and utilization or imaginary, absent, or hypothetical audiences, when real or socially present audiences are inimical or inhibitory, increases the probability of creativity. Respect for one's own voluntary fantasy and ability to withdraw are the principal cases in point; these must of course be distinguished from compulsory fantasy and worry.

. . . . .

10. Increasing the variety and range of a person's experience increases his potentiality for creativity, providing a richer fund of materials and a broader base for creativity. . . .

. . . . .

12. Creativity operates under a law of increasing returns, in that each episode of creativity increases the potentiality for future creativity. Providing people with experiences of creativity on a small scale increases the probability of more extensive creativity on a larger scale in the future.

13. Interpersonal activities and orientations which are genuinely playful are favorable to creativity. Competition and conflict (where competitors are matched and consequences limited and not serious), satire, parody, and burlesque of cherished values; humor; the playful juxtaposition of incongruities; the playful cultivation of illogicality, fantasy, and the mixture of the real and the unreal are among the kinds of playfulness favorable to creativity. . . .

14. Cultivation of an aesthetic orientation toward activity ("do it because it pleases you") as opposed to a utilitarian practical orientation ("do it because it is good for you") increases the probability of creativity. . . .

9 | A SUMMARY DESCRIPTION OF FIFTY "NORMAL" WHITE MALES

JULES GOLDEN, NATHAN MANDEL,

BERNARD C. GLUECK, JR., AND ZETTA FEDER

Can tension be productive as well as destructive? Can it move a person to resolve conflict and to grow personally? In selection 23, Selye describes both disastrous and constructive consequences of stress. What is the total personality of a normal, relaxed, satisfied person without conflict? Who is he? What does he think about? What does he want? Does he achieve? How does he compare with his more harried, neurotic, agitated peers? This study is based on follow-up tests and interviews with a small group of "normal" men some 12 years after they had distinguished themselves as ninth-grade students by achieving unblemished scores on a battery of psychological tests. The stability they demonstrated in the ninth grade appears to have been a permanent characteristic leading to remarkably stable, if placid, lives.

. . . . .

Personality research in general, and psychiatric research in particular, has been seriously handicapped by the lack of uniformly accepted standards of normality.

In the past 15 years several very comprehensive studies have been reported, coming mainly from the highly selected groups represented by college students. In 1945 Heath gave one of the first reports on the Grant Study, describing the general plan of this study of Harvard College sophomores. He states that 60 per cent of the men examined had well integrated basic personalities, while the remaining 40 per cent showed various symptoms such as shyness, mood fluctuations, autonomic

Excerpts reprinted from *The American Journal of Psychiatry*, CXIX (July, 1962), 48–55, by permission of the authors and the publisher.

instability, asocial behavior, and incomplete integration of basic personality. It is interesting to note that only 6 per cent of the group were felt to be motivated toward creative activity. Heath concludes that normal means a "perpendicular and balanced" personality.

In 1952 Earl Bond reported on 64 of 66 student council members in 3 colleges in the Philadelphia area. In spite of the opinion of one of the college presidents, "It is as normal a group as you will get," only 39 of these students were judged to be well balanced, or to have such strong assets as to outweigh their liabilities. Sixteen of the group showed extraordinary ability and important neurotic traits, "success at the price of unhappiness." Nine of the group were described as gifted, but with serious personality problems: schizoid, depressive, etc. Bond concluded that 57 per cent would benefit from psychiatric help, while 14 per cent were in urgent need of help. In discussing the concept of normality Bond stresses a number of negatives, things that normal is not: e.g., "normal does not mean average—normal does not mean uninteresting—normal is not per-

fect—a normal person is not one who has no problems."

This study of "normal" young males was undertaken primarily to provide a reference group for a study of 100 psychiatric patients, part of a project studying "The Skilled Clinician's Assessment of Personality." We were able to draw upon a large group of young adult males who had first been studied 12 years previously, as part of a project on delinquency being conducted by Monachesi and Hathaway of the University of Minnesota. They had obtained a self-descriptive evaluation, by means of the MMPI, of all ninth grade students in the Minneapolis public schools. These individuals have been followed periodically in the succeeding 12 years, so that those developing known mental illness or delinquency patterns have been identified, and were readily eliminated from our sample. We took as our basic group those individuals who, on self-description at approximately age 14, had indicated an absence of psychopathology in any of the areas measured by the MMPI. This is indicated on the MMPI results by a profile with no score above 55 (Figure 1).

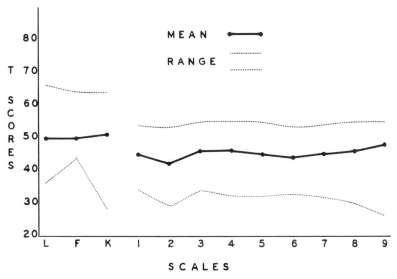

ORIGINAL MMPI

Figure 1.

Of 1,953 male students tested, 73 gave no indication of significant pathology. Of these 73 potential subjects, 23 were excluded from the study for the following reasons: 13 had moved out of the state, 7 were not locatable, one was deceased, one could not leave his job in a distant part of the state to come in for interview, and one subject refused to cooperate. Of the 50 remaining subjects, all but 5 agreed quite readily to assist in the project. These 5 were primarily concerned about the economic loss occasioned by leaving their jobs, and were persuaded quite readily when they were told they would be recompensed for the time spent in the interviews.

Each subject was seen for evaluation at the University. The following procedures were carried out:

1. A 1½-hour unstructured psychiatric interview in which current adjustment, description of home of origin, personal history and aspirations, and mental status were appraised.

2. Examination on additional material to cover an extensive check list type of psychiatric history.

3. A structured mental status examination (check list).

4. A social adjustment rating (MSAS).

5. Psychometrics: (a) repeat of the Minnesota Multiphasic Personality Inventory (MMPI); and (b) Projective drawings (House-Tree-Person) (HTP).

6. A home visit and unstructured interview with the wife, which included the wife's evaluation of her husband, and the interviewer's evaluation of the wife. (The MMPI, MSAS, and HTP were administered to the wife as well.) The wives of 38 of the 40 married men in the sample were interviewed.

FINDINGS

Our first impression, and one that has continued through subsequent evaluation of the data obtained, was of a re-

markable consistency and uniformity in the sample of 50 men. On most of the items in the extensive psychiatric history, these men were rated either identically, or within one step, on the variables involved. Some of the similarities were directly influenced by the choice of subjects; for example, 49 of the 50 subjects were born and raised in the Middle West, all were in the 25- to 26-year age range, 48 were currently living in a large metropolitan area.

Some diversity occurs when the current adaptational patterns are examined: 11 men were engaged in professional or semiprofessional technical work, 2 were in executive positions, 12 were clerical, sales, or other white collar workers, 13 were craftsmen, skilled workers or foremen, and 12 were operatives and semi-skilled workers. None was in the unskilled, laboring, service, or domestic categories. A narrower spread is observed in their income levels. Only one man was in the $10,000 to $14,000 a year class, 14 were in the $6,000 to $10,000 category, 34 were in the $3,000 to $6,000, and only one was earning under $3,000 a year. All of the men had completed high school, 15 had some college education, while 7 had postgraduate education.

The spread becomes somewhat wider when the observers' evaluations of these individuals enter into the picture. On the mental status examination these men were rated as having a spread of from 6 to 40 positive items, with a mean of 22.3 items. This contrasted with a spread of from one to 5 negative items, with a mean of .52 negative items per subject.

The social adjustment of the subjects was assessed quantitatively by using the Mandel Social Adjustment Scale, which gives a quantitative measure of the extent to which an individual meets the overt societal norms of his society. A score of 5 on each of the subcategories of this scale would mean a perfect adjustment. These men had a mean score of 4.43 on the

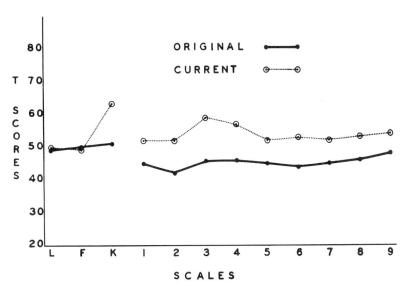

Figure 2. Comparison of original and current near profiles, N = 50.

combined 7 scales, with a low of 3.84 on the scale measuring religious adjustment, and a high of 4.80 on the scale measuring health adjustment. This compares favorably with the scores obtained on 3 other groups of subjects as indicated in Table 1.

The current MMPI profiles of the subjects were rated by a panel of 5 psychologists, again on a 5-point scale, with a rating of 5 indicating the most healthy end, and a rating of 1 as the most pathological end. Three subjects were rated 5, 23 between 4 and 5, 18 between 3 and 4, 5 between 2 and 3, and 1 between 1 and 2, with a group mean of 3.82.

An appraisal of the overall adjustment of the married subjects, based on the data obtained from the interview with their spouses, was made independently by 3 social workers. Identical ratings were given 19 of the subjects, another 18 subjects were rated identically by 2 of the 3 judges, and only one step off by the third, while in only one case was there lack of agreement between at least 2 of the 3 raters. Two of the men were not rated due

TABLE 1. COMPARISON OF MSAS MEAN SCORES	Scale	Study subjects	U. of M. students[1]	R-E-S-T patients[2]	Hospital patients[3]
	I. Occupational adjustment	4.79	4.40	3.84	3.53
	II. Family life adjustment	4.39	4.39	3.62	3.52
	III. Economic adjustment	4.36	4.41	3.45	3.06
	IV. Health adjustment	4.80	4.53	3.42	2.41
	V. Religious adjustment	3.84	3.98	3.81	3.46
	VI. Residence adjustment	4.71	4.17	4.35	2.86
	VII. Community and social adjustment	4.0	4.11	3.08	2.95
	TOTAL SCALE SCORE	4.43	4.28	3.66	3.11
	TOTAL SUBJECTS	50	29	58	51

[1] University of Minnesota undergraduate students in Family Life course.
[2] Post-regressive electric shock treatment psychiatric patients from University of Minnesota Hospitals.
[3] University of Minnesota Hospital psychiatric inpatients.

to insufficient information, and none of the 10 unmarried subjects was evaluated. The mean rating obtained was 3.16 on a 5-point scale, with a rating of 5 being the ideal, again showing relatively good adjustment. The subjective impression of the 3 raters was that they were confronted with a particularly "normal group of people."

A global evaluation of the subjects based on all of the above information resulted in the distribution by diagnostic categories shown in Table 2.

DISCUSSION

Looking at the last table, showing the distribution of the men by diagnostic categories, one might question the validity of the selection process described above for choosing these men. We would like to raise the question, however, as to whether the "range of normal personality" should not include 47 of the 50 men examined. If we evaluate these individuals on the basis of the various definitions of normality described earlier in this pa-

per, we believe that all but 3 of the men would fall within the normal groupings given by the various authors. . . . One subject with a current history of peptic ulcer, and 2 subjects who showed some antisocial patterns, particularly in traffic violations, might . . . [indicate the presence of] social and occupational maladaptation. . . . Only 2 men, one with moderately severe pseudoneurotic schizophrenia, one with an obsessive-compulsive pattern, could be said to have definitely structured psychiatric symptoms . . . . Thus, 45 of the men in our sample would probably be considered . . . to be emotionally healthy, within the broad range encompassed by . . . use of that term.

The major focus of interest of the subjects appears to be in the home. Those who were married expressed a high order of contentment with their wives and children. There were no separations or broken marriages; with one outstanding exception, the men tended to idealize their wives and the wives were, again with one exception, content with their husbands as stable, responsible, dependable,

TABLE 2. DIAGNOSTIC CATEGORIES	No significant symptomatology		23
	Psychoneurotic		9
	Minimal	(5)	
	Mild	(4)	
	Neurotic character disorders		9
	Minimal	(5)	
	Mild	(4)	
	Psychosomatic disorders		4
	Minimal	(3)	
	Mild	(1)	
	Character disorders (acting out)		2
	Minimal	(1)	
	Mild	(1)	
	Pseudoneurotic schizophrenia		2
	Mild	(1)	
	Moderate	(1)	
			49

One subject not included as he had Addison's Disease, with psychological symptoms, 3 years before study.

TABLE 3.
DESCRIPTIVE
CATEGORIES

I. Contentment with vocational position: Satisfaction with job level and activities.

II. Enjoyment of occupation: Extent of pleasure derived from job and associated activities.

III. Vocational ambition: Vocational goals and aspirations (in relation to estimated abilities and opportunities).

IV. Parents' previous concern with subject's vocational development: Parent's role in influencing subject's vocational choice and progress.

V. Contentment with spouse: Satisfaction with choice and relationship with spouse.

VI. Compatibility with spouse: Comfort in relationship with spouse.

VII. Effectiveness as a husband: Assumption and performance of the role of head of the household.

VIII. Effectiveness as a parent: Assumption and performance of parental role.

IX. Means of handling anger: Mode of expressing assertion and dissatisfaction.

X. Symptoms: Manifestations or organized psychopathology.

XI. Wishes for 10 years hence: "What would you wish in 10 years if you could write your own ticket?"

XII. Use of unlimited finances: "What would you do if you were given $5 million with no strings attached?"

XIII. Breadth of interests and pleasures: Range of pleasure yielding activities.

XIV. Richness of personality: Subject's positive social stimulus value.

XV. Overall mental health: Degree of adaptational behavior, considering both personality assets and deficits.

supportive individuals. If the findings of . . . [researchers] that suggest that the emotional health of children is influenced primarily by the nature of the conjugal relationship are applied to our married men and women, we would predict that the children of the married subjects should develop in a healthy fashion, since the conjugal relationship seems to be so satisfactory in 39 of the 40 married couples.

The marked vocational and residential stability which is characteristic of this group, and the general lack of significant psychopathology, may perhaps be achieved at the price of a more creative, spontaneous type of personality organization. These men were found to have little imagination, and generally limited interests and social activities. They indicate limited educational and vocational aspirations for themselves, and also for their children. This was reflected in the ratings given on various subitems of the psychiatric interviews, with richness of personality and breadth of interests and pleasures being the 2 lowest ratings of the 15 descriptive categories. Contentment with spouse and compatibility with spouse were the two highest ratings, with enjoyment of occupation, and contentment with vocational position also being very high on the list.

CONCLUSION

All of the above raises in our minds a question which has been stated in a number of different ways in the past concerning the balance between the needs and the wants of individuals on the one hand —in this group apparently very much in balance—and the various factors that have been considered to be part of the richer, more creative, spontaneous type of personality. Does "normality," as evidenced by lack of intrapsychic tension,

	Descriptive Categories	N	$\bar{X}$	SD
TABLE 4.	I. Contentment with vocational position	47	3.53[1]	.66
MEAN RATINGS OF	II. Enjoyment of occupation	47	3.74	.49
SUBJECTS ON	III. Vocational ambition	47	3.79	.62
DESCRIPTIVE	IV. Parents' previous concern with subjects'			
CATEGORIES DERIVED	vocational development	47	2.92	.55
FROM PSYCHIATRIC	V. Contentment with spouse[2]	38	3.89	.61
INTERVIEWS	VI. Compatibility with spouse[2]	38	3.82	.32
	VII. Effectiveness as a husband[2]	38	3.43	.69
	VIII. Effectiveness as a father[2]	38	3.48	.77
	IX. Expression of anger	47	3.57	.65
	X. Symptoms	47	3.77	.92
	XI. Wishes (for 10 years hence)	47	3.0	.74
	XII. Use of unlimited finances ($5 million)	47	3.39	.62
	XIII. Breadth of interests and pleasures	47	2.40	.74
	XIV. Richness of personality	47	2.30	.69
	XV. Overall mental health	47	3.32	.66

[1] 5-point scale, with 5 indicating the healthiest or the ideal.
[2] Only married subjects rated, 2 subjects not rated as wives not seen.

adequate social, economic, and familial adaptation, and harmonious integration with other individuals at all levels, necessarily imply a lack of creativity, imagination, and spontaneity? Our data are suggestive of this conclusion. Confirmation would be dependent upon a study of those individuals in the original sample of 1,953 male ninth-graders, who have subsequently been more creative, although they showed evidence of some disturbance at that time as measured by their MMPI profiles; at the very least.

It is our opinion that the 23 subjects described in this study as being free of symptomatology and as having made a stable, successful adaptation, represent a very normal, healthy, socially acceptable and desirable group of individuals. We would feel that an additional 12 subjects represent the broader "range of normal," which allows for some degree of intra-psychic tension and some minimal adaptational difficulties, none serious enough to interfere with a basically adequate and successful social and economic adjustment. The remainder of the group, with 2 exceptions, while having somewhat greater difficulty in making an adaptation, are still quite successful in most areas and will probably continue to make a successful adaptation without psychiatric help, although perhaps at the cost of greater tension and psychic stress and strain than might otherwise be the case.

10 | CLOSE-UP OF THE "NORMAL" WIFE

RENA CORMAN

Whom do placid, comfortable, satisfied, home-loving men marry? The low divorce rate observed in the group of "50 normal men" led investigators to wonder about the wives of "normal men." Do they run the gamut of personality types, or do they resemble one another in certain important dimensions of personality? This article summarizes the study of the wives of the men described in the previous selection.

Having examined these paragons (and how few, alas, there were), the investigators were naturally curious as to what kind of women such men marry. Thirty-eight amenable wives (40 of the men were married) were subjected to examination similar to that undergone by the husbands. The results showed 30 of these women to be not only completely free of emotional disturbance, but so well-adjusted to their lives and marriages and so contented in their little homes on their little plots of ground that they saw their prosaic husbands as ideal, their moderate incomes as highly satisfactory, and their futures as requring little more than an extra bedroom. To the psychiatrists and psychologists who tested them, they were not just normal but "astonishingly so."

What kind of people were they, these normal young women? Very like their husbands, for one thing. They had the same level of estimated intelligence (an average I.Q. of about 110), were very close to them in age, and had just about the same amount of education (high school, for the most part). They came from the same geographical area—a Midwestern city of 500,000—and the same kind of socio-economic background—their fathers were typically semiskilled or skilled workers.

Of the 38, only two had married without their parents' blessings, and most of them had had a conventional religious ceremony. They say things like—as one of them said—"I'd always dreamed of that long white dress with a train, and how my husband would lift my veil to kiss me."

Most of the women had been virgins when they were married, and almost without exception they were convinced—and rightly—of their husbands' fidelity. . . .

. . . . .

In the years that these wives had been dwelling in marital bliss—only five had been married for more than five years—only one had even considered a separation or divorce, although, according to recent estimates, divorce rates hit their peak in the second year of marriage. Only two of the wives had any doubts at all about their faith, and in only five families was there a difference in religion which produced even "mild contention."

There were few other departures from the wholesome, virtuous, healthy pattern. Only six of the 38 women showed a deplorable tendency to rule the roost. And only five were not truly contented with their sexual lives.

In spite of this small sprinkling of sour notes, in spite of the fact that some of them could not be awarded the gold star of complete medical normality, all the women, it was found, make marvelous wives and mothers. Indeed, the investigators lavished praise on both sets of spouses: "Our data indicate that they experience what we consider some of life's deepest and most meaningful pleasures in their stable relationships with each other as well as in raising their children. Such a population would promote stability and a firm backbone for our country."

But the praise is mixed with regret. Although the women rate high in "contentment with spouse," and "effectiveness as a parent"; although their "residence adjustment" is ideal, and all their other "adjustments"—occupational, family life, economic, health, religious, community, and social—are very close to perfect; although they got lots of credits for such items as neat appearance, relaxed demeanor, and a warm, cooperative attitude, their marks fall considerably when they are judged for "breadth of interests and pleasures" and "richness of personality." Granting that richness of personality involves a value judgment, Dr. Golden explains his group's standards for gauging this quality:

We thought of a person like Eleanor Roosevelt as the epitome of a rich personality. And at the other extreme, representing the barren personality, was the housewife who simply takes care of her home, doesn't socialize at all, and is quite contented at the end of the day merely by having finished her chores.

The investigators thus were forced to conclude: "These couples' lives seem essentially mundane and dull." Not only were most of the women well below average in range of interests and richness of personality, they also failed to meet the inquisitors' standards for imagination.

In attempting to measure this elusive attribute, the investigators asked, "What would you do if given $5,000,000?" A 22-year-old woman, pregnant for the first time and living in a new home, gave a typical reply: "Well, we'd pay off this house and get all the furniture we need for it right away, instead of a piece at a time. Joe [her husband] would get a new car, too. . . . I guess we'd invest the rest. Maybe we'd need it for the future. . . . Of course, we'd give to charities, too, and our church. . . . And maybe Joe would retire and we'd travel some."

The investigators felt that much more imaginative responses came from some former juvenile deliquents, one of whom said, "Gosh, I'd never thought of more than *one* million. But I have plenty of things I'd like to do with it. First of all, I'd hire a French chef and get me a Rolls-Royce. And I'd hire a special attorney just to 'fix' my traffic tickets. I'd set up a public golf course, and endow a museum, and build a hospital for crippled children, and—say, Doc, do you think you could up the ante to 10 million?"

The fact that the satisfied women in this study had no such grandiose desires emphasizes the lack of stress and stimulation in their lives. The typical wife caught in Dr. Golden's net leads a placid, calm

existence. She doesn't yearn for a French chef, because her family is satisfied with the meat and potatoes she cooks. She doesn't care about a golf course or a museum, because her world is bounded by the neat grass plot surrounding her home.

Home, for this woman, is a ranch-type, clapboard house on a small piece of treeless ground in a new development. It is still rather sparsely furnished with colonial-style furniture, decided on and purchased together with her husband. Typically, one wife confided, "Bill used to want blond modern, but we talked it over, and then one day he came home and told me about a beautiful maple bedroom set he'd seen. And we went right out and bought it."

Her nest, then, contains early-American furniture, ruffled chintz curtains, a TV set, and not much else. The walls are bare, and the only books are left over from required school reading. She subscribes to a woman's magazine, though, and *Look*, and her husband buys *Popular Mechanics* from time to time for inspiration in his workshop tinkering.

Reading opens no magic casements to delight for either of them. Nor does dining out or going to the theater. And they feel no passionate urge to join any particular organization. But he loves hunting and fishing, and spends about one weekend out of three in pursuit of these pleasures; and as a dutiful wife, she often goes along. Then, when they visit their friends or their families, he can sit with the men and review their sportive accomplishments, while she, of course, sits with the women and confers about their children.

What goes on amidst the madding crowd outside her home, however, isn't nearly so important as what happens inside, every day, all the time. At 24, our normal housewife has been married four years and has two children. She stopped working when she became pregnant, and has never regretted it. She doesn't feel she is biding her time, nor does she think of herself as a "trapped housewife." The possibility of returning to work when her children are grown doesn't cross her mind even though wives and mothers make up more than half of today's 24,-000,000 working women.

She and her family live comfortably on her husband's $6,000-a-year salary, and she is content to minister to his needs (she makes his breakfast and packs his lunch, too), run the house, and give her children the love and attention she feels they require. (This doesn't, of course, mean reading to them, or taking them to an art museum or a children's concert. These children, who also "give evidence of an emotionally healthy adjustment," are not being subjected to the pressures of an upward-striving, education-oriented family.)

The normal housewife's home and children are important and satisfying, and when she is sharing them with her husband her cup overfloweth. As one woman said, "When Johnny [her 3-year-old son] laughs over some funny thing my husband has done with him, and I see both of them enjoying each other like that, I get all mushy inside."

When she's alone with her husband, in bed, our normal wife finds nothing to complain of either. He is, she feels, a considerate and satisfactory lover, and if she achieves a climax about half the time, that's all she expects.

According to our scientific scrutinizers, then, these housewives are stable, contented homebodies—blithely conventional, cheerfully unambitious, happily in a rut. . . . The words "happiness" and "adjustment" are used almost interchangeably in the literature of mental health. And study after study draws a portrait of the well-adjusted wife which might be a carbon copy of Dr. Golden's normal woman.

As Dr. Emily Mudd, professor of family study in psychiatry at the University of Pennsylvania, regretfully sums up the situation:

Unfortunately, the definition of mental health in the last decade, with its emphasis on adjustment, precludes the extremes in imagination and creativity. In fact, I'm afraid that if we try to raise our children rigidly in accordance with that definition, we'll be breeding for mediocrity.

Thus, normality would seem to be bound inextricably to conformity, and these women are snugly ensconced within the bonds. And yet, conformity doesn't necessarily produce normality—or does it? Is it possible that these contented, adjusted, unimaginative, conventional women are not only normal, but average as well?

Statistically, it is true, in a few scattered facts, they do come close to being average. According to the 1961 U. S. Statistical Abstract, these women are among the 70 per cent of the population inhabiting urban areas; their schooling matches the median educational level for women of their age (slightly more than 12 years); and the incomes of their husbands are very like the annual mean income for males 25 years and over, who have completed high school (just over $5,500). But beyond these numerical similarities, is their satisfaction median or typical, too? On this aspect, a conflict again arises.

Dr. Mudd thinks this may be the case, and suggests a possible explanation. She feels that "people who haven't gone beyond high school, in our culture, have much more stereotyped goals, and their whole horizon is perforce much more confined."

And yet, even for high school graduates with simple goals, their field of view seems too narrow, their smug satisfaction with the four walls of home too rare to be typical. At least one survey, reported by Morton Hunt in "Her Infinite Variety," shows that their housewifely happiness is not average: interviews with a group of high-school girls indicated that although 90 per cent wanted to marry, 85 per cent did *not* want to be housewives.

The lack of concern over the future seems unusual as well. According to "Americans View Their Mental Health," a nationwide interview survey prepared for the Joint Commission on Mental Illness and Health, people making from $3,000 to $6,000 a year (34 of the 50 men in the Golden study were in that income bracket) report not only financial worries but also particularly strong aspirations to higher incomes. And the freedom from any kind of worry and stress is clearly shown to be atypical by the mammoth "Midtown" mental-health study of a section of Manhattan by Cornell University Medical College. The findings of this study were that 75 per cent of the people interviewed, whatever their status, showed significant symptoms of anxiety.

Even the average American housewife, it would appear, is subject to worry, discontent and—horror of horrors—neurosis. These golden few may be normal only because they have neither education, nor stimulation, nor stress, nor imagination. In fact, perhaps they are not only few but on their way to becoming extinct.

11 | THE FAMILY IN THE U.S.S.R.

KENT GEIGER AND ALEX INKELES

This discussion presents a brief but interesting picture of family relationships in a totalitarian society. The Soviet revolution not only changed the ownership and control of wealth, but also revolutionized the Russian family and its child-rearing customs.

The evidence at hand points to an increasingly pronounced and widespread orientation toward equality as between husband and wife. Among the peasantry, of course, and among some of the ethnic groups where male and age prerogatives are deeply embedded in the traditional way of life, the woman can hardly be said to have reached equality with her husband. However, patriarchal patterns are looked upon by both the government and the urban population as backward and unenlightened "remnants" of an outmoded way of life. Equality of power and authority within the family between husband and wife is also supported by law. No distinctions whatsoever are made on the basis of sex in re-

Excerpts reprinted from *Marriage and Family Living*, XVI, No. 4 (November, 1954), 403–4, by permission of the authors and The National Council on Family Relations.

gard to legally enforceable rights and duties in the family. Husband and wife enjoy full freedom of choice as to their individual occupation and place of residence. Neither may compel the other to change his place of residence or occupation; the wife need not "follow the husband." Further, each spouse is required to support the other if he or she is in need and unable to work, and husband and wife are jointly responsible for the support and upbringing of the children.

Although in many respects the husband-wife relationship tends to be markedly symmetrical, there still remain spheres of specialization which are sex-typed. The primary responsibility of the husband is seen as that of providing for the material security of the family, and the care of young children, the preparation of food, washing of clothes, etc., are regarded as the wife's responsibilities. In some families the bulk of the daytime care of young children is delegated to in-laws, older children, or servants in the case of upper class families. This is not always possible, however, and even where such aid is available it is only a partial answer to the problem of the divided role of the Soviet woman. Therefore most Soviet women must be both wives and mothers on the one hand, and full-time workers on the other, a fact which introduces a definite element of strain to their lives and in turn into the family.

As to relations between parents and children in the Soviet family, children definitely appear to be desired and cherished, and while they are young much attention is paid to them. Soviet parents seem as a rule to prefer to keep their children at home while they are young rather than send them to the public nurseries for the entire day. Since many families have no one at home to care for them, however, a large number of children must spend most of their waking hours in these government sponsored institutions. This is a start of a series of experiences outside the home controlled and dominated almost completely by the state. Children enter the regular primary school at the age of seven. The requirement for compulsory education is four years for the entire U.S.S.R., but in the more settled and urban areas it involves a seven year minimum. In addition to the ideas and training which children absorb at school at appropriate ages they enter the Soviet youth organizations—the Octobrists, the Pioneers, and the Komsomol—which are organizationally integrated with the schools but controlled and directed by representatives of the Communist Party. This early and intensive training of children to be loyal Soviet patriots reflects back on family relationships, and as the children grow up some tension between parents and children in the form of parent-youth conflict quite frequently develops.

Conflict in the family between parents and children in the U.S.S.R. was especially common in the early years of Soviet history when the tendency was to look upon all the established institutions of pre-Revolutionary society with a jaundiced eye and when the revolutionary fervor of the youth often got out of control. At present the family is accepted and promoted as a "basic unit of socialist society," but certain socially structured modes of conflict with the older generations still persist. Under the influence of a utopian, monothematic ideology, inculcated by the school and youth organizations, and with very limited opportunities to temper ideas with experience, the Soviet child is apt to take the official propaganda and agitation seriously and quite literally. In many cases young people become fanatically devoted to the ruling regime and its goals, and rebel against their more detached or even hostile parents, who, they feel, are old-fashioned and not socially conscious. Differences in religious orientation, for instance, are particularly likely to be a basis for conflict and tensions. In the schools and youth organizations the children are taught that religion is nonscientific and at best mistaken, whereas in the home, especially in the case of peasant and worker families, traditional religious attitudes often predominate. While the denunciation of parents by children is clearly a rare and exceptional occurrence, particularly in recent times, there is no doubt that parent-child differences of this order are quite widespread and severe, and parents often report marked hesitation to let their children know their real feelings on many issues.

A final aspect of interpersonal relationships in the Soviet family is related to the fact that the U.S.S.R. is a totalitarian social system in which the government chronically carries out large scale repressive activities against the people. The presence of the powerful secret police, and the wholesale political arrests and purges have created throughout Soviet society an atmosphere of distrust and insecurity so that large parts of the population constantly feel exposed and anxious. Family life serves for many as an especially gratifying counterbalance to this kind of atmosphere, for that element of trust and stability which is conspicuously absent in the larger society can often be found in the interpersonal relationships within the family. For those who have not identified with the goals and symbols of the ruling regime, therefore—and it appears that there are many who fall in this category—the family serves as a refuge or retreat from a threatening life situation.

In conclusion it can be said that the general direction of change and the lines of development indicated for the Soviet family in the future are broadly similar to those which have already occurred in Western industrial countries. The family will probably become smaller in size, more mobile geographically, more isolated from the larger kinship system, and other patterns inherited from a peasant cultural background will be increasingly replaced by those demanded by an urban industrial system. Greater stress on educational preparation of children and on the development of characteristics leading to the possibility of occupational mobility are probable developments in the realm of values and attitudes; and a general trend toward equalitarianism in social relationships between husband and wife and parents and children is indicated on the interpersonal relations dimension of family life.

12 | THE ANCIENT FAMILY IN ISRAEL: DAVID AND ABSALOM

II SAMUEL 13–15, 18

No book contains more dramatic incidents involving love and loyalty, courage and despair, envy and hate, rape and murder than the Holy Bible. The passages below relate some tragic events in the family of King David.
Although his children were guilty of serious crimes, David did not punish or reprimand them. Nor did he summon a meeting of the village board or call the police, priest, or psychiatrist. Instead, he "tare his garments and lay on the earth . . . and wept very sore." Today many would consider this kind of behavior infantile; others would regard it as the healthiest way to express one's grief.

CHAPTER 13

And it came to pass . . . , that Absalom the son of David had a fair sister, whose name was Tamar; and Amnon the son of David loved her. And Amnon was so vexed, that he fell sick for his sister Tamar; for she was a virgin; and Amnon thought it hard for him to do anything to her. But Amnon had a friend, whose name was Jonadab, the son of Shimeah David's brother: and Jonadab was a very subtil man. And he said unto him, Why art thou, being the king's son, lean from day to day? wilt thou not tell me? And Amnon said unto him, I love Tamar, my brother Absalom's sister. And Jonadab said unto him, Lay thee down on thy bed, and make thyself sick: and when thy father cometh to see thee, say unto him, I pray thee, let my sister Tamar come, and give me meat, and dress the meat in my sight, that I may see it, and eat it at her hand.

So Amnon lay down, and made himself sick: and when the king was come to see him, Amnon said unto the king, I pray thee, let Tamar my sister come, and make me a couple of cakes in my sight, that I may eat at her hand. Then David sent home to Tamar, saying, Go now to thy brother Amnon's house, and dress him meat. So Tamar went to her brother Amnon's house; and he was laid down. And she took flour, and kneaded it, and made cakes in his sight, and did bake the cakes. And she took a pan, and poured them out before him; but he refused to eat. And Amnon said, Have out all men from me. And they went out every man from him. And Amnon said unto Tamar, Bring the meat into the chamber, that I may eat of thine hand. And Tamar took the cakes which she had made, and brought them into the chamber to Amnon her brother. And when she had brought them unto him to eat, he took hold of her, and said unto her, Come lie with me, my sister. And she answered him, Nay, my brother, do not force me; for no such thing ought to be done in Israel: do not thou this folly. And I, whither shall I cause my shame to go? and as for thee, thou shalt be as one of the fools in Israel. Now therefore, I pray thee, speak unto the king; for he will not withhold me from thee. Howbeit he would not hearken unto her voice: but, being stronger than she, forced her, and lay with her.

Then Amnon hated her exceedingly; so that the hatred wherewith he hated her was greater than the love wherewith he had loved her. And Amnon said unto her, Arise, be gone. And she said unto him, There is no cause: this evil in sending me away is greater than the other that thou didst unto me. But he would not hearken unto her. . . .

· · · · ·

. . . When King David heard of all these things, he was very wroth. And Absalom spake unto his brother Amnon neither good nor bad: for Absalom hated Amnon, because he had forced his sister Tamar.

Now Absalom had commanded his servants, saying, Mark ye now when Amnon's heart is merry with wine, and when I say unto you, Smite Amnon; then kill him, fear not: have not I commanded you? be courageous, and be valiant. And the servants of Absalom did unto Amnon as Absalom had commanded. Then all the king's sons arose, and every man gat him up upon his mule, and fled.

And it came to pass, while they were in the way, that tidings came to David, saying, Absalom hath slain all the king's sons, and there is not one of them left. Then the king arose, and tare his garments, and lay on the earth; and all his servants stood by with their clothes rent. And Jonadab, the son of Shimeah David's brother, answered and said, Let not thy lord suppose that they have slain all the young men the king's sons; for Amnon only is dead: for by the appointment of Absalom this hath been determined from the day that he forced his sister Tamar. Now therefore let not my lord the king take the thing to his heart, to think that all the king's sons are dead: for Amnon only is dead. . . . And it came to pass, as soon as he had made an end of speaking, that, behold, the king's sons came, and lifted up their voice and wept: and the king also and all his servants wept very sore.

But Absalom fled, and went to Talmai, the son of Ammihud, king of Geshur. And David mourned for his son every day. So Absalom fled, and went to Geshur, and was there three years. And the soul of King David longed to go forth unto Absalom: for he was comforted concerning Amnon, seeing he was dead.

CHAPTER 14

Now Joab the son of Zeruiah perceived that the king's heart was toward
Absalom. And Joab sent to Tekoah, and
fetched thence a wise woman, and said
unto her, I pray thee, feign thyself to be
a mourner, and put on now mourning
apparel, and anoint thyself with oil, but
be as a woman that had a long time
mourned for the dead: And come to the
king, and speak on this manner unto
him. So Joab put the words in her
mouth.

And when the woman of Tekoah spake
to the king, she fell on her face to the
ground, and did obeisance, and said,
Help, O king.

. . . . .

For we must needs die, and are as
water spilt on the ground, which cannot be gathered up again; neither doth
God respect any person: yet doth he
devise means, that his banished be not
expelled from him. Now therefore that I
am come to speak of this thing unto my
lord the king . . . . For the king will
hear, to deliver his handmaid out of the
hand of the man that would destroy me
and my son together . . . . Then thine
handmaid said, The word of my lord the
king shall now be comfortable: for as an
angel of God, so is my lord the king to
discern good and bad: therefore the LORD
thy God will be with thee.

Then the king answered and said unto
the woman, Hide not from me, I pray
thee, the thing that I shall ask thee. And
now speak. And the king said, Is not the
the woman said, Let my lord the king
hand of Joab with thee in all this? And
the woman answered and said, As thy
soul liveth, my lord the king, none can
turn to the right hand or to the left from
ought that my lord the king hath spoken:
for thy servant Joab, he bade me, and he
put all these words in the mouth of thine
handmaid: To fetch about this form of

speech hath thy servant Joab done this
thing: and my lord is wise, according to
the wisdom of an angel of God, to
know all things that are in the earth.

And the king said unto Joab, Behold
now, I have done this thing: go therefore,
bring the young man Absalom again. And
Joab fell to the ground on his face, and
bowed himself, and thanked the king:
and Joab said, To day thy servant knoweth that I have found grace in thy sight,
my lord, O king, in that the king hath
fulfilled the request of his servant. So
Joab arose and went to Geshur, and
brought Absalom to Jerusalem. And the
king said, Let him turn to his own house,
and let him not see my face. So Absalom
returned to his own house, and saw not
the king's face.

But in all Israel there was none to be so
much praised as Absalom for his beauty:
from the sole of his foot even to the
crown of his head there was no blemish
in him.

And when he polled his head, (for it
was at every year's end that he polled
it: because the hair was heavy on him,
therefore he polled it:) he weighted the
hair of his head at two hundred shekels
after the king's weight. . . .

So Absalom dwelt two full years in
Jerusalem, and saw not the king's face.
Therefore Absalom sent for Joab, to have
sent him to the king; but he would not
come to him: and when he sent again
the second time, he would not come.
Therefore he said unto his servants, See,
Joab's field is near mine, and he hath
barley there; go and set it on fire. And
Absalom's servants set the field on fire.
Then Joab arose, and came to Absalom
unto his house, and said unto him,
Wherefore have thy servants set my field
on fire? And Absalom answered Joab,
Behold, I sent unto thee, saying, Come
hither, that I may send thee to the king,
to say, Wherefore am I come from Geshur?
it had been good for me to have been
there still: now therefore let me see the

king's face; and if there be any iniquity in me, let him kill me. So Joab came to the king, and told him: and when he had called for Absalom, he came to the king, and bowed himself on his face to the ground before the king: and the king kissed Absalom.

CHAPTER 15

And it came to pass after this, that Absalom prepared him chariots and horses, and fifty men to run before him. And Absalom rose up early, and stood beside the way of the gate: and it was so, that when any man that had a controversy came to the king for judgment, then Absalom called unto him, and said, Of what city art thou? And he said, Thy servant is of one of the tribes of Israel. And Absalom said unto him, See, thy matters are good and right; but there is no man deputed of the king to hear thee. Absalom said moreover, Oh that I were made judge in the land, that every man which hath any suit or cause might come unto me, and I would do him justice! And it was so, that when any man came nigh to him to do him obeisance, he put forth his hand, and took him, and kissed him. And on this manner did Absalom to all Israel that came to the king for judgment: so Absalom stole the hearts of the men of Israel.

And it came to pass after forty years, that Absalom said unto the king, I pray thee, let me go and pay my vow, which I have vowed unto the LORD, in Hebron. For thy servant vowed a vow while I abode at Geshur in Syria, saying, if the LORD shall bring me again indeed to Jerusalem, then I will serve the LORD. And the king said unto him, Go in peace. So he arose, and went to Hebron.

But Absalom sent spies throughout all the tribes of Israel, saying, As soon as ye hear the sound of the trumpet, then ye shall say, Absalom reigneth in Hebron. And with Absalom went two hundred men out of Jerusalem, that were called; and they went in their simplicity, and they knew not anything. And Absalom sent for Ahithophel the Gilonite, David's counseller, from his city, even from Giloh, while he offered sacrifices. And the conspiracy was strong; for the people increased continually with Absalom.

And there came a messenger to David, saying, The hearts of the men of Israel are after Absalom. And David said unto all his servants that were with him at Jerusalem, Arise, and let us flee; for we shall not else escape from Absalom: make speed to depart, lest he overtake us suddenly, and bring evil upon us, and smite the city with the edge of the sword.

· · · · ·

CHAPTER 18

· · · · ·

So the people went out into the field against Israel: and the battle was in the wood of Ephraim; Where the people of Israel were slain before the servants of David, and there was there a great slaughter that day of twenty thousand men. For the battle was there scattered over the face of all the country: and the wood devoured more people that day than the sword devoured.

And Absalom met the servants of David. And Absalom rode upon a mule, and the mule went under the thick boughs of a great oak, and his head caught hold of the oak, and he was taken up between the heaven and the earth; and the mule that was under him went away. And a certain man saw it, and told Joab, and said, Behold, I saw Absalom hanged in an oak. And Joab said unto the man that told him, And, behold, thou sawest him, and why didst thou not smite him there to the ground? and I would have given thee ten shekels of silver, and a girdle. And the man said unto Joab, Though I should receive a thousand shekels of silver in mine hand, yet would I

not put forth mine hand against the
king's son: for in our hearing the king
charged thee and Abishai and Ittai, saying, Beware that none touch the young
man Absalom. Otherwise I should have
wrought falsehood against mine own life:
for there is no matter hid from the king,
and thou thyself wouldest have set thyself against me. Then said Joab, I may
not tary thus with thee. And he took
three darts in his hand, and thrust them
through the heart of Absalom, while he
was yet alive in the midst of the oak. And
ten young men that bare Joab's armour
compassed about and smote Absalom,
and slew him.

. . . . .

. . . And, behold, Cushi came; and
Cushi said, Tidings, my lord the king: for
the LORD hath avenged thee this day of
all them that rose up against thee. And
the king said unto Cushi, Is the young
man Absalom safe? And Cushi answered,
the enemies of my lord the king, and all
that rise against thee to do thee hurt, be
as that young man is.

And the king was much moved, and
went up to the chamber over the gate,
and wept: and as he went, thus he said,
O my son Absalom, my son, my son
Absalom! Would God I had died for thee,
O Absalom, my son, my son!

13 | THE MODERN FAMILY IN ISRAEL: THE KIBBUTZ

YONINA TALMON-GARBER

*Israel today is very different from the Israel of David's time. There are
cities and farms, cooperative communities and collective settlements,
and the family structure in each is different. The peoples of Europe and
Africa stream into this new democracy, bringing with them a wide
variety of customs and family relationships.*

*But the Kibbutz is an institution peculiar to modern Israel. Children
see their parents as friends, while nurses and teachers function as
disciplinarians. This system is organized in the hope of preventing
children from hating their parents with the kind of consequences seen
above in David's family. If the child must be angry with someone, it will
be with the nurse or teacher.*

Melford E. Spiro, in his book Children of the Kibbutz, *describes
the Kibbutz as carefully planned to make the entire community
responsible for each and every one of its children.*

The disposition to establish new types of
family organization prevailed mainly
among immigrants to whom immigration
entailed a conscious and voluntary break
with former social structure. Many of the

Excerpts reprinted from *Marriage and Family
Living*, XVI, No. 4 (November, 1954), 346–49,
by permission of the author and The National
Council on Family Relations.

founders of the Cooperative and Communal Settlements were members of youth
movement groups and arrived in the
country as young, unattached individuals.
To many of them the cohesion of the
new primary group and the identification
with its values replaced the family they
had left behind—hence a strong communal organization and a redefinition of

the position of the family within the community.

. . . . .

The basic features of the Collective Settlements (Kibbutz)* are common ownership of all property, except for a few personal belongings, communal organization of production, consumption and the care of children. The Community is run as one economic unit and as one household. The family has ceased to be an autonomous group from the point of view of the division of labor.

Husband and wife have independent jobs. Roles are allotted to individual members by a central committee elected yearly by the general assembly. Main meals are taken in the communal dining hall and are served from a common kitchen. Members' needs are provided for by communal institutions. Families look after their own rooms but have few other household responsibilites.

In most of the Collectives, children live apart from their parents and are attended mainly by members assigned to this task. From their birth on they sleep, eat and study in special houses. Each age group leads its own life and has its autonomous arrangements. Almost every activity in the age group is supervised by an elected committee and many issues are settled by open discussion between the youngsters and the adults in charge of them. Committees work under the guidance of adults but children are given some experience in self-government and get some preparation for active participation in adult institutions. Living conditions and the number of members assigned to look after the children depend on the economic situation of the settle-

ment. But in all communities the standard of living of the children is noticeably higher than that of their parents. Children lead a sheltered life and are not allowed to suffer any want. They start to do some work early, but only at the age of eighteen to twenty years do they enter the adult division of labor and work full-time.

The age groups lead their own social and cultural life. On festive occasions they do not participate in the general celebration but arrange special festivities in which parents participate as passive observers. The only important exception is the culminating feast of the year (Passover) when parents and children participate alike. It is mainly through the age group that children come into definite and structured relations with the adult world.

Children meet their parents and their siblings every day in off hours. They spend the afternoons and early evenings with them. Parents put their young children to sleep. On Saturdays and on holidays children are with their parents most of the time except for short intervals when they take their separate meals. There are thus frequent and intensive relations between parents and children, but the main socializing agencies are the peer age groups and specialized nurses, instructors and teachers. The age group is a solidary unit and it substitutes the sibling unit. It duplicates the structural lines of the community and inculcates communal norms. Basically the children belong to the community as a whole.

The family has delegated most of its functions to the community. The main emphasis lies therefore on affective ties and personal relationships within it. The family is the only sphere in which both children and parents are free from routine tasks. It is mainly within the family that the individual members have intimate relations unpatterned by their position in the community. In so far as the nuclear family has ceased to be the prime social-

---

* There are 227 Collective Settlements in Israel. Population in the Collective Settlements was 69,089 in 1952. The total population of Israel was around two million, indicating only 3 or 4 per cent of the population was using the special child-rearing arrangements described here.—Eds.

izing agency it avoids the inevitable ambivalence towards the agents of socialization. Parents do not have to combine the contrasting tasks of providing the child's needs for security and unconditional love on the one hand with thwarting their wishes on the other hand. They can afford to be permissive and the authoritarian element in child-parent relationships is thus minimized. The emotional attachment to parents is intensive for yet another reason. The child's position outside the family is ascribed only to a small extent. He has to compete for a position in his age group and he has to compete with his age peers for the approval of the adults in charge of them. All the children in the same age group have the same claim to attention. It is only in their family that they get special individualized treatment.

As mentioned before, the Collectives were established by solidary primary groups of young and single individuals. The formation of families within the community has inevitably weakened the primary group characteristics of the community and the families tend to become a competing focus of intensive primary group relations. Diversification of social and economic structure and routinization entailed some re-definition of the relations of the family and the community. There is a growing tendency to allow the family a little more independence and privacy. In some Collectives they have even tried to change certain aspects of the care of children. Children in those Collectives spend the whole day with their age group, but come home to sleep in their parents' flats. In spite of a slight shift in the position of the family the Collective Settlements still represent an extreme "non-familistic" division of labor.

The main trend of change of demographic standards in the Collectives is a considerable decrease in the age at marriage and a small increase of fertility. Average age at marriage in 1949 was 26.5 for males and 23.5 for females, as compared with 30.7–25.1 for the whole country. The birth rate was 30.1 per thousand as compared with 29.3 in towns and 31.9 in the whole country. Divorce rate was 3.54. Establishment of a family in the Collectives does not entail the setting up of a separate household, consequently members can marry as early as they choose. In spite of the fact that the birth of children does not have a direct or immediate effect on the standard of living of the family and does not entail much additional work for the parents, fertility remains comparatively low. The economic factor is not eliminated and the size of family is planned more or less consciously with due consideration of the economic position of the community. . . .

14 | FRENCH PARENTS TAKE THEIR CHILDREN TO THE PARK

MARTHA WOLFENSTEIN

Are European children "civilized" as compared to American youngsters? Or, as many Europeans have said—putting it generously—are American children more "active" than their European counterparts?

This delightful description, from a book filled with wonderfully lively studies, may raise—and partially answer—any number of questions about the behavior of children in different cultures.

In Parisian families it is a regular routine to take the children to the park. This is a good situation in which to observe how French children play, their relations with one another and with the adults who bring them to the park. In the summer of 1947 and again in the summer of 1953 I had occasion to make such observations in various parks in Paris. . . .

THE "FOYER" IN THE PARK

For the French each family circle is peculiarly self-inclosed, with the family members closely bound to one another and a feeling of extreme wariness about intrusion from outside. This feeling is carried over when parents take their children to play in the park. The children do not leave their parents to join other children in a communal play area. In fact, there are few communal play facilities—an occasional sand pile, some swings and carrousels, to which one must pay admission and to which the children are escorted by the parents. The usual procedure is for the mother (or other adult who brings the children to the park) to establish herself on a bench while the children squat directly at her feet and play there in the sand of the path. Where there is a sand pile, children frequently fill their buckets there and then carry the sand to where mother is sitting and deposit it at her feet. . . .

. . . . .

There seems to be a continual mild anxiety that possessions will get mixed up in the park. Mothers are constantly checking on the whereabouts of their children's toys and returning toys to other mothers. One woman hands a toy shovel to another, saying: *C'est à vous, madame?* Toys seem to be regarded as

Reprinted from Margaret Mead and Martha Wolfenstein, *Childhood in Contemporary Cultures*, by permission of The University of Chicago Press. Copyright 1955 by The University of Chicago.

the possessions of the parents, and mislaid ones are usually restored to them. While parents are concerned to keep track of their own child's toys, they seem particularly upset if their child has picked up something belonging to another and are apt to slap the child for it. This happens regardless of whether there has been any dispute and where the owner may be quite unaware that another child has picked up something of his.

The following incidents illustrate these attitudes. A girl of about two is holding a celluloid fish belonging to a boy of about the same age. Though the boy makes no protest, the attendant of the girl scoldingly tells her to give it to him, pushes her forward, and after the girl has handed the fish to the boy, hustles her back to her own bench.

A girl of about two has picked up a leather strap from a neighboring group. Her nurse reproves her, takes her by the hand, and returns the strap. A little later a boy of about the same age, belonging to this neighboring family, plays with the little girl, picks up her pail, and keeps it while the little girl is fed by her nurse. The boy's grandmother becomes aware that he has the pail, hits him on the buttocks, scolds, and, taking him by the hand, returns the pail to the girl's nurse. In front of the nurse she repeatedly hits the boy about the head and ears.

. . . . .

Among American children issues of ownership versus sharing tend to arise when two children dispute about the use of a toy. What is considered desirable is that the child should learn to share his playthings, which are his property, with others. French children seem to be taught something quite different. Toys are familial property, and those belonging to each family must be kept separate. Just as the children with their parents or other familial adults form a close little circle in the park, so their belongings should remain within the circle. The child who brings into this circle something from outside seems to be introducing an intrusive object, which arouses all the negative sentiments felt, but from politeness not directly expressed, toward outsiders. At the same time it is an offense to the outsiders, whose belongings are thus displaced, and restitution and apologies to them are required. Also, as French adults are much preoccupied with property and with increasing their own, they have to ward off the temptation to do so by illegitimate means. The child's easy way of picking up others' things may evoke in adults impulses to take which they strive to repress in themselves and which they therefore cannot tolerate in the child.

Friendly behavior between children of different families is not encouraged by the adults. . . .

SECRET SOLIDARITY OF BROTHERS

In the following incident one can observe the friendly relation of two brothers which becomes more outspoken when they get by themselves, away from the adults. The two boys, of about six and seven, very neat, dressed alike in blue jerseys and white shorts, are playing together in the sand of the path. Their father sits talking with two women, who appear to be friends of the family, and the boys' sister, about a year older, sits on a bench with her doll. As the younger boy moves into the father's field of vision, the father slaps his hands and face, presumably because he has got himself dirty. This puts an end to the sand play; the two boys sit down, subdued, on the bench, and, as the father turns away, the older presents the younger with a cellophane bag—a gesture of sympathy and compensation. After a time the father suggests to the girl that the children take a walk around the park, and they im-

mediately set out. On their walk the boys keep close together, leaving the girl to herself. As they get farther away from the father, the boys begin putting their arms around each other's shoulders. They become much more animated and point things out to each other as they go. As they get nearer to the father again on the return path, they drop their arms from each other's shoulders, drift apart, and again become more subdued. Having returned, they seat themselves quietly again on the bench.

ACCEPTANCE OF THE LITTLE ONES

French children show a great readiness to play with children younger than themselves, in a way which contrasts strikingly with the behavior of American children. It is typical of American boys particularly to be intolerant of the "kid brother" who wants to tag along and get into the big boys' game when he isn't good enough. An American boy of seven will complain that he has no one of his own age to play with; the neighbors' little boy is six. In America there tends to be a strict age-grading, which the children themselves feel strongly about.

In contrast to this, French children appear interested in younger children and ready to accept them in their games. A boy of eight or nine will play ball with a smaller boy, a five-year-old or even a two-year-old, without showing any impatience at the ineptitude of the younger one. The two children may be brothers or may belong to families that know each other. A slender blond boy of about seven seems completely absorbed in a little girl of two or three whom he follows around, bending over to speak to her. The mothers of the two children are acquainted with each other, and the boy and his mother both shake hands with the little girl's mother when she leaves the park. The boy looks quite disconsolate without his little friend; eventually, at his mother's suggestion, he picks up his scooter and slowly pushes off on it.

Such interest, particularly on the part of boys, in younger children differs markedly from the American pattern, where interest in babies becomes strictly sex-typed for girls only and out of keeping with the boy's ideal of masculine toughness.

. . . . .

. . . Where the American child is expected from an early age to become a member of a peer group outside the family, for the French child the family and the contacts which the adults make with other families remain decisive. While, from the American point of view, this may appear restrictive, it also facilitates friendly relations between older and younger children, including notably affectionate quasi-paternal feelings of older boys toward small children.

. . . . .

GROWNUPS STOP CHILDREN'S AGGRESSION

French children are not taught to fight their own battles, to stick up for their rights, in the American sense of these terms. If one child attacks another, even very mildly, the grownups regularly intervene and scold the aggressor. The child who is attacked is likely to look aggrieved or to cry, to look toward his mother or go to her. He does not hit back, nor is he encouraged to do so. An attack is thus not a challenge which must be met by the attacked to save his self-esteem. It is a piece of naughty behavior to be dealt with by the adults.

In the following instances one can see how quickly adults intervene in even very slight manifestations of aggression. Among a group of small children playing on a sand pile, a girl of about two and a half takes a shovel away from her four-year-old sister and walks away with it, looking back in a mildly provocative way. The older girl remains seated and simply looks dismayed. The younger one is already going back to return the shovel when the mother comes over and scolds her, calling her *vilaine*. The little one gives back the shovel, and the two resume their digging.

. . . . .

In [another] incident . . . , where a little girl stepped on a little boy's sand pie, the boy looked toward his grandmother with an expression of amazement and distress. The grandmother promptly launched into a biting verbal attack on the little girl: *Vilaine! Vilaine fille! Tu commences maintenant à faire des sottises!* A little later when another girl was throwing sand into the sand pile, the grandmother scolded her repeatedly, telling her it could get into children's eyes. The girl's mother, a little way off, then chimed in and told the girl to stop. Protective as she was of her little grandson, the grandmother was equally ready to interfere in an aggressive act of his. Thus, when he was pushing another boy, who did not seem to notice the rather gentle pressure, the grandmother called to him to stop, that he would make the other boy get a *bo-bo*, and the grandson stopped.

Thus what French children learn is not the prized Anglo-Saxon art of self-defense or the rules that determine what is a fair fight. What they learn is that their own aggression is not permissible.

A consequence of the prohibition against physical aggression is that verbal disputes are substituted for it. . . .

RESTRAINT IN MOTOR ACTIVITY

To an American visitor it is often amazing how long French children stay still. They are able to sit for long periods on park benches beside their parents. A typical position of a child in the park is squatting at his mother's feet, playing in the sand. His hands are busy, but his total body position remains constant. Children are often brought to the park in quite elegant (and unwashable) clothes, and they do not get dirty. The squatting child keeps his bottom poised within an inch of the ground but never touching, only his hands getting dirty; activity and getting dirty are both restricted to the hands. While sand play is generally permissible and children are provided with equipment for it, they seem subject to intermittent uncertainty whether it is all right for their hands to be dirty. From time to time a child shows his dirty hands to his mother, and she wipes them off.

Among some children between two and three I noticed a particularly marked tendency to complete immobility, remaining in the same position, with even their hands motionless, and staring blankly or watching other children. A French child analyst suggested that this is the age when children are being stuffed with food and are consequently somewhat stuporous. Occasionally one could see children of these ages moving more actively and running about. But the total effect contrasted with the usual more continuous motor activity which one sees in American children. Also, French children seemed more often to walk where American children run.

. . . . .

The relation between restraint on aggression and on large-muscle activity was remarked upon by another French child analyst, who had treated both French and American children. She observed that an American child in an aggressive mood would throw things up to the ceiling, while a French child would express similar angry impulses by making little cuts in a piece of clay.

Forceful activity on the part of children is apt to evoke warning words from the adults: "Gently, gently." Two brothers about nine and six were throwing a rubber ball back and forth. The younger had to make quite an effort to throw the ball the required distance; his throws were a bit badly aimed but did not come very close to any bystanders. His mother and grandmother, who were sitting near him, repeatedly cautioned him after every throw: *Doucement! Doucement!* I had the feeling that it was the strenuousness of his movements which made them uneasy, though they may also have exaggerated the danger of his hitting someone. Similarly, when two little girls about four and five were twirling around, holding each other's hands, an elderly woman seated near by kept calling to the older girl: *Doucement, elle est plus petite que toi.* To which the child answered that they were not going very fast. The implication here seems to be that any rapid or forceful movement can easily pass into a damaging act.

. . . . .

On the same occasion the play of another boy whom I observed, with a paper airplane, seemed to demonstrate very nicely the feeling about remaining within a small space. When American boys make planes out of folded paper, these planes are generally long and narrow, with a sharp point, with the aim of their being able to fly as fast and far as possible. In contrast to this prevailing American style, the French boy had folded his paper plane in a wide-winged, much less pointed shape. It moved more slowly through the air and did not go any great distance, but within a small space described many complicated and elegant loops.

Another time I observed a game where an active chase was led up to by elaborate preliminaries in which action was slight. This seemed comparable to the protracted talk postponing action. Five children (of about six to nine) were playing together with a young nursemaid. The nurse-maid sat on a bench while the children performed charades in front of her, the performance being preceded by consider-able consultation among themselves as to the subject they would enact. As the nursemaid ventured various guesses, the children interrupted their act several times to explain the exact rules of the game to her. When she finally uttered the right word, this was the signal for them to run and her to chase them. Any child she caught before they reached a certain tree then joined her on the bench and helped to guess and to chase the next time round. But before the next brief chase there were again the consultations and the pantomine. Other children's games in which an introductory ritual precedes a chase are common, but I am not familiar with any in which the less active prepara-tory phase is so elaborate, where talk and small movements occupy such a large part of the game and the chase comes only as a brief finale.

THE CHILD ALONE

French children manifest a greater toler-ance for being alone than American chil-dren do. Just as they do not show the urge to be incessantly in motion, which one sees in American children, so also they do not show the need to be constantly with other children. When I speak of a child being alone, I mean alone with the adult who has brought him to the park. But this may mean in effect being very much alone, since, as a rule, the adult pays little attention to him. There is usually little interchange in the park between adults and children over one and a half. While mothers and nurses direct a good deal of affectionate talk to a baby in a carriage, they tend to ignore the three-year-old squatting at their feet or sitting on the bench beside them. . . .

. . . . .

Where there is a choice of either play-ing alone or with others, playing alone may be preferred (which again I think would be very rare among American chil-dren). Three girls of about thirteen were playing near one another, each with the kind of toy which is whirled into the air from a string and caught again, a game requiring considerable skill. The three of them, all quite proficient, continued this play, each by herself, for at least an hour before they joined together and began passing the whirling object from one to another.

. . . . .

It may be added that for the French the mere presence of others, even if there is no overt interaction with them, appears to constitute a valued form of sociability. This would apply to the child who plays by himself alongside other children in the park as well as to the adult who sits alone with his drink and his newspaper at a café table.

. . . . .

ADULTS ARE ABOVE THE EMOTIONS OF CHILDREN

Adults seem to look down from a con-siderable height on both the griefs and the joys of children. Childhood and adulthood are two very distinct human conditions. From the vantage point of the adult, the emotions of the child do not seem serious: they are not, after all, about anything very important. The adult is likely to be detached in the face of the child's distress. Where the child is elated, the adult, though sympathetic, may regard the child humorously, per-haps a bit mockingly: how he overesti-mates these little childish things!

On an occasion when a mother pun-ished a little boy, she appeared quite unconcerned about his rage and grief and was amused when he later came to fling his arms around her. . . .

. . . . .

For the French, adulthood is decidedly the desirable time of life. Simply assuming the role of adults as he knows them is gratifying to a French child; no extraneous glamour need be added. At the same time, the adults in their role of authority rouse impulses of rebellious mockery in children, which they express in parodying the adults among themselves. This motive is liable to persist and to be permitted much stronger expression when the children grow up, in the mockery of authority figures, particularly in the political sphere, which is so prominent in French life.

. . . . .

CHILDHOOD IS NOT FOR FUN

For the French, enjoyment of life is the prerogative of adults. Childhood is a preparation. Then everything must be useful, not just fun; it must have an educational purpose. The hard regime of French school children, with its tremendous burden of work, is well known. Probably nothing in later life is such a terrible ordeal as the dreaded *bachot* (the examination at the conclusion of secondary school). It is a real *rite de passage*, a painful test to which youths on the verge of maturity are subjected by their elders.

The attitude that everything for children, even the very young, must serve a useful purpose and not be just amusing is well exemplified around the carrousel in the Luxembourg Gardens. There are various rides for the children, among them rows of large rocking horses. A sign describes these as: *Chevaux hygiéniques. Jeu gymnastique pour les enfants développant la force et la souplesse.*

At the carrousel, as soon as the ride began, an old woman with spectacles and red hair done up in a bun on top of her head and wearing an old-fashioned gray coat (she seemed to me a benevolent witch), handed out to each child in the outer circle a stick (*baguette*). She then held out to them a contraption which dispensed rings and encouraged them to catch the rings on their sticks. Throughout the duration of the ride, the old woman directed to the children an incessant didactic discourse, urging them to pay attention and work very hard to catch the rings. *Attention! Regarde ton travail! Regarde bien, chou-chou! Au milieu,* indicating with her finger the middle of the ring at which the child should aim. *Doucement!* When a child used his stick to beat time instead of to catch rings, the old woman scolded him for this frivolity. . . . Thus, even on the carrousel, children have a task to perform. The elders direct, commend, and rebuke them. They are not there just for fun.

The paradox from the American point of view is that the French grow up with a great capacity for enjoyment of life. The adult enters fully into the pleasures which have not been permitted to the child. There seems to be a successful realization that pleasure is not taboo, but only postponed. The song of Charles Trenet, *Quand j'étais petit,* ends with the triumphant, *On n'est plus petit!*—everything is now permitted. It remains one of the puzzles of French culture how this effect is achieved: that the restraints to which children are subjected have only a temporary influence and do not encumber the adult with lasting inhibitions.

If we compare Americans and French, it seems as though the relation between childhood and adulthood is almost completely opposite in the two cultures. In America we regard childhood as a very nearly ideal time, a time for enjoyment, an end in itself. The American image of the child, whether envisaged in the classical figures of Tom Sawyer and Huckleberry Finn, or in the small hero of the recent film *The Little Fugitive,* who achieves self-sufficient existence at Coney Island, is of a young person with great resources for enjoyment, whose present life is an end in itself. . . . With the French, as I have said, it seems to be the other way around. Childhood is a period of probation, when everything is a means to an end; it is unenviable from the vantage point of adulthood. The image of the child is replete with frustration and longing for pleasures of the adults which are not for him. It is in adulthood that the possibility of living in the moment is achieved. Not that this precludes much scheming and planning as far as careers or business advantage is concerned. But this is not allowed to interfere with sensuous pleasures, which are an end in themselves. The attainment of these end-pleasures, notably in eating and in love-making, is not a simple matter. Much care and preparation are required, and changing stimuli may be needed to keep pleasure intense. Concern with such pleasures and ingenuity in achieving them are persistent in adult life. It is with the prospect of these pleasures that the individual has served his hardworking childhood, and it is now, as an adult, that he can lose himself in the pleasures of the moment.

15 | THE FAMILY IN INDIA

S. CHANDRASEKHAR

This brief description of the family in India indicates that institutions in that newly freed country are slowly evolving away from long-held customs—large families, early marriage, low status for women, etc.— toward more modern patterns. The poverty and despair throughout the large and complex nation and the illiteracy of most of the population hinder progress, of course, and, in many ways, the culture of India remains as it has for centuries.

The Indian sex ratio for the whole country is an adverse one, for in 1951 there were 947 females per 1000 males. The rural sex ratio is 966:1000, while the urban sex ratio is 860:1000. This sex ratio has been more or less the same during the last fifty years.

. . . . .

The Indian pattern of marital status presents an interesting picture. According to Indian law (the Child Marriage Restraint Act of 1929 popularly known as the Sarda Act) child marriages (of males under 18 and females under 14) are punishable. But according to the 1951 Census, there were 2,833,000 married males, 6,180,000 married females, 66,000 widowers and 134,000 widows—all between the ages of 5 and 14! This simply means that the Sarda Act has failed in its objective of restraining early marriages.

The universality of the married state in India is well known. In the country as a whole, every other male is married, while three out of five females—of all ages—are married. In other words, 49.1 per cent of all males are either married men or widowers and 61.2 per cent of all females are either married women or widows. Only 6.4 per cent of all females aged fifteen and over were unmarried. But even this 6.4 per cent will not remain unmarried long for they are bound to get married within a few years. In other words, between the ages 35-44, only 0.1 per cent

Excerpts reprinted from *Marriage and Family Living*, XVI, No. 4 (November, 1954), 336–41, by permission of the author and The National Council on Family Relations.

of the total population of women remain unmarried. The problem of spinsters does not exist or at any rate is very insignificant in India.

In 1951 there were 5 widowers to 100 males and 12.8 widows to 100 females. But since widowers are permitted to and very often do marry, they constitute no social problem, unlike the widows who are not expected to and invariably do not marry. (There is no legal barrier to widow remarriage, nor is Hinduism opposed to second marriage of Hindu women or widows, but all Hindu males seem to prefer virgins.) The total number of widows of all ages according to the 1951 census was nearly 25 million.

. . . . .

THE HINDU JOINT FAMILY

The traditional Hindu joint family is larger than the conjugal or the biological family. The unit is not the husband, wife and children, but the larger family group. It is at once a corporate, economic, religious and social unit. In a joint family when sons grow up to manhood and marry, they do not leave the parental household and set up their own separate houses, but occupy different rooms in the parental, rather ancestral, residence, along with their children and children's children. Correspondingly, the womenfolk also, the mother, the daughters-in-law, unmarried daughters, granddaughters, and sometimes great-granddaughters, live under the same roof. The daughters of the family, on getting married, of course leave their parental home and become members of the joint families to which their husbands belong. And so, naturally, the number of those who live together under the same roof may be very large and sometimes may even run to more than fifty. The household servants, many of whom often grow up with the family, have their recognized place, and their attachment to the master members of the

family is often deep and cordial. To accommodate all these, it need hardly be added that the house has to be very large indeed.

The father and mother have their places of honor in these joint families. (Hence the absence of state-supported homes for old people in India; it is difficult to say whether there is no need for such homes today though the number of old people is small.) The father, being the oldest and most experienced, is nominally the head of the family. Under ordinary circumstances it is he who controls, guides and directs the whole family, unless he is very old or disabled, in which case the eldest son or the eldest member in the nearest line of male descent—maternal or paternal uncle—takes his place. The mother always has her say. Though grownup sons live in the family with their wives, the respect and consideration shown by all members of the family to the old mother is very great. And it may be safely asserted that no important measure of domestic concern will be approved or carried out without the final, if formal, sanction of the mother.

In the family, food and property are held in common and jointly owned, and the actual share to which each member is entitled if there be separation diminishes or increases with each birth or death. This arrangement is normally not disturbed even if some members of the family have to reside far away from the home in different parts of the country by virtue of their calling. (The prolonged sojourn in a distant place outside the joint family has been a factor in recent years for the breakup of the joint family.) When at home, all share the food prepared in a single common kitchen. In fact, in popular parlance, the chief criterion of the joint nature of the commensal family arises largely from the fact of the common kitchen. The saying is "Ek hi chule ka pakka khate hain," or "they eat food cooked in one and the same kitchen."

The ancestral property and the income arising from it, along with the earnings of the individual members, constitute the the common family fund, out of which the expenses of the whole family are met. Often an earning member of the joint family who happens to live outside the common family out of town or village remits a part of his income to the common family pool, a system resembling that of the pre-Revolution peasant family in Russia. The funds—money, land, houses, jewelry and cattle—like other family affairs, are looked after by the father or the eldest son or some senior male relative. But in financial matters, all adult members are usually consulted before any major item of expenditure is granted. Every earning member contributes his share to the family fund. And the necessary and legitimate needs of all the family members are generally met. Thus, all earning members — mostly male — contribute in proportion to their income, and all members—men, women, married, widowed and children—whether earning or not, enjoy the common family resources. In practice, it sometimes happens that an unemployed brother, his wife and children may consume more from the family funds than a childless brother whose income may be considerable. This arrangement of give and take demands a great deal of mutual tolerance, affection, accommodation and understanding on the part of all the members. This traditional system in which all are entitled to be maintained from the family funds according to their needs is, in practice, a recognized socialist unit, though not necessarily secular in spirit. All the adult members follow the principle, "Give what you can and take what you need."

In a word, the joint family is simply the common ownership of the means of production and the common enjoyment of the fruits of labor. In practice, the system has through the centuries led to both beneficial and harmful effects on the Indian social and economic structure.

BETROTHAL AND MARRIAGE

The most important event in any family is marriage and the place of the married householder, particularly for a woman, in the Hindu cultural milieu, is an exalted one. The Hindu view of marriage is that it is a sacramental duty and that every man and woman must perforce enter into it, as the married state is one of the fourfold stages—*ashramas*—in an individual's life. Therefore, the first desideratum of a good life, according to Hindu scriptures, is that all should marry, marry young, and stay married. Hence the universality of the married state in India. One does not take a wife for sexual pleasure, or companionship necessarily, but one marries a daughter-in-law to help the family and hand down the torch of life to generations yet unborn to thus perpetuate the family line. As the young man or woman does not marry to suit his or her fancy, the choice of the partner does not rest with the individual. The parents and interested relatives—in fact, the whole joint family —choose the bride without any particular consideration of the groom's tastes or views. The bride, on her side, is consulted even less by her parents and relatives.

The Hindu scriptural injunction has been in favor of pre-puberty betrothal and marriage. In practice, however, while girls today may be betrothed before puberty, marriage after puberty has become common. The law, as well as enlightened public opinion, has veered in this direction, but exceptions are not wanting, as pointed out in our analysis of recent census statistics. It is difficult to be precise on this question, for the exact age of an individual, particularly in the village, is still largely a matter of guess. It is possible that parents arrange the marriage of their daughters at an age well past puberty to ease their consciences, but give out a lower age for the bride as a matter of misplaced pride and esteem in the community. Therefore, while early marriage does exist, physical consummation and living together is, by and large, a post-puberty affair.

As I have pointed out elsewhere: In Western countries, romance (or love as a pre-requisite to marriage), economic considerations, prolonged education and training and eagerness for personal and social advancement contribute to the postponement of marriage to a comparatively late date. Religion not only does not condemn celibacy but has a kind word for it. The current social attitudes do not disapprove of those who never enter the married state. Many therefore do not marry just for the sake of marriage. The pressure of these considerations may and sometimes does result in many remaining bachelors and spinsters.

But in India there is no chance for love to play any significant part in marriage. Marriages, by and large, are arranged by the parents and the majority are herded into the married state in a routine fashion. Economic stability of the bridegroom has never been an important consideration in contracting a marriage. Of course, the parents-in-law are anxious to see that the son-in-law is well employed or otherwise settled in life, but unemployment is not a positive disqualification since the resources of the joint family are available for the initial support of the newly married couple. Besides, there is the dowry that the bride brings. Religion does not encourage celibacy, for a Hindu, if he be a strict one, must have at least one son. But perhaps it is not really the fear of religious ostracism that is behind this urge to get married. It is the social disapproval of the unmarried state that explains the universal prevalence of the married state.[1]

---

[1] S. Chandrasekhar, *India's Population: Fact and Policy* (2d ed.; Madras, 1951).

DIVORCE AND WIDOWHOOD

As factual data on family disorganization are unavailable, it is difficult to estimate the nature and extent of desertion, separation, divorce, annulment and widowhood. However, the problem of family disorganization, with the exception of widowhood, is not acute in India.

As pointed out already, social attitudes are opposed to widow remarriage. Since most widowers marry and since they cannot, or rather do not, marry widows, they have to seek wives among girls much their juniors. If a widower aged forty or fifty wants to marry, he cannot marry a woman aged thirty, for a woman at that age is likely to be either married and living with her husband, or a widow. So he will have to marry a girl between the ages of fourteen and twenty. This unequal combination from the point of view of age leads to an increasing number of widows, for the relatively old husband soon passes away, leaving behind his young wife a widow. And she cannot, of course, remarry.

The paucity of females keeps up the custom of early marriage for girls. Early marriages customarily involve considerable disparity in age between husband and wives. This difference in age increases widowhood. Since widows cannot remarry, widowhood increases the shortage of eligible brides, which accentuates the paucity of females. Thus the vicious wheel whirls on.

    · · · · ·

As a rule, marriages in India are deprived of both premarital meeting (in the sense of meeting, dating and courtship) and postmarital dissolution (such as separation, annulment and divorce) in case the marriage is a failure. Both these safety valves are denied to the Hindus. By and large, they do not know what they are getting into, and once in it, good, bad or indifferent, there is no easy way out. There is no special effort of adjustment on the part of the husband to make his marriage a success; the effort is almost one-sided, always on the part of the wife. And yet ninety-five per cent of the Hindu marriages appear successful and it is difficult to assess the factors behind this apparent stability. It may be that the partners endure such difficulties as they encounter as an inevitable part of the married state, or they may not be aware of anything better. As for the average wife, she is conditioned by upbringing not to expect anything better and to be ready for the worst. After all, in a sense, Hindu marriage is a sustained blind date. Secondly, the fact that there is no acceptable and socially approved way out, compels the partners to reconcile themselves to the situation. Or it may be that all these marriages are really happy and successful, based on mutual understanding, affection and goodwill.

. . . . .

MODERN TRENDS IN
THE INDIAN FAMILY

What are the present trends which are likely to mould the future of the family in India? Marriage is ordinarily limited to a member's own caste, sub- and even sub-sub caste. With the growth of Western contact, modern education and the spread of coeducational colleges and universities, young people are able to meet, get to know one another and fall in love beyond the purview of parental supervision. When young people fall in love across caste lines and when such inter-caste love becomes serious the first major obstacle is parental objection. When the couple in question are serious and when they have some measure of economic security in the sense of some private means or a job, they tend to oppose the parental and family objections and brave the world. But this is not al-

ways easy, for in India, one's private life is very much the public concern! (Such marriages in India are called "love marriages" as opposed to the traditional Hindu concept where you "marry and love" and not "love and marry.") These marriages are still so few in number that they elicit public comment.

And yet it is possible that inter-caste and even inter-religious marriages might become the pattern of future Indian society. Two powerful aids in this direction are that no one today seriously upholds caste in public, for it has come to be agreed that the caste system is opposed to democratic ideals. Secondly, all great Indian leaders and social reformers from Ram Mohan Roy down to Gandhi and Nehru have disapproved of the caste system as practiced and have not only approved but have set examples of inter-caste marriages by letting their children marry outside the caste. Once the system of permitting an individual to choose his or her partner gets under way, the caste system will disappear; this process might eventually evolve that rare species of *Indians*, for today there are no Indians, in the strict sense, but only Bengalis and Andhras, Tamils and Gujiaratis, high and low caste Hindus.

Second, educational facilities for women with their accompanying right to employment and economic freedom have already led to the beginning of a conflict between traditional marriage and a socially useful and lucrative career (this does not imply that marriage and a career for a woman ought always to conflict). What is more, even in marriage, Indian women are beginning to assert their rights and want to decide when and how many children they shall have. India is witnessing such rapid changes that Indian women are beginning to demand contraceptive knowledge.

Third, now that India is free, the Government itself is aiding in the evolution

of Hindu law on marriage, divorce, succession, property rights, etc. in conson-
ance with modern thought and needs.
When the comprehensive Hindu Code
Reform Bill, which is now on the anvil

of the Indian Parliament, is passed into
law, India will have taken a great step
towards   modernizing   her   domestic
law. . . .

16 | RELATION OF CHILD TRAINING
TO SUBSISTENCE ECONOMY

HERBERT BARRY, III, IRVIN L. CHILD,

AND MARGARET K. BACON

*This study of 104 societies indicates that child-rearing practices are
closely related to the way in which the child's parents earn a living.
In societies that accumulate food resources, with herds or crops, there is
strong pressure toward responsibility, conformity, and obedience—
and pressure against independence, self-reliance, and achievement. But
in societies primarily made up of hunters and fishers, the opposite
"virtues" are desired: self-reliance and initiative rather than obedience and
conformity.*

Cross-cultural research on child training
has generally grown out of an interest
in how the typical personality of a people
is brought into being. The customary
child training practices of a group are
thought to be one important set of influences responsible for the typical personality, and hence an important clue in
tracing its causal background. But the
typical personality may also be viewed as
an existing set of conditions which may
exert an influence on later child training
practices. Indeed, any present feature of
culture may influence future child training practices, either directly or through an
influence on typical personality. Thus
child training may just as well, and with
equal interest of another sort, be viewed
as effect in a series of cultural events,
rather than as cause (being in fact, we pre-

sume, both at once). Moreover, even while
considering child training as a cause of the
typical personality of a people, one is led
to inquire: Why does a particular society
select child training practices which will
tend to produce this particular kind of
typical personality? Is it because this
kind of typical personality is functional
for the adult life of the society, and
training methods which will produce it
are thus also functional?

By a variety of routes, then, the student of child training is led to inquire
into the relation of child training to the
basic patterns of social life—to those
aspects of culture, whatever they be,
which set the scene for the rest of culture. Among the features likely to hold
this sort of dominant or controlling position is the general nature of the subsistence economy, and it is to this aspect
of culture that we will here relate child
training practices.

. . . . .

Excerpts reprinted from *American Anthropologist*,
61, No. 1 (February, 1959), 51–63, by permission of the authors and publishers.

AN HYPOTHESIS ABOUT ECONOMIC ROLE AND TYPE OF SUBSISTENCE

Earlier anthropological writers classified economies in accordance with a notion of uniform sequences in cultural development from primitive to civilized. As a result of further research, this attempt has given way to more objective bases of classification. One such objective classification is that of Forde (1934). While stressing the limited usefulness of any classificatory scheme, in view of the great overlap between categories and the variation of economic practices within any one category, Forde does propose the following categories for dominant economy of a society: collecting, hunting, fishing, cultivation, and stock-raising. The usefulness of these categories has been affirmed by Herskovits (1952:86) and Murdock (1957).

In considering the relation of economy to adult role, and hence to child training, we felt that perhaps a variable of great significance is the extent to which food is accumulated and must be cared for. At one extreme is dependence mainly upon animal husbandry, where the meat that will be eaten in coming months and years, and the animals that will produce the future milk, are present on the hoof. In this type of society, future food supply seems to be best assured by faithful adherence to routines designed to maintain the good health of the herd. Agriculture perhaps imposes only slightly less pressure toward the same pattern of behavior. Social rules prescribe the best known way to bring the growing plants to successful harvest, and to protect the stored produce for gradual consumption until the next harvest. Carelessness in performance of routine duties leads to a threat of hunger, not for the day of carelessness itself but for many months to come. Individual initiative in attempts to improve techniques may be feared be-cause no one can tell immediately whether the changes will lead to a greater harvest or to disastrous failure. Under these conditions, there might well be a premium on obedience to the older and wiser, and on responsibility in faithful performance of the routine laid down by custom for one's economic role.

At an opposite extreme is subsistence primarily through hunting or fishing, with no means for extended storing of the catch. Here individual initiative and development of high individual skill seem to be at a premium. Where each day's food comes from that day's catch, variations in the energy and skill exerted in food-getting lead to immediate reward or punishment. Innovation, moreover, seems unlikely to be so generally feared. If a competent hunter tries out some change in technique, and it fails, he may still have time to revert to the established procedures to get his catch. If the change is a good one, it may lead to immediate reward.

We recognize, of course, that there will not be a perfect correlation between the dominant type of food-getting and such aspects of the economic role. Agricultural and herding societies may produce a sufficient food surplus to allow some individuals to experiment with new techniques. Some hunting and fishing societies have means of preserving their catch, and this should increase the pressure for conformity to rules for ensuring preservation. Hunting and fishing may be done by teamwork, so that success depends partly upon responsible performance of the special duties assigned to each member. Some societies regard their hunting lands as a resource which must be protected by rigid conformity to conservation rules. A better picture of the relation of economy to socialization could surely be obtained through an analysis of such details of economic activity.

ECONOMY AND CHILD TRAINING

We have outlined above an hypothesis about economic behavior as an adaptation to the general type of subsistence economy. If economic role tends to be generalized to the rest of behavior, predictions might be made about the typical character or personality of adults in societies with different subsistence economies. In societies with low accumulation of food resources, adults should tend to be individualistic, assertive, and venturesome. By parallel reasoning, adults should tend to be conscientious, compliant, and conservative in societies with high accumulation of food resources.

If economic role and general personality tend to be appropriate for the type of subsistence economy, we may expect the training of children to foreshadow these adaptations. The kind of adult behavior useful to the society is likely to be taught to some extent to the children, in order to assure the appearance of this behavior at the time it is needed. Hence we may predict that the emphases in child training will be toward the development of kinds of behavior especially useful for the adult economy.

As a method for testing the hypothesis of adaptation to subsistence economy, societies with different types of economy may be compared in adult economic roles, general adult personality, and child training. In the present paper, societies which differ in economy are compared in child training, not in adult economic role or adult personality, because child training seems to have the most indirect connection with economy. If appropriate differences in child training are found, we may infer that the adaptation to economy includes a wide sphere of social behavior.

PROCEDURE

In the preliminary version of a recent article, Murdock (1957) classified the subsistence economy of societies into six categories, designated by the letters A, F, G, H, P, and R. We have considered societies as likely to be . . . high in accumulation of food resources, by our definition, if they were classified by Murdock as predominantly pastoral (P) or as agricultural with animal husbandry also important (A). Societies were considered likely to be . . . low in accumulation if Murdock designated them as predominantly hunting (H) or fishing (F).

Societies were considered intermediate in accumulation if Murdock designated them as predominantly agricultural, with either grain (G) or root (R) crops, with animal husbandry not important. . . .

Several other cultural variables, to be used somewhat incidentally later in the paper, were also taken from Murdock's analyses (1957, and preliminary unpublished version).

The authors of the present paper obtained ratings on several aspects of child training practices by their own analysis of ethnographic documents. The methods used are described in detail in Barry, Bacon and Child (1957). Societies were rated separately for boys and for girls with respect to six aspects of training.

1. Obedience training.

2. Responsibility training, which usually was on the basis of participation in the subsistence or household tasks.

3. Nurturance training, i.e., training the child to be nurturant or helpful toward younger siblings and other dependent people.

4. Achievement training, which was usually on the basis of competition, or imposition of standards of excellence in performance.

5. Self-reliance training, defined as training to take care of oneself, to be independent of the assistance of other people in supplying one's needs and wants.

6. General independence training. This was defined more generally than self-reliance training, to include training not only to satisfy one's own needs but also toward all kinds of

freedom from control, domination, and super-vision. Ratings of general independence train-ing were highly correlated with ratings of self-reliance training, but were not identical to them.

For each of these six aspects of train-ing, societies were rated on strength of socialization, which was defined as the combined positive pressure (rewards for the behavior) plus negative pressure (punishments for lack of the behavior). The ratings were for the stage of child-hood, from age 4 or 5 years until shortly before puberty. Each rating was made by two separate judges, working inde-pendently, and the sum of their two judgments was used.

The results to be reported are on 104 societies which are included in two sep-arate samples: Murdock's sample of over 500 societies classified on economy and social organization, and 110 societies rated on socialization by Bacon and Barry. Most of these 104 societies are nonliterate, and they are distributed all over the world. Many cultures were omitted from some of the ratings because of insufficient information; such omissions are much more frequent for the so-cialization variables than for Murdock's variable.

RESULTS

Economy and Specific Variables of Socialization

. . . Figure 1 shows the average ranking of our six socialization variables for the societies classified according to sub-sistence economy. Societies with ex-tremely high accumulation, compared to those with extremely low accumulation, tend to show higher pressure toward re-sponsibility and obedience and lower pressure toward achievement, self-re-liance and independence. Nurturance is the only child training variable which has approximately the same average ranking in both groups of societies. The associa-tion of each variable with accumulation is in the same direction for boys and girls.

. . . . .

It is apparent from Figure 1 that child training practices are correlated with amount of accumulation of food re-

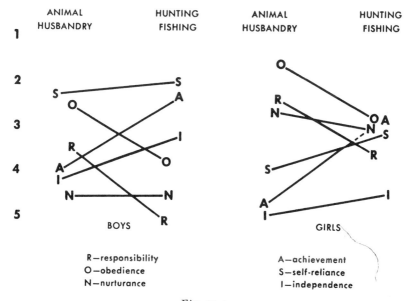

R—responsibility
O—obedience
N—nurturance

A—achievement
S—self-reliance
I—independence

Figure 1.

sources. For example, strong pressure toward responsibility (i.e., high ranking) tends to occur more frequently in societies which have high accumulation of food resources. If this correlation were perfect, so that societies high in responsibility were always high in accumulation and vice versa, the coefficient of association would be +1.00. If societies high in responsibility, and those low in responsibility were each divided equally between high and low accumulation, the association coefficient would be zero (0.00). If the correlation were in the reverse direction, so that societies high in responsibility were always low in accumulation, the association coefficient would be negative but again of maximum size (−1.00). Thus the size of the association coefficient gives a measure of the consistency of the relationship between two variables; the plus or minus sign shows the direction of the relationship.

The results portrayed in Figure 1 have been expressed in coefficients of association in Table 1. As Table 1 shows, responsibility and obedience are positively correlated with accumulation of food resources; achievement, self-reliance, and independence are negatively correlated with accumulation. Nurturance shows . . . results . . . of small magnitude and [not] statistically significant. . . .

These results are all substantially alike for the training of the two sexes. The correlations between economy and child training are in the same direction for boys and girls for all the variables except nurturance. There seems to be no consistent difference between the sexes in size of the correlations. However, it is worth noting in Figure 1 that the variables which ranked higher in societies with high accumulation of food resources (obedience and responsibility) were emphasized more strongly in the training of girls than boys, whereas the variables which ranked higher in societies with low accumulation of food resources (achievement, self-reliance and independence) were emphasized more strongly in the training of boys than girls. A further description of sex differences for the same group of societies may be found in a recent paper by Barry, Bacon and Child (1957).

. . . . .

Economy and a General Variable of Socialization

In their relation to economy, the socialization variables (if we omit nurturance) fall into two distinct groups. This fact suggests that a single more general variable might be extracted for presentation of data on individual societies and for further exploration of results. We have called this variable pressure toward compliance vs. assertion. It is based on the separate socialization variables, and was derived in the following way: The sum of the rankings of responsibility and obedience training, for both boys and

TABLE 1.

RELATION OF CHILD TRAINING PRACTICES TO ACCUMULATION OF FOOD RESOURCES (EXPRESSED AS COEFFICIENTS OF ASSOCIATION)

	Boys	Girls
Responsibility	+.74**	+.62**
Obedience	+.50**	+.59**
Nurturance	−.01	+.10
Achievement	−.60**	−.62**
Self-reliance	−.21	−.46*
Independence	−.41*	−.11

* $p < .05$ } Two-tail tests, based on the Mann-
** $p < .01$ } Whitney U (Siegel 1956: 116–127).

girls, was subtracted from the sum of the rankings of achievement and self-reliance, for both boys and girls. A plus score meant that responsibility and obedience were ranked higher (i.e., were assigned lower numbers) than achievement and self-reliance, and for purposes of calculating a coefficient of association any plus score was designated as predominant pressure toward compliance. A zero or minus score was designated as predominant pressure toward assertion. We dealt with cases of missing information as follows: In the several societies in which the achievement rating was not made, general independence was substituted for it in deriving this general measure of pressure toward compliance vs. assertion. In the two societies where the obedience rating was not made, the responsibility rating was substituted for it. Eleven societies were omitted because some or all of the ratings had been made only for one sex.

Table 2 presents a list of societies, divided according to predominant economy and arranged in order of their score on relative predominance of compliance vs. assertion in child training pressures. The correlation portrayed in this table is very consistent. Societies with high accumulation of food resources almost always had predominant pressure toward compliance, whereas societies with low accumulation almost always had predominant pressure toward assertion; 39 societies conformed to this result and only seven had high accumulation with assertion or low accumulation with compliance. The association coefficient for this relationship is .94, (P), and P is less than .001, measured by the Mann-Whitney U Test (Siegel 1956: 116-117).

It is not surprising, of course, that economy shows a higher correlation with the combined measure of socialization pressures than with any of the separate child training measures from which it is derived. The magnitude of the correlation is, however, surprising. We may conclude that a knowledge of the economy alone would enable one to predict with considerable accuracy whether a society's socialization pressures were primarily toward compliance or assertion.

Relation to Other Cultural Variables

We have suggested that child training practices are shaped by the behavioral requirements of the adult economic roles. This implies a fairly direct causal relation between economy and child training. It is quite possible, however, that the causal connection might be much more indirect. The subsistence economy may have a pervasive influence on many other aspects of culture, and some of these other aspects of culture may be more directly responsible for influencing child training practices. As a first check on this possibility, we decided to explore the relation of pressure toward compliance vs. assertion, and of subsistence economy, to nine other major cultural variables for which Murdock . . . has prepared analyses from the ethnographic literature for these same societies.

For five of these variables, it was possible to treat Murdock's categories as falling along an ordered scale: these are the first five variables listed in Table 3. For three additional variables (the rest of those appearing in Table 3), Murdock's categories were divided into two groups to form a reasonable dichotomy. Clearly these eight variables show some consistency in their relation both to our economic measure and to pressure toward compliance vs. assertion. . . .

[However,] pressure toward compliance vs. assertion shows [a] higher correlation with accumulation of food resources (.94) . . . than with any of the other cultural variables. These other cultural variables are mostly related more closely to accumulation than to compliance vs. assertion.

TABLE 2.	EXTREMES IN ACCUMULATION	
RELATION OF SUBSISTENCE ECONOMY TO GENERAL PRESSURE TOWARD COMPLIANCE VS. ASSERTION IN CHILD TRAINING	*High* (animal husbandry)	*Low* (hunting, fishing)
	Aymara (+ 13½)	
	Tepoztlan (+13½)	
	Lepcha (+11½)	
	Swazi (+8½)	
	Tswana (+8½)	
	Nyakyusa (+8)	
	Sotho (+8)	
	Nuer (+7)	
	Tallensi (+7)	
	Lovedu (+6½)	
	Mbundu (+6½)	
	Venda (+6½)	
	Kikuyu (+6)	
	Zulu (+6)	
	Pondo (+4½)	
	Chagga (+4)	
	Ganda (+3)	
	Chamorro (+2½)	Teton (+4)
	Masai (+2½)	Yahgan (+1)
	Chukchee (+1)	Hupa (+½)
	Tanala (0)	Chiricahua (0)
	Thonga (−2½)	Murngin (0)
	Araucanian (−3)	Paiute (0)
	Balinese (−3)	Arapaho (−2)
		Kwakiutl (−2)
		Cheyenne (−2½)
		Kaska (−2½)
		Klamath (−2½)
		Ojibwa (−2½)
		Ona (−3)
		Aleut (−4)
		Jicarilla (−6½)
		Western Apache (−10)
		Siriono (−10½)
		West Greenland Eskimo (−11)
		Aranda (−12)
		Comanche (−12)
		Crow (−13½)
		Manus (−15)

The societies are grouped in columns on the basis of economy and are listed within each column in descending order of degree of pressure toward compliance as compared with pressure toward asser-tion. The number in parentheses after each society indicates the degree of preponderance of compliance (plus scores) or of assertion (minus scores).

TABLE 3.
RELATION OF
OTHER CULTURAL
VARIABLES TO
PRESSURE TOWARD
COMPLIANCE VS.
ASSERTION, AND TO
ACCUMULATION OF
FOOD RESOURCES,
SEPARATELY FOR
TWO GROUPS OF
SOCIETIES

TABLE 3. RELATION OF OTHER CULTURAL VARIABLES TO PRESSURE TOWARD COMPLIANCE VS. ASSERTION, AND TO ACCUMULATION OF FOOD RESOURCES, SEPARATELY FOR TWO GROUPS OF SOCIETIES

Cultural Variable	Relation to Accumulation	Relation to Pressure toward Compliance
Size of permanent settlement unit	+.52	+.43
Degree of political integration	+.76	+.63
Complexity of social stratification	+.74	+.56
Greater participation by women in predominant subsistence activity	+.60	+.48
Extent of approach to general polygyny	+.25	—.08
Presence of bride-price or bride-service	+.84	+.86
Unilinearity of descent	+.83	+.49
Residence fixed or neolocal, rather than shifting or bilocal	+.32	+.35

The measure given here is the index of order association, for which see Wallis and Roberts, 1956:282–284; where both variables are dichotomous, this measure reduces to the more familiar coefficient of association. Pressure toward compliance, and accumulation of food resources, have been treated here as dichotomous variables; the other variables have from two to seven ordered categories. A plus or minus sign indicates whether the variables are positively or negatively related to high accumulation and high pressure toward compliance.

. . . Therefore it is plausible that the relation of compliance vs. assertion to the variables listed in Table 3 is principally due to their common relation to accumulation of food resources.

. . . . .

Intermediate Accumulation of Food Resources. [*]

The high correlations we have reported between subsistence economy and child training were applied only to societies which are extremely high or extremely low in accumulation of food resources. A large group of predominantly agricultural societies do not fit into either category but might still show considerable variation in accumulation of food resources. The question remains whether the correlations found among the extreme cases would also be found in this more intermediate group of societies. Furthermore, the data shown in Table 3 suggest the possibility that the

high correlation between accumulation of food resources and pressure toward compliance is found only in societies where the subsistence economy is consistently linked with a group of other cultural variables.

In order to answer these questions, we divided the predominantly agricultural societies into two groups. Those with little or no hunting or fishing (15 societies) were considered as having high accumulation of food resources, and those which rely on hunting or fishing for an important part of their food (18 societies) were considered as having low accumulation of food resources. Here as in the extreme comparison, societies with high accumulation of food resources tend to emphasize responsibility and obedience training, and show high overall pressure toward compliance in child training; societies with low accumulation of food resources tend to emphasize achievement, self-reliance and independence training, and show low overall pressure toward compliance in child training. The associa-

---

[*] This section, preceding the conclusion, has been added to the original article by the authors.

tion coefficient between accumulation of food resources and pressure toward compliance is .93 ($p < .02$). Accumulation of food resources shows low and inconsistent relationships to all of the cultural variables listed in Table 3, with the exception of the last one (residence fixed or neolocal, rather than shifting or bilocal). Therefore the high positive correlation between accumulation of food resources and pressure toward compliance in child training is found among our entire sample of societies and does not depend upon the group of cultural variables which are linked with the extreme variations in accumulation of food resources.

DISCUSSION

Some readers may feel that our main results are obvious, to the extent of being therefore trivial. We believe that this is not the case, that we have instead obtained strong evidence for one hypothesis where some other quite different hypothesis might seem more obvious in advance. For example, let us start the other way around and think of child training as the basic given. Pressure toward self-reliance and achievement should produce strongly independent people who hate to be dependent on others. This character tendency should render very rewarding all features of economic behavior that make it easier to avoid being dependent on others. Among such features, one of the most conspicuous might be the possession by each individual or family of an accumulated food supply (such as herd or crop), which ensures that an unlucky hunt will not leave one dependent upon the neighbor's catch. Hence child training pressure toward assertion should moti-

vate (perhaps unconsciously) the quest for high accumulation techniques of subsistence. But according to our findings, it evidently does not. If any such process operates to a slight degree, it appears to be completely obscured by the much more important process to which our results point.

Our findings then are consistent with the suggestion that child training tends to be a suitable adaptation to subsistence economy. Pressure toward obedience and responsibility should tend to make children into the obedient and responsible adults who can best ensure the continuing welfare of a society with a high-accumulation economy, whose food supply must be protected and developed gradually throughout the year. Pressure toward self-reliance and achievement should shape children into the venturesome, independent adults who can take initiative in wresting food daily from nature, and thus ensure survival in societies with a low-accumulation economy.

REFERENCES CITED

BARRY, HERBERT III, MARGARET K. BACON, AND IRVIN L. CHILD. A cross-cultural survey of some sex differences in socialization. Journal of Abnormal and Social Psychology, 1957, 55:327–332.

FORDE, C. DARYLL. Habitat, economy and society. London, Methuen, 1934.

HERSKOVITS, MELVILLE J. Economic anthropology. New York, Alfred A. Knopf, 1952.

MURDOCK, GEORGE PETER. World ethnographic sample. American Anthropologist, 1957, 59:664–687.

SIEGEL, SIDNEY. Nonparametric statistics for the behavioral sciences. New York, McGraw-Hill, 1956.

WALLIS, W. ALLEN AND HARRY V. ROBERTS. Statistics, a new approach. Glencoe, Illinois, Free Press, 1956.

GEORGE BERNARD SHAW

Perhaps Shaw's essential greatness—as a playwright, as a critic of the arts, and as a critic of society as well—lay in his capacity to cut through pretense and shatter hypocrisy. What special childhood experiences enabled him to develop this ability?

In these autobiographical sketches, Shaw describes his childhood and family with mixed contempt and admiration for the values of his people. Is this the kind of person we would want?

MY MOTHER AND HER RELATIVES

My mother was the daughter of a country gentleman, and was brought up with ruthless strictness to be a paragon of all ladylike virtues and accomplishments, by her grand aunt, whom I remember from my very early childhood as a humpbacked old lady with a pretty face, whose deformity seemed to me quaintly proper to her as a beneficent fairy. Had she known the magically favorable impression she made on me, she would perhaps have left me her property; and I now believe I was brought to her in the hope I should attract her to this extent. But I was a failure. She had brought my mother up to make such a distinguished marriage as would finally wipe out an unmentionable stain on her pedigree; for though on her parents side her extraction was everything that could be desired, her grandfather was a mysterious master spirit whose birth was so obscure that there was some doubt as to whether he ever had any legal parents at all.

．．．．．

Nature, expelled with a fork, came back again and wrecked the life plans of her fairy aunt. When my mother grew up, she knew thoroughbass as taught by her musicmaster Johann Bernhard Logier

Reprinted from *Sixteen Self Sketches* (Dodd, Mead & Company, 1949) by permission of The Public Trustee as Executor of the Estate of George Bernard Shaw, Deceased, and of The Society of Authors, London.

(famous in Dublin as the inventor of the chiroplast, a mechanical finger exerciser which set his piano pupils all wrong); she could repeat two of La Fontaine's fables in French with perfect pronunciation; she could carry herself with complete dignity; and she could have worked as a ragpicker without losing her entire conviction that she was a lady, of a species apart from servants and common persons. But she could not housekeep on a small income; she had no notion of the value of money; she detested her grand aunt and regarded all that had been taught her as religion and discipline as tyranny and slavery. Consequently, as she was naturally very humane, she abandoned her own children to the most complete anarchy. Both my parents, as it happened, were utterly uncoercive.

In due time she was floated in Dublin society to get married. Among other persons with whom she came in contact was George Carr Shaw, an apparently harmless gentleman of forty, with a squint and a vein of humor which delighted in anti-climax, and would have made him an appreciative listener for Charles Lamb. He was a member of a large family which spoke of itself as "the Shaws," and got invited, on the strength of a second cousinship, to Bushy Park, the seat of the bachelor Sir Robert Shaw, Bart., as to whom see Burke's *Landed Gentry*. George Carr Shaw seemed very safe company for my carefully guarded mother, because nobody could conceive his having the audacity, the enterprise, nor the means, to marry anybody, even if it could be supposed that his years or his squint could appeal to so well brought-up a female as Miss Lucinda Elizabeth Gurly. He was therefore well spoken of by her relatives as a quite eligible person to know in a general social way. They forgot that, having never been taught what marriage really means, nor experienced impecuniosity, she might marry any adventurer without knowing how much she was doing.

Her tragedy came about by external pressure of a sort that nobody could have foreseen.

Her widowed father was most unexpectedly married again; this time the penniless daughter of an old friend of his whose bills he had backed with ruinous consequences. The alliance did not please the family of his first wife, especially his brother-in-law, a Kilkenny squire, to whom he owed money, and from whom he concealed his intention to marry again.

Unfortunately my mother innocently let out the secret to her uncle. The consequence was that my grandfather, going out on his wedding morning to buy a pair of gloves for the ceremony, was arrested for debt at the suit of his brother-in-law. One can hardly blame him for being furious. But his fury carried him beyond all reason. He believed that my mother had betrayed him deliberately so as to stop the marriage by his arrest. My mother, who was on a visit to some relatives in Dublin at the time, had to choose between two homes to return to. One was the house of a stepmother and an enraged father. The other was to the house of her aunt, which meant the old domestic slavery and tyranny.

It was at this moment that some devil, perhaps commissioned by the Life Force to bring me into the world, prompted my father to propose marriage to Miss Bessie Gurly. She caught at the straw.

She had heard that he had a pension of £60 a year; and to her, who had never been allowed to have more than pocket money nor the housekeep, £60 seemed an enormous and inexhaustible sum. She calmly announced her engagement, dropping the bombshell as unconcernedly as if it were a colored glass ball from her solitaire board. People played solitaire in those days.

Finding it impossible to make her see the gravity of the pecuniary situation, or to induce her to cancel her engagement on such ground, her people played another card. They told her that George Carr Shaw was a drunkard. She indignantly refused to believe them, reminding them that they had never objected to him before. When they persisted, she went to him straightforwardly and asked him was it true. He assured her most solemnly that he was a convinced and life-long teetotaller. And she believed him and married him. But it was not true. He drank.

Without attempting to defend my father for telling this whopper, I must explain that he really was in principle a convinced teetotaller. Unfortunately it was the horror of his own experience as an occasional dipsomaniac that gave him this conviction, which he was miserably unable to carry into practice.

I can only imagine the hell into which my mother descended when she found out what shabby-genteel poverty with a drunken husband is like. She told me once that when they were honeymooning in Liverpool (of all places) she opened her bridegroom's wardrobe and found it full of empty bottles. In the first shock of the discovery she ran away to the docks to get employed as a stewardess and be taken out of the country. But on the way she was molested by some rough docklanders and had to run back again.

I have elsewhere recorded how, when my father, taking me for a walk, pretended in play to throw me into the canal, he very nearly did it. When we got home I said to my mother as an awful and hardly credible discovery "Mamma: I think Papa is drunk." This was too much for her. She replied "When is he anything else?"

It is a rhetorical exaggeration to say that I have never since believed in anything or anybody; but the wrench from my discovery that he was a hypocrite and a dipsomaniac was so sudden and violent that it must have left its mark on me.

. . . . .

Under all the circumstances it says a great deal for my mother's humanity that she did not hate her children. She did not hate anybody, nor love anybody. The specific maternal passion awoke in her a little for my younger sister, who died at twenty, but it did not move her until she lost her, nor then noticeably. She did not concern herself much about us; for she had never been taught that mothering is a science, nor that it matters in the least what children eat or drink; she left all that to servants whose wage was £8 a year and could neither write nor read. She had no sense of the value of her own training, and gave it no credit for its results, which she may have regarded as gifts of nature; but she had a deep sense of its cruelties. As we grew up and had to take care of ourselves unguided, we met life's difficulties by breaking our shins over them, gaining such wisdom as was inevitable by making fools of ourselves.

. . . . .

My father was impecunious and unsuccessful: he could do nothing that interested her; and he did not shake off his miserable and disgraceful tippling (he did eventually) until it was too late to make any difference in their relations. Had there not been imagination, idealization, the charm of music, the charm of lovely seas and sunsets, and our natural kindliness and gentleness, it is impossible to say what cynical barbarism we might not have grown into.

My mother's salvation came through music. She had a mezzosoprano voice of extraordinary purity of tone; and to cultivate it she took lessons from George John Vandaleur Lee, already well established in Dublin as an orchestral conductor, an organizer of concerts, and a teacher of singing so heterodox and original that he depended for his performances on amateurs trained by himself, and was detested by his professional rivals, whom he disparaged as voice wreckers, as indeed they mostly were. He extended this criticism to doctors, and amazed us by eating brown bread instead of white, and sleeping with the window open, both of which habits I acquired and have practised ever since. His influence in our household, of which he at last became a member, accustomed me to the scepticism as to academic authority which still persists in me.

He not only made my mother sing by a method that preserved her voice perfectly until her death at over eighty but gave her a Cause and a Creed to live for.

Those who know my play *Misalliance*, in which the lover has three fathers, will note that I also had a natural father and two supplementaries, making three varieties for me to study. This widened my outlook very considerably. Natural parents should bear in mind that the more supplementaries their children find, at school or elsewhere, the better they will know that it takes all sorts to make a world. Also that though there is always the risk of being corrupted by bad parents, the natural ones may be—probably ten per cent. of them actually are—the worst of the lot.

Then there was my maternal Uncle Walter. During my boyhood he was a ship's surgeon on the Inman line (now the American), visiting us between voyages. . . . In spite of his excesses, which were not continuous, being the intermittent debauches of a seafarer on shore, he was an upstanding healthy man until he married an English widow in America and settled as a general practitioner in Leyton, Essex, then a country district on the borders of Epping Forest. His wife tried to make him behave himself according to English lights, to go to church; to consult the feelings and prejudices of his patients; to refrain from the amusement of scandalizing their respectability; or at least to stint himself in the item of uproarious blasphemy. It was quite useless: her protests only added to the zest of his profanities.

. . . . .

The children of Bohemian Anarchists are often in such strenuous reaction against their bringing-up that they are the most tyrannically conventional of parents. The problem of how much and when children can be kindly and safely left to their own devices, and how much guided and ordered, is the most difficult part of parental policy. Prince Peter Kropotkin, a comprehensive thinker, far above the average in wisdom and kindliness, said of children "You can only look on." My mother, if she had ever thought about the matter at all would have said "You can only go your own way and let the children go theirs."

. . . . .

IN THE DAYS OF MY YOUTH

All autobiographies are lies. I do not mean unconscious, unintentional lies: I mean deliberate lies. No man is bad enough to tell the truth about himself during his lifetime, involving, as he must, the truth about his family and his friends and colleagues. And no man is good enough to tell the truth to posterity in a document which he suppresses until there is nobody left alive to contradict him.

. . . . .

I am in the further difficulty that I have not yet ascertained the truth about myself. For instance, how far am I mad, and how far sane? I do not know. My specific talent has enabled me to cut a figure in my profession in London: but a man may, like Don Quixote, be clever enough to cut a figure, and yet be stark mad.

A critic recently described me as having "a kindly dislike of my fellow creatures." Dread would have been nearer the mark than dislike; for a man is the only animal of which I am thoroughly and cravenly afraid. I have never thought much of the courage of a lion tamer. Inside the cage he is at least safe from other men. There is less harm in a well-fed lion. It has no ideals, no sect, no party, no nation, no class: in short, no reason for destroying anything it does not want to eat.

. . . . .

My father was an Irish Protestant gentleman of the down-start race of younger sons. He had no inheritance, no profession, no manual skill, no qualification of any sort for any definite social function. He must have had some elementary education; for he could read and write and keep accounts more or less inaccurately; and he spoke and dressed like an Irish educated gentleman and not like a railway porter. But he certainly had not a university degree; and I never heard him speak of any school or college of which he could claim to be an alumnus. He had, however, been brought up to believe that there was an inborn virtue of gentility in all Shaws as partisans of William the Conqueror. . . . My father was a second cousin of the baronet, and was privileged to hire a carriage and attend the Bushy Park funerals, beside having a right to an invitation to certain family parties there. Necessarily all the Shaws were Protestants and snobs. . . .

I believe Ireland, as far as the Protestant gentry is concerned, to be the most irreligious country in the world. I was christened by my uncle; and as my god-father was intoxicated and did not turn up, the sexton was ordered to promise and vow in his place, precisely as my uncle might have ordered him to put more coals on the vestry fire. I was never confirmed; and I believe my parents never were either. Of the seriousness with which English families took this rite I had no conception; for Irish Protestantism was not then a religion: it was a side in political faction, a class prejudice, a conviction that Roman Catholics are socially inferior persons who will go to hell when they die and leave Heaven for the exclusive possession of Protestant ladies and gentlemen. In my childhood I was sent every Sunday to a Sunday school where genteel little children repeated texts, and were rewarded with cards inscribed to them. After an hour of this we were marched into the adjoining church (the Molyneux in Upper Leeson Street), to sit around the altar rails and fidget there until our neighbors must have wished the service over as heartily as we did. I suffered this, not for my salvation, but because my father's respectability demanded it. When we went to live in Dalkey we broke with the observance and never resumed it.

. . . . .

Imagine being taught to despise a workman, and to respect a gentleman, in a country where every rag of excuse of gentility is stripped off by poverty! Imagine being taught that there is one God, a Protestant and a perfect gentleman, keeping Heaven select for the gentry against an idolatrous impostor called the Pope! Imagine the pretensions of the English peerage on the incomes of the English middle class! I remember Stopford Brooke one day telling me that he discerned in my books an intense and contemptuous hatred for society. No wonder!

. . . . .

And now, what power did I find in Ireland religious enough to redeem me from this abomination of desolation? Quite simply, the power of Art. My mother, as it happened, had a considerable musical talent. In order to exercise it seriously, she had to associate with other people who had musical talent. My first doubt as to whether God could really be a good Protestant was suggested by the fact that the best voices available for combination with my mother's in the works of the great composers had been unaccountably vouchsafed to Roman Catholics. Even the divine gentility was presently called in question; for some of these vocalists were undeniably shop-keepers. If the best tenor, undeniably a Catholic, was at least an accountant, the buffo was a frank stationer.

There was no help for it: if my mother was to do anything but sing silly ballads in drawing rooms, she had to associate herself on an entirely unsectarian footing with people of like artistic gifts without the smallest reference to creed or class. She must actually permit herself to be approached by Roman Catholic priests, and at their invitation to enter that house of Belial, the Roman Catholic chapel, and sing the Masses of Mozart there. If religion is that which binds men to one another, and irreligion that which sunders, then must I testify that I found the religion of my country in its musical genius, and its irreligion in its churches and drawing rooms.

Let me add a word of gratitude to that cherished asylum of my boyhood, the National Gallery of Ireland. I believe I am the only Irishman who has ever been in it, except the officials. But I know that it did much more for me than the two confiscated medieval Cathedrals so magnificently "restored" out of the profits of the drink trade.

PART TWO
INFANCY
SATISFYING FUNDAMENTAL NEEDS:
SOME DIMENSION OF LOVE

Man has always tried to explain the differences among individuals of his species. Some people work hard, others are agile; some become football players, others, criminals. How do we explain an Einstein and a Hitler? Learned men offer explanations in terms of genes, psychological traits, or sociological structures. For the biologist, our behavior is caused— or at least limited—by our inherited nature. For the psychologist, our behavior is determined by our drives, wishes, impulses, or attitudes. And for the sociologist, we behave according to the traditions, values, and cultural, class, or racial standards of our group.

Essentially, such views see man as a neutral object, completely at the mercy of forces either inside or outside him, and not as a decision-maker. For George Herbert Mead and his followers, however, man is the actor, that is, it is he who acts, not his drives, attitudes, values, or social position. The basic concept in this theory is the *self*, which intercedes between man and his situations, observing, interpreting, and weighing the consequences of alternative actions before action itse   s taken.

At birth the infant has no self. Rather, he is a neutral object, acting in response to his internal drives, needs, and wants, and in response to external conditions such as heat, cold, and noise. At three months, he is still unaware that there is a world outside and apart from him. He has no self to address, to which he might indicate, "This is me that is not me." By his first or second year, however, he has developed a self and is differentiating it from the external world; and since there are literally millions of interactions between an infant and adults in the first two or three years of the infant's life, the opportunities for each child to develop a unique self are great.

Our question is, "What happens to the self which causes the child to die in infancy or to grow up hopelessly ill or a criminal?" The theory underlying many of the selections in this part suggests that the infant who has been badly treated by the adults in his world has learned that the world is not a fit place for him to live, or that people are no good. If, on the other hand, he is in pain from cold, hunger, or other distress, and each time an adult appears the pain is replaced by pleasure, the infant might indicate to himself that the world and its inhabitants are good.

What are the fundamental needs of the infant, and how can they be satisfied? What is motherly love, and how much of it does the infant need? The selections that follow explore these questions and provide some provocative answers. Montagu reveals that some infants are born already handicapped by the deficiencies or diseases of the mother. Can it be said therefore that the infant needs love even before birth? The experiments of Clara Davis demonstrate one way in which love may be shown an infant; in terms of his dietary needs, it is to provide for him a wide variety of natural foods and to allow him to eat as he pleases.

What are the laws that govern growth? Breckenridge and Vincent present several of the principles that regulate this complex process; the developmental patterns described in selection 18, which show the kinds of behavior children are capable of at different age levels, should serve as a useful guide to the study of all of the articles.

Harlow's early experiments suggest that for the infant monkey, a supply of warm milk and a clean soft form to clutch provide the infant's essential needs. However, Harlow's more recent findings indicate that when the monkey is provided with an inanimate parent substitute which is more constant and patient than a living parent can be, a severely disturbed new generation is formed.

The investigations of ecologists, exemplified here by the experiments of Hess, introduce the concepts of imprinting and critical period, showing the close interrelationship of the rapidly-developing infant and the external world. Selye's selection provides a more specific understanding of the physiological functions of animals in their struggle for survival, while the research of Thomas and his associates points up the important part that organic factors play in the determination of each child's psychological individuality.

Of the pioneering researches investigating the needs of infants, most claim that early separation from his mother has an irreversible detrimental impact upon the infant's life, his intellectual and emotional development, and his ability to survive at all. Qualifications to these conclusions are offered by later studies suggesting more subtle, important factors than simple separation. Thus, for example, Prugh and Harlow broaden the concept of maternal deprivation to include various debilitating experiences suffered by children who are not separated from their mothers.

Early studies of mother-child separation in addition to Bowlby's (selection 26), by Spitz (1949) and Goldfarb (1955), revealed that children reared in orphanages or similar institutions were so severely damaged intellectually and emotionally, were so destructive, uncontrollable, sick, and unhappy, and suffered such high death rates, that orphanages were for the most part closed down, their occupants being placed instead in foster homes. In the typical orphanage, the attendants were trained more in maintaining cleanliness than they were in "mothering," and the ratio of attendants to infants was usually one to ten. In the foster home, on the other hand, a husband and wife are paid a small fee to rear the infant along with their other children, in the expectation that such a setting will enable the foster child to develop normally.

In sharp contrast to the conclusions of Bowlby, Spitz, Ribble, and Goldfarb, Dennis and Najarian's (1957) studies of infants reared in institutions provide evidence that they may develop normally. In the succeeding eight years, more than a hundred studies that deal with some of the questions enumerated below have been published. The answers accompanying the questions are supported by current research but must be considered tentative until more conclusive evidence is available. The

most comprehensive survey of the literature to date has been made by
Mary D. Ainsworth in *Deprivation of Maternal Care* (1962).

1. *What are some of the elements found to be important in adequate
mothering of a human infant before the age of two?* Physical presence of
an adult nearby when the infant is awake. Proper food given when the infant
is hungry, and other comforts given as needed. Gentle physical contact,
sounds of pleasant and varying tones of the human voice, antigravity
play. Avoidance of heat and cold. Soft, dry clothing and a quiet,
comfortable place to sleep. Encouragement to explore self and surroundings.

Maternal deprivation may be defined as the absence of one or more
of these experiences, an indication that all human beings are deprived
to some extent, since the mother cannot always be certain that the
infant is hungry, that all foods are proper, or that other comforts are
not needed.

In the institutions studied by Spitz, Ribble, and Goldfarb, infants
were not only deprived of the presence of their mothers but also of several
of the other elements mentioned here. For example, they might cry
for hours in their cold wet diapers. We remain ignorant as to whether
the serious damage they reported was the result of separation from
mother or denial of these other necessities.

2. *What are some other elements in adequate mothering of a
two-to-five-year-old child?* Toys, pencils, paper, crayons, scissors,
conversations, games, songs, reading poems and stories, and trips to the
store, zoo, beach, and park.

3. *If a child is separated from its mother, how long must the separation
be to cause damage to the child?* Most studies suggest that the longer
the separation, the greater the damage.

4. *What forms of disturbance may be exhibited by infants separated
from their mothers and deprived of "adequate mothering"?* A high death
rate, retarded intellectual development, poor speech, apathy, depression,
inability to feel close to others and to trust others, undisciplined or
criminal, asocial, nonconforming behavior.

5. *May these same symptoms occur even if the child is not physically
separated from the mother?* Yes, if the mother neglects the child or
develops a distorted relationship with him.

6. *May these disturbances be reversed or are they permanent?* They
may be reversed or may be permanent depending on age at separation,
adequacy of the mother-substitute, and the inherent vitality and adaptability
of the infant. Psychotherapy may bring about dramatic improvement.

7. *What is an adequate mother substitute?* Infants have different needs
at different ages. Even a feeble-minded girl may provide comfort and
intellectual stimulation to a severely retarded infant traumatized by
maternal deprivation; but feeble-minded girls might be unable to provide
intellectual stimulation to older children.

8. *Is the age of the infant an important factor in determining susceptibility
to damage?* It appears that children can be separated from their mothers

before the age of five months, provided they have an adequate substitute.
Between the ages of six months and three years, separation is more
likely to be traumatic because by six months the child recognizes and
has become attached to the parent. After the fourth year, he seems
to be able to withstand the separation.

9. *Is the worst natural mother better for the infant than a good foster
home?* A good foster home is better than a depriving or distorting home.
The practice today is to remove severely neglected or disturbed children
from their natural homes and to place them in good foster homes. The
effects of such placement appear highly individualized, some being
very successful, others not.

10. *Are frequent changes in placement from one foster home to another
beneficial in supplying the infant with many varied experiences, or are
such changes disruptive?* Overwhelming evidence at this time indicates
that frequent changes are correlated with severe disturbance. Sometimes
a child is transferred from home to home because he is so badly
disturbed no one wants him around.

11. *Is physical separation from the mother the major kind of maternal
deprivation of the infant?* Probably much more frequent than physical
separation are experiences in which the infant feels neglected or rejected by
the mother who is physically present but emotionally distant. Obviously
it is easier to study the effects of physically distant mothers than of
emotionally distant mothers. The child is either with his mother or
separated from her, with her for some months, separated for some months.
Separation here can be measured in terms of days. But the typical child
remains with his mother, living in the same home. How can one measure
whether the child suffers from maternal deprivation in these circumstances?
Part Five in this book includes a number of studies of distorted lives
associated with distorted relationships between the mother and the child
who live together.

12. *If the mother is present in an average well-equipped home, what
are some of her activities which seem to help the child to grow emotionally
and intellectually?* Encouraging him to explore; taking him on trips;
smiling or showing other approval when he learns to sit up or to walk
or to climb; encouraging him to try the crayons on the paper, to try
riding the tricycle, to play ball, to use the typewriter, telephone, radio,
phonograph, to help set the table and wash the dishes, to make his
bed and sweep his room; and protecting him from activities that might
be very harmful, such as running out in the street or playing with matches.

13. *What may a mother do that would interfere with the child's normal
growth?* Discourage normal exploration of himself and his surroundings
by saying "don't do this" and "don't do that" more frequently than
"do this" and "do that." Of course, the mother will not want the child
sticking his finger in the electric socket; when he does it, she takes his
hand, walks him over to another part of the room, and gives him
something more interesting to do such as playing with a toy, a book, a ball.
Most distressing to a small child is the requirement that he sit quietly
and do nothing, which for some mothers seems to be the mark of a
"good" child. A good child moves about a great deal, is much more active

than the adult, is constantly exploring, and is trying new muscles and powers. To squelch all of his movement is just as devastating as permitting him complete freedom to be destructive or tyrannical. To learn, the child must be free to try new activities, and have his errors corrected.

BIBLIOGRAPHY

AINSWORTH, MARY D., *et al. Deprivation of Maternal Care*, Public Health Papers, No. 14 (Geneva: World Health Organization, 1962).

BOWLBY, J. "Childhood Mourning and Its Implications for Psychiatry," *J. Child Psychol. Psychiat.*, 1960.

————, AINSWORTH, M., BOSTON, M., AND ROSENBLUTH, D. "The Effects of Mother-Child Separation: A Follow-up Study," *Brit. J. med. Psychol.*, XXXIX (1956), 211.

BURLINGHAM, D., AND FREUD, A. *Infants without Families* (London: Allen & Unwin, 1944).

DENNIS, W., AND NAJARIAN, P. "Infant Development under Environmental Handicap," *Psychol. Monogr.*, LXXI (1957).

GOLDFARB, W. "Emotional and Intellectual Consequences of Psychologic Deprivation in Infancy: A Re-evaluation." *In* Hock, P. and Zubin, J., eds., *Psychopathology of Childhood* (New York: Grune and Stratton, 1955), p. 192.

RHEINGOLD, H. L., AND BAYLEY, N. "The Later Effects of an Experimental Modification of Mothering," *Child Develop.*, XXX (1959), 363.

RIBBLE, M. A., *The Rights of Infants* (New York: Columbia University Press, 1943).

SKODAK, M., AND SKEELS, H. M. "A Final Follow-up Study of One Hundred Adopted Children," *J. genet. Psychol.*, LXXV (1949), 85.

SPITZ, R. A. "Motherless Infants," *Child Develop.*, XX (1949), 144.

————. "Discussion of Dr. Bowlby's Paper." In *Psychoanalytical Study of the Child* (New York: International Universities Press), II, 313.

18 | DEVELOPMENT PATTERNS: BIRTH TO FIVE YEARS

NATALIE R. HAIMOWITZ

Is the process by which children grow larger, change in proportion, and master new controls a random process, or a uniform, purposeful one? Is it largely determined by a plan concealed in the child, pressing to elaborate itself, or by accidental external forces in the environment which now facilitate, now impede? Years of careful observations of the growth patterns in thousands of normal and abnormal children made by Gesell and other pioneering observers have led to the establishment of the norms for growth and development with which this selection deals. They have led us to think in terms of chains of sequential events, of the unfolding of patterns that are external correlates of internal physiological changes occurring within the child. And they have provided us with a comprehensive framework for understanding a life process that is amazingly predictable.

Like so many parts of our universe, growth and development patterns are orderly and predictable and occur with such universality within the human species that they have come to be known as "laws," repeating themselves in the life history of every child. Some of these laws may be summarized as follows:

1. Growth is continuous from conception till death, but occurs at an ever declining rate. After 15, the increment of growth declines significantly.

2. Although the child is continuously growing, he is growing in a number of different ways. He is becoming larger, heavier, and, through muscular development, stronger. His body proportions are changing, and his motor control and coordination are improving. His command of language is growing, and his mastery of the social techniques of his group is also altering significantly.

3. While the child's growth is continuous, he is not developing in all ways simultaneously. His mental growth alternates with his physical and social growth. At any given moment, the kind of growth that is occurring may not be visible to the naked eye or to the unskilled observer. The best single measure of developmental maturity is the carpal bone age, which is assessed through careful x-ray study.

4. Growth is orderly, with sequences in which the growth of more simple and localized controls precede other, more complicated skills and controls. For example, sitting up always precedes walking, and walking precedes bicycle-riding and dancing.

5. Development proceeds in a outward direction from the brain. Therefore, neuromuscular control of the head and face precedes control in the arms and hands, followed by the beginning of controls in the feet.

6. Within each body member or system, development proceeds from the body in an outward direction to the extremities. Thus, control of the arms precedes skillful use of the fingers.

THE CONCEPT OF PACE

Development for each child takes place at a relatively consistent rate, a pace established and maintained from birth until adolescence. Some children develop more slowly than their peers, others more rapidly, although the sequences followed by both the slow child and the advanced child are usually the same; they are also orderly and lawful in expression of the laws outlined above. For practically all children, the slow as well as the fast developers, sitting upright precedes standing, smiling precedes talking, and all of these precede repeating television commercials, drawing, and writing. When we observe a child's current level of mastery in the developmental sequence, we can usually tell what he will next achieve, although we can tell nothing of his age nor how soon he will develop the next level of skill. To determine the latter, we must know a good deal about this individual child, his characteristic pace, and his individual speed.

Most children proceed at rates similar to one another. Most one-year-old babies can do just about what other one-year-old babies can do. They are beginning to talk, capable of saying one or two words; they can finger-feed themselves and can smile and wave goodbye. They are almost able to walk, and most will walk successfully at 14 months of age. These commonly exhibited masteries and the age at which they usually happen have come to be known as "norms," that is, they represent "average" expectations and are a measure of developmental conformity. Norms change: What is expected of an average child varies with the age and the social milieu. The social demands made upon children in urban middle-class society today are vastly different from those made upon children a decade ago.

If junior is average, that is, if he is proceeding at the rate most other children are proceeding, he can be expected to arrive at a particular point in his sequential pattern at the age when most of his peers are also arriving at it. Thus, he can be expected to delight everyone by being able to say "mama" or "daddy" or "bye-

bye" or "more" when he is a year old. If he is developing at a more rapid rate than most children, he will have passed this landmark sooner (possibly at nine months of age) and can be expected to pass most future landmarks one-quarter sooner than his age mates. In fact, a child's future achievements and the date they will appear may be reliably predicted once his rate is established. The premise is that the amount of deviation from the norm remains proportionately constant through life. Barring the intervention of traumatic accidents, certain specific diseases, or some special kind of progressive retardation, the child who is half-way behind his peers will probably continue half-way behind them throughout his development. Four weeks of retardation at the age of 8 weeks lengthens into 12 weeks of retardation at the age of 24 weeks, and into 2 years of retardation at the age of 4. Similarly, rates of acceleration remain constant. A child who at one year demonstrates the skills of an average 18-month-old can be expected to perform like a child of 15 years when he is 10 years old.

The chart on pages 122–123 contains some of the established norms, that is, specific skills and the age at which they are expected to appear.

THE INTELLIGENCE QUOTIENT

Developmental rate is usually stated in statistical and mathematical form, namely, as Intelligence Quotient or Developmental Quotient. The latter term is usually used in appraising infants and children under the age of three. Both I.Q. and D.Q. represent a mathematical ratio between the child's level of skill mastery (his Mental Age) and his actual age (Chronological Age). This is expressed in the ratio

$$\text{I.Q.} = \frac{\text{Mental Age}}{\text{Chronological Age}} \times 100$$

(The fraction is multiplied by 100 to facilitate the expression of small differences with arithmetic ease.)

In an average child, the I.Q. fraction will reduce itself to 1 x 100. In a brighter than average child, the fraction may be 1.3 x 100. (yielding an I.Q. of 130) or 1.15 x 100 (yielding an I.Q. of 115). If a child is demonstrating less skill than his age mates, he is "slower," and the Mental Age : Chronological Age ratio will be less than 1. If it is .89, his I.Q. will be 89.

Sixty-eight per cent of the population achieve Intelligence Quotients within the 90-110 range. This is called "average" intelligence. Thirty-two per cent (or nearly one-third of the population) are developmentally deviant. Some (26 per cent) deviate by a small margin; 6 per cent deviate grossly (I.Q.'s below 70 or above 140), and are referred to as "exceptional children."

EXCEPTIONAL CHILDREN

The Gifted (I.Q. above 140)

The reader is referred to selections 72 and 73 for a detailed description of gifted children, who presumably make up 3 per cent of the population. In both studies, Terman and Lewis refute some of the common misconceptions about the physical and emotional fragility of mentally gifted children and correct the misconceptions about their successes being brief and transient. The reader is referred also to selection 82, in which Mary Cover Jones discusses some of the social and psychological rewards that come with early maturation to adolescent boys, contrasting with the penalties that are associated with early maturation of adolescent girls.

The Retarded (I.Q. below 70)

Some of the 3 per cent of children who are functioning less adequately than their peers are healthy, otherwise normal, often happy children of low intelligence. They are usually, but not always, the children

Age	Perceptual–Motor Behavior	Language Development	Personal–Social–Cultural Development
Birth	Motor behavior highly variable and transient. Wakefulness not sharply differentiated from sleep. Incapable of sustained posture. Tight (arboreal) grasp. Babinski reflex. Respiration and temperature variable and unsteady. Swallowing and peristalsis under precarious directional control. Vomits easily.	Startles, cries easily and frequently. Yawns.	Drowsy, frequently irritable, and fretful. Sleeps about 20 hours a day. Urination about 18 times daily, defecation 4 to 7 times daily. Occasional penis erection.
4 weeks	Head sags when not supported, hand fisted. Stares at surroundings. Some restricted eye-following.	Small throaty sounds. When a bell is rung, becomes inactive to "attend."	Looks at faces.
16 weeks	Head steady. Hands open and close. Reaches for objects closeby but can't quite get them. Contemplates objects held in hand. Recognizes bottle. Eyes follow more distant objects. Plays with hands and clothing.	Coos, laughs, gurgles, smiles.	Sleeps less. Looks around while nursing. May be fed from spoon or cup but loses half of food.
28 weeks	Sits for a while, leaning forward. Holds head up, grabs objects successfully, puts them in mouth. Becomes more able with hands. Transfers toy from one hand to the other when offered a second one. When a desired object is removed from sight, forgets it immediately. Some attempts at crawling.	Crows, vocalizes eagerness, listens to own vocalizations.	Plays with toys. Expectant in feeding. Morning and afternoon nap. Takes 4 meals a day. Has one bowel movement a day in diaper.
40 weeks	Sits up easily. Pulls up to standing. Uses index finger. Can combine two objects in play. Can place one toy or block on top of another. If desired object is removed from sight, will look for it.	Says one word. Heeds his own name. Expressive. Communicates a wide variety of ideas and feelings.	Can use spoon with much spilling. Can put spoon in cup. Plays simple nursery games. Likes adults to play with him. Plays pat-a-cake. Rolls ball. Feeds self cracker.

Age	Perceptual–Motor Behavior	Language Development	Personal–Social–Cultural Development
1 year	Walks with support. Can release objects and enjoys dropping objects from high chair. Uses thumb and forefinger with ease.	Can use one or two words. Comprehension good. Gestures, mimics, waves bye-bye.	Cooperates in dressing. Gives toy when asked. Finger feeds. Mastering use of cup. Eats a wide variety of table foods. Sleeps 14 hours a day. Aware of strangers and often balky at being handled by them.
18 months	Walks alone. Seats self. Runs in clumsy fashion with much falling. Unwraps gifts and removes toys from bag. Pulls and pushes mobile toys. Can bang on toys and make a drum of objects. Can hold crayon and imitate stroke. Can build tower of 2 or 3 blocks.	Uses nouns. Uses jargon. Names pictures.	Can take off shoes and mittens. Sweeps with broom. Needs much supervision. Exploratory and active.
2 years	Walks well. Runs fairly well. Kicks ball. Can turn pages one at a time. Can build a tower of 3 blocks. Can imitate circular stroke.	Says over 200 words. Can point to correct toy when its name is given, and to parts of his body.	Can play alone. Grabs toys away from other children. Plays mama and daddy, feeding teddy bears and dolls and wiping their noses. Can be stubborn and strong-willed.
3 years	Stands on one foot. Rides tricycle. Builds bridge of 3 blocks. Imitates cross and can draw a circle. Can pour from pitcher. Buttons and unbuttons.	Talks in sentences. Answers simple questions.	Uses spoon well. Puts on shoes but cannot fasten them. Takes turns and can sometimes wait and share.
4 years	Skips on one foot. Draws man. Builds gate of 5 blocks.	Uses conjunctions, understands prepositions.	Can wash and dry face and hands. Goes on errands. Plays cooperatively.
5 years	Skips on alternate feet. Tries to skate, jump rope, and swim, usually with awkwardness. Counts 10 pennies. Can string beads, control a pencil or crayon fairly well.	Speaks without infantile articulation. Asks "why?" Asks meaning of words. Enjoys a vocabulary of about 2,000 words.	A "little man" or "little lady." Dresses self, eats well, can help set table or clear off. Can dry dishes. Plays organized games, taking different roles. Believes anything he is told.

of healthy parents of low intelligence. They can be expected to grow, develop, hold jobs, marry, and lead normal lives. Contrary to popular misconception, they usually look like other children and cannot be diagnosed as retarded from factors of expression or countenance. The retardation in such children may be a consequence of disease, inherited or contracted, such as encephalitis or paresis, or from glandular disorders, such as mongolism or cretinism. Some children who appear normal at birth and begin to develop at an average rate suffer, however, from inborn errors of metabolism. In phenylketoneuria, one such metabolic disease, children are unable to metabolize certain common foods which, when ingested, liberate toxic substances that permanently damage the brain. Other retarded children are suffering from convulsive disorders, of which there are more than 60 identifiable varieties, some of them "progressive." While many persons of gifted intelligence suffer from convulsive seizures all through their lives without apparent progressive damage to the brain and central nervous system, others sustain brain damage from each seizure and have a disease that is progressively debilitating.

Persons with I.Q.'s below 30 are termed "idiots," and rarely develop controls beyond those of the average 28-week-old baby. Persons who achieve I.Q.'s between 30 and 50 are termed "imbeciles." Those who achieve I.Q.'s between 50 and 60 are classified as "morons." Adult morons generally function with the mental capacity of average children within the 7- to 11-year range. These psychometric definitions of mental deficiency vary from legal definition in different states. From the standpoint of the law, a mentally deficient person in most states is one who because of "demonstrated inadequate judgment" will always require special supervision or external control for his own and social welfare.

THE "ORGANIC" CHILD

The vast majority of children experience some brain damage through the process of birth. Almost all first-born children sustain intracranial hemorrhages as a consequence of the birth process. However, the plasticity and the flexibility of the human organism, its tendency to substitute and compensate for lost functions, and its adaptive capacity are such that few of these children ever show later symptoms. Those who do show later symptoms tend to be of three types: those who sustain massive, severe structural damage; those whose adaptive capacities as organisms are somehow impaired so that they cannot, out of their own resiliency, "recover"; or those whose environmental situation is so unfavorable as to add sufficiently to the stress and strain of an already mildly impaired central nervous system. Encephalographic study of random samples of the general, adequate, symptom-free population usually reveals that 15 per cent exhibit abnormal brain wave patterns, evidence of some organic dysfunction which has failed to lead to distressing symptoms. Apparently, the environmental factors within their lives are so compatible with health, or their own organisms are so adaptive, as to result in their functioning on a normal, nonconspicuous, symptom-free basis.

Of the three types of "organic" children, the first, those with severe damage, are usually identifiable through medical, neurological, or encephalographic examination. Damage may be in the form of a growth or tumor, a lesion (opening or break) where there should be continuity of tissue, the loss of tissue through external trauma (accident or injury), oxygen lack (anoxia), or other chemical or surgical damage. The second and third types of "organicity" are more difficult to diagnose, largely because the symptoms resemble those of emotionally disturbed children, because the more mild and transient pathology often eludes diagnostic procedures, and because the environments of such children are often also contributory, although to an unknown degree.

Those "organic" children with reduced energy, reduced vigor, or reduced adaptive capacity may be exhibiting a kind of dysfunction not based on structure at all, but on faulty integration between individual parts of the nervous system that appear to be intact structurally. As with other parts of the body, the nervous system operates by an intricate interaction of cooperative antagonisms, a delicately balanced process by which the dominance of one function requires the accommodation of another in relinquishing its dominance. Impaired functioning is often the result of faulty coordination, some failure among the parts. When well coordinated, they enable the individual to behave in a unified and selective manner, permitting him, for example, to decide to attend to certain stimuli and to shut out others, as when he "listens carefully" or "studies hard." When the normal balance between alternating, shifting dominance patterns is disturbed, possibly because of impairment in the usual lines of communication present in other well-integrated persons, then a lack of synergy, neurological symptoms, and learning and behavior problems result.

There has been increasing interest in children whose organic dysfunction takes the form of perceptual handicaps. The integrating mechanisms of some "organic" children appear to be impaired in such a fashion that, unlike other children, they perceive the world around them as being chaotic or poorly organized. Their powers of fine discrimination may be impaired. Reading, writing, and making the subtle distinctions required for the acquisition of language skills become far more difficult for such children. Recently, special educational procedures have proven helpful in enabling them to master some of the fundamentals of reading, writing, and arithmetic with which they would otherwise labor unsuccessfully, and toward which they would build up tremendous secondary resistances and expectations of failure.

TESTS, NORMS, AND THE CULTURAL MILIEU

Because tests and norms offer rewards and recognition for certain abilities and skills, thereby indicating a preference for these over others, such measuring devices are reflective of our culture's values. Thus, the person who scores highly on an I.Q. test not only demonstrates his intelligence, but also a high degree of compatibility between the abilities he has at his command and those that his culture currently esteems. The formalized norms represent, in mathematical form, an appraisal of this compatibility. Persons are appraised highly who not only have achieved a high degree of skill in those qualities the culture values, but who also display these abilities in a fashion approved of and prescribed by the culture. (Our culture values a high degree of motivation, drive, reliability in performing, cheerfulness, respect, and so on.) Those who arouse favorable reactions in their contemporaries and in "the appraisers" come away with better scores. Those who have eaten recently and well get better scores, as do those who share cultural values with the appraisers. Although an Eskimo may know more than 50 different words that refer to qualities of snow, a kind of adaptive intelligence in his own culture, he would receive no credits for this knowledge on the standard intelligence tests currently in use. Similarly, an Indian lad's knowledge of variations in footprints and of many different words for greenery would be of little value in our culture and go unnoticed. On the other hand, if he could tell what a diamond is and what "join" means (Wechsler Intelligence Scale for Children Vocabulary Test), it is likely that he would come away from a test evaluation with a better score.

Thus, the I.Q. is a function of a number of things, in addition to basic capacity and pace. It usually assumes the child's orientation to an urban, middle-class, highly technological culture. In fact, the increased value placed on innovation and creativity in our culture, especially within the last decade, has called attention to a quality of intelligence, problem-solving, and adaptation previously ignored. Studies of creative persons have led to the discovery that such persons often did not do well on standard I.Q. tests, and their brilliant and unconventional ways of thinking often eluded their teachers and occasionally even antagonized them.

Thus, the attempts to assess an individual's development potentials continue to pose very difficult and not yet solved problems. The physical endowment seems most validly assessed before the age of one year, for after that time the social-cultural-emotional factors become so important in the life and development of every person, so varied from person to person, and so difficult to quantify as to make the problem of assessing each person's developmental potentials a "complex one." Thus, tests probably more accurately predict present and future achievement than potential achievement.

19 | CONSTITUTIONAL AND PRENATAL FACTORS IN INFANT AND CHILD HEALTH

M. F. ASHLEY MONTAGU

Dr. Montagu's knowledgeable and provocative article gives new significance to the term "environment." An impressive amount of evidence is presented regarding the interplay between the mental-emotional state of the mother and her unborn child, the mechanisms by which stress, tension, and anxiety are transferred from mother to child in utero. That many children are born handicapped by parental deprivations reveals the profound influence of socio-economic, biological, and psychological factors on the individual even before he is born.

INTRODUCTION

This review of the materials relating to constitutional and prenatal factors in infant and child health should be regarded as of suggestive rather than of determinative value. That is to say, it

Excerpts reprinted from *Symposium on the Healthy Personality*, Milton J. Senn, ed. (Josiah Macy Jr. Foundation, 1950), pp. 148–69, by permission of the author and publisher.

should be read as suggesting areas for research to research workers, and to parents it should suggest something of the nature of the care and caution they need to exercise even before the baby is born. In short, most statements made in this review should be read with the phrase, "The evidence suggests . . ." mentally affixed.

It is important to bear in mind that much of our knowledge of what conditions affect the unborn fetus is drawn from the field of disease, from pathology. This fact should not cause the reader to develop an exaggerated view of the dangers to which the fetus is exposed nor to marvel at what might seem the surprising fact that so many human beings have survived unmarred. The pathological cases are fortunately in the minority. Their value, and their use here, lies in the fact that they show, as it were, in high relief the kind of conditions which can influence the development of the fetus, as well as something of the probable mode of action of the more normal conditions. They also show us how the development of the fetus can be influenced for better or for worse. Indeed, if there is one important lesson to be learned from the findings which are discussed in this paper, it is that we can do much to make the prenatal development of the infant a satisfactory one.

· · · · ·

CONSTITUTION, HEREDITY, AND ENVIRONMENT

Constitution is the sum total of the structural, functional, and psychological characters of the organism. It is in large measure an integral of genetic potentialities influenced in varying degrees by internal and external environmental factors. What, in fact, we are concerned with here is the answer to the following questions: (1) What are the inherited genetic potentialities (the genotype) of the organisms? (2) How are these influenced by the internal and external environmental factors during prenatal life? and (3) What role does each of these factors play in influencing the subsequent physical and mental health of infant and child?

What we mean by these questions is what we mean by "constitution," for constitution is at first a series of operative questions that even by the time of birth have not yet become final declarative answers. Indeed, there is little that is final about constitution, for constitution is a *process* rather than an unchanging entity. In brief, it is important to understand at the outset that constitution is not a biologically *given* structure predestined by its genotype to function in a predetermined manner. The manner in which all genotypes function is determined by the interaction of the genotype with the environment in which it undergoes development. What, so to speak, the genotype—the complex of genetic potentialities with which the organism is endowed—asks is: What kind of responses are going to be made to my autocatalytic enzymatic (chemically accelerating) overtures, my tentative advances? How will I impress? How will I be impressed? For the outcome of all this will be my constitution.

The point that must be emphasized here is that every genotype is a unique physicochemical system comprising particular kinds of potentialities having definite limits. These limits vary from individual to individual, so that were the genotype to be exposed to identical environmental conditions its interactive expression would nevertheless continue to vary from individual to individual. But in point of fact the environmental conditions never are the same for two individuals, not including single-egg or so-called "identical" twins. This fact renders it necessary for us to recognize that heredity is not merely constituted by the genotype, but by the genotype as modified by the environment in which it has developed. It is necessary to grasp clearly the fact that what the organism inherits is a genotype *and* an environment. That heredity is the dynamic integral of the genotype and the environment—the resultant of the dynamic interaction between the two.

If it is true that the organism inherits a genotype and an environment, and that the resultant of the interaction between the two is heredity, then it follows that it would be possible to influence the heredity of the developing organism by controlling its environment. This we know to be true by virtue of numerous experiments involving plants and nonhuman animals, and we have good evidence that it is also true for man. The question of an earlier day which asked whether heredity was more important than environment or vice versa has been dismissed by some experts as a spurious question. It has been said that heredity and environment are equally important, since both are necessary if the genes are to develop, or rather if the genes are to produce development. Genes always act within the conditioning effects of an environment. Some have gone further and stated that the genotype is more important than the environment, and others have asserted the opposite.

Clearly, the genotype is fundamental in that it is biologically determined as a complex of potentialities with inherent limitations for development. But since those potentialities are always considerably influenced by the environment, the question of importance becomes a relative one, depending upon whether one takes the view that the genotype can be favorably influenced by controlled environmental factors or that it cannot. Since it is through its environment alone that the developing "human" organism can be influenced, it seems clear that it is the most important means through which we can work to secure the optimum development of the genotype in its final expression in what we see, which we call the phenotype. The importance of the genotype is affirmed as potentiality or potentialities, a statement which implies the necessity of emphasizing its complementary, the importance of the developer of those potentialities—the environment.

Genes determine, not characters nor traits, but responses of the developing organism to the environment. Since the expression of the genotype is a function of the environment, it is to a certain extent amenable to human control. The practical significance of this statement cannot be overemphasized for those of us who are interested in understanding, and to some extent controlling, the character and influence of prenatal factors upon the developing fetus and their effects upon the health of infant and child.

INHERITED POTENTIALITIES AND ENVIRONMENTAL INFLUENCES

We may now turn to our three questions and the answers to them. The first two questions are best answered together.

What are the inherited genetic potentialities of the organism, and how are these influenced by internal and external environmental factors during prenatal life?

The inherited genetic potentialities are contained in the genes in the 24 chromosomes transmitted from the mother and in the 24 chromosomes transmitted from the father. Three different observers (Ashley Montagu, 1945; Spuhler, 1948; Evans, 1949), by three different methods, have independently estimated the number of genes in man to be somewhere in the vicinity of 30,000. Genes are autocatalytic, enzymatic, self-duplicating giant protein molecules of great complexity. That is to say, genes are the organic catalysts which accelerate essential chemical reactions, the original builders of the body which they serve to differentiate according to the type of medium and other conditions which surround them in their interactive chemical relations (Muller, 1947). These chemical relations are inherent in the chemical properties of the genes and will be *more or less* broadly realized according to a determinate pattern under all environments. The *more* or the *less* will depend upon the nature of the environment in which the genes find themselves. The important point to understand, however, is that the same genes may be influenced to express themselves differently and to have different end effects as a consequence of the different environments in which they function. It is in this way, we believe, that the different parts of the body come to be developed by essentially the same genes. Furthermore, from fertilization onward small random or accidental changes in the environment of the egg or embryo may be operative and can have a decisive effect upon development. A gene on the verge of expressing itself may be affected by random variations in the constitution of the cell substance (Dahlberg, 1948). Variations in the prenatal environment during the limited period of the action of certain genes may substantially affect their manifestation.

A great many constitutional defects in children are believed to be owing to disturbances during the prenatal development of the organism. The evidence for this is in part derived from experimental studies on nonhuman animals and in part from the factual data for man himself.

Is There a Connection between the Nervous Systems of Mother and Child?

Until recently there has been a widespread belief that the fetus is so well insulated in the womb and so well protected by the placental barrier that it lives a nirvana-like existence completely sufficient unto itself. Some have described this condition as a state of uterine bliss. According to them this uterine state of bliss leaves its mark upon the mind of the organism and, unconsciously recollected in later life, usually in anything but tranquillity, determines the person's search for such a state of bliss. This "Maginot Line" view of uterine existence is no longer in agreement with the facts. Indeed, we begin to perceive that there is more than a modicum of truth in the remark, uttered by Samuel Taylor Coleridge more than a hundred years ago, "Yes, the history of man for the nine months preceding his birth, would, probably, be far more interesting, and contain events of greater moment, than all the threescore and ten years that follow it."

A still widely prevalent belief has it that there is no connection between the nervous systems of mother and fetus. This notion is based on a very narrow conception of the nervous system. It is through the neurohumoral system, the system comprising the interrelated nervous and endocrine systems acting through the fluid medium of the blood (and its oxygen and carbon-dioxide contents), that nervous changes in the mother may affect the fetus. The common endocrine pool of the mother and fetus forms a neurohumoral bond between them. The endocrine systems of mother and fetus complement each other.

All this is not to say that there is anything at all in the old wives' tale of "maternal impressions." The mother's "impressions," her "psychological states" as such, cannot possibly be transmitted to the fetus. What are transmitted are the gross chemical changes which occur in the mother and, so far as we know at the present time, nothing more.

While it is believed that some hormonal molecules are not small enough to pass through the placenta, there is no doubt that many maternal hormones are composed of molecules of small enough size to be able to pass very readily through the placenta (Needham, 1931; Windle, 1940; Flexner, 1947).

Are the Mother's Emotional States Communicated to the Fetus? If So, How? Possible Effects.

The answer to this compound question is: Yes, there is good evidence that the mother's emotional states are, at least in chemical form transmitted to the fetus. The Fels Institute workers at Antioch College, Yellow Springs, Ohio, have found that emotional disturbances in the pregnant mother produce a marked increase in the activity of the fetus. Mothers undergoing periods of severe emotional distress have fetuses which show considerably increased activity. Moreover, the Fels workers have found that mothers having the highest rates for the functioning of that part of the nervous system which is mostly under unconscious control, and is concerned with the regulation of visceral activities, the autonomic nervous system in such measures as skin conductance, resting heart rate, respiration rate, variability of respiration and variability of heart rate under basic conditions, have the most active fetuses. In view of these facts, it has been postulated "that the psychophysiological state of the mother exerts an influence upon the behavior pattern of the normal fetus" (Sontag, 1944, page 152).

The Fels Institute workers have observed that fatigue in the pregnant mother will also produce hyperactivity in the fetus. Supporting these observations, other observers have found that the activity of the fetus is greatest in the evening (Harris and Harris, 1946).

How are the mother's emotional states capable of effecting the fetus?

Through the neurohumoral system, which has already been defined as being composed of the interrelated nervous and endocrine systems acting through the fluid medium of the blood. For example,

stimuli originating in the cerebral cortex (the external gray matter of the brain) may set up reflexes which pass directly into the autonomic nervous system (through the autonomic representation in the cerebral cortex) or are mediated through the feeling-tone center or relay station known as the thalamus to the lower autonomic centers of the hypothalamus, the great coordinating center of the autonomic nervous system situated at the base of the brain. By whatever route such reflexes travel, the autonomic nervous system acts upon the endocrine glands and these pour their secretions into the blood. In the pregnant mother such secretions are known to be capable of passing through the placenta to the fetus, with the possible exception of some of the hormones of the pituitary gland. Stimuli originating in the central nervous system of the mother can therefore indirectly produce changes in the fetus. Acetylcholine, which is a substance given off along the course of a nerve fiber during the passage of a nerve impulse, and adrenaline, the secretion of the glands situated on top of the kidneys, the adrenal glands, are almost certainly two among the many substances involved. But we may well consider this under the heading of the third part of our question: What are the possible effects of the mother's emotional states upon the fetus?

The infants of mothers who were emotionally disturbed during pregnancy frequently exhibit evidences of an irritable and hyperactive autonomic nervous system. The cases observed by Sontag presented disturbances in gastrointestinal motility, tone, and function manifested by excessive regurgitation, dyspepsia, and perhaps diarrhea. In some cases there is increase in heart rate, increased vasomotor irritability (irritability of the blood vessels in terms of construction and dilation), and changes in respiratory pattern. Sontag says:

Irritable or poorly balanced adrenergic-cholinergic systems probably constitute an important part of the rather poorly defined syndrome commonly labeled constitutional inadequacy or nutritional diaphysis. Early feeding difficulties based on motor and sensory abnormalities of the gastrointestinal system are in many instances of automatic origin. The presence of feeding difficulties of a motor or secretory nature from birth must presume their etiology and basic disturbances during intrauterine life. In prenatal development of such a condition, prolonged nervous and emotional disturbances of the mother during the later months of pregnancy seem to be important (Sontag, 1941, page 1001).

The suggestion is that the autonomic nervous system of the fetus becomes sensitized through the hyperactivity of the mother's neurohumoral system.

In connection with hyperirritability and gastrointestinal disturbances, Halliday has recently mentioned:

The clinical impression (which has not yet been subjected to clinical testing) that patients who develop recurring depressive states in adult life frequently provide a history—if this can be obtained and confirmed—showing that the mother was grievously disturbed emotionally during the intrauterine phase of the patient. Similar biographical findings, though to a less spectacular degree, are not uncommon in duodenal ulcer. (Halliday, 1948, pages 91–92).

. . . . .

Sontag (1941) has observed an association between prenatal stimulation of the fetus and postnatal feeding difficulties. The drugs used by the pregnant mother, her nutrition, her endocrine status, emotional life, and activity level may very likely contribute to the shaping of the physical status, the behavior patterns, and the postnatal progress of the child.

The Fels Institute workers have found that if the mother undergoes severe emotional stresses during pregnancy, especially during the latter part of pregnancy, her child will be born as, and develop as, a hyperactive, irritable, squirming infant who cries for his feeding every two or three hours instead of sleeping through the four-hour interval between feedings. The irritability of such infants involves the control of the gastrointestinal tract, causing emptying of the bowel at frequent intervals, as well as regurgitation of food. As Sontag puts it:

He is to all intents and purposes a neurotic infant when he is born—the result of an unsatisfactory fetal environment. In this instance he has not had to wait until childhood for a bad home situation or other cause to make him neurotic. It has been done for him before he has even seen the light of day (Sontag, 1944, pages 1–5).

Greenacre (1945) has suggested that the evidence indicates the possible existence of preanxiety reactions in fetal life without, necessarily, any psychic content. She suggests that traumatic stimuli, such as sudden sounds, vibrations, umbilical-cord entanglements, and the like, may produce a predisposition to anxiety which, whether combined or not with constitutional and traumatizing birth experiences, might be an important determinant in producing the severity of any neurosis.

That the fetus is capable of being conditioned . . . has long been thought to be a possibility. The possibility has now been turned into a certainty. Spelt (1948) has shown that the fetus in utero during the last two months of pregnancy can be taught to respond to the secondary association of a primary original stimulus. . . .

These are important findings, for they indicate that the potentialities for conditioning and probably learning (the ability to increase the strength of any act through training) are already present in the unborn fetus, as well as the possibility of its acquiring certain habits of response while still in the womb.

Other environmental factors which may affect the prenatal development of the organism may be considered under the following eight headings: (I) physical agents, (II) nutritional effects, (III) drugs, (IV) infections, (V) maternal dysfunction; (VI) maternal sensitization, (VII) maternal age, (VIII) maternal parity.

I. PHYSICAL AGENTS | The fetus will respond to sounds originating outside the mother's body at the thirtieth week, when, for example, a doorbell buzzer is held opposite its head (Sontag and Richards, 1938). Under such conditions the fetal responses are of a convulsive nature. The startle reflex is easily elicited. It has been found that very slight tapping upon the amnion at the time of hysterectomy under local anesthesia will result in quick fetal movements at a much earlier period in prenatal life (Windle, 1940, page 189). Tapping indirectly, as upon the side of a bathtub in which a pregnant woman was lying, induced a sudden jump on the part of the fetus thirty-one days before it was born. Orchestral or piano music or the vibration of a washing machine, during the last two months of pregnancy, resulted in marked increase in fetal activity. It is now known that the human fetus *in utero* is capable of being stimulated by, and responding to, a wide range of tones (Bernard and Sontag, 1947).

It is believed that the ability to receive stimuli originating within the organism, the proprioceptive sense, is developed very early in the fetus, and that muscle-joint responses are capable of being produced not only by proprioceptive but also by stimuli originating outside the organism (exteroceptive stimulation) (Windle, 1940, page 186). Differences in pressure *in utero,* whether induced through internal or external forces; differences in position, umbilical-cord entanglements, and similar factors may more or less adversely affect the development of the organism. Deformity may be caused by faulty position, mechanical shaking, temperature changes; asymmetry of the head may be produced by pressure of the head downward upon the thorax; wryneck (torticollis) has been observed, and pressure atrophy of the skin indicates the kind of continuous stimulation to which the fetus may be exposed.

Exposure to massive doses of x-rays within the first two months of pregnancy will, in many cases, produce abortion of the embryo (Goldstein and Wexler, 1931). Where abortion does not follow, serious injury has been found to result in a large percentage of cases. Thus, Murphy (1929) found that in a series of 74 recorded cases of therapeutic maternal irradiation, there were only 36 normal children born; there were 23 imbeciles with heads of abnormal size and 15 offspring otherwise malformed or diseased. In other words, 51.3% of the children were abnormal.

A series of experiences which may seriously affect the fetus is the process of birth itself. The severity of the birth process as measured by length and difficulty of labor, presentation, forceps delivery, primiparity, and similar factors is highly correlated with nutritional disturbances in the infant. A large proportion of such infants develop condensations of bone which show in x-rays of one-month-old infants in the form of fine white striae in the tarsal bones of the foot. Sontag and Harris (1938) conclude that these striae "are the result of disturbances in growth produced by the process of birth itself and influenced by such factors as maternal health and nutrition." They write:

We believe that shock of birth is an important factor and that it is determined by the severity of the birth process plus the physical condition of the infant. We consider the mechanism comparable to that involved when striae are laid down in the long bones of growing children as a result of a surgical procedure or of a severe illness.

Greenacre has already been quoted to the effect that in the process of birth:

where there has been considerable disproportion between an increased sensory stimulation and a limited motor discharge over a period of time such tension may conceivably be incorporated into the working balance of the individual and become temporarily or permanently a characteristic of his makeup.

Greenacre adds:

where this is true, a sudden increase or decrease in the established tension level of the individual contributes to symptoms of anxiety. There is, however, in each individual, a unique primary organization and level of tension that is determined, in some measure, by the birth experience, furnishing an important element in the patterning of the drive and energy distribution of that individual (1945).

It may be that the trauma of birth is not experienced as a trauma by all fetuses; there is good evidence that it is so experienced by some. In these latter cases the experience may, to a more or less important extent, influence the later psychic development of the organism.

Physical agents which may be operative before or at birth to influence the subsequent health of infant and child are such factors as abnormal physical or instrumental delivery. Injury sustained by the fetus by these means may be crippling for life. Apart from purely physical injuries, permanent damage may be done to the mental faculties. In the New York State Schools for Mental Defectives, Malzberg (1950) has calculated that approximately 6% of all first admissions are due to injuries sustained at birth.

II. NUTRITIONAL EFFECTS | From the standpoint of the physical growth and development of the organism, it is known that such environmental factors as are produced by the mother's nutrition and occupation during all stages of pregnancy, her health, general hygiene, and sanitation can affect the development of the fetus (Sanders, 1934; Warkany, 1947). These conditions generally reflect the socioeconomics status or the nutritional status of the mother. Festuses and infants of mothers of low socioeconomic status are smaller and have a higher mortality rate than those of mothers of higher socioeconomic status. In itself small size is not necessarily a handicap, but in many cases it is a symptom of basic organic deficiencies which will play an important role in the later developmental history of the organism. Children who may otherwise appear to be normal will usually exhibit evidences of deficient intrauterine environment in the form of radio-opaque white striae which may be seen in the tarsal bones by the end of the first postnatal month (Sontag and Harris, 1938). These striae, corresponding to the lines of retarded growth seen in the long bones of older children and adults and caused by periods of prolonged illness, indicate that disturbances in nutrition, from whatever cause, during prenatal life are capable of inscribing their effects very substantially upon the structure of the developing organism.

Experiments reported by Warkany (1947) suggest that maternal nutrition in the early stages of fetal growth is a decisive factor in the production of certain physical abnormalities. It is not at present clear how the damage is done, but the evidence strongly indicates that it is owing to a lack of certain vitamins or proteins, or to some complex toxic disturbance occasioned by the mother's state of malnutrition. Recent studies indicate that emotional stress may severely disturb the nutritional economy of the individual (Sieve, 1949). In the pregnant mother malnutrition so induced may seriously affect the development of the fetus.

Murphy (1947) found that the fetuses of pregnant women suffering from renal hypertension and albuminuria showed no more serious defects than fetuses of a random sample of pregnant women. He did, however, find that diets deficient in calcium, phosphorus, and vitamins B, C, and D were common in pregnant women with a high frequency of malformed fetuses. Fetal rickets as a consequence of the depletion of the mineral reserves of starved mothers is a well-known phenomenon. It is also known that vitamin D deficiency during pregnancy predisposes the child to early rickets (M'Gonigle and Kirby, 1936).

Ebbs and his co-workers (1942) and Tisdall (1945) have demonstrated the substantive importance of an adequate maternal diet during pregnancy for the health of the infant and the adult it grows to be—*if* it survives to be an adult. An important point which should be underscored here is that not one of the 120 women in the poor-diet group studied by these investigators showed the slightest sign of any deficiency diseases. As these workers found, and as Burke and his co-workers (1943) found in an independent investigation, when nutrition during pregnancy is inadequate the fetus suffers more than the mother. If the mother's diet is good during pregnancy, then the infant is usually in excellent condition at birth. In Ebbs' Canadian study 120 pregnant women on a poor diet were compared with 90 pregnant women of the same socioeconomic status whose diet had been made good. In every way the mothers and their offspring who were on a good diet did better than the mothers and their offspring who were on a poor diet.

The facts set out in Table 1 are striking. They show that a diet which was inadequate, although good enough not to produce any recognizable clinical conditions in the mother, seriously interfered with the efficiency of the pregnant mother but affected the fetus more than it did her.

These findings were abundantly confirmed by the group of workers at Harvard (Burke *et al.*, 1943). In their study, carried out on 216 mothers and their infants during 1930–1941, they found that every stillborn, every infant dying during the first few days after birth, with one exception (the majority with congenital defects) all prematures, and all functionally immature infants were born to mothers who had had inadequate diets during pregnancy. The effects of maternal malnutrition upon the infant were very evident in babies born in Europe during World War II. Birth weight and length of infant decreased (Smith, 1947); premature births and stillbirths increased (Antonov, 1947), as did cases of severe rickets, severe anemais, and tuberculosis (Heseltine, 1948). Where the food intake was rigidly and scientifically controlled, as in England, the health of children improved. Unfortunately, in other countries food shortages were not so intelligently handled. The fact that well-nourished mothers tend to have well-nourished babies (Beilly and Kurland, 1945), and poorly nourished mothers, poorly nourished babies (Ebbs *et al.*, 1942; Burke *et al.*, 1943), as well as all the evidence known to us, indicates, as Macy (1946) has said, "that the well-being of the child before and after birth is influenced by the nutrition of the mother before and at the time of conception, and by the adequacy of her diet during pregnancy."

On the actual contributory side one can say that not only must great care be taken to see to it that the pregnant mother's diet is an optimum one but also that her meals are properly spaced. The

TABLE 1.

		DIET	
		Poor	*Good*
Prenatal maternal record	*Poor-Bad*	36.0%	9.0%
Condition during labor	*Poor-Bad*	24.0%	3.0%
Duration of the first stage of labor	*Primapara*	20.3 hours	11.1 hours
	Multipara	15.2 hours	9.5 hours
Convalescence	*Poor-Bad*	11.5%	3.5%
Record of babies during first two weeks	*Poor-Bad*	14.0%	0.0%
Illness of Babies during First Six Months			
Frequent colds		21.0%	4.7%
Bronchitis		4.2%	1.5%
Pneumonia		5.5%	1.5%
Rickets		5.5%	0.0%
Tetany		4.2%	0.0%
Dystrophy		7.0%	1.5%
Anemia		25.0%	9.4%
Deaths		3.0%	0.0%
Miscarriages and Infant Deaths			
Miscarriages		7.0%	0.0%
Stillbirths		4.0%	0.0%
Deaths:			
Pneumonia		2.0%	0.0%
Prematurity		1.0%	0.0%
Prematures		9.0%	2.0%

evidence (Tompkins, 1948) indicates that six small meals rather than two or three large ones daily tend to reduce or eliminate the severe nausea and vomiting of early pregnancy and to eliminate fatigue and other untoward symptoms.

We may conclude this section on nutrition with the words of a distinguished student of the subject, H. D. Kruse (1950), to the effect that many environmental factors, inside as well as outside the body, exert influences upon nutrition which in turn reflect in health and welfare. In this relationship nutrition is seen to signalize the influence of environment on health and welfare and to occupy a key and paramount position as the crucial medium between them.

In connection with the nutrition of the fetus, it should be added here that the fetus swallows amniotic fluid at least as early as the fifth month, and though its nutritional value may under ordinary circumstances be slight, significant changes in its composition may affect the fetus. By artificially sweetening the amniotic fluid, it has been possible to induce the fetus to swallow more actively, thus reducing the girth and other unpleasant symptoms of polyhydramnios (excessive amniotic fluid) in the pregnant mother (De Snoo, 1937). Saccharine was subsequently demonstrated in the umbilical vein blood and in the first urine of these infants. Methylene blue injected with the saccharine appeared in the urine of the hydramniotic mothers, at times coinciding with increased fetal activity. It was concluded that the fetus spends most of its time in sleep and that, becoming wakeful, it begins to move and drink the sweet amniotic fluid.

Swallowing and gastrointestinal activity in the fetus have been demonstrated by many other means (Windle, 1940, page 101). The whole gastrointestinal system appears to be prepared and ready to function quite early in fetal life. That the fetal gastrointestinal tract may be seriously disturbed as a result of severe emotional distress experienced by the pregnant mother has already been noted. There may be other conditions which may produce similar effects, but this in an area of fetal physiology concerning which we know very little.

III. DRUGS | Drugs taken by the pregnant mother may seriously affect the fetus. Many cases of congenital deafness have been traced to the mother's use of quinine for malaria during pregnancy. Morphinism has been reported in the infants of mothers who were morphine addicts. Inhalation of amyl nitrite by the mother for a few seconds induced an increase in fetal heart rate, beginning during the third minute following the mother's inhalation. Subsequent inhalations produced a diphasic (excitor-depressor) response (Rech, 1931, 1933; Sontag and Richards, 1938).

The obstetrical practice of dosing the pregnant mother with barbiturates and similar drugs prior to delivery may so overload the fetal blood stream as to produce asphyxiation in the fetus at birth, with either permanent brain damage or subtle damage of such a kind as to lead to mental impairment. Fortunately, the trend today is away from heavy sedation.

It is known that a barbiturate derivative such as "sodium seconal," usually prescribed as a sedative, when given to the pregnant mother will pass into the blood stream of the fetus and cause a cortical electrical depression in its brain

waves which can be measured at, and persists for some time after, birth (Hughes et al., 1948).

. . . . .

Is there any evidence that the pregnant mother's smoking affects the fetus? There is. It has been found that the smoking of one cigarette generally produced an increase in the heart rate, sometimes a decrease in the heart rate. The maximum individual increase in fetal heart beats per minute was 39.6, the greatest drop 16.8 (Sontag and Wallace, 1935; Sontag and Richards, 1938). The maximum effect is observed between the eighth and twelfth minutes after the cigarette, and the cardiovascular response is more marked after the eighth month. It is quite possible that the products of tobacco may adversely affect not only the heart of the fetus but its whole cardiovascular system, not to mention the possibility of many other organs. This is a subject upon which we need more research. At the present time we have no definite evidence that the mother's intake of tobacco smoke actually harms the fetus. This is a question which further research alone can settle.

IV. INFECTIONS | Some virus and bacterial diseases can be transmitted from pregnant mother to fetus, with considerable damage to the latter. Rubella (German measles) is an example of a virus disease which, contracted by the mother in early pregnancy, may produce cataract and deafness with mental defect (Gregg, 1941).

Swan (1948) has shown that if the mother contracts rubella during the first four months of pregnancy she has a three to one chance of giving birth to a congenitally defective child. Equine encephalomyelitis, fortunately very rare, is another virus disease which can cause changes in the fetus which produce idiocy. Smallpox, chickenpox, measles, mumps, scarlet fever, erysipelas, and recurrent fever have long been known to be transmissible from mother to fetus (Goodpasture, 1942). There is also good experimental evidence indicating that the virus of *influenza A* can produce serious deformities in the developing embryo (Hamburger and Habel, 1947). The bacterium of congenital syphilis, *Treponema pallidum,* can actually enter the embryo. If this happens, miscarriage occurs (Dippel, 1945). If the bacterium enters at a later fetal age, the child is born with signs of congenital syphilis, or the disease may not show itself till later, as congenital paresis. Tuberculosis is also transmissible to the fetus from the mother by means of the *Bacillum tuberculosis.* The fetal death rate from tuberculosis is high, while those infants who are born with the disease usually die within the first year (Elizalde and Latienda, 1943). Malarial parasites are known to be transmissible from mother to fetus. Protozoal parasites, such as *Toxoplasma,* can be transmitted from mother to fetus and produce such conditions as meningoencephalomyelitis, microphthalmos, bilateral choreoretinitis, hydrocephalus, microcephalus, convulsions, and idiocy or mental retardation. Malignant melanoma has been transmitted by mother to fetus (Holland, 1949). Retrolental fibroplasia (Terry, 1943, 1945), or, as it is sometimes called, congenital encephalo-ophthalmic dysplasia (Krause, 1946; Ingalls, 1948; Owens and Owens, 1949), is a condition in which the fetus usually prematurely born, exhibits a retrolental mass, often with secondary glaucoma and cataract, and recurrent retinal and vitreous hemorrhages. Microphthalmos and strabismus is common. The cause is unknown, but the condition probably develops as a result of changes during the sixth and seventh months of pregnancy. These changes are almost certainly due to maternal environmental conditions. Unfortunately, what the precise nature of these may be is at present unknown.

V. MATERNAL DYSFUNCTION | By maternal dysfunction is meant noninfectious functional disease in the pregnant mother. Such disorders in the mother may seriously affect the development of the fetus. Pregnant women suffering from hypertensive disease (high blood pressure) show a very high rate both of fetal loss and of maternal mortality, as well as of other serious conditions. Chesley and Annetto (1947) have reported that in 301 pregnancies in 218 women with essential hypertension (disease due to no known cause), the gross fetal loss in the first hypertensive pregnancy reached the staggeringly high figure of 38% and increased with the increase in blood pressure. There were thirteen maternal deaths, or a total of 4.3%, some 200 times higher than occurs in general obstetrical practice. Gasper (1945) found that out of 49 deliveries in 45 pregnant diabetics there were 19 stillbirths and 6 neonatal deaths, in other words a fetal mortality rate of 51%!

VI. MATERNAL SENSITIZATION | Instances in which the genotype of the mother and fetus differ in the substances borne on the surfaces of the red blood corpuscles, the mother may become sensitized and produce antibodies inimical to fetal development. This usually results in causing anemia at a relatively late fetal age. The Rh incompatibilites constitute a well-known example of this. When the blood of the rhesus monkey is injected into rabbits or guinea pigs, a special serum is obtained. The serum will "clump" the blood of about 85% of all white persons. The factor in the blood which makes it clump in response to the serum is the Rh factor. Persons who have this type of blood are said to be Rh positive. Persons who do not are Rh negative. The exact way in which the Rh factor is inherited is extremely complicated. Three distinct Rh factors are known, and at least six major genes are involved. These result in twenty-one combinations of genotypes which produce eight Rh blood types.

Understanding how the Rh factor operates and how it is inherited is extremely important in biology and medicine. And the practical implications for human health are great.

When a woman who is Rh negative marries a man who is Rh positive, the first-born child of such a marriage is usually normal. However, during following pregnancies the fetus may be lost by miscarriage. Or it may be born in such an anemic and jaundiced state that it lives only a few hours after birth. The infant usually dies from a disease called erythroblastosis. The name means that the red blood corpuscles—the erythrocytes—have been subject to wholesale destruction.

The disease is caused by the fact that the fetus has inherited an Rh positive gene from its father. The fetus produces Rh positive substances called antigens in its blood. These substances pass through the placenta into the mother's blood, where the antigens stimulate the production of large numbers of antibodies. These antibodies in turn pass through the placenta into the blood system of the fetus. There they start destroying the red blood corpuscles of the fetus.

Fortunately this disease does not occur as often as the facts of heredity might lead us to expect. Erythroblastosis takes place in about one out of every two hundred pregnancies. Actually, about one in twelve pregnancies involve an Rh negative mother carrying an Rh positive fetus. Therefore, in theory we should have children suffering from erythroblastosis born in one out of twelve instead of one out of two hundred pregnancies. If we omit firstborn children—who are seldom affected—this figure would work out to one in seventeen or eighteen pregnancies.

This fortunate discrepancy may be caused by the fact that in many cases the antigens from the fetus may not pass through the placenta. In other cases some mothers may not respond to the actions of the antigens from the fetus. And there is also a possibility that the chemical incompatibility between the blood of the mother and that of the unborn child may result in other harmful effects than the ones commonly expected.

Recent research indicates that mental deficiency may be caused by a lack of oxygen in the developing brain. Such an oxygen lack could result from the destruction of the oxygen-carrying red blood corpuscles in the absence of the Rh factor. Thus, if the brain of the fetus is deprived of oxygen during an important stage of its development, the brain may be permanently damaged. This may partly explain how mentally deficient children sometimes occur in families in which there is no previous record of mental deficiency.

Understanding the importance of the Rh factor is of great practical importance. Every woman planning marriage should consult her physician to find out the Rh types both of herself and of her prospective husband. There are various ways in which the evil effects of clashing Rh factors may be partially averted if doctors know about them beforehand.

Endocrine disturbances in the mother may affect the development of the fetus in many ways, but our knowledge of this subject is at present very meager. It is known that in diabetic mothers the fetus grows very rapidly, owing possibly to her excessive pituitary secretion. The fetus may reach the average birth weight of the newborn long before it reaches term, and thus present considerable obstetrical difficulty. It is of interest to note that the birth weights of babies whose mothers subsequently develop diabetes are greater than the average normal birth weight (Barns and Morgans, 1948). It is quite possible that a certain proportion of such mothers are supported relatively free of diabetes during pregnancy by the insulin secretion of the fetus. It has already been noted that the mortality rates of fetuses and infants of diabetic mothers are extremely high (Gaspar, 1945).

VII. MATERNAL AGE | There is a high correlation between age of mother and maldevelopment of the fetus. The cause of this is obscure. Half the known cases of Mongolism were born to mothers of thirty-eight years of age or more (Penrose, 1949; Malzberg, 1950). Congenital hydrocephalus is also significantly correlated with late maternal age. Indeed, statistically speaking abnormal conditions appear with significantly higher frequency in the infant of the older .mother (Kuder and Johnson, 1944) than in any other group. The incidence of two-egg twinning also increases with maternal age. The evidence is now fairly complete that infant and maternal mortality rates, prematurity, stillbirths, and miscarriage rates are highly correlated with age of mother (Montagu, 1946). The optimum period for childbearing seems to lie between the years of twenty-three and twenty-nine. Before twenty-three years of age, on the average, the younger the mother—and after twenty-nine years of age, the older the mother—the higher are the maternal and infant mortality rates. In the younger mothers the responsible factor appears to be inadequate development of the reproductive system. In the older mothers the progressive decline in the functions of that system is almost certainly responsible. Since these functions are largely endocrine in nature, it is likely that in some cases the fetus is adversely affected developmentally.

VIII. PARITY (number of previous pregnancies of mother) | There is evidence that first-born children, as well as those born at the end of a long series of pregnancies, are less viable than those born in between, irrespective of maternal age. Fetal malformations are slightly more common in the children of mothers having their first pregnancies (primiparae) than in those of the second and third. It is known that disturbances due to sensitization become more marked with increasing age of the mother, but the reason for this is at present unknown.

It should be remembered that these are statistical findings, and that there are plenty of first-born and last-born children, as well as children who were born well after their mother's thirty-eighth birthday, who are in every way perfectly healthy. . . .

The question has been asked whether some children from birth are more likely than others to find the achievement of healthy personality development difficult. Some of the facts already mentioned in the preceding pages should make it quite clear that the answer to this question is in the affirmative.

Excluding physical malformations from our discussion in the present connection, the indications are that a child which as a fetus was traumatized by such factors as have already been discussed is likely to find the achievement of healthy personality development more difficult, other things being equal, than a child who as a fetus was not so traumatized. Some children, as Sontag has pointed out, are born "neurotic" as a result of their intrauterine experiences.

The "neurotic" newborn is generally hyperactive, irritable, restless, squirming, a crier, and a feeding problem. It is interesting to note that in those cases in which the evidence for the birth trauma is strong, as in children who have had to be instrumentally delivered, some 50% of such children at school age exhibited general hyperactivity in the form of ir-ritability, restlessness, and distractibility, as compared to only 25% who showed such hyperactivity but were spontan-eously born (Wile and Davis, 1941). Also significant in this connection is the "prematurity syndrome" exhibited by prematurely born children. In the nursery age group prematurely born children exhibit a significantly higher sensory acuity than term children, and in com-parison are somewhat retarded in lingual and manual motor control, and in pos-tural and locomotor control. Control of bowel and bladder sphincters is achieved later and with difficulty; the attention span is short, such children being highly emotional, jumpy, anxious, and usually shy (Shirley, 1939; Hirschl *et al.*, 1948). Furthermore, prematurely born children show a significantly higher incidence of nasopharyngeal and respiratory infec-tions, especially during the first year. Be-havior disorders, especially with regard to feeding, are more frequent in prema-ture infants (Drillien, 1947, 1948).

REFERENCES

ANTONOV, A. N., "Children Born During the Siege of Leningrad in 1942," *J. Pediat.*, 50, 250–259 (1947).

BARNS, H. H. F., AND MORGANS, M. E., "Pre-diabetic Pregnancy," *J. Obst. & Gynec. Brit. Emp.*, 55, 449–454 (1948).

BEILLY, J. S., AND KURLAND, I. I., "Relation-ship of Maternal Weight Gain and Weight of Newborn Infant," *Am. J. Obst. & Gynec.*, 50, 202–206 (1945).

BERNARD, J., AND SONTAG, L. W., "Fetal Reactivity to Fetal Stimulation: A Preliminary Report," *J. Genet. Psychol.*, 70, 205–210 (1947).

BRYANT, E. R., "Heredity and Length of Gestation," *J. Hered.*, 24, 339 (1943).

BURKE, B. S., BEAL, V. A., KIRKWOOD, S. B., AND STUART, H. C., "Nutrition Studies During Pregnancy," *Am. J. Obst. & Gynec.*, 46, 38–52 (1943).

CHESLEY, L. C., AND ANNETTO, J. E., "Preg-nancy in the Patient with Hypertensive Dis-ease," *Am. J. Obst. & Gynec.*, 53, 372–381 (1947).

DAHLBERG, C., "Environment, Inheritance and Random Variation with Special Reference to Investigations on Twins," *Acta Genetica et Statistica Medica*, 1, 104–114 (1948).

DE SNOO, K., "Das Trinkende Kind im Uterus," *Monatschrift fur Geburtshulfe und Gynekologie*, 105, 88–97 (1937).

DIPPEL, A. L., "The Relationship of Con-genital Syphilis to Abortion and Miscarriage, and the Mechanism of Intrauterine Protec-tion," *Am. J. Obst. & Gynec.*, 47, 369–379 (1945).

DRILLIEN, M. C., "Studies in Prematurity, Stillbirth and Neonatal Death, Factors Affect-ing Birth-Weight and Outcome; Delivery and Its Hazards," *J. Obst. & Gynaec. Brit. Emp.*, 54, 300–323, 443–468 (1947).

DRILLIEN, M. C., "Studies in Prematurity; Development and Progress of Prematurely Born Child in Pre-School Period," *Arch. Dis. Childhood*, 23, 69–83 (1948).

EBBS, J. H. BROWN, A., TISDALL, F. F. MOYLE, W. J., AND BELL, M., "The Influence of Improved Prenatal Nutrition upon the In-fant," *Canad. M.A.J.*, 46, 6–8 (1942).

EBBS, J. H., TISDALL, F. F., AND SCOTT, W. A., "The Influence of Prenatal Diet on the Mother and Child," *The Milbank Memorial Fund Quarterly*, 20, 35–36 (1942).

ELIZALDE, P. I., AND I. LATIENDA Y RAMAN, "Tuberculosis Prenatal," *Arch. Soc. argent. anat. Norm. y. Pat.*, 5, 576–596 (1943).

EVANS, R. D., "Quantitative Inferences Con-cerning the Genetic Effects of Radiation on Human Beings," *Science*, 109, 299–304 (1949).

GASPAR, J. L., "Diabetes Mellitus and Preg-nancy," *West. J. Surg.*, 53, 21 (1945).

GATES, R. R., *Human Genetics* (New York: Macmillan, 1946), 2 vols.

GOLDSTEIN, I., AND WEXLER, D., "Rosette Formation in the Eyes of Irradiated Human Embryos," *Arch. Ophth.*, 5, 591 (1931).

GOODPASTURE, E. W., "Virus Infection of the Mammalian Fetus," *Science*, 99, 391–396 (1942).

GREENACRE, P., "The Biological Economy of Birth," *The Psychoanalytic Study of the Child*, ed. O. Fenichel *et al.* (New York: In-ternational Universities Press), 1, 31–51 (1945).

GREGG, N. MC A., "Congenital Cataract Following German Measles," *Tr. Ophth. Soc. Australia*, 3, 35 (1941).

HALLIDAY, J. L., *Psychosocial Medicine* (New York: W. W. Norton, 1948).

HAMBURGER, V., AND HABEL, K., "Teratogenic and Lethal Effects of Influenza-A and Mumps Viruses on Early Chick Embryos," *Proc. Soc. Exper. Biol. & Med.*, 66, 608 (1947).

HARRIS, D. B., AND HARRIS, E. S., "A Study of Fetal Movements in Relation to Mother's Activity," *Human Biol.*, 18, 221–237 (1946).

HESELTINE, M., "The Health and Welfare of the World's Children," *J. Am. Dietet, A.*, 24, 91–95 (1948).

HIRSCHL, D., LEVY, H., AND LITVAK, A. M., "The Physical and Mental Development of Premature Infants: A Statistical Survey with Five-Year Follow-up," *Arch. Pediat.*, 65, 648–653 (1948).

HOLLAND, E., "A Case of Transplacental Metastasis of Malignant Melanoma from Mother to Foetus," *J. Obst. & Gynaec. Brit. Emp.*, 56, 529 (1949).

HUGHES, J. G., EHMANN, B., AND BROWN, U. A., "Electroencephalography of the Newborn," *Am. J. Dis. Child*, 76, 626–633 (1948).

INGALLS, T. H., "Congenital Encephalo-ophthalmic Dysplasia; Epidemiologic Implications," *Pediatrics*, 1, 315 (1948).

KRAUSE, A. C., "Congenital Encephalo-ophthalmic Dysplasia," *Arch. Ophth.*, 36, 387–444 (1946).

KRUSE, H. D., "Malnutrition: Its Nature, Cause, and Significance," *Biological Foundation of Health Education* (New York: Columbia University Press, 1950), pp. 10–31.

KUDER, K., AND JOHNSON, D. G., "The Elderly Primipara," *Am. J. Obst. & Gynec.*, 47, 794–807 (1944).

MACY, I. G., *The Science of Nutrition* (New York: Nutrition Foundation, 1946).

M'GONIGLE, G. C. M., AND KIRBY, J., *Poverty and Public Health* (London: Gollancz, 1936).

MALZBERG, B., "Some Statistical Aspects of Mongolism," *Am. J. Ment. Deficiency*, 54, 266–281 (1950).

MONTAGU, M. F. ASHLEY, *Adolescent Sterility* (Springfield, Ill.: C. C. Thomas, 1945).

MULLER, H. J., "Genetic Fundamentals: The Work of the Genes," *Genetics, Medicine and Man* (Ithaca, N.Y.: Cornell University Press, 1947), p. 16.

MURPHY, D. P., "The Outcome of 625 Pregnancies in Women Subjected to Pelvic Radium Roentgen Irradiation," *Am. J. Obst. & Gynec.*, 18, 179–187 (1929).

MURPHY, D. P., *Congenital Malformation*, 2nd. ed. (Philadelphia: University of Pennsylvania Press, 1947).

OWENS, W. C., AND OWENS, E. H., "Retrolental Fibroplasia in Premature Infants," (1) *Am. J. Ophth.*, 32, 1–21 (1949); (2) *ibid.*, 1631–1637.

PENROSE, L. S., *The Biology of Mental Defect* (London: Sidgwick & Jackson, 1949).

RECH, W., "Untersuchungen uber die Herstatigkeit des Fetus," *Archiv. fur Gynakologie*, Teil I, 145, 714–737 (1931); Teil II, 147, 8–94 (1931); Teil III, 54, 47–57 (1933).

SANDERS, B. S., *Environment and Growth* (Baltimore: Warwick & York, 1934).

SHIRLEY, M., "A Behavior Syndrome Characterizing Prematurely-Born Children," *Child Development*, 10, 115–128 (1939).

SIEVE, B. F., "Vitamins and Hormones in Nutrition. V: Emotional Upset and Trauma," *Am. J. Digest. Dis.*, 16, 14–25 (1949).

SMITH, G. A., "Effects of Maternal Undernutrition upon the Newborn Infant in Holland (1944–45)," *J. Pediat.*, 30, 229–243 (1947).

SONTAG, L. W., AND WALLACE, R. F., "The Effect of Cigarette Smoking During Pregnancy upon the Fetal Heart Rate," *Am. J. Obst. & Gynec.*, 29, 3–8 (1935).

SONTAG, L. W., AND HARRIS, L. M., "Evidence of Disturbed Prenatal and Neonatal Growth in Bones of Infants Aged One Month," *Am. J. Dis. Child.*, 56, 1248–1255 (1938).

SONTAG, L. W., AND RICHARDS, T. W., "Studies in Fetal Behavior," *Monographs of the Society for Research in Child Development*, 3, x–72 (1938).

SONTAG, L. W., "The Significance of Fetal Environmental Differences," *Am. J. Obst. & Gynec.*, 42, 996–1003 (1941).

SONTAG, L. W., "Differences in Modifiability of Fetal Behavior and Physiology," *Psychosomatic Medicine*, 6, 151–154 (1944).

SONTAG, L. W., "War and the Fetal Maternal Relationship," *Marriage and Family Living*, 6, 1–5 (1944).

SPUHLER, J. N., "On the Number of Genes in Man," *Science*, 10, 279–280 (1948).

SWAN, C., "Rubella in Pregnancy as an Aetiological Factor in Congenital Malformation, Stillbirth, Miscarriage and Abortion," *J. Obst. & Gynaec. Brit. Emp.*, 56, 341–363, 591–605 (1949).

TERRY, T. L., "Fibroplastic Overgrowth of Persistent Tunica Vasculosa Lentis in Premature Infants; Etiologic Factors," *Arch. Ophth.*, 29, 36–38 (1943).

TERRY, T. L., "Retrolental Fibroplasia in Premature Infants; Further Studies in Fibroplastic Overgrowth of Persistent Tunica Vasculosa Lentis," *Arch. Ophth.*, 33, 203–208 (1945).

TISDALL, F. F., "The Role of Nutrition in Preventive Medicine," *The Milbank Memorial Fund Quarterly*, 23, 1–15 (1945).

TOMPKINS, W. T., "The Clinical Significance of Nutritional Deficiencies in Pregnancy," *Bull. New York Acad. Med.*, 24, 376–388 (1948).

WARKANY, J., "Etiology of Congenital Malformations," *Advances in Pediatrics* (New York: Interscience Publishers, 1947), 2, 1.

WILE, I. S., AND DAVIS, R., "The Relation of Birth to Behavior," *Am. J. Orthopsychiat.*, 11, 320–324 (1941).

WINDLE, W. F., *Physiology of the Fetus* (Philadelphia: Saunders, 1940).

20 | WHAT ARE SOME OF THE LAWS WHICH GOVERN GROWTH?

MARIAN E. BRECKENRIDGE AND E. LEE VINCENT

The child is not a miniature adult. His brain and optic nerve are not developed. He cannot see as well as an adult, and his muscular development and bone growth are not complete. Regardless of how much training and practice he gets, the average three-year-old cannot read or write, ride a bicycle or swim, do arithmetic, whip up a soufflé, or play the violin. It goes without saying that it may be damaging to the child to expect behavior at a particular age level which he is not physically or intellectually able to perform. Conversely, it may be damaging to discourage learning when a child is "ready" for it.

Experiments have shown that children specially trained much earlier than usual in such skills as walking, climbing stairs, reading, and writing master these skills at about the same age as ordinary children. For example, since most children are physically and psychologically mature enough to learn to read at the age of six, the average child of four who gets special reading lessons will take two years to learn to read, while a six-year-old will learn in a few weeks.

Breckenridge and Vincent present here some laws which govern human growth and development—laws which control the "readiness" for learning social and intellectual skills.

GROWTH IS BOTH QUANTITATIVE AND QUALITATIVE

"Growth" includes two aspects of change. They are not interchangeable but, nev-

Reprinted from *Child Development* (W. B. Saunders Company, 1955), pp. 5–16, by permission of the authors and publisher.

ertheless, are inseparable. It is said that a child "grows" and "grows up." He "grows" in size; he "grows up" or matures in structure and function. In maturing he passes through successive changes, which indicate his progress. These indicators are called maturity indicators. Ultimately, as he has passed through each successive stage of growth he reaches the end point of this process, which is called maturity.

There are many illustrations of this maturing or "growing up" process which accompanies growth in size. The baby's digestive tract, for example, not only grows in size, but also changes in structure. This permits digestion of more complex foods and increases its efficiency in converting foods into simpler forms which the body can use. The child, therefore, can widen his experiences with foods as he grows, and this will in turn contribute to his physical well-being and his social development. The structure and functional efficiency of many of the internal organs change with development.

Younger children are not only smaller than older ones; they are also simpler organisms, both physically and psychologically. The young baby, for example, learns motor controls over his larger muscles first. Only gradually can he master such fine coordinations as are required for reading and writing. Reasoning too, in children of preschool age is, of necessity, relatively simple and uncomplicated. Only later, when his nervous system has developed more complex organization and when accumulated experience exists as a basis, can the child attempt more complex forms of reasoning.

Emotions are simpler, the younger the child. Babies feel things "with all of themselves," being completely joyous or completely miserable about rather simple things. Differentiation of structure and accumulation of experience produce more and more complex emotional reactions to more and more complicated situations. If we permit children to go on expressing "full-blast" emotions about simple, babyish things instead of growing into greater controls and more "civilized" responses to more "grown up" situations, we are not helping them to live up to their growth potentialities.

Some people, failing to understand this double aspect of growth, do not realize that children's intellectual capacity and character traits are essentially different from those of adults. We cannot without disaster expect the motor skills, intellectual complexities or character insights from children that we expect from adults, or from younger children that we expect from older children. They have simply not "grown up," any more than they have "grown."

These aspects of "growing up" are discussed later under the effect of maturation upon learning. We have many experiments to prove that children cannot learn what they are not ready through growth or maturity to learn.

GROWTH IS A CONTINUOUS AND ORDERLY PROCESS

Growth is a continuous process which moves with an urgency supplied from deep inner sources. We may well ask how the relatively helpless, unskilled, uncontrolled infant finally reaches a level of maturity at which he can meet the tests of life just discussed. The answer is that he does it by an orderly sequence of acquisitions. He will grow because of a strong impulse to grow which is inherent in the organism; and his growth will be orderly—the product of his innate gifts of inheritance, enhanced or modified by his experience.

This should comfort us, since we realize that we do not need to make him grow. He will do that anyway. Only severe neglect or abuse will seriously disrupt his growth. Because growth is continuous we must realize that what happens at one stage carries over into and influences the next and ensuing stages.

Even the seemingly sudden spurts in tempo of growth lead into and grow out of quieter, less dramatic periods. It may be possible that in the quieter periods the child is mobilizing his forces for ensuing spurts. Parents rightly celebrate the appearance of baby's first tooth, the first independent step in walking, or the first word spoken, the first evidence of reading ability, or the first "date" with a girl (or boy) in adolescence. Each of these noticeable changes is a sort of graduation from the school of preliminary developments. The first step in walking cannot be taken until a long chain of learnings in bodily control has preceded. This is also true of the first word spoken, the first evidence of successful adjustment to other children, or any other conspicuous event in growth. Each of them is a milestone which marks progress in a long process.

Fortunately for students of child development these milestones appear in an orderly sequence. It is not difficult to chart the steps by which growth takes place or to describe the patterns which it follows. No child, for example, learns to walk without having first learned to stand, nor does any child speak clearly before he has passed through the babble stage of syllables in language. As Gesell[1] so delightfully puts it: Each child "sits before he stands; he babbles before he talks; he fabricates before he tells the truth; he draws a circle before he draws a square; he is selfish before he is altruistic; he is dependent on others before he achieves dependence on self." For the great mass of children, these patterns or stages of learning follow each other in so fixed a sequence, and parallel certain birthdays so consistently that standards of what to expect at each age have been set up.

THE TEMPO OF GROWTH IS NOT EVEN

These sequences of development do not move along in time at a steady pace.

[1] A. L. Gesell and F. Ilg, *The Child from Five to Ten* (Harper Bros., 1943).

Maturity indicators do not appear at regular intervals. There are periods of accelerated growth and periods of decelerated growth. During infancy and the early preschool years growth moves swiftly and the maturity indicators of each of the various aspects of growth appear in rapid succession. During the later preschool and school years the rate of growth slackens. But this does not mean that significant changes are not taking place. Before puberty certain phases of growth become accelerated before they taper off to the adult level. Figure 1 illustrates the change in tempo of growth. It shows the growth profiles of height for a boy and demonstrates the rapid growth in infancy, the slower growth during the preschool and school years before pubescence, and the pubescent acceleration followed by the tapering off of growth during adolescence. Profile A shows the general trend of his growth; Profile B shows his growth rate during successive periods. This pattern, with the exception of the pubescent spurt, would be as evident in typical intelligence growth curves.

DIFFERENT ASPECTS OF GROWTH DEVELOP AT DIFFERENT RATES

Not all aspects of growth develop at the same rate at the same time; that is, they do not proceed along an even front. For example, parents often worry because children characteristically speak three to five words at twelve months of age, but in the next three or four months they seldom acquire new words and often even forget the ones they knew. Language growth slows up for the time being because the child's physical energy and enthusiasm for learning are thoroughly occupied with the thrills of upright locomotion. Development in general bodily skill spurts ahead at this time, apparently leaving little growth energy (if we may use such a phrase) for

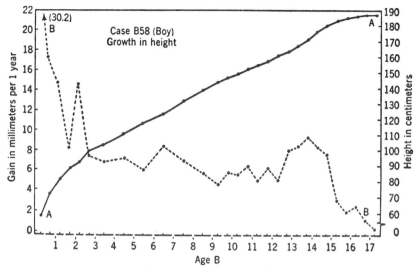

Figure 1. Growth in height of a boy, expressed in Profile A as height at successive chronologic years and in Profile B as growth rate during successive periods, illustrates the changes in tempo of growth. From H. R. Stolz and L. M. Stolz, *Somatic Development of Adolescent Boys* (New York: The Macmillan Company, 1951).

language development. Similarly, school work sometimes suffers a slump while children's growth energy is being expended on the rapid increase in height and weight characteristic of pubescence. It is important to know which aspects of growth can be expected to absorb much of the child's capacity for growth at any given time of his life. We do not now in our public schools, for example, make provisions for the fact that physical development proceeds rapidly during pubescence. Academic loads are stepped up rather than reduced in junior and senior high school, extracurricular activities, home work, and rapidly increasing social interests frequently replace the extra hours of sleep which rapid physical growth requires. It is slight wonder that we have in this country so high a tuberculosis rate among adolescent children.

Figure 2 shows how some of the different parts of the body develop at different rates at given ages. We have no comparable charts to show tempo of growth in intellect and character. We can see that the nervous system develops rapidly in earlier years. This parallels rapid acquisition of control over the body, and rapid expansion of intellectual capacities. Children probably learn more new things in the first five years of life than in any comparable period during the rest of their lives. On the other hand, we can see that the most rapid development of the genital system occurs during pubescence. Certain definite social interests and emotional capacities increase concurrently or soon afterward.

BOTH RATE AND PATTERN OF GROWTH CAN BE MODIFIED BY CONDITIONS WITHIN AND WITHOUT THE BODY

Although the impulse to grow is strong through innate force and even though patterns are fairly definite for all children, both rate and exact pattern can be changed when the child's environment is not fulfilling the fundamental needs of the child. Nutrition, activity, rest, psychologic challenge, opportunity to learn, se-

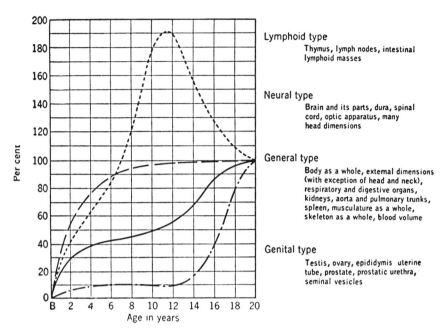

Figure 2. A graph showing the major types of postnatal growth of the various parts and organs of the body. The several curves are drawn to a common scale by computing their values at successive ages in terms of their total postnatal increments (to twenty years). From R. E. Scammon and J. A. Harris, The Measurement of Man (Minneapolis: University of Minnesota Press, 1930).

curity in affection, an adequate and understanding discipline and many other circumstances are of great importance in determining how fast and to what extent the potentialities of the child will be realized.

Around the world there are children who have been so poorly fed during their growing years that they have been unable to achieve healthy growth. Psychologic deprivations are also producing damaged personalities. Physical and psychologic scars incurred by conditions during World War II, such as lack of food, separation of families, loss of parents, destruction of home and communities, have in many cases become permanent when the deprivations were very severe and of long duration. The resilience of the growing mind and body has its limitations if environmental conditions prove to be too unfavorable for growth. In ad-

dition to such conditions as those resulting from war or other crises there are also dramatic evidences of modification in the changes in growth produced by such things as lack of iodine in community drinking water, which results in an increase of cretinism (dwarfism due to inadequate thyroid secretion) in the population concerned. The disease called rickets, which results from deficiency in diet or sunshine or both, may leave permanent evidences on the body in the form of flat chests or deformed pelves, and crooked backs, all of which interfere with the efficient functioning of the body. Similarly, deficiencies in affection and security in childhood may leave permanent scars on the personality in the form of explosive tempers, "grudges," fears, and other severe handicaps to the adequate functioning of personality. Poor methods of teaching reading or other primary school subjects may leave a child with a resistance to all academic work.

On the other hand, if a child's inheritance is good, and if he has adequate diet, security in love, good teaching and other favorable circumstances he will flourish in his growth, and will develop in excellent health, with a keen intellect and a well-balanced and likable personality. We cannot, however, set up "ideal" environments, even if we wished to do so. Human nature has its weaknesses; germs exist in abundance; accidents will happen. Fortunately, the body and the personality have great resiliency. They can make up for temporary retardations, provided the disturbing factors are removed in time or the accidental damage is not too devastating. We must, in fact, consciously avoid an attempt to set up a too protected environment, since if the child is reared in early years in an aseptic (germ free) atmosphere he develops no immunity to life's ordinary germs; if he is protected and coddled too much he becomes what is known as a spoiled child; if he struggles for nothing he gains no moral strength.

EACH CHILD GROWS
IN HIS OWN UNIQUE WAY

Some children are tall and some short, some slender, others stocky. Some are physically strong, others are weak; some are intellectually keen, others are dull.

There are the energetic and the phlegmatic, the agile and the awkward, the courageous and the fearful, the outgoing and the ingoing in personality. Almost every trait measured by any scale scatters individuals along a distribution known as "the normal probability curve," or "the range of normal probability." Figures 3 and 4 show the idea of normal distribution of traits. We can see from this that there is a midpoint, or theoretical average. It is quite possible that no given person in any group would measure exactly at the theoretic average for his group in any given trait. The great mass of "average" people spread over a certain span of measurement called "the normal range," within which development or growth may be considered desirable. The extremes may or may not be undesirable. In weight measurements, for example, excessive overweight or underweight is considered detrimental to health at any age. On the other hand, on the "mental age" scale people are usually desirous of belonging in the most extreme upper brackets of accomplishment where one is referred to as in the "genius" class. There is some discussion in the literature, however, as to whether even in this trait it is not possible to rank too far from the average of the population to be understood easily by others or happily adjusted to them.

An example of how widely these differences vary within the same age range can be found in Meredith's[2] study of eighteen anthropometric measurements on Iowa City boys between birth and eighteen years in whom he noted wide individual differences. The lightest boy at eighteen years was no heavier than the heaviest boy at eight years. The lightest boy at eight years weighed hardly as much as the heaviest two-year-old. These, of course, represent extremes but

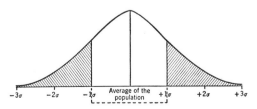

Figure 3. Normal probability curve. Range within which the great mass of "normal" people lie. Shaded areas represent extremes, in either direction.

---

[2] H. V. Meredith, "The Rhythm of Physical Growth," *University of Iowa Studies, Child Welfare,* 11 (3): 1936.

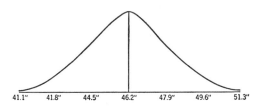

41.1"   41.8"   44.5"   46.2"   47.9"   49.6"   51.3"

Figure 4. Normal probability curve of height in inches for six-year-old boys. Average and standard deviation taken from K. Simmons and T. W. Todd, "Growth of Well Children: Analysis of Stature and Weight 3 Months to 13 Years," *Growth*, 1938, Vol. 2, No. 2.

are warnings to us in using chronologic age scales too rigidly in classifying children.

While all children pass through the sequence of maturity stages, some may omit some of the intermediate steps. For example, some children walk upright without creeping or crawling, even though most children crawl, creep, walk in sequence. Then again, a sequence may be disturbed because of a structural defect. Such may be the case of deaf children who sometimes learn to read and write before they learn to speak or understand spoken language, this being a reversal of the usual order of development.

Some children also differ in their rate of development, going through the sequential steps as expected but at a slower or faster rate than average children. Thus there are *slow growers* and *fast growers*. The period of adolescence initiated by the beginning of pubescent changes illustrates dramatically these differences. For some it begins early; for some it begins late. Stolz and Stolz[3] give a range of at least five and one-half years in the chronologic age at which adolescence began for the boys in the

California Adolescent Study and at least four and one-half years at which it ended.

Thus one boy may be entering adolescence at age ten years while he is in the high fifth grade, while for an age peer classmate childhood may continue until he is fifteen and a half years old and in the low eleventh grade (p. 423).

There are also definite *differences between boys and girls*. Figure 5, representing growth in weight of boys and girls from three months to seventeen years shows that boys generally exceed girls in weight in the early years and after fourteen years of age. In the early school years they are somewhat similar in weight, but between nine and fourteen years girls, because they mature earlier than boys and therefore pass through the pubescent spurt of growth earlier than boys, are temporarily heavier than boys. Within each sex, there is considerable difference in the ages at which children arrive at maturity.

There seems to be very little differences between boys and girls in general intellectual capacity, but there are certain definite differences in interests and behavior, as we shall see later. Whether these differences in interests and behavior are innate or a product of the way we rear children is not clear, but much depends upon which interest or which trait is under discussion.

Goodenough and Maurer[4] after a comparison of a number of types of tests of preschool children and test performances at later years found that in nearly all instances girls' scores showed a more consistent correlation between early and later tests than boys' scores.

---

[3] H. R. Stolz and L. M. Stolz, *Somatic Development of Adolescent Boys* (New York: The Macmillan Company, 1951).

[4] F. L. Goodenough and K. M. Maurer, *The Mental Growth of Children from Two to Fourteen Years: A Study of the Predictive Value of the Minnesota Preschool Scale*, (Minneapolis: University of Minnesota Press, 1947).

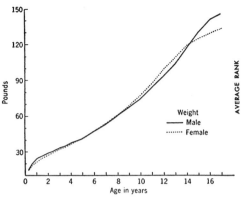

Figure 5. Curves showing the growth in weight of boys and girls from three months to seventeen years. From K. Simmons, "The Brush Foundation Study of Child Growth and Development: II. Physical Growth and Development," *Monograph for the Society for Research in Child Development,* Vol. 9, No. 1.

Thus girls showed a reliable tendency toward greater stabilization of performance on tests than boys in the early years. They discuss this by saying:

Although it is possible that sex difference represents an earlier stabilization of mental level in females than in males it is probably more reasonable to assume that better cooperation and greater docility in the test situations—characteristics in which a number of girls are likely to exceed boys—provide sufficient explanation for the differences found. Nevertheless, the other possibility is by no means excluded. Because of the theoretical significance of the problem further investigation is desirable.

We must understand these unique aspects of each individual child's growth if we are to treat children intelligently. A tall, slender child does not put on weight at the same rate, nor does he weigh as much for his height, as does a stocky child. Some parents create unnecessary feeding problems in their attempt to achieve "standard" weight gains. Certain intellectually fast growing children have the physical stamina and so-

cial maturity to enter school at five and one-half years of age. Other children of the same chronologic and mental ages will be quite unable physically or socially to stand the competition of other first graders. Some children seem "slow to catch on" in school for several years, yet prove later to be excellent students. Forcing the pace of growth at any stage will not produce good results in the long run, and may incur serious damage along the way. Forcing children into any pattern of growth which is not in harmony with their natural potentialities is likely to result in tragedy both for the child and for the misguided adult. Fathers, for example, should not try to make "go getters" out of sensitive, artistic boys; nor should Susie be compelled to try to make Phi Beta Kappa because her older sister did.

GROWTH IS COMPLEX.
ALL OF ITS ASPECTS ARE
CLOSELY INTERRELATED

The many failures in attempting to discover simple causal relationships in development speak for the fact that growth is an extremely complex process, the various aspects of which are intimately interrelated. It is impossible to understand the physical child without understanding him at the same time as a thinking and feeling child. It is likewise impossible to understand his mental development without a real knowledge of his physical body and its needs. There is a close relationship, for example, between his total adjustment to school and his emotions, his physical health and his intellectual adequacy. Such simple things as fatigue or hunger may influence his behavior. An emotional disturbance may contribute to difficulties in eating or sleeping. An illness may be an incubation period for a behavior problem. A physical defect may have been the starting point for certain attitudes and social adjustments. It is important to an adolescent not to be too tall, too short or obese. It makes a difference in the total picture of the child whether he is en-

ergetic or phlegmatic. The posture of a child may express his physical well-being or the reverse, and also may reveal something of his attitudes. . . .

. . . . .

21 | IMPRINTING

ECKHARD H. HESS

Newly hatched sea birds or chicks are in a few hours ready to follow the mother away from the nest. Imprinting, or the development of an attachment to the mother-object, occurs during these few critical hours. What is there about the mother that binds the infant to her? This article describes experiments showing that the infant makes profound and enduring attachments to its mother, to the species, or even to a football—any object which moves during the critical imprinting period. The attachment has little to do with the kindly responses from the loved object or with its suitability. The infant seems to be so urgently in need of a mother that it will make one out of almost anything. Imprinting appears also to be related to the ability to walk and to the development of fear.

It should be pointed out, however, that the infant also stimulates the mother, not only after birth but even before. For example, it has been discovered that if a gull has laid two or three eggs, and if one or two are removed, the gull will continue to lay. If all are removed, she will stop laying, and if there are four or five eggs, she will stop laying. Apparently the stimulation of feeling created by one or two eggs activates the ovaries while no eggs or five or six deactivates them.

The very idea of imprinting as an early experience during which a young animal forms a strong social attachment to a mother-object has been responsible for firing the imagination of many workers who have become increasingly aware of the fact that early experiences of many

Excerpts reprinted from "Ethology: An Approach toward the Complete Analysis of Behavior," in R. Brown, E. Galanter, E. Hess, and G. Mandler, *New Directions in Psychology*, Vol. I, pp. 224–46. Copyright © 1962, Holt, Rinehart and Winston, Inc. Reprinted by permission of the publishers. Figures 1–5 are reprinted from E. H. Hess, "Imprinting," *Science*, CXXX (1959), 133–41, by permission; figures 7–9, from E. H. Hess, "Two Conditions Limiting Critical Age for Imprinting," *Journal of Comparative Physiology and Psychology*, LII (1959), 515–18.

kinds can have permanent effects on an animal's behavior. This, together with the many ways in which the imprinting phenomenon differs from the simple association learning processes commonly studied in the psychological laboratory, has resulted in the arousal and maintenance of a great deal of interest and research in imprinting in the North American continent.

Unfortunately, however, some of the research in the past has been robbed of potential usefulness, because the prevalence of the conceptual framework of association learning in experimental psychology caused a Procrustean effort to fit the imprinting phenomenon into the association learning framework. Although the intensive effort to find and formulate laws of learning (in hopes of accounting for the causal bases of all behaviors) did show that certain behaviors once thought to be instinctive were indeed modifiable by learning, the realization is growing that there are still certain behaviors that are so persistent in character and resistant to modification by reinforcement that they cannot be satisfactorily explained by conventional laws of learning. In such cases, and imprinting is one of them, other explanatory devices must be constructed. This does not mean that untestable hypotheses concerning the nature of imprinting must be devised, for the good work carried out by many investigators, including H. James, Peter Klopfer, Howard Moltz, and M. Schein, has demonstrated that such is not the case. Thus, the gap between ethologically oriented and behavioristically oriented researchers has recently narrowed, and common areas of agreement are being formed. Recent reviews on the topic of imprinting have been made by Hess (1959 a, b, c) and Moltz (1960).

Konrad Lorenz was the first to bring widespread attention to this phenomenon of imprinting, and he gave it its name (1935). In a broad sense, imprinting refers to an early experience that has a profound influence on the later adult social and sexual behavior of an animal with respect to the choice of objects for these behaviors. Although earlier workers noted this phenomenon, Lorenz was the first to point out that it appeared to occur at a critical period, early in the life of an animal. He postulated that the first object to elicit a social response on the part of a young animal later released not only that response but also related responses such as sexual behavior. Imprinting, therefore, was important in the consideration not only of animal behavior, but also of the wider problems of biological evolution and speciation. For example, Craig (1908) reported Whitman's unpublished experiments with wild pigeons, in which he found that in order to be able to cross two different pigeon species, he had first to rear the young of one species with foster parents of the other species. After such an upbringing, these animals actually preferred to mate with the other species. Such inter-species sexual fixations have been observed since then in other birds, some fishes, and two mammals—the alpaca and vicuña.

Heinroth and his wife (1924–1933) raised by hand the young of almost every species of European birds, and noted that many of the social responses of these birds were transferred to their human caretaker as a result of this experience.

Although imprinting has been studied mainly in birds, it also has been observed in other animals. Instances of imprinting have been reported in insects (Thorpe, 1944), in fish (Baerends and Baerends-van Roon, 1950), and in some mammals. These mammals in which the phenomenon has been found—alpaca and vicuña (Hodge, 1946), sheep (Grabowski, 1941, Murie, 1944), deer (Darling, 1938), zebra and buffalo (Hediger, 1938)—are all animals in which the young are mobile almost immediately after birth. Controlled experimental work with mammals, however, has just begun.

It is now thought that processes very much like imprinting exist in every social species, particularly those in which there are parent-young relationships. However, in the case of species in which there are extended periods of parental care, it is apparent that the period of primary socialization occurs over a more extended length of time than it does in, say, chickens or ducks. Dogs, for example, cannot be made into pets if they have not had contact with human beings during the period of primary socialization. Freedman, King, and Elliott (1961) have found that the age of three and a half to nine-to-thirteen weeks of age approximates a critical period in dogs for socialization to human beings, with the age of seven weeks being the most sensitive time. Similarly, if kittens are not handled during the period after the eyes are open up to the time of weaning, they always remain somewhat wild and fearful of people. Finally, it is evident (Goldfarb, 1943, Bowlby, 1951, and others) that orphaned children can grow up to be incurably unsocialized, being unable to maintain friendships or to establish permanent social relationships, and so on, if not given the opportunity to undergo normal socialization at an early age, due to lack of contact with people.

The first systematic investigations on imprinting were published in 1951. Independently, in this country and in Europe, the work of Ramsay (1951) and Fabricius (1951 a, b) gave the first indications of some of the important factors in the process. Most of Ramsay's experiments dealt with exchange of parents and young, although he also imprinted some waterfowl on such objects as a football or a green box. He noted the importance of the auditory component in the imprinting situation, the effect of changes in coloring in parental recognition as well as the recognition of the parents by the young. His findings also showed that color is an essential element in recognition, while size or form seemed to be of less importance. Fabricius carried out experiments with several species of ducklings and was able to approximate the critical age at which imprinting was most successful in several species of ducks.

Since 1951, my associates and I have carried out a program in imprinting at McDonogh and Lake Farm Laboratories, Maryland, and at our laboratories at the University of Chicago. Many thousands of animals, including many different breeds and species, have been used. Most of them mallard ducklings and chickens.

METHODOLOGY

Our birds (ducks and chicks) were incubated and hatched right in our laboratory. They hatched in the dark, and each animal was placed in an individual box marked with the exact hour at which the animal hatched. The bird, in the box, was kept in a still-air incubator and kept there until it was to be imprinted. After the animal had undergone the imprinting experience, it was returned to the box and kept there until testing. Only after testing was completed was the young bird placed in daylight and given food and water.

The apparatus we used in the imprinting procedure consisted of a circular runway, about five feet in diameter, and is pictured in Figure 1. A mallard duck decoy was suspended from a rotating arm and was internally outfitted with a heating element and a loudspeaker which played an arbitrarily chosen rendition of *GOCK, gock, gock, gock*. The animal was placed, in the dark, about one foot away from the decoy, a pulley arrangement opening the bird's box. The experimenter placed himself behind a one-way screen and turned on the lights and sound. After a short interval the model began to move around for a specified amount of time, usually less than one hour. After the lights were again turned off, the animal was returned to its box until it was to be tested. No human contact was needed, since a trap door arrangement dropped the animal into its home box.

The testing procedure consisted of giving the young animal a choice between going to the male decoy to which it had been imprinted or going to a female decoy alike in shape but different in color. The male model made the *gock* call while the female model gave the call of a real mallard female calling her young. Four test conditions followed each other in immediate succession, and

Figure 1. The apparatus used by Hess in his studies on imprinting. It consists principally of a circular runway around which a decoy, suspended from a moving arm, rotates. Here a duckling is shown following the decoy. The controls of the apparatus are in the foreground. Normally a curtain or a one-way screen is placed between the apparatus and its controls so as to prevent the duckling from seeing the experimenter.

the choice of the animal in each condition was noted. If the duckling gave the positive response of walking to or staying with the object to which it had been imprinted—the male decoy—in all four of the tests, then imprinting was regarded as complete, or 100 percent. These tests involved choices between (1) stationary and silent male and female models, (2) stationary and calling male and female models, (3) silent male model, calling female model, both stationary, and (4) stationary and silent male model, calling and moving female model.

IMPRINTING VERSUS LEARNING

The most salient feature of the imprinting phenomenon is its many differences from simple association learning. There is now a wealth of experimental evidence to show that imprinting differs fundamentally from association learning in several respects, and to demonstrate the problems in dealing with behaviors that owe a great deal to genetic factors

rather than exclusively to environmental ones.

For example, a principal distinguishing feature of the imprinting phenomenon is its *critical period,* which, as Lorenz postulated, means that there is a particular time in the life of the animal during which exposure to the mother-object will have the most extensive and lasting effects on that animal's social behavior. This fact is one which must be considered in distinguishing imprinting from ordinary association learning, as there is no critical period for association learning.

Our experimentation with imprinting in ducklings and chicks offers ample evidence for the existence of the critical period (Hess, 1957). To determine the age at which an imprinting experience is most effective, we imprinted our ninety-two ducklings at various ages after hatching. In this series of experiments the imprinting experience was standard: the duckling followed the model one hundred and fifty to two hundred feet around the runway during a period of ten minutes. Figure 2 shows the scores made by ducklings in the different age groups. It appears that some imprinting

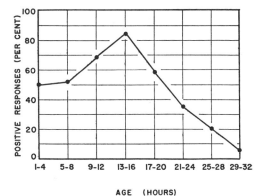

Figure 2. The critical period in which ducklings are most easily imprinted is demonstrated by this graph, which shows the mean test scores made by ducklings in each group that had been imprinted at different ages, calculated in hours from the time of hatching.

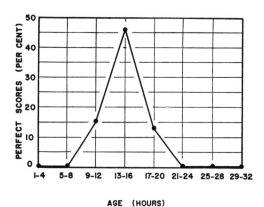

Figure 3. Another way of demonstrating the critical age is by plotting the percentage of animals in each age group that made perfect test scores, or 100%.

occurs immediately after hatching, but a maximum score is consistently made only by those ducklings in the thirteen-to-six-teen-hour-old group. This result is indi-cated in Figure 3, which shows the per-centage of animals in each age group that made perfect imprinting scores.

There is another difference between imprinting and association learning. Learning a visual discrimination problem with food reward is quicker and more stable when practice trials are spaced than when they are massed. That such is not the case with imprinting is shown by the following experimental study we car-ried out.

We decided to vary independently the factors of length of exposure time and the actual distance traveled by the duck-lings during the imprinting period. Since a ten-minute period had been found sufficient to produce testable results, we ran a series of animals varying the dis-tance traveled but keeping the time con-stant at ten minutes. Each group of duck-lings followed the model for different distances, these distances being one foot, twelve and a half feet, twenty-five feet, fifty feet, and one hundred feet. All ducklings were imprinted between twelve and seventeen hours of age to

keep constant the variable of the critical period of sensitivity. The results showed that increasing the distance over which the duckling had to follow the imprint-ing object increased the strength of im-printing. A leveling-off of this effect ap-pears to occur after a distance of about fifty feet (Hess, 1957). These results are shown in Figure 4.

We also investigated the effects of the length of exposure time to the model when the distance followed was kept constant. Since the distance of twelve and a half feet could be traveled by the duck in periods of two minutes, ten min-utes, and thirty minutes, we used this as a unit. Imprinting scores made by ani-mals in each of these three groups were essentially identical. We also found that there is no significant difference between ducklings allowed to follow for a dis-tance of one hundred feet during ten minutes and those allowed thirty min-utes to cover the same distance (Hess, 1957). Both of these results are shown in Figure 5.

It is very clear, therefore, that the strength of imprinting is apparently de-pendent not on the duration of the im-

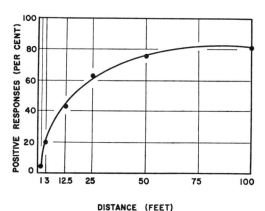

Figure 4. Mean test scores made by groups of ducklings that followed the model for dif-ferent distances but that all had the same amount of exposure time. The strength of imprinting is thus a function of the distance traveled during the imprinting experience.

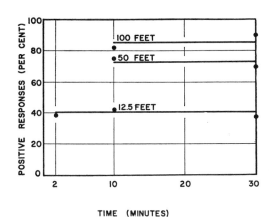

Figure 5. Mean test scores made by groups of ducklings that followed the model for different distances and different amounts of exposure time. It is apparent that the ducklings that followed the model for the same distance but during different amounts of time showed the same degree of imprinting strength; therefore, time in itself had little effect on the strength of imprinting when the distance traveled was held constant.

printing period, but on the effort expended by the duckling in following the imprinting object. We did other supplementary experiments that confirmed this notion. For example, if the ducklings had to follow the model up an inclined plane, this resulted in greater imprinting than in ducklings following the same distance on level ground. We concluded that we could even write an equation for imprinting: the strength of imprinting is equal to the logarithm of the effort expended by the animal in following the imprinting object during the imprinting experience, or $I_s = \log E$.

Another example of the fact that it is the effort expended by the animal that is crucial in determining the effectiveness of the imprinting experience during the critical period in ducklings is offered by our attempts to produce imprinting by means of presenting auditory stimulation to mallard eggs. The sound of a female mallard calling her young was played for forty-eight hours before hatching. When tested after hatching, these young did not choose this sound any more frequently than they chose the *gock* call used in our experiments. Therefore, auditory imprinting, while the mallard is still in the egg, is considered unlikely on the basis of these results, particularly in view of the fact that it is not possible for the animals still in the eggs to exert much effort toward the source of sound (Hess, 1959a).

It is well known that in discrimination learning, recency in experience is more effective for retention of learning. In imprinting, however, primacy of experience is the maximally effective factor. This difference is demonstrated by the following experiment. Two groups of eleven ducklings each were imprinted to two different imprinting objects. Animals of Group I were first individually imprinted to a male mallard model, and then to a female model. Group II, on the other hand, was first imprinted to a female model, and subsequently to a male model. Fourteen of the twenty-two ducklings, when tested with both models present, preferred the model to which they first had been imprinted, showing primacy. Only five preferred the model to which they had been imprinted last, showing recency, and three showed no preference at all (Hess, 1959b).

The administration of punishment or painful stimulation is well known to result in avoidance of the associated stimulus in discrimination learning. But in imprinting, such aversive stimulation actually causes an enhancement of the effectiveness of the imprinting experience. For example, it has been repeatedly observed that a young mallard duckling whose toes are stepped on while he is being imprinted to a human being during his critical period does not run away with fear; on the contrary, he stays even closer to the punitive imprinting object. This naturalistic observation has been substantiated in recent unpublished experiments by J. Kovach in our laboratory. It was found that the administration of electric shock in the imprinting situation during the critical period enhances the following tendency in chicks, whereas it diminishes imprintability *after* the critical period. Thus, the use of electric shocks results in an even more sharply defined critical period for imprintability, and the notion of the critical period is thereby resubstantiated independently. Figure 6 gives a representative set of figures from the pilot study. Each subgroup had at least ten animals.

We have carried out experimentation with chicks in which we found that the administration of meprobamate (Miltown) or carisoprodol (Soma) had no effect on the ability of these animals to learn a simple color discrimination problem with food reward when they were under the influence of either drug, as compared with animals that had not been given either drug. All three groups learned equally efficiently, and furthermore, animals run the next day, after the effects of the drugs had worn off completely, all showed the same degree

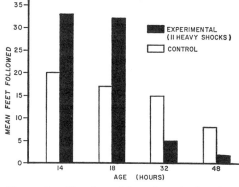

Figure 6. Number of feet that chicks of two different major treatment groups, one shocked and the other not shocked, followed the imprinting object, by age at first exposure to the imprinting situation. The shocked chicks were given eleven heavy shocks of 3 mamp. intensity, ½ sec. duration, during the imprinting experience; the nonshocked control chicks were given none.

of retention. However, the effects of these drugs in the case of imprinting are very different (Hess, 1960, and Hess, Polt, and Goodwin, 1959).

We became interested, a few years ago, in the effect of tranquilizers on imprinting behavior, because we found that the end of the critical period was accompanied by the development of innate or unlearned fear responses during the imprinting situation. We thought that perhaps tranquilizers would extend the critical period by removing these animals' fear. First, we used meprobamate on ducklings, and found that it did indeed render the animals fearless when they were under its influence in the imprinting situation. But when the animals were tested, they showed no effect of the imprinting experience.

In the face of this most surprising result, we had to look for an explanation. The explanation, we decided, lay in the Law of Effort and the muscle-relaxant effects of meprobamate. So we tried another drug, carisoprodol (Soma) which is a congener, or chemical derivative, of meprobamate. It is an almost pure muscle relaxant, without the tranquilizing effects of meprobamate.

We ran three groups out of a total of forty-two mallard ducklings and eighty-nine "Vantress Broiler" chicks. One group was imprinted while under the influence of meprobamate, another while under the influence of carisoprodol, and a third group served as a control, having been given distilled water in order to equalize effects of fluid intake and the necessary handling for administration. We found that both drugs, particularly carisoprodol, interfered with the retention of imprinting when these animals were tested after the effects of the drugs had worn off, twenty-four hours later.

That the drugs interfered with the *process* of imprinting and not with its retention was shown by another condition to which some animals in these groups were subjected: they were imprinted normally and tested under the influence of a drug. This procedure had no effect whatever on the retention of the imprinting experience: the animals behaved normally.

The hypothesis of ours that the interfering effects of these drugs lies in their muscle-relaxant effect is further supported by other investigations (Hess, 1957) in which we found that perfectly good imprinting can be obtained when the animals are under the influence of chlorpromazine.

So far, in our treatment of the topic of imprinting and its differences from association learning, we have concentrated on the reaction of following a certain model, as an indicator of the progress of imprinting during the first exposure to this object and also as an indicator of the effectiveness of this experience. However, while the animal is being imprinted, he also engages in other innate activities which can be observed and recorded. For example, the animal may emit "distress notes," or "contentment tones," remain silent, or fixate an object. This suggests that it is worthwhile to study these other behaviors in order to gain information about the imprinting process, and indeed, this is the case.

For example, "distress notes" and "contentment tones" can be used as indicators of the state of fearfulness in the animal being imprinted. It is quite easy to differentiate between these two calls in chickens, for the "distress notes" are a series of high-intensity, medium-pitch tones, of one-quarter-second duration and little pitch modulation, while "contentment tones," on the other hand, are a series of high-pitch, low-intensity notes, of one-twelfth-second duration or less, and considerable pitch modulation. The names that have been given to these calls are purely labels and their meanings should not necessarily be taken literally.

The presence or absence of fear be-havior, together with other behaviors engaged in by the chick, is an important indicator of the developmental changes that would account for the limits of the critical period. Why should the critical period occur when it does, and what causes it to end?

We noted, as indicated in our studies on the effects of drugs, that the end of the critical period was accompanied by the development of innate fear responses. It is obvious that fear will prevent an animal from engaging in the kinds of social behavior that are necessary for imprinting to occur. Fabricius (1951b), in his early laboratory work on imprinting, as well as other investigators since then, observed that there is a steady increase in the amount of fear shown by a duckling during the first hours of life when he is confronted with an imprinting object.

But even if increasing fear is correlated with the end of the period of imprintability, at this point we still do not know what factors enter into the limitation of the beginning of the critical period. Why is it that newly hatched ducklings or chicks do not imprint just as well as those that have reached the age of thirteen to sixteen hours? Anyone who has observed newly hatched animals will notice at once that they do not walk as well or as fast as the older animals. Perhaps, then, we should look for an explanation of the beginning of the critical period in our Law of Effort. If a young animal is not able to follow the imprinting object, then of course it cannot expend as much effort in actual following as one that walks well. If the model is moving, the young bird will lose it. However, imprintability at the time of hatching is not zero, since the model may return to the young bird, and it can expend effort in trying to follow it.

With these two propositions in mind, we studied the development of fear responses and of locomotor ability in chicks from the time of hatching to the age of thirty-six hours (Hess and Schaefer, 1959). First we took 137 White Rock chicks and divided them into nine age groups. Each was observed individually in an imprinting experience. If an animal emitted distress notes in the presence of the model or moved away from it, it was considered to have shown fear. We then tabulated the number of animals in each age group that had shown fear while exposed to the imprinting object. We found that among the different age groups, the number of fearful animals in each group increased steadily with increasing age. During the very early hours of their lives, from the time of hatching up to about the age of thirteen to sixteen hours, these animals show little or no fear. After that time, the number of animals showing fear increases sharply, until the age of about thirty-three to thirty-six hours, when all chicks in that age group showed fear. These results are summarized in Figure 7.

Then we took another group of sixty Vantress Broiler chicks of White Rock stock, divided them into six different age groups, and studied the development of increasing locomotor ability (Hess, 1959c). We gave each chick three trials

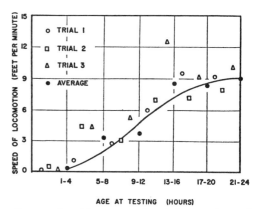

Figure 8. *Mean speed of locomotion of Vantress Broiler chicks of different ages and with different degrees of prior practice.*

within one hour so as to observe the effects of practice as well as of developmental stage. We found that groups consisting of chickens between the fourth and sixteenth hour after hatching showed improvement in locomotion during the three trials. However, the conditions of the experiment were such that after the sixteenth hour after hatching, a relative plateau of locomotion was reached, since there was great fluctuation between trials and a leveling of average speed. In addition, there was a clear increase in the ability to locomote with increasing age between the fourth and sixteenth hours. The results of this experiment are graphically illustrated in Figure 8.

If we arrange our data on a graph so that the percentage of animals showing fear and the percentage of animals able to move at the rate of at least three feet per minute or more are drawn, the area under these two curves resembles the area under the curve for the critical period for the same breed, with the peaks coincident at exactly the same age period—thirteen to sixteen hours after hatching. This is shown in Figure 9.

There are probably several reasons why the empirical curve for imprintability is consistently lower than the theoret-

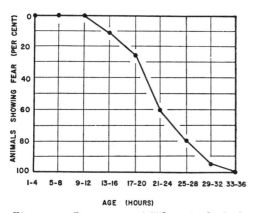

Figure 7. *Percentage of White Rock chicks in each group that showed fear responses to a potential imprinting object.*

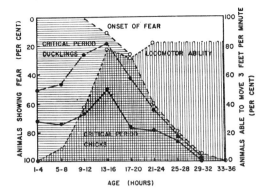

Figure 9. The hypothetical period of imprinting sensitiveness as determined by the superposition of the fear and locomotion curves, together with actual curves of imprintability in chicks and mallard ducklings as a function of age, as shown by mean test scores.

ical curve for imprintability as determined by the development of fearfulness and locomotor ability. For example, the suitability of a potential imprinting object may not be the same for all species, and the imprintability of the breed is another limiting factor. Since some breeds and species have higher imprintability than others, the area under their empirical curves of imprintability would be greater than those for the other breeds, and also more closely approach the theoretical curve. For example, our experimentation has shown that wild mallards display a much greater degree of imprintability than do any breed of chickens. The curve of imprintability for these mallards is also shown in Figure 9 and it can be seen that it agrees much more closely with the theoretical curve. However, the important aspect of our results is that on the basis of the data we obtained with our chicks, the curve of imprintability should be very much like a normal distribution curve, with a peak at a certain hour after hatching and lower points before and after that time. The curves for the critical period that have been established in our laboratories for

chicks and ducklings have exactly that shape. The fact of interest to emphasize here is not the absolute identity of the points of the theoretical and empirical curves, but the resemblances between them.

The correlation between the termination of the critical period and the maturing of the fear response is an important finding. This has already been singled out by Ramsay and Hess (1954) and Hess (1957) as relevant to the imprinting process. In fact, as the stage of our present knowledge indicates, it seems likely that all animals showing the phenomenon of imprinting will have a critical period that ends with the onset of fear. Thus we can predict, in a series of animals, knowing only the time of onset of fear responsiveness, the end of imprintability for that species. Freedman, King, and Elliott (1961) have recently verified that such is the case for dogs. Even in the human being one could thus theoretically place the end of maximum imprintability at about five and a half months of age, since observers have placed the onset of fear at about that time (Bridges, 1932; Spitz and Wolf, 1946). Weidmann (1958) has recently mentioned the possibility that the onset of the fear response may limit the duration of the critical period for imprinting in ducks while Gray (1958) has proposed a similar scheme for humans.

The importance of fear in relation to the imprinting phenomenon has been documented by Moltz, Rosenblum, and Halikas (1959). They found that while the tendency of Peking ducklings to follow a mother-object closely declines with age, in accordance with the increasing independence from the protection of the mother, the arousal of anxiety would cause them to seek close proximity to the mother-object and to follow it around even when they were at an age when they normally would not do so.

Furthermore, they found that ducklings in the presence of a model to which they had been imprinted were less susceptible to startles and other fear responses. This they attribute to the model's having acquired anxiety-reducing properties for the ducklings.

In summary, the notion of the critical period is a rather important one in considering the imprinting phenomenon. Not only do animals show different degrees of imprintability according to their age, in hours after hatching, but the critical period is also correlated with other behaviors in the chick, the ability to locomote, and the appearance of the innate fear response to strange objects. The idea of the critical period also has been substantiated by the fact that punishment or painful stimulation (within limits), such as electric shocks, actually will cause the young animal to imprint more intensively on the mother-object— but only if it is at the stage of maximum imprintability; otherwise, the punishment will decrease any disposition the animal might have to follow the mother-object.

The critical period concept, however, has met with resistance on the part of some researchers. The principal reason for this is that animals can often be trained to lose their fear of an alien species (or of their own species, if never before encountered) when they are past their critical period, and even to follow members of this species. This is one reason imprinting has been thought by some to be association learning of the species to which the young animal belongs. Further, the critical period can occur so early in the life of the animal that it may not be noticed by experimenters.

In addition, conflicting reports regarding the location of the critical period arise because different measures are used. To cite one instance, Jaynes (1957) stated that whereas the greatest follow-ing of a mother-object during the initial imprinting exposure occurs early in the first day of life, animals exposed to an imprinting object for the first time during the second day of life showed the strongest amount of following when tested ten days later. The use of the degree of following of a mother-object during a much later age thus led Jaynes to different conclusions regarding the location of the critical period from those Hess (1957) was led to. Hess's conclusions were arrived at on the basis of the choice, made twenty-four hours after the imprinting experience, by animals exposed to the object to which they had been imprinted as well as to another they had not seen before.

When a young animal is tamed during a period later than the critical period, this is an association learning process, and conforms to all the classical laws of association learning: it can be erased, it is stronger with increased training, and so on. The fact that animals can be tamed is the source of the occasional confusion between imprinting and association learning. However, taming can occur at almost any time during the life of an animal, whereas imprinting can occur only during a very limited period. In addition, the effects of imprinting are relatively permanent, even when it has taken place in quite a brief period of time, in contrast with the extensive training often necessary for complete taming. It appears, then, that imprinting results in a more truly social bond than taming does, inasmuch as imprinting can determine what objects constitute social or sexual partners for an animal, whereas taming does not. Finally, the social bond created by the imprinting process is extremely difficult to erase, since an animal raised by a particular species during the sensitive period usually will not dissociate himself from them even when treated cruelly. The faithful mistreated dog is an excellent example of this. The point is that the imprinting experience during the critical period establishes in the animal an image of the species to which it belongs. Thus the mistreated dog who stays close to his oppressive master does so because he is closely bound emotionally to the human species, having had close contact with human beings during his critical period of primary socialization. In fact, it would seem as if he considers himself more of a human being than a dog, as indicated by his failure to detach himself from the company of his owner.

REFERENCES

BAERENDS, G. P., AND J. M. BAERENDS-VAN ROON. An introduction to the study of ethology of cichlid fishes. *Behaviour Suppl.*, 1950, *1*, 1–243.

BOWLBY, J. *Maternal care and mental health.* Geneva, World Health Organization, 1951.

BRIDGES, K. M. B. Emotional development in early infancy. *Child Developm.*, 1932, *3*, 342–341.

CRAIG, W. The voices of pigeons regarded as a means of social control. *Amer. J. Sociol.*, 1908, *14*, 86–100.

DARLING, F. F. *Wild country.* London: Cambridge University Press, 1938.

FABRICIUS, E. Some experiments on imprinting phenomena in ducks. *Proc. 10th Int. Ornith. Kongr.*, 1951a, 375–379.
———. Zur Ethologie junger Anatiden, *Acta Zool. Fennica*, 1951b, *68*, 1–178.

FREEDMAN, D. G., J. A. KING, AND O. ELLIOTT. Critical period in the social development of dogs. *Science*, 1961, *133*, 1016–1017.

GOLDFARB, W. The effects of early institutional care on adolescent personality. *J. exp. Educ.*, 1943, *12*, 106–129.

GRABOWSKI, U. Prägung eines Jungscafs auf den Menschen. *Zeit. f. Tierpsychol.*, 1941, *4*, 326–329.

GRAY, P. H. Theory and evidence of imprinting in human infants. *J. Psychol.*, 1958, *46*, 155–166.

HEDIGER, H. *Wild animals in captivity.* London: Butterworth, 1938.

HEINROTH O., AND M. HEINROTH. *Die Vögel Mitteleuropas.* Berlin: Lichterfelde, 1924–1933.

HESS, E. H. Effects of meprobamate on imprinting in waterfowl. *Ann. N. Y. Acad. Sci.*, 1957, *67*, 724–732.
———. Imprinting. *Science*, 1959a, *130*, 133–141.
———. The relationship between imprinting and motivation. In *Nebraska Symposium on Motivation*, M. R. Jones, ed., 1959b. 44–77.
———. Two conditions limiting critical age for imprinting. *J. comp. physiol. Psychol.*, 1959c, *52*, 515–518.
———. Effects of drugs on imprinting behavior. *Drugs and behavior*, editors, L. Uhr, and J. G. Miller. New York: Wiley and Sons, 1960. 268–271.
———, J. M. POLT, AND E. GOODWIN. Effects of carisoprodol on early experience and learning. In *The pharmacology and clinical usefulness of carisoprodol*, ed., J. G. Miller, Detroit: Wayne State University Press, 1959. 51–85.
———, AND H. H. SCHAEFER. Innate behavior patterns as indicators of the "critical period." *Zeit. f. Tierpsychol.*, 1959, *16*, 155–160.

HODGE, W. H. Camels of the clouds. *The Nat. Geogr. Mag.*, 1946, *89*, 641–656.

JAYNES, J. Imprinting: the interaction of learned and innate behavior. II. The critical period. *J. comp. physiol. Psychol.*, 1957, *50*, 6–10.

LORENZ, K. Z. Der Kumpan in der Umwelt des Vogels. *J. f. Ornith.*, 1935, *83*, 137–213, 289–413.

MOLTZ, HOWARD. Imprinting: empirical basis and theoretical significance. *Psychol. Bull.*, 1960, *57*, 291–314.
———, L. A. ROSENBLUM, AND N. HALIKAS. Imprinting and level of anxiety. *J. comp. physiol. Psychol.*, 1959, *52*, 240–244.

RAMSAY, A. O. Behaviour of some hybrids in the mallard group. *Animal Behaviour*, 1961, *9*, 104–105.
———. Familial recognition in domestic birds. *Auk*, 1951, *68*, 1–16.
———, AND E. H. HESS. A laboratory ap-

proach to the study of imprinting. *Wilson Bull.*, 1954, *66*, 196–206.

SPITZ, R. A., AND K. M. WOLF. The smiling response: a contribution to the ontogenesis of social relations. *Genet. Psychol. Monogr.*, 1946, *34*, 57–125.

THORPE, W. H. Some problems of animal learning. *Proc. Linn. Soc. Lond.*, 1944, *156*, part 2, 70–83.

WEIDMANN, U. Verhaltensstudien an der Stockente, II. Versuche zur Auslösung und Prägung der Nachfolge- und Anschlussreaktion. *Zeit. f. Tierpsychol.*, 1958, *15*, 277–300.

22 | PECKING ORDER AND SOCIAL BEHAVIOR

MORRIS L. HAIMOWITZ

In Supervisory and Executive Development,[*] Norman R. F. Maier reports a problem that was brought to notice when an insurance company investigated a large number of truck accidents resulting in broken ankles. The investigation revealed that the men who most frequently broke their ankles were those who jumped over the tail gate of a truck in order to open it for others inside the truck. The accidents could have been easily prevented by having the man sitting with the driver in the front seat come out to open the tail gate; however, this adjustment was difficult to make because the pecking order among the truck crew would not permit it. The man sitting in the front seat with the driver was the foreman, the high man in the pecking order, whereas the man who jumped over the tail gate and occupied the hard bench next to the rear opening—the coldest spot in the winter and otherwise the dustiest and most uncomfortable—was low man in the pecking order. How could the top man be expected to do the job of the bottom man without jeopardizing the former's status? Efforts to establish a pecking order may be observed in a wide range of human activities—competitive sports, monopolistic business mergers, wars, and in the great anger of children or childish adults who lose a game. In this selection, the relevance of pecking order in the behavior of many species of animals is described.

In the year 1922, T. Schjelderup-Ebbe, a Norwegian psychologist, discovered a social hierarchy among chickens, which he identified as a pecking order. He noticed that a flock of chickens acted toward one another in a very definite order. If there were ten chickens in the flock, the number one chicken could peck any of the other nine; the number two chicken could peck any of the other eight, but not number one, and so on. The number ten chicken could be pecked by any of the nine others but he himself could peck none of them. Even before this great discovery, most men who had observed chickens knew that the top chicken had first choice of food and dusting and roosting places and that she was active, alert, and healthy, with a fine proud upright posture; on the other hand, the bottom chicken in the line was slow, drooping, dirty, the last to be permitted access to food or water, and sometimes so frequently pecked by the hens and mounted by the roosters that her neck and back feathers were torn out,

[*] New York: John Wiley and Sons, 1957, ch. 3.

leaving the sore flesh exposed. This sickly chicken laid few eggs, if any, and lived a short miserable life.

The pecking order among chickens is usually established by nine or ten weeks after hatching. If ten chickens, strangers to one another, are put together, each of the ten may fight with each of the others. Two hens will pair off, raise their heads high with a gesture of dominance, and have, perhaps, a bloody bout; or one may quickly turn away and leave an easy victory to the other. The flock will thus have engaged in 50 to 100 such encounters to form the pecking order.

Once the order is established, a certain degree of peace reigns, but it is the peace of the barnyard jungle, in which might makes right, and the more powerful, more aggressive, more agile members prevail. Occasionally the peace is disturbed when, for example, the number six hen threatens the number five hen. Or if a strange hen is introduced into the flock, it must fight each resident, usually with the result that it tires before too many clashes and retires to a low position in the order. Most upsetting to the order, however, is the introduction of five or ten new chickens into the flock. Such a disruption, so unsettling as to cause the flock's egg production to fall, would require that each of the old timers fight each of the newcomers, resulting in the formation of a new pecking order.

Pecking order has been found to be influenced by any of the factors affecting the health or feeling of confidence of animals. Thus, male sex hormones increase aggression and female hormones decrease it. Because cocks don't usually peck hens, each sex will have its own pecking order. Capons are more submissive and fight with less intensity, but even they form pecking orders.

In all-male flocks, dominant cocks will mount for sexual purposes other cocks in lower positions. Indeed, the lowest-ranking males may be so frequently trodden and pecked that they are killed. Similarly, in all-female flocks, dominant hens will tread on lower-ranking hens, but will respond normally to males that enter the flock. In mixed flocks, the more dominant male will be most successful in mating with the hens and will therefore father the most chickens.

The top hens in a flock of thirty or forty females are less likely to be receptive to male advances. Thus, the roosters will mate more frequently with the lower-order hens and may not mount the number one hen at all. But if the flock is divided into three groups—the top third, the middle third, and the bottom third of the pecking order—so that each hen has fewer birds to dominate or to be dominated by, then the hens in the upper third become more receptive to male advances, while those in the middle and bottom thirds become less submissive.

Nearly every species of bird is affected by pecking order. For example, if fifteen blue jays share an area of trees, the fifteen establish a pecking order. However, the blue jay's mating patterns, unlike those of the chicken, follow this order: the top-ranking males mate with the top-ranking females, and the number seven male with perhaps the number six, seven, or eight female.

The great zoologist Konrad Lorenz, who has described in detail the life patterns of geese, states that if a chief gander is removed, those strongly attached to him—his family—would search for him and would become much less aggressive, showing, as a consequence, a drop in pecking order relative to other families. Pecking order of geese is partly determined by the size of the family. If the dominant bird in a flock of Canadian geese has his eggs eaten by a predator, and his next inferior has a brood of five husky sons, the rank order of the two families will shift, the family with five sons overcoming the family deprived of its offspring.

The one species of bird that apparently does not form a pecking order is the starling. Unable to distinguish one of his species from another, he therefore does not fight.

Age is a central factor in pecking order, not only in birds but in many other species. When he is seven years old, the young male baboon may be ready to compete for lead position in his troop. The bull elephant and the cockrell each has his time. A three-year-old child may kick and bite his daddy, but he is no real threat in most families until he is thirteen or fourteen.

TERRITORIALITY

Two years before Schjelderup-Ebbe discovered pecking order in chickens, Eliot Howard, who studied the warbler and the English bunting, noticed a pattern of behavior which he identified as "territoriality" (*Territory of Birds*, 1920). Most animals establish not only a pecking order but also territorial rights. One territory is secured for food gathering, another for nesting, and a third for mating. After seals and warblers have migrated, for example, the males are the first to arrive at the new location and establish their territory by threatening or fighting off other males; then the females arrive. In the process of establishing territory, bloody battles between males will often occur in many species such as walrus, turtles, sheep, and rabbits; moose, deer, and elk, with horns locked in combat, may starve to death. Mice, chipmunks, and squirrels not only fight but try with occasional success to bite off the testicles of their rivals. The first official duty of the queen bee is to kill off all the virgin queens in the hive. The official feeding territory of a flock of gulls or a troop of baboons may extend for several miles; the mating territory of a wren may be only one or two backyards, the nesting territory, only a few inches.

If two vertebrates of one species, two animals unknown to each other, are put together, either in their home cage or tank or one resembling it, it is very likely that they will fight. If they are in a strange place, they may withdraw. Two cichlids put together in a tank that looks like their home tank will fight. If put in a strange tank, they flock together and their color becomes their nonfighting color.

FIGHTING, SEX, AND FLEEING

Intensive studies of a small tropical fish, the sunfish-like cichlid, reveal that although cichlids don't peck, they do threaten or bite or strike one another with their tails. One of the studies of the apparent drives of this fish, by Beatrice Oehlert, illuminates the relationship of aggression to other drives, specifically, sex and withdrawal. When two cichlids meet, it is difficult for the human observer to distinguish which of the three tendencies is dominant, since the three always seem to be activated simultaneously. Swimming broad-on signifies aggression, while swimming with head downward and quivering signifies sex; turning tail and fleeing signifies withdrawal. After observing cichlids for many months, Oehlert was able to predict what an individual would do at any given moment. She discovered that although each sex possessed the same three drives, the combination of them was different in each. Thus, the male was capable of performing sexual movements toward the female at the same time that he was indicating aggression toward her. But if the female was even slightly threatening, he was incapable of sexual movements. The female, on the other hand, could signify withdrawal and still perform sexually, but she was unable to combine the sexual and aggressive drives. Lorenz had reported this same pattern of complex interrelationship of drives in many animals, including doves, ruffled grouse, ravens, and jackdaws. It has also been observed as a problem of many human beings seeking the assistance of marriage counsellors.

THE TRIUMPH CEREMONY

The tendency or drive to fight, which most vertebrates of the same species exhibit, has survival value for the species in defending offspring, spacing out territory, and selecting out the strongest, the fastest, or the cleverest members. But in those species in which both parents are required to stay together after mating, mechanisms have been evolved that prevent the partners from attacking each other without, however, inhibiting them from fighting other members of the species. Thus, the cichlid may start out to attack its mate, but at the last moment swerves to attack another fish or simply the empty water. If the mated couple are alone in a tank, they will sooner or later attack each other, but their fight is just a kind of ceremony in which no injury is done.

The coot, a small diving duck, possesses a similar mechanism. When in a threatening situation, the coot displays the white patch on its forehead, a signal to another coot, also displaying the white patch, that a fight is imminent. When, however, two coots approach each other sexually, they bend their necks forward so that the white patches disappear below the surface of the water, thereby inhibiting their fighting responses.

The beginning-to-attack-but-changing-midway behavior among webfooted birds has been called "the triumph ceremony" by Lorenz. When two partners pass each other, each may threaten the other but they do not attack; but if a third party is present, it will be attacked. The partners may threaten each other for some time, during which each species performs a ceremony unique to it. Cranes "dance" at each other, and if no third party is present for them to attack, they may pick up a piece of wood and shake it excitedly. Some species have intricate honking routines, which are more intense in the mating than in the molting season. The ceremony may last only a few seconds in some species or a few minutes in others.

The triumph ceremony is apparently rigid and mechanical, and, once started, cannot be interrupted. For example, having just fought, a goose may rush back to his mate to perform the triumph ceremony. But because he is compelled to complete the ceremony without interruption, a rival may take the opportunity to move in with his mate. A deserted goose may seek a new mate with which to perform the ceremony, and while he is doing so, the original mate may try to intercede to get him back.

During the mating period, or when the offspring are hatched, the triumph ceremony provides the parents with the excitement, energy, and intensity to attack much larger animals that may threaten the young.

The beginning-to-attack-but-changing-midway behavior of cichlids, geese, and ducks is suggestive of the background of human ceremonies. When a pair of human beings come together, tendencies to fight, to withdraw, and to copulate may be stimulated simultaneously. It is possible that the inhibited or bottled-up drives, when released, are more intense than they were originally. When human beings congregate in large groups they often behave ritualistically. They pledge allegiance, sing, dance, light candles, or wave spears, suggesting that such behaviors are ways of avoiding conflicts. We assume, however, that human behavior differs from that of other animals, the latter being controlled by instinct, the former by the self. That is, although the human being may sense a drive, longing, desire, or feeling, he tends to act according to his assessment of the situation. For example, he may feel very hungry in a fine restaurant, but being without funds decides to delay eating for a while. Or he may face an inferior enemy he could subdue without difficulty, but because of other considerations, matters of judgment, or talking it over with himself, he chooses to walk away.

FACTORS AFFECTING PECKING ORDER

Separation from the Mother

In selection 25 of this book, the mentally damaging effects of maternal separation on children are described. Are infant animals affected by separation from their mothers in similar ways? To investigate this in the laboratory, Liddell selected twin pairs of sheep and goats; one twin was tested with its mother; the other, given the same tests, without the mother. One test involved dimming the lights—frightening to a sheep—for ten seconds, followed by mild electric shock to the foreleg. Twenty of these darkness signals spaced two minutes apart and each followed by shock comprised the daily session of fifty minutes. In every case, the infant with its mother showed no restriction of locomotion during the tests—it would run to her, then jump on her and cuddle up. The twin separated from the mother soon became immobilized, paralyzed by fear. Liddell writes,

We conditioned ten kids in isolation at four to fourteen hours of age for just one session of about an hour with twenty darkness signals at two minute intervals. Of the ten, two died within a week. All but one of the remaining eight died in the summer at less than a year of age. . . .

We also conditioned ten pairs of twin kids at one month of age, five in isolation and five with the mother. Four of the five in isolation died within the year, while only one of the five conditioned with the mother died within the year. . . .

We had under observation 22 control kids in which there was no separation from the mother and 21 experimental kids separated from the mother five minutes following birth and kept away from her, alone for half an hour to two hours. Nineteen of the 21 experimental kids died at less than a year of age. Only two of the 22 control kids died. None of these 43 had any form of conditioning.

Although much more evidence is needed, these experiments do suggest that separation of kids from their mothers not only reduces pecking order but is disastrous.

Experimental Frustration

If a chicken sees a worm, the chicken will usually walk over and eat it. But Erich von Holst has noticed that chickens have a special place in their brain which, when stimulated electrically by an electrode inserted into the brain, causes the chicken to become afraid, look alarmed, and try to run away. If the chicken becomes attracted to the worm and then is given a very light electrical stimulation through the electrode, the chicken walks around the worm, is attentive to it, but afraid. When the electricity is turned off, the chicken rebounds with a rush at the worm and eats it with much more intensity than he had previously without the fear stimulation.

Another set of experiments by Liddell could be entitled "Waiting for the Other Shoe." A sheep is shocked with a very mild, tickling current, which alarms the animal when it is strapped down and unable to escape. Just before the shock is administered, a metronome beats 60 times per minute. When the clicking has continued for five to ten seconds on ten occasions, a conditioned reflex, or prejudice, will have been formed, though not firmly. After experiencing 100 coincidences of the metronome beats and the shocks to its foreleg, the sheep will be prejudiced against the sound of the metronome for life, unable ever again to listen to the metronome with equanimity. Indeed, the clicking of a typewriter visibly disturbs it.

The metronome is then set to click twice as fast, 120 beats per minute, but no shock is administered to the animal, which is very alert to the sound and ready to be shocked. After several days of hearing the metronome without being shocked, the animal is severely agitated, easily startled, bleats, urinates and defecates frequently, and shows irregular rapid respiration and heart action. In addition, its rest at night is disturbed and normal gregariousness severely damaged. When returned to the flock, it no longer moves along with the other sheep and becomes an easy prey to marauding dogs.

If the animal is then returned to the laboratory and experiences 72 beats per minute, then 60 beats per minute without shock, and then shock is administered, instead of eliciting the slight foreleg movement that occurred at 60 beats per minute earlier, the shock now elicits an explosive leap upward, followed by relief of tension. This reaction is similar to that of the hen with the worm, described above. It appears that the animal expected the shock, and when it did not occur, became agitated. Slowing down the beat from 120 to 72, closer to the 60-beat rate at which shock was conditioned, had the effect of raising tension, so that when a shock finally was given, all of the accumulated tension was released at once. Those who live in apartment houses where the tenant upstairs throws down the first shoe, and then the second shoe, each night before going to bed can understand the tension that builds up some night when the second shoe is not heard, and the relief when it is finally dropped.

Animals may be taught to starve themselves to death. Experiments were performed with a fish, placed in a tank with a glass plate separating it from its food, so that every time it swam towards the food it bumped its nose. After many trials, it stopped trying to obtain the food even when the glass plate was removed. This behavior is analogous to that of the people who were seeking jobs during the depression, only to be turned down time after time. Then, when jobs became available, they were afraid to ask for them. In this sense, frustration reduces action and pecking order. Many experiments show that children's position in the classroom or

pecking order may be changed by the activities of the teacher. (See Part Five.)

PECKING ORDER AND NEUROSIS

Masserman has produced experimental neuroses in monkeys, cats and dogs, which severely impaired their behavior. (See also selection 51 in this book which describes the effects of frustration on rats.) The animal was made neurotic by first teaching it to obtain food by operating a switch or a lever, jumping at a signal, or moving in a certain direction. After learning to do this, the animal was then frightened by an electric shock, a blast of air, or a toy snake, just at the moment it expected to receive the food. Thus, the animal was first rewarded for its act by being given food, and then punished for the very same act. When the animal was first traumatized in this way, depending on its degree of hunger, the possibility of escape, and other factors, it would become startled, proceed to work the switches again, and with some hesitation open the food box. When traumatized again—two to seven times in cats or dogs, and more in monkeys—a pattern of aberration became clearly present: the animal would be startled easily, develop asthmatic breathing, anorexia, flatulence, diarrhea, muscular tics, markedly diminished heterosexual interest, and increased homosexual or masturbatory activities. Each animal had its own pattern, but the general anxiety, tension, perspiration, raised blood pressure, crouched body posture, irregular increased pulse, dilatated pupils, and increased coagulability of the blood were common in all. (See selection 23 in this volume for an analysis of these symptoms in human beings.) Masserman states that "alterations in social conduct generally took the form of inertia and withdrawal from competition, with consequent loss of position in the group hierarchy." Overt hostility toward group-mates appeared only in neurotic animals that had been dominant. When experimentally frustrated, they turned upon their successful rivals with displaced fury.

Gerard reports that when chimpanzees were reared in total darkness for the first months of their lives, the animals never acquired the ability to use pattern vision, even though their eyes and brains were unmolested. Because the animals were deprived of the opportunity to function in a normal environment during the maturation process, their nervous systems developed in a direction other than in the normally guided one, and it was then too late to establish the correct connections. Something very similar to this undoubtedly happens in the child with strabismus, who suppresses the visual image. Here, as in imprinting, time is of the essence: if the divergence from normal is caught at the beginning, it can be corrected; later, it is irremediable. For Gerard, important molecular, chemical, or electrical changes accompany many mental diseases, and he feels specific chemical or electrical therapies will be developed some day to cure or reduce such illness.

Masserman has pointed out how important it is for us to know the meaning of a particular behavior to an animal before we can understand that behavior. "For example, monkeys who ordinarily like bananas could be made to show avoidance reactions by having even the odor of the fruit associated with some unpleasant occurrence. Conversely, cats taught to depress a switch which gave them a mild electric shock signalling food could be made so eager to administer increasingly severe electric shocks to themselves even without the reward that their behavior would almost invariably be called 'masochistic' by observers unaquainted with their histories."

We would expect this kind of behavior to be discontinued by the process of extinction, whereby a behavior pattern learned through reward is discontinued when rewards are stopped; yet this "masochistic" behavior may continue throughout the lives of neurotic animals and human beings without ever being extinguished.

SEX AND PECKING ORDER

As noted earlier, roosters do not usually peck hens. Indeed, throughout the animal world, and even the plant world, sex differences are recognized, except in algae and certain bacteria. Although two microscopic animals in a drop of slime may look identical to us, they themselves recognize sex differences and mate accordingly. How plants recognize differences in sex we do not know at this time, but we do know that animals can tell by size, shape, sound, color, odor, taste, or feel. Fireflies, for example, react by signal lights. The female's sign of approval is a signal light she flashes just two seconds after the male flashes his. After each signal, the male flies closer to the inviting female. In some species, the male is larger, as the walrus, sea lion, moose, but for most species the female is larger, though the male is more active. Regardless of the size of the respective mates, the ova is always much larger than the sperm, which are always microscopic salt-water swimmers.

The only mammals capable of distinguishing differences through color are the primates, although this ability is most common among day-active birds, fish, and lizards. Insects are sensitive to colors not visible to man, such as ultraviolet rays, just as rats, dogs, birds, porpoises, and bats are sensitive to sounds that man can not hear. Apparently each species is most highly sensitive to the coloring, odor, or sounds of its own potential mates; some snakes and insects are very sensitive to a point or two of difference in temperature.

In the spring, when robins and warblers return from the south, the males usually come first, establish a territory by fighting off other males, and announce their readiness for mating by singing a song that says to other males, "Keep off!" and to females, "Here I am, you lucky girl!" The male yellow-throat warbler recognizes other males by their black mask-like markings. Experiments in which a stuffed female bird had been painted with a black mask resulted in the male's pecking and ripping her to pieces. Similar experiments indicated that a black mustache on the flicker and a blue stripe on the fence lizard are the special signs of maleness, while the yellow face on the spotted turtle seems to be the crucial sign of femaleness.

Gecko lizards seem to have no pecking order and do not establish territorial claims. They may be so crowded on the tree trunk that in attempting to mate, one male may clasp another, but the reluctant male will shake himself free. Apparently this reptile cannot distinguish male from female, although when its nostrils are plugged, courtship stops, suggesting that an odor stimulates mating. The lion, the tomcat, the bull moose, the woodpecker, the frog, the cricket, the cicada, and even the spider make sounds to attract females and frighten off males.

COOPERATION

After pecking order is established, animals spend more time in cooperating than in fighting. They bring each other gifts, especially during the mating season, build nests for their families, and bring food to their offspring. A shelf of books could be written on the cooperative behavior of flies, turtles, bowerbirds, newts, elephants, baboons, and human beings. Most of animal behavior is purely instinctual, with a specific color, act, odor or feel giving rise to a specific response. Every cell and every local neighborhood inside every cell knows how to respond to every electrical and chemical situation. The human animal is unique in being able to mediate some of these reactions and in learning to resist some of its instinctual responses. The whole march of civilization depends on man's learning about these instincts in the other animals and in himself, and in learning to cooperate more than to fight. The human baby is one of the slowest of all animals in becoming independent. In this very long period of dependence he can be taught by his parents, teachers, and neighbors how to help, how to hurt, how to be creative, how to be a drudge, how to be a slave, or how to be free.

Today man is at the head of the pecking order, having outfought or outwitted every other animal, and much of mankind is busy, from the age of two or three, struggling for power with other men. This is evident in the rivalries of little children and big business tycoons, in negotiations around the conference table and in presidential elections, in the PTA and sandlot baseball. Civilization, which involves the art of being civil, accommodates better to power struggles through speech-making than through cobalt bombs. The civil-rights revolution means that those who have been outside the struggle are entering it. If men cannot control their hostile tendencies toward each other, it is likely that the new head of the pecking order may be the insects.

REFERENCES

GERARD, RALPH W., "Material Aspects of Mental Disease," *Diseases of the Nervous System* (May, 1959).

GUHL, A. M., "Psychophysiological Interrelations in the Social Behavior of Chickens," *Psychological Bulletin*, (1964), pp. 277–85.

LIDDELL, HOWARD, "The Biology of the Prejudiced Mind," in Jordan M. Sher, ed., *Theories of the Mind* (Glencoe, Ill.: Free Press, 1962).

LORENZ, KONRAD, *King Solomon's Ring* (New York: Thomas Y. Crowell Co., 1952).

MASSERMAN, JULES H., *Science and Psychoanalysis*, Vol. III (New York: Grune and Stratton, 1959).

MILNE, L. J., and M. J. MILNE, *The Mating Instinct* (Boston: Little, Brown and Co., 1950).

SCHAFFNER, BERTRAM, ed., *Group Processes* (New York: Josiah Macy, Jr., Foundation, 1959).

TINBERGEN, N., "Psychology and Ethology as Supplementary Parts of a Science of Be-havior," in Bertram Schaffner, ed., *Group Processes* (New York: Josiah Macy, Jr., Foundation, 1959).

OEHLERT, BEATRICE, "Kampf und Paarbildung bei einigen Cichliden," *Ztschr f. Tierpsychol.*

SHER, JORDON M., ed., *Theories of the Mind* (Glencoe: The Free Press, 1962).

23 | THE STRESS OF LIFE

HANS SELYE

When one steps on a splinter, a vast complex of interrelated reactions occurs. The pituitary gland emits notices; the adrenal cortex releases hormonal messengers which influence the lymphatic system to contract, the heart to beat faster, the stomach to ulcerate; and these in turn instigate still other changes. How does the pituitary gland know when to secrete its hormones; how does the lymphatic system know when and how much to contract; and how does the heart know when to beat faster? Toward the end of his book The Stress of Life, *Dr. Selye offers some fascinating explanations for these phenomena, speculating on the possibilities that every cell in the body has a "mind" of its own, with its individual memory, several ways of receiving and interpreting messages, and the ability to react in one or more of several possible ways. The selection from* The Stress of Life *that follows summarizes some of the remarkable discoveries made since 1935 by this modern Pasteur, who is director of the Institute of Experimental Medicine and Surgery at the University of Montreal.*

What is stress? The soldier who sustains wounds in battle, the mother who worries about her soldier son, the gambler who watches the races, the horse and the jockey he bet on: they are all under stress. The beggar who suffers from hunger and the glutton who overeats, the little shopkeeper with his constant fears of bankruptcy and the rich merchant struggling for yet another million: they are also all under stress. Stress is not always due to something bad, nor is it always bad for you. Stress is the rate at which we live at

Reprinted from Hans Selye, *The Stress of Life.* Copyright © 1956 by Hans Selye and used by permission of the publisher, McGraw-Hill Book Company; and from Hans Selye, "The Two-Edged Sword of Stress," *Canada's Health and Welfare*, May, 1964, by permission of the author.

any one moment. All living beings are constantly under stress and anything, pleasant or unpleasant, that speeds up the intensity of life, causes a temporary increase in stress, the wear and tear exerted upon the body. A painful blow and a passionate kiss can be equally stressful.

The word "stress" has long been used by laymen to designate tension, fatigue or exhaustion, but it was not until recently that physicians began to realize that stress can be scientifically analyzed and objectively appraised by certain characteristic changes in the structural and chemical composition of the body. At the same time, we learned that stress does not consist merely of damage, but also adaptation to damage, irrespective of what causes wear and tear.

It might help to explain the essence of stress as we now understand it in medicine, if I briefly related the circumstances under which I first stumbled upon what I later called the "*Stress Syndrome.*" (A syndrome is a group of changes which tend to appear conjointly.)

In 1925, I had just completed the preclinical subjects required at that time in medical schools as preparation before ever seeing a patient. Then finally came the great day when we were to hear our first lecture in internal medicine and see how a patient should be examined. By way of introduction, we were shown several instances of the earliest stages of various infectious diseases.

SIGNS OF ILLNESS

Each of these patients felt and looked ill, had a coated tongue, complained of fatigue, with more or less diffuse aches and pains in the joints, intestinal disturbances, loss of weight and appetite, etc. All this was quite evident to me, but the professor attached very little significance to any of it. He enumerated only a few "characteristic signs" which might help us in the diagnosis of disease. These I could not see. They were either still absent or at least so inconspicuous that my untrained eye could not distinguish them. Yet, we were told that these were the important changes to which we would have to give all our attention. The professor explained that, at this early stage, most of the specific, typical diagnostic signs were not yet evident and until they appeared not much could be done. Without them, we could not tell precisely what the patient suffered from and, hence, it was quite impossible to recommend any efficient, specific treatment. I was struck by the fact that the many features of disease which were already manifest even to me, did not interest our teacher merely because they

were "nonspecific," that is, not characteristic of any one disease.

I realized that we had to find typical disease manifestations in order to identify the particular cause of disease in any one patient. This was obviously indispensable before we could prescribe any medicines having the specific effect of killing the germs or neutralizing the poisons that made these people sick. But what impressed me, the novice, much more was that apparently only few signs are actually characteristic of any one disease; most of them are apparently quite common to many, or perhaps even to all diseases.

I wondered why such widely different disease-producing agents as those of measles, scarlet fever or tuberculosis, share the property of evoking the nonspecific manifestations, just mentioned. I also wondered why medicine concentrated all its efforts upon the recognition of individual diseases and the discovery of specific remedies for them, without giving any attention to the much more obvious "*syndrome of just being sick.*" The patients we had just seen had a syndrome, but this seemed to be the syndrome that characterized disease as such, not any one particular disease. Would it be possible, I asked myself, to analyze the mechanism of this ubiquitous syndrome and perhaps even to find drugs which act against the nonspecific factor in disease?

. . . . .

HOW TO QUESTION NATURE

The Urge to Learn

What is disease—not any one disease, just disease in general? This question lingered on in my mind. . . .

. . . . .

What is disease?—What is stress?

I did not know how to ask the first of these questions; I did not even think of asking the second.

Not until about ten years after hearing my first lecture in internal medicine did these same problems confront me again, although now under entirely different circumstances. At the time, I was working as a young assistant in the Biochemistry Department of McGill University in Montreal, on an entirely unrelated subject: the sex hormones. Still, I must say something about this work because it led me right back to the "syndrome of being sick."

Great Hopes

Various extracts prepared from the ovaries (the female sex glands) and the placenta (the highly vascular afterbirth through which the embryo gets nourishment from the mother's womb) are very rich in female sex hormones.

A *hormone* is a specific chemical messenger-substance, made by an endocrine gland and secreted into the blood, to regulate and coordinate the functions of distant organs. Sex hormones are coordinators of sexual activities, including reproduction.

An *extract* is made by mixing tissue (say, the ovaries of cows) with solvents (water, alcohol, etc.) and taking what goes into solution. The extract is pure when it contains only the desired substance (for instance, a hormone) and impure when it also contains contaminants (for instance, unwanted and perhaps damaging ovarian substances).

Several sex hormones had already been prepared by that time (1935), but I thought there was still another one to be discovered. . . . To prove my point, I injected rats with various ovarian and placental extracts to see whether the organs of these animals would show such changes as could not be due to any known sex hormone.

Much to my satisfaction, such changes were produced in my rats even by my first and most impure extracts:

1. There was a considerable enlargement of the *adrenal cortex*.

The *adrenals* are two little endocrine glands which lie just above the kidneys, on both sides. Each of them consists of two portions, a central part, the medulla, and an outer rind, the cortex. Both of these parts produce hormones, but not the same kind. My extracts seemed to stimulate the cortex, without causing much of a change in the medulla. The cortical portion of the adrenals was not only enlarged, but it also showed the microscopic features of increased activity (such as cell-multiplication and discharge of stored secretion droplets into the blood).

2. There was an intense shrinking (or atrophy) of the thymus, the spleen, the lymph nodes, and of all other lymphatic structures in the body.

The *lymphatic structures* are made up of innumerable, small white blood cells, similar to the *lymphocytes*, which circulate in the blood. . . .

The *lymphocytes* are made in the lymph nodes, little nodules in the groins, under the armpits, along the neck, and in various other parts of the body. Lymphocytes also make up most of the tissue in the *thymus* and *spleen*: that is why these organs are called *lymphatic tissues* or *thymicolymphatic system*. The thymus is a huge lymphatic organ just in front of the heart in the chest. In children it is very well developed but, after puberty, it tends to shrink, presumably under the influence of sex hormones.

When I saw that the lymphatic organs had so rapidly disintegrated in the rats, I naturally also examined the lymphocytes in the blood. Their number had also diminished under the influence of my tissue extracts, but while studying them I accidentally found an even more striking change in the blood picture: the almost complete disappearance of the *eosinophil cells*.

These are somewhat larger white blood cells, which have received their name because they stain very easily with a dye called *eosin*. . . . The function of the eosinophils is also still debated, but they seem to be related to allergy, because their number increases remarkably when a person suffers from asthma, hay fever, or allied conditions.

3. There appeared bleeding, deep *ulcers* in the lining of the stomach, and that uppermost part of the gut, just after the stomach, which we call the duodenum.

These three types of changes formed a definite syndrome, because they were closely interdependent in some way. When I injected only a small amount of extract, all these changes were slight; when I injected much extract, they were all very pronounced. But with no extract could I ever produce one of these three changes without the others. This interdependence of lesions is precisely what makes them a syndrome.

· · · · ·

. . . To me, the most important thing was that no ovarian hormone, or combination of ovarian hormones, known at that time ever produced adrenal enlargement, thymicolymphatic involution, and ulcers in the intestinal tract. It seemed rather obvious that we were dealing with a *new* ovarian hormone.

You may well imagine my happiness! At the age of 28, I seemed to be already on the track of a new hormone. . . .

Grave Doubts

Unfortunately, this happiness was not to last long. Not only ovarian, but placental, extracts also produced our triad. This did not worry me very much at first; after all, we knew that both the ovaries and the placenta can produce female sex hormones. I began to be somewhat confused, however, when it turned out subsequently that even pituitary extracts produced the same syndrome.

The *pituitary* (or hypophysis) is a little endocrine gland embedded in the bones of the skull, just below the brain. It produces a number of hormones, but, as far as we know, no ovarian hormones.

Yet, even this was not too disturbing, since mine was supposed to be a new hormone and (who knew?) perhaps the pituitary could manufacture this one.

But I really became puzzled when I found, a little later, that extracts of the kidney, spleen, or any other organ would produce the same triad. Was the causative factor some kind of general "tissue hormone" that could be produced by almost any cell?

Another inexplicable fact was that all efforts to purify the active extracts led to a diminution of their potency. The crudest preparations—the most impure ones—were invariably the most active. This did not seem to make sense.

The Great Disappointment

I shall never forget one particularly dark, rainy afternoon during the spring of 1936, when the great disappointment came. . . .

It was then that a horrible thought occurred to me: for all I knew, this entire syndrome might be due merely to the toxicity of my extracts, to the fact that I did not purify them well enough.

In this case, of course, all my work meant nothing. I was not on the track of a new ovarian hormone; indeed, I was not even dealing with any specific ubiquitous "tissue hormone," but merely with damage as such.

As I thought of this, my eyes happened to fall upon a bottle of Formalin [an extremely toxic and irritating fluid] on a shelf in front of my desk.

· · · · ·

Now, I thought, if my syndrome is really due only to tissue-damage, I should be able to reproduce it by injecting rats with a dilute Formalin solution. The cells in immediate contact with the Formalin would be precipitated and killed and considerable tissue-damage would result. This seemed to be a good way to formulate the question I wanted to ask: can even a toxic fluid not derived from any living tissue also produce my syndrome?

I immediately undertook such experiments and, within 48 hours, when I examined the organs of my animals, the answer was only too clear. In all the rats there was even more adrenocortical enlargement, thymicolymphatic atrophy, and intestinal-ulcer formation than I had ever been able to produce with any of my tissue-extracts.

I do not think I have ever been more profoundly disappointed! Suddenly all my dreams of discovering a new hormone were shattered. All the time and all the materials that went into this long study were wasted. . . . I became so depressed that for a few days I could not do any work at all. I just sat in my laboratory, brooding about how this misadventure might have been avoided and wondering what was to be done now.

. . . . .

THE BIRTH OF THE G.A.S.

A New Point of View

As I repetitiously continued to go over my ill-fated experiments and their possible interpretation, it suddenly struck me that one could look at them from an entirely different angle. If there was such a thing as single nonspecific reaction of the body to damage of any kind, this might be worth study for its own sake. Indeed, working out the mechanism of this kind of stereotyped "syndrome of response to injury as such" might be much more important to medicine than the discovery of yet another sex hormone.

As I repeated to myself, "a syndrome of response to injury as such," gradually, my early classroom impressions of the clinical "syndrome of just being sick" be-

gan to reappear dimly out of my subconsciousness, where they had been buried for over a decade. Could it be that this syndrome in man (the feeling of being ill, the diffuse pains in joints and muscles, the intestinal disturbances with loss of appetite, the loss of weight) were in some manner clinical equivalents of the experimental syndrome, the triad (adrenocortical stimulation, thymicolymphatic atrophy, intestinal ulcers) that I had produced with such a variety of toxic substances in the rat?

If This Were So . . .

If this were so, the general medical implications of the syndrome would be enormous! Some degree of nonspecific damage is undoubtedly superimposed upon the specific characteristics of any disease, upon the specific effects of any drug.

. . . . .

It had long been learned by sheer experience that certain curative measures were nonspecific, that is, useful to patients suffering from almost any disease. Indeed, such measures had been in use for centuries. One advises the patient to go to bed and take it easy; one tells him to eat only very digestible food and to protect himself against drafts or great variations in temperature and humidity.

Furthermore, there were all these nonspecific treatments that we had learned about in medical school, such as injection of substances foreign to the body, fever therapy, shock therapy, or bloodletting. They were unquestionably useful in certain cases. The trouble was that often they did not help, and sometimes they did much harm; since one knew nothing about the mechanism of their action, using them was like taking a shot in the dark.

. . . . .

A Change of Mind

I was simply fascinated by these new possibilities and immediately decided to reverse my plans for the future. Instead of dropping the stress problem and returning to classical endocrinology, I was now prepared to spend the rest of my life studying it. . . .

Discouragement

. . . I remember one senior investigator whom I admired very much and whose opinion meant a great deal to me. I knew he was a real friend who seriously wanted to help me with my research efforts. One day . . . he asked me into his office for a good heart-to-heart talk . . . to convince me that I must abandon this futile line of research. . . .

I met [his] remarks with my usual outbursts of uncontrolled youthful enthusiasm for the new point of view; I outlined again the immense possibilities inherent in a study of the nonspecific damage which must accompany all diseases and all but the mildest medications.

When he saw me thus launched on yet another enraptured description of what I had observed in animals treated with this or that impure, toxic material, he looked at me with desperately sad eyes and said in obvious despair, "But, Selye, try to realize what you are doing before it is too late! You have now decided to spend your entire life studying *the pharmacology of dirt!*"

. . . . .

Encouragement

In such moments of doubt I derived considerable strength and courage from the fact that, right from the beginning, one of the most respected Canadian scientists, Sir Frederick Banting, was manifestly interested in my plans. . . .

. . . . .

I often wonder whether I could have stuck to my guns without his encouragement.

Plans for Future Research

The next point to decide was how to go about studying *the new syndrome*. . . . "Just how nonspecific is this syndrome?" Up to now, I had elicited it only by injecting foreign substances (tissue-extracts, Formalin). Subsequent experiments showed that one can produce essentially the same syndrome with purified hormones, for instance, with adrenaline (a hormone of the adrenal medulla), or with insulin (a hormone of the pancreas). One can also produce it with physical agents, such as cold, heat, x-rays, or mechanical trauma; one can produce it with hemorrhage, pain, or forced muscular exercise; indeed, *I could find no noxious agent that did not elicit the syndrome*. . . .

. . . . .

The First Publication
on the Stress Syndrome

My first paper, in which I endeavored to show that the syndrome of stress can be studied independently of all specific changes, happened to come out on . . . July 4, in 1936. It was published as a brief note of only 74 lines in a single column of the British journal *Nature*, under the title, "A Syndrome Produced by Diverse Nocuous Agents."

. . . . .

The Three Stages

In this . . . paper I . . . suggested the name *alarm reaction* for the initial response—that is, in the previously mentioned triad—because I thought that this syndrome probably represented the bodily expression of a generalized call to arms of the defensive forces in the organism.

But this alarm reaction was . . . not the whole response. My . . . experiments showed that upon continued exposure to any noxious agent capable of eliciting this alarm reaction (unless it killed immediately), a stage of adaptation or resistance followed. . . . If survival is possible . . . , this alarm reaction is necessarily followed by a second stage, which I called the *stage of resistance.*

The manifestations of this second stage were quite different from, and in many instances the exact opposite of, those which characterized the alarm reaction. For instance, during the alarm reaction, the cells of the adrenal cortex discharged their microscopically visible granules of secretion (which contain the hormone) into the blood stream. Consequently, the stores of the gland were depleted. Conversely, in the stage of resistance, the cortex accumulated an abundant reserve of secretory granules. In the alarm reaction, the blood became concentrated and there was a marked loss of body-weight; but during the stage of resistance, the blood was diluted and the body-weight returned toward normal. . . .

. . . After still more prolonged exposure to any of the noxious agents I used, this acquired adaptation was eventually lost. The animal entered into a third phase, the *stage of exhaustion,* the symptoms of which were, in many respects, strikingly similar to those of the initial alarm reaction. At the end of a life under stress, this was a kind of premature aging due to wear and tear. . . .

All these findings made it necessary to coin an additional all-embracing name for the entire syndrome. Since the latter appeared to be so evidently related to adaptation, I called the entire nonspecific response the *general adaptation syndrome.* This is usually abbreviated as G. A. S. . . .

. . . . .

DISSECTION OF STRESS

. . . . .

. . . *Stress is defined as the state which manifests itself by the G.A.S.* The latter comprises: adrenal stimulation, shrinkage of lymphatic organs, gastrointestinal ulcers, loss of body-weight, alterations in the chemical composition of the body, and so forth. All these changes form a syndrome, a set of manifestations which appear together.

In tissues more directly affected by stress, there develops a *local adaptation syndrome* (L.A.S.); for instance, there is inflammation where microbes enter the body.

L.A.S. and G.A.S. are closely coordinated. Chemical *alarm signals* are sent out by directly stressed tissues, from the L.A.S. area to the centers of coordination in the *nervous system* and to endocrine glands, especially the *pituitary* and the *adrenals,* which produce *adaptive hormones,* to combat wear and tear in the body. Thus the generalized response (G.A.S.) acts back upon the L.A.S. region.

Roughly speaking, the adaptive hormones fall into two groups: the *anti-inflammatory hormones* (ACTH, cortisone, COL), which inhibit excessive defensive reactions, and the *proinflammatory hormones* (STH, aldosterone, DOC), which stimulate them. The effects of all these substances can be modified, or conditioned, by other hormones (adrenalines, or the thyroid hormone), nervous reactions, diet, heredity, and the tissue-memories of previous exposures to stress. Derailments of this G.A.S.-mechanism produce wear-and-tear-diseases, that is, *diseases* of *adaptation.*

In a nutshell, the response to stress has a tripartite mechanism, consisting of: (1) the direct effect of the stressor upon the body; (2) internal responses which stimulate tissue-defense; and (3) internal responses which stimulate tissue-surrender by inhibiting defense. *Resistance and adaptation depend on a proper balance of these three factors.*

Surgical Techniques

. . . In our Institute last year, we used about 400 rats a week for research. . . . In a standard experiment a rat is anesthetized with ether, or some other anesthetic, until it is completely unconscious and unable to move or feel pain. Then the experimenter can expose a gland and remove it to learn how the rat will react to stress without this organ. Similarly the experimental surgeon can transect a sensory nerve if, for his studies, he wants to render a certain region of the body insensitive to pain. He can diminish the blood-flow through an artery by putting a constricting loop of thread around it, and so forth. After the operation, the animal wakes up and is then ready for observation.

. . . . .

Chemical Techniques

There is much we can learn only through the application of chemical methods. For instance, if we want to study the actions of corticoids, we can get large quantities of beef-adrenals from the slaughterhouse and extract hormones from these glands. . . .

Morphologic Techniques

Morphology literally means "the science of shape" (from Greek *morphē*, shape, form, plus *-logy*, science of). . . . By merely looking at [the structure or cellular pattern of tissues] through a microscope we can learn much about the function of certain organs. For example, the resting adrenal is laden with small fat-droplets—readily visible under the microscope—which contain the fat-soluble hormones; the active gland discharges its reserves into the blood and, therefore contains no such droplets.

. . . . .

During stress we noticed changes in all these tissues, but we did not know how —through what pathways—they were produced. As far as we could tell, when we began this work, the thymus might have produced some hormone which stimulates the adrenals. But this possibility was soon ruled out. After surgically removing the thymus (point 4 in the preceding figure) of rats, their adrenals (point 2) still became enlarged and overactive during stress. Conversely, however, after the adrenals were removed, the thymus no longer showed the changes characteristic of the stress-reaction. Finally, we found that injections of adrenal extracts (rich in corticoid hormones) produced typical stress-changes in the thymus, even after adrenalectomy. Obviously the pathway went from adrenal to thymus and not from thymus to adrenal.

Now the question arose, "How does the adrenal know when there is stress and, therefore, a need for large amounts of corticoid hormone?" In other words, what is the immediately preceding link in this sequence of events? After unsuccessfully trying various other possibilities, we removed the pituitary and found that, after interruption of the biologic chain-reaction at this point (point 1), exposure to stress now no longer stimulated the adrenal glands (point 2). On the other hand—even without stress, and even in the absence of the pituitary—injection of a pituitary hormone, ACTH, . . . caused typical stress-changes in the adrenal. It became enlarged and produced a great excess of its own hormones. Evidently, the adrenal was a relay station between point 1 and certain points farther down the chain.

It is easy to see how—using this sketch as a blueprint for the dissection of stress—the whole complex endocrine network of the G.A.S. became amenable to scientific analysis. We merely had to interrupt the network by the removal of a gland and then correct the resulting defect by the injection of the gland's special hormone.

This kind of work is still in progress and will have to continue for quite some time. We, like hundreds of other investigators, are busy trying to disentangle the many still mysterious complexities of the stress-machinery. But now let us take stock and see what we have managed to find out about it so far.

. . . . .

. . . The pituitary gland is embedded in bones at the base of the skull and regulates the production of corticoids through its *adrenocorticotrophic hormone* or ACTH. It does not matter that the adrenals are placed above the kidneys, at a great distance from the pituitary, because hormones are carried equally to all organs through the blood. When the pituitary produces ACTH, this trophic (from Greek *trephein,* to nourish) hormone incites the cells of the adrenal cortex to transform all suitable raw materials into corticoids. These are then also discharged into the blood so that they can act throughout the body wherever they are needed.

. . . . .

. . . We have seen, for instance, that if one rat is exposed to intense sound, another to severe cold, and yet another to scalding of a paw, there is a moderate adrenal enlargement in each of them.

There is a definite limit to the adrenal stimulation that can be produced by any one agent, say scalding a small area, no matter how severely. On the other hand, if a rat is exposed to sound, cold, and scalding simultaneously, the resulting adrenal enlargement will be much greater than that produced by any one of these stressors. Obviously these three distinct agents must have had some common effect through which their actions upon the adrenal could be added.

It is apparently the discharge of alarm signals that makes stress the common denominator of the most diverse reactions to all kinds of agents.

The Course of the Stress-Response Is Triphasic

If we follow the development of the G.A.S. in time, we can see that it goes through a typical triphasic course. . . . If an animal is continuously exposed to some stressor (say cold), the adrenal cortex first discharges all its microscopic fat-granules which contain the cortical hormones (alarm reaction), then it becomes laden with an unusually large number of fat-droplets (stage of resistance) and finally it loses them again (stage of exhaustion). As far as we can see, the same triphasic course is followed by most, if not all, of the manifestations of the G.A.S.

The next figure illustrates this graphically, using general resistance to injury as an indicator.

In the acute phase of the alarm reaction (A.R.), general resistance, to the particular stressor with which the G.A.S. had been elicited, falls way below normal. Then, as adaptation is acquired, in the stage of resistance (S.R.), the capacity to resist rises considerably above

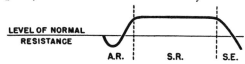

normal. But eventually, in the stage of exhaustion (S.E.), resistance drops below normal again.

You may well ask, "How does one find out about such things?"

We exposed large numbers of rats to various stressors over long periods of time and tested the resistance of sample groups among these animals at repeated intervals. For instance, in one experiment we placed a hundred rats in a refrigerated room where the temperature was near freezing. Thanks to their fur coats, they could stand this quite well, although during the first 48 hours they developed the typical manifestations of the alarm reaction. This was proved by killing ten animals at the end of the second day; all of them had large fat-free adrenals, small thymuses, and stomach ulcers.

At this same time—after 48 hours of exposure—twenty other rats were also removed from the cold-room to test their resistance to low temperatures. They were now placed in a still colder chamber, together with normal rats which up to then had lived at room temperature. It turned out that the rats which had already developed an alarm reaction due to moderate cold were even less than normally resistant to excessive cold.

Five weeks later another sample of rats was taken from the cold-room. By that time they had fully adapted themselves to life at low temperature and were in the stage of resistance of the G.A.S. When these animals were placed in the still more refrigerated chamber, they survived temperatures which nonpretreated animals could never withstand. Evidently their resistance had risen above the normal level.

Yet, after several months of life in the cold, this acquired resistance was lost again, and the stage of exhaustion set in. Then the animals were not even capable of further surviving in the comparatively moderate cold of the refrigerated chamber in which they had spent so much time in a state of perfect well-being, even since the initiation of the experiment.

The three waves in the curve (down, up, and down again) represent a summary of many such observations, because this type of experiment was repeated with various other stressors (forced muscular work, drugs, infections) and the result was always the same.

Adaptability can be well trained to serve a special purpose, but eventually it runs out; its amount is finite.

This was not what I had expected. I should have thought that once an animal has learned to live in the cold, it could go on resisting low temperatures indefinitely. Why shouldn't it, as long as it received enough food to create the internal heat necessary for the maintenance of a normal body-temperature? . . .

Similar experiments have . . . revealed that the same loss of acquired adaptation also occurs in animals forced to perform intense muscular exercise, or in those given toxic drugs and other stressors over long periods of time. . . .

The Defense Is Antagonistic

There are two principal ways of defending yourself against aggression: to advance and attack the foe or to retreat and run out of his reach. Both these techniques are also used by the defensive forces of our tissues against foes inside the body. For instance, there are serologic mechanisms which can defend us against invading microbes. When a germ gets into the blood stream it can be killed by these purely aggressive, chemical substances which we call *antibodies*. There is no element of retreat, no flight in this response. Conversely, if I accidentally put my hand on a hot plate, my muscles will immediately pull the burned hand back. This happens whether I want it to or not, because it is an involuntary reflex of flight. There is nothing aggressive about this; I make no effort to destroy the source of my injury, but merely draw away from it.

To my mind, it is one of the most characteristic features of the G.A.S. that its various defensive mechanisms are always based on combinations of these two types of response: advance and retreat. . . .

Survival depends largely upon a correct blending of advance, retreat, and standing one's ground. . . .

The principal coordinating systems of the body are the nervous and the hormonal systems. In both of these we have pairs of antagonists. As far as the fight for survival is concerned, we might call them the *pro-* and the *antidefense factors.* The former carry the message to act or to advance, the latter to relax or to retreat.

As regards the *nervous system* this had been known for a long time. The voluntary muscles of our limbs are innervated by antagonistic nerve fibers; so are the many involuntary muscles which innervate the stomach, intestines, blood vessels, and other internal organs.

How do nerves act this way? Interestingly, in the final analysis even they act through hormones. At the minute endpoints of each nerve-branch, hormone-like chemical substances are discharged, and it is these which act upon the tissues, for instance, upon the muscles to cause contraction.

. . . . .

The nerve hormone which acts as an antagonist of the adrenalines is called *acetylcholine.* As far as we know, it is not produced and secreted into the general blood stream by any endocrine gland; it is liberated only at nerve-endings.

The *adrenal cortex* makes a large number of hormones. Some of these are sex hormones, . . . [which are] quite similar to those produced by the sex glands. They have little or nothing to do with stress research, but may cause severe sexual derangements. For instance, most of the bearded women who exhibit themselves in circuses, are suffering from an excessive production of male hormones by their adrenals. Three- to four-year-old little girls may develop mature breasts and other sexual characteristics of adult women merely as a result of excessive female-hormone production by their adrenals.

. . . . .

At first it was thought that the adrenal cortex produced only one kind of vital hormone; this was called *cortine.* But further research showed that there are at least two types of such hormones. It was at that time—some fifteen years ago —that I proposed the term *corticoid hormones,* as a collective name for this group.

The outstanding effect of one type of corticoid is to inhibit inflammation. Inflammation is a defense reaction of the tissues; so this type of hormone can be regarded as an antidefense hormone, in that it prevents a defensive reaction. There are several such hormones. Let us call them *anti-inflammatory corticoids* (A-Cs). To this group belong cortisone and cortisol, which have become so generally known because of their conspicuous beneficial effects in rheumatoid arthritis, allergic inflammation, inflammation of the eyes, and other inflammatory diseases.

The opposite kind are quite naturally designated as the *proinflammatory corticoids* (P-Cs). These are less well known by the general public, because we are just beginning to learn something about their role in clinical medicine. Aldosterone and desoxycorticosterone are two such proinflammatory hormones.

. . . . .

If, for the sake of simplicity, we group them this way, we must constantly bear in mind, however, that these terms are merely symbols; they do not tell the whole story. First, it is only under certain conditions that the two types of corticoids inhibit or stimulate inflammation. Second, they do many other things besides acting on inflammation. For instance, the anti-inflammatory corticoids can also raise the blood sugar; therefore, biochemists prefer to call them *glucocorticoids* (from glucose). On the other hand, one of the most outstanding chemical effects of proinflammatory corticoids is to influence mineral metabolism; they are *mineralocorticoids* in that they cause a retention of sodium and an excretion of potassium.

. . . . .

Finally, it must be kept in mind that although the anti- and proinflammatory corticoids do, under certain conditions, diametrically oppose each other's effects on inflammation, this is not always so; nor are these hormones necessarily antagonistic as regards their other actions. In some respects they may actually be synergistic, that is, they may work together and mutually increase each other's effects.

. . . . .

STRESS AND INFLAMMATION

Forms of Inflammation

Inflammation has been defined as "a local reaction to injury." It can occur almost anywhere in the body and it can take many forms; yet it is always the same kind of reaction. When fully developed it is always characterized by swelling, reddening, heat, and pain.

If a particle of dust gets under your eyelid, there will be some pain, with reddening and swelling . . . ; we call it *conjunctivitis.*

If a child develops a sore throat, what usually happens is that certain microbes proliferate in his tonsils and cause local swelling, reddening, heat, and pain. This is an inflammation of the tonsils; we call it *tonsillitis.*

A patient may come down suddenly with violent pain in his abdomen because microbes have gotten out of control in one small part of his intestine, the appendix, and caused swelling, heat, reddening, and pain there; this is *appendicitis.* . . .

The disorders which I have just mentioned are very different, indeed; yet all of them are examples of . . . *inflammation.* In medicine it became customary to add the suffix -*itis* after the name of the organ affected, to indicate that an inflammation had developed in it. . . . Inflammation of the liver is *hepatitis*; of the kidney, *nephritis*; of the joints, *arthritis*; of the nerves *neuritis*; . . . of the heart, . . . *endocarditis*; of the stomach, . . . *gastritis*; and of the skin, . . . *dermatitis.*

From all this it is evident that virtually any agent can cause inflammation in virtually any part of the body, and the resulting conditions present the most varied aspects. Yet when you examine the affected organs under the microscope, the cellular changes in them are essentially the same in every case.

Surely this gives food for thought. No one can look upon this list of disorders without feeling the need for some unifying explanation. How could so many conditions be so vastly different and yet be the same, in the sense that they are all inflammations? This is undoubtedly a striking instance of nonspecificity in bodily reactions. . . .

The Structure of Inflammation

We have said, "Inflammation is a reaction to injury." If so, it must be something active; it is not merely the passive result of injury, but a positive reaction against it. By calling it a *reaction,* we also imply that it has a purpose; apparently its object is to repulse the aggressor and mend whatever damage has been caused.

But what is its structure? . . . The reddening and heat are due to a dilatation of the blood vessels in the inflamed area. The swelling is caused, partly, by the leakage of fluids and cells from the dilated blood vessels into the surrounding solid tissues, and, partly, by an intense proliferation of the fibrous connective tissue, whose cells rapidly multiply in response to irritation. The pain is due to an irritation of the sensory nerve-endings which are caught in and invaded by this inflammatory process.

These cardinal signs have long been known to physicians. They were first clearly described in the Third Book of the famous *Treatise on Medicine,* which Aurelius Cornelius Celsus, the great Roman physician, wrote just a few years before the birth of Christ. This volume contains what is probably the most quoted sentence in medical writing: "Indeed, the signs of inflammation are four, redness and swelling with heat and pain." To this was later added: "and interference with function," because the swelling and the pain always diminish the functional efficiency of inflamed organs.

The parts of the body work in a very similar way. We have seen, for instance, that if a dirty splinter of wood gets under your skin, the tissues around it swell up and become inflamed. You develop a boil or an abscess. This is a useful, healthy response, because the tissues forming the wall of this boil represent a barricade which prevents any further spread throughout the body of microbes or poisons that may have been introduced with the splinter. But sometimes the body's reactions are excessive and quite out of proportion to the fundamen-

tally innocuous irritation to which it was exposed. . . .

. . . . .

The Diseases of Adaptation

. . . If the adrenal must produce an excess of corticoids to maintain life during stress, it is quite probable that the resulting hormone-excess in itself may have dangerous consequences. It is a well-known fact that flooding the body with any hormone produces disease. When the thyroid secretes too much of its hormones, metabolism is unduly accelerated. When the pituitary manufactures huge amounts of STH, the result is gigantism. When the adrenal medulla discharges an excess of its adrenalines, the pulse quickens and the blood pressure rises dangerously. It was quite natural to ask, therefore, "What would happen if the adrenal secreted an excess of corticoids?" It obviously does so during stress. But this question could not be answered by just examining a patient in stress; in him it would be impossible to distinguish between the effects of the corticoids and those of stress itself.

. . . . .

Naturally, the thing to do was to give enormous amounts of corticoids to normal experimental animals and just see what happened. But, in 1941 when we reached this point in our work, only one corticoid, DOC (one of the P-C hormones) was available in adequate amounts for such experiments, and even it was very scarce and expensive. Besides, most of the common experimental animals are singularly resistant to DOC. If one just injects this hormone into the usual laboratory animals nothing seems to happen; and, of course, at that time nobody knew how to sensitize or condition the body for this substance. Curiously, even now, after some fifteen years of research, I have found no animal which would be more sensitive to DOC (without special conditioning) than the newly hatched chick. This is why it was fortunate that, by sheer accident, I happened to use young chicks for my first experiments.

. . . . .

To start with, I bought 24 three-day-old white Leghorn chicks. . . . When we were satisfied that our birds were well taken care of, we divided them into two groups: twelve received daily injections of DOC, and the other twelve acted as untreated controls. During the first ten days I could see no difference between the two groups. Then all the DOC-treated chicks began to drink much more water than the controls, and gradually they developed a kind of dropsy. Their bodies became enormously swollen with fluid-accumulations under the skin and they began to breathe with difficulty, gasping for air, just like certain cardiac patients.

On the twentieth day, we killed both the DOC-treated and the control pullets to examine their internal organs. Upon dissection it was striking that, under the influence of the hormone, large amounts of fluid had also accumulated in their body-cavities and especially within the sac that surrounds the heart (the pericardium). The heart itself was much enlarged and the walls of the blood vessels had become thick and rigid; they looked very much like those of patients suffering from high blood pressure. The most pronounced changes occurred in the kidneys, which were swollen and had an irregular, discolored surface. . . .

. . . . .

Clearly here, in an experimental animal, we had reproduced all the six major features of Bright's disease: (1) characteristic structural changes in the kidneys, (2) enlargment of the heart muscle; (3) thickening and hardening of the arteries; (4) high blood pressure; (5) general-ized dropsy; and (6) elimination of albumin into the urine.

. . . . .

This started . . . a great controversy in medical literature. Hypertensive kidney disease is one of the most common fatal maladies of man; and since nothing was known about its cause, naturally any clue had to be carefully analyzed. Physicians were particularly reluctant to accept my view, because, in the whole of endocrinology, there was no precedent of any such inflammatory or degenerative disease caused by hormones. . . .

Can Corticoids Produce Renal and Cardiovascular Diseases in Mammals?

The first question which now arose was whether an experimental Bright's disease could be produced by corticoids only in chicks or also in mammals. The structure of the kidney is similar in man and in other mammals, but in birds it is quite different. Naturally we wanted to repeat our experiments on mammals. In this we failed. When DOC was injected into rats, guinea pigs, dogs, or cats, no obvious changes were noted either in the kidneys or the heart or the blood vessels. . . .

It was at this time that the idea of some special "conditioning" for corticoids began to take shape. Could we identify the factor which renders chicks particularly sensitive to an excess of corticoids? Would this same factor participate in the development of corticoid-overdosage diseases in man?

Medical experience had shown long ago that patients suffering from Bright's disease cannot stand much salt. . . .

With this in mind, we proceeded to give newly-hatched chicks dilute solutions of sodium chloride as a drinking fluid; half of them, the controls, received no hormone treatment; the other half were given injections of DOC. It turned out that surprisingly small doses of DOC can produce Bright's disease in birds kept on dilute sodium-chloride solutions which caused no damage in themselves.

We had proved that the experimental DOC disease resembled clinical Bright's disease in that both were aggravated by salt-supplements.

An interesting by-product of this work grew out of the observation that, on more concentrated solutions of sodium chloride, baby chicks develop a kind of Bright's disease, even without any hormone-treatment. This malady is well known to farmers and veterinarians as a spontaneous disease of pullets. . . .

Corticoids Can Produce Renal and Cardiovascular Diseases in Mammals

. . . In rats forced to drink 1 per cent sodium chloride, instead of water, DOC did produce nephrosclerosis and hypertension. Yet very large doses of hormone had to be injected for many weeks, and even so the changes were rather mild.

We than argued that the immature pullet may not have sufficient safety margin of renal function to adjust itself well to overdosage with salt and corticoids. If so, perhaps we could further augment the DOC-sensitivity even in mammals by simply taking out one of their kidneys.

In the next experimental series we removed the right kidney in a group of rats which were then forced to drink 1 per cent sodium chloride while receiving DOC. Here the hormone produced extremely marked and rapidly fatal nephrosclerosislike changes in the kidney, enlargement of the heart, hardening and inflammation (arteritis) of the blood vessels, as well as a pronounced rise in blood pressure. Most of these rats died from coronary lesions and cardiac infarcts.

. . . . .

This was an important turning point in the analysis of these diseases. Within the next few months it could be shown that,

after suitable conditioning (removal of one kidney and administration of salt-supplements), DOC also produces similar renal and cardiovascular changes in other mammals, such as the mouse, guinea pig, cat, dog, and even in the monkey . . . .

INFLAMMATORY DISEASES

The Basic Problems

. . . We have seen that the principal purpose of inflammation is to put a strong barricade of activated, connective tissue around a territory invaded, or at least damaged, by some disease-producer, thereby sharply *demarcating the sick from the healthy.*

If the invader is dangerous and threatens life because the causative agent could spread into the blood and throughout the body, then—and only then—this reaction is useful.

. . . Inflammation causes swelling, pain and interference with the function of the affected parts. All this is a small price to pay, however, when this reaction is our only means of maintaining health or even life: that is why inflammation is essentially a useful, adaptive response to injury.

But, *if the invader is harmless,* there is no point in reacting at all. An inoffensive plant-pollen, for instance, does not damage the tissues directly, and it could not invade the body as a whole. If we react to it with allergic inflammation, this is merely a sign of morbid hypersensitivity. Here the inflammation itself is actually what we experience as disease. In such cases we are not being injured, we merely injure ourselves. . . .

The Inflammatory-Pouch Test

In patients suffering from consumption, it is often useful to inject air (or some other gas) into the chest-cavity, so as to collapse a diseased lung and give it a rest to promote healing. Since, on the other hand, any kind of stress is particularly bad for tuberculous patients, I was interested in finding out exactly how stressful the air-injection itself would be. To determine this, I injected air into the chest-cavity in rats, with the intention of then measuring their adrenal-response as an indicator of stress.

It so happened while I was doing this, that a group of Brazilian physicians who visited our Institute, were shown into my lab by one of my assistants. As I turned around to greet them, my needle slipped out of the chest-cavity of the rat I was just injecting and all the air went under the skin; there it formed a perfectly regular, roughly egg-shaped connective-tissue sac. Why not *use air as a mold* with which to force connective tissue to form a sac of predictable size and shape? Air is very elastic and it need not be removed to permit fluid accumulation in the pouch. I then made such air-sacs on purpose, and injected some irritant (usually croton oil) into the cavity, so as to transform the lining connective tissue into an inflammatory barricade. It became a useful technique by which to study inflammation.

. . . . .

How is it possible that general stress sometimes cures and sometimes aggravates a local disease condition? Various shock therapies and other nonspecific treatments have clearly shown that general stress can cure certain diseases; yet we also know that so often a latent disease-tendency is transformed into a manifest malady by too much stress and strain. Could we not use the inflammatory-pouch test as a simple model with which to analyze this apparent paradox?

This is what the pouch looks like on a rat.

I took two groups of rats, in which an inflammatory pouch was produced under exactly identical conditions, except that in one group I put a weak irritant (dilute croton oil), in the other a strong irritant (more concentrated croton oil) into the air-sac. Shortly afterwards both these groups of animals were exposed to a general stressor in the form of a frustrating experience. . . . In such tests, the animals are forcefully immobilized, so that they cannot run around freely; this causes them to struggle and to become very angry. A rat wants to have his own way, just like a human being, and does not like to be prevented from doing what he wants to do. I thought that this kind of frustration and struggle would come about as close to the most common human stress-situations as we can come in rats, and wondered how it would influence local tissue-reactions to irritants.

. . . . .

In the rats which received the weak irritant, there was little inflammation and the general stress actually cured the local disease by inhibiting this tissue-response. The irritant was not strong enough to destroy the covering skin in any case, so it did not matter whether the substance was allowed to spread or not. Inflammation was the whole disease here and, by inhibiting it, the rat was cured.

In the animals treated with the strong irritant, there was much more inflammatory-barricade formation and fluid formation; still the adjacent tissues remained healthy, because the inflammatory barricade prevented the strong croton oil from spreading into the surroundings. Under the influence of general stress, however, the skin and all the adjacent tissues were infiltrated and destroyed by the spreading concentrated croton-oil solution. This was the crucial experiment showing that stress can either cure or aggravate a disease, depending upon whether the inflammatory response to a local irritant is necessary or superfluous.

. . . . .

. . . Using certain combinations of irritants and microbes in rats, we finally managed to produce a syndrome characterized, among other things, by an inflammation of the heart valves (endocarditis), very similar to that which occurs in children suffering from rheumatic fever. . . . The proinflammatory and anti-inflammatory hormones can modify the whole focal syndrome and . . . an excess of salt in the diet, after removal of one kidney, selectively aggravates the nephritis in the remaining kidney. . . .

The Experimental Arthritis Tests

Chronic inflammation of the joints (arthritis) is one of the most common, crippling, wear-and-tear diseases of man. We still had no adequate procedure for reproducing this condition in animals for the study of its mechanism and for the assay of hormones or drugs which may be used to treat it.

In searching for such a test, I noted that if we inject a drop of some irritant solution (Formalin, croton oil) under the skin of the sole into a hind paw of a rat, there develops a *local experimental arthritis* . . . . First there is acute swelling at the site of injection, and then this gradually transforms itself into a chronic arthritis of the many small joints in the paw and, particularly, of the ankle joint. This arthritis, due to local stress, becomes a permanently crippling disease for the rat, because the joints stiffen with hard connective tissue, so that they can no longer be moved. On the other hand, if the rat develops an alarm reaction due to some stressor or if anti-inflammatory hormones (for instance, ACTH, cortisone, or COL) are given at the right time— during the critical period of development—the arthritis can be completely

suppressed and here again the proinflammatory hormones (STH, DOC) have an opposite, aggravating effect.

This test proved to be useful, among other things, in the routine screening of new hormone derivatives and other anti-arthritic drugs, especially now that so many university laboratories and pharmaceutical companies are making such compounds. . . .

One disadvantage of this test is that an arthritis produced by the local injection of irritants into a joint is not quite comparable to the kind of arthritis that people develop. It was a great step forward, therefore, when Dr. Gaëtan Jasmin—while working for his Ph.D. degree at our Institute in 1955—discovered a more natural type of *multiple experimental arthritis*. . . . Drs. A. Horava and A. Robert, had noticed that a peculiar inflammatory fluid was produced by certain experimental tumors, when they were grown in the inflammatory pouch of the rat. Dr. Jasmin found that if one injects a single, cubic centimeter of this tumor-fluid into the blood of a rat, within a few days a pronounced inflammation appears in many of the joints, most frequently in the ankles, wrists, elbows, knee joints, and the many little joints between the vertebrae of the spinal column. It is impossible to say whether or not this experimental disease is closely related to the rheumatic or rheumatoid arthritis of man, but they certainly resemble each other in many respects. It was extremely instructive, therefore, to learn that this induced generalized arthritic tendency of the rat also depends upon the function of the pituitary-adrenal defense mechanism. The principal findings were these:

1. In intact rats—which can respond to stress by anti-inflammatory hormone-production—comparatively large amounts of tumor-fluid must be used to produce this arthritis.

2. In adrenalectomized rats maintained exclusively on the proinflammatory DOC, small amounts of fluid suffice to produce very pronounced and widespread arthritic changes.

3. In adrenalectomized rats treated only with the anti-inflammatory COL, even the largest doses of tumor-fluid produce little or no arthritis.

4. In adrenalectomized rats treated with both COL and DOC, the anti-inflammatory effect of the former is neutralized by the latter hormone.

Rheumatic and Rheumatoid Diseases of Man

. . . Rheumatic fever and rheumatoid arthritis . . . are typical inflammatory maladies; their essence is inflammation in the joints, the heart valves, and other tissues. These diseases are not identical with the experimental conditions which we produced in rats—no spontaneous malady of man is identical with its artificial counterpart in animals—but they are certainly very closely related and presumably governed by the same general laws. . . .

This was perhaps most clearly demonstrated by Professor Philip S. Hench and his associates at the Mayo Clinic in 1949, when ACTH and cortisone became available in sufficiently large amounts to be tested on patients. These investigators found that rheumatic and allied inflammations can be largely suppressed by anti-inflammatory hormones. Their observation opened the way for the clinical use of this type of treatment.

The extent to which such inflammatory diseases depend upon an insufficient mobilization of the body's alarm system is particularly well illustrated by such observations as those made by Drs. Wilhelm Brühl and Hans-Jürgen Jahn, at the Civic Hospital in Korbach, Germany. These physicians wanted to put the concept of stress therapy to practical use in patients suffering from very severe rheumatoid arthritis which did not respond to treatment with the usual anti-inflammatory drugs. They wondered whether the combined effect of naturally produced anti-inflammatory hormones and the conditioning action of stress could not help here. In order to produce stress, they used a modified type of insulin shock which proved very effective in otherwise rather hopeless cases of this type. For instance, they describe the case of a 44-year-old woman, bedridden and crippled by an intense chronic rheumatoid arthritis in the joints of the hands, feet, and knees. After a series of insulin shocks, she was able to get up and walk about for the first time in three years. The German doctors ascribed this success to the production of an alarm reaction, with a discharge of ACTH and anti-inflammatory corticoids by the patient's own endocrine glands. Many similar observations have been published by other physicians who used different

. . . . .

Inflammatory Diseases of the Skin and the Eyes

. . . . .

The great majority of all the skin and eye diseases are essentially inflammations, and many of them are caused by agents which would not be particularly harmful if the body did not react to them with unduly violent inflammatory responses. Here again we are apparently dealing with maladaptations, senseless overreactions to cutaneous or ocular injuries. It had long been noted that during periods of intense general stress the predominantly inflammatory diseases of the skin and eyes tended to become better. Various nonspecific therapies have therefore been devised to combat such conditions and, more recently, even more striking improvements have been obtained by the use of anti-inflammatory adaptive hormones (ACTH, cortisone, COL).

Of course, an excess of any hormone has harmful side-effects, and in this respect the adaptive hormones are no exceptions. For instance, a patient heavily overdosed with cortisone tends to become very prone to infections and may develop high blood pressure, insomnia, gastrointestinal disturbances, and so forth. Indeed, often it is impossible to give enough cortisone to cure an inflammatory disease without automatically producing the unpleasant side-effects of hormone overdosage. But, in the cutaneous and ocular diseases, cortisone or COL may be applied locally, through ointments and eye drops, so that a great concentration can be achieved in the diseased area without much getting into the blood. . . .

Infectious Diseases

. . . . .

That the balance between proinflammatory hormones is of paramount importance, even in tuberculosis, has clearly been shown by experiments performed in our Institute by Dr. Paul Lemonde. The rat is normally resistant to the human type of tuberculosis, but it can be made very sensitive to it by overdosage with cortisone. Dr. Lemonde found that this artificially induced sensitivity to tuberculosis is in turn abolished if, simultaneously with the cortisone, large amounts of the proinflammatory STH are injected. In other words, the natural tuberculosis-resistance of the rat can be abolished by an anti-inflammatory hormone and restored again by a proinflammatory one.

It would be difficult to furnish more eloquent proof of the important role played by adaptive hormones in determining disease-susceptibility. It is an old and well-established fact that stress and strain predispose to tuberculosis. That is why patients suffering from this disease are advised to take long rest cures, in order to recover their resistance against tubercle bacilli. The analysis of the stress-mechanism helped us to understand why this is so. Apparently, the anti-inflammatory hormones, which are produced in excess during stress, remove the protective barricades around the foci of tubercle bacilli and thereby permit them to spread.

. . . . .

. . . All kinds of infections are met by the body with an inflammatory response which tends to delimit them. Therefore, the hormones regulating inflammation are evidently important in determining the course of various infections. Even the *saprophytes* (microbes which live in our lungs, gastrointestinal system, and on our skin without ever causing any disease) can become dangerous disease-producers when our normal defenses against them are broken down by anti-inflammatory hormones. I have seen, for instance, that in rats treated with large amounts of ACTH, cortisone, or COL, such saprophytes can invade the blood and produce considerable tissue-destruction, finally resulting in death. STH prevents all this.

These findings confirm the role of the hormones in determining just what microbe is a disease-producer. Almost no germ is unconditionally dangerous to man; its disease-producing ability depends upon the body's resistance.

Allergic and
Hypersensitivity Diseases

. . . In 1937 I injected rats with a variety of drugs and assessed the resulting stress by the adrenal enlargement and by other signs of the G.A.S. . . . One group of rats was injected with egg-white, just to see how much stress this foreign protein would produce. Much to my surprise, egg-white did not act merely as a stressor, but produced a very specific and strange syndrome. Immediately after the injection the rats seemed to be quite all right, but soon afterwards they started to sneeze and sat up on their haunches, scratching their snouts with the forepaws. A few minutes later, their noses and lips became greatly swollen and red, giving the animals a very peculiar appearance. A friend of mine suffered from hay fever at that time, and the resemblance. . . . Well, in any case, this seemed to be a new experimental disease, due to some innate hypersensitivity of the rat to egg-white.

To follow this up, I then injected other animals (guinea pigs, rabbits, dogs) with egg-white, but they did not respond in this singular fashion. Apparently, just as among people there are some who do and some who do not respond with hay fever to certain plant-pollens, so among animals, the rat is sensitive to egg-white, while most other species are not. This seemed to offer interesting possibilities for the study of what we call *allergic* and *anaphylactic hyper-sensitivity* reactions. . . .

Even some twenty years ago, when cortisone and COL were not yet available, it was quite easily proved that this inflammatory reaction also depended somehow upon adrenal hormones. We merely removed the adrenals of rats and then injected the egg-white, to see how the absence of corticoids would affect the reaction. The result was most spectacular. The rats which had no adrenals showed a much more intense reaction, the swollen parts became bluish because of engorgement with venous blood, and within hours all these animals died, but rats with adrenals enlarged by stress, tolerated egg-white perfectly well. . . . This type of anti-inflammatory effect is fundamentally the same as that of insulin

shock in patients with rheumatoid arthritis; it is due to the increased secretion of ACTH and COL-like hormones by the endocrine glands.

Of course, now that we have highly potent, purified preparations of ACTH and of anti-inflammatory corticoids, it is much simpler to administer these than to expose a patient to stress and make his own endocrine glands produce the proper adaptive hormones. In fact, it is common knowledge that, in a variety of diseases due to hypersensitivity, treatment with anti-inflammatory hormones proved to be very effective. This was so, for instance, in many cases of hay fever and asthma, as well as in certain types of dermatitis and conjunctivitis, which are due respectively to allergic irritation of the skin and eyes.

. . . . .

Nervous and Mental Diseases

It is common knowledge that *maladaptation plays an important part in nervous and mental diseases.* Such expressions as, "This work gives me a headache" or "drives me crazy" are not without real significance. . . .

I have been . . . interested in . . . *relationships between abnormal mental reactions and the objectively measurable features of the G.A.S.* Again—as in so many other investigations described in this book—my attention was called to this possibility by the accident of a spoiled experiment.

In 1951 I was working on the effects of various adrenal and ovarian hormones upon the sex organs. For this purpose I injected rats with DOC and with progesterone (an ovarian hormone chemically related to DOC). These injections were given under the skin of the animals in the usual manner and, after a few weeks of treatment, the sex organs were removed for microscopic study. Eventually, I handed this work over to a technician who had just then joined our laboratory, but much to my surprise the next day she reported that all the animals were dead. Since I had given the same amount of the same hormones before without any trouble, I thought she must have made some mistake in preparing her solutions and merely told her to repeat the experiment more carefully. But next day all her rats died again. I could not imagine what might have gone wrong, so I asked the technician to inject another group of rats in my presence. It turned out that, being unacquainted with our techniques, she injected the hormones into the belly (the peritoneal cavity) of the rats. . . . While we discussed the point, all the rats became extremely excited and ran around in the cage as if they were intoxicated. After a time they fell asleep, just as if they had received a strong anesthetic, and . . . all of them died.

Now this was very odd, and I repeated the experiment several times, using smaller doses of hormones. Always there was an initial stage of excitement, followed by deep anesthesia; but after injection with smaller amounts the animals woke up within a couple of hours and were perfectly all right. Here we were dealing with a true hormonal anesthesia, with sleep induced by natural products of our endocrine glands. There remained no doubt that hormones can affect consciousness and that, at least under our experimental conditions, they act very much like an excess of alcohol, ether, and certain narcotics, which tend to cause excitement followed by depression.

Could the corticoids secreted under stress influence mental activity? Could the delirium of fever be related to adrenocortical activity? Could we use such hormones in man as sleeping pills, or for the treatment of mental derangements, or perhaps even for the induction of surgical anesthesia? A multitude of problems was raised by this incidental

observation and hundreds of medical publications have since dealt with experiments designed to answer them. Here are a few of the more outstanding facts which have come to light:

1. Various species, including man, can be anesthetized with hormones. . . .
2. Adaptive hormones can combat convulsions. . . .
3. Under certain conditions an excess of DOC can produce brain lesions such as are often seen in old people. . . .
4. Perhaps adaptive hormones may even be used as tranquilizing agents in mental patients. . . .
5. DOC-like hormones can cause spells of periodic paralysis. . . .

Sexual Derangements

That animals in which intense and prolonged stress is produced by any means suffer from sexual derangements was one of the first observations on the G.A.S. During stress the *sex glands* shrink and become less active in proportion to the enlargement and increased activity of the adrenals. The sex glands are stimulated by gonadotrophic hormones of the pituitary, just as the adrenals are activated by adrenocorticotrophic hormone (ACTH). It seemed probable, therefore, that during stress, when the pituitary has to produce so much ACTH to maintain life it must cut down on the production of other hormones which are less urgently needed in times of emergencies. . . . Our explanation seemed all the more likely, since other functions which depend upon the pituitary are likewise diminished during stress. For instance, young animals cease to grow and lactating females produce no milk during intense stress. It will be recalled that growth and milk-secretion are also governed by hormones of the pituitary.

. . . . .

In 1931 Dr. R. T. Frank described the *premenstrual syndrome,* a condition which tends to develop in women just before their monthly periods. It is characterized, among other things, by nervous tension and the desire to find relief in foolish actions which are difficult to restrain. Many of Dr. Frank's patients also suffered from migraine headaches and swelling of the face, hands, and feet, with a definite increase in weight due to water-retention. Other signs of the syndrome are: pain in the back and in the breasts, small hemorrhages in the skin, a feeling of stuffiness in the nose, asthma, and (very rarely) epilepsylike seizures. All these symptoms disappear suddenly at the onset of the monthly cycle, but recur again as the next period approaches.

This long overlooked syndrome is actually very common. A statistical study by Drs. W. Bickers and M. Woods revealed that, in one American factory employing 1,500 women, 36 per cent applied for treatment in the premenstrual phase; and Dr. S. L. Israel calculates that symptoms of this kind occur in 40 per cent of otherwise healthy women. The derangement deserves very serious attention also because it is frequently accompanied by a number of disturbing mental changes such as: periods of abnormal hunger, general emotional instability, and, occasionally, a morbid increase in the sexual drive. It is particularly noteworthy that, according to extensive statistical studies, 79 per cent (J. H. Morton and coworkers) to 84 per cent (W. R. Cooke) of all crimes of violence committed by women occur during, or in the week before their periods, [and most automobile accidents involving women seem to occur at this time].

· · · · ·

Is there any relationship between premenstrual tension and stress? The great tendency to retain water, the predisposition for various allergic and hypersensitivity reactions, the occasional occurrence of convulsive seizures, vascular dis-turbances, and rheumaticlike pains are, of course, very reminiscent of the DOC-intoxication syndrome. I might add that our DOC-overdosed monkeys also probably suffered from sick headaches prior to the convulsive fits. At least I think so, because they usually retired to a corner of the cage, holding their heads between their hands; the facial expression was one of pain.

Ulcers

. . . People who have been severely burned often develop bleeding duodenal ulcers within a day or two after the accident. . . . It always remained a mystery just why and through what pathways a skin-burn could so affect the intestinal lining. During World War II, veritable epidemics of "air-raid ulcers" occurred in people living in some of the heavily blitzed cities in Great Britain. Immediately after an intense bombardment, an unusual number of people would appear in hospital, with bleeding gastric or duodenal ulcers which developed virtually overnight. Many of the affected persons had not been physically hurt in any way during the attack but, of course, they suffered the great stress of extreme emotional excitement.

With this background, it was not quite unexpected that, when ACTH and cortisone were introduced into clinical practice, in patients receiving large amounts of these stress hormones—say, for an inflammatory disease—preexistent gastrointestinal ulcers often became worse, and sometimes actually perforated through the gut. . . .

This revived my interest in the *mechanism through which the lining of the stomach defends itself against self-digestion.* Meat is digested in the stomach; why does the gastric juice not digest the lining itself? This problem has occupied many generations of physiologists, but no definite solution was found. . . .

· · · · ·

I first took some rats and made air-sacs on their backs—in the usual manner, but without introducing an irritant. Immediately after this, I injected 5 cc of fresh gastric juice. The adjacent tissue of the skin was digested within a few hours. This proved that normal living tissue can be attacked by gastric juice.

Then I made a similar air-sac, but injected some croton oil into it, so as to transform the lining into an inflammatory barricade before introducing the gastric juice into the cavity. Now no digestion of adjacent tissue occurred. This proved that the inflammatory tissue itself is an adequate barricade to protect against gastric digestion. Obviously, an inflammatory barricade, such as always paves the crater of gastric ulcers, is in itself adequate protection against digestion, under normal conditions.

Next I repeated exactly the same experiment (introducing the gastric juice into an inflammatory pouch whose lining was transformed into an inflammatory barricade by pretreatment with croton oil), but then exposed the animals to the frustrating immobilization test. Now I witnessed the singular phenomenon of a perforating peptic ulcer on the back of the rat. During stress—presumably due to the secretion of anti-inflammatory hormones—the barricade became so weakened that the gastric juice digested it easily. Apparently in man chronic gastric ulcers, which normally are well under control, also perforate during stress, because an excess of anti-inflammatory stimuli breaks down the resistance of the barricade.

Finally, to prove this theory, I repeated the last-mentioned experiment on adrenalectomized rats. Here the condition was exactly the same as before (an irritated pouch possessing a well-developed inflammatory barricade was exposed to the general stress of frustrating immobilization), but these animals had

no adrenals which might have responded by increased anti-inflammatory hormone-secretion. Here the pouch remained unaffected by the digestive juices even during stress. This was definite proof of adrenal-participation in this type of tissue-breakdown.

General Stress and Local Stress

. . . It was found that the picture of general stress in the body, the G.A.S. has a local counterpart. This is the L.A.S., which can be appraised by exposing many parts of the body selectively to many locally applied agents. The changes which any agent can produce virtually anywhere in the body constitute the syndrome of local stress. Inflammation and degeneration of cells were found to be the chief components of this picture.

Finally it was discovered that the G.A.S. *and the L.A.S. are interdependent.* General stress can influence local stress-reactions, for instance, through hormones (particularly corticoids), which regulate inflammation. Conversely, local stress, if strong enough, can produce general stress and thereby mobilize defensive organs located far from the site of injury. Through chemical messengers (the *alarm signals*) each of the many local stress-reactions, which happen to go on in the various parts of the body at any one time, has a voice in determining the extent of the general counterstress measures to be taken. This procedure of "regulation by majority decision" is very necessary. For instance, a small splinter entering the skin may create great local demands for anti-inflammatory corticoids, but the limited local inflammation caused by this minor irritant may not justify the exposure of the entire body to an excess of corticoids. The central organs of defense must consider the interests of the whole and, of course, to do so judiciously, they have to be constantly informed of the requirements of all parts. It was chiefly the recognition of these close interactions between the G.A.S. and the L.A.S. which made it possible to outline a sketch for a unified theory of medicine.

. . . . .

A child or a hysterical person can snap out of a tantrum if you splash cold water in his face. A phonograph needle stuck in a groove . . . can snap out of it if you just give it a jerk. Well, the body of a patient can also be shaken out of habitually responding in the same senseless manner if you expose it to the stress of some intense shock therapy, such as, electroshock, Metrazol shock, insulin shock, or injection of toxic foreign proteins.

Another way to deal with essentially the same problems is to provide complete rest, which gives the body time to "forget" stereotyped somatic reactions to stress. Prolonged sleep (e.g., that induced by barbiturates), artificial hibernation, and treatment with such quieting drugs as chlorpromazine and extracts of the Rauwolfia root appear to act largely through this mechanism.

. . . . .

PSYCHOSOMATIC IMPLICATIONS

To Know Thyself

The ancient Greek philosophers clearly recognized that, in governing human conduct, the most important, but perhaps also the most difficult, thing was "to know thyself." It takes great courage even just to attempt this honestly. As Logan Pearsall Smith says, "How awful to reflect that what people say of us is true!" Yet it is well worth the effort and humiliation, for most of our tensions and frustrations stem from compulsive needs to act the role of someone we are not. . . .

. . . . .

. . . Most people fail to realize that "to know thy body" also has an inherent curative value. Take a familiar example. Many people have joints which tend to crack at almost every movement; by concentrating upon this unexplained condition, a person can talk or worry himself into a crippling arthritis. If, on the other hand, some understanding physician just explains to him that his cracking sensations are caused by slight, inconsequential irregularities in the joint-surfaces, and have no tendency to become worse, the disease is practically cured—just by the knowledge of its trifling nature.

. . . . .

. . . Looking fit helps one to *be* fit. A pale, unshaven tramp, who wears dirty rags and is badly in need of a bath, actually does not resist either physical or mental stresses as well as he would after a shave, a bit of sunburn, a good bath, and some crisp new clothes have helped to rehabilitate his external appearance.

None of this is new. Intuitively, and merely on the basis of experience throughout centuries, these facts have long been recognized. That is why, to strengthen morale, armies insist on the spotless appearance of their men. That is also why opposite procedures are used (in some countries) for breaking down the physical and mental resistance of prisoners.

I was first introduced to these truths at the age of six, by my grandmother, when she found me desperately crying, I no longer recall about what. She looked at me with that particularly benevolent and protective look that I still remember and said, "Anytime you feel that low, just try to smile with your face, and you'll see . . . soon your whole being will be smiling." I tried it. It works.

. . . . .

On Being Keyed Up

Everybody is familiar with the feeling of being keyed up from nervous tension; this process is quite comparable to raising the key of a violin by tightening the strings. We say that our muscles limber up during exercise and that we are thrilled by great emotional experiences; all this prepares us for better peak-accomplishments. On the other hand, there is the tingling sensation, the jitteriness, when we are too much keyed up. This impairs our work and even prevents us from getting a rest.

Just what happens to us when we are alerted? Being keyed up is a very real sensation which must have a . . . chemical basis. . . . We know that at times of tension our adrenals produce an excess, both of adrenalines and of corticoids. We also know that taking either adrenalines or corticoids can reproduce a very similar sensation of being keyed up. . . . A person who is given large doses of cortisone in order to treat some allergic or rheumatoid condition often finds it difficult to sleep. He may even become abnormally euphoric, that is, carried away by an unreasonable sense of well-being and buoyancy, which is not unlike that caused by being slightly drunk. Later a sense of deep depression may follow.

. . . . .

What can we do about this? Hormones are probably not the only regulators of our emotional level. Besides, we do not yet know enough about their workings to justify any attempt at regulating our emotional key by taking hormones.

Still, it is instructive to know that stress stimulates our glands to make hormones which can induce a kind of drunkenness. Without knowing this, no one would ever think of checking his conduct as carefully during stress as he does at a cocktail party. Yet he should. The fact is that *a man can be intoxicated with his own stress hormones.* I venture to say that this sort of drunkenness has caused much more harm to society than the other kind. . . . In all our actions throughout the day we must consciously look for signs of being keyed up too much—and we must learn to stop in time. To watch our critical stress-level is just as important as to watch our critical quota of cocktails. More so. . . .

How to Tune Down

It is not easy to tune down when you have reached your stress-quota. Many more people are the helpless slaves of their own stressful activities than of alchohol. Besides, simple rest is no cureall. Activity and rest must be judiciously balanced, and *every person has his own characteristic requirements for rest and activity.* To lie motionless in bed all day is not relaxation for an active man. . . .

All work and no play is certainly harmful for anyone at any age; but then, what is work and what is play? Fishing is relaxing play for the business executive, but it is hard work for the professional fisherman. The former can go fishing to relax, but the latter will have to do something else, or simply take a rest, in order to relax.

. . . . .

Stress as an Equalizer of Activities

It seems to be one of the most fundamental laws regulating the activities of complex living beings that no one part of the body must be disproportionately overworked for a long time. Stress seems to be the great equalizer of activities within the body; *it helps to prevent one-sided overexertion.*

To carry a heavy suitcase for a long time without fatigue, you have to shift it from one hand to the other occasionally. Here, local stress, manifested as muscular fatigue, is the equalizer; it acts by way of the nervous system which experiences the feeling of fatigue and thereby suggests the change-over.

. . . . .

. . . To put this into the simplest terms, we might say that the stress-quotient to be watched is:

$$\frac{\text{local stress in any one part}}{\text{total stress in the body}}$$

If there is proportionately too much stress in any one part, you need diversion. If there is too much stress in the body as a whole, you must rest.

24 | BEHAVIOR INDIVIDUALITY IN EARLY CHILDHOOD

ALEXANDER THOMAS, STELLA CHESS,

HERBERT G. BIRCH, MARGARET E. HERTZIG,

AND SAM KORN

In selection 19, Professor Montagu explored the influence of the prenatal environment on the unborn child in producing important differences among infants at birth. The selection that follows adds valuable evidence to support Professor Montagu's observations as well as the theories of organicists, who hold that what a person is constitutionally influences his later life and that this leads him to act upon his environment rather than vice versa. The nine behavioral traits described below give a working definition of the word "temperament," suggesting that temperament from birth to two years (and possibly throughout childhood and life) is fairly constant. This implies that child-rearing practices suitable for one child would not be so for another. Articles by Chess and Thomas in Parents Magazine, *1964 and 1965, state, for example, that some children can be comfortably trained to use a potty at nine or ten months; others, not until thirty months. "The infant who can be trained early is one who has a regular bowel movement at a predictable time and is comfortable sitting still." But if the infant's bowel movement is irregular and he is squirmy, training may have to wait until he is ready. Later on, in elementary school, great differences in attention span, activity level, and other temperamental traits may make it important that the teacher discover and make use of these individual differences in working with each child.*

The research program of which this monograph represents a part starts out

Excerpts reprinted from Alexander Thomas *et al., Behavior Individuality in Early Childhood* (New York: New York University Press, 1963), by permission.

with the basic conviction that inborn temperamental characteristics of the infant make a fundamental contribution to the development of psychological individuality. . . . The data available for exploring the process of interaction have been insufficient because most investigations in both developmental psychology and child psychiatry have tended to focus one-sidedly upon the environmental contributions to development. . . .

Especially in the United States, the primary emphasis has been placed upon the environmental or experiential determination of individuality. The tendency to seek the source of individuality in environmental influences on the developing child is not limited to any one school of thought. . . .

. . . Until quite recently, little or no systematic attention has been focused upon the initial biologic characteristics of infants as significant factors in determining the development of psychological individuality. Over the last few years, however, a number of studies have reported observations on individual differences in the infant and young child in specific discrete areas such as sensory threshold, motility, perceptual responses, sleeping and feeding patterns, drive endowment, quality and intensity of emotional tone, social responsiveness, autonomic response patterns, biochemical individuality, and electroencephalographic patterns. These various reports have emphasized that certain individual differences potentially important for behavioral functioning appear to be present at birth or shortly thereafter and are not the result of postnatal experience.

Despite their limited character, the findings of these studies were in accord with the view that important individual differences in responsiveness did exist in young infants. However, the pertinence of these characteristics for later development was unknown. What appeared to be necessary was detailed longitudinal information on the relation of early reactivity to later functioning. . . .

The present investigation is concerned with identifying characteristics of individuality in behavior during the first months of life and with exploring the degree to which these characteristics are persistent and influence the development of later psychological organization. This inquiry is being carried out through the longitudinal study of a group of 130 children from the first months of life onward. Although the study proper is now in its eighth year, the present report concerns itself only with the first two years of life. . . .

The present report is concerned with the data collected on the first 80 of the 130 children whose behavioral development has been followed from the first months of life. These 80 children are those of the group who had passed their second birthdays at the time the present analysis was undertaken. Thirty-nine of the children were girls and 41 were boys.

The families of all the children represent a fairly homogeneous middle- and upper-middle-class urban and suburban group. . . .

A content analysis was . . . performed on the interview protocols of the first 22 children studied. In the course of this analysis the protocol data were distributed against a wide variety of formal behavioral attributes. It was found that nine categories of functioning could be scored continuously throughout the protocols. Further, the distributions of scores in each of these categories were sufficiently wide to permit differentiation among individuals within each category. Although various amounts of data were available for additional categories of functioning, their distributions failed to satisfy either the requirement of ubiquitousness (being scorable and present in all protocols), or of sufficient variability to permit of interindividual comparison. The content analysis, therefore, resulted in the adoption of the following nine categories for the assessment of individuality in behavioral functioning.

ACTIVITY LEVEL

This category describes the extent to which a motor component exists in the child's functioning. In scoring, all data in the protocol concerned with motility were utilized. Some examples of representative behaviors that were scored as high activity are: "He moves a great deal in his sleep," "I can't leave him on the bed or couch because he always wriggles off." "He kicks and splashes so in the bath that I always have to mop up the floor afterward," "Dressing him becomes a battle, he squirms so," "He runs around so, that whenever we come in from the park I'm exhausted," "He crawls all over the house," and "Whenever I try to feed him he grabs for the spoon." Examples of low activity behaviors are: "In the bath he lies quietly and doesn't kick," "In the morning he's still in the same place he was when he fell asleep. I don't think he moves at all during the night," and "He can turn over, but he doesn't much."

RHYTHMICITY

This category based itself upon the degree of rhythmicity or regularity of repetitive functions. Information concerning rest and activity, sleeping and waking, eating and appetite, and bowel and bladder function was utilized in the scoring.

A child's sleep-wake cycle was considered to be regular if the child fell asleep at approximately the same time each night and awoke at approximately the same time each morning. The child's functioning was considered to be irregular if there was a marked difference in the time of retiring and arising from day to day.

Information concerning the rest and activity periods of the child was derived from the protocol data on napping behavior. The child was scored as regular if he napped for the same length of time each day, and irregular if there was no discernible time pattern of function established.

Eating and appetite behavior was scored as regular if the protocol reported that the child demanded or accepted food readily at the same time each day and consumed approximately same amount of food on corresponding diurnal occasions. The child was scored as irregular if his intake fluctuated widely from day to day, or if he could be induced to eat at times which differed widely from day to day.

Bowel function was scored as regular if the protocol indicated that the number and time of evacuations were constant from day to day, and irregular if the time and number were not readily predictable.

In all of these areas behavior was considered variable if there was evidence in the protocol that the child had established a pattern of functioning, but that there was some deviation from this pattern on occasion. This designation stands in contrast to a score of irregular, which denoted the failure to establish even a partial pattern.

APPROACH OR WITHDRAWAL

This category describes the child's initial reaction to any new stimulus pattern, be it food, people, places, toys, or procedures. A few examples of initial approach responses are: "He always smiles at a stranger," "He loves new toys. He plays with one so much he often breaks it the first day," and "The first time he had his hair cut he sat on his father's lap and laughed through the whole thing." Withdrawal responses are illustrated by: "When I gave him his orange juice the first time he made a face. He didn't cry but he didn't suck it as eagerly as he does milk," "Whenever he sees a stranger he cries," "When we went to the doctor's for the first time he started to cry in the waiting room and didn't stop until we got home again," and "It takes him a long time to warm up to a new toy; he pushes it away and plays with something more familiar."

ADAPTABILITY

When considering adaptability, one is of necessity concerned with the sequential course of responses that are made to new or altered situations. In contrast to the previous category, it is not with the initial response that one is concerned. Rather, emphasis is on the ease or difficulty with which the initial pattern of response can be modified in socially desirable directions. Examples of adaptive behavior may be found in the following excerpts from parental interviews: "He used to spit out cereal whenever I gave it to him, but now he takes it fairly well, although still not as well as fruit," "Now when we go to the doctor's he doesn't start to cry till we undress him, and he even stops then if he can hold a toy," "At first he used to hold himself perfectly stiff in the bath, but now he kicks a little and pats the water with his hand," and "Every day for a week he'd go over to this stuffed lion someone gave him and say 'I don't like it,' but today he started playing with it and now you'd think it was his best friend."

Nonadaptive behavior can be illustrated by the following examples: "During the summer she used to nap in her carriage outside, and now that it's cold I've tried to put her in the crib, but she screams so I have to take her out and wheel her up and down the hall before she falls asleep," "Every time he sees the scissors he starts to scream and pull his hand away, so now I cut his nails when he's sleeping," "Whenever I put his snowsuit and hat on he screams and struggles,

and he doesn't stop crying till we're outside," and "He doesn't like eggs and makes a face and turns his head away no matter how I cook them."

INTENSITY OF REACTION

In this category interest is in the energy content of the response, irrespective of its direction. A negative response may be as intense or as mild as a positive one. Scorable items for this category were provided by descriptions of behavior occurring in relation to stimuli, to preeliminations straining, to hunger, to repletion, to new foods, to attempts to control, to restraint, to diapering and dressing, to the bath, and to play and social contacts.

Examples of intense reactions are the following: "He cries whenever the sun shines in his eyes," "Whenever she hears music she begins to laugh and to jump up and down in time to it," "When he is hungry he starts to cry, and this builds up to a scream, and we can't distract him by holding or playing with him," "When she is full she spits the food out of her mouth and knocks the spoon away," "The first time we gave him cereal he spit it out and started to cry," "If we tell him 'No' he starts to cry," "Dressing is such a problem, he wriggles around so, and when I hold him so that he can't move he screams," and "She loves her bath so, that as soon as she hears the water running she tries to climb into the tub even if she's still fully dressed."

Examples of mild responses are: "He squints at a bright light but doesn't cry," "To a loud noise he jumps and startles a little but he doesn't cry," "If he's hungry, he starts to whimper a bit, but if you play with him he won't really cry," "When she's had enough she turns her head away, and I know that it is time to stop," "If he does not like a new food he just holds it in his mouth without swallowing and then lets it drool out," "When we tell her 'No' she looks and smiles and then goes right on doing what she wants," "Now it's a pleasure to dress him, he stands up when you tell him to, and holds still when he has to," and "When other children take a toy away from him, he plays with something else, he doesn't try to get it back or cry."

THRESHOLD OF RESPONSIVENESS

This category refers to the intensity level of stimulation that is necessary to evoke a discernible response. The explicit form of response that occurs is irrelevant and may be of any quality, e.g., approaching or withdrawing, intense or mild. What is fundamental is the intensity of stimulus that had to be applied before a response of any kind could be elicited. The behaviors utilized were those concerning responses to sensory stimuli, environmental objects, and social contacts. We were also interested in the magnitude of difference between similar stimuli that had to obtain before the child showed evidences of discrimination.

Examples of the types of descriptions that were scored in this category are the following: "You can shine a bright light in his eyes and he doesn't even blink, but if a door closes he startles and looks up." This would be scored as high threshold for visual stimulation and low threshold for auditory stimuli. "I can never tell if he's wet except by feeling him, but if he has a bowel movement he fusses and is cranky until I change him." The statement indicates high threshold with respect to wet, but low threshold to the tactual complex associated with a bowel movement. "He loves fruit, but if I put even a little cereal in with it he won't eat it at all." This was scored as a low threshold response because it demonstrated the ability to discriminate small taste or textural differences. "He doesn't pay any attention to new people; he doesn't cry, but he doesn't really respond to them, either." This is an example of a high threshold in the area of social relations, as contrasted with "He laughs and smiles at a stranger, and starts to cry if they don't play with him," which was scored as low threshold. "He always cries when he sees a man wearing a hat even if it's his father," is illustrative of effective discrimination and was scored as a low threshold statement. "He makes himself at home anywhere, and runs around a strange house as if it were his," was scored as high threshold, while "He notices any little change. When we got new curtains for his room he spent a whole day crawling over to the window and pulling on them," received a low threshold score.

QUALITY OF MOOD

This category describes the amount of pleasant, joyful, friendly behavior as contrasted with unpleasant, crying, unfriendly behavior. Consequently, statements which indicated crying behavior and unfriendly behavior were scored as negative mood statements, as in the following: "Whenever we put him to bed he cries for about five or ten minutes before falling asleep," "He cries at almost every stranger, and those that he doesn't cry at he hits," "I've tried to teach him not to knock down little girls and sit on them in the playground, so now he knocks them down and doesn't sit on them," and "Every time he sees food he doesn't like he starts to fuss and whine until I take it off the table." Examples of positive mood statements are: "Whenever he sees me begin to warm his bottle he begins to smile and coo," "He loves to look out of the window. He jumps up and down and laughs," "He always smiles at a stranger," and "If he's not laughing and smiling I know he's getting sick."

DISTRACTIBILITY

This category refers to the effectiveness of extraneous environmental stimuli in interfering with, or in altering the direction of, the ongoing behavior. If the course of a child who is crawling toward an electric light plug can be altered by presenting him with a toy truck, he would be considered distractible. If such attempts to alter his behavior are unsuccessful, he would be considered nondistractible. A child who is crying because he is hungry but stops when he is picked up is distractible, as opposed to the child who continues to cry until he is fed.

ATTENTION SPAN AND PERSISTENCE

This category refers to the definition of a direction of functioning and to the difficulty with which such an established direction of functioning can be altered. We were concerned with descriptions that gave information as to the attention span and the persistence of the child. By attention span is meant the length of time a particular activity was pursued. For example, if a two-year-old child could pour water from one cup to another for a half-hour, he would be scored as possessing a long attention span. If he engaged in this activity for five minutes, his attention span would be short. The attention span can be measured with regard to self-initiated activities, such as the above example of pouring water, as well as the child's participation in planned activities, such as listening to a story or listening to music. By persistence we mean the maintaining of an activity by a child in the face of ob-

stacles and the continuation of the activity direction. Obstacles may be maternal. In the case of our child pouring water, if his mother comes along and says "No" and he continues to do it, he would be considered persistent. The obstacles may be much more directly related to the child's abilities. For example, the child who continually attempts to stand up although he always falls down would be scored as persistent, as would the child who struggles with a toy he can't make perform properly and not asking for help. The category, therefore, is an omnibus one which includes selectivity, persistence, and at a later age level frustration tolerance.

RESULTS

A longitudinal analysis of the first two years of life has been made of the behavioral characteristics of the eighty children in our sample who are now over two years of age. This analysis had two objectives:

1. To determine whether children are discriminably different in the patterning of behavioral reactivity in early infancy.

2. To analyze the degree to which features of behavioral reactivity identifiable in early infancy continue to characterize the child during his first two years.

. . . Examination of Table 1 suggests that the pattern of scores in each category may reveal features of individuality of the children, as well as characteristics of the behavioral attributes under examination. To begin with, the analysis of the persistence of the hierarchical pattern of scores in each category reveals some variation among the nine behavior categories. For example, 74 of the 80 children studied (92.5 percent), maintained a consistent pattern of responses in mood, 65 percent in rhythmicity, and 27.5 percent in activity. The variation

TABLE 1.	Category	Percent of Cases with Interperiod Stability
RESULTS OF FRIEDMAN TWO-WAY		
ANALYSIS OF VARIANCE	Activity	27.5
	Rhythmicity	65.0
	Adaptability	83.8
	Approach	81.2
	Threshold	41.2
	Intensity	87.5
	Mood	92.5
	Distractibility	36.2
	Persistence	65.0

among categories may be attributable to the developmental characteristics of the particular aspects of behavior included in each response category. Perhaps mood exhibits one particular developmental trend, activity another, and so on. However, this factor is apparently compounded with some additional source of individuality of the children; there is also variation in the number of categories each child maintained with a reliable, recurrent order. On the average, the number of rank patterns maintained consistently was 5.8. Therefore, almost two thirds of the nine categories were sustained by each child. However, as indicated in Table 2, one child maintained consistency in all nine categories, nine children in eight of the categories, etc. All in all, 78 of the 80 children maintained a statistically reliable rank pattern over the first two years in four or more of the nine categories. Thus part of the overall variation in the regularity of recurrence of the order of scored items

may be a function of the behavior characteristics involved, but part may be dependent on characteristics of individuality of the children. The latter may be a function of both intrinsic and environmental factors that need further elaboration.

Using the percent-rank index findings, we sought to determine the persistence of individual differences in reactivity over the period of the first two years of life. In order to treat the data longitudinally, rank order correlations were calculated among all combinations of the five periods into which the two-year span was divided. . . .

. . . The treatment of interperiod relations resulted in ten correlation coefficients for each period of reactivity. For four of these categories—rhythmicity, adaptability, threshold, and intensity— seven or more of the ten interperiod comparisons resulted in significant levels of positive correlation. For the remaining categories the findings were six signifi-

TABLE 2.	Total Number of Consistent Categories	Number of Children
CONSISTENCY OF RANK		
PATTERN IN PERIODS I–V	9	1
	8	9
	7	13
	6	23
	5	21
	4	11
	3	1
	2	1
	44	80

cant positive intercorrelations for mood, five for activity, and three for approach. The most striking stability was found for intensity, for which category all ten of the intercorrelations resulted in coefficients significant at less than the .01 level of confidence.

PRACTICAL IMPLICATIONS

Any study of the sources of psychological individuality has practical implications. The finding that each child has an individual pattern of primary reactivity, identifiable in early infancy and persistent through later periods of life, must be considered seriously by everyone with responsibility for effective socialization of the child.

In general, this finding of initial and persisting reactivity patterns implies that all the infants will not respond in the same fashion to a given environmental influence. Rather, given constancy of environmental factors, the reaction will vary with the characteristics of the child upon whom the relatively constant stimulus is brought to bear. Specifically, the tactics utilized by parents or others in child rearing will have different behavioral results depending on the nature of the child to whom they are applied. This holds true for all aspects of the child's functioning: his response to feeding, sleep routines, and bath in the first year of life; his interaction with parents, siblings, and playmates as he grows older; and his reaction to situations of special stress, such as illness, radical changes in living conditions, or abrupt shifts in geographic environment. Whether weaning is early or late, toilet training is rigid or permissive, his mother hostile or overprotective, the characteristics of the child's behavior will be influenced by his primary reaction pattern as well as by his environment. In each new situation he faces his behavior will depend, in part at least, on whether his

reactive style is primarily positive or negative, mild or of high intensity, rhythmic or arhythmic. This view of the child stands in contrast to the assumption that environmental influences as such have determinative effects.

. . . Differences between children, whether they be well-adjusted kindergartners or angry adolescents, have been assumed to be almost exclusively the result of their parents, or a combination of this central parental force with especially stressful environmental factors.

Underlying the environmental approach is the assumption that all children will tend to react similarly to the same developmental influences. This has resulted in a search for the right set of rules, or no-rules, for bringing up baby. Our findings suggest that exclusive emphasis on the role of the environment in child development tells only part of the story and that responses to any regimen will vary in accordance with primary patterns of reactivity. It follows, therefore, that there can be no universally valid set of rules that will work equally well for all children everywhere.

Two case histories serve to illustrate the manner in which primary reactive characteristics may affect the infant's organization of behavior in feeding under self-demand conditions. One neonate fell asleep after two and a half ounces and was awake and crying in three and a half hours. His crying stopped only for a moment when he was picked up; it continued until the bottle was introduced into his mouth. At other times he might cry in between feedings; he would be found to be wet or soiled, and if changed, he would go back to sleep. Whether the last evening bottle was given as usual or was held off in the hopes of a larger meal and a longer sleep, the baby woke after the same three-and-a-half- to four-hour interval and cried until fed. The implications for child care practices are clear. This infant has a rhythmical pattern; he is intense, persistent, and nondistractible. The sooner the mother trains herself to follow his pattern of rhythmicity and to identify his needs, the sooner will her nurturing become more effective and satisfying to the infant.

A second infant fed inconsistently. Sleep was irregular. When he cried he could be quieted by stimuli such as rocking or holding. Frequently it was difficult to identify his need when he cried, since he was not wet, soiled, or apparently hungry, overclothed, or cold. For this infant optimum care practices could not be identical with those optimal for the first. Since the child did not have good rhythmicity or specific responses to defined conditions of need, it would be exceedingly difficult, if not impossible, for the mother to train herself to follow his rhythms or identify his needs. When an attempt was made to pursue a self-demand feeding schedule, the result was chaos and a complete disruption of family life. Peace was restored upon instituting a strictly scheduled regimen. When a measured amount of food was given and strict timing of meals observed, he rapidly formed habit patterns which were consistent with normal parental and societal requirements.

Fortunately for the parents the majority of the children in our group showed patterns involving adaptability with reactions of moderate and graded intensity. Our evidence suggests that within broad limits such babies did well with differing child care practices, as long as a given parent was consistent in approach. Accordingly, the application of a self-demand regimen resulted in the ready acquisition of acceptable patterns of socialization. It would be anticipated, however, that the course of habit acquisition and the development of desired behaviors and skills in the modal group of children would have been acquired with comparable ease had a more structured

regimen been applied. Very likely it is this group of children that represents the substantial basis for the support of claims made concerning the efficacy of different child-rearing strategies.

From decade to decade child care practices have varied widely, and all in their time have been advocated by authorities as being clearly applicable to children's needs. While there has always tended to be a small group of youngsters whose behavior was not in keeping with the predicted outcome, a striking variety of practices seems to have been assimilated equally well by children of different periods, cultures, and classes. . . .

In certain respects a variety of child care practices may be equally helpful with an equal proportion of youngsters. However, the small proportion of children who fail to adapt and thrive with one type of child care practice may be totally different from those who fail to thrive with another type of practice. During the centuries when infants were fed whenever they were hungry, most children apparently adapted to this approach. When feeding by the clock according to a predetermined schedule became the advocated pattern, most children adapted to this. When once again it was decided to feed children when they were hungry—now called "self-demand feeding"—in response to the awareness that a small group of children did not adapt to clock feeding, again most, but not all, children adapted to this method. While it is likely that those who failed to adapt to clock feeding had idiosyncratic behavioral characteristics dissimilar to those who failed to adapt to demand feeding, the majority of infants can adapt to either type of timing.

The enormous variety of child care practices which have succeeded in maintaining the race does not, however, attest to the equality of excellence. With the understanding that no general rule of child care practice will be appropriate for every child, it nevertheless can be argued that some general rules will be optimal for a higher percentage of children than other modes of practice. Defining such optimal practices still remains a goal, even though it will always be necessary to deviate from such general rules with some children.

The youngsters for whom the prescribed child care practice proves to be incompatible require an analysis of their primary characteristics of reactivity and an individually planned modification of the favored practice. It should be borne in mind that, while the unadaptable, irregular child of negative mood is a departure from the average, such a child is not thereby pathologic.

Awareness of characteristics of primary reactivity is particularly important when working with youngsters who present behavioral disturbances. Maladaptation of children, expressed in behavior disorders, is frequently discussed in terms of defensive reactions to inappropriate parental handling. But when one has succeeded in describing primary behavioral characteristics of given children, it becomes possible to examine the patterns that preceded the problem behavior. In the children of the present study it has been noteworthy that the maladaptive patterns have represented in many cases a caricature of the premorbid pattern; in others there has been a reversal of specific behaviors that had been characteristic prior to the appearance of disturbance in functioning. At times, in the same child, one characteristic has been extended to the point of caricature while another has been reversed. These findings carry their own implications for child care practices, and consequently have been examined for clues as to the sequences and causes of their occurrence.

The caricature maladaptation was most clearly seen in those children whose normal pattern included initial withdrawal to new situations followed by positive approach after acclimatization. As demands multiplied for involvement with new groups of children or new places, the length of time needed for acclimatization often proved too great for productive interaction—the visit was almost over, the time allotment for the class activity came to an end, the other children were tired of the activity and went on to a different one before a shift from withdrawal to approach had occurred. In place of experiencing positive involvement, with the period of initial withdrawal being a negligible aspect, the child experienced instance after instance in which he was the outsider and onlooker. In time his behavior came to be characterized more by withdrawal than by participation.

It is apparent, too, from our study that the child's primary reaction pattern may influence not only his own behavior but also his parents' immediate and persistent attitude toward him. Where the child's primary pattern has made his care easy, the mother has often shown a much quicker and more intense development of positive attitudes than is manifested where the child's primary reactions have made his care more difficult and time-consuming. This influence of the child on the parental attitude has been most dramatically evident in two families whose twin children showed differences in initial and subsequent patterning of reactivity. In each family the mother started with the same general maternal attitude toward the two infants but developed increasingly dissimilar affective bonds and responses to them as they grew older. In large part these differences in attitude could be accounted for by the mother's reaction to initial differences in reactivity.

These findings raise several interesting questions about the interrelation of general parental attitude and child characteristics in the evolution of the parent-child relationship. Given any degree of ambivalence toward the parental role, the characteristics of the child may foster and reinforce a specific direction of parental attitude and practice. It is easy to mother a mildly active, positively responsive, highly adaptive, rhythmic child whose mood is predominantly cheerful. It is quite another matter to sustain the same positive maternal responses toward a highly active, negatively responsive, nonadaptive, arhythmic child whose mood is expressed by a preponderance of crying. The reciprocal dynamics of the parent-child interrelation have been insufficiently explored in child development and represent a most fruitful area for investigation.

The knowledge that certain characteristics of their child's development are not primarily due to parental malfunctioning has proven helpful to many parents. Mothers of problem children often develop guilt feelings because they assume that they are solely responsible for their children's emotional difficulties. This feeling of guilt may be accompanied by anxiety, defensiveness, increased pressures on the children, and even hostility toward them for "exposing" the mother's inadequacy by their disturbed behavior. When parents learn that their role in the shaping of their child is not an omnipotent one, guilt feelings may lessen, hostility and pressures may tend to disappear, and positive restructuring of the parent-child interaction can become possible.

25 | CHILD CARE AND THE GROWTH OF LOVE

JOHN BOWLBY

When the third session of the Social Commission of the United Nations decided to arrange for a study of homeless children, Dr. Bowlby was appointed by the World Health Organization to carry out the project. He surveyed the scientific literature dealing with children without mothers and journeyed to many countries, observing and discussing their problems. He found general agreement among persons and agencies having contact with large numbers of children that the mental health of children is tragically damaged by separation from their mothers.

Some of the immediately bad effects of deprivation on young children and some of the short-term after-effects have now been discussed, and note taken that those without training in mental health are apt either to deny the existence of such responses or to waive them aside as of no consequence. In this chapter, the

Excerpts reprinted from *Child Care and the Growth of Love*, edited by Margery Fry (Penguin Books Ltd., 1953), pp. 33–49, by permission of the publisher.

tremendous weight of evidence will be reviewed which makes it clear that those who view these responses with concern, so far from crying wolf, are calling attention to matters of grave medical and social significance.

During the late 1930s, at least six independent workers were struck by the frequency with which children who committed numerous delinquencies, who seemed to have no feelings for anyone and were very difficult to treat, were found to have had grossly disturbed relationships with their mothers in their early years. Persistent stealing, violence, egotism, and sexual misdemeanors were among their less pleasant characteristics.

. . . . .

Between 1937 and 1943 there were many papers on this subject, several of which originated independently and some of which were completed in ignorance of the work of others. The unanimity of their conclusions stamps their findings as true. With monotonous regularity each observer put his finger on the child's inability to make relationships as being the central feature from which all the other disturbances sprang, and on the history of long periods spent in an institution or, as in the case quoted, of the child's being shifted about from one foster-mother to another as being its cause. So similar are the observations and the conclusions—even the very words— that each might have written the others' papers:

The symptom complaints are of various types. They include, frequently, aggressive and sexual behaviour in early life, stealing, lying, often of the fantastic type, and, essentially, complaints variously expressed that indicate some lack of emotional response in the child. It is this lack of emotional response, this shallowness of feeling that explains the difficulty in modifying behaviour.

Early in the work a third group of girls was recognized who were asocial [i.e., unaware of obligations to others], but not obviously neurotic, and with whom no treatment methods seemed of any avail. Later it became clear that the feature common to them was an inability to make a real relationship with any member of the staff. There might seem to be a good contact, but it invariably proved to be superficial. . . . There might be protestations of interest and a boisterous show of affection, but there was little or no evidence of any real attachment having been made. In going over their previous history, this same feature was outstanding. . . . [These girls] have ap-

parently had no opportunity to have a loving relationship in early childhood [and] seem to have little or no capacity to enter into an emotional relation with another person or with a group.

All the children [twenty-eight in number] present certain common symptoms of inadequate personality development chiefly related to an inability to give or receive affection; in other words, inability to relate the self to others. . . . The conclusion seems inescapable that infants reared in institutions undergo an isolation type of experience, with a resulting isolation type of personality.

Two special problems were referred to the ward from two child-placing agencies. One came from an agency [in which] there is a feeling that no attachment should be allowed to develop between the child and the boarding home, so that by the time the child is five years old, he has no attachment to anybody and no pattern of behaviour. . . . Another special group consisted of children placed in infancy [who] are given the best pediatric care . . . but have been deprived of social contacts and play materials. . . . These children are unable to accept love, because of their severe deprivation in the first three years. . . . They have no play pattern, cannot enter into group play and abuse other children. . . . They are overactive and distractible; they are completely confused about human relationships. . . . This type of child does not respond to the nursery group and continues overactive, aggressive and asocial.

"Imperviousness and a limited capacity for affective relationships" characterize children who have spent their early years in an institution. "Can it be that the absence of affective relationship in infancy made it difficult or even unnecessary for the institution children to participate later in positive emotional relationships . . . ?"

These communications came from across the Atlantic: meanwhile quite independent observations by Dr. Bowlby in London led to exactly the same conclusions:

Prolonged breaks [in the mother-child relationship] during the first three years of life leave a characteristic impression on the child's personality. Such children appear emotionally withdrawn and isolated. They fail to develop loving ties with other children or with adults and consequently have no friendships worth the name. It is true that they are sometimes sociable in a superficial sense, but if this is scrutinized we find that there are no feelings, no roots in these relationships. This, I think, more than anything else, is the cause of their hard-boiledness. Parents and school-teachers complain that nothing you say or do has any effect on the child. If you thrash him he cries for a bit, but there is no emotional response to being out of favour, such as is normal to the ordinary child. It appears to be of no essential consequence to these lost souls whether they are in favour or not. Since they are unable to make genuine emotional relations, the condition of relationship at a given moment lacks all significance for them. . . . During the last few years I have seen some sixteen cases of this affectionless type of persistent pilferer and in only two was a prolonged break absent. In all the others gross breaches of the mother-child relation had occurred during the first three years, and the child had become a persistent pilferer.

Since these early papers there have been several careful "retrospective studies," namely, studies made by specialists who were called upon to treat nervous symptoms and disturbances of behaviour, who by working back into the children's histories, unearthed the common factors of lack of care-caused either by their being in institutions, or being posted, like parcels, from one mother-figure to another.

One doctor in a large New York hospital had some 5,000 children under her care from 1935 to 1944. She found that from 5 per cent to 10 per cent of them showed the characteristics which have already been described.

There is an inability to love or feel guilty. There is no conscience. Their inability to enter into any relationship makes treatment or even education impossible. They have no idea of time, so that they cannot recall past experience and cannot benefit from past experience

or be motivated to future goals. This lack of time concept is a striking feature in the defective organization of the personality structure. . . .

Ten of the children referred to were seen five years later. They "all remained infantile, unhappy, and affectionless and unable to adjust to children in the schoolroom or other group situation."

Dr. Bowlby, writing of the children he dealt with in London, described how in some of their histories it was possible to find how the child had reacted to some startling and painful happening. He laid especial emphasis on the tendency of these children to steal. Dividing all the cases he had seen at a child guidance clinic into those who had been reported as stealing and those who had not, he compared a group of forty-four thieves with a control group, similar in number, age, and sex, who although emotionally disturbed did not steal. The thieves were distinguished from the controls in two main ways. First, there were among them fourteen "affectionless characters," while there were none in the control group. Secondly, seventeen of the thieves had suffered complete and prolonged separation (six months or more) from their mothers or established foster-mothers during their first five years of life; only two of the controls had suffered similar separations. Neither of these differences can be accounted for by chance. Two further points of great importance were that the "affectionless characters" almost always had a history of separation, and that they were far more delinquent than any of the others.

The results showed that bad heredity was less frequent amongst the "affectionless" thieves than amongst the others: of the fourteen children who came into this class only three could be said to have had a bad heredity (i.e., parents or grandparents with serious psychological ill-health), but twelve of them had histories of separation from their mothers.

Thus there can be no doubting that for the affectionless thief nurture not nature is to blame.

Dr. Bowlby concludes:

There is a very strong case indeed for believing that prolonged separation of a child from his mother (or mother substitute) during the first five years of life stands foremost among the causes of delinquent character development.

Among the cases described is one of a boy who was believed to have had a good relation to his mother until the age of eighteen months, but who was then in hospital for nine months, during which time visiting by his parents was forbidden. Other cases suggest that hospitalization and changes of mother-figure as late as the fourth year can have very destructive effects in producing the development of an affectionless psychopathic character given to persistent delinquent conduct and extremely difficult to treat.

Other retrospective studies touch on this problem. Thus the record of some 200 children under the age of twelve seen at a child-guidance clinic in London during the years 1942–6, whose troubles seemed to have been caused or aggravated by the war, showed that in one-third of the cases the trouble had been caused by evacuation. Almost all the difficult and long treatment cases were due to evacuation, not, it must be emphasized, to experience of bombing. No less than two-thirds of the children who presented problems after evacuation had been under the age of five when first evacuated. Since the number of young children evacuated in proportion to older ones was small, the figures make clear the extent to which it is especially the young child who is damaged by experiences of this kind.

Again, studies of adult patients have often led their authors to the conclusion that love deprivation is the cause of their psychological condition. Writing of hysterical patients, one doctor puts forward the view that

regardless of the nature of the individual's inborn tendencies, he will not develop hysteria unless he is subjected during childhood to situations causing him to crave affection.

Among such situations he lists the death of a parent and separation of child from parents. Another doctor who collected information on 530 prostitutes in Copenhagen, found that one-third of them had not been brought up at home, but had spent their childhood under troubled and shifting conditions.

Three per cent were brought up by close relations, 3 per cent were boarded out or sent to a home, 27 per cent were raised under combined conditions, partly in homes or almshouses, partly in institutions for the feeble-minded or epileptics, partly at home or with relatives.

Sometimes they had three or four different foster-homes during the course of their childhood. Seventeen per cent of the total were illegitimate.

The objection to all these retrospective studies is, of course, that they are concerned only with children who have developed badly and fail to take into account those who may have had the same experience, but have developed normally. We now come to studies of especial value, since they take a group of children placed as infants in institutions and seek to discover how they have turned out.

One very careful investigation carried out by a New York psychologist, Dr. Goldfarb, was scientifically planned from the beginning to test the theory that the experience of living in the highly impersonal surroundings of an institution nursery in the first two or three years of life has an adverse effect on personality development. What he did was to compare the mental development of children, brought up until the age of about three in an institution and then placed in foster-homes, with others who had gone straight from their mothers to foster-homes, in which they had remained. In both groups the children had been handed over by their mothers in infancy, usually within the first nine months of life. Dr. Goldfarb took great care to see that the two groups were of similar heredity. The children most thoroughly studied consisted of fifteen pairs who, at the time of the examination, ranged in age from ten to fourteen years. One set of fifteen was in the institution from about six months of age to three and a half years, the other set had not had this experience. Conditions in the institution were of the highest standards of physical hygiene, but lacked the elementary essentials of mental hygiene:

Babies below the age of nine months were kept in their own little cubicles to prevent the spread of epidemic infection. Their only contacts with adults occurred during these few hurried moments when they were dressed, changed, or fed by nurses.

Later they were members of a group of fifteen or twenty under the supervision of one nurse, who had neither the training nor the time to offer them love or attention. As a result they lived in "almost complete social isolation during the first year of life," and their experience in the succeeding two years was only slightly richer. Dr. Goldfarb has gone to great pains to ensure that the foster-homes of the two groups are similar, and shows further that, in respect of the mother's occupational, educational, and mental standing, the institution group was slightly superior to the controls. Any differences in the mental states of the two groups of children are, therefore, almost certain to be the result of their differing experiences in infancy. We must remember that none of the children had had the advantage of a quite unbroken home life. All had been in their foster-homes for six or seven years. Yet the differences between the groups are very marked and painfully full of meaning.

The two groups of children were studied by a great variety of tests. In intelligence, in power of abstract thinking, in their social maturity, their power of keeping rules or making friends, the institution group fell far below those who had stayed with their mothers for some months and then gone straight to the care of foster-mothers. Only three of the fifteen institution children were up to the average in speech, whilst all fifteen of the others reached this level. This continuing backwardness of speech has been noticed by many other observers— it looks as though the art of speech must be learnt at the right time and in the right place.

Whilst it will be seen that in most respects Dr. Goldfarb's conclusions are much like those of other observers, it must be noted that in two respects they differ from Dr. Bowlby's. First, the New York children "craved affection" and the London ones are observed to be "affectionless." This contrast is probably more apparent than real. Many affectionless characters crave affection, but none the less have a complete inability either to accept or reciprocate it. The poor capacity of all but two of Goldfarb's children for making relationships clearly confirms other work. The fact that only one of this group of Goldfarb's institution children stole and none truanted is, however, surprising in view of Bowlby's findings. The difference is probably valid and needs explanation: perhaps it can be explained this way. All of Goldfarb's cases had been institutionalized from soon after birth until they were three years old. None of Bowlby's had—they were all products of deprivation for a limited period, or of frequent changes. It may well be that their stealing was an attempt to secure love and gratification and so reinstate the love relationship which they had lost, whereas Goldfarb's cases, never having experienced anything of the kind, had nothing to reinstate. Certainly it would appear that the more complete the deprivation is in the early years the more indifferent to society and isolated the child becomes, whereas the more his deprivation is broken by moments of satisfaction the more he turns against society and suffers from conflicting feelings of love and hatred for the same people.

Before we leave the subject of Dr. Goldfarb's writings, we must make it clear that we must not take it for granted that all infants and toddlers in institutions have similar experiences. Not only is it clear that they do not, but the more one studies all the evidence on the subject the more one becomes convinced that the outcome is to a high degree dependent on the exact nature of the psychological experience. If further research is to be fruitful, it must pay minute attention not only to the ages and periods of deprivation, but also to the quality of the child's relation to his mother before deprivation, his experiences with mother-substitutes, if any, during separation, and the reception he gets from his mother or foster-mother when at last he becomes settled again.

There are several other follow-up studies which, though far less thorough, show similar results. An American psychiatrist, Dr. Lowrey, studied a group of children comprising among others twenty-two unselected cases who, with one exception, had been admitted to an institution before their first birthday and had remained there until they were three or four, when they were transferred to another society for fostering. They were examined when they were five years of age or older. All of them showed severe personality disturbances centering on an inability to give or receive affection. Symptoms, each of which

occurred in half or more of them, included aggressiveness, negativism (contrariness or obstinacy), selfishness, excessive crying, food difficulties, speech defects, and bedwetting. Other difficulties only a little less frequent included overactivity, fears, and soiling.

Both Dr. Goldfarb and Dr. Lowrey report 100 per cent of children institutionalized in their early years to have developed very poorly; other studies show that many such children achieve a tolerable degree of social adaptation when adult. Though this finding is in accordance with the expectations of the man in the street, it would be a mistake to build too much on it, since it is known that very many people who are psychologically disturbed are able to make an apparent adjustment for long periods. Moreover, these other studies show a large proportion of obvious mental ill-health which the authors regard as confirming the harmfulness of institutional conditions for young children.

As long ago as 1924, a comprehensive study was made in America of the social adjustment as adults of 910 people who had been placed in foster-homes as children. A particularly interesting comparison is made between ninety-five of them who had spent five years or more of their childhood in institutions and eighty-four who had spent the same years at home (in 80 per cent of cases in bad homes). Not only had all the children of both groups, later, been placed in foster-homes of similar quality and at similar ages, but so far as could be determined the heredity of the two groups was similar. The results show that those brought up in an institution adjusted significantly less well than those who had remained during their first five years in their own homes. Since the two groups were of similar heredity, the difference cannot be explained in this way. The fact that no less than one-third of the institution children turned out to be "socially incapable," of which nearly half were troublesome and delinquent, is to be noted.

It will be remarked, however, that, despite the institutional experience in the early years, two-thirds turned out "socially capable." So far as it goes this is satisfactory, but, as no expert examination was carried out, psychological troubles not leading to social incompetence were not recorded.

So far all the evidence has pointed in but one direction. It is now time to consider the three studies which present evidence which calls these conclusions in question. It may be said at once that none of them is of high scientific quality. One is a brief note, questioning the accuracy of Dr. Lowrey's 100 per cent bad results in some institutions, by another specialist who states that he has seen some sixteen children coming from the same institution and having had the same experiences as Lowrey's group, and and that only two showed adverse features of personality. No details are given and there appears to have been no systematic investigation of the individual cases.

Another critic compares a group of 100 boys aged nine to fourteen years living in an institution with another 100 of the same age living at home in bad surroundings, where broken homes and family discords predominate. Using questionnaires, he shows that the two groups are similar in mental ill-health. Not only is a questionnaire an unsatisfactory way of measuring mental health, but no evidence is given regarding the age at which the children entered the institution.

The most recent of the three studies was carried out by a group of child-guidance workers in England. They compared the "social maturity" of two groups of fifteen-year-old children: fifty-one who had spent the previous three years or more in an institution, and a comparable fifty-two who had lived at home. They showed that, although the institution children have a lower score than the family children, when the cases are regrouped according to their heredity an exactly similar difference is to be seen. On the basis of these figures they conclude that the case of those who argue that any social or personal retardation is attributable exclusively or mainly to environmental influences is weakened, and that constitutional factors are at least as important as environmental factors in the growth of social maturity.

These conclusions are ill-judged and certainly cannot be sustained by the evidence presented. In addition to technical criticism of the methods used in the enquiry, it is pointed out that some of the institution children did not enter until they were quite old, the average age of admission being four years; while, even more serious, of the family children in the control group, no less than twenty-two had been evacuated from their homes during the war, the average length of time being one year and nine months. Work with so many shortcomings cannot be accepted as calling in question the almost unanimous findings of the workers already quoted.

There is one other group of facts which is sometimes quoted as casting doubt on these findings—that from the Jewish communal settlements in Israel known as Kibbutz (plural, Kibbutzim). In these settlements, largely for ideological reasons, children are brought up by professional nurses in a "Children's House." Babies are reared in groups of five or six, and are later merged at the age of three years into larger groups numbering twelve to eighteen. The emphasis is throughout on communal rather than family care. Is not this, it may be asked, a clear example that communal care can be made to work without damaging the children? Before answering this question it is necessary to look more carefully at the conditions in which the children are raised. The following account is taken partly from the report of an American psychiatric social worker who recently visited Israel, and partly from a personal communication from the Lasker Child Guidance Centre in Jerusalem. Both describe life in certain of the non-religious Kibbutzim. The former remarks:

Separation is a relative concept and separation as it appears in the Kibbutz should not be thought of as identical with that of children who are brought up in foster-homes or institutions away from their parents. . . . In the Kibbutz there is a great deal of opportunity for close relationship between child and parents.

Not only does the mother nurse the baby and feed him in the early months, but, to follow the Lasker Centre's description:

once the suckling tie between mother and child is abandoned, the daily visit of the child to the room of the parents becomes the focus of family life for the child, and its importance is scrupulously respected. During these few hours the parents, or at least one of them, are more or less completely at the disposal of the children; they play with them, talk to them, carry the babies about, take the toddlers for little walks, etc.

The time spent with the children "may amount to as much as two to three hours on working days and many more on the Sabbath."

Here, then, is no complete abandonment of parent-child relations. Though the amount of time parents spend with their young children is far less than in most other Western communities, the report makes it clear that "the parents are extremely important people in the children's eyes, and the children in the parents'." It is interesting to note, too, that the trend is steadily towards parents taking more responsibility. Formerly parents had to visit the children in the Children's House—now the children come to the parents' room and the parents even prepare light meals for them; feasts are now celebrated in the parents' room as well as communally in the Children's House; mothers are asserting themselves and demanding to see more of their children.

Finally, it is by no means certain that the children do not suffer from this regime. While both observers report good and co-operative development in adolescence, the Lasker Centre think there are signs of a somewhat higher level of insecurity among Kibbutz children than among others, at least until the age of seven years. They also point out that the strong morale and intimate group life of the Kibbutz are of great value to the older child and adolescent, and that these may offset some of the unsettlement of earlier years.

From this brief account it is evident that there is no evidence here which can be held to undermine our conclusions. The conditions provide, of course, unusually rich opportunities for research in child development, and it is to be hoped that these will not be missed.

OBSERVATIONS OF WAR ORPHANS AND REFUGEES

Evidence of the adverse effects on children of all ages of separation from their families was provided on a tragic scale during the Second World War, when thousands of refugee children from occupied lands in Europe were cared for in Switzerland and elsewhere. Owing to the scale of the problem, there was little time for systematic research, and in any case the children had been submitted to such diverse and often horrifying experiences that it would have been almost impossible to have isolated the effects of separation from those of other experiences. A summary of the findings of medical, educational, and relief workers emphasizes that "while the reports tell of disturbances in character resulting from war, they show also the fundamental part played in their causation by rupture of the family tie." Of experiences with refugree children at the Pestalozzi Village at Trogen, Switzerland, we read:

No doubt remains that a long period without individual attention and personal relationships leads to mental atrophy; it slows down or arrests the development of the emotional life and thus in turn inhibits normal intellectual development. We have observed that acute psychical traumata [damaging experiences], however serious, do not result in such deep injury as chronic deficiencies and prolonged spiritual solitude.

In 1944 a small comparative study was made of ninety-seven Jewish refugee children in homes in Switzerland and 173 Swiss children of about the same age (eleven to seventeen years). All the children were asked to write an essay on "What I think, what I wish, and what I hope." From a scrutiny of these essays it appeared that for the refugees separation from their parents was evidently their most tragic experience. In contrast, few of the Swiss children mentioned their parents, who were evidently felt to be a natural and inevitable part of life. Another great contrast was the refugee children's preoccupation with their suffering past, or with frenzied and grandiose ideas regarding the future. The Swiss children lived happily in the present, which for the refugee was either a vacuum or at best an unsatisfying transition. Deprived of all the things which had given life meaning, especially family and friends, they were possessed by a feeling of emptiness.

Another psychologist also studied refugee children in Switzerland and others in a concentration camp. He describes such symptoms as bedwetting and stealing, an inability to make rela-tions and a consequent loss of ability to form ideals, an increase of aggression, and intolerance of frustration.

In the Netherlands after the war, a group of psychiatrists studied some thousands of children whose parents had been deported in 1942 and 1943 and who had been cared for in foster-homes, often from earliest infancy. They report that frequent changes of foster-home almost always had very adverse effects, leading the child to become withdrawn and apathetic. This was sometimes accompanied by a superficial sociability and, later, promiscuous sex-relationships. Some young children managed to weather a single change, but others could not stand even this, and developed symptoms such as anxiety, depression, excessive clinging, and bedwetting. Many of the children were still emotionally disturbed when examined after the war and in need of treatment. It was noted that those who had had good family relationships before separation could usually be helped to an adjustment, but that for those with a bad family background the outlook was poor.

Finally may be noted an extensive psychological and statistical study undertaken in Spain following the civil war on over 14,000 cases of neglected and delinquent children housed in the environs of Barcelona. Once again there is confirmation of the decisive and adverse role in character development played by the break-up of the family and the vital importance of family life for satisfactory social and moral development. Particularly interesting is the confirmation of Dr. Goldfarb's findings regarding impaired mental development. The intelligence levels of the neglected and delinquent children are much below those of a control group. Lessened capacity for abstract thought is also noted—the evidence, in the investigator's opinion, pointing to the existence of a strong link between the development of the abstract mental faculties and the family and social life of the child. He notes especially the following characteristics of the neglected and delinquent child:

Feeble and difficult attention due to his great instability. Very slight sense of objective realities, overflowing imagination and absolute

lack of critical ability. Incapacity for strict abstraction and logical reasoning. Noteworthy backwardness in the development of language. . . .

The similarity of these observations on war orphans and refugees to those on other deprived children will not fail to impress the reader.

26 | "MASKED DEPRIVATION" IN INFANTS AND YOUNG CHILDREN

DANE G. PRUGH AND ROBERT G. HARLOW

Separations between parents and children are not always physical; they may also be psychological. Far more numerous than physically separated children are those who reside at home with their parents, but fail to experience the usual emotional exchange with them. The deterioration of the mother-child relationship may be even more devastating to the child than physical separation. In fact, in many cases, social agencies intervene in the family to separate mother and child. The following article explores some of the factors that appear so pathoformic as to warrant such a radical procedure.

It is the purpose of this [article] to . . . discuss the effects of various sorts of covert, subtle, or "masked" emotional deprivation which may result for the child in otherwise intact parent-child relationships, as opposed to those effects seen as a result of flagrant and gross physical separation of mother and child during the early years.

. . . . .

In regard to the . . . question of whether "affectionless characters" develop only as a result of gross maternal deprivation, clinical observations at least would lend ample support to the thesis that such is not the case. The work of Aichhorn, Lippman, and others (including the present

Excerpts reprinted from *Deprivation of Maternal Care: A Reassessment of Its Effects*, Public Affairs Papers, No. 14 (Geneva: World Health Organization, 1962), pp. 9–29. By permission of the authors.

writers) provides a number of case examples of children in . . . chronic difficulty with the authorities, with the parents always available to plead the child's case for him, in spite of their ambivalent or hostile feelings towards him in other respects. . . . It would seem that early institutionalization or prolonged separation from parents does not *necessarily* lead to specific effects upon personality in later life, and that these personality patterns, when they are observed, are not *always* due to a particular set of early experiences.

. . . . .

A further conclusion that has sometimes been [erroneously] drawn is that any home setting is better than any institutional placement. Case studies by Du Pan and Roth and by many other workers . . . attest to the fact that the physical presence of a parent or a foster-parent does not guarantee emotional satisfaction to the child, especially if that parent is unable to tolerate any disturbance in behaviour on the part of the child. If a foster-home setting is involved, a train of events leading to repetitive shifts in home settings, with serious emotional consequences for the child, may be set in motion. . . .

Finally, misplaced emphasis given to Bowlby's earlier statements can lead to the facile conclusion that any child at any age is better off in his own home than in a foster-home, hospital, or other institutional setting. It is true that most children are happier with their own parents, no matter how disturbed or unsatisfying the parent-child relationships may be. However, recent experiences in nurseries and residential treatment centres, which have admitted disturbed children from physically intact but seriously disturbed families, have indicated that the home may not always be the most favourable environment for a child's development. On the contrary, it is sometimes seen that only when the child is removed from the home is he able to begin to mature and develop. [It is the position of the writers] that the subtle effects of less obvious disruptions or distortions in the parent-child relationship may have as devastating effects upon emotional development as the more gross maternal deprivations highlighted by Bowlby. Further, it is to be emphasized that instances of "masked" or covert deprivation, of a virtually "complete" nature, may occur frequently in intact families, giving rise to clinical pictures in children which may equal in pathological intensity those deprived from overt deprivations. . . . With the provision of satisfying mother-substitute relationships or with the use of direct psychotherapeutic work with the mother, such retardation appears to be reversible. This more subtle, but apparently equally potent, psychological "separation" or deprivation seems to deserve re-emphasis at this time and to

require more careful description and dynamic formulation.

CLINICAL OBSERVATIONS

We shall now consider some clinical examples from or own experience of parent-child relationships which involve no actual or physical separation but which may be said to involve emotional separation or deprivation. . . .

. . . At least two major ways of perceiving and relating to the child appear to exist. The first involves the situation in which the child has a specific but distorted meaning for the parent; hence a relationship develops in which the child is not viewed as an individual with integrity in his own right, but rather, in some way, as a being responding to the needs, wishes, and feelings of the parent, with the result that his emotional needs are not met adequately. This situation will be termed "distorted relatedness." The second way in which the child may be perceived by his parents, leading to pathological development, is one in which the child does not have any such specific meaning to the parent; the parent, however, is so involved in his own concerns, whether of a transient or of an enduring nature, that he is unable to provide adequate emotional supplies or, more broadly, adequate parenting for the infant. This situation we shall call "insufficient relatedness." We shall attempt to provide, subsumed under each of these categories, examples of different sorts of reaction in the parent—i.e., the varying affects experienced by the parent figures, the different ways in which these affects are expressed, and what seems to be the answering response in the behaviour patterns of the children.

Distorted Relatedness

(1) The mother (or father) may be unable to perceive the child as an individual separate from herself (or himself)

and may handle the child accordingly, with little or no regard for the child's own needs.

(*a*) In extreme examples the parent may be completely confused as to the identity of the child and the child essentially undifferentiated from the parent.

EXAMPLE   A chronically psychotic woman, living at home with her husband, gave birth to a female infant who she said was the incarnation of her mother. She had previously been confused as to whether she was herself or her mother. This confusion was revived and, instead of feeding her infant, she often lay down beside the infant, opening her mouth and saying, "Feed me." In spite of the urgings of her husband, an ineffectual person, she was unable to feed the infant more than occasionally but refused frequently to permit her husband to feed her. Although the husband managed to give the infant some surreptitious feedings, her nutritional state became precarious over the course of several months. The mother could not accept either medical care for the infant or psychiatric hospitalization for herself. Finally the neighbours, seeing the infant's marasmic state, forced the husband to steal the baby away from the mother and take her to a hospital.

(*b*) Less extreme, but still deeply pathological, examples involve situations in which a relationship is established wherein either the parents' or the child's needs can only be gratified through the other's response. Hence each is dependent upon the other's actions for his or her own satisfactions. This represents the so-called symbiotic or complementary relationship.

EXAMPLE   A markedly obese girl had been constantly fed large amounts of food by the mother, who had adopted her in early infancy. Here the mother's need to offer this child nutritional supplies appeared to operate in part as a substitute for her incapacity to provide emotional supplies of a satisfying nature, because of her own conflicts in the role of woman and mother. Her associated need to keep the girl, whom she called "Baby," in a state of infantile dependence

upon her appeared to derive in part from her unsatisfying and unsuccessful marital relationship with an immature, alcoholic husband. At a deeper level, she regarded the girl as a part of herself which needed gratification, but was also dependent upon the girl's clinging response to her. In spite of the mother's constant feeding, over-protective and controlling behavior towards the girl, she readily permitted her to be placed in a convalescent hospital for nearly a year, and her underlying hostility towards the girl showed in her reluctance to have her return to the home. The girl at the age of 12 presents the picture of a firmly entrenched passive-aggressive personality disorder, with markedly unsatisfied emotional needs and the tendency to over-eat as a substitute for healthier gratifications.

(2) In other instances, while the child may be perceived as a separate person, the parent may still respond in terms of his or her own needs.

(*a*) In some instances, the significant parent may identify the child with certain aspects of himself or of other persons; the interaction with the child may then take place in terms of these projected personality attributes or partial identifications.

EXAMPLE   A mother had experienced deep anger at her own father for his coolness towards her. She permitted her infant daughter's rebellion towards her husband, identifying the daughter with herself and her husband with her father. When the little girl stole objects from her father, the mother laughed and thought her behavior "cute," while superficially criticizing her. She could only relate warmly to the girl when she acted out towards her husband, at other times pushing her off, saying she was "too busy" to talk to her. The girl became delinquent, stealing from boys and becoming involved sexually with a series of men, without any real gratification in such relationships.

EXAMPLE   A woman gave birth to her first child, a boy, in a setting of considerable marital conflict. She had made a neurotic choice in her marriage and could neither accept nor leave her husband, being bound to him in a hostile-dependent relationship. From the first she seemingly projected the hostility she felt towards the father on to this infant. She said that she could not accept him and paid him little attention except during feeding. When he refused food, she became openly angry and would take his plate away, expressing openly her dislike of him. The child ate very poorly, developing a picture of extreme undernourishment, with the result that he weighed only 19 lb. at 4½ years and was the size of a two-year-old. Gradually his state of nutrition and hydration became precarious, necessitating medical treatment. With psychiatric help, the mother was finally able to place him in another setting, whereupon he gained 15 lb. within a few weeks.

(b) Parents may, in addition, possess irrational and distorted perceptions of their children, arising not from identification but from basic attitudes, acquired values and standards, or other aspects of their previous experience.

EXAMPLE   A boy was regarded from infancy as mentally retarded by the mother because of his initial lack of responsiveness to her. Although she hovered constantly around him in a protective fashion, she remained emotionally isolated and withdrawn from him and looked on him as a family disgrace. The boy in turn became increasingly withdrawn, with shallow relationships. Gradually he conformed to the mother's perception of him as retarded, by his complete lack of scholastic achievement despite high average to superior intellectual endowment.

Insufficient Relatedness

(1) The parent may, because of unhealthy characterological or deeply neurotic or psychotic trends, quite independent of the child, be unable to relate warmly to the infant.

(a) The mother may be a cold and isolated personality, with little or no ability to "give" emotionally to her child.

EXAMPLE   A mother, an attractive but seriously inhibited and cold young woman, felt completely unable to respond to her first-born infant, a boy. She went through the motions

of his care, but was consciously aware that she felt no warmth towards him and took no pleasure in him at any time. Although she remained close to him physically, she let him play alone for many hours in his playpen during the first year of life, withdrawing into herself or reading and paying only occasional attention to his safety. During the latter part of the boy's second year, the father became alarmed at the child's lack of responsiveness or interest in the environment, and upon psychiatric study an autistic psychotic picture was apparent.

(b) The parents may be so involved in their own narcissistic needs or pleasures that any emotional warmth for the child is precluded, even though physical care is provided.

EXAMPLE   In a particular family, the father was an expert bowler, who spent all his spare time in this activity. As a result of his need to prove himself in competition, he took no interest in his eldest son, even when the boy grew old enough to imitate his father, leaving his care completely to the mother. The mother was a helpless and dependent person, who was frightened of the boy's healthy aggression as an infant and of his growing masculinity. She could set no limits on his aggressive behavior, "washing her hands" of him in early childhood, although she continued to care for his physical needs. The boy became an impulsive and antisocial personality, with inability to control his hostile and destructive impulses and with no adequate identification with a father figure.

(2) In other instances, situational factors involving current reality problems may produce psychological disorders in the parent which may affect detrimentally the development processes of the infant.

EXAMPLE   A young mother experienced the death of her own mother during the latter part of her pregnancy with her second child. Although still able to minister to the physical needs of the infant, she felt that she had "nothing left to give" to him. During the first eight months of the infant's life, the father was able to offer significant emotional support to the mother, although she remained definitely depressed without a feeling of warmth for the infant. The father became ill suddenly, however, and temporarily lost his job, so that he also became depressed and apathetic and could no longer offer support to the mother. At this point, the infant developed diarrhea of a non-infectious nature, showing an associated refusal of food, without underlying physical abnormalities. The combined loss of body fluids and the lack of nutritional intake produced a picture resembling that of marasmus. Intensive medical therapy was of no avail, but the infant responded, with a cessation of diarrhea and a resumption of feeding, to the assignment in the hospital of one warm and "giving" nurse to his principle care. Supportive psychotherapy for the parents enabled the mother to lose her depression and the father to conquer his apathy and secure a job. Upon returning home under these circumstances, the infant resumed normal development with no subsequent difficulties over a number of years.

. . . It is also evident that "masked deprivation" can be involved in the production of a variety of symptomatic pictures or personality disorders in the child, including examples of the so-called "affectionless character" described by Bowlby. No one symptom complex or personality pattern appears to predominate in persons whose early life was characterized by "masked deprivation." These conclusions, when taken in conjunction with the studies cited earlier, cast further doubt upon the specificity of the development of any personality configuration in response to any specific antecedent event.

It is proposed now to discuss some of the variables which may be important in determining the child's reaction to traumatic events during his early development. Because of the intensely unique quality of each parent-child diad, . . . any event, whether it be actual separation, psychological estrangement from the parents, or some other significant happening, may have greatly varying effects on both parent and child. . . . Current conceptualizations

also point up the importance to the mother of the infant's capacity to respond pleasurably to her ministrations. Some mothers have extreme difficulty in adjusting to a role in which they "give" but in which there tends to be little "return" for this giving—e.g., the infant who fails to smile responsively or who refuses to accept the breast or bottle. This maternal reaction to the child's lack of response, or "feedback," . . . "feeds back" to the child, and a cycle of resentment and frustration in the mother-infant relationship tends to be established.

Variations in the capacity of the mother to satisfy the infant's affective needs may arise from her own neurotic problems, reflecting earlier unsolved conflicts, or from current difficulties in carrying out her maternal functions—e.g., disturbances in the marital relationship or in the balance of interpersonal forces within the family unit. On the parent's part, individual inborn or acquired differences in responsiveness may exist, as demonstrated by Bergmann and Escalona and Fries, thus affecting the quality of the "feedback" of satisfactions to the mother. . . .

In regard to separation, actual or psychological, it is already apparent that the effects of such experience upon the infant will vary according to its nature and length of duration, as well as to the quality of substitute maternal relationships available. (In some instances of "masked deprivation," arising particularly from insufficient relatedness between mother and infant, an other female member of the family, or even occasionally the father, may provide adequate substitute relationships.)

An additional variable is represented by the age or stage of development of the infant or young child when separation or equivalent emotional trauma occurs. Most studies indicate that actual or symbolic separation from the mother during the first two or three months of life rarely disturbs the infant seriously if an adequate mother-substitute figure is provided. Separation after this time, when the infant has at hand the developmental capacities to begin to develop a definite object relationship with the mother, may be more disturbing, with disturbances appearing during the second quarter of the first year, as Fischer has indicated, and involving "anaclitic depression," described by Spitz and Wolf. A particular point of vulnerability seems to be the period during the second half of the first year of life when the infant begins to be involved in differentiating himself from the mother and in developing a primitive body image, albeit in the context of an extremely dependent relationship. . . .

A further variable which must be considered concerns the meaning of the child's trauma to the mother. Because of the extreme closeness of the parent-child unit, the mother's conflicts concerning and reaction to events may determine, in part, particularly for the older infant and young child, the way in which the child accepts, deals with, and reacts to such things as separation, injuries, or the introduction of siblings into the family. Numerous cases in the literature and in the authors' experience, for example, suggest that the parent's reaction to the child's hospitalization for an operation is a factor of great importance in determining the response of the child to this situation, even though other variables are, of course, involved.

In summary, it would seem that the child's response to separation, as a representative potential trauma, is a complex process, influenced by its nature and duration, the quality of mothering before and after the experience, the age and stage of development of the child, and the emotional conflicts with which he is principally dealing. Also important are such factors as the child's physical health, his integrative or other ego capacities, the reaction of salient figures around him to the experience, and the nature of important later events. The influence of other variables such as the inborn or acquired biological capacities of the child are more difficult to assess but must also be considered.

. . . . .

It seems important to emphasize that the state of our knowledge is such, at this time, that conclusions regarding the effects of early experience can be drawn only tentatively and then in quite general terms. No one symptom complex seems to eventuate consistently from one set of prior experiences, nor does any particular early event necessarily mark all those who experience it similarly. Significant trauma to the child may occur as a function of physical separation from the mother. This does not always occur, however, as the telling examples cited by Caplan and J. Mann of the *Kibbutzim* in Israel demonstrate, nor is this trauma always more severe in its effects than "psychological" separation with its consequent "masked deprivation."

27 | THE NATURE OF LOVE

HARRY F. HARLOW

Although the fact that mortality and morbidity rates for children separated from their mothers are higher than those for children who are not maternally deprived has been clearly established, exactly what essential factors the mother provides remain unknown.
Certainly there must be factors other than food, clothing, and warmth, since these are provided for infants in institutions.
The ingenious series of experiments described in this article

*show that baby monkeys "love" something soft and warm, that
ever-present soft, warm artificial mothers seemed initially to be superior
to natural mothers. Anyone who has seen how chickens, kittens,
mice, or sheep huddle together, even on warm days, or who has observed
the strong attachment an infant can develop to a tattered old blanket
or a doll, can verify this snuggling response.*

   *Perhaps any old rag will do as well as an actual mother—and
better than some—but final demonstration of this remains to be completed.
Further evidence provides some surprises in the next selection.*

The position commonly held by psychologists and sociologists is quite clear: The basic motives are, for the most part, the primary drives—particularly hunger, thirst, elimination, pain, and sex—and all other motives, including love or affection, are derived or secondary drives. The mother is associated with the reduction of the primary drives—particularly hunger, thirst, and pain—and through learning, affection or love is derived.

It is entirely reasonable to believe that the mother through association with food may become a secondary-reinforcing agent, but this is an inadequate mechanism to account for the persistence of the infant-material ties. There is a spate of researches on the formation of secondary reinforcers to hunger and thirst reduction. There can be no question that almost any external stimulus can become a secondary reinforcer if properly associated with tissue-need reduction, but the fact remains that this redundant literature demonstrates unequivocally that such derived drives suffer relatively rapid experimental extinction. Contrariwise, human affection does not extinguish when the mother ceases to have intimate association with the drives in question. Instead, the affectional ties to the mother show a lifelong, unrelenting persistence and, even more surprising, widely expanding generality.

Oddly enough, one of the few psychologists who took a position counter to modern psychological dogma was John B. Watson, who believed that love was an innate emotion elicited by cutaneous stimulation of the erogenous zones. . . .

The psychoanalysts have concerned themselves with the problem of the nature of the development of love in the neonate and infant, using ill and aging human beings as subjects. They have discovered the overwhelming importance of the breast and related this to the oral erotic tendencies developed at an age preceding their subjects' memories. Their theories range from a belief that the infant has an innate need to achieve and suckle at the breast to beliefs not unlike commonly accepted psychological theories. There are exceptions, as seen in the recent writings of John Bowlby, who attributes importance not only to food and thirst satisfaction, but also to "primary object-clinging," a need for intimate physical contact, which is initially associated with the mother.

As far as I know, there exists no direct experimental analysis of the relative importance of the stimulus variables determining the affectional or love responses in the neonatal and infant primate. Unfortunately, the human neonate is a limited experimental subject for such researches because of his inadequate motor capabilities. By the time the human infant's motor responses can be precisely measured, the antecedent determining conditions cannot be defined, having been lost in a jumble and jungle of confounded variables.

Excerpts reprinted from *The American Psychologist*, XIII (December, 1958), 673–85, by permission of the author and the American Psychological Association.

Many of these difficulties can be resolved by the use of the neonatal and infant macaque monkey as the subject for the analysis of basic affectional variables. It is possible to make precise measurements in this primate beginning at two to ten days of age, depending upon the maturational status of the individual animal at birth. The macaque infant differs from the human infant in that the monkey is more mature at birth and grows more rapidly; but the basic responses relating to affection, including nursing, contact, clinging, and even visual and auditory exploration, exhibit no fundamental differences in the two species. Even the development of perception, fear, frustration, and learning capability follows very similar sequences in rhesus monkeys and human children.

Three years' experimentation before we started our studies on affection gave us experience with the neonatal monkey. We had separated more than 60 of these animals from their mothers 6 to 12 hours after birth and suckled them on tiny bottles. The infant mortality was only a small fraction of what would have obtained had we let the monkey mothers raise their infants. Our bottle-fed babies were healthier and heavier than monkey-mother-reared infants. We know that we are better monkey mothers than are real monkey mothers thanks to synthetic diets, vitamins, iron extracts, penicillin, chloromycetin, 5% glucose, and constant, tender, loving care.

During the course of these studies we noticed that the laboratory-raised babies showed strong attachment to the cloth pads (folded gauze diapers) which were used to cover the hardware-cloth floors of their cages. The infants clung to these pads and engaged in violent temper tantrums when the pads were removed and replaced for sanitary reasons. Such contact-need or responsiveness had been reported previously by Gertrude van Wagenen for the monkey and by Thomas

Figure 1. Response to cloth pad by one-day-old monkey.

McCulloch and George Haslerud for the chimpanzee and is reminiscent of the devotion often exhibited by human infants to their pillows, blankets, and soft, cuddly stuffed toys. Responsiveness by the one-day-old infant monkey to the cloth pad is shown in Figure 1, and an unusual and strong attachment of a six-month-old infant to the cloth pad is illustrated in Figure 2. The baby, human or monkey, if it is to survive, must clutch at more than a straw.

We had also discovered during some allied observational studies that a baby monkey raised on a bare wire-mesh cage floor survives with difficulty, if at all, during the first five days of life. If a wire-mesh cone is introduced, the baby does

Figure 2. Response to gauze pad by six-month-old monkey used in earlier study.

better; and, if the cone is covered with terry cloth, husky, healthy, happy babies evolve. It takes more than a baby and a box to make a normal monkey. We were impressed by the possibility that, above and beyond the bubbling fountain of breast or bottle, contact comfort might be a very important variable in the development of the infant's affection for the mother.

At this point we decided to study the development of affectional responses of neonatal and infant monkeys to an artificial, inanimate mother, and so we built a surrogate mother which we hoped and believed would be a good surrogate mother. In devising this surrogate mother we were dependent neither upon the capriciousness of evolutionary processes nor upon mutations produced by chance radioactive fallout. Instead, we designed the mother surrogate in terms of modern human-engineering principles (Figure 3). We produced a perfectly proportioned, streamlined body stripped of unnecessary bulges and appendices. Redun-

dancy in the surrogate mother's system was avoided by reducing the number of breasts from two to one and placing this uni-breast in an upper-thoracic, sagittal position, thus maximizing the natural and known perceptual-motor capabilities of the infant operator. The surrogate was made from a block of wood, covered with sponge rubber, and sheathed in tan cotton terry cloth. A light bulb behind her radiated heat. The result was a mother, soft, warm, and tender, a mother with infinite patience, a mother available twenty-four hours a day, a mother that never scolded her infant and never struck or bit her baby in anger. Furthermore, we designed a mother-machine with maximal maintenance efficiency since failure of any system or function could be resolved by the simple substitution of black boxes and new component parts. It is our opinion that we engineered a very superior monkey mother, although this position is not held universally by the monkey fathers.

Before beginning our initial experiment we also designed and constructed a second mother surrogate, a surrogate in which we deliberately built less than the maximal capability for contact comfort. This surrogate mother is illustrated in Figure 4. She is made of wire-mesh, a substance entirely adequate to provide postural support and nursing capability, and she is warmed by radiant heat. Her body differs in no essential way from that of the cloth mother surrogate other than in the quality of the contact comfort which she can supply.

In our initial experiment, the dual mother-surrogate condition, a cloth mother and a wire mother were placed in different cubicles attached to the infant's living cage as shown in Figure 4. For four newborn monkeys the cloth mother lactated and the wire mother did not; and, for the other four, this condition was reversed. In either condition the

Figure 3. Cloth mother surrogate.

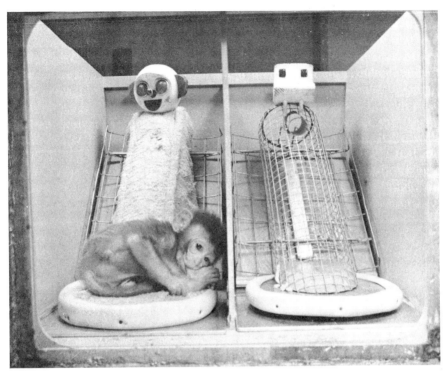

Figure 4. Wire and cloth mother surrogates.

infant received all its milk through the mother surrogate as soon as it was able to maintain itself in this way, a capability achieved within two or three days except in the case of very immature infants. Supplementary feedings were given until the milk intake from the mother surrogate was adequate. Thus, the experiment was designed as a test of the relative importance of the variables of contact comfort and nursing comfort. During the first 14 days of life the monkey's cage floor was covered with a heating pad wrapped in a folded gauze diaper, and thereafter the cage floor was bare. The infants were always free to leave the heating pad or cage floor to contact either mother, and the time spent on the surrogate mothers was automatically recorded. Figure 5 shows the total time spent on the cloth and wire mothers under the two conditions of feeding. These data make it obvious that contact comfort is a variable of over-

whelming importance in the development of affectional responses, whereas lactation is a variable of negligible importance. With age and opportunity to learn, subjects with the lactating wire mother showed decreasing responsiveness to her and increasing responsiveness to the nonlactating cloth mother, a finding completely contrary to any interpretation of derived drive in which the mother-form becomes conditioned to hunger-thirst reduction. The persistence of these differential responses throughout 165 consecutive days of testing is evident in Figure 6.

One control group of neonatal monkeys was raised on a single wire mother, and a second control group was raised on a single cloth mother. There were no differences between these two groups in amount of milk ingested or in weight gain. The only difference between the groups lay in the composition of the feces, the softer stools of the wire-mother

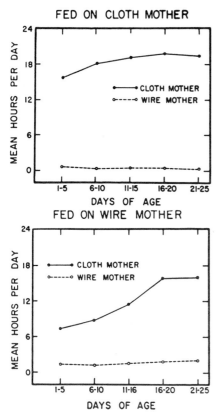

Figure 5. Time spent on cloth and wire mother surrogates.

subsequently talked to her, her face brightened with sudden insight: "Now I know what's wrong with me," she said, "I'm just a wire mother." Perhaps she was lucky. She might have been a wire wife.

We believe that contact comfort has long served the animal kingdom as a motivating agent for affectional responses. Since at the present time we have no experimental data to substantiate this position, we supply information which must be accepted, if at all, on the basis of face validity.

. . . . .

One function of the real mother, human or sub-human, and presumably of a mother surrogate, is to provide a haven of safety for the infant in times of fear and danger. The frightened or ailing child clings to its mother, not its father; and this selective responsiveness in times of distress, disturbance, or danger may be used as a measure of the strength of affectional bonds. We have tested this kind of differential responsiveness by presenting to the infants in their cages, in the presence of the two mothers, vari-

infants suggesting psychosomatic involvement. The wire mother is biologically adequate but psychologically inept.

We were not surprised to discover that contact comfort was an important basic affectional or love variable, but we did not expect it to overshadow so completely the variable of nursing; indeed, the disparity is so great as to suggest that the primary function of nursing as an affectional variable is that of insuring frequent and intimate body contact of the infant with the mother. Certainly, man cannot live by milk alone. Love is an emotion that does not need to be bottle- or spoon-fed, and we may be sure that there is nothing to be gained by giving lip service to love.

A charming lady once heard me describe these experiments; and, when I

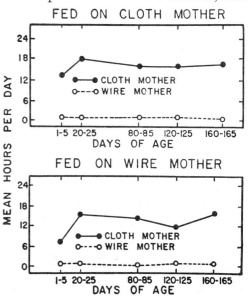

Figure 6. Long-term contact time on cloth and wire mother surrogates.

Figure 7.   Typical fear stimulus.

ous fear-producing stimuli such as the moving toy bear illustrated in Figure 7. A typical response to a fear stimulus is shown in Figure 8, and the data on differential responsiveness are presented in Figure 9. It is apparent that the cloth mother is highly preferred over the wire one, and this differential selectivity is enhanced by age and experience. In this situation, the variable of nursing appears to be of absolutely no importance: the infant consistently seeks the soft mother surrogate regardless of nursing condition.

Similarly, the mother or mother surrogate provides its young with a source of security, and this role or function is seen with special clarity when mother and child are in a strange situation. At the present time we have completed tests for this relationship on four of our eight baby monkeys assigned to the dual mother-surrogate condition by introducing them for three minutes into the strange environment of a room measuring six feet by six feet by six feet (also called the "open-field test") and contain-

ing multiple stimuli known to elicit curiosity-manipulatory responses in baby monkeys. The subjects were placed in this situation twice a week for eight weeks with no mother surrogate present during alternate sessions and the cloth mother present during the others. A cloth diaper was always available as one

Figure 8.   Typical response to cloth mother surrogate in fear test.

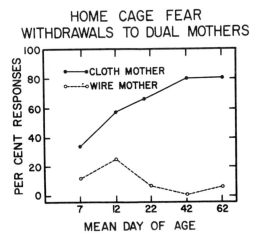

Figure 9.   Differential responsiveness in fear tests.

Figure 10. Response to cloth mother in the open-field test.

Figure 12. Response in the open-field test in the absence of the mother surrogate.

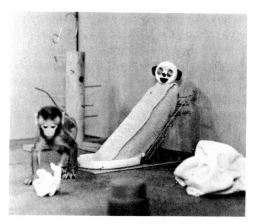

Figure 11. Object exploration in presence of cloth mother.

Figure 13. Response in the open-field test in the absence of the mother surrogate.

of the stimuli throughout all sessions. After one or two adaptation sessions, the infants always rushed to the mother surrogate when she was present and clutched her, rubbed their bodies against her, and frequently manipulated her body and face. After a few additional sessions, the infants began to use the mother surrogate as a source of security, a base of operations. As is shown in Figures 10 and 11, they would explore and manipulate a stimulus and then return to the mother before adventuring again into the strange new world. The behavior of these infants was quite different when the mother was absent from the room. Frequently they would freeze in a crouched position, as is illustrated in Figures 12 and 13. Emotionality indices such as vocalization, crouching, rocking, and sucking increased sharply. . . . Total emotionality score was cut in half when the mother was present. In the absence of the mother some of the experimental monkeys would rush to the center of the room where the mother was customarily placed and then run rapidly from object to object, screaming and crying all the while. Continuous, frantic clutching of their bodies was very common, even when not in the crouching position. These monkeys frequently contacted and clutched the cloth diaper, but this action never pacified them. The same behavior occurred in the presence of the wire mother. No difference between the cloth-mother-fed and wire-mother-fed infants was demonstrated under either condition. Four control infants never raised with a mother surrogate showed the same emotionality scores when the mother was absent as the experimental infants showed in the absence of the mother, but the controls' scores were slightly larger in the presence of the mother surrogate than in her absence.

. . . . .

Affectional retention was . . . tested in the open field during the first 9 days after separation and then at 30-day intervals, and each test condition was run twice at each retention interval. The infant's behavior differed from that observed during the period preceding separation. When the cloth mother was present in the post-separation period, the babies rushed to her, climbed up, clung tightly to her, and rubbed their heads and faces against her body. After this initial embrace and reunion, they played on the mother, including biting and tearing at her cloth cover; but they rarely made any attempt to leave her during the test period, nor did they manipulate or play with the objects in the room, in contrast with their behavior before maternal separation. The only exception was the occasional monkey that left the mother surrogate momentarily, grasped the folded piece of paper (one of the standard stimuli in the field), and brought it quickly back to the mother. It appeared that deprivation had enhanced the tie to the mother and rendered the contact-comfort need so prepotent that need for the mother overwhelmed the exploratory motives during the brief, three-minute test sessions. No change in these behaviors was observed throughout the 185-day period. When

the mother was absent from the open field, the behavior of the infants was similar in the initial retention test to that during the preseparation tests; but they tended to show gradual adaptation to the open-field situation with repeated testing and, consequently, a reduction in their emotionality scores.

In the last five retention test periods, an additional test was introduced in which the surrogate mother was placed in the center of the room and covered with a clear Plexiglas box. The monkeys were initially disturbed and frustrated when their explorations and manipulations of the box failed to provide contact with the mother. However, all animals adapted to the situation rather rapidly. Soon they used the box as a place of orientation for exploratory and play behavior, made frequent contacts with the objects in the field, and very often brought these objects to the Plexiglas box. The emotionality index was slightly higher than in the condition of the available cloth mothers, but it in no way approached the emotionality level displayed when the cloth mother was absent. Obviously, the infant monkeys gained emotional security by the presence of the mother even though contact was denied.

Affectional retention has also been measured by tests in which the monkey must unfasten a three-device mechanical puzzle to obtain entrance into a compartment containing the mother surrogate. All the trials are initiated by allowing the infant to go through an unlocked door, and in half the trials it finds the mother present and in half, an empty compartment. The door is then locked and a ten-minute test conducted. In tests given prior to separation from the surrogate mothers, some of the infants had solved this puzzle and others had failed. . . . On the last test before separation there were no differences in total manipulation under mother-present and mother-absent conditions, but striking differences exist between the two conditions throughout the post-separation test periods. Again, there is no interaction with conditions of feedings.

The over-all picture obtained from surveying the retention data is unequivocal. There is little, if any, waning of responsiveness to the mother throughout this five-month period as indicated by any measure. It becomes perfectly obvious that this affectional bond is highly resistant to forgetting and that it can be retained for very long periods of time by relatively infrequent contact reinforcement. During the next year, retention tests will be conducted at 90-day intervals, and further plans are dependent upon the results obtained. It would appear that affectional responses may show as much resistance to extinction as has been previously demonstrated for learned fears and learned pain, and such data would be in keeping with those of common human observation.

. . . . .

We have already described the group of four control infants that had never lived in the presence of any mother surrogate and had demonstrated no sign of affection or security in the presence of the cloth mothers introduced in test sessions. When these infants reached the age of 250 days, cubicles containing both a cloth mother and a wire mother were attached to their cages. There was no lactation in these mothers, for the monkeys were on a solid-food diet. The initial reaction of the monkeys to the alterations was one of extreme disturbance. All the infants screamed violently and made repeated attempts to escape the cage whenever the door was opened. They kept a maximum distance from the mother surrogates and exhibited a considerable amount of rocking and crouching behavior, indicative of emo-

tionality. Our first thought was that the critical period for the development of maternally directed affection had passed and that these macaque children were doomed to live as affectional orphans. Fortunately, these behaviors continued for only 12 to 48 hours and then gradually ebbed, changing from indifference to active contact on, and exploration of, the surrogates. The home-cage behavior of these control monkeys slowly became similar to that of the animals raised with the mother surrogates from birth. Their manipulation and play on the cloth mother became progressively more vigorous to the point of actual mutilation, particularly during the morning after the cloth mother had been given her daily change of terry covering. The control subjects were now actively running to the cloth mother when frightened and had to be coaxed from her to be taken from the cage for formal testing.

. . . . .

Consistent with the results on the subjects reared from birth with dual mothers, these late-adopted infants spent less than one and one-half hours per day in contact with the wire mothers, and this activity level was relatively constant throughout the test sessions. Although the maximum time that the control monkeys spent on the cloth mother was only about half that spent by the original dual mother-surrogate group, we cannot be sure that this discrepancy is a function of differential early experience. The control monkeys were about three months older when the mothers were attached to their cages than the experimental animals had been when their mothers were removed and the retention tests begun. Thus, we do not know what the amount of contact would be for a 250-day-old animal raised from birth with surrogate mothers. Nevertheless, the magnitude of the differences and the fact that the contact-time curves for the mothered-from-birth infants had remained constant for almost 150 days suggest that early experience with the mother is a variable of measurable importance.

. . . . .

Before the introduction of the mother surrogate into the home-cage situation, only one of the four control monkeys had ever contacted the cloth mother in the open-field tests. In general, the surrogate mother not only gave the infants no security, but instead appeared to serve as a fear stimulus. The emotionality scores of these control subjects were slightly higher during the mother-present test sessions than during the mother-absent test sessions. These behaviors were changed radically by the fourth post-introduction test approximately 60 days later. In the absence of the cloth mothers the emotionality index in this fourth test remains near the earlier level, but the score is reduced by half when the mother is present, a result strikingly similar to that found for infants raised with the dual mother-surrogates from birth. The control infants now show increasing object exploration and play behavior, and they begin to use the mother as a base of operations, as did the infants raised from birth with the mother surrogates. However, there are still definite differences in the behavior of the two groups. The control infants do not rush directly to the mother and clutch her violently; but instead they go toward, and orient around her, usually after an initial period during which they frequently show disturbed behavior, exploratory behavior, or both.

That the control monkeys develop affection or love for the cloth mother when she is introduced into the cage at 250 days of age cannot be questioned. There is every reason to believe, however, that this interval of delay depresses the intensity of the affectional response below that of the infant monkeys that were surrogate-mothered from birth onward. In interpreting these data it is well to remember that the control monkeys had had continuous opportunity to observe and hear other monkeys housed in adjacent cages and that they had had limited opportunity to view and contact surrogate mothers in the test situations, even though they did not exploit the opportunities.

During the last two years we have observed the behavior of two infants raised by their own mothers. Love for the real mother and love for the surrogate mother appear to be very similar. The baby macaque spends many hours a day clinging to its real mother. If away from the mother when frightened, it rushes to her and in her presence shows comfort and composure. As far as we can observe, the infant monkey's affection for the real mother is strong, but no stronger than that of the experimental monkey for the surrogate cloth mother, and the security that the infant gains from the presence of the real mother is no greater than the security it gains from a cloth surrogate. Next year we hope to put this problem to final, definitive, experimental test. But, whether the mother is real or a cloth surrogate, there does develop a deep and abiding bond between mother and child. In one case it may be the call of the wild and in the other the McCall of civilization, but in both cases there is "togetherness."

In spite of the importance of contact comfort, there is reason to believe that other variables of measurable importance will be discovered. Postural support may be such a variable, and it has been suggested that, when we build arms into the mother surrogate, 10 is the minimal number required to provide adequate child care. Rocking motion may be such a variable, and we are comparing rocking and stationary mother surrogates and inclined planes. The differential responsiveness to cloth mother and cloth-covered inclined plane suggests that clinging as well as contact is an affectional variable of importance. Sounds, particularly natural, maternal sounds, may operate as either unlearned or learned affectional variables. Visual responsiveness may be such a variable, and it is possible that some semblance of visual imprinting may develop in the neonatal monkey. There are indications that this becomes a variable of importance during the course of infancy through some maturational process.

John Bowlby has suggested that there is an affectional variable which he calls "primary object following," characterized by visual and oral search of the mother's face. Our surrogate-mother-raised baby monkeys are at first inattentive to her face, as are human neonates to human mother faces. But by 30 days of age ever-increasing responsiveness to the mother's face appears—whether through learning, maturation, or both—and we have reason to believe that the face becomes an object of special attention.

Our first surrogate-mother-raised baby had a mother whose head was just a ball of wood since the baby was a month early and we had not had time to design a more esthetic head and face. This baby had contact with the blank-faced mother for 180 days and was then placed with two cloth mothers, one motionless and one rocking, both being endowed with painted, ornamented faces. To our surprise the animal would compulsively rotate both faces 180 degrees so that it viewed only a round, smooth face and never the painted, ornamented face. Furthermore, it would do this as long as the patience of the experimenter in reorienting the faces persisted. The monkey showed no sign of fear or anxiety, but it showed unlimited persistence. Subsequently it improved its technique, compulsively removing the heads and rolling them into its cage as fast as they were returned. We are intrigued by this observation, and we plan to examine systematically the role of the mother face in the development of infant-monkey affections. Indeed, these observations suggest the need for a series of ethological-type researches on the two-faced female.

Although we have made no attempts thus far to study the generalization of infant-macaque affection or love, the techniques which we have developed offer promise in this uncharted field. Beyond this, there are few if any technical difficulties in studying the affection of the actual, living mother for the child, and the techniques developed can be utilized and expanded for the analysis and developmental study of father-infant and infant-infant affection.

Since we can measure neonatal and infant affectional responses to mother surrogates, and since we know they are strong and persisting, we are in a position to assess the effects of feeding and contactual schedules; consistency and inconsistency in the mother surrogates; and early, intermediate, and late maternal deprivation. Again, we have here a family of problems of fundamental interest and theoretical importance.

28 | SOCIAL DEPRIVATION IN MONKEYS

HARRY F. HARLOW AND MARGARET K. HARLOW

Just as contradiction often occurs in the process of exploring complex phenomena, so further study into the effects of the "prefabricated mothering" described in the previous selection brought a wealth of qualifications. The Harlows watched their infants mature into adults, and did a "follow-up" study, comparing the social, sexual, and maternal behavior of the adult monkeys who had been reared by monkey mothers with those reared by ever-present mother surrogates. The Harlows' study reveals some surprising long-term pathological consequences of artificial mothering.

In almost all other respects, the behavior of these monkeys at ages ranging from three to five years is indistinguishable from that of monkeys raised in bare wire cages with no source of contact comfort other than a gauze diaper pad. They are without question socially and sexually aberrant. No normal sex behavior has been observed in the living cages of any of the animals that have been housed with a companion of the opposite sex. In exposure to monkeys from the breeding colony not one male and only one female has shown normal mating behavior and only four females have been successfully impregnated. Compared with the cage-raised monkeys, the surrogate-raised animals seem to be less aggressive, whether toward themselves or other monkeys. But they are also younger on the average, and their better dispositions can be attributed to their lesser age.

Thus the nourishment and contact comfort provided by the nursing cloth-covered mother in infancy does not produce a normal adolescent or adult. The surrogate cannot cradle the baby or communicate monkey sounds and gestures. It cannot punish for misbehavior or attempt to break the infant's bodily attachment before it becomes a fixation. The entire group of animals separated from their mothers at birth and raised in individual wire cages, with or without surrogate, must be written off as potential breeding stock. Apparently their early social deprivation permanently impairs their ability to form effective relations

Reprinted from *Scientific American*, November, 1962, by permission.

with other monkeys, whether the opportunity was offered to them in the second six months of life or in the second to the fifth year of life.

One may correctly assume that total social isolation, compared with the partial isolation in which these subjects were reared, would produce even more devastating effects on later personality development. Such disastrous effects have been reported in the rare cases of children who have been liberated after months or years of lonely confinement in a darkened room. We have submitted a few monkeys to total isolation. Our purpose was to establish the maximum of social deprivation that would allow survival and also to determine whether or not there is a critical period in which social deprivation may have irreversible effects.

In our first study a male and a female were housed alone from birth for a period of two years, each one in its own cubicle with solid walls. Their behavior could be observed through one-way vision screens and tested by remote control. The animals adapted to solid food slowly, but they had normal weight and good coats when they were removed from the isolation boxes at the end of two years. Throughout this period neither animal had seen any living being other than itself.

They responded to their liberation by the crouching posture with which monkeys typically react to extreme threat. When placed together, each one crouched and made no further response to the other. Paired with younger monkeys from the group raised in partial isolation, they froze or fled when approached and made no effort to defend themselves from aggressive assaults. After another two years, in which they were kept together in a single large cage in the colony room, they showed the same abnormal fear of the sight or sound of other monkeys.

We are now engaged in studying the effects of six months of total social isolation. The first pair of monkeys, both males, has been out of isolation for eight months. They are housed, each monkey in its own cage, in racks with other monkeys of their age that were raised in the partial isolation of individual wire cages. For 20 minutes a day, five days a week, they are tested with a pair of these monkeys in the "playroom" of the laboratory. This room we designed to stimulate the young monkeys to a maximum of activity. It was not until the 12th and 27th week respectively that the two totally deprived monkeys began to move and climb about. They now circulate freely but not as actively as the control animals. Although frequently attacked by the controls, neither one has attempted to defend itself or fight back; they either accept abuse or flee. One must be characterized as extremely disturbed and almost devoid of social behavior. The other resembles a normal two-month-old rhesus infant in its play and social behavior, and the indications are that it will never be able to make mature contacts with its peers.

A considerably more hopeful prognosis is indicated for two groups of four monkeys raised in total isolation for the much shorter period of 80 days. In their cubicles these animals had the contact comfort of a cloth-covered surrogate. They were deficient in social behavior during the first test periods in the playroom. But they made rapid gains; now, eight months later, we rate them as "almost normal" in play, defense and sex behavior. At least seven of the eight seem to bear no permanent scars as the result of early isolation.

Our first few experiments in the total isolation of these animals would thus appear to have bracketed what may be the critical period of development during which social experience is necessary for normal behavior in later life. We have additional experiments in progress, involving a second pair that will have been isolated for six months and a first pair that will have been isolated for a full year. The indications are that six months of isolation will render the animals permanently inadequate. Since the rhesus monkey is more mature than the human infant at birth and grows four times more rapidly, this is equivalent to two or three years for the human child. On the other hand, there is reason to believe that the effects of shorter periods of early isolation, perhaps 60 to 90 days or even more, are clearly reversible. This would be equivalent to about six months in the development of the human infant. The time probably varies with the individual and with the experiences to which it is exposed once it is removed from isolation. Beyond a brief period of neonatal grace, however, the evidence suggests that every additional week or month of social deprivation increasingly imperils social development in the rhesus monkey. Case studies of children reared in impersonal institutions or in homes with indifferent mothers or nurses show a frightening comparability. The child may remain relatively unharmed through the first six months of life. But from this time on the damage is progressive and cumulative. By one year of age he may sustain enduring emotional scars and by two years many children have reached the point of no return.

In all of these experiments in partial and total isolation, whether unwitting or deliberate, our animals were deprived of the company of their peers as well as of their mothers. We accordingly undertook a series of experiments designed to distinguish and compare the roles of mother-infant and infant-infant relations in the maturation of rhesus monkey behavior. Our most privileged subjects are two groups of four monkeys each, now two years old, that were raised with their mothers during the first 18 and 21 months respectively and with peers from the first weeks. Each mother-infant pair occupied a large cage that gave the infant access to one cell of a four-unit playpen. By removing the screens between the playpens we enabled the infants to play together in pairs or as foursomes during scheduled observation periods each day. In parallel with these two groups we raised another group of four in a playpen setup without their mothers but with a terrycloth surrogate in each home cage.

From the time the mothers let them leave their home cages, after 20 or 30 days, the mothered infants entered into more lively and consistent relations with one another than did the four motherless ones. Their behavior evolved more rapidly through the sequence of increasingly complex play patterns that reflects the maturation and learning of the infant monkey and is observed in a community of normal infants. The older they grew and the more complex the play patterns became, the greater became the observable difference between the mothered and the motherless monkeys. Now, at the end of the second year, the 12 animals are living together in one playpen setup, with each original group occupying one living cage and its adjoining playpen. All are observed in daily interaction without the dividing panels. The early differences between them have all but disappeared. Seven of the eight mothered animals engage in normal sexual activity and assume correct posture. The deviant is a male, and this animal was the social reject in its all-male group of four. Of the two motherless males, one

has recently achieved full adult sexual posture and the other is approaching it. The two motherless females appear normal, but it remains to be seen whether or not their maternal behavior will reflect their lack of mothering.

Observation of infants with their mothers suggests reasons for the differences in the early social and sexual behavior of these playpen groups. From early in life on, the infant monkey shows a strong tendency to imitate its mother; this responding to another monkey's behavior carries over to interaction with its peers. It is apparent also that sexual activity is stimulated by the mother's grooming of the infant. Finally, as the mother begins occasionally to reject its offspring in the third or fourth month, the infant is propelled into closer relations with its peers. These observations underlie the self-evident fact that the mother-infant relation plays a positive role in the normal development of the infant-infant and heterosexual relations of the young monkey.

That the mother-infant relation can also play a disruptive role was demonstrated in another experiment. Four females that had been raised in the partial isolation of individual wire cages—and successfully impregnated in spite of the inadequacy of their sexual behavior— delivered infants within three weeks of one another. This made it possible to set up a playpen group composed of these "motherless" mothers and their infants. The maternal behavior of all four mothers was completely abnormal, ranging from indifference to outright abuse. Whereas it usually requires more than one person to separate an infant from its mother, these mothers paid no attention when their infants were removed from the cages for the hand-feeding necessitated by the mothers' refusal to nurse. Two of the mothers did eventually permit fairly frequent nursing, but their apparently closer maternal relations were accompanied by more violent abuse. The infants were persistent in seeking contact with their mothers and climbed on their backs when they were repulsed at the breast. In play with one another during the first six months, the infants were close to the normally mothered animals in maturity of play, but they played less. In sexual activity, however, they were far more precocious. During the eight months since they have been separated from their mothers, they have exhibited more aggression and day-to-day variability in their behavior than have the members of other playpen groups. The two male offspring of the most abusive mothers have become disinterested in the female and occupy the subordinate position in all activities.

More study of more babies from motherless mothers is needed to determine whether or not the interrelations that characterize this pilot group will characterize others of the same composition. There is no question about the motherless mothers themselves. The aberration of their maternal behavior would have ensured the early demise of their infants outside the laboratory. As for the infants, the extremes of sexuality and aggressiveness observed in their behavior evoke all too vivid parallels in the behavior of disturbed human children and adolescents in psychiatric clinics and institutions for delinquents.

Another pilot experiment has shown that even normal mothering is not enough to produce socially adequate offspring. We isolated two infants in the exclusive company of their mothers to the age of seven months and then brought the mother-infant pairs together in a playpen unit. The female infant took full advantage of the play apparatus provided, but in three months the male was never seen to leave its home cage, and its mother would not permit the female to come within arm's reach. Social interaction of the infants was limited to

an occasional exchange of tentative threats. For the past two months they have been separated from their mothers, housed in individual cages and brought together in the playroom for 15 minutes each day. In this normally stimulating environment they have so far shown no disposition to play together. Next to the infants that have been raised in total isolation, these are the most retarded of the infants tested in the playroom.

It is to the play-exciting stimulus of the playroom that we owe the unexpected outcome of our most suggestive experiment. The room is a relatively spacious one, with an eight-foot ceiling and 40 square feet of floor space. It is equipped with movable and stationary toys and a wealth of climbing devices, including an artificial tree, a ladder and a burlap-covered climbing ramp that leads to a platform. Our purpose in constructing the playroom was to provide the monkeys with opportunities to move about in the three-dimensional world to which, as arboreal animals, they are much more highly adapted than man. To assess the effects of different histories of early social experience we customarily turn the animals loose in the room in groups of four for regularly scheduled periods of observation each day.

The opportunities afforded by the playroom were most fully exploited by two groups of four infants that otherwise spent their days housed alone in their cages with a cloth surrogate. In terms of "mothering," therefore, these monkeys were most closely comparable to the four that were raised with surrogates in the playpen situation. These animals were released in the playroom for 20 minutes a day from the first month of life through the 11th, in the case of one group, and through the second year in the case of the other. In contrast with all the other groups observed in the playroom, therefore, they did their "growing up" in this environment. Even though their exposure to the room and to one another was limited to 20 minutes a day, they enacted with great spirit the entire growth pattern of rhesus-monkey play behavior.

They began by exploring the room and each other. Gradually over the next two or three months they developed a game of rough-and-tumble play, with jumping, scuffling, wrestling, hair-pulling and a little nipping, but with no real damage, and then an associated game of flight and pursuit in which the participants are alternately the threateners and the threatened. While these group activities evolved, so did the capacity for individual play exploits, with the animals running, leaping, swinging and climbing, heedless of one another and apparently caught up in the sheer joy of action. As their skill and strength grew, their social play involved shorter but brisker episodes of free-for-all action, with longer chases between bouts. Subsequently they developed an even more complex pattern of violent activity, performed with blinding speed and integrating all objects, animate and inanimate, in the room. Along with social play, and possibly as a result or by-product, they began to exhibit sexual posturing—immature and fleeting in the first six months and more frequent and adult in form by the end of the year. The differences in play activity that distinguish males and females became evident in the first two or three months, with the females threatening and initiating rough contact far less frequently than the males and withdrawing from threats and approaches far more frequently.

Thus in spite of the relatively limited opportunity for contact afforded by their daily schedule, all the individuals in these two groups developed effective infant-infant play relations. Those observed into the second year have shown the full repertory of adult sexual behavior. At the same chronological age these motherless monkeys have attained as full a maturity in these respects as the infants raised with their mothers in the playpen.

Another group of four motherless animals raised together in a single large cage from the age of two weeks is yielding similar evidence of the effectiveness of the infant-infant affectional bond. During their first two months these animals spent much of their time clinging together, each animal clutching the back of the one just ahead of it in "choo-choo" fashion. They moved about as a group of three or four; when one of them broke away, it was soon clutched by another to form the nucleus of a new line. In the playroom the choo-choo linkage gave way to individual exploratory expeditions. During periods of observation, whether in their home cage or in the playroom, these animals have consistently scored lower in play activity than the most playful groups. We think this is explained, however, by the fact that they are able to spread their play over a 24-hour period. At the age of one year they live amicably together. In sex behavior they are more mature than the mother-raised playpen babies. No member of the group shows any sign of damage by mother-deprivation.

Our observations of the three groups of motherless infants raised in close association with one another therefore indicate that opportunity for optimal infant-infant interaction may compensate for lack of mothering. This is true at least in so far as infant-infant and sexual relations are concerned. Whether or not maternal behavior or later social adjustment will be affected remains to be seen.

29 | RESULTS OF SELF-SELECTION OF DIETS BY YOUNG CHILDREN

CLARA M. DAVIS

The late Dr. Davis experimentally concluded that, given a variety of natural foods from which to choose, infants can properly select their own healthy diets. Unfortunately, her classic study has often been misquoted, and unwarranted implications have been drawn from it; many "experts" have concluded that children possess a natural wisdom in their appetites and that they therefore should be permitted to eat whatever and whenever they please. But in the experiment described here care was taken to omit processed foods—such as refined sugar, candy, jams, cookies, macaroni, and soft drinks—and food was offered only three times a day, at definite mealtimes.

A similar study observing older children whose appetites had been "perverted" and who were allowed to roam freely in an environment filled with popsicles, soft drinks, etc., as well as natural foods, might be an important sequel to the observations presented here.

The self-selection of diet experiment had for its subjects infants of weaning age, who had never had supplements of the ordinary foods of adult life. This age was chosen because only at this age could we have individuals who had neither had experience of such foods nor could have been influenced by the ideas of older persons and so would be without preconceived prejudices and biases with regard to them. The children concerned were studied for six years.

The list of foods used in the experiment was made up with the following considerations in mind. It should comprise a wide range of foods of both animal and vegetable origin that would adequately provide all the food elements, amino-acids, fats, carbohydrates, vitamins and minerals known to be necessary for human nutrition. The foods should be such as could generally be procured fresh in the market the year around. The list should contain only natural food materials and no incomplete foods or canned foods. Thus, cereals were whole grains; sugars were not used nor were milk products, such as cream, butter or cheese.

The preparation of the foods was as simple as possible. All meats, vegetables and fruits were finely cut, mashed or ground. Most of the foods were served only after being cooked, but lettuce was served only raw, while oat meal, wheat, beef, bone marrow, eggs, carrots, peas, cabbage and apples were served both raw and cooked. Lamb, chicken and glandular organs, all of local origin and not Federal inspected, were cooked as a measure of safety. Cooking was done without the loss of soluble substances and without the addition of salt or seasonings. Water was not added except in the case of cereals. Combinations of food materials such as custards, soups or bread were not used, thus insuring that each food when eaten was chosen for itself alone.

Reprinted from *Canadian Medical Association Journal*, XLI (1939), 257–61, by permission of the author and publisher.

The list of foods was as follows:

1. Water	18. Potatoes
2. Sweet milk	19. Lettuce
3. Sour (lactic) milk	20. Oatmeal
4. Sea salt (Seisal)	21. Wheat
5. Apples	22. Corn meal
6. Bananas	23. Barley
7. Orange juice	24. Ry-Krisp
8. Fresh pineapple	25. Beef
9. Peaches	26. Lamb
10. Tomatoes	27. Bone marrow
11. Beets	28. Bone jelly
12. Carrots	29. Chicken
13. Peas	30. Sweetbreads
14. Turnips	31. Brains
15. Cauliflower	32. Liver
16. Cabbage	33. Kidneys
17. Spinach	34. Fish (haddock)

The entire list could not, of course, be gotten ready and served at one time and was therefore divided and served at three (in the early weeks, four) meals a day, this arrangement providing a wide variety at each meal. Both sweet and sour (lactic) milk, two kinds of cereals, animal protein foods, and either fruits or vegetables were served at each meal according to a fixed schedule. Each article, even salt, was served in a separate dish, salt not being added to any, nor was milk poured over the cereal. All portions were weighed or measured before serving and the remains weighed or measured on the return of the tray to the diet kitchen.

Food was not offered to the infant either directly or by suggestion. The nurses' orders were to sit quietly by, spoon in hand, and make no motion. When, and only when, the infant reached for or pointed to a dish might she take up a spoonful and, if he opened his mouth for it, put it in. She might not comment on what he took or did not take, point to or in any way attract his attention to any food, or refuse him any for which he reached. He might eat with his fingers or in any way

he could without comment on or correction of his manners. The tray was to be taken away when he had definitely stopped eating, which was usually after from twenty to twenty-five minutes.

The results of this six-year study of self-selection of diet by young children from the time of weaning on may, for the purpose of this discussion, be conveniently grouped under three heads: (1) The results in terms of health and nutrition of the fifteen children; (2) the adequacy of the self-chosen diets as judged by nutritional laws and standards; (3) the contributions made by the study to our understanding of appetite and how it functions.

Like the lives of the happy, the annals of the healthy and vigorous make little exciting news. There were no failures of infants to manage their own diets; all had hearty appetites; all throve. Constipation was unknown among them and laxatives were never used or needed. Except in presence of parenteral infection, there was no vomiting or diarrhoea. Colds were usually of the mild three-day type without complications of any kind. There were a few cases of tonsillitis but no serious illness among the children in the six years. Curiously enough, the only epidemic to visit the nursery was acute glandular fever of Pfeiffer with which all the children in the nursery came down like ninepins on the same day. During this epidemic when temperatures of 103 to 105° F. prevailed, as with colds, etc., trays were served as usual, the children continuing to select their own food from the regular list. This led to the interesting observation that just as loss of appetite often precedes by twenty-four to forty-eight hours every other discoverable sign and symptom of acute infection, so return of appetite precedes by twelve to twenty-four hours all other signs of convalescence, occurring when fever is still

high and enabling the observer to correctly predict its fall. This eating of a
hearty meal when fever is still high is
often not in evidence when children are
put on restricted diets during such illness, but the correctness of the observation has been amply confirmed in the
Children's Memorial Hospital where a
modification of the self-selective method
of feeding prevails. During convalescence unusually large amounts of raw
beef, carrots and beets were eaten. The
demand for increased amounts of raw
beef and carrots can be easily accounted
for but we are still curious about that for
beets, and inclined to wonder whether
they may furnish an anti-anaemic substance (iron?) from the fact that beets
were eaten by all in much larger
quantities in the first six months or year
after weaning than ever again save after
colds and acute glandular fever.

Some of the infants were in rather
poor condition when taken for the experiment. Four were poorly nourished
and underweight; five had rickets. Two
of these five had only roentgenological
signs of rickets, and one mild clinical
rickets as well, while the other two were
typical text-book cases. The first infant
received for the study was one of the
two with severe rickets, and, bound by
a promise to do nothing or leave nothing undone to his detriment, we put a
small glass of cod liver oil on his tray
for him to take if he chose. This he did
irregularly and in varying amounts until
his blood calcium and phosphorus became normal and x-ray films showed his
rickets to be healed, after which he did
not take it again. He had taken just over
two ounces in all. No other of the 15
children had any cod liver oil, viosterol,
treatment by ultra-violet rays or other
dietary adjuvants at any time during the
study, and all four of the other cases of
rickets were healed in approximately the
same length of time as was the first. Regardless, however, of their condition

when received, within a reasonable
time the nutrition of all, checked as it
was at regular and frequent intervals by
physical examinations, urine analyses,
blood counts, haemoglobin estimations
and roentgenograms of bones, came up
to the standard of optimal so far as
could be discovered by examinations.

However, as I may be thought to have
been unduly biased in my estimate of
this rollicking, rosy-cheeked group, Dr.
Joseph Brennemann's appraisal of them
may be of interest. In his article, "Psychologic aspects of nutrition," published in
an early number of the *Journal of
Pediatrics*, he says, "I saw them on a
number of occasions and they were the
finest group of specimens from the
physical and behavior standpoint that I
have ever seen in children of that age."

. . . . .

QUANTITIES OF FOOD EATEN

The average daily calories furnished by
the diets during each six months' period
were in every instance found to be
within the limits set by scientific nutritional standards for the individual's age.
So, too, were the average daily calories
per kilogram of body weight, except in
the few instances in which infants, un-
dernourished before weaning, exceeded
the standard in their first six months'
period on the experiment. Finally, the
law of the decline of calories, per kilogram of body weight, with growth was
followed without exception and in orderly fashion as shown by curves made
on a monthly basis. Quite possibly it is
the close conformity of the diets to these
quantitative laws and standards that accounts for the fact that there were after
the first six months' period of each child
no noticeably fat or thin children, but a
greater uniformity of build than often
obtains among those of the same
family.

. . . . .

THE DISTRIBUTION OF CALORIES

As yet no statistical analysis of the diets has been made for their vitamin and mineral contents, but with all vegetables fresh, all cereals whole grains, ground by the old stone process, eggs, liver and kidney eaten freely, fresh fruits eaten in amazingly large quantities, and the salt used, an unpurified sea salt containing all the minerals found in the body, the probability of any deficiency in vitamins or minerals is slight indeed. In fact, the quantities of fresh fruit, carrots and potatoes and of eggs, liver and kidneys in practically all the diets preclude, on the basis of their known vitamin content, any shortage of Vitamins A, B, C and G. For the adequacy in vitamin D and calcium of the diets of children who took none or little milk for considerable periods of time we cannot speak so surely from an off-hand consideration of the quantities of foods eaten. We can, however, call in evidence the roentgenograms of these children's bones which showed as excellent calcification as those of the others.

Regarding the calcification of bones in the group, Dr. W. E. Anspach, Roentgenologist of the Children's Memorial Hospital, has written in a personal communication to your essayist, "The beautifully calcified bones in roentgenograms of your group of children stand out so well that I have no trouble in picking them out when seen at a distance." That such "beautiful calcification" of bones was achieved by all, regardless of whether or not they had rickets when admitted, would seem difficult to account for, had adequate calcium or vitamin D been lacking.

The diets, then, were orthodox, conforming to nutritional laws and standards in what they furnished. The children actually were as well nourished as they looked to be.

Such successful juggling and balancing of the more than thirty nutritional essentials that exist in mixed and different proportions in the foods from which they must be derived suggests at once the existence of some innate, automatic mechanism for its accomplishment, of which appetite is a part. It is certainly difficult to account for the success of the fifteen unrelated infants on any other grounds.

Also, such success with the nutritional essentials suggests the possibility that appetite indicated one orthodox diet in terms of foods and the quantities of them, comparable to the diet lists of paediatricians and nutritionists. But to this possibility the self-chosen diets give not a scintilla of support. In terms of foods and relative quantities of them they failed to show any orthodoxy of their own and were wholly unorthodox with respect to paediatric practice. For every diet differed from every other diet, fifteen different patterns of taste being presented, and not one diet was the predominantly cereal and milk diet with smaller supplements of fruit, eggs and meat, that is commonly thought proper for this age. To add to the apparent confusion, tastes changed unpredictably from time to time, refusing as we say "to stay put," while meals were often combinations of foods that were strange indeed to us, and would have been a dietitian's nightmare—for example, a breakfast of a pint of orange juice and liver; a supper of several eggs, bananas and milk. They achieved the goal, but by widely various means, as Heaven may presumably be reached by different roads.

This seemingly irresponsible and erratic behavior of appetite with respect to selection of foods from which the essentials were obtained stamps it as the same Puckish fellow we have always known it to be. Why, then, were his pranks beneficent in the experiment when so often harmful elsewhere? Or to put it baldly, as I hope many of you are doing, what was the trick in the experiment? This brings us to the discussion of what we learned about appetite and its workings, that throws light on the question of its competencies and fallibilities.

Selective appetite is, primarily, the desire for foods that please by smelling or tasting good, and it would seem that in the absence of such sensory information, i.e., if one had never smelled or tasted a food, he could not know whether he liked or disliked it. Such proved to be the case with these infants. When the large tray of foods, each in its separate dish, was placed before them at their first meals, there was not the faintest sign of "instinct" directed choice. On the contrary, their choices were apparently wholly random; they tried not only foods but chewed hopefully the clean spoon, dishes, the edge of the tray, or a piece of paper on it. Their faces showed expressions of surprise, followed by pleasure, indifference or dislike. All the articles on the list, except lettuce by two and spinach by one, were tried by all, and most tried several times, but within the first few days they began to reach eagerly for some and to neglect others, so that definite tastes grew under our eyes. Never again did any child eat so many of the foods as in the first weeks of his experimental period. Patterns of selective appetite, then, were shown to develop on the basis of sensory experience, i.e., taste, smell, and doubtless the feeling of comfort and well-being that followed eating, which was evidenced much as in the breast-fed infant. In short, they were developed by sampling, which is essentially a trial and error method. And it is this trial and error method, this willingness to sample, that accounts for the most glaring fallibility of appetite. From time immemorial adults as well as children have eaten castor oil beans, poisonous fish, toad stools and

nightshade berries with fatal results. Against such error, only the transmission of racial experience as knowledge can protect. Such error affords additional proof that in omnivorous eaters there is no "instinct" pointing blindly to the "good" or "bad" in food. And since every trial and error method involves the possibility of error, the problem of successful eating by appetite is that of reducing possible errors to those that are most trivial by a prior selection of the foods that are made available for eating.

Appetite also appears to have fallibilities with processed foods which have lost some of their natural constituents and which have become such important features of modern diet, e.g., sugar and white flour. Certainly their introduction into previously sound primitive diets has invariably brought with it a train of nutritional evils, and their wide-spread excess in civilized diets is decried by nutritional authorities. Whether the evils are due to innate fallibilites of appetite with respect to these products, or whether appetite in such cases is merely overruled by extraneous considerations of novelty, cheapness, ease of procurement and preparation, etc., has not been determined.

We had hoped to investigate this problem in a small way by an experiment with newly weaned infants in which both natural foods and their processed products were simultaneously served, but the depression dashed this hope.

By this time you have all doubtless perceived that the "trick" in the experiment (if "trick" you wish to call it) was in the food list. Confined to natural, unprocessed and unpurified foods as it was, and without made dishes of any sort, it reproduced to a large extent the conditions under which primitive peoples in many parts of the world have been shown to have had scientifically sound diets and excellent nutrition.

Errors the children's appetites must have made—they are inherent in any trial and error method—but the errors with such a food list were too trivial and too easily compensated for to be of importance or even to be detected.

The results of the experiment, then, leave the selection of the foods to be made available to young children in the hands of their elders where everyone has always known it belongs. Even the food list is not a magic one. Any of you with a copy of McCollum's or H. C. Sherman's books on nutrition and properties of foods, could make a list quite different and equally as good. Self-selection can have no, or but doubtful, value if the diet must be selected from inferior foods. Finally, by providing conditions under which appetite could function freely and beneficently as in animals and primitive peoples, the experiment resolved the modern conflict between appetite and nutritional requirements. It eliminated anorexia and the eating problems that are the plague of feeding by the dosage method.

PART THREE
CHILDHOOD
THE CHILD VIEWS HIS WORLD

The well-known fable of the four blind men and the elephant illustrates one important psychological principle—the individual's view of his world often depends upon his particular position in it. The world seen by adults, for example, is vastly different from that seen by the child. How do children see their mothers and sisters; their schools, teachers, paints, and pencils; and their friends on the street? The meaning of a child's interactions with his world depends, of course, upon his perceptions of this world.

The articles reprinted in this part demonstrate some aspects of the child's world gained through inference from and careful analysis of children's behavior. Piaget's ideas on children's thought and logic are reviewed, as are Bruner's observations on cognitive growth. The selections from *Patterns of Child Rearing* offer conclusions based on both children's and mothers' behavior. Wolfenstein and Buhler interpret the child's view from his jokes and drawings, while Child's article analyzes children's textbooks; responding to his conclusions, some readers may want to run out and quickly rewrite the books. The last three studies in this part discuss the interaction of the child with his group and teacher, showing how changes in either may effect definite changes in how the child feels about his world and how he behaves.

30 | HOW TO STUDY CHILDREN

HORACE B. ENGLISH

The best way to understand how a child views his world is to talk to one and to observe and study him. Some students will make a case study for laboratory experience in their psychology course. Professor English in this selection answers the questions: How do you find a child to study? How do you observe him? How do you write up the report?

"FIRST CATCH YOUR HARE"

Few of you are so unfortunate, one hopes, as to study child psychology in a region where there are no children. There is, therefore, much to be said for the idea that "the way to begin is to be-

gin"—just pick a child and start in studying him. Experience shows, however, that there are a few principles which should be brought to your attention, not as rigid prescriptions but as suggestive guide lines.

First of all, the child selected should usually *not* be a "problem child." Of course, every child presents a problem to the teacher who has any imagination.

Reprinted from *Child Psychology*, pp. 15–31, by permission of Henry Holt and Company, Inc. Copyright 1951.

But the term *problem child* has become something of a technical term for a badly adjusted child in need of specialized psychological treatment. You will occasionally have such a child in your class and may—unfortunately—have to deal with him or her without the professional psychological help that is really called for. Your first need, however, is to learn to deal with "normal" children. Most of your problems—and your most important ones—will be *normal* problems. It would be one of the worst possible results of a study of child psychology to get in the habit of trying to find something "abnormal" in every puzzling behavior, or of seeing a "problem child" beneath every curly head.

There is another and eminently practical reason, moreover, why it is wise to select a typical child. When we are asked why this child is being picked for study, we must be able to say with complete honesty that he is chosen because he is just an ordinary, everyday specimen.

MAKING CONTACT WITH THE SCHOOL | In most cases you should begin by a preliminary visit to the school. It is true, as we have insisted, that the child's school behavior cannot be fully understood in terms of only what happens in the classroom, but it is equally true that much that happens at home is unintelligible without an understanding of what is happening to the child in school. Since, moreover, most of you are planning to be teachers, it is perfectly proper that you *start* with the problem as it presents itself in the classroom; we merely insist that you should not stop there.

There is a very practical reason, also, for starting with the school. We obviously need the cooperation of parents, and the investigation of Johnny will seem less mysterious if presented as a school project rather than as a "case study."[1] Very often the principal can obtain the good will and cooperation of enough parents to supply an entire psychology class with subjects.

As a rule, then, your instructor will have broached the matter to the principal for you. Nonetheless, your first step is to present yourself to the principal and obtain his explicit permission to begin observation in his school. You must remember that the principal is legally and morally responsible for the conduct of school matters; it is only fair that he be kept fully informed of what is going on. Your call at his office, even if you should get no instructions and no information, is an elementary professional courtesy.

Because, however, she stands so much closer to the child, the cooperation of the classroom teacher is even more vital. One of the student's first obligations is thus to insure that the teacher understands the purposes of the investigation and is prepared to forward it. Many teachers, especially older ones, tend to feel a little on the defensive when their classes are being visited by students who are full of enthusiasm for new ways. It has been my experience that it helps to emphasize that your purpose is not so much to observe the class routine as it is to observe the individual child, that you are not at all interested for the time being in methods of teaching but only in the behavior of the child. Nor does it do

---

[1] As a matter of fact, you would probably do well not to get in the habit of talking about your "case study." Educated parents may look for too much, uneducated ones are likely to be made to feel rather uncomfortable; too many of them have had experience with relief case workers.

For similar reasons it is better not to make much mention of psychology. People are apt to expect miracles of anything called psychology but also to be unduly skeptical of more mundane findings. "Child study" is a fairly accurate statement of our purposes and is less likely to be misunderstood.

any harm to show that you realize you are making extra work for the teacher and shall be very grateful for any help extended.

MAKING INITIAL CONTACTS WITH THE HOME | If there is a sound tradition of friendly parent-teacher relations in the community, there should be no difficulty about an occasional visit to the child's home. The exact approach to the parents will have to depend on how one is introduced by the school. In general, it is to be hoped that the observer will have the way prepared for him by the principal of the school. Here various means have been tried. Sometimes the parents have been asked to come to the school to talk the whole program over with the representatives of the college. Sometimes the principal has written the parents a letter which is sent home with the child, asking their cooperation. A few principals have been generous enough to talk individually with each parent. Sometimes the student has merely been furnished the name of the parents and must introduce himself and make his own arrangements.

Should you make an appointment or should you go unannounced to your first interview? Middle-class housewives —and most of your subjects will come from middle-class homes—are likely to be embarrassed if a "visitor" comes unannounced. They prefer to go to a lot of wholly unnecessary trouble to have things "looking nice." You, of course, would much prefer to see a normal everyday situation, but the choice is not yours. Moreover, the mother will talk more freely when she is confident of the appearance of the house and of herself; for your first visit that is more important than seeing the usual routine of the home. If, then, the family has a telephone, it is generally best to try to make an appointment. If you can wangle an

invitation in general terms ("Any afternoon this week except Thursday"), so much the better. If there is no telephone in the home, have the child carry a message, written or oral. The lack of a telephone, however, is often an index of a lack of middle-class concern with appearances, so an unannounced visit may be risked.

In all cases you must remember that you occupy a rather delicate position. In the first place you are inevitably a representative both of the college and of the school. You have thus an opportunity to learn how to conduct yourself in a professional and tactful manner. In seeking your first appointment, for example, you should put yourself at the parents' disposal rather than seek your own convenience. We know, of course, that students, no less than the parents, have other appointments to meet. But in arranging for a mutually convenient meeting, you can manage to convey the impression that the parents' convenience has first consideration—as, indeed, it should have.

If the general plan has been outlined to the parent by the school, you should not elaborate much upon the statements already made. You can say quite simply that you are taking a course in child study in preparation for teaching, that the college considers a better understanding of children of great importance for effective teaching and has sought an opportunity for each prospective teacher to become thoroughly familiar with a typical, normal child. This child has been selected, not because he is a problem in school but simply because he represents the kind of child you will have to deal with when you become a teacher.

At this point it is generally well to allow the parent to ask questions. These questions should be answered frankly and directly. If the parents do not ask any questions, you might continue somewhat as follows; "Naturally it is impossible to understand a child without knowing how he has developed, so I should like to have you tell me something about his earlier years. And one thing that we certainly need to understand, better than teachers usually do, is how the child acts with his brothers and sisters around home." You would like permission, therefore, to come home from school with the child some day and notice how he acts there. You will try not to be too obvious, but if the child asks what you are doing, the mother may simply tell him that you are a student who is trying to get better acquainted with children in order to become a better teacher.

You should admit smilingly that neither the school nor the parent is likely to be very greatly enlightened by your study of the child. You will, of course, be quite glad to discuss with the mother anything that you find, but you are, after all, just a beginner in this field, and the purpose of this study is mainly your own improvement. You hardly expect to discover anything that the mother does not already know. As some slight return, however, for any bother you occasion, you will be happy to act as a "sitter" some evening while the parents are away.[2] And you may also indicate that if the parents are willing, you would like to take the child with you to a concert or motion picture or some such treat to see how he reacts there.

You should not volunteer any estimate of how much of the parent's time you will take, but if you are asked you should say: "Why, of course, I shall take only such time as you find it possible to give me. However, there seems to be no need, unless something unusual should develop, to take up more than an hour,

or perhaps two hours at the most. I should like to be around the home somewhat longer just playing or talking with Suzanne, but I should certainly not expect to take up very much of your time in any direct way."

Be careful at this time to ask no questions about the parents themselves; the first approach should concern the child. When you are on a more familiar footing it may (or may not) be possible to ask a few questions about the family situation.

Just because some of the above directions take the form of direct quotation, you are not to make a prepared talk along these lines! There could be no greater mistake than to memorize these words and deliver them as a mechanical speech.

On the contrary it is desirable to get the *parent* to talk freely to you. It does no harm to let the conversation range very widely—even to "cabbages and kings." You will be at once learning something about the child's home and parents and cultivating an easy relationship. And, be assured, the conversation will presently come back to the child or can be very gently steered back.[3]

Only one thing is essential: a simple, friendly, unassuming approach. Most parents will be cooperative and quite understanding of your mission. A few will be suspicious and doubtful at the start, but they will readily accept you if you are friendly and tactful. Only a very small number will prove so uncooperative that it is advisable to start over with another family.

CONTACT WITH THE CHILD | The approach to the child can be made with the utmost simplicity. Children, of course, are very curious, but their curiosity as a rule is easily satisfied. In general, the best thing is just to make a plain statement:

---

[2] Need it be pointed out that this is a chance not merely to repay the parents but to further your study of the child!

[3] In the exceptional case where this is not true, it is likely to be symptomatic of the relationship between parent and child.

"I am studying to become a teacher (or to make myself a better teacher), and so I want to know children better. You see, if I am to be a good teacher I have to know what children are like." This simple statement seldom fails to satisfy the child, and it has the merit of being direct—and, strangely enough, true. If, however, the child has any further questions, these can be answered frankly and with similar simplicity. If the child asks, "Why pick on me?" answer that the teacher suggested that he was a perfectly "regular" sort of a child to become acquainted with. If the child wants to know what you are going to do, say that you will come around and play with him sometimes, get acquainted with his father and mother, find out about his health when he was a little boy and things like that. Suggest that perhaps you and he will go to a movie sometime or that you may take him to a concert or a museum (or something that will seem attractive). Do not offer to help him with his schoolwork; if he asks whether you will, say that you might look over some of his schoolwork sometime to see how he is getting on. This aspect, however, should not be emphasized. You will be surprised to find how readily children accept this whole proceeding, especially where several in the same room have what they are likely to call "My college girl."

To emphasize the necessity for sympathy and understanding of the child's feelings, we adapt from Teagarden eleven rules for the guidance of case workers which you will do well to ponder and observe. Lest you be worried about having to memorize them, Teagarden, and I, hasten to add that they are only a code of good sense.

1. Remember that the child may be uncomfortable. Make the situation as easy for him as possible. Unless you are so old that it makes you feel uncomfortable to do so, you should have the child call you by your first name. You are not at this time, you see, to act the teacher.

2. Be kindly but objective—not effusive.

3. Don't talk too much. Get the child to talk.

4. Don't "talk down" to the child.

5. Don't ask questions until rapport has been established.

6. Don't try to get too much the first time.

7. Don't follow any outline or interviewing device woodenly.

8. Don't take notes obviously.

9. Don't show shock at anything the child tells you. (If he "tries you out" with obscenity, let him see you know what he is up to and are unimpressed.)

10. Don't try to handle problems that require expert handling in a particular field.

11. Don't betray confidences. You should repeat what you hear only where by doing so you may actually be giving help or protection. The child should never be allowed to feel imposed on.[4]

Naturally the approach to both parents and child will differ somewhat in the case of teachers actually in service, especially if they are dealing with a child in their own class. In other cases, also, it will be necessary to adapt your procedures to suit individual circumstances.

PLANNING OBSERVATION

LIMITING THE FIELD | There is practically no limit to the number of things which can be observed about any child of any age. A detailed and exhaustive study of a child's family relationships alone would take many weeks to complete. And even then it would be necessary to check every conclusion against further observations in order to insure that the study was based on permanent attitudes rather than chance occurrences. For a brief study such as you are about to make, it is especially necessary to discover as soon as possible what are likely to be the

4 Modified from Florence M. Teagarden, *Child psychology for professional workers*, rev. ed. Copyrighted, New York: Prentice-Hall, 1946.

most important factors in the life of the child under observation.

It is impossible, however, to set up a rigid list of the "most important factors." What is most significant for one child may have very little significance for another. Thus, health is undoubtedly important; but health may play a very small part in the school adjustment of the child who has average health and vitality, whereas it may be the outstanding fact in the adjustment of another. Almost anything may be the most important factor in the child you are studying. We can, however, make certain rather general suggestions.

One of the most important areas to explore is the child's relationships with other people, especially members of the immediate family. Unfortunately, you will not have much opportunity to observe such relationships because of the limits of your study and prohibitory social conventions. A child's relations with his teacher are much more accessible and open to observation; and, so, in general, are the influences of schoolmates and neighborhood friends. In some cases a certain child may identify himself with a person not in the immediate family; his relations with that person are of prime importance.

Anything that makes the child a little different is always interesting and important: differences in physical size or appearance, in racial stock, in culture, in interests, in religion. You should be particularly alert to discover anything in the child's behavior that is unusual or that is personally characteristic.

Your preliminary observations, then, and your early interviews will provide you with certain "information" and, unless you are different from most persons, with certain rather vague impressions. These should be neither accepted nor rejected at this time. Instead, they should be "put on ice."

FIRST-IMPRESSIONS RECORD | For this purpose, it may be well to follow a suggestion I owe to Dr. Fritz Redl and write out a fairly detailed thumbnail sketch of the child very early in your relation with him—say after your second observation. Tell what you saw and heard, what seemed likely to you to be his chief characteristics, his chief problems, his probable background, and—here you must be honest!—how you felt toward the child. If he seems unattractive, don't be afraid that you are telling on yourself if you say so. While you should not lose contact with reality and write a merely imaginary sketch, you are encouraged *for just this once* to give way to your "hunches." This *first-impressions* record should be put aside and *not referred to again* until after the case history is finally written.

Then—and then only—bring out your *first-impressions* record and compare it with the conclusions of your study. This should be done in writing, and both the original note and the comparison included in the appendix to your study.

A word of warning. If, for just this once, you are encouraged to "let yourself go" in these initial "hunches," you are not thereby encouraged to take them seriously. Or perhaps I should urge that you be seriously skeptical of them. Too frequently we see only those things in another person's behavior that are in accord with our initial impressions. This is especially true when we have written down impressions, for then anything that contradicts the impressions means that "we were wrong." It may amuse as well as interest you to observe how readily you spring to your own defense, but you won't catch yourself unless you are constantly on the alert to do so. My purpose in having you commit your first impressions to writing is to have you become sufficiently aware of them that you will also beware! Don't let them blind you. Moreover, the accuracy or inaccuracy of your first impressions, as shown by the comparison in your appendix, is no indication of the excellence of your case study. The first impressions of even experienced personnel workers, psychiatrists, and psychologists are open to error. On the other hand, some few things turn out to be correct, maybe more than a few. Only a complete study can tell which judgments are which. Use the first-impressions record, then, as merely an informal experiment. Do not worry if your final comparisons shows that you are either right or wrong in some or all of your first notions.

If however, your final conclusions are to be sound, your tentative conclusions must be checked and rechecked *continuously*. We speak of "final" conclusions only because all human enterprises must have an end sometime. Otherwise, quite clearly what is called your "final" conclusion is only the last in a series of tentative conclusions. In the next section is outlined a method of checking these conclusions which is much less formidable than its title indicates.

GETTING PRELIMINARY HYPOTHESES | The great physicist Michael Faraday was once asked to observe an experiment. "Before we begin," he responded, "just what am I expected to see?" He knew better than to believe himself capable of detecting, offhand and without guidance, the essential features of a complicated machine.

Now you are about to begin observing the most complicated "machine" on earth. You, too, need the guidance of certain preliminary hypotheses. Faraday, please note, hoped to get his preliminary hypothesis from someone who already understood something of the problem. And we believe that you, too, are likely to make progress more quickly in the early stages if you turn to the persons who know the child. Accordingly, after a brief visit to the class merely to acquaint yourself with the object of your investigation, you should talk with parent or teacher.

Certain precautions, however, are very important if you are to get off on the right foot. We have already noted that you will gain friendly rapport with an "interviewee" in proportion as you succeed in getting him or her to talk freely. Such free conversation also serves your purpose of learning what seem to be the child's outstanding characteristics and qualities. You should not, therefore, attempt to dominate the interview. Instead, cultivate the art of listening. If it is possible, avoid direct questioning and elicit the interviewee's spontaneous remarks. To keep him going and to show your interest, it is occasionally wise to say something which indicates your understanding, putting the matter in question form: "Do you mean that Harold seemed very happy when his sister was born?" Or you may somewhat direct the trend by such a question as: "He got over the measles rather easily?" Usually it will not be long before the interviewee has revealed his or her own major understandings of the child.

Now these understandings must be taken very tentatively. Suppose you are having your first interview with the child's teacher, who tells you that Robert seems to be neither a leader nor a follower but cooperates with his playmates and sometimes leads, other times follows. This statement, *carefully dated and duly ascribed to its author*, may be entered in your notes as a tentative hypothesis. Very tentative, in fact, for your next interview may be with a former teacher who was very enthusiastic about Robert and tells you that in her class Robert was always a leader. Here you have a problem, with several possible solutions.

It may be that the present teacher has been inaccurate in her observations and that Robert leads in most of his activities. Or, it is possible that the former teacher was incorrect and believed as she did mainly because she liked him so much. And it is quite possible that Robert may have been very much of a leader while in the former teacher's room, but at present is just as his present teacher describes him, cooperative but leading only when he is especially proficient in the activity. Before accepting one of these three interpretations as a conclusion, all three should be kept written down in your notes as something to be checked against further observations.

Your next observation may be of Robert on the playground. It is tempting to plan to spend your time in confirming or rejecting the tentative hypothesis that you may have set up with respect to Robert's leadership. Since, however, this is your first direct observation of Robert on the playground you should not spend all your time in this way. In the first place, perhaps we hear a little too much about leadership in child study; it is an important characteristic but not the only one. In any case, the question of leadership cannot be solved unless it is seen in relationship to other variable factors, for example, health. Thus, if you were thinking only of how much Robert leads, it would be quite possible that you would fail to note that he hangs back and does not initiate activities because he is out of breath or suddenly very tired; these are the characteristics of a child somewhat lacking in health or physical vigor. So for your early observation, even though eager to check on the leadership hypothesis, you must work more toward a certain broad understanding, a bird's-eye overview.

In other words, at this stage, your observations should be directed *by the behavior you are witnessing* rather than

by any preconceived questions you have formulated. Note *what* the child has been doing, *with whom* he is doing it, and *how* in general he seems to conduct himself. Note also the reactions of other children or adults to him and how he reacts to them.

In both these preliminary approaches —that is, in the first interview and in the first direct observations—make sure that you are seeing and hearing correctly what the other person or the child is saying and doing. The observation needs to be very concrete, very objective and factual, very precise. Any appraisal or judgment not only may be, but should be, rather vague and indefinite. Yet out of all this there should emerge certain *tentative* hypotheses.

KEEPING AN OPEN MIND | At this point there is grave danger of taking these hypotheses too seriously. First, even when they are correct, they may be stated in too general a form. In Robert's case, for example, your information is derived from the school situation—that is, from the teachers' reports and from what you saw on the school playground. This may justify some statement about leadership, but it certainly does not justify a broad generality. It is not at all unusual to find a child a leader at school and a follower at home. Your tentative hypothesis should therefore not concern "leadership" but "leadership at school."

And secondly, there is the question of the correctness of the hypothesis. The behavior may not have been correctly observed or interpreted, or the behavior may not be typical. For these reasons, you will do better to frame your hypotheses in the form of *questions* instead of statements or conclusions. All of us are too prone to take direct statements as conclusions and read them into all our further observations, whereas the questions serve to remind us that the issue is still open.

USING HYPOTHESES TO DIRECT OBSERVA-
TION | But, in order that they take on a
definite enough form to guide your observing, your hypotheses should be put
in writing—early in your work with the
child. *Before and after* each observation
you should look over your notes, notice
what seems *on the way* to confirmation,
what seems disproved, which hypotheses need modification.

This part of scientific method seems
time-consuming and is often neglected.
Actually it is time-saving, since it enables
you to get a greater wealth of really usable fact from your observations. The
greatest vice of most child-study observation is *aimlessness,* dependence upon mere
impressionism. Scientific observation is
pointed, intensive search, not aimless
gazing. Even in the first two or three
observations you are not just looking
around purposelessly; you are searching
for your starting points. Hence I lay
down one of the few rigid rules contained in this guide: Before beginning an
observation period, formulate definitely
the one or two questions or hypotheses
with which your observation is to be particularly concerned. Ask yourself—in advance—what kinds of behavior will throw
light on the hypothesis. After the observation is finished, report with respect to
these questions (*a*) what you found, (*b*)
what you did not find, and (*c*) what you
should look for another time. All this
must be very concrete and specific.

After a conference with a teacher a
student wrote:

James's teacher says he is always cutting
into the discussion in a way which she thinks
is an attention-getting device. I noticed myself
that his interruption was not to the point as
it would be if it came from interest in the
topic. I must see what I can observe in the
home that bears on this. Does Mrs. T. tend to
ignore him? Is there rivalry with Donny? Or
at the other end, is he encouraged to be
"cute"? If these leads fail, I'll try to find the
cause of attention-getting in the school.

Note that the student has accepted
someone else's interpretation—always a
bit dangerous, though in this case fairly
well supported. At any rate, having accepted the hypothesis, she begins an active *search* for relevant information to
validate or invalidate it. How much more
enlightening her observation of the home
situation is likely to be when she goes
with a definite searching attitude.

Should one ignore facts that do not
bear on the hypothesis? By no means!
Whatever else you observe and report is
an "extra dividend." The *rule* given
above is rigid, but *you* should be flexible
and adaptable and sensitive to all sorts
of child behavior. The whole situation
may become radically unfavorable to
finding out anything about the kind of
behavior you had planned to study. A
rapid change of plan is then called for.
But there should still be a plan, a real
search, not just aimless gazing.

KEEPING THE RECORDS

Adequate records are essential if your
case study is to be acceptable, but they
have a wider value. To an extent often
not realized, the attempt to put fleeting
observations in words clarifies them and
brings out their significance. I believe in
the value of direct experience; otherwise
I should not be concerned with having
you observe children. But even the
lower animals can observe children;
dogs, notably, are excellent observers. It
is only when we can verbalize that we
reach the human level.

WHO   Make clear who is the source of your
information. If you are reporting your
own direct observation, let that be
clear.

WHAT   Clearly set off facts from interpretation.

HOW   Describe how the facts were gathered
—by what methods in what circumstances.

WHEN   Date every record.

And be sure your record is complete. The Big Four of sound journalism apply here as well. Make clear *who* is the source of your information. If it was your own direct observation, let that be clear. If you are reporting what someone told you, be crystal clear as to just who told you what. The methods and circumstances of gathering the information must be given. If you observed the event, it is not too difficult to tell *how* you observed it. But if you are retelling something you learned secondhand, you have a double obligation. You must report how you got the information from your informant; and you must tell how your informant got it—if you can. Finally, tell where and when the event occurred.

As a double-check, you should always indicate when you wrote the report.

TAKING NOTES | While observing the child in class, you can generally take notes freely. In interviewing the teacher you will be expected to take notes. Many parents, on the other hand, are made nervous if you bring out a pencil and notebook. When you have become well acquainted with them, or when certain objective facts are being given (such as the date of Harold's attack of measles), you might ask permission to jot down a memo. If anyone seems concerned about your taking notes and asks for an explanation, you will find it best to say frankly that you are making notes merely to help you think things through afterward. It is obvious that only rarely may you write down things in the child's presence, though in case of need you can tell the child you are writing yourself a reminder of something to do. (A friend of mine who overworked this device in a group situation became known to the children as "that man who is always remembering something he's *forgotten*." They thought him queer in that respect, but took it in their stride.)

If you have been unable to take notes during the observation, write them as soon as possible thereafter. In every instance record the time (day and hour), the circumstances of the observation, the place, the purpose you had in mind in making the observation, and the time elapsing between observation and writing. All five of these essentials are illustrated in the following:

Jan. 7, '51. 10 A.M. Record made at the time at school. Class at work painting. Originally planned to study Mary's initiative in recitation. In light of the program, changed to observing extent of physical activity and distractibility.

FIELD NOTES | The notes you thus take on the spot or write down immediately afterward are known as *Field Notes* and should be included in the appendix of your final report to the instructor. *Unless they are very illegible or untidy, they need not be copied.* It is desirable, however, that they be uniform in size and in plan. We suggest that you use full $8\frac{1}{2} \times 11$ paper. This can be conveniently folded in half or quarter for "on-the-spot" notes and still fit in with the rest of your written or typed report. Make sure that the field notes are uniform in size and securely fastened together, so that they do not get out of order.

THE DISTINCTION BETWEEN FACT AND INTERPRETATION

While it is impossible to keep the human or personal element out of your observations, it must be your constant effort to reduce it to a minimum. This implies that you must distinguish what actually happened (observed fact) from how the fact impressed you (interpretation or meaning of the fact).

For present purposes we may think of observed fact as a percept—something seen, heard, smelled, touched, or tasted. As a rough criterion, whatever an actor directly conveys is observable. If he strides up and down, we actually observe a "nervous manner." Similarly we can observe a child's "happy smile" or "puzzled frown." These are the basic materials of observation.

In reacting to such "facts," however, we almost invariably indulge in a certain amount of interpretation. Several levels of interpretation may be usefully distinguished.

Consider the following statements:

(1) He replied, when his mother spoke to him, in a very cross tone. (2) He was irritated by the interruption to his work. (3) Besides that, his mother tends to nag him quite a lot and that makes him snappy in his replies. (4) This habit of making cross replies is getting to be general; he might be described as a cross or surly boy. (5) No wonder he is unpopular.

A SCALE OF CLOSENESS TO THE IMMEDIATE FACTS | The first statement is reasonably factual. You observed a cross tone—although it may be difficult to state what, in physical terms, a cross tone is.

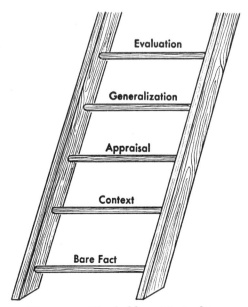

Figure 1. The ladder of factuality.

The second statement goes somewhat beyond the bare fact; it is obviously an interpretation or explanation of the fact. But the explanation is stated in terms of the immediate setting of the event and is necessary if the event is to have any meaning. We may call this a *meaning* or *context* interpretation. Unless it is obvious, it should always be given as a part of the observation. Without it the bare fact would be too bare.

The third statement goes beyond the immediate situation; it is an *appraisal* in terms of quite a number of facts which have previously been observed and in the light of quite a complex psychological theory. (The hypothesis that a nagging mother leads to snappy replies seems so self-evidently true that we forget that it is only an hypothesis or theory.)

The fourth statement even more obviously goes beyond the immediate facts. It implies enough observations to warrant a judgment that the behavior in question is habitual or characteristic. This may be called generalization from the facts.[5] And once more we see a theory as to cause-and-effect relationships.

The last statement involves us in another theory and obviously implies moral and social evaluation as well.

We have here, then, a sort of scale of closeness to the immediate facts of experience: first, *observed fact;* second, fact plus immediate *context* or meaning; third, *appraisal* of the fact; fourth, *generalization* from the fact; fifth, *evaluation.*

Now perhaps all of this is justifiable. In a full study of an individual we have

[5] Generalization *from* the fact must be distinguished from generalization *of* the facts. The latter may be illustrated by such statement as: "He answered crossly every time his mother spoke to him the entire afternoon." Generalization *of* the facts is not interpretation at all but simply a short way of stating them.

to come to rather far-reaching judgments; that, in a sense, is what the study is for. But most of this interpretation has no place in what purports to be a record of *factual observation*. The field notes should therefore give only a minimum of interpretation; any interpretation we do make should be clearly distinguished from the facts, and its tentative nature made clear. Let us see how the above statements might appear in your field notes.

Replied to mother's question in very cross tone. [Apparently irritated by interruption to his work. *Query:* Does his mother nag him a lot? Does this make him irritable in relation to his mother? Or irritable in general? Wonder if this explains the unpopularity of which his teacher spoke.]

Note that the statement about interruption (the meaning) is set forth as a positive statement, though it is enclosed in brackets to show that it is your interpretation not your observation. But the wider interpretations, the judgments or generalizations and evaluations, are set down as questions for further investigation.

Particularly troublesome is that form of interpretation which consists in attributing some "trait" of character or personality to the child—as in (4) above, where the child is said to be "surly." Since "traits" are always a matter of inference and not of observed fact, they have no place in a factual report.

Such trait descriptions, moreover, cover up our lack of full knowledge. A child is said to have shown "strong will" because for three hours he refused a half stick of gum when he had asked of a whole piece. But saying this was "strong will" merely says he persisted in his refusal. It does not tell us *why*. It does not give us a clue as to how often or cunningly he was tempted with the half stick. It does not tell us what he gained from the refusal.

Compare the usefulness of these two reports:

1. Chester is very quick tempered, as was seen in the way he acted when his sister jogged his elbow while he was working on a model airplane.

2. While Chester was working on a model airplane, his sister accidentally jogged his elbow. He was instantly angry and pushed her away. [Of course, the model is fragile and very dear to him and his sister did endanger it. Yet I wondered whether that was the whole story. Does she pester him a lot? Or what is his relation to her? Does he think she is mother's pet just because she is young and rather doll-like? Does he feel that he must defend his possessions against her? I shall have to watch closely for indications that will bring out this. I wonder whether his mother has insight and objectivity enough to know. I think I shall not ask her directly, but she may have some evidence for me.]

The writer of the second report is looking for facts, the writer of the first found a ready-made conclusion.

31 | PERCEIVING

BERNARD BERELSON AND GARY A. STEINER

The world becomes known to us through perception. It is the manner in which human beings organize experience to establish order and meaning in the world. The Austrian psychologist Wilhelm Wundt initiated the study of perception in 1879 in his Psychological Institute at the University of Leipzig, to give birth to modern experimental psychology. The following selection enumerates the laws of perception discovered since then.

How people come to know and interpret their world is fundamental to the understanding of human behavior, since behavior, as distinct from sheer motion, is action that takes the environment into account.

Two basic starting points are: (1) all knowledge of the world depends on the senses and their stimulation, but (2) the facts of raw sensory data are insufficient to produce or to explain the coherent picture of the world as experienced by the normal adult. The first of these statements is axiomatic: a philosophical assumption not empirically verifiable but certainly not contradicted by any known facts. The second is an empirical finding that will be documented at length in these pages. Indeed, the study of perception is largely the study of what must be added to and subtracted from raw sensory input to produce our picture of the world.

Throughout the discussion we illustrate mainly by reference to vision, man's most important and most widely studied sense. But although the preponderance of evidence comes from visual experiments, the general propositions apply to the other senses as well.

· · · · ·

SENSATION

· · · · ·

Let us begin with some basic and general findings regarding the relationship between physical stimuli . . . and the experience they produce . . . . This is part of the field of *psychophysics*, . . . which attempts to establish quantitative relationships between the *psycho*logical dimensions of experience (loudness, pitch, color, etc.) and the *physical*

characteristics of stimuli (wave length, amplitude, intensity, etc.).

Perhaps the most general proposition on the mechanics of the sensory process is this:

A1 Sensation itself is fundamentally a matter of energy change or differentiation: a perfectly homogeneous environment or an absolutely unchanging one, regardless of the strength of its sensory input, is equivalent to none at all.

A perfectly homogeneous visual field, for example, is lost to the eye. A smooth surface of one color that completely surrounds the viewer loses its solidity and location: it may be six inches away, but all that appears is endless "film" or space. Even a simple differentiated shape quickly becomes imperceptible unless it plays continuously on different receptors in the retina. In one study, for example, an experimenter was able, by means of a mirror arrangement actually attached to the eye, to project an image on a given constant spot in the retina with no fluctuation whatsoever due to normal eye movements. Under such conditions the image disappears in a matter of seconds (Ditchburn *et al.*, 1959). More than that:

A1.1 A certain amount of differentiated input seems necessary for normal orientation and even for mental balance in the human being.

Experiments in sensory deprivation drastically reduce input and/or variability of input and in doing so produce marked deterioration in various capacities.

In a typical experimental situation, subjects were isolated in a cubicle; they wore translucent goggles to eliminate visual variability, and had their fingers separated by cotton and their hands cuffed in cardboard to reduce tactual stimulation.

Abridged from Bernard Berelson and Gary A. Steiner, *Human Behavior: An Inventory of Scientific Findings*, pp. 87–131. Copyright © 1964 by Harcourt, Brace and World, Inc., and reprinted with their permission.

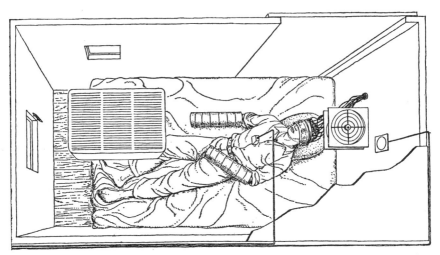

The experimental cubicle. Reprinted from W. Heron, "Cognitive and Physiological Effects of Perceptual Isolation," in Philip Solomon, *Sensory Deprivation* (Cambridge, Mass.: Harvard University Press, 1961), p. 9 by permission of the publisher. Copyright 1961 by the President and Fellows of Harvard College.

Tests during and after the two- to three-day isolation period showed impaired effectiveness in diverse intellectual and problem-solving abilities, including verbal, mathematical, and spatial skills. In addition, subjects exhibited greater susceptibility to propaganda introduced while in isolation.

. . . . .

Furthermore:

Twenty-five of the 29 subjects reported some form of hallucinatory activity. Typically, the hallucinations progressed from simple to complex. The first symptom would be a lightening of the visual field. Dots of light or lines would then occur. Next would appear geometrical figures and patterns, generally composed of reduplicated figures, followed by isolated objects against a homogeneous background. Finally, full-blown scenes would appear. These seemed to be in front of the subjects. If they wanted to examine part of a scene more closely, they found that they could do so more easily by moving their eyes in the appropriate direction, as they would do if they were looking at a picture.

They had little control over the content of their hallucinations (one subject, for instance, could see nothing but eyeglasses, however

hard he tried), nor were they able to start or stop them. They were often vivid as to prevent the subject from sleeping, and one man left the experimental situation because he was disturbed by their persistence [Heron, 1961, pp. 17–18].

. . . . .

Two other fundamental topics in perceptual investigation deal with the minimal stimulus values capable (1) of being sensed at *all* (the absolute threshold) and (2) of being told *apart* (the differential threshold). And as we shall see, the findings seem to have implications far beyond the psychological laboratory. The overriding generalization with respect to absolute and differentiated thresholds is this:

A2 Human sensitivity changes as it needs to: when there is abundant or superfluous input (e.g., brilliant illumination, very loud sound), the senses ignore—in fact, are incapable of detecting—small intensities or differences. As the available input decreases and becomes sparse, the sensitivity to detect intensity and difference increases tremendously, until man attains his maximum sensitivity under conditions of minimal stimulation.

This process not only provides more sensitivity when demanded but also protects the organism, via decreased sensitivity, from damaging, disruptive, or irrelevant bombardment when the input is high. Such accommodation in levels of sensitivity as external conditions vary is probably among the most general and far-reaching principles of human behavior, and we shall encounter it in various forms in subsequent chapters. Here, then, in somewhat greater specificity, are its foundations in the sensory thresholds.

The Absolute Threshold

Actually, there is some question as to whether an absolute threshold exists in a truly absolute sense—that is, whether a minimum value of energy can be established even under the most carefully controlled conditions. There is always some "noise" in the environment, i.e., stimulation unrelated to the input being measured; and there is always some unrelated activity in the sensory machinery being tested. Beyond that, it is necessary to distinguish *awareness* of stimulation ("I *see* it") from the ability to make better-than-chance guesses as to whether or not a "signal" is present. These and other technical considerations have given rise to a reformulation of the threshold notion in more statistical and probabilistic terms (known as "detection theory"). But at any rate:

A3 Up to the point of maximum sensitivity, the absolute threshold of a sense becomes progressively lower (that is, sensitivity, or the ability to detect stimuli, increases) with disuse or rest. The longer in total darkness, the more sensitive vision becomes ("sensory adaptation").

Just as a rough indication of the magnitude of this effect: the eye at its most sensitive, after a prolonged period in total darkness, will respond to a stimulus 1/100,000 as intense as that required when the eye is least sensitive, after sustained, strong exposure. As this suggests, under ideal conditions human receptors—especially in the case of vision—can be extremely sensitive.

Measured under the best possible conditions, the absolute thresholds for various stimuli are amazingly low. . . . Thus, for example, it has been estimated that the physical energy equivalent to *one pin dropping one inch* would, if converted to light energy and properly distributed, be sufficient to stimulate *every one* of the more than four billion human eyes on earth! [Krech and Crutchfield, 1958, p. 51.]

Sensory adaptation stems directly from properties of the individual receptor cells that initiate sensory impulses—in the case of vision, the rods and cones in the retina. Within limits, the sensitivity of such neurons is directly related to the time since last fired. Immediately after firing, there is a brief period during which the cell is entirely incapable of being activated, regardless of the strength of bombardment; beyond this recovery period, stimuli of ever decreasing intensity will be adequate to fire the cell, until ultimate sensitivity is reached.

. . . . .

A3.1 Under conditions of constant stimulation, receptors initially exhibit decreasing sensitivity; experience becomes less intense over time as input remains constant.

Hence the familiar experiences of "getting used to" a hot bath, a cold shower, the bright sun, the odor in a room.

A4 Conscious sensation is not always equivalent to the threshold as measured at the receptor end. Many stimuli strong enough to fire one or more receptor cells are too weak to create awareness, and some stimuli have measurable effects on behavior, not just on receptor cells, even though they are too weak or too brief to be consciously "seen" or "heard."

Thus, the threshold for awareness or conscious recognition may be higher than the threshold for effective perception as measured by more sensitive indicators. This process is called "subliminal perception" because the stimulus is beneath the threshold or "limen" of awareness, though obviously not beneath the absolute threshold of the receptors involved.

In one study, for example, subjects gave heightened involuntary responses of an emotional character (GSR, for "galvanic skin response") to nonsense syllables that had previously been paired with electric shock, when the syllables were later exposed at subthreshold speeds, i.e., at exposures too rapid for conscious recognition and report. Neutral syllables not previously shock-associated showed far smaller effects (Lazarus and McCleary, 1951). Similarly, emotionally loaded words, subliminally exposed, elicit higher galvanic skin responses than do neutral words.

. . . . .

There is some theoretical controversy about the exact nature of the process and the measurements that demonstrate it, but the fact remains that subjects can give evidence that some stimulus material is getting through at thresholds beneath those required to produce the response "I see such-and-such," or even the response "I see something." In this sense, "unrecognized" stimuli do have effects—not just on the retina, but on feelings and thoughts as well.

A4.1 There is no scientific evidence that subliminal stimulation can initiate subsequent action, to say nothing of commercially or politically significant action. And there is nothing to suggest that such action can be produced "against the subject's will," or more effectively than through normal, recognized messages.

An important review of the matter recently concluded:

One fact emerges from all of the above. Anyone who wishes to utilize subliminal stimulation for commercial or other purposes can be likened to a stranger entering into a misty, confused countryside where there are but few landmarks. Before this technique is used in the market place, if it is to be used at all, a tremendous amount of research should be done, and by competent experimenters [McConnell et al., 1958, p. 237].

In short, while super hidden-persuasion may be something to fear, it is first something to document.

The Differential Threshold

Next, with respect to the minimal difference that can be detected between stimuli, usually designated "differential threshold" or "jnd" (for "just noticeable difference"): the differential threshold varies not only with (a) the sensitivity of the receptor and with (b) the type of stimuli but also, and importantly, with (c) the absolute intensity of the stimuli being compared. This last introduces a fundamental principle:

A5 The size of the least detectable change or increment in intensity is a function of the initial intensity: the stronger the initial stimulus, the greater the difference needs to be. More specifically, where I is the intensity of the stimulus, ΔI the jnd, and k a constant for the particular type of stimuli:

$$\frac{\Delta I}{I} = k$$

This formulation is known as *Weber's Law.*

Suppose the problem is to determine the differential threshold for unmarked weights, lifted by hand. What is the smallest difference that can be detected?

If one weight is 300 grams, it may take an increment of 6 grams, or a comparison weight of 306 grams, before the subject detects a difference. But given a weight of 600 grams, a 6-gram increment is undetectable. According to Weber's Law, it now takes a 12-gram increment, or a comparison weight of 612 grams, to produce a just noticeable difference:

$$\frac{6}{300} = \frac{1}{50} \quad \text{and} \quad \frac{12}{600} = \frac{1}{50}$$

Thus, k ("Weber's constant," or "Weber's fraction") in this case would equal $\frac{1}{50}$ or .02, and any two weights would be discriminable if they differed at least by the ratio 51:50.

Weber's Law holds for all the senses, and for almost all intensities—in the case of vision and hearing, over more than 99.9 per cent of the usable stimulus range. When stimuli approach minimal intensity (the absolute threshold), the fraction may become considerably larger (discrimination is less acute); similarly, k may also increase for extremely intense stimuli. Thus, the relative power to discriminate is highest in the broad, normal range of intensities (although the general proposition holds for the extremes as well).

Here is a table of minimal Weber fractions for different sensory discriminations, obtained under ideal laboratory conditions. They provide a rough index as to the relative sensitivity and discriminating power of the various senses: the smaller the fraction, the greater the differential sensitivity.

Weber's Law stands as a milestone in psychological research. It is one of the first psychological laws worthy of the name, and it may prove to be of far greater and more general significance than the differential threshold problems that provided its initial formulation. In effect, it establishes a law of psychological relativity: subjective discriminations are not bound to absolute characteristics of stimuli but to relations between them.

This has been demonstrated in a number of diverse situations, from human judgments of aesthetic objects to the rat's ability to differentiate the length of two pathways in a maze (Yoshioka, 1929). Weber's Law has also been applied in economic utility theory (Stigler, 1950), stock-market analysis (Osborne, 1959), and consumer attitudes towards prices (Webb, 1961). In addition, everyday observation lends credibility to the notion that Weber's Law taps something quite general: a grocery store two

	Weber ratio	Weber fraction
Deep pressure, from skin and subcutaneous tissue, at about 400 grams	0.013	$\frac{1}{77}$
Visual brightness, at about 1000 photons	0.016	$\frac{1}{62}$
Lifted weights, at about 300 grams	0.019	$\frac{1}{53}$
Tone, for 1000 cycles per second, at about 100 db above the absolute threshold	0.088	$\frac{1}{11}$
Smell, for rubber, at about 200 olfacties	0.104	$\frac{1}{10}$
Cutaneous pressure, on an isolated spot, at about 5 grams per mm	0.136	$\frac{1}{7}$
Taste, for saline solution, at about 3 moles per liter concentration	0.200	$\frac{1}{5}$

Reprinted from S. S. Stevens, "Sensation and Psychological Measurement," in E. G. Boring, H. S. Langfeld, and H. P. Weld, *Foundations of Psychology* (John Wiley, 1948), by permission of the publisher

blocks away seems much further than one around the corner, but Los Angeles seems about as far from Chicago as San Francisco does; the difference between one and two hours appears great, but the difference between a month and thirty-two days is negligible; a five-cent increase in the cost of a newspaper is quite noticeable, whereas one or two hundred dollars in the price of a house may be of little concern, and so on. As Thoreau once observed: "If you wish to give a man a sense of poverty, give him a thousand dollars—the next 100 he gets will not be worth more than the 10 he used to get."

More recently, continued psychophysical investigation has yielded still another and more general law, regarding the relationship between the magnitudes of the stimulus and the resulting sensation:

If you shine a faint light in your eye, you have a sensation of brightness—a weak sensation, to be sure. If you turn on a stronger light, the sensation becomes greater. . . . But how, precisely, does the output of the system (sensation) vary with the input (stimulus)? Suppose you double the stimulus, does it then look twice as bright?

The answer to that question happens to be no. It takes about nine times as much light to double the apparent brightness, but this specific question, interesting as it may be, is only one instance of a wider problem: what are the input-output characteristics of sensory systems in general? Is there a single, simple, pervasive psychophysical law?

Unlikely as it may seem, there appears to be such a law. . . . Within a first-order approximation, there appears to be no exception to the principle that equal stimulus *ratios* correspond to equal sensation *ratios*. . . .

The psychophysical power law relating the psychological magnitude ψ to the physical stimulus a can be written

$$\psi = k(a - a_0)^n$$

where k is a constant determined by the choice of units. The exponent n varies with the modality, and also with such parameters as adaptation and contrast. Generally speaking, each modality has its characteristic exponent, ranging from about 0.33 for brightness to about 3.5 for electric shock [Stevens, 1962, pp. 29–30].

. . . . .

PERCEPTION

Against the background of these findings on sensation, a basic—perhaps *the* basic—generalization on perception mentioned at the outset now takes on more meaning; the remainder of this section will elaborate it further.

B1 The facts of raw sensory data are themselves insufficient to produce or to explain the coherent picture of the world as the normal adult experiences it.

The raw units of sensory experience are bits of on-or-off information transmitted by discrete neural fibers, each originating in a specific receptor location and ending in a specific location in the brain. Literally, then, the sensory world consists of an almost infinite number of discrete impulses, in an ever changing pattern. In this sense, no man can have the same sensation twice.

But no one, fortunately, sees the world so fragmented. The perceived visual world, for example, contains many objects, not millions of discrete pinpoint impressions. In addition, the objects and the world they are in remain remarkably constant, even though the sensory input that represents them is always changing.

B1.1 There are some experiences with no corresponding sensory input.

Extreme and complicated examples are dreams and hallucinations. More simply, consider the apparent motion that occurs when two successive, slightly different stimuli are alternated (the so-called phi phenomenon, on which moving pictures are based). Lights A and B turned on and off at the appropriate rate are seen as one light moving back and forth between these points; the light actually appears at *C* and all other intermediate positions as it travels. There is corresponding retinal stimulation at *A* and *B*, but none whatsoever between them.

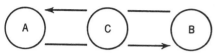

Note that phi is not due to movement of the eye—it can occur simultaneously in many directions, as in a motion picture. The phenomenon also appears in other senses: in touch, for example, two successive light pressures at nearby points produce a sensation of movement along the path.

B1.2 Many sensory stimuli normally fail to be represented in conscious experience.

For example, your nose: close the left eye and you see it with the right; close the right eye and you see it with the left; open both and where is it?

In short, sensory information does not correspond simply to the perception that it underlies. The fundamental reason for the difference between sensory data and perception is that sensory impulses do not act on an empty organism; they interact with certain predispositions and states already there, and immediate experience is the result of that interaction. The nature of experience, then, depends on two interacting sets of contributions: those of the environment, in the form of physical stimulation, and those of the observer himself, which we now review under the general headings of selection, organization, and interpretation.

Selection

First of all, the observer exercises selection regarding *what* aspects of the environment will be perceived.

B2 Of all possible stimuli—i.e., all bits of energy actually capable of firing re-ceptors at any given moment—only a small portion become part of actual experience; and that portion is not a random sample of what is objectively available.

To begin with, the observer, of course, plays an active part in determining what will be allowed to stimulate the receptors at all: we look *at* some things, ignore others, and look *away* from still others ("selective exposure"). Beyond that, only a fraction of those stimuli that have gained effective entry to a receptor ever reach awareness ("selective awareness"). For example, at this moment you are mainly aware of the paragraph in front of you and, most of all, of this particular phrase. Yet the objects actually reflected in effective visual stimuli extend above, below, and well to the sides of the book. As this sentence calls them to your attention, objects on the periphery may enter awareness. Such selective awareness occurs between as well as within the various senses: you may also have been unaware of various noises, smells, pressures on the skin that have been present while you were reading.

B3 Which stimuli get selected depends upon three major factors: the nature of the stimuli involved; previous experience or learning as it affects the observer's expectations (what he is prepared or "set" to see); and the motives in play at the time, by which we mean his needs, desires, wishes, interests, and so on—in short, what the observer wants or needs to see and not to see. Each of these factors can act to heighten or to decrease the probability of perceiving, and each can act on both exposure and awareness.

B3.1 With regard to the stimulus factors, differential intensity or quality is a major determinant.

A cannon shot on a quiet street or sudden silence in the midst of a din gets attention whether or not anyone expects it or wants to hear it. Thus contrast, as illustrated by THIS word, is one of the most attention-compelling attributes of a stimulus.

B3.2 With regard to expectations, other things equal, people are more likely to attend to aspects of the environment they anticipate than to those they do not, and they are more likely to anticipate things they are familiar with.

Thus the difference between the trained observer and the layman is largely a matter of differential selectivity: the pathologist examining a microscope slide concentrates on the crucial (familiar and expected) microbe, while the novice sees an undifferentiated mass. Conversely, novel aspects of the environment—those that conflict sharply with expectations (e.g., a bearded lady)—will also get more notice than those unrelated to what is expected.

B3.3 With regard to motives, not only do people look for things they need or want; but the stronger the need, the greater the tendency to ignore irrelevant elements.

A hungry man looks for food and seeks out signs of it; but beyond that, at given levels of exposure, awareness of motive-relevant stimuli exceeds that for neutral ones. For example, words that have sexual as well as nonsexual connotation (e.g., fairy, screw) are more quickly identified in unclear carbon copies when they have recently been experienced in the sexual, rather than the neutral, context (Wiener, 1955).

In general, then, there is heightened awareness of relevant stimuli and depressed awareness of irrelevant ones. The adaptiveness of this mechanism is evident when it fails to operate, as in the case of the hypochondriac who is acutely aware of various inner sensations that most people ignore. . . .

. . . . .

Finally, pleasant or sympathetic scenes and messages are sought out, while painful or threatening ones are actively avoided; thus, the typical audience for partisan speeches or propaganda is weighted with those already sympathetic, as we shall see in the chapter on mass communication.

B3.3a There may also be decreased awareness of stimuli it is important *not* to see, once exposure has taken place ("perceptual defense"); that is, threatening or otherwise damaging materials may be *less* apt to reach consciousness than neutral materials at the same level of exposure.

In several experiments, threatening pictures or words are found to have higher thresholds of recognition and/or are described less accurately at given levels of exposure than are neutral materials. One such study used "Blacky Pictures," in which a small dog is found in a variety of situations, some rich in sexual significance. When two threatening scenes ("masturbation guilt," "oral sadism") and two neutral ones were flashed at near threshold speeds, the subjects took longer locating the threatening pictures than the neutral controls. Moreover, threatening pictures also made more of an impression (i.e., were reported to "stand out more") when exposure time was far beneath threshold.

. . . . .

The tendency to be more open to some experiences and to shut out others seems to extend, literally, to the pupil of the eye.

B3.4 When looking at interesting or pleasant materials, as compared to neutral ones, the pupil dilates measurably. Conversely, looking at distasteful or disliked materials produces contraction.

Here are some illustrative results showing how men and women respond to various pictures:

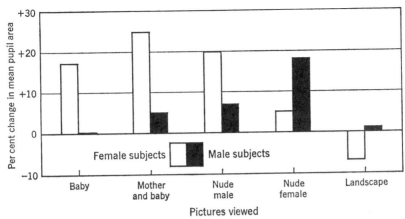

Changes in mean pupil size, in terms of percentage of decrease or increase in area, from size during viewing of control patterns, in response to various pictures. Reprinted from E. H. Hess and James Polt, "Pupil Size as Related to Interest Value of Visual Stimuli," *Science*, Vol. 123, 1960, p. 350, by permission of the authors and publisher.

Or, again, acknowledged homosexuals were discriminated from normals simply by their differential pupillary response to photographs of homosexuals versus female pin-ups:

Five normal males, five normal females, and five admitted homosexual males were shown three abstract paintings, six pictures of men and six pictures of women. Scores were obtained in terms of deviation from the mean change of the pupil in response to all twelve critical pictures. No normal male showed a total negative response to the six pictures of women. No homosexual or woman showed a positive response to the six pictures of women. There is no overlap between normal male and homosexual male subjects in their responses to the two categories of pictures. While the females and the homosexuals gave similar responses, the homosexuals showed a much greater rejection of pictures of women than did the female subjects [Hess, 1963].

The extent to which the response relates to the degree of interest versus the degree of liking has not yet been established. In addition, pupil dilation seems to signal sheer mental activity, e.g., working arithmetic problems mentally even when the materials thought about are not visually presented. Further:

B3.4a The response is not under conscious control or awareness. Subjects can neither report nor manipulate the pupillary response at will.

Thus, under certain circumstances, pupil reaction may be a more accurate index of subjective response to visual materials than verbal reports, e.g., when subjects might conceal or distort their real feelings. Thus this recent development may provide an objective measure of subjective state.

Guillaume de Salluste once called the eyes "these windows of the soul." Even if the eyes are not the "windows of the soul," it has become increasingly apparent that the eyes, more specifically the pupil, register directly certain activities of the nervous system, including, but not restricted to, the effects of visual stimulation. Our evidence so far indicates that deeply rooted personal attitudes may be laid bare by the activities of the pupils [Hess, 1963].

Organization

B4 Even the simplest experiences are organized by the perceiver; and the perceived characteristics of any part are a function of the whole to which it appears to belong.

The principles of organization, first developed and stressed by Gestalt psychologists (*Gestalt* is German for configuration or pattern), are best illustrated by visual demonstrations, but they apply to other senses as well. Here are some of the basic ones, as they become progressively more complex:

B4.1 *Figure and ground:* The simplest differentiated experience consists of a figure on a ground. The figure appears well defined, at a definite location, solid, and in front of the ground. In contrast, the ground appears amorphous, indefinite, and continuous behind the figure. The common contour of figure and ground appears to belong to the figure rather than to the ground:

These distinctions are not inherent in the stimulus material, as is demonstrated by reversible figure-ground patterns:

The Peter-Paul goblet. What do you see, the goblet or the famous twins? Whichever you

see, try to find the other. Then, when you have found the other, try to turn the perception back to what it was at first. Reprinted from E. B. Newman, "Perception," in E. G. Boring, H. S. Langford, and H. P. Wells, *Foundations of Psychology*, Wiley, 1948, p. 277, by permission of the publisher.

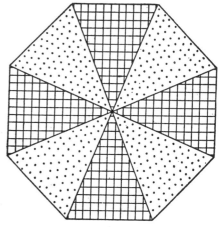

A reversible cross. Keep your eyes fixed near the center of the figure, and note whether you see an × *or a* +. *Maintain your fixation and see how long the cross at which you are looking lasts.* Reprinted from E. B. Newman, "Perception," in E. G. Boring, H. S. Langfeld, and H. P. Weld, *Foundations of Psychology*, Wiley, 1948, p. 277, by permission of the publisher.

In these figures the *same* stimuli serve alternately as figure and ground, changing their perceptual characteristics as they fluctuate. But the basic relationship between figure and ground remains.

The tendency for people to organize their perceptions into figure-ground is apparently innate, although learning affects what will be perceived as figure and what as ground. On gaining sight, congenitally blind adults exhibit figure-ground organization before many other visual abilities (Senden, 1932).

B4.2 *Grouping:* Elements in experience are automatically and almost irresistibly grouped—other things equal—according to proximity, similarity, and continuity.

Proximity

You see a row of small slanted groups $\left(\begin{smallmatrix} & \cdot \\ \cdot & \end{smallmatrix}\right)$ going from lower left to upper right. That is, if we label the dots as follows, you see

$$c \qquad f \qquad i \qquad l$$
$$b \qquad e \qquad h \qquad k \quad \text{etc.,}$$
$$a \qquad d \qquad g \qquad j$$

the form *abc/def/ghi/. . . .* The opposite organization,

ceg/fhj/. . . , is not seen, and is impossible to achieve simultaneously in the entire series for most people.
  Or, further, in

you see the triads *abc/def/ . . .* and not one of many other theoretically possible groupings.
  Reprinted from M. Wertheimer, "Principles of Perceptual Organization," in David C. Beardslee and M. Wertheimer, *Readings in Perception*, Van Nostrand, 1958, p. 117, by permission of the publisher.

Similarity

Similar grouping by proximity in hearing can be illustrated by the auditory stimuli of the Morse code (right).
  Below, greater horizontal similarity tends to overcome greater vertical proximity.

@   @   @   @   @   @
*   *   *   *   *   *
@   @   @   @   @   @
*   *   *   *   *   *

Continuity

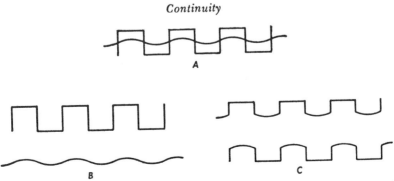

A

B   C

Reprinted from M. Wertheimer, "Principles of Perceptual Organization," in David C. Beardslee and M. Wertheimer, *Readings in Perception*, Van Nostrand, 1958, pp. 128–29, by permission of the publisher.

A appears as composed of the elements in *B* rather than of those in *C;* the straight lines and arcs are grouped to produce the greater continuity.

B4.3 *Closure:* Experience tends to be organized into whole, continuous figures. If the stimulus pattern is incomplete, the perceiver tends to fill in missing elements.

For example, this is one dog, not twenty discrete blotches:

Reprinted from R. F. Street, *A Gestalt Completion Test: A Study of a Cross-Section of Intellect,* Columbia University Press, 1931, p. 41, by permission of the publisher.

And here, closure tends to overcome proximity:

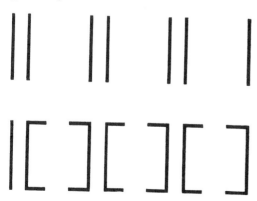

An example of the competition between grouping by proximity and grouping by closure. The seven lines above tend to fall "naturally" into three pairs and one isolate, by virtue of proximity relations. But the same lines below, with the addition of the short

horizontal lines, tend to be grouped by closure with the more distant partner, overriding the influence of proximity. Reprinted from D. Krech and R. S. Crutchfield, *Elements of Psychology,* Knopf, 1958, p. 93, by permission of the authors.

B4.4 *"Good" figures:* When stimuli can be organized in various ways, the "best" one tends to win out perceptually— "best" in terms of similarity, continuity, proximity, closure, symmetry, and so on.

For example, note how difficult it is to find *A* in *B, C,* and *D:*

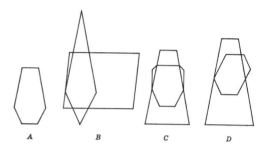

Reprinted from M. Wertheimer, "Principles of Perceptual Organization," in David C. Beardslee and M. Wertheimer, *Readings In Perception,* Van Nostrand, 1958, p. 131, by permission of the publisher.

or *E* in *F:*

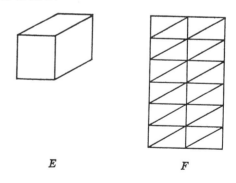

Reprinted from W. D. Ellis, *A Sourcebook of Gestalt Psychology,* Harcourt, Brace & World, 1938, p. 118, by permission of the publisher.

This principle is used in camouflage: a figure is destroyed, perceptually, by incorporation into a better one.

B5 People tend to perceive homogeneity in the internal characteristics of figures. Within the boundaries of a given figure, differences (up to a point) are ironed out ("assimilated").

For example, this circle, a "good" and whole figure, is a uniform shade of gray:

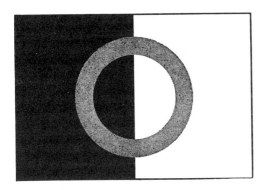

Reprinted from C. E. Osgood, *Method and Theory in Experimental Psychology*, p. 235. Copyright 1953 by Oxford University Press, Inc. Reprinted by permission.

Now dissect it vertically with a pencil, producing two figures: the right one is considerably darker than the left because of contrast effects with the respective backgrounds (discussed below). Slide the pencil slowly to one or the other side, and note how the appropriate shade is dragged into the other sector. Each portion, now a separate figure, tends to be perceived homogeneously within its boundaries.

Whether some of these organizational tendencies reflect learning or intrinsic properties of the perceptual machinery

is a matter of theoretical dispute. For example, is grouping by continuity automatic, or does it come from the fact that experience with the real world has taught us that the figure $ is more likely to be composed of the elements in *A* than the elements in *B?*

In any case, holding constant the characteristics of the stimulus:

$$\text{S}\|\qquad\qquad ¶ ⋮ ♭$$

$$A\qquad\qquad\qquad B$$

B6 Perceptual organization, as well as perceptual selection, is affected by expectations based on experience and by motives.

For example, because of our experience, the word "jump" will be organized like this:

jump

and not like this (Wertheimer, 1958, p. 132):

ji un rp

And a more familiar stimulus pattern is likely to be seen as figure under conditions where a less familiar one would be ground—as when black figures such as these

become ground for this:

With regard to motives, how a reversible figure-ground pattern will be seen can be influenced by prior pleasant or painful associations with one or the other figure in isolation. The effect is such as to increase the likelihood that subjects will see the neutral or pleasant perceptual organization rather than the painful one. For example, when subjects have previously been shocked in association with one or the other figure in a reversible figure-ground pattern, they are more apt to report the nonshocked resolution than the shocked one when the reversible pattern is briefly exposed.

In the present case, 164 unshocked and 101 shocked faces were reported for the A-B figure, and 98 unshocked and 81 shocked for the C-D figure, i.e., the same direction in both cases. In short, while purely "figural" factors were of importance, the shock procedure clearly had effect [Smith and Hochberg, 1954, p. 85].

Some of these principles of perceptual organization seem appropriate to more general and complex phenomena than the simple examples presented here for purposes of illustration. The need for "closure," for example, may apply to the tension that accompanies interruption of a task and the satisfaction and relief that come from its completion (i.e., attainment of the whole figure). Similarly, factors that impede creative problem-solving have been analyzed in terms of the "camouflage" of ideas, the necessary innovation being imperceptible by reason of its incorporation in a more familiar or "better" figure. Or again:

The perception of individuals as belonging to a common group is achieved according to some of the principles made familiar by Gestalt psychology: similarity, proximity, good continuation, closure, etc. That is, we group together those of similar appearance, clothing, or mannerisms, assuming more congeniality, perhaps, than the similarity assures; we tend to see those who live near together or who associate together as sharing common values or beliefs (including "guilt by association"); we structure the social environment into figure and ground as we do the impersonal environment. When a figure appears, the boundaries are sharpened, and the distinction between what belongs to the figure and what belongs to the ground becomes clear; we may thus structure the world into the "free world" and the "Communist world," ignoring many of the other differences between nations and governments [Hilgard, 1962, pp. 552–53].

Finally, these organizational demonstrations are perhaps the simplest instances of a highly general proposition applicable almost everywhere in human behavior: people respond neither to discrete elements one at a time nor to the sum total of discrete elements, they respond to the relationships between them. And this serves as an introduction to perceptual interpretation, where this proposition is further documented.

Interpretation and Judgment

Stimuli, or patterns of stimuli, are often ambiguous; that is, there is no inherent or constant relationship between the sensory input and the stimulus objects it represents. Sometimes stimuli are physically weak or incomplete, as when something is dimly illuminated, partly obscured, briefly exposed, and so on. But even when the stimulus pattern is physically strong, the mechanics of sensation are such that no automatic, invariant conclusions about what is "out there" come from sensory input alone, because (1) even the simplest objects can produce an infinite variety of stimuli (e.g., a book held at varying distances, at different angles, under different conditions of illumination); and, conversely, (2) different objects can produce the same stimuli (e.g., a big disc far away and a small one nearby; an eighty-piece symphony orchestra and a twelve-inch hi-fi speaker). As a consequence, perception imposes the task of interpretation, of deciding what objects or events the sensory pattern actually does represent. Such interpretation is not usually a matter of conscious thinking-through but an instantaneous perceptual response. Accordingly:

B7 The greater the ambiguity of the stimulus, the more room and need for interpretation.

This is, in fact, the principle behind many diagnostic devices (projective tests) in which interpretations of ambiguous stimuli—for example, the ink blots of the Rorschach test—are taken to reveal something about the observer, on the basis that, again, the general determinants of interpretation (beyond the constant characteristics of the stimulus) are expectations from previous experience and motives, needs, and interests in play at the time.

B8 In interpreting ambiguous stimuli, the observer typically assumes that the most likely object(s) capable of producing the pattern are the ones actually in-

volved. Further, the relative familiarity with alternatives is one of the strongest determinants of what will be considered likely. Thus:

B8.1 Familiar objects retain their perceived size, color, shape, etc., though their sensory projections fluctuate tremendously ("perceptual constancy").

This capacity to maintain constant perceptions in the face of widely and continually fluctuating sensations is highly adaptive because it is realistic: objects usually *do* remain the same size and shape as they change in angle of regard or in distance. But the same process will prove illusory when that is not the case.

For example, in an otherwise darkened room, when an oversized playing card is displayed considerably behind an undersized football, they are seen as the normal-sized objects in the reversed positions; each is perceived at the distance the normal-sized counterpart would have to be to project the observed pattern. The sensory pattern is interpreted as stemming from familiar objects at inverted distances rather than from the actual but unfamiliar objects at their true distances.

Or, again, rapidly exposed playing cards with reversed color-suit combinations (black hearts, red spades) will be distorted toward the familiar. The color or suit may be entirely misperceived as the expected one or, short of that, "compromised" with reality so that a black heart is seen as "purple" (Bruner and Postman, 1949).

Perhaps a more complex offshoot that may affect human relationships is the fact that people attribute some of the traits of familiar persons to strangers whose photographs resemble them ("parataxis"), whether or not they are aware of the connection. A recent review of studies in which subjects draw inferences from or interpret the photographs of others concluded that such generalization from the familiar is an important source of distortion:

In the perception of strangers or the perception of photographic representations of them, two conflicting pressures concerning parataxis exist. On the one hand, there is not much involvement in the contemporary interpersonal situation; thus little pressure toward parataxic distortion is produced. On the other hand, the relative ambiguity of the perceptual situation tends to force the perceiver to utilize his past experience in forming impressions. Perhaps the crucial factor tending to produce parataxic distortion in particular situations is the degree of similarity of physiognomic, behavioral, or situational cues concerning the stranger to those concerning some significant other [Secord, 1958, p. 308].

B8.2 Familiarity with various possible alternatives is not the only determinant of "likelihood"; expectations regarding what is likely in the specific situation are also involved.

For example, on rapid exposure, ambiguous words (e.g., "chack") are interpreted in line with experimentally induced expectations: "chick," when subjects are led to expect names of animals; "check," when expecting travel-related terms (Siipola, 1935).

So, too, expectations or stereotypes regarding what specific people will be like are important determinants of how their subsequent behavior will actually be interpreted, at least on first impressions. [The table, p. 271, top, shows] how student descriptions of the same instructor after the same class session varied, according to whether he had previously been described as "very warm" or "rather cold" in a brief written introduction.

B9 As the ambiguity of the stimulus increases and/or as the strength of motivation or subjective importance increases, people's interpretations will move in the "relevant" direction—that is, they will tend to see things as they want or need to see them.

For example, hungry subjects report more food objects in vague "pictures" (actually, just smudges) than do less hungry subjects [table, p. 271, bottom].

When the goal is positive, the distinction between want and need collapses; when one is hungry, food is both necessary and pleasant to find. However, when a negative or threatening object is involved, e.g., an enemy sniper or the sound of an airplane engine faltering over the ocean, detection may be necessary—but it is certainly not pleasant. Does interpretation in such cases lean toward what is needed or toward what is wanted? The relationship and relative strength of the two tendencies is not clearly established. Sometimes protection against recognition of the threat seems to be dominant, as in the perceptual-defense studies. At other times, vigilance predominates—as when anxious people see threat everywhere. One hypothesis is that if the threat can realistically be averted, vigilance is a normal reaction; whereas perceptual defense comes into play when nothing could be done, even if the threat were recognized. In any case, as a complex example, anti-Semites as well as Jews rate a larger percentage of photographs as Jewish than do people not so concerned with the issue, in either direction:

Two groups of S's, 118 Jewish and 194 non-Jewish, labeled a group of 100 photographs as Jewish and non-Jewish. In addition, each S selected 30 of the 100 that appeared to be the most Jewish-looking. The photographs included 30 Jews and, in the non-Jewish group, 30 Americans, 20 Northern Europeans and 20 Southern Europeans. Each subject was also administered the California F scale.

In both groups high F scores ["authoritarian," and "ethnocentric"] labeled more photographs as Jewish than low F scorers, but in neither group was there a significant difference in accuracy between high and low scorers. There was no significant relationship in either group between response bias and accuracy. With respect to between-group differences Jews were more accurate than non-

	COMPARISON OF "WARM" AND "COLD" OBSERVERS IN TERMS OF AVERAGE RATINGS GIVEN STIMULUS PERSONS		Average rating		Level of signifi-cance of warm-cold differ-ence	Asch's data (1946): per cent of group assigning quality at low end of our rating scale[*]	
Item	Low end of rating scale	High end of rating scale	Warm (N = 27)	Cold (N = 28)		Warm	Cold
1	Knows his stuff	Doesn't know his stuff	3.5	4.6			
2	Considerate of others	Self-centered	6.3	9.6	.01		
3 †	Informal	Formal	6.3	9.6	.01		
4 †	Modest	Proud	9.4	10.6			
5	Sociable	Unsociable	5.6	10.4	.01	91	38
6	Self-assured	Uncertain of himself	8.4	9.1			
7	High intelli-gence	Low intelli-gence	4.8	5.1			
8	Popular	Unpopular	4.0	7.4	.01	84	28
9 †	Good natured	Irritable	9.4	12.0	.05	94	17
10	Generous	Ungenerous	8.2	9.6		91	08
11	Humorous	Humorless	8.3	11.7	.01	77	13
12	Important	Insignificant	6.5	8.6		88	99
13 †	Humane	Ruthless	8.6	11.0	.05	86	31
14 †	Submissive	Dominant	13.2	14.5			
15	Will go far	Will not get ahead	4.2	5.8			

[*] Given for all qualities common to Asch's list and this set of rating scales.
† These scales were reversed when presented to the subjects.
Reprinted from H. H. Kelley, "The Warm-Cold Variable in First Impressions of Persons," *Journal of Personality*, XVIII (1950), by permission of the publisher.

MEAN NUMBER OF FOOD-RELATED RESPONSES PER SUBJECT OUT OF POSSIBLE FOUR-TEEN[*] FOR THREE DEGREES OF STRENGTH OF THE HUNGER DRIVE	Hours food depriva-tion	N	Average rated drive strength	σm	Strength of drive	Mean food related R's	σm	$P_{diff.}$ occurring by chance with	
								4-hour	16-hour
	1	44	3.30	.17	weak	2.14	.24	<.10	<.002
	4	24	2.02	.17	medium	2.88	.36		<.42
	16	40	1.90	.14	strong	3.22	.23		

[*] Counting three possible responses for the item which asked for three objects, any or all of which could be food-related.
Reprinted from D. C. McClelland and J. W. Atkinson, "The Projective Expression of Needs I: The Effects of Different Intensities of the Hunger Drive in Perception," *Journal of Psychology*, XXV (1948), by permission of the publisher.

Jews and manifested a tendency to label more photographs as Jewish [Scodel and Austrin, 1957, p. 280].

Another study correlated ethnic prejudice with the tendency to cling to "familiar" interpretations when the sensory evidence begins to depart from the familiar; if a series of pictures gradually moves from dog to cat, people prejudiced against minority groups are slower than others to recognize the change and to switch their identification to the latter. Thus, people who tend to hold rigid social stereotypes are also more apt than others to cling to "stereotypic" perception in the laboratory, suggesting that the two processes do, in fact, have something in common. The author speculates that

it may well turn out upon further evidence that intolerance of perceptual ambiguity is related to a broader psychological disturbance of which prejudice—itself often a deviation from the prevalent code, especially in school —is but another manifestation [Frenkel-Brunswik, 1949, p. 128].

JUDGMENT OF QUANTITY

A special case of perceptual interpretation is the judgment of quantities: How big? How bright? How far? Often such judgments are equivalent to interpreting *what* the object is—midget or giant, model or real. Usually, however, they are independent of the designation of objects, at least to some extent: the perceived color, brightness, size, distance, and speed of a car do not affect its essential identification. A great deal of investigation has been given this matter, as a special case of perceptual interpretation. As in the more general finding:

B10 Interpretations of quantities are affected by expectations and motives.

For example, with reference to *expectations,* if a small wooden block weighs

the same as a much large one, the weight of the smaller will be grossly overestimated when subjects are told the correct weight of the larger and allowed to lift them both—apparently by contrast with the expected lighter weight of the smaller. Among one hundred military officers, the average overestimate was 2.5 times the correct weight, and in some cases the error reached sevenfold. And the illusion persists even after subjects are allowed to weigh both blocks, and know that they are identical in weight (Crutchfield *et al.,* 1955).

The operation of *motivation* or subjective importance is illustrated by a classic study which found that children overestimate the sizes of coins as compared with discs of the same size, and poor children by more than wealthy children—presumably because of the greater value the coins have for the former.

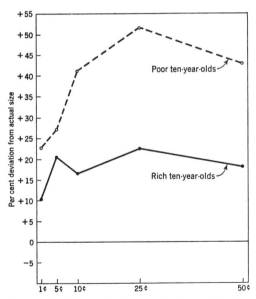

Size estimations of coins made by well-to-do and poor ten-year-olds (method of average error). Reprinted from J. S. Bruner and C. C. Goodman, "Value and Need as Organizing Factors in Perception," *Journal of Abnormal and Social Psychology,* Vol. 42, 1947, p. 40, by permission of the authors and publisher.

This interpretation gains support from a later experiment where overestimation of the size of poker chips was experimentally induced in children by making the chips redeemable for candy (Lambert *et al.*, 1949).

In addition to, and interacting with, these effects of expectations and motives, judgments are made in accordance with the general proposition that perception is determined by relationships rather than absolutes:

B11 Judgments of magnitude are made within a frame of reference established by the total range of relevant stimuli.

For example, when the total range of luminosity varies from x to $2x$, a stimulus at $2x$ will be considered white. When the total range goes from $2x$ to $4x$, $2x$ will be seen as black and $4x$ as white. The facts that a white shirt appears white under all degrees of illumination ("brightness constancy"), that receding telephone poles are recognized as the same height ("size constancy"), that a book appears rectangular regardless of the angle of vision ("shape constancy") —all of these are due not only to familiarity with the objects involved but also to this principle. In each case, not only the specific object but the others surrounding it vary accordingly, so that the *relationship* between them remains constant. The black suit as well as the white shirt reflects less light at night: the luminosity relationship, and thus perceived whiteness, remains constant.

B11.1 The characteristic(s) differentiating a clearly defined figure from surrounding figures or from the background tend to be accentuated ("contrast").

Which is to say that figures are judged partially by reference to their surroundings. The question of whether this constitutes distortion is definitional. For ex-

ample, all these heads are cut from the same gray paper.

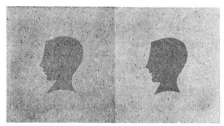

Reprinted from D. Krech and R. S. Crutchfield, *Elements of Psychology*, Knopf, 1958, p. 79, by permission of the authors.

Which of them represents the "real" appearance of this shade of gray? Cutting out the silhouette and holding it up "by itself" is no solution, since it will then also be against *some* background.

Again, the two center circles are the same size, though the surrounding circles suggest not, to our perception of them:

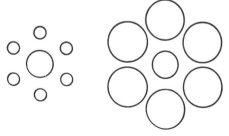

Contrast is thus the converse of assimilation, discussed above, in which differences within a figure are minimized. The relationship between the two processes is demonstrated in the following experiment.

A subject faces a blank wall that is differentially illuminated, gradually going from very bright to dim. It appears as a homogeneous, "average" brightness throughout (assimilation). If a very thin vertical line now separates the wall in two halves, one appears dark and the other light; each appears homogeneous within itself, but contrasts with the other. This shows the intimate relationship between organization (what will be perceived as "figure") and judgment (what characteristics will be attributed to the figure). In fact, the distinction between organization and interpretation or judgment, like many distinctions in this book, is one of convenience in analysis, and not one that can be rigorously maintained.

Experimentation with contrast and assimilation has been applied to behavior as complex as attitude formation. For example, information differing significantly from a stereotype tends either to be ignored or distorted to fit the stereotype (assimilation), or exaggerated and perceived as far more different than it really is (by contrast with the stereotype). As we shall see in a later chapter, differences in platform within a political party tend to be minimized by the partisan (assimilated), whereas differences between the party platforms are exaggerated (contrasted). So, also, if two people are perceived simultaneously, and both are liked but in unequal degrees, the difference tends to be leveled (assimilated). But if one is disliked and the other liked, both reactions become more extreme (contrast) (Peak, 1958).

Further, the comparison with "surrounding" characteristics can be temporal as well as spatial. An orange tastes sweet after a lemon but sour after sugar; a black silhouette (or negative after-image) appears before the eyes after exposure to a brilliant stimulus. Such contrasts are largely a matter of sensory adaptation: the sour receptors are relatively insensitive after heavy bombardment by the lemon, and the same is true for the sweet receptors after sugar. But more generally, and beyond the effects of purely sensory adaptation:

B11.2 People develop an "adaptation level" with respect to given stimulus magnitudes (e.g., temperature, light intensity, size of cars) based on the range of values that has been present in the relevant series.

That is, a stimulus will be judged in relation to the temporal series of which it is a recognized member; and values in the middle (not necessarily the arithmetic center or average) will appear to be "normal," "average," "neutral." Such values are said to be *at* adaptation level. Values that depart from the adaptation level produce one-sided experiences: they feel or appear hot, large, bright, and so on.

For example, a subject is asked to rate each of a series of unmarked weights as "heavy" or "light." The first few judgments appear to be arbitrary, but soon an adaptation level develops such that some actually feel heavy and others light. The point at which judgments divide is normally not the center of the range nor the average of the series. A series ranging from 200 to 400 grams, for example, divides at about 250 grams (recall Weber's Law). Adding new stimuli outside the previous range will shift the adaptation level and thus in turn will shift judgments of specific stimuli. A 300-gram weight that felt heavy in the original series becomes light when weights in the 600-gram range are added.

B11.3 Which stimuli become part of a series is partly a matter of organization, e.g., proximity, similarity, and so forth (as above), and partly a conceptual decision about the meaning attached to various stimuli through learning.

When an adaptation level has been established by a series of weights, as in the illustration just above, the surreptitious addition of another weight outside the series will shift it; but picking up an "irrelevant" object of equivalent weight (a tray, a cup of coffee) has no effect. This shows that something beyond sheer sensory adaptation is involved, since the muscles are subject to the same effects in either case.

The importance and implications of the notion of adaptation level rest on the fact that such judgments are not simply intellectual recognitions of relativity but matters of immediate perceptual experience. The weight *feels* heavy or light; cars *appear* large or small—but always depending on the rest of the series. The first warm day of spring feels much warmer than the first cool day of fall, though it may in fact be many degrees cooler, just as surely and directly as the heads on page 273 appear to be different shades of gray.

Thus, human perceptual judgments are inexorably under the control of the particular background brought to the judgment. Perceptually, as well as logically, there is no absolute correlate of any perceived magnitude. Even the distinction between black and white, which we normally take as the prototype of an absolute qualitative dichotomy, is perceptually a matter of degree. White immediately turns to black if and when the area surrounding it becomes more brilliantly illuminated—which is exactly how areas of black on a white movie screen are produced. Thus from the simplest sensory experiences, as we have seen, to the most complicated judgments of social norms and values, as we shall see, man responds relatively—by making comparisons that detect similarities and differences and little, perhaps nothing, more.

Finally, before leaving this section, we should say something about the question of how "realistic" perception is, given the observer's influences on interpretation. To what extent do the effects of learning and motives on interpretation "distort" perception?

With respect to learning, it is clear that these effects usually act to resolve stimulus ambiguity in a realistic way; in a normal environment, past experience ordinarily helps in the interpretation of the present. It is mainly when faced with "abnormal" (unusual or changing) stimulus conditions, as in illusions, that these learned assumptions produce erroneous interpretations.

Motives or subjective importance, however, may often "bend" interpretation, as when poor children overestimate the size of coins; there is no particular reason to expect a close match between what people need and/or want and the way the world actually is. But the distortion becomes pronounced only when stimulus ambiguity and/or motivation level is unusually high. The major effect of motives upon perception, under normal conditions, is through *what* will be seen—i.e., selection—rather than on *how* it will be seen—i.e., interpretation.

With regard to other than normal conditions, we conclude with two striking instances of human behavior, hypnosis and extrasensory perception. Both have been subjected to a good deal of scientific investigation. One has come through as well substantiated, the other is still controversial.

REFERENCES

BRUNER, JEROME S., AND LEO J. POSTMAN. "On the Perception of Incongruity: A Paradigm," *J. Pers.*, 18, 1949, pp. 206-23.

CRUTCHFIELD, RICHARD S., D. G. WOODWORTH, AND R. A. ALBRECHT. *Perceptual Per-*

formance and the Effective Person. U.S. Air Force Personnel and Training Research Center, 1955.

DITCHBURN, R. W., D. H. FENDER, AND STELLA MAYNE. "Vision with Controlled Movements of the Retinal Image," *J. Physiol.*, 145, 1959, pp. 98–107.

FRENKEL-BRUNSWIK, ELSE. "Intolerance of Ambiguity as an Educational and Perceptual Personality Variable," *J. Pers.*, 18, 1949, pp. 108–43.

HERON, WOODBURN. "Cognitive and Physiological Effects of Perceptual Isolation," in Philip Solomon *et al.*, eds., *Sensory Deprivation*, a symposium at the Harvard Medical School. Harvard U. Press, 1961, pp. 6–33.

HESS, ECKHARD H. Personal communication, 1963.

HILGARD, ERNEST R. *Introduction to Psychology.* 3rd ed. Harcourt, Brace & World, 1962.

KRECH, DAVID, AND RICHARD S. CRUTCHFIELD. *Elements of Psychology.* Knopf, 1958.

LAMBERT, W. W., R. L. SOLOMON, AND P. D. WATSON. "Reinforcement and Extinction as Factors in Size Estimation," *J. Exper. Psychol.*, 39, 1949, pp. 637–41.

LAZARUS, RICHARD S., AND ROBERT A. MC CLEARY. "Autonomic Discrimination Without Awareness: A Study of Subception," *Psychol. Rev.*, 58, 1951, pp. 113–22.

MC CONNELL, JAMES V., RICHARD L. CUTLER, AND ELTON B. MC NEIL. "Subliminal Stimulation: An Overview." *Amer. Psychologist*, 13, 1958, pp. 229–42.

OSBORNE, M. F. "Brownian Motion in the Stock Market," *Operations Research*, 7, 1959, pp. 145–73.

PEAK, HELEN. "Psychological Structure and Psychological Activity," *Psychol. Rev.*, 65, 1958, pp. 325–47.

SCODEL, ALVIN, AND HARVEY AUSTRIN. "The Perception of Jewish Photographs by Non-Jews and Jews," *J. Abnorm. Soc. Psychol.*, 54, 1957, pp. 278–80.

SECORD, PAUL F. "Facial Features and Inference Processes in Interpersonal Perception," in Renato Tagiuri and Luigi Petrullo, eds., *Person Perception and Interpersonal Behavior.* Stanford U. Press, 1958, pp. 300–315.

SMITH, DONALD E., AND JULIAN E. HOCHBERG. "The Effect of 'Punishment' (Electric Shock) on Figure-Ground Perception," *J. Psychol.*, 38, 1954, pp. 83–87.

STEVENS, S. S. "The Surprising Simplicity of Sensory Matrics," *Amer. Psychologist*, 17, 1962, pp. 29–39.

STIGLER, GEORGE J. "The Development of Utility Theory, II," *J. Political Economy*, 58, 1950, p. 373.

WEBB, EUGENE. "Weber's Law and Consumer Prices," *Amer. Psychologist*, 63, 1961, p. 450.

WERTHEIMER, MICHAEL. "Principles of Perceptual Organization," in David C. Beardslee and Michael Wertheimer, eds., *Readings in Perception.* Van Nostrand, 1958, pp. 115–35.

YOSHIOKA, J. G. "Weber's Law in the Discrimination of Maze Distance by the White Rat," *U. of California Publications in Psychology*, 4, 1929, pp. 155–84.

32 | COGNITION IN CHILDHOOD

JEAN PIAGET AS INTERPRETED BY

ALFRED L. BALDWIN

One of the most creative and productive investigators of children's thinking is the French psychologist Jean Piaget, the understanding of whom in this country has been handicapped by difficulties in translation. The selection by the distinguished Cornell University professor Alfred Baldwin is more an independent interpretation than a translation. It is partly Piaget, partly Baldwin. These experiments Baldwin describes may be duplicated very easily. The reader is encouraged to

try them on some infants and young children, and, while doing so,
to keep in mind the genius of Piaget in observing, reporting,
and generalizing, in bringing order to what was a chaotic semblance
of impressions and anecdotes, and in discovering for mankind how some
of our thinking sequences develop during infancy and childhood.

The Development of Cognition of Space

Before we can truly say that a cognitive representation of the external world exists, the child must demonstrate certain behavioral signs of cognition. First, the object must be cognized as a permanent object that exists outside the child and that continues to exist even when the child does not perceive it. Secondly, the child must distinguish between properties of the object and its spatial relations. Properties such as size, weight, color, etc., are unchanged when the object is moved around, whereas its spatial position is changed by movements. The independence of these two kinds of properties is required for the object to have permanence. Thirdly, the child must have some knowledge of movements in space. It is very important for him to know that locomotions in space and also turning movements of an object around an axis are reversible, and that any movement can be reversed. Also, he must recognize that, to find an object, he does not need to take the same path it did to reach its present location. If the location is known, any path to that point will locate the object.

Fourthly, the various senses—vision, touch, etc.—must be integrated so that they give the person information about a single external world. Fifthly, the child must have recognized that objects and movements occur outside of himself, and he must distinguish between the movements in the external world, which he

observes, and his own movements, which are adapted to the world. It is obvious, as soon as we think of it, that it must not be easy for the child to distinguish between the actions that have external effects, such as hitting, moving, etc., and the actions that have no effect, such as looking or listening. Lastly, and this may be the same as the fourth, the child must have some cognition of himself in this space that he cognizes. He must be one of the objects in his cognitive map.

Piaget has described the stages in the infant's development of cognition of the external world and has described the parallel developments of cognition and goal-directed behavior.

STAGES 1 AND 2 | During the first two stages of infancy, which correspond to the period before the child is able to reach for a visually perceived object, none of these criteria for a cognitive map is met. The permanence of perceived objects is best investigated by studying the child's reaction to the disappearance of an object. During this period the child does not search for an object that is gone, nor does he anticipate where it might have gone. At best, he continues to feel or look at the place where it disappeared —*i.e.*, he continues doing what he was doing at the time it disappeared. During this period, there is some integration of the senses. The child learns to look at an object that is making a noise; he can tie together tactual sensations from the hand, kinaesthetic sensations from limbs, and tactual sensations from the mouth. He can put what he touches into his mouth and suck it.

This is not yet space or object perception, but it is the beginning of them.

When the same object is involved in two different schemata, or behavior patterns, so that it is touched by the hands and also sucked, the child gets two sources of information about it. Gradually this recognition that something fits into all the various schemata leads to its being unified into an object, but this does not happen for some time.

STAGE 3 | Moving on now to stage 3, corresponding to the period between the acquisition of visual motor prehension and the ability to engage in goal-directed means-end behavior, we find that the various senses are much better integrated than before. This is one of the characteristics signified by visually guided reaching for an object. This same behavior also puts the child in the position to observe the relationship between two objects rather than merely the relation of an object to his own actions.

Secondary circular reactions imply the same thing. The child produces a causal sequence in the external world and is able to reproduce it. This attracts his attention to the external events and makes him more sensitive to them. Secondary circular reactions are also part of stage 3 of infancy.

The child in stage 3 still does not search for an object that has disappeared, but he does show some behavior patterns which indicate that he is beginning to conceive of an external object. Piaget describes Jacqueline's behavior when she holds an object that is slowly pulled away from her. If this process causes the hand to follow the movement of the object, then when she finally loses contact with it, she may continue groping along the trajectory she has already begun. If, however, the object is jerked away rapidly or made to disappear by screening it, there is no search for it. Similarly, the eyes may follow a falling object in the first part of its fall. If this movement

is begun, then when the child loses sight of it, he continues the downward movement of the eyes and eventually may rediscover the fallen object. This depends, however, according to Piaget, upon the eye movement's or the hand movement's having been initiated by the moving object. The searching is merely an extension of the activity that was going on at the time the object disappeared.

The child also shows an advance in another respect. If the object is not hidden completely by a screen, but is left so that a tiny portion protrudes, the child can at this stage recognize it and retrieve the partially hidden object. When it disappears completely, however, it is not recovered. It is not that the child's search fails; he does not even miss the object, as the following striking observation shows (Piaget, 1954):

At the age of 6 months and 19 days, Laurent was whimpering and fussing because it was just before a meal. When Piaget showed him his bottle, Laurent immediately began to cry lustily. Now Piaget repeatedly hid the bottle, either under a table or behind his hand. As soon as the bottle was out of sight, Laurent stopped crying; as soon as it reappeared he began to cry once more. Each time there was calm as long as the bottle could not be seen. After he had been teased this way several times, Laurent became very angry. His anger was in a sense a response to the frustration even though his motive to have the bottle disappeared when the bottle was invisible. If he had in any way cognized the bottle under the table, his behavior would have been quite different, as illustrated by the effect of making only part of the bottle disappear. When Piaget partly covered the bottle, Laurent's cries remained strong; if anything, they increased in strength.

Further observations show clearly the

peculiar situation that exists in the child's cognition at this time. Laurent is unable to turn the bottle around if the nipple is invisible. As long as the nipple can be seen, he is quite capable of rotating it to get the nipple to his mouth, but if he sees only the bottom of the bottle, he does not turn it around but tries to suck from the bottom. Similarly, he recognizes the bottle no matter which part of it protrudes from under the cloth; it does not need to be the nipple in order to set off the crying. Thus, Laurent recognizes that the bottle is to suck and he wants it. If the nipple is visible at all, he recognizes that it is there and he must suck; but, if the nipple cannot be seen, he then sucks the bottom as though he does not recognize that the bottle has a nipple or that a nipple is necessary for effective sucking.

STAGE 4; SEARCH FOR ABSENT OBJECTS | As well as failing to attribute permanence to objects, the infant in stage 3 does not recognize the paths an object may follow. He acts as though the only movement an object could make is in the direction of the child's movement at the time it disappeared. In stage 4 we observe true searching behavior when an object disappears. This corresponds to the period when the child puts two behavior patterns together in a means-end relationship. At this time the child's search for a vanished object is, in a sense, halfway to a full understanding of disappearing objects.

The procedure in one of Piaget's observations can be described as follows: The object is hidden at point a—i.e., it is put out of sight at that point but the action is visible to the child. The child then searches for it at a and finds it. Now the object is hidden at point b before the child's eyes. Although the child has continued to watch the object and has seen it disappear at b, he immedi-ately looks for it at point a (Piaget, 1954).

At 0:10(3) Jacqueline looks at the parrot on her lap (a toy parrot). I place my hand on the object; she raises it and grasps the parrot. I take it away from her and before her eyes, I move it away very slowly and put it under a rug 40 centimeters away. Meanwhile, I place my hand on her lap again. As soon as Jacqueline ceases to see the parrot, she looks at her lap, lifts my hand and hunts beneath it. The reaction is the same during three sequential attempts.

Here we see a conflict between repeating the behavior that was previously successful and searching for the toy where it was last seen.

STAGE 5 | In the next stage this conflict is resolved. The child attributes permanence to the object, which means that he looks for it at the place where it last disappeared rather than at places where it has previously been found. We must recognize that looking in the customary place for an object is well-adjusted behavior, if one has not observed it put somewhere else.

Along with the achievement of true searching behavior we find that the child's understanding of possible movements of the object is much enlarged. At this time the child can do such things as throwing an object in back of him in one direction and turning around in the other direction to look for it. He can follow the trajectory of an object and look for it where it probably came to rest. Part of the information for such an adjustment may come from one sense modality and part from another; there is an integration of the various modalities.

The Appearance of True Cognition

This is not the end of development during infancy. The final step, according to Piaget, is stage 6, marked by the achievement of a cognition that contains representations of absent objects, events that no longer exist, events that represent possibilities but were never observed, or events that would produce desired effects if they were carried out. In other words, the child is capable of memory, of imagination, of pretending, of hypothesizing about an unknown event, of planning events and foreseeing effects. This cognition takes place only at the level of action and only under simple circumstances, but it nevertheless represents quite an achievement.

Let us look at the evidence for these statements about children in the sixth stage of infancy, which usually occurs close to the age of eighteen months.

DEFERRED IMITATION | How can we find evidence for the cognitive picturing of past events? This implies more than recognizing familiar objects, more than profiting by past experience, more than repeating a past action to produce the same effect. One type of evidence for the cognitive picture of a past event is the existence of deferred imitation. If the child can imitate a model after the model is no longer present, Piaget argues that the guidance for the behavior must come from a cognitive picture, a mental image of the model.

PRETENDING | Pretending appears for the first time in this same period of childhood. The play behavior that occurs earlier in infancy consists of repeating schemata or behavior patterns after they have been mastered, because such patterns are interesting or fun. When the schema is repeated in an inappropriate context but with the recognition that it is inappropriate, then pretending has occurred. For example, Jacqueline had a ritual about going to sleep. It was a schema that was evoked by the situation of going to bed. In stage 6, Jacqueline performed this going-to-sleep ritual in a

play situation when she was not going to sleep. That it was not merely a mistake was indicated by the fact that she did it in a playful way, having fun with her pretense. To pretend implies a cognitive representation of a pattern that is copied outside of situations where it is recognized to be appropriate.

RECONSTRUCTION OF AN INVISIBLE EVENT | A third line of evidence of the development of cognition in this period of life is the child's ability to conceive of a movement that was unobservable but that might have happened. For example, Piaget tried the following experiment when Jacqueline was eighteen months and sixteen days old: First, he put a ring in his hand and showed it to her. Then he closed his hand upon it. She opened his hand to find the object with a great deal of enjoyment.

Now, he placed the ring in his left hand, pressed his left hand against his right hand and extended both closed hands to Jacqueline. She searched in his left hand, did not find the ring, and said, "Ring, ring, where is it?"

On the next trial, however, and thereafter, she was not content to look in the hand where the ring had been hidden. She looked there first, but then looked in the other hand to find the ring. Now Piaget put the ring in his hand and then his hand into a beret lying on the table. Then he took his closed hand out of the beret. It took Jacqueline a number of trials to discover the possibility that the ring was left in the beret rather than kept in the hand. Later, she performed much more complicated searches when the closed hand was put under several different objects so that there were a number of possible locations of the hidden object.

INSIGHTFUL PROBLEM SOLVING | Finally, let us examine the problem solving that becomes possible once the child is able to picture cognitively nonexistent happenings. The result is an insightful solution to problems without having to try out every possible action to see what its consequence will be.

The following observations show how Laurent at stage 6 discovered how to use a stick as a tool for retrieving objects (Piaget, 1952). The history of Laurent's eventual insight into the use of a stick as a tool goes back to the beginning of stage 3. At that age he sometimes shook the stick, sometimes rubbed it against the side of his crib, and once he accidentally hit a suspended toy with it. He immediately repeated the action, but despite all Piaget's efforts, Laurent could not learn that schema consistently. Later he could use a stick to hit objects, but during stages 4 and 5 he never used the stick as a tool to pull something toward him or to push it away. Jacqueline and Lucienne learned to use the stick as a tool during stage 5, but Laurent did not do so. He hit aimlessly with it and pushed it around with his finger, but did not use it as a tool.

At the age of 12 months, 5 days, Laurent was amusing himself with a small cane. He was obviously much surprised to observe the relationship between movements of one end of the cane and movements of the other end. He moved the cane in various directions, letting the free end drag and watching its movements intently. Still, however, he did not use the stick as a tool.

When he was 14 months, 25 days, he had mastered other relations which are at the same level of difficulty but still could not solve stick problems. Finally, when he was 16 months, 5 days old, Piaget placed a crust of bread in front of him but out of his reach. To the right, Piaget placed a stick. Laurent, who was seated at a table, first tried to reach the bread directly. Then Piaget placed the stick directly in front of him, but not so that it touched the bread. Laurent again

looked at the bread, then at the stick, then seized the stick and guided it toward the bread. Unfortunately he had picked it up near the middle so that it was too short to reach the object. He put it down again and tried fruitlessly to reach the bread directly. Then he picked up the stick by one end—we cannot know whether it was by intention or by accident—and drew the bread toward him by the stick. At first he merely touched the bread, then pushed it to the right, and finally drew it in.

CONCEPTUAL THINKING
IN THE PRESCHOOL PERIOD

A review of the characteristics of stage 6 in infancy might lead us to believe that the infant has little farther to go. He is able to solve problems through mental experimentation without the necessity for actually discovering solutions through trial-and-error procedures. He is able to recognize objects when he sees them from different points of view; he is able to perceive the relationships among external objects, such as the relation between an object and its support. . . .

But this is true only under very limited conditions. The preschool child, despite the fact that he is past stage 6, does not show all the characteristics of maturity. The following characteristics mark a preschool child's behavior as being less mature than an older child's.

Egocentrism with Respect to Remote Objects

Although the preschool child can respond to objects outside of his immediate environment and can even copy models whose presence is not communicated by cues, the range of objects to which he can respond is still relatively limited. While he can recognize in behavioral terms the different aspects of objects, so that each object has an individual identity, he does not show the same recognition of distant objects.

We have seen that the infant nearing the age of two can recognize his bottle or a toy even when he sees it from a variety of angles. This ability seems to depend upon two conditions: first, the object must not be very remote; secondly, it must have been observed in a variety of situations in which its identity has been confirmed by actual manipulation. The baby has turned the toy around and discovered quite directly that the same toy looks different from different angles.

When this same problem is presented in more abstract terms, as when Piaget (1948) asked children whether a mountain would look different from a different point of view, he found that children of four and five years had no appreciation of the fact that the mountain would look different from the opposite side. The mountain is much more remote than the bottle or toy and it cannot be quickly turned around, so its different aspects are not easily revealed. In order to apply to the problem of the mountain the principles implicit in turning a toy around to see the other side, the principles themselves need to be explicitly recognized and abstracted from any specific concrete situation.

Representation Limited to Concrete Objects

Three beads are strung on a wire that is fastened at both ends and mounted on a board that can be lifted and moved around. The wire goes through a tube, or tunnel, so that when the beads are moved from one end to the other they can all be hidden by the tube. The beads have been placed on the wire in the following order: red, yellow, and blue. They are all moved into the tube and the child is asked to draw a picture of them as they would look in the tube. This is to reinforce his memory of the order of the colors. Then he is asked which color will be the first to come out of the tube if the

beads are pushed on through the tube, emerging at the other end. Nearly all preschool children are able to make the correct prediction.

Then the beads are pushed back in the tube and the child is asked in what order they will come out if they are pushed back through the tube so they emerge from the same end from which they entered. It is more difficult for the child to recognize the fact that they will come out in the opposite order. Piaget reports that children of less than four years are unable to solve this problem.

If the child solves this second problem correctly, the experiment is repeated after the entire board on which the wire is strung is turned through a 180° angle while the beads are in the tube. Then the child is asked in what order they will emerge if they are pushed out of the tube in either direction. Some of the children are unable to solve this problem. A child may feel that since the red one came out first on the first trial and the blue one on the second, now it is the yellow one's turn to come out first.

Even if the child can predict correctly the result of one reversal, he may be unable to generalize. If he answers the third problem correctly, then the board is reversed more and more times, one half turn, one full turn, one and one-half turns, and so on. Finally the child is asked which would come out first if the board were turned around thirteen times. The difficulty in imagining the result of many turns demonstrates the limitations of the child's mental representations. In order to obtain the correct prediction for large numbers of reversals, it is necessary to appreciate in some way that any number of full turns is equivalent to no turn at all, and that any odd number of half turns is equivalent to one half turn. Thus, there has to be some representation of the abstraction, *any number of full turns.* This conceptual ability, according to

Piaget's results, occurs only after the beginning of school age.

Logical Thinking in the Preschool Period

One question concerning the thinking of children that has been answered differently by different psychologists is whether the child is pre-logical in his thinking or is logical enough in his reasoning but is so hampered by his lack of information that his logical thinking frequently results in the incorrect answer.

In order to understand this question we must look first at some of the properties of logical thinking. It is quite possible for logical thinking to be inaccurate and for illogical thinking to result in an accurate conclusion. It is, for example, completely logical to conclude that because all laboring men are Democrats, because Democrats vote for the Democratic candidate, and because there are enough laborers to hold the balance of power, therefore, the Democratic candidate will be elected. The trouble with such a conclusion is not that it is illogical but that the premises are inaccurate. On the other hand, it is illogical to reason that: a brick falls to the ground; a brick is an object; a piece of iron is an object; therefore, a piece of iron will fall to the ground. The accuracy of the conclusion does not mean that the reasoning is logical.

COGNITION OF A CLASS OF EVENTS | Let us look at a very simple example of child's thinking. At the age of thirty months Jacqueline and her father went on a walk each day to look at some slugs (worms) that were of great interest to her. Piaget asked Jacqueline one morning whether or not they would see a slug today. She answered, "Yes, because it is not sunny." The next morning she responded to the same question with, "No, because it's sunny." Slugs, like

angleworms, actually do appear more frequently on cloudy days or after a rain. These answers of Jacqueline's could be arrived at by a very logical procedure. We see slugs on all cloudy days; today is cloudy; therefore, we shall see slugs today. In order for her to follow this line of reasoning, she must in some way be able to recognize the fact that this cloudy day is a member of a "class" that includes all cloudy days.

Now, it is not necessary for her answer to have been arrived at through a recognition of class membership that requires that the individual be able to conceive of a class containing a number of separate events. If we look back to the experiment of Watson that showed how Albert, a child of eleven months, learned to fear furry objects, we recall that the experimenter made a loud noise that frightened the baby at the moment when he was shown a white rabbit. After a few such experiences Albert showed fear of rats, rabbits, even white pieces of fur. We are justified in saying that the similarity of the various objects was sufficient for them all to evoke the same response. It was not necessary for Albert to conceive of "the class of white furry objects," in order to respond as he did.

Jacqueline might have been expecting slugs in much the same way that Albert was afraid of white objects—because of the similarity between this cloudy day and the other days on which slugs were found. Even so, considerably more maturity is required than was necessary for Albert's behavior. One way we might check, therefore, upon whether Jacqueline was reasoning logically or responding on the basis of mere similarity would be to study her response to a class of objects that are not all alike.

COMPARISON OF WHOLE AND PART | Piaget (1952) reports an experiment, not on Jacqueline, which shows some of the problems that arise when children are asked to consider the relationship between the members of a class and the class as a whole. He places about twenty beads in a box. Each bead is a wooden one and the subject agrees that they are "all made of wood." Most of these beads are brown, but a few of them are colored white. In terms of classes there is a class of "wooden beads" that includes all of the beads. The members of this class are not all alike, but are in turn divided into two classes, brown beads and white beads. Now the child is asked, "In this box which are there more of, brown beads or wooden beads?" Up to the age of seven, according to Piaget's results, the children nearly always say that there are more brown ones than wooden ones. Why? "Because there are only two or three white ones." Piaget then questions the child further, along the following lines: "Are all the brown ones made of wood?"—"Yes"—"If I take away all the wooden ones will there be any left?"— "No, because they are all made of wood."—"If I take away all the brown ones, will there be any left?"—"Yes, the white ones." Then the original question is asked again, "Which are there more of, the brown beads or the wooden ones?" Again the answer, "The brown ones—because there are so few white ones."

Piaget explains this curious behavior by saying that the child is unable to consider simultaneously the brownness that distinguishes the two colors and the woodenness that constitutes the basis for the whole class. When the child focuses on one of the subclasses, the brown beads, he cannot simultaneously compare it with the whole class, wooden beads, which includes the subclass itself.

A similar problem arises when preschool children must recognize that they can be in a city and at the same time in the state in which the city is located. Such statements as, "We are *not* in Wichita, we are in Kansas," are very commonly heard from preschool children. Then, if the child is informed that he can be in Wichita and at the same time in Kansas because Wichita is a city in Kansas, the next time the argument may be, "We are not in Kansas, we are in Wichita." Somehow, the idea of being included in a class that is in turn a part of a bigger class demands a double reference and a shifting frame of reference that is hard for the child to understand.

In some case it is quite clear that the child considers the members of a class to be all the same object. When Jacqueline went for a walk before the one described above, she was looking for slugs, but actually she was looking for "the slug." "There it is" she cried when she spied one. Then when she came upon another about ten yards up the road she said, "There's the slug again." Her father asked her if it wasn't another one. They went back to look at the first one. "Is it the same one?"—"Yes."— "Another slug?"—"Yes."—"Another or the same?" The question meant nothing to Jacqueline.

FOCUS ON ONE ASPECT OF A PROBLEM | We have seen in the experiment with wooden beads the difficulty that the child gets into because he tends to focus upon only one aspect of a situation. This effect can be further seen in the following episode that occurred in a school for six- and seven-year-olds:

The children were "going to have a wedding" and there was much talk as to whether Priscilla would marry Frank or Dan, who are the two rivals for her affection.—Frank said, "You can't marry Dan, because daddy must be bigger than mommy." They argue about this and appealed to Mrs. I. as to whether "daddies are always bigger than mommies," She said, "Well, let's ask everyone about it," and we asked each child in turn whether his mommy or his daddy was the bigger. The others all agreed that "daddies *must* be bigger than mommies." Dan then said, stamping his foot, "Yes, you see, I *shall* be bigger than Priscilla."

Here the logic should proceed from the premise, men are bigger than their wives, to the minor premise, Dan is not bigger than Priscilla, to the conclusion, Dan cannot marry Priscilla. Dan was, however, centered upon what he wanted in the situation; so for him the reasoning—if it was reasoning at all—went, I shall marry Priscilla, men are bigger than their wives, so I shall be bigger than Priscilla. . . . One might well argue that Dan's reasoning about his marrying Priscilla was not defective in logical structure, but reflected merely that Dan made his major premise that he would marry Priscilla. Given that assumption, his logic was faultless. . . .

The problem, then, is to account for the sort of errors that the child does make, and also to account for the fact that he makes no errors in many situations that require reasoning. The distortion in these errors can be seen to derive from the child's being bound to some aspect of the situation that is immediate and that frequently is of great interest. Dan wanted to marry Priscilla; this motivation distorted the whole structure of the situation. The more mature person would have seen the entire structure, including the major premise, in the objective properties of the situation, regardless of his motivation. His perception of the real world would enable him to withstand the pressure of the motivation that focused his attention on the goal.

The lack of motivational focus is shown in the example of the reasoning about shaving. Jacqueline was here disinterested, and, furthermore, it seems likely that she was anticipating the act of shaving without any especial logic. The reasoning that would have been necessary to deduce shaving would have, in fact, been incorrect. Father does not always shave every time he draws water into the basin.

Whether, aside from the distortion due to focusing on one aspect of a situation, the thinking of the child is logical depends upon just what is meant by logical. It is certainly as logical as many an adult's decisions in which he does not explicitly reason from premise to conclusion. When the child is asked to reason explicitly under controlled conditions he seems unable, at this age, to do so. The story of the brown and white beads illustrates this point. Explicit reasoning demands the cognitive representation of the abstract principles of logic, divorced of any specific content. If this be accepted, then the child at this level of maturity cannot reason. If, however, the correct prediction of results in a concrete situation, which might have been arrived at by logical deduction, is a reasoning process, then the child does reason, and does it quite frequently.

33 | THE COURSE OF COGNITIVE GROWTH

JEROME S. BRUNER[1]

How do children think? What thinking processes can be identified for various age groups, and how are these processes related to the use of language and tools? Our fragmentary knowledge of the development of cognition shows that in order to develop, human beings require external stimuli just as much as do animals. These intriguing experiments suggest the awkward, painful struggle to understand man's unique capacity to think.

I shall take the view in what follows that the development of human intellectual functioning from infancy to such perfection as it may reach is shaped by a series of technological advances in the use of mind. Growth depends upon the mastery of techniques and cannot be understood without reference to such mastery. These techniques are not, in the main, inventions of the individuals who are "growing up"; they are, rather, skills transmitted with varying efficiency and success by the culture—language being a prime example. Cognitive growth, then, is in a major way from the outside in as well as from the inside out.

Two matters will concern us. The first has to do with the techniques or technologies that aid growing human beings to represent in a manageable way the recurrent features of the complex environments in which they live. It is fruitful, I think, to distinguish three systems of processing information by which human beings construct models of their world: through action, through imagery, and through language. A second concern is with integration, the means whereby acts are organized into higher-order ensembles, making possible the use of larger and larger units of information for the solution of particular problems.

Let me first elucidate these two theoretical matters, and then turn to an examination of the research upon which they are based, much of it from the Center for Cognitive Studies at Harvard.

On the occasion of the One Hundredth

[1] The assistance of R. R. Olver and Mrs. Blythe Clinchy in the preparation of this paper is gratefully acknowledged.

Excerpts reprinted from *The American Psychologist*, XVIV (January, 1964), 1–15, by permission of the American Psychological Association and the author.

Anniversary of the publication of Darwin's *The Origin of Species*, Washburn and Howell (1960) presented a paper at the Chicago Centennial celebration containing the following passage:

It would now appear . . . that the large size of the brain of certain hominids was a relatively late development and that the brain evolved due to new selection pressures *after* bipedalism and consequent upon the use of tools. The tool-using, ground-living, hunting way of life created the large human brain rather than a large brained man discovering certain new ways of life. [We] believe this conclusion is the most important result of the recent fossil hominid discoveries and is one which carries far-reaching implications for the interpretation of human behavior and its origins. . . . The important point is that size of brain, insofar as it can be measured by cranial capacity, has increased some threefold subsequent to the use and manufacture of implements. . . . The uniqueness of modern man is seen as the result of a technical-social life which tripled the size of the brain, reduced the face, and modified many other structures of the body [p. 49 f.].

This implies that the principal change in man over a long period of years—perhaps 500,000 thousand—has been alloplastic rather than autoplastic. That is to say, he has changed by linking himself with new, external implementation systems rather than by any conspicuous change in morphology—"evolution-by-prosthesis," as Weston La Barre (1954) puts it. The implement systems seem to have been of three general kinds—*amplifiers of human motor capacities* ranging from the cutting tool through the lever and wheel to the wide variety of modern devices; *amplifiers of sensory capacities* that include primitive devices such as smoke signaling and modern ones such as magnification and radar sensing, but also likely to include such "software" as those conventionalized perceptual shortcuts that can be applied to the redundant sensory environment; and finally *amplifiers of human ratiocinative capacities* of infinite variety ranging from language systems to myth and theory and explanation. All of these forms of amplification are in major or minor degree conventionalized and transmitted by the culture, the last of them probably the most since ratiocinative amplifiers involve symbol systems governed by rules that must, for effective use, be shared.

Any implement system, to be effective, must produce an appropriate internal counterpart, an appropriate skill necessary for organizing sensorimotor acts, for organizing percepts, and for organizing our thoughts in a way that matches them to the requirements of implement systems. These internal skills, represented genetically as capacities, are slowly selected in evolution. In the deepest sense, then, man can be described as a species that has become specialized by the use of technological implements. His selection and survival have depended upon a morphology and set of capacities that could be linked with the alloplastic devices that have made his later evolution possible. We move, perceive, and think in a fashion that depends upon techniques rather than upon wired-in arrangements in our nervous system.

Where representation of the environment is concerned, it too depends upon techniques that are learned—and these are precisely the techniques that serve to amplify our motor acts, our perceptions, and our ratiocinative activities.

As for integration, it is a truism that there are very few single or simple adult acts that cannot be performed by a young child. In short, any more highly skilled activity can be decomposed into simpler components, each of which can be carried out by a less skilled operator.

What higher skills require is that the component operations be combined. Maturation consists of an orchestration of these components into an integrated sequence. The "distractability," so-called, of much early behavior may reflect each act's lack of imbeddedness in what Miller, Galanter, and Pribram (1960) speak of as "plans." These integrated plans, in turn, reflect the routines and subroutines that one learns in the course of mastering the patterned nature of a social environment. So that integration, too, depends upon patterns that come from the outside in—an internalization of what Roger Barker (1963) has called environmental "behavior settings."

If we are to benefit from contact with recurrent regularities in the environment, we must represent them in some manner. To dismiss this problem as "mere memory" is to misunderstand it. For the most important thing about memory is not storage of past experience, but rather the retrieval of what is relevant in some usable form. This depends upon how past experience is coded and processed so that it may indeed be relevant and usable in the present when needed. The end product of such a system of coding and processing is what we may speak of as a representation.

MODES OF REPRESENTATION

I shall call the three modes of representation mentioned earlier enactive representation, iconic representation, and symbolic representation. Their appearance in the life of the child is in that order, each depending upon the previous one for its development, yet all of them remaining more or less intact throughout life—barring such early accidents as blindness or deafness or cortical injury. By enactive representation I mean a mode of representing past events through appropriate motor response. We cannot, for example, give an adequate description of familiar sidewalks or floors over which we habitually walk, nor do we have much of an image of what they are like. Yet we get about them without tripping or even looking much. Such segments of our environment—bicycle riding, tying knots, aspects of driving—get represented in our muscles, so to speak. Iconic representation summarizes events by the selective organization of percepts and of images, by the spatial, temporal, and qualitative structures of the perceptual field and their transformed images. Images "stand for" perceptual events in the close but conventionally selective way that a picture stands for the object pictured. Finally, a symbol system represents things by design features that include remoteness and arbitrariness. A word neither points directly to its referent here and now, nor does it resemble it as a picture. The lexeme "Philadelphia" looks no more like the city so designated than does a nonsense syllable. The other property of language that is crucial is its productiveness in combination, far beyond what can be done with images or acts. "Philadelphia is a lavender sachet in Grandmother's linen closet," or $(x + 2)^2 = x^2 + 4x + 4 = x\,(x + 4) + 4$.

An example or two of enactive representation underlines its importance in infancy and in disturbed functioning, while illustrating its limitations. Piaget (1954) provides us with an observation from the closing weeks of the first year of life. The child is playing with a rattle in his crib. The rattle drops over the side. The child moves his clenched hand before his face, opens it, looks for the rattle. Not finding it there, he moves his hand, closed again, back to the edge of the crib, shakes it with movements like those he uses in shaking the rattle. Thereupon he moves his closed hand back toward his face, opens it, and looks. Again

no rattle; and so he tries again. In several months, the child has benefited from experience to the degree that the rattle and action become separated. Whereas earlier he would not show signs of missing the rattle when it was removed unless he had begun reaching for it, now he cries and searches when the rattle is presented for a moment and hidden by a cover. He no longer repeats a movement to restore the rattle. In place of representation by action alone—where "existence" is defined by the compass of present action—it is now defined by an image that persists autonomously.

A second example is provided by the results of injury to the occipital and temporal cortex in man (Hanfmann, Rickers-Ovsiankina, & Goldstein, 1944). A patient is presented with a hard-boiled egg intact in its shell, and asked what it is. Holding it in his hand, he is embarrassed, for he cannot name it. He makes a motion as if to throw it and halts himself. Then he brings it to his mouth as if to bite it and stops before he gets there. He brings it to his ear and shakes it gently. He is puzzled. The experimenter takes the egg from him and cracks it on the table, handing it back. The patient then begins to peel the egg and announces what it is. He cannot identify objects without reference to the action he directs toward them.

The disadvantages of such a system are illustrated by Emerson's (1931) experiment in which children are told to place a ring on a board with seven rows and six columns of pegs, copying the position of a ring put on an identical board by the experimenter. Children ranging from 3 to 12 were examined in this experiment and in an extension of it carried out by Werner (1948). The child's board could be placed in various positions relative to the experimenter's: right next to it, 90 degrees rotated away from it, 180 degrees rotated, placed face to face with it so that the child has to turn full around to make his placement, etc. The older the child, the better his performance. But the younger children could do about as well as the oldest so long as they did not have to change their own position vis-à-vis the experimenter's board in order to make a match on their own board. The more they had to turn, the more difficult the task. They were clearly depending upon their bodily orientation toward the experimenter's board to guide them. When this orientation is disturbed by having to turn, they lose the position on the board. Older children succeed even when they must turn, either by the use of imagery that is invariant across bodily displacements, or, later, by specifying column and row of the experimenter's ring and carrying the symbolized self-instruction back to their own board. It is a limited world, the world of enactive representation.

. . . If an adult subject is made to choose a path through a complex bank of toggle switches, he does not form an image of the path, according to Mandler (1962), until he has mastered and over-practiced the task by successive manipulation. Then, finally, he reports that an image of the path has developed and that he is now using it rather than groping his way through.

Our main concern in what follows is not with the growth of iconic representation, but with the transition from it to symbolic representation. For it is in the development of symbolic representation that one finds, perhaps, the greatest thicket of psychological problems. The puzzle begins when the child first achieves the use of productive grammar, usually late in the second year of life. Toward the end of the second year, the child is master of the single-word, agrammatical utterance, the so-called holophrase. In the months following, there occurs a profound change in the use of language. Two classes of words appear

—a pivot class and an open class—and the child launches forth on his career in combinatorial talking and, perhaps, thinking. Whereas before, lexemes like *allgone* and *mummy* and *sticky* and *bye-bye* were used singly, now, for example, *allgone* becomes a pivot word and is used in combination. Mother washes jam off the child's hands; he says *allgone sticky*. In the next days, if his speech is carefully followed (Braine, 1963), it will be apparent that he is trying out the limits of the pivot combinations, and one will even find constructions that have an extraordinary capacity for representing complex sequences—like *allgone bye-bye* after a visitor has departed. . . .

DOUBLE CLASSIFICATION MATRIX

Let me begin with an experiment by Bruner and Kenney (in press) on the manner in which children between 5 and 7 handle a double classification matrix. The materials of the experiment are nine plastic glasses, arranged so that they vary in 3 degrees of diameter and 3 degrees of height. They are set before the child initially, as in Figure 1, on a 3 × 3 grid marked on a large piece of cardboard. To acquaint the child with the matrix, we first remove one, then

Matrix Procedure

Figure 1. Array of glasses used in study of matrix ordering. Bruner and Kenney, in press.

two, and then three glasses from the matrix, asking the child to replace them. We also ask the children to describe how the glasses in the columns and rows are alike and how they differ. Then the glasses are scrambled and we ask the child to make something like what was there before by placing the glasses on the same grid that was used when the task was introduced. Now we scramble the glasses once more, but this time we place the glass that was formerly in the southwest corner of the grid in the southeast corner (it is the shortest, thinnest glass) and ask the child if he can make something like what was there before, leaving the one glass where we have just put it. That is the experiment.

The results can be quickly told. To begin with, there is no difference between ages 5, 6, and 7 either in terms of ability to replace glasses taken from the matrix or in building a matrix once it has been scrambled (but without the transposed glass). Virtually all the children succeed. Interestingly enough, *all* the children rebuild the matrix to match the original, almost as if they were copying what was there before. The only difference is that the older children are quicker.

Now compare the performance of the three ages in constructing the matrix with a single member transposed. Most of the 7-year-olds succeed in the transposed task, but hardly any of the youngest children. Figure 2 presents the results graphically. The youngest children seem to be dominated by an image of the original matrix. They try to put the transposed glass "back where it belongs," to rotate the cardboard so that "it will be like before," and sometimes they will start placing a few glasses neighboring the transposed glass correctly only to revert to the original arrangement. In several instances, 5- or 6-year-olds will simply try to reconstitute the old matrix, building right over the transposed glass. The 7-year-old, on the

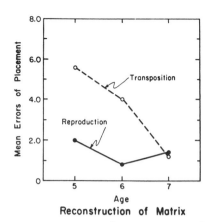

Figure 2. Mean number of errors made by children in reproducing and transposing a 3 × 3 *matrix.* Bruner and Kenney, in press.

other hand, is more likely to pause, to treat the transposition as a problem, to talk to himself about "where this should go." The relation of place and size is for him a problem that requires reckoning, not simply copying.

Now consider the language children use for describing the dimensions of the matrix. Recall that the children were asked how glasses in a row and in a column were alike and how they differed. Children answered in three distinctive linguistic modes. One was *dimensional*, singling out two ends of an attribute—for example, "That one is higher, and that one is shorter." A second was *global* in nature. Of glasses differing only in height the child says, "That one is bigger and that one is little." The same words could be used equally well for diameter or for nearly any other magnitude. Finally, there was *confounded* usage: "That one is tall and that one is little," where a dimensional term is used for one end of the continuum and a global term for the other. The children who used confounded descriptions had the most difficulty with the transposed matrix. Lumping all ages together, the children who used confounded descriptions were twice as likely to fail on the transposition task as those who used either dimensional or global terms. *But the language the children used had no relation whatsoever to their performance in reproducing the first untransposed matrix.* Inhelder and Sinclair in a [personal] communication also report that confounded language of this kind is associated with failure on conservation tasks in children of the same age, a subject to which we shall turn shortly.

The findings of this experiment suggest two things. First, that children who use iconic representation are more highly sensitized to the spatial-qualitative organization of experience and less to the ordering principles governing such organization. They can recognize and reproduce, but cannot produce new structures based on rule. And second, there is a suspicion that the language they bring to bear on the task is insufficient as a tool for ordering. If these notions are correct, then certain things should follow. For one thing, *improvement* in language should aid this type of problem solving. This remains to be investigated. But it is also reasonable to suppose that *activation* of language habits that the child has already mastered might improve performance as well—a hypothesis already suggested by the findings of Luria's students (e.g.,

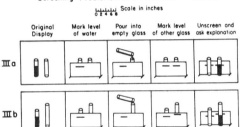

Screening Prediction and Feedback : Part III

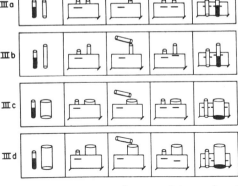

Figure 4. One procedure used in study of effect of language activation on conservation. Frank, in press.

Abramyan, 1958). Now, activation can be achieved by two means: One is by having the child "say" the description of something before him that he must deal with symbolically. The other is to take advantage of the remoteness of reference that is a feature of language, and have the child "say" his description in the absence of the things to be described. In this way, there would be less likelihood of a perceptual-iconic representation becoming dominant and inhibiting the operation of symbolic processes. An experiment by Françoise Frank (in press) illustrates this latter approach —the effects of saying before seeing.

Piaget and Inhelder (1962) have shown that if children between ages 4 and 7 are presented two identical beakers which they judge equally full of water, they will no longer consider the water equal if the contents of one of the beakers is now poured into a beaker that is either wider or thinner than the original. If the second beaker is thinner, they will say it has more to drink because the water is higher; if the second beaker is wider, they will say it has less because the water is lower. Comparable

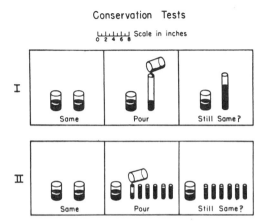

Figure 3. Two Geneva tests for conservation of liquid volume across transformations in its appearance. Piaget and Inhelder, 1962.

results can be obtained by pouring the contents of one glass into several smaller beakers. In Geneva terms, the child is not yet able to conserve liquid volume across transformations in its appearance. Consider how this behavior can be altered.

CONSERVATION EXPERIMENTS

Françoise Frank first did the classic conservation tests to determine which children exhibited conservation and which did not. Her subjects were 4, 5, 6, and 7 years old. She then went on to other procedures, among which was the following. Two standard beakers are partly filled so that the child judges them to contain equal amounts of water. A wider beaker of the same height is introduced and the three beakers are now, except for their tops, hidden by a screen. The experimenter pours from a standard beaker into the wider beaker. The child, without seeing the water, is asked which has more to drink, or do they have the same amount, the standard or the wider beaker. The results are in Figure 5. In comparison with the unscreened pre-

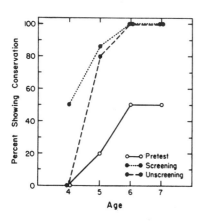

Conservation and Screening

Figure 5. Percentage of children showing conservation of liquid volume before and during screening and upon unscreening of the displays. Frank, in press.

test, there is a striking increase in correct equality judgments. Correct responses jump from 0% to 50% among the 4s, from 20% to 90% among the 5s, and from 50% to 100% among the 6s. With the screen present, most children justify their correct judgment by noting that "It's the same water," or "You only poured it."

Now the screen is removed. All the 4-year-olds change their minds. The perceptual display overwhelms them and they decide that the wider beaker has less water. But virtually all of the 5-year-olds stick to their judgment, often invoking the difference between appearance and reality—"It looks like more to drink, but it is only the same because it is the same water and it was only poured from there to there," to quote one typical 5-year-old. And all of the 6s and all the 7s stick to their judgment. Now, some minutes later, Frank does a posttest on the children using a tall thin beaker along with the standard ones, and no screen, of course. The 4s are unaffected by their prior experience: None of them is able to grasp the idea of invariant quantity in the new task. With the 5s, instead of 20% showing conservation, as in the pretest, 70% do. With both 6s and 7s, conservation increases from 50% to 90%. I should mention that control groups doing just a pretest and posttest show no significant improvement in performance.

A related experiment of Nair's (1963) explores the arguments children use when they solve a conservation task correctly and when they do not. Her subjects were all 5-year-olds. She transferred water from one rectangular clear plastic tank to another that was both longer and wider than the first. Ordinarily, a 5-year-old will say there is less water in the second tank. The water is, of course, lower in the second tank. She had a toy duck swimming in the first container, and when the water was poured into the new container, she told the child that "The duck was taking his water with him."

Three kinds of arguments were set forth by the children to support their judgments. One is perceptual—having to do with the height, width, or apparent "bigness" of the water. A second type has to do with action: The duck took the water along, or the water was only poured. A third one, "transformational" argument, invokes the reversibility principle: If you poured the water back into the first container, it would look the same again.[2] Of the children who thought the water was not equal in amount after pouring, 15% used nonperceptual arguments to justify their judgment. Of those who recognized the equality of the water, two-thirds used nonperceptual arguments. It is plain that if a child is to succeed in the conservation task, he must have some internalized verbal formula that shields him from the overpowering appearance of the visual displays much as in the Frank experiment. The explanations of the children who lacked conservation suggest how strongly oriented they were to the visual appearance of the displays they had to deal with.

Consider now another experiment by Bruner and Kenney (in press) also designed to explore the border between iconic and symbolic representation. Children aged 5, 6, and 7 were asked to say which of two glasses in a pair was fuller and which emptier. "Fullness" is an interesting concept to work with, for it involves in its very definition a ratio or proportion between the volume of a container and the volume of a substance

contained. It is difficult for the iconically oriented child to see a half-full barrel and a half-filled thimble as equally full, since the former looms larger in every one of the attributes that might be perceptually associated with volume. It is like the old riddle of which is heavier, a pound of lead or a pound of feathers. To make a correct judgment of fullness or emptiness, the child must use a symbolic operation, somewhat like computing a ratio, and resist the temptation to use perceptual appearance—Figure 6 contains the 11 pairs of glasses used, and they were selected with a certain malice aforethought.

There are four types of pairs. In Type I (Displays 4, 9a, and 9b), the glasses are of unequal volume, but equally,

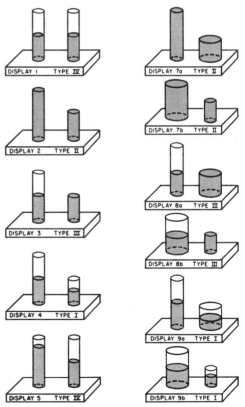

Figure 6. Eleven pairs of glasses to be judged in terms of which glass is fuller and which emptier. Bruner and Kenney, in press.

---

[2] Not one of the 40 children who participated in this experiment used the compensation argument—that though the water was lower it was correspondingly wider and was, therefore, the same amount of water. This type of reasoning by compensation is said by Paiget and Inhelder (1962) to be the basis of conversation.

though fractionally, full. In Type II (Displays 2, 7a, and 7b) again the glasses are of unequal volume, but they are completely full. Type III (Displays 3, 8a, and 8b) consists of two glasses of unequal volume, one filled and the other part filled. Type IV consists of identical glasses, in one case equally filled, in another unequally (Displays 1 and 5).

All the children in the age range we have studied use pretty much the same criteria for judging *fullness,* and these criteria are based on directly observable sensory indices rather than upon proportion. That glass is judged fuller that has the greater apparent volume of water, and the favored indication of greater volume is water level; or where that is equated, then width of glass will do; and when width and water level are the same, then height of glass will prevail. But now consider the judgments made by the three age groups with respect to which glass in each pair is *emptier.* The older children have developed an interesting consistency based on an appreciation of the complementary relation of filled and empty space—albeit an incorrect one. For them "emptier" means the glass that has the largest apparent volume of unfilled space, just as "fuller" meant the glass that had the largest volume of filled space. In consequence, their responses seem logically contradictory. For the glass that is judged fuller also turns out to be the glass that is judged emptier—given a large glass and a small glass, both half full. The younger children, on the other hand, equate emptiness with "littleness": That glass is emptier that gives the impression of being smaller in volume of liquid. If we take the three pairs of glasses of Type I (unequal volumes, half filled) we can see how the judgments typically distribute themselves. Consider only the errors. The glass with the larger volume of empty space is called emptier by 27% of the erring 5-year-olds, by 53% of the erring

6-year-olds, and by 72% of erring 7-year-olds. But the glass with the smallest volume of water is called emptier by 73% of the 5-year-olds who err, 47% of the 6s, and only 28% of the 7s. When the children are asked for their reasons for judging one glass as emptier, there is further confirmation: Most of the younger children justify it by pointing to "littleness" or "less water" or some other aspect of diminutiveness. And most of the older children justify their judgments of emptiness by reference to the amount of empty space in the vessel.

The result of all this is, of course, that the "logical structure" of the older children seems to go increasingly awry. But surely, though Figure 7 shows that contradictory errors steadily increase with age (calling the same glass fuller and emptier or equally full but not equally empty or vice versa), the contradiction is a by-product of the method of dealing with attributes. How shall we interpret these findings? Let me suggest that what

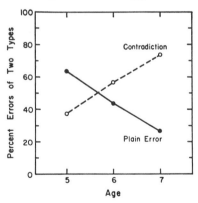

Proportion of
Two Types of Error

Figure 7. Percentage of children at three ages who make contradictory and plain errors in judging which of two glasses is fuller and which emptier. A contradictory error is calling the same glass both fuller or emptier or calling them equally full but not equally empty or vice versa. A plain error is calling one glass fuller and the other emptier, but incorrectly. Bruner and Kenney, in press.

is involved is a translation difficulty in going from the perceptual or iconic realm to the symbolic. If you ask children of this age whether something can be fuller and also emptier, they will smile and think that you are playing riddles. They are aware of the contrastive nature of the two terms. Indeed, even the very young child has a good working language for the two poles of the contrast: "all gone" for completely empty and "spill" or "tippy top" for completely full. Recall too that from 5 to 7, there is perfect performance in judging which of two identical beakers is fuller and emptier. The difference between the younger and the older child is in the number of attributes that are being attended to in situations involving fullness and emptiness: The younger child is attending to one—the volume of water; the older to two—the volume of filled space and the volume of empty space. The young child is applying a single contrast pair—full-empty—to a single feature of the situation. The older child can attend to two features, but he does not yet have the means for relating them to a third, the volume of the container per se. To do so involves being able to deal with a relation in the perceptual field that does not have a "point-at-able" or ostensive definition. Once the third term is introduced—the volume of the glass—then the symbolic concept of proportion can come to "stand for" something that is not present perceptually. The older child is on the way to achieving the insight, in spite of his contradictions. And, interestingly enough, if we count the number of children who justify their judgments of fuller and emptier by pointing to *several* rather than a single attribute, we find that the

proportion triples in both cases between age 5 and age 7. The older child, it would seem, is ordering his perceptual world in such a way that, shortly, he will be able to apply concepts of relationship that are not dependent upon simple ostensive definition. As he moves toward this more powerful "technology of reckoning," he is led into errors that seem to be contradictory. What is particularly telltale is the fact, for example, that in the Type III displays, younger children sometimes seem to find the judgment easier than older children—pointing to the fuller by placing their finger on the rim of the full member and pointing to the emptier with the remark that "It is not to the top." The older child (and virtually never the younger one) gets all involved in the judgment of "fuller by apparent filled volume" and then equally involved in the judgment of "emptier by apparent empty volume" and such are his efforts that he fails to note his contradiction when dealing with a pair like Display 8b, Figure 6.

We have said that cognitive growth consists in part in the development of systems of representation as means for dealing with information. The growing child begins with a strong reliance upon learned action patterns to represent the world around him. In time, there is added to this technology a means for simultanizing regularities in experience into images that stand for events in the way that pictures do. And to this is finally added a technology of translating experience into a symbol system that can be operated upon by rules of transformation that greatly increase the possible range of problem solving. One of the effects of this development, or possibly

TABLE 1.

PERCENTAGE OF CHILDREN WHO JUSTIFY JUDGMENTS OF "FULLER" AND "EMPTIER" BY MENTIONING MORE THAN A SINGLE ATTRIBUTE

Age	"Fuller" judgments	"Emptier" judgments	N
5	7.2%	4.1%	30
6	15.6%	9.3%	30
7	22.2%	15.6%	30

one of its causes, is the power for organizing acts of information processing into more integrated and long-range problem solving efforts. To this matter we turn next.

ORGANIZING PERCEPTION

Consider in rapid succession three related experiments. All of them point, I think, to the same conclusion.

The first is by Huttenlocher (in press), a strikingly simple study, performed with children between the ages of 6 and 12. Two light switches are before the child; each can be in one of two positions. A light bulb is also visible. The child is asked to tell, on the basis of turning only one switch, what turns the light on. There are four ways in which the presentations are made. In the first, the light is off initially and when the child turns a switch, the light comes on. In the second, the light is on and when the child turns a switch, it goes off. In the third, the light is on and when the child turns a switch, it stays on. In the fourth and final condition, the light is off and when the child turns a switch, it stays off. Now what is intriguing about this arrangement is that there are different numbers of inductive steps required to make a correct inference in each task. The simplest condition is the off-on case. The position to which the switch has just been moved is responsible for the light going on. Intermediate difficulty should be experienced with the on-off condition. In the on-off case, two connected inferences are required: The present position achieved is rejected and the original position of the switch that has been turned is responsible for lighting the bulb. An even larger number of consecutive acts is required for success in the on-on case: The present position of the turned switch is rejected, the original position as well and the present position of the *other* switch is responsible. The

off-off case requires four steps: rejecting the present position of the turned switch, its original position, and the present position of the other switch, finally accepting the alternative position of the unturned switch. The natures of the individual steps are all the same. Success in the more complex cases depends upon being able to integrate them consecutively.

Huttenlocher's results show that the 6-year-olds are just as capable as their elders of performing the elementary operation involved in the one-step case: the on-off display. They, like the 9s and 12s, make nearly perfect scores. But in general, the more inferential steps the 6-year-old must make, the poorer his performance. By age 12, on the other hand, there is an insignificant difference between the tasks requiring one, two, three, or four connected inferences.

An experiment by Mosher (1962) underlines the same point. He was concerned with the strategies used by children from 6 to 11 for getting information in the game of Twenty Questions. They were to find out by "yes-no" questions what caused a car to go off the road and hit a tree. One may distinguish between connected constraint-locating questions ("Was it night-time?" followed up appropriately) and direct hypothesis-testing questions ("Did a bee fly in the window and sting the man on the eye and make him go off the road and hit the tree?"). From 6 to 11, more and more children use constraint-locating, connected questioning. Let me quote from Mosher's account.

We have asked children . . . after they have played their games, to tell us which of two questions they would rather have the answer to, if they were playing the games again— one of them a typical constraint-seeking question ("Was there anything wrong with the man?") and the other a typical discrete test of an hypothesis ("Did the man have a heart attack?"). All the eleven-year-olds and all the eight-year-olds choose the constraint-seeking question, but only 29% of the six-year-olds do [p. 6].

The questions of the younger children are all one-step substitutes for direct sense experience. They are looking for knowledge by single questions that provide the answer in a finished form. When they succeed they do so by a lucky question that hits an immediate, perceptible cause. When the older child receives a "yes" answer to one of his constraint-locating questions, he most often follows up by asking another. When, on the rare occasions that a younger child asks a constraint question and it is answered "yes," he almost invariably follows it up with a specific question to test a concrete hypothesis. The older child can accrete his information in a structure governed by consecutive inference. The younger child cannot.

Potter's (in press) study of the development of perceptual recognition bears on the same point. Ordinary colored photographs of familiar scenes are presented to children between 6 and 12, the pictures coming gradually into focus. Let me sum up one part of the results very briefly. Six-year-olds produce an abundance of hypotheses. But they rarely try to match new hypotheses to previous ones. "There is a big tower in the middle and a road over there and a big ice cream cone through the middle of the tower and a pumpkin on top." It is like a random collage. The 9-year-old's torrent of hypotheses, on the other hand, shows a sense of consistency about what is likely to appear with what. Things are in a context of likelihood, a frame of reference that demands internal consistency. Something is seen as a merry-go-round, and the child then restricts later hypotheses to the other things to be found in an amusement park. The adolescent operates under even more highly organized sequential constraints: He occasionally develops his initial hy-potheses from what is implied by the properties of the picture, almost by intersection—"It is red and shiny and metallic: It must be a coffee-pot." Once such constraints are established, the order of hypotheses reflects even more the need to build up a consistent world of objects—even to the point of failing to recognize things that do not fit it.

What shall we make of these three sets of findings—that older children are able to cumulate information by asking questions in a directed sequence leading to a final goal, and that they are capable of recognizing visual displays in a manner governed by a dominating frame of reference that transcends momentary and isolated bits of information? Several points seem apparent. The first is that as children mature, they are able to use indirect information based on forms of information processing other than the act of pointing to what is immediately present. They seem, in short, to make remote reference to states and constraints that are not given by the immediate situation, to go beyond the information given. Second, and this is a matter that has already been discussed, they seem to be able to cumulate information into a structure that can be operated upon by rules that transcend simple association by similarity and contiguity. In the case of Twenty Questions, the rule is best described as implication—that knowing one thing implies certain other things and eliminates still others. In the experiments with the light switches, it is that if the present state does not produce the effect, then there is a system for tracing back to the other states that cause the light to go on. Where perceptual recognition is concerned, the rule is that a piece of information from one part of the display implies what other parts might be. The child, in sum, is translating redundancy into a manipulable model of the environment that is governed by rules of implication. It is this model of the environment that permits him to go beyond the information before him. I would suggest that it is this new array of cognitive equipment that permits the child to transcend momentaneity, to integrate longer sequences of events.

Let me urge, moreover, that such a system of processing environmental events depends upon the translation of experience into symbolic form. Such a translation is necessary in order for there to be the kind of remoteness of reference as is required when one deals with indirect information. To transcend the immediately perceptual, to get beyond what is vividly present to a more extended model of the environment, the child needs a system that permits him to deal with the nonpresent, with things that are remote in space, qualitative similarity, and time, from the present situation. Hockett (1959), in describing the design features of language includes this feature as crucial. He is referring to human speech as a system of communication. The same point can be made about language as an instrument of thought. That humans have the *capacity* for using speech in this way is only part of the point. What is critical is that the capacity is *not* used until it is coupled with the technology of language in the cognitive operations of the child.

In children between 4 and 12 language comes to play an increasingly powerful role as an implement of knowing. Through simple experiments, I have tried to show how language shapes, augments, and even supercedes the child's earlier modes of processing information. Translation of experience into symbolic form, with its attendant means of achieving remote reference, transformation, and combination, opens up realms of intellectual possibility that are orders of magnitude beyond the most powerful image forming system.

What of the integration of intellectual activity into more coherent and intercon-

nected acts? It has been the fashion, since Freud, to see delay of ratification as the principal dynamism behind this development—from primary process to secondary process, or from assimilation to accommodation, as Piaget would put it today. Without intending to question the depth of this insight, let me suggest that delay of immediate gratification, the ability to go beyond the moment, also depends upon techniques, and again they are techniques of representation. Perhaps representation exclusively by imagery and perceptual organization has built into it one basic operation that ties it to the immediate present. It is the operation of pointing—ostensiveness, as logicians call it. (This is not to say that highly evolved images do not go beyond immediate time and given place. Maps and flow charts are iconic in nature, but they are images that translate prior linguistic and mathematical renderings into a visual form.) Iconic representation, in the beginning, is built upon a perceptual organization that is tied to the "point-at-able" spatioqualitative properties of events. I have suggested that, for all its limitations, such representation is an achievement beyond the earlier stage where percepts are not autonomous of action. But so long as perceptual representation dominates, it is difficult to develop higher-order techniques for processing information by consecutive inferential steps that take one beyond what can be pointed at.

Once language becomes a medium for the translation of experience, there is a progressive release from immediacy. For language, as we have commented, has the new and powerful features of remoteness and arbitrariness: It permits productive, combinatorial operations in the *absence* of what is represented. With this achievement, the child can delay gratification by virtue of representing to himself what lies beyond the present, what other possibilities exist beyond the clue that is under his nose. The child may be *ready* for delay of gratification, but he is no more able to bring it off than somebody ready to build a house, save that he has not yet heard of tools.

The discussion leaves two obvious questions begging. What of the integration of behavior in organisms without language? And how does language become internalized as a vehicle for organizing experience? The first question has to be answered briefly and somewhat cryptically. Wherever integrated behavior has been studied—as in Lehrman's (1955) careful work on integrated instinctive patterns in the ringdove, it has turned out that a sustaining external stimulus was needed to keep the highly integrated behavior going. The best way to control behavior in subhuman species is to control the stimulus situation. Surely this is the lesson of Lashley's (1938) classic account of instinctive behavior. Where animal learning is concerned, particularly in the primates, there is, to be sure, considerable plasticity. But it too depends upon the development of complex forms of stimulus substitution and organization—as in Klüver's (1933) work on equivalence reactions in monkeys. If it should seem that I am urging that the growth of symbolic functioning links a unique set of powers to man's capacity, the appearance is quite as it should be.

As for how language becomes internalized as a program for ordering experience, I join those who despair for an answer. My speculation, for whatever it is worth, is that the process of internalization depends upon interaction with others, upon the need to develop corresponding categories and transformations for communal action. It is the need for cognitive coin that can be exchanged with those on whom we depend. What Roger Brown (1958) has called the Original Word Game ends up by being the Human Thinking Game.

If I have seemed to underemphasize the importance of inner capacities—for example, the capacity *for* language or *for* imagery—it is because I believe that this part of the story is given by the nature of man's evolution. What is significant about the growth of mind in the child is to what degree it depends not upon capacity but upon the unlocking of capacity by techniques that come from exposure to the specialized environment of a culture. Romantic clichés, like "the veneer of culture" or "natural man," are as misleading if not as damaging as the view that the course of human development can be viewed independently of the educational process we arrange to make that development possible.

REFERENCES

ABRAMYAN, L. A. Organization of the voluntary activity of the child with the help of verbal instruction. Unpublished diploma thesis, Moscow University, 1958. Cited by A. R. Luria, *The role of speech in the regulation of normal and abnormal behavior.* New York: Liveright, 1961.

BARKER, R. G. On the nature of the environment. Kurt Lewin Memorial Address presented at American Psychological Association, Philadelphia, September 1963.

BRAINE, M. D. On learning the grammatical order of words. *Psychol. Rev.*, 1963, 70, 323–348.

BROWN, R. *Words and things.* Glencoe, Ill.: Free Press, 1958.

BRUNER, J. S., AND KENNEY, HELEN. The development of the concepts of order and proportion in children. In J. S. Bruner, *Studies in cognitive growth.* New York: Wiley, in press.

CHOMSKY, N. *Syntactic structures.* S'Gravenhage, Netherlands: Mouton, 1957.

EMERSON, L. L. The effect of bodily orientation upon the young child's memory for position of objects. *Child Develpm.*, 1931, 2, 125–142.

FRANK FRANÇOISE. Perception and language in conservation. In J. S. Bruner, *Studies in cognitive growth.* New York: Wiley, in press.

HANFMANN, EUGENIA, RICKERS-OVSIANKINA, MARIA, AND GOLDSTEIN, K. Case Lanuti: Extreme concretization of behavior due to damage of the brain cortex. *Psychol. Monogr.*, 1944, 57(4, Whole No. 264).

HOCKETT, C. F. Animal "languages" and human language. In J. N. Spuhler, *The evolution of man's capacity for culture.* Detroit: Wayne State Univer. Press, 1959. Pp. 32–39.

HUTTENLOCHER, JANELLEN. The growth of conceptual strategies. In J. S. Bruner, *Studies in cognitive growth.* New York: Wiley, in press.

KLÜVER, H. *Behavior mechanisms in monkeys.* Chicago: Univer. Chicago Press, 1933.

LA BARRE, W. *The human animal.* Chicago: Univer. Chicago Press, 1954.

LASHLEY, K. S. Experimental analysis of instinctive behavior. *Psychol. Rev.*, 1938, *45*, 445–472.

LEHRMAN, D. S. The physiological basis of parental feeding behavior in the ring dove (*Streptopelia risoria*). *Behavior*, 1955, *7*, 241–286.

LURIA, A. R. *The role of speech in the regulation of normal and abnormal behavior.* New York: Liveright, 1961.

MANDLER, G. From association to structure. *Psychol. Rev.*, 1962, *69*, 415–427.

MARTSINOVSKAYA, E. N. Research into the reflective and regulatory role of the second signalling system of pre-school age. Collected papers of the Department of Psychology, Moscow University, undated. Cited by A. R. Luria, *The role of speech in the regulation of normal and abnormal behavior.* New York: Liveright, 1961.

MILLER, G. A. Some psychological studies of grammar. *Amer. Psychologist*, 1962, *17*, 748–762.

MILLER, G. A., GALANTER, E., AND PRIBRAM, K. H. *Plans and the structure of behavior.* New York: Holt, 1960.

MOSHER, F. A. Strategies for information gathering. Paper read at Eastern Psychological Association, Atlantic City, N. J., April 1962.

NAIR, PATRICIA. An experiment in conservation. In Center for Cognitive Studies, *Annual Report.* Cambridge, Mass.: Author, 1963.

OLVER, ROSE R. A developmental study of cognitive equivalence. Unpublished doctoral dissertation, Radcliffe College, 1961.

PIAGET, J. *The construction of reality in the child.* (Trans. by Margaret Cook) New York: Basic Books, 1954.

PIAGET, J., AND INHELDER, BÄRBEL. *Le développement des quantitiés physiques chez l'enfant.* (2nd rev. ed.) Neuchâtel, Switzerland: Delachaux & Niestlé, 1962.

POTTER, MARY C. The growth of perceptual recognition. In J. S. Bruner, *Studies in cognitive growth.* New York: Wiley, in press.

RIGNEY, JOAN C. A developmental study of cognitive equivalence transformations and their use in the acquisition and processing of information. Unpublished honors thesis, Radcliffe College, Department of Social Relations, 1962.

VYGOTSKY, L. S. *Thought and language.* (Ed. & trans. by Eugenia Hanfmann & Gertrude Vakar) New York: Wiley, 1962.

WASHBURN, S. L., AND HOWELL, F. C. Human evolution and culture. In S. Tax, *The evolution of man.* Vol. 2. Chicago: Univer. Chicago Press, 1960.

WEIR, RUTH H. *Language in the crib.* The Hague: Mouton, 1962.

WERNER, H. *Comparative psychology of mental development.* (Rev. ed.) Chicago: Follett, 1948.

34 | INDUSTRY VERSUS INFERIORITY

ERIK H. ERIKSON

We have all frequently heard things described as being "as easy as child's play." Just how "easy" is child's play?

This selection provides some notion of what play means to children and to adults and of the close interrelationships of play, industriousness, self-esteem, and the feeling of mastery.

One might say that personality at the first stage crystallizes around the conviction "I am what I am given," and that of the second, "I am what I will." The third can be characterized by "I am what I can imagine I will be." We must now approach the fourth: "I am what I learn." The child now wants to be shown how to get busy with something and how to be busy with others.

This trend, too, starts much earlier, especially in some children. They want to watch how things are done and to try doing them. If they are lucky they live near barnyards or on streets around busy people and around many other children of all ages, so that they can watch and try, observe and participate, as their capacities and their initiative grow in tentative spurts. But now it is time to "go to school." In all cultures, at this stage, children receive some systematic instruction, although it is by no means always in the kind of school which literate people must organize around teachers who have learned how to teach literacy. In preliterate people much is learned from adults who become teachers by acclamation rather than by appointment; and very much is learned from older children. What is learned in more primitive surroundings is related to the basic skills of *technology* which are developed as the child gets ready to handle the utensils, the tools, and the weapons used by the big people: he enters the technology of his tribe very gradually but also very directly. More literate people, with more specialized careers, must prepare the child by teaching him things which first of all make him literate. He is then given the widest possible basic education for the greatest number of possible careers. The

greater the specialization, the more indistinct the goal of initiative becomes; and the more complicated the social reality is, the vaguer the father's and mother's role in it appears to be. Between childhood and adulthood, then, our children go to school; and school seems to be a world all by itself, with its own goals and limitations, its achievements and disappointments.

Grammar school education has swung back and forth between the extreme of making early school life an extension of grim adulthood by emphasizing self-restraint and a strict sense of duty in doing what one is *told* to do, and the other extreme of making it an extension of the natural tendency in childhood to find out by playing, to learn what one must do by doing steps which one *likes* to do. Both methods work for some children at times but not for all children at all times. The first trend, if carried to the extreme, exploits a tendency on the part of the preschool and grammar school child to become entirely dependent on prescribed duties. He thus learns much that is absolutely necessary and he develops an unshakable sense of duty; but he may never unlearn again an unnecessary and costly self-restraint with which he may later make his own life and other people's lives miserable, and in fact spoil his own children's natural desire to learn and to work. The second trend, when carried to an extreme, leads not only to the well-known popular objection that children do not learn anything any more but also to such feelings in children as are expressed in the by now famous remark of a metropolitan child who apprehensively asked one morning: "Teacher, *must* we do today what we *want* to do?" Nothing could better express the fact that children at this age *do* like to be mildly coerced into the adventure of finding out that one can learn to accomplish things which one would never have thought of by oneself,

Selections reprinted from "Growth and Crises" in *Symposium on the Healthy Personality*, edited by Milton J. Senn (Josiah Macy, Jr. Foundation, 1950), 127–34, by permission of the author and publisher.

things which owe their attractiveness to the very fact that they are *not* the product of play and fantasy but the product of reality, practicality, and logic; things which thus provide a token sense of participation in the world of adults. In discussions of this kind it is common to say that one must steer a middle course between play and work, between childhood and adulthood, between old-fashioned and progressive education. It is always easy (and it seems entirely satisfactory to one's critics) to say that one plans to steer a middle course, but in practice it often leads to a course charted by avoidances rather than by zestful goals. Instead of pursuing, then, a course which merely avoids the extremes of easy play or hard work, it may be worth while to consider what play is and what work is, and then learn to dose and alternate each in such a way that play is play and work is work. Let us review briefly what play may mean at various stages of childhood and adulthood.

The adult plays for purposes of recreation. He steps out of his reality into imaginary realities for which he has made up arbitrary but none the less binding rules. But an adult must not be a playboy. Only he who works shall play—if, indeed, he can relax his competitiveness.

The playing child, then, poses a problem: whoever does not work shall not play. Therefore, to be tolerant of the child's play the adult must invent theories which show either that childhood play is really the child's work or that it does not count. The most popular theory, and the easiest on the observer, is that the child is nobody yet and that the nonsense of his play reflects it. According to Spencer, play uses up surplus energy in the young of a number of mammalians who do not need to feed or protect themselves because their parents do it for them. Others say that play is either preparation for the future or a

method of working off past emotion, a means of finding imaginary relief for past frustrations.

It is true that the content of individual play often proves to be the infantile way of thinking over difficult experiences and of restoring a sense of mastery, comparable to the way in which we repeat, in thought and endless talk, experiences that have been too much for us. This is the rationale for play observation, play diagnosis, and play therapy. In watching a child play, the trained observer can get an impression of what it is the child is "thinking over," and what faulty logic, what emotional dead end he may be caught in. As a diagnostic tool such observation has become indispensable.

Play has its crisis, too (which, in fact, makes its observation an even better clinical tool). Let us consider the activity of building and destroying a tower. Many a mother thinks that her little son is in a "destructive stage" or even that he has a "destructive personality" because, after building a big, big tower, the boy cannot follow her advice to leave the tower for Daddy to see but instead *must* kick it and make it collapse. The almost manic pleasure with which children watch the collapse in a second of the product of long play labor has puzzled many, especially since the child does not appreciate it at all if his tower falls by accident or by a helpful uncle's hand. He, the builder, must destroy it himself. This game, I should think, arises from the not so distant experience of sudden falls at the very time when standing upright on wobbly legs afforded a new and fascinating perspective on existence. The child who consequently learns to *make* a tower "stand up" enjoys causing the same tower to waver and collapse: it helps *to do to somebody or something what was done to oneself;* it makes one feel stronger to know that there is somebody weaker—and towers, unlike little sisters, can't cry and call Mummy. But since it is the child's still precarious mastery over space which is thus to be demonstrated, it is understandable that watching somebody else kick one's tower may make the child see himself in the tower rather than in the kicker: all fun evaporates. Later, circus clowns afford satisfaction and amusement to the child when they obligingly fall and tumble about from mere ineptness and yet continue to challenge gravity and causality with ever renewed innocence: there are, then, even big people who are funnier, dumber, and wobblier. Some children, however, find themselves too much identified with the clown. They cannot bear to see his downfalls; to them they are "not funny." This example throws light on the beginning of many an anxiety in childhood, anxiety aroused when the child's attempt at mastery in play finds unwelcome "support" from adults who treat him roughly or amuse him with exercises which he likes only if and when he himself has initiated them.

The child's play begins with, and centers in, his own body. It begins before we notice it as play, and it consists first in the exploration by repetition of sensual perceptions, of kinesthetic sensations, and of vocalizations. (The handling of the genitals often begins as play and becomes "serious" only because of the adults' frightened attitude.) Next, the child plays with available persons and things. He may playfully cry to see what wave length serves best to make the mother reappear, or he may indulge in experimental excursions on her body and on the protrusions and orifices of her face. This is the child's first geography, and the basic maps acquired in such interplay with the mother no doubt remain guides for the first impressions of the "world."

The small world of manageable toys is a second harbor which the child establishes, returning to it when he needs to overhaul his ego. But the thing-world has its own laws: it may resist rearrangement or it may simply break to pieces; it may prove to belong to somebody else and be subject to confiscation by superiors. Often the microsphere seduces the child into an unguarded expression of dangerous themes and attitudes which arouse anxiety and lead to sudden *play-disruption*. This is the counterpart, in waking life, of the anxiety dream; it can keep children from trying to play just as the fear of night terror can keep them from going to sleep. If thus frightened or disappointed, the child may regress into daydreaming, thumb-sucking, masturbating. On the other hand, if the first use of the thing-world is successful and guided properly, the pleasure of mastering toy things becomes associated with the *mastery of the conflicts* which were projected on them and with the *prestige* gained through such mastery.

Finally, at nursery school age playfulness reaches into the world shared with others. At first these others are treated as things; they are inspected, run into, or forced to "be horsie." Learning is necessary in order to discover what potential play content can be admitted only to fantasy or only to play by and with oneself; what content can be successfully represented only in the world of toys and small things; and what content can be shared with others and even forced upon them.

As this is learned, each sphere is endowed with its own sense of reality and mastery. For quite a while, then, solitary play remains an indispensable harbor for the overhauling of damaged emotions after periods of rough going on the social seas.

What is infantile play, then? We saw that it is not the equivalent of adult play, that it is not recreation. The playing adult steps sideward into another, an artificial reality; the playing child advances forward to new stages of real mastery. This new mastery is not restricted to the technical mastery of toys and *things;* it also includes an infantile way of mastering *experience* by meditating, experimenting, and planning.

While all children at times need to be left alone in solitary play, or later in the company of books and radio, motion pictures and video, all of which, like the fairy tales of old, at least *sometimes* seem to convey what fits the needs of the infantile mind, and while all children need their hours and days of make-believe in games, they all, sooner or later, become dissatisfied and disgruntled without a sense of being useful, without a sense of being able to make things and make them well and even perfectly: this is what I call the *sense of industry.* Without this, the best entertained child soon acts exploited. It is as if he knows and his society knows that now that he is psychologically already a rudimentary parent, he must begin to be somewhat of a worker and potential provider before becoming a biological parent. With the oncoming latency period, then, the normally advanced child forgets, or rather "sublimates" (that is, applies to more useful pursuits and approved goals) the necessity of "making" people by direct attack or the desire to become papa and mamma in a hurry: he now learns to win recognition by producing things. He develops industry, that is, he adjusts himself to the inorganic laws of the tool world. He can become an eager and absorbed unit of a productive situation. To bring a productive situation to completion is an aim which gradually supersedes the whims and wishes of his idiosyncratic drives and personal disappointments. As he once untiring strove to walk well, and to throw things away well, he now wants to make things well. He develops the pleasure of work completion by steady attention and persevering diligence.

The danger at this stage is the development of a sense of *inadequacy and inferiority.* This may be caused by an insufficient solution of the preceding conflict: he may still want his mummy more than knowledge; he may still rather be the baby at home than the big child in school; he still compares himself with his father, and the comparison arouses a sense of guilt as well as sense of anatomical inferiority. Family life (small family) may not have prepared him for school life, or school life may fail to sustain the promises of earlier stages in that nothing that he has learned to do well already seems to count one bit with the teacher. And then, again, he may be potentially able to excel in ways which are dormant and which, if not evoked now, may develop late or never.

Good teachers, healthy teachers, relaxed teachers, teachers who feel trusted and respected by the community, understand all this and can guide it. They know how to alternate play and work, games and study. They know how to recognize special efforts, how to encourage special gifts. They also know how to give a child time, and how to handle those children to whom school, for a while, is not important and rather a matter to endure than to enjoy; or the child to whom other children are much more important than the teacher and who shows it.

Good parents, healthy parents, relaxed parents, feel a need to make their children trust their teachers, and therefore to have teachers who can be trusted. It is not my job here to discuss teacher selection, teacher training, and the status and payment of teachers in their communities—all of which is of indirect importance for the development and the maintenance in children of a *sense of industry* and of a positive identification with those who *know* things and know how to *do* things. Again and again I have observed in the lives of especially gifted people that one teacher, somewhere, was able to kindle the flame of hidden talent.

The fact that the majority of teachers in the elementary schools are women must be considered here in passing, because it often leads to a conflict with the "ordinary" boy's masculine identification, as if knowledge were feminine, action masculine. Both boys and girls are apt to agree with Bernard Shaw's statement that those who can, do, while those who cannot, teach. The selection and training of teachers, then, is vital for the avoidance of the dangers which can befall the individual at this stage. There is, first, the above-mentioned sense of inferiority, the feeling that one will never be any good—a problem which calls for the type of teacher who knows how to emphasize what a child *can* do, and who knows a psychiatric problem when she sees one. Second, there is the danger of the child's identifying too strenuously with a too virtuous teacher or the teacher's pet. What we shall presently refer to as his sense of identity can remain prematurely fixed on being nothing but a good little worker or a good little helper, which may not be all he *could* be. Third, there is the danger (probably the most common one) that throughout the long years of going to school he will never acquire the enjoyment of work and the pride of doing at least one kind of thing well. This is particularly of concern in relation to that part of the nation who do not complete what schooling is at their disposal. It is always easy to say that they are born that way; that there must be less educated people as background for the superior ones; that the market needs and even fosters such people for its many simple and unskilled tasks. But from the point of view of the healthy personality (which, as we proceed, must now include the aspect of playing a constructive role in a healthy society), we must consider those who

have had just enough schooling to appreciate what more fortunate people are learning to do but who, for one reason or another, have lacked inner or outer support of their stick-to-itiveness.

It will have been noted that, regarding the period of a developing sense of industry, I have referred to outer hindrances but not to any crisis (except a deferred inferiority crisis) coming from the inventory of basic human drives. This stage differs from the others in that it does not consist of a swing from a violent inner upheaval to a new mastery. The reason why Freud called it the latency stage is that violent drives are normally dormant at that time. But it is only a lull before the storm of puberty.

On the other hand, this is socially a most decisive stage: since industry involves doing things beside and with others, a first sense of division of labor and of equality of opportunity develops at this time. When a child begins to feel that it is the color of his skin, the background of his parents, or the cost of his clothes rather than his wish and his will to learn which will decide his social worth, lasting harm may ensue for the *sense of identity*. . . .

. . . . .

CONCLUSION

At this point, then, I have come close to overstepping the limits (some will say I have long and repeatedly overstepped them) that separate psychology from ethical philosophy. But in suggesting (in an admittedly most tentative manner) that parents, teachers, and doctors must learn to discuss matters of human relations and of community life if they wish to discuss their children's needs and problems, I am only insisting on a few basic psychological insights, which I shall try to formulate briefly in conclusion.

While we have, in the last few

decades, learned more about the development and growth of the individual and about his motivations (especially unconscious motivations) than in the whole of human history before us (excepting, of course, the implicit wisdom expressed in the Bible or Shakespeare), increasing numbers of us come to the conclusion that a child and even a baby —perhaps even the fetus—sensitively reflects the quality of the milieu in which he grows up. Children feel the tensions, insecurities, and rages of their parents even if they do not know their causes or witness their most overt manifestations. Therefore, you cannot fool children. To develop a child with a healthy personality, a parent must be a genuine person in a genuine milieu. This, today, is difficult because rapid changes in the milieu often make it hard to know whether one must be genuine *against* a changing milieu or whether one may hope for a chance to do one's bit in the way of bettering stabilizing conditions. It is difficult, also, because in a changing world we are trying out—we must try out—new ways. To bring up children in personal and tolerant ways, based on information and education rather than on tradition, is a very new way: it exposes parents to many additional insecurities, which are temporarily increased by psychiatry (and by such products of psychiatric thinking as the present paper). Psychiatric thinking sees the world so full of dangers that it is hard to relax one's caution at every step. I, too, have pointed to more dangers than to constructive avenues of action. Perhaps we can hope that this is only an indication that we are progressing through one stage of learning. When a man learns how to drive a car, he must become conscious of all the things that

might happen; and he must learn to hear, see, and read all the danger signals on his dashboard and along the road. Yet he may hope that some day, when he has outgrown this stage of learning, he will be able to glide with the greatest ease through the landscape, enjoying the view with the confident knowledge that he will react to signs of mechanical trouble or road obstruction with automatic and effective speed.

We are now working toward, and fighting for, a world in which the harvest of democracy may be reaped. In order to make the world safe for democracy, we must make democracy safe for the healthy child. In order to ban autocracy, exploitation, and inequality in the world, we must realize that the first inequality in life is that of child and adult. Human childhood is long, so that parents and schools may have time to accept the child's personality in trust and to help it to be human in the best sense known to us. This long childhood exposes the child to grave anxieties and to a lasting sense of insecurity which, if unduly and senselessly intensified, persists in the adult in the form of vague anxiety—anxiety which, in turn, contributes specifically to the tension of personal, political, and even international life. This long childhood exposes adults, in turn, to the temptation to exploit thoughtlessly and often cruelly the child's dependence by making him pay for the psychological debts owed to them by others, by making him the victim of tensions which they will not, or dare not, correct in themselves or in their surroundings. We have learned not to stunt a child's growing body with child labor; we must now learn not to break his growing spirit by making him the victim of our anxieties.

35 | GAMES PEOPLE PLAY

ERIC BERNE

Games, whether fun or not even desirable, are learned in childhood.
In some games, everyone wins; in others, nobody wins. A brilliant
observer analyzes games that he has discovered to be for many
the substance of their lifelong contact with people. Features common
to all "games" seem to be the deception of self and the
exploitation of others.

As far as the theory of games is concerned, the principle which emerges here is that any social intercourse whatever has a biological advantage over no intercourse at all. This has been experimentally demonstrated in the case of rats through some remarkable experiments by S. Levine in which not only physical, mental and emotional development but also the biochemistry of the brain and even resistance to leukemia were favorably affected by handling. The significant feature of these experiments was that gentle handling and painful electric shocks were equally effective in promoting the health of the animals.

. . . . .

THE STRUCTURING OF TIME

Granted that handling of infants, and its symbolic equivalent in grown-ups, recognition, have a survival value. The question is, What next? In everyday terms, what can people do after they have exchanged greetings, whether the greeting consists of a collegiate "Hi!" or an Oriental ritual lasting several hours? After stimulus-hunger and recognition-hunger comes *structure-hunger*. The perennial problem of adolescents is: "What do you say to her (him) then?" And to many people besides adolescents, nothing is

more uncomfortable than a social hiatus, a period of silent, unstructured time when no one present can think of anything more interesting to say than: "Don't you think the walls are perpendicular tonight?" The eternal problem of the human being is how to structure his waking hours. In this existential sense, the function of all social living is to lend mutual assistance for this project.

Social programing results in traditional ritualistic or semi-ritualistic interchanges. The chief criterion for it is local acceptability, popularly called "good manners." Parents in all parts of the world teach their children manners, which means that they know the proper greeting, eating, emunctory, courting and mourning rituals, and also how to carry on topical conversations with appropriate strictures and reinforcements. The strictures and reinforcements constitute tact or diplomacy, some of which is universal and some local. Belching at meals or asking after another man's wife are each encouraged or forbidden by local ancestral tradition, and indeed there is a high degree of inverse correlation between these particular transactions. . . .

As people become better acquainted, more and more *individual programing* creeps in, so that "incidents" begin to occur. These incidents superficially appear to be adventitious, and may be so described by the parties concerned, but careful scrutiny reveals that they

Excerpts reprinted from Eric Berne, M.D., *Games People Play: The Psychology of Human Relationships* (New York: Grove Press, Inc., 1964). Copyright © 1964 by Eric Berne.

tend to follow definite patterns which are amenable to sorting and classification, and that the sequence is circumscribed by unspoken rules and regulations. . . .

Such sequences, which in contrast to pastimes are based more on individual than on social programing, may be called *games*. Family life and married life, as well as life in organizations of various kinds, may year after year be based on variations of the same game.

To say that the bulk of social activity consists of playing games does not necessarily mean that it is mostly "fun" or that the parties are not seriously engaged in the relationship. On the one hand, "playing" football and other athletic "games" may not be fun at all, and the players may be intensely grim; and such games share with gambling and other forms of "play" the potentiality for being very serious indeed, sometimes fatal. On the other hand, some authors, for instance Huizinga, include under "play" such serious things as cannibal feasts. Hence calling such tragic behavior as suicide, alcohol and drug addiction, criminality or schizophrenia "playing games" is not irresponsible, facetious or barbaric. The essential characteristic of human play is not that the emotions are spurious, but that they are regulated. This is revealed when sanctions are imposed on an illegitimate emotional display. Play may be grimly serious, or even fatally serious, but the social sanctions are serious only if the rules are broken.

Pastimes and games are substitutes for the real living of real intimacy. Because of this they may be regarded as preliminary engagements rather than as unions, which is why they are characterized as poignant forms of play. Intimacy begins when individual (usually instinctual) programing becomes more intense, and both social patterning and ulterior

restrictions and motives begin to give way. It is the only completely satisfying answer to stimulus-hunger, recognition-hunger and structure-hunger. Its prototype is the act of loving impregnation.

. . . . .

. . . When one is a member of a social aggregation of two or more people, there are several options for structuring time. In order of complexity, these are: (1) Rituals (2) Pastimes (3) Games (4) Intimacy and (5) Activity, which may form a matrix for any of the others. The goal of each member of the aggregation is to obtain as many satisfactions as possible from his transactions with other members. The more accessible he is, the more satisfactions he can obtain. Most of the programing of his social operations is automatic. Since some of the "satisfactions" obtained under this programing, such as self-destructive ones, are difficult to recognize in the usual sense of the word "satisfactions," it would be better to substitute some more non-committal term, such as "gains" or "advantages."

. . . . .

The most gratifying forms of social contact, whether or not they are embedded in a matrix of activity, are games and intimacy. Prolonged intimacy is rare, and even then it is primarily a private matter; significant social intercourse most commonly takes the form of games, and that is the subject which principally concerns us here. For further information about time-structuring, the author's book on group dynamics should be consulted.

. . . . .

. . . A *ritual* is a stereotyped series of simple complementary transactions programed by external social forces. . . . Of more significance as an introduction to game analysis are informal rituals, and among the most instructive are the American greeting rituals.

1A: "Hi!" (Hello, good morning.)
1B: "Hi!" (Hello, good morning.)
2A: "Warm enough forya?" (How are you?)
2B: "Sure is. Looks like rain, though." (Fine. How are you?)
3A: "Well, take cara yourself." (Okay.)
3B: "I'll be seeing you."
4A: "So long."
4B: "So long."

It is apparent that this exchange is not intended to convey information. Indeed, if there is any information, it is wisely withheld. It might take Mr. A fifteen minutes to say how he is, and Mr. B, who is only the most casual acquaintance, has no intention of devoting that much time to listening to him. This series of transactions is quite adequately characterized by calling it an "eight-stroke ritual." If A and B were in a hurry, they might both be contented with a two-stroke exchange, Hi-Hi. If they were old-fashioned Oriental potentates, they might go through a two-hundred stroke ritual before settling down to business. . . .

This ritual is based on careful intuitive computations by both parties. At this stage of their acquaintance they figure that they owe each other exactly four strokes at each meeting, and not oftener than once a day. . . . Let us now consider Mr. C and Mr. D, who pass each other about once a day, trade one stroke each—Hi-Hi—and go their ways. Mr. C goes on a month's vacation. The day after he returns, he encounters Mr. D as usual. If on this occasion Mr. D merely says "Hi!" and no more, Mr. C will be offended, "his spinal cord will shrivel slightly." By his calculations, Mr. D and he owe each other about thirty strokes. . . .

1D: "Hi!" (1 unit.)
2D: "Haven't seen you around lately." (2 units.)
3D: "Oh, *have* you! Where did you go?" (5 units.)

4D: "Say, *that's interesting*. How was it?" (7 units.)
5D: "Well, you're sure looking fine." (4 units.) "Did your family go along?" (4 units.)
6D: "Well, glad to see you back." (4 units.)
7D: "So long." (1 unit.)

The inverse case is also worth considering. Mr. E and Mr. F have set up a two-stroke ritual, Hi-Hi. One day instead of passing on, Mr. E stops and asks: "How are you?" The conversation proceeds as follows:

1E: "Hi!"
1F: "Hi!"
2E: "How are you?"
2F (*Puzzled.*): "Fine. How are you?"
3E: "Everything's great. Warm enough for you?"
3F: "Yeah." (*Cautiously.*) "Looks like rain, though."
4E: "Nice to see you again."
4F: "Same here. Sorry, I've got to get to the library before it closes. So long."
5E: "So long."

As Mr. F hurries away, he thinks to himself: "What's come over him all of a sudden? Is he selling insurance or something?" In transactional terms this reads: "All he owes me is one stroke, why is he giving me five?"

An even simpler demonstration of the truly transactional, business-like nature of these simple rituals is the occasion when Mr. G says "Hi!" and Mr. H passes on without replying. Mr. G's reaction is "What's the matter with him?" meaning: "I gave him a stroke and he didn't give me one in return." If Mr. H keeps this up and extends it to other acquaintances, he is going to cause some talk in his community.

. . . . .

DEFINITION OF GAMES

A game is an ongoing series of complementary ulterior transactions progressing to a well-defined, predictable outcome.

Descriptively it is a recurring set of transactions, often repetitious, superficially plausible, with a concealed motivation; or, more colloquially, a series of moves with a snare, or "gimmick." Games are clearly differentiated from procedures, rituals, and pastimes by two chief characteristics: (1) their ulterior quality and (2) the payoff. Procedures may be successful, rituals effective, and pastimes profitable, but all of them are by definition candid; they may involve contest, but not conflict, and the ending may be sensational, but it is not dramatic. Every game, on the other hand, is basically dishonest, and the outcome has a dramatic, as distinct from merely exciting, quality.

It remains to distinguish games from the one remaining type of social action which so far has not been discussed. An *operation* is a simple transaction or set of transactions undertaken for a specific, stated purpose. If someone frankly asks for reassurance and gets it, that is an operation. If someone asks for reassurance, and after it is given turns it in some way to the disadvantage of the giver, that is a game. Superficially, then, a game looks like a set of operations, but after the payoff it becomes apparent that these "operations" were really *maneuvers;* not honest requests but moves in the game.

In the "insurance game," for example, no matter what the agent appears to be doing in conversation, if he is a hard player he is really looking for or working on a prospect. What he is after, if he is worth his salt, is to "make a killing." The same applies to "the real estate game," "the pajama game" and similar occupations. Hence at a social gathering, while a salesman is engaged in pastimes, particularly variants of "Balance Sheet," his congenial participation may conceal a series of skillful maneuvers designed to elicit the kind of information he is professionally interested in. There are dozens of trade journals devoted to improving commercial maneuvers, and which give accounts of outstanding players and games (interesting operators who make unusually big deals). Transactionally speaking, these are merely variants of *Sports Illustrated, Chess World,* and other sports magazines.

. . . . .

What we are concerned with here, however, are the unconscious games played by innocent people engaged in duplex transactions of which they are not fully aware, and which form the most important aspect of social life all over the world. Because of their dynamic qualities, games are easy to distinguish from mere static *attitudes,* which arise from taking a position.

The use of the word "game" should not be misleading. As explained in the introduction, it does not necessarily imply fun or even enjoyment. Many salesmen do not consider their work fun, as Arthur Miller made clear in his play *The Death of a Salesman.* And there may be no lack of seriousness. Football games nowadays are taken very seriously, but no more so than such transactional games as "Alocholic" or "Third-Degree Rapo."

The same applies to the word "play," as anyone who has "played" hard poker or "played" the stock market over a long period can testify. The possible seriousness of games and play, and the possibly serious results, are well known to anthropologists. The most complex game that ever existed, that of "Courtier" as described so well by Stendhal in *The Charterhouse of Parma,* was deadly serious. The grimmest of all, of course, is "War."

A TYPICAL GAME

The most common game played between spouses is colloquially called "If It

Weren't For You," and this will be used to illustrate the characteristics of games in general.

Mrs. White complained that her husband severely restricted her social activities, so that she had never learned to dance. Due to changes in her attitude brought about by psychiatric treatment, her husband became less sure of himself and more indulgent. Mrs. White was then free to enlarge the scope of her activities. She signed up for dancing classes, and then discovered to her despair that she had a morbid fear of dance floors and had to abandon this project.

This unfortunate adventure, along with similar ones, laid bare some important aspects of the structure of her marriage. Out of her many suitors she had picked a domineering man for a husband. She was then in a position to complain that she could do all sorts of things "if it weren't for you." Many of her women friends also had domineering husbands, and when they met for their morning coffee, they spent a good deal of time playing "If It Weren't For Him."

. . . . .

But there was more to it than that. His prohibitions and her complaints frequently led to quarrels, so that their sex life was seriously impaired. And because of his feelings of guilt, he frequently brought her gifts which might not otherwise have been forthcoming; certainly when he gave her more freedom, his gifts diminished in lavishness and frequency. . . .

. . . . .

. . . In its most dramatic form, IWFY at the social level is a Parent-Child game.

Mr. White: "You stay home and take care of the house."

Mrs. White: "If it weren't for you, I could be out having fun."

At the psychological level . . . the relationship is . . . quite different.

Mr. White: "You must always be here when I get home. I'm terrified of desertion."

Mrs. White: "I will be if you help me avoid phobic situations."

. . . . .

Moves

The moves of a game correspond roughly to the strokes in a ritual. As in any game, the players become increasingly adept with practice. Wasteful moves are eliminated, and more and more purpose is condensed into each move. "Beautiful friendships" are often based on the fact that the players complement each other with great economy and satisfaction, so that there is a maximum yield with a minimum effort from the games they play with each other. Certain intermediate, precautionary or concessional moves can be elided, giving a high degree of elegance to the relationship. The effort saved on defensive maneuvers can be utilized in flourishes and endless variations.

. . . . .

THE GENESIS OF GAMES

From the present point of view, child rearing may be regarded as an educational process in which the child is taught what games to play and how to play them. He is also taught procedures, rituals and pastimes appropriate to his position in the local social situation, but these are less significant. His knowledge of and skill in procedures, rituals and pastimes determine what opportunities will be available to him, other things being equal; but his games determine the use he will make of those opportunities, and the outcomes of situations for which he is eligible. As elements of his script, or unconscious life-plan, his favored games also determine his ultimate destiny (again with other things being equal): the payoffs on his marriage and career, and the circumstances surrounding his death.

While conscientious parents devote a great deal of attention to teaching their children procedures, rituals and pastimes appropriate to their stations in life, and with equal care select schools, colleges and churches where their teachings will be reinforced, they tend to overlook the question of games, which form the basic structure for the emotional dynamics of each family, and which the children learn through significant experiences in everyday living from their earliest months. Related questions have been discussed for thousands of years in a rather general, unsystematic fashion, and there has been some attempt at a more methodical approach in the modern orthopsychiatric literature; but without the concept of games there is little possibility of a consistent investigation. Theories of internal individual psychodynamics have so far not been able to solve satisfactorily the problems of human relationships. These are transactional situations which call for a theory of social dynamics that cannot be derived solely from consideration of individual motivations.

· · · · ·

Tanjy, age 7, got a stomach-ache at the dinner table and asked to be excused for that reason. His parents suggested that he lie down for a while. His little brother Mike, age 3, then said, "I have a stomach-ache, too," evidently angling for the same consideration. The father looked at him for a few seconds and then replied, "You don't want to play that game, do you?" Whereupon Mike burst out laughing and said, "No!"

If this had been a household of food or bowel faddists, Mike would also have been packed off to bed by his alarmed parents. If he and they had repeated this performance several times, it might be anticipated that this game would have become part of Mike's character, as it so often does if the parents cooperate. Whenever he was jealous of a privilege granted to a competitor, he would plead illness in order to get some privileges himself. . . .

THE FUNCTION OF GAMES

. . . It should be remembered that the essential feature of a game is its culmination, or payoff. The principal function of the preliminary moves is to set up the situation for this payoff, but they are always designed to harvest the maximum permissible satisfaction at each step as a secondary product. Thus in "Schlemiel" (making messes and then apologizing) the payoff, and the purpose of the game, is to obtain the forgiveness which is forced by the apology; the spillings and cigarette burns are only steps leading up to this, but each such trespass yields its own pleasure. The enjoyment derived from the spilling does not make spilling a game. The apology is the critical stimulus that leads to the denouement. Otherwise the spilling would simply be a destructive procedure, a delinquency perhaps enjoyable.

· · · · ·

Beyond their social function in structuring time satisfactorily, some games are urgently necessary for the maintenance of health in certain individuals. These people's psychic stability is so precarious, and their positions are so tenuously maintained, that to deprive them of their games may plunge them into irreversible despair and even psychosis. Such people will fight very hard against any antithetical moves. This is often observed in marital situations when the psychiatric improvement of one spouse (i.e., the abandonment of destructive games) leads to rapid deterioration in the other spouse, to whom the games were of paramount importance in maintaining equilibrium. Hence it is necessary to exercise prudence in game analysis.

Fortunately, the rewards of game-free intimacy, which is or should be the most perfect form of human living, are so great that even precariously balanced personalities can safely and joyfully relinquish their games if an appropriate partner can be found for the better relationship.

On a larger scale, games are integral and dynamic components of the unconscious life-plan, or script, of each individual; they serve to fill in the time while he waits for the final fulfillment, simultaneously advancing the action. Since the last act of a script characteristically calls for either a miracle or a catastrophe, depending on whether the script is constructive or destructive, the corresponding games are accordingly either constructive or destructive. In colloquial terms, an individual whose script is oriented toward "waiting for Santa Claus" is likely to be pleasant to deal with in such games as "Gee You're Wonderful, Mr. Murgatroyd," while someone with a tragic script oriented toward "waiting for *rigor mortis* to set in" may play such disagreeable games as "Now I've Got You, You S.O.B."

It should be noted that colloquialisms such as those in the previous sentence are an integral part of game analysis, and are freely used in transactional psychotherapy groups and seminars. The expression "waiting for *rigor mortis* to set in" originated in a dream of a patient, in which she decided to get certain things done "before *rigor mortis* set in." A patient in a sophisticated group

pointed out what the therapist had overlooked: that in practice, waiting for Santa Claus and waiting for death are synonymous. . . .

· · · · ·

TYPES OF GAMES
Alcoholic

THESIS | In game analysis there is no such thing as alcoholism or "an alcoholic," but there is a role called the Alcoholic in a certain type of game. If a biochemical or physiological abnormality is the prime mover in excessive drinking —and that is still open to some question —then its study belongs in the field of internal medicine. Game analysis is interested in something quite different—the kinds of social transactions that are related to such excesses. Hence the game "Alcoholic."

In its full flower this is a five-handed game, although the roles may be condensed so that it starts off and terminates as a two-handed one. The central role is that of the Alcoholic—the one who is "it"—played by White. (The one who is "it" is generally referred to as the "agent," or is given the name of "White," while the other party is called "Black.") The chief supporting role is that of Persecutor, typically played by a member of the opposite sex, usually the spouse. The third role is that of Rescuer, usually played by someone of the same sex, often the good family doctor who is interested in the patient and also in drinking problems. In the classical situation the doctor successfully rescues the alcoholic from his habit. After White has not taken a drink for six months they congratulate each other. The following day White is found in the gutter.

The fourth role is that of the Patsy, or Dummy. In literature this is played by the delicatessen man who extends credit to White, gives him a sandwich on the cuff and perhaps a cup of coffee, without either persecuting him or trying to rescue him. In life this is more frequently played by White's mother, who gives him money and often sympathizes with him about the wife who does not understand him. In this aspect of the game, White is required to account in some plausible way for his need for money—by some project in which both pretend to believe, although they know what he is really going to spend most of the money for. Sometimes the Patsy slides over into another role, which is a helpful but not essential one: the Agitator, the "good guy" who offers supplies without even being asked for them: "Come have a drink with me (and you will go downhill faster)."

The ancillary professional in all drinking games is the bartender or liquor clerk. In the game "Alcoholic" he plays the fifth role, the Connection, the direct source of supply who also understands alcoholic talk, and who in a way is the most meaningful person in the life of any addict. The difference between the Connection and the other players is the difference between professionals and amateurs in any game: the professional knows when to stop. At a certain point a good bartender refuses to serve the Alcoholic, who is then left without any supplies unless he can locate a more indulgent Connection.

In the initial stages of "Alcoholic," the wife may play all three supporting roles: at midnight the Patsy, undressing him, making him coffee and letting him beat up on her; in the morning the Persecutor, berating him for the evil of his ways; and in the evening the Rescuer, pleading with him to change them. . . .

Present experience indicates that the *payoff* in "Alcoholic" (as is characteristic of games in general) comes from the aspect to which most investigators pay least attention. In the analysis of this game, drinking itself is merely an incidental pleasure having added advantages, the procedure leading up to the real culmination, which is the hangover. It is the same in the game of Schlemiel: the mess-making, which attracts the most attention, is merely a pleasure-giving way for White to lead up to the crux, which is obtaining forgiveness from Black.

For the Alcoholic the hangover is not as much the physical pain as the psychological torment. The two favorite pastimes of drinking people are "Martini" (how many drinks and how they were mixed) and "Morning After" (Let me tell you about *my* hangover). "Martini" is played, for the most part, by social drinkers; many alcoholics prefer a hard round of psychological "Morning After," and organizations such as A.A. offer him an unlimited opportunity for this.

Whenever one patient visited his psychiatrist after a binge, he would call himself all sorts of names; the psychiatrist said nothing. Later, recounting these visits in a therapy group, White said with smug satisfaction that it was the psychiatrist who had called him all those names. The main conversational interest of many alcoholics in the therapeutic situation is not their drinking, which they apparently mention mostly in deference to their persecutors, but their subsequent suffering. The . . . object of the drinking, aside from the personal pleasures it brings, is to set up a situation where the Child can be severely scolded not only by the internal Parent but by any parental figures in the environment who are interested enough to oblige. Hence the therapy of this game should be concentrated not on the drinking but on the morning after, the self-indulgence in self-castigation. There is a type of heavy drinker, however, who does not have hangovers, and such people do not belong in the present category.

There are a variety of organizations involved in "Alcoholic," some of them national or even international in scope, others local. Many of them publish rules for the game. Nearly all of them explain how to play the role of Alcoholic: take a drink before breakfast, spend money allotted for other purposes, etc. They also explain the function of the Rescuer. Alcoholics Anonymous, for example, continues playing the actual game but concentrates on inducing the Alcoholic to take the role of Rescuer. Former Alcoholics are preferred because they know how the game goes, and hence are better qualified to play the supporting role than people who have never played before. Cases have been reported of a chapter of A.A. running out of Alcoholics to work on; whereupon the members resumed drinking, since there was no other way to continue the game in the absence of people to rescue.

There are also organizations devoted to improving the lot of the other players. Some put pressure on the spouses to shift their roles from Persecutor to Rescuer. The one which seems to come closest to the theoretical ideal of treatment deals with teen-age offspring of alcoholics; these young people are encouraged to break away from the game itself, rather than merely shift their roles.

The psychological cure of an alcoholic also lies in getting him to stop playing the game altogether, rather than simply change from one role to another. In some cases this has been feasible, although it is a difficult task to find something else as interesting to the Alcoholic as continuing his game. Since he is classically afraid of intimacy, the substitute may have to be another game rather than a game-free relationship. Often so-called cured alcoholics are not very stimulating company socially, and possibly they feel a lack of excitement in their lives and are continually tempted to go back to their old ways. The criterion of a true "game cure" is that the former Alcoholic should be able to drink socially without putting himself in jeopardy. The usual "total abstinence" cure will not satisfy the game analyst.

. . . . .

Debtor

THESIS | "Debtor" is more than a game. In America it tends to become a script, a plan for a whole lifetime, just as it does in some of the jungles of Africa and New Guinea. There the relatives of a young man buy him a bride at an enormous price, putting him in their debt for years to come. Here the same custom prevails, at least in the more civilized sections of the country, except that the bride price becomes a house price, and if there is no stake from the relatives, this role is taken on by the bank.

Thus the young man in New Guinea with an old wrist watch dangling from his ear to ensure success, and the young man in America with a new wrist watch wrapped around his arm to ensure success, both feel that they have a "purpose" in life. The big celebration, the wedding or housewarming, takes place not when the debt is discharged, but when it is undertaken. What is emphasized on TV, for example, is not the middle-aged man who has finally paid off his mortgage, but the young man who moves into his new home with his family, proudly waving the papers he has just signed and which will bind him for most of his productive years. After he has paid his debts—the mortgage, the college expenses for his children and his insurance —he is regarded as a problem, a "senior citizen" for whom society must provide not only material comforts but a new "purpose." . . .

Most young Americans, however, take their mortgages very seriously only in times of stress. If they are depressed, or the economic situation is bad, their obligations keep them going and may prevent some of them from committing suicide. Most of the time they play a mild game of "If It Weren't for the Debts," but otherwise enjoy themselves. Only a few make a career out of playing a hard game of "Debtor."

"Try and Collect" (TAC) is commonly played by young married couples, and illustrates how a game is set up so that the player "wins" whichever way it goes. The Whites obtain all sorts of goods and services on credit, petty or luxurious, depending on their backgrounds and how they were taught to play by their parents or grandparents. If the creditor gives up after a few soft efforts to collect, then the Whites can enjoy their gains without penalty, and in this sense they win. If the creditor makes more strenuous attempts, then they enjoy the pleasures of the chase as well as the use of their purchases. The hard form of the game occurs if the creditor is determined to collect. In order to get his money he will have to resort to extreme measures. These usually have a coercive element— going to White's employers or driving up to his house in a noisy, garish truck labeled in big letters COLLECTION AGENCY.

At this point there is a switch. White now knows that he will probably have to pay. But because of the coercive element, made clear in most cases by the "third letter" from the collector ("If you do not appear at our office within 48 hours. . . ."), White feels peremptorily justified in getting angry; he now switches over to a variant of "Now I've Got You, You Son of a Bitch." In this case he wins by demonstrating that the creditor is greedy, ruthless and untrustworthy. The two most obvious advantages of this are (1) it strengthens White's existential position, which is a disguised form of "All creditors are grasping," and (2) it offers a large external social gain, since he is now in a position to abuse the creditor openly to his friends without losing his own status as a "Good Joe." He may also exploit further internal social gain by confronting the creditor

himself. In addition, it vindicates his taking advantage of the credit system: if that is the way creditors are, as he has now shown, why pay anybody?

"Creditor," in the form "Try and Get Away With It" (TAGAWI), is sometimes played by small landlords. TAC and TAGAWI players readily recognize each other, and because of the prospective transactional advantages and the promised sport, they are secretly pleased and readily become involved with each other. Regardless of who wins the money, each has improved the other's position for playing "Why Does This Always Happen To Me?" after it is all over.

. . . . .

ANTITHESIS | The obvious antithesis of TAC is to request immediate payment in cash. But a good TAC player has methods for getting around that, which will work on any but the most hardboiled creditors. The antithesis of TAGAWI is promptness and honesty. Since hard TAC and TAGAWI players are both professionals in every sense of the word, an amateur stands as much chance playing against them as he does playing against professional gamblers. While the amateur seldom wins, he can at least enjoy himself if he becomes involved in one of these games. Since both are by tradition played grimly, nothing is more disconcerting to the professionals than to have an amateur victim laugh at the outcome. In financial circles this is considered strictly Out. In the cases reported to this writer, laughing at a debtor when one encounters him on the street is just as bewildering, frustrating and disconcerting to him as playing anti-"Schlemiel" is to a Schlemiel.

Kick Me

THESIS | This is played by men whose social manner is equivalent to wearing a sign that reads "Please Don't Kick Me."

The temptation is almost irresistible, and when the natural result follows, White cries piteously, "But the sign says '*don't* kick me.'" Then he adds incredulously, "Why does this always happen to me?" (WAHM). . . .

. . . . .

An interesting form of WAHM occurs in well-adapted people who reap increasing rewards and successes, often beyond their own expectations. Here the WAHM may lead to serious and constructive thinking, and to personal growth in the best sense, if it takes the form "What did I really do to deserve this?"

Now I've Got You, You S.O.B.

THESIS | This can be seen in classic form in poker games. White gets an unbeatable hand, such as four aces. At this point, if he is a NIGYSOB player, he is more interested in the fact that Black is completely at his mercy than he is in good poker or making money.

White needed some plumbing fixtures installed, and he reviewed the costs very carefully with the plumber before giving him a go-ahead. The price was set, and it was agreed that there would be no extras. When the plumber submitted his bill, he included a few dollars extra for an unexpected valve that had to be installed—about four dollars on a four-hundred-dollar job. White became infuriated, called the plumber on the phone and demanded an explanation. The plumber would not back down. White wrote him a long letter criticizing his integrity and ethics and refused to pay the bill until the extra charge was withdrawn. The plumber finally gave in.

It soon became obvious that both White and the plumber were playing games. In the course of their negotiations, they had recognized each other's potentials. The plumber made his pro-vocative move when he submitted his bill. Since White had the plumber's word, the plumber was clearly in the wrong. . . .

NIGYSOB is a two-handed game which must be distinguished from "Ain't It Awful?" (AIA). In AIA the agent seeks injustices in order to complain about them to a third party, making a three-handed game: Aggressor, Victim, Confidant. AIA is played under the slogan "Misery Loves Company." The confidant is usually someone who also plays AIA. WAHM is three-handed, too, but here the agent is trying to establish his pre-eminence in misfortune and resents competition from other unfortunates. NIGYSOB is commercialized in a three-handed professional form as the "badger game." It may also be played as a two-handed marital game in more or less subtle forms.

ANTITHESIS | The best antithesis is correct behavior. The contractual structure of a relationship with a NIGYSOB player should be explicitly stated in detail at the first opportunity, and the rules strictly adhered to. In clinical practice, for example, the question of payment for missed appointments or cancellations must be settled clearly at once, and extra precautions must be taken to avoid mistakes in bookkeeping. If an unforeseen contretemps arises, the antithesis is to yield gracefully without dispute, until such time as the therapist is prepared to deal with the game. In everyday life, business dealings with NIGYSOB players are always calculated risks. The wife of such a person should be treated with polite correctness, and even the mildest flirtations, gallantries or slights should be avoided, especially if the husband himself seems to encourage them.

See What You Made Me Do

THESIS | In its classical form this is a marital game, and in fact is a "three-star marriage buster," but it may also be played between parents and children and in working life.

(1) First-Degree SWYMD: White, feeling unsociable, becomes engrossed in some activity which tends to insulate him against people. Perhaps all he wants at the moment is to be left alone. An intruder, such as his wife or one of his children, comes either for stroking or to ask him something like, "Where can I find the long-nosed pliers?" This interruption "causes" his chisel, paintbrush, typewriter or soldering iron to slip, whereupon he turns on the intruder in a rage and cries, "See what you made me do." As this is repeated through the years, his family tends more and more to leave him alone when he is engrossed. Of course it is not the intruder but his own irritation which "causes" the slip, and he is only too happy when it occurs, since it gives him a lever for ejecting the visitor. . . .

. . . . .

The professional player who pays his psychological way with SWYMD will use it also in his work. In occupational SWYMD the long-suffering look of resentment replaces words. The player "democratically" or as part of "good management" asks his assistants for suggestions. In this way he may attain an unassailable position for terrorizing his juniors. Any mistake he makes can be used against them by blaming them for it. Used against seniors (blaming them for one's mistakes), it becomes self-destructive and may lead to termination of employment or, in the army, to transfer to another unit. In that case it is a component of "Why Does This Always Happen To Me?" with resentful people, or of "There I Go Again" with depressives —(both of the "Kick Me" family).

Almost any game can form the scaffolding for married life and family

living, but some, such as "If It Weren't for You," flourish better or, like "Frigid Woman," are tolerated longer, under the legal force of contractual intimacy. Marital games, of course, can only be arbitrarily separated from sexual games. . . . Those games which characteristically evolve into their most full-blown forms in the marital relationship include "Corner," "Courtroom," "Frigid Woman" and "Frigid Man," "Harried," "If It Weren't for You," "Look How Hard I've Tried" and "Sweetheart."

Corner

THESIS | Corner illustrates more clearly than most games their manipulative aspect and their function as barriers to intimacy. Paradoxically, it consists of a disingenuous refusal to play the game of another.

1. Mrs. White suggests to her husband that they go to a movie. Mr. White agrees.

2a. Mrs. White makes an "unconscious" slip. She mentions quite naturally in the course of conversation that the house needs painting. This is an expensive project, and White has recently told her that their finances are strained; he requested her not to embarrass or annoy him by suggesting unusual expenditures, at least until the beginning of the new month. This is therefore an ill-chosen moment to bring up the condition of the house, and White responds rudely.

2b. Alternatively: White steers the conversation around to the house, making it difficult for Mrs. White to resist the temptation to say that it needs painting. As in the previous case, White responds rudely.

3. Mrs. White takes offense and says that if he is in one of his bad moods, she will not go to the movie with him, and he had best go by himself. He says if that is the way she feels about it, he will go alone.

4. White goes to the movie (or out with the boys), leaving Mrs. White at home to nurse her injured feelings.

There are two possible gimmicks in this game:

A. Mrs. White knows very well from past experience that she is not supposed to take his annoyance seriously. What he really wants is for her to show some appreciation of how hard he works to earn their living; then they could go off happily together. But she refuses to play, and he feels badly let down. He leaves filled with disappointment and resentment, while she stays at home looking abused, but with a secret feeling of triumph.

B. White knows very well from past experience that he is not supposed to take her pique seriously. What she really wants is to be honeyed out of it; then they would go off happily together. But he refuses to play, knowing that his refusal is dishonest: he knows she wants to be coaxed, but pretends he doesn't. He leaves the house, feeling cheerful and relieved, but looking wronged. She is left feeling disappointed and resentful.

In each of these cases the winner's position is, from a naïve standpoint, irreproachable; all he or she has done is take the other literally. This is clearer in (B), where White takes Mrs. White's refusal to go at face value. They both know that this is cheating, but since she said it, she is cornered.

The most obvious gain here is the external psychological. Both of them find movies sexually stimulating, and it is more or less anticipated that after they return from the theater, they will make love. Hence whichever one of them wants to avoid intimacy sets up the game in move (2a) or (2b). This is a particularly exasperating variety of "Uproar." The "wronged" party can, of course, make a good case for not wanting to make love in a state of justifiable indignation, and the cornered spouse has no recourse.

ANTITHESIS | This is simple for Mrs. White. All she has to do is change her mind, take her husband by the arm, smile and go along with him. . . . It is more difficult for Mr. White, since she now has the initiative; but if he reviews the whole situation, he may be able to coax her into going along with him, either as a sulky Child who has been placated or, better, as an Adult.

. . . . .

An everyday form of "Corner" which is played by the whole family and is most likely to affect the character development of the younger children occurs with meddlesome "Parental" parents. The little boy or girl is urged to be more helpful around the house, but when he is, the parents find fault with what he does—a homely example of "damned if you do and damned if you don't." This "double-bind" may be called the Dilemma Type of "Corner."

"Corner" is sometimes found as an etiological factor in asthmatic children.

LITTLE GIRL: "Mommy, do you love me?"
MOTHER: "What is love?"

This answer leaves the child with no direct recourse. She wants to talk about mother, and mother switches the subject to philosophy, which the little girl is not equipped to handle. She begins to breathe hard, mother is irritated, asthma sets in, mother apologizes and the "Asthma Game" now runs its course. This "Asthma" type of "Corner" remains to be studied further.

. . . . .

Closely allied to "Corner" on the one hand, and to "Threadbare" on the other, is the marital game of "Lunch Bag." The husband, who can well afford to have lunch at a good restaurant, nevertheless makes himself a few sandwiches every morning, which he takes to the office in a paper bag. In this way he uses up crusts of bread, leftovers from dinner and paper bags which his wife saves for him. This gives him complete control over the family finances, for what wife would dare buy herself a mink stole in the face of such self-sacrifice? The husband reaps numerous other advantages, such as the privilege of eating lunch by himself and of catching up on his work during lunch hour. In many ways this is a constructive game which Benjamin Franklin would have approved of, since it encourages the virtues of thrift, hard work and punctuality.

. . . . .

Courtroom

THESIS . . . | "Courtroom" can be played by any number, but is essentially three-handed, with a plaintiff, a defendant and a judge, represented by a husband, a wife and the therapist. If it is played in a therapy group or over the radio or TV, the other members of the audience are cast as the jury. The husband begins plaintively, "Let me tell you what (wife's name) did yesterday. She took the . . ." etc., etc. The wife then responds defensively, "Here is the way it really was . . . and besides just before that he was . . . and anyway at the time we were both . . ." etc. The husband adds gallantly, "Well, I'm glad you people have a chance to hear both sides of the story, I only want to be fair." . . .

. . . . .

ANTITHESIS . . . | After sufficient clinical material has been gathered to clarify the situation, the game can be interdicted by a maneuver which is one of the most elegant in the whole art of antithetics. The therapist makes a rule prohibiting the use

of the (grammatical) third person in the group. Thenceforward the members can only address each other directly as "you" or talk about themselves as "I," but they cannot say, "Let me tell you about him" or "Let me tell you about her." At this point the couple stop playing games in the group altogether, or shift into "Sweetheart," which is some improvement, or take up "Furthermore," which is no help at all. . . .

. . . . .

In its *everyday* form, "Courtroom" is easily observed in children as a three-handed game between two siblings and a parent. "Mommy, she took my candy away." "Yes, but he took my doll, and before that he was hitting me, and anyway we both promised to share our candy."

. . . . .

Frigid Woman

THESIS | This is almost always a marital game, since it is hardly conceivable that an informal liaison would present the required opportunities and privileges over a sufficient length of time, or that such a liaison would be maintained in the face of it.

The husband makes advances to his wife and is repulsed. After repeated attempts, he is told that all men are beasts, he doesn't really love her, or doesn't love her for herself, that all he is interested in is sex. He desists for a time, then tries again with the same result. Eventually he resigns himself and makes no further advances. As the weeks or months pass, the wife becomes increasingly informal and sometimes forgetful. She walks through the bedroom half dressed or forgets her clean towel when she takes a bath so that he has to bring it to her. If she plays a hard game or drinks heavily, she may become flirtatious with other men at parties.

At length he responds to those provocations and tries again. Once more he is repulsed, and a game of "Uproar" ensues involving their recent behavior, other couples, their inlaws, their finances and their failures, terminated by a slamming door.

This time the husband makes up his mind that he is really through, that they will find a sexless *modus vivendi*. Months pass. He declines the negligee parade and the forgotten towel maneuver. The wife becomes more provocatively informal and more provocatively forgetful, but he still resists. Then one evening she actually approaches him and kisses him. At first he doesn't respond, remembering his resolution, but soon nature begins to take its course after the long famine, and now he thinks he surely has it made. His first tentative advances are not repulsed. He becomes bolder and bolder. Just at the critical point, the wife steps back and cries: "See, what did I tell you! All men are beasts, all I wanted was affection, but all you are interested in is sex!" The ensuing game of "Uproar" at this point may skip the preliminary phases of their recent behavior and their in-laws, and go right to the financial problem.

It should be noted that in spite of his protestations, the husband is usually just as afraid of sexual intimacy as his wife is, and has carefully chosen his mate to minimize the danger of overtaxing his disturbed potency, which he can now blame on her.

In its *everyday* form this game is played by unmarried ladies of various ages, which soon earns them a common slang epithet. With them it often merges into the game of indignation, or "Rapo."

ANTITHESIS | This is a dangerous game, and the possible antitheses are equally dangerous. Taking a mistress is a gamble. In the face of such stimulating competition, the wife may give up the game and try to initiate a normal married life, perhaps too late. On the other hand, she may use the affair, often with the help of a lawyer, as ammunition against the husband in a game of "Now I've Got You, You, You S.O.B." . . .

Harried

THESIS | This is a game played by the harried housewife. Her situation requires that she be proficient in ten or twelve different occupations; or, stated otherwise, that she fill gracefully ten or twelve different roles. From time to time semi-facetious lists of these occupations or roles appear in the Sunday supplements: mistress, mother, nurse, housemaid, etc. Since these roles are usually conflicting and fatiguing, their imposition gives rise in the course of years to the condition symbolically known as "Housewife's Knee" (since the knee is used for rocking, scrubbing, lifting, driving and so forth), whose symptoms are succinctly summarized in the complaint: "I'm tired."

. . . . .

The thesis of this game is simple. She takes on everything that comes, and even asks for more. She agrees with her husband's criticisms and accepts all her children's demands. If she has to entertain at dinner, she not only feels she must function impeccably as a conversationalist, chatelaine over the household and servants, interior decorator, caterer, glamor girl, virgin queen and diplomat; she will also volunteer that morning to bake a cake and take the children to the dentist. If she already feels harassed, she makes the day even more harried. Then in the middle of the afternoon she justifiably collapses, and nothing gets done. She lets down her husband, the children and their guests, and her self-reproaches add to her misery. After this happens two or three times her marriage is in jeopardy, the children are confused, she loses weight, her hair is untidy, her face is drawn and her shoes are scuffed. Then she appears at the psychiatrist's office, ready to be hospitalized.

ANTITHESIS | The logical antithesis is simple: Mrs. White can fill each of her roles in succession during the week, but she must refuse to play two or more of them simultaneously. When she gives a cocktail party, for example, she can play either caterer or nursemaid, but not both. . . .

If she is actually playing a game of "Harried," however, it will be very difficult for her to adhere to this principle. In that case the husband is carefully chosen; he is an otherwise reasonable man who will criticize his wife if she is not as efficient as he thinks his mother was. . . .

When the position becomes untenable, often because of official school intervention on behalf of the unhappy offspring, the psychiatrist is called in to make it a three-handed game. Either the husband wants him to do an overhaul job on the wife, or the wife wants him as an ally against the husband. The ensuing proceedings depend on the skill and alertness of the psychiatrist. Usually the first phase, the alleviation of the wife's depression, will proceed smoothly. The second phase, in which she will give up playing "Harried" in favor of playing "Psychiatry," is the decisive one. It tends to arouse increasing opposition from both spouses. Sometimes this is well concealed and then explodes suddenly, though not unexpectedly. If this stage is weathered, then the real work of game analysis can proceed.

. . . . .

Sweetheart

THESIS | This is seen in its fullest flower in the early stages of marital group therapy, when the parties feel defensive; it can also be observed on social occasions. White makes a subtly derogatory remark about Mrs. White, disguised as an anecdote, and ends: "Isn't that right, sweetheart?" Mrs. White tends to agree for two ostensibly Adult reasons: (a) because the anecdote itself is, in the main, accurately reported, and to disagree about what is presented as a peripheral detail (but is really the essential point of the transaction) would seem pedantic; (b) because it would seem surly to disagree with a man who calls one "sweetheart" in public. The psychological reason for her agreement, however, is her depressive position. She married him precisely because she knew he would perform this service for her: exposing her deficiencies and thus saving her from the embarrassment of having to expose them herself. Her parents accommodated her the same way when she was little.

Next to "Courtroom," this is the most common game played in marital groups. The more tense the situation, and the closer the game is to exposure, the more bitterly is the word "sweetheart" enunciated, until the underlying resentment becomes obvious. On careful consideration it can be seen that this is a relative of "Schlemiel," since the significant move is Mrs. White's implicit forgiveness for White's resentment, of which she is trying hard not to be aware. Hence anti-"Sweetheart" is played analogously to anti-"Schlemiel": "You can tell derogatory anecdotes about me, but please don't call me 'sweetheart.' " This antithesis carries with it the same perils as does anti-"Schlemiel." A more sophisticated and less dangerous antithesis is to reply: "Yes, *honey!*"

In another form the wife, instead of agreeing, responds with a similar "Sweetheart" type anecdote about the husband, saying in effect, "You have a dirty face too, dear."

Sometimes the endearments are not actually pronounced, but a careful listener can ‑ hear them even when they are unspoken. This is "Sweetheart," Silent Type.

. . . . .

Schlemiel

THESIS | The term "schlemiel" does not refer to the hero of Chamisso's novel, who was a man without a shadow, but to a popular Yiddish word allied to the German and Dutch words for cunning. The Schlemiel's victim, who is something like the "Good-Natured Fellow" of Paul de Kock, is colloquially called the Schlemazl. The moves in a typical game of "Schlemiel" are as follows:

1W. White spills a highball on the hostess's evening gown.

1B. Black (the host) responds initially with rage, but he senses (often only vaguely) that if he shows it, White wins. Black therefore pulls himself together, and this gives him the illusion that he wins.

2W. White says: "I'm sorry."

2B. Black mutters or cries forgiveness, strengthening his illusion that he wins.

3W. White then proceeds to inflict other damage on Black's property. He breaks things, spills things and makes messes of various kinds. After the cigarette burn in the tablecloth, the chair leg through the lace curtain and the gravy on the rug, White's Child is exhilarated because he has enjoyed himself in carrying out these procedures, for all of which he has been forgiven, while Black has made a gratifying display of suffering self-control. Thus both of them profit from an unfortunate situation, and Black is not necessarily anxious to terminate the friendship.

As in most games, White, who makes the first move, wins either way. If Black shows his anger, White can feel justified in returning the resentment. If Black restrains himself, White can go on enjoying his opportunities. The real payoff in this game, however, is not the pleasure of destructiveness, which is merely an added bonus for White, but the fact that he obtains forgiveness. This leads directly into the antithesis.

ANTITHESIS | Anti-"Schlemiel" is played by not offering the demanded absolution. After White says "I'm sorry," Black, instead of muttering "It's okay," says, "Tonight you can embarrass my wife, ruin the furniture and wreck the rug, but please don't say 'I'm sorry.'" Here Black switches from being a forgiving Parent to being an objective Adult who takes the full responsibility for having invited White in the first place.

The intensity of White's game will be revealed by his reaction, which may be quite explosive. One who plays anti-"Schlemiel" runs the risk of immediate reprisals or, at any rate, of making an enemy.

· · · · ·

Uproar

THESIS | The classical game is played between domineering fathers and teen-age daughters, where there is a sexually inhibited mother. Father comes home from work and finds fault with daughter, who answers impudently; or daughter may make the first move by being impudent, whereupon father finds fault. Their voices rise, and the clash becomes more acute. The outcome depends on who has the initiative. There are three possibilities: (a) father retires to his bedroom and slams the door (b) daughter retires to her bedroom and slams the door (c) both retire to their respective bedrooms and slam the doors. "Uproar" offers a distressing but effective solution to the sexual problems that arise between fathers and teen-age daughters in certain households. Often they can only live in the same house together if they are angry at each other, and the slamming doors emphasize for each of them the fact that they have separate bedrooms.

In degenerate households this game may be played in a sinister and repellent form in which father waits up for daughter whenever she goes out on a date, and examines her and her clothing carefully on her return to make sure that she has not had intercourse. The slightest suspicious circumstance may give rise to the most violent altercation, which may end with the daughter being expelled from the house in the middle of the night. In the long run nature will take its course—if not that night then the next, or the one after. Then the father's suspicions are "justified," as he makes plain to the mother, who has stood by "helplessly" while all this went on.

In general, however, "Uproar" may be played between any two people who are trying to avoid sexual intimacy. For example, it is a common terminal phase of "Frigid Woman." It is relatively rare between teen-age boys and their female relatives, because it is easier for teen-age boys to escape from the house in the evening than for other members of the family. At an earlier age brothers and sisters can set up effective barriers and partial satisfactions through physical combat, a pattern which has various motivations at different ages, and which in America is a semi-ritualistic form of "Uproar" sanctioned by television, pedagogic and pediatric authorities. In upper-class England it is (or was) considered bad form, and the corresponding energies are channeled into the well-regulated "Uproar" of the playing fields.

ANTITHESIS | The game is not as distasteful to the father as he might like to think, and it is generally the daughter who makes the antithetical move through an early, often premature or forced marriage. If it is psychologically possible, the mother can make the antithetical move by relinquishing her . . . frigidity. The game may subside if the father finds an outside sexual interest, but that may lead to other complications. In the case of married couples, the antitheses are the same as for "Frigid Woman" or "Frigid Man."

. . . . .

Many games are played most intensely by disturbed people; generally speaking, the more disturbed they are, the harder they play. Curiously enough, however, some schizophrenics seem to refuse to play games, and demand candidness from the beginning. In everyday life games are played with the greatest conviction by . . . the Sulks . . . .

The Sulk is a man who is angry at his mother. On investigation it emerges that he has been angry at her since early childhood. He often has good "Child" reasons for his anger: she may have "deserted" him during a critical period in his boyhood by getting sick and going to the hospital, or she may have given birth to too many siblings. Sometimes the desertion is more deliberate; she may have farmed him out in order to remarry. In any case, he has been sulking ever since. He does not like women, although he may be a Don Juan. Since sulking is deliberate at its inception, the decision to sulk can be reversed at any period of life, just as it can be during childhood when it comes time for dinner. The requirements for reversing the decision are the same for the grown-up Sulk as for the little boy. He must be able to save face, and he must be offered something worthwhile in exchange for the privilege of sulking. . . .

36 | PATTERNS OF CHILD REARING

ROBERT R. SEARS, ELEANOR E. MACCOBY,

AND HARRY LEVIN

Should a child be breast fed? What are the causes of bed-wetting?
How frequently do children express aggression against their parents, and
what patterns does such aggressive behavior take?

These passages from Patterns of Child Rearing *offer*
interpretations of the descriptions of child-rearing practices by
379 New England suburban mothers. The entire book presents evidence
that middle-class mothers are more permissive than those of the lower class.

Allison Davis and Robert J. Havighurst,* however, concluded
in their studies that middle-class mothers were more restrictive—completing
weaning and toilet training earlier and being more rigid in
feeding. They also found, as did Kinsey, that middle-class children
masturbate more often and concluded that this was due to the
tensions resulting from the restrictions imposed on them. Whiting and
Child,† who studied child rearing throughout the world, have
claimed that children of the American middle class are among the
most restricted anywhere.

. . . Breast feeding and self-demand scheduling have received the most interested public discussion in recent years. Militant enthusiasts for both have generated more excitement than facts. They have reasoned, in effect, that the "natural way" is best, and that a deep insecurity is created in infancy by bottle-propping or rigid scheduling or other methods of impersonalizing the feeding experience. They have talked much of *good* and *bad* consequences of various infant care practices without sure evidence that there are any consistent consequences at all. It is worth reviewing what we have discovered about these matters.

Sixty per cent of the mothers in this sample did not breast-feed their children. Their reasons were various, ranging from genuine physical disability to frankly emotional rejection of the nursing function. If we may judge by the experience of other cultures, actual incapacity could have accounted for a very small proportion of these cases. In between the extremes were a host of explanations which may or may not have been the major reasons.

. . . . .

Now as to the effects of breast feeding. There have been very few careful studies of the question. None so far has demonstrated any important and consistent relationship between breast feeding and any later quality of the personality. Our own data, reported in this chapter, add nothing new to this negative state of affairs. None of the children's characteristics, as judged by the mothers' descriptions of them, were different for the two groups, the breast-fed and the non-breast-fed. . . .

. . . . .

What have we found out about the self-demand *vs.* rigid scheduling controversy?

---

* Allison Davis and Robert J. Havighurst, *Father of the Man* (Boston: Houghton Mifflin Co., 1947).

† J. W. M. Whiting and I. L. Child, *Child Training and Personality: A Cross-Cultural Study* (New Haven: Yale University Press, 1953).

Excerpts reprinted from *Patterns of Child Rearing* (Row, Peterson & Co., 1957), by permission of the publisher and authors.

There is a clear indication in the mothers' reports that rigid scheduling is infrequent. So is complete self-demand, which is not surprising, for most infants develop some kind of schedule for themselves. Even the mother who is most solicitous of the baby's needs has some kind of schedule for her own household activities and probably in subtle ways tends to transfer this to the child. The range on this practice is quite wide in this group of mothers, but it tends clearly toward a child-oriented policy.

The findings with respect to weaning fit well with what was already known and add a few new items. The range of ages at which weaning to the cup was begun by this group of mothers was wide, but the central tendency was to begin early, well under the age of one year. This is very early, compared with the practices of nonliterate cultures. But the amount of emotional disturbance produced was not great, and the earlier the change was made, the less the upset. This accords with previous findings, which have suggested that the strength of the sucking habit, and the need to get food by sucking, are increased by more practice at sucking. The stronger such a drive or need is, the greater the severity of emotional upset when its actions are frustrated.

We have known, also, that upset is least when there is extensive preparation for the new mode of eating before the final step is taken that makes the child totally dependent on it. We can now add a new finding, that once the weaning has started, the emotional disturbance connected with it is most severe if the transition takes a long time.

It is always risky to give advice on the basis of group findings, but mothers have to make decisions on weaning anyway, and it may help to spell out what these facts suggest. If the goal is to have as little emotional disturbance as possible—and this is a big *if*, because there may be other goals that are more important, and would be better reached by doing some-

thing else—then it appears wisest to begin weaning before the end of the first year or else wait until the end of the second. If the longer period is used, the child obviously will have long since gone on a solid diet and will be taking many of his liquids by cup anyway. Secondly, there should be all possible preparation for the new mode of eating—orange juice, water, and especially some sips of milk by cup from the very beginning of life. Thus the new mode is not a shock and the skill is available. Giving attention to this preparation is obviously more important if weaning is to be done early. Thirdly, once the decision is made to wean—not just to prepare for it—the transition should be made as expeditiously as possible. There is no kindness in keeping a child on tenterhooks. If serious weaning is not undertaken until after the second year, there is always a good chance the baby will have weaned himself before the mother starts.

Finally, there is the matter of feeding problems in the preschool years. None of the infant-feeding practices we have examined—whether severe or gentle—appear to have been related to the later development of such problems. On the other hand, there was evidence that finickiness and other more severe reactions were related to harsh and restrictive methods of discipline. The relation is not a strong one, but it is consistent among the scales we examined.

. . . . .

TOILET TRAINING

Why is it that some children have so much difficulty in this area, others so little? It is likely that there are physiological differences between children which are important, but in the present context we are concerned with the influence of methods of training, and the emotional relationships within the home environment.

The most obvious matter to examine first is the toilet-training method itself.

The age at the beginning of training was of no significance ($r = .08$), so we can turn to *severity*. Our ratings on severity of toilet training took into account both bowel training and prevention of bed-wetting. From Table 1 it can be seen that the severity of the entire toilet-training process did have some bearing on children's tendencies to be late bed-wetters. When they were scolded and punished in the training process, they were somewhat more likely to be late bed-wetters than if their mothers were milder in their treatment.

As was the case with emotional reaction to the training process itself, however, simple severity of training does not tell the whole story. Again we find that the disruptive effects of severe training occurred with some mothers but not with others. As one can see from comparing the top and bottom lines of Table 1, severe training apparently had a kind of "kill or cure" effect so far as bed-wetting was concerned. When severely trained, the child either learned to be dry before he was two years old or he tended not to learn before he was five or six. Relatively few of the severely-trained children learned in the middle period.

Which children were "killed" and which "cured?" The answer is a curious one and we cannot pretend to have any theoretical explanation for it. Three things were related to late persistence of bed-wetting.

One was the severity of toilet training, and another was the mother's affectional warmth. Both of these, it will be recalled, were also related to the amount of emotional upset during training. But a third factor is new—the mother's sex anxiety. We saw earlier that this quality in the mother was somewhat connected with whether she breast-fed her baby or not, and with whether she started bowel training early. Now we find it positively associated with persistent bed-wetting. The combination of high sex anxiety, a relatively cold and undemonstrative attitude toward the child, and severe toilet training were most efficient for producing prolonged bed-wetting. This is the "kill" prescription. The "cure" combination, that gave unusually high probability of the child's achieving night dryness before he was two years old, also included high sex anxiety, but in this instance it was associated with a warm and affectionate attitude toward the child, and with gentle toilet training. Perhaps an easier way of saying this is that both warmth of affection and gentleness of training were positively related to early night dryness, while their opposites led to night wetting. But both dimensions were much more influential, in their respective ways, in mothers who were rated as having high sex anxiety.

Bed-wetting is a problem, of course, and the connection of severe toilet training with problem behavior has a familiar ring.

TABLE 1.		SEVERITY OF TOILET TRAINING			
BED-WETTING:	AGE AT WHICH CHILD	*Not at All Severe*	*Slight Pressure*	*Moderate Pressure*	*Quite Severe*
RELATIONSHIP	STOPPED WETTING BED				
TO THE SEVERITY					
OF TOILET	Before two years old	38%	49%	42%	45%
TRAINING	Between two and three years	30	21	27	11
	Between three and five years	4	5	6	9
	Before age five; not ascertained just when	11	10	6	4
	Still wets bed	17	15	19	31
	TOTAL	100%	100%	100%	100%
	NUMBER OF CASES	54	117	129	75

$$p < .01 \ (r = .18)$$

. . . [Earlier], we reported that children with feeding problems seemed to have had more severe toilet training, also. This raises the question as to whether children who had feeding problems also tended to be late bed-wetters, or whether problems in the feeding area (loss of appetite, refusal of certain foods) and bed-wetting are two possible *alternative* reactions to severe parental discipline. If the latter is so, the child who had one of these modes of response would not have had the other. There is some evidence that this was the case. Among the severely trained children, a child was less likely to wet the bed if he had feeding problems, and vice versa. Among the severely trained children who had *some* feeding problems, 22 per cent were late bed-wetters, while among the severely trained children who had *no* feeding problems, 47 per cent were late bed-wetters.

· · · · ·

Viewed even from a cross-cultural standpoint, the range of ages at which the mothers began toilet training was wide. An anthropologist might have difficulty in defining just what *the* American custom is. The modal age was between nine and eleven months, but there were quite a number of mothers who started within the child's first half-year and a good many more who waited until well after the first birthday.

Did these variations make any difference? From the mother's standpoint, yes. By and large, the later the training was started, the more quickly it was accomplished. Likewise, from the child's standpoint, training begun after twenty months produced emotional upset in relatively few of the children. These facts sound like arguments for a late beginning, especially when one notes the high proportion of upsets in those cases in which training began in the fifteen- to nineteen-month range.

There are other aspects of the situation

to be kept in mind, however. First there is the fact that mothers who began bowel training at the moderately early age of five to nine months found this procedure as successful as a very late start, in the sense that their children accepted the training with few signs of disturbance.

· · · · ·

Within the limits of our two measures —duration and upset—we conclude that either of two periods may be chosen for training with an expectation of reasonable comfort. These are the second six months of the child's life and the time after twenty months. The training evidently goes more quickly at the later time and produces little upset. The earlier period is also not immediately upsetting to the child, though the process takes longer. We do not know, of course, whether there are later consequences, in the child's personality, resulting from the choice between these two age periods.

A word is in order about the fifteen- to nineteen-month period. One reason that bowel training in this period may be upsetting to the child is that the *wrong* habits have become deeply ingrained. There has been little or no experience with the *right responses*. In other words, he has been practicing elimination in a diaper, lying down or walking, and in rooms that are not in the future to be appropriate for sphincter release. He has not been practicing in the presence of such correct cues as sitting on the potty, being undressed, hearing his mother talk about toileting, and so on. A further problem is that if training is begun after the child is old enough to run around, he will resist being kept in one place long enough for evacuation to occur and for him to be rewarded. A nine-months-old baby who is not yet walking, and who is still content to be confined to a play pen for reasonable lengths of time, will also sit happily on the potty for five or ten minutes, especially if someone stays with him. If he is at all regular in his bowel movements this is usually enough time for his bowel movement to coincide. His mother can then follow it with rewards and praise. The child of a year and a-half, however, finds it confining to be required to sit still, even for five minutes. He is likely to struggle or cry—activity which can in itself prevent sphincter release. Even if it does occur, the child's emotional state is such that his mother has difficulty making the experience rewarding to him, no matter how much she praises and smiles.

In contrast with these various doubts and queries about the most appropriate age for beginning toilet training, there is considerable certainty about the effects of the dimension of severity. The introduction of pressure, impatience, irritability and punishment into toilet training produces resentment, recalcitrance, and emotional upset in the child. It does not serve to speed his learning in the slightest, and may, if the mother is rather cold in her relations with him, serve to initiate a prolonged period of bed-wetting.

Severe training may be an almost inevitable maternal reaction to external conditions, of course. A child gone balky because he has gotten started wrong in his attempts to gain control is difficult to handle gently under the best of circumstances. A siege of illness in either the mother or child at a critical part of the training can prolong the process and be quite frustrating.

. . . . .

DEPENDENCY

Even though we must maintain a cautious attitude toward the validity of our measure of dependency, these findings provide a consistent picture of the sources of dependency. . . .

Mothers who repeatedly demonstrate their affection for children are providing many supports for whatever actions the children have performed in order to ob-

tain such demonstrations. These actions often involve following the mother around, touching her, smiling at her and talking, and keeping some kind of contact with her. These are the actions, of course, that we have labeled dependency.

Once the child has developed these habitual ways of acting—and all children develop some—he may be expected to use them as devices for reassuring himself that his mother does love him. That is to say, if she shows signs of rejection, if she uses withdrawal of love to discipline him, and if she is punitive toward his aggression, he may be expected to double his efforts to secure her affection. This will simply increase the frequency and persistence of the acts we have defined as dependent, and hence the mother will describe more of them.

The influence of affectionate demonstrativeness, if we may suggest a theoretical point, is an influence on the *learning* of dependency and aggression, and other behaviors that threaten the child's security, is an effect on performance or *action*. Therefore, the actual amount of dependency observed and reported by a mother is a product of both factors. It follows that the most dependent children should be those whose mothers express openly their affection for the child but repeatedly threaten the affectional bond by withholding love as a means of discipline and by being punitive toward his displays of parent-directed aggression.

These relationships are exactly what we have found, but just which way the cause-and-effect arrows point is impossible to say. We are skeptical that there is any single direction of cause-and-effect relations in the child-rearing process. True, the mother's personality comes first, chronologically, and she starts the sequence of interactive behavior that culminates in the child's personality. But once a child starts to be over-dependent—or is *perceived* as being so by his mother—he becomes a stimulus to the mother and influences her behavior toward him. Perhaps, within the present group of mothers, over-dependency of their children increased the mothers' rejective feelings, made them more angry and hence more punitive for aggression. The whole relationship could be circular. An enormous amount of painstaking research will be required to untangle these phenomena.

. . . . .

AGGRESSION

The control of aggression in the home is obviously not a simple matter. Every mother in our group had had to cope with angry outbursts or quarreling at one time or another, and 95 per cent of them reported instances of strong aggression that had been directed at the parents themselves. It seems evident that the conditions of living are such that all children develop aggressive motivation. It is equally certain that very few parents can tolerate as much hostility in the home as the children are instigated to display.

One can distinguish two important themes in the control of children's aggression. One is what we have called "non-permissiveness"—the tendency for a parent to believe that aggression by a child toward his parents is wrong, and to accompany this belief by action designed to prevent aggressive outbursts or stop them when they occur.

The other theme has to do with the amount of punishment a child receives for being aggressive toward his parents. The two dimensions are obviously not independent, for some parents express their non-permissive attitude primarily through punishment which they administer during or after a child's dislay of temper. But other parents express their non-permissiveness in such a way as to *prevent* the aggressive outburst's occurring; under such circumstances, punishment is not necessary. Still other parents have non-punitive ways of dealing with the child's aggression

once it does occur. Thus, not all non-permissive parents are to be found among the group who do a great deal of punishing for aggression.

Our findings suggest that the way for parents to produce a non-aggressive child is to make abundantly clear that aggression is frowned upon, and to stop aggression when it occurs, but to avoid punishing the child for his aggression. Punishment seems to have complex effects. While undoubtedly it often stops a particular form of aggression, at least momentarily, it appears to generate more hostility in the child and lead to further aggressive outbursts at some other time or place. Furthermore, when the parents punish—particularly when they employ physical punishment—they are providing a living example of the use of aggression at the very moment they are trying to teach the child not to be aggressive. The child, who copies his parents in many ways, is likely to learn as much from this example of successful aggression on his parents' part as he is from the pain of punishment. Thus, the most peaceful home is one in which the mother believes aggression is not desirable and under no circumstances is ever to be expressed toward her, but who relies mainly on non-punitive forms of control. The homes where the children show angry, aggressive outbursts frequently are likely to be homes in which the mother has a relatively tolerant (or careless!) attitude toward such behavior, or where she administers severe punishment for it, or both.

. . . . .

THE DEVELOPMENT OF CONSCIENCE

According to the theory of identification, the child imitates the mother, and adopts her standards and values as his own, in order to assure himself of her love. This suggests that a high conscience would develop most readily if the mother relied largely on those disciplinary techniques that involved *giving or withholding love*

| TABLE 2. | | Percentage of Children Rated | |
| HIGH CONSCIENCE: | | | |
RELATIONSHIP TO	Parents	High on Conscience	Number of Cases
TECHNIQUES OF	High in their use of praise	32%	181
DISCIPLINE	Low in their use of praise	$r = .18$ 17%	192
EMPLOYED BY	High in their use of isolation	29%	152
THE PARENTS	Low in their use of isolation	$r = .00$ 17%	167
	High in use of withdrawal of love	27%	81
	Low in use of withdrawal of love	$r = .09$ 24%	107
	High in their use of reasoning	30%	192
	Low in their use of reasoning	$r = .18$ 16%	91
	High in use of tangible rewards	20%	188
	Low in use of tangible rewards	$r = -.04$ 28%	181
	High in use of deprivation of privileges	18%	213
	Low in use of deprivation of privileges	$r = -.07$ 33%	156
	High in use of physical punishment	15%	175
	Low in use of physical punishment	$r = -.20$ 32%	197

as a means of rewarding or punishing child behavior. Conversely, we would expect that the children of mothers who used such materialistic methods as deprivation of privileges, physical punishment, and tangible rewards, would develop conscience control more slowly. Children do learn to adapt themselves somewhat to the prevailing climate of the family environment. If love is used as a reward, a child learns to do what will bring him love. If his mother withholds love, he will even learn to give himself love, and he will do as she does to avoid the pain of having her separate herself from him. On the other hand, if the mother uses physical punishment, a child is understandably reluctant to confess his misdeeds or to admit, when asked, that he has done wrong. He may use hiding or flight or counter-aggression as devices to avoid punishment.

In Table 2, we have compared the six dimensions which describe these two classes of disciplinary techniques. The first three—praise, isolation, and withdrawal of love—are ones that make use of love-oriented behavior by the mother. We have added "reasoning" to the table,

too, because it was associated with these love-oriented techniques. In each instance, the high use of such methods is accompanied by a greater number of "high conscience" children than the lesser use. The second group of three—tangible rewards, deprivation, and physical punishment—is more materialistic, and in each case the more frequent use is accompanied by a smaller number of "high conscience" children. Again, as with our previous analyses, the statistical reliabilities of the relationships are meagre. Indeed, in four of the seven cases, the correlation coefficients which express the size of the relationships are approximately zero. However, six of the seven are in the theoretically expected direction. And in every case the percentage of extreme cases ("high conscience") shows a rather substantial difference between high and low groups. The consistency of these findings, rather than the amount of influence of each separate dimension, gives us some confidence in the significance of the final results.

In general, our findings support our theory of identification. They provide a little more information on the way in which parents' child-rearing practices influence the child's character. We can say with some degree of conviction that mothers who love and accept their children, and who use love-oriented techniques of discipline rather than material or physical techniques, produce relatively more children with high conscience. We can say, too, that girls develop this inner control, and adopt their appropriate sex-role qualities, earlier and faster than boys.

In some ways these are discomforting discoveries. They mix up our adult values a little. Ordinarily, we think of *acceptance* as a good thing; a rejecting mother is thought of as unfair and unkind. The words *love-oriented techniques of discipline* have a good sound, too, especially when they are put in contrast with physical punishment—at least . . . this is true for a good many mothers. But when we examine these love-oriented techniques more closely, and find that they include *withdrawal of love* as a means of control or punishment, we realize that we are dealing with a form of maternal behavior that is as much derogated as is rejection. Yet both *acceptance* and *withdrawal of love* appear to produce a strong conscience. Is this a good outcome or a bad outcome of child training?

Some degree of inner control of sex, aggression, and other powerful impulses is clearly necessary if a society is to survive. On the other hand, these impulses do exist in every child and in every adult. Too severe inner control can prevent any direct expression of them and can produce a quite unnecessary degree of guilt and anxiety. Too much conscience can destroy the happiness and productivity of the individual, just as too little can destroy the peace and stability of society.

The problem can be approached in a different way, however. We have discussed here only the *strength* of conscience, saying nothing of its content. In our interviews we asked about the signs of conscience, not what kinds of behavior

the child prevented himself from doing, or felt guilty about after doing. The *content* of conscience appears to be the important thing, both from the individual's standpoint and from society's. A strong inner control of impulses to kill other people, or to make indiscriminate sexual advances to many potential partners, is not severely limiting to the individual's initiative. But if these inhibitions extend to *all* aggressive or sexual actions, the person may be crippled in his efforts to live a normal and productive life. American society is competitive and the American culture tolerates, indeed demands, a good deal of interpersonal aggression. In the sexual sphere, both males and females—in their respective fashions—must take initiative in seeking a marriage partner, and marriage can be misery for those whose inhibitions prevent them from yielding fully to the physical expression of love.

· · · · ·

THE MOTHER'S WARMTH

Perhaps the most pervasive quality we attempted to measure was the warmth of the mother's feelings for her child. Although our main measure of this was the single rating scale called *warmth*, the quality itself seems to have been an underlying contributor to several of the scales (and, indeed, appeared as Factor C in the factor analysis).

Warmth proved equally pervasive in its effects on the child. Maternal *coldness* was associated with the development of feeding problems and persistent bed-wetting. It contributed to high aggression. It was an important background condition for emotional upset during severe toilet training, and for the slowing of conscience development. Indeed, the only one of our measures of child behavior with which warmth was not associated was dependency, and even in that instance the closely related scale for *affectionate demonstrativeness* was slightly correlated.

There is no clear evidence in our findings to explain why warmth should have such widespread influence. We can speculate, on the basis of our general theory of the learning process, about the possibility that it may play several roles. A warm mother spends more time with her child. She offers him more rewards, technically speaking, and gives him more guidance. He develops stronger expectancies of her reciprocal affection, and thus is more highly motivated to learn how to behave as she wants him to. He becomes more susceptible to control by her, for he has more to gain and more to lose. It seems likely, too, that he gets proportionately more satisfaction and less frustration from his growing desire for affection. We offer the hypothesis, for further research, that the children of warm mothers mature more rapidly, in their social behavior, than those of cold mothers.

PUNISHMENT

In our discussion of the training process we have contrasted punishment with reward. Both are techniques used for changing the child's habitual ways of acting. Do they work equally well? The answer is unequivocally "no"; but to be truly unequivocal, the answer must be understood as referring to the kind of punishment we were able to measure by our interview method. We could not, as one can with laboratory experiments on white rats or pigeons, examine the effects of punishment on isolated bits of behavior. Our measures of punishment, whether of the object-oriented or love-oriented variety, referred to *levels of punitiveness* in the mothers. That is, the amount of use of punishment that we measured was essentially a measure of a personality quality of the mothers. Punitiveness, in contrast with rewardingness, was a quite ineffectual quality for a mother to inject into her child training.

The evidence for this conclusion is overwhelming. The unhappy effects of punishment have run like a dismal thread through our findings. Mothers who punished toilet accidents severely ended up with bed-wetting children. Mothers who punished dependency to get rid of it had more dependent children than mothers who did not punish. Mothers who punished aggressive behavior severely had more aggressive children than mothers who punished lightly. They also had more dependent children. Harsh physical punishment was associated with high childhood aggressiveness and with the development of feeding problems.

37 | CHILDREN'S HUMOR: JOKING AND ANXIETY

MARTHA WOLFENSTEIN

A most interesting way to discover how a child views his world is to study his jokes. Scientifically analyzed, every act has a cause, and every joke therefore has a meaning—or, indeed, many meanings, most of which are not funny at all.

It is fascinating to read the speculations about children's humor presented here. Miss Wolfenstein's interpretations are clearly the product of a creative mind. By questioning her particular views and discovering others, the reader can do some creative speculating of his own.

At a quarter past three there was only one child left in the kindergarten classroom, the others having been called for by mothers or maids or older brothers or sisters. The teacher came over to where the little boy sat quietly and asked with some solicitude: "Who is calling for you today, Eugene? Your mother? Or Betty?" The boy smiled: "My mother is coming, and Betty is coming, and Kay is coming—the whole family is coming except me because I'm here already." He laughed.

In this joke the little boy transformed an anxious feeling into one of amusement. Let us see how this has come about. He takes the teacher's question as an occasion for reversing the situation, as if to say: It is only you and not I who is worried whether anyone is coming to call for me—and how ridiculous you are to doubt it. He is helped to this retort by a rather precocious tendency to turn what the teacher says into nonsense. Here he says something nonsensical himself (I am not coming because I am already here) in order to make nonsense of the teacher's concern.

But to understand Eugene's little joke more fully we must know that his father has died in the past year. The thought "the whole family is coming" contains the wish: and my father too. This is immediately renounced with the word "except": the whole family is coming except one. But what would have been a direct expression of the sad reality is in its turn warded off with the substitution of himself for his father. Instead of "all except Daddy because he is dead," he produces "all except me because I'm here already." This gives the impression of being nonsense as he pretends to convey information while what he says is self-evident. The little boy's substitution of himself for his father in the joke repeats what has happened in life: the father has died and the

Excerpts reprinted from *Children's Humor—A Psychological Analysis* (The Free Press, 1954), chapter I, by permission of the publisher.

five-year-old boy has been left alone with the mother and two older sisters. The nonsense in the joke expresses the thought: But it is nonsense to suppose that I could take my father's place. As in the case of nonsense in dreams, it represents opposed wishes: I did and did not wish for my father's death. Thus the nonsense has a double application: the boy disposes of the doubt—which he imputes to the teacher—that anyone is coming for him; and, on a deeper level, he repudiates the wish to take his father's place. In yet another way this joke may have served to ward off anxiety. Waiting for his mother or sister the little boy may indeed have wondered whether they were ever coming, whether they might not also be dead. And this may have evoked fears of his own death. In saying, "I am here," he is affirming: I am alive.

The human capacity to transform suffering into an occasion for mirth is thus already at work in a five-year-old. Under the strain of separation from the mother and sisters with whom he expected to be reunited at this moment, and which evokes the tragic and permanent separation from the father, he is able to joke. He might instead have been overwhelmed with anxiety; he might have cried in the teacher's arms. Or he might have struggled to repress his painful feelings, to be apathetic. But he wants to continue to feel, and he insists on feeling something pleasant. He might then have forgotten his actual situation and become absorbed in play. He does not do this either; he remains aware of his situation of lonely waiting. While confronting this reality, he transforms his feeling about it from pain to enjoyment. This retaining of contact with a disappointing reality combined with the urgent demand to continue to feel, but to feel something pleasant, is decisive for joking. However, the little boy could not have achieved this transformation of emotion if the teacher had not been there. She offers him sympathy which he refuses to accept, preferring to mock her. Repudiating the teacher's pity, he is able to ward off self-pity.

. . . . .

A twelve-year-old boy draws a picture titled, "Custer's Last Stand": it shows a man with a fruit stand. Here . . . the horror of annihilation is transformed into, or mistaken for, oral gratification. The boy wards off the image of the piled up corpses and substitutes an appetizing heap of fruit. Custer who led his men into bloody death becomes a kindly provider of food. In playing on the word "stand," the boy pretends to have mistaken its meaning. It is as if he said: Stand?—ah, you mean a fruit stand. The wish to transform the grievous into the gratifying finds expression in a pretended misunderstanding. It is true that for the unconscious oral gratification and death may be equated, in the persistent infantile fantasy of blissful merging with the mother's breast which is also annihilation. But on the conscious level this thought is disparaged. The boy who makes the joking picture knows very well that Custer's last stand was not a fruit stand; he only pretends to confuse the two. The unconscious fusing of opposites, subjected to the light of conscious criticism, appears as an absurd mistake.

. . . . .

The obstacles which oppose the satisfaction of human wishes are manifold. Not only outer circumstances but inner constraints prove obstructive, constraints which are related to a fear of one's own impulses. Many wishes can obtain only an imaginary satisfaction, in a dream, a story, a joke. One of the specific nuances of the joke is the assurance that impulses are harmless. The joker does not intend to carry out any damaging action; he is only joking. Robert, another ten-year-old boy, is obsessed with destructive fantasies. He composes a story about a bad boy, Jack, in which various chapters are

titled: "Jack wrecks the house," "Jack wrecks father," "Jack wrecks mother," "Jack wrecks everything," "Nothing stops Jack." Family life in this story is a series of quarrels frequently giving way to free-for-all fights. But the fighting has a slapstick quality: on the one hand the violence is abrupt and extreme, on the other hand no real damage is done. The combatants always emerge unscathed. Through his hero, Jack, who so brazenly wages war on his parents, Robert tries to reduce his disturbance about his own destructive impulses: it is all very funny. As he plans a new episode in which the chandelier will fall on father's head, or Jack will push mother through a hole in the floor, or will make a bomb to blow up the house, Robert's usually troubled face lights up and he laughs over it. As he writes, he repeatedly asks for my reassurance: "It is funny, isn't it?" He also insists that his parents read over what he has written and laugh about it. He wants the assurance that they do not condemn him for his destructive wishes. If they find the story funny it means that they regard his impulses as harmless. Since Robert's doubts on this point persist, he requires an amused response to his story over and over again. He reads it to his aunts, to his little brother, to his class in school. We can see in this one of the motives of the habitual joker, who requires ever renewed assurance that the impulses he expresses are innocuous. We can also understand the joker's distress when he fails to obtain an amused reaction. He then feels that his underlying bad wishes have been perceived and condemned.

Under the pressure of conflicting wishes children discover a joking way of dealing with them. The conflict may be translated into a contradiction which they then regard with a lofty reasonableness as if to say: But that's absurd! In this way they gain a momentary respite from inner stress. Six-year-old John is an intellectually ambitious little boy, eager to learn to read and write. His father discusses scientific subjects with him and John strives anxiously and pridefully to master them. At the same time he has intense longings in the opposite direction. When he sees his parents carry his baby sister in their arms he is overwhelmed with the yearning to be carried in this way himself. However, when he pleads with his parents to carry him, they protest that he is now too big. At such moments he must wonder what is the good of his intellectual attainments; growing up only debars him from what he wants most. John makes up this riddle which he considers funny: "Why did the moron write on a piece of paper?—'Cause he couldn't walk yet." The combination of being able to write but not being able to walk, so that one would have to be carried, represents the fulfilment of both of John's opposed wishes. In making a joke of this impossible consummation, he stresses its paradoxical character: What an absurd idea to be able to write and not to be able to walk yet! He uses his critical reasoning powers to devalue his frustrated wishes. We shall see how often children, in their joking, attempt to free themselves from impossible wishes by picturing their fulfilment as ridiculous.

. . . . .

A five-year-old little girl, Nora, turns an oedipal wishfulfilment fantasy into a funny story in this way. She says that she will tell me "a very silly poem. It's a joke. One day my grandfather went out walking. He met a lamb. Haha. He said to the lamb, 'Will you marry me?' Haha. And the lamb said, 'Baah,' because it didn't know what to say. That's a funny one. A silly one." Here the child has disguised the characters in her oedipal drama, substituting her grandfather for her father and turning herself into a little lamb. Such disguises occur frequently in myths and fairy tales, where the closest, incestuous relations are transformed into relations

between remote creatures, as here a human being and an animal. The disguise serves to avoid the guilt and fear which would be roused in acknowledging the true identity of the protagonists. The little girl who, while availing herself of this disguise, finds it funny, has proceeded to take the fantasy literally: How absurd it would be for grandfather to propose marriage to a little lamb. Thus having indulged in a dream-like fantasy, she turns upon what she has produced with a reasonable, realistic criticism. The comic effect is achieved by a shift of level, from fantasy which uses a symbolic mode of expression to literal-minded everyday thinking. By this shift the fantasied wishfulfilment is laughed off as ridiculous. The child has used a further defense against her wishes; she has projected them onto the father-figure in her little story. The grandfather is the one who proposes the improper alliance to the little lamb. The lamb remains demure and only emits a noncommital "Baah." Thus the little girl suppresses her own response to the tempting situation which she has conjured up, blanking it out with a meaningless sound. But again, taking it literally, she finds this dialogue comic: What kind of answer is that to a proposal of marriage if one can only say, "Baah?" It is in effect a mocking response. The little girl, in the guise of the lamb, brushes off the gratifying advances of the father. The comic treatment of the wishfulfilment fantasy consists in repudiating the gratification momentarily offered in imagination but in fact unavailable. The pathos of the unobtainable is transformed into the absurdity of the improbable.

. . . . .

Another joking fantasy plays with the image of the pregnant mother. Five-year-old Ann, having listened to the story of the man whose hat was as big as the world, was inspired to compose a story about an old lady whose house was as big as the world. The same consequence follows that no one can get out of this house. The bigness of the house (house being a frequent symbol of the female body) becomes a nuisance not only to others but to the lady herself, who is unable to get out of the house. Ann mocks the pregnant mother by stressing her incapacitation, in part projecting onto the mother her own frustration and distress. She transforms an enviable situation into one of comic annoyance. The wished-for is laughed off by playing up and exaggerating its inconvient aspects. Here is Ann's story: "Once there was an old lady who lived in a house. A great big house as big as the world. That's why everybody had to walk straight in her house. Every time they tried to walk out of her house they couldn't. Because their house was in her house too. Every time they tried to play a game they had to play in her house of course. Every time they tried to move their bed out of her house they couldn't. This old lady did not like that. Every time she got cross every person she got cross at would try to get out, to get out the window. They couldn't. The window was too small. And when she went shopping she had to go shopping at her house. And when she ate, she couldn't eat at a restaurant. The restaurants were all in her house. Now this old lady got too tired one day. And she said to someone: 'Why do I have to do all these things in my house?' And one day she got much too tired and she said: 'I guess I'll get out of this house.' But she went over to the door and it was locked. It was no use. . . ."

Here the little girl, who has envied her mother's recent pregnancy and cherished the impossible wish to be pregnant herself, transforms the wished-for into a nuisance. The mother's body (house) is so big that she cannot go anywhere. There is also the question so puzzling to children: how does the baby get out? . . . In Ann's story, the pregnant mother, confined to the house, is condensed with the baby in the womb: neither the mother nor the other people (babies) can get out. There is also probably her own wish to escape from the mother (to get out of the house) which she is unable to realize.

. . . . .

The envied procreative powers of the parents may be made fun of by exaggeration, for instance, in fantasies of a family with hundreds of children. Just as the great size of the father's phallus or of the body of the pregnant mother were made ridiculous by being blown up beyond belief, so the baby which the child hopelessly longs to produce becomes less desirable by being multiplied a hundredfold. Also the power of the parents here passes into loss of control: They cannot stop making babies. A six-year-old girl tells the following: "Once there was a little girl. A lady. And she had three hundred children in one year. And they all went to school and they all had the same group and they were all the same age. They all did the same things at school. Wasn't that sil-lee? They all had dirty faces. They all had pimples on their lips. And they all had the same age. They all had dresses on. Some were boys but they had dresses on too, hee, hee, hee. . . . Then they all said the same thing at the same time. And they all sang. The only song they knew was: Abbadabbadabba. . . . Their names were Jimmy and Mary and Cocky" (she laughs) "and Ellen and Frances and Jonathan . . . Timmy and Bimmy and Kisser. The End."

One baby is an object of longing, but at the prospect of three hundred babies all singing "Abbadabbadabba" in unison motherly sentiment is dissipated. Thus a transformation of feeling is achieved by the multiplication of its objects. The little girl uses additional devices to devalue the babies: they are dirty and diseased (they have pimples on their lips), the boys are castrated (wearing dresses), and they have silly or naughty names (Cocky, Kisser). Another motive behind such a fantasy is the child's anxious concern with how many more children the mother may have. The motive of rivalry with possible brothers and sisters complicates the wish to compete with the mother. In producing the fantasy that the mother will have three hundred children in one year, which she knows is impossible, the little girl reassures herself: nothing is going to happen.

. . . . .

We have seen how children find ways of making fun of the bigness, power, and prerogatives of the grown-ups whom they envy. There is another imposing aspect of adults, which is often oppressive and fearful to children, namely their moral authority; and here too children seek relief through mockery. They seize with delight on opportunities to show that the grown-ups are not infallibly good, or to expose the grown-ups' demands as absurdly impossible, or to distort the meaning of a prohibition into a permission. A little girl of five was very fond of using words for more or less taboo body parts, such as "bottom." If her mother happened to say, "I think I put this or that in the bottom drawer," the child would shout delightedly: "You said 'bottom'!" Thus she pretended to catch her mother in the same naughtiness to which she herself was prone. In a joking way she attempted to make out that her mother was not so very good, and so to relieve herself from the pressure of a too ideal model.

In rebellion against adults' demands, children may try to reduce these demands to absurdity. A six-year-old girl tells me that her teacher said something funny. "She said we couldn't get up from our chairs until we'd finished eating. It sounded as if we'd have to sleep there all night!" In her wish to demonstrate that adults' demands are excessive, the little girl retorts mockingly in her own mind to what the teacher has said: And suppose we don't finish? Then you mean we'll have to stay here all night? By distorting the teacher's demand into something so unreasonable as to be ridiculous, the child exempts herself from feeling bound by it.

Children become skillful in misinterpreting what adults say, to find sanctions for naughtiness or exemption from chores. A teacher says to a four-year-old little girl: "Are you going to help me to put down the beds?" The little girl replies playfully, pretending to have misheard: "Yes, I'm going to help you to take off your head." Thus she pretends that the teacher has requested an all-out expression of the child's aggressive impulses, and she, being a nice little girl, will gladly comply. In the classroom of the six-year-olds, the teacher is teaching the children how to tell time. She has a large clock, the hands of which she places in various positions as she asks the children what time it is. As she puts the clock hands to three o'clock, she asks again: "What time is it now?" The children shout: "Three o'clock! Goodbye, teacher!" In an uproar of laughter they rush to put on their hats and coats and are half-way out the door before the teacher can stop them. Thus they pretend not to have understood the hypothetical character of the teacher's question, and to believe that she is pointing out the actual time to them, three o'clock, the end of the school day. They distort the teacher's meaning in such a way that it becomes an exemption from further work; it is she who sets the clock hands forward and lets them out of school. The embodiment of restrictions is transformed by their joking pretense into an agent of release.

. . . . .

The relation of the comic world to inadequate moral authorities is particularly evident when these authorities appear as characters in the drama. In

Charlie Chaplin's *City Lights,* the little tramp encounters by chance an eccentric millionaire who befriends him. The millionaire's benevolence is, however, unpredictable. When he is drunk, he is extravagantly friendly to the little tramp, embracing him, feeding and clothing him, giving him an expensive car. But when he is sober, he fails to recognize the little fellow, has him thrown out of the house and abandons him to the police. Thus for the bewildered little tramp the world is presided over by a capricious deity.

. . . . .

How decisive the image of parental authority is for comedy or tragedy may be seen in the alternative interpretations of the *Merchant of Venice.* The comic or tragic effect depends on how the character of Shylock is regarded. Shylock is a father-figure who has been wronged and who claims vengeance. The issue is whether his claim is a righteous one. The comic impact, which the play originally had, depended on taking Shylock as an unworthy and ludicrous character; his pretense to justice could be unmasked as low vindictiveness. To the extent to which more recent interpretations of the play have tended to attribute justice to Shylock's position, and to see him as cheated of his due, he becomes invested with the paternal right to punish and the play loses its comic effect.

. . . . .

Eugene showed a precocious tendency to mock adults. By demonstrating how silly they were he reduced their impressiveness; the huge beings of his frightening fantasies for the moment dwindled away. With his teacher he used the technique of taking her words more literally than they were intended and so making out that she had said something foolish. When the teacher told another boy to put on his shoes, Eugene remarked: "He doesn't have shoes, he has sneakers." The **teacher** corrected herself: "I meant, 'Put on your sneakers.'" To this Eugene retorted: "I already have my sneakers on." By thus reducing an authority figure to absurdity Eugene seemed to be reassuring himself that the adults were harmless and that he had nothing to fear from them.

. . . . .

In a joking story Katherine takes a different approach to her family problems. "Once there was a girl named Sissy and a boy named Heinie. They lived in a house made of brown stuff, and not logs I'm telling you! . . . Their mother was called BM. . . . One day they went into the woods to seek their fortune. They crawled to the mouth of the great world. . . . Mrs. BM was very unhappy at the sad turn of events because the two youngsters ran away. So she went looking for them. . . . When she found them sleeping contentedly at the bottom of the toilet and took them back and—shooosh! If you guessed everything up to now you'll guess that's the toilet flushing. And the family went to live downstairs, in a little brown house. The end." . . . The children with their comically naughty names, "Sissy" (urine) and "Heinie" (behind), are not objects of sympathy. Katherine had previously told me that she would not like it if her younger sister called her "Sissy," "because it means coward and second you know what." "Heinie" is the name of the hero in a series of jokes very popular with children of this age; he keeps getting lost and his mother goes around asking everyone: "Have you seen my Heinie?" In her story Katherine makes both Sissy and Heinie excreta. She expresses in a joking way her early wish that her mother would throw her little sister out, flush her down the toilet. Children originally value highly their own body products and do not want to part with them. Later they learn that these products are to be despised. Children also frequently imagine that babies are born through the bowel, and equate babies with feces. Following this line of thought, Katherine says in effect: Mother was just as foolish to want to keep the baby as I used to be when I wanted to preserve my bowel movements. But the child who wants to throw out the baby readily imagines that she will be punished with a similar fate. Or the child has the fantasy that, to separate the younger one from the mother, the two children will run away from home together. This is what happens in Katherine's story. Katherine also reverses the idea that the children are the mother's excreta: the mother is also nothing but a BM. Thus she expresses the feeling: I am just as foolish to want that worthless mother as she was to keep the baby. Where in her serious story Katherine evokes her longing for love from her parents, in the joking one she makes light of this wish by devaluing its object. . . .

38 | INTERPRETATION OF PROJECTIVE DEVICES

CHARLOTTE BUHLER, FAITH SMITTER, SYBIL RICHARDSON, AND FRANKLYN BRADSHAW

The development and use of projective techniques flourished after Freud's theories of unconscious motivation were publicized. Since the child unwittingly expresses his unconscious self in countless ways, a trained observer may learn many things by studying the child's behavior, his speech, his jokes, his reactions to ink drawings, pictures, or cloud formations, his dreams, his stories, and his drawings. The psychologist acts like a detective; he slowly assembles bits of information, like a jigsaw puzzle, into a picture of the child's personality.

This selection demonstrates some interpretations of children's drawings by experts.

The main objection to projective techniques has been the difficulty of reliable interpretation of an individual's projections. Because of this difficulty there is danger of abusing projective methods.

People with empathy, intuition, and imagination often feel that they can interpret another's feelings and motives. Although they succeed often, their interpretations are far from reliable. Children's drawings, for instance, seem to offer an

Excerpts reprinted from Charlotte Buhler, Faith Smitter, Sybil Richardson, and Franklyn Bradshaw, *Childhood Problems and the Teacher*, by permission of Henry Holt and Company, Inc. Copyright 1952.

almost irresistible invitation to interpretation. For the alert and interested teacher, the temptation to think of the child who uses gay colors as gay, and to find clues to the child's personality in certain contents, is very great. But this should be done only with extreme caution unless the teacher has had clinical training. In order to interpret projective self-expression, the examiner must recognize that there are unique personal features in self-expression which exist only in this individual's "private world." Such features are understood only if one knows something about the individual's history. To the experienced worker, the detection of these unique features becomes an important clue to the discovery of emotionally traumatic experiences.

An interesting example is the little three-year-old girl who evidently had some problem in connection with the use of her hands. She went around the room touching things so that they fell down, but she never used her hands directly. She touched objects by pushing her doll's head toward the toys.

Later this same child built a stable for a toy cow and built it almost like a hand with blocks protruding like fingers. But there were six, not five blocks.

This child had been born with the anomaly of six fingers on one hand. Although operated on as a baby, she no doubt had heard about it and had also raised questions regarding the scar on her hand.

Another interesting example is the forty-one-year-old man who saw injured birds in the Rorschach ink blots in seven places in which most people saw quite different things. After the test, when the examiner asked whether he had any particular experience with birds, the subject was astonished by the question—he had not been conscious of seeing so many birds. Then he began to think and suddenly exclaimed that indeed as a boy of seven he had accidentally stepped on a little bird and crushed it. The incident bothered him for many years, after which he forgot it completely.

In addition to such unique experiences, projective techniques also show general human trends. These recurring content or form characteristics of projective productions have been submitted to standardizing procedures and can be interpreted generally as will be shown in the following.

SAMPLES OF PROJECTIVE MATERIAL

Drawings and Paintings

For the teacher, drawings and paintings, including finger paintings, are so much a part of her experience and interest that a sampling of this important material is given here.

Figure 1.

A good example is *Vigdis* whose drawings (Figure 1) were reproduced with a short explanation of her problem. . . .

She is quite *conscious* of the fact that she loves her teacher more than her grandparents; she wants her teacher to love her and to take her away from her grandparents into her own new home; Vigdis hopes to be welcome to the new husband also. She wants to be their child. She is *unconscious* of the fact that her drawings make a plea to the teacher to take her into her married life and into her new home as her child.

She gives a *direct* picture of herself with her grandparents and herself with the new couple. By the symbol of hand-holding she also *indirectly* expresses being close to the teacher and the husband but not to the grandparents.

In five-year-old *Tommy's* picture (Figure 2), there is an equally complex pattern of his conscious longing for the mother to be home, his unconscious fear and loneliness, his direct picture of the children at

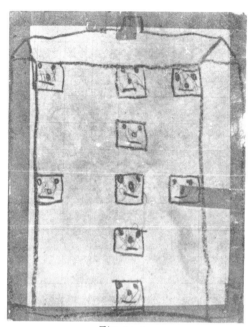

Figure 2.

the windows, and his symbolic multiplication of many faces expressing the urgency he feels.

The deeper a child's problem, the more unconscious and unrealistic becomes the symbolism that expresses his disturbance. When *Frick* . . . ties the house he draws to a tree, he forgets reality in which houses are never tied to trees. He just expresses his fear and his wish concerning his home's stability.

The relationship between *Leigh's* apple tree (Figure 3) and himself was even deeper. When Leigh came to therapy . . . he was deeply disturbed by his soiling. The "ugly brown leaves" of the tree as well as the "dirty balls" of sand were semi-conscious references to the soiling which shamed him. The leaves had to be burned; the balls to be buried. But the tree also had nice green leaves, and the tree must not burn. This was an unconscious reference to himself, to his good potentialities, and his wish that not Leigh but his shameful deeds be abolished.

This symbolic self-expression is deep because Leigh is not aware that his drawings and his sand formations relate to himself, or that he tells the therapist his problem by means of these products.

The therapist may or may not explain this symbolism to the child. Psychoanalysts formerly considered these interpretations to be essential. At present the prevailing tendency is to refrain from many interpretations, especially with younger children, and to achieve a certain amount of insight without making the child conscious of the way in which he revealed himself.

Leigh's apple tree is an *individual symbol* which refers to his private world. Leigh has been much interested in the burning of old leaves in his parents' back yard where grows this apple tree which he loves and climbs and which he identified with his home and himself. Other symbols are much more general and repetitious.

In spontaneous drawings of young children, the *house* appears most frequently. There seems to be a strong feeling about the protection that his home gives to the child. The strong identification of family and house is shown in one of the drawings that Wolff collected. At his

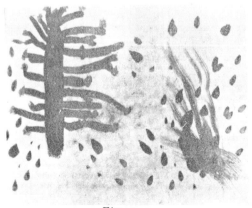

Figure 3.

Figure 4.

Figure 5.

Figure 6.

instruction to "draw your family," a number of children drew the family beside their house.

In their drawings many children surround their houses with fences, whether or not their own houses and yards have fences. The *fence* is another of the most frequently used symbols—to fence out potential aggressors or to imprison "bad" people.

Charlie, age eleven, makes a self-protective fence (Figure 4). So does nine-year-old *Henry* (Figure 5). *Henk*, an eight-year-old boy with severe anxieties caused by a very strict and punitive father, at first expresses his feelings that his house is a prison by painting barred windows. Then (Figure 6), probably becoming fearful that someone will guess how he feels, he covers the windows with paint, but expresses his feeling about lack of freedom everywhere by enclosing every object in his world—the trees, the flowers, even the sun and garden. There is only one hope, the boat with which to escape outside.

The most unhappy feeling seems expressed in *Hallie's* drawing (Figure 7). The whole world is only fence and sky. It is empty of people, of things, of anything to have fun with—an empty prison.

The depth of feelings of imprisonment and the need for self-protection cannot be decided by looking at the drawings. The interpreter has to know more about the

Figure 7.

child, his background and history, his symptoms, and his ability or inability to project his feelings appropriately.

In remedial release work, children will quite frequently draw jails or witches. This need not always mean deep feelings of deprivation and hatred. Sometimes these drawings may express only acute anger and acute unhappiness. It is helpful, whenever possible, to have the child's comments on his drawings.

. . . . .

To the child, the *human figure* is as important as the *house*. The Goodenough "Draw-a-Man" test, originally devised for the purpose of testing intelligence, finds increasing application as a projective technique, because the attributes given to the human figure are often more expressive of the child's emotional responses than they are of his intellectual responses.

Children's self-portraits are also of great interest, revealing as they do children's attitudes toward their personalities and their moods. A frequent self-portrait is of the "lonely" child (Figure 8), done with unusually painstaking care.

Many of the examples we have used

here show that *contents* as well as *formal* characteristics can be used for projection. This is as true of drawings as of other projective techniques, for example, the Rorschach and World tests. Protective fences, rigid schemation, confused disarrangements, over- or underemphasis of items, repetitions, worry over or disregard of detail—all are formal characteristics produced by an individual similarly in all these techniques.

. . . . .

An unconscious formal symptom of importance is the child's worry over much detail and his overconscientious efforts to produce the most careful detail. This is almost always a sign of excessive worry and of an emotionally disturbing perfectionism.

. . . *Paulinke's* flower garden (Figure 9), which is a happy content but, even so, not a release from worry, *Dagny's* detailed work on the girl in the snow (Figure 8), and *Henry's* detail on the garden fence (Figure 5) all belong in the same category.

A frequent content symbol used by little five- and six-year-old girls is the lonely child, as Dagny, age five, paints herself in the snow (Figure 8). "I want to stand all by myself," said another little girl who made such a drawing. Older lonely children paint "lonely" landscapes without people, sometimes without a sign of life,

Figure 8.

Figure 9.

as *Ingrid* does in her second picture, "Road in the Sun" (Figure 10), or *Jerry* does in "The Desert" (Figure 11). Older children also sometimes express their distrust of people by choosing animals, particularly horses, as their friends.

It would be wrong to assume that all children's paintings refer to emotionally disturbing events. Six-year-old *Irma's* "Happy Birthday" (Figure 12) and ten-year-old *Paulinke's* "Flower Garden" (Figure 9) project happy feelings, and drawings such as "The Battle of Hastings" (Figure 13) by *Douglas*, age nine, represent intellectual and artistic interests.

Figure 10.

Figure 12.

Figure 11.

Figure 13.

IRVIN L. CHILD, ELMER H. POTTER,

AND ESTELLE M. LEVINE

*One of the many ways in which children learn cultural values and
expectations is through the stories they read. In grammar school the
average child reads or has read to him thousands of stories, each
of which carries its own message about right and wrong, what will be
rewarded and what punished.*

*The findings in this important monograph analyzing 914 third-grade
stories are startling. Under most conditions, the stories show that
initiative and original thinking are punished—rather than rewarded.
Unlike real life, nearly every story has a happy ending, and the
child in the story always wins the competition. Thus the stories
offer few positive suggestions to aid their readers in facing the problems
of failure or aggression with which most children must cope in real life.*

The specific objective of this study is the
analysis of certain content of the world of
ideas which confronts children in the process of education, from the point of view
of the probable effect of that content on
the motivation of their behavior. Just what
that means will be made clear through
the discussion, in the rest of this chapter,
of the way the content was analyzed.

SELECTION OF MATERIAL

The Books Chosen

The material chosen for analysis consisted
of certain portions of the content of general readers intended for use in the
third grade. Printed material was selected,
rather than the content of what was said
by teachers in classrooms, because of the
accessibility of printed material, and be-

Excerpts reprinted from *Psychological Monographs*, LX, No. 3 (1946), Whole No. 279, 1–7,
43–53, by permission of the authors and the
American Psychological Association.

cause a manageable sample of it must of
necessity reflect accurately certain educational practices in the country at large.
The choice of the third-grade level was
made on the grounds of convenience for
the purpose of this study: textbooks for
the first and second grades have such very
simple content that few passages are susceptible of the kind of analysis that we
have undertaken, while readers from the
fourth grade up, on the other hand, begin
to have such complex material that the
analysis would be more laborious and less
reliable.

We chose for our purpose all of the
general third-grade readers we were able
to find which had been published since
1930. (Excluded were third-grade readers
intended primarily to teach special topics
such as science, social studies, or arithmetic, and one reader which deviated
greatly from all the others in containing
considerable material on religion.) In all,
30 books were included in the analysis.

Selection of Content from the Books

The first step in the process of analysis of the readers was the selection of those stories which were to be analyzed. Since the purpose of the analysis was to determine what effect the readers might have on the socialization of the child, only those stories were chosen in which the content could conceivably affect the child's behavior. The general criterion for selection was that the story contain characters in action, since the child's behavior would be affected only by his generalizing from that of individuals in the stories to his own behavior. This resulted in the exclusion of three types of material.

· · · · ·

The content which was included in the analysis was, then, those stories in which characters appeared who presented distinctive behavior that could be analyzed according to the method described below. The material analyzed included well over three quarters of the content of the books. Altogether, 914 stories were analyzed.

A story is often, however, a cumbersome and complex unit for analysis and comparison. Sometimes a story contains several incidents whose context is very different. Or, in a single incident very different things will be happening to two or more important characters, or one character may be showing more than one significant kind of behavior. The unit for analysis, therefore, was not the story but the *thema*. A thema is a sequence of psychological events consisting of (1) a situation or circumstances confronting a person, (2) the behavior (internal and external) with which the person responds, (3) the consequences of the behavior as felt by the person himself. In the 914 stories used, 3409 thema were found and analyzed, an average of almost 4 thema per story. In the presentation of quantitative data in the rest of this monograph, the number of thema is always the basic quantity dealt with.

METHOD OF ANALYSIS

The method of analysis applied to the thema found in the readers was based on the following considerations:

It is assumed that in reading a story, a child goes through symbolically, or rehearses to himself, the episode that is described. The same principles, then, are expected to govern the effect of the reading on him as would govern the effect of actually going through such an incident in real life. The principles that seemed important for this study are those of reinforcement and of avoidance learning.

It is assumed that when a sequence of behavior is shown as leading to reward, the effect will be to increase the likelihood of a child's behaving in that way under similar conditions in the future. Among the kinds of behavior that may be learned in this way are motives, for they are to be regarded as being produced largely by a subject's own behavior.

When, on the other hand, a sequence of behavior is shown as leading up to punishment, it is expected that the incident will contribute to the probability of the subject's avoidance of such behavior in the future. Again, among the effects of such avoidance can be the reduction of the strength or the likelihood of the appearance of a motive.

This reasoning suggested the analysis of the content in accordance with the following general scheme:

1. *Character* whose behavior is represented in the thema
2. *Behavior* displayed by the character
3. *Circumstances* surrounding the behavior
4. *Consequences* of the behavior (for the character himself)
5. *Type of story* in which the incident occurs.

The way that each of these aspects was analyzed will now be presented in turn.

Characters

If the effect of an incident upon a child depends upon his identification with the character whose behavior is being described, then the effect is likely to vary according to the ease of identification with the given character. Boys, for example, may be more likely to identify with boys, and girls with girls. Children may be more likely to identify with children than with adults, or perhaps less likely.

It was first necessary to decide which characters were those with which identification was most likely. Many characters were easily and reliably chosen on this basis. They were the *central characters*, the characters from whose point of view the story was written. In most cases a single individual or group of individuals clearly stood out as the central character of the story. In some cases there seemed to be two or three such figures, and in that case each one was dealt with separately.

There was a second group of figures who appeared in stories as the villainous antagonists of central characters, *anti-social characters* who injured or threatened the wealth or happiness of the central characters. It might be supposed at first glance that identification with these anti-social characters is not likely. We believe, however, that it is likely. Much behavior which is rarely shown as performed by social characters is shown as performed by anti-social characters, and the punishment that follows may indeed produce an effect on the child who reads the story.

Characters are first of all, then, divided into central and anti-social ones. For most of the categories of behavior dealt with, the number of anti-social characters is small and they are not treated separately. For certain categories of behavior, however, distinctive facts about the anti-social characters will be mentioned.

For each character, regardless of whether central or anti-social, a further classification was made as follows:

1. Children (divided into boys, girls, and groups of mixed sex)
2. Adults (men, women, and groups of mixed sex)
3. Animals (including in this single cate-

TABLE 1. CATEGORIES OF BEHAVIOR EMPLOYED IN ANALYZING THE CONTENT OF THIRD-GRADE READERS, WITH THE NUMBER OF THEMA IN WHICH EACH CATEGORY WAS FOUND	Category	Number of Thema in Which It Appears	Category	Number of Thema in Which It Appears
	Objectless Behavior		Altruistic Social Behavior	
	Activity	264	(generally leading to	
	Passivity	89	simultaneous gratification	
	Sentience	82	of other person's needs)	
	Elation	55	Affiliation	364
	Behavior Primarily in		Nurturance	266
	Relation to Things		Succorance	176
	and Events		Deference	184
	Cognizance	351	Egoistic Social Behavior	
	Achievement	221	(generally competing with	
	Construction	75	other person's needs)	
	Imaginality	31	Aggression	206
	Acquisition	177	Dominance	152
	Retention	33	Recognition	175
	Order	43	Autonomy	122
			Rejection	21
			Avoidance Behavior	
			Harmavoidance	212
			Blameavoidance	
			Infavoidance	38

gory both animals who are portrayed realistically and those who are shown as behaving like human beings)

4. Fairies (used here as a convenient short name for all supernatural creatures, including fairies in the strict sense, giants, dwarfs, gods, and inanimate objects imbued with life).

It is this classification of characters that has been most significant in connection with the analysis of behavior and that will be referred to in reporting on almost every behavioral category.

· · · · ·

Summary of Procedure

The outline of the analysis given above will now be briefly summarized, together with some indication of the actual technique used in recording the data.

The first step was to read each story in a given book and determine whether it was suitable for the purposes of the analysis. If it was suitable, the second step was to identify all the separate thema in the story that fitted the pattern of analysis. When these thema were identified, a file card was prepared for each one. It was labeled appropriately to identify the story and the book and then the following information was entered on it:

1. The type of story
2. Whether the character was central or anti-social
3. The classification of the character according to age, sex, humanity, etc.
4. The behavior displayed, classified according to Murray's system of needs
5. Notes on the circumstances surrounding the behavior
6. The classification of the consequences of the behavior.

OVERALL FINDINGS AND DISCUSSION

Cultural Forces Influencing Personality

The observations that have been reviewed on the treatment of various categories of behavior in children's readers can leave no doubt that this treatment is such as to encourage the development of certain motives and to discourage others. A tabulation of the percentage of reward, punishment, and no consequence for the various categories of behavior, presented in Table 2, brings out this general point quite clearly. The categories are arranged here in order of relative frequency of reward, and this order may be taken as one indication of the degree of encouragement or discouragement of the development of each one. In considerable part, of course, this order reflects general cultural norms —for example, in the high value placed on affiliation, nurturance and cognizance, and in the frequent punishment of aggression, retention and rejection. To this extent the analysis of the contents of the readers does not stand alone but is useful as symptomatic of probable characteristics of other kinds of content of the world of ideas that reach children—what teachers say to them in classes, morals that their parents point up to them, the content of stories they read elsewhere.

But the entire impact of cultural forces on personality manifested in these readers is not shown in a simple listing of the treatment of the several categories separately. There are also certain generalities which can be found running through the whole series of categories, generalities about particular ways of achieving ends which are most likely to lead to success or to failure.

Perhaps the most striking case of this sort is the repeated reward of effort or work as a way of reaching goals. In the discussion of acquisition, it was shown that effortful ways of acquiring things are the most frequently rewarded; similar observations were made in connection with achievement and construction. Even in the case of the relatively objectless need for activity, the more purposeful instances of activity which require more work are more frequently rewarded. Here certainly are some of the forces leading to the development of a motive to work or put forth

TABLE 2.

PERCENTAGE OF REWARD, PUNISHMENT, AND

NO CONSEQUENCE FOR EACH CATEGORY OF BEHAVIOR

(IN ALL OF THE 3409 THEMA WHICH WERE ANALYZED)

Category of Behavior	Percent of Thema in Which the Behavior Is Rewarded	Percent of Thema in Which the Behavior Is Punished	Percent of Thema in Which Behavior Results in No Consequence (i.e., Neither Rewarded nor Punished)
Construction	96	1	3
Sentience	96	4	0
Elation	95	4	1
Cognizance	86	9	5
Succorance	84	10	6
Affiliation	82	8	9
Nurturance	82	5	12
Achievement	80	10	9
Recognition	79	13	8
Activity	74	9	16
Dominance	74	16	8
Blameavoidance	71	15	14
Imaginality	71	6	23
Order	70	2	28
Acquisition	64	31	3
Passivity	54	26	20
Deference	52	10	38
Harmavoidance	49	39	12
Autonomy	48	40	12
Retention	42	48	10
Aggression	35	52	11
Rejection	14	62	24
Infavoidance	8	74	18
All categories	71	17	12

effort. This motive is sometimes very important in adults or older children, and may activate them for a long time, even when the effort leads to no external reward. It needs explanation, because of marked contrast with the general tendency for human beings and other organisms to avoid work or effort when it is not necessary. The motive is doubtless developed in large part through social learning, and we have in this reading matter an example of the kinds of social influences that lead to its development.

Another special emphasis is on the acquisition of skills, on learning. This is, of course, evident in the first place from the high frequency of cognizant behavior and its high proportion of reward. It also appears in the treatment of achievement; there it was observed that the most frequently rewarded mode of achievement was by the acquisition of new skills, even more frequently rewarded than achievement through the display of skills formerly acquired.

Despite the emphasis on learning, there

is in these third-grade readers little encouragement of intellectual activity as such. The cognizance is usually directed at simple isolated information rather than a quest for understanding. Sentience, as it appears in the readers, is only rarely concerned with esthetic appreciation which goes beyond the admiration of simple man-made objects or of nature. Activity is ordinarily physical, and in only one case intellectual in nature. The achievements, even those involving the acquisition of a skill, can in most cases hardly be spoken of as intellectual. Similarly in constructive behavior: only one story about construction concerns a non-material product, a poem.

It should be noted, moreover, that the acquisition of skills or knowledge which is rewarded is generally that which is dependent upon other persons in a superior position—for example the gaining of knowledge by children through questioning parents or teachers. In this sense, too, there is less emphasis on intellectual activity than might appear, since there is relatively little encouragement of original thinking on the part of the central character.

A distinction is also made between satisfying needs in socially approved ways, which tends to be rewarded, and satisfying them in disapproved ways, which tends to be punished. For example, in the case of retention, retention which is defined as socially or individually useful and permissible, such as saving money, is rewarded; on the other hand, retention which is defined as selfish is punished. Similarly for recognition: there is heavy reward for exhibiting one's capacities so long as social rules are followed; but when rules are broken, as by exhibiting oneself at the wrong time or making claims about one's powers that are not justified, then the behavior is punished. Dominance and aggression provide examples of other modes of behavior where social rules set down certain conditions as making the behavior permissible and certain other conditions as not. In these cases the conditions have to do with what other needs, if any, are served at the same time; if dominance or aggression does not serve some other approved purpose, or if it serves other disapproved purposes such as selfish acquisition or retention, it is punished.

Problems of Adjustment

In the ways that have just been indicated, material such as that in the readers provides lessons to children, encouraging or discouraging the development of motives in a way that on the whole is likely to lead to more satisfactory adjustment in our society. But at the same time there are certain respects in which this material is failing to contribute to good adjustment.

A major defect of the readers from this point of view is what might be called their unrealistic optimism. Behavior directed at affiliation and nurturance, for example, is almost always rewarded in the readers. There are very few cases of failure. It is impossible to compare the proportion of success here with that obtaining in children's everyday life. Yet from the point of view of contributing to the solution of problems of everyday life, failures ought to receive a larger proportion of attention, for it is they that pose problems.

It may indeed be true that the encouragement of affiliative and nurturant needs in this reading is of little consequence, because the much stronger pressures from the real environment are already working in that same direction, and the contribution from here can be little more. But there is a very great opportunity for reading matter, such as in these textbooks, to point up possible solutions for frustrations often encountered by the child in seeking for gratification of these needs. In that case, such reading matter should include a larger number of accounts of how children get around obstacles in their attempts to satisfy affiliative and nurturant needs—

stories in which expression of these needs first meets with punishment or rebuff and only attains success when some new method of approach more suited to the environment is hit upon.

For children who have encountered failure in their everyday life, the easy attainment of goals such as nurturance and affiliation in the readers may be so unrealistic as to have little effect in strengthening their desire for such goals. Suggestions as to how these needs may be satisfied despite serious difficulties might, on the other hand, through their realism to such children, contribute to strengthening the needs.

A similar sort of unrealism was commented on in the discussion of avoidance. While the content of these readers might do a great deal towards strengthening a desire for achievement in competitive success, there is very little about those children—perhaps the majority—who frequently experience failure in competition, and few suggestions about how such children can find some satisfactory way of adjusting to their failure. Such material might be more beneficial than what is actually found in contributing to the better adjustment of those children whose present adjustment is unsatisfactory.

A similar failure to make positive suggestions is found in the treatment of aggression and acquisition. Here are two needs, certainly universally present in children, which lead to serious problems of adjustment because of their frequent interference with desires of other and more powerful persons.

Children's reading matter might be quite useful in furthering satisfactory adjustment if it were able to pose models for the child of ways to satisfy these needs when they are prevented from the most direct and immediately satisfactory expression. While there are certainly some incidents which might be useful in this way, the general tendency in the readers is, instead, for these needs simply to be overlooked in the child characters. It is as though the writers were inclined to solve problems of aggression and acquisition in children by trying to convince children that they do not have these needs, that they are experienced only by adults, animals and supernatural creatures. To a certain extent the child's real social environment may be cooperating with the readers in this direction, through a tradition that children do not hate or covet and are basically nice unless they are led to be otherwise. But the fact probably is that every child does hate and does covet, and that in his efforts to do so he is being repeatedly rebuffed by the more powerful persons in his environment. Those persons are apt often not to have the psychological insight necessary for redirecting these interests of the child into channels where they can have more success. Here then is a valuable potential role of children's reading matter.

Another possible inadequacy of the reading matter, one much more difficult to judge, is concerned with maturity. It is notable in the content of these readers that independent action initiated by child characters, and indeed by anyone, is more likely to be punished than similar behavior which is performed under the direction of a superior. Cognizance, for example, is rather frequently punished when it is undertaken on the child's own initiative and leads to pursuit of knowledge directly by the child's own exploratory behavior, whereas it is almost always rewarded if knowledge is gained through dependence upon authority. Autonomous behavior, too, is generally punished except in the case where the kind of autonomy is that desired by the child's elders. (There is an exception to this in the case of nurturance, which is more often rewarded when it is spontaneously initiated by the character himself.)

There can be no doubt that if children continue to be trained in this way as they grow older, the effect on their potentialities as adults will be a bad one. It may indeed be that a considerable proportion of adult maladjustment in marriage and occupational life is due to the discouragement of autonomy and independence by the educational system up to the point where an adolescent or young adult leaves it. On the other hand, it may of course be argued that the amount of independence encouraged by the content of these readers is quite appropriate for the particular age level at which the readers are directed. Certainly the development towards autonomy must be a gradual process and a considerable amount of dependence on superiors is necessary, not only at this age but even on into adult life. It is for this reason that it is impossible to make a conclusive judgment about the wisdom of this aspect of the content of the readers.

Differential Treatment of the Sexes

Perhaps the most striking single finding of this study is the extent to which a differentiation is made between the roles of male and female in the content of these readers. To the extent that boys identify with male characters, and girls with female characters, this difference both in itself and as a reflection of facts that hold true of many other sources of influence on children, must have a profound significance on the differential development of personality in the two sexes.

Some of the differentiation can be seen in the mere frequency with which the two sexes appear among the characters displaying the various categories of behavior. Female characters, for example, are relatively more frequent among those displaying affiliation, nurturance, and harmavoidance. On the other hand, females are less frequent, relatively, among characters displaying activity, aggression, achievement, construction, and recognition. Girls and women are thus being shown as sociable, kind and timid, but inactive, unambitious and uncreative.

This picture is further added to by con-

sidering the relative proportion of male and female characters among the subsidiary characters who are objects related to the satisfaction of the needs of the central characters. The most important findings here refer to nurturance and cognizance. The persons nurtured by a central character are in the majority female, suggesting that females are in a relatively helpless position.

The persons who supply information to central characters who are seeking for knowledge are, in contrast, predominantly male. It will be recalled that even among unrelated adults who supply knowledge to children, the majority are male despite the obvious fact that the most important such persons of the real environment are the child's teachers, who are mostly women. Males, in short, are being portrayed as the bearers of knowledge and wisdom, and as the persons through whom knowledge can come to the child.

In all of these respects, a distinction in role is being made between the sexes which may indeed have a certain validity as of our society of the present time, but which seems much more a survival of former practices. The many schoolgirls who will at some future time have to make their own living are failing, if they identify with female characters, to receive the same training in the development of motives for work and achievement that boys are receiving. To the extent that this distinction is characteristic of many other aspects of the training the child receives from his environment, it should cause little wonder that women are sometimes less fitted for creative work and achievement than men of similar aptitude, for there is certainly much difference in the motivational training they receive for it. It has been a common assumption that the education of the two sexes is virtually the same in American public schools, except for differences in vocational training. Here is clear evidence that the education is not the same, even at early levels of grammar school and even when the boys and girls are mixed together, as they usually are, in the same classroom. Not only does the informal training of boys and girls at home and in the community differ, but even the formal education they are receiving in the classroom differs.

It has been shown in several instances that the differential treatment of the sexes goes further than mere correspondence with this stereotype of different categories of behavior as being more conspicuous in a particular sex. There are several striking instances where females are shown as being definitely inferior from a moral point of view. In the discussion of passivity it was shown that female characters are portrayed as lazy twice as often, relatively, as male characters. In the discussion of acquisition it was seen that female characters are shown as acquiring in socially disapproved ways much more often, relatively, than males, and much less frequently by the most approved routes of work and effort.

In view of the social values of our society, it can also be said that the facts already cited above are relevant here. Insofar as female characters are shown as not often achieving, constructing, obtaining recognition or engaging in activity, they are being shown in an unfavorable light by the general standards of our society. But on the other hand, in that female characters are being shown as more frequently affiliative, nurturant, or unaggressive, they may perhaps be said to be receiving the more favorable treatment. While it is not true, then, that female characters are uniformly shown in a more unfavorable light, the balance is certainly in that direction.

The most striking single fact of all, however, about the difference between the sexes is that female characters do simply tend to be neglected. Of all the central characters in all these thema (excluding central characters who consist of a group of mixed sex), 73% are male and only 27%

are female. Male characters are thus over two and a half times as frequent as female ones. The same tendency is found, though not so strikingly, in the characters who are objects of, or cooperators in, the satisfaction of the needs of the central characters; here the proportion of males is 63% and of females 37%.

There can be no excuse for this greater attention to males in the claim that males have achieved more in society and hence that there is more to write about them. These stories are, with few exceptions, not about individuals of outstanding achievement but simply about the life of everyday people. The implication of this difference for a girl is that being female is a pretty bad thing, that the only people even in everyday life who are worth writing about or reading about are boys and men. If the content of these readers is typical of other social influences, small wonder that girls might develop for this reason alone an inferiority complex about their sex.

Differential Treatment of Adults and Children

The human characters in the stories were readily divisible into two groups according to age—adults and children. The treatment of these two groups differed markedly, and in ways that raise interesting problems about the effect of these stories on the children who read them.

There are, first of all, great differences in the relative frequency of the various categories of behavior. Children are much lower than adults in the incidence of aggression and acquisition. In adults, aggression and acquisition are the most frequently appearing categories of behavior, whereas in children these two are of very low incidence.

It is of interest that this contrast should show the children as conforming more closely than adults to socially approved behavior. The same tendency is found in certain other comparisons that can be made between children and adults.

In the discussion of acquisition, retention and aggression, it was shown in each case that child characters more frequently exhibit the more approved forms of these needs and that adult characters more frequently exhibit the most disapproved forms. Thus even within some of the separate categories of behavior, children are shown as more socialized than adults.

That children are shown as more socialized is demonstrated also by the relative frequency of different kinds of rewards. It was noted in connection with several categories of behavior, especially affiliation and nurturance, that children are shown as more frequently receiving only internal rewards. This generalization holds true for all of the behavior in the readers taken as a whole. A summary of the percent of each type of reward in all four types of character is presented in Table 3. It appears there that children receive internal rewards in more than twice as large a proportion as do adults. When the separate categories of behavior are considered, it is found that the proportion of internal rewards is higher in children than in adults in all but one of the fourteen most frequent categories. Now internal rewards are dependent upon socialization, for they are rewards that a person administers to himself because he is well socialized, because he is able to feel good or virtuous at having done the right thing, even if no reward is offered by an external agency.

That children are shown as more socialized than adults, perhaps points up more clearly than anything else the role that the content of these readers must be more or less consciously intended to play in the moral education of children. If the readers are intended for inculcating proper behavior in children, then it must seem only natural at first glance that it is the child characters who especially should be shown as displaying the desired forms of behavior. But a serious question may be raised as to whether the readers are likely to accomplish the purpose in this way. A more sophisticated consideration of the probable effect of the content of these readers would suggest that there is considerable probability that children pattern their behavior more after that of the adult characters than after that of the child characters. There is ample reason to suppose that children imitate adults, especially their parents, much more than they do their age-mates, and particularly with reference to deep-seated motivational tendencies. If this be true, then for purposes of the moral education of the children who read these stories, the adult characters should be shown as at least as well socialized as the child characters.

Whether this criticism is justified does, of course, depend upon factual determination of whether children are more likely to be influenced by the behavior portrayed in adult characters than in child characters. But on general psychological grounds, this does seem so likely as to give the criticism considerable weight.

The content of the readers, then, is likely to point out to children certain rewards and punishments that, for them, follow upon the display of approved or disapproved behavior, but to suggest that these rewards and punishments may stop

TABLE 3. KINDS OF REWARDS FOR ALL CATEGORIES OF BEHAVIOR: PERCENTAGE DISTRIBUTION IN EACH CHARACTER TYPE	CHARACTER TYPE	PERCENTAGE DISTRIBUTION OF KINDS OF REWARD IN EACH CHARACTER TYPE			
		Internal	*Social*	*Material*	*Automatic*
	Children	34	23	36	6
	Adults	16	26	53	4
	Animals	24	18	50	8
	Fairies	16	34	43	8

when they grow up to be adults. Such a lesson, which to be sure is also often made in a child's everyday life, may be satisfactory for the short-sighted parent or teacher, who knows that his immediate responsibility for the child will cease when

the child becomes an adult. But as a background for educational policy it seems deficient to anyone who looks at child-rearing or education as a task of preparing children to become adequate adults.

40 | AN EXPERIMENTAL STUDY OF LEADERSHIP AND GROUP LIFE

RONALD LIPPITT AND RALPH K. WHITE

This is one of the most famous experiments in child psychology. It attempts to make specific the meaning of such terms as "democratic," "autocratic," and "laissez-faire" in a leader-follower situation. Children's reactions to leaders who are autocratic and to those who are democratic and laissez-faire are compared, and the changes in attitude and behavior when the leadership shifts from one type to another are described.

The study here reported, conducted in 1939 and 1940, attempted in an explora-

Reprinted from *Readings in Social Psychology*, Third Edition, edited by Eleanor E. Maccoby, Theodore M. Newcomb, and Eugene L. Hartley. By permission of Henry Holt and Company, Inc. Copyright 1958. Prepared by the authors from data more fully reported in (1) Kurt Lewin, Ronald Lippitt, and Ralph K. White, "Patterns of Aggressive Behavior in Experimentally Created 'Social Climates,'" *J. Soc. Psychol.*, 1939, X, 271–299; (2) Ronald Lippitt, "An Experimental Study of Authoritarian and Democratic Group Atmospheres" in *Studies in Topological and Vector Psychology, I, University of Iowa Studies in Child Welfare*, No. 16, 1940; (3) Ronald Lippitt, "An Analysis of Group Reactions to Three Types of Experimentally Created Social Climates" (Unpublished doctoral thesis, State University of Iowa, 1940); (4) Ronald Lippitt, "Field Theory and Experiment in Social Psychology: Authoritarian and Democratic Group Atmospheres," *Am. J. Sociol.*, 1939, XLV, 26–49; (5) Ronald Lippitt, "The Morale of Youth Groups," in Goodwin Watson (ed.), *Civilian Morale* (Boston: Published for Reynal & Hitchcock by Houghton Mifflin Co., 1942); and (6) Ronald Lippitt and Ralph K. White, "The 'Social Climate' of Children's Groups," in Roger Barker, Jacob Kounin, and Herbert Wright, *Child Development and Behavior* (New York: McGraw-Hill Book Co., 1943).

tory way to discover the extent to which various aspects of leadership behavior and of total group life could be fruitfully studied by experimental procedures of controlled matching and planned variation in conditions. The study had as its objectives:

1. To study the effects on group and individual behavior of three experimental variations in adult leadership in four clubs of eleven-year-old children. These three styles may be roughly labeled as "democratic," "authoritarian" and "laissez-faire."

2. To study the group and individual reactions to shifts from one type of leadership to another within the same group.

3. To seek relationships between the nature and content of other group memberships, particularly the classroom and family, and the reactions to the experimental social climates.

4. To explore the methodological problems of setting up comparative "group test situations," to develop adequate techniques of group process recording, and to discover the degree to which experimental conditions could be controlled and ma-

nipulated within the range of acceptance by the group members.

The major experimental controls may be described briefly as follows:

1. PERSONAL CHARACTERISTICS OF GROUP MEMBERS | Because a large group of volunteers were available from which to select each of the small clubs, it was possible to arrange for comparability of group members on such characteristics as intelligence, and on such social behaviors (measured by teachers' ratings) as obedience, amount of social participation, leadership, frequency of quarreling, amount of physical energy, etc.

2. THE INTERRELATIONSHIP PATTERN OF EACH CLUB | In each group, by the use of a sociometric questionnaire in each classroom, it was possible to select groups which were very closely matched in terms of patterns of rejection, friendship, mutuality of relationship, and leadership position.

3. PHYSICAL SETTING AND EQUIPMENT | All clubs met in the same clubroom setting, two at a time in adjacent meeting spaces, with a common equipment box.

4. ACTIVITY INTERESTS | It was important to know the extent to which initial interest in the planned activities might be responsible for differences in degree of involvement in activity during the experiment. Therefore it was ascertained in the beginning that all groups of boys were comparably interested in the range of craft and recreational activities in which they would later be engaged.

5. ACTIVITY CONTENT | It is clear that the structure and content of an activity often exerts a powerful influence on the patterns of interdependence, cooperation, competition, etc. in group life. Therefore, it was important that activity content should be equated in these three types of leadership situations. In order to insure this, the clubs under democratic leadership met first in time during the week, and the activities which were selected by those clubs were automatically assigned to the parallel clubs under authoritarian leadership. In the laissez-faire situation, there were a number of potential activities of the same type as that selected by the "democratic clubs."

6. THE SAME GROUP UNDER DIFFERENT LEADERSHIP | The experimental design also made it possible to have a perfect matching of club personnel on the same analysis by comparing the same club with itself under three different leaders.

	Period 1 (7 weeks)	Period 2 (7 weeks)	Period 3 (7 weeks)
Treatment Club Leader	Autocracy Sherlock Holmes I	Autocracy Sherlock Holmes IV	Democracy Sherlock Holmes II
Treatment Club Leader	Autocracy Dick Tracy II	Democracy Dick Tracy III	Autocracy Dick Tracy I
Treatment Club Leader	Democracy Secret Agents III	Autocracy Secret Agents II	Democracy Secret Agents IV
Treatment Club Leader	Democracy Charlie Chan IV	Democracy Charlie Chan I	Autocracy Charlie Chan III

EXPERIMENTAL VARIATIONS

In the beginning the experimenters had planned for only two major variations in adult leader behavior: an authoritarian pattern and a democratic pattern. Later it was decided that it would be more fruitful to add a third variation of "laissez-faire" adult behavior, although with the four available clubs it would make the experimental design less rigorous. The method of systematic rotation can be noted in the above chart, which refers to the earlier experiment (the same method was followed in the later experiment).

The three types of planned variation were as follows:

1. THE SEQUENCE OF SOCIAL CLIMATES | A number of the hypotheses focused upon the effect of a particular type of group history in determining the reactions of a group to a present pattern of leadership. The chart indicates the variety of group history sequences which were selected for exploratory study.

2. "LEADER ROLE" AND "LEADER PERSONALITY" | There was a question as to the extent to which certain basic personality characteristics of the adult leaders would be important determinants in the individual and group behavior patterns which resulted. To study this variable, four adults with very different personality patterns were selected as leaders and all of them after proper indoctrination took two or three different leadership roles with different groups during the course of the experiment as indicated on the chart. This made it possible to discover whether certain of the leaders induced common reaction patterns which could be traced to their "personality" as contrasted to their "leadership role."

3. THE THREE PLANNED LEADERSHIP ROLES | The three variations in leader role which were worked through in careful detail by the four club leaders may be summarized as follows:

Plan for authoritarian leadership role. Practically all policies as regards club activities and procedures should be determined by the leader. The techniques and activity steps should be communicated by the authority, one unit at a time, so that future steps are in the dark to a large degree. The adult should take considerable responsibility for assigning the activity tasks and companions of each group member. The dominator should keep his standards of praise and criticism to himself in evaluating individual and group activities. He should also remain fairly aloof from active group participation except in demonstrating.

Plan for the democratic leadership role. Wherever possible, policies should be a matter of group decision and discussion with active encouragement and assistance by the adult leader. The leader should attempt to see that activity perspective emerges during the discussion period with the general steps to the group goal becoming clarified. Wherever technical advice is needed, the leader should try to suggest two or more alternative procedures from which choice can be made by the group members. Everyone should be free to work with whomever he chooses, and the divisions of responsibility should be left up to the group. The leader should attempt to communicate in an objective, fact-minded way the bases for his praise and criticism of individual and group activities. He should try to be a regular group member in spirit but not do much of the work (so that comparisons of group productivity can be made between the groups).

Plan for laissez-faire leadership role. In this situation, the adult should play a rather passive role in social participation and leave complete freedom for group or individual decisions in relation to activity and group procedure. The leader should make clear the various materials which are available and be sure it is understood that he will supply information and help when asked. He should do a minimum of taking the initiative in making suggestions. He should make no attempt to evaluate negatively or positively the behavior or productions of the individuals or the group as a group, although he should be friendly rather than "stand-offish" at all times.

The data below will indicate the extent

to which these planned variations were carried out and the pattern of social stimulation which was represented by the leader behavior in each of the clubs.

THE THREE PATTERNS OF LEADER BEHAVIOR

From the great variety of observations recorded on the behavior of each leader it was possible to compute quantitative profiles of leader performance which could be compared to see the extent to which the three different types of leadership role were different and the degree to which the adults carrying out the same role were comparable in their behavior patterns. Figure 1 illustrates some of the major differences in the patterns of behavior of the three leadership roles. Most of the comparisons on the graph meet the test of statistical significance. The "average leader" comparisons are based on four democratic, four authoritarian, and two laissez-faire leader roles. The first three classifications of behavior, "leader orders," "disrupting commands" and "nonconstructive criticism," may be thought of as representing adult behavior which has a limiting effect upon the scope and spontaneity of child activity. About 60 percent of all of the behavior of the average authoritarian leader was of these types as compared to 5 percent for the democratic and laissez-faire leaders. The data show that the authoritarian leader usually initiated individual or group activity with an order, often disrupted on-going activity by an order which started things off in the new direction not spontaneously chosen, and fairly frequently criticized work in a manner which carried the meaning, "It is a bad job because I say it is a bad job" rather than, "It is a poor job because those nails are bent over instead of driven in."

The next three behavior classifications, "guiding suggestions," "extending knowledge," "stimulating self-guidance," may be thought of as extending individual and

group freedom and abilities. We note here some of the major differences between the democratic and the laissez-faire leadership role. Whereas the democratic leader took the initiative (where he felt it was needed in making guiding suggestions) much more frequently than the laissez-faire leader, a major proportion of the latter leadership role was giving out information when it was asked for. It is clear, however, that the democratic leader did not take initiative for action away from the group as indicated by the fact that the average democratic leader showed a greater proportion of "stimulating self-guidance" than even the laissez-faire leader. The category of "stimulating self-guidance" was made up of three main items: "leader's requests for child's opinions on individual and group plans," "use of child judgment as criterion," and "taking consensus of opinion." The data indicate that the democratic leaders stimulated child independence eight times as often as the authoritarian leader and about twice as often as the laissez-faire leader, although the latter two types of adults showed about the same proportion of this behavior in their total pattern of activity.

The classification on the graph entitled, "praise and approval" is made up of such behavior items as "praising," "giving credit," "giving O.K.s," etc. It indicates largely the functioning of the adult as a dispenser of social recognition. The authoritarian adult was significantly more active in this regard than either of the other two types of leaders.

The extent to which the adult discussed personal matters unrelated to the club situation (home, school, etc.), and also joked on a friendly basis with the club members, is indicated by the "jovial and confident" classification. The democratic leader had social interactions of this type with the group members about eight times as often as either the authoritarian or laissez-faire leaders. This is perhaps one of the best indices of the extent to which the democratic leaders were "on the same level" as the club members.

The last classification on Figure 1, "matter of fact," indicates one measurement of the extent to which the various social atmospheres were "fact-minded" as compared to "personal-minded" as far as the behavior of the adults was concerned.

The degree to which all the adult leaders, delegated to assume a given leadership role, behaved in a comparable fashion on these major aspects of leadership role is indicated by the fact that, on all comparisons differentiating major characteristics of the three roles, there is no overlapping of the behavior of any representative of one role with any representative of a different role. Thus it is possible to conclude that three clearly different leadership patterns were created with a

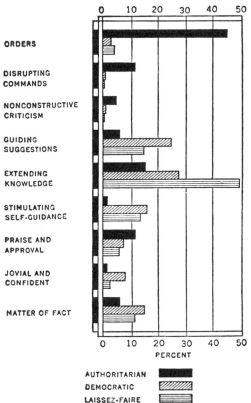

Figure 1. Comparison of behavior of average authoritarian, democratic, and laissez-faire leader.

much smaller range of individual differences in leader behavior within each pattern than between the patterns.

Leadership Role and Personality Style

An examination of the behavior patterns of the different leadership roles by the same individuals . . . reveals that on the items of leader behavior there is no greater similarity between the different performance patterns of the same individual than between those of different individuals. If we turn to the data of the three interviews with each club member in which at each transition stage in their club life they compared their leaders and talked very fully about them, we find again that there is no evidence of any adult personalities being rated favorably or unfavorably independently of their particular leadership role (i.e., authoritarian, democratic, laissez-faire). All leaders stood high as well as low for one group or another and all the comments about their "personalities" were concerned with attributes of their leadership roles which had been measured.

The following excerpts from interviews of club members who had just completed six months of club life which included an authoritarian, a laissez-faire, and a democratic leader (in that sequence) indicate rather clearly the aspects of "leadership personality" which were perceived as important.

"RW (democratic) was the best leader and DA (laissez-faire) was the poorest. RW has good ideas and goes right to the point of everything . . . and always asked us what to do next time the club met, which was very nice. . . . DA gave us no suggestions like RW did, and didn't help us out at all, though he was very nice to us . . . but let us figure things out too much. I liked RL (authoritarian) pretty well for that kind of work."

"RL (authoritarian) was best, and then RW (democratic) and DA (laissez-faire). RL was the strictest and I like that a lot. DA and RW let us go ahead and fight, and that isn't good, though RW didn't do it as much as DA did. DA just didn't give us much to do. RW was OK, but he didn't have so many ideas as RL did. RW wanted to do what we did; RL didn't want to go with us lots of times, and he decided what we were to do."

"I liked RW (democratic) best, then DA (laissez-faire) and then RL (authoritarian). RW was a good sport, works along with us and helps us a lot; he thinks of things just like we do and was just one of us—he never did try to be the boss, and wasn't strict at all, but we always had plenty to do (the golden mean). DA didn't do much, just sat and watched; there wasn't much I didn't like about him, but he didn't help us much . . . not like with RW when we had regular meetings and that was very good. RL was all right mostly; he was sort of dictator like, and we had to do what he said pretty nearly; he helped us work but he was sort of bossy."

"I liked RW (democratic) the best and RL (authoritarian) the least. RW was in between DA and RL. I like everything about him. I once said I didn't want to change from DA but I'm glad we changed. We could do what we pleased with DA but he was too easy going, not hard enough nearly, but he's a real nice person. With RL we always had something to do, and we did get a lot of things done, but I didn't like anything about him; he was much too strict. He was not cross, but very direct."

"I'd take RW (democratic) for a club leader, and DA (laissez-faire) was the worst. RW is just the right sort of combination; RL (authoritarian) was just about as good as RW, but he was kind of cross once in a while. RW had interesting things to do, he was just about right in everything. DA was too easy; he didn't know anything about the club—didn't know about its ways. He didn't understand us boys at all. . . . I didn't like him as well as RL because he had too few things for us to do."[1]

Another indirect indication that indi-

vidual personality characteristics were not of any great significance in influencing group life in this study might be inferred from the finding that the total patterns of group reactions of different clubs to the same atmosphere tend to be remarkably homogeneous in spite of differences in adult leadership.

DATA COLLECTION AND ANALYSIS

Before continuing to summarize the individual and group behaviors which resulted from these three variations in leadership role, we will indicate briefly the types of data collection and analysis in the total study.

Eight types of club records were kept on each group, of which the four most important were kept by four different observers as follows.

1. A quantitative running account of the social interactions of the five children and the leader, in terms of symbols for directive, compliant, and objective (fact-minded) approaches and responses, including a category of purposeful refusal to respond to a social approach.

2. A minute-by-minute group structure analysis giving a record of activity subgroupings, the activity goal of each subgroup, whether the goal was initiated by the leader or spontaneously formed by the children, and rating on degree of unity of each subgrouping.

3. An interpretive running account of strikingly significant member actions and changes in the atmosphere of the group as a whole.

4. Continuous stenographic records of all conversation.

These data were synchronized at minute intervals so that placed side by side they furnished quite a complete and integrated picture of the on-going life of the group.

Five other types of data covering the lives of the club members were collected, the three most important being:

1. Interviews with each child by a friendly "non-club" person during each transition period from one kind of group atmosphere

---

[1] Beside indicating the leadership characteristics perceived as important by the boys, the reader will note that one boy in this club (an army officer's son) preferred his authoritarian leader and that the other four split in that two preferred their authoritarian leader second best and two liked their laissez-faire leader second best.

and leader to another. These interviews elicited comparisons of the various club leaders with one another, with the teacher and with parents as well as other data about how the club could be run better, who were the best and poorest types of club members, what an ideal club leader would be like, etc.

2. Interviews with the parents, concentrating on kinds of discipline used in the home, status of the child in the family group, personality ratings on the same scales used by the teachers, discussion of the child's attitude toward the club, school and other group activities.

3. Talks with the teachers concerning the transfer to the schoolroom of behavior patterns acquired in the club and vice versa.

The reliability of the eleven trained observers ranged from .78 to .95 with an average reliability of .84. Another reliability computation on the coding of three thousand units of conversation into twenty-three categories of behavior showed a percent agreement of 86. The analyses of what constituted a "group life unit" showed reliabilities ranging from .90 to .98. A number of methodological researches carried on since the date of this study seem to suggest that it is possible to get much more meaningful and reliable observation data than has been generally believed if much more time and effort are spent on a careful "calibration" of psychologically well-trained observers.

Comparative Group Test Situations

The experimenters also postulated that a fruitful way to discover some of the major differences between the three types of group atmosphere would be to arrange comparable "test episodes" in each club. So at regular intervals the following situations occurred:

1. Leader arrives late.
2. Leader called away for indeterminate time.
3. Stranger ("janitor" or "electrician") arrives while leader is out and carries on critical attack of work of individual group member, then of group as a whole.

THE FOUR RESULTANT STYLES OF GROUP LIFE

Some of the major findings, summarized from stenographic records and other case material which are elsewhere reproduced, are as follows: Two distinct types of reaction were shown to the same pattern of authoritarian leadership. All of the data, including the documentary films, indicate that three of the clubs responded with a dependent leaning on the adult leader, relatively low levels of frustration tension, and practically no capacity for initiating group action, while the fourth club demonstrated considerable frustration and some degree of channelized aggression toward the authoritarian leader. (This latter pattern is much more comparable to the behavior of the club under authoritarian leadership in a previous experimental study of two clubs.)

Figure 2 indicates the major differences in the relations which developed between the group members and the adult leaders in the four resultant social atmospheres.

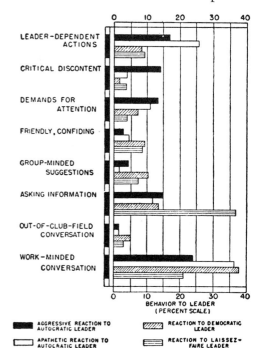

Figure 2. Four patterns of group reaction to the three different types of leadership.

In both types of authoritarian atmosphere the members were markedly more dependent upon the leader than in either the democratic or laissez-faire situations, dependence being somewhat greater in the more passive clubs. All other clubs showed a somewhat greater feeling of discontent in their relations with the adult leader than did the members of the democratic clubs, members of the "aggressive autocracy" being outstanding in their expression of rebellious feelings. There is evidence from other sources that the actual "felt discontent" in the "apathetic autocracies" was somewhat higher than indicated by the conversation which was considerably more restricted than was that of the democratic and laissez-faire club members.

In both types of authoritarian situations the demands for attention from the adult were greater than in the other atmospheres. It seemed clear that getting the attention of the adult represented one of the few paths to more satisfactory social status in the authoritarian situation where all of the "central functions" of group life were in the hands of the dominator.

The category "friendly, confiding" indicates that the members of the democratic and laissez-faire clubs initiated more "personal" and friendly approaches to their adult leaders, and the data on "out-of-club-field conversation" further indicate the more spontaneous exchanging of confidences about other parts of one's life experience in the democratic club atmosphere.

The data on "group-minded suggestions" to the leader show that the members in the democratic atmosphere felt much freer and more inclined to make suggestions on matters of group policy than in the other three group atmospheres. It is clear from other data that the lower level of suggestions in the laissez-faire situation is not because of any feeling of restricted freedom but because of a lack of a cooperative working relationship between the adult and the other group members.

The much greater responsibility of the members of the laissez-faire clubs to get their own information is shown by the fact that about 37 percent of their behavior toward their leader consisted of asking for information, as compared to about 15 percent in the other three club situations.

The final category in Figure 2, "work-minded conversation," indicates that a considerably larger proportion of the initiated approaches of the club members to their leaders were related to on going club activity in the democratic and in the apathetic authoritarian situations than in the other two types of social climate.

Resultant Relationships of Club Members

The relationships between the club members also developed along quite different lines in the four social climates. Expressions of irritability and aggressiveness toward fellow members occurred more frequently in both the authoritarian atmospheres and the laissez-faire situation than in the democratic social climates. Unlike the relationships of high interpersonal tension and scapegoating which developed in the previous aggressive autocracy the club in this experiment seemed to focus its aggression sufficiently in other channels (toward the leader and toward the outgroup) so that in-group tension did not rise to a dangerously high point.

There were more requests for attention and approval from fellow club members to each other in the democratic and laissez-faire situations than in the two authoritarian climates. It seems clear that the child members depended upon each other to a great extent for social recognition and were more ready to give recognition to each other in the democratic and laissez-faire situations.

It is interesting to find nearly as high a level of interpersonal friendliness in the authoritarian situations as in the democratic and laissez-faire atmospheres. The underlying spirit of rebellion toward the leader and cooperation in out-group aggression seem to be the "cohesive forces" in aggressive autocracy, while in apathetic autocracy with its much lower level of felt frustration, the shared submissiveness seemed to do away with all incentive to competition for social status.

Intermember suggestions for group action and group policy were significantly lower in both types of autocracy than in the laissez-faire and democratic atmospheres. The dissatisfactions arising from any lack of feeling of real progress in the laissez-faire situation led to a high frequency of expression of ideas about "something we might do." Contrary to the democratic situation, these suggestions seldom became reality because of the lack of the social techniques necessary for group decision and cooperative planning. The group achievement level, as contrasted to the "wish level," was far lower in laissez-faire than in any of the other three atmospheres.

Other Differences

By having the leaders arrive a few minutes late at regular intervals in each club life, it was possible to discover that in the five authoritarian situations no group initiative to start new work or to continue with work already under way developed, as contrasted with the democratic situations where leaders who arrived late found their groups already active in a productive fashion. The groups under the laissez-faire leaders were active but not productive. Figure 3 shows the percentage of total club time in each of the four social atmospheres which was spent in giving major attention to some planned club project. For each atmosphere there is a comparison between the time when the leader was in the room, the time when the leader had been called out for planned experimental periods, and the unit of time just after the leader returned. The data here give striking evidence of the extent to which work motivation was leader-

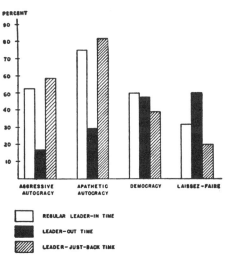

Figure 3. Percent of time spent in high activity involvement.

induced in the two types of authoritarian situation. "Working time" dropped to a minimum with the leader out, and most of what was done was in the minutes just after the leader had left the room. We see that in the democratic atmosphere the absence or presence of the leader had practically no effect. The apparent increase in group productive time with the laissez-faire leader out of the room may or may not be a meaningful result. Two or three times it was noted that when the adult left, one of the boys exerted a more powerful leadership and achieved a more coordinated group activity than when the relatively passive adult was present.

The behavior of the groups under authoritarian domination after their transition to a freer social atmosphere provided a very interesting index of unexpressed group tension. In Figure 4 it can be noted that both of these apathetic authoritarian clubs showed great outbursts of horseplay between the members on the first day of their transitions to a laissez-faire and a democratic group situation. This need to "blow off" disappeared with more meetings in the freer atmosphere.

It will be recalled that in certain situations all groups were subject to the same frustration of hostile criticism by a strange

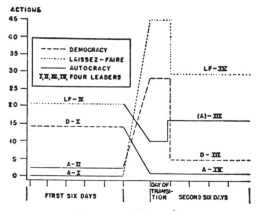

Figure 4. Horseplay.

adult (e.g., "janitor") while the adult leader was gone. Under the different types of leaders, the groups handled these frustrations differently. Members of the apathetic authoritarian clubs tended to accept individually and to internalize the unjust criticism or, in one or two cases, they "blew off steam" in aggressive advances toward an out-group (the other club meeting in the adjacent clubroom; see Figure 5). In the aggressive authoritarian situation, the frustration was typically channeled in aggression toward the out-group, although in several cases there was some

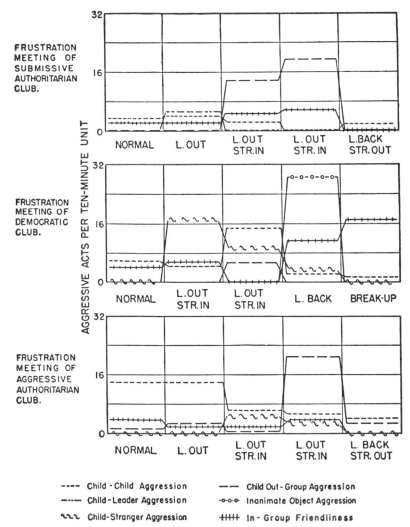

Figure 5. Channels of group tension release in clubs of eleven-year-old boys under different types of leadership.

direct reaction to the source of frustration, the hostile stranger (see Figure 5). In the democratic atmospheres there was evidence of a greater readiness to unite in rejection of the real source of frustration, the stranger, and to resist out-group aggression. Figure 5 shows an interesting case of a democratic club which first expressed its aggression directly against the stranger, then showed a slight rise in intermember tension, followed by an aggressive outburst against a sheet of three-ply wood with hammer and chisels accompanied by a striking rise in in-group friendliness and a quick return to cooperative harmony. It was particularly interesting to discover that the clubs under democratic leaders resisted scapegoating as a channel of aggressive release.

The data indicate that the democratic type of adult role resulted in the greatest expression of individual differences, and that some type of uniformity-producing forces brought about a slightly lessened individual variability in the laissez-faire situation, and a much reduced range of individuality in the authoritarian clubs. Figure 6 gives an example of this analysis for the same group of individuals under three different leaders.

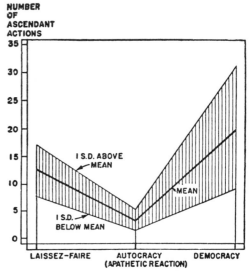

Figure 6.   The effect of changed atmosphere upon the range of individual differences within the same group.

41 | THE INFLUENCE OF THE GROUP
ON THE JUDGMENTS OF CHILDREN

RUTH W. BERENDA

In the tale of "The Emperor's New Clothes," one child dares to see and admit reality, while others "see" the emperor as elegantly clothed. How much are the individual's perceptions influenced by others? What happens when reports of others contradict what a child actually sees?

In the series of ingenious experiments reported here, Dr. Berenda discovered that the influence of the group on children's judgments was greatest when the material to be evaluated was ambiguous and least where the material was clear-cut.

The fact that the most serious problems of our time are complicated and ambiguous—the elimination of war, poverty, crime, and racial tensions, for example, as well as the age-old questions concerning the metaphysical bases of existence—may perhaps explain why so many adults today are satisfied to accept the group's values and judgments.

FORMULATION OF THE PROBLEM AND PROCEDURE

This study is an attempt to analyze the effect that group pressure has on judgments of children between the ages of seven to thirteen. We are trying to understand the nature of this "pressure," the conditions under which it is effective in modifying judgments, and the child's conception of such situations and his reaction to them.

The general character of our procedure was to place an individual child in contradiction to a group and to observe the effect quantitatively and qualitatively.

. . . . .

The group was at all times composed of members of the child's class.

In some cases the majority was made up of the child's brightest classmates (Experiment I), and in other cases (Experiments III and IV) they were all the other children in his class—bright and dull.

Systematic investigation would require that tasks differing in structural clarity be investigated. We therefore used tasks that were extremely clear and also others that were somewhat varied with regard to this quality. The subjects were required to estimate the lengths of lines, compare lines with a standard and to match lines.

EXPERIMENT I: A GROUP VERSUS A MINORITY OF ONE

Problem and Procedure

What would be the effect on the judgment of an individual child when a majority of the group of which he is a member unanimously gives wrong judgments regarding simple perceptual materials?

Excerpts reprinted from *The Influence of the Group on the Judgments of Children* (New York: King's Crown Press, 1950), by permission of the author.

Would such a child yield to group influence and change his judgments or would he conform to the group? What would be the reaction of a child to such a situation?

From a total of 240 children who participated in the control experiment only 90 of these children, ranging in age from seven to thirteen years and selected from grades two to seven, served as critical subjects in this experiment. Thirty-eight of these children came from classes with an average I.Q. whereas 52 were taken from the so-called "opportunity classes" where the I.Q. was 130 and above. Of the nine classes that participated the 8 bright children in each class served as the "majority." The 10 "minority" subjects of each class were selected by their teacher, 5 for such personality traits as leadership and independence and the remaining 5 for submissiveness and meekness. The two sexes were equally represented.

The children were presented successively with twelve pairs of cards, a standard containing a single line and a comparison card with three lines, one of which was equal in length to the standard. The task consisted in identifying that comparison line which was equal to the standard. The lines were made by pasting black tape, ¼ inch wide, on white cards, 17½ by 6 inches. The three lines of a comparison card were numbered from left to right. In each case a standard and a comparison card were presented on the ledge of a blackboard, 3 feet apart, the standard to the right.

Previously, these children had performed the same task in control experiments with their respective classes. Now, the same task was repeated with one essential change in the conditions. Eight of these children, or the so-called "majority," were under instruction to give false answers on seven out of the twelve lines. These seven lines will be referred to as "critical lines." In Table 1 are given the

TABLE 1. LENGTHS OF STANDARD AND COMPARISON LINES AND THE RESPONSES OF THE CO-OPERATING GROUP

TRIALS	LENGTH OF STANDARD LINE	LENGTH OF COMPARISON LINES			CORRECT ANSWERS	GROUP ANSWERS[a]
		First	*Second*	*Third*		
1	7½	5	5¾	7½	3	3
2	5	6½	7	5	3	3
3	8	8	7	6	1	*2*
4	3½	3¾	5	3½	3	*1*
5	9	7	9	11	2	2
6	6½	6½	5¼	7½	1	*3*
7	5½	4½	5½	4	2	*1*
8	1¾	2¾	3¼	1¾	3	3
9	2½	4	2½	3⅜	2	*3*
10	8½	8½	10¼	11	1	*2*
11	1	3	1	2¼	2	2
12	4½	4½	3½	5½	1	*3*

[a] The italic figures in this column refer to the false responses of the group.

lengths of the lines as well as the incorrect answers of the majority.

On the day of the experiment those children who were to serve as critical subjects were sent to another classroom and were told by their teacher to stay there all day for special work. The experimenter then led the eight majority children to another classroom while the teacher remained with those who were not participating in the experiment.

To the majority the experimenter explained the purpose and procedure of the experiment and stressed the need for their full co-operation. To the child who was usually selected by the group as the most reliable and careful the experimenter gave a typewritten copy of the answers he was to give in their sequence. The other seven children were instructed to follow him in their responses. All were given copies[1] of the questions they were to ask in the discussion that was to follow the judgments. The experiment as well as the discussion were carefully rehearsed.

Each critical subject was brought by a monitor to the experimental room where he found the eight majority children waiting in line outside of the room, with their books under their arms. The impression was thus created that the entire group was just entering the classroom. The child in the fifth seat had been instructed to make sure that the minority child was seated in the seat beside him, the sixth.

Presenting the first pair of cards, the experimenter addressed the group, saying: "You will remember I showed you these lines before. I have here at the right one line. On the other side I have a card with three lines. You see that the three lines are not the same size. You also see that the lines are numbered one, two, and three. There is one line among these three that is just as long as the one line on this card [pointing to standard]. When I put up the two cards, you will not write your answers as you did last time, but each of you will stand up and give his answer out loud."

The twelve pairs of cards were thus presented and the responses of each child were recorded on a previously prepared chart.[2] After all the judgments had been given, the experimenter opened the discussion.

[1] These copies were used for purposes of instruction but were not in evidence during the experiment.

[2] Of course, only the answers of the minority children were tabulated, those of the majority having been prearranged.

If the minority child did not follow the group, the experimenter started by saying: "Was this a hard test?" Invariably receiving a negative reply to this, the experimenter continued: "Yes, these are simple lines, and yet you didn't all agree. What happened?" At this point the majority children, as previously instructed, turned upon the minority child with the following:

1. "You gave different answers."
2. "What was the matter?"
3. "Why did you give these answers?"
4. "Who do you think was right, you or we?"

If the minority child said he was right, he was confronted with the question: "Was everyone else wrong?" If, on the other hand, the child said he was wrong, the majority demanded that he explain why he did not give their answers. In the interest of spontaneity the exact order of the questions could not be rigidly set in advance, since they depended so much upon the replies and the behavior of the critical child.

If the minority child would not admit that the group was wrong, the experimenter said: "You were right and they were wrong seven times." The reaction to this information was observed, and then the actual purpose of the experiment was revealed.

If the minority child had responded with the group, the experimenter started the discussion by saying: "Were you all sure of your answers? Was there any time when you felt like giving a different answer?" If the minority child did not reply to these questions, the experimenter put up two or three of the pairs on which the child followed the group and said to the minority child: "I am not sure I got all your answers right. Only you answer now." When the answers were recorded and the child's behavior noted, the experimenter took him out of the room and said: "Before you go back, I would like to ask you a few questions about this test. Let's go into this room." The experimenter then asked some of the following questions: "Were you sure of your answers? You gave different answers now than you did before. Which were right? If the other children were not there, would you have given the same answers? Why did you give the same answers? Did you doubt what you saw? How did you feel?"

At the end of the interview the experimenter explained the purpose of the experiment and observed the pupil's reaction to this information. The experimenter elicited from each critical child a promise[3] to keep the secret and led him back to his own classroom.

Before we present the quantitative results, it will be relevant to describe the atmosphere of the group experiments. By frankly discussing with each majority group, even the very young ones, the purpose and the implications of the experiment, we were able to secure their enthusiastic and complete co-operation. These children felt honored being chosen to help and realized the importance of their role in the experiment. They offered many suggestions, often valuable ones, on procedure, and when the teacher proved a poor judge in the selection of the minority children, the majority objected and by a vote designated those to be called in as critical subjects. They were also the ones who by a vote decided whether a child was reliable and could be trusted with the "secret" (purpose) of the experiment. True, to the younger children the procedure remained a game, but a very serious one indeed. They watched with interest and concern the behavior of each minority child and expressed disappointment when one whom they consid-

---

[3] Five out of the total number of critical subjects admitted having heard about the "secret." The dynamics of the experimental situation were so strong that this knowledge in no way affected their behavior.

ered very bright yielded to group pressure. In the group discussion the majority turned with considerable fervor and such force on the dissenter that the latter was often brought to tears or to an open accusation that the majority gave wrong answers. As one youngster of eight put it when pressed by the group: "I wouldn't have took the answers if I didn't think it was right. Why are you asking me all these questions?" Or another: "I was just making up my mind. At least you must give a guy a chance to make up his mind."

If, as was often the case among the younger ones, the minority child admitted being right but could not bring himself to say that the majority was wrong, the others would challenge him on his lack of logic, pointing out that if he believed the others to be right he should have given their answers. The few who stubbornly insisted that theirs were the right answers were really put to test by their classmates who would point out indignantly that eight could not be wrong and

one alone right. This led on several occasions to spontaneous discussions of a more general nature.

With all classes the experimental situation was so real and so dynamic that even among the older children there was never a trace of suspicion nor any doubt that the situation was serious and important, even though very puzzling and strange.

Results

. . . . .

It will be helpful to examine first how strongly the individual children were affected by the group conditions. The relevant results are reported in Table 2. In this table we include the frequencies with which the children followed the group. The corresponding results are presented graphically in Figure 1.

It will be noted that the effect of group conditions was indeed strong. Table 2 shows further that the effect of the majority was more pronounced on the younger than on the older children. Out

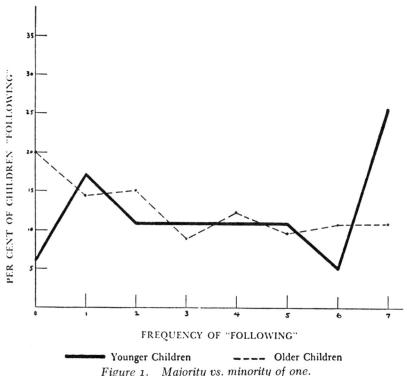

Younger Children   - - - - Older Children

Figure 1. Majority vs. minority of one.

TABLE 2. FREQUENCY OF "FOL-LOWING" RESPONSES ON CRITICAL LINES: EXPERI-MENT I	NUMBER OF TIMES "FOLLOWING"	YOUNGER CHILDREN SEVEN TO TEN		OLDER CHILDREN TEN TO THIRTEEN		TOTAL "FOLLOWING"	
		Number	Per Cent	Number	Per Cent	Number	Per Cent
	0	3	7	11	20	14	15.5
	1	7	18	7	13	14	15.5
	2	4	11	8	15	12	13
	3	4	11	4	8	8	9
	4	4	11	6	12	10	11
	5	4	11	4	8	8	9
	6	2	5	6	12	8	9
	7	10	26	6	12	16	18
	TOTAL	38	100	52	100	90	100
	AVERAGE	3.5		2.5		2.7	

of the maximum score of seven, the younger children followed the group 3.5 times on the average, the older children 2.5 times. Fully 26 per cent of the younger children followed the group throughout with only 7 per cent remaining independent in all their responses. Of the older group, on the other hand, only 12 per cent gave the incorrect group answers throughout and 20 per cent never followed. Considering the extremely clear character of the task and also the relatively high accuracy of the children's judgments under the control conditions, we have to conclude that the group exerted an effect of considerable magnitude.

An examination of the percentages of correct responses to the lines considered individually adds support to our preceding conclusions. These are reported in Tables 3 and 4 and represented graphically in Figures 2 and 3.

The critical lines were responded to correctly by 93 per cent of the younger children under control conditions and by only 43 per cent of the same children under the pressure of the group. Of the older group, 94 per cent gave correct answers to the critical lines in the control experiment, whereas only 54 per cent did so in the critical experiment.

If we consider first the results concerning the younger group (see Table 3 and Figure 2), the following conclusions seem warranted.

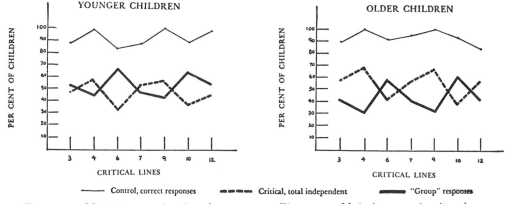

Figure 2. *Majority vs. minority of one.*   Figure 3. *Majority vs. minority of one.*

TABLE 3.

DISTRIBUTION OF "GROUP" RESPONSES TO EACH

CRITICAL LENGTH; YOUNGER CHILDREN, 7 TO 10 (N=38)

	CONTROL EXPERIMENT				CRITICAL EXPERIMENT					
Critical Lines in Order of Presentation	Correct Answers		Independent Correct		Group Answer		Independent Incorrect		Total Independent[a]	
	Number	Per Cent	Number	Per Cent	Number	Per Cent	Number	Per Cent	Number	Per Cent
Third	34	89	13	34	20	53	5	13	18	47
Fourth	38	100	21	55	17	45	0	0	21	55
Sixth	32	84	12	32	26	68	0	0	12	32
Seventh	34	89	19	50	18	47	1	3	20	53
Ninth	38	100	20	53	16	42	2	5	22	58
Tenth	34	89	14	37	24	63	0	0	14	37
Twelfth	37	97	15	40	21	55	2	5	17	45
AVERAGE		93		43		53		37		43

	Correct Answers		Independent Correct		Group Correct		Independent Incorrect	
Noncritical Lines in Order of Presentation	Number	Per Cent	Number	Per Cent	Number	Per Cent	Number	Per Cent
First	38	100	0	0	38	100	0	0
Second	38	100	0	0	38	100	0	0
Fifth	31	82	0	0	38	100	0	0
Eighth	37	97	0	0	38	100	0	0
Eleventh	38	100	0	0	38	100	0	0
AVERAGE		95				100		

[a] This column is the sum of the "Independent Correct" and the "Independent Incorrect" columns. For purposes of the experiment answers different from those of the majority were termed "Independent" whether correct or incorrect.

1. All lengths were affected by the group conditions. Table 3 shows more errors for each length under critical than under control conditions.

2. The frequency of incorrect group responses in the critical experiment is as great as the frequency of all other categories of responses, 53 per cent as against 47 per cent.

3. The different lines are differently affected by the experimental conditions. It is of interest to note that the lengths most sensitive to the group factor were also those that under control conditions produced the greatest incidence of errors. . . .

The Effect of Age

An examination of the preceding tables and figures reveals certain differences between the younger and older groups. There seems to be a tendency for the younger children to be more affected by the group pressure, and this tendency applies to each of the critical lines.

I.Q. and Following

. . . . .

There is no significant difference in the frequency of following between the younger children with I.Q.s of 130 and above and those of average I.Q. (t = .93). Nor is this difference significant for the older bright and average children (t = .61). The critical ratio between the older children from the opportunity classes and the younger ones from average classes is larger (t = 1.30) but still not significant. Twenty-eight per cent of the older bright children never followed the group and only 4 per cent followed throughout. Of the average younger children none remained entirely independent of the group, and as many as 55 per cent completely yielded to group pressure. Here again, as in Table 2, we note however, a remarkable range of individual differences especially in the middle of the distribution.

Teacher's Choice and Frequency of Following

Will children who were judged to be independent by their teachers follow less than those found to be submissive? . . . Those judged submissive in the classroom situation often exhibited more independent behavior than some of the children

TABLE 4.

DISTRIBUTION OF "GROUP" RESPONSES TO EACH

CRITICAL LENGTH; OLDER CHILDREN, 10 TO 13 (N=52)

	CONTROL EXPERIMENT				CRITICAL EXPERIMENT					
Critical Lines in Order of Presentation	Correct Answers		Independent Correct		Group Answer		Independent Incorrect		Total Independent[a]	
	Number	Per Cent	Number	Per Cent	Number	Per Cent	Number	Per Cent	Number	Per Cent
Third	47	90	25	48	21	41	6	11	31	59
Fourth	52	100	36	69	16	31	0	0	36	69
Sixth	48	92	21	41	31	59	0	0	21	41
Seventh	50	96	31	59	21	41	0	0	31	59
Ninth	52	100	35	67	17	33	0	0	35	67
Tenth	49	94	20	38	32	62	0	0	20	38
Twelfth	44	85	31	59	21	41	0	0	31	59
AVERAGE		94		54		44		1.5		56

Noncritical Critical Lines in Order of Presentation	Correct Answers		Independent Correct		Group Correct		Independent Incorrect	
	Number	Per Cent	Number	Per Cent	Number	Per Cent	Number	Per Cent
First	52	100	0	0	52	100	0	0
Second	52	100	0	0	52	100	0	0
Fifth	49	94	0	0	50	96	2	4
Eighth	51	98	0	0	52	100	0	0
Eleventh	52	100	0	0	52	100	0	0
AVERAGE		98				99		

[a] See note to Table 3.

known for their leadership and self-reliance. Of course, the number of cases is too small to draw any conclusions from our resutls.

Qualitative Differences between Younger and Older Children

Our observations of the behavior of the two groups seems to correspond to the quantitative results on the younger and older children. Among the younger children of seven to ten years there was little if any personal involvement—the situation at all times remaining remote. It was noted that whereas the older children would, for many days, discuss the experiment, the younger children, upon their return to their classrooms, did not talk about it either among themselves or with their respective teachers. Some of the younger children in the majority, in spite of the fact that they understood the directions and the purpose of the experiment, found it very difficult to give the wrong, prescribed answers.

On two occasions, when the objective situation was particularly clear, three children in the two lower grades found themselves compelled to give the correct response saying later: "I just couldn't help it." It is interesting to note that these three children were among the brightest pupils in the class.

A greater dependence on the group was noted among the younger children than among the older ones (see quantitative results).

This is well expressed in the answers given by the two age groups to the question: "Why did you give the same wrong answers as the group?" The most frequently heard explanations offered by the younger children were: "They all said the same number"; "I thought I should give the same answers as the other children"; or "If so many people said it, it might be right."

. . . . .

It was almost impossible for a younger child to admit, even under pressure, that he "copied," whereas among the older ones many readily conceded that they did. The fear of copying was found to be very strong, especially among the younger children.[4] It was also among the older children that the tendency to doubt the adequacy of one's eyes was observed. A youngster of twelve remarked: "My eyes could be different." Another said: "Maybe I don't see so good; maybe I need glasses." The younger children never expressed such doubts.

Discussion

Despite the prevailing hypothesis that it is natural and easy to follow a group, we found quite the contrary to be the fact. It was *not* easy for these children to "follow." It was interesting to observe the reaction of the minority children to the wrong answers of the group. Lulled into security by the first two correct responses, each met the third (first wrong) answer with shock and bewilderment. Many a child would stand up in his seat, rub his eyes, look at all the others and then at the lines with a puzzled, embarrassed, and frightened expression on his face. Each child, without exception, felt ill at ease, fidgeted in his seat, or smiled uncomfortably at the others and at the experimenter. Many would whisper the right answer and turn to a neighbor for assurance. Some, after a few wrong group answers, would grow apathetic and look at the others in the group for the answer rather than at the lines. The situation was too puzzling; and being unable to explain it,

---

[4] It is interesting to note that copying as such was not considered bad in itself but definitely dependent on the general atmosphere in the classroom and the teacher's role in it. Thus, in two grades (the third and sixth) where the respective teachers were considered unfair and incompetent by the children, the pupils prided themselves on copying and not being caught.

they resigned themselves to it. There was always a note of relief when the majority gave a correct response.

. . . . .

Here are some of the comments made by the children in answer to the question "How did you feel during the test?"

A seven year old said: "I felt funny. I know it will be silly, but when they said an answer and I didn't think it was right, I felt like my heart-beat went down." A little girl of eight who followed the group completely said: "I didn't feel right. I kinda felt like giving my own but I don't know why I didn't." A more sophisticated eleven-year-old boy explained: "After I gave the answers, I felt like changing but didn't think it was proper." A boy of eight and one-half who gave all the wrong group answers offered this explanation in his own defense: "I know they were wrong, but it was like a jury—we were nine and I was the only one against eight. The majority wins. Besides, how could I prove I was right?" A girl of eleven said: "I had a funny feeling inside. You know you are right and they are wrong and you agree with them. And you still feel you are right and you say nothing about it. Once I gave the answer they didn't give. I thought they would think I was wrong. I just gave their answers. If I had the test alone, I wouldn't give the answers I gave." A nine-year-old boy who remained independent in his judgments in spite of group pressure said in the discussion: "I wanted to be like the rest, but then I thought it was correct to say the right answer. It would have been easier to give the same, but then it didn't look right." The same boy tried to explain why many children would follow under these conditions: "If you do too much disagreeing, people will think that you always disagree and get the wrong impression."

. . . . .

There was also the question of the children's faith in the ability of either the entire group or in particular members of the group. We must not forget that the majority was composed of the eight brightest children in each class! The minority child, therefore, had to meet the impact of a unanimous majority, one that was composed of people whom he knew to be "smart." Also, this majority did give right answers sometimes! This was especially difficult for those who in the opinion of the class and the teachers were the brightest in their class. They, irrespective of age, were brought to tears during the discussion and the interview, and were the only ones to become most personally involved. For them not only membership in the group was at stake, but their position in it was endangered. Even after the purpose of the experiment was revealed, they did not feel relieved.

Contrary to the classical hypothesis that a majority is always felt to be right, most of our minority children admitted upon questioning that the majority was giving wrong answers and that they fully realized it but that they couldn't understand why their classmates whom they knew to be "smart people" should give wrong answers on such simple material. Among the older children reference was often made to a particular member of the majority who was especially noted for being smart and right most of the time.

. . . . .

Following, as we have seen from the quantitative results, also depended on the clarity of the objective situation and was a function of the ease of discrimination of the lines presented for judgment. . . . A thirteen year old commented: "When I wasn't sure of myself, then I was inclined to agree with them." . . . In other words, where the situation is ambiguous and not very clear-cut, one is more apt to *accept* the opinion of a unanimous majority than when the situation is clearly structured. In the first instance in fact, the children did not feel that they "copied" or "followed." They merely admitted that they were uncertain of the right answer. It is only in the clear-cut situations that "copying" as such was admitted.

. . . . .

In conclusion we must say that though the children did follow the group significantly, in doing so they were affected by very real factors in the situation and not by blind faith in the majority or an instinct to imitate.

42 | GROUP LEADERSHIP AND INSTITUTIONALIZATION

FERENC MEREI

This study compares the strength of the leader with that of the group.
When a child who is a leader in one group is placed in another,
he attempts to be the leader there also. Although he cannot change the
new group's customs, he may ascend to leadership by accepting
and utilizing its traditional values.

PRELIMINARIES TO THE EXPERIMENT

The problem we set ourselves concerns the relationship between leader and group. To tackle it, we took the following steps.

Children suitable to form a group were selected. Previous observation showed that from the age of 5 upward, in spontaneously formed groups, the sexes as a rule do not mix. Hence, the groups had to be homogeneous as to sex. They had to be homogeneous as to age, too, because, as our observations showed, in spontaneous groupings the age differences seldom exceed two years. Homogeneity was desirable also regarding the ties between members, e.g., children had to be chosen who had no strong likes or dislikes for one another. Finally, for the most pertinent purpose of our experiment, we tried to select children with an average capacity for leadership and social influence.

To rate the individual on these scores,

Reprinted from *Human Relations*, II (1949), 23–39. First published in Hungarian, this material was translated and prepared in its present form by Mrs. David Rappaport for *Human Relations*, which journal granted permission for its use.

we made some preliminary observations. We saw the children of two day nurseries for 35 to 40 minutes each day for a period of two weeks. Two people worked simultaneously and afterward unified their notes. The observations were not selective: everything that occurred in the nursery during that period was chronologically and fully recorded. On the basis of these observations we picked out those children whose social qualities were an average for that nursery group and who were *not* leaders. Children were selected in whom the frequency of: (*a*) "following orders" greatly outnumbered "giving orders"; (*b*) imitation outnumbered being imitated; (*c*) participation in group play was an average in number as well as in degree of cooperation; and (*d*) acts of attacking, crying, telling on each other, were about the average of the group. Furthermore, their ties to one another had to be no more solid or lasting than to other members of the nursery.

The children were formed into a group. An assembly was considered a group when it developed a relatedness, with permanent rules, habits, traditions, entirely of its own.

The children chosen were put in a separate room. Their field was permanent: the same set of furniture, toys, and tools every day. In this room they spent 30 to 40 minutes each day. Their actions were fully recorded by two observers who later synchronized and combined their notes. The observers were completely passive.

The group thus met until a tendency to "institutionalization" became noticeable, and their habits and traditions appeared to become lasting. Only such habits were considered traditions as were not found in the day nurseries, but had developed during the experimental period. This gave us an objective criterion of the point at which an assembly constituted a group. To form a tradition from three to six meetings were needed.

The children formed traditions such as permanent seating order (who should sit where); permanent division of objects (who plays with what); group ownership of certain objects, ceremonies connected with their use, expressions of belonging together; returning to certain activities; rituals; sequence of games; forming a group jargon out of expressions accidentally uttered, etc.

A leader was placed in the group so formed. The leader was chosen from the same day nursery. He was a child who the nursery-school teachers—they had spent many days with him—considered to have initiative and directing power, who was older than the members of the group, and who, during the preliminary observation, more often gave than followed orders, more often was imitated than imitating, and more often was the attacker than the attacked.

Thus the leader was chosen because he was older, domineering, imitated, aggressive rather than submissive, and because he had initiative.

After the group had formed fixed traditions we added such a leader. The place, the objects remained the same. Recording went on as before.

What did we expect to learn from the experiment thus set up? Our question was: Do group habits and traditions change with the appearance of a leader? Does the leader introduce new habits, and does the group accept them? Does the group follow the leader, or does it force its traditions upon him? We see the group through its traditions—the objective expressions of the existing relationship. Hence, the vector of forces between the stronger leader and the group of weaker individuals is determined not by *who* gives the orders but by *what* the orders are. The question is not whether they accept leadership, but whether they give up their traditions by accepting what the leader initiates, whether they form new habits, rules, traditions, under his influence.

By carrying out this experiment we hoped to get the answer to our question.

THE EXPERIMENTAL PLAN

The experimental plan used the method of *varying the situation.* Individuals who scored high on leadership were observed in three situations:

1. In a larger group, where the members had no particular relationship with each other and where the leader's influence was felt by the group as a whole;

2. In a more closely knit group of the pre-social stage formed through evolving group traditions; and

3. In a group with strong traditions of its own, facing a leader stronger than any one group member.

To record the entire process, we needed an adequate technique. We evolved a system of 76 symbols, each representing one complex act. The five people taking the notes synchronized them at 5-minute intervals.

Further variation was afforded through the objects in the room. By giving as many toys as there were children, we weakened group activity, since each could find something to do. By giving one object only we strengthened group activity, since all had to congregate around it. Setting a concrete task also strengthened the group. If an object familiar only to the leader was given, he was strengthened and the group weakened.

The choice of objects offers further possible variations which we have not sufficiently explored as yet.

We tried out many objects. Finally, the younger children (4 to 7 years) were given a tin toy house and a box of building blocks, the older ones (8 to 11 years), cardboard, picture magazines, scissors, crayons, paste, and paint brushes, and the instruction, "we want to make an exhibition." Of the latter objects there were fewer than there were children in the group, so that some manner of collaboration was required.

Most groups consisted of three children plus the leader, with some groups of four and six as well. The number chosen was determined by previous observations which showed that spontaneously formed groups, up to the age of 7, lasted longer when consisting of three to four children, and, between the ages of 7 to 10, of three to six children. Larger groups easily disintegrated.

We worked with twelve groups. In them we tried out the power of penetration of twenty-six children capable of leadership. The ages of all children ranged from 4 to 11 years. The difference within a group never exceeded two years. In every case but one the leader was older than any group member.

THE CONQUERED CONQUEROR

Let us now see the results of this experiment.

To summarize schematically, the same definite tendencies could be observed in all the experimental units: the group absorbed the leader, forcing its traditions on him. The leader takes over the habits and traditions of children who are younger than himself and who in the day nursery had been his underlings following his guidance. Now he engages in those activities which the group had developed before he entered it. His own undertakings either remain unsuccessful or gain acceptance only in a modified form suiting the traditions of that group.

Examples from our material demonstrate the point.

The table below will be understood from the following definitions:

Modeling is one of the most important types of social behavior. When a child's act or behavior is spontaneously imitated by some others, the child, we say, is *modeling*. When a child, even if unintentionally, imitates another—as members of a group do to take over each other's mode of behavior and thereby form common habits—we say that he is *being modeled*. We avoid the word "imitation" because it has a connotation of intention.

The ratio of *modeling* to *being modeled* is a measure of the social penetrating power of a person.

The table shows the ratio *modeling/being modeled* of four children (Nos. 13, 15, 25, 10). In the day nursery all four

MODELING: BEING MODELED			IN THE EXPERIMENTAL SITUATION	
	SUBJECT NO.	IN THE NURSERY	*Without Leader*	*With Leader*
	13	3:4	17:5	10:5
	15	1:4	3:8	1:2
	25	1:5	1:11	3:4
	10	2:8	0:2	0:3
	20 (leader)	6:3		5:11

tended to follow some model, rather than to serve as a model to others. It was for just this behavior that we selected them.

When they became members of a separate group forming its own traditions, a change occurred: one of the four children (No. 13) took on the modeling role, while the others went on being modeled.

It was after this change had taken place that the leader (No. 20) joined the group. In the day nursery he did the modeling: he served as a model six times, but followed another model only three times, making this ratio of social penetration 6 : 3 (Column 2 "In day nursery" shows an inverse ratio for all the others in this group.)

In the experimental situation—when the leader was confronted with a developed group—his ratio changed: his power of social penetration diminished. Formerly he was *modeling* (6 : 3), but now he was *being modeled* (5 : 11)—that is, the others did not take over his mode of action, but he took over the habits developed by the group. In other words, he followed those who in the day nursery had followed him.

In other groups and with other leaders a similar tendency was observed. The ratio *modeling/being modeled* of an extremely influential and willful leader in the day nursery changed from 9 : 5 to 0 : 8. For another such child the ratio changed from 6 : 2 to 1 : 6.

This portion of our results shows that, in a group possessing traditions, the leader introduced does not become the source of new habits and rules; rather, he will be the one to take over existing group traditions and thus to follow a model. This happens in spite of the fact that in the larger social formation (day nursery) he had served as a model to every member of the group.

Since "forming traditions" was our criterion of social influence, we came to the conclusion that, *confronted by a group having its own traditions, the leader*

proves weak; this in spite of the fact that when confronting them singly he is stronger than any one member of the group—stronger precisely as to his social penetrating power.

PLAY OF FORCES

The last paragraph is only a schematic summary of our results. Reality is richer and more varied; what we see in reality is a wide variety of *tendencies*—a pull of the group force facing other pulls in other directions.

What does this mean? Though the group generally assimilates the leader, we find that it does so only on certain conditions and within certain limits. We find that the leading personality, while accepting the traditions and habits of the group, also influences and changes them. Let us then inquire into the modes of this influence, into the conditions which allow the assimilated leader to become that group's leader.

On the twenty-six leaders of the experiment the group force acted in varied ways.

At one extreme is the case where the group entirely assimilated the child who previously showed definite capacity to lead. This occurred in a group that possessed particularly strict traditions, and had well established and meticulously carried out rituals of activity. One such group played with a doll house and two dolls. In the course of three play periods they worked out a ritual of activity of playing around the house and of taking the dolls for a walk. The leader, one and a half years their senior, joining the group at its fourth meeting, tried to introduce something new (fourth and fifth play periods). He suggested a circle game and group singing. He was not followed. When he started singing alone they followed him for a few moments, then returned to their old game. The third time he came (sixth play period), the leader joined in the group's original game. Only for a few moments, here and there, did he start new activities, but he was followed by no one. At the seventh and eighth play periods no sign was left that this child had once (before these same children had developed a group habit) been a leader among them.

At the other extreme is the case of the child who proved to be stronger than the group: he broke its traditions. There was one such case. The leader, a little girl (a year and a half older than the members) completely reorganized the group. She gave orders, she modeled, she decided what to do and how to play. The rules she introduced took the place of those the group had had.

This group's history is important: it was subjected to increasing difficulties, while the leader was given virtual training in leadership. After the group had formed its habits, each day a different leader was introduced. In three days three different leaders tried to foist their initiative upon it and to change its rituals. Against these three leaders the group was able to preserve its customs, rejecting their suggestions, in the face of all the enticing and aggression these leaders tried out on it. However, the struggle exhausted the group and it began to weaken. This weakening showed itself in that the children more often played by themselves, less often played their old organized games, playing instead merely side by side. The traditions were still formally there, but the members of the group tended to observe them singly, by themselves. The group lost much of its coherence.

These are borderline cases. *In the overwhelming majority of our cases the leader was forced to accept the group's traditions—that is, he proved weaker than the group but still managed to play the role of leader.* We observed each leader's ways of doing this.

1. THE ORDER-GIVER | The group whose data on "modeling" and "being modeled" was given above had fully developed customs when the leader was introduced. The new boy, older, more experienced, and more of a leader than any member of the group, attempted to take over. He gave orders, made suggestions, bossed everybody. The children carefully avoided him, ignored his orders, and carried on in their traditions.

Soon the leader found himself alone. Suddenly his behavior changed, he joined the group in its activities and quickly learned its rituals. He learned their expressions, their habits, their games. During his second play period with them, he again gave orders. Though keeping within the frame of activities he had just learned from them, and according to their rules, he told the children what to do—that is, he ordered them to do exactly what they would have done anyway. He appropriated the leadership without being able to change the group's traditions. The members accepted this situation by following his orders, since this did not change their habitual activities.

The data on the frequency of group activity shows this. The following table contains the proportion of *order-giving* to *order-following*.

Four members of the group (Nos. 13, 15, 25, 10) were *order-followers* in the day nursery. After they had formed a separate homogeneous group, one of them (No. 15) became an *order-giver*. When group habits were developed and a leader (No. 20) was added, all followed the leader's orders, as in the day nursery. In the group with a tradition, the leader became just as much of an order-giver (11 : 3) as he was in the day nursery (12 : 2). Regarding order-giving, then, the leader was stronger than the group (he gave orders—they accepted them). At the same time, however, he was the one to copy the others; he took over their ways (his

ORDER-GIVING; ORDER-FOLLOWING

EXPERIMENTAL SUBJECT NO.	IN DAY NURSERY	IN EXPERIMENTAL SITUATION Without Leader	With Leader
13	3:5	3:6	1:4
15	1:2	8:1	0:2
25	1:4	0:2	2:5
10	2:3	0:3	0:3
20	12:2		11:3

modeling proportion changed from 6 : 3 to 5 : 11).

If a person should observe the group for only a short period of time, for example by the Goodenough 1-minute or 5-minute method, he would see a leader giving orders and a group obeying. A prolonged observation of the group plus its history would, however, soon disclose the inner workings of this *order-giving*: the leader gives such orders as have reference to the group's traditional activities; he expropriates the leadership without changing the group's traditional modes of activity.

The leader is weaker than the group because he takes over its traditions and because his own suggestions do not take root. At the same time he is also stronger because everyone follows his orders.

The gist of the phenomenon lies just in this dichotomy.

The leader is stronger than any one group member. (He gives orders—they obey.) He is weaker than *group traditions* and is forced to accept them. He is stronger than the individual member, weaker than the "plus" which a group is over and above the sum of the individuals in it. He is stronger than the members, weaker than the formation.

In the relationship between group and leader, two factors stand out: (1) the group as a particular order of quality, whose strength is expressed by the change of the leader's modeling proportion (from 6 : 3 to 5 : 11); and (2) the members,

whose *weakness* is expressed by the constancy (12 : 2 to 11 : 3) of the leader's ratio of *order-giving/order-following*.

Thus the curious situation obtains where the order-giver imitates, while the models follow the orders of their imitator.

What appears here is the "group plus" —the unique reality of a group—experimentally verified.

2. THE PROPRIETOR | A second way in which leadership may express itself is ownership: the leader joining the developed group takes possession of all the objects in the room. They continue being used according to group tradition; the games played with them remain the same. The leader joins in these games, but all the objects "belong" to him. The following table presents the data on this phenomenon, concerning the group discussed before.

The frequency of taking possession of objects sharply falls for group members, and rises for the leader.

Into some groups, after traditions had been formed, outstanding leading personalities were placed—leaders obeyed in the day nursery by everyone, virtual dictators to more than thirty children. Let us follow one of them. If a child's behavior displeased him, he beat up that child; he allowed no opposition, and always had to have his way. The group into which he was put consisted of children younger than himself, children who in the day nursery always obeyed him. The result

FREQUENCY OF OBJECT APPROPRIATION (BORROWS OR TAKES AWAY FROM ANOTHER CHILD)	EXPERIMENTAL SUBJECT NO.	IN THE EXPERIMENTAL SITUATION	
		Without Leader	With Leader
	13	21	1
	15	9	0
	25	7	1
	10	3	1
	20		12

was unexpected: this structured group virtually swallowed him. (His proportion of modeling changed from 9 : 5 to 0: 8). He followed the group's every activity, accepted its every custom, while his own suggestions were *never* followed.

However, his exceptional personality still asserted itself with the group. The children gave him every object without his asking, and with that acknowledged his authority. The group had two traditional activities: using blocks they built a train, and using chairs they built a bridge. The leader soon learned these constructions and used the objects acquired to build just these. From time to time the group gathered around him, eloquently praising whatever he did. They praised his beautiful creation, his skill, the wonderful things he made (which he had learned from them), as if to placate some dangerous genie. At the same time they followed him in nothing; on the contrary they drew him into their own activities and caused him to accept their habits. Their play remained unchanged; the same game with the same toys. They talked of the toys as they did before—Johnny's blocks, Tom's box—but occasionally they said; "The blocks belong to Andrew" (Andrew was the leader), or: "Tom's box belongs to Andrew." The owners of the objects became their users, while the right of ownership was given over, voluntarily or otherwise, to the new leader.

Observation over only a short period would lead to mistaken conclusions. One might see only that one child has all the toys, while the others surround and admire him. Only prolonged observation would show that those are but scenes of ceremonial offerings with which the children purchase, as it were, the leader's continued trust, with which they protect their traditions.

Again we see that apparently the leader is stronger than *the members* of the group (he appropriates their belongings), but weaker than *the group* because he is forced to accept its customs, traditions, and forms of activity.

3. THE DIPLOMAT | The third way of asserting leadership, as observed in our experimental situation, is quite devious. The cases belonging here are peculiar. The leader, having a greater force of social penetration than the group members, attempts to force upon them a new mode of activity. He fails. However, the leader, for reasons as yet unclear to us—perhaps through his personality, perhaps because of the tense situation—does not get lost in the group, nor take over its habits, as did those leaders who complied in order to rule or in order to take possession of the toys.

This type of leader takes a roundabout course: he accepts the traditions of the group in order to change them.

Into old forms he pours new contents. What takes place here is a veritably dramatic struggle. We had one group with particularly strong traditions and institutionalization. This group rose to the highest level of spontaneous organization of games: to the level of division of roles.

One of the children, who in the day nursery showed no leadership, in this narrower group developed into a leader: games he suggested were followed, and their various parts became traditional with the group. It was at this point that a new leader was added. He tried to suggest new games but was not accepted. Then he joined their traditional game and slowly took over the leadership. The first day there were only two instances in which he led, the second day there were already nine. However, he was the one being modeled, taking over the group's habits. He accepted those habits but introduced minute changes. For example, he joined in the block game traditional with the group, but he demanded that always the red side of a block be on top. He was being modeled, he imitated, but he also introduced changes; then he became the leader of the traditional activities thus changed.

The third time he was with the group he again suggested new activities. One was "hide and seek." (They had a game involving hiding, and this feature attracted the leader.) The group did not accept the suggestion and played instead another traditional game they called "acting with hats."

The leader yielded, joined the "hat game" and instantly began to organize it, in the course of which he made changes so as to combine with it the hide-and-seek game he had suggested. He was *being modeled* to the group, but he also *modeled* the group; he accepted their traditions but changed them.

His roundabout road to leadership is clear here:

1. He tries to do away with the group traditions and lead it on to new ones.
2. He is rejected.

3. He accepts the traditions and quickly learns them.
4. Within the frame of those traditions he soon assumes leadership, and, though reluctantly, the group follows him because he does a good job.
5. He introduces insignificant variations, loosening the tradition.
6. He then introduces new elements into the ritual already weakened by variation.

In this case accepting the traditions is a roundabout way to introducing new ones. This is a very active process in which the leader plays an important role. Only children with exceptional social influence and a great deal of initiative could act this way.

Thus, between the extremes of total assimilation and total conquest, we find three types of behavior. In the experimental situation the leader either (1) is being modeled—but gives orders; or (2) is being modeled—but obtains possession of the toys; or again (3) is being modeled—but he also models the others.

It has to be emphasized that in all these cases the leader must accept the traditions and can give orders only within their framework. The following is a nice example: into a well-developed group of children, 4 to 5 years old, a leader of 6½ with a strong personality was introduced. The group had traditional ways of using the toys. It was exactly determined who would play with what. Each toy, though they might exchange them for a while, traditionally constituted the possession of a certain child.

The leader was unable to change this rule of ownership. Yet he found himself a place in the system. At the beginning of the play period he distributed the objects, giving each child the one that "belonged to him." The children continued to ask the "owners" for the blocks or boxes when they wanted to play with them; they continued to exchange toys as before. Only now the blocks, house, or boxes were distributed by the leader at the beginning of the period. Thus he found himself a role in an order which was there when he first arrived, though unable essentially to change the existing traditions.

THE FORMING OF TRADITION

We have examined the influence of the group on a new leader. We have seen that the group forces its traditions on the leader; and that with varying circumstances the process involves changes, while the basic tendency remains the same. We have seen that the capitulating leader still makes his superior personality felt. Even though he accepts the group's traditions, he exerts an influence. Even in the case of total assimilation of the leader we find changes in the group's life which can be ascribed to his influence.

For example, one group always built trains out of blocks. The leader followed this activity. He too built trains, only he put a chimney on his locomotive. The others followed suit.

Another group's traditional game was to climb up and hang on to the top edge of a wardrobe and to swing there. The leader —of the type that gives orders but is being modeled—soon joined the game. Only one child at a time could swing on the wardrobe. On each side stood a chair to climb up on. Shortly after the leader joined the group he introduced a "one-way traffic." Everything went on as before with the exception that the children had to climb up one side and down the other. This innovation added color to the game without changing its structure. Such phenomena occurred often. Almost every leader, just as soon as he met the group, reorganized it, introducing direction and order.

In other cases this coloring lent by the leader pertained rather to the contents, as when a fitting little story was introduced. One group that played with a small house said: "This is the mailman's house—in the evening he comes home—in the morning he leaves." In the game itself there was no mailman. The children put nothing into the house. The mailman was not even symbolically represented. The words were merely additional coloring. On this the leader elaborated: "The mailman brings coal—they put it on wagons and trucks, etc." The others took over these little themes and their activity, though undamaged, became more colorful.

Often the leader would step up the pace of activity. This is another way to impose his will on the group. He would dictate a very fast tempo, driving them. A certain type of leader is needed to create this acceleration of pace: a child who is very active, who has many interests, whose attention is divided, and who has a stormy temperament. Such leaders busy themselves with several things at once, join several games at once, and with their "swing" accelerate the group's life.

An interesting influence of the leader is the *widening of the terrain*. The group's accustomed space becomes larger: a group that has worked in one portion of the room will, after the leader appears, expand into the entire room. The way this occurs clearly shows the relationship between a developed group and a new leader.

One group would play around a table in the middle of the room. From time to time they would go to the wardrobe in one corner of the room and try to climb up. Then the new leader appropriated the table, whereupon a migration to the wardrobe took place where they started the game of climbing up. The leader followed them and started organizing that game. Slowly the children shifted back to the table, but the leader was on their trail. The result was a pendulum-like movement between the table and wardrobe. Then one child went to a new place and started doing something there. At once the leader extended his pendulum motion to that place. A veritable pilgrimage began.

Everywhere the leader was being modeled: he was the one who adjusted to the others' mode of activity.

Another frequent influence of the leader is that he changes the degree of concerted action. The degree of group action is not to be confused with the degree of creative activity of a person. When a presocial formation of four people sit together, one reading a philosophical treatise, the other solving a mathematical problem, the third writing an ode, etc., without having anything in common with each other, the group is of a lower social level than a foursome playing bridge.

During our investigations we observed that in some cases the leader brings a presocial group to a higher degree of concerted action, in other cases to a lower one. If, for example, a group that has merely congregated around a set of toys is organized into one with a division of roles, the group level has been raised. It will be lowered if group activity is reduced to mere side-by-side play. Such raising or lowering of group level depends mostly on the personal qualities of the leader, especially on his capacity to organize. The capacity consists of the bent to remember every custom, to see to it that objects are returned where they belong and that the rituals are observed, even if these were learned from the group. The leader who has this quality raises the group level even if he totally submits to the group's traditions.

THE POWER OF THE GROUP

Our question was: Which is stronger, the group made up of individuals of average social penetration, or the individual of high degree of social penetration but alien to the group?

Our criterion was, not the relationship between the new leader and the individual group members, but that "plus" arising from "groupness" which raises the power of the group above the aggregate strength of its members. This "plus" shows in the habits, customs, rules, and relationships making for institutionalization. Accordingly, the individual is the stronger of the two if he can change those traditions; but the group is the stronger if it assimilates the leader.

Couching our inquiry in these terms lent decisive importance to the ratio *modeling/being modeled.*

Our investigations have shown that the group with a tradition is stronger than the leader (though he is stronger than any one group member).

The play of forces between leader and group resulted in the following graduations:

1. The leader is totally assimilated;
2. The leader is being modeled but gives orders;
3. The leader is being modeled but gains possession of the toys;
4. The leader is being modeled but modifies the traditions;
5. The leader destroys the group's traditions and introduces new ones. It is rare that the leader should become not only the center of the group but also the maker of its rules.

Which of these five situations will obtain depends on:

1. The degree of crystallization of traditions;
2. The extent of collaborative play;
3. The degree of group cohesion (the marginal child included).

These conditions issue from the nature of the group. It is no doubt important what kind of person, what character type the new leader is. It may be that in the child who expropriates the toys in order to set himself up as leader a desire for acquisition asserts itself; it may be that the child who gives orders is driven by narcissism and aggression. However, our investigation did not extend to these motivations.

Even the leader who is forced to accept existing traditions makes his superiority felt: he may lend color to activities, step up the pace, widen the field, or change the group level by influencing cohesion.

In our experiment, individuals of strong social penetrating power seldom became changers of traditions; however, being modeled to the existing traditions, they influenced them.

We were thus able to experience that "plus" which makes the group more than and different from the aggregate of its members: as in cases where the new leader conquered everyone, where each child followed his orders—as long as *what* he ordered was in agreement with the group's traditions.

It is in this peculiar strength of tradition that this group "plus" appears. Its carriers are the individuals constituting the group. By belonging to the group each is "more" and stronger. This became clear when children who in the day nursery were *being modeled* by leaders there, became the models of these leaders in the organized group.

Thus the group "plus" is not some substance hovering above the group: it is the hold their customs and habits have on the members; it is tradition, the carrier of which is the individual, who, in turn, is strengthened by it. Conceivably, the feeling of heightened intensity always evoked by group experience is the experiencing of just this "plus."

Why does the leader accept the group's traditions? Is it because he is weaker than its members, or more suggestible? No. We have seen him in the day nursery, modeling the others. Is it because he is in a new situation where the group members have the advantage of being familiar with the situation? This is contraindicated by the behavior of leaders who give orders quite without inhibition. The dichotomy is clear: the leader is supraordinated since he gives orders; but he is also subordinated since he is being modeled. He has the upper hand *vis à vis* the members but has to bow to group tradition.

Thus the reaction of the group to the new leader clearly brings into view the power of the group "plus." It is this "plus" that is stronger than the leader, who is stronger than any one group member.

With this we can discard all hypotheses which deny the uniqueness of the group, and which attempt fully to account for the group by assessing its members.

Our experiment refutes the prejudice of metaphysical social psychology that the group, through an evening effect, lowers the level of the individual. We observed exactly the opposite: the strength of the group strengthens its members. Group experience not only pleases, it also strengthens.

PART FOUR
DISTORTED VIEWS

Some children's views of the world are distorted views, views which may give rise to deviant behavior. If we may assume that all behavior is purposive and aimed at coping with the environment, deviant behavior and normal behavior must follow the same principle.

When its environment is too demanding or unpredictable or overly unrewarding or cruel, the organism, bearing the scars of many unfortunate experiences, comes to expect the imminent recurrence of similar events or conditions. One may view life as a lovely garden—or as a jungle filled with wild beasts, where one devours or is devoured. Through early experiences, each of us develops attitudes and expectations which we may carry throughout life. We all assume postures that we believe necessary to get along in particular circumstances or with particular people, and often these attitudes continue long after the original pressures causing them have disappeared.

The studies in this part deal with some of the anxious behavior patterns developed by children in order to secure comfort and avoid pain, patterns adaptive at one period in life but maladaptive and ineffective at later periods, or patterns which never were adaptive. Several of the articles contain emphatic and insightful descriptions of unrealistic expectations and feelings in disturbed children. Some discuss the people and situations to which a particular child was forced to adjust, with crippling results. The last two articles describe laboratory attempts to recreate such stressful conditions.

If antisocial behavior is to be controlled and ability to handle stress effectively is to be increased, understanding of the nature, causes, and possibilities for altering distorted perceptions is necessary.

43 | THE CASE OF PETER

ERIK H. ERIKSON

Distorted views are often private and unique interpretations of events with peculiar meanings understood only by those who hold them. This description of some private meanings which threaten the life of a small child, and of the thinking processes of an eminent psychologist who magnificently uncovers the secret distortions, reads like a detective story.

I had been told that Peter was retaining his bowel movements, first for a few days

Reprinted from Erik H. Erikson, *Childhood and Society*, by permission of W. W. Norton & Company, Inc. Copyright 1950 by W. W. Norton & Company, Inc.

at a time, but more recently up to a week. I was urged to hurry when, in addition to a week's supply of fecal matter, Peter had incorporated and retained a large enema in his small, four-year-old body. He looked miserable, and when he thought nobody watched him he leaned his bloated abdomen against a wall for support.

His pediatrician had come to the conclusion that this feat could not have been accomplished without energetic support from the emotional side, although he suspected what was later revealed by X-ray, namely that the boy indeed had by then an enlarged colon. While a tendency toward colonic expansion may initially have contributed to the creation of the symptom, the child was now undoubtedly paralyzed by a conflict which he was unable to verbalize. The local physiological condition was to be taken care of later by diet and exercise. First it seemed necessary to understand the conflict and to establish communication with the boy as quickly as possible so that his co-operation might be obtained.

It has been my custom before deciding to take on a family problem to have a meal with the family in their home. I was introduced to my prospective little patient as an acquaintance of the parents who wanted to come and meet the whole family. The little boy was one of those children who make me question the wisdom of any effort at disguise. "Aren't dreams wonderful?" he said to me in the tone of a hostess as we sat down to lunch. He then improvised a series of playful statements which, as will be clear presently, gave away his dominant and disturbing fantasy. It is characteristic of the ambivalent aspect of such sphincter problems that the patients surrender almost obsessively the very secret which is so strenuously retained in their bowels. I shall list here some of Peter's dreamy statements and my silent reflections upon them which emerged during and after luncheon.

"I wish I had a little elephant right here in my house. But then it would grow and grow and burst the house."—The boy is eating at the moment. This means his intestinal bulk is growing to the bursting point.

"Look at that bee—it wants to get at the

sugar in my stomach."—"Sugar" sounds euphemistic, but it does transmit the thought that he has something valuable in his stomach and that somebody wants to get at it.

"I had a bad dream. Some monkeys climbed up and down the house and tried to get in to get me."—The bees wanted to get the sugar in his stomach; now the monkeys want to get at him in his house. Increasing food in his stomach—growing baby elephant in the house—bees after sugar in his stomach—monkeys after him in the house.

After lunch coffee was served in the garden. Peter sat down underneath a garden table, pulled the chairs in toward himself as if barricading himself, and said, "Now I am in my tent and the bees can't get at me."—Again he is inside an enclosure, endangered by intrusive animals.

He then showed me his room. I admired his books and said, "Show me the picture you like best in the book you like best." Without hesitation he produced an illustration showing a gingerbread man floating in water toward the open mouth of a swimming wolf. Excitedly he said, "The wolf is going to eat the gingerbread man, but it won't hurt the gingerbread man because [loudly] he's not alive, and food can't feel it when you eat it!" I thoroughly agreed with him, reflecting in the meantime that the boy's playful sayings converged on the idea that whatever he had accumulated in his stomach was alive and in danger of either "bursting" him or of being hurt. To test this impression I asked him to show me the picture he liked next best in any of the other books. He immediately went after a book called "The Little Engine That Could" and looked for a page which showed a smoke-puffing train going into a tunnel, while on the next page it comes out of it—its funnel not smoking. "You see," he said, "the train went into the tunnel and in the dark tunnel it went dead!"—Something alive went into a dark passage and came out dead. I no longer doubted that this little boy had a fantasy that he was filled with something precious and alive; that if he kept it, it would burst him and that if he released it, it might come out hurt or dead. In other words, he was pregnant.

The patient needed immediate help, by interpretation. I want to make it clear that I do not approve of imposing sexual enlightenment on unsuspecting children before a reliable relationship has been established. Here, however, I felt experimental action was called for. I came back to his love for little elephants and suggested that we draw elephants. After we had reached a certain proficiency in drawing all the outer appointments and appendages of an elephant lady and of a couple of elephant babies, I asked whether he knew where the elephant babies came from. Tensely he said he did not, although I had the impression that he merely wanted to lead me on. So I drew as well as I could a cross section of the elephant lady and of her inner compartments, making it quite clear that there were two exits, one for the bowels and one for the babies. "This," I said, "some children do not know. They think that the bowel movements and the babies come out of the same opening in animals and in women." Before I could expand on the dangers which one could infer from such misunderstood conditions, he very excitedly told me that when his mother had carried him she had had to wear a belt which kept him from falling out of her when she sat on the toilet; and that he had proved too big for her opening so she had to have a cut made in her stomach to let him out. I had not known that he had been born by cesarean section, but I drew him a diagram of a woman, setting him straight on what he remembered of his mother's explanations. I added that it seemed to me that he thought he was pregnant; that while this was impossible in reality it was important to understand the reason for his fantasy; that, as he might have heard,

I made it my business to understand children's thoughts and that, if he wished, I would come back the next day to continue our conversation..He did wish; and he had a superhuman bowel movement after I left.

There was no doubt, then, that once having bloated his abdomen with retained fecal matter this boy thought he might be pregnant and was afraid to let go lest he hurt himself or "the baby." But what had made him retain in the first place? What had caused in him an emotional conflict at this time which found its expression in a retention and pregnancy fantasy?

The boy's father gave me one key to the immediate "cause" of the deadlock. "You know," he said, "that boy begins to look just like Myrtle." "Who is Myrtle?" "She was his nurse for two years; she left three months ago." "Shortly before his symptoms became so much worse?" "Yes."

Peter, then, has lost an important person in his life: his nurse. A soft-spoken Oriental girl with a gentle touch, she had been his main comfort for years because his parents were out often, both pursuing professional careers. In recent months he had taken to attacking the nurse in a roughhousing way, and the girl had seemed to accept and quietly enjoy his decidedly "male" approach. In the nurse's homeland such behavior is not only not unusual, it is the rule. But there it makes sense, as part of the whole culture. Peter's mother, so she admitted, could not quite suppress a feeling that there was something essentially wrong about the boy's sudden maleness and about the way it was permitted to manifest itself. She became alerted to the problem of having her boy brought up by a stranger, and she decided to take over herself.

Thus it was during a period of budding, provoked, and disapproved masculinity that the nurse left. Whether she left or was sent away hardly mattered to the child. What mattered was that he lived in a social class which provides paid mother substitutes from a different race or class. Seen from the children's point of view this poses a number of problems. If you like your ersatz mother, your mother will leave you more often and with a better conscience. If you mildly dislike her, your mother will leave you with mild regret. If you dislike her very much and can provoke convincing incidents, your mother will send her away—only to hire somebody like her or worse. And if you happen to like her very much in your own way or in her own way, your mother will surely send her away sooner or later.

In Peter's case, insult was added to injury by a letter from the nurse, who had heard of his condition and who was now trying her best to explain to him why she had left. She had originally told him that she was leaving in order to marry and have a baby of her own. This had been bad enough in view of the boy's feelings for her. Now she informed him that she had taken another job instead. "You see," she explained, "I always move on to another family when the child in my care becomes too big. I like to tend babies." It was then that something happened to the boy. He had tried to be a big boy. His father had been of little help because he was frequently absent, preoccupied with a business which was too complicated to explain to his son. His mother had indicated that male behavior in the form provoked or condoned by the nurse was unacceptable behavior. The nurse liked babies better.

So he "regressed." He became babyish and dependent, and in desperation, lest he lose more, *he held on.* This he had done before. Long ago, as a baby, he had demonstrated his first stubbornness by holding food in his mouth. Later, put on the toilet and told not to get up until he had finished, he did not finish and he did not get up until his mother gave up. Now he

held on to his bowels—and to much more, for he also became tight-lipped, expressionless, and rigid. All of this, of course, was one symptom with a variety of related meanings. The simplest meaning was: I am holding on to what I have got and I am not going to move, either forward or backward. But as we saw from his play, the object of his holding on could be interpreted in a variety of ways. Apparently at first, still believing the nurse to be pregnant, he tried to hold on to her by becoming the nurse and by pretending that he was pregnant too. His general regression, at the same time, demonstrated that he too, was a baby and thus as small as any child the nurse might have turned to. Freud called this the overdetermination of the meaning of a symptom. The overdetermining items, however, are always systematically related: the boy identifies with *both partners of a lost relationship;* he is the nurse who is now the child and he is the baby he once was. Identifications which result from losses are like that. We become the lost person *and* we become again the person we were when the relationship was at its prime. This makes for much seemingly contradictory symptomatology.

Our boy, however, concerned himself with the fantasy of being pregnant. Once it looked as if he did indeed have the equivalent of a baby in him, he remembered what his mother had said about birth and about dangers to mother and child. He could not let go.

The interpretation of this fear to him resulted in a dramatic improvement which released the immediate discomfort and danger and brought out the boy's inhibited autonomy and boyish initiative. But only a combination of dietetic and gymnastic work with many interviews with mother and child could finally overcome a number of milder setbacks.

44 | CRIMINALS ARE MADE, NOT BORN

MORRIS L. HAIMOWITZ

How does a nasty, trouble-making child evolve into a professional criminal? Where does he learn his trade? When is graduation day?

This paper describes some of the crucial experiences which lead a boy into a criminal career. The changes in self-image that accompany the progress of this "nobody" to the status of a criminal "somebody" appear to develop during his interaction with the responsible persons in his community. Paradoxically, the boy who is frequently told, "Don't be a bad boy," very often comes to feel that only by being very, very bad can he maintain his self-respect, dignity, and integrity.

I. INTRODUCTION

A number of theories attempt to explain how people become professional criminals: poverty causes crime; "bad" neighborhoods cause crime; movies, TV, comic books, or radio crime stories cause crime; criminal associates cause crime; broken homes cause crime; race, nationality, neuroses, or crowded housing cause crime. These theories do not explain why most poor people never become professional criminals. Nor do most people from bad neighborhoods, or most children of broken homes, or most members of any race or nationality, or most neurotics become criminals. If crowded housing caused crime, all Eskimos would be criminals; actually, very few are.

Some studies show these factors to be associated with criminality. But science aims at generalizations which account for *all* cases, and not one of these theories accounts for even a majority of cases. What they do indicate is some *associated* factors, not the *causes* of crime. Let us illustrate the difference. Suppose we didn't know how a child is conceived and were seeking an explanation. We might make a survey and find the following factors associated with having children: poverty, illiteracy, race, religion, marriage, wed-

Revised from *Teleclass Study Guide, Social Science 101,* 1958, by Francis Gaul, by permission of The Chicago Board of Education.

ding rings, rural dwellings. Could we therefore state that poverty, illiteracy, and so on, were the causes of conception? Such a conclusion would completely overlook the crucial role of the sperm and ovary. Marriage is an associated factor, but it is not the cause of conception. The theories that poverty or race cause crime are as untrue as the ones that poverty or a wedding ring cause conception.

II. HYPOTHESIS

This paper seeks to develop the hypothesis that the only way a person can become a professional criminal is by getting the idea that he is expected to be an outlaw by those whom he takes seriously: his parents, friends, neighbors, teachers, clergymen, police, social workers, or judges. He must form a mental picture of himself as different from others, different in a way requiring a different vocational career and requiring that he associate with persons ostracized as he is.

This hypothesis refers to professional criminals, not to occasional lawbreakers or alcoholics, or persons who murder or steal in a passionate outbreak. It applies to those persons who belong to professional criminal societies and whose trade or occupation is criminal, with "professional" standards or skills. It is not always easy to tell which criminal is the professional and which is the amateur because many criminals have conflicting self-conceptions. And it is not easy to study the professional because he rarely goes to jail. Our jails are filled by the amateurs or neurotics, who play cops and robbers, who get a kick out of tearing up a place or doing something to get caught.

We like to think that there are two classes of occupations, the legal and the illegal, but the actual situation is not so simple. There are many gradations between the strictly honest and the strictly criminal. Many activities of business or professional men, repairmen, or governmental workers fall into criminal categories. In addition, there are other activities, not definitely criminal, nor yet definitely honest, in the shady or unethical category. Moreover, there are perfectly legal activities which are of questionable value, such as manufacturing, advertising, or selling hydrogen bombs, white flour, candy, alcohol, tobacco, patent medicines, or firearms, and which may be declared illegal in the future. Finally there are ideas which may be considered dangerous or illegal because they are new or different.

Some parents teach their children methods of stealing, but the usual delinquent cannot be explained so easily. Usually, his mother is frightened and embarrassed by his notoriety, even though she also may be secretly proud of her little rascal. This seems to be especially true of the mother whose husband is dead, divorced, or absent. The lonely mother is titillated by the adventures of her two-, three-, ten-, or twenty-year-old boy, and subtly encourages them by her exciting laughter or other reactions. Some criminals put on a "tough-baby" mask with an exaggerated masculinity.[1]

It is popular to explain socially disapproved behavior by labeling it neurotic.

Suppose a man steals or damages property and finds himself waiting, terrified and yet wanting to be caught. He may experience an anxiety, like the child playing hide-and-seek, with excitement reaching a climax when he is discovered. Such a person would be a neurotic criminal. However, one can not say all criminals are neurotic, especially the one who performs his acts because he, his family, and his associates consider them proper and desirable. Furthermore, criminal law changes from time to time and is differently enforced from place to place. Betting is illegal in Chicago; legal in the suburbs. George Washington was a hero in America; a criminal in England.

III. THE SETTING: SOME FACTORS ASSOCIATED WITH CRIME

When we study criminals we find certain factors statistically associated with crime.

Most delinquents are found in the slums, yet most slum children never become delinquents. Most delinquents come from broken homes, yet most children from broken homes never become delinquents. Most delinquents are of a different racial or ethnic stock than the majority, yet race or ethnic affiliation is no guarantee of law-abiding or criminal behavior. Most delinquents are probably neurotic, but so are most non-delinquents. Most delinquents, finally, come from low-income families, but most persons with low incomes are law-abiding. A recent study of 2,000 white teenagers by Nye and Short showed that delinquency was not as closely related to income, religion, or to broken homes, as to the feeling, "My parents hate me."

Most people who steal are not professional criminals. The act of stealing something probably involves a conscious decision. But the act of becoming a professional criminal appears to involve a long series of experiences in which a pattern of behavior occurs, a drifting into an

---

[1] See M. K. Bacon, Irvin L. Child, and Herbert Barry III, "A Cross-Cultural Study of Correlates of Crime," *Journal of Abnormal and Social Psychology*, LXVI (1963), 291–300.

unplanned habit of life which could have only one ending. The criminal may never have made a conscious decision to enter on a career of crime.

The people living in the slums and rooming house areas of the city are different from others not only in being on the average less well educated, earning less money, having higher mortality and morbidity rates, in appearing to have a higher rate of criminality, but also in being of different ethnic, racial, or national stocks. They are the newcomers. The immigrants usually settle in the slums; they bring with them not only poverty but also opinions as to what's right and what's wrong which were appropriate in the environment from which they came. It is a crime for the newcomer in Chicago to throw his garbage out the window; but home in the South it was perfectly proper to so feed the chickens and hogs. Prohibition was incomprehensible to Europeans accustomed to wine with dinner.

The rapid growth of the factories and of the slums housing the factory workers, the high rate of immigration, and the rapid technological developments have made this country, as well as other countries of our time, an area of cultural ferment, with rapidly changing ideas of what is criminal and what is proper. What is legal today may be criminal tomorrow.

All children get into mischief. Technically, you could say they violate the law. A little boy two years old pulls down the curtains in the living room. When they fall they knock over a lamp, dust flies all over the room, and his mother, hearing the commotion, runs in from the kitchen and helps him out of difficulty. He has behaved in utter disregard for life and property and is thus a lawbreaker, but no one calls him a criminal. His mother is caring for him all the time, getting him out of the refrigerator, turning off the gas which he has turned on, rescuing his toy rabbit from the toilet bowl. Like adults, all little children err, but few become gangsters.

Not all children, especially slum children, have a mother at home caring for them. They live in the "zones of transition," called such because these areas are changing from big homes to rooming houses, from residential to business, from native citizens to immigrants, from white to Negro to Mexican and Puerto Rican. But in one way such a zone is not changing. It always has had the highest crime rate of any area in the city. When the father is sick, dead, in jail, or shut out of home because he is unable to find a job and bring home money, the mother has to work, and cannot be home supervising the children; or perhaps she is sick or doesn't like caring for children.

A very high proportion of professional criminals come from the slums. Occasionally they come from nicer neighborhoods, but here too we find the unsupervised child. The child who steals and is caught and arrested is delinquent; if he steals and is not caught or not arrested, he is not delinquent. Of course, police act more courteously to accused children of middle class or wealthy families. The policeman here says "naughty, naughty." He neither wants to give the child a record nor be sued for false arrest.

There are many ways a child may react to the fears and loneliness resulting from parental neglect. He can become a dreamer; he can become sick or develop an inferiority complex; or he can become a fighter, and demand attention, stating in effect, "Love me or fear me." The self-conception he forms is determined by the way he perceives certain crucial experiences.

IV. THE CRUCIAL EXPERIENCES

WITH PARENTS | Let's see what happens. A boy is involved in an incident during which someone is hurt or property is damaged or stolen. The injured party usually talks to the boy or his parents, and they make an amicable settlement. But sometimes the injured party feels frightened, angry with himself and his neighbors, and unable to deal with the situation alone, and so he calls the police. The boys see the police, and they all run away. One who did not run away, or was too slow, or had nothing to do with it, or has a bad reputation is caught. The parents are called in and they protect or spank the boy and everyone is satisfied. Or for some reason parents and sons are brought in for questioning. What concerns us is how the child learns that people expect him to be untrustworthy.

There are many ways parents may tell their children they are not to be trusted. They may be direct and say, "You are becoming a little hoodlum." Or they may be subtle and say, "My boy is good," and the boy knows they mean, "He is bad."

Here is an example of this. A juvenile officer was told that a fifteen-year-old boy had been committing delinquencies with a girl of his age. The girl had admitted relations with him. So the boy, accompanied by his mother, was brought in for questioning.

POLICE OFFICER: Did you see Miss X on December 15?
MOTHER: No, he didn't.
POLICE OFFICER: Did you meet Miss X after school that day?
MOTHER: No, why don't you leave him alone?
POLICE OFFICER: Did you have relations with her?
MOTHER: Why do you keep picking on him? He's a good boy; he would never do such a thing!
POLICE OFFICER: Why don't you let him talk for himself. I've been asking him questions for thirty minutes and you haven't let him answer once.

Was this mother so convinced of her son's innocence? It is natural for a mother to defend her son. Her words said, "He is a good boy," but her manner said, "He can't be trusted to speak; he is either too stupid to say the right thing, or he is terribly guilty." Thus she became an accessory to the crime.

And how would the boy feel in a spot like this? "To die, to sink through the floor, where can I hide? It's even harder when she lies. Why don't the police mind their own business?"

When persons important to the child don't trust him, he may come to distrust himself. The conception of oneself as a law-violator, or just a hateful, worthless, public nuisance does not usually develop full-blown in a few minutes. We don't know precisely how it happens. Little children interact thousands of times with others, thereby learning what is expected of them. Little children of two, three, or four years like to help their mothers in the kitchen—wash the dishes, peel the potatoes, string the beans, crack the nuts, mop the floor. They like to help their father repair the clock, fix the furnace, paint the chairs, drive the car. Some mothers and fathers find this "help" more than they can bear. They tell the child, "Go away! You can't wash the dishes, you'll break them; you can't paint the furniture; you can't mop the floor, scram!"

We have observed eleven-year-old children who could not clear the table or wash a dish ("She might break them," the mother would say); and we have observed other children, five years old, who could clear the table and wash and dry the dishes. One mother expects the child to break the dishes; the other mother expects the child to do a good job. Both children do what is expected of them, and by doing so, each is developing a self-conception.

Parents are very worried when their children are destructive. One mother who asked us for help could not understand her child: "Come see for yourself; that little boy was impossible." We went to her home, and she was right. He was impossible. But he wasn't learning how to be impossible all by himself; he was getting lots of help from his mother, and from his older brothers. During the hour of the visit we heard them tell him forty times,

"Don't break the wall down; don't tear up your clothes; don't scream so loud; don't sweep the floor; don't be a bad boy; don't run; don't carry the tray. For God's sake, don't be impossible!" The boy told us, "I just wanted to help, and every time I try to help they make me do it wrong." His family wanted him to be good; but they told him they expected him to be bad. It appears that some children are more likely to act as people *expect* them to act than as they want to act. How many times a day may a parent tell the child, "I expect you to be bad." One hundred? and how many times by the child's sixth birthday? One hundred thousand? Some parents are more patient and can even enjoy the child's attempts to be useful. When the child strings one bean, they say, "Thank you," because they consider the child's age when judging his craftsmanship.

What is important is not so much just what words the parents say to the child as the way they act and the way their acts are interpreted by the child. The parents may say, "You are bad," but act as though the child were the most precious object in the world. Both the words and the other feelings are communicated. So the child may feel, "I am capable, but my parents are sometimes impatient."

If neglect, cruelty, or constant criticism indicate to the child he is the least *precious* object in the world, he will learn to see himself as no good. It may happen because the child is often neglected, left uncared for, unfed. Or no one takes time for the child or every time the child wants to help wash dishes, they say, "Go away, dishes are not for you, you just make a mess." This may happen thousands of times between his second and sixth year. And one day his mother decides he is now old enough to help, and she calls him in —but now he has learned "Dishes are not for me." He refuses to help wash the dishes, or gets a headache, or has to go to the bathroom. More extreme situations, such as the parent's leaving the child alone for days at a time, or beating him frequently, convey to him a sense of his worthlessness or undesirability.

WITH POLICE | Sometimes the boy is unsupervised, out on the streets. His parents prefer earning money to staying home and taking care of him. Something happens. He borrows a friend's bicycle, rides to the grocery store, goes inside, and buys an ice cream bar. As he comes out some bigger boys, wanting to share the ice cream, are waiting for him; he runs away from them, leaving the bicycle.

Meanwhile, the owner of the bicycle starts screaming, "Someone stole my bike." Fred says, "Tommy took it. I saw him." They find Tommy. He says he left it at the grocery store, but it is no longer there. The police are called. They try to locate Tommy's parents, but they are not at home. Now it is up to the police.

Usually the policeman is friendly but firm; he has children of his own who might have done the same thing, and he wouldn't want anyone roughing them up. He tells the boy, "You're a good boy. I know it was an accident. Be more careful next time," and lets him go. If he has the time and the desire, if he is well trained, if he has been assigned to that neighborhood long enough to know it well, if he is patient, the policeman will talk to the natural leaders of the boys to convert the leaders from delinquent to productive activities. The policeman knows that most leaders of boys' gangs will cooperate if they are given a chance to participate in the planning and that these leaders can influence their followers better than anyone else. Or the policeman may recognize the need for community aid for these boys and will talk to local adult leaders—the clergyman, teacher, school principal, businessman, YMCA, or Lions Club officials for the purpose of getting more supervised activities underway. A number of studies have shown that participation in supervised activities deters juvenile delinquency. Even when such facilities are available, however, some supervisors refuse to permit delinquents to participate.

Often the policeman can't do these things. He doesn't have the time or the training. Perhaps he is under strain because it has happened several times before, or the citizen wronged is very angry or influential, or the policeman was recently reprimanded for being lax, or another child hit him in the ear with a snowball ten minutes earlier. Or, most important of all, the lad is impertinent. Then our young citizen—five, ten, fifteen years old—may be taken in and detained. The policeman may feel less likely to get into trouble by such action. Or he may feel, "Today I am starting a boy off on the wrong road, but I can't help it."

Until this time the boy is like all the other kids; full of energy, going through many different kinds of activities all day long, singing, jumping, screaming, playing cops and robbers, tearing clothes, crying, fighting—just like everyone else. But once arrested he becomes different. He is asked questions which imply a difference— name, father's name, religion, age, father's occupation, nationality, race. Ordinary things become extraordinary. He never thought about such things before. He was just like everyone else until now. He wonders about himself. He is frightened but also may be very impressed with the whole procedure and perhaps with his own importance. He wants his mother. He is taken to a social worker. She is expected to ask questions. Tell me about your home, your father and mother, the implication being something is wrong with them. She might even go home and find out for herself. He is taken to a psychologist or sociologist. His intelligence is measured. His emotions are wondered at. He is taken to a judge: he hears lawyers talking about him. He is getting an education that his brothers and sisters and neighbors never dreamed about. Being in a detention home

or jail can terrify a child. Everyone is saying, "Something's wrong with you."

He may be interrogated. Did you ever hear a policeman interrogating a teenager alleged to be guilty of a crime? The policeman acts and speaks as though the prisoner is guilty. It's his duty to clear up the crime. He is usually courteous, but sometimes he is filthy with insults, especially if the boy is a member of an ethnic group the policeman doesn't trust:

POLICE: What were you doing at that house?
BOY: I went there to collect $5.00 a man owed me.
POLICE: Don't you know they're a pack of thieves?
BOY: I didn't know that.
POLICE: If you sleep in a stable, you will smell like—.
BOY: I just went to collect my $5.00.
POLICE: Who did you lend it to?
BOY: Fred Johnson.
POLICE: Fred Johnson! He's an old-timer. Been in jail a dozen times. Why did you lend him $5.00?
BOY: He asked me for it. He lent me money when we were in school together.
SECOND POLICE: Oh boy! what a tale! [Sarcastically] They were planning another A&P job.
BOY: I never had anything to do with any A&P. I go to Brundy School.
POLICE: Who went through the transom, you or Fred?
BOY: I never robbed any store in my life!
POLICE: [All laugh] You're a damned liar! [Boy cries.][2]

Some policemen treat him like a son. Others, like a step-son. The policeman has a tough job. It sounds easy, "Just enforce law and order." But what does he do when John Doe, age eight, is caught for the third time stealing a bike? Scold him, let him go, arrest him? There must be an answer.

---

[2] This dialogue is quoted verbatim. Only names and obscenity are changed. The writer is grateful to many policemen in Chicago and prison officials in New York whose cooperation helped to formulate the ideas here.

Why should a poorly paid, often semi-trained policeman be permitted to bear the burden of such a major decision? Many people are involved; many should help decide—maybe a community council, including teenagers as well as adults. One thing the police could do to give the boy some idea of the problems of policemen would be to invite delinquents to patrol the city a few hours a week in a police squad car. Most cities have enough squad cars to keep many delinquents occupied several hours a week. It might work, properly supervised so that the officers are instructed to try to be friendly, courteous, to explain their jobs, to listen to the problems of the boys as a sort of get-acquainted, how-do-you-do gesture, or as a long-term intensive activity.

IN COURT | The boy may be taken to court. What happens in the court room? The state's attorney may appear if enough publicity is involved, and he makes a speech, such as: "[Crime] by teen-agers must be stopped. The energetic measures taken by police to deal with *these future hoodlums* will be backed to the limit by the state's attorney's office." (In this particular case, the judge in Boy's Court ordered bond increases from $100 to $4,000 for each of the six young men arrested.) The state's attorney continued his speech. "Either those boys will have a chance to reflect in jail while they are waiting trial, or their parents, through the expense of getting them out on bond, will realize that *parental irresponsibility doesn't pay*."[3] His speech was longer. The boys might remember part of it, but we are sure they would like to forget that such a prominent man considered them "future hoodlums" and publicly proclaimed that not only they, but their parents as well, are tainted. Could the boys think: "He's important; he says we'll be criminals. He ought to know. I never thought I'd be a

criminal; but he's a very important man." The public doesn't expect the state's attorney to furnish adequate homes, parents, playgrounds, and psychologists for these boys. But the public doesn't expect him to teach these boys that they are permanent public enemies either.

The judge at the Boy's Court has many problems. Among some boys who had been arrested for participating in a riot, two were dismissed. Here's what the newspapers said about these two: "John ——, 21, of Chicago, a laborer, and his brother, 19, of Chicago, unemployed, were dismissed. They said they merely stopped nearby to see what the trouble was and were arrested. Judge —— told the defendants: 'We're going to give you a break. We operate on the theory that every dog is entitled to one bite.' "[4] Here were two bystanders arrested, taken to jail, and then instead of getting an apology for being inconvenienced, the judge says he will invoke a canine justice. But this is no dog's court. These boys, like the judge, are human. What can the judge do? The police say, "They are guilty—we saw them rioting." The boys say, "We broke no law." Citizens, relatives, and neighbors testify, orate, hiss, and applaud both sides. The judge doesn't know who is right or what to do. The boys are our concern here. They may get the impression: "We are not like other human beings. We are bad."

What can the judge do? The voters are angry because there was a riot; the police are angry because the boys were not convicted; the boys, because they were arrested and scolded; the judge, because he too is on public trial in a difficult situation. Because of this many judges try to protect themselves and the public by utilizing medical, sociological, psychological, or other professional advice. Sometimes, though, they lose their tempers.

The writer has no quarrel with these officials. Thousands of such items appear

[3] Chicago Sunday *Tribune*, August 23, 1953, part 1, p. 25.

[4] Chicago *Daily News*, August 17, 1953. p. 3.

in the papers every year. The point is that the police, state's attorney, and judges may not lead the defendants to expect honest, law-abiding behavior of themselves. If this were the end of it, probably the defendants would go back home and be upright citizens. The suggestions from the officials that they are disreputable might not be taken seriously. But this may not be the end.

Why should a solitary judge with fifty to one hundred cases in one day be permitted to make such vital decisions? Crime hurts everyone. These decisions are too important for any one person to make.

BACK HOME | The boy goes back home. Whether or not he was found guilty, he is not quite like his friends any more, but is an object of curiosity: "What did they do to you?" "My lawyers defended me," he says. "I saw the judge." An object of adoration: his picture was in the paper; he has had his IQ measured; he has talked to lots of policemen. An object of scorn—he was arrested, put in jail with crooks—he is vicious. For some of his friends he is a hero; for others he must never be played with again. If he should see them, they turn away: "My mother says not to play with you. The state's attorney says you're a hoodlum."

Little boys soon forget. They play together as usual, except for those whose mothers are constantly reminding them, protecting them from the "criminal," the bad apple in the neighborhood. Then something happens again. The newspapers have a heyday. Who did it? The citizens are upset and impatient. They put pressure on the police. The police have to do something. Well, everyone knows who did it. Didn't someone just leave the detention home? Wasn't his name in the paper? It makes no difference that he was at school or visiting in another city when it happened. He is apprehended because he is convenient. He is found not guilty, but everyone suspects him just the same.

He is getting a reputation, and a self-conception.

Lots of boys find their home life uncomfortable. Pick a child up off the street some night—say, at midnight. Take him home and you will see why he doesn't want to be home. His home may be physically repulsive; or it may be a lovely house but a miserable home. To say that it's the parent's fault misses the point. Most parents of delinquents are helpless, sorely in need of psychological, medical, religious, or economic aid. Responsibility lies not with irresponsible parents but with the community.

We assume that parents mean well but many just do not have the energy and skills necessary to win the confidence of their children and to make plans together. Parents expect their children to mature gradually and become independent. That this can be done gracefully is proved by many happy parents who help their children settle on their own. Even in the better neighborhoods a barrier often develops between the parents and children. Most children on the street go home after a while and play inside, but some can't go home. In many instances help for the parents would prevent a child from going to the street.

ON THE STREET | Our young citizen may find friends on the street where things are more pleasant, where he can be a hero. We assume everyone wants to be liked; everyone wants a word of praise, and if it is not available at home and is available on the street, then one goes to the street. A little boy knows where he is afraid to breathe and where he is a regular guy like all the rest.

The boys he plays with on the street may like to play volleyball. They have a volleyball and play all the time. They don't get into trouble. Or they may not have a volleyball. Slum children have less equipment than other children. What can you do on the street?

Everyone needs someone to idealize, someone to be like, someone to dream he is like. These street children could idealize their parents, but it is not likely since they don't enjoy their parents. Their hero could be a policeman who saves a man's life; but not if the policeman hurts them or depreciates them. We don't know enough about whom the street boys idealize. Maybe it's a famous boxer who can beat anyone in the whole world; or a cowboy movie star. These boys can't be cowboys; but they can fight, they can be brave, not afraid of their parents, not afraid of the police. They can learn to be tough.

If the street boy could get along with his mother, he might be home with her, learning to keep his room straight: "Freddie, hang up your clothes. Freddie, wash your hands; Freddie shine your shoes this minute. Freddie, here's some new crayons. That's a sweet boy." His mother cannot be at ease until she knows he is responding to her attempts at socialization.

The boys on the street are learning a different moral code: Who can throw the stone the straightest. Who can run faster. Who is a sissy. Who can do things and not get caught. Hundreds of times a day a boy is learning the code of the street: Be loyal to friends—never betray a comrade. Find out who you can trust. Avoid the police.

Street boys go to school. The teacher knows they have been in trouble and if anything out of the ordinary occurs in the classroom, she knows who is to blame. Even if they are not really to blame, she can guess who were the agitators. Because the street boys have more than average trouble at home, they may be more restless than the average pupils and not perform well in school. You can't want to please a teacher if this makes you a sissy, especially if this teacher is always picking on you or your friends. The teacher is not going to be his ideal or model. She could if she had a class of fifteen children instead of thirty to sixty and if her salary made it unnecessary to hold down an extra job or two, and if teachers had high morale, and if she had time to consult with parents, social workers, religious workers, a physician, a psychologist, a reading specialist, to discuss the boy's problems, and if she had professional training and attitudes. Sometimes she can do it without all these. But aren't we foolish to expect miracles of semitrained overworked teachers?

It takes most people years to settle down to one ego ideal. Little boys play at being policemen or cowboys or gangsters. When they are growing up they decide to be truck drivers or ambulance drivers or doctors. In school they want to be teachers or janitors or a principal or the coach. In college they want to be lawyers or scientists or philosophers or businessmen. After they leave college, they are deciding one day this, one day that. Who do I want to be like? What am I going to do? It takes years for the average citizen to decide.

Lots of people are helping the street boy to decide on his career. His mother and father and his home life are unbearable to him, so he joins the street boys. His friends on the street give him fellowship and praise for doing a good job. His teacher tells him he is too jumpy. The police suggest that he is a liar. The social worker suggests his family is tainted. The psychologist tells him he is not like other boys. The judge says, "Every dog deserves one bite." The state's attorney says, "You are the future hoodlums." Can one's career be that of a hoodlum?

REFORM SCHOOL | One day he is arrested, found guilty and goes to reform school. He is frightened and angry. He wishes he were home. He wants to find out: "Who are my friends and who are enemies?" He learns that some of the inmates are regular guys; others snitch on you. The guards, the hired hands around the place, can't be trusted; they are against you. "What are you here for?" a friend asks.

"I grabbed a pocketbook and ran." "Is that all? Boy! I robbed five filling stations! You know that kid with the glasses, the tall blond one? He killed a policeman! When he says something, you'd better jump."

How do you rob a filling station? What do you do with the tires? Which lawyers will help you if you get caught? Which is the easiest way to rob the A&P? How do you steal a car? Where can you sell it? Who buys the parts? How can you be successful? This sounds like an exciting career. He never realized so many people are in this business. The reform school teaches much about crime, but little about reform.

The guards are afraid the boys will run away, hurt each other or hurt the guards. The superintendent has his job to do. He has to keep the boys clean, working, in school, has to buy the groceries, get a new psychologist to replace the one leaving for a better job, get three new attendants, make out dozens of reports, read what the wardens at other schools are doing, go to meetings, see visitors from the Rotary Club, decide what to do about a boy who is always fighting. If he is strict, the boys hate him more. If he is less strict, the place gets dirty and citizens complain; newspapers take pictures. There is never enough money. The superintendent does what he can. The boys are learning a career. They can't help it, and he can't help it. And the respectable citizens back home are not aware of the fact that they are paying $500 to $5,000 per year to train each child to become a more professional criminal. Foster homes may be a better risk, especially if foster parents get special training in ways to handle these children, however it's hard to find parents who will take disturbed children.

AFTER REFORM SCHOOL | When the boy leaves the reform school, he goes home. He has been a disgrace to the family, and his welcome is thin: "Your mother is ashamed to walk down the street!" "We

hope they reformed you." He is now perhaps nine, twelve, or fifteen years old. His sister says, "You have ruined my life." He wonders who his friends are. Maybe a brother is friendly to him. Maybe his mother. She gives him a new necktie. But can she give him what will save him from the electric chair or from a life sentence? If she can give him the trust and patience and ability to be responsible, and skill in holding a job—what every boy needs much and he needs immensely—she can save him. Usually she cannot, any more than she could before reform school. If he is to be helped, it will be by foster parents or officials of the institutional kingdoms, school, church, scouts, PTA, settlement house, working as an integrated unit. Today these kingdoms often work in competition and at odds with one another.

It is easy in the neighborhood to tell who can be trusted. Plenty of guys make nasty remarks. They go to school; they go to Sunday school; they brush their teeth and say, "Good afternoon," to the corner policeman. When their mothers see the returned "criminal" in the drug store, they say: "Look who's out! If I see my boy playing with you I'll call the police. Stay away." You can understand that such mothers are trying to protect their own boys. But they are helping another boy to become a criminal. If good boys won't play with him, who will? Underworld characters?

Other mothers don't know much about him. They are working or sick or preoccupied. Their sons are the street boys. The boys want to know about reform school. Did they beat you? Let me show you what I learned. Let's pull a job tonight. I'll show you how to do it. I can chin with one hand.

He has to go to school. That's the law. The principal talks to him, the teacher talks to him, some kids talk to him, and what they say adds up to one thing: They are not his friends. They expect him to start something. It doesn't have to be that way. They could invite him to join the Scouts, or write on the school paper, or sing in the choir, or play on the team. If they did, it might save him.

His mother wants him to go to church. She has talked to the clergyman, who says he needs religion. He may not be as clean, as well dressed as the next boy—or he may be cleaner. The boy out of reform school wonders how his new clothes look. They feel strange. The people in Sunday school may not feel hostile toward him, but they are strangers. One looks at him in a friendly way; another says, "He just got out of reform school."

There is still a chance he won't go back to reform school or graduate into prison, but the chance is slim. Let a window be broken, a store burglarized, a car stolen, and the neighbors will know who to blame. A nice neighborhood finds it easy to blame someone for its troubles, not only because the accused may be guilty, but because he is the one expected to perform such acts in this community. If he does not expect of himself what they expect of him, he will go straight, perhaps leaving the community, perhaps even changing the community, but that is unlikely.

Even after he comes to expect vicious or criminal behavior of himself, he may still act like a good citizen most of the time. But it appears that the self-concept, the picture of himself inside, is more powerful than anything else in determining his behavior. Here is part of an interview between a prisoner and a prison counselor to illustrate this:

PRISONER: Why do I keep getting in trouble? I want to go straight, but I'll go out and before you know it I'm with the same crowd. I know it's wrong and yet there I am.

COUNSELOR: Maybe you are forced back to the old crowd.[5] Have you ever been treated like an ex-con?

PRISONER: I was going with a girl and couldn't get the nerve to tell her I'd been in the pen. I knew she'd find out sooner or later. I kept wanting to give her up, I finally did in a way. I took to drinking.

COUNSELOR: You had to. It's too much to bear. You knew she wouldn't understand.

PRISONER: I began to hate her. She kept asking what was wrong and all that. In fact I don't think I minded it too much when I had to leave her, knowing what she would think of me.

COUNSELOR: It's hard to love a person when you expect her to hate you.

PRISONER: You know, she still comes to see me, so I was wrong about how she would feel.

The prisoner could not bring himself to tell his girl friend that he had been in jail for fear that she would hate him. Since it was not true that she hated him, we must conclude that the hatred was in himself, that he hated himself because he felt he was a criminal or because he expected her to hate him because he was a criminal. Of course, it is difficult for one who has been arrested many times to feel, "I'm an honest and respected man." He wanted to go straight but felt he was not honest. In not telling the girl, he was in fact dishonest. If he had felt he was an honest man, it would have been much easier for him to say, "I was convicted of a crime and spent some time in jail, but now I am honest." But his self-conception must have been: "I'm a criminal. She would hate criminals like everyone else hates them, perhaps even as I myself do. So I can't tell her." With such a self-conception, he could not be comfortable around law-abiding citizens.

Gradually, over the years, if he comes to expect of himself what his neighbors expect of him, he becomes a professional criminal. But if along the way he can find satisfactions and social approval from

---

[5] In trying to be sympathetic, the counselor may be destructive. He suggests that the prisoner is not responsible for his behavior. A more con-

structive response would be, "Let's outline activities you can do when you leave the prison," although this would not be successful until the prisoner and counselor are involved with one another.

legitimate activities, he will obey the law. When he has learned over and over again that he can find no satisfaction this way, he welcomes the greetings of his professional associates in the underworld. As a professional criminal, he has standards of performance to live up to, friends who will help him when in trouble, visit him in prison, send him presents at Christmas, give him a home when he is sick, tell him where the police are lax and where strict—hideouts, fences, and lawyers. At twelve, fourteen, sixteen, or eighteen he has come to a conclusion about his career that ordinary boys may not make until they are twenty or even forty. And he could not have drifted into this career without the help of his family and neighbors who sought a scapegoat and unwittingly suggested to him that he become an outlaw.

V. IMPLICATIONS

When a crime is committed in a community, it is, in a sense, caused by everyone. No one grows up and lives alone; the criminal grows up with people. He is affected by his social experiences. If he wants to murder, people have made him want to murder; if he wants to break school windows, his environment has taught him how and given him a reason. And if he is punished by the community, it is because the community feels guilty for his crime, for failing to provide positive experiences in schools, for not protecting him from severe cruelty, neglect, starvation, and rejection. Those in the community who most demand his punishment are usually those who feel most guilty for their own failures, real or imaginary. They punish the criminal as they have been punished themselves. If they could forgive themselves, accept themselves, they could forgive the delinquent, accept and teach him, and, in so doing, convert him before he becomes a hardened unconvertible criminal. This conversion

process is usually too big a job for any one school, teacher, policeman, judge, psychologist or social worker. It takes many people to make an ordinary little boy into a hardened criminal. It will take a lot of people to make a criminal into a good citizen. Every little boy or girl in trouble should be examined by a physician, a psychologist, a reading specialist, a social worker, and his home and neighborhood should be studied. Intelligent steps can then be taken by this team of people working with the community council, with the cooperation of the boy and taking into consideration his preferences, to give this boy what everybody needs: security, affection, adventure, a chance to get recognition, to learn, and to give to others the best that he has to give.

Every city and hamlet has some special programs for handling delinquents. Every program in every city is different from the next. Naturally, some are more effective than others. Study and systematic evaluation of these programs are required to find out what works and what does not.

Statistics show considerable increase in juvenile crime, just as they show increase in divorce rate. This is not clear evidence of increase in juvenile crime or in broken marriages. The first could be a result of more accurate reporting or because there are more policemen; the second, of greater resort to legal processes because there is more money for divorce lawyers. In a rural community or village where everyone is known, the community is aware when a child takes another child's bicycle and tries private means to have it returned. No police are notified. In the secular, impersonal, anonymous city, a bicycle theft is more likely to be reported to the police. As our society becomes more secular, the official agencies are used more often. Two hundred years ago, divorce was rare: When a couple could not get along they either separated, the husband left, the wife ran away, they lived together but did not speak to one another, or they took lovers.

The rise in the divorce rate does not necessarily mean a rise in unsuccessful marriages. In a friendly neighborhood, when children at play break a window, the parents may talk it over and decide who pays; but in an anonymous neighborhood, they may call the police. The two misdeeds are the same, but the "crime rate" is higher in one place than another.

PUNISHMENT

Sometimes a youth commits a crime which so angers the community that letting him go without "punishment" is impossible. Punishment in our society is either a fine, imprisonment, or the death penalty. There are no other punishments within our legal system. When I ask some of my legal advisers why we might not try out some other forms of punishment, they ask me to name one. I name several: for the youth who breaks windows and street lights, let him pick up glass and other debris from the streets for a few days. For the youth who breaks someone's jaw, let him take care of patients who have been injured. For those bigots who have been involved in racial demonstrations, let them meet with bigots on the other side. The attorney said about picking up debris, "That would be involuntary servitude, which would be illegal." Zing Yang Kiro's experiments showed that baby cats, dogs, rats, and birds can grow up to be friends, to eat together in peace if their misbehavior is punished. Animals that pushed at lunch went to the end of the line. Dogs that bit had water sprayed on their faces. Punishment properly used is effective.

The problem is that what is punishment to one person may be reward to another. Sending a person to jail may be just what he has been hoping for, an opportunity to get away from his mother or wife or gang, relax, and get three square meals a day.

A good deal of evidence is accumulating to show that the majority of juvenile delinquents and criminals have been neglected or otherwise punished as infants and children. What will reduce crime, therefore, will be prevention of such punishment of these infants and small children, for it seems that by the age of four or five a child may believe "I am no good; people are no good; it is a dog-eat-dog world, and I'll take what I can get. The only mistake is getting caught." Those of us who assume that delinquency is an act of free will might contemplate this: We know a great deal about how persons become delinquent, and how delinquents may be converted into law-abiding citizens.[6] We know that if someone accepts the delinquent and is sufficiently persuasive in attempts to redirect him, the delinquent may discover a new self and a new model to follow. We know that if the delinquent is educated and trained in salable skills, and if opportunities for dignified work at acceptable wages are available, he will go to work.

If we know how to turn a delinquent into a law-abiding citizen—by voting more money for schools and for mental health research, by helping the Boy Scouts and the Girl Scouts, by providing parks and playgrounds supervised by professionally trained personnel, by volunteering our services as tutor or referee or big brother, by helping the parents of the potentially delinquent find suitable training and jobs—if we know this and refuse to act, arguments about free will fall on deaf ears. If we are free to cure the delinquent and do not, how ghastly incredible is our crime. Only determinism theory exonerates us: We are not free to change the delinquent even though we know how, just as he is not free to change himself unless we help him.

[6] See William Glasser, *Reality Therapy* (New York: Harper and Row, 1965) for a description of highly skilled teams that convert the most delinquent girls and 20-year veterans of psychoses into responsible citizens. Excerpts from *Reality Therapy* make up selection 86 in this volume.

45 | CHILDREN WHO HATE

FRITZ REDL

What are delinquents? Are they simply average children who are misunderstood, who have had bad breaks, but are ready to become good, smiling little boys and girls if given half a chance? Or are they thoroughly lost children for whom there is no hope?

Redl presents some enlightening views growing out of his work at Pioneer House, a home for incorrigible boys. He describes with brilliant insight how delinquent children try to gratify antisocial impulses and to avoid the burden of a guilty conscience. His analysis gives new meaning and power to the concepts of the id, ego, and superego in dynamic conflict.

THE CONCEPT OF "EGO" AND OUR CLINICAL TASK

Psychoanalytic theory has different names for what is . . . called, with intended colloquial looseness, the "control system." The psychoanalysts would relegate the "control" of impulsivity to two separate "systems," which constitute special "parts of our personality," the superego and the ego. Sometimes there is a third one described in psychiatric literature, the "ego ideal," but we think we can safely adopt a widespread custom of considering it as a special part of the ego and reduce the basic issue to just the two. For the non-psychiatric reader it may be explained that the "superego" is more or less the same as the "conscience." It is that part of the personality whose job it is to remind us of value issues that arise in daily living. The "ego" is supposed to "keep us in touch with reality," a statement whose specific meaning will soon be amplified. The distinction between "ego" and "superego" is not as difficult as it is made out to be. If a youngster doesn't take a dollar which just fell out of his mother's purse because he is afraid of being caught and getting thrashed, then we would say that it was his "ego" which limited his possessive urge

Excerpts reprinted from *Children Who Hate* (Glencoe, Ill.: The Free Press, 1951) by permission of the publisher.

along the line of "reality consequences." If a youngster doesn't take that dollar, even though he is certain nobody would ever find out, because he would feel bad to do anything which he considers to be a sin, such as stealing, then we would credit his "superego" with the success in impulse control. The concept of superego will be discussed more fully later. First, that peculiar agent within us which was given the name "ego" long ago by Sigmund Freud will be examined.

. . . . .

Freud himself developed this concept of the ego only late and gradually and subjected its conception to many changes and improvements. . . . It was primarily his daughter, Anna Freud, who elevated the ego and its mechanisms of defense to a respected place in therapy, especially in work with children. Since then, speculations about the intimate and not always peaceful interrelationship between the "ego" and the superego and many other details have taken increasing space in psychoanalytic literature. The growing interest of psychoanalysts in work with schizophrenics has given "ego" psychology another boost, and the need to bring psychoanalytic conceptualization closer to the action scene, which was especially increased through the development of all sorts of "group therapy," has added its push. Foregoing the fascination of portraying those details and what they mean for the therapist, we shall be satisfied with attempting to sketch what, today, we usually conceived as the "tasks of the ego."

From what Freud and his followers said, and from what can be inferred from the way they use the term in context when applying it to clinical observations, the "ego" actually is expected to fulfill at one time or another, the following functions:

I. Cognitive Function

A. COGNITIVE FUNCTION, EXTERNALIZED | It has always been conceived as one of the main tasks of the ego to establish contact with the "outside world." In this respect, it seems to be the job of the ego to size up just what the "world around us" is like, and to give adequate signals about its imminent promises or dangers to our well-being. This vague notion of "sizing up outside reality" must, of course, today be replaced by a much more specific breakdown into at least two sides of this "outside world." One is what we may call the "Physical Reality." That means, it is the job of the ego to estimate actual dangers or advantages inherent in physical situations. "I don't want to go to that dentist today," says my anxiety-ridden and comfort-greedy id. "You had better get there fast. Remember what they found out about tooth decay and dentist bills if you wait too long?" my ego is supposed to chime in. The other side of "reality demands" to which we are subject in this world might be shortly and rather crudely summarized as "Social Reality." By this is meant that the behavior of other people, individually or in groups, directly or through their institutionalized laws, customs, pressures, etc., is also a factor to be reckoned with. It is obviously also the function of the ego to become aware of existing reality limitations from that source and to give appropriate warning signals, should our behavioral urges threaten to

run into conflict with them. Even a child who is clearly delinquent in his value identification, that means, one with little "superego" at all, would be expected to have his ego make a careful assessment of just in which case stealing is "safe," in which other case the very openly enjoyed and guilt-free act of stealing had better be omitted because of "reality risks" involved in discovery, capture, too threatening legal consequences, or difficulty in getting rid of the loot. In short, it is the ego's job to size up the world around us, in its physical or social aspects, and to give danger signals if any one of our desires is too seriously in conflict with the "reality outside." . . .

B. COGNITIVE FUNCTION, INTERNALIZED | In the earlier definitions of the ego, its function of "establishing contact with the world around us," was usually emphasized. From the way the concept is now being used, though, it is obvious that an emphasis on a "cognitive appraisal of what is going on inside us" is an equally important job. In fact, some of the basic definitions of the role of psychoanalytic therapy are based on that very issue, namely, on the assumption that some id-contents cannot be got hold of by the ego, because they are repressed, that means, not even accessible to the conscious perception by the ego. If the ego doesn't even know what is going on, how can it get hold of it? This was the underlying tenor of the thinking even in the early stages of theory development leading to the demand that the repressed be made conscious. We can portray the situation implied in the following way:

COGNITIVE APPRAISAL OF ITS OWN ID | By this we mean the awareness by the ego of the most important impulses, urges, desires, strivings, fears, etc., that obviously motivate our behavior, but are not necessarily always known to us. To know as much as possible about what is really going on "in the cellar of our unconscious" always has been a primary job of the ego, if it wants to retain or regain its health.

In other words, it seems that all insights, including those into ourselves, are a function of the "ego."

COGNITIVE APPRAISAL OF ITS OWN SUPER-EGO | It is also one of the tasks of the ego to register "value demands" coming from within, not only to register "reality threats" coming from without. It is the job of the ego to know which behavior would run counter to what the specific personality "believes in," what its own superego considers fair or decent, or which behavior would, if allowed to go through, produce the horror of deep shame and nagging guilt. Ample evidence was produced in later psychoanalytic work to show that superego particles, too, can be unconscious and repressed. In those cases, it is the ego's job to become aware of the voice of its own conscience, and the therapist's task to help the ego onto that road. In short, "know thyself" does not only mean "know what your most secret strivings would make you do if they had a chance," but also "know what price you would have to pay in guilt feelings, should you give in to them."

II. The Power-Function of the Ego

Though not always implied in the definitions, it has always been assumed that the task of an ego that is in good working order is not only to "know" what reality demands are, but also to exert some force, so as to influence behavioral strivings in line with that knowledge. Or, in other words, if my ego is smart enough to tell me I "ought" to go to the dentist today, but not "strong" enough to get me there, it does only half its job and is not much help to me really. This "Power Function" of the ego is a most fascinating metapsychological problem, because we have so far wondered and speculated a good deal as to just where the ego is supposed to get the "power" to suppress impulses and drives. This problem was a difficult one in the early phases of theory, when the ego was

supposed to be little more than a "voice" telling us about the world outside. We have come a long way since then. We have to assume, for any usable conception of the ego, that it somewhere has access to a power system and then can use whatever energies it has at its disposal to enforce the dictates of its insights upon our pleasure-greedy impulse system. By the way, this is what we should mean when we say an ego is "weak." Unfortunately, the term "weak" is also used freely to indicate simply that an ego doesn't function well. We shall limit our use of the term "ego weakness" only to those situations where a disturbance of its power function is clearly meant.

III. The Selective Function of the Ego

When confronted with an outside danger or an inner conflict, it is not enough to know what the situation is and to be ready to block inadmissible impulses—the ego has a few other decisions to make. For there is usually more than one way to react. The old idea that all the ego has to do is to decide whether an impulse can be afforded or not is an oversimplification which needed debunking long ago. Even in the most flash-like and simple situation, where the ego resorts to ready-made, stereotyped, reflex-like "defense mechanisms," it still has to select one from quite a number. Let's assume that a child suddenly becomes aware that the rest of his pals are engaged in some "dirty talk" which seems highly status-loaded in their gang but of which he doesn't understand a word because of parental overprotection and lack of sophistication. He has a variety of ways in which to react to the emerging conflict. He can deny his desire to be in on the talk. He can add "reaction formation" to this trick to make it more foolproof. Then he will get very indignant at the very insinuation that he might want to know about things like this and will even ward off his friendly therapist's help along the line of sex information. He may, on the other hand, simply withdraw, and this he may do on different levels and with varying scope. He may, for instance, simply avoid being near those bad boys; he may try not to have to play with them. On the other hand, he may ask to be transferred to a different group. Or he may have to cement his withdrawal with wild accusations and gossip propaganda against these youngsters. Finally, he may not do any of these things. He may successfully repress during daytime what is going on inside him, only to be flooded with bad dreams or night terrors, or plagued by insomnia or anxiety attacks.

Of course, our youngster doesn't have to resort to these automatic defense mechanisms at all. In that case he has to meet the problem on a reality level. Then, his ego has to make even more far-reaching decisions. Maybe he simply can tell his father and have a man-to-man talk and ask him what all those things the kids are talking about mean. Maybe he can ask another boy or his counselor. Or maybe his group skills are so well developed that he simply forces or inveigles the others into "cutting him in on it," swallowing the unavoidable transitional razzing he will get in order to solve the problem once and for all. In these cases, too, his ego will have quite a job to do. It will not only have to appraise just which of these paths are open to it but it will have to "inspect the tool by which reality is being met" as to its potential ability to solve the problem. It will have something like a "tool selection job in terms of efficiency appraisal" to perform.

IV. The Synthetic Function of the Ego

The concept of a synthetic function, a much later addition to ego psychology, has led into fascinating but also specifically metapsychological speculations. One of the latest studies around this issue is that of Nunberg. Here, we do not want to enter into such metapsychological speculations. We are using the term "synthetic function" in a somewhat simplified way. This is what we have in mind: if we assume that there are a number of "parts of the personality" at work, each one apparently equipped with some "influence" in the internal household affairs, then the job of putting them all together and keeping them in some sort of balance with each other must somewhere be ascribed to "somebody" in the picture. We suggest that the ego be given this task. In other words, it is also the ego's job to decide just how much a personality shall be predominantly influenced by the demands of the impulse system, the demands of outside reality, the dictates of its own conscience. It seems that "personality disbalance" can result from any one of a number of "wrong" assortments of power distribution. For instance, if the superego is allowed to dominate far beyond what an individual can sacrifice and still remain healthy and happy, you get a virtuous person, who will finally break down under his own frustrations or have to become hostile and nasty for the same reason. On the other hand, if impulsivity is entirely rampant, the present state of happiness will soon be destroyed by the conflict with the "outside world" which may result in lifelong incarceration, or by the "nagging guilt" from within, if too strongly established value issues are allowed to be violated by a too little vigilant ego. In brief, it is the job of the ego to balance the various demand systems and to keep this balance "reasonable" on all sides. We think, by the way, that the term "balanced personality" should be reserved for this issue rather than be used as widely as is currently the custom. The most glaring illustration of a one-sided handling of the synthetic function by the ego is the one which will engage us soon, namely, the case where the ego throws its weight entirely on the side of impulsivity or of a delinquency-identified superego—a situational distortion for which we plan to use the term "delinquent ego."

THE EGO AND THE CONCEPT OF
DELINQUENCY

. . . . .

When we talk about the "delinquent ego"
here, we have two things in mind:

1. We use the term "delinquent" in its
cultural meaning—referring to any behavior which runs counter to the dominant
value system within which the child's
character formation takes place. Thus, we
would include his insistence on "hate without cause," even where no clearly legally
punishable act was involved. We mean all
the attitudes which will be developed in a
child who is about to drift into a "delinquent style of life."

2. As far as the "ego" side of the picture
goes, we want to describe the ego in those
situations in which it is bent on *defending
impulse gratification at any cost*. In short,
instead of performing its task of looking
for a synthesis between desires, reality
demands, and the impact of social values,
the ego is, in those moments, totally on the
side of impulsivity. It throws all its weight
into the task of making impulse gratification possible, against the outside world as
well as against whatever remainders of
the voice of its own conscience may be
left. The amazing spectacle which we have
before us in the children who hate lies
right here: Sometimes these children seem
to act wrong and confused simply because
their ego is inefficient and cannot, as
described before, manage the onrush of
impulsivity in complex life situations.
At other times, the situation is different
indeed. Far from being helpless, the ego
of these children is suddenly a rather
shrewd appraiser of that part of reality
which might be dangerous to their impulsive exploits and becomes an efficient
manipulator of the world around them as
well as an energetic protector of delinquent fun against the voice of their own
conscience. Just which specific task the
"delinquent ego," by which we mean from
now on the ego's effort to secure guilt-free

and anxiety-free enjoyment of delinquent
impulsivity, may have to fulfill, will depend upon other details of a youngster's
personality. Some, for instance, are identified with a delinquent behavior code
anyway. Their own superego being delinquency identified already, guilt feelings
won't bother them. The task of their ego
is primarily to make it possible to "get
away with things" and to defend their delinquency against the threat of the world
around them. Others are not quite that
advanced. They still have mighty, chunks
of their value-identified superego intact;
the voice of their conscience still tries to
make itself heard. In that case, the "delinquent ego" has the additional task of
"duping its own superego," so that delinquent impulsivity can be enjoyed tax-free
from feelings of guilt. In still another case,
neither value-identified nor delinquent
superego allegiances are very strongly
developed. Those children are like a "bun-
dle of drives," and their ego seems to have
primarily a "reality manipulative task."
These details are fascinating but irrelevant
here. In all three cases we shall receive
the full brunt of an efficient ego, bent on
the task of impulse protection, when we
try to educate or treat such children. Far
from acting delinquent out of helplessness
or just because of an occasional onrush of
unusual impulse intensity, these children
have an organized system of defenses well
developed and meet the adult who tries
to change them with a consistent and well-
planned barrage of counter-techniques.

. . . . .

Once a child has part of its ego so clearly
throwing its weight toward the side of the
defense of delinquency, we are saddled
with an entirely new task. In order to
"free" the youngster of his delinquent
urges, we have to take the hurdle of strategic impulse defense by their ego. With
such children, therefore, the exact study
of just how their ego goes about to defend
their impulsivity against their own con-

science, as well as against the outside world, becomes a matter of prime importance. Since the material gained from the psychiatric treatment of the basically neurotic delinquent has produced little insight into the "tough defense machinery" we are referring to here, it is worth while to give it our full attention. Indeed, the development of a successful "total treatment strategy" in a residential treatment design hinges upon this very ability to know their *ego strengths as well as their ego disturbances.* The detailed tracing of the machinations of the delinquency-protective ego of our Pioneers would run into several volumes. We have to restrict ourselves here, therefore, to a mere listing of the most discernable "ego functions in the service of impulse defense."

THE STRATEGY OF TAX EVASION

Our Pioneers did not fall into the category of children who simply have "no superego at all," or who are harmoniously identified with a totally delinquent neighborhood code, as the classical "healthy delinquent" is supposed to be. In fact, we never met a child who would fit that description. Even the toughest children with whom we had to deal would reveal, upon closer inspection, that the aggressive front of behavior with which they would surround themselves needed many "special tricks" to be maintained at all. Below the behavioral surface, there would be a great number of little "value islands" left—stemming out of isolated remainders of earlier childhood identification, from the automatic absorption of non-delinquent elements in the general "code of behavior" which even a delinquent neighborhood still has sprinkled around, or out of occasional real ties or dependencies with people which couldn't quite be avoided after all. In short, even the ego of the toughest delinquent doesn't have quite as simple a job as we might assume. While visibly expert in the task of producing delinquent be-

havior without much concern, it has quite a job to perform in order to keep all phases of that behavior from being "tax exempt" from feeling of guilt. The children we talk about have many such "value islands" in their personalities, and consequently their ego spends much time seeing to it that what they do can be enjoyed without the price of guilt feelings. In fact, they have little trouble "getting away" with a good deal of behavior for the moment. To really "get away" with doing all this without feeling bad about it afterwards, however, seems to be an additional job. It is fascinating to watch the special machinery these children's ego has developed in order to secure their behavior against post-situation guilt feelings.

. . . . .

The following is a fairly cursory list of such "tax evasion from guilt feelings" techniques which we could amply observe at Pioneer House as well as at camp:

Repression of Own Intent

Some of our youngsters have an enviable skill of repressing, right after an incident happens, its actual emotional gain and of course everything that would betray their basic motivation to begin with. This repression accomplished, they can now afford to remember, relate or brag about any other detail of the incident without having to fear that the voice of their conscience might be raised in this process.

One of the youngsters at camp had stolen a wallet from a counselor whom he actually liked a lot, and whose "fairness toward him" he had openly and repeatedly recognized before. The specific child had a perfectly "delinquent" superego as far as stealing as such was concerned, but his own value standard would reject as very "unfair" "to be mean to somebody who had been nice to you." When confronted with his misdeed, he had no trouble remembering, admitting, and discussing freely the details of his theft. When challenged, not along the line of having stolen, but of having been mean to somebody who had been so nice to him, he blocked entirely, couldn't remember a thing about just "why" he might have wanted to do a thing like that, assuring us that he didn't mean to hurt the adult, he just needed the cash in the wallet. As long as he could keep up this separation of issues for himself, he was perfectly safe. He would have liked nothing better than to be punished for the delinquent side of the act, so as to be sure not to be confronted with the real "guilt" as far as he was concerned. It took considerable interview work in this specific case until, much later, the child was able to allow himself to become aware of the full impact of his own love for the adult, of the specific fantasies which had gone into the theft, and could be helped to cope with the feelings of guilt which then, post-situationally, suddenly arose.

By the way, it is our experience that sudden *blocking* in a "grilling" interview does not always mean an attempt to hide from discovery. The inability of children to produce at all, when challenged in a way similar to that of the example, is sometimes a direct indication that we have hit upon an area in which real value sensitivity might still be intact.

He Did It First

We do not mean the case, here, where a youngster tries to ward off blame by shoving it off onto somebody else. We actually mean that the mere fact that "somebody else did it first" would really constitute a chance not to have to feel guilty for something he did. We have pointed at this basic principle of "exculpation magics through the initiatory act" before. We do not claim that we can explain it, but have to state it as a simple matter of fact: Conscience can be assuaged at times by the simple awareness that the guilt-producing behavior was entered in only after somebody else had already openly done what one only intended to do. Needless to point out, this is a most "illogical" way of thinking, and no system of ethics we could conceive of actually supports such argument. For the Uncon-

scious, however, it seems to be a fact that, for "intramural use" so to speak, priority of somebody else's guilt takes away the tax burden of guilt feelings quite well.

For a long time, at camp, we were fooled by considering the youngsters with the most patent trend to accuse others, as the more "delinquent ones." For some of them that is still correct. We had to learn, though, that sometimes this actually works the other way around. The great need to find somebody who did it first need not come from a need to be revengeful or accusatory, but may, on the contrary, point to the very intact part of the youngster's superego. Only because he would really have to feel guilty for what he did, does a child sometimes seek so hard to find somebody else to blame.

Everybody Else Does Such Things Anyway

This is a well-known device even among adult sinners, and easily enters the "self-apologetic" argument of otherwise honorable people, especially where obligations to larger issues are involved. Many people who wouldn't steal one cent from another person's pocket find their morals crumbling if something can be pointed out as "general business practice." This kind of "logic," again, is equally indicative of two facts: that this special person's superego can be easily punctured, and also that there is still something that needs puncturing by a special trick.

. . . . .

We Were All In On It

. . . . .

On one occasion the whole Pioneer group had been involved in a very dangerous and destructive episode of throwing bricks from the top of the garage. We decided to have individual interviews with each of the boys to "rub-in" the total unacceptability of such behavior. Andy, especially, was fascinating in his real indignation at even being approached on the subject. Tearfully he shouted at the Director who was doing the interviewing,

"Yeah, everybody was doing it and you talk to me. Why is it my fault?" When it was pointed out to him that we were not saying it was all his fault but that he was responsible for his individual share in the matter, he was still unable to admit the point: "But we were all in on it. Why talk to me?"

But Somebody Else Did That Same Thing to Me Before

As an open argument, such a statement seems incredible and void of all sense. An efficient delinquent ego, though, knows to what wonderful use it can be put, when the task of warding off guilt feelings arises. In fact, we had many children, after long interview work, really come out with this "theory of exculpation" in open declaration. After we had finally crowded them enough so that they could not any longer ward off the guilt issue involved in what they did, they found a last refuge, in arguing with themselves and with us, in this device. They really tried to prove that their stealing was all right because "somebody swiped my own wallet two weeks ago." Needless to add, only a rather primitive ego can still afford to get away with an alibi trick like that.

. . . . .

Two items need to be stressed to avoid a misunderstanding of what we have tried to point out in this whole section on the strategy of tax evasion. One is, again, the importance of differentiating between the mechanisms described here and a use of any such "arguments" in order to fool authority figures or as a semi-legalistic device to soften the punitive implication of a misdeed for which one has been caught. Wherever the latter is being done, the same arguments quoted here may be used, but we then have to deal with an entirely different layer of "defenses of the delinquent ego." . . . What we have in mind in the section on tax evasion is an actual attempt of the ego to ward off *inner* conflict between the children's own conscience and what they do. That is, their ego uses these devices to make delinquent behavior possible and to keep it guilt free, not to ward off outside consequences. The existence and usability of such defenses always prove both the energetic effort of the child's ego to protect his delinquency from his own "better self," and the existence of some parts of an intact conscience or superego—for the really "valueless" youngster wouldn't need any of this at all, and would simply enjoy his delinquent fun with a defiant "so what?" attitude. As in the case of the emergence of resistance in the treatment of neurotics, the defenses employed here prove both the existence of pathology and the functioning of the ego defending it. Thus, the careful study of such "alibi tricks" would help us in the diagnosis of what the enemy of our treatment effort is doing and, at the same time, also offer us additional insight into those parts of a child's superego which are still intact. The clinician, as well as the educator, might welcome both.

The other item to be stressed here and elaborated upon later on is, of course, the great impact of all this for practice. And this part is relevant not only for the educator of the disturbed child, but also for the parent and educator of his normal age mate. For, what is disturbance later on usually was a perfectly legitimate phase of development at an earlier time. The very type of "alibi tricks" children have to employ in the defense of their search for happiness which will irritate adults gives us a wonderful picture of just which level of superego development they have achieved, which is still to be entered into, where potential distortions might lurk. For the therapist of a disturbed child, the implications of all this are equally serious —for it means that in those cases the problem is not one of "ego support" but one of *superego support* and ego *repair*. The areas in which children act in the way we described are not the ones where their ego is "weak" or "disturbed." On the contrary, these seem to be hypertrophically developed ego functions—only applied in the service of the wrong goal. The result of these hypertrophic ego skills applied for the wrong goal must not be confused with the evidence of other areas in which the ego is weak or disturbed in its functioning, though any one child may, and usually does, show a mixture of both. . . .

CONSCIENCE ON SECOND BOULEVARD

The statement that a specific child simply has no conscience or superego at all is being bandied about rather freely these days. In fact, some quite elaborate terminology has been invented to label such far-reaching claims. Frankly, we think that this is the bunk. Among all the hundreds of children who were supposed to be without a conscience and with whom we lived quite closely for varying lengths of time, we haven't yet found one to whom such an exaggerated diagnosis would apply. We admit, though, that we were often tempted to make such a statement about a particular child, especially when we were angry at him, when our own middle-class sensitivities were rubbed the wrong way by what he said or did, when our lack of familiarity with his natural habitat made us blind to the fact that his conscience simply talked to him in a language different from the one ours would use, including four letter words. . . .

1. Peculiarities in Value Content

As far as the content of specific values goes, our youngsters showed three clearly differentiated peculiarities rather than just an "absence of superego." The first one might be described as *clear identification areas with a delinquent neighborhood code.* By this we imply that our youngsters have accepted some value demands from parents and from their surrounding community, but it so happens that these value demands are themselves of a delinquent nature. From the outside, this may make our children look as though they had "no values at all," but the clinical difference between that and what we really had before us is enormous and of great relevance. Some of their proud display of crude violence, which the middle-class clinician finds so embarrassing to watch, and some of their open bragging about acts of theft or about their deceit in "getting away" with thefts are openly contradictory to the value system by which we would judge. And often enough such behavior simply meant that our youngsters were "value blind" or "value defiant." It would be too easy, though, to shift the whole problem onto this simple explanation. We observed many instances where we were quite certain that such attitudes were *not* expressive of value defiance against the system in which they operated, but that their behavior was really "innocent." By this we mean that they acted that way because they felt in line with the value scale of their own parents and their natural habitat. Thus, when bragging about crude and unjust violence and when proud of a cleverly gotten away with theft, these children were sometimes not only not rebellious, but actually value-conforming as far as their natural habitat goes. Doing things like these, they did what any good child, obedient to his elders and conforming to the mores of the community, would do. The only trouble was that the parental and communal values themselves were out of focus with the general middle-class value scale. Clinically speaking, though, this makes such acts not acts of value rebellion but acts of value conformism. The conflict in those cases was between the standards of their natural habitat and ours, not between the child's impulse and his superego. . . .

In other moments of their lives, our youngsters did not give the impression of nearly total value absence or conflict.

Sometimes they showed a sudden emergence of what we might term *"childhood value islands"* which was surprising to watch.

This means that, tough as they were, they would suddenly display very obviously non-delinquent, quite middle-class-like value issues which emerged out of nowhere. The fact seems to be that even a delinquent neighborhood in which children may grow up is not so consistently delinquent in its behavior code, so far as children are concerned, as it may be in its adult affairs. Toward their own children even the adults from tough neighborhoods sometimes practice a much more "civilian" type of behavior code than in their own lives. Also, the fact that children were rejected, had nobody to love and identify with, is rarely true to as high a degree as such overgeneralized statements seem to imply. It seems that even neglected children rescue some one or other "relationship memory" out of the debris of their infancy, and that occasional "identification loopholes" pierce the seemingly impenetrable wall of human coldness and disinterest.

As far as our Pioneers go, there were moments in our otherwise conflict-studded life with them, when individual youngsters would suddenly come through with unexpectedly value-identified statements or attitudes. "You see, that comes from not doing what Emily told you," one of the otherwise most recalcitrant ones would be overheard saying to his pal. Sometimes one of them would suddenly be ashamed when caught in some especially vehement swearing, and would explain his feelings by saying that "Kids aren't supposed to say such things in front of adults." Occasionally, the appearance of a visitor, which usually led to a great display of exhibitionistic toughness, would surprisingly throw the group or individual members of it into scenes of "Let's introduce our guest to our dear housemother, who is so kind to us all." Especially in moments of child-adult happiness, primarily focused around child-housemother, or child-cook, relationships, real value concern or guilt around an act of unfairness would crop up freely, seemingly from nowhere. Such value islands would emerge much too early for us to think that we produced them. They obviously had been there all the time, and now began to emerge out of the debris of general value warfare, as a remainder from earlier times.

. . . . .

2. Inadequacy of the Signal Function

The pathology of a sick conscience does not necessarily have to lie in the inadequate value content coverage. It may have its main trouble in a disturbance of the job of "giving value danger signals." These, indeed, were often very weak in our children. Where a normal child would feel some anticipatory pangs of conscience, even before he decided how he would act, our youngsters would have only a very dim awareness that what they were about to do wasn't so good. Thus, even in areas which were covered by value identifications, the very weakness of the voice of their conscience would often mean that it remained unheard amidst the noise of temptational challenge. This made it easy for their ego to ignore it entirely whenever feasible. Sometimes our youngsters seemed to suffer also from another incapacity of a sick conscience, but one which is more often found in the neurotic rather than the delinquent child. They seemed to have what we might term a "post-action conscience." A superego suffering from this disease is of no help at all. It is value identified, all right. But it does not raise its voice in a moment of temptation. It confines itself to screaming all the more loudly after the deed has been committed. Colloquial usage tends to throw this type of disturbance in together with the previous one, referring to both as a "weak conscience." Yet, clinically speaking, we have obviously an entirely different disturbance before us. This type of conscience acts, in fact, as many of the parents of such children acted earlier in their lives. They were, initially, too disinterested or rejective to care much how their children fared, or to give them any help to go straight. Then, if something went wrong, they would literally descend upon the child with the full blast of their revenge for the discomfort the child had caused them. This, in turn, would be followed by another stretch of disinterest, of lack of supervision and care. In some moments of their lives, the conscience of our youngsters would react in exactly the same way. It would produce some feelings of guilt after a too obvious misdeed, but would still give no anticipatory value danger signal in the next temptational situation. This special disease of "post-action conscience" constitutes an important challenge to the task of superego repair. While the behavioral results are the same as with the child who has no conscience to begin with, its cure needs to take an entirely different path.

THE COMPLEXITY
OF SUPEREGO REPAIR

In this chapter we have isolated the "superego" or "conscience" of the child as though it were a part all by itself. This was unavoidable for the purpose of a crude sketch and rough outline of its main functions and their disturbance types. Before we forget the real complexity of our clinical task, though, we had better hasten to put things into context again. For, were only the superego of our children disturbed, the task would be comparatively simple. In fact, most normal and neurotic children also show isolated disturbances of their conscience as we have described them here, and we can often cope with them along the line of re-education, case

work, and psychiatric treatment. The children who hate constitute a special problem over and beyond all that. Their deficient and sick conscience happens to coincide with a deficient or delinquent ego. That makes for a combination which seems to defy our usual treatment channels, and which taxes even the most ingenious "total treatment strategy" to the utmost.

Let us assume for a moment that we were lucky or skillful and discovered an old value island or even inserted a new value identification into Danny's life. What a clinical triumph that would constitute all by itself! Yet, where would it lead us if we achieved that much before we were able to bring his "ego" up to par? If Danny, for instance, suddenly feels guilty for acting "so mean" toward us— and what a healthy feeling that would be —what does it get us, so long as his ego cannot cope with even a normal feeling of guilt? From our description of that type of ego disturbance we can easily forecast the chaos in which this will result. Feeling guilty for having been unfair to us, Danny will have to have an anxiety attack or a temper tantrum, or he will have to destroy things which remind him of this obligation or guilt toward us. So the behavior result will be wild, even though we obviously scored a great therapeutic success so far as his superego goes. Or, to raise another complication, let's assume that we "strengthen" Joe's ego enough so that it suddenly is able to be more perceptive of the reality around him than it has been before. Where does that get us unless we also give his conscience more power over his life? For ego strength per se is a small gain, as our chapter on the "delinquent ego and its techniques" ought to have shown. On the other hand, how can we get Joe even to see the implication of his earlier deeds unless his ego is first strengthened to be self-perceptive enough of his own motives and to be socially sensitive enough to stop his delusional persecutory fantasies by which he defends himself from the impact of love?

The worst combination of all, though, is not that of superego deficiency and ego deficiency, but of superego deficiency and delinquency-identified ego strength. With the children who simply suffer from a maldeveloped conscience, we would have only one area of sickness to combat. With the children who combine such pathology with the impressive ego strength of the "delinquent ego and its defenses," . . . we have an indeed formidable combination arrayed against us. How can we ever get "value identifications" across against such hypertrophically developed defensive skills? What good would the breakdown of such defenses be to our clinical goals if we could not pull the value switch equally fast? Breaking down their ego defenses without supplying them with livable values at the same time will only leave us with ego-deficient children, not with the product we are supposed to deliver.

---

46 | THE WAY OF ALL FLESH

SAMUEL BUTLER

The novelist, in creating the characters for his story, may reach back into his own intimate experience and thus reveal a great deal about his relations with those who were close to him. Butler's novel, from which these excerpts are taken, is reputed to be autobiographical, the parents being patterned after those of the author. Butler's insistence that the novel be published only after his death indicates that his hatred of his father, however strong, was tempered by feelings of compassion and guilt.

INTRODUCTION

. . . The worst misfortune that can happen to any person, says Butler, is to lose his money; the second is to lose his health; and the loss of reputation is a bad third. He seems to have regarded the death of his father as the most fortunate event in his own life; for it made him financially independent. He never quite forgave the old man for hanging on till he was eighty years old. He ridiculed the Bishop of Carlisle for saying that we long to meet our parents in the next world. "Speaking for myself, I have no wish to see my father again, and I think it likely that the Bishop of Carlisle would not be more eager to see his than I mine." Melchisedec "was a really happy man. He was without father, without mother, and without descent. He was an incarnate bachelor. He was a born orphan."

CHAPTER XX

The birth of his son opened Theobald's eyes to a good deal which he had but faintly realised hitherto. He had had no idea how great a nuisance a baby was. Babies come into the world so suddenly at the end, and upset everything so terribly when they do come: why cannot they steal in upon us with less of a shock to the domestic system? His wife, too, did not recover rapidly from her confinement; she remained an invalid for months; here was another nuisance and an expensive one, which interfered with the amount which Theobald liked to put by out of his

Excerpts reprinted from Samuel Butler, *The Way of All Flesh*, Everyman's Library, by permission of E. P. Dutton & Co., Inc.

income against, as he said, a rainy day, or to make provision for his family if he should have one. Now he was getting a family, so that it became all the more necessary to put money by, and here was the baby hindering him. Theorists may say what they like about a man's children being a continuation of his own identity, but it will generally be found that those who talk in this way have no children of their own. Practical family men know better.

About twelve months after the birth of Ernest there came a second, also a boy, who was christened Joseph, and in less than twelve months afterwards, a girl, to whom was given the name of Charlotte. A few months before this girl was born Christina paid a visit to the John Ponti-fexes in London, and, knowing her condition, passed a good deal of time at the Royal Academy exhibition looking at the types of female beauty portrayed by the Academicians, for she had made up her mind that the child this time was to be a girl. Alethea warned her not to do this, but she persisted, and certainly the child turned out plain, but whether the pictures caused this or no, I cannot say.

Theobald had never liked children. He had always got away from them as soon as he could, and so had they from him; oh, why, he was inclined to ask himself, could not children be born into the world grown up? If Christina could have given birth to a few full-grown clergymen in priest's orders—of moderate views, but inclining rather to Evangelicism, with comfortable livings and in all respects facsimiles of Theobald himself—why, there might have been more sense in it; or if people could buy ready-made children at a shop of whatever age and sex they liked, instead of always having to make them at home and to begin at the beginning with them —that might do better, but as it was he did not like it. He felt as he had felt when he had been required to come and be married to Christina—that he had been

going on for a long time quite nicely, and would much rather continue things on their present footing. In the matter of getting married he had been obliged to pretend he liked it; but times were changed, and if he did not like a thing now, he could find a hundred unexceptionable ways of making his dislike apparent.

It might have been better if Theobald in his younger days had kicked more against his father: the fact that he had not done so encouraged him to expect the most implicit obedience from his own children. He could trust himself, he said (and so did Christina), to be more lenient than perhaps his father had been to himself; his danger, he said (and so again did Christina), would be rather in the direction of being too indulgent; he must be on his guard against this, for no duty could be more important than that of teaching a child to obey its parents in all things.

He had read not long since of an Eastern traveller, who, while exploring somewhere in the more remote parts of Arabia and Asia Minor, had come upon a remarkably hardy, sober, industrious little Christian community—all of them in the best of health—who had turned out to be the actual living descendants of Jonadab, the son of Rechab; and two men in European costume, indeed, but speaking English with a broken accent, and by their colour evidently Oriental, had come begging to Battersby soon afterwards, and represented themselves as belonging to this people; they had said they were collecting funds to promote the conversion of their fellow tribesmen to the English branch of the Christian religion. True, they turned out to be impostors, for when he gave them a pound and Christina five shillings from her private purse, they went and got drunk with it in the next village but one to Battersby; still, this did not invalidate the story of the Eastern traveller. Then there were the Romans—whose greatness was probably due to the wholesome authority exercised by the head of a family over all its members. Some Romans had even killed their children; this was going too far, but then the Romans were not Christians, and knew no better.

The practical outcome of the foregoing was a conviction in Theobald's mind, and if in his, then in Christina's, that it was their duty to begin training up their children in the way they should go, even from their earliest infancy. The first signs of self-will must be carefully looked for, and plucked up by the roots at once before they had time to grow. Theobald picked up this numb serpent of a metaphor and cherished it in his bosom.

Before Ernest could well crawl he was taught to kneel; before he could well speak he was taught to lisp the Lord's prayer, and the general confession. How was it possible that these things could be taught too early? If his attention flagged or his memory failed him, here was an ill weed which would grow apace, unless it were plucked out immediately, and the only way to pluck it out was to whip him, or shut him up in a cupboard, or dock him of some of the small pleasures of childhood. Before he was three years old he could read and, after a fashion, write. Before he was four he was learning Latin, and could do rule of three sums.

As for the child himself, he was naturally of an even temper; he doted upon his nurse, on kittens and puppies, and on all things that would do him the kindness of allowing him to be fond of them. He was fond of his mother, too, but as regards his father, he has told me in later life he could remember no feeling but fear and shrinking. Christina did not remonstrate with Theobald concerning the severity of the tasks imposed upon their boy, nor yet as to the continual whippings that were found necessary at lesson times. Indeed, when during any absence of Theobald's the lessons were entrusted to her, she found to her sorrow that it was the only thing to do, and she did it no less effectually than Theobald himself; nevertheless she was fond of her boy, which Theobald never was, and it was long before she could destroy all affection for herself in the mind of her first-born. But she persevered.

CHAPTER XXI

Strange! for she believed she doted upon him, and certainly she loved him better than either of her other children. Her version of the matter was that there had never yet been two parents so self-denying and devoted to the highest welfare of their children as Theobald and herself. For Ernest, a very great future—she was certain of it—was in store. This made severity all the more necessary, so that from the first he might have been kept pure from every taint of evil. She could not allow herself the scope for castle building which, we read, was indulged in by every Jewish matron before the appearance of the Messiah, for the Messiah had now come, but there was to be a millennium shortly, certainly not later than 1866, when Ernest would be just about the right age for it, and a modern Elias would be wanted to herald its approach. Heaven would bear her witness that she had never shrunk from the idea of martyrdom for herself and Theobald, nor would she avoid it for her boy, if his life was required of her in her Redeemer's service. Oh, no! If God told her to offer up her first-born, as He had told Abraham, she would take him up to Pigbury Beacon and plunge the—no, that she could not do, but it would be unnecessary—some one else might do that. It was not for nothing that Ernest had been baptised in water from the Jordan. It had not been her doing, nor yet Theobald's. They had not sought it. When water from the sacred stream was wanted for a sacred infant, the channel had been found through which it was to flow from far Palestine over land and sea to the door of the house where the child was lying. Why, it was a miracle! It was! It was! She saw it all now. The Jordan had left its bed and flowed into her own house. It was idle to say that this was not a miracle. No miracle was effected without means of some kind; the difference between the faithful and the unbeliever consisted in the very fact that the former could see a miracle where the latter could not. The Jews could see no miracle even in the raising of Lazarus and the feeding of the five thousand. The John Pontifexes would see no miracle in this matter of the water from the Jordan. The essence of a miracle lay not in the fact that means had been dispensed with, but in the adoption of means to a great end that had not been available without interference; and no one would suppose that Dr. Jones would have brought the water unless he had been directed. She would tell this to Theobald, and get him to see it in the . . . and yet perhaps it would be better not. The insight of women upon matters of this sort was deeper and more unerring than that of men. It was a woman and not a man who had been filled most completely with the whole fulness of the Deity. But why had they not treasured up the water after it was used? It ought never, never to have been thrown away, but it had been. Perhaps, however, this was for the best too—they might have been tempted to set too much store by it, and it might have become a source of spiritual danger to them—perhaps even of spiritual pride, the very sin of all others which she most abhorred. As for the channel through which the Jordan had flowed to Battersby, that mattered not more than the earth through which the river ran in Palestine itself. Dr. Jones was certainly worldly—very worldly; so, she regretted to feel, had been her father-in-law, though in a less degree; spiritual, at heart, doubtless, and becoming more and more spiritual continually as he grew older, still he was tainted with the world, till a very few hours, probably, before his death, whereas she and Theobald had given up all for

Christ's sake. *They* were not worldly. At least Theobald was not. She had been, but she was sure she had grown in grace since she had left off eating things strangled and blood—this was as the washing in Jordan as against Abana and Pharpar, rivers of Damascus. Her boy should never touch a strangled fowl nor a black pudding—that, at any rate, she could see to. He should have a coral from the neighbourhood of Joppa—there were coral insects on those coasts, so that the thing could easily be done with a little energy; she would write to Dr. Jones about it, etc. And so on for hours together day after day for years. Truly, Mrs. Theobald loved her child according to her lights with an exceeding great fondness, but the dreams she had dreamed in sleep were sober realities in comparison with those she indulged in while awake.

When Ernest was in his second year, Theobald, as I have already said, began to teach him to read. He began to whip him two days after he had begun to teach him.

"It was painful," as he said to Christina, but it was the only thing to do and it was done. The child was puny, white and sickly, so they sent continually for the doctor who dosed him with calomel and James's powder. All was done in love, anxiety, timidity, stupidity, and impatience. They were stupid in little things; and he that is stupid in little will be stupid also in much.

Presently old Mr. Pontifex died, and then came the revelation of the little alteration he had made in his will simultaneously with his bequest to Ernest. It was rather hard to bear, especially as there was no way of conveying a bit of their minds to the testator now that he could no longer hurt them. As regards the boy himself anyone must see that the bequest would be an unmitigated misfortune to him. To leave him a small independence was perhaps the greatest injury which one could inflict upon a young man. It would cripple his energies, and deaden his desire for active employment. Many a youth was led into evil courses by the knowledge that on arriving at majority he would come into a few thousands. They might surely have been trusted to have their boy's interests at heart, and must be better judges of those interests than he, at twenty-one, could be expected to be: besides if Jonadab, the son of Rechab's father—or perhaps it might be simpler under the circumstances to say Rechab at once—if Rechab, then, had left handsome legacies to his grandchildren— why Jonadab might not have found those children so easy to deal with, etc. "My dear," said Theobald, after having discussed the matter with Christina for the twentieth time, "my dear, the only thing to guide and console us under misfortunes of this kind is to take refuge in practical work."

EDITORS' SUMMARY OF
CHAPTERS XXXVIII AND XXXIX

[Ernest became very fond of a remarkably pretty servant girl named Ellen, who, it was discovered, was very ill—and pregnant. There was no question about what should be done with Ellen: she should receive her wages and be packed off immediately. The only question was, who did it? Ernest? The mother thought about it. When innocent Ernest found out that Ellen was gone, almost penniless, he ran after the carriage, caught it—all out of breath—and gave Ellen his watch and the few shillings he had. Of course, this made Ernest late for dinner. What should he tell his parents? The truth? Oh, no! They would surely punish him. So he told them he had lost his watch, and was looking for it. His conscience troubled him deeply.]

CHAPTER XL

. . . Next day and for many days afterwards he fled when no man was pursuing, and trembled each time he heard his father's voice calling for him. He had

already so many causes of anxiety that he could stand little more, and in spite of all his endeavours to look cheerful, even his mother could see that something was preying upon his mind. Then the idea returned to her that, after all, her son might not be innocent in the Ellen matter—and this was so interesting that she felt bound to get as near the truth as she could.

"Come here, my poor, pale-faced, heavy-eyed boy," she said to him one day in her kindest manner; "come and sit down by me, and we will have a little quiet confidential talk together, will we not?"

The boy went mechanically to the sofa. Whenever his mother wanted what she called a confidential talk with him she always selected the sofa as the most suitable ground on which to open her campaign. All mothers do this; the sofa is to them what the dining-room is to fathers. In the present case the sofa was particularly well adapted for a strategic purpose, being an old-fashioned one with a high back, mattress, bolsters and cushions. Once safely penned into one of its deep corners, it was like a dentist's chair, not too easy to get out of again. Here she could get at him better to pull him about, if this should seem desirable, or if she thought fit to cry she could bury her head in the sofa cushion and abandon herself to an agony of grief which seldom failed of its effect. None of her favourite manœuvres were so easily adopted in her usual seat, the armchair on the right hand side of the fireplace, and so well did her son know from his mother's tone that this was going to be a sofa conversation that he took his place like a lamb as soon as she began to speak and before she could reach the sofa herself.

"My dearest boy," began his mother, taking hold of his hand and placing it within her own, "promise me never to be afraid either of your dear papa or of me; promise me this, my dear, as you love me, promise it to me," and she kissed him again and again and stroked his hair. But with her other hand she still kept hold of his; she had got him and she meant to keep him.

The lad hung down his head and promised. What else could he do?

"You know there is no one, dear, dear Ernest, who loves you so much as your papa and I do; no one who watches so carefully over your interests or who is so anxious to enter into all your little joys and troubles as we are; but, my dearest boy, it grieves me to think sometimes that you have not that perfect love for and confidence in us which you ought to have. You know, my darling, that it would be as much our pleasure as our duty to watch over the development of your moral and spiritual nature, but alas! you will not let us see your moral and spiritual nature. At times we are almost inclined to doubt whether you have a moral and spiritual nature at all. Of your inner life, my dear, we know nothing beyond such scraps as we can glean in spite of you, from little things which escape you almost before you know that you have said them."

The boy winced at this. It made him feel hot and uncomfortable all over. He knew well how careful he ought to be, and yet, do what he could, from time to time his forgetfulness of the part betrayed him into unreserve. His mother saw that he winced, and enjoyed the scratch she had given him. Had she felt less confident of victory she had better have foregone the pleasure of touching as it were the eyes at the end of the snail's horns in order to enjoy seeing the snail draw them in again —but she knew that when she had got him well down into the sofa, and held his hand, she had the enemy almost absolutely at her mercy, and could do pretty much what she liked.

"Papa does not feel," she continued, "that you love him with that fulness and unreserve which would prompt you to have no concealment from him, and to tell him everything freely and fearlessly as your most loving earthly friend next only

to your Heavenly Father. Perfect love, as we know, casteth out fear: your father loves you perfectly, my darling, but he does not feel as though you loved him perfectly in return. If you fear him it is because you do not love him as he deserves, and I know it sometimes cuts him to the very heart to think that he has earned from you a deeper and more willing sympathy than you display towards him. Oh, Ernest, Ernest, do not grieve one who is so good and noble-hearted by conduct which I can call by no other name than ingratitude."

Ernest could never stand being spoken to in this way by his mother: for he still believed that she loved him, and that he was fond of her and had a friend in her— up to a certain point. But his mother was beginning to come to the end of her tether; she had played the domestic confidence trick upon him times without number already. Over and over again had she wheedled from him all she wanted to know, and afterwards got him into the most horrible scrape by telling the whole to Theobald. Ernest had remonstrated more than once upon these occasions, and had pointed out to his mother how disastrous to him his confidences had been, but Christina had always joined issue with him and showed him in the clearest possible manner that in each case she had been right, and that he could not reasonably complain. Generally it was her conscience that forbade her to be silent, and against this there was no appeal, for we are all bound to follow the dictates of our conscience. Ernest used to have to recite a hymn about conscience. It was to the effect that if you did not pay attention to its voice it would soon leave off speaking. "My mamma's conscience has not left off speaking," said Ernest to one of his chums at Roughborough; "it's always jabbering."

When a boy has once spoken so disrespectfully as this about his mother's conscience it is practically all over between him and her. Ernest, through sheer force of habit, of the sofa, and of the return of the associated ideas, was still so moved by the siren's voice as to yearn to sail towards her, and fling himself into her arms, but it would not do; there were other associated ideas that returned also, and the mangled bones of too many murdered confessions were lying whitening round the skirts of his mother's dress, to allow him by any possibility to trust her further. So he hung his head and looked sheepish, but kept his own counsel.

"I see, my dearest," continued his mother, "either that I am mistaken, and that there is nothing on your mind, or that you will not unburden yourself to me: but, oh, Ernest, tell me at least this much; is there nothing that you repent of, nothing which makes you unhappy in connection with that miserable girl Ellen?"

Ernest's heart failed him. "I am a dead boy now," he said to himself. He had not the faintest conception what his mother was driving at, and thought she suspected about the watch; but he held his ground.

I do not believe he was much more of a coward than his neighbours, only he did not know that all sensible people are cowards when they are off their beat, or when they think they are going to be roughly handled. I believe that if the truth were known, it would be found that even the valiant St. Michael himself tried hard to shirk his famous combat with the dragon; he pretended not to see all sorts of misconduct on the dragon's part; shut his eyes to the eating up of I do not know how many hundreds of men, women and children whom he had promised to protect; allowed himself to be publicly insulted a dozen times over without resenting it; and in the end, when even an angel could stand it no longer, he shilly-shallied and temporised an unconscionable time before he would fix the day and hour for the encounter. As for the actual combat it was much such another *wurra-wurra* as Mrs. Allaby had had with the young man who had in the end mar-

ried her eldest daughter, till after a time, behold, there was the dragon lying dead, while he was himself alive and not very seriously hurt after all.

"I do not know what you mean, mamma," exclaimed Ernest anxiously and more or less hurriedly. His mother construed his manner into indignation at being suspected, and being rather frightened herself she turned tail and scuttled off as fast as her tongue could carry her.

"Oh!" she said, "I see by your tone that you are innocent! Oh! oh! how I thank my heavenly Father for this; may He for His dear Son's sake keep you always pure. Your father, my dear"—(here she spoke hurriedly but gave him a searching look) "was as pure as a spotless angel when he came to me. Like him, always be self-denying, truly truthful both in word and deed, never forgetful whose son and grandson you are, nor of the name we gave you, of the sacred stream in whose waters your sins were washed out of you through the blood and blessing of Christ," etc.

But Ernest cut this—I will not say short—but a great deal shorter than it would have been if Christina had had her say out, by extricating himself from his mamma's embrace and showing a clean pair of heels. As he got near the purlieus of the kitchen (where he was more at ease) he heard his father calling for his mother, and again his guilty conscience rose against him. "He has found all out now," it cried, "and he is going to tell mamma—this time I am done for." But there was nothing in it; his father only wanted the key of the cellaret. Then Ernest slunk off into a coppice or spinney behind the Rectory paddock, and consoled himself with a pipe of tobacco. Here in the wood with the summer sun streaming through the trees and a book and his pipe the boy forgot his cares and had an interval of that rest without which I verily believe his life would have been insupportable.

47 | MATERNAL OVERPROTECTION

DAVID M. LEVY

*This study of "spoiled" children and their long-suffering parents reveals
that both are trapped by circumstances in narrowing, mutually
coercive, exasperating servitude. Levy observes the relationships of
twenty overprotected children to their overprotecting parents,
to school, and to other children; he also describes the relationships of
the parents to each other and discusses the later adjustments
of these children to adult life.*

The most frequent clinical type of maternal overprotection . . . is found in the group in which the overprotection masks or is compensatory to a strong rejection. It will be considered separately.

There remain a number of mild and mixed forms that require description. Early overprotection followed by rejection is an example. Theoretically, a frank rejection of a child may be followed by "pure" overprotection. . . . A mother absorbed in a first child and indifferent to the second may, after a dangerous illness of the second child has necessitated much nursing care on her part, shift about in her attitudes. Such cases are of the guilt-overprotection form. There are children, also, who experience temporary periods of overprotection, or alternating periods of overprotection and rejection, or mixtures of overprotection and severity. In this connection, those children also should be included who are seen by their mothers for brief periods of time during the day, yet, in the time available, receive strongly overprotective care. They are often children of professional women. The latter act as though they must make up for their hours of absence from the child through the intensity of their devotion in every minute of contact.

"Mild" maternal overprotection is presumably an attenuated form and very

common. A quantitative distribution of overprotective manifestations would show, no doubt, a graduated progressive series. In the mild forms, however, many extraneous problems complicate evaluation and selection. Since we are dealing with mothers of various cultural backgrounds and of different economic and social groups, patterns of maternal behavior with children, correctly estimated as overprotective in one group, may in another group be typical phenomena. Breast feeding over a period of two years, for example, may be a symptom of overprotection. On the other hand, it may be typical behavior in certain cultural groups.

. . . . .

A clinical classification of overprotection includes 1. *pure*, 2. *guilt*, 3. *mixed*, 4. *mild*, and 5. *nonmaternal* forms.

Here are three examples of Group I, the "pure" form:

Case 1 (Male, 8 Years)

EXCESSIVE CONTACT | When he was an infant, mother could never leave him for an instant. When he was two years old, she had moods of despondency because she could not get away from him. She feels worried and unhappy when patient is out of her sight. Has been sleeping with him the past six months because he has called her. Lies down with him at night. Extra nursing care has been required because of his frequent colds. Mother says they are attached together like Siamese twins.

Excerpts reprinted from *Maternal Overprotection* (New York: Columbia University Press, 1943), by permission of the publisher.

PROLONGATION OF INFANTILE CARE | Mother dresses him every day (age 8), takes him to school every morning and calls for him every afternoon. When at school in the morning she pays the waiter for his lunch and tells waiter what to give him. Breast fed 13 months. Mother fed him the first five years. Mother still goes to the bathroom with him and waits for him. Mother insists on holding his hand when they walk together. Resents his walking alone.

PREVENTION OF INDEPENDENT BEHAVIOR | He has one friend whom mother takes him to see every two weeks. Mother does not allow him to help in housework for fear he'll fall and break a dish, etc.

MATERNAL CONTROL | Mother must have a light burning for him until he falls asleep. He goes to bed at 10 P. M. Mother always gives in to him; does everything for him; is dominated by him. He spits at her and strikes her.

. . . . .

Case 5 (Male, 13 Years)

EXCESSIVE CONTACT | Mother has slept with him the past three years. Up to age 7, she never let him go out with any adult (even father) except herself.

PROLONGATION OF INFANTILE CARE | When the patient is disobedient she puts him to bed in the afternoon, even now. She still prepares special food for him when he refuses to eat. She still sits by and coaxes.

PREVENTION OF INDEPENDENT BEHAVIOR | Mother delayed his schooling until he was seven because she did not like him to leave her. She blocks the plan of sending him to boarding school. She kept him from having friends or learning bad things from other children. When he was sent to camp at 14, the mother visited him on the second day, found that his feet were wet and took him home.

MATERNAL CONTROL | General obedient, submissive response to maternal domination. Uses aggressive methods to maintain his dependency on the mother, insisting she walk to school with him, et cetera.

. . . . .

Case 10 (Male, 12 Years)

EXCESSIVE CONTACT | There is frequent kissing and fondling. The mother practically never let him alone during infancy. She kept him away from all but a few adults because she was afraid of infection. Patient still sleeps with the mother when father is out of town (continued to age 13).

PROLONGATION OF INFANTILE CARE | Patient was breast fed 12 months. Mother still waits on him, gets water for him, butters his bread, etc.

PREVENTION OF INDEPENDENT BEHAVIOR | Mother has prevented his bicycling, making his own friends, and has generally prevented the development of responsibility.

MATERNAL CONTROL | The patient is disrespectful and impudent to the parents. He constantly demands mother's service, and had a temper tantrum at the age of twelve because she didn't butter his bread for him. He resents giving up his chair for mother. He leaves the table and refuses to eat when he doesn't get the biggest piece.

. . . . .

PLAYMATES

A tabulation of the number of playmates of children of overprotecting, rejecting and "other" mothers has been made. Divided into groups of "none or one" and "few or many," the table shows a trend of increasing number of playmates as we go from the "over-protecting" mothers, to "rejecting," and to "neither."

A study was also made to determine if there is a relationship between the number of companions of parents and children. The study revealed a distinct tendency towards increase in number of companions of the child with increase in the number of social contacts of the parents.

The findings are consistent also with the observation that in case of pure overprotection the mother narrows down her social life to the child.

EXCESS OF CONTACT

Excessive contact is manifested in continuous companionship of mother and child, prolonged nursing care, excessive fondling, and sleeping with the mother long past infancy. The twenty "pure" cases (Group I) contained six boys who slept with their mothers long past infancy, three of them during adolescence. Of the latter, two showed overt evidence of direct sexual response or conflict, though none showed overt incestuous behavior. Of the former, one showed active incestuous behavior. In the remaining fourteen cases of Group I, no overt sexual response to the mother was revealed.

INFANTILIZATION

. . . . .

The data of infantilization concern feeding, dressing, bathing, washing, punishing and various kinds of behavior typical for children of younger years. Glaring examples are shown by a mother who helps her thirteen-year-old son dress; and by another who still butters bread and gets water for a twelve-year-old; by another who punishes a thirteen-year-old son by putting him to bed in the afternoon. Such examples are typical of many others illustrating the behavior of mothers who have prolonged the infantile method of handling into the older years.

Mothers in Group I demonstrate singly or in combination three types of infantilizing activity. Commonest is the continuation of breast feeding, a prolongation of the mother-infant relationship. Five mothers showed this type of infantilization with little or no evidence of the other forms. Six mothers gave evidence of prolonged breast feeding in combination with other forms.

The other two types of infantilization show a difference of degree, in which the child has a greater measure of control. A mother may wait on her child "hand and foot," yet may allow him to bathe and dress himself. In the gradual relinquishing of infantile care, breast feeding first gives way, then bodily care, and finally, the "waiting on" the child for services he can perform himself. The last form of infantilization includes services that adults may perform for each other, services that some of our overprotected children demand. Yet the same children may prevent the mother's insistent efforts to continue bathing and dressing them.

MATERNAL CONTROL

. . . . .

Under *maternal control* are included all available data of maternal discipline. Such control in Group I mothers is manifested by exaggerations of normal maternal domination or indulgence of the child, and described as overdomination and overindulgence.

Overindulgence consists in yielding to wishes or actions of a child or submitting to his demands to an extent not tolerated by most parents. Overindulgence appears in active form through willing catering to the child's whims or wishes, and in passive form through surrender to the child's demands. Overindulgence in its extreme form would be manifested by complete maternal surrender to the child.

Both phases of maternal activity in the control of children can be studied most conveniently in an indirect way; *i.e.*, by collection of data on the response of children in this phase of maternal overprotection. Since children of overindulgent mothers display various rebellious symptoms disturbing to parents, they are more likely to be referred for treatment than children of overdominating mothers, since the latter are obedient and submissive.

In the Group I cases, nine children appear to be overdisciplined. All but one have been infantilized also to some degree. The absence of infantilization in the one case leads to a doubt of its proper inclusion in a group of so-called "pure" cases, since instances of maternal overdomination, without other evidence of overprotection, represent an essentially different type of mother-child relationship.

The activity of the child in initiating maternal overprotection appears more striking in the overindulgent than in any other phase of overprotection.

Eleven of the twenty Group I mothers who overindulge show numerous instances of submission to the tyranny of infantile demands. . . . In spite of long citations of what they had to endure, only three of the eleven overindulgent mothers sought help directly.

THE MOTHER-FATHER RELATIONSHIPS

As potent sources of increased maternal longing for a child, varieties of experience threatening the possibility of successful termination of pregnancy were gathered from the records of the overprotecting mothers. Of the 20, 13 yielded such instances: long periods of sterility (5); death of offspring (3); spontaneous miscarriages (3); and serious complications of pregnancy (3), preceding the birth of the patient.

An attempt was made to determine from available data whether unconscious wishes for the state of sterility operated in the instances given. It appeared likely

in one case. The question was considered as to whether overprotection of any variety must be considered a neurosis, a compensatory reaction to unconscious hostility to the child, based on feelings of guilt and resembling obsessional neurosis. It was argued that such a position would refute the possibility of a normal maternal response, since if a normal response may be assumed, its increase in the presence of stronger stimuli must also be assumed.

Sixteen instances of sexual maladjustment were found in the group, a relatively high frequency as compared with check groups. In itself the difficulty was regarded as a strengthening factor of the overprotection, by the method of simple compensatory increase in mother love through blocking other channels of expression.

Fifteen instances were found in which there was little social life in common among the parents of the overprotected child. Of the five remaining cases in which there was a good general social relationship, two were sexually incompatible. The severe curtailment in mutual social activity, as in the mother's own general activity, was determined in most instances primarily by the mother-child relationship. Where the mother's social life was limited almost entirely to the child, the overprotecting data appeared especially striking with regard to infantilization and to attempts to prevent the child from making friends with other children.

Of the 20 overprotecting mothers, severe privation of parental love in their childhood was found in 16. Of these the death of one or both parents occurred in nine. Of the four cases in which an affectionate relationship with parents was recorded, there was evidence of some impoverishment of affection in terms of contact in three. The privation of all those positive feelings implicit in parental love, called "affect hunger," was regarded as an important consideration in understanding the overprotecting relationship, since the child could be utilized as a means of satisfying the abnormal craving for love resulting from affect hunger.

All but two of the 20 overprotecting mothers (Group I) were responsible, stable, and aggressive. The responsible attitude was manifested in stability of work, measured by steadiness of employment, and also in active helping out. The active or aggressive feature of the responsible behavior was regarded as a distinctly maternal type of behavior; it characterized the lives of 18 of the 20 overprotecting mothers since childhood.

Though evidence of thwarted ambitions for a career occurred in 12 instances in the group, the number checked by studies of contrast groups was not considered, in itself, significant.

. . . . .

As in humans, variations in the component maternal drives occur in animals, even in virgin rats, and are measurable. They show also a high degree of plasticity in the presence of external stimuli, in fact, to such a degree that, for example, the lactation period in the rat has been prolonged twenty times the normal by supplying the mother with successive litters of young. Two instances of maternal overprotection in monkeys were cited.

. . . . .

The fathers of the overprotected children studied were, in general, submissive, stable husbands and providers who played little or no authoritative role in the lives of their children. They made a ready adjustment to the maternal monopoly of the child, some adding to the infantilizing care (three cases). Twelve, in all, maintained an affectionate relationship with the child, five showed little or no affection, and the remaining three were out of contact due to divorce, desertion, and absence from the home.

A consistent pattern of submissive adaptation was revealed in the backgrounds of the fathers. Seven were obedient and favorite children, five were obedient sons of dominating mothers, and three, obedient sons of dominating fathers. Of the 18 fathers interviewed, there was only one instance in which evidence of difficulty as a husband was due to aggressive behavior towards the wife. With two exceptions, all the fathers in the group were stable and responsible workers. The group of parents represent a logical choice of dominating maternal women and submissive responsible men.

The usual patterns of interfering relatives were found in the group. In five cases their activities were important in the life of the child, and consisted chiefly in adding to the indulgence of the mother, and weakening her discipline.

. . . . .

BEHAVIOR OF THE OVERPROTECTED

The behavior of the indulged overprotected children was featured by disobedience, impudence, tantrums, excessive demands, and varying degrees of tyrannical behavior. The characteristics described were thought to represent accelerated growth of the aggressive components of the personality, and related directly to maternal indulgence. Limitations in the production of extreme tyrannical and possessive behavior at home was explained by varying degrees of parental modification, and external factors.

Most of the indulged overprotected children presented no special problems in school adjustment. This discrepancy between behavior at home and at school was explained by an exceptional and disciplinary attitude towards schoolwork on the part of the mothers; by satisfactions in the classroom related to high intelligence, verbal skill, and help through coaching on the part of the children; also, possibly, to their fear of the school group and a gratification in playing an obedient role. In any event, the adjustment of highly indulged children to classroom discipline indicates a high degree of flexibility in their personalities. When difficulties in classroom behavior occurred, they were consistent with the type of difficulty manifested at home.

Three boys who were disciplinary problems in the classroom were less intelligent than the others and their mothers less concerned about schoolwork.

In contrast with the indulged group, the dominated group responded well to the requirements of classroom behavior in every instance, regardless of I.Q. or of school success.

In all instances but one, difficulties in making friendships with other children occurred. The aggressive children showed, with one exception, "domination" or egocentric difficulties, that is, bossy, selfish, show-off, or cocky behavior. The submissive children showed in all cases but one timidity and withdrawal. There was a remarkable similarity of all the children's difficulty in relationship with their mothers and other children.

Successful adjustment of the indulged overprotected child to camp, as to school, would indicate that his difficulty with playmates could be improved, despite maternal overprotection, if opportunity were afforded for early social experience with children. Difficulties in making friendships were attributed to paucity of contact with children in the preschool age and lack of skill in play and sports, besides the problems inherent in the mother-child relationship. Follow-up studies indicated improvement in this regard during adolescence.

Some form of overt sexual behavior in childhood was noted in six instances, all in the indulged group. No problem in sex abnormality was present. The entire group showed nothing unusual in the frequency or form of masturbation.

Despite the very close attachment, including six cases in which children slept with their mothers long past infancy, follow-up studies into late adolescence or adult life failed to reveal an instance of sex abnormality. The theoretical aspect of this finding was discussed and the inference drawn that in maternal indulgent overprotection, the development of heterosexual behavior was hastened rather than delayed, because of lessened inhibitions.

The main outside interest of the overprotected group consisted in reading. There was a notable lack of interest in sports.

Feeding problems occurred in 12 of the 20 cases. The usual variety was manifested; in the form of bad table manners, refusal to eat on schedule, insistence on being fed or coaxed, finickiness, and refusal to eat certain foods. There was no instance of inappetence. Practically all the indulged overprotected were included in this group. The problems were consistent with maternal indulgence in regard to the feeding.

Nothing unusual was found in regard to sleeping difficulties. Problems related to sleep were in the form of refusal to go to bed, on time or without mother's company. Seven of the eight children who manifested such behavior were in the indulged overprotected group.

No problems in soiling occurred. There were but two cases of enuresis. The number was much less frequent than in other Institute cases. This difference was explained by the greater care exerted by overprotecting mothers. The assumption that the vast majority of problems in enuresis are originally due to neglect in training was supported by special data.

Information regarding cleanliness and care of possessions was available for 11 cases. The four who were very careless in this regard were all in the indulged group. Those noted as neat and careful were all in the dominated group.

Physical examinations revealed that the group of 20 overprotected children was taller and heavier than other groups, in keeping with the high degree of maternal care. Of the group, two only may be regarded as quite obese.

Errors of refraction were found in 11 cases. The inference that this relatively large number may have been due to excessive reading could not be determined, through lack of comparable data.

Treatment of organic difficulties seemed clearly related to improvement of social adjustment in two cases. In two others, organic factors were apparently reinforcing to the maternal over-protection. In three cases, findings during the physical examination served to overcome maternal apprehension. It was followed in one case by withdrawal of interest in the entire study.

In the cases presented, maternal over-protection appeared to be related directly to increased breast feeding, early bladder control, frequency of tonsillectomy, good nutrition, and probably obesity. It appeared to be related, indirectly, to correction of errors of visual refraction.

Manifestations of personality difficulties were revealed during the physical examination in 14 of the 20 cases. They were seen chiefly in the form of dependency on the mother, sensitivity, shyness, and bids for the examiner's attention.

48 | A STUDY OF PREJUDICE IN CHILDREN

ELSE FRENKEL-BRUNSWIK

Persons in authority both comfort and frustrate us from our first moments of life. Each person works out some pattern of adjustment to this authority. Some spend all their lives in revolt while others cling to authority persons. The latter attempt to produce over and over again relationships in which there is a strong, punitive, cold authority-person whose word is law. Such persons are called "authoritarian." They prefer dominator-submitter, leader-follower relationships rather than relationships in which all are equal; they want to look up to people or down on them.

The preference of many people for relationships which allow them to be dependent rather than self-reliant—to let others make their decisions—is reflected in attitudes such as those of many Americans at election time. "My vote means nothing," they say, and they do not go to the polls. Apparently, their natural impulses to learn, to strive, and to participate in the events of democratic life have been beaten down, twisted, and broken by autocratic parents, friends, teachers, and employers.

This history-making article describes the feelings of prejudiced children toward their parents and toward their upbringings. A considerable amount of research has shown that the less educated express more prejudice than those with more schooling; moreover, persons in the lower socio-economic classes—perhaps because theirs is a more threatened position without security—have been shown to be more authoritarian than middle-class individuals.

A RESEARCH PROJECT ON ETHNIC PREJUDICE IN CHILDREN AND ADOLESCENTS

. . . A research project designed to throw light on the determinants of susceptibility to racial or ethnic prejudice and allied forms of undemocratic opinions and attitudes in children is being conducted at the Institute of Child Welfare of the University of California in Berkeley.

The age levels studied range from eleven to sixteen. The source of our present report includes attitude and personality tests as well as interviews with children and their parents. A total of about 1,500 boys and girls of varied socio-economic background was studied, and 120 of those found extremely prejudiced or unprejudiced were interviewed according to a schedule prepared in advance. The parents of the children interviewed were visited and likewise interviewed.

In general, the results indicate that already at these age levels children's reactions to statements about men and society as well as their spontaneous formulations about these topics form a more or less consistent pattern. This pattern, in turn, seems to be related to certain personality features of the child. Though there can be little doubt about the existence of these relationships, there is evidence that they are not as consistent and rigid as those found with adults in an earlier, similarly conceived Public Opinion Study, also conducted in Berkeley.

We shall point out the differences in the personalities of the ethnically prejudiced and unprejudiced child. It will turn out that such prejudice is but one aspect of a broader pattern of attitudes. At the same time, we shall try to discover areas of possible modifiability in the personality structure of the prejudiced child. As a first

Reprinted from *Human Relations*, I, No. 3 (1948), 295–306, by permission of the Executor of the Estate of Else Frenkel-Brunswik, and the publisher.

step, a description will be given of the social and political beliefs of such children. Next, we shall present a composite picture of their personality structure. An attempt will be made to study their social opinions and attitudes in relation to their basic personality needs.

ESTABLISHMENT AND TESTING OF OPPOSITE EXTREMES

The initial classification of subjects was made on the basis of responses to a series of about fifty slogans of racial prejudice or tolerance as well as statements pertaining to more general social attitudes. A prejudice scale was thus constructed with items regarding the attitude of children toward five minority groups: Jews, Negroes, Japanese, Mexicans, and "outgroups" in general. It proceeds along established lines in that it covers such situations as eating in the same restaurant, living in the same neighborhood, participating at the same social affairs, letting in or keeping people out of the country, and stereotypical accusations of minority members such as cruelty of the Japanese, laziness of the Negroes, or radicalism and moneymindedness of the Jews.

It was found that some of the children tend to reveal a stereotyped and rigid glorification of their own group and an aggressive rejection of outgroups and foreign countries. The scale yielded split-half correlations of from .82 to .90 (uncorrected for length of test), indicating that ethnic prejudice is a consistent and firmly established pattern not later than at the earliest of the age levels studied. In the present paper, the term "unprejudiced" (or "liberal") refers to those 25 per cent of the children who were found to be in greatest agreement with tolerant statements, whereas those in the opposite extreme quartile will be called "prejudiced" or "ethnocentric." The last two terms especially are to be understood to refer not only to racial or ethnic prejudice in the narrower sense of the word, but to a certain extent also to include its usual accompaniments, such as clannishness or national chauvinism and even glorification of family and self, in correspondence with the varying scope of what is being experienced as "ingroup" in any given context.

The disjunctive statements made in this paper concerning other attitudes or personality traits found predominantly in one or the other of the two extreme groups are all based on quantitative material gained from other tests or from the interviews. The tests involved were constructed on the basis of initial clinical data gathered from children with extreme standing on the prejudice scale. Aside from a separate scale for more general social attitudes, there was a personality test containing about 150 items. The interviews were evaluated in terms of a system of categories which had proved themselves to be especially relevant in this context. Statistical significance (often at as high a level as 1 per cent or better) is established for all differences referred to in this paper between the two extreme groups, with respect to test items and in most cases also with respect to overall interview ratings. Quotations of answers to interview questions are added informally by way of illustration. It must also be kept in mind that the results presented here are limited to extremes only. Furthermore, they may well be less pronounced in cultures or subcultures in which the choice between alternative ideologies of the type involved here is less clearcut.

In addition to revealing prejudice toward specific ethnic groups, the children classified as ethnocentric are in marked disagreement with such more general statements, also included in the defining scale, as the following:

Different races and religions would get along better if they visited each other and shared things.

America is a lot better off because of the foreign races that live here.

The liberal children endorse most of such statements with a considerable approximation to unanimity.

GENERAL SOCIAL ATTITUDES OF PREJUDICED AND UNPREJUDICED CHILDREN

Along similar lines are the children's spontaneous reactions in the interviews to the question: "What is America's biggest problem today?" The liberal children can more readily remove themselves from their immediate needs and think in terms of a far-reaching social good. Examples of the problems they list are:

". . . the starving people in Europe, because the people in our country won't think of them and they should," or,
"The atom bomb; how to do things about the atom bomb to keep peace in the world."

Ethnocentric children, on the other hand, are more concerned with things that affect their immediate welfare. They tend to give greatest prominence to such problems as:

"Taxes on everything, and the cost of living."

The question "How would you change America?" is answered similarly. Ethnocentric children tend to mention external things:

"Clean up the streets—all that garbage lying around! See that everything is in order."

Liberal children, on the other hand, tend to mention such things as:

"So the Negroes wouldn't be beaten up like they are down South," or
"We should have a world police so that there would be no more wars."

We now turn to the test intended to ascertain even broader social attitudes. In this scale, as well as in the personality scales to be discussed next, differentiations are much more clearcut at the later age levels studied. Study of the interviews suggests that this is in part due to a comprehension factor, but that there is also a genuine absence of the relationship in the younger children.

The following statements in this scale differentiate to a particularly significant degree between the prejudiced and unprejudiced children, with the prejudiced more often endorsing them:

If we keep on having labor troubles, we may have to turn the government over to a dictator who will prevent any more strikes.

It is better to have our government run by business men rather than by college professors.

The government is interfering too much with private business.

Paralleling the rejection of the outgroup is a naïve and selfish acceptance of the ingroup. Thus above age 11 approximately two-fifths of the prejudiced extreme but only a scattered few of the opposite extreme group subscribe to the following two statements:

People who do not believe that we have the best kind of government in the world should be kicked out of the country.

Refugees should be thrown out of this country so that their jobs can be given to veterans.

A particularly narrow form of ethnocentrism is revealed in the tendency, prominent in the prejudiced child, to agree with the following statement:

Only people who are like myself have a right to be happy.

The selfish orientation toward their own country and the indifference and hostility against other countries is furthermore expressed in the agreement of almost half of the ethnocentric children with the following statement:

We should not send any of our food to foreign countries, but should think of America first.

The rejection of foreign countries by the ethnocentric child, and the projection of his own hostility onto them, may be considered to contribute to his affinity toward war. Thus, our ethnocentric children subscribe almost twice as often as the liberal to the statement:

Most of the other countries of the world are really against us, but are afraid to show it.

There is, furthermore, the conviction—apparently deep-rooted in the personality structure of the prejudiced child—that wars are inevitable. Comparatively often he tends to endorse the following statement:

There will always be war, it is part of human nature.

In the interviews, where the children are able to express their opinions spontaneously, the ethnocentric children make remarks such as the following about war:

"One happens in every generation," or,
"The Bible says there will always be wars," or;
"Sure, we will have another war. Wars never end."

ANTI-WEAKNESS ATTITUDE OF THE PREJUDICED CHILD

The aggression of the ethnocentric children is not limited to minority groups and other countries but is part of a much more generalized rejection of all that is weak or different. Statements from additional scales help to assess such more general personality traits. Thus the prejudiced child agrees more often than the unprejudiced with the statement:

The world would be perfect if we put on a desert island all of the weak, crooked and feeble-minded people.

It is especially the prejudiced girl who tends to disagree with the following statement:

It is interesting to be friends with someone who thinks or feels differently from the way you do.

The ingroup feeling is clearly expressed by her tendency to endorse the following statement:

Play fair with your own gang, and let the other kids look out for themselves.

DICHOTOMY OF SEX ROLES

Ethnocentric children tend to conceive of the other sex as outgroup, and tend toward segregation from, and resentment against, the other sex. Associations of masculinity vs. femininity with strength vs. weakness need no further elaboration.

Around adolescence, the prejudiced of both sexes tend to agree with the statement:

Girls should only learn things that are useful around the house.

On the whole, ethnocentric children tend toward a rigid, dichotomizing conception of sex roles, being intolerant of passive or feminine manifestations in boys and masculine or tomboyish manifestations in girls. Thus an ethnocentric girl, asked how girls should act around boys, answers:

"Act like a lady, not like a bunch of hoodlums. Girls should not ask boys to date. It's not lady-like."

Two of the liberal boys reply to the same question as follows:

"It depends on their age; the girls should not be so afraid of the boys and not be shy," and,
"Talk about the things you like to talk about, about the same as another boy would."

Asked what is the worst occupation for a woman, one of the ethnocentric boys answers:

"To earn her own living, usually the man does that."

On the other hand, a boy low on ethnocentrism answers to the same question

"What she doesn't like to do."

The intolerance the ethnocentric child tends to show toward manifestations of the opposite sex in himself or in others makes for bad heterosexual adjustment, as was also found in the study of adults. The rigid and exaggerated conception of masculinity and femininity further tends to lead to a strained relation to one's own sex role. Thus the few children who, in reaction to some indirect questions, show envy of the role of the other sex, are ethnocentric.

The liberal child, on the other hand, tends, as does the liberal adult, to have a more flexible conception of the sex roles as well as to face conflicts in this direction more openly. Boys in this group show less repression of feminine, girls less repression of masculine trends. At the same time there is on the whole a better heterosexual development and less rejection of the opposite sex. Tolerance toward the other sex and the equalitarian relationship between the two sexes seems to be an important basis for tolerance in general and thus should be fostered by coeducational measures. This is one of the places where thinking in dichotomies has to be broken down.

POWER AND MONEY

The contempt the ethnocentric child has for the weak is related to his admiration of the strong, tough, and powerful, *per se.* He tends to disagree with the statement:

Weak people deserve consideration; the world should not belong to the strong only.

And he relatively often agrees with the statements:

Might makes right; the strong win out in the end.
A person who wants to be a man should seek power.

The latter statement shows the ideal aspired to by the typical ethnocentric boy and demanded in men by the typical ethnocentric girl. This pseudo-masculine ideal often prevents a humanitarian outlook which is sometimes considered as soft and "sissified." The fear of weakness is expressed in the tendency of the ethnocentric boy to agree with a statement like:

If a person does not watch out somebody will make a sucker out of him.

In the same context belongs the orientation toward money as a means of obtaining power, material benefits, and sometimes even friends. In the interviews of prejudiced children appear such statements as the following:

"It means something if you want to buy a house or a car or a fur coat for your wife. No dollar, no friend; have a dollar, got a friend."

The over-libidinization of money leads not only to an exaggeration of its importance but also to an unrealistic fear of it as something evil. The following is typical of the statements made by some of the ethnocentric children:

"It helps make enemies. Money is the root of all evil, they say."

AMBIVALENT SUBMISSION TO PARENTS AND TEACHERS

The admiration the ethnocentric child tends to have for success, power, and prestige may be assumed to result from submission to authority based on his fear of punishment and retaliation. The originally forced submission to parental authority apparently leads to a continued demand for autocratic leadership, strict discipline and punishment, as exercised not only by parents but also by parent substitutes. Thus ethnocentric children, especially girls, tend to agree more often than liberal ones with the statements

Teachers should tell children what to do and not try to find out what the children want.

It would be better if teachers would be more strict.

This attitude is also mirrored in their spontaneous statements made in the interviews while talking about parents and teachers. They tend to refer to the authoritarian aspects of the parent-child relationship whereas liberal children tend to emphasize the cooperative aspects of this relationship.

Though there tends to be a surface submission to authority in the ethnocentric, there is often, at the same time, an underlying resentment against authority. Apparently, this resentment is repressed for two reasons: first, because of a fear of retaliation for any open expression of resentment; and second, because of a fear of being deprived of the material benefits which persons in authority can give, and upon which the typical prejudiced child seems especially dependent. For the ethnocentric more than for the liberal, parents and other adults are conceived of as the deliverers of goods.

The following quotations illustrate the attitude of the ethnocentric child toward the parents as well as toward teachers. Asked to describe the perfect father, one of the boys in this group says:

"Does not give you everything you want, isn't very strict with you, doesn't let you do the outrageous things that you sometimes want to."

Typical of these children is the use of the negative in the characterization of the perfect parent and the references to the punitive and restrictive aspects. Others of these boys say about the perfect father:

"He spanks you when you are bad and doesn't give you too much money,"

or;

"When you ask for something he ought not to give it to you right away. Not soft on you, strict."

Similar is the description of the perfect teacher by another ethnocentric boy:

"She is strict, treats all children the same, won't take any nonsense of them, keeps them organized in the playground, in class, in lines."

About teachers who are not liked an ethnocentric boy says:

"Those who tell you in a nice way instead of being strict and they don't make you mind."

The same group of children when asked how they would like to change their father sometimes reveal resentment and feelings of being deprived and victimized. One of the ethnocentric boys says:

"He wouldn't smoke a pipe, would not eat too much, wouldn't take all the food away from his son."

Along the same lines is the answer of an ethnocentric boy to the question, "For what should the hardest punishment be administered?";

"Should be for talking back to parents, it should be a whipping."

One of the girls in this group says:

"Naturally for murder, the next is for not paying attention to her mother and father. She should be sent to a juvenile home for not paying attention to her parents."

Another ethnocentric boy asks for punishment too:

"Talking back, not minding, for example, if you are supposed to saw a certain amount of wood in one hour and don't do it you should be punished for it."

Methodical clinical ratings of the interviews confirm the impressions gained from these quotations. The ethnocentric children tend to think in the category of strictness and harshness when telling about their fathers, the liberal children tend to think primarily in terms of companionship. The ratings also seem to indicate that ethnocentric children tend to complain more about neglect by their fathers. The interview ratings bear out the fearful submission to harsh punishment on the part

of the typical ethnocentric child and the ability of the typical liberal child to assimilate punishment which is explained to them and for which their understanding is thus assured. Fear and dependency not only seem to prevent the ethnocentric child from any conscious criticism of the parents but even lead to an acceptance of punishment and to an "identification with the aggressor." The fact that the negative feelings against the parents have to be excluded from consciousness may be considered as contributing to the general lack of insight, rigidity of defense, and "narrowness of the ego." Since the unprejudiced child as a rule does not seem to have had to submit to stern authority in childhood (according to the interviews at least), he can afford in his later life not to long for strong authority, nor does he need to assert his strength against those who are weaker. The "anti-weakness" attitude referred to above seems thus to be directly related to the fearful submission to authority.

PARENTS' CONCERN WITH SOCIAL STATUS, RIGID RULES AND DISCIPLINE

The hypothesis may be offered that it is this repressed resentment toward authority which is displaced upon socially inferior and foreign groups. As may be seen from the interviews with the parents, the liberal child, in contrast to the ethnocentric child, is more likely to be treated as an equal and to be given the opportunity to express feelings of rebellion or disagreement. He thus learns at home the equalitarian and individualized approach to people, as the ethnocentric child learns the authoritarian and hierarchical way of thinking. Interviews with parents of ethnocentric children show an exaggerated social status-concern. This may well be assumed to be the basis of a rigid and externalized set of values. What is socially accepted and what is helpful in the climbing of the social ladder is considered good, and what deviates, what is different, and what is socially inferior is considered bad.

The parents of the ethnocentric children are often socially marginal. The less they can accept their marginality, the more urgent becomes the wish to belong to the privileged groups. This leads to the development of a kind of collective ego which is very different from genuine group identification and which must be assumed to contribute to ethnocentrism. With this narrow and steep path in mind such parents are likely to be intolerant of any manifestation on the part of the children which seems to deter from, or to oppose, the goal decided upon. The more urgent the social needs of the parents, the more they are apt to view the child's behavior in terms of their own instead of the child's needs. Since the values of the parents are outside the children's scope, yet are rigorously enforced, only a superficial identification with the parents and society can be achieved. The suppressed instinctive and hostile tendencies are apt to become diffuse and depersonalized and to lead an independent, autonomous life. In line with this the overall clinical ratings seem to indicate the more diffuse and explosive nature of the aggression of ethnocentric children, as compared with milder and more ego-acceptable forms of aggression in the typical liberal child. Thus fascism and war must have a special appeal to ethnocentric children and adults, who expect liberation of their instincts in combination with approval by authorities.

MORALISM AND CONFORMITY

The influence of the parents must be considered at least a contributing factor to the tendency, observed in the ethnocentric child, to be more concerned with status values than are liberal children. He expects—and gives—social approval on the basis of external moral values, including cleanliness, politeness, and the like. He condemns others for their nonconformity to such values, conformity being an all-or-none affair. The functioning of his superego is mainly directed toward punishment, condemnation, and exclusion of others, mirroring thus the type of discipline to which he was exposed. Interview ratings show a tendency toward more moralistic condemnation on the part of the prejudiced child and greater permissiveness toward people in general on the part of the unprejudiced.

The trend to conformity of the ethnocentric child is expressed in his greater readiness to agree with the following statements:

There is only one right way to do anything.
Appearances are usually the best test.
One should avoid doing things in public which seem wrong to others even though one knows that these things are really all right.

Politeness, cleanliness, good manners appear again and again among the requirements of prejudiced children, especially the girls, for a perfect boy or perfect girl. Interview ratings indicate that ethnocentric children tend to mention in this connection purity, cleanliness and what corresponds to a conventional conception of good personality, whereas the liberal children tend to mention companionship and fun.

In the light of what has been said before about the attitude of the typical ethnocentric child toward parents, we may assume that the conformity to approved social values is based on fear of retaliation by society for disobedience rather than on a real incorporation of those values. In order to conform, he demands a set of inflexible rules which he can follow, and he is most at ease when he can categorize and make value judgments in terms of good or bad.

INTOLERANCE OF AMBIGUITIES

Analysis of the interviews indicates that this inflexibility of the ethnocentric child is part of a broader texture of rigidity and incapacity to face ambiguous situations. Intolerance of ambiguity has been found above in his conception of the parent-child relationship and in his conception of the sex roles. It is also present in the organization of the perceptual and cognitive field.

That this rigidity represents a more generalized approach to the solving of problems even in fields where there is no social or emotional involvement has been experimentally demonstrated by Rokeach. In solving arithmetic problems ethnocentric children show greater resistance to changing a given set which interferes with the direct and simple solution of a new task. Thus even in children rigidity tends to be a pervasive trait. It must be added that it is rigidity in thinking that is related to ethnocentrism, and not intelligence, *per se*; the IQ was found to be only very slightly (negatively) correlated with ethnocentrism.

Our interpretation then could be that ideas and tendencies which are nonconforming and which do not agree with rigid, simple and prescribed solutions (such as submission to the strong) have to be repressed and displaced. When displaced into the social sphere, this is expressed in an overly moralizing, authoritarian or generally destructive manner, and it is here that the ethnocentric child becomes a potential fascist. The choice of simple solutions apparently helps to reduce some of the repressed anxieties. These anxieties are often more directly expressed in the liberal child, since he does not tend as much to deny possible weakness or shortcomings in himself and his group as does the ethnocentric child.

CATASTROPHIC CONCEPTION OF THE WORLD

The anxieties and insecurities of the ethnocentric child are expressed more indirectly, e.g., in a greater readiness to conceive of dangers and catastrophes in the outside world, to feel helplessly exposed to external powers and to subscribe to bizarre and superstitious statements. Thus the ethnocentric child (as also in this instance the ethnocentric adult) relatively often tends to answer in the affirmative to the following three statements:

Some day a flood or earthquake will destroy everybody in the whole world.

There are more contagious diseases nowadays than ever before.

If everything would change, this world would be much better.

The tendency to wish for a diffuse and all-out change rather than for definite progress indicates how relatively poorly rooted the typical ethnocentric child is in the daily task of living and in his object relationships. Behind a rigid facade of conformity there seems to be an underlying fascination by the thought of chaos and destruction. A leader will thus be welcome who gives permission to this type of license. The ideal solution for this type of child and adult is to release what is dammed up, and thus remains unintegrated, under the protection of a leader representing the externalized superego.

We find dependency not only upon external authority but also upon inanimate external forces. Thus ethnocentric children subscribe significantly more often to such superstitious statements as:

The position of the stars at the time of your birth tells your character and personality.

It is really true that a black cat crossing your path will bring bad luck.

You can protect yourself from bad luck by carrying a charm or good luck piece.

It seems to be important for the typical ethnocentric child to use devices by which he can get evil dangerous forces to join him on his side as a substitute for an undeveloped self-reliance. In general, his attitudes tend to be less scientifically oriented and rational than that of the liberal child, and he is likely to explain events for which he has no ready understanding in terms of chance factors.

COMPARATIVE FLEXIBILITY OF ETHNOCENTRISM IN CHILDREN

As indicated above, the personality structure of the ethnocentric child is similar to that of the ethnocentric adult. But while this personality pattern seems quite firmly established in the adult, it appears in the child as incipient, or as a potential direction for development. This is indicated by correlations which are all-round lower than the analogous ones in adults. For instance, we often find in ethnocentric adults a highly opportunistic, exploitative and manipulative attitude toward other people. The ethnocentric child, however, in spite of showing tendencies in the same direction, still generally seeks more primary satisfaction of his psychological needs. Thus not only liberal minded children, but to a great extent children in general, tend to choose their friends from the standpoint of good companionship and "fun," whereas the ethnocentric adult tends to be more exclusively oriented toward status in his choice of friends. Furthermore, the ethnocentric child is more accessible to experience and reality than the ethnocentric adult who has rigidly structured his world according to his interests and desires. Finally, the child's position as a comparative underdog constitutes a possible resource for expanding the experimental basis for his sympathy for other underdogs.

In spite of all the differences between the ethnocentric and liberal child, it must be pointed out that with respect to many of the features mentioned above, such as superstition or conformity, children in general have more of a touch of the ethnocentric than of the liberal adult. In turn, the ethnocentric adult may be considered as more infantile than is the liberal adult with respect to these variables. The older the children become, the greater the differences between the ethnocentric and the liberal child. All this seems to indicate that some of the trends which are connected with ethnocentrism are natural stages of development which have to be overcome if maturity is to be reached.

OVERALL PICTURE AND CONCLUSIONS

Let us review once more the personality structure and the background of the ethnocentric child and compare this with that of the liberal child. As mentioned before, the parents of the ethnocentric child are highly concerned with status. They use more harsh and rigid forms of discipline which the child generally submits to rather than accepts or understands. Parents are seen simultaneously as the providers of one's physical needs and as capricious arbiters of punishment. On the surface the ethnocentric child tends, especially in his more general statements, to idealize his parents. There are, however, indications that the parent-child relationship is lacking in genuine affection. In many ethnocentric children underlying feelings of being victimized are revealed by specific episodes, told by the children, of neglect, rejection and unjust punishment. The pressure to conform to parental authority and its externalized social values makes it impossible for the child to integrate or to express his instinctual and hostile tendencies. This lack of integration makes for a narrow and rigid personality. Thus instinctual tendencies cannot be utilized for constructive purposes, such as genuine ability for love, or creative activities, for which both more permissiveness and more guidance on the part of the adult would be needed. Since the ethnocentric child often gets neither of these he presents the dual aspects of being too inhibited, on the one hand, and of having the tendency to join wild and rough games, on the other. The gang-oriented child may later conform to an "adult gang" without having acquired an internalized conscience which would control the direct and indirect expressions of aggression. When the inhibition is more pronounced we have to do with the conventional pattern of ethnocentrism. Whenever disinhibition dominates the picture, we have to do with the delinquent variety of the ethnocentric. Since, however, delinquency also often looms behind the surface of rigid conventionality the affinity of the two patterns should not be overlooked.

By contrast, the liberal child is more oriented toward love and less toward power than is the ethnocentric child. He is more capable of giving affection since he has received more real affection. He tends to judge people more on the basis of their intrinsic worth than does the ethnocentric child who places more emphasis on conformity to social mores. The liberal child, on the other hand, takes internal values and principles more seriously. Since he fears punishment and retaliation less than does the ethnocentric child, he is more able really to incorporate the values of society imposed upon him. The liberal child employs the help of adults in working out his problems of sex and aggression, and thus can more easily withstand hateful propaganda both in the forms of defamation of minorities and of glorification of war. By virtue of the greater integration of his instinctual life he becomes a more creative and sublimated individual. He is thus more flexible and less likely to form stereotyped opinions about others. The interview ratings point toward a better developed, more integrated and more internalized superego. The unprejudiced child seems to be able to express disagreement with, and resentment against, the parents more openly, resulting in a much greater degree of independence

from the parents and from authorities in general. At the same time there is love-oriented dependence on parents and people in general which constitutes an important source of gratification.

This is not to say that the liberal child is necessarily always socially or personally better adjusted. He has more open anxieties, more directly faced insecurities, more conflicts. For the reduction of these conflicts he does not as a rule use the simple though, in the last analysis, inappropriate and destructive methods characteristic of the ethnocentric child. It may be precisely this lack of displacement and projectivity which enables the liberal child and adult to evaluate social and political events in a more realistic and adequate fashion. This makes it less likely that the paradoxical attitudes of depersonalizing human relationships and personally tinting political and social events will be developed. Glorification of the ingroup and vilification of the outgroup in the ethnocentric child recurs in the dimensions of power-weakness, cleanliness-dirtiness, morality-immorality, conformance-difference, fairness-unfairness, etc., thus mirroring some of the basic dimensions of their outlook and personality dynamics. Above and beyond this, stereotypes provide the individual enough latitude to project onto outgroups his specific problems, such as aggression, underlying weakness, or preoccupation with sex. Different minority groups thereby seem to lend themselves to different types of accusations.

From the point of view of society as a whole, the most important problem therefore seems to be the child's attitude toward authority. Forced submission to authority produces only surface conformity countermanded by violent underlying destructiveness, dangerous to the very society to which there seems to be conformity. Only a frightened and frustrated child will tend to gain safety and security by oversimplified black-white schematizations and categorizations on the basis of crude, external characteristics. Deliberately planned democratic participation in school and family, individualized approach to the child, and the right proportion of permissiveness and guidance may be instrumental in bringing about the attitude necessary for a genuine identification with society and thus for international understanding.

49 | THE CHILDREN'S FORM OF THE MANIFEST ANXIETY SCALE

ALFRED CASTANEDA, BOYD R. McCANDLESS, AND DAVID S. PALERMO

How does the anxious child feel? How does the world look to him, by day and by night? What lurking dangers does he see within himself and in the outside environment?

The scale presented here is an attempt to describe and measure manifest anxiety in children, using items based on the subjective experiences and symptoms that accompany the disturbance. The paper thus illustrates some of the steps necessary in developing a personality scale.

An earlier version of the present scale was administered to approximately 60 subjects for the purposes of obtaining information regarding possible difficulties in the instructions for its administration and the comprehensibility of the items. A total of 42 anxiety items were selected and modified, and 11 additional items designed to provide an index of the subject's tendency to falsify his responses to the anxiety items were included in the present form of the test. A similar set of items was included by Taylor from the L scale of the MMPI for the same purpose, hence these 11 items will also be referred to as the L scale. All of these items were then submitted to two elementary school system officials for a final check on their comprehensibility for the population for which they were intended. The 42 anxiety items,

constituting the anxiety scale of the present test, are reproduced in Table 1 with their appropriate ordinal numbers as they appear in the present form of the test. The index of the level of anxiety is obtained by summing the number of these items answered "yes."

The 11 L scale items are reproduced in Table 2 with their appropriate ordinal numbers as they appear in the present form of the test. Items 10 and 49, if answered "no" contribute to the L scale score as do the remaining nine items if answered "yes." The index of the subject's tendency to falsify his responses to the anxiety items, then, is the sum of these items answered in the designated manner.

Copies of this test were distributed to the classroom teacher who administered it to her class on a group basis. The only instructions provided the teacher were those which appeared on the test itself and which she read to the class. The instructions were, "Read each question carefully. Put a circle around the word YES if

Excerpts reprinted from *Child Development*, XXVII (1956), 317–26, by permission of the authors and the Society for Research in Child Development.

TABLE 1.

ANXIETY ITEMS
INCLUDED IN THE
ANXIETY SCALE AND
NUMBERED AS THEY
APPEAR IN THE PRESENT
FORM OF THE TEST

1. It is hard for me to keep my mind on anything.
2. I get nervous when someone watches me work.
3. I feel I have to be best in everything.
4. I blush easily.
6. I notice my heart beats very fast sometimes.
7. At times I feel like shouting.
8. I wish I could be very far from here.
9. Others seem to do things easier than I can.
11. I am secretly afraid of a lot of things.
12. I feel that others do not like the way I do things.
13. I feel alone even when there are people around me.
14. I have trouble making up my mind.
15. I get nervous when things do not go the right way for me.
16. I worry most of the time.
18. I worry about what my parents will say to me.
19. Often I have trouble getting my breath.
20. I get angry easily.
22. My hands feel sweaty.
23. I have to go to the toilet more than most people.
24. Other children are happier than I.
25. I worry about what other people think about me.
26. I have trouble swallowing.
27. I have worried about things that did not really make any difference later.
28. My feelings get hurt easily.
29. I worry about doing the right things.
31. I worry about what is going to happen.
32. It is hard for me to go to sleep at night.
33. I worry about how well I am doing in school.
35. My feelings get hurt easily when I am scolded.
37. I often get lonesome when I am with people.
38. I feel someone will tell me I do things the wrong way.
39. I am afraid of the dark.
40. It is hard for me to keep my mind on my school work.
42. Often I feel sick in my stomach.
43. I worry when I go to bed at night.
44. I often do things I wish I had never done.
45. I get headaches.
46. I often worry about what could happen to my parents.
48. I get tired easily.
50. I have bad dreams.
51. I am nervous.
53. I often worry about something bad happening to me.

you think it is true about you. Put a circle around the word NO if you think it is not true about you." Space was provided on the test sheet for the subject to identify himself by name, grade, sex and school. Approximately one week later the classroom teacher re-administered the test. A total of 15 classrooms from four different

schools participated in the study. A total of 386 children participated in the first administration of the test. However, due primarily to absences, only 361 of these children were tested on the second administration. One week re-test reliabilities averaged at about .90 for the anxiety scale and at about .70 for the L scale. Inter-

TABLE 2.

ITEMS INCLUDED IN THE L SCALE AND NUMBERED AS THEY APPEAR IN THE PRESENT FORM OF THE TEST

5. I like everyone I know.
10. I would rather win than lose in a game.
17. I am always kind.
21. I always have good manners.
30. I am always good.
34. I am always nice to everyone.
36. I tell the truth every single time.
41. I never get angry.
47. I never say things I shouldn't.
49. It is good to get high grades in school.
52. I never lie.

correlations between the anxiety scale and the L scale clustered around the zero value. Girls were found to score significantly higher than boys on both scales. Significant differences on the L scale were found to be associated with grade.

50 | COMPLEX LEARNING AND PERFORMANCE AS A FUNCTION OF ANXIETY IN CHILDREN AND TASK DIFFICULTY

ALFRED CASTANEDA, DAVID S. PALERMO,

AND BOYD R. MCCANDLESS

This study, using the Manifest Anxiety Scale described in selection 49, compares the problem-solving ability of anxious children with that of less disturbed children. It shows that a high degree of anxiety helps children learn to solve simple problems but hinders them seriously when the problems become more difficult.

This approach seems more constructive than that which stops after simply diagnosing a disorder. Since anxious children probably will become anxious adults, an attempt to describe and understand the limits of their abilities seems useful. Today's society presents a great variety of tasks to be performed, and it is helpful to have some idea of who can do what.

The present study is concerned with the performance of fifth grade children on a complex learning task as a function of the relative difficulty of the various components comprising the task and of their scores on a scale of manifest anxiety adapted for children from Taylor's adult form.

METHOD

SUBJECTS | The 37 Ss in the present study were from among those who participated in the standardization of the children's

Excerpts reprinted from *Child Development*, XXVII (1956), 328–32, by permission of the authors and the Society for Research in Child Development.

form of the anxiety scale . . . and who, in addition, participated in a complex learning experiment . . . a year previously. The present study, then, reports the relationship between the anxiety scale scores of these Ss and their performance in the experiment of the previous year. Although the conventional practice with the adult form is to select Ss whose scores fall within the upper or lower 20th percentiles of the distribution the small number of Ss available in the present study precluded such a procedure. The anxiety scores of the present Ss ranged from a low of three to a high of 33, hence a score of 18 or above was arbitrarily designated as falling in the high anxious category and a score of 17 or below in the low anxious category. The high anxious group, then, consisted of 21 Ss, 9 boys and 12 girls and the low anxious group was composed of 16 Ss, 6 boys and 10 girls. . . .

APPARATUS | . . . In essence, the apparatus consisted of a rectangularly shaped box approximately 9 x 18 x 9 in., painted flat black. A response panel containing five linearly arranged push buttons projected from the box. Centered 3 in. above the response panel was a 1 in. diameter aperture of flashed opal glass. Behind the aperture were five pilot lamps colored either dark red, green, amber, blue or light red. All controls used by E were situated to the back of the apparatus. By a simple switching arrangement E could actuate any single light and set any push button so that depressing it turned off the light. Depression of any other of the four remaining buttons did not affect the light.

PROCEDURE | All Ss had to learn the same five light button combinations. These five combinations had been previously determined on a random basis. Each single light was presented five times and randomly interspersed within the total 25 presentations. All Ss were allowed to continue responding until the correct button

had been depressed at which time the next light was presented. Ss were merely instructed that the task required learning which buttons were associated with which colored lights and in case of an error to select another button until the correct one had been depressed. The particular buttons depressed and the order in which they were depressed for each presentation was recorded for each S.

RESULTS AND DISCUSSION

Studies with the adult form of the anxiety scale have indicated that the differential performance of high and low anxious Ss can differ depending on the particular characteristics of the task. For example, the tendency for the high anxious Ss to perform more poorly in comparison to low anxious Ss increases as the difficulty of the task increases . . . Conversely, if the difficulty of the task can be sufficiently decreased, differences in anxiety level may result to the benefit of the high anxious Ss. . . . Hence, these studies indicate that the difficulty existing either among several different tasks or among the various components comprising a given task . . . should be assessed, preferably on some basis independent of the performance of the high and low anxious groups which are being studied. Therefore, in order to determine the possibility that the five light button combinations in the present task may not have been equal with respect to the ease with which they could be learned, 20 Ss from among those who had participated in the previous experiment, and for whom anxiety scores were not available, were drawn at random and their performance on each of the five combinations was determined. The index of the difficulty of learning a given combination was the number of times, out of five, the first response to the light was the correct one, or more simply, the number of errorless trials.

. . . . .

TABLE 1.	GROUP	DIFFICULTY LEVEL			
MEAN NUMBER OF ERRORLESS TRIALS		*Easy*		*Hard*	
ON THE EASY AND DIFFICULT		M	SD	M	SD
COMBINATIONS FOR THE HIGH AND	High Anxious	5.00	2.41	3.33	1.29
LOW ANXIOUS GROUPS SEPARATELY	Low Anxious	4.38	2.13	4.81	2.66

Table 1 presents the number of errorless trials for the high and low anxious groups for the easy and difficult combinations separately. It is apparent, on the basis of these data, that the high anxious children performed better, in comparison to the low anxious children, on the easy combinations, but more poorly on the difficult combinations. It can be noted that the performance of the high anxious children appeared to be more affected by the differences in the difficulty of the two sets of combinations than for the low anxious children.

. . . . .

Of great interest is the significant interaction between anxiety and task difficulty. This interaction may be interpreted to indicate that the effects of anxiety are dependent on the degree of difficulty involved in the task. This is in accord with the data presented in Table 1, showing that the position of superiority of the high anxious children on the easy combinations, in comparison to the low anxious children, is completely reversed on the more difficult combinations. Tests of the simple effects indicated that only the difference between the low and high anxious children on the difficult combinations was significant at beyond the .05 level ($F = 4.99$, df $= 1.35$).

. . . The present results support the notion that the effects of anxiety can be more profitably studied if the characteristics of the task can be specified. . . .

51 | EXPERIMENTALLY INDUCED ABNORMAL BEHAVIOR

NORMAN R. F. MAIER

The startling conclusions of this paper have important implications in regard to the issue of when to punish and when not to punish children. Working with animals, Maier and many others have observed that punishment of undesirable behavior in an animal already under severe stress leads to continual rigid repetition of the undesirable behavior. There is a great deal of evidence indicating that this is also true of human beings.

Most of what we know about abnormal behavior has been learned from the study of mental patients and the way they respond to various forms of therapy. There are, however, a number of problems con-

Excerpts reprinted from *The Scientific Monthly*, XLVII (September, 1948), 210–16, by permission of the author and the American Association for the Advancement of Science.

cerning the nature of the abnormal that can only be solved by experimental procedures with animals. One of these is to determine whether neurosis is a disease peculiar to man. This raises the question of whether man is so subject to the disease because of his superior mentality or whether the disease is primarily the product of man's way of living. It has been said that it takes imagination and intelligence of a high order to experience conflicts and that personality disorders require a complex personality structure. Obviously, the ability to produce true neurosis in animals will make it possible to answer this question.

The second problem concerns the relation of the symptom to the cause of the symptom. Has nature supplied man with protective mechanisms—processes whereby the organism develops certain unusual responses that serve to prevent a worse condition? Thus, if a patient develops hysterical blindness, is this symptom a means for protecting the patient from seeing something in his environment that causes his anxiety and conflict? Further, does a psychosis represent a patient's escape from reality and hence serve as a solution when reality is too stressful? If one deals only with studies of case histories, one can find support for this thesis, because the many events in a case history permit one to find a logical connection between the symptom and some problem in the patient's life. Further, when a child has enuresis, should one seek in this behavior some reason, or some way in which he thereby solves a problem? Could bedwetting give him attention he desires? Could it be a way of striking back at strict parents? Only when we control the life histories of individuals and purposely produce symptoms can the relationship between a symptom and its cause be studied.

Animal studies permit one to secure the necessary case-history data for such investigation, but in order to use lower animals one must be able to produce behavior disorders comparable to those found in man. Thus, one of the first steps in animal studies of abnormal behavior was acquiring the ability to produce abnormal symptoms under laboratory conditions.

When our work was begun, success already had been achieved in this field. By the use of the conditioning method, Pavlov produced what he called an "experimental neurosis" in the dog. Liddell's laboratory at Cornell followed this line of attack, and Liddell used sheep and pigs as well as dogs in his research. At Johns Hopkins University, Gannt established a laboratory to continue the type of research initiated by Pavlov. These studies clearly showed that stressful and conflictual situations caused basic behavior disruptions. The disturbance was apparent from the facts that training on discrimination problems was lost, the animal became emotionally unstable (struggled and bit at restraining harnesses), and, in general, the docile animal became most unco-operative. Many symptoms akin to those observed in human patients (such as disturbances in heart rate, and peculiar fears) were seen, but their appearance was difficult to separate from reactions of normal individuals. At the time that our work with rats was begun at the University of Michigan, there was some doubt as to whether the changes produced in the animal were a "true" neurosis. The symptoms were regarded as not sufficiently profound to be convincing, and some psychiatrists argued that neurosis in subhuman animals was impossible because animals below man lacked sufficient imagination, they could not have sex conflicts, or they did not undergo permanent personality changes. Even though some of these criticisms seem to depend upon specialized definitions of neurosis, which exclude the disease from lower animals by defining it as a human disease, it seemed at the time that part of the failure to accept neurosis in animals was based upon the facts that the behavior disturbances observed were not profound enough and that the behavior was produced by a specialized aspect of the conditioning method.

It is probable that the attention our study received in 1938 was influenced by the fact that the disturbance produced in the rat was extremely violent and left no doubt about its being abnormal. The abnormal behavior was in the form of a seizure in which the rat ran madly in a circular pattern. This running was so violent that the nails of the feet became torn. It was not a typical fear pattern, because shelter was not sought and the animal often ran into table legs and walls. The running phase frequently was followed by a convulsion, which was similar to that produced by drugs; since then we have actually found that the convulsions produced by metrazol have a good deal in common with those produced in the training situation. After the active part of the seizure had passed (one or more minutes), the rat became very passive and its righting reflexes were either absent or greatly depressed. During this period the animal could be molded into almost any position, where it would remain for several minutes—sometimes as long as twenty minutes.

The situation for producing this behavior was built around our interpretation of the conditioning studies. It seemed that behavior disturbances in the earlier studies arose when an animal was trained to give a certain response to a signal and to withhold the response when a different signal was given. When these signals were made more and more alike, the animal had difficulty in determining whether to express or withhold the response. By the presentation of a signal that was as much like the withholding signal as the arousal signal, the animal was stimulated to express and withhold the response at the same time. This was a conflict between doing and not doing which we regarded as a basic conflict.

To incorporate this condition in our experiment, we trained rats to discriminate between . . . two cards in the apparatus. . . . The rat was trained to jump to the cards, and when it chose the correct card (the one with a white circle) this card yielded to the jump and gave the rat access to food. When the rat jumped to the wrong card (the one with the black circle), this card remained in place and the animal received a bump on the nose and fell into a protective net below. Under these conditions animals soon learn always to choose the reward card and to avoid the punishment card. After the discrimination is well learned the situation is changed so that only one of the cards is presented. If this card happens to be the punishment card, the animal, as may be expected, refuses to jump. In order to cause the animal to jump to the punishment card, it is necessary to drive him. This is done by using a jet of air and directing it on the rat. When released, the air makes a hissing noise and is irritating to the rat; consequently the resistance to jumping is broken. The condition of driving the rat to make a response to a card it has been trained to avoid was considered a conflict between doing and not doing, and it was the condition under which the violent seizures most frequently were produced.

These experiments raised two interesting questions: Was the seizure produced by the conflict, or by the sound of the air? Is the seizure akin to an epileptic attack and, therefore, an abnormality other than a neurosis? The implication of the second question is that the symptoms observed are too profound to be considered a neurosis.

Experimental studies concerning these and other points have been numerous. Our laboratory alone has contributed more than 25 studies, and a total of perhaps 150 studies have been published on some aspects of the rat's abnormal behavior. The studies include the effects of diet, drugs, heredity, emotionality, and brain injury on seizure susceptibility, as well as studies directed toward determining the nature of the abnormality.

At the present time it seems quite clear that the basic condition for producing the disturbance is conflict. The same auditory conditions, with and without the element of conflict, produce different results. The delay in settling this issue was due to the fact that auditory stimuli, such as the hiss of air, the sound of buzzers and bells, the jingling of keys, supersonic tones, and pure tones of low pitch all produce seizures in some animals. To explain these seizures it was necessary to show that these conditions also produce conflict. Certain sounds are irritants and arouse generalized escape behavior. However, when the animal is confined it is driven to escape, but at the same time its escape is blocked. Thus the animal is trapped in a situation which demands responses and yet inhibits those responses. It has been shown by Dr. Marcuse, of Cornell University, that seizures do not occur when the sound source is fastened to the animal. Under these conditions the escape behavior is permitted even though escape is not accomplished. It also has been shown that the type of confinement and the type of responses made during auditory stimulation influence the appearance of seizures. These facts indicate that auditory stimulation as mere sound stimulation is inadequate for producing seizures. Rather, other conditions must be present, and these other conditions determine whether behavior tensions are built up without permitting a release through some avenue of behavior. It is when these tensions become too great that they break forth as a seizure. The fact that smoke, water spray, and electric shock (applied during conflict) also produce seizures under proper conditions indicate that sound is not unique in its seizure-producing qualities. Since the expression of escape behavior prevents seizures, one is led to conclude that behavior must be blocked while irritants are applied.

The mere fact that conflict and unresolved tensions seem to be essential for producing seizures makes the seizure appear to be a form of neurosis rather than the epileptic attack of a defective organism. Perhaps Dr. Goldstein's classification, "catastrophic reaction," is more adequate than neurosis, since this term implies a form of disorganized behavior which occurs when the environment places demands on the organism that it is incapable of handling. Either "neurosis" or "catastrophic reaction," however, places the emphasis on the abnormality as being one that is situation-induced rather than the response of an injured or defective organism.

Because of the profound nature of the seizure, other aspects of the abnormality reported in our rats frequently have been overlooked. The conflict situation in the rat was highly frustrating and produced nervousness which extended outside the situation. Experimental rats become less likely to breed, and they develop a retiring nature. These behavior alterations are akin to personality changes, since they extend outside the test situation. Further, and more important, is the fact that the frustrating situation produced compulsive behavior in many of the rats, particularly those not showing seizures. Compulsive behavior commonly appears in neurosis and is one of the most difficult to explain. A classical illustration of compulsive behavior is Lady Macbeth's repeated handwashing, which is regarded as an effort to cleanse herself from guilt. Because compulsive behavior is a fundamental type of abnormality, it was selected for special study. Thus, from the outset, our studies of abnormal behavior in the rat have dealt with two distinct forms of abnormality.

When a rat is placed in the card-discrimination problem situation in which reward and punishment are applied in a random order, the animal is confronted with an insoluble problem. This fact is soon recognized by the animal, and it expresses its recognition of such a difficult problem by refusing to choose between cards. This refusal is so intense that hunger is not sufficient to cause the animal to take a 50–50 chance on happening to strike the reward card. In order to overcome this resistance, the animal is driven with a blast of air, as described earlier. Occasionally seizures are produced in this situation, but more commonly the animal jumps at one of the cards, and soon its choices follow a consistent pattern. Usually the rat chooses a card on a position basis, i.e., it chooses the card on the right (or left) side, regardless of which of the cards it is. Once the rat ceases trying out various possibilities and makes its choice on a position basis, this way of choosing becomes the response to the insoluble problem, and the animal never deviates from this procedure once it is established. In practicing the position response, the animal is punished on half its choices and rewarded on the other half, since these are applied in random order. Such a condition should not establish a preferred way of responding, yet under frustration a highly specific response becomes established.

Other animals can be *trained* to show similar position responses. This is accomplished by rewarding animals for choosing the cards on a position basis. Such animals are *motivated* to express position responses, whereas the animals in the insoluble problem situation express their position responses as a consequence of *frustration*.

The question now is, Are responses established under frustration different from those established through motivational training?

It is found that animals that acquire their responses under frustration cannot substitute them for other responses. In other words, they cannot learn new responses even when the situation ceases being insoluble. Not only are they unable to adopt new responses, but they are unable to drop their inadequate position responses. This is true even if they are punished each time they express their old responses. As a matter of fact, punishing them for making their former responses makes them *more* likely to repeat them in the future. Animals with such frustration-induced position responses will choose the punishment cards whenever they are placed on the side of the animals' position preferences. They will even refuse to jump to an open window in which food is clearly displayed when its position does not correspond with their position reaction. . . .

This rigid behavior is in contrast to that of animals that have acquired their position responses under conditions of motivation. These animals readily learn new responses when training conditions are changed, and they are constructively influenced when being punished for errors. If punished too severely, however, they, too, may become frustrated, and they then behave like the above-mentioned animals.

Because frustration makes behavior rigid and unchangeable, we have called the responses acquired under frustration "abnormal fixations" to distinguish them from normal habits. The adjective "abnormal" is used because the strength of the response does not follow the principles of learning in establishing or fixating habits.

Abnormal fixations not only are rigid but they have a compulsive character. This trait can be demonstrated in the following manner. Suppose that after a period of frustration a rat's jump to the card with the white circle is always rewarded, whereas a jump to the card with the black circle is always punished. In this situation a rat with a right-positional fixation will receive punishment whenever the card with the black circle is on the right side, and reward whenever the card with the white circle is on the right side. After a time in this situation, the rat begins to hesitate to jump whenever the punishment card is on the right, or position, side. When forced to jump it strikes the card with its rump to avoid a bump on the nose. When the reward card is on the right side, however, the animal jumps readily and hits the card with its nose and forepaws.

It is evident that the animal knows which card punishes and which card rewards, and, although it expresses its knowledge of the difference in the cards by the way it jumps, it does not choose the card to jump to on this basis. The right-position fixation apparently prevents the rat from making an adaptive response to the situation, so it is forced to take punishment even though it knows better. This unadaptive behavior is in contrast to that of animals with normal position habits. As soon as they learn which card punishes and which card rewards, they abandon their position responses and, instead, follow the reward card from right to left.

Behavior similar to the abnormal fixations in rats has been demonstrated in college students by Dorothy Marquart, one of our graduate students. After mild frustration in any insoluble problem, the time required by students to learn a simple problem is greatly increased. Since all learning requires the acquisition of a new response, any resistance to change that is produced by frustration results in retarded learning. As might be expected, individual differences were apparent. Some of the students were not frustrated by the mild shock and learned at the normal rate. Those that were frustrated, however, required many more trials than the slowest of the normal learners.

The abnormal fixation is akin to rigid responses found in human beings. Accounts of compulsive behavior, such as is found in kleptomania, phobias, and alcoholism, are common in the literature of abnormality. So-called ritualistic behaviors, in which the person must repeat a senseless routine of activities, are further examples. The fact that some attitudes are rigid and not subject to modification, regardless of how senseless they are from a logical point of view, suggests that they are fixated. Of interest are the facts that rigid attitudes are emotionally loaded and are commonly associated with objects that are threats to a person's security. These observations support the suggestion that rigid attitudes have their basis in frustration. Thus, attitudes on socioeconomic topics, racial questions, and religious questions are least subject to modification, and these attitudes are most rigid during periods of frustration and stress.

The studies of abnormal behavior in the rat lead to a new theory of frustration. They demonstrate that behavior elicited during a state of frustration has certain unique properties, and that these properties make frustration-induced behavior different in kind from that produced in a motivated state. This basic separation between motivated and frustrated behavior is in contrast to the view which postulates that all behavior has a motive. When it is assumed that all behavior is motivated, it follows that any behavior expressed is a *means* to some *end*. Thus, one is led to assume that if a child steals he is doing it to achieve some goal, or end. It is said that he is solving the problem of satisfying his wants or needs, even though he may be going contrary to some other needs, such as being accepted by society. From this point of view it follows that if we make stealing unattractive (punishing for the act), such behavior will be deterred. If, on the other hand, we recognize that there are two different kinds of behavior, then it follows that there may be two kinds of stealing, one that is motivated and solves the problem of gratifying needs, and one that is frustration-instigated and compulsive in nature. The latter type of behavior solves no problem and has no goal to direct it. It may occur in children from broken homes in which the child has adequate spending money. This type of stealing may involve the theft of objects for which the child has no need or interest. Such behavior is similar to vandalism, in which objects are destroyed rather than taken. The fact that stealing increases with frustration indicates that we must distinguish between the various forms of stealing. The separation of behavior into frustration-instigated and goal-motivated behavior permits just such a distinction.

Once we accept the belief that behavior produced under frustration follows different principles from behavior motivated by goals, we can reorganize our knowledge of the subject of frustration. For example, it is known that destructive (aggressive or hateful) behavior is associated with frustration and that a frustrated person attacks his enemy. This behavior may appear to be problem-solving in nature, but difficulty is encountered in explaining why people who are frustrated so often strike out at innocent bystanders. One can see how the destruction of one's enemies would achieve objectives, but the fact is that frustrated persons do not always express their hates in such a manner as to solve problems. Instead, they create more problems by their hateful behavior. Thus, frustrated parents abuse their children and rationalize that they are training them. The children return the hatred or direct it toward society through delinquent behavior.

It seems useless to probe for problems which hate behavior solves. Instead, our theory suggests that frustration produces hate, and the hatred is directed toward anything that is convenient or is in the individual's attention during his frustration. Some of the animal experiments show that the type of behavior expressed in frustration is determined by its availability to the individual rather than by its effectiveness.

Another form of behavior associated with frustration is that of regression, which represents a type of behavior more childish than the individual's level of development warrants. Thus, bed-wetting in an eight-year-old is a sign of regression. A child that has learned to walk may temporarily revert to creeping when frustrated. Believers in the theory that all behavior is motivated have difficulty in explaining such senseless regressive behaviors. What problem is solved by this type of behavior? Frequently, it is said that the child desires attention. The attention he receives from bed-wetting, however, may be a spanking and degradation. Is this activity solving a problem for the child, or is it aggravating a condition that is already bad? If, however, we assume that frustration produces regression and that this simplification of behavior is a direct result of frustration, then our problem is to seek the source of frustration. The child that regresses may feel rejected. Punishment makes him feel more rejected. On the other hand, love and understanding reduce the state of frustration. It then follows that a child is most likely to be cured if he is given treatment that reduces his frustration, and this is frequently what the practicing psychiatrist recommends. He suggests love and attention because they work. Nevertheless, from a motivation point of view, rewarding a bad response with love should strengthen it. Yet both aggressive and regressive behaviors are reduced when treated with understanding and love.

From our point of view it follows that the behavior expressed gives no clue as to what the frustrated individual needs. A child that is insecure may develop a form of ritualistic behavior and so show signs of fixation; he may whine excessively, wet the bed, and have difficulty in learning, thereby showing signs of regression; he may become destructive with toys or be a bully in school, thereby showing aggressive symptoms; or he may show behaviors that are combinations of fixation, regression, and aggression. Regardless of which behaviors are expressed, however, the underlying cause may be the same. If the insecure or rejected child is to be made to feel secure, therapy is achieved in the same way, regardless of the specific symptoms that a given child exhibits.

To show more clearly the difference between motivated and frustrated behavior, we have listed in Table 1 those char-

TABLE 1.	*Motivation-Induced*	*Frustration-Instigated*
CHARACTERIS- TICS OF MOTI- VATED AND FRUSTRATED BEHAVIOR	Goal-oriented	Not directed toward a goal
	Tensions reduced when goal is reached	Tensions reduced when behavior is expressed, but increased if behavior leads to more frustration
	Punishment deters action	Punishment aggravates state of frustration
	Behavior shows variability and resourcefulness in a problem situation	Behavior is stereotyped and rigid
	Behavior is constructive	Behavior is nonconstructive or destructive
	Behavior reflects choices influenced by consequences	Behavior is compulsive
	Learning proceeds and makes for development and maturity	Learning is blocked and behavior regresses

acteristics of each that seem to be sufficiently common to warrant inclusion (although there may be many others).

The differences in behavior listed in the table are basic, and failure to make these distinctions seems only to lead to inconsistencies and confusion. If these differences are recognized it means that the first step in diagnosis is to determine which condition an individual is in when one attempts to correct behavior. The nonfrustrated person is subject to training because he is responsive to training methods, and he can be attracted to substitute goals.

The frustrated individual, however, needs relief from frustration. Can the situation be corrected? If so, then such correction is a form of therapy. Another possibility is to treat the *individual* rather than the *situation*. Can the state of frustration be relieved without making it necessary to change the situation? Actually the expression of a frustrated response reduces the state of frustration. An act of aggression such as writing a hateful letter achieves relief even if the letter is not mailed. Crying (a regressive response to frustration) reduces frustration and the person need not receive the

concessions that tears sometimes attain. Rats which showed tendencies to have seizures when frustrated, had fewer seizures when they developed fixations. Thus the various frustration-induced responses seem to relieve the state of frustration, but it must not be supposed that the anticipation of such relief is an essential cause of the behavior. To make this supposition would deny the basic evidence which differentiates motivated and frustration-instigated behavior.

Unfortunately, the expression of frustration-instigated responses frequently leads to further frustration. When one strikes another or verbally abuses him, the other person strikes back and so creates a further problem. Thus the value of the relief gained through expression is offset by the fact that the end the expression has served is one which leads to new frustration. It is for this reason that therapy must permit harmless forms of aggression. Such harmless forms of aggression are encouraged in play therapy and in counselling situations. These permit children and adults to express hostility without having the behavior challenged.

We thus find that the experimentation

with animals leads us to a theory of frustration which reorganizes the facts of human behavior and reinterprets the meaning and importance of certain forms of therapy. It has supplied us with certain basic principles which have a firm foundation in that the principles are experimentally derived. Whether the experimentation can proceed to aid us in answering many of our perplexing problems remains to be seen.

52 | THE MAMMAL AND HIS ENVIRONMENT

D. O. HEBB

Hebb describes some of the fascinating research with dogs, chimpanzees, and students that is being discussed currently. He concludes that perceptual restriction produces low intelligence and reports that dogs in an environment of low stimulation express their excitement in overactivity.

Bowlby, reporting similar results in experiments with children, would agree with these findings. Hebb, however, declares that such dogs do not become "neurotic" in the human or clinical sense.

The original intention in this paper was to discuss the significance of neurophysiological theory for psychiatry and psychology, and to show, by citing the work done by some of my colleagues, that the attempt to get at the neural mechanisms of behavior can stimulate and clarify purely behavioral—that is, psychiatric and psychological—thinking. The research to be described has, I think, a clear relevance to clinical problems; but its origin lay in efforts to learn how the functioning of individual neurons and synapses relates to the functions of the whole brain, and to understand the physiological nature of learning, emotion, thinking, or intelligence.

In the end, however, my paper has simply become a review of the research referred to, dealing with the relation of the mammal to his environment. The question concerns the normal variability of the sensory environment and this has been studied from two points of view. First, one may ask what the significance of perceptual activity is during growth; for this purpose one can rear an animal with a considerable degree of restriction, and see what effects there are upon mental development. Secondly, in normal animals whose development is complete, one can remove a good deal of the supporting action of the normal environment, to discover how far the animal continues to be dependent on it even after maturity.

THE ROLE OF THE ENVIRONMENT DURING GROWTH

The immediate background of our present research on the intelligence and personality of the dog is the work of Hymovitch (6) on the intelligence of rats. He reared laboratory rats in 2 ways: (1) in a psychologically restricted environ-

Reprinted from a paper read at the 110th annual meeting of the American Psychiatric Association (St. Louis, Mo., May 3–7, 1954) and published in *American Journal of Psychiatry*, CXI (1955), 826–31, by permission of the author and publisher.

ment, a small cage, with food and water always at hand and plenty of opportunity for exercise (in an activity wheel), but with no problems to solve, no need of getting on with others, no pain; and (2) in a "free" environment, a large box with obstacles to pass, blind alleys to avoid, other rats to get on with, and thus ample opportunity for problem-solving and great need for learning during growth. Result: the rats brought up in a psychologically restricted (but biologically adequate) environment have a lasting inferiority in problem-solving. This does not mean, of course, that environment is everything, heredity nothing: here heredity was held constant, which prevents it from affecting the results. When the reverse experiment is done we find problem-solving varying with heredity instead. The *same* capacity for problem-solving is fully dependent on both variables for its development.

To take this further, Thompson and others have been applying similar methods to dogs (9). The same intellectual effect of an impoverished environment is found again, perhaps more marked in the higher species. But another kind of effect can be seen in dogs, which have clearly marked personalities. Personality —by which I mean complex individual differences of emotion and motivation— is again strongly affected by the infant environment. These effects, however, are hard to analyze, and I cannot at present give any rounded picture of them.

First, observations during the rearing itself are significant. A Scottish terrier is reared in a small cage, in isolation from other Scotties and from the human staff. Our animal man, William Ponman, is a dog lover and undertook the experiment with misgivings, which quickly disappeared. In a cage 30 by 30 inches, the dogs are "happy as larks," eat more than normally reared dogs, grow well, are physically vigorous: as Ponman says, "I never saw such healthy dogs—they're

like bulls." If you put a normally-reared dog into such a cage, shut off from everything, his misery is unmistakable, and we have not been able to bring ourselves to continue such experiments. Not so the dog that has known nothing else. Ponman showed some of these at a dog show of national standing, winning first-prize ribbons with them.

Observations by Dr. Ronald Melzack on pain are extremely interesting. He reared 2 dogs, after early weaning, in complete isolation, taking care that there was little opportunity for experience of pain (unless the dog bit himself). At maturity, when the dogs were first taken out for study, they were extraordinarily excited, with random, rapid movement. As a result they got their tails or paws stepped on repeatedly—but paid no attention to an event that would elicit howls from a normally reared dog. After a few days, when their movements were calmer, they were tested with an object that gave electric shock, and paid little attention to it. Through 5 testing periods, the dog repeatedly thrust his nose into a lighted match; and months later, did the same thing several times with a lighted cigar.

A year and a half after coming out of restriction they are still hyperactive. Clipping and trimming one of them is a 2-man job; if the normal dog does not stand still, a cuff on the ear will remind him of his duty; but cuffing the experimental dog "has as much effect as if you patted him—except he pays no attention to it." It seems certain, especially in view of the related results reported by Nissen, Chow, and Semmes (7) for a chimpanzee, that the adult's perception of pain is essentially a function of pain experience during growth—and that what we call pain is not a single sensory quale but a complex mixture of a particular kind of synthesis with past learning and emotional disturbance.

Nothing bores the dogs reared in restriction. At an "open house," we put 2 restricted dogs in one enclosure, 2 normal ones in another, and asked the public to tell us which were the normal. Without exception, they picked out the 2 alert, lively, interested animals—not the lackadaisical pair lying in the corner, paying no attention to the visitors. The alert pair, actually, were the restricted; the normal dogs had seen all they wanted to see of the crowd in the first 2 minutes, and then went to sleep, thoroughly bored. The restricted dogs, so to speak, haven't the brains to be bored.

Emotionally, the dogs are "immature," but not in the human or clinical sense. They are little bothered by imaginative fears. Dogs suffer from irrational fears, like horses, porpoises, elephants, chimpanzees, and man; but it appears that this is a product of intellectual development, characteristic of the brighter, not the duller animal. Our dogs in restriction are not smart enough to fear strange objects. Things that cause fear in normal dogs produce only a generalized, undirected excitement in the restricted. If both normal and restricted dogs are exposed to the same noninjurious but exciting stimulus repeatedly, fear gradually develops in the restricted; but the normals, at first afraid, have by this time gone on to show a playful aggression instead. On the street, the restricted dogs "lead well," not bothered by what goes on around them, while those reared normally vary greatly in this respect. Analysis has a long way to go in these cases, but we can say now that dogs reared in isolation are not like ordinary dogs. They are both stupid and peculiar.

Such results clearly support the clinical evidence, and the animal experiments of others (1), showing that early environment has a lasting effect on the form of adjustment at maturity. We do not have a great body of evidence yet, and before we generalize too much it will be particularly important to repeat these ob-servations with animals of different heredity. But I have been very surprised, personally, by the lack of evidence of emotional instability, neurotic tendency, or the like, when the dogs are suddenly plunged into a normal world. There is, in fact, just the opposite effect. This suggests caution in interpreting data with human children, such as those of Spitz (8) or Bowlby (3). Perceptual restriction in infancy certainly produces a low level of intelligence, but it may not, by itself, produce emotional disorder. The observed results seem to mean, not that the stimulus of another attentive organism (the mother) is necessary from the first but that it may become necessary only as psychological *dependence* on the mother develops. However, our limited data certainly cannot prove anything for man, though they may suggest other interpretations besides those that have been made.

THE ENVIRONMENT AT MATURITY

Another approach to the relation between the mammal and his environment is possible: that is, one can take the normally reared mammal and cut him off at maturity from his usual contact with the world. It seems clear that thought and personality characteristics develop as a function of the environment. Once developed, are they independent of it? This experiment is too cruel to do with animals, but not with college students. The first stage of the work was done by Bexton, Heron, and Scott (2). It follows up some work by Mackworth on the effects of monotony, in which he found extraordinary lapses of attention. Heron and his co-workers set out to make the monotony more prolonged and more complete.

The subject is paid to do nothing 24 hours a day. He lies on a comfortable bed in a small closed cubicle, is fed on request, goes to the toilet on request.

Otherwise he does nothing. He wears frosted glass goggles that admit light but do not allow pattern vision. His ears are covered by a sponge-rubber pillow in which are embedded small speakers by which he can be communicated with, and a microphone hangs near to enable him to answer. His hands are covered with gloves, and cardboard cuffs extend from the upper forearm beyond his fingertips, permitting free joint movement but with little tactual perception.

The results are dramatic. During the stay in the cubicle, the experimental subject shows extensive loss, statistically significant, in solving simple problems. He complains subjectively that he cannot concentrate; his boredom is such that he looks forward eagerly to the next problem, but when it is presented he finds himself unwilling to make the effort to solve it.

On emergence from the cubicle the subject is given the same kind of intelligence tests as before entering, and shows significant loss. There is disturbance of motor control. Visual perception is changed in a way difficult to describe; it is as if the object looked at was exceptionally vivid, but impaired in its relation to other objects and the background—a disturbance perhaps of the larger organization of perception. This condition may last up to 12 or 24 hours.

Subjects reported some remarkable hallucinatory activity, some which resembled the effects of mescal, or the results produced by Grey Walter with flickering light. These hallucinations were primarily visual, perhaps only because the experimenters were able to control visual perception most effectively; however, some auditory and somesthetic hallucinations have been observed as well.

The nature of these phenomena is best conveyed by quoting one subject who reported over the microphone that he had just been asleep and had a very vivid dream and although he was awake, the dream was continuing. The study of dreams has a long history, and is clearly important theoretically, but is hampered by the impossibility of knowing how much the subject's report is distorted by memory. In many ways the hallucinatory activity of the present experiments is indistinguishable from what we know about dreams; if it is in essence the same process, but going on while the subject can describe it (not merely hot but still on the griddle), we have a new source of information, a means of direct attack, on the nature of the dream.

In its early stages the activity as it occurs in the experiment is probably not dream-like. The course of development is fairly consistent. First, when the eyes are closed the visual field is light rather than dark. Next there are reports of dots of light, lines, or simple geometrical patterns, so vivid that they are described as being a new experience. Nearly all experimental subjects reported such activity. (Many of course could not tolerate the experimental conditions very long, and left before the full course of development was seen.) The next stage is the occurrence of repetitive patterns, like a wallpaper design, reported by three-quarters of the subjects; next, the appearance of isolated objects, without background, seen by half the subjects; and finally, integrated scenes, involving action, usually containing dream-like distortions, and apparently with all the vividness of an animated cartoon, seen by about a quarter of the subjects. In general, these amused the subject, relieving his boredom, as he watched to see what the movie program would produce next. The subjects reported that the scenes seemed to be out in front of them. A few could, apparently, "look at" different parts of the scene in central vision, as one could with a movie; and up to a point could change its content by "trying." It was not, however, well under control. Usually, it would disappear if the subject were given an interesting task, but not when the subject described it, nor if he did physical exercises. Its persistence and vividness interfered with sleep for some subjects, and at this stage was irritating.

In their later stages the hallucinations were elaborated into everything from a peaceful rural scene to naked women diving and swimming in a woodland pool to prehistoric animals plunging through tropical forests. One man saw a pair of spectacles, which were then joined by a dozen more, without wearers, fixed intently on him; faces sometimes appeared behind the glasses, but with no eyes visible. The glasses sometimes moved in unison, as if marching in procession. Another man saw a field onto which a bathtub rolled: it moved slowly on rubber-tired wheels, with chrome hub caps. In it was seated an old man wearing a battle helmet. Another subject was highly entertained at seeing a row of squirrels marching single file across a snowy field, wearing snowshoes and carrying little bags over their shoulders.

Some of the scenes were in 3 dimensions, most in 2 (that is, as if projected on a screen). A most interesting feature was that some of the images were persistently tilted from the vertical, and a few reports were given of inverted scenes, completely upside down.

There were a few reports of auditory phenomena—one subject heard the people in his hallucination talking. There was also some somesthetic imagery, as when one saw a doorknob before him, and as he touched it felt an electric shock; or when another saw a miniature rocket ship maneuvering around him, and discharging pellets that he felt hitting his arm. But the most interesting of these phenomena the subject, apparently, lacked words to describe adequately. There were references to a feel-

ing of "otherness," or bodily "strangeness." One said that his mind was like a ball of cottonwool floating in the air above him. Two independently reported that they perceived a second body, or second person, in the cubicle. One subject reported that he could not tell which of the 2 bodies was his own, and described the 2 bodies as overlapping in space—not like Siamese twins, but 2 complete bodies with an arm, shoulder, and side of each occupying the same space.

THEORETICAL SIGNIFICANCE

The theoretical interest of these results for us extends in 2 directions. On the one hand, they interlock with work using more physiological methods, of brain stimulation and recording, and especially much of the recent work on the relation of the brain stem to cortical "arousal." Points of correspondence between behavioral theory and knowledge of neural function are increasing, and each new point of correspondence provides both a corrective for theory and a stimulation for further research. A theory of thought and of consciousness in physiologically intelligible terms need no longer be completely fantastic.

On the other hand, the psychological data cast new light on the relation of man to his environment, including his social environment, and it is this that I should like to discuss a little further. To do so I must go back for a moment to some earlier experiments on chimpanzee emotion. They indicate that the higher mammal may be psychologically at the mercy of his environment to a much greater degree than we have been accustomed to think.

Studies in our laboratory of the role of the environment during infancy and a large body of work reviewed recently by Beach and Jaynes (1) make it clear that psychological development is fully dependent on stimulation from the environment. Without it, intelligence does not develop normally, and the personality is grossly atypical. The experiment with college students shows that a short period—even a day or so—of deprivation of a normal sensory input produces personality changes and a clear loss of capacity to solve problems. Even at maturity, then, the organism is still essentially dependent on a normal sensory environment for the maintenance of its psychological integrity.

The following data show yet another way in which the organism appears psychologically vulnerable. It has long been known that the chimpanzee may be frightened by representations of animals, such as a small toy donkey. An accidental observation of my own extended this to include representations of the chimpanzee himself, of man, and of parts of the chimpanzee or human body. A model of a chimpanzee head, in clay, produced terror in the colony of the Yerkes Laboratories, as did a life-like representation of a human head, and a number of related objects such as an actual chimpanzee head, preserved in formalin, or a colored representation of a human eye and eyebrow. A deeply anesthetized chimpanzee, "dead" as far as the others were concerned, aroused fear in some animals and vicious attacks by others (4).

I shall not deal with this theoretically. What matters for our present purposes is the conclusion, rather well supported by the animal evidence, that the greater the development of intelligence the greater the vulnerability to emotional breakdown. The price of high intelligence is susceptibility to imaginative fears and unreasoning suspicion and other emotional weaknesses. The conclusion is not only supported by the animal data, but also agrees with the course of development in children, growing intelligence being accompanied by increased frequency and strength of emotional problems—up to the age of 5 years.

Then, apparently, the trend is reversed.

Adult man, more intelligent than chimpanzee or 5-year-old child, seems not more subject to emotional disturbances but less. Does this then disprove the conclusion? It seemed a pity to abandon a principle that made sense of so many data that had not made sense before, and the kind of theory I was working with—neurophysiologically oriented—also pointed in the same direction. The question then was, is it possible that something is concealing the adult human being's emotional weaknesses?

From this point of view it became evident that the concealing agency is man's culture, which acts as a protective cocoon. There are many indications that our emotional stability depends more on our successful avoidance of emotional provocation than on our essential characteristics: that urbanity depends on an urbane social and physical environment. Dr. Thompson and I (5) reviewed the evidence, and came to the conclusion that the development of what is called "civilization" is the progressive elimination of sources of acute fear, disgust, and anger; and that civilized man may not be less, but more, susceptible to such disturbance because of his success in protecting himself from disturbing situations so much of the time.

We may fool ourselves thoroughly in this matter. We are surprised that children are afraid of the dark, or afraid of being left alone, and congratulate ourselves on having got over such weakness. Ask anyone you know whether he is afraid of the dark, and he· will either laugh at you or be insulted. This attitude is easy to maintain in a well-lighted, well-behaved suburb. But try being alone in complete darkness in the streets of a strange city, or alone at night in the deep woods, and see if you still feel the same way.

We read incredulously of the taboo rules of primitive societies; we laugh at the superstitious fear of the dead in primitive people. What is there about a dead body to produce disturbance? Sensible, educated people are not so affected. One can easily show that they are, however, and that we have developed an extraordinarily complete taboo system—not just moral prohibition, but full-fledged ambivalent taboo—to deal with the dead body. I took a poll of an undergraduate class of 198 persons, including some nurses and veterans, to see how many had encountered a dead body. Thirty-seven had never seen a dead body in any circumstances, and 91 had seen one only after an undertaker had prepared it for burial; making a total of 65% who had never seen a dead body in, so to speak, its natural state. It is quite clear that for some reason we protect society against sight of, contact with, the dead body. Why?

Again, the effect of moral education, and training in the rules of courtesy, and the compulsion to dress, talk and act as others do, adds up to ensuring that the individual member of society will not act in a way that is a provocation to others—will not, that is, be a source of strong emotional disturbance, except in highly ritualized circumstances approved by society. The social behavior of a group of civilized persons, then, makes up that protective cocoon which allows us to think of ourselves as being less emotional than the explosive 4-year-old or the equally explosive chimpanzee.

The well-adjusted adult therefore is not intrinsically less subject to emotional disturbance: he is well-adjusted, relatively unemotional, as long as he is in his cocoon. The problem of moral education, from this point of view, is not simply to produce a stable individual, but to produce an individual that will (1) be stable in the existing social environment, and (2) contribute to its protective uniformity. We think of some persons as being emotionally dependent, others not; but it looks as though we are all completely dependent on the environment in a way and to a degree that we have not suspected.

BIBLIOGRAPHY

1. BEACH, F. A., AND JAYNES, J. Psychol. Bull., 51:239, 1954.
2. BEXTON, W. H., HERON, W., AND SCOTT, T. H. Canad. J. Psychol., 8:70, 1954.
3. BOWLBY, J. Maternal Care and Mental Health. Geneva: WHO Monogr. #2, 1951.
4. HEBB, D. O. Psychol. Rev., 53:259, 1946.
5. HEBB, D. O., AND THOMPSON, W. R. in Lindzey, G. (Ed.), Handbook of Social Psychology. Cambridge: Addison-Wesley, 1954.
6. HYMOVITCH, B. J. Comp. Physiol. Psychol., 45:313, 1952.
7. NISSEN, H. W., CHOW, R. L., AND SEMMES, JOSEPHINE. Am. J. Psychol., 64:485, 1951.
8. SPITZ, R. A. Psychoanalytic Study of the Child, 2:113, 1946.
9. THOMPSON, W. R., AND HERON, W. Canad. J. Psychol., 8:17, 1954.

PART FIVE

PLANNED INTERVENTION

Parents and teachers usually assume that they know better than their children what the latter should become, and they usually also assume that they have the power and moral right to act as manipulators of their children's destinies. However, having decided just what they would like their children to become, they are still faced with the question of what methods to use in asserting influence.

Although in its youth, the science of psychology has already produced a wealth of information and advice on influencing people, helping people in trouble, and teaching people. Numerous "schools"—from Freud and Watson to Rogers and Skinner—each with a body of practice and theory, compete for public support.

This part presents some concepts which might be regarded as tools in skillful personal relationships, the power of the conditioned response, psychoanalysis, client-oriented therapy, group work, and reality therapy.

One extreme in child-rearing advice was advocated for centuries: spank the child every time he does something wrong. After Freud showed the misery and damage caused by this practice when confusingly administered, the other extreme developed: don't punish or correct the child because he may become neurotic and hate his parents. Most of us today feel that children grow to accept more and more freedom, thus expanding their areas of responsibility, and that they learn to satisfy their needs for affection by seeing the world as it is. If you want to do well at the piano, you must practice. If you want people to believe you, tell them the truth. If you want to be successful, you must discipline yourself. The parent who is a good model and who cares enough for his child to praise his efforts and to help him correct his errors wins the respect and love of his child and may expect him to grow up to be a responsible citizen.

53 | RETRAINING A CHILD TO EAT

ELIZABETH CADY AND EVELYN M. CARRINGTON

Experiments with animals and observations of children have shown that if they have learned that eating will result in punishment, they will refuse to eat, allowing themselves to starve to death even when food is present in the immediate environment. This study describes a child who would eat only through a tube until—by gentle handling, rocking, and singing, and then by forced feeding—she was taught to accept oral feeding.

In February, 1956 when the senior writer first saw Sammie, she was a lethargic, pale four-year-old, swaying back and forth in her bed, gritting her teeth. . . . She had no speech, but at times made a mumbling sound. Occasionally, she smiled a lopsided grin.

The previous June, Sammie had entered the Children's Medical Center with the diagnosis of tubercular infection. Shortly thereafter, she developed meningitis, the encephalopathy being widespread with greatest dominance in the left posterior frontal region. She had difficulty in using her right leg, her right arm and hand were limp, and the left side of her face showed some paralysis.

· · · · ·

During all this time, Sammie had been given through a tube a special formula which supplied her daily nutritional needs.

· · · · ·

Since a psychologic evaluation in February showed Sammie's mental functioning to be at the eight-month level, the psychologist decided to treat her as an eight-month-old. When she rocked and sang to her, Sammie appeared relaxed and happily made humming noises. However, when her formula was given her in a bottle, the child was unable to suck and violently pushed it away. . . . Realizing that Sammie needed to be retrained to eat with her mouth, the dietetic intern took the case as a special project, working with the little girl from 30 min. to 1 hr. each day.

FIRST DAY | Sammie was rocked and an attempt was made to feed her applesauce. She looked suspiciously at the spoon and cup of fruit, keeping her teeth clamped together. . . .

Excerpts reprinted from the *Journal of the American Dietetic Association*, XXXIII (1957), 605–6, by permission of the authors and publisher.

THIRD DAY | It was decided to force feed Sammie, as she must taste food before she could conceive of what she was missing. Under protest, Sammie took some applesauce in her mouth. . . . She was laid on her back and her formula in a thickened form was spooned into her mouth. Several tablespoons were swallowed.

FOURTH DAY | It was decided to use applesauce exclusively in the training sessions because it is easily swallowed, has a pleasant taste, and has enough fiber to induce chewing.

FIFTH DAY | Sammie voluntarily opened her mouth and took a teaspoon of applesauce which she chewed and swallowed. . . .

· · · · ·

NINTH DAY | The sugar was removed from Sammie's formula as she has vomited after her tube feedings for several days. This eliminated the vomiting. She also took one teaspoonful of applesauce.

TENTH DAY | She was quite fussy today. She was fed some strained apricots, which were sent by mistake. The apricots seemed to interest her, but did not stay in her mouth well. She still showed no interest in learning to eat, batting at the spoon.

THIRTEENTH DAY | After a half hour of encouragement, Sammie took a teaspoonful of applesauce. . . .

SEVENTEENTH DAY | All tube feedings have been discontinued and three times a day in spite of crying and flaying hands and feet, Sammie is given puréed vegetables, meat, and fruit. She tolerates the vegetables, regurgitates the meat, and takes the sweets with mild relaxation. Today she went into the kitchen, took out a box of dry cereal and played with it. However, she made no effort to eat any.

. . . . .

TWENTY-THIRD DAY | . . . All the food was taken orally and retained. Vomiting has stopped completely, and there has been no constipation. All strained foods are diluted with Protenum.

TWENTY-EIGHTH DAY | For the first time Sammie is eating while sitting in a high chair. She is still resistant to oral feedings and spits out any food she does not want. . . .

TWENTY-EIGHTH DAY | Sammie is no longer resistant to oral feedings. In fact, she not only eats her regular meal, but begs for additional food. . . . The accompanying personality changes are just this side of miraculous. The little girl is 100 per cent happier and more demonstrative. She is now on a regular diet, with puréed foods eliminated. Self-feeding will be the next training problem.

ANALYSIS OF THE PROBLEM

This feeding problem was complicated by several factors: (a) prolonged tube feeding, (b) paralysis of right facial muscles, and (c) mental regression due to severe illness. . . .

54 | THE POWERFUL PLACEBO

HENRY K. BEECHER, M.D.

Suppose a force could be found within each person that would enable him to resist pain, diminish fatigue, and lessen discomfort? And suppose that force were psychological, specifically, human suggestibility? Of what incredible assistance this force could be in bringing comfort and relief to those suffering the pain of physical as well as emotional illness. This study attempts to learn the ways in which a universal psychological phenomenon, human suggestibility, may be used in a controlled and predictable manner to bring relief to those in pain.

Placebos have doubtless been used for centuries by wise physicians as well as by quacks; but it is only very recently that recognition of an enquiring kind has been given the clinical circumstance where the use of this tool is essential "to distinguish pharmacological effects from the effects of suggestion, and . . . to obtain an unbiased assessment of the result of experiment." It is interesting that Pepper (1945) could say, . . . "apparently there has never been a paper published discussing primarily the important subject of the placebo."

Gaddum (1954) says,

Such tablets are sometimes called placebos, but it is better to call them dummies. According to the Shorter Oxford Dictionary the word "placebo" has been used since 1811 to mean a medicine given more to please than to benefit the patient. Dummy tablets are not particularly noted for the pleasure which they give to their recipients. One meaning of the word dummy is "a counterfeit object." This seems to me the right word to describe a form of treatment which is intended to have no effect and I follow those who use it. A placebo is something which is intended to act

Excerpts reprinted from *The Journal of the American Medical Association*, CLIX (1955), 1602–6. Copyright 1955 by the American Medical Association.

through a psychological mechanism. It is an aid to therapeutic suggestion, but the effect which it produces may be either psychological or physical. It may make the patient feel better without any obvious justification, or it may produce actual changes in such things as the gastric secretion. . . . Dummy tablets may, of course, act as placebos, but, if they do, they lose some of their value as dummy tablets. They have two real functions, one of which is to distinguish pharmacological effects from the effects of suggestion, and the other is to obtain an unbiased assessment of the result of experiment.

One may comment on Gaddum's remarks: Both "dummies" and placebos are the same pharmacologically inert substances, lactose, saline, starch, and so on. Since they appear to be differentiable chiefly in the *reasons* for which they are given and only at times distinguishable in terms of their effects, it seems simpler to use the one term, "placebo," . . . whose two principal functions are well stated in Professor Gaddum's last sentence quoted above.

Reasons for the use of the placebo can be indicated by summarizing . . . its common purposes: as a psychological instrument in the therapy of certain ailments arising out of mental illness, as a resource of the harassed doctor in dealing with the neurotic patient, to determine the true effect of drugs apart from suggestion in experimental work, as a device for eliminating bias not only on the part of the patient but also, when used as an unknown, of the observer, and finally as a tool of importance in the study of the mechanisms of drug action. Moreover, as a consequence of the use of placebos, those who react to them in a positive way can be screened out to advantage under some circumstances and the focus sharpened on drug effects. For example, Jellinek (1946) in studying 199 patients with headache found that 79 never got relief from a placebo, whereas 120 did. . . .

. . . . .

We can take an example from our own work where placebos have relieved pain arising from physiological cause (surgical incision) and show how useful the screening out of placebo reactors can be. We (Beecher, Keats, Mosteller and Lasagna, 1953) administered analgesics by mouth to patients having steady, severe postoperative wound pain and found that when we took all patients and all data we could not differentiate between certain combined acetylsalicylic acid data and narcotic (morphine and codeine) data; however, when we screened out the placebo reactors, a sharp differential emerged in favor of the acetylsalicylic acid administered orally as opposed to the narcotics administered orally. Observations of these kinds were enough to give us an interest in the placebo reactor as such. We made a study of him and of the placebo response (Lasagna, Mosteller, von Felsinger and Beecher, 1954) in a group of 162 patients having steady, severe postoperative wound pain. We found that there were no differences in sex ratios or in intelligence between reactors and non-reactors. There were however significant differences in attitudes, habits, educational background, and personality structure between consistent reactors and non-reactors. . . .

Lasagna, Mosteller, von Felsinger and Beecher (1954) found in their study of severe postoperative wound pain that the number of placebo doses was correlated highly with the total number of doses of all kinds. Fifteen patients with one placebo dose showed 53 per cent relief from the placebo; 21 patients with two placebo doses got 40 per cent relief from the placebo; in 15 patients with three placebo doses 40 per cent gave relief, and of 15 patients with four or more placebo doses, 15 per cent gave relief. There was a significant correlation between number of doses and per cent relief. This same study gave an opportunity to examine the consistency of the placebo response: 69 patients received two or more doses of a placebo. Fifty-five per cent (38 patients) of these behaved inconsistently, that is to say, sometimes the placebo produced relief and sometimes not. Fourteen per cent (10 patients) were consistent reactors, that is, all placebo doses were effective. Thirty-one per cent (21 patients) were consistent non-reactors; the placebo doses were never effective. It is impossible to predict the efficacy of subsequent placebos from the response to the initial dose of saline. . . .

It must not be supposed that the action of placebos is limited to "psychological" responses. Many examples could be given of "physiologic" change, objective change, produced by placebos. . . .

MAGNITUDE OF THE THERAPEUTIC EFFECT OF PLACEBOS

. . . . .

. . . Fifteen illustrative studies have been chosen at random (doubtless many more could have been included). . . . These are not a selected group: all studies examined that presented adequate data have been included. Thus in 15 studies (seven of our own, eight of others) involving 1082 patients, placebos are found to have an average significant effectiveness of 35.2 ± 2.2 per cent, a degree not widely recognized. The great power of placebos provides one of the strongest supports for the view that drugs which are capable of altering subjective responses, symptoms, do so to an important degree through their effect on the reaction component of suffering.

TOXIC AND OTHER SUBJECTIVE SIDE EFFECTS OF PLACEBOS

Not only do placebos produce beneficial results, but like other therapeutic agents they have associated toxic effects. In a consideration of 35 different toxic effects of placebos which we had observed in one or more of our studies (Denton and Beecher, 1949; Keats and Beecher, 1952; Lasagna and Beecher, 1954 a,b), there is a sizable incidence of effect attributable to the placebo as follows: dry mouth, 7 subjects out of 77, or 9 per cent; nausea, 9 subjects out of 92, or 10 per cent; sensation of heaviness, 14 subjects out of 77, or 18 percent; headache, 23 subjects out of 92, or 25 per cent; difficulty concentrating, 14 subjects out of 92, or 15 per cent; drowsiness, 36 subjects out of 72, or 50 per cent; warm glow, 6 subjects out of 77, or 8 per cent; relaxation, 5 subjects out of 57, or 9 per cent; fatigue, 10 subjects out of 57, or 18 per cent; sleep, 7 subjects out of 72, or 10 per cent. The effects mentioned were recorded as definite but without the subject's or observer's knowledge that only a placebo had been administered.

Wolf and Pinsky (1954) made an interesting study of placebos and their associated toxic reactions. They found in studying a supposedly effective drug and a placebo (lactose) in patients with anxiety and tension as prominent complaints that these symptoms were made better in about 30 per cent of 31 patients. It is interesting to observe that the improvement rate was greater on the subjective side as just given than it was when objective signs of anxiety, such as tremulousness, sweating, and tachycardia were considered. In this case (objective signs) about 17 per cent were made better.

In these patients of Wolf and Pinsky there were various minor complaints, but three of the 31 patients had major reactions to the placebo: one promptly had overwhelming weakness, palpitation, and nausea both after taking the placebo and also after the tested (therapeutically ineffective) drug. A diffuse rash, itchy, erythematous and maculopapular, developed in a second patient after the placebo. It was diagnosed by a skin consultant as dermatitis medicamentosa. The rash quickly cleared after the placebo administration was stopped. Since the placebo was a small quantity of lactose taken orally, it is hardly possible that it could have produced a real dermatitis. In a third patient within ten minutes after taking her pills, epigastric pain followed by watery diarrhea, urticaria and angioneurotic edema of the lips developed. These signs and symptoms occurred twice more after getting the pills and again when the batch of pills was shifted; thus she had the reaction after both the (therapeutically ineffective) drug as well as after the placebo. *These powerful placebo effects are objective evidence that the reaction phase* (Beecher 1956) *of suffering can produce gross physical change. . . .*

DISCUSSION

An interesting discussion of the use of the placebo in therapy was presented by Gold and others in one of the Cornell Conferences on Therapy (1946). At this particular . . . conference, DuBois commented that although scarcely mentioned in the literature, placebos are more used than any other class of drugs. . . . Wolff pointed out that the placebo as a symbol of the doctor says in effect "I will take care of you." . . . Gold made a strong plea for "pure" placebos; i.e., placebos that do not contain any element that could have a direct effect on the body's cells, otherwise the physician is likely to deceive himself. . . .

In studies of *severe*, steady postoperative wound pain extending over a considerable number of years we have found that rather constantly 30 per cent or more of these individuals get satisfactory pain relief from a placebo. The effectiveness of a placebo does vary in

this work . . . from one group to another, but is always at an impressively high level, generally above the 30 per cent mentioned.

Certainly in these and . . . other studies, . . . the validity of the thesis presented here (namely, that the placebo can have powerful therapeutic effect) much hinges on the definition of "satisfactory relief." In each of the studies referred to, this has been carefully defined. For example, in our pain work satisfactory relief is defined as "50 per cent or more relief of pain" at two checked intervals, 45 and 90 minutes after administration of the agent. (This is a reproducible judgment patients find easy to make.) Each author has been explicit and some have required even greater success than indicated above. For example, Gay and Carliner (1949) required for a positive effect, complete relief of seasickness within 30 minutes of administration of the placebo. The important point here is that in each of these representative studies, patients and observers alike, working with unknowns (usually "double blind" technique) have concluded that a real therapeutic effect has occurred. The implication of this for an uncontrolled study is clear.

The constancy of the placebo effect $(35.2 \pm 2.2 \text{ per cent})$ as indicated by the small standard error of the mean in a fairly wide variety of conditions, pain, nausea, mood changes and so on, suggests that a common fundamental mechanism is operating in these several cases, one that surely deserves further study. . . . Many "effective" drugs have power only a little greater than that of a placebo. To separate out even fairly great true effects above those of a placebo is manifestly difficult to impossible on the basis of clinical impression. Many a drug has been extolled on the basis of clinical impression when the only power it had was that of a placebo. . . .

Placebos provide an opportunity for

attacking problems not possible of study with specifically effective drugs (like morphine on pain) since with these drugs one can never be sure that the original sensation was not altered by drug action. The placebo effect of active drugs is masked by their active effects. The power attributed to morphine is then presumably a placebo effect plus its drug effect. The total "drug" effect is equal to its "active" effect plus its placebo effect: 75 per cent of a group in severe postoperative pain are satisfactorily relieved by a large dose of morphine (15 mg. of the salt per 70 kg. body weight); but 35 per cent are relieved by the placebo.

SUMMARY AND CONCLUSIONS

1. It is evident that placebos have a high degree of therapeutic effectiveness in treating subjective responses, decided improvement, interpreted under the unknowns technique as a real therapeutic effect, being produced in 35.2 ± 2.2 per cent of cases. This is shown in over a thousand patients in 15 studies covering a wide variety of areas: wound pain, the pain of angina pectoris, headache, nausea, phenomena related to cough and to drug induced mood changes, anxiety and tension and finally the common cold; a wide spread of human ailments where subjective factors enter. The relative constancy of the placebo effect over a fairly wide assortment of subjective responses suggests that a common fundamental mechanism is operating, one that deserves more study. *Evidence is presented that placebos are most effective when the stress is greatest.* This supports the concept of the reaction phase as a very important site of drug action. . . .

2. Placebos not only have remarkable therapeutic power but also toxic effects. These are both subjective and objective. Examples are given of the power of the reaction (psychological) component of suffering to produce gross physical

change. It is plain that not only the therapeutic power of a drug under study must in most cases be hedged about by the controls described under (3) below, but studies of side effects must also be subjected to the same controls.

3. When subjective responses, symptoms, are under study, it is apparent that the high order of effectiveness of placebos must be recognized. Clearly, arbitrary criteria of effectiveness of a drug must be set up. Preservation of sound judgment both in the laboratory and in the clinic requires the use of the "double blind" technique, where neither the subject nor the observer is aware of *what* agent was used or indeed *when* it was used. This latter requirement is made possible by the insertion of a placebo, also as an unknown, into the plan of study. A standard of reference should be employed for comparison with new agents or techniques. Randomization of administration of the agents tested is important. The use of correlated data (the agents compared are tested in the same patients) is essential if modest numbers are to be worked with. Mathematical validation of observed difference is often necessary. Whenever judgment is a component of appraisal of a drug or a technique, and this is certainly very often the case, conscious or unconscious bias must be eliminated by the procedures just mentioned. . . . These requirements have been discussed in detail elsewhere (Beecher, 1955).

REFERENCES

BEECHER, H. K.: "The appraisal of drugs intended to alter subjective responses, symptoms." Special Report of the Council on Pharmacy and Chemistry of the American Medical Association. *J.A.M.A. 158*: 399–401, 1955.

———: "The subjective response and reaction to sensation. The reaction phase as the site of effective drug action." *Am. J. Med. 20*: 107–113, 1956.

————, KEATS, A. S., MOSTELLER, F., AND LASAGNA, L.: "The effectiveness of oral analgesics (morphine, codeine, acetylsalicylic acid) and the problem of placebo 'reactors' and 'non-reactors.'" *J. Pharmacol. & Exper. Therap. 109*: 393–400, 1953.

DENTON, J. E., AND BEECHER, H. K.: "New analgesics. III. A comparison of the side effects of morphine, methadone and methadone's isomers in man." *J.A.M.A. 141*: 1148–1153, 1949.

GADDUM, J. H.: "Clinical Pharmacology." *Proc. Roy. Soc. Med., 47*: 195–204, 1954.

GAY, L. M., AND CARLINER, P. E.: "The prevention and treatment of motion sickness." *Johns Hopkins Bull. 84*: 470–487, 1949.

JELLINEK, E. M.: "Clinical tests on comparative effectiveness of analgesic drugs." *Biometrics Bull. 2*: 87–91, 1946.

KEATS, A. S., AND BEECHER, H. K.: "Analgesic potency and side action liability in man of heptazone, WIN 1161-2, 6-methyl dihydromorphine, Metopon, levo-isomethadone and pentobarbital sodium, as a further effort to refine methods of evaluation of analgesic drugs." *J. Pharmacol. & Exper. Therap. 105*: 109–129, 1952.

————, AND BEECHER, H. K.: "The analgesic effectiveness of codeine and meperidine (Demerol)." *J. Pharmacol. & Exper. Therap. 112*: 306–311, 1954a.

————: "The analgesic effectiveness of nalorphine and nalorphine-morphine combinations in man." *J. Pharmacol. & Exper. Therap. 112*: 356–363, 1954b.

LASAGNA, L., MOSTELLER, F., VON FELSINGER, J. M., AND BEECHER, H. K.: "A study of the placebo response." *Am. J. Med. 16*: 770–779, 1954.

PEPPER, O. H. P.: "A note on the placebo." *Transactions and Studies of the College of Physicians of Philadelphia. 13*: 81–82, 1945.

WOLF, S., AND PINSKY, R. H.: "Effects of placebo administration and occurrence of toxic reactions." *J.A.M.A. 155*: 339–341, 1954.

55 | RELIGIOUS HEALING

JEROME D. FRANK

Psychotherapy is one of the oldest professions, appearing in modern, complex, technological, and secular societies such as our own as well as in stone-age, primitive, sacred societies throughout the world. It appears that there are always some unhappy people. Dr. Frank, who has examined elements common to the practice of therapy in a variety of settings, here explores factors which appear to be common to the art of healing for mankind everywhere.

Examination of religious healing in so-called primitive societies and in Western society illuminates certain aspects of human functioning that are relevant to psychotherapy. Methods of supernatural healing . . . also bring out the parallel between inner disorganization and disturbed relations with one's group, and indicate how patterned interaction of patient, healer, and group within the

framework of a self-consistent . . . world can promote healing. Certain properties of healing rituals in primitive societies . . . show interesting resemblances to naturalistic psychotherapeutic methods that may serve to increase understanding of both.

The view that illness can be caused and cured by the intervention of supernatural forces stretches back to furthest antiquity and continues to be important, though often in attenuated form, in most modern cultures. It is possible to make all kinds of distinctions in regard

Excerpts reprinted from Jerome D. Frank, *Persuasion and Healing* (Baltimore: Johns Hopkins Press, 1961), pp. 36–64, by permission.

to the type of supernatural theories invoked, as to whether they dominate a society or are believed only by deviant groups, and in regard to the social acceptance and status of the healers. We shall consider primarily those theories that are integral parts of the religion of the total society or of a respectable and numerous portion of it, and in which the healing rituals are public and socially sanctioned. . . .

ILLNESSES IN PRIMITIVE SOCIETIES

The world views of primitive societies regard illness as a misfortune involving the entire person, with direct consequences on his relationships with the spirit world and with other members of his group. Although they recognize different kinds of illness, their classifications often bear no relation to those of Western medicine. In particular, they may not distinguish sharply between mental and bodily illness, or between that due to natural and that due to supernatural causes.

Illnesses tend to be viewed as symbolic expressions of internal conflicts or of disturbed relationships to others, or both. Thus they may be attributed to soul loss, possession by an evil spirit, the magical insertion of a harmful body by a sorcerer, or the machinations of offended or malicious ancestral ghosts. It is usually assumed that the patient laid himself open to these calamities through some witting or unwitting transgression against the supernatural world, or through incurring the enmity of a sorcerer or someone who has employed a sorcerer to wreak revenge. The transgression need not have been committed by the patient himself. He may fall ill through the sin of a kinsman.

Although many societies recognize that certain illnesses have natural causes, this does not preclude the simultaneous role of supernatural ones. A broken leg may be recognized as caused by a fall from a tree, but the cause of the fall may have been an evil thought or a witch's curse.

Because of the high mortality rates among primitive peoples, diseases in primitive tribes represent a greater threat to the patient than they do in countries with highly developed means of treatment. The longer the illness lasts, the greater the threat becomes. In societies subsisting on a marginal level, illness is a threat to the group as well as to the invalid. It prevents the invalid's making his full contribution to the group's support and diverts the energies of those who must look after him from group purposes. Therefore, it seems likely that every illness has overtones of anxiety, despair, and similar emotions, mounting as cure is delayed. That is, persons for whom healing rituals are performed probably are experiencing emotions that aggravate their distress and disability, whatever their underlying pathological condition may be. The invalid, then, is in conflict within himself and out of harmony with his group. The group is faced with the choice of abandoning him to his fate by completing the process of extrusion, or of making strenuous efforts to heal him, thereby restoring him to useful membership in his community.

Before considering the healing of illness in primitive societies, it seems appropriate to examine a type of personal disaster that can befall members of certain groups and that may have a counterpart in civilized societies. This is the so-called taboo death, which apparently results from noxious emotional states.

Anthropological literature contains anecdotes of savages who, on learning that they have inadvertently broken a taboo, go into a state of panic and excitement that eventuates in death in a few hours. Unfortunately in none of these cases can more mundane causes of rapid death, such as overwhelming infection, be entirely excluded. The evidence that members of certain tribes may pine away and die within a brief period after learning that they have been cursed is more fully documented and more convincing. The *post hoc* nature of the explanations cannot be overlooked, especially since in groups where this type of death occurs, practically all illness and death is attributed to having been cursed. Nevertheless, the process has been observed in sufficient detail in different tribes to make the explanation highly plausible.

The most convincing examples are those in which a native at the point of death from a curse rapidly recovers when the spell is broken by a more powerful one, as in the following anecdote, which can be multiplied many times:

Some years ago my father, who lived in Kenya, employed a Kikuyu garden "boy," of whom we were all fond. Njombo was gay, cheerful and in the prime of life. He was paying goats to purchase a wife and looking forward to marriage and a bit of land of his own. One day we noticed he was beginning to lose weight and looked pinched and miserable. We dosed him with all the usual medicines to no avail. Then we persuaded him, much against his will, to go into a hospital. Three weeks later he was back with a note from the doctor: "There is nothing wrong with this man except that he has made up his mind to die."

After that Njombo took to his bed, a heap of skins, and refused all food and drink. He shrank to nothing and at last went into a coma. Nothing we could do or say would strike a spark, and all seemed to be up with him.

As a last resort, my father went to the local chief and threatened him with all sorts of dreadful penalties if he did not take action to save Njombo's life. This was largely bluff, but the chief fell for it. That evening we saw a man with a bag of stoppered gourds entering Njombo's hut. We did not interfere, and no doubt a goat was slaughtered. Next morning, Njombo allowed us to feed him a little beef tea. From that moment he started

to rally—the will to live was restored. We asked no questions, but learned some time later that Njombo had had a serious quarrel over the girl and that his rival had cursed him. Only when the curse was removed could he hope to survive.

In certain societies, the victim's expectation of death may be powerfully reinforced by the attitudes of his group. For example, in the Murngin, a North Australian tribe, when the theft of a man's soul becomes general knowledge, he and his tribe collaborate in hastening his demise. Having lost his soul, he is already "half dead." Since his soul is in neither this world nor the next, he is a danger to himself as a spiritual entity and also to his tribe because his soul, not having been properly laid away, is likely to cause illness and death among his kin. All normal social activity with him therefore ceases and he is left alone. Then, shortly before he dies, the group returns to him under the guidance of a ceremonial leader to perform mourning rites, the purpose of which is "to cut him off entirely from the ordinary world and ultimately place him . . . in . . . the . . . world . . . of the dead." The victim, concomitantly, recognizes his change of status: ". . . the wounded feudist killed by magic dances his totem dance to . . . insure his immediate passage to the totem well. . . . His effort is not to live but to die." The writer concludes: "If all a man's near kin . . . business associates, friends, and all other members of the society, should suddenly withdraw themselves because of some dramatic circumstance . . . looking at the man as one already dead, and then after some little time perform over him a sacred ceremony believed with certainty to guide him out of the land of the living . . . the enormous suggestive power of this twofold movement of the community . . . can be somewhat understood by ourselves."

Although this account stresses the

role of group influences, the major source of the victim's decline is probably the emotional state induced by his conviction—grounded in his belief system—that he has lost his soul. In this example the group's withdrawal reinforces this conviction. It is conceivable, however, that the victim would have died even if surrounded by their loving care if his conviction that the situation was hopeless were sufficiently strong. Calling attention to the interpersonal forces involved in the process should not be taken as minimizing the importance of intrapersonal ones.

Plausible speculations based on work with animals have been offered to explain the physiological mechanism of death in these cases. One hypothesis is that it might be due to prolonged adrenal overexcitation caused by terror, leading to a state analogous to surgical shock. Another, based on studies of physiological changes in wild rats who give up and die when placed in a stressful situation after their whiskers have been clipped, suggests that the emotional state is more one of despair than terror, and that the mechanism of death is stoppage of the heart resulting from overactivity of the vagus nerve. This view is supported by fascinating and suggestive parallels between this phenomenon in wild rats and taboo deaths in primitive peoples—for example, prompt recovery even at the point of death if the stress is suddenly removed. Both hypotheses are plausible, and each may account for a particular variety of emotionally caused death—the first for the rapid form, if it occurs, and the second for the slower variety.

In civilized as well as primitive societies a person's conviction that his predicament is hopeless may cause or hasten his disintegration and death. For example, the death rate of the aged shortly after admission to state mental hospitals is unduly high, and with these and other age groups often no adequate cause of death is found at autopsy, raising the possibility that some of these deaths are caused by hopelessness, aggravated by abandonment by the patient's group. Similarly, some young schizophrenics may go into overactive panic states in which they exhaust themselves and die. This fortunately rare reaction usually occurs in conjunction with the patient's admission to the hospital; that is, at the moment when his family withdraws and he feels most alone. Sometimes it can be successfully interrupted if a member of the treatment staff succeeds in making contact with the patient and getting across to him, by one means or another, that someone still cares about him.

Descriptions of the "give-up-itis" reaction of American prisoners of war of the Japanese and Koreans suggest a similar interaction of hopelessness and group isolation to produce death. A former prisoner of war well describes this reaction. He lists the major factors that had to be dealt with in order to survive as: "the initial shock and subsequent depression induced by being taken prisoner by Oriental people; the feeling of being deserted and abandoned by one's own people; the severe deprivation of food, warmth, clothes, living comforts, and sense of respectability; the constant intimidation and physical beatings from the captors; loss of self-respect and the respect of others; the day-to-day uncertainty of livelihood and the vague indeterminable unknown future date of deliverance." It will be noted that physical and psychological threats are placed on the same footing. Under these circumstances: "Occasionally an individual would . . . lose interest in himself and his future, which was reflected in quiet or sullen withdrawal from the group, filth of body and clothes, trading of food for cigarettes, slowing of work rate . . . and an expressed attitude of not giving a damn. . . . If this attitude were not met with firm resistance . . . death inevitably resulted."

This is clearly a description of hopelessness. It could be successfully combatted by "forced hot soap-and-water bathing, shaving and delousing, special appetizing food, obtaining a few days rest in camp . . . a mixture of kindly sympathetic interest and anger-inducing attitudes. Victory was assured with the first sign of a smile or evidence of pique." It is of interest that successful measures may include anger-arousing as well as nurturant behavior. As another observer reports: "One of the best ways to get a man on his feet initially was to make him so mad, by goading, prodding, or blows, that he tried to get up and beat you. If you could manage this, the man invariably got well." Thus it may be that any kind of emotional stimulus, whether pleasant or not, may successfully counteract lethal despair if it succeeds in breaking through the victim's isolation, demonstrates that his comrades care about him, and implies that there are things he can do to help himself.

HEALING IN PRIMITIVE SOCIETIES: THE HEALING CEREMONY

Healing in primitive societies utilizes both individual and group methods. It may be conducted by the shaman with the patient alone, analogous to the pattern of Western medicine. The shaman makes a diagnosis by performing certain acts and then offers a remedy, which may be a medication or the performance of suitable incantations. . . . The healing power of these procedures probably lies in the patient's expectation of help, based on his perception of the shaman as possessing special healing powers, derived from his ability to communicate with the spirit world.

Other forms of primitive healing involve a long-term two-person relationship between shaman and patient, which

seems to show certain analogies to long-term psychotherapy. The only available descriptions, however, are too sketchy to warrant consideration here.

This section considers a third type of primitive healing, which has been adequately described by anthropologists and which bears on psychotherapy—the group healing ceremonial. These rituals may involve ancestral or other spirits, for example, and are intensive, time-limited efforts aimed at curing specific illness and involving members of the patient's family. As a result, they cast little, if any, light on certain features that may be of central importance in long-term individual psychotherapy, such as the development and examination of transference reactions between patient and therapist. On the other hand, they throw certain aspects of long-term therapy into relief, as it were, by compressing them into a brief time span, and highlight the healing role of group and cultural forces, the effect of which may be underestimated in individual therapy because they are present only implicitly. With these considerations in mind, it may be instructive to consider a healing ceremony in some detail—the treatment of "espanto" in a sixty-three-year-old Guatemalan Indian woman. This was her eighth attack. Her symptoms seem similar to those that would lead an American psychiatrist to diagnose an agitated depression. The Indians attribute it to soul loss.

The treatment began with a diagnostic session attended not only by the patient but by her husband, a male friend, and two anthropologists. The healer felt her pulse for a while, while looking her in the eye, then confirmed that she was suffering from "espanto." He then told her in a calm, authoritative manner that it had happened near the river when she saw her husband foolishly lose her money to a loose woman, and he urged her to tell the whole story. After a brief period of reluctance, the patient "loosed a flood of words telling of her life frustrations and anxieties. . . . During the recital . . . the curer . . . nodded non-committally, but permissively, keeping his eyes fixed on her face. Then he said that it was good that she should tell him of her life." Finally they went over the precipitating incident of the present attack in detail. In essence, she and her husband were passing near the spot where he had been deceived by the loose woman. She upbraided him, and he struck her with a rock.

The curer then told her he was confident she could be cured and outlined in detail the preparations that she would have to make for the curing session four days later. She was responsible for these preparations, which involved procuring and preparing certain medications, preparing a feast, persuading a woman friend or kinsman to be her "servant" during the preparatory period and healing session, and persuading one of the six chiefs of the village to participate with the medicine man in the ceremony.

The ceremony itself began at four in the afternoon and lasted until five the next morning. Before the healer arrived, the house and the house altar had been decorated with pine boughs, and numerous invited guests and participants had assembled. After they were all present, the healer made his entrance, shook hands all around, and checked the preparations carefully. Then there was a period of light refreshment and social chitchat, which apparently helped to organize a social group around the patient and to relax tension.

After dusk the healer, chief, and others of the group went off to church, apparently to appease the Christian deities in advance, since "recovery of a soul involves dealing with renegade saints and familiar spirits certainly not approved of by God Almighty." When they returned, a large meal was served. The patient

did not eat, but was complimented by all present on her food. Then the healer carried out a long series of rituals involving such activities as making wax dolls of the chief of evil spirits and his wife, to whom the healer appealed for return of the patient's soul, and elaborate massage of the patient with whole eggs, which were believed to absorb some of the sickness from the patient's body. The curer, the chief, two male helpers, and the ever-present anthropologists next took the eggs and a variety of paraphernalia, including gifts for the evil spirits, to the place where the patient had lost her soul, and the healer pleaded with various spirits to restore her soul to her.

On their return they were met at the door by the patient, who showed an intense desire to know whether the mission had been successful. The curer spoke noncommittal but comforting words. This was followed by much praying by the healer and the chief before the house altar and a special ground altar set up outside, and by rites to purify and sanctify the house. Some of these activities were devoted to explaining to the household patron saint why it was necessary to deal with evil spirits. All this took until about 2 A.M., at which time the ceremony came to a climax. The patient, naked except for a small loin cloth, went outside. Before the audience, the healer sprayed her entire body with a magic fluid that had been prepared during the ritual and that had a high alcoholic content. Then she had to sit, naked and shivering, in the cold air for about ten minutes. Finally she drank about a pint of the fluid. Then they returned indoors, the patient lay down in front of the altar, and the healer massaged her vigorously and systematically with the eggs, then with one of his sandals. She then arose, put on her clothes, lay down on the rustic platform bed, and was covered with blankets. By this time she was thoroughly relaxed.

Finally, the healer broke the six eggs used in the massage into a bowl of water one by one, and as he watched their swirling whites he reviewed the history of the patient's eight "espantos," pointing out the "proofs" in the eggs. The sinking of the eggs to the bottom of the bowl showed that all the previous "espantos" had been cured and that the present symptoms would shortly disappear. The healer "pronounced the cure finished. The patient roused herself briefly on the bed and shouted hoarsely, 'That is right.' Then she sank back into a deep snoring sleep." This ended the. ceremony and everyone left but the patient's immediate family.

The patient had a high fever for the following few days. This did not concern the healer, whose position was that everyone died sooner or later anyway, and if the patient died, it was better for her to die with her soul than without it. He refused to see her again, as his work was done. The anthropologist treated her with antibiotics, and she made a good recovery from the fever and the depression. The author notes that for the four weeks he was able to observe her "she seemed to have developed a new personality. . . . The hypochondriacal complaints, nagging of her husband and relatives, withdrawal from her social contacts, and anxiety symptoms all disappeared."

This example illustrates certain generalizations about religious healing which, if not universal, are at least widely applicable. It should be noted that healing rituals are not undertaken lightly. Usually they are resorted to only after simpler healing methods have failed. The analogy springs to mind that in America patients are often referred for psychiatric treatment only after all other forms of treatment have failed to relieve their suffering. In any case, this suggests that the state of mind of a patient receiving a healing ritual and that of one receiving psychotherapy may often resemble each other in some respects. Both types of patient are apt to be discouraged and apprehensive about their condition, while at the same time hopeful for relief from the treatment.

That the mythology of the shaman does not correspond to objective reality does not matter. The patient believes in it and belongs to a society that believes in it. The protecting spirits, the evil spirits, the supernatural monsters and magical monsters are elements of a coherent system which are the basis of the natives' concept of the universe. The patient accepts them, or rather she has never doubted them. What she does not accept are the incomprehensible and arbitrary pains which represent an element foreign to her system but which the shaman, by invoking the myth, will replace in a whole in which everything has its proper place.

The conceptual scheme is validated and reinforced by the rituals that it prescribes. In the above example this occurred especially when the healer examined the eggs swirling in the water and pointed out to the assembled group the "proofs" of the patient's previous illnesses. The scheme, moreover, cannot be shaken by failure of the ritual to cure the patient. If this one had died, the ceremony would still have been regarded as successful in restoring her soul.

The shaman's activities validate his supernatural powers. In this example his manner in the diagnostic interview and especially his revelation to the patient of an event that she did not know he knew, and that he therefore presumably learned about through magic, must have had this effect. In other rituals the shaman may start by reciting how he got his "call" or citing examples of the previous cures, to which others present may add confirmation. He may resort to legerdemain, as in the Kwakiutl, but most authorities agree that this is not regarded as trickery, even when the audience knows how it is done. They seem to give emotional assent to the proposition that the bloody bit of cotton is the patient's illness and has been extracted from his body, while at another level they know perfectly well that it is only a piece of cotton. Perhaps their state of mind is analogous to that of partakers of communion, for whom in one sense the bread and wine are the body and blood of Christ while in another they are just bread and wine. In any case, the healing ritual reinforces the image of the shaman as a powerful ally in the patient's struggle with the malign forces that have made him ill.

Rituals often involve a preparatory period, which represents a dramatic break in the usual routine of daily activities. In the case of "espanto" it served to jolt the patient out of her usual routines, heighten her sense of personal importance by letting her have a "servant," and start the process of rallying family and group forces to her aid. Also, like the rest of the ritual, it gave her something to do to combat her illness, in itself a powerful allayer of anxiety and strengthener of the expectancy of cure.

That patient's family, as well as respected representatives of the tribe, convey their concern for him by participating in the ritual. As they represent a healthy group, they are not likely to reinforce the patient's pathological trends, as may occur, for example, in a mental hospital.

Many rituals have an altruistic quality. All the participants try to help the patient by performing parts of the ritual, interceding for him with the powers he has presumably offended, or defending the patient to them. Sometimes the patient also performs services for the group. In our example, the patient was responsible for preparing the feast. The performance of services to others may help to counteract the patient's morbid self-absorption and enhance his sense of self-

worth by demonstrating that he can still be of use to them. It also contributes to the meritorious quality of the ritual.

In those ceremonies that involve confession, atonement, and forgiveness, the gaining of merit is especially apparent. The fact that confession is required for cure implies a close link between illness and transgression, as discussed earlier. Impersonalized forms of confession and repentance, as in some Christian liturgies, serve the purpose of general purification.

Some healing rituals elicit confessions of specific personal transgressions based on detailed review of the patient's past history with special emphasis on the events surrounding his illness. In addition to its confessional . . . aspect, this procedure brings the patient's vague, chaotic, conflicting, and mysterious feelings to the center of his attention and places them in a self-consistent conceptual system. Thus they are "realized in an order and on a level which permits them to unfold freely and leads to their resolution."

It may be noted in passing that the shaman's technique of eliciting this type of confession may also be a way of demonstrating his powers as in the example cited. That is, he warns the patient that the spirits have already told him what the true facts are and that they cannot be hidden. As the patient confesses, the shaman confirms that this is what he already knew and urges the patient to confess further. Often the other participants jog the patient's memory or bring up episodes with the patient in which they too transgressed, or even crimes ostensibly unrelated to the patient's illness. Thus the process further cements the group, and participants other than the patient may gain virtue from it. The confession may be followed by intercession with the spirit world on behalf of the patient by the whole group as well as by the shaman, heightening the patient's hope that forgiveness will be forthcoming.

Thus confession may have many implications. It helps the patient to make sense of his condition, counteracts his consciousness of sin, brings him into closer relationship with his group, impresses him with the shaman's powers, and improves the relationship of all concerned with the spirit world. In these ways it counteracts his anxiety, strengthens his self-esteem, and helps him to resolve his conflicts.

Healing ceremonies tend to be highly charged emotionally. The shaman may act out a life-and-death struggle between his spirit and the evil spirit that has possessed the patient. The patient may vividly re-enact past experiences or act out the struggles of spirit forces within himself. The emotional excitement may be intensified by rhythmic music, chanting, and dancing. It frequently mounts to the point of exhausting the patient and not infrequently is enhanced by some strong physical shock. In our example, it will be recalled, the patient was sprayed by an alcoholic liquid, which gave her a bad chill.*

Finally, many rituals make a strong aesthetic appeal. The setting may be especially decorated for the occasion, and participants may be elaborately costumed, may perform stylized dances, and may draw sand paintings and the like. Since these trappings and activities have symbolic meanings, they not only are soothing and inspiring aesthetically but they represent tangible reinforcements of the conceptual organization that the ritual endeavors to impose on the patient's inchoate sufferings. Participation of the whole group either actively or as attentive spectators fosters group solidarity.

In short, methods of primitive healing

involve an interplay between patient, healer, group, and the world of the supernatural, which serves to raise the patient's expectancy of cure, help him to harmonize his inner conflicts, reintegrate him with his group and the spirit world, supply a conceptual framework to aid this, and stir him emotionally. In the process they combat his anxiety and strengthen his sense of self-worth.

RELIGIOUS HEALING IN THE WESTERN WORLD: LOURDES

From its inception, Christianity has included the notion of healing through divine intervention. Starting with the healing miracles of Christ, this form of curing has come down through the centuries to the present. Today healing sects like Christian Science and shrines of miraculous healing have millions of devotees. Since the rituals of these groups and places parallel religious healing in primitive societies in many ways, it may be of interest to take a look at one of them. The great modern shrine of Lourdes seems particularly suitable because it has been well described and because the cures of severe illness that have occurred there are exceptionally well documented and have received careful critical scrutiny.

The history of Lourdes, starting with the visions of Bernadette Soubirous in 1858, is too well known to require retelling here. It is perhaps odd, in view of subsequent developments, that the apparition that appeared to Bernadette and told her where to dig for the spring said nothing about its healing powers. Be that as it may, miraculous cures following immersion in the spring were soon reported, and today over two million pilgrims visit Lourdes every year, including over thirty thousand sick.

The world view supporting Lourdes, like those on which religious healing in primitive tribes is based, is all-inclusive

---

* See selection 23 on the therapeutic value of stress.—Eds.

and is shared by almost all the pilgrims to the shrine. While cures are regarded as validating it, failures cannot shake it. Those who seek help at Lourdes have usually been sick a long time and have failed to respond to medical remedies. Like the primitives who undergo a healing ritual, most are close to despair. Being chronic invalids, they have had to withdraw from most or all of their community activities and have become burdens to their families. Their activities have become routinized and constricted, their lives are bleak and monotonous, and they have nothing to anticipate but further suffering and death.

The decision to make the pilgrimage to Lourdes changes all this. The preparatory period is a dramatic break in routine. Collecting funds for the journey, arranging for medical examinations, and making the travel plans requires the cooperative effort of members of the patient's family and the wider community. Often the congregation contributes financial aid. Prayers and masses are offered for the invalid. Members of the family, and often the patient's physician or a priest, accompany him to Lourdes and serve as tangible evidence of the interest of the family and larger group in his welfare. Often pilgrims from many communities travel together, and there are religious ceremonies while the train is en route and at every stop. In short, the preparatory period is emotionally stirring, brings the patient from the periphery of his group to its center, and enhances his expectation of help. It is interesting in this connection that, except for the original cures, Lourdes has failed to heal those who live in its vicinity. This suggests that the emotional excitement connected with the preparatory period and journey to the shrine may be essential for healing to occur.

On arrival at Lourdes after an exhausting, even life-endangering journey, the sufferer's expectation of help is further strengthened. He is plunged into "a city of pilgrims, and they are everywhere; people who have come from the four corners of the earth with but one purpose: prayer, and healing for themselves or for their loved ones. . . . One is surrounded by them, and steeped in their atmosphere every moment of existence in Lourdes." Everyone hopes to witness or experience a miraculous cure. Accounts of previous cures are on every tongue, and the pilgrim sees the votive offerings and the piles of discarded crutches of those who have been healed. Thus the ritual may be said to begin with a validation of the shrine's power, analogous to the medicine man's review of his cures in primitive healing rites.

The pilgrims' days are filled with religious services and trips to the Grotto, where they are immersed in the ice-cold spring. Every afternoon all the pilgrims and invalids who are at Lourdes at the time, and they number forty or fifty thousand, gather at the Esplanade in front of the shrine for the procession that is the climax of each day's activities. The bedridden are placed nearest the shrine, those who can sit up are behind them, the ambulatory invalids behind them, while the hordes of visitors fill the rest of the space. The enormous emotional and aesthetic impact of the procession is well conveyed by the following quotation:

At four the bells begin to peal—the Procession begins to form. The priests in their varied robes assemble at the Grotto. . . . The bishop appears with the monstrance under the sacred canopy. The loud-speakers open up. A great hymn rolls out, the huge crowd joining in unison, magnificently. The Procession begins its¯long, impressive way down one side and up the other of the sunny Esplanade. First the Children of Mary, young girls in blue capes, white veils . . . then forty or fifty priests in black cassocks . . . other priests in white surplices . . . then come the Bishops in purple . . . and finally the officiating Archbishop in his white and gold robes under the golden canopy. Bringing up the rear large numbers of men and women of the different pilgrimages, Sisters, Nurses, members of various religious organizations; last of all the doctors. . . . Hymns, prayers, fervent, unceasing. In the Square the sick line up in two rows. . . . Every few feet, in front of them, kneeling priests with arms outstretched praying earnestly, leading the responses. Nurses and orderlies on their knees, praying too. . . . Ardor mounts as the Blessed Sacrament approaches. Prayers gather intensity. . . . The Bishop leaves the shelter of the canopy, carrying the monstrance. The Sacred Host is raised above each sick one. The great crowd falls to its knees. All arms are outstretched in one vast cry to Heaven. As far as one can see in any direction, people are on their knees, praying. . . .

What are the results of the tremendous outpouring of emotion and faith? The great majority of the sick do not experience a cure. However, most of the pilgrims seem to derive some psychological benefit from the experience. The pilgrimage is regarded as meritorious in itself and the whole atmosphere of Lourdes is spiritually uplifting. In this connection, the altruism of all involved is especially worthy of note. Physicians, brancardiers (who serve the sick), and helpers of all sorts give their time and effort freely, and throughout the ceremonies the emphasis is on self-forgetfulness and devotion to the welfare of others. The pilgrims pray for the sick and the sick for each other, not themselves. Therefore, the words attributed to an old pilgrim may well be largely true: "Of the uncured none despair. All go away filled with hope and a new feeling of strength. The trip to Lourdes is never made in vain."

The evidence that an occasional cure of advanced organic disease does occur at Lourdes is as strong as that for any other phenomenon accepted as true. The reported frequency of such cures varies widely depending on the criteria used.

The piles of crutches attest to the fact that many pilgrims achieve improved functioning, at least temporarily. In many of these cases, however, improvement is probably attributable to heightened morale, enabling them to function better in the face of an unchanged organic handicap. Fully documented cures of unquestionable and gross organic disease are extremely infrequent—probably no more frequent than similar ones occurring in secular settings.

In the century of the shrine's existence, less than a hundred cures have passed the stringent test leading the Church to declare them miraculous. This figure may well be much too low, as many convincing cases fail to qualify because they lack the extensive documentary support required. But even several thousand cures of organic disease would represent only a small fraction of one per cent of those who have made the pilgrimage. As a sympathetic student of spiritual healing writes: ". . . there is probably no stream in Britain which could not boast of as high a proportion of cures as the stream at Lourdes if patients came in the same numbers and in the same psychological state of expectant excitement."

Inexplicable cures of serious organic disease occur in everyday medical practice. Every physician has either personally treated or heard about patients who mysteriously recovered from a seemingly fatal illness. One surgeon has recently assembled from the literature ninety cases of unquestionable cancer that disappeared without adequate treatment. Had these cures occurred after a visit to Lourdes, many would have regarded them as miraculous. Since no physician sees enough of these phenomena to acquire a sufficient sample for scientific study, and since they cannot be explained by current medical theories, the fascinating questions they raise have tended to be pushed aside.

The processes by which cures at Lourdes occur do not seem to differ in kind from those involved in normal healing, although they are remarkably strengthened and accelerated. Careful reading of the reports reveals that healing is not instantaneous, as is often claimed, but that, like normal healing, it requires time. It is true that the consciousness of cure is often (not always) sudden and may be accompanied by immediate improvement in function—the paralyzed walk, the blind see, and those who had been unable to retain food suddenly regain their appetites. But actual tissue healing takes hours, days, or weeks, and persons who have lost much weight require the usual period of time to regain it, as would be expected if healing occurred by the usual processes. Moreover, gaps of specialized tissues such as skin are not restored but are filled by scar formation as in normal healing. No one has regrown an amputated limb at Lourdes.

It should be added that cures at Lourdes involve the person's total personality, not merely his body. The healed, whatever they were like before their recovery, all are said to be possessed of a remarkable serenity and a desire to be of service to others.

Rivers of ink have been spilled in controversy over whether or not the cures at Lourdes are genuine, based on the erroneous assumption that one's acceptance or rejection of them is necessarily linked to belief or disbelief in miracles or in the Catholic faith. Actually, it is perfectly possible to accept some Lourdes cures as genuine while maintaining skepticism as to their miraculous causation, or to be a devout Catholic while rejecting modern miracles. The world is full of phenomena that cannot be explained by the conceptual schemes current at a particular time. Today these include inexplicable cures of fatal illnesses, in secular as well as religious settings. Depending on one's theoretical predilections, one may choose to believe that all, none, or a certain class of these are miraculous. The mere fact of their occurrence leaves the question of their cause completely open.

A not implausible assumption, in the light of our review of primitive healing, is that Lourdes cures are in some way related to the sufferers' emotional state. This view is supported by the conditions under which the cures occur, and the type of person who seems most apt to experience them. Although they can occur en route to Lourdes, on the return journey, or even months later, most cures occur at the shrine and at the moments of greatest emotional intensity and spiritual fervor—while taking communion, or during immersion in the spring or when the host is raised over the sick at the passing of the sacrament during the procession. The persons who have been cured include the deserving and the sinful, believers and apparent skeptics, but they tend to have one common characteristic: they are "almost invariably simple people—the poor and the humble; people who do not interpose a strong intellect between themselves and the Higher Power." That is, they are not detached or critical. It is generally agreed that persons who remain entirely unmoved by the ceremonies do not experience cures.

The skeptics who have been cured had a parent or spouse who was highly devout, suggesting either that their skepticism was a reaction-formation against an underlying desire to believe, or at least that the pilgrimage involved emotional conflict. In this connection, all cured skeptics have become ardent believers.

In short, the healing ceremonials at Lourdes, like those of primitive tribes, involve a climactic union of the patient, his family, the larger group, and the supernatural world by means of a dramatic, emotionally charged, aesthetically rich ritual that expresses and reinforces a shared ideology.

MAGICAL HEALING, CULTS, AND CHARLATANS

In most societies, in addition to institutionalized, public, "respectable" forms of religious healing, there are more-or-less clandestine, private forms of trafficking with supernatural forces, involving small, sometimes secret, groups, or a strictly private arrangement between patient and healer. Despite the large following of cults and quacks, which suggests that they must help many persons, they do not repay extended attention because of their enormous variety and the lack of dispassionate, objective information about most of them.

The main interest of such cults for us is that their success seems to rest on their ability to evoke the patient's expectancy of help, a factor also involved in religious healing. Two sources of this expectancy are discernible. The first is the personal magnetism of the healer, often strengthened by his own faith in what he does. As an investigator who interviewed many such healers writes: "The vast majority of the sectarians sincerely believe in the efficacy of their practices . . . the writer has talked to [chiropractors] whose faith was . . . nothing short of evangelistic, whose sincerity could no more be questioned than that of Persia's 'whirling dervishes.'" However, the success of peddlers of obviously worthless nostrums and gadgets attests to the fact that the healer need not necessarily believe in the efficacy of his methods to be able to convince his patients of their power.

Another source of the patient's faith is the ideology of the healer or sect, which offers him a rationale, however absurd, for making sense of his illness and the treatment procedure, and places the healer in the position of transmitter or controller of impressive healing forces. In this he is analogous to the shaman. Often these forces are supernatural, but the healer may pose as a scientist who has discovered new and potent scientific principles of healing, thus surrounding himself with the aura that anything labeled scientific inspires in members of modern Western societies. These healers characteristically back up their pretensions with an elaborate scientific-sounding patter and often add an imposing array of equipment complete with dials, flashing lights, and sound effects.

The apparent success of healing methods based on all sorts of ideologies and methods compels the conclusion that the healing power of faith resides in the patient's state of mind, not in the validity of its object. At the risk of laboring this point, an experimental demonstration of it with three severely ill, bedridden women may be reported. One had chronic inflammation of the gall bladder with stones, the second had failed to recuperate from a major abdominal operation and was practically a skeleton, and the third was dying of widespread cancer. The physician first permitted a prominent local faith healer to try to cure them by absent treatment without the patients' knowledge. Nothing happened. Then he told the patients about the faith healer, built up their expectations over several days, and finally assured them that he would be treating them from a distance at a certain time the next day. This was a time in which he was sure that the healer did *not* work. At the suggested time all three patients improved quickly and dramatically. The second was permanently cured. The other two were not, but showed striking temporary responses. The cancer patient, who was severely anemic and whose tissues had become waterlogged, promptly excreted all the accumulated fluid, recovered from her anemia, and regained sufficient strength to go home and resume her household duties. She remained virtually symptom free until her death. The gall bladder patient lost her symptoms, went home, and had no recurrence for several years. These three patients were greatly helped by a belief that was false—that the faith healer was treating them from a distance—suggesting that "expectant trust" in itself can be a powerful healing force.

SUMMARY

This review of religious healing, with a side glance at its questionable fringes, emphasizes the profound influence of emotions on health and suggests that anxiety and despair can be lethal, confidence and hope, life-giving. The modern assumptive world of Western society, which includes mind-body dualism, has had difficulty incorporating this obvious fact and has therefore tended to underemphasize it.

Part of the deleterious effect of all illness, especially if prolonged, results from the emotional states it fosters. Constant misery, forced relinquishment of the activities and roles that give significance to life, the threat of dissolution, all may intensify feelings of anxiety and despair, and these may be further enhanced by reactions of anxiety, impatience, and progressive withdrawal in those around the patient, especially when his illness threatens their security as well as his own. Thus illness may lead to a vicious circle by fostering emotional states that aggravate it.

Methods of religious healing may evoke emotions that are equally intense and perhaps as distressing as those produced by the illness itself, but they do it in a different context. The sufferings of a debilitated invalid caused by the rigors of the trip to Lourdes, and cul-

minating in an icy bath, must often be very severe. This suggests that the effects of strong emotions on one's well-being depend on their meaning or context. If they imply hopelessness and lead to progressive isolation of the patient from his usual sources of support, they may kill him. If they are aroused in a setting of massive human and supernatural encouragement and can be discharged through organized activities in a context of hopefulness, they can be healing.

The core of the effectiveness of methods of religious and magical healing seems to lie in their ability to arouse hope by capitalizing on the patient's dependency on others. This dependency ordinarily focuses on one person, the healer, who may work privately with the patient or in a group setting. In either case, the patient's expectation of help is aroused partly by the healer's personal attributes, but more by his paraphernalia, which gains its power from its culturally determined symbolic meaning. Even in private forms of healing, group and cultural factors are implicit.

This becomes explicit in healing ceremonies, in which the healer acts as the mediator between the patient, his group, and the supernatural world, and the patient's faith in him rests largely on his institutionalized role and the powers attributed to him by the group. The role of the healer may be diffused among many persons, as at Lourdes, where it resides in the participating priests.

The patient's hope is enhanced by a set of assumptions about illness and healing that he shares with his society and a ritual based on it. The theory cannot be shaken by failures, while every repetition of the ritual validates and reinforces it. Thus knowledge of previous failures need not diminish the patient's belief that he will be helped.

The ideology and ritual supply the patient with a conceptual framework for organizing his chaotic, mysterious, and vague distress and give him a plan of action, helping him to regain a sense of direction and mastery and to resolve his inner conflicts. To the extent that the ritual includes participation of the group and healer, it heightens the patient's hope by demonstrating to him that he has allies.

Methods of religious healing also have aspects that heighten the patient's sense of self-worth. Performance of the ritual is usually regarded as meritorious in itself—all involved gain virtue by participating. The patient becomes the focus of the group's attention and, by implication, worthy of the invocation of supernatural forces on his behalf. If he is cured, this may be taken as a mark of divine favor, permanently elevating his value in his own and the group's eyes. In fact, one factor in maintaining a cure may be the changed attitude of the group, which continually reinforces it. That is, if the patient relapsed, he would be letting the group down.

An aspect of the interplay of patient and group in religious cures that deserves special comment is the emphasis on mutual service. Often the patient does things for the group, and the group intercedes for the patient. At Lourdes, pilgrims pray for each other, not for themselves. This stress on service counteracts the patient's morbid self-preoccupation, strengthens his self-esteem by demonstrating that he can do something for others, and cements the tie between patient and group.

Many religious healing rituals include a detailed review of the patient's past life, with especial emphasis on the events surrounding his illness, usually coupled with some form of confession and forgiveness. These activities can be helpful in several ways. By bringing certain feelings and problems to the forefront of the patient's attention, they help him to conceptualize, clarify, and re-integrate them. They also strengthen the patient's bonds with his group and with the supernatural world, in that the members of the group, after hearing the worst, still stand by him and join their pleas for supernatural forgiveness with his. Finally, in religious healing, relief of suffering and production of attitude change are inseparable. Healing is accompanied not only by a profound change in the patient's feelings about himself and others, but by a strengthening of previous assumptive systems or, sometimes, conversion to new ones.

56 | ON BECOMING A PERSON

CARL R. ROGERS

Despite the many elaborate doctrines of psychotherapeutic procedure, success in this field remains largely a result of artistry and merchandising, for psychotherapy is an undeveloped science. Some patients experience tremendous relief and show very great progress; others benefit less or not at all. A portion of the latter group "go shopping" among practitioners, seeking ones who appear more promising and who arouse in them hope and expectation. Honest and thoughtful practitioners who wish to be more effective continually rework the basic concepts that guide them. Here, one of the pioneering researchers in psychotherapy guides us through his exploration of the purpose and methods of psychotherapy and, in a broader sense, the meaning of life.

. . . What are the characteristics of those relationships which *do* help, which do facilitate growth? And at the other end of the scale is it possible to discern those characteristics which make a relationship unhelpful, even though it was the sincere intent to promote growth and development? It is to these questions, particularly the first, that I would like to take you with me over some of the paths I have explored, and to tell you where I am, as of now, in my thinking on these issues.

. . . . .

Most [research] studies throw light on the attitudes . . . of the helping person which make a relationship growth-promoting or growth-inhibiting. Let us look at some of these.

A careful study of parent-child relationships made some years ago by Baldwin and others at the Fels Institute contains interesting evidence. Of the various clusters of parental attitudes toward children, the "acceptant-democratic" seemed most growth-facilitating. Children of these parents with their warm and equalitarian attitudes showed an accelerated intellectual development (an increasing I.Q.), more originality, more emotional security and control, less excitability than children from other types of homes. Though somewhat slow initially in social development, they were, by the time they reached school age, popular, friendly, non-aggressive leaders.

Where parents' attitudes are classed as "actively rejectant" the children show a slightly decelerated intellectual development, relatively poor use of the abilities they do possess, and some lack of originality. They are emotionally unstable, rebellious, aggressive, and quarrelsome.

Excerpts reprinted from Carl R. Rogers, *On Becoming a Person*, pp. 41–46, 50–56, 107–22, 215–22, 352. Copyright © 1961 by Carl R. Rogers. Reprinted by permission of the publisher, Houghton Mifflin Company.

The children of parents with other attitude syndromes tend in various respects to fall in between these extremes.

. . . . .

Let me turn to another careful study in a very different area. Whitehorn and Betz investigated the degree of success achieved by young resident physicians in working with schizophrenic patients on a psychiatric ward. They chose for special study the seven who had been outstandingly helpful, and seven whose patients had shown the least degree of improvement. Each group had treated about fifty patients. The investigators examined all the available evidence to discover in what ways the A group (the successful group) differed from the B group. Several significant differences were found. The physicians in the A group tended to see the schizophrenic in terms of the personal meaning which various behaviors had to the patient, rather than seeing him as a case history or a descriptive diagnosis. They also tended to work toward goals which were oriented to the personality of the patient, rather than such goals as reducing the symptoms or curing the disease. It was found that the helpful physicians, in their day by day interaction, primarily made use of active personal participation—a person-to-person relationship. They made less use of procedures which could be classed as "passive permissive." They were even less likely to use such procedures as interpretation, instruction or advice, or emphasis upon the practical care of the patient. Finally, they were much more likely than the B group to develop a relationship in which the patient felt trust and confidence in the physician.

Although the authors cautiously emphasize that these findings relate only to the treatment of schizophrenics, I am inclined to disagree. I suspect that similar facts would be found in a research study of almost any class of helping relationship.

Another interesting study focuses upon the way in which the person being helped perceives the relationship. Heine studied individuals who had gone for psychotherapeutic help to psychoanalytic, client-centered, and Adlerian therapists. Regardless of the type of therapy, these clients report similar changes in themselves. But it is their perception of the relationship which is of particular interest to us here. When asked what accounted for the changes which had occurred, they expressed some differing explanations, depending on the orientation of the therapist. But their agreement on the major elements they had found helpful was even more significant. They indicated that these attitudinal elements in the relationship accounted for the changes which had taken place in themselves: the trust they had felt in the therapist; being understood by the therapist; the feeling of independence they had had in making choices and decisions. The therapist procedure which they had found most helpful was that the therapist clarified and openly stated feelings which the client had been approaching hazily and hesitantly.

There was also a high degree of agreement among these clients, regardless of the orientation of their therapists, as to what elements had been unhelpful in the relationship. Such therapist attitudes as lack of interest, remoteness or distance, and an over-degree of sympathy, were perceived as unhelpful. As to procedures, they had found it unhelpful when therapists had given direct specific advice regarding decisions or had emphasized past history rather than present problems. Guiding suggestions mildly given were perceived in an intermediate range—neither clearly helpful nor unhelpful.

Fiedler, in a much quoted study, found that expert therapists of differing orientations formed similar relationships with their clients. Less well known are the elements which characterized these relationships, differentiating them from the relationships formed by less expert therapists. These elements are: an ability to understand the client's meanings and feelings; a sensitivity to the client's attitudes; a warm interest without any emotional over-involvement.

A study by Quinn throws light on what is involved in understanding the client's meanings and feelings. His study is surprising in that it shows that "understanding" of the client's meanings is essentially an attitude of desiring to understand. Quinn presented his judges only with recorded therapist statements taken from interviews. The raters had no knowledge of what the therapist was responding to or how the client reacted to his response. Yet it was found that the degree of understanding could be judged about as well from this material as from listening to the response in context. This seems rather conclusive evidence that it is an attitude of wanting to understand which is communicated.

As to the emotional quality of the relationship, Seeman found that success in psychotherapy is closely associated with a strong and growing mutual liking and respect between client and therapist.

An interesting study by Dittes indicates how delicate this relationship is. Using a physiological measure, the psychogalvanic reflex, to measure the anxious or threatened or alerted reactions of the client, Dittes correlated the deviations on this measure with judges' ratings of the degree of warm acceptance and permissiveness on the part of the therapist. It was found that whenever the therapist's attitudes changed even slightly in the direction of a lesser degree of acceptance, the number of abrupt GSR deviations significantly increased. Evidently when the relationship is experienced as less acceptant the organism organizes against threat even at the physiological level.

Without trying fully to integrate the

findings from these various studies, it can at least be noted that a few things stand out. One is the fact that it is the attitudes and feelings of the therapist, rather than his theoretical orientation, which is important. His procedures and techniques are less important than his attitudes. It is also worth noting that it is the way in which his attitudes and procedures are *perceived* which makes a difference to the client, and that it is this perception which is crucial.

Let me turn to research of a very different sort, some of which you may find rather abhorrent, but which nevertheless has a bearing upon the nature of a facilitating relationship. These studies have to do with what we might think of as manufactured relationships.

Verplanck, Greenspoon, and others have shown that operant conditioning of verbal behavior is possible in a relationship. Very briefly, if the experimenter says "Mhm," or "Good," or nods his head after certain types of words or statements, those classes of words tend to increase because of being reinforced. It has been shown that using such procedures one can bring about increases in such diverse verbal categories as plural nouns, hostile words, statements of opinion. The person is completely unaware that he is being influenced in any way by these reinforcers. The implication is that by such selective reinforcement we could bring it about that the other person in the relationship would be using whatever kinds of words and making whatever kinds of statements we had decided to reinforce.

Following still further the principles of operant conditioning as developed by Skinner and his group, Lindsley has shown that a chronic schizophrenic can be placed in a "helping relationship" with a machine. The machine, somewhat like a vending machine, can be set to reward a variety of types of behaviors. Initially it simply rewards—with candy, a cigarette, or the

display of a picture—the lever-pressing behavior of the patient. But it is possible to set it so that many pulls on the lever may supply a hungry kitten—visible in a separate enclosure—with a drop of milk. In this case the satisfaction is an altruistic one. Plans are being developed to reward similar social or altruistic behavior directed toward another patient, placed in the next room. The only limit to the kinds of behavior which might be rewarded lies in the degree of mechanical ingenuity of the experimenter.

Lindsley reports that in some patients there has been marked clinical improvement. Personally I cannot help but be impressed by the description of one patient who had gone from a deteriorated chronic state to being given free grounds privileges, this change being quite clearly associated with his interaction with the machine. Then the experimenter decided to study experimental extinction, which, put in more personal terms, means that no matter how many thousands of times the lever was pressed, no reward of any kind was forthcoming. The patient gradually regressed, grew untidy, uncommunicative, and his grounds privilege had to be revoked. This . . . pathetic incident would seem to indicate that even in a relationship to a machine, trustworthiness is important if the relationship is to be helpful.

. . . . .

HOW CAN I CREATE A HELPING RELATIONSHIP?

I believe each of us working in the field of human relationships has a similar problem in knowing how to use such research knowledge. We cannot slavishly follow such findings in a mechanical way or we destroy the personal qualities which these very studies show to be valuable. It seems to me that we have to use these studies, testing them against our own experience and forming new and further personal hypotheses to use and test in our own further personal relationships.

So rather than try to tell you how you should use the findings I have presented I should like to tell you the kind of questions which these studies and my own clinical experience raise for me, and some of the tentative and changing hypotheses which guide my behavior as I enter into what I hope may be helping relationships, whether with students, staff, family, or clients. Let me list a number of these questions and considerations.

1. Can I *be* in some way which will be perceived by the other person as trustworthy, as dependable or consistent in some deep sense? Both research and experience indicate that this is very important, and over the years I have found what I believe are deeper and better ways of answering this question. I used to feel that if I fulfilled all the outer conditions of trustworthiness—keeping appointments, respecting the confidential nature of the interviews, etc.—and if I acted consistently the same during the interviews, then this condition would be fulfilled. But experience drove home the fact that to act consistently acceptant, for example, if in fact I was feeling annoyed or skeptical or some other non-acceptant feeling, was certain in the long run to be perceived as inconsistent or untrustworthy. I have come to recognize that being trustworthy does not demand that I be rigidly consistent but that I be dependably real. The term "congruent" is one I have used to describe the way I would like to be. By this I mean that whatever feeling or attitude I am experiencing would be matched by my awareness of that attitude. When this is true, then I am a unified or integrated person in that moment, and hence I can *be* whatever I deeply *am*. This is a reality which I find others experience as dependable.

2. A very closely related question is this: Can I be expressive enough as a person that what I am will be communi-

cated unambiguously? I believe that most of my failures to achieve a helping relationship can be traced to unsatisfactory answers to these two questions. When I am experiencing an attitude of annoyance toward another person but am unaware of it, then my communication contains contradictory messages. My words are giving one message, but I am also in subtle ways communicating the annoyance I feel and this confuses the other person and makes him distrustful, though he too may be unaware of what is causing the difficulty. When as a parent or a therapist or a teacher or an administrator I fail to listen to what is going on in me, fail because of my own defensiveness to sense my own feelings, then this kind of failure seems to result. It has made it seem to me that the most basic learning for anyone who hopes to establish any kind of helping relationship is that it is safe to be transparently real. If in a given relationship I am reasonably congruent, if no feelings relevant to the relationship are hidden either to me or the other person, then I can be almost sure that the relationship will be a helpful one.

One way of putting this which may seem strange to you is that if I can form a helping relationship to myself—if I can be sensitively aware of and acceptant toward my own feelings—then the likelihood is great that I can form a helping relationship toward another.

Now, acceptantly to be what I am, in this sense, and to permit this to show through to the other person, is the most difficult task I know and one I never fully achieve. But to realize that this *is* my task has been most rewarding because it has helped me to find what has gone wrong with interpersonal relationships which have become snarled and to put them on a constructive track again. It has meant that if I am to facilitate the personal growth of others in relation to me, then I must grow, and while this is often painful it is also enriching.

3. A third question is: Can I let myself experience positive attitudes toward this other person—attitudes of warmth, caring, liking, interest, respect? It is not easy. I find in myself, and feel that I often see in others, a certain amount of fear of these feelings. We are afraid that if we let ourselves freely experience these positive feelings toward another we may be trapped by them. They may lead to demands on us or we may be disappointed in our trust, and these outcomes we fear. So as a reaction we tend to build up distance between ourselves and others—aloofness, a "professional" attitude, an impersonal relationship.

I feel quite strongly that one of the important reasons for the professionalization of every field is that it helps to keep this distance. In the clinical areas we develop elaborate diagnostic formulations, seeing the person as an object. In teaching and in administration we develop all kinds of evaluative procedures, so that again the person is perceived as an object. In these ways, I believe, we can keep ourselves from experiencing the caring which would exist if we recognized the relationship as one between two persons. It is a real achievement when we can learn, even in certain relationships or at certain times in those relationships, that it is safe to care, that it is safe to relate to the other as a person for whom we have positive feelings.

4. Another question the importance of which I have learned in my own experience is: Can I be strong enough as a person to be separate from the other? Can I be a sturdy respecter of my own feelings, my own needs, as well as his? Can I own and, if need be, express my own feelings as something belonging to me and separate from his feelings? Am I strong enough in my own separateness that I will not be downcast by his depression, frightened by his fear, nor engulfed by his dependency? Is my inner self hardy enough to realize that I am not destroyed by his anger,

taken over by his need for dependence, nor enslaved by his love, but that I exist separate from him with feelings and rights of my own? When I can freely feel this strength of being a separate person, then I find that I can let myself go much more deeply in understanding and accepting him because I am not fearful of losing myself.

5. The next question is closely related. Am I secure enough within myself to permit him his separateness? Can I permit him to be what he is—honest or deceitful, infantile or adult, despairing or overconfident? Can I give him the freedom to be? Or do I feel that he should follow my advice, or remain somewhat dependent on me, or mold himself after me? In this connection I think of the interesting small study by Farson which found that the less well adjusted and less competent counselor tends to induce conformity to himself, to have clients who model themselves after him. On the other hand, the better adjusted and more competent counselor can interact with a client through many interviews without interfering with the freedom of the client to have a personality quite separate from that of his therapist. I should prefer to be in this latter class, whether as parent or supervisor or counselor.

6. Another question I ask myself is: Can I let myself enter fully into the world of his feelings and personal meanings and see these as he does? Can I step into his private world so completely that I lose all desire to evaluate or judge it? Can I enter it so sensitively that I can move about in it freely, without trampling on meanings which are precious to him? Can I sense it so accurately that I can catch not only the meanings of his experience which are obvious to him, but those meanings which are only implicit, which he sees only dimly or as confusion? Can I extend this understanding without limit? I think of the client who said, "Whenever I find someone who understands a *part* of me at the time,

then it never fails that a point is reached where I know they're *not* understanding me again. . . . What I've looked for so hard is for someone to understand."

For myself I find it easier to feel this kind of understanding, and to communicate it, to individual clients than to students in a class or staff members in a group in which I am involved. There is a strong temptation to set students "straight," or to point out to a staff member the errors in his thinking. Yet when I can permit myself to understand in these situations, it is mutually rewarding. And with clients in therapy, I am often impressed with the fact that even a minimal amount of empathic understanding—a bumbling and faulty attempt to catch the confused complexity of the client's meaning—is helpful, though there is no doubt that it is most helpful when I can see and formulate clearly the meanings in his experiencing which for him have been unclear and tangled.

7. Still another issue is whether I can be acceptant of each facet of this other person which he presents to me. Can I receive him as he is? Can I communicate this attitude? Or can I only receive him conditionally, acceptant of some aspects of his feelings and silently or openly disapproving of other aspects? It has been my experience that when my attitude is conditional, then he cannot change or grow in those respects in which I cannot fully receive him. And when—afterward and sometimes too late—I try to discover why I have been unable to accept him in every respect, I usually discover that it is because I have been frightened or threatened in myself by some aspect of his feelings. If I am to be more helpful, then I must myself grow and accept myself in these respects.

8. A very practical issue is raised by the question: Can I act with sufficient sensitivity in the relationship that my behavior will not be perceived as a threat? The work we are beginning to do in studying the physiological concomitants of psychotherapy confirms the research by Dittes in indicating how easily individuals are threatened at a physiological level. The psychogalvanic reflex—the measure of skin conductance—takes a sharp dip when the therapist responds with some word which is just a little stronger than the client's feelings. And to a phrase such as, "My you *do* look upset," the needle swings almost off the paper. My desire to avoid even such minor threats is not due to a hypersensitivity about my client. It is simply due to the conviction based on experience that if I can free him as completely as possible from external threat, then he can begin to experience and to deal with the internal feelings and conflicts which he finds threatening within himself.

9. A specific aspect of the preceding question but an important one is: Can I free him from the threat of external evaluation? In almost every phase of our lives —at home, at school, at work—we find ourselves under the rewards and punishments of external judgments. "That's good"; "that's naughty." "That's worth an A"; "that's a failure." "That's good counseling"; "that's poor counseling." Such judgments are a part of our lives from infancy to old age. I believe they have a certain social usefulness to institutions and organizations such as schools and professions. Like everyone else I find myself all too often making such evaluations. But, in my experience, they do not make for personal growth and hence I do not believe that they are a part of a helping relationship. Curiously enough a positive evaluation is as threatening in the long run as a negative one, since to inform someone that he is good implies that you also have the right to tell him he is bad. So I have come to feel that the more I can keep a relationship free of judgment and evaluation, the more this will permit the other person to reach the point where he recognizes that the locus of evaluation, the center of re-

sponsibility, lies within himself. The meaning and value of his experience is in the last analysis something which is up to him, and no amount of external judgment can alter this. So I should like to work toward a relationship in which I am not, even in my own feelings, evaluating him. This I believe can set him free to be a self-responsible person.

10. One last question: Can I meet this other individual as a person who is in process of *becoming*, or will I be bound by his past and by my past? If, in my encounter with him, I am dealing with him as an immature child, an ignorant student, a neurotic personality, or a psychopath, each of these concepts of mine limits what he can be in the relationship. Martin Buber, the existentialist philosopher of the University of Jerusalem, has a phrase, "confirming the other," which has had meaning for me. He says, "Confirming means . . . accepting the whole potentiality of the other. . . . I can recognize in him, know in him, the person he has been . . . *created* to become. . . . I confirm him in myself, and then in him, in relation to this potentiality that . . . can now be developed, can evolve." If I accept the other person as something fixed, already diagnosed and classified, already shaped by his past, then I am doing my part to confirm this limited hypothesis. If I accept him as a process of becoming, then I am doing what I can to confirm or make real his potentialities.

It is at this point that I see Verplanck, Lindsley, and Skinner, working in operant conditioning, coming together with Buber, the philosopher or mystic. At least they come together in principle, in an odd way. If I see a relationship as only an opportunity to reinforce certain types of words or opinions in the other, then I tend to confirm him as an object—a basically mechanical, manipulable object. And if I see this as his potentiality, he tends to act in ways which support this hypothesis. If, on the other hand, I see a relationship as an

opportunity to "reinforce" *all* that he is, the person that he is with all his existent potentialities, then he tends to act in ways which support *this* hypothesis. I have then —to use Buber's term—confirmed him as a living person, capable of creative inner development. Personally I prefer this second type of hypothesis.

. . . . .

WHAT IT MEANS
TO BECOME A PERSON

In my work at the Counseling Center of the University of Chicago, I have the opportunity of working with people who present a wide variety of personal problems. There is the student concerned about failing in college; the housewife disturbed about her marriage; the individual who feels he is teetering on the edge of a complete breakdown or psychosis; the responsible professional man who spends much of his time in sexual fantasies and functions inefficiently in his work; the brilliant student, at the top of his class, who is paralyzed by the conviction that he is hopelessly and helplessly inadequate; the parent who is distressed by his child's behavior; the popular girl who finds herself unaccountably overtaken by sharp spells of black depression; the woman who fears that life and love are passing her by, and that her good graduate record is a poor recompense; the man who has become convinced that powerful or sinister forces are plotting against him.

. . . . .

As I follow the experience of many clients in the therapeutic relationship which we endeavor to create for them, it seems to me that each one is raising the same question. Below the level of the problem situation about which the individual is complaining—behind the trouble with studies, or wife, or employer, or with his own uncontrollable or bizarre behavior, or with his frightening feelings, lies one central search. It seems to me that at bottom each person is asking, "Who am I, *really?* How can I get in touch with this real self, underlying all my surface behavior? How can I become myself?"

· · · · ·

In this attempt to discover his own self, the client typically uses the relationship to explore, to examine the various aspects of his own experience, to recognize and face up to the deep contradictions which he often discovers. He learns how much of his behavior, even how much of the feeling he experiences, is not real, is not something which flows from the genuine reactions of his organism, but is a façade, a front, behind which he has been hiding. He discovers how much of his life is guided by what he thinks he *should* be, not by what he is. Often he discovers that he exists only in response to the demands of others, that he seems to have no self of his own, that he is only trying to think, and feel, and behave in the way that others believe he *ought* to think, and feel, and behave.

In this connection, I have been astonished to find how accurately the Danish philosopher, Søren Kierkegaard, pictured the dilemma of the individual more than a century ago, with keen psychological insight. He points out that the most common despair is to be in despair at not choosing, or willing, to be oneself; but that the deepest form of despair is to choose "to be another than himself." On the other hand "to will to be that self which one truly is, is indeed the opposite of despair," and this choice is the deepest responsibility of man. As I read some of his writings I almost feel that he must have listened in on the statements made by our clients as they search and explore for the reality of self—often a painful and troubling search.

This exploration becomes even more disturbing when they find themselves involved in removing the false faces which they had not known were false faces. They

begin to engage in the frightening task of exploring the turbulent and sometimes violent feelings within themselves. To remove a mask which you had thought was part of your real self can be a deeply disturbing experience, yet when there is freedom to think and feel and be, the individual moves toward such a goal.

· · · · ·

I would like to say something more about this experiencing of feeling. It is really the discovery of unknown elements of self. The phenomenon I am trying to describe is something which I think is quite difficult to get across in any meaningful way. In our daily lives there are a thousand and one reasons for not letting ourselves experience our attitudes fully, reasons from our past and from the present, reasons that reside within the social situation. It seems too dangerous, too potentially damaging, to experience them freely and fully. But in the safety of the therapeutic relationship, they can be experienced fully, clear to the limit of what they are.

· · · · ·

Let us pursue a bit further this question of what it means to become one's self. It is a most perplexing question and again I will try to take from a statement by a client, written between interviews, a suggestion of an answer. She tells how the various façades by which she has been living have somehow crumpled and collapsed, bringing a feeling of confusion, but also a feeling of relief. She continues:

You know, it seems as if all the energy that went into holding the arbitrary pattern together was quite unnecessary—a waste. You think you have to make the pattern yourself; but there are so many pieces, and it's so hard to see where they fit. Sometimes you put them in the wrong place, and the more pieces mis-fitted, the more effort it takes to hold them in place, until at last you are so tired that even that awful confusion is better than holding on any longer. Then you discover that left to themselves the jumbled pieces fall quite naturally into their own places, and a living pattern emerges without any effort at all on your part. Your job is just to discover it, and in the course of that, you will find yourself and your own place. You must even let your own experience tell you its own meaning; the minute *you* tell it what it means, you are at war with yourself.

Let me see if I can take her poetic expression and translate it into the meaning it has for me. I believe she is saying that to be herself means to find the pattern, the underlying order, which exists in the ceaselessly changing flow of her experience. Rather than to try to hold her experience into the form of a mask, or to make it be a form or structure that it is not, being herself means to discover the unity and harmony which exists in her own actual feelings and reactions. It means that the real self is something which is comfortably discovered in one's experiences, not something imposed upon it. . . .

I have been trying to suggest what happens in the warmth and understanding of a facilitating relationship with a therapist. It seems that gradually, painfully, the individual explores what is behind the masks he presents to the world, and even behind the masks with which he has been deceiving himself. Deeply and often vividly he experiences the various elements of himself which have been hidden within. Thus to an increasing degree he becomes himself—not a façade of conformity to others, not a cynical denial of all feeling, nor a front of intellectual rationality, but a living, breathing, feeling, fluctuating process —in short, he becomes a person.

I imagine that some of you are asking, "But what *kind* of a person does he become? It isn't enough to say that he drops the façades. What kind of person lies underneath?" Since one of the most obvious facts is that each individual tends to become a separate and distinct and unique person, the answer is not easy. However

I would like to point out some of the characteristic trends which I see. No one person would fully exemplify these characteristics, no one person fully achieves the description I will give, but I do see certain generalizations which can be drawn, based upon living a therapeutic relationship with many clients.

OPENNESS TO EXPERIENCE

First of all I would say that in this process the individual becomes more open to his experience. This is a phrase which has come to have a great deal of meaning to me. It is the opposite of defensiveness. Psychological research has shown that if the evidence of our senses runs contrary to our picture of self, then that evidence is distorted. In other words we cannot see all that our senses report, but only the things which fit the picture we have.

Now in a safe relationship of the sort I have described this defensiveness or rigidity tends to be replaced by an increasing openness to experience. The individual becomes more openly aware of his own feelings and attitudes as they exist in him at an organic level, in the way I tried to describe. He also becomes more aware of reality as it exists outside of himself, instead of perceiving it in preconceived categories. He sees that not all trees are green, not all men are stern fathers, not all women are rejecting, not all failure experiences prove that he is no good, and the like. He is able to take in the evidence in a new situation, *as it is*, rather than distorting it to fit a pattern which he already holds. As you might expect, this increasing ability to be open to experience makes him far more realistic in dealing with new people, new situations, new problems. It means that his beliefs are not rigid, that he can tolerate ambiguity. He can receive much conflicting evidence without forcing closure upon the situation. This openness of awareness to what exists at *this moment* in *oneself* and in *the situation* is, I believe, an important element in the description of the person who emerges from therapy.

Perhaps I can give this concept a more vivid meaning if I illustrate it from a recorded interview. A young professional man reports in the 48th interview the way in which he has become more open to some of his bodily sensations, as well as other feelings.

c: It doesn't seem to me that it would be possible for anybody to relate all the changes that you feel. But I certainly have felt recently that I have more respect for, more objectivity toward my physical makeup. I mean I don't expect too much of myself. This is how it works out: It feels to me that in the past I used to fight a certain tiredness that I felt after supper. Well, now I feel pretty sure that I really *am tired*—that I am not making myself tired—that I am just physiologically lower. It seemed that I was just constantly criticizing my tiredness.

t: So you can let yourself *be* tired, instead of feeling along with it a kind of criticism of it.

c: Yes, that I shouldn't be tired or something. And it seems in a way to be pretty profound that I can just not fight this tiredness, and along with it goes a real feeling of *I've* got to slow down, too, so that being tired isn't such an awful thing. I think I can also kind of pick up a thread here of why I should be that way in the way my father is and the way he looks at some of these things. For instance, say that I was sick, and I would report this, and it would seem that overtly he would want to do something about it but he would also communicate, "Oh, my gosh, more trouble." You know, something like that.

t: As though there were something quite annoying really about being physically ill.

c: Yeah, I'm sure that my father has the same disrespect for his own physiology that I have had. Now last summer I twisted my back, I wrenched it, I heard it snap and everything. There was real pain there all the time at first, real sharp. And I had the doctor look at it and he said it wasn't serious, it should heal by itself as long as I didn't bend too much. Well this was months ago—and I have been noticing recently that—hell, this is a real pain and it's still there—and it's not my fault.

t: It doesn't prove something bad about you—

c: No—and one of the reasons I seem to get more tired than I should maybe is because of this constant strain, and so— I have already made an appointment with one of the doctors at the hospital that he would look at it and take an X-ray or something. In a way I guess you could say that I am just more accurately sensitive—or objectively sensitive to this kind of thing. . . . And this is really a profound change as I say, and of course my relationship with my wife and two children is—well, you just wouldn't recognize it if you could see me inside—as you have—I mean— there just doesn't seem to be anything more wonderful than really and genuinely—really *feeling* love for your own children and at the same time receiving it. I don't know how to put this. We have such an increased respect—both of us—for Judy and we've noticed just —as we participated in this—we have noticed such a tremendous change in her—it seems to be a pretty deep kind of thing.

t: It seems to me you are saying that you can listen more accurately to yourself. If your body says it's tired, you listen to it and believe it, instead of criticizing it; if it's in pain, you can listen to that; if the feeling is really loving your wife or children, you can *feel* that, and it seems to show up in the differences in them too.

Here, in a relatively minor but symbolically important excerpt, can be seen much of what I have been trying to say about openness to experience. Formerly he could not freely feel pain or illness, because being ill meant being unacceptable. Neither could he feel tenderness and love for his child, because such feelings meant being weak, and he had to maintain his façade of being strong. But now he can be genuinely open to the experiences of his organism—he can be tired when he is tired, he can feel pain when his organism is in pain, he can freely experience the love he feels for his daughter, and he can also feel and express annoyance toward her, as he goes on to say in the next portion of the interview. He can fully live the experiences of his total organism, rather than shutting them out of awareness.

TRUST IN ONE'S ORGANISM

A second characteristic of the persons who emerge from therapy is difficult to describe. It seems that the person increasingly discovers that his own organism is trustworthy, that it is a suitable instrument for discovering the most satisfying behavior in each immediate situation.

If this seems strange, let me try to state it more fully. Perhaps it will help to understand my description if you think of the individual as faced with some existential choice: "Shall I go home to my family during vacation, or strike out on my own?" "Shall I drink this third cocktail which is being offered?" "Is this the person whom I would like to have as my partner in love and in life?" Thinking of such situations, what seems to be true of the person who emerges from the therapeutic process? To the extent that this person is open to all of his experience, he has access to all of the available data in the situation on which to base his behavior. He has knowledge of his own feelings and impulses, which are often complex and contradic-

tory. He is freely able to sense the social demands, from the relatively rigid social "laws" to the desires of friends and family. He has access to his memories of similar situations, and the consequences of different behaviors in those situations. He has a relatively accurate perception of this external situation in all of its complexity. He is better able to permit his total organism, his conscious thought participating, to consider, weigh and balance each stimulus, need, and demand, and its relative weight and intensity. Out of this complex weighing and balancing he is able to discover that course of action which seems to come closest to satisfying all his needs in the situation, long-range as well as immediate needs.

In such a weighing and balancing of all of the components of a given life choice, his organism would not by any means be infallible. Mistaken choices might be made. But because he tends to be open to his experience, there is a greater and more immediate awareness of unsatisfying consequences, a quicker correction of choices which are in error.

It may help to realize that in most of us the defects which interfere with this weighing and balancing are that we include things that are not a part of our experience, and exclude elements which are. Thus an individual may persist in the concept that "I can handle liquor," when openness to his past experience would indicate that this is scarcely correct. Or a young woman may see only the good qualities of her prospective mate, where an openness to experience would indicate that he possesses faults as well.

In general then, it appears to be true that when a client is open to his experience, he comes to find his organism more trustworthy. He feels less fear of the emotional reactions which he has. There is a gradual growth of trust in, and even affection for the complex, rich, varied assortment of feelings and tendencies which exist in him at the organic level. Consciousness, instead of being the watchman over a dangerous and unpredictable lot of impulses, of which few can be permitted to see the light of day, becomes the comfortable inhabitant of a society of impulses and feelings and thoughts, which are discovered to be very satisfactorily self-governing when not fearfully guarded.

AN INTERNAL LOCUS
OF EVALUATION

Another trend which is evident in this process of becoming a person relates to the source or locus of choices and decisions, or evaluative judgments. The individual increasingly comes to feel that this locus of evaluation lies within himself. Less and less does he look to others for approval or disapproval; for standards to live by; for decisions and choices. He recognizes that it rests within himself to choose; that the only question which matters is, "Am I living in a way which is deeply satisfying to me, and which truly expresses me?" This I think is perhaps *the* most important question for the creative individual.

Perhaps it will help if I give an illustration. I would like to give a brief portion of a recorded interview with a young woman, a graduate student, who had come for counseling help. She was initially very much disturbed about many problems, and had been contemplating suicide. During the interview one of the feelings she discovered was her great desire to be dependent, just to let someone else take over direction of her life. She was very critical of those who had not given her enough guidance. She talked about one after another of her professors, feeling bitterly that none of them had taught her anything with deep meaning. Gradually she began to realize that part of the difficulty was the fact that she had taken no initiative in *participating* in these classes. Then comes the portion I wish to quote.

c: Well now, I wonder if I've been going around doing that, getting smatterings of things, and not getting hold, not really getting down to things.

t: Maybe you've been getting just spoonfuls here and there rather than really digging in somewhere rather deeply.

c: M-hm. That's why I say—(*slowly and very thoughtfully*) well, with that sort of a foundation, well, it's really up to *me.* I mean, it seems to be really apparent to me that I *can't depend on someone else* to give me an education. (*Very softly*) I'll really have to get it myself.

t: It really begins to come home—there's only one person that can educate you— a realization that perhaps nobody else *can give* you an education.

c: M-hm. (*Long pause—while she sits thinking*) I have all the symptoms of fright. (*Laughs softly*)

t: Fright? That this is a scary thing, is that what you mean?

c: M-hm. (*Very long pause—obviously struggling with feelings in herself*).

t: Do you want to say any more about what you mean by that? That it really does give you the symptoms of fright?

c: (*Laughs*) I, uh—I don't know whether I quite know. I mean—well it really seems like I'm cut loose (*pause*), and it seems that I'm very—I don't know—in a vulnerable position, but I, uh, I brought this up and it, uh, somehow it almost came out without my saying it. Is seems to be—it's something I let out.

t: Hardly a part of you.

c: Well, I felt surprised.

t: As though, "Well for goodness sake, did I say that?" (*Both chuckle.*)

c: Really, I don't think I've had that feeling before. I've—uh, well, this really feels like I'm saying something that, uh, *is* a part of me really. (*Pause*) Or, uh, (*quite perplexed*) it feels like I sort of have, uh, I don't know. I have a feeling of *strength,* and yet, I have a feeling of—realizing it's so sort of fearful, of fright.

T: That is, do you mean that saying something of that sort gives you at the same time a feeling of, of strength in saying it, and yet at the same time a frightened feeling of *what* you have said, is that it?

C: M-hm. I am feeling that. For instance, I'm feeling it internally now—a sort of surging up, or force or outlet. As if that's something really big and strong. And yet, uh, well at first it was almost a physical feeling of just being out alone, and sort of cut off from a—a support I had been carrying around.

T: You feel that it's something deep and strong, and surging forth, and at the same time, you just feel as though you'd cut yourself loose from any support when you say it.

C: M-hm. Maybe that's—I don't know—it's a disturbance of a kind of pattern I've been carrying around, I think.

T: It sort of shakes a rather significant pattern, jars it loose.

C: M-hm. (*Pause, then cautiously, but with conviction*) I, I think—I don't know, but I have the feeling that then I am going to begin to *do* more things that I know I should do. . . . There are so many things that I need to do. It seems in so many avenues of my living I have to work out new ways of behavior, but—maybe—I can see myself doing a little better in some things.

I hope this illustration gives some sense of the strength which is experienced in being a unique person, responsible for oneself, and also the uneasiness that accompanies this assumption of responsibility. To recognize that "I am the one who chooses" and "I am the one who determines the value of an experience for me" is both an invigorating and a frightening realization.

WILLINGNESS TO BE A PROCESS

I should like to point out one final characteristic of these individuals as they strive to discover and become themselves. It is that the individual seems to become more content to be a *process* rather than a *product*. When he enters the therapeutic relationship, the client is likely to wish to achieve some fixed state: he wants to reach the point where his problems are solved, or where he is effective in his work, or where his marriage is satisfactory. He tends, in the freedom of the therapeutic relationship, to drop such fixed goals, and to accept a more satisfying realization that he is not a fixed entity, but a process of becoming.

One client, at the conclusion of therapy, says in rather puzzled fashion, "I haven't finished the job of integrating and reorganizing myself, but that's only confusing, not discouraging, now that I realize this is a continuing process. . . . It's exciting, sometimes upsetting, but deeply encouraging to feel yourself in action, apparently knowing where you are going even though you don't always consciously know where that is." One can see here both the expression of trust in the organism, which I have mentioned, and also the realization of self as a process. Here is a personal description of what it seems like to accept oneself as a stream of becoming, not a finished product. It means that a person is a fluid process, not a fixed and static entity; a flowing river of change, not a block of solid material; a continually changing constellation of potentialities, not a fixed quantity of traits.

. . . . .

A CHANGED VIEW OF SCIENCE

The major shortcoming [is], I believe, in viewing science as something "out there," something spelled with a capital S, a "body of knowledge" existing somewhere in space and time. In common with many psychologists I thought of science as a systematized and organized collection of tentatively verified facts, and saw the methodology of science as the socially approved means of accumulating this body of knowledge, and continuing its verification. It has seemed somewhat like a reservoir into which all and sundry may dip their buckets to obtain water—with a guarantee of 99% purity. When viewed in this external and impersonal fashion, it seems not unreasonable to see Science not only as discovering knowledge in lofty fashion, but as involving depersonalization, a tendency to manipulate, a denial of the basic freedom of choice which I have met experientially in therapy. I should like now to view the scientific approach from a different, and I hope, a more accurate perspective.

SCIENCE IN PERSONS

Science exists only in people. Each scientific project has its creative inception, its process, and its tentative conclusion, in a person or persons. Knowledge—even scientific knowledge—is that which is subjectively acceptable. Scientific knowledge can be communicated only to those who are subjectively ready to receive its communication. The utilization of science also occurs only through people who are in pursuit of values which have meaning for them. These statements summarize very briefly something of the change in emphasis which I would like to make in my description of science. Let me follow through the various phases of science from this point of view.

THE CREATIVE PHASE

Science has its inception in a particular person who is pursuing aims, values, purposes, which have personal and subjective meaning for him. As a part of this pursuit, he, in some area, "wants to find out." Consequently, if he is to be a good scientist, he immerses himself in the relevant experience, whether that be the physics laboratory, the world of plant or animal life, the hospital, the psychological laboratory or clinic, or whatever. This immer-

sion is complete and subjective, similar to the immersion of the therapist in therapy, described previously. He senses the field in which he is interested, he lives it. He does more than "think" about it—he lets his organism take over and react to it, both on a knowing and on an unknowing level. He comes to sense more than he could possibly verbalize about his field, and reacts organismically in terms of relationships which are not present in his awareness.

Out of this complete subjective immersion comes a creative forming, a sense of direction, a vague formulation of relationships hitherto unrecognized. Whittled down, sharpened, formulated in clearer terms, this creative forming becomes a hypothesis—a statement of a tentative, personal, subjective faith. The scientist is saying, drawing upon all his known and unknown experience, that "I have a hunch that such and such a relationship exists, and the existence of this phenomenon has relevance to my personal values."

What I am describing is the initial phase of science, probably its most important phase, but one which American scientists, particularly psychologists, have been prone to minimize or ignore. It is not so much that it has been denied as that it has been quickly brushed off. Kenneth Spence has said that this aspect of science is "simply taken for granted."[*] Like many experiences taken for granted, it also tends to be forgotten. It is indeed

---

[*] It may be pertinent to quote the sentences from which this phrase is taken. ". . . the data of all sciences have the same origin—namely, the immediate experience of an observing person, the scientist himself. That is to say, immediate experience, the initial matrix out of which all sciences develop, is no longer considered a matter of concern for the scientist qua scientist. He simply takes it for granted and then proceeds to the task of describing the events occurring in it and discovering and formulating the nature of the relationships holding among them." Kenneth W. Spence, in *Psychological Theory*, ed. by M. H. Marx (New York: Macmillan, 1951), p. 173.

in the matrix of immediate personal, subjective experience that all science, and each individual scientific research, has its origin.

CHECKING WITH REALITY

The scientist has then creatively achieved his hypothesis, his tentative faith. But does it check with reality? Experience has shown each one of us that it is very easy to deceive ourselves, to believe something which later experience shows is not so. How can I tell whether this tentative belief has some real relationship to observed facts? I can use, not one line of evidence only, but several. I can surround my observation of the facts with various precautions to make sure I am not deceiving myself. I can consult with others who have also been concerned with avoiding self-deception, and learn useful ways of catching myself in unwarranted beliefs, based on misinterpretation of observations. I can, in short, begin to use all the elaborate methodology which science has accumulated. I discover that stating my hypothesis in operational terms will avoid many blind alleys and false conclusions. I learn that control groups can help me to avoid drawing false inferences. I learn that correlations, and t tests and critical ratios and a whole array of statistical procedures can likewise aid me in drawing only reasonable inferences.

Thus scientific methodology is seen for what it truly is—a way of preventing me from deceiving myself in regard to my creatively formed subjective hunches which have developed out of the relationship between me and my material. It is in this context, and perhaps only in this context, that the vast structure of operationism, logical positivism, research design, tests of significance, etc. have their place. They exist, not for themselves, but as servants in the attempt to check the subjective feeling or hunch or hypothesis of a person with the objective fact.

And even throughout the use of such rigorous and impersonal methods, the important choices are all made subjectively by the scientist. To which of a number of hypotheses shall I devote time? What kind of control group is most suitable for avoiding self-deception in this particular research? How far shall I carry the statistical analysis? How much credence may I place in the findings? Each of these is necessarily a subjective personal judgment, emphasizing that the splendid structure of science rests basically upon its subjective use by persons. It is the best instrument we have yet been able to devise to check upon our organismic sensing of the universe.

THE FINDINGS

If, as scientist, I like the way I have gone about my investigation, if I have been open to all the evidence, if I have selected and used intelligently all the precautions against self-deception which I have been able to assimilate from others or to devise myself, then I will give my tentative belief to the findings which have emerged. I will regard them as a springboard for further investigation and further seeking.

It seems to me that in the best of science, the primary purpose is to provide a more satisfactory and dependable hypothesis, belief, faith, for the investigator himself. To the extent that the scientist is endeavoring to prove something to someone else—an error into which I have fallen more than once—then I believe he is using science to bolster a personal insecurity, and is keeping it from its truly creative role in the service of the person.

In regard to the findings of science, the subjective foundation is well shown in the fact that at times the scientist may refuse to believe his own findings. "The experiment showed thus and so, but I believe it is wrong," is a theme which every scientist has experienced at some time or other. Some very fruitful discoveries have grown out of the persistent *disbelief,* by a scientist, in his own findings and those of others. In the last analysis he may place more trust in his total organismic reactions than in the methods of science. There is no doubt that this can result in serious error as well as in scientific discoveries, but it indicates again the leading place of the subjective in the use of science.

COMMUNICATION OF SCIENTIFIC FINDINGS

Wading along a coral reef in the Caribbean this morning, I saw a large blue fish —I think. If you, quite independently, saw it too, then I feel more confident in my own observation. This is what is known as intersubjective verification, and it plays an important part in our understanding of science. If I take you (whether in conversation or in print or behaviorally) through the steps I have taken in an investigation, and it seems to you too that I have not deceived myself, and that I have indeed come across a new relationship which is relevant to my values, and that I am justified in having a tentative faith in this relationship, then we have the beginnings of Science with a capital S. It is at this point that we are likely to think we have created a body of scientific knowledge. Actually there is no such body of knowledge. There are only tentative beliefs, existing subjectively, in a number of different persons. If these beliefs are not tentative, then what exists is dogma, not science. If on the other hand, no one but the investigator believes the finding then this finding is either a personal and deviant matter, an instance of psychopathology, or else it is an unusual truth discovered by a genius, which as yet no one is subjectively ready to believe. This leads me to comment on the group which can put tentative faith in any given scientific finding.

COMMUNICATION TO WHOM

It is clear that scientific findings can be communicated only to those who have agreed to the same ground rules of investigation. The Australian bushman will be quite unimpressed with the findings of science regarding bacterial infection. He knows that illness truly is caused by evil spirits. It is only when he too agrees to scientific method as a good means of preventing self-deception, that he will be likely to accept its findings.

But even among those who have adopted the ground rules of science, tentative belief in the findings of a scientific research can only occur where there is a subjective readiness to believe. One could find many examples. Most psychologists are quite ready to believe evidence showing that the lecture system produces significant increments of learning, and quite unready to believe that the turn of an unseen card may be called through an ability labelled extrasensory perception. Yet the scientific evidence for the latter is considerably more impeccable than for the former. Likewise when the so-called "Iowa studies" first came out, indicating that intelligence might be considerably altered by environmental conditions, there was great disbelief among psychologists, and many attacks on the imperfect scientific methods used. The scientific evidence for this finding is not much better today than it was when the Iowa studies first appeared, but the subjective readiness of psychologists to believe such a finding has altered greatly. A historian of science has noted that empiricists, had they existed at the time, would have been the first to disbelieve the findings of ·Copernicus.

It appears then that whether I believe the scientific findings of others, or those from my own studies, depends in part on my readiness to put a tentative belief in such findings. One reason we are not particularly aware of this subjective fact is that in the physical sciences particularly, we have gradually adopted a very large area of experience in which we are ready to believe any finding which can be shown to rest upon the rules of the scientific game, properly played.

THE USE OF SCIENCE

But not only is the origin, process, and conclusion of science something which exists only in the subjective experience of persons—so also is its utilization. "Science" will never depersonalize, or manipulate, or control individuals. It is only persons who can and will do that. That is surely a most obvious and trite observation, yet a deep realization of it has had much meaning for me. It means that the use which will be made of scientific findings in the field of personality is and will be a matter of subjective personal choice —the same type of choice as a person makes in therapy. To the extent that he has defensively closed off areas of his experience from awareness, the person is more likely to make choices which are socially destructive. To the extent that he is open to all phases of his experience we may be sure that this person will be more likely to use the findings and methods of science (or any other tool or capacity) in a manner which is personally and socially constructive. There is, in actuality then, no threatening entity of "Science" which can in any way affect our destiny. There are only people. While many of them are indeed threatening and dangerous in their defensiveness, and modern scientific knowledge multiplies the social threat and danger, this is not the whole picture. There are two other significant facets. (1) There are many persons who are relatively open to their experience and hence likely to be socially constructive. (2) Both the subjective experience of psychotherapy and the scientific findings regarding it indicate that individuals are motivated to change, and may be helped to change, in the direction of greater openness to experience, and hence in the direction of behavior which is enhancing of self and society, rather than destructive.

To put it briefly, Science can never threaten us. Only persons can do that. And while individuals can be vastly destructive with the tools placed in their hands by scientific knowledge, this is only one side of the picture. We already have subjective and objective knowledge of the basic principles by which individuals may achieve the more constructive social behavior which is natural to their organismic process of becoming.

. . . . .

. . . Recent clinical findings from the field of psychotherapy give us hope. It has been found that when the individual is "open" to all of his experience . . . then his behavior will be creative, and his creativity may be trusted to be essentially constructive.

The differentiation may be put very briefly as follows. To the extent that the individual is denying to awareness (or repressing, if you prefer that term) large areas of his experience, then his creative formings may be pathological, or socially evil, or both. To the degree that the individual is open to all aspects of his experience, and has available to his awareness all the varied sensings and perceivings which are going on within his organism, then the novel products of his interaction with his environment will tend to be constructive both for himself and others. To illustrate, an individual with paranoid tendencies may creatively develop a most novel theory of the relationship between himself and his environment, seeing evidence for his theory in all sorts of minute clues. His theory has little social value, perhaps because there is an enormous range of experience which this individual cannot permit in his awareness. Socrates, on the other hand, while also regarded as "crazy" by his contemporaries, developed novel ideas which have proven to be socially constructive. Very possibly this was because he was notably nondefensive and open to his experience.

57 | PREVENTING FAILURE BY REMOVING RESISTANCE

PRESCOTT LECKY

What should be done about the child who is failing in his studies?
He may be forced to study, kept in after school until his work is done.
Or he may be bribed with promises of a dime, a dollar, or a
convertible if he passes.

The writings of the late Prescott Lecky, a brilliant theorist,
provide some indication of how ineffectual force or bribery can be.
Lecky contends that the individual fails because he expects himself to
fail; failure thus leads to expectation of renewed failure, in an
almost unbreakable cycle. Lecky suggests that the most effective way
to help the student, who, in failing, is actually resisting success,
is by altering his conception of self.

These findings have been confirmed in the editors' frequent
experiences as counselors to failing students. The students described
how their parents or teachers pressed them again and again to
study, to pass; eventually, it seemed that only by failing could the
students preserve their integrity. To pass would mean to surrender.

Ever so often, a child who has formerly been deficient in a certain subject suddenly seems to find himself, and rises toward the top of the class. Such cases present an interesting problem. Are we confronted by a miracle, or do these spontaneous changes only seem miraculous because their study has been neglected? More important still, assuming a clearer understanding of what takes place in these rare cases, is it possible to bring about similar results among large numbers of children? These are by no means idle questions. With approximately half of the pupils in our schools already below grade in either reading or mathematics, to say nothing of other subjects, the problem of what to do is an urgent one. Either we must devise some effective method of raising the level of accomplishment, or lower our educational standards.

Previous intepretations of spontaneous improvement have usually been stated in terms of increased interest or readiness. Since there seems to be nothing to do about readiness except to wait for it to develop, however, and since no practical method of increasing interest beyond the present level seems to be available, these diagnoses turn out to be little more than truisms which lead to no constructive action. This point is borne out by the fact that in the actual treatment of deficient pupils there seems to be no alternative except to send the child to remedial classes or recommend outside tutoring. These remedies are apparently based on the belief that children need additional instruction for some reason in order to help them to form the habits which they failed to form in the class room. But even if our present remedial methods were successful in every case, the expense of tutoring so many pupils would make this approach impracticable.

Reprinted from *Self-Consistency: A Theory of Personality* (Island Press Cooperative, 1951), pp. 245–55, by permission of the publisher.

THE THEORY OF SELF-CONSISTENCY

The method described in this report is based on a different conception of the problem; namely, that the cause of most failures in school is not insufficient or inadequate instruction, but active resistance on the part of the child. To make this point clear, we must give a brief description of the theory of self-consistency, from which the method is derived.

The part of the theory which interests us here is the concept of the mind. According to self-consistency, the mind is a unit, an organized system of ideas. All of the ideas which belong to the system must seem to be consistent with one another. The center or nucleus of the mind is the individual's idea or conception of himself. If a new idea seems to be consistent with the ideas already present in the system, and particularly with the individual's conception of himself, it is accepted and assimilated easily. If it seems to be inconsistent, however, it meets with resistance and is likely to be rejected. This resistance is a natural phenomenon; it is essential for the maintenance of individuality.

Thus the acceptability of an idea to any particular pupil is determined by his needs as an individual. In order to understand the environment, he must keep his interpretations consistent with his experience, but in order to maintain his individuality, he must organize his interpretations to form a system of ideas which is internally consistent. This consistency is not objective, of course, but subjective, private, and wholly individual. It is difficult to understand resistance unless this point is borne in mind.

From this standpoint, learning cannot be understood as a process of forming separate habits, but only in terms of the development of the entire personality. It follows that no type of subject matter is interesting merely for its own sake. It is interesting only when an individual happens to be interested in it, because of the way he interprets it in relation to his problem. Indeed, though learning and resistance seem to point in opposite directions, they really serve the same purpose.

In the one case we are supporting the system by the assimilation of consistent ideas, while in the other we are protecting the system from inconsistency and conflict. Both are necessary in order that the unity of the system may be preserved.

If the pupil shows resistance toward a certain type of material, this means that from his point of view it would be inconsistent for him to learn it. If we are able to change the self-conception which underlies this viewpoint, however, his attitude toward the material will change accordingly. With the resistance eliminated, he learns so rapidly that tutoring is often unnecessary.

Such a change in the pupil's attitude often results in improvement which is quite astonishing. A high school student who misspelled 55 words out of a hundred, and who failed so many subjects that he lost credit for a full year, became one of the best spellers in the school during the next year, and made a general average of 91. A student who was dropped from another college and was later admitted to Columbia was graduated with more than 70 points of "A" credits. A boy failing in English, who had been diagnosed by a testing bureau as lacking aptitude for this subject, won honorable mention a year later for the literary prize at a large preparatory school. A girl who had failed four times in Latin, with marks between 20 and 50, after three talks with the school counselor made a mark of 92 on the next test and finished with a grade of 84. She is now taking advanced Latin with grades above 80.

Two of the poorest spellers in the High School of Clifton, N.J., were used to demonstrate this method before a university class in psychology. Given twenty words to spell, one missed all twenty and the other nineteen. The school counselor, continuing the use of the method, reports that both are now excellent spellers and have taken up spelling as a sort of hobby. The results reported are taken from the work of three different counselors, showing that the method lends itself to general use in the school system.

These examples are selected to show how little we are justified in judging the future potentialities of the pupil by the record he has made in the past. In the majority of cases, of course, the improvement, if any, is much less spectacular. But the fact that such extraordinary results can be obtained at all, and by means of a method which is still in the experimental stage, show that an optimistic attitude in regard to the possibilities of the school population in general is not unreasonable. The greatest handicap to constructive action is the well-entrenched, though perhaps unconscious, dogma that learning is the direct result of teaching, a mechanical reaction to the school environment instead of a purposive achievement.

PREDICTIONS BASED ON THE HABIT THEORY ARE UNRELIABLE

The methods that we use, in other words, reflect the theory that we accept. In psychology and education, theories are often accepted merely because they seem plausible. In the physical sciences, however, the value of a theory is judged by its ability to make predictions that are later verified by experience. Let us apply this test to the theory that learning is a process of habit formation.

Most of us have been taught that habits are fixed by exercise and the satisfaction obtained by practicing them, and that predictions based on this theory can be relied upon. Actually, however, such predictions often turn out to be highly unreliable. A good example is thumb-sucking. Certainly the child who sucks his thumb gives the act plenty of exercise and gets enough satisfaction from it to fix the act indelibly. Therefore if the habit theory is true, we should be able to predict absolutely that the child will continue to suck his thumb for the rest of his life. But what really happens? Every year millions of children who have industriously sucked their thumbs since birth, and who have successfully resisted every effort to force them to change their behavior, quit the practice spontaneously when they are five or six years old. The reason is that they are beginning at this age to think of themselves as big boys or girls, and they recognize that thumb-sucking is inconsistent with the effort to maintain this new idea. The changed conception of who they are, and the necessity of making good in the new role they have accepted, furnishes them with a new standard to which their behavior must now conform. If a child continues to think of himself as a baby, due perhaps to prolonged illness or overprotection by the parents, the necessary standard is lacking and the thumb-sucking will continue. Parents often invoke the "big boy" standard deliberately in the effort to change the child's behavior in many other situations.

WHY BOYS ARE SLOWER THAN GIRLS IN LEARNING TO READ

The behavior of the child in the classroom must also be understood in terms of the standards he is trying to maintain. Let us take, for example, the well known fact that boys on the average are slower than girls in learning to read. Educational textbooks usually explain this by saying that girls have more native ability in respect to reading than boys. In terms of self-consistency, however, the explanation is that to most boys the reading material in elementary readers seems infantile and effeminate. The boy from six to eight years old, just beginning to learn to read, is mainly concerned with maintaining the conception of himself as manly. He likes to play cowboy, G-man and Indian. He tries not to cry when he gets a bump. The greatest possible insult would be to call him a sissy. Yet this boy, when the reading lesson begins, must stand up before his companions and read that "The little red hen says 'Cluck! Cluck! Cluck!' "—or something equally inconsistent with his standards of how he should behave. If a boy is trying to maintain a standard of manliness on the playground, he does not abandon that standard merely because he walks from the playground into the class-room. When boys are given books about railroads and airplanes, the resistance disappears, and they learn just as rapidly and have as much "native ability" as girls.

Thus the pupil's resistance to learning certain subjects is really resistance to behaving in a manner which is inconsistent with his personal standards. Eagerness to learn, on the other hand, is due to the pupil's effort to maintain and support his standards. But he is not conscious of these standards, and explains his failures and successes either in terms of ability, or as due to likes and dislikes over which he has no control.

STANDARDS RESPONSIBLE FOR FAILURE

Now suppose that a pupil thinks of himself as a poor speller or reader, or as one of those unfortunates who "just haven't got a mathematical mind." Is he merely lacking a standard to maintain? Not at all. This conception, so long as he believes it to be true, is just as definite as any other, and the standard is just as positive. Though he seems to be saying "I can't," he is really asserting "I won't try." Many people find it hard to believe that a person will defend and strive to maintain an idea which is not to his advantage. But the evidence allows of no other conclusion.

For example, if we examine the letters or themes written by a poor speller, we find that he seems to have a standard of how many words he should misspell per page. Often a word will be spelled both correctly and incorrectly in the same theme, but the average number of mistakes per page remains approximately constant. If we give him two spelling tests of the same length and equal difficulty, we find approximately the same number of errors on each of the tests. If we tutor him in spelling, the effect often wears off within a few weeks, and he returns to his characteristic level. As one student said, "I can remember how a word is spelled all right, but I can't remember whether it is the right way or the wrong way." The presence of a standard is also shown by the fact that many poor spellers in English have no more difficulty than others in spelling foreign languages.

In a study of remedial instruction in reading made in the New York schools last year, ten per cent of the pupils who were tutored actually retrogressed in reading ability, though their average I.Q. was slightly higher than that of the group which made normal progress. How could this be explained except in terms of the pupil's resistance to changing his standards?

Perhaps the most striking illustration of resistance is the complete inability to read which is known as congenital word-blindness. Word-blind pupils are suffering not from a visual handicap, but a mental one. They can see other things, including letters, but they cannot "see" words. In many cases they have I.Q.'s above normal, and often are proficient in non-reading subjects such as arithmetic. But they think of themselves as unable to read, and maintain this standard by rejecting the ideas necessary for reading, for these ideas are inconsistent with their self-conception and consequently cannot be assimilated. "None are so blind as those that will not see."

The reliability of a child's behavior, as indicated either by tests or by general observation, is thus explained by self-consistency as the outward expression of relatively fixed internal standards. It is often argued that the reliability of a test proves that the test is measuring the child's ability. All that any test can measure, however, is the level of performance which is characteristic of the child at the time when the test is given. It is not the test which is reliable, but the child. We cannot interpret the score simply as a measure of ability unless we disregard the problem of resistance entirely, and assume not only the presence of specific abilities, but also the motive to use them to the limit.

CHANGING STANDARDS BY AROUSING CONFLICTS

The problem of how to remove the deficiency, then, is really the problem of how to remove the standard responsible for it. We cannot remove it ourselves, of course, but if we can show the pupil that the standard in question is inconsistent with his other standards, and endangers the unity of the system as a whole, he will have to alter it himself. It can safely be taken for granted, in the majority of cases, that the "big boy" or "big girl" idea of childhood has developed and reached a more mature level, and hence that the pupil now thinks of himself as self-reliant and independent. Obviously, the childish standard which is causing the resistance does not belong in the same system with these mature standards. The pupil has not recognized the inconsistency, however, because he has always managed to keep the conflicting ideas apart. Reorganization is temporarily painful, and in order to avoid it he has resorted to private logic and rationalized the conflict away.

Our method must therefore aim to break down the structure of rationalization and bring the contradictory ideas into intimate relationship. There is nothing novel in this plan. All of us use it frequently. But it has to be used with skill and understanding if we hope to circumvent the pupil's effort to preserve the status quo in spite of us.

A pupil whose unconscious standards are preventing his development in certain directions is really caught in a trap. He set up the standard originally as a means of avoiding conflict. By defining himself as unable or unwilling to master a subject which seemed to be difficult, he protected himself from the pain of contradiction by making it seem consistent to fail. As a result, he finds himself increasingly handicapped in the effort to maintain other standards whose preservation is imperative; for example, the idea that he is normally intelligent and respected by others as an equal. But the longer he maintains the standard, and the greater the handicap becomes, the greater the difficulty he has in escaping from his own defenses.

To free himself, it would be necessary to set up a new and higher standard supported by consistency alone. This is by no means impossible, in spite of the influence of past experience. But he cannot make up his mind to this step because he is not clearly aware of the nature of the problem. The picture of himself as caught in a trap is hidden from his view. Hence he not only clings to the inhibiting idea, but defends it by rationalizing to the effect that since every one has his weaknesses, it is foolish to worry about them. The rationalization masks the problem so cleverly that the pupil sees no inconsistency to be corrected, and hence has no motive for changing his attitude. As long as they are protected by their parents and enjoy their customary social status, such pupils as a rule take an optimistic view of the future, anticipate a lenient and sympathetic attitude on the part of others, and expect to be successful in spite of their deficiency. Indeed, this attitude is necessary for defense.

In applying the method, we first explain to the pupil that his deficiency is not due to lack of ability, but to a standard which he created himself. We must make it clear that the standard is unconscious, since this explains why he has continued to maintain it. It is most important that the interpretation of his difficulty be offered in a friendly and uncritical manner. The attitude should be that this is not our problem, but his.

The next step is to demonstrate that the pupil also has other standards which likewise must be maintained; for example, the conception of himself as self-reliant, independent, socially acceptable, and able to solve his problems by his own effort.

Finally, we call attention without criticism to the inconsistency between mature and immature standards. We make the conflict as clear as possible. In this way we take advantage of the need for consistency and make it work in the pupil's favor instead of against him.

Many counselors make the mistake of trying to influence the pupil by appealing to practical or material motives, such as the need of arithmetic and spelling in business. Our experience has shown that these appeals have little or no effect. We can influence the pupil to change his behavior in order to preserve his mental integrity, but not in order to prepare himself to make a material success.

58 | CASES ILLUSTRATING PSYCHOANALYTIC CONTRIBUTIONS TO THE PROBLEMS OF READING DISABILITIES

PHYLLIS BLANCHARD

Sometimes Johnny can't read because his father has told him over and over again that he is a poor reader. Sometimes he can't read because the words remind him that his mother has left him; or they remind him that he is angry or afraid or curious. Remedial reading often fails to help, because before the child can learn to read he must resolve these underlying emotional problems.

This article discusses several cases in which reading difficulties were treated by helping children understand their own feelings rather than tutoring them in the actual reading skills.

For purposes of brevity, the following illustrations will not be complete case summaries but will consist of material selected chiefly to clarify points made in the preceding general discussion. Since the selection has been made for research purposes and to illustrate theoretical concepts, no implications as to therapeutic methods and techniques are intended. In some instances, longer case reports have been published previously (in papers referred to in reviewing the literature on reading disabilities). Perhaps it should be stated that the children were seen at the clinics, appointments being once or twice weekly for varied periods of time. When the children were living in their own homes, case work with the parents was quite as important as psychotherapy for the children.

The first case illustrates a chronically unfavorable parent-child relationship in which the child was under constant emotional strain. For some three years prior

Reprinted from *Psychoanalytic Study of the Child*, Vol 11, (International Universities Press, Inc., 1946), by permission of the author and publisher.

to his referral to clinic, the boy had been the object of his father's anxiety and criticism, focused upon the subject of reading. Why the boy developed difficulty in reading and other neurotic symptoms should be self-evident from the case material presented below.

CASE 1

Matthew was a twelve-year-old boy who was repeating fifth grade and still failing the work. He was considered mentally deficient by parents, teachers and classmates but psychological examination showed that he actually was of superior intelligence, with an IQ of 133.

The boy's father had had considerable difficulty in his vocational adjustments and had often been unemployed. He displaced anxiety from himself onto worry about the boy's future, stressing success in school as a preparation for later vocational success. When the boy was in third grade, the father began to supervise his school work. Although Matthew's teachers gave him good marks in reading, his father decided that he was poor in this subject. The father came to this conclusion after asking Matthew to read matter that was far too advanced for a third grade pupil. From that time, however, the father centered his anxiety upon the boy's reading and began to tutor him in it. Invariably, he scolded and criticized the boy during these home lessons, so that they always ended with Matthew in tears and his father in a temper. It is not strange, therefore, that the boy made no further progress in reading between the third and fifth grades or that by the time he was in fifth grade, he had a serious reading disability. By then, also, he was so sensitive to criticism that he would burst into tears at the slightest reprimand from a teacher and would fight with any child who said a teasing word to him.

Neither remedial teaching nor psychotherapy helped in this case so long as

the boy remained at home, for the father was unable to change in his relationship to the boy, continued to displace anxiety onto him, and could not be induced to forego tutoring him. When the boy went to a boarding school and was thus freed from his father's anxiety and criticisms, he was able to learn to read with the help of individual remedial teaching.

Unfavorable comparisons with a brother or sister have been mentioned in the literature as another type of chronic family situation leading to neurotic conflicts and trouble with reading, in some instances. In the next case, comparisons between a living child and brother who had died were intimately associated with the reading disability.

CASE 2

Patrick was a nine-year-old boy, of normal intelligence (IQ 105) but was unable to read. Remedial teaching provided at school was unsuccessful in helping him to learn reading. There had been three children in the family—a first son who had died, Patrick, and a younger sister.

In his interviews with the therapist, Patrick soon spoke of the death of his older brother as having occurred shortly before he himself started first grade. A little more than a year later, Patrick said, he received a book as a birthday gift but he had not liked it, for when the stories were read to him, they proved to be about people who were killed. He had hated the stories and cried whenever he saw the book. After hearing those stories, he felt that he never wanted to hear a book read again nor did he ever want to read one himself.

At first, during his interviews, he stressed his love for his mother and his dead brother and dwelt upon wishes always to be good and kind to people. However, he soon became jealous of other patients, was angry with them for coming and with the therapist for seeing them. He complained that the therapist was just like his teachers, preferring other boys to him. After awhile, he began to accuse his mother of never having loved him as much as his dead brother. He told how she often talked about the dead child, saying that he had learned to read very quickly and criticizing Patrick for not being as apt at reading. "I wouldn't want to be like my brother," Patrick asserted contemptuously, "maybe he could read but he couldn't stand up for himself with the other kids. I'm a good fighter. They don't dare pick on me."

Patrick also told of his mother's weekly visits to his brother's grave and the tears that she shed each time she went there. Discarding his desire to be good and kind, he went on to express his wishes to dig up the brother's body and bury it somewhere so far away that his mother would never be able to find the grave and visit it. Or better yet, he would burn the body, destroying it completely. He then told how he hated his mother when he believed that she was behaving as if she wished his brother had lived and he had died. Similarly, he hated his teachers and his therapist when he thought that they might prefer other boys to him.

The mother, in the above case, had brought the boy to the clinic at the insistence of the school; she rarely kept her appointments with the social worker but sent the boy alone for his interviews with the therapist; finally, she withdrew him from therapy before it was completed. The material is therefore of interest only in connection with the etiology of the boy's reading disability. Obviously, when he first came to therapy, his conflicts about his mother and brother had been unconscious and he had repressed his resentment and hostility. His wishes to be good and kind were defenses by which he maintained the repression. The book with stories about people being killed naturally stirred up the repressed aggressive drives

and threatened to bring them into his conscious experience. In turn, this aroused feelings of guilt and anxiety (shown in his weeping whenever he saw the book) as he came closer to awareness of his hostility toward his mother and his dead brother. Thus another defense and way of maintaining the repressions was refusal to learn to read, for he feared that reading content might release aggressive impulses. Self-assertion through being different from his brother was indicated by his stating his preference for being a good fighter rather than a good reader and his desire not to be like his brother. This was another motive influencing his negative attitude toward reading. Again, not learning to read was a disguised expression of hostility toward the mother who wanted him to be clever in this respect. He identified the teachers who wanted him to read with the mother and also rebelled against learning to read to please them. Indeed he transferred his jealousy of his mother and brother to the teacher and other pupils at school, and to the therapist and other patients at the clinic, always neurotically recreating for himself the unpleasant and painful family situation which he was trying to repress from consciousness.

In the following case, we see how a later event may reactivate the unconscious feelings that surrounded an earlier traumatic one.

CASE 3

Thomas was an eleven-year-old boy, failing fifth grade for the second time. He had made low ratings on group tests given at school. Individual tests showed that he had an IQ of 108 but was handicapped in doing both group tests and school work by a reading disability. He dated the start of his trouble with reading from the first part of third grade, when a teacher whom he liked very much had to go to the hospital for an operation. Since she did not return to school, Thomas assumed she had died. He explained that he was so worried over the teacher's absence and her supposed death that he could not keep his mind on his work and so fell behind in reading.

This preoccupation with the question of the teacher's possible death becomes more intelligible if we know that when the boy was five years old, his mother had been away in a hospital, for an operation. He did not recall these circumstances about his mother's hospitalization, even when they were mentioned to him; he only remembered about the teacher.

In some of his therapeutic interviews, Thomas wanted to read aloud. It then became obvious that the content of reading often brought up his unconscious emotional conflicts. He would be reading fairly well when suddenly he would begin to make many errors until he stopped and talked of personal matters suggested to him by something he had read. After speaking out what had come into his mind, he could resume reading without excessive mistakes. For example, in reading a story about a dog, Thomas began making errors and continued to do so until he had paused to talk about a dog he once had owned. He had loved his dog very much indeed, he said, but he had not been permitted to keep it. After his dog was given away, he was very lonely; he cried and cried because he wanted his dog back and because he did not know what might be happening to it. "I was afraid my dog might die without my knowing about it," he explained. "It is awful to be wondering whether someone you love is alive or dead."

By the time his therapy ended, he could read without breaking down as described above. According to follow-up reports, during the next two years, his school progress was satisfactory.

The circumstances of the teacher's going to a hospital for an operation evidently revived the boy's feelings about his mother's hospitalization even though he had repressed the memory of his mother's operation and his anxiety about it. Reactivation of the emotional trauma was not the only reason for his trouble with reading, however, for from his interviews it was evident that reading content too frequently tended to stir up his unconscious conflicts. It does not take a very vivid imagination to realize that his feelings about his dog, for instance, were like those he had experienced when his mother was in the hospital. These feelings quite obviously were brought closer to consciousness when he read the story about the dog, even though it was a very cheerful one, just because the content contained the word dog many times repeated.

Both case 2 and case 3 illustrate the statements in the preceding general theoretical formulation concerning the ease with which reading content becomes associated with a child's unconscious emotional conflicts, leading to a break-down in reading skill, or to an aversion to reading.

An immediate effect of an emotional trauma connected with separation from the mother at a time when the child is entering school is illustrated by the next case.

CASE 4

When Ethel was nearly six years old, her mother was forced to place her in a boarding school. Ethel's father had died two years previously and now the mother had to go to work so that she could no longer keep the child with her. At the school, Ethel seemed to have little appetite and would refuse to eat very much except when her mother visited and brought her food, which she would eat heartily. She did not learn to read during two years in first grade. She was brought to the clinic at the age of eight years, unable to read, still refusing food and having lost weight to the point where she seemed weak and ill and had to be kept in bed for considerable periods. Medical examinations could detect no physical basis for her symptoms.

In her interviews at the clinic, both her refusal to eat and her failure in learning to read soon appeared as symptoms of her unconscious conflicts over being sent away to school by her mother. At first she spoke of how much she loved her mother but soon in her play she began to dramatize her other attitudes of anger and hostility. She portrayed a mother doll sending her little girl doll away to school. The little girl doll was then angry with the mother, would not let the mother have anything to eat because she wanted to starve her mother to death, a fate that would serve her right for sending the little girl away to school. Immediately afterward, however, the little girl was punished for being so bad to her mother and also was described as being unable to eat and feeling weak and ill. Another drama with the dolls showed the little girl refusing to study or to read at school. Her poor school reports were sent to the mother doll, who decided that the school was no good and came to take the little girl home.

After this play with the dolls, Ethel could talk about how she felt when her mother placed her in the boarding school. She became aware of her idea that if she became ill or did not do well in her school work, she could force her mother to take her home again. At this point, she went on to explain that in reality, her mother could not take her because she no longer had a home. Since her father was no longer alive to take care of her mother and herself, her mother had to work to support them. She worked hard to earn money to pay for Ethel's school and her clothing. Ethel then felt very sympathetic toward her mother, who was tired from her hard work, and she was sorry that she had worried her mother by not eating and

not learning to read. She announced that she was eating all right now but she had not been able to learn to read at school and she wished she could have someone to help her with reading. This request was seen as indicative of a change in attitude toward reading and special teaching was provided. Ethel worked hard with her tutor. She learned to read and began to make regular progress in school. At the time of the last follow-up report she was in seventh grade. None of her symptoms had recurred.

We might ask why this girl reacted so much more violently to being placed in boarding school by her mother than to her father's death. We can only guess at the possible reasons. Many children have less conflict over the loss of a parent through death than over separation from a parent through placement. Apparently placement is often taken as an act of aggression and rejection from the parent and therefore stimulates anger and resentment as well as grief. When a parent dies, love and grief over the loss need not necessarily come into conflict with other attitudes of anger and resentment. Serious conflicts over the death of a parent of course do occur when there was so much hostility toward the parent that a child feels guilty because of the hostile wishes before the parent died, as if they were responsible for the event. Thus a parent's death may or may not be a source of conflict to a child, depending upon the relationship that preceded it. On the other hand, placement often arouses conflict because it engenders hostility toward the parent while at the same time love and wishes to be reunited with the parent still persist.

While the next case also involves a child's conflicts over placement by the mother, it was selected for presentation primarily because it illustrates how errors in reading may provide a disguised expression and gratification of repressed wishes and drives, as was suggested in the more theoretical explanations of reading difficulties.

CASE 5

Benjamin was an eight-year-old boy who had remained for two years in the first half of first grade without learning to write or read words. His efforts to write them consisted of reversals of letters or sequence, seemingly meaningless combinations of letters, or a series of peculiar marks. Other symptoms were a solitary withdrawal from social relationships and wetting and soiling himself, although when still living with his own mother, he had established bladder and bowel control. Regression to wetting and soiling began when he was about three years of age after the mother placed him.

Repeated medical examinations revealed no physical basis for his symptoms. There was no left-handedness nor left or mixed eye-hand dominance connected with his tendency to reversals in writing words. At the age of three years, before his neurotic symptoms appeared, he achieved an IQ of 95. When tested by the same psychologist at five and seven years of age, he achieved IQ's of 75 and 74. At the end of therapy, after he had recovered from his severe neurosis, he was retested and his IQ then was 95.

Benjamin was placed in a foster home after birth of a sister. Both children were illegitimate but the mother married the father of the second one. He did not wish to take the child by a former lover into their home, so the mother turned the boy over to a placement agency and then deserted him completely.

Benjamin was seen for nearly a year and a half, mostly twice a week. During these appointments, emotional conflicts about having been deserted by his mother were very evident. His feelings toward the mother were transferred to the therapist, whom he often reproached for sending him to live with strange people and

causing his illness symptoms, saying, "I hate you for what you have done to me." He had various fantasy explanations of why his mother had deserted him. Since she placed him at the time of his sister's birth, he sometimes imagined that she had given him away because she loved girls better than boys. At other times, he suspected that she stopped loving him when she began to love the man she married, for it was after she had known this man that she gave up Benjamin. He hated his mother because he felt that placement was a proof of her ceasing to love him more than because of the placement per se. His hatred was expressed in certain fantasies associated with the symptoms of wetting and soiling; for example, he pictured burning up his mother with his hot urine or poisoning her by making her eat his feces. On the other hand, fantasies of being a baby, living with his mother and cared for tenderly by her, were also closely connected with his enuresis and soiling. Thus these symptoms concealed his love as well as his hostility and afforded gratification of ambivalent feelings toward his mother. Both his resentment toward his mother and his longing for her love had been repressed and were permitted an outlet only through his symptoms.

Benjamin regarded reading as evidence of being grown-up, but was blocked in his wishes to grow up because of fantasies that this could be achieved only by eating the father to gain his traits in magic manner. He was very guilty about such aggressive desires. But Benjamin's errors in writing words, like his other symptoms, were similarly disguised expressions of feelings toward his mother. He sometimes explained his mother's desertion as due to her not being Jewish, like himself, for he had heard that Christians were cruel to Jews. If his mother was not Jewish, the English language that they wanted him to write at school must be her language and he hated her so much that he **did not** want to learn it; instead, he wished to learn Hebrew, the language of Jewish people. He was unable to write Hebrew but he knew that it is written in the opposite direction to English; he explained that he tried to turn the English taught at school into Hebrew by writing it backwards. This was the reason for his reversals in writing words.

He called the peculiar marks that he sometimes made for words his "Chinese writing." He knew that the Chinese made peculiar marks to represent words; he had heard that Chinese tortured people whom they hated. When he hated his mother for deserting him, he elaborated, he felt like torturing her the way she had tortured him by letting him love her and then sending him away from her. His "Chinese writing" was a magic spell that would cause his mother to be tortured with sharp knives or in other ways and to be eaten by fierce animals.

These two types of errors in writing words—the reversals and the peculiar marks—were thus symbolic of his anger toward his mother, and his wish to hurt her. His other errors, in which he combined letters into what seemed nonsense, were symbolic of the love he still felt for his mother. For instance, he once wrote the following letter combinations—"As ur mor," which stood for the words, "Ask your mother." It developed that what he wanted to ask her (and the therapist, too) was to have a baby for him, as a proof that his love was returned. Then he need no longer fear that his mother loved the man she had married better than him.

It was only after he had produced all his imaginary explanations for his mother's having placed him and had become conscious of his repressed ambivalent feelings toward her, that he could realize there might be a different reason for the placement than those he had fantasied. Finally he accepted the reality that his mother had placed him because she could no longer take care of him. He then decided that he no longer needed to hate his mother, adding that this permitted him to love other women, too—his foster mother and his teachers at school. He explained that when he hated his own mother, he had hated all women, and so he had never wanted to do a single thing that his foster mother or his teachers asked of him. Now that he could love women, he wanted to do as they expected, so he would not have any more trouble with school work.

In thus describing how he felt about doing things for people because he loved them, this boy was confirming the psychoanalytic theory that the child first learns to please adults whom he loves. Of special interest was the fact that the reversals in writing words, often explained on a physical basis, in this instance were symbolic expressions of hostility and aggression. In two more recent clinic cases, reversals in reading and writing were similarly disguised forms of negative attitudes toward parents and teachers, accompanied by aggressive, destructive fantasies.

In reviewing the literature, there was a reference to a statement by Pearson and English concerning an inhibition of reading after a child had been forbidden peeping activities by parents. Our last case is that of a boy whose expressions of sexual curiosity and also of aggression had been stringently restricted. This case shows a reading disability developing from too severe limitations of instinctive drives.

CASE 6

Jonathan, eight years old when referred to the clinic, had been living in the same foster home since infancy. He had for some time been a tense, hyperactive child, hardly ever still. After two years in school, he had not learned to read. At first it was difficult to maintain contact with him or carry on any connected conversation because of his extreme motor restlessness. He was always running around the room and never continued any one play activity or topic of conversation for more than a few minutes. It was soon observed that he often hunted among the therapist's books, as if searching for something in particular, but he never would tell what he was looking for, saying that he did not know, which was probably quite true. One day as he rummaged through the books, he came upon *Growing Up*. He seized it with the exclamation, "That's what I wanted," but immediately replaced it upon the shelf, saying he could not read it. When asked if he would like it read to him, he hastily disclaimed any such wish.

For some time after this episode, the interviews were taken up with some of his conflicts about living in a foster home and having no parents of his own. At first he tried to protect himself from the anxiety aroused by the knowledge that his own parents had died when he was a small child, by fantasies that the foster parents were his own. After a while he gave up this defense and admitted the insecurity he felt at having no "real" parents like other children at school. Instead of running aimlessly around the room, he now began to do carpentry, liking to fashion swords, knives and guns out of wood. From his talk about these weapons, it was clear that they were symbols of both masculinity and aggressive tendencies, but he often had to leave them with the therapist because he was sure that his foster mother would object to his having them. Actually, when he did get courage to take home a sword he had made, his foster mother took it away from him. As he complained, she wanted him to act like a girl. His complaint had foundation in the fact, for the foster mother told us that she had wanted the placement agency to give her a girl (although she had never mentioned this to the agency) and when

receiving a boy instead, she had dressed him like a girl as long as he would tolerate it and still expected him to be feminine in his behavior.

After he had found some relief from the repression of aggression and masculinity imposed by the foster mother, he again sought out the book *Growing Up* and looked at the pictures, asking the therapist to read some of the pages. He was guilty about this until he had talked over how his foster father once read him this book—but behind locked doors and with a stern warning that Jonathan must never talk about these sex education matters with the foster mother or anyone else except the foster father himself. This was only one aspect of the foster father's need to assure himself the sole intimate relationship with the boy; he did not permit Jonathan to play after school with other children, visit them or invite them to his home. Once Jonathan had thrown aside the restriction his foster father had placed upon his speaking of sex matters to other people, his next interviews with the therapist were full of questions and talk about sex and babies, including repetition of all the slang words and phrases he had heard. He concluded this series of interviews by saying, "I wish I could have asked my mother these things and talked about them with her, but I didn't dare because it would have made my father so angry that maybe he wouldn't have kept me. I was afraid he would give me back to the agency." He also told how he had been eager to learn to read when he first went to school, so that he could read *Growing Up* by himself, only he was fearful that the foster father would not have liked his reading it, for he always kept the book locked in his desk.

After the therapy was completed, Jonathan was able to learn to read at school without remedial teaching. By then, too, he was ready for a move to another foster home where masculine and aggressive strivings were acceptable. Followup reports from the agency indicated that he was developing along normal masculine lines thereafter and when a young adolescent, he was seen for educational guidance tests and interview. At this later date, he could never have been recognized as the same repressed, effeminate boy who had come to the clinic years earlier.

It is interesting to raise a question as to whether this boy would have developed his reading disability as the result of limitation of sexual curiosity alone. To be sure, he was so guilty over wanting to read *Growing Up* and talk about it with his foster mother that he had to resist all reading, but it would seem that repression of aggression was also involved in his avoidance of reading. At least, it was plain in the therapeutic interviews that he could only admit his interest in sex questions, in defiance of his foster father's prohibitions, after relaxation of the repression of masculine, aggressive strivings. Apparently reading was not simply a way of acquiring knowledge but also was an activity that represented aggressive rebellion against the foster father's restrictions, and against his desire to keep the boy to himself. The boy realized that aggression of any kind would meet with disapproval from the foster mother, on whom he had been very dependent as a young child. He was afraid also that the foster father might punish rebellious resistance to his domination by refusing to give him a home any longer. Hence it is little wonder that the boy had to repress aggression so completely.

CONCLUSION

In the clinical cases just presented to illustrate reading disabilities of a psychogenic nature, it seems possible to interpret the material in the light of psychoanalytic theories of reading and learning. But it also appears that there is no single situation or personality maladjustment which can be isolated to explain the development

of a reading disability as one of the child's neurotic symptoms. The background may be either traumatic or may reveal chronically unfavorable experiences; the personality difficulties may be severe (as in the case of Ethel who made herself ill by refusing food, or Benjamin who was withdrawn from social relationships and had other serious neurotic symptoms, or Jonathan who was inhibited, passive and effeminate); or maladjustments other than the trouble with reading may be mild enough to be masked from ordinary observation and may become fully apparent only to the professional eye in therapeutic work with the child. These statements might not seem warranted as generalizations on the basis of the comparatively small number of cases included in this paper or reported in previous ones, except for the fact that other investigators have arrived independently at the same conclusions by accumulating statistical data on large numbers of cases.

Both our individual case studies and the statistical findings of other psychologists suggest that a complexity of factors came together in a focal point around reading, particularly where the disability is of emotional origin. In this respect, the neurotic reading disability conforms to the psychoanalytic concept of neurotic symptoms generally as being overdetermined. It also conforms otherwise to psychoanalytic theories of symptom-formation: for the repression of instinctive drives and existence of emotional conflicts forms the setting for the reading disability as well as for other neurotic symptoms; errors in reading may serve as disguised ways of gratifying repressed impulses just as illness-symptoms serve this purpose; failure in reading may represent a hidden antagonism to adults expressed in passive resistance rather than in openly rebellious behavior, and thus may also conceal repressed attitudes. To be sure, at other times the failure may result from a wish to avoid reading because it has previously stirred up feelings of guilt or anxiety, but here, too, it closely resembles a well-known neurotic tendency toward avoidance of imaginary dangers.

In considering that reading disabilities tend to appear as a center of convergence for several emotional factors, we probably need to take into account the timing of this occurrence. It is reasonable to believe that reading is most apt to become involved in a child's emotional conflicts when these concur with the period of learning the fundamentals of the reading process in the early school grades. Once a firm foundation has been acquired, further proficiency in reading depends more upon enlarging the reading vocabulary than

learning new processes so that disability for this subject is less likely to begin in higher grades, although it may have remained undetected until then. It is possible, therefore, that the time element may have a bearing on whether a special educational disability will be for reading or for some other subject. Since in many cases personality maladjustments of children begin by the time they enter school or soon afterward, this may be one reason why reading disabilities are more frequent than others. But an equally valid reason, already mentioned, is the ease with which reading content, either directly or symbolically, can become associated with unconscious emotional conflicts.

59 | FAMILY PATHOLOGY, FAMILY DIAGNOSIS, AND FAMILY THERAPY WITH A CHILD WELFARE FOCUS

OTTO POLLAK

Theoretically it has long been accepted that disturbance in a child is symptomatic of a disturbed family. Pollak and his associates have been in the forefront of the attempts to apply this theoretical understanding practically—to focus treatment on the entire family unit rather than on only the child or only the mother and child.

In the following selection, Pollak describes how his clinic analyzes and deals with the forces and personalities within the family— including a family doctor who discouraged psychotherapy.

There seems to be very little recognition, and even less acceptance, in diagnostic and therapeutic emphasis, of the fact that the *family of procreation*—the biological and reproductive unit of the parents and child—need not be identical with the *family of orientation*—the sum total of

Excerpts reprinted from *Integrating Sociological and Psychoanalytic Concepts* (Russell Sage Foundation, 1956), pp. 31–34, 127–38, and from *Social Science and Psychotherapy for Children* (Russell Sage Foundation, 1952), pp. 42–43, by permission of the author and publisher.

persons who form continuing members of the household in which the child grows up, that is, the primary group at the home. There may be aunts and uncles, grandparents, or even boarders, who are in daily-living contact with the child for periods extending over the whole stretch of his formative years.

Perhaps the basic fact about the presence of "other persons" in the home is that they are not acceptable equally to all members of the family of procreation. They may be acceptable to the child, or to the parents, or to one parent and the child, and so on, but not to the other or others. The presence of an adult relative, particularly if childless, invariably means the presence of an active competitor with the parent of the same sex as the relative for the child's affection. This competition may be overt or it may be subtle or insidious. Or the adult relative is not included in the rules or regime which the parent imposes upon the others in the family; hence this adult, no matter how circumspect his behavior may be, appears to the child as a challenge to the parent's authority, or as a refuge or comfort which the child may seek. A good many domestic situations might be summarized in the statement that the presence of a younger adult in the family means a potential competitor for the affection of the child; and the presence of an older person, a potential competitor for his control. The problem, of course, is often less simple than such a summary suggests. Adults who live with other families tend often to be problem adults. A parent's brother or sister who is not married, or who has been married but not successfully, or who cannot get along with other people, or who is too sick or too feeble to live by himself—these constitute a good proportion of the adults who live with "their" families. Taking in a relative is often the assumption of a burden and a problem. Parents may assume such an obligation with the philosophy of maturity or the resignation of despair, but to the child the newcomer is as he is, without the comfort of compensating philosophy.[1]

This may arise particularly in situations where a member of the family of orientation, such as an old and feeble grandfather, competes with the child for the attention and care of the mother and thus actually starts something equivalent to sibling rivalry between himself and the grandchild.

Thus in psychodynamic terms all members of the family of orientation may become partners to emotionally significant interrelationships with the child and influ-

ence his growth process. Dynamic consideration of all persons living in the household in which the child grows up may give a now lacking measure of assurance that an important relationship is not overlooked, minimized, or perceived in its full impact only after considerable treatment time has been lost. Of course, treatment of the child's environment must admit the treatment needs of such persons as well as the treatment needs of the mother.

. . . . .

It helped us to free ourselves from the perceptual trap presented by the dichotomy of patient and environment and actually to see the total family as a unit of diagnostic and therapeutic concern. It provided a permanent challenge to strive for a psychodynamic understanding of all the members of the family, to see the social interaction among them as based on these individual psychodynamic pictures, and to base therapeutic planning on such understanding. In essence, it helped us shift our orientation from child psychotherapy to family psychotherapy with child welfare focus and to experiment with procedures which such an orientation demanded. In response to this challenge of reorientation we attempted wherever possible to perform three tasks. First of all, we tried to formulate a clinical, a genetic, and a dynamic diagnosis of every family member in whom we encountered pathology. Essentially this was only an accumulation of individual diagnostic procedures which had been practiced before regularly as far as the mother and the child were concerned. To be sure, the extension of this procedure to other members of the family as well was burdensome because of its demand on the worker's time. It also proved technically difficult because of the concern that such an extension of the diagnostic inquiry might on occasion interfere with the establishment of a relationship between the worker and the individual patient. Still,

---

[1] James H. Bossard, *The Sociology of Child Development* (New York: Harper and Bros., 1948), pp. 59–60.

this was from the point of view of theory simply an additive process of gaining information.

The next step in our team thinking, however, presented theoretical difficulties which we did not fully overcome and which suggest a fruitful field of further research. To identify pathology in the various members of a family on an individual basis and even to gain an understanding of pathological interaction between two of them is one thing. To gain and formulate an understanding of pathological interaction patterns among three, four, or even more members of a household on which to base therapeutic planning on such an understanding is more difficult, because this presents problems of another order, namely, problems of formulating a family diagnosis and planning a family therapy. The solution of these problems requires specific conceptual tools and specific therapeutic practices which have been hardly yet developed, although the need for advance in that direction has been recognized and some promising beginnings have been made.

Thus, our own attempts at formulating a family diagnosis represent only one phase in a development of thought which apparently goes in this direction. They were characterized not only by an effort to keep a balance between our psychodynamic understanding of individuals and the observation of interactional patterns but by an effort to achieve an integration between these two orientations. We tried to see how the intrapsychic difficulties of the individuals involved determined their interaction patterns and how these interaction patterns in turn determined the development, persistence, or abating of their intrapsychic difficulties. Furthermore, we attempted to make these analyses not on a two-person but on a real family basis, which always involved more than two persons. Finally, we evaluated the nature and effect of the interaction patterns which we found operating in a family in

terms of family functions and family tendencies as seen from an institutional angle.

Our third effort was concerned with the development of a family treatment plan. Owing to the very nature of our family diagnoses, these treatment plans had to express concern with pluralities greater than dualities. They had to be directed at the change of more than one interaction pattern. In consequence, frequently more than two persons had to be considered for treatment. Furthermore, because of trying to think in terms of families rather than in terms of two-person fragments thereof, we had to be reluctant about dividing cases. While it still may be possible to keep treatment procedures pursued by two workers integrated, the chances for maintaining such an integration where three workers are involved obviously are slight. In consequence, we found it fruitful to have the same worker see all the members of the family as actual or potential patients to be treated by herself until such time as special counterindications became apparent. The latter actually happened very infrequently.

Our attempts to treat families as totalities rather than only in terms of two-person fragments also strengthened our awareness of the limitation of goals. We became better aware of the fact that such limitations are determined not only by the intensity of intrapsychic difficulties in one or the other member of a family, but also by the nature and the level of common concern in the family unit. In this respect the child welfare focus of the agency proved to be helpful in keeping the various courses of therapy with the individual members of the family on a concerted plane.

It will be noticed that in this report the term "child focus" is replaced by the term "child welfare focus." This substitution of terms represents a postproject conceptualization. In our actual team discussions we had retained the term "child focus." In retrospect it appears, however, that the use of this term created a number of difficulties. It failed to express conceptually the reorientation which our situational approach implied. For this reason, it caused perceptual pitfalls and logical inconsistencies with which we had to struggle a great deal and against which the term "child welfare focus" promises to furnish a measure of protection.

By focusing upon the child as an individual, perception is likely to be restricted and the dynamic forces in his environment are likely to be blurred. Under the impact of such a terminology clinical consideration of the mother on an equal footing with the child is indeed an advance. By focusing on the welfare of a child, however, the perception of the plurality of factors involved is promoted and clinical emphasis upon the mother-child relationships as encountered in routinized practice appears to be fragmentation rather than comprehensiveness. Child welfare focus, furthermore, makes it difficult to single out one child from a number of siblings as the only receiver of clinical concern. It directs attention to the siblings rather than to a sibling. By doing so it is likely to enhance effectiveness in the prevention function of child guidance work. The concept of child welfare focus also promises to keep family therapy from disintegrating into a number of treatments which serve only the individuals involved for their own sake rather than gearing the therapeutic efforts to a common social interest. Thus, the concept may serve as an orchestrating principle in the management of the various individual lines of therapy which compose the family treatment, and it seems to anchor the clinical effort in a recognized area of social concern.

. . . . .

THE CASE OF EDWARD N.

Presenting Symptoms

Edward's mother was referred to the Child Guidance Institute by a psychologist. He was an only child, described as destructive at home and aggressive to other children. He pulled at their genitals, threw rocks at girls, and pulled boys off bicycles. At other times he showed completely withdrawn behavior. As a result of these difficulties in relating to other children, he had no friends. He was also aggressive to his mother who, the psychologist reported, was overprotective toward the definite history of respiratory allergies, apparently accentuated at four years of age. He also complained frequently of abdominal distress. The family background showed a history of asthma in a maternal aunt. In the father's opinion, the boy was infantile, secretive, and had temper outbursts. The mother feared the boy's sexual interests. She worried lest he be "abnormal" like herself or a maternal aunt who had undergone psychiatric treatment.

Edward's health history revealed infantile colic, pneumonia at fifteen weeks, two and one-half-years, and at three and one-half years, with frequent respiratory discomfort, eventually developing into known allergy at about the age of four. At six he had an ear infection with hearing difficulties, relieved by adenoidectomy. At nine, just before direct therapy, he developed a fourth attack of pneumonia. A number of medical specialists had been involved by consultation, and a general practitioner occupied the foremost role in caring for the boy's allergies, as well as advising the mother on matters of child-rearing.

The mother suffered from recurrent depressions with obsessional thoughts and anxieties throughout her life history. An exacerbation of her depressions had occurred during and subsequent to her pregnancy, a further increase at the time of her menopause, which was prior to treatment at the Clinic. She had seen a psychiatrist twice during her postpartum depression, but had reacted with great apprehension and resisted psychiatric help for herself. She was the youngest of a large family, brought to the United States at the age of fifteen by an elder brother. She relied on the oldest sister in a very dependent way. As a child, she had been exposed to the rages of her father, and her pattern had been to withdraw from these scenes. The maternal grandmother was described as a frail, sweet-tempered woman who had tried to protect her daughters from the outbursts of their father by keeping them out of his way as much as possible.

Edward's father, an engineer, appeared to be more composed, and handled his wife's depressive moods with extreme patience. This served to increase guilt feelings and perpetuate her lack of effective effort. He recognized the difficulty of the mother-child relationship, was concerned about Edward's social adjustment and emotional attitudes, but had never taken any initiative in seeking professional help for the mother's difficulties. The contacts which the mother had attempted to make in this direction had been initiated by herself.

For many years it had been the stated policy of the Child Guidance Institute of the Jewish Board of Guardians not to accept children for psychotherapy if psychosomatic conditions were so severe that ambulatory medical treatment had to go on apace with psychotherapy. It was felt that such cases would best be served in hospital clinics where total treatment, providing close cooperation between the departments of psychiatry and those representing other medical specialties, could be given to the patients. However, the appearance of severe emotional disturbance in the mother-child relationship, which the social work therapist readily perceives as important, plus the pressure of the initial referral source, plus the wishes of the medical practitioner himself, lead frequently to a decision for exploration in our Clinic. In many instances, this leads to dramatic supportive help, despite questions as to the effectiveness of the use

of our time and personnel. In the case of Edward, these pressures had also exerted themselves.

Ambivalence of Mother

The mother was offered an interview shortly after application, but she was already away on summer vacation with her son. Intake was completed in the fall, and there then ensued another wait considerably longer than the first one because an assignment to a therapist could not be made. Throughout this time the mother, while ambivalent and depressed, had telephoned the Clinic on occasions and indicated her wish to keep the application open. When we informed her that we could offer a therapist, she reported that Edward had facial twitching and had suffered another siege of pneumonia which curtailed his summer vacation. The boy had responded well to a brief separation in the hospital, but had suffered recurrent colds thereafter. The mother realized that there was definite correlation between her own symptomatology and the boy's demanding behavior with her. Medical treatment consisted of periodic hypodermic injection of nonspecific vaccine to clear up his infectious bronchitis. The family physician had advised her not to send the boy to school because of his debilitated condition and had expressed also the opinion that Edward would not be ready to receive psychotherapy for four more months. The mother did not want the Clinic to close the case, however, and asked the worker to give her a month to decide.

Ambivalence of the Intake Worker

The long delay from first application to a second intake reevaluation in this case was contrary to practice. It was in part related to the problems of the Clinic and in part to the disturbed mother-child relationships. The mother always left a tentative line of approach open, but at times used the physician-child relationship to sustain her own mixed feelings. This seems to be more characteristic of mothers whose children have allergic discomforts than of mothers whose children show other types of maladjustments. As far as the Clinic was concerned there also seemed to have existed ambivalence on the part of the intake worker as to whether this case should be accepted for treatment or not. Apparently the worker's conflict between our general policy not to accept psychosomatic cases in which ambulatory medical treatment has to go on simultaneously and the pressure to offer some help in this severely disturbed situation had remained unresolved. When the case came up for discussion in the project seminar, the uncertainty underlying the original decision to take on Edward's case for exploration had again to be solved. The seminar group expressed the idea that previous indecision of the intake staff regarding acceptability had itself now become a factor in the mother's own hostile reactions toward Edward.

After we had decided to take on the case for research purposes and contact with the mother was planfully established, Mrs. N. appeared depressed, anxious, and easily threatened. She gave much detail of Edward's illnesses, but was protective about his behavioral disturbances. Although she did not conceal the boy's destructiveness, she tried to see in it only a way of self-expression. Admitting that he also showed other difficulties in his behavior at home, she was inclined to present things as improving in that area. She stated her chief concern to be not Edward's behavior at home but his rejection by other children. She indicated a deep sense of brooding responsibility rather than love for Edward. She was deeply dependent upon her husband's patience and devotion to the family to prevent worsening of her depressive moods, serious obsessional thoughts, and her anxiety. She felt "heavy," slept excessively during the daytime, retiring into her bedroom from the family activities.

At these times she ate excessively, and her brooding and irritability were more marked toward Edward.

Ambivalence of the Family Physician

Initially, Mrs. N. saw the Child Guidance Institute as a place for help with Edward's behavioral problems, apart from the physical factors. This definition of the situation on her part appeared to be influenced by the family physician who apparently wanted Edward to come to the Clinic for treatment but thought that his coming for help would have to wait until his physical distress was considerably lessened. The general practitioner had previously resisted suggestions by specialists for testing gastrointestinal factors in the allergic condition. The mother's utilization of the family physician seemed to serve her own need to infantilize the child by excessive physical care, occasioning long school absences and curtailment of his social activities. In addition, she satisfied her own dependency needs by the authoritative, guiding figure of the physician. On the other hand, the worker gained the impression that the mother herself had some questions as to whether Edward's problems could be strictly divided into physical and behavioral problems and whether his physical difficulties were not in part the result of his emotional difficulties.

At any rate, the mother's dependency on the judgment of the family physician required that considerable attention be paid to him in any attempt to establish a common frame of reference among all persons involved in the situation. The next problem on which the seminar discussion focused, therefore, was that of consulting the family physician. The values of such a contact were seen in his ability to clarify fully the medical history of the child and to help the mother cooperate in providing psychotherapy for the boy. It was agreed that the physician seemed to be a person of power in the situation. On the negative side, it was mentioned that the schedule of the doctor as well as that of the worker might prevent their getting together for a conference. The thought was also expressed that the mother might regard this contact as a criticism of her, with the result that her feelings of inadequacy and self-reproach might increase. In the discussion which ensued, the psychiatrist pointed out that it was dangerous to develop set attitudes against approaching another professional person. Such an attitude would in and by itself preclude any possibility of exploring potentially available opportunities of arriving at a common frame of reference in many situations. Doctors often had the notion that a physical condition should be cleared up first and that only afterward should a child receive psychotherapy. His opinion was that only an attempt to interchange experiences could offset this and particularly in this type of case.

Following seminar discussion, several interesting developments occurred. Instead of a possible heightening of the mother's feelings of inadequacy, the therapist's request to see the family doctor occasioned surprise and pleasure—proof of the therapist's interest in Edward. The mother also felt that it would be good for the doctor to gain an idea of the Clinic's treatment procedure inasmuch as he might then feel that it would not endanger Edward's physical status. In other words, the mother herself felt that the physician needed a new frame of reference within which to view the feasibility and potential of psychotherapy for Edward.

The doctor, finally reached by telephone after several unsuccessful calls, refused a conference. He could only talk over the telephone because of his lack of time. He said Edward had just had a really old-fashioned lobar pneumonia, and that his allergies had acted as a hindrance to his recovery. Psychotherapy should be postponed until February. He thought that Edward needed the Clinic's help for "en-vironmental and behavioral reasons" and did not allow the therapist to explain the aims and nature of the psychotherapy. In our seminar discussions, it was felt that the physician by his advice to postpone therapy until February, a time when the boy's medical history indicated frequent recurrence of increased respiratory difficulties, might have revealed unconscious hostile trends toward psychotherapy.

Ambivalence of the Father

Quite apart from our position that an integration of the concept of the family of orientation with psychodynamic concepts required contact with the father in principle, such a contact seemed particularly indicated in this situation. In some cases which we carried in our seminar, the correctness of our belief in the necessity of seeing the father was substantiated only after the contact has been established. In Edward's case, however, the need to make such a contact seemed to be factually determined before the worker even met Mr. N. First of all, there were the mother's serious condition of depression and the boy's physical distress which was likely to restrict the parental power of seeing his problems in their totality. There was further the doctor's attitude which would not be supportive. Finally, there were some remarks by the mother that Edward showed traits which reminded her of Mr. N. All these factors suggested that the father was a key figure in this situation and that without his support it was unlikely that we would be permitted to render meaningful services in this case. From the angle of preparing the case for treatment, it seemed imperative that we should find out what the father thought of the mother's depression, what he thought of the condition of the boy, how he viewed the position taken by the family physician, and what his ideas were regarding the treatment of his wife and son in the Clinic.

When the worker mentioned her interest

in seeing Edward's father to Mrs. N., the latter accepted this without any trace of resistance and made an appointment for her husband. On the next day she confirmed the appointment by telephone. Mr. N., on his arrival, stated at first that he was on his way to his office and hard pressed for time. He could not stay more than five minutes. He said that he had come in only to tell us about his agreement with his wife that Edward should come to our Clinic for treatment. He was willing to give it a chance. His original attitude thus seemed to be one of submission to a proposition which he questioned and in which he did not see a reason for becoming personally involved. The worker, however, was able to convey to him interest in his personal thinking so effectively that Mr. N. quickly changed his mind and decided to stay for a discussion of the situation. In the course of this discussion, he was helped by the worker to reveal his true concerns and in doing so showed how justified we were in assuming that his cooperation would require an effort of the Clinic to give him an appropriate frame of reference within which to view the potential of our service.

First of all, Mr. N. gave expression to the idea that he might have been under a misapprehension as to the nature of our service. He had had the impression that the Clinic was intended to help only mentally dull children. He felt, however, that Edward was a bright boy and had wondered whether—if this was so—our Clinic was the right place for his son. After the worker cleared up with Mr. N. this misconception and had freed him from his concern in this respect, Mr. N. gave vent to another concern. He felt that his wife could use psychiatric treatment but he did not think that Edward needed it. In his understanding, Edward's troubles were essentially "health problems" and they were improving. He felt that if Edward's organic discomforts were removed, the boy would not need psychotherapy. As Mr. N. elaborated this theme he became increasingly aware of the fact that his boy's difficulties were not confined to the organic area. He began to mention the conflicts between Edward and his mother, his difficulties in getting along with other children, and particularly his physical aggressiveness. This development of his own train of thought apparently led Mr. N. to question his original position that Edward needed help only in the physical area, because he concluded his description of the boy's difficulties by asking how our Clinic operated. In reply to this question the worker used directness similar to the procedure followed in the preceding case. She explained to Mr. N. our efforts to build up a positive relationship between a child and his worker, our methods of gaining access to his ideas and problems by plan and discussion, and of coming to agreement with the child about the purpose of his therapy in terms which the child can understand and use. Finally, she clarified with Mr. N. the nature of the emotional learning and un-learning which children experience in therapy.

After having established a common frame of reference with the father along these lines, the worker engaged him in a discussion of Edward's history of physical difficulties in the course of which the father himself broached the topic of the attitude of the family physician toward Edward's treatment. Mr. N. seemed to appreciate the physician's concern for Edward's physical condition, but showed signs of an increasing readiness to separate himself from the doctor's judgement. He felt there might be some reality in the doctor's wish to see psychotherapy for Edward postponed until he had built up his physical condition after his last bout with pneumonia. Mr. N. thought, however, that the boy had been well now for six weeks and that probably he had recovered sufficiently to start coming without further delay. When the worker suggested that she would want to discuss this again with the mother and the doctor, the father remarked that the physician was too busy to pay much attention to Edward beyond that required for giving him his injections. He thought it unlikely that the doctor would be able to tell the worker much about the boy's problems for that reason. With regard to his wife, he felt definitely that treatment at the Clinic would be helpful to her. Maybe she could find here some release from the emotional tension which made her so irritable at home and in turn affected the boy.

Toward the end of the interview, Mr. N. summed up the experience of his discussion with the worker by saying that at first he had not been convinced of the soundness of the idea of therapy for Edward. Now, however, and particularly in view of what the worker had told him about the type of child who received help here, he was in favor of Edward's coming to the Clinic for psychotherapy.

Planning a Restructuring
of the Situation

When we reviewed our attempts at preparing this case for treatment up to this point, it became clear in our seminar discussions that again we had encountered extrafamilial as well as familial factors. Our identification of interpersonal relationships within the family of orientation, our appraisal of the relationships between the family physician and the parents, and our consideration of the physical manifestations of Edward's problems had suggested that three main factors in the situation had been dealt with so far.

The dependency needs of the mother which we had come to recognize in her use of the authoritarian attitude of the physician, in her beginning contacts with the worker, and in her relationship with her husband suggested that Mrs. N.'s narcissistic demands on the worker's patience and acceptance would be extreme. We had

come to the decision, however, that these demands would have to be met if a positive relationship between Mrs. N. and the worker was to be established, and the existing pressures in the mother-child relationship were to be eased.

The father's misconception of therapy for the boy had been clarified. Since he had thought that therapy was only for dull children and since Edward was obviously bright, it was apparent that it was chiefly his concern for his wife's depression that had led him even to consider psychotherapy for the boy. The clarification of a more appropriate frame of reference for Mr. N., therefore, was of great importance. Without it, he might easily have become a silent antagonist with a truly masochistic participation until his wife was helped. With clarification, however, the father seemed to lend support to the idea of psychotherapy for Edward—for Edward's sake. Secondly, he had also shown a measure of independence from the judgement of the family physician with regard to the start of this type of help for the boy.

Establishing a contact with the family doctor, while not assuring cooperation, was of great value to the family attitude and our planning. Interestingly enough, the negative character of the contact with the family physician proved to be one of the cornerstones of our plan. It is tempting in our cultural value system to expect that a contact between representatives of two different professional disciplines will produce teamwork. When this cultural expectation is not fulfilled, the contact is considered as having resulted in failure. In therapeutic situations such a failure is then considered as an obstacle to treatment. This tendency to view open conflict as essentially negative may well lead to a certain avoidance tendency on the part of psychotherapists with regard to organically oriented physicians. Our experience in this case suggested, however, that a negative outcome of an attempt to establish a common frame of reference with a family physician and failure to enlist his cooperation can also be turned into constructive channels. Only the actual contact and the worker's personal experience of the attitude of the doctor toward psychotherapy gave an opportunity for a full appraisal of the force with which we had to deal in this physician. The comprehension of this force made it clear to us that we were faced with an impossibility of psychotherapy for Edward so long as the doctor's opposition maintained its dynamic power within the field of social realities in which we had to operate.

It had been clarified that an alignment of perception among all the persons who composed this field of forces was impossible. In order to provide a therapeutic milieu, this field of forces, therefore, had to be restructured in terms of a different composition rather than in terms of a different frame of reference for the persons who composed it originally. A beginning in that direction had been made by helping the father to visualize psychotherapy for Edward without complete dependence on the approval of the general practitioner. The mother, however, was not yet ready to view the situation independent of the physician's judgement. We felt, however, that the authoritative and magical meaning with which Mrs. N. had vested his opinion could be discussed by her and the therapist with a chance of developing some independence of judgement also on the mother's part. This required, of course, that the relationship between the mother and the worker be given a chance to develop. In consequence, we decided to initiate treatment first with the mother, emphasizing, however, from the start that this was done on the basis of her child's difficulties and with a view of working toward an improvement also of the latter.

The mother's treatment initially continued to reveal more and more her deep dependency needs, and the relationship with the worker provided great satisfaction of the needs on the basis of a "good mother" transference. Mrs. N. became less depressed after confiding to the worker her severe emotional difficulties of rage, overeating, and oversleeping. She recognized her infantilization of the boy, her concerns about his sexual interests, and her fears of his sadistic nature. She related her own family relationships, appreciated her resentment against her sister who had occupied an ambivalent mother role with her, and she was able to secure work as a professional person. This had coincided with the oft-expressed reassuring wish of her husband that when Edward would become older she would be able to spend less time with him. After four months of interviews, she was able to bring the boy in for treatment.

60 | NON-DIRECTIVE PLAY THERAPY

VIRGINIA MAE AXLINE

The non-directive client-centered approach is but one of the many methods of dealing with a child who is nervous, unmanageable, aggressive, or speechless. These excerpts from the book Play Therapy *discuss some of the major principles of the non-directive approach to disturbed children. The student may observe that some of the rules presented here appear to be violated by the writers of other articles in this section—yet those writers also claim successful therapeutic results.*

INTRODUCTION

By Carl R. Rogers

Some will read [these selections] and say, "It can't be true. Children are not like this. Bad children do not have within them the positive forces that are shown here. The whole thing is too good to be true!" To such skeptics I can only say that results such as are portrayed in this book do occur when the principles which are set forth are faithfully followed. Not only can I vouch for the fact that Miss Axline achieves such results, but that many others without as much native tolerance, without such an intuitive understanding, can also achieve such outcomes. I might also suggest the final and conclusive test— that the skeptic try to put these principles into practice himself, and closely observe developments. Even though the therapy is carried on in blundering fashion because of the skepticism, there are likely to be highly rewarding experiences. School would become a very different institution, with markedly different effects upon the child, if even a few teachers undertook to deal with youngsters in the manner described in the chapters which follow.

NON-DIRECTIVE THERAPY

Non-directive therapy is based upon the assumption that the individual has within himself, not only the ability to solve his own problems satisfactorily, but also this growth impulse that makes mature behavior more satisfying than immature behavior.

PLAY THERAPY

Non-directive play therapy may be described as an opportunity that is offered to the child to experience growth under

Excerpts reprinted from *Play Therapy: The Inner Dynamics of Childhood* (Boston: Houghton Mifflin Company, 1947), by permission of the author and publisher.

the most favorable conditions. Since play is his natural medium for self-expression, the child is given the opportunity to play out his accumulated feelings of tension, frustration, insecurity, aggression, fear, bewilderment, confusion.

By playing out these feelings he brings them to the surface, gets them out in the open, faces them, learns to control them, or abandon them. When he has achieved emotional relaxation, he begins to realize the power within himself to be an individual in his own right, to think for himself, to make his own decisions, to become psychologically more mature, and, by so doing, to realize selfhood.

The play-therapy room is good growing ground. In the security of this room where the child is the most important person, where he is in command of the situation and of himself, where no one tells him what to do, no one criticizes what he does, no one nags, or suggests, or goads him on, or pries into his private world, he suddenly feels that here he can unfold his wings; he can look squarely at himself, for he is accepted completely; he can test out his ideas; he can express himself fully; for this is his world, and he no longer has to compete with such other forces as adult authority or rival contemporaries or situations where he is a human pawn in a game between bickering parents, or where he is the butt of someone else's frustrations and aggressions. He is an individual in his own right. He is treated with dignity and respect. He can say anything that he feels like saying—and he is accepted completely. He can play with the toys in any way that he likes to—and he is accepted completely. He can hate and he can love and he can be as indifferent as the Great Stone Face—and he is still accepted completely. He can be as fast as a whirlwind or as slow as molasses in January—and he is neither restrained nor hurried.

Quotations of what children have actually said in describing the play-therapy experience as the remarks came out spontaneously are more indicative of what it means to the child than anything the therapist can say.

Three boys, aged eight, were experiencing group-therapy sessions. During the eighth interview, Herby suddenly asked the therapist, "Do you have to do this? Or do you like to do this?" Then he added, "I wouldn't know how to do this." Ronny asked, "What do you mean? You play. That's all. You just play." And Owen agreed with Ronny. "Why, sure you do," he said. But Herby continued the discussion. "I mean I wouldn't know how to do what she does. I don't even know what she does. She doesn't seem to do anything. Only all of a sudden, I'm free. Inside me, I'm free." (He flings his arms around.) "I'm Herb and Frankenstein and Tojo and a devil." (He laughs and pounds his chest.) "I'm a great giant and a hero. I'm wonderful and I'm terrible. I'm a dope and I'm so smart. I'm two, four, six, eight, ten people, and I fight and I kill!" The therapist said to Herby, "You're all kinds of people rolled up in one." Ronny added, "And you stink, too." Herby glared at Ronny, and replied, "I stink and you stink. Why, I'll mess you up." The therapist continued to speak to Herby—"You're all kinds of people in here. You're wonderful and you're terrible and you're dopey and you're smart." Herby interrupted exultantly, "I'm good and I'm bad and still I'm Herby. I tell you I'm wonderful. I can be anything I want to be!" Apparently Herby felt that during the therapy hour he could express fully all of the attitudes and feelings that were an expression of his personality. He felt the acceptance and permissiveness to be himself. He seemed to recognize the power of self-direction within himself.

Another boy, aged twelve, commented during a first therapy session: "This is all so different and so strange. In here you say I can do what I want to do. You don't tell me what to do. I can mess up a picture if I want to. I can make a clay model of

my art teacher and let the crocodile eat her." He laughed. "I can do anything. I can be me!"

Feeling their way, testing themselves, unfolding their personalities, taking the responsibility for themselves—that is what happens during therapy.

. . . . .

Oscar had no sense of security at all. Some of the helpers mistreated him. He became one of the most maladjusted children imaginable. He was aggressive, belligerent, negative, insecure, defiant, dependent. He was a masterpiece of conflicting feelings. His mother, erratic and nervous, brought him to the psychologist. This is an excerpt from the initial contact.

MOTHER: This is Oscar. Heaven only knows what you can do with him! But here he is.

THERAPIST: Would you like to come over to the playroom with me?

OSCAR: No! Shet up! [*Yells.*]

MOTHER [*also yelling*]: Oscar! Now you be polite. Stop that sass!

OSCAR [*louder than ever*]: No! No! No!

MOTHER: Well, you are! What do you think I brought you up here for? The ride?

OSCAR [*whimpering*]: I don't wanta!

The beginning therapist asks herself at this point, "Now what?" Cajole him into the playroom? "We have such nice toys over in the playroom. You're such a nice big boy now. You come with me and I'll show you what there is to play with." That is not accepting Oscar exactly as he is. He doesn't want to come. Or should she say, with a note of regret in her voice, "Your mother brought you all the way up here and you don't want to come into the playroom with me!" That is a reflection of feeling, but it also carries subtle condemnation. There is an implied "My, aren't you an ungrateful little brute!" If the therapist wants to reflect his feeling only, what should she say? "You don't want to come with me." The therapist tries that.

THERAPIST: You don't want to come with me.

OSCAR: No! [*Makes face at therapist and folds up fists.*] Shet up!

MOTHER: If you don't go over there, I'll leave you here forever.

OSCAR [*attaching self to mother, whimpering*]: Don't leave me. Don't leave me. [*Sobs hysterically.*]

THERAPIST: Oscar is scared when Mother threatens to leave him here. [*This is a recognition of Oscar's feeling, but condemnation of Mother, who flares up.*]

MOTHER: Well, I've got to do something. Honest to God, Oscar, if you don't shut up and go with this lady, I will leave you! Or give you away!

OSCAR: You wait for me? [*Pitifully.*] You be here when I come back.

MOTHER: Of course I will—if you behave.

OSCAR [*transferring death-like grip from Mother's skirt to therapist's skirt*]: You wait?

THERAPIST: You want Mother to promise you that she will wait.

OSCAR: You promise?

MOTHER: I promise!

[*Therapist and Oscar go into the playroom. Therapist starts to close the door.*]

OSCAR [*screaming*]: Don't shet the door! Don't shet the door! [*Tears roll down his checks.*]

THERAPIST: You don't want me to shut the door. You're afraid to stay here with me if I shut the door. Very well. We'll leave the door open and you close the door when you feel like it.

[*This leaves the responsibility up to Oscar. It is up to him to make the choice. Oscar looks around the playroom. As he thaws out, he becomes aggressive.*]

OSCAR: I'll bust up everything in here!

What about limitations? Should the therapist say, "You can play with the toys

in here any way you want to, but you can't bust them up." Or, "Other children use these toys, too, so you can't bust them up." That is not responding to Oscar's expressed feeling. That is succumbing to the trap of responding to content rather than feeling back of content.

THERAPIST: You're feeling tough now.

OSCAR [*glaring at therapist*]: I'll bust you up, too.

THERAPIST: You're still feeling tough.

OSCAR: I'll—— [*suddenly laughs*] I'll—— [*He wanders around the playroom and picks up the toy telephone.*] What's this?

Accepting the Child Completely

Jean is brought into the clinic by her mother. Jean, aged twelve, is getting completely out of hand. She shows no respect for her mother, quarrels with her younger brother, will not have anything to do with the other children in her class at school. After introductions, Jean goes to the playroom with the therapist. The therapist attempts to structure the situation verbally. "You may play with any of the toys in here any way that you want to, Jean. There are paints, clay, finger paints, puppets." The therapist smiles at Jean, who stares back at the therapist in obvious boredom. The therapist waits for a few moments. Jean sits down and maintains her stony silence. The therapist, anxious to get things moving, speaks again. "Don't you know just what to do first? Oh, and there is a family of dolls over in the doll house. Do you like to play with dolls?"

Jean shakes her head negatively. The therapist pursues her quarry. "You don't like to play with dolls. Don't you see anything in here that you would like to play with? You may play with any of these things in here in any way that you want to." Jean still maintains the icy silence. Then the therapist says, "You don't want to play. You just want to sit here." Jean nods agreement. "Very well," says the therapist. She, too, sits down and silence descends upon both of them. But the therapist is tense. "Would you rather just talk?" she asks hopefully. "No," says Jean. The therapist taps her pencil on her barren notebook. She taps her foot. She looks a little annoyed at Jean. This silence is maddening. There is a silent battle going on between the two, of which Jean is surely aware.

If the girl has been fighting for acceptance outside the clinic, why must she continue here? If it is obvious that she does not want to play or talk, why not be accepting and permissive to the extent of letting her sit there in silence? After explaining the situation clearly enough so that she understands that she might play with any of the things in the playroom, or use the hour any way she desires, the accepting therapist would go along with the child and, if silence was the order of the hour, then silence it would be. It would seem well to include in the preliminary explanation to the girl that it is her privilege either to play or not to play as she desires, to talk or not to talk, and, after the girl has made the decision, the therapist should abide by it. The therapist might busy herself with notes—or with doodling if she feels that she must do something. She should be on the alert to reflect any feeling the girl might express. A deep sigh, a longing glance out the window, might safely be reflected to her——"It is boring to just sit here with me. Perhaps you would rather be outside." At that understanding, Jean might relax a little.

Establishing a Feeling of Permissiveness

During the first hour the child explores the materials and is very alert to the therapist's attitude. That is why words alone are not enough. Permissiveness is established by the therapist's attitude toward the child, by facial expressions, tone of voice, and actions.

If the child spills water deliberately and the therapist immediately wipes it up, the action more or less cancels the verbal expression of permissiveness.

If the therapist, thinking the child's problem is centered around family relationships, pushes the doll family toward the child with, "See the doll family? Wouldn't you like to play with them?" she is not granting permissiveness of choice to the child.

If the child picks up the ball of clay and rolls it idly between indecisive hands, the therapist will do well to refrain from commenting, "You don't know what to make." Such a remark might be taken by the child to indicate that the therapist is not satisfied to have the child roll the clay aimlessly back and forth. Permissiveness implies choice to use or not to use the materials according to the child's wishes.

There should be no attempt made to guide the actions or conversation of the child. That implies that there must be no probing questions directed toward the child.

For example, five-year-old May, who has been referred to the clinic for therapy because of a traumatic hospital experience, is playing with the family of dolls. She picks up the girl doll, places her in the toy wagon and pushes her across the floor. The therapist, thinking to capture the crucial experience, says, "Is the little girl going to the hospital?" "Yes," says the child. "Is she afraid?" "Yes." "Then what happens?" asks the therapist. The child gets up, goes over to the window, turns her back on the therapist and doll family. "How much longer?" she asks. "Is the time up yet?" Thus the child wards off the probing. The child is not yet ready to explore the experience that has been so upsetting. She has not yet been accepted as she is. She has not been granted the permissiveness to open that door when she felt adequate to face what was beyond it.

When he feels so securely accepted by

the therapist that he can beat up the mother doll, or bury the baby in the sand, or lie down on the floor and drink from a nursing bottle even though he is nine, ten, or eleven years old, and yet can do these things without a feeling of shame or guilt, then the therapist has established a feeling of permissiveness. The child is free to express his feelings. He gives vent to his most aggressive and destructive impulses. He screams, yells, throws the sand all over the place, spits water on the floor. He gets rid of his tensions. He becomes emotionally relaxed. Then, it seems, the groundwork for more constructive behavior has been laid.

Recognition and Reflection of Feelings

One day Jack went home for a visit. He had been planning on this visit for a long time. He wanted to get his toys. He had been coming for play-therapy contacts for five weeks before the home visit. This was his first day back.

JACK: Well, I went home. [*He sat down at the paint table and drew a clean sheet of paper toward him, opened the box of paints, and began to paint, still grinning happily.*] I saw my father and my brother. And do you know why they hadn't come to see me?

THERAPIST: No.

JACK: Because they thought it would make me feel sad to see them and then have them leave me here. That's what my father said. And they took me on a picnic and we had ice cream and candy and a boat ride. I told my father I wanted to bring my toys back. I asked about my gun. And we went out in the country one day, too. [*All the time Jack was relating the story of his visit back home, he was painting a tiny green spot in the middle of the paper and all round the green spot a growing expanse of black. Finally the paper was covered over with the black paint.*] Yep, I went home all right. But

I didn't get my toys. And my brother had broken my gun. And he had lots of his own toys. He has fun all the time. He stays there.

THERAPIST: You went home, but you were disappointed in your visit. [*This statement is interpretation. The therapist is drawing a conclusion from what Jack had said.*] You didn't get the toys you went after and your gun had been broken.

JACK: Yes. [*He got up from the table and went over to the shelf and got the nursing bottle. He brought it back to the table and sat down across from the therapist.*] I told him a thing or two. I told him I wanted my toys. [*He seemed very close to tears. He looked at the therapist.*] Me baby [*sucking on the nursing bottle*].

THERAPIST: Now you are a baby. You don't think they treated you very nice when you went home. [*This, too, is interpretation, going beyond what the child expressed. In reality, it seems to be what the therapist feels about the home situation, but it was close enough to Jack's feelings to be acceptable by him.*]

[*Jack filled his mouth with water. He leaned over and spat it on the floor.*]

JACK: Look. I spit on my home.

THERAPIST: You spit on your home.

[*Jack jerked off the nipple and filled his mouth again and once more spat on the floor.*]

JACK: I spit on my brother. I spit on my father. I spit right in their very faces. They wouldn't give me my toys. He broke my gun. I'll show them. I'll spit on them. [*Again and again he filled his mouth with water and spat it on the floor.*]

THERAPIST: You are very angry with your brother and your father. You would like to spit right in their faces because of the way they have treated you.

In this case the boy progresses from a

polite verbalization about his trip home to a violent display of his true feelings. It is interesting to note how he releases his feelings with deeper significance as he receives recognition for each feeling that he does express.

. . . . .

No more fearful or inadequate child than Jerry ever came into the play-therapy room. He was four years old, mentally retarded, physically undersized. He could not talk, was very poorly co-ordinated, and seemed to be absolutely lacking in self-direction. He was brought in for play therapy because of his unreasonable fears, because he was a feeding problem, and because the mother thought that Jerry might learn how to talk as a result of this therapy experience.

When the therapist first met Jerry, she saw a whimpering, insecure, bewildered little fellow who didn't know what it was all about. He muttered and staggered around in circles when the therapist reached for his hand to take him into the playroom.

FIRST CONTACT

Jerry gazed around him at the toys in the playroom. Then he began to pick up the toys, look at them briefly, and drop them on the floor. He grunted and muttered, but said nothing intelligible. He picked out the army truck, smiled a very fleeting smile, dropped the truck on the floor. He lifted down the cardboard box containing the doll family. One by one he picked them up and dropped them down on the floor. Then he went to the box of blocks and repeated his activity, strewing the blocks aimlessly around the floor. During all this play, he grunted and muttered in a very subdued manner. His movements were nervous, quick, uncoordinated. Things fell out of his feeble grasp and he made no effort to pick them up again. Then he picked up the hammer

and began to pound on the peg-board set, but he could not control the hammer. After a very short interval of hammering, he pushed it away and took the toy knives, forks, and spoons and strewed them across the floor. Finally, everything in the room that he could handle was on the floor. Jerry got the little wagon and pushed it across the floor.

During this play, whenever he laughed the therapist said, "Jerry likes to do that," or, "Jerry thinks that is funny." Occasionally he would hold up a toy truck or a doll and grunt at the therapist. She would name the object that he held up. Jerry seemed to get a great deal of satisfaction out of this. He began to center his actions around that type of activity. He would hold up the toy, look at the therapist, she would name it, he would smile, lay it down, and pick up something else.

After a while he began to select the truck every other time. The therapist continued to repeat the names of the toys, especially "truck," the toy which he intermittently held up. Finally, Jerry said "truck" himself as he held up the toy. He seemed to keep his eyes closed most of the time and to fumble among the toys rather than to attempt any real play with them.

Finally he went back to the wagon and pushed it. The therapist said, keeping up with his activity, "Jerry is pushing the wagon," "Jerry is shooting the gun," "Jerry is smashing the trucks together." Then Jerry began to yell. He banged the trucks together harder and harder and yelled something that sounded very much like "Truck smash!"

Then a fire engine went by the building. Jerry immediately dropped what he was doing, whimpered, ran over to the therapist, and took her hand. "Jerry is afraid of the noise," said the therapist. Jerry suddenly smiled.

Then Jerry took the therapist's hand and tried to convey some message to her. He said, "Do! Do!" very emphatically.

"You want me to do something," said the therapist. Jerry pulled harder and repeated "Do!" He seemed to understand what the therapist said to him. Finally the therapist got up, Jerry led her over to the box of toys on the floor, and, by taking her hand, putting it down in the toy box and then putting a toy in her hand and guiding it over to his hand, finally conveyed the idea to the therapist that he wanted her to hand him the toys. The therapist did, one toy at a time, each of which he promptly dropped on the floor. He still tugged at the therapist's hand as though he wanted her to do something else. The therapist started to name the toys as she handed them to Jerry, and that was what he

wanted. He began to smile. Finally he began to jabber and laugh and yell. Occasionally he would yell out "Truck!"

The mother reported a noticeable change in Jerry's behavior after the first contact. He had become more self-assertive in his non-verbal fashion. Previously he had been very docile, and stayed where he was put, doing nothing but crawling aimlessly around the baby pen that she kept him in. He now tried to climb out of the baby pen. The mother let him out. Then she noticed other improvements as time passed. He tried to talk. He said a few words that all could understand. He said "trucks," "streetcar," "ducks," and "cow."

61 | ON EDUCATION

ALBERT EINSTEIN

Albert Einstein's was surely one of the greatest and liveliest minds of the ages. This statement of his views on education is filled with stimulating ideas. Particularly interesting are his remarks that intellectual work can be a source of pleasure.

A day of celebration generally is in the first place dedicated to retrospect, especially to the memory of personages who have gained special distinction for the development of the cultural life. This friendly service for our predecessors must indeed not be neglected, particularly as such a memory of the best of the past is proper to stimulate the well-disposed of today to a courageous effort. But this should be done by someone who, from his youth, has been connected with this State and is familiar with its past, not by one who like a gypsy has wandered about

Translation by Lina Arronet of an address at the tercentenary celebration of higher education in America (Albany, New York, October 15, 1936); reprinted from *Out of My Later Years* (Philosophical Library, 1950), by permission of the Executor of the Estate of Albert Einstein.

and gathered his experiences in all kinds of countries.

Thus, there is nothing else left for me but to speak about such questions as, independently of space and time, always have been and will be connected with educational matters. In this attempt I cannot lay any claim to being an authority, especially as intelligent and well-meaning men of all times have dealt with educational problems and have certainly repeatedly expressed their views clearly about these matters. From what source shall I, as a partial layman in the realm of pedagogy, derive courage to expound opinions with no foundations except personal experience and personal conviction? If it were really a scientific matter, one would probably be tempted to silence by such considerations.

However, with the affairs of active human beings it is different. Here knowledge of truth alone does not suffice; on the contrary this knowledge must continually be renewed by ceaseless effort, if it is not to be lost. It resembles a statue of marble which stands in the desert and is continuously threatened with burial by the shifting sand. The hands of service must ever be at work, in order that the marble continue lastingly to shine in the sun. To these serving hands mine also shall belong.

The school has always been the most important means of transferring the wealth of tradition from one generation to the next. This applies today in an even higher degree than in former times, for through modern development of the economic life, the family as bearer of tradition and education has been weakened. The continuance and health of human society is therefore in a still higher degree dependent on the school than formerly.

Sometimes one sees in the school simply the instrument for transferring a certain maximum quantity of knowledge to the growing generation. But that is not right. Knowledge is dead; the school, however, serves the living. It should develop in the young individuals those qualities and capabilities which are of value for the welfare of the commonwealth. But that does not mean that individuality should be destroyed and the individual become a mere tool of the community, like a bee or an ant. For a community of standardized individuals without personal originality and personal aims would be a poor community without possibilities for development. On the contrary, the aim must be the training of independently acting and thinking individuals, who, however, see in the service of the community their highest life problem. So far as I can judge, the English school system comes nearest to the realization of this ideal.

But how shall one try to attain this ideal? Should one perhaps try to realize this aim by moralizing? Not at all. Words are and remain an empty sound, and the road to perdition has ever been accompanied by lip service to an ideal. But personalities are not formed by what is heard and said, but by labor and activity.

The most important method of education accordingly always has consisted of that in which the pupil was urged to actual performance. This applies as well to the first attempts at writing of the primary boy as to the doctor's thesis on graduation from the university, or as to the mere memorizing of a poem, the writing of a composition, the interpretation and translation of a text, the solving of a mathematical problem or the practice of physical sport.

But behind every achievement exists the motivation which is at the foundation of it and which in turn is strengthened and nourished by the accomplishment of the undertaking. Here there are the greatest differences and they are of greatest importance to the educational value of the school. The same work may owe its origin to fear and compulsion, ambitious desire for authority and distinction, or loving interest in the object and a desire for truth and understanding, and thus to that divine curiosity which every healthy child possesses, but which so often is weakened early. The educational influence which is exercised upon the pupil by the accomplishment of one and the same work may be widely different, depending upon whether fear of hurt, egoistic passion, or desire for pleasure and satisfaction is at the bottom of this work. And nobody will maintain that the administration of the school and the attitude of the teachers do not have an influence upon the molding of the psychological foundation for pupils.

To me the worst thing seems to be for a school principally to work with methods of fear, force, and artificial authority. Such treatment destroys the sound sentiments, the sincerity, and the self-confidence of the pupil. It produces the submissive subject. It is no wonder that such schools are the rule in Germany and Russia. I know that the schools in this country are free from this worst evil; this also is so in Switzerland and probably in all democratically governed countries. It is comparatively simple to keep the school free from this worst of all evils. Give into the power of the teacher the fewest possible coercive measures, so that the only source of the pupil's respect for the teacher is the human and intellectual qualities of the latter.

The second-named motive, ambition or, in milder terms, the aiming at recognition and consideration, lies firmly fixed in human nature. With absence of mental stimulus of this kind, human cooperation would be entirely impossible; the desire for the approval of one's fellow-man certainly is one of the most important binding powers of society. In this complex of feelings, constructive and destructive forces lie closely together. Desire for approval and recognition is a healthy motive; but the desire to be acknowledged as better, stronger, or more intelligent than a fellow being or fellow scholar easily leads to an excessively egoistic psychological adjustment, which may become injurious for the individual and for the community. Therefore the school and the teacher must guard against employing the easy method of creating individual ambition, in order to induce the pupils to diligent work.

Darwin's theory of the struggle for existence and the selectivity connected with it has by many people been cited as authorization of the encouragement of the spirit of competition. Some people also in such a way have tried to prove pseudo-scientifically the necessity of the destructive economic struggle of competition between individuals. But this is wrong, because man owes his strength in the struggle for existence to the fact that he is a socially living animal. As little as a battle between single ants of an ant hill is essential for survival, just so little is this the case with the individual members of a human community.

Therefore one should guard against preaching to the young man success in the customary sense as the aim of life. For a successful man is he who receives a great deal from his fellowmen, usually incomparably more than corresponds to his service to them. The value of a man, however, should be seen in what he gives and not in what he is able to receive.

The most important motive for work in the school and in life is the pleasure in work, pleasure in its result, and the knowledge of the value of the result to the community. In the awakening and strengthening of these psychological forces in the young man, I see the most important task given by the school. Such a psychological foundation alone leads to a joyous desire for the highest possessions of men, knowledge and artist-like workmanship.

The awakening of these productive psychological powers is certainly less easy than the practice of force or the awakening of individual ambition but is the more valuable for it. The point is to develop the childlike inclination for play and the childlike desire for recognition and to guide the child over to important fields for society; it is that education which in the main is founded upon the desire for successful activity and acknowledgment. If the school suceeds in working successfully from such points of view, it will be highly honored by the rising generation and the tasks given by the school will be submitted to as a sort of gift. I have known children who preferred school-time to vacation.

Such a school demands from the teacher that he be a kind of artist in his province. What can be done that this spirit be gained in the school? For this there is just as little a universal remedy as there is for an individual to remain well. But there are certain necessary conditions which can be met. First, teachers should grow up in such schools. Second, the teacher should be given extensive liberty in the selection of the material to be taught and the methods of teaching employed by him. For it is true also of him that pleasure in the shaping of his work is killed by force and exterior pressure.

If you have followed attentively my meditations up to this point, you will probably wonder about one thing. I have spoken fully about in what spirit, according to my opinion, youth should be instructed. But I have said nothing yet about the choice of subjects for instruction, nor about the method of teaching. Should language predominate or technical education in science?

To this I answer: in my opinion all this is of secondary importance. If a young man has trained his muscles and physical endurance by gymnastics and walking, he will later be fitted for every physical work. This is also analogous to the training of the mind and the exercising of the mental and manual skill. Thus the wit was not wrong who defined education in this way: "Education is that which remains, if one has forgotten everything he learned in school." For this reason I am not at all anxious to take sides in the struggle between the followers of the classical philologic-historical education and the education more devoted to natural science. On the other hand, I want to oppose the idea that the school has to teach directly that special knowledge and those accomplishments which one has to use later directly in life. The demands of life are much too manifold to let such a specialized training in school appear possible. Apart from that, it seems to me, moreover, objectionable to treat the individual like a dead tool. The school should always have as its aim that the young man leave it as a harmonious personality, not as a specialist. This in my opinion is true in a certain sense even for technical schools, whose students will devote themselves to a quite definite profession. The development of general ability for independent thinking and judgment should always be placed foremost, not the acquisition of special knowledge. If a person masters the fundamentals of his subject and has learned to think and work independently, he will surely find his way and besides will better be able to adapt himself to progress and changes than the person whose training principally consists in the acquiring of detailed knowledge.

Finally, I wish to emphasize once more that what has been said here in a somewhat categorical form does not claim to mean more than the personal opinion of a man, which is founded upon *nothing but* his own personal experience, which he has gathered as a student and as a teacher.

62 | MOBILE CHILDREN NEED HELP

WILLIAM W. WATTENBERG

Most of the data in this article were published twenty years ago; yet a study conducted in 1958 and 1959 by the editor and his students strongly confirmed them.

Two thousand pupils in a midwestern city were asked to fill out questionnaires telling how many schools they had attended and describing their problems in moving from school to school. Their teachers were asked to insert reading and arithmetic achievement scores. The average sixth-grade child had attended about four schools; some had attended as many as fifteen; and very few, only one. The more frequently a child had moved, the lower were his reading and

arithmetic achievement scores and the higher his age in a particular
school grade; in some eighth-grade classes the average age was
sixteen years and the average reading and arithmetic achievement only
that of the third or fourth grade. These findings were more valid
for working-class than for middle-class neighborhoods.

Among the problems in the actual moving, the children reported
their difficulties in making new friends and understanding new
teachers and stated that their parents tended to be disagreeable at
moving time.

The sad reality is that, however clearly this article and the editors'
study indicate that mobile children need help, they very probably
will not get it in the near future, unless we organize to provide assistance
to each one who needs it.

In this article we shall deal with one, and it is only one, of the factors which may contribute directly or indirectly to maladjustments among children and, when those children reach adulthood, among adults. We shall try to indicate a few, and they are only a few, ways in which schools may help children to cope with that factor. The problem we have selected is mobility.

We know from extreme cases that when families move, when children are uprooted, the resultant events may lead to problems. These are most manifest in city areas where many families are transient. Such areas uniformly have high delinquency rates, and high insanity rates, symptoms of maladjustment.

Before going into greater detail on effects or possible counteracting measures, we first should appraise the scope of mobility affecting children. For a long time we have suspected that Americans' traditionally great mobility involved many children, but have had no accurate measures for the nation as a whole. How many children have to go through an adjustment, with their families, to a drastic change of setting, with all that means in terms of finding new friends and learning new neighborhood customs?

During the past year, the Census Bureau has released its statistics, gathered during the 1940 enumeration, of the number and ages of migrants. The census takers, in 1940, had to supply on their schedules, the answer to this question: "In what place did this person live on April 1, 1935? If the 1940 address was in a different city or different county from the 1935 address, the individual was considered a migrant.

We are particularly interested in this 1935–40 period because it was a period of comparative normality, the pattern of which may be expected to be duplicated with comparatively minor variations in the immediate future. By 1935, the strong back-to-the-farm movement of the early 1930's had spent itself. The shifts to war plants and the post-war adjustment which uprooted 5,940,000 families, at least 3,600,-000 of them containing children, between April, 1940, and February, 1946, had barely started.

During the period, 1935 to 1940, some 1,052,291 children of elementary school age (5 to 13) in 1940 were involved in migration and another 437,681 of high school age (14 to 17) had migrated. In percentage of the total population of their age groups, these young people represented eleven per cent of all children of elementary school age and nine per cent of all youth of high school age. That is, in a comparatively stable period,

Excerpts reprinted from the article in *The Educational Forum* (March, 1948), 336–39, by permission of the author and Kappa Delta Pi.

TABLE 1.
TYPE OF MIGRATION,
BY AGE GROUPS

Type of Migration	*5 to 13* Year Group	*14 to 17* Year Group
Urban to Urban	707,432	281,926
Urban to Non-Farm Rural	378,471	138,014
Urban to Farm Rural	152,477	69,438
Non-Farm Rural to Urban	198,783	87,636
Non-Farm Rural to Non-Farm Rural	214,532	78,338
Non-Farm Rural to Farm Rural	79,279	32,678
Farm Rural to Urban	104,804	49,521
Farm Rural to Non-Farm Rural	121,863	48,449
Farm Rural to Farm Rural	383,853	164,017

roughly one out of every ten young people of school age was involved in a migration and had to make an adjustment to strange surroundings, form new friendships and, if going to school, learn a more or less novel school routine. How many of these young people made more than one move we have no way of knowing.

The nature of the shift is indicated partially by the analysis, in Table 1, of the

TABLE 2.
MIGRATION OF YOUNG PEOPLE
IN AND OUT OF LARGE
CITIES, 1935–40

City	*5 to 13* Year Group	*14 to 17* Year Group
New York City		
In-Migrants	19,029	9,346
Out-Migrants	49,778	18,260
Chicago		
In-Migrants	15,721	6,791
Out-Migrants	37,987	13,305
Philadelphia		
In-Migrants	7,841	3,089
Out-Migrants	15,607	6,359
Detroit		
In-Migrants	14,249	5,828
Out-Migrants	33,065	11,121
Los Angeles		
In-Migrants	30,385	13,827
Out-Migrants	30,259	11,822
Cleveland		
In-Migrants	4,620	1,994
Out-Migrants	15,933	6,266
Baltimore		
In-Migrants	5,206	2,088
Out-Migrants	7,352	3,127
St. Louis		
In-Migrants	6,275	2,754
Out-Migrants	15,144	5,749
Boston		
In-Migrants	4,346	1,678
Out-Migrants	10,718	3,269
Pittsburgh		
In-Migrants	3,427	1,486
Out-Migrants	9,693	3,968

TABLE 3. DISTANCES OF MIGRATIONS AFFECTING YOUNG PEOPLE, 1935–40	Distance of Migration	5 to 13 Year Group	14 to 17 Year Group
	Within a state	1,553,608	639,520
	Between contiguous states	494,683	195,951
	Between noncontiguous states	434,665	175,647

type of community which the young people left and the type to which they went.

Two facts revealed by this table are striking: First, a very substantial number of these moves were between quite different types of community. This means that the young folks and their families had to undergo a marked change in patterns of living and recreation. Second, the number of urban children who had to adjust to rural settings was surprisingly great. In part, this represented a suburban trend. However, in some cases the moves to "non-farm rural" communities involved the growth of unorganized settlements, including trailer camps, on the fringe of metropolitan areas. In other cases, the move to farm communities meant just what it says: a child brought up in city streets had to learn the patterns of farm life. In short, mobile children are not merely a problem of big city schools; rural schools have an equal load in this respect.

Table 2 gives more complete statistics for the movement of young people in and out of the ten largest cities of the United States.

It is clearly apparent that, although large city schools still had to absorb considerable numbers of migrant children, the basic trend was outward to smaller communities. To a child, the change from city life to rural ways could involve as much confusion and as many problems as the adjustment to city patterns on the part of rural migrants.

In addition to change in patterns of living, many migrant children had to contend with sectional differences. As Table 3 shows, many of the moves were over long distances, and brought children in contact with somewhat different customs and patterns of climate.

Contrary to popular assumption, migration was not confined to poorly skilled laborers and dispossessed farmers. All economic levels were affected. In fact, the most mobile group during 1935–40 were professional people, some 25 per cent of whom had made at least one change of residence during the five-year period. Table 4 gives the detailed figures on migration of the major occupational groups. We cite figures for men only, to give an indication of the economic status of families involved.

Up to this point we have been dealing with migration between communities. To complete the picture, however, we must take into account the restlessness of city

TABLE 4. OCCUPATIONAL LEVEL OF MALE MIGRANTS, 1935–40	Occupational Group	Number	Number of Migrants	%
	Professional and semiprofessional workers	1,875,387	476,162	25.4
	Farmers and farm managers	4,991,715	410,793	8.2
	Proprietors, managers and officials	3,325,767	511,235	15.4
	Clerical, sales and kindred workers	4,360,648	690,950	15.8
	Craftsmen, foremen and kindred workers	4,949,132	661,613	13.4
	Operatives and kindred workers	6,205,898	784,476	12.6
	Domestic service workers	142,231	24,798	17.4
	Service workers, except domestic	2,196,695	393,239	17.9
	Farm laborers and foremen	2,770,005	441,994	16.0
	Laborers, except farm	3,210,427	383,825	12.0

families which, until their movements were hampered temporarily by the housing shortage, frequently moved from house to house, and from neighborhood to neighborhood. No over-all figures on such intracity mobility are available.

However, a study of Rochester, New York gives a clue to the extensiveness of such movements. The city was divided into fourteen large areas and an analysis made of changes of residence between 1930 and 1940. In the median area, approximately one out of every five families had moved from one area to another, and an additional one out of seven families had changed addresses within the area. In the most stable area of the city, 77.0 per cent of the families had lived at the same address for ten years; in the most unstable area, only 48.5 per cent had stayed put for that long.

63 | SUCCESS AND FAILURE IN THE CLASSROOM

ROGER G. BARKER

A number of studies have suggested that one way a child—or an adult—may respond to repeated failure is by dreaming he is successful. The mental hospitals are filled with victims of the more extreme forms of this dream.

Barker summarizes current research on the problems of failure and suggests some constructive ways of coping with them.

Of the numerous rôles which the classroom teacher plays, that of dispenser of success and failure is undoubtedly the most impressive and worrisome to the pupils, and one of the most crucial for their present and future adjustment. It is also the rôle in which many teachers meet their severest conflicts; to fail John or not to fail him, whichever is done, frequently leaves feelings of guilt and anxiety. Clearly an understanding of the conditions and effects of success and failure would be of greatest value to teachers.

When does a child experience success? When does he experience failure? In what ways do these experiences affect behavior? Do the schools make it possible for children to achieve a sufficient number of important success experiences? If not, what can be done about it? A small but very important body of verified knowledge is now available bearing upon these crucial questions. In this article only a very small segment of these data can be presented.

Professor Kurt Lewin, then at the University of Berlin, and his student Ferdinand Hoppe initiated an experimental approach to these questions in the late 1920's.[1] Hoppe first considered the fundamental problem of when a person experiences success and when failure. He presented his adult subjects with simple motor and intellectual tasks such as hanging 16 rings upon as many hooks as they passed upon a rapidly moving belt, and solving puzzles. During each trial with the tasks, Hoppe observed the subjects secretly and after the completion of each trial he interviewed them thoroughly in an effort to find out the circumstances under which they experienced success and failure. One result was clearly apparent:

Reprinted from *Progressive Education*, XIX (1942), 221–24, by permission of the author and publisher.

[1] Hoppe, F., "Erfolg und Misserfolg," *Psychol. Forsch.*, 1930, 14, 1–62.

The experiences of success and failure were unrelated to the actual achievements of the individual. One subject might experience success when he placed 4 rings on the hooks; another experienced failure when he placed 15 correctly. In addition, for a particular person, the achievement experienced as success (or failure) continually changed; at one time a single ring correctly placed might give rise to an experience of success, while on a later occasion the placing of 6 rings would result in an experience of failure. These findings led Hoppe to a conclusion which seems very obvious once it is stated, but one that is so fundamental that it has very wide implications: The occurrence of success and failure experiences is independent of actual achievement; it is determined, rather, by the goals, expectations, and aspirations of the person at the time of the action. These expected achievements Hoppe called the level of aspiration.

It is obvious that the level of aspiration is important, for on it depends the occurrence of success and failure. Hoppe therefore directed his study to the effects of success and failure experiences on the level of aspiration. He found that after success the level of aspiration is usually raised (that is, a new and higher goal is set after a lower one is achieved), and that after failure the level of aspiration is usually lowered (that is, a new and lower goal is set after a high one has not been achieved). He found, in other words, that the level of aspiration shifts in such a way that, whatever the actual achievement of the person, the frequency of his success and failure experiences remains fairly constant. This means that the level of aspiration operates as a mental hygiene factor of great significance. It constitutes a sort of governor; it protects the person against continual failure on the one hand, and against easy achievements which do not give the feeling of success, on the

other hand. This fact is behind the frequent observation that feelings of success accompany the process of achieving but disappear after attainment.

Sometimes, however, this mechanism is thrown out of balance and it fails to perform this protective function. In some cases, aspirations are maintained consistently above achievement. The individual is then subjected to continual failure with its disastrous consequences for adjustment and happiness. In other cases, aspirations are placed consistently below achievement with resulting lack of ambition, exaggerated caution, broken morale, cynicism, and so forth. In both instances very serious personal and social difficulties may develop. It is of the greatest importance, therefore, to determine why the level of aspiration does not function protectively for these persons.

Hoppe suggested that the level of aspiration is set as a compromise between two conflicting tendencies: (a) the desire to avoid the hurt accompanying failure, operating to force aspirations safely below the level of achievement; and (b) the desire to succeed at the highest possible level; operating to push goals above achievement levels. Subsequent investigations suggested that the latter tendency derives from social pressures to do what is most highly approved by society, irrespective of a realistic assessment of one's own capabilities. This conflict between fear of failure and desire to maintain goals that are socially approved results, usually, in a level of aspiration at or near the upper limit of one's ability range.

If this interpretation is correct, it would be expected that an increase in social pressure should alter the level of aspiration. This is, in fact, the case. Subsequent investigations have shown that pupils at the low end of the class achievement distribution aspire, on the average, above the level of their achievement possibilities (and therefore experience failure), while those at the upper end of the achievement distribution set their aspirations below their level of achievement (and therefore experience success).

Although the differences between aspiration and achievement are not great in a quantitative sense, they are psychologically very important. So far as success and failure are concerned, "a miss is as good as a mile." This difference in relation of aspiration to achievement appears to mean that the social pressures of the school situation may operate to throw off balance the protective mechanism of the level of aspiration, thus subjecting children to exaggerated failure and success experiences.

It is not difficult to understand why these pressures arise in many schools. Social acceptability in an intimate group such as a school class requires a high degree of conformity to group standards in all sorts of public behavior. The first step in achieving such acceptability is to set goals in accordance with the group standards. In schools where evaluation is largely on the basis of academic achievements this means that poor students are forced, by the social pressure of the classroom, to admit that they are mavericks; both are undesirable alternatives from a mental hygiene viewpoint. There is pressure upon bright students, also, to set their goals in conformity with the achievements of their roommates, rather than with their own.

Adults on the other hand are infrequently subjected to such pressures for long periods of time, for adults are able with considerable success to hide from others certain crucial symbols of their divergence from what is considered good or desirable (such as age, income, family background), and they are able to withdraw when the pressures become too great. Furthermore, achievement in most adult activities is not estimated with the precision that is attempted in many schools. Doctors, lawyers, plumbers, and bakers can vary within a considerable range of effectiveness and no one is wiser; they are still adequate. This gives a fundamental security which is denied to pupils who are frequently and publicly evaluated, that is, acclaimed or humiliated by an authority from whose decisions there is no recourse and in a group from which there is no escape.

Middle-class pupils are unusually sensitive to these pressures. They are, in effect, subjected to the demands of a single dominating institution, for the family supports the demands of the school. This means that the pressures, the demands, the rewards, the punishments, the successes, and the failures of the school are frequently of overwhelming importance to these children. No one with influence will question the righteousness of the school's verdicts or the correctness of its values. If the school is one in which the rewards are all centered about a very limited variety of achievements, for example, academic achievements, the child who is relatively dull or uninterested in academic activities must experience continual failure. He will fail even though he is kind, or good looking, or has a sense of humor, or has physical prowess, even though he is full of energy, graceful, courageous, friendly, or with mechanical abilities. He will fail in school even though these behavior characteristics are very highly valued by many other institutions, until in adolescence he becomes sufficiently independent to establish affiliations with other groups which do reward nonacademic achievement.

Compared with life outside school, many schools distribute success and failure in an extremely unrealistic way. Adults, for example, are inevitably influenced by various pressures, and rewarded according to conflicting values of a variety of institutions and social groups (family, vocation, clique, church, lodge, union, and so on), and these influences are likely to be of somewhat equal potency in their lives. This means that the adult can to some extent balance the failures in one region of his life by successes in other regions. The effects of vocational failures may be mitigated by successes in family and recreational relationships where quite different achievements are valued. In schools that emphasize academic achievement, this kind of balancing is impossible for middle-class children.

What is the consequence of the chronic failure and success that many schools enforce upon great numbers of pupils? We do not know a great amount from scientific experiment but what we do know is very suggestive.

Sears[2] studied the level of aspiration of a group of fifth grade children who had long histories of chronic school failure in reading and arithmetic, and another group with equally consistent histories of school success in reading and arithmetic. She found that the children who had experienced continual success set their aspirations at a realistic level, that is, at a level where success was frequently achieved. The children with a history of chronic failure, on the other hand, set their aspirations with little regard for their achievements. Of those in this latter group, some children apparently lived almost exclusively in terms of their aspirations, ignoring completely the fact that their achievements were entirely out of line with their expectations. In these cases the desire for respectability may have

forced the children to an imaginary world where the mere gesture of achieving by setting high goals was accepted in lieu of real achievement. The seriousness of this behavior is sufficiently obvious to need no special emphasis. The institutionalized person for whom a gesture is sufficient to convince him he is Napoleon has traveled further along the same path.

The cases where the children failed to set goals even at the level of their poor achievement may involve withdrawal from the activity in any except a very peripheral sense; they may be cases of extreme caution or they may represent attempts to depreciate the importance of the activity by refusing to take it seriously. None of these outcomes of educational effort are desirable.

What can schools do to avoid throwing out of gear the protective mechanism of the level of aspiration with the resulting unfortunate consequences for the success and failure experiences of pupils? The answers are implied in the discussion, but they may be summarized as follows: (a) broaden the basis for evaluating pupils; (b) reduce to a minimum the prominence of the relative standing of the pupils; (c) allow maximum freedom to pupils to set their own goals and to alter them as their success and failure experiences require; that is, make success possible at all levels of achievement; (d) reduce the dominance of the teacher.

These conditions can be achieved in different ways. It is interesting to note, however, that they can hardly be avoided if democratic teaching procedures are used, if the interests of the child are followed, and if group undertakings are an important part of school activities.

---

[2] Sears, P. S., "Levels of Aspiration in Academically Successful and Unsuccessful Children," *Journal of Abnormal and Social Psychology*, 1940, 35, 498–536.

64 | EXPERIMENTAL STUDIES OF FRUSTRATION IN YOUNG CHILDREN

ROGER G. BARKER, TAMARA DEMBO, KURT LEWIN,

AND M. ERIK WRIGHT

What happens when young children are unable to get what they want or need? Anyone who has ever tried to maneuver a child who is tired or hungry, or who is angry because something he wants has just been taken away, knows how unreasonable the child can be, how unwilling he can be to adapt himself.

The experiments described here reveal that such frustrations result in impaired intellectual functioning, restlessness, destructiveness, increased intra-group unity (clannishness), and aggression against the out-group.

Frustration occurs when an episode of behavior is interrupted before its completion, i.e., before the goal appropriate to the motivating state of the individual is reached. It is well established that frustration has widely ramifying effects upon behavior; the behaving person is not like a rolling billiard ball that remains motionless when its movement is stopped. However, what these effects are and how they are produced have not yet been determined. To frustration has been attributed most of what is valued and deplored in individual and group behavior: delinquency, neurosis, war, art, character, religion. This, however, is speculation. It is of greatest importance that these questions be removed from the realm of speculation, that the conditions of frustration be conceptualized, that its degree and effects be measured and that systematic experimental studies be made. It is with these problems that the studies here reported are concerned. They constitute an effort to measure the degree of frustration and its effects upon intellectual and emotional behavior and social interaction.

This has been done by comparing the behavior of children in a nonfrustrating play situation with their behavior in a frustrating play situation. Children were observed on two occasions: first, in a standardized playroom under conditions of unrestricted free play; second, in the same room with the same toys, but with a number of more attractive, but inaccessible, toys present. The latter were provided by replacing a wall of the original room with a wire-net partition through which the subjects could easily see the fine toys but through which they could not move. The subjects were children who attended the preschool laboratories of the Iowa Child Welfare Research Station. They ranged in age from 2 to 6 years.

Two series of experiments were performed. In the first series, by Barker, Dembo, and Lewin, 30 children were studied individually with the objective of determining some of the effects of frustration on intellectual and emotional behavior. In the second series, by Wright, 78 entirely different children were taken in pairs with the main emphasis upon the effects of frustration on social behavior. The second series of experiments served, also, as a check upon the first so far as

Reprinted from *Readings in Social Psychology*, edited by Theodore M. Newcomb and Eugene L. Hartley. By permission of Henry Holt and Company, Inc. Copyright 1947.

effects on intelligence and emotion were concerned.

THE NONFRUSTRATING SITUATION | On the floor of the experimental room in the nonfrustrating play situation there were three squares of paper, each 24 by 24 inches. A set of standardized play materials was placed on each square. After entering the experimental room with the child or pair of children, the experimenter demonstrated the toys and gave complete freedom to play. The child (or children) was left to play for a 30-minute period. During this time the experimenter, as if occupied with his own work, sat at his table in the corner and made records of the behavior occurring.

THE FRUSTRATING SITUATION | Three parts of the frustration experiment can be distinguished in the temporal order of their occurrence: the prefrustration period, the frustration period and the postfrustration period.

In the prefrustration period the dividing partition was lifted so that the room was twice the size it had been in the nonfrustrating situation. The squares were in their places, but all toys except the crayons and paper had been incorporated into an elaborate and attractive set of toys in the part of the room that had been behind the partition. In all cases the children showed great interest in the new toys and at once started to investigate them. Each child was left entirely free to explore and play as he wished. If, after several minutes, the child had played with only a limited number of toys, the experimenter demonstrated the others. The experimenter returned to his place and waited until the child had become thoroughly involved in play; this took from 5 to 15 minutes. The prefrustration period was designed to develop highly desirable goals for the child which he could later be prevented from reaching. This was a prerequisite to creating frustration.

The transition from prefrustration to frustration was made in the following way. The experimenter collected in a basket all the play materials which had been used in the nonfrustrating free-play session and distributed them, as before, on the squares of paper. He then approached the child and said, "Now let's play at the other end," pointing to the "old" part of the room. The child went or was led and the experimenter lowered the wire partition and fastened it by means of a large padlock. The part of the room containing the new toys was now physically inaccessible, but it was visible through the wire-net partition. With the lowering of the partition, the frustration period began. This part of the experiment was conducted exactly as was the nonfrustrating session. The experimenter wrote at his table, leaving the child completely free to play or not as he desired. The child's questions were answered, but the experimenter remained aloof from the situation in as natural a manner as possible.

Thirty minutes after the lowering of the partition, the experimenter suggested that it was time to leave. After the experimenter had made sure that the child was willing to leave, the partition was lifted. Usually the child was pleasantly surprised and, forgetting his desire to leave, joyfully hurried over to the fine toys. If the child did not return spontaneously, the experimenter suggested his doing so. The lifting of the partition at the end of the frustration period was designed to satisfy the desire of the child to play with the toys and to obviate any undesirable after-effects. The child was allowed to play until he was ready to leave.

Both the nonfrustrating and frustrating situations produced two general kinds of behavior: occupation with accessible goals, and activities in the direction of inaccessible goals. We shall call the first *free activities* and the second *barrier and escape behavior*. Playing with the available toys, turning on the light, and talking with each other or with the experimenter are examples of free activities. Trying to leave the experimental situation and attempting to reach the inaccessible toys behind the barrier or talking about them are examples of barrier and escape behavior.

A subject could be involved in more than one activity simultaneously, e.g., he might ask to have the barrier raised while swinging the fish line. In these cases we speak of *overlapping situations*. A type of overlapping situation of special importance occurred when play and nonplay activities took place simultaneously. We have called this *secondary play*. *Primary play*, on the other hand, occurred when the subject seemed to give play his complete attention.

SAMPLE RECORD | A part of a record is given below to acquaint the reader with the sequence and content of the course of events. This is the type of material with which we had to work.

Subject #22 is a girl fifty-three months old. Her I.Q. is 122. Each unit of action is numbered consecutively. At the end of each unit the length in seconds and the constructiveness rating are given. Constructiveness rating is discussed in the section immediately following.

Nonfrustrating Situation

1. Subject: "Here," to the experimenter, "you make me something from this clay." She takes the clay to Square 1 and asks, "Where are the other things?" (Referring to toys present in another experiment.) "I want you to play with me." The experimenter continues recording. (45; 2)

2. Subject throws clay onto Square 2. "This is an elephant." Then, finding a small peg on the floor, "Look what I found. I'll put it at his eyes." Looks at it. Makes elephant sit up. (70; 6)

3. Subject starts to draw. "I'm going to draw a picture. Do you know what I'm going to draw? That will be a house. That is where you go in." (45; 7)

4. Someone moves in another room. Subject: "Who is that?" (10)

5. Subject goes to Square 1, shakes phone, and examines it. Manipulates phone, pretends conversation but does not use words. "How do . . ." are the only words that experimenter can distinguish. (30; 5)

6. Subject sits on chair and looks around. "I guess I'll sit here and iron." Repeats, then says gaily, "See me iron." (45, 5)

Frustrating Situation

1. Subject watches experimenter lower the partition. She asks, "I will not play on the other side again?" Experimenter answers, "You can play here now." Subject faces the experimenter for about 15 seconds with hands behind her neck. (25)

2. Subject looks around. (5)

3. Subject goes to Square 3 and examines sailboat and fish pole. (15; 2)

4. Subject stands at Square 3 and looks at barrier. (5)

5. Turning to the play material on Square 3, Subject takes the fish line and dangles it about sailboat. (20; 2)

6. Subject goes to the barrier and reaches through the meshes of the screen. (5)

7. Subject turns around, looks at the experimenter, laughs as she does so. (15)

8. Subject goes to Square 3, takes the fish pole, and returns to the barrier. She asks, "When are we going to play on that side?" Experimenter does not answer. Then, in putting the fish pole through the barrier, Subject says, "I guess I'll just put this clear back." She laughs and says, "Out it comes!" Takes pole out again. (35; 2)

9. Subject walks to experimenter's table. (10)

10. Subject goes to Square 2 and manipulates clay. (10; 2)

11. From Square 2 she looks at the objects behind the barrier and says, "I do like the balloon." Then she asks, "Who put that house there?" Experimenter answers, "Some of my friends." (35)

CONSTRUCTIVENESS OF PLAY | From this example, the reader will gain an impression of the richness of the play which oc-

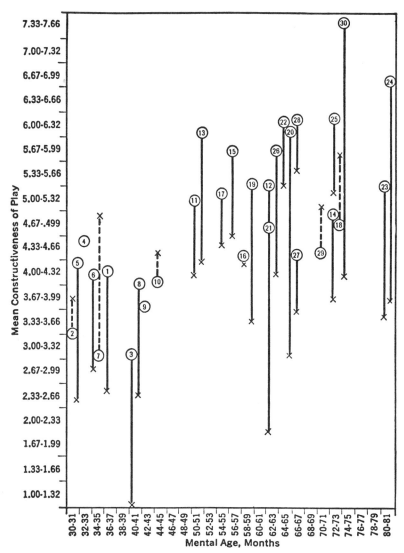

Figure 1. The relation between mean constructiveness of play and mental age in the nonfrustrating and the frustrating play situations. (1) The mean constructiveness of primary and secondary play in the nonfrustrating situation is indicated by circles. (2) The mean constructiveness of play in the frustrating situation is indicated by crosses. (3) Change in the constructiveness of play from the nonfrustrating to the frustrating situation is designated by solid lines when constructiveness decreases in frustration, and by broken lines when it increases. The absence of a cross indicates no change in constructiveness.

curred. It is possible to use such manifold material for many purposes. In the first experiments we were most interested in phases of the play related to the intellectual aspects of the child's behavior. For this purpose we made an analysis of the play activities on the basis of their constructiveness. One can distinguish variations in the type of play on a continuum ranging from rather primitive, simple, little-structured activities to elaborate, imaginative, highly developed play. We speak in the former case of low constructiveness; in the latter, of high constructiveness. In our first experiment, constructiveness was rated on a 7-point scale (2 to 8) devised to be applicable to play with all the toys. Examples of its use are given in the preceding sample record. The mean constructiveness of play for an experimental session was determined by assigning the proper scale value to each play unit, multiplying by the duration of the unit, summing these values for the whole record, and dividing by the total time of play during the session. The mean constructiveness ratings had an estimated reliability cofficient of .88. Their validity as an indicator of intellectual level is indicated by a correlation with mental age of .73.

RESULTS

AVERAGE CONSTRUCTIVENESS OF PLAY IN THE NONFRUSTRATING AND FRUSTRATING SITUATIONS | The mean constructiveness of the play of each child in the nonfrustrating and frustrating situations is shown in the correlation chart. These data include all play, both primary and secondary. The mean constructiveness of play in the non-frustrating situation is 4.99 and in the frustrating situation 3.94. The mean regression in constructiveness of play is 4.39 times its standard error. Stated in terms of mental-age equivalents, i.e., in terms of the regression of constructiveness upon mental age, the mean regression amounts to 17.3 months of mental age. Twenty-two of the subjects regressed in the constructiveness of their play, three did not change, and with five subjects the constructiveness of play increased in frustration.

These data establish rather definitely the fact that a frustrating situation of the kind considered here reduces, on the average, the constructiveness of play below the level upon which it normally occurs in a nonfrustrating, free-play situation. Further analysis showed that regression in the constructiveness of play occurred when only primary play and only play units of the same length in the nonfrustrating and frustrating situations were compared.

These results indicate that frustration not only affects actions involved in achieving inaccessible goals, such as attempts to find roundabout routes or aggression against physical or social barriers, but that it may also affect behavior not directly frustrated or involved in overcoming the frustration. The findings show the importance of the total situation for promoting or hindering a child's creative achievement, and they suggest that the level of intellectual functioning is dependent upon the immediately existing situation.

MEASUREMENT OF STRENGTH OF FRUSTRATION | The technical arrangements of the experiment were planned to create frustration and nonfrustration. Inevitably, these results were not secured in all cases, inasmuch as we had control over only the immediate, experimental situation and not over the expectations and attitudes which the children brought to the experiment. In some instances frustration occurred in the nonfrustration situation and in others there was no frustration in the frustration situation. In addition, all degrees of strength of frustration occurred. Thus far in the analysis we have proceeded as if the technical arrangements had functioned with all subjects as was intended. The data have been classified according to the intention of the experimenters rather than according to the psychological realities of the situations for the subjects. We turn now to an analysis of some quantitative differences in the dynamic properties of the existing psychological situations.

We have taken as a measure of strength of frustration the proportion of the total experimental period occupied by barrier and escape behavior. Inasmuch as we are here concerned with the *changes* in strength of frustration from the nonfrustration to the frustration situations, we have limited ourselves to a consideration of the *difference* in the amount of time occupied with barrier and escape actions in the two settings. Using this difference as a measure of increase in frustration, it turned out that 20 subjects were relatively strongly frustrated and 10 subjects relatively weakly frustrated.

Considering these two groups of subjects, we find that there is a highly significant reduction in the constructiveness of play in the case of the strongly frustrated subjects amounting to $1.46 \pm .15$ constructiveness points when both primary and secondary play are considered, and $1.11 \pm .15$ constructiveness points when primary play alone is included. The first is equivalent to a regression of twenty-four months' mental age, the latter to a regression of nineteen months' mental age. With the weakly frustrated subjects, on the other hand, there is a small and not statistically significant reduction in constructiveness, amounting to 0.23 constructiveness points for primary and secondary play and 0.12 points for primary play. All subjects showing an increase in constructiveness of play in frustration fall in the weakly frustrated group.

From these results it is clear that regression in level of intellectual functioning is determined by dynamic situational factors that are subject to measurement.

EMOTION | *Pari passu* with the shift in constructiveness of play there occurred a change in emotional expression. In frustration there was a marked decrease in the happiness of the mood (e.g., less laughing, smiling and gleeful singing), there was an increase in motor restlessness and hypertension (e.g., more loud singing and talking, restless actions, stuttering, and thumb sucking); and there was an increase in aggressiveness (e.g., more hitting, kicking, breaking, and destroying). The changes were greater with the strongly frustrated than with the weakly frustrated subjects.

SOCIAL INTERACTION IN THE NONFRUSTRATING SITUATION | In order to describe the changes in social interaction from nonfrustration to frustration, it was first necessary to distinguish various types of social behavior. Five main categories of social interaction were differentiated: *Cooperative actions* included those in which both children strove towards a common goal and helped each other to achieve that goal. *Social parallel* behavior covered activities in which both children, separately, pursued almost the same goals but watched each other closely. *Sociable* actions were those in which the goal seemed to be maintenance of the social contact itself. *Social matter-of-fact* interactions were impersonal contacts made primarily for information about ownership or other property rights. *Conflict* actions occurred when children were aggressive toward each other; acts of aggression ranged in intensity from verbal teasing to physical violence.

The most typical form of social interaction in the nonfrustration situation was friendly in character; 67.2 per cent of all social interaction was spent either in cooperative or sociable behavior. However, 14.9 per cent of the time was spent in inter-child conflict.

There were two important shifts in social behavior from nonfrustration to frustration: Cooperative behavior increased from 38.2 per cent to 50.4 per cent of total interaction, and social conflict decreased from 14.9 per cent to 6.9 per cent. These changes are significant at the 2 per cent and 1 per cent levels, respectively. There were no statistically significant changes in the amount of time spent in sociable, social parallel, or matter-of-fact social interactions. The two shifts which occurred point toward increased interdependence and unity under the influence of frustration.

TABLE 1.
PERCENT OF HOSTILE AND
FRIENDLY BEHAVIOR TOWARD
THE EXPERIMENTER WHICH
OCCURRED AS SOCIAL AND
SOLITARY ACTION

SITUATION	HOSTILE		FRIENDLY	
	Social	Solitary	Social	Solitary
Nonfrustration	99	1	26	74
Frustration	82	18	51	49

STRENGTH OF FRIENDSHIP AND SOCIAL INTER-
ACTION | On the basis of their behavior
in the nursery school, 18 of the pairs of
subjects were judged to be strong friends
and 21 weak friends. The strong and weak
friends resembled each other very closely
in their social interaction in the nonfrustrating situation. However, the changes
in social behavior in frustration were more
marked for the strong friends than for the
weak friends. Cooperativeness increased
and conflict decreased significantly for
these subjects while they did not change
significantly for the weak friends. When
the weak and strong friends were compared with each other in the frustrating
situation the strong friends were found to
exhibit significantly more cooperative
behavior and significantly less conflict
behavior than the weak friends.

Under the relatively calm, stable conditions with low level of emotional tension
that existed in the nonfrustrating situation,
the social behavior of strong and weak
friends was not observably different.
When the environmental surroundings
became precarious, however, when frustration occurred, and when there was a
heightening of emotional tension, the influence of the pre-existing friendship relation became apparent. A greater
cohesiveness and unity tended to occur
under stress with the strong friends than
with the weak friends.

In nonfrustration, the contacts with
the experimenter were predominantly
friendly: 80 per cent of all experimenter-
directed behavior was of this nature. A
marked change took place in frustration.
There was a 30 per cent rise in the
amount of hostile action toward the ex-

perimenter and a 34 per cent decrease in
friendly approaches. Although friendly
contacts were still more frequent than hostile ones, the situation in frustration could
no longer be characterized as predominantly friendly. It will be noted from the
tabulation above that hostile actions
against the experimenter were predominantly social in character in both nonfrustration and frustration, while friendly
actions were not predominantly social.
This suggests that the children may have
felt more powerful and able to cope with
hostile forces when in social contact than
when alone. This interpretation is supported by the fact that in nonfrustration
there was a great amount of solitary,
friendly contact with the experimenter,
while in the frustrating situation, where
the power of the experimenter had become much stronger, the proportion of
friendly, solitary actions toward the
experimenter decreased, and the proportion of friendly social action increased. It
appears that under frustration the children needed social support to make even
a friendly approach to the powerful,
implicitly hostile adult.

In general, only when the individuals
combined did they feel strong enough to
attack the superior adult power. We
should expect that the stronger and more
cohesive the group, the more capable they
would feel of challenging the power of
the experimenter. This interpretation is
substantiated by the data on hostile actions toward the experimenter in the
frustrating situation. The strong friends
showed more hostile action against the
experimenter than did the weak friends
(47 per cent and 31 per cent respectively)

and the difference was even more marked when direct physical attack on the experimenter was considered: 26 per cent for the strong friends and 4 per cent for the weak friends. Furthermore, only the strong friends went so far as to hit the experimenter with blocks, tear his records, throw him off his chair, scratch at him, etc. The weak friends stopped at touching the experimenter while calling him names.

DISCUSSION

The main findings of the studies reported may be summarized as follows: Frustration, as it operated in these experiments, resulted in an average regression in the level of intellectual functioning, in increased unhappiness, restlessness, and destructiveness, in increased intra-group unity, and in increased out-group aggression. The amount of intellectual regression and the amount of increase in negative emotionality were positively related to strength of frustration. The degree of intra-group unity and of out-group aggression were positively related to strength of friendship. These findings present important and difficult problems for social-psychological theories.

Theory in science has two main functions: to account for that which is known, and to point the way to new knowledge. It does this by formulating hypotheses as to the essential nature of the phenomenon under consideration. The fruitfulness of a theory lies in the unknown facts and relations it envisions which can then be tested, usually by experiments. A fruitful theory gives birth, as it were, to new knowledge which is then independent of its theoretical ancestry.

The main results of the present experiments were predicted on the basis of a theory. Originally the experiments were designed to test the hypothesis that strong frustration causes tension which leads to emotionality and restlessness, to de-differentiation of the person, and hence to behavioral regression. These results were obtained. It is probable that not only the changes in the constructiveness of play, but also the greater cohesiveness of the strong friends under frustration can be interpreted as regression. In the nonfrustrating situation the social interactions of the strong and the weak friends did not differ, but under the tensions created by frustration the previously existing, fundamental structure of interpersonal relations was revealed. De-differentiation of the person from diffusing tension would be expected to reduce the variety and complexity of both intellectual and social behavior and leave the strongest structures intact. In the case of the strong friends, this basic structure was one that led to a friendly, cooperative interrelation.

However, the experiments suggest that other factors probably enter also. In the frustrating situation, the subject's future time perspective and security were shattered by the superior power of the experimenter. This could easily have two results: first, to interfere with long-range planning, and this would certainly result in lowered constructiveness of play; second, to lead to a mobilization of power by the subject directed at increasing his security. Counter-aggression on the part of the subjects was clear in the shift toward hostility in their relations with the experimenter. It seems likely that the greater cohesiveness occurring in the frustrating situation is one aspect of the efforts of the subjects to increase their power *vis-à-vis* the experimenter. This is particularly likely in view of the predominantly social character of all hostile actions against the experimenter, and the greater hostility of the strong friends.

65 | A STUDY OF CHILDREN'S REACTIONS TO FAILURE AND AN EXPERIMENTAL ATTEMPT TO MODIFY THEM

MARY E. KEISTER AND RUTH UPDEGRAFF

Although no human being is impervious to frustration, it undoubtedly has more destructive effects on some individuals than on others. How can those whose reactions to frustration are extreme be helped to respond more constructively?

This article describes the way in which two psychologists identified children whose responses to frustrations were ineffective and then helped them to handle difficult problems in a more self-reliant manner.

Psychologists and educators believe that it is important for an individual to respond adequately in situations involving failure or great difficulty. After his first attempt meets failure, the individual's subsequent, possibly characteristic, reaction is related not only to his emotional adjustment but also to his ability to learn and to profit by experience.

It is natural for a young child to be confronted with many situations which are not readily resolved. Moreover, in his attempts to meet and overcome difficulties as they arise lie the child's opportunities to learn. In general, mental hygienists and educators have considered it desirable for a child to attack a difficult problem with composure, to try out one possibility after another in an attempt to reach a solution. It is usually considered that he is not meeting the situation desirably if he retreats from the problem, if he rationalizes, if he leans heavily on an adult for assistance, if he attacks the problem with such emotional accompaniments as crying, sulking, and tantrums.

Even the most casual observation of young children reveals wide differences in such responses. In the face of a difficult

situation, some children make attempts at their own solution, intently and without emotion. There are others, however, who under many circumstances, immediately ask for the help of an adult or another child; some retreat from the scene of action when they discover difficulty; some cry or become angry; some rationalize.

Given, then, a variability from child to child (and in some cases the occurrence of modes of behavior which are undesirable from the standpoint of the future as well as of the present), the problem becomes one of discovering the existence of an undesirable pattern and of modifying that pattern if possible. Such was the problem of this study, the purpose of which may be summarized as follows:

1. To devise tests by means of which one may discover what responses a child of preschool age gives when faced with failure.
2. To select a group of children evidencing undesirable models of response.
3. To attempt to modify, by special help or individual training, the responses of the children in this group.

Mental hygienists have employed the concept of failure in two ways. They have used it in connection with a situation which is ultimately impossible for the individual to overcome because of his own incapacity; under such circumstances it is

Reprinted from *Child Development*, VIII (1937), 241–48, by permission of the authors and the Society for Research in Child Development.

important for him to realize this fact and adjust himself to the idea of the impossibility. In the second sense, failure has been thought of as a step in the process of solving a problem, as involved in the individual's working his way out of a difficulty. It is with behavior of the latter type that this study is concerned. Failure, as defined here, is the child's lack of immediate success following an attempt to contend with a situation, the situation being one in which he sees some relation to himself as an instrument of his own success or failure.

A preliminary survey of suitable approaches indicated the inapplicability of the observational method, at least in the beginning stages of the study. Not only did it become apparent that failure situations occurred in the nursery school with such infrequency that the time-sampling method was too extensive, but also controls of motivation and of the difficulty of the tasks were lacking. Accordingly, plans were made for presenting failure in experimental situations. The decision was made to confront the child with one situation somewhat in the form of a puzzle, with another which challenged his physical strength, and with a third which offered social obstacles. Among the criteria for setting up the experiments were the following:

1. They must be possible of accomplishment and yet of such difficulty that the child does not succeed immediately.
2. They must provide situations which are natural, in the sense that the difficulties are not obviously or forcibly imposed.
3. The average child should be able to see for himself that he has failed and to see in the situation some relation to himself as an instrument of his success or failure.

As a result of preliminary study, two test situations were believed adequate for use. The first, the puzzle box test, confronted the subject with a small, lidded, colored box, 9 by 7 by 1½ inches. The box being opened, it was found to have a false bottom within ¼ inch from the top. On this lay ten small, colored figures, of irregular shape, ½ inch thick, representing various objects of interest to children, such as a sailboat and an engine. Because of their form they fitted rather closely into the available space. The experimenter then removed the figures and gave the test instructions which invited the child to put the blocks into the box so that the lid could go down again. In spite of the fact that there were several ways in which the blocks could be fitted into the space, the task was quite a difficult one to complete in the fifteen minutes allowed. There was no question of its being an interesting one to children.

The weighted box test consisted of a five-sided box, weighted at the ends and through the middle with from 60 to 90 pounds of iron weights. These weights were adjustable. The box was placed in the middle of a room upside down over a group of attractive toys. When the subject entered the box was raised slightly, then lowered. Instructions indicated that the toys could be played with if the box could be lifted in order to obtain them. Ten minutes was the time allowed.

The same scheme for recording behavior, a system of controlled observation with time divisions of minutes, was used for both tests. The type of behavior observed is indicated in the tables.

The subjects in this study, 82 children (38 boys and 44 girls) aged three to six years, were enrolled in the preschool laboratories of the Iowa Child Welfare Station. The mean intelligence quotient was 122. Because the tests evidenced no statistically significant age differences, marked individual differences being apparent at all ages, the data have not been classified into age groups. Comparative frequency of various types of responses in the two tests is indicated in Tables 1 and 2. In each test the most frequent response of the group as a whole was "attempts to solve alone" although "interest"

TABLE 1.
MEAN NUMBER OF MINUTES
DURING WHICH RESPONSES
OCCURRED DURING PUZZLE BOX
TEST $(N = 81)$[a]

Behavior	Mean	Standard Deviation
No overt attempt	2.2	3.2
Attempts to solve alone	11.1	4.2
Asks another to solve	1.2	2.3
Asks help	1.5	2.1
Destructive behavior	.1	.5
Rationalizes	1.2	1.8
Interest	10.2	4.7
No emotional manifestations	1.6	2.9
Indifference	.2	1.4
Smiles	.2	.9
Laughs	.1	.2
Sulks	.2	.6
Cries	.3	1.2
Whines	.8	2.0
Yells	.1	.4
Motor manifestations of anger	.04	.3

[a] Mean length of experimental period: 13.3 minutes.

ran a close second. That requests for either partial or complete help and rationalizations were more common than disgruntled emotional responses proved to be the case.

Inasmuch as it was the purpose of these tests to differentiate between those subjects giving undesirable or immature responses and those responding more desirably, the extent to which this end was achieved was first to be determined. To describe the process briefly, certain objective criteria were set up in terms of test behavior. Five kinds of behavior occurring for at least a minimum amount of time were listed and definitely stated quantitatively. If a child's behavior fell into two or more of these classifications on either or both tests, he was judged to have given an immature response. In brief, these five types were as follows: (1) giving up attempts to solve the puzzle box in less than five minutes or to solve the weighted box in less than two minutes, (2) requesting help during more than

TABLE 2.
MEAN NUMBER OF MINUTES
DURING WHICH RESPONSES
OCCURRED DURING WEIGHTED
BOX TEST $(N = 74)$[a]

Behavior	Mean	Standard Deviation
No overt attempt	3.4	2.8
Attempts to solve alone	5.7	2.7
Asks another to solve	.4	3.6
Asks help	1.1	1.9
Rationalizes	1.0	1.5
Interest	5.7	3.2
No emotional manifestations	2.1	2.6
Indifference	.1	.9
Smiles	.3	.8
Laughs	.1	.4
Sulks	.2	1.0
Cries	.3	.9
Whines	.7	1.7

[a] Mean length of experimental period: 9.1 minutes.

one half the total time of the test, (3) manifesting destructive behavior, (4) making more than two rationalizations, (5) evidencing exaggerated emotional responses.

Analysis of the test records showed a total of fifteen children (18 per cent) who fell into the immature group.

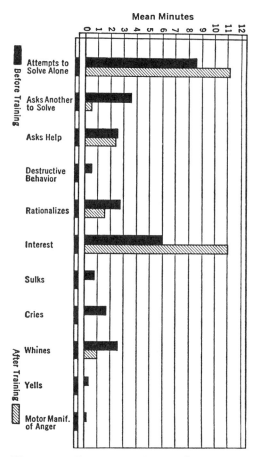

Figure 1. *Responses of trained group on puzzle box text before and after training.*

The diagnostic value of the tests is illustrated by contrasting frequencies of behavior as shown in Tables 3 and 4, in which it is apparent that real differences do exist between the groups as classified by this means.

The next step in the study was the training program. In this, twelve out of the fifteen children participated.

The basic philosophy underlying the training assumed that children can learn to meet difficulty in a controlled manner and acceptably if they know from experience what type of behavior is most likely to bring success or satisfaction. It was the aim of the training program to raise the responses of the immature group nearer to the level of desirability. Specifically, in the training an attempt was made to teach the child to persist longer in the face of difficult tasks (which were, however, not impossible ones), to teach him to depend less upon an adult for help, and to attack a problem and see it through with some composure.

The method of training consisted in introducing the child to a series of problems which grew progressively more difficult as the program of training proceeded. The problem situations reflected the following criteria:

1. The tasks should be graded in difficulty so that the child experiences success in the earlier ones and gradually works up to problems which are difficult for him.

2. The later tasks must be of such difficulty that the child does not succeed immediately but is forced to persevere, to continue to try if he is to attain success.

3. The child must be able to see his progress and previous successes.

In describing the two training situations briefly[1] it may be said that they were similar in type but differed in the specific materials used. For the first, four picture-puzzle books were prepared, each one in the series more difficult than the one preceding and each one of graduated difficulty from beginning to end. For these, interesting, colorful and appropriate story books were cut up. The pictures were mounted on 4-ply wood, varnished, cut into puzzles, and the book was rebound on loose rings. The experimenter read

---

[1] Detailed descriptions of all the materials used in this study may be obtained from the Iowa Child Welfare Research Station, Iowa City, Iowa.

TABLE 3. MEAN AND STANDARD DEVIATION OF RESPONSES IN MINUTES FOR TWO GROUPS OF SUBJECTS ON PUZZLE BOX TEST	BEHAVIOR	GROUP SHOWING UNDESIRABLE OR IMMATURE RESPONSE (N = 15)		REMAINDER OF TOTAL GROUP (N = 54)	
		Mean	Standard Deviation	Mean	Standard Deviation
	No overt attempt	6.0	3.7	1.6	2.3
	Attempts to solve alone	8.5	4.2	13.0	3.0
	Asks another to solve	3.6	3.4	.8	1.6
	Asks help	2.5	2.4	1.5	2.1
	Destructive behavior	.6	1.1		
	Rationalizes	2.8	2.5	1.0	1.4
	Interest	6.0	3.8	12.4	3.9
	No emotional manifestations	2.5	2.4	1.7	3.2
	Sulks	.8	1.3		
	Cries	1.7	2.4		
	Whines	2.6	2.9	.5	1.5
	Yells	.3	.8		
	Motor manifestations of anger	.2	.5		

the story to the child. As she reached a part illustrated by one of the pictures, she stopped for him to put the puzzle together before continuing the story. After the first picture was completed she covered it with cellophane, so that both she and the child could refer to it later, and resumed the story until the next picture. Each book contained four to six pictures.

In the second situation a "block boy" was built. Copied from a drawn pattern hung on the wall, he was to be made of colored blocks placed upon each other so that having attained first feet, then legs, then trunk and arms, then head, he stood approximately three feet high, a somewhat precarious figure and a frequently exasperatingly unsteady one. Usually several attempts were necessary in order to complete him. After a successful production his builder had the task of devising a hat from a wide variety of materials provided.

The entire program of training was handled by one person. Training periods varied in length from eight to thirty-three minutes, depending largely upon the difficulty of the tasks and the child's behavior. To subject the twelve children to all of the training took approximately six weeks.

TABLE 4. MEAN AND STANDARD DEVIATION OF RESPONSES IN MINUTES FOR TWO GROUPS OF SUBJECTS ON WEIGHTED BOX TEST	BEHAVIOR	GROUP SHOWING UNDESIRABLE OR IMMATURE RESPONSE (N = 15)		REMAINDER OF TOTAL GROUP (N = 50)	
		Mean	Standard Deviation	Mean	Standard Deviation
	No overt attempt	5.2	2.9	3.4	2.4
	Attempts to solve alone	4.2	2.9	6.5	2.3
	Asks another to solve	.7	1.6	.3	.9
	Asks help	2.2	2.3	.9	1.7
	Rationalizes	1.7	1.2	.8	1.5
	Interest	3.5	3.0	6.8	2.9
	Sulks	1.0	2.0		
	Cries	1.0	1.6	.1	.4
	Whines	2.3	2.3	.3	1.2

Behavior during the training program underwent a gradual improvement as is shown by both objective and subjective estimate. In order to study post-training behavior objectively, two approaches were utilized; first, retests by means of a similar but not identical puzzle box were given the trained subjects (Figure 1); second, also retested were an equal number of children, not in the trained group, who during the initial tests had shown some undesirable behavior (Figure 2).

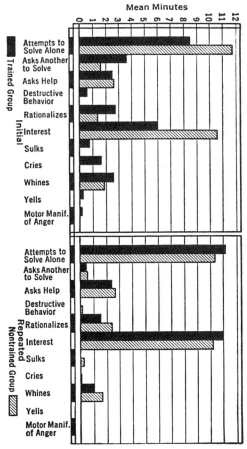

Figure 2. Responses of trained and untrained groups on puzzle box test.

It is evident from a study of Figure 1 that the behavior of the children after training was remarkably different from their behavior prior to training. Differences in the three items *attempts to solve alone, interest,* and *cries* are statistically significant. Excepting in the case of the item *asks help,* the remaining differences closely approximate significance. The differences were in form of the response given in the retest and indicate that a reasonable improvement was effected in the trained group. The exaggerated emotional responses of sulking and crying dropped out entirely in this group.

Figure 2 concerns responses of the trained and the compared nontrained group before and after training. The two groups differed in the responses *no overt attempt, attempts to solve alone, interest, sulks,* and *cries.* All of the differences were in favor of the trained subjects in spite of the fact that previous to training the difference lay in the opposite direction.

The results of this study, hopeful as they are, must be interpreted in the light of the specific conditions. The entire program was carried out by the experimenter, who also gave the retests. Further study, at present underway, must determine the extent to which the more desirable behavior occurs in other situations and with other persons. There is evidence that behavior of children in difficulties has been similar in two test situations; it would be valuable to make observations in other situations and under circumstances of a more social nature. Probably the most important contribution of the present study is its indication of the marked effect of this training program. After training, children tried longer, manifested more interest in solving problems themselves, and completely eliminated emotional behavior. Evidently this improvement was not a function of age or other training. Of particular interest to teachers and psychologists may be the fact that the program of training was neither arduous nor time-consuming.

66 | A LABORATORY STUDY OF FEAR: THE CASE OF PETER

MARY COVER JONES

This famous experiment followed the conditioning experiments of Ivan Pavlov with dogs and those of Watson with children. It demonstrates how a child developed fear of an object which never hurt him and how this fear spread to other objects with similar characteristics. The process followed in eventually "unconditioning" Peter provides valuable ideas of how children may be helped to overcome certain fears.

As part of a genetic study of emotions, a number of children were observed in order to determine the most effective methods of removing fear responses.

The case of Peter illustrates how a fear may be removed under laboratory conditions. His case was selected from a number of others for the following reasons:

1. Progress in combating the fear reactions was so marked that many of the details of the process could be observed easily.

2. It was possible to continue the study over a period of more than three months.

3. The notes of a running diary show the characteristics of a healthy, normal, interesting child, well adjusted, except for his exaggerated fear reactions. A few descriptive notes show something of his personality:

Remarkably active, easily interested, capable of prolonged endeavor. . . . A favorite with the children as well as with the nurses and matrons . . . Peter has a healthy passion for possessions. Everything that he lays his hands on is his. As this is frequently disputed by some other child, there are occasional violent scenes of protest. These disturbances are not more frequent than might be expected in a three-year-old, in view of the fact that he is continually forced to adjust to a large group of children, nor are they more marked in Peter's case than in others of his age. Peter's IQ at the age of 2 years and 10 months was 102 on the Kuhlmann Revision of the Binet. At the same time he passed 5 of the 3 year tests on the Stanford Revision. In initiative and constructive ability, however, he is superior to his companions of the same mental age.

4. This case is a sequel to one recently contributed by Dr. Watson and furnished supplementary material of interest in a genetic study of emotions. Dr. Watson's case illustrated how a fear could be produced experimentally under laboratory conditions. A brief review follows: Albert, eleven months of age, was an infant with a phlegmatic disposition, afraid of nothing "under the sun" except a loud sound made by striking a steel bar. This made him cry. By striking the bar at the same time that Albert touched a white rat, the fear was transferred to the white rat. After seven combined stimulations, rat and sound, Albert not only became greatly disturbed at the sight of a rat, but this fear had spread to include a white rabbit, cotton wool, a fur coat, and the experimenter's hair. It did not transfer to his wooden blocks and other objects very dissimilar to the rat.

In referring to this case, Dr. Watson says, "We have shown experimentally that when you condition a child to show fear of an animal, this fear transfers or spreads in such a way that without separate con-

Reprinted from *Journal of Genetic Psychology*, XXXI (1924), 308–15, by permission of the author and The Journal Press.

ditioning he becomes afraid of many animals. If you take any one of these objects producing fear and uncondition, will fear of the other objects in the series disappear at the same time? That is, will the unconditioning spread without further training to other stimuli?"

Dr. Watson intended to continue the study of Albert in an attempt to answer this question, but Albert was removed from the hospital and the series of observations was discontinued.

About three years later this case, which seemed almost to be Albert grown a bit older, was discovered in our laboratory.

Peter was 2 years and 10 months old when we began to study him. He was afraid of a white rat, and this fear extended to a rabbit, a fur coat, a feather, cotton wool, etc., but not to wooden blocks and similar toys. An abridgment of the first laboratory notes on Peter reads as follows:

Peter was put in a crib in a play room and immediately became absorbed in his toys. A white rat was introduced into the crib from behind. (The experimenter was behind a screen.) At sight of the rat, Peter screamed and fell flat on his back in a paroxysm of fear. The stimulus was removed, and Peter was taken out of the crib and put into a chair. Barbara was brought to the crib and the white rat introduced as before. She exhibited no fear but picked the rat up in her hand. Peter sat quietly watching Barbara and the rat. A string of beads belonging to Peter had been left in the crib. Whenever the rat touched a part of the string he would say "my beads" in a complaining voice, although he made no objections when Barbara touched them. Invited to get down from the chair, he shook his head, fear not yet subsided. Twenty-five minutes elapsed before he was ready to play about freely.

The next day his reactions to the following situations and objects were noted:

Play room and crib———Selected toys, got into crib without protest
White ball rolled in———Picked it up and held it

Fur rug hung over crib———Cried until it was removed
Fur coat hung over crib———Cried until it was removed
Cotton———Whimpered, withdrew, cried
Hat with feathers———Cried
Blue woolly sweater———Looked, turned away, no fear
White toy rabbit of rough cloth———No interest, no fear
Wooden doll———No interest, no fear

This case made it possible for the experiment to continue where Dr. Watson had left off. The first problem was that of "unconditioning" a fear response to an animal, and the second, that of determining whether unconditioning to one stimulus spreads without further training to other stimuli.

From the test situations which were used to reveal fears, it was found that Peter showed even more marked fear responses to the rabbit than to the rat. It was decided to use the rabbit for unconditioning and to proceed as follows: Each day Peter and three other children were brought to the laboratory for a play period. The other children were selected carefully because of their entirely fearless attitude toward the rabbit and because of their satisfactory adjustments in general. The rabbit was always present during a part of the play period. From time to time Peter was brought in alone so that his reactions could be observed and progress noted.

From reading over the notes for each session it was apparent that there had been improvement by more or less regular steps from almost complete terror at sight of the rabbit to a completely positive response with no signs of disturbance. New situations requiring closer contact with the rabbit had been gradually introduced and the degree to which these situations were avoided, tolerated, or welcome, at each experimental session, gave the measure of improvement. Analysis of the notes on Peter's reactions indicated the following progressive steps in his degrees of toleration.

A. Rabbit anywhere in the room in a cage causes fear reactions.
B. Rabbit 12 feet away in cage tolerated.
C. Rabbit 4 feet away in cage tolerated.
D. Rabbit 3 feet away in cage tolerated.
E. Rabbit close in cage tolerated.
F. Rabbit free in room tolerated.
G. Rabbit touched when experimenter holds it.
H. Rabbit touched when free in room.
I. Rabbit defied by spitting at it, throwing things at it, imitating it.
J. Rabbit allowed on tray of high chair.
K. Squats in defenseless position beside rabbit.
L. Helps experimenter to carry rabbit to its cage.
M. Holds rabbit on lap.
N. Stays alone in room with rabbit.
O. Allows rabbit in play pen with him.
P. Fondles rabbit affectionately.
Q. Lets rabbit nibble his fingers.

These "degrees of toleration" merely represented the stages in which improvement occurred. They did not give any indications of the intervals between steps, nor of the plateaus, relapses, and sudden gains which were actually evident. To show these features a curve was drawn by using the seventeen steps given above as the Y axis of a chart [p. 556] and the experimental sessions as the X axis. The units are not equal on either axis, as the "degrees of toleration" have merely been set down as they appeared from consideration of the laboratory notes with no attempt to evalute the steps. Likewise the experimental sessions were not equi-distant in time. Peter was seen twice daily for a period and thence only once a day. At one point illness and quarantine interrupted the experiments for two months. There is no indication of these irregularities on the chart. For example, along the X axis, 1 represents the date December 4 when the observation began. Eleven and 12 represent the dates March 10 A. M. and

P. M. (from December 17 to March 7, Peter was not available for study).

The question arose as to whether or not the points on the Y axis which indicated progress to the experimenter represented real advance and not merely idiosyncratic reactions to the subject. The "tolerance series" as indicated by the experimenter was presented in random order to six graduate students and instructors in psychology to be arranged so as to indicate increase in tolerance, in their judgment. An average correlation of 70 with the experimenter's arrangement was found for the six ratings. This indicates that the experimenter was justified from an *a priori* point of view in designating the steps to be progressive stages.

The first seven periods show how Peter progressed from a great fear of the rabbit to a tranquil indifference and even a voluntary pat on the rabbit's back when others were setting the example. The notes for the seventh period [see (a) on chart] read:

Laurel, Mary, Arthur, Peter playing together in the laboratory. Experimenter put rabbit down on floor. Arthur said, "Peter doesn't cry when he sees the rabbit come out." Peter, "No." He was a little concerned as to whether or not the rabbit would eat his kiddie car. Laurel and Mary stroked the rabbit and chattered away excitedly. Peter walked over, touched the rabbit on the back, exulting, "I touched him on the end."

At this period Peter was taken to the hospital with scarlet fever. He did not return for two months.

By referring to the chart at (b), it will be noted that the line shows a decided drop to the early level of fear reaction when he returned. This was easily explained by the nurse who brought Peter from the hospital. As they were entering a taxi at the door of the hospital, a large dog, running past, jumped at them. Both Peter and the nurse were very much frightened, Peter so much that he lay back in the taxi pale and quiet, and the nurse

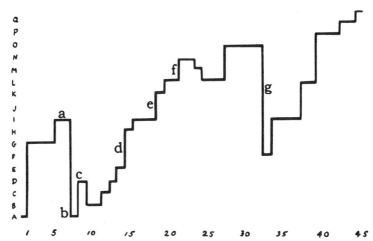

debated whether or not to return him to the hospital. This seemed reason enough for his precipitate descent back to the original fear level. Being threatened by a large dog when ill, and in a strange place and being with an adult who also showed fear, was a terrifying situation against which our training could not have fortified him.

At this point (b) we began another method of treatment, that of "direct conditioning." Peter was seated in a high chair and given food which he liked. The experimenter brought the rabbit in a wire cage as close as she could without arousing a response which would interfere with the eating. Through the presence of the pleasant stimulus (food) whenever the rabbit was shown, the fear was eliminated gradually in favor of a positive response. Occasionally also, other children were brought in to help with the "unconditioning." These facts are of interest in following the charted progress. The first decided rise at (c) was due to the presence of another child who influenced Peter's reaction. The notes for this day read:

Lawrence and Peter sitting near together in their high chairs eating candy. Rabbit in cage put down 12 feet away. Peter began to cry. Lawrence said, "Oh, rabbit." Clambered down, ran over and looked in the cage at him. Peter followed close and watched.

The next two decided rises at (d) and (e) occurred on the day when a student assistant, Dr. S., was present. Peter was very fond of Dr. S. whom he insisted was his "papa." Although Dr. S. did not directly influence Peter by any overt suggestions, it may be that having him there contributed to Peter's general feeling of well being and thus indirectly affected his reactions. The fourth rise on the chart at (f) was, like the first, due to the influence of another child. Notes for the 21st session read:

Peter with candy in high chair. Experimenter brought rabbit and sat down in front of the tray with it. Peter cried out, "I don't want him," and withdrew. Rabbit was given to another child sitting near to hold. His holding the rabbit served as a powerful suggestion; Peter wanted the rabbit on his lap, and held it for an instant.

The decided drop at (g) was caused by a slight scratch when Peter was helping to carry the rabbit to his cage. The rapid ascent following shows how quickly he regained lost ground.

In one of our last sessions, Peter showed no fear although another child was present who showed marked disturbance at sight of the rabbit.

An attempt was made from time to time to see what verbal organization accompanied this process of "unconditioning."

Upon Peter's return from the hospital, the following conversation took place:

E. [experimenter]. What do you do upstairs, Peter? [The laboratory was upstairs].
P. I see my brother. Take me up to see my brother.
E. What else will you see?
P. Blocks.

Peter's reference to blocks indicated a definite memory as he played with blocks only in the laboratory. No further response of any significance could be elicited. In the laboratory two days later (he had seen the rabbit once in the meantime), he said suddenly, "Beads can't bite me, beads can only look at me." Toward the end of the training an occasional "I like the rabbit," was all the language he had to parallel the changed emotional organization.

Early in the experiment an attempt was made to get some measure of the visceral changes accompanying Peter's fear reactions. On one occasion Dr. S. determined Peter's blood pressure outside the laboratory and again later, in the laboratory while he was in a state of much anxiety caused by the rabbit's being held close to him by the experimenter. The diastolic blood pressure changed from 65 to 80 on this occasion. Peter was taken to the infirmary the next day for the routine physical examination and developed there a suspicion of medical instruments which made it inadvisable to proceed with this phase of the work.

Peter has gone home to a difficult environment but the experimenter is still in touch with him. He showed in the last interview, as on the later portions of the chart, a genuine fondness for the rabbit. What has happened to the fear of the other objects? The fear of the cotton, the fur coat, feathers, was entirely absent at our last interview. He looked at them, handled them, and immediately turned to something which interested him more. The reaction to the rats and to the fur rug with the stuffed head was greatly modified and improved. While he did not show the fondness for these that was apparent with the rabbit, he had made a fair adjustment. For example, Peter would pick up the tin box containing frogs or rats and carry it around the room. When requested, he picked up the fur rug and carried it to the experimenter.

What would Peter do if confronted by a strange animal? At the last interview the experimenter presented a mouse and a tangled mass of angleworms. At first sight, Peter showed slight distress reactions and moved away, but before the period was over he was carrying the worms about and watching the mouse with undisturbed interest. By "unconditioning" Peter to the rabbit, he has apparently been helped to overcome many superfluous fears, some completely, some to a less degree. His tolerance of strange animals and unfamiliar situations has apparently increased.

The study is still incomplete. Peter's fear of the animals which were shown him was probably not a directly conditioned fear. It is unlikely that he had ever had an experience with white rats, for example. Where the fear originated and with what stimulus, is not known. Nor is it known what Peter would do if he were again confronted with the original fear situation. All of the fears which were "unconditioned" were transferred fears, and it has not yet been learned whether or not the primary fear can be eliminated by training the transfers.

Another matter which must be left to speculation is the future welfare of the subject. His "home" consists of one furnished room which is occupied by his mother and father, a brother of nine years and himself. Since the death of an older sister, he is the recipient of most of the unwise affection of his parents. His brother appears to bear him a grudge because of this favoritism, as might be expected. Peter hears continually, "Ben is so bad and so dumb, but Peter is so good and so smart!" His mother is a highly emotional individual who can not get through an interview, however brief, without a display of tears. She is totally incapable of providing a home on the $25 a week which her husband steadily earns. In an attempt to control Peter she resorts to frequent fear suggestions. "Come in Peter, someone wants to steal you." To her erratic resorts to discipline, Peter reacts with temper tantrums. He was denied a summer in the country because his father "forgets he's tired when he has Peter around." Surely a discouraging outlook for Peter.

But the recent development of psychological studies of young children and the growing tendency to carry the knowledge gained in the psychological laboratories into the home and school induce us to predict a more wholesome treatment of a future generation of Peters.

67 | BRAVE NEW WORLD

ALDOUS HUXLEY

If children can be conditioned to fear and not to fear, they can also be conditioned to hate and love, to admire one kind of "ism" and reject another. In fact, it might be possible for an entire society to be so conditioned; perhaps many societies—possibly including our own—have been.

Mr. Huxley imaginatively and starkly describes the methods which might be used for an almost totally effective conditioning of a future society.

. . . The love of servitude cannot be established except as the result of a deep, personal revolution in human minds and bodies. To bring about that revolution we require, among others, the following discoveries and inventions. First, a greatly improved technique of suggestion—through infant conditioning and, later, with the aid of drugs, such as scopolamine. Second, a fully developed science of human differences, enabling government managers to assign any given individual to his or her proper place in the social and economic hierarchy. (Round pegs in square holes tend to have dangerous thoughts about the social system and to infect others with their discontents.) Third (since reality, however utopian, is something from which people feel the need of

taking pretty frequent holidays), a substitute for alcohol and the other narcotics, something at once less harmful and more pleasure-giving than gin or heroin. And fourth (but this would be a long-term project, which it would take generations of totalitarian control to bring to a successful conclusion) a foolproof system of eugenics, designed to standardize the human product and so to facilitate the task of the managers. In *Brave New World* this standardization of the human product has been pushed to fantastic, though not perhaps impossible, extremes. Technically and ideologically we are still a long way from bottled babies and Bokanovsky groups of semi-morons. But by A.F. 600, who knows what may not be happening? Meanwhile the other characteristic features of the happier and more stable world —the equivalents of soma and hypnopaedia and the scientific caste system—are

Excerpts reprinted from *Brave New World* (Modern Library Edition), pp. 20–24, 27, 28–31, by permission of the author.

probably not more than three or four generations away. Nor does the sexual promiscuity of *Brave New World* seem so very distant. There are already certain American cities in which the number of divorces is equal to the number of marriages. In a few years, no doubt, marriage licenses will be sold like dog licenses, good for a period of twelve months, with no law against changing dogs or keeping more than one animal at a time. As political and economic freedom diminishes, sexual freedom tends compensatingly to increase. And the dictator (unless he needs cannon fodder and families with which to colonize empty or conquered territories) will do well to encourage that freedom. In conjunction with the freedom to daydream under the influence of dope and movies and the radio, it will help to reconcile his subjects to the servitude which is their fate.

All things considered it looks as though Utopia were far closer to us than anyone, only fifteen years ago, could have imagined.

· · · · ·

INFANT NURSERIES. NEO-PAVLOVIAN CONDITIONING ROOMS, announced the notice board.

The Director opened a door. They were in a large bare room, very bright and sunny; for the whole of the southern wall was a single window. Half a dozen nurses, trousered and jacketed in the regulation white viscose-linen uniform, their hair aseptically hidden under white caps, were engaged in setting out bowls of roses in a long row across the floor. Big bowls, packed tight with blossom. Thousands of petals, ripe-blown and silkily smooth, like the checks of innumerable little cherubs, but of cherubs, in that bright light, not exclusively pink and Aryan, but also luminously Chinese, also Mexican, also apoplectic with too much blowing of celestial trumpets, also pale as death, pale with the posthumous whiteness of marble.

The nurses stiffened to attention as the D.H.C. came in.

"Set out the books," he said curtly.

In silence the nurses obeyed his command. Between the rose bowls the books were duly set out—a row of nursery quartos opened invitingly each at some gaily coloured image of beast or fish or bird.

"Now bring in the children."

They hurried out of the room and returned in a minute or two, each pushing a kind of tall dumbwaiter laden, on all its four wire-netted shelves, with eight-month-old babies, all exactly alike (a Bokanovsky Group, it was evident) and all (since their caste was Delta) dressed in khaki.

"Put them down on the floor."

The infants were unloaded.

"Now turn them so that they can see the flowers and books."

Turned, the babies at once fell silent, then began to crawl towards those clusters of sleek colours, those shapes so gay and brilliant on the white pages. As they approached, the sun came out of a momentary eclipse behind a cloud. The roses flamed up as though with a sudden passion from within; a new and profound significance seemed to suffuse the shining pages of the books. From the ranks of the crawling babies came little squeals of excitement, gurgles and twitterings of pleasure.

The Director rubbed his hands. "Excellent!" he said. "It might almost have been done on purpose."

The swiftest crawlers were already at their goal. Small hands reached out uncertainly, touched, grasped, unpetaling the transfigured roses, crumpling the illuminated pages of the books. The Director waited until all were happily busy. Then, "Watch carefully," he said. And, lifting his hand, he gave the signal.

The Head Nurse, who was standing by a switchboard at the other end of the room, pressed down a little lever.

There was a violent explosion. Shriller and even shriller, a siren shrieked. Alarm bells maddeningly sounded.

The children started, screamed, their faces were distorted with terror.

"And now," the Director shouted (for the noise was deafening), "now we proceed to rub in the lesson with a mild electric shock."

He waved his hand again, and the Head Nurse pressed a second lever. The screaming of the babies suddenly changed its tone. There was something desperate, almost insane, about the sharp spasmodic yelps to which they now gave utterance. Their little bodies twitched and stiffened; their limbs moved jerkily as if to the tug of unseen wires.

"We can electrify that whole strip of floor," bawled the Director in explanation. "But that's enough," he signalled to the nurse.

The explosions ceased, the bells stopped ringing, the shriek of the siren died down from tone to tone into silence. The stiffly twitching bodies relaxed, and what had become the sob and yelp of infant maniacs broadened out once more into a normal howl of ordinary terror.

"Offer them the flowers and the books again."

The nurses obeyed; but at the approach of the roses, at the mere sight of those gaily-coloured images of pussy and cock-a-doodle-doo and baa-baa black sheep, the infants shrank away in horror; the volume of their howling suddenly increased.

"Observe," said the Director triumphantly, "observe."

Books and loud noises, flowers and electric shocks—already in the infant mind these couples were compromisingly linked; and after two hundred repetitions of the same or a similar lesson would be wedded indissolubly. What man has joined, nature is powerless to put asunder.

"They'll grow up with what the psychol-ogists used to call an 'instinctive' hatred of books and flowers. Reflexes unalterably conditioned. They'll be safe from books and botany all their lives." The Director turned to his nurses. "Take them away again."

Still yelling, the khaki babies were loaded on to their dumb-waiters and wheeled out, leaving behind them the smell of sour milk and a most welcome silence.

. . . . .

"The principle of sleep-teaching, or hypnopædia, had been discovered." The D.H.C. made an impressive pause.

The principle had been discovered; but many, many years were to elapse before that principle was usefully applied.

. . . . .

"These early experimenters," the D.H.C. was saying, "were on the wrong track. They thought that hypnopædia could be made an instrument of intellectual educa-tion . . ."

(A small boy asleep on his right side, the right arm stuck out, the right hand hanging limp over the edge of the bed. Through a round grating in the side of a box a voice speaks softly.

"The Nile is the longest river in Africa and the second in length of all the rivers of the globe. Although falling short of the length of the Mississippi-Missouri, the Nile is at the head of all rivers as regards the length of its basin, which extends through 35 degrees of latitude . . ."

At breakfast the next morning, "Tommy," some one says, "do you know which is the longest river in Africa?" A shaking of the head. "But don't you remember something that begins: The Nile is the . . ."

"The-Nile-is-the-longest-river-in-Africa-and-the-second-in-length-of-all-rivers-of-the-globe . . ." The words come rushing out. "Although-falling-short-of . . ."

"Well now, which is the longest river in Africa?"

The eyes are blank. "I don't know."

"But the Nile, Tommy."

"The-Nile-is-the-longest-river-in-Africa-and-second . . ."

"Then which river is the longest, Tommy?"

Tommy bursts into tears. "I don't know," he howls.)

That howl, the Director made it plain, discouraged the earliest investigators. The experiments were abandoned. No further attempt was made to teach children the length of the Nile in their sleep. Quite rightly. You can't learn a science unless you know what it's all about.

"Whereas, if they'd only started on *moral* education," said the Director, leading the way towards the door. The students followed him, desperately scribbling as they walked and all the way up in the lift. "Moral education, which ought never, in any circumstances, to be rational."

"Silence, silence," whispered a loud speaker as they stepped out at the fourteenth floor, and "Silence, silence," the trumpet mouths indefatigably repeated at intervals down every corridor. The students and even the Director himself rose automatically to the tips of their toes. They were Alphas, of course; but even Alphas have been well conditioned. . . .

Fifty yards of tiptoeing brought them to a door which the Director cautiously opened. They stepped over the threshold into the twilight of a shuttered dormitory. Eighty cots stood in a row against the wall. There was a sound of light regular breathing and a continuous murmur, as of very faint voices remotely whispering.

A nurse rose as they entered and came to attention before the Director.

"What's the lesson this afternoon?" he asked.

"We had Elementary Sex for the first forty minutes," she answered. "But now it's switched over to Elementary Class Consciousness."

The Director walked slowly down the long line of cots. Rosy and relaxed with sleep, eighty little boys and girls lay softly breathing. There was a whisper under every pillow. The D.H.C. halted and, bending over one of the little beds, listened attentively.

"Elementary Class Consciousness, did you say? Let's have it repeated a little louder by the trumpet."

At the end of the room a loud speaker projected from the wall. The Director walked up to it and pressed a switch.

". . . all wear green," said a soft but very distinct voice, beginning in the middle of a sentence, "and Delta children wear khaki. Oh no, I don't want to play with Delta children. And Epsilons are still worse. They're too stupid to be able to read or write. Besides they wear black, which is such a beastly colour. I'm *so* glad I'm a Beta."

There was a pause; then the voice began again.

"Alpha children wear grey. They work much harder than we do, because they're so frightfully clever. I'm really awfully glad I'm a Beta, because I don't work so hard. And then we are much better than the Gammas and Deltas. Gammas are stupid. They all wear green, and Delta children wear khaki. Oh, no, I *don't* want to play with Delta children. And Epsilons are still worse. They're too stupid to be able. . . ."

The Director pushed back the switch. The voice was silent. Only its thin ghosts continued to mutter from beneath the eighty pillows.

"They'll have that repeated forty or fifty times more before they wake; then again on Thursday, and again on Saturday. A hundred and twenty times three times a week for thirty months. After which they go on to a more advanced lesson."

Roses and electric shocks, the khaki of Deltas and a whiff of asafoetida—wedded indissolubly before the child can speak. But wordless conditioning is crude and wholesale; cannot bring home the finer distinction, cannot inculcate the more complex courses of behavior. For that there must be words, but words without reason. In brief, hypnopaedia.

"The greatest moralizing and socializing force of all time."

68 | THE SCIENCE OF LEARNING AND THE ART OF TEACHING

B. F. SKINNER

If conditioning can be used to teach a dog to salivate or a child to fear rabbits, or to teach pigeons, cats, chickens, and other animals all kinds of complex tricks, why not use it to teach spelling or arithmetic?

Professor Skinner has carefully examined two aspects of such teaching: determining what is to be taught and discovering adequate ways of rewarding (reinforcing) correct responses. Here he discusses the problem of reinforcement and describes a mechanical teaching device which he invented. Thousands of teaching machines and programmed learning materials have resulted from this theory, which, despite technological imperfections and the need for narrow and rigid content, may yet prove to be more influential in changing educational methods than any other theory in history.

Perhaps the most serious criticism of the current classroom is the relative infrequency of reinforcement. Since the pupil is usually dependent upon the teacher for being right, and since many pupils are usually dependent upon the same teacher, the total number of contingencies which may be arranged during, say, the first four years, is of the order of only a few thousand. But a very rough estimate suggests that efficient mathematical behavior at this level requires something of the order of 25,000 contingencies. We may suppose that even in the brighter student a given contingency must be arranged several times to place the behavior well in hand.

Excerpts reprinted from *Harvard Educational Review*, XXIV (1954), 86–87, and *Current Trends in Psychology and the Behavior Sciences* (University of Pittsburgh Press, 1955), 38–58, by permission of the author and the University of Pittsburgh Press.

The responses to be set up are not simply the various items in tables of addition, subtraction, multiplication, and division; we have also to consider the alternative forms in which each item may be stated. To the learning of such material we should add hundreds of responses concerned with factoring, identifying primes, memorizing series, using short-cut techniques of calculation, constructing and using geometric representations or number forms, and so on. Over and above all this, the whole mathematical repertoire must be brought under the control of concrete problems of considerable variety. Perhaps 50,000 contingencies is a more conservative estimate. In this frame of reference the daily assignment in Arithmetic seems pitifully meagre.

The result of all this is, of course, well known. Even our best schools are under criticism for their inefficiency in the teaching of drill subjects such as arithmetic.

The condition in the average school is a matter of widespread national concern. Modern children simply do not learn arithmetic quickly or well. Nor is the result simply incompetence. The very subjects in which modern techniques are weakest are those in which failure is most conspicuous, and in the wake of an ever-growing incompetence come the anxieties, uncertainties, and aggressions which in their turn present other problems to the school. Most pupils soon claim the asylum of not being "ready" for arithmetic at a given level or, eventually, of not having a mathematical mind. Such explanations are readily seized upon by defensive teachers and parents. Few pupils ever reach the stage at which automatic reinforcements follow as the natural consequences of mathematical behavior. On the contrary, the figures and symbols of mathematics have become standard emotional stimuli. The glimpse of a column of figures, not to say an algebraic symbol or an integral sign, is likely to set off—not mathematical behavior—but a reaction of anxiety, guilt, or fear.

The teacher is usually no happier about this than the pupil. Denied the opportunity to control via the birch rod, quite at sea as to the mode of operation of the few techniques at her disposal, she spends as little time as possible on drill subjects and eagerly subscribes to philosophies of education which emphasize material of greater inherent interest. . . .

There would be no point in urging these objections if improvement were impossible. But the advances which have recently been made in our control of the learning process suggest a thorough revision of classroom practices and, fortunately, they tell us how the revision can be brought about. This is not, of course, the first time that the results of an experimental science have been brought to bear upon the practical problems of education. The modern classroom does not, however, offer much evidence that research in the field of learning has been respected or used. This condition is no doubt partly due to the limitations of earlier research. But it has been encouraged by a too hasty conclusion that the laboratory study of learning is inherently limited because it cannot take into account the realities of the classroom. In the light of our increasing knowledge of the learning process we should, instead, insist upon dealing with those realities and forcing a substantial change in them. Education is perhaps the most important branch of scientific technology. It deeply affects the lives of all of us. We can no longer allow the exigencies of a practical situation to suppress the tremendous improvements which are within reach. The practical situation must be changed.

There are certain questions which have to be answered in turning to the study of any new organism. What behavior is to be set up? What reinforcers are at hand? What responses are available in embarking upon a program of progressive approximation which will lead to the final form of the behavior? How can reinforcements be most efficiently scheduled to maintain the behavior in strength? These questions are all relevant in considering the problem of the child in the lower grades.

In the first place, what reinforcements are available? What does the school have in its possession which will reinforce a child? We may look first to the material to be learned, for it is possible that this will provide considerable automatic reinforcement. Children play for hours with mechanical toys, paints, scissors and paper, noise-makers, puzzles—in short, with almost anything which feeds back significant changes in the environment and is reasonably free of aversive properties. The sheer control of nature is itself reinforcing. This effect is not evident in the modern school because it is masked by the emotional responses generated by aversive control. It is true that automatic reinforcement from the manipulation of the environment is probably only a mild reinforcer and may need to be carefully husbanded, but one of the most striking principles to emerge from recent research is that the *net* amount of reinforcement is of little significance. A very slight reinforcement may be tremendously effective in controlling behavior if it is wisely used.

If the natural reinforcement inherent in the subject matter is not enough, other reinforcers must be employed. Even in school the child is occasionally permitted to do "what he wants to do," and access to reinforcements of many sorts may be made contingent upon the more immediate consequences of the behavior to be established. Those who advocate competition as a useful social motive may wish to use the reinforcements which follow from excelling others, although there is the difficulty that in this case the reinforcement of one child is necessarily aversive to another. Next in order we might place the good will and affection of the teacher, and only when that has failed need we turn to the use of aversive stimulation.

. . . . .

. . . We have every reason to expect, that the most effective control of human learning will require instrumental aid. The simple fact is that, as a mere reinforcing mechanism, the teacher is out of date. This would be true even if a single teacher devoted all her time to a single child, but her inadequacy is multiplied many-fold when she must serve as a reinforcing device to many children at once. If the teacher is to take advantage of recent advances in the study of learning, she must have the help of mechanical devices.

The technical problem of providing the necessary instrumental aid is not particularly difficult. There are many ways in which the necessary contingencies may be arranged, either mechanically or electrically. An inexpensive device which solves most of the principal problems has already been constructed. It is still in the experi-

mental stage, but a description will suggest the kind of instrument which seems to be required. The device consists of a small box about the size of a small record player. On the top surface is a window through which a question or problem printed on a paper tape may be seen. The child answers the question by moving one or more sliders upon which the digits 0 through 9 are printed. The answer appears in square holes punched in the paper upon which the question is printed. When the answer has been set, the child turns a knob. The operation is as simple as adjusting a television set. If the answer is right, the knob turns freely and can be made to ring a bell or provide some other conditioned reinforcement. If the answer is wrong, the knob will not turn. A counter may be added to tally wrong answers. The knob must then be reversed slightly and a second attempt at a right answer made. (Unlike the flash-card, the device reports a wrong answer without giving the right answer.) When the answer is right, a further turn of the knob engages a clutch which moves the next problem into place in the window. This movement cannot be completed, however, until the sliders have been returned to zero.

The important features of the device are these: Reinforcement for the right answer is immediate. The mere manipulation of the device will probably be reinforcing enough to keep the average pupil at work for a suitable period each day, provided traces of earlier aversive control can be wiped out. A teacher may supervise an entire class at work on such devices at the same time, yet each child may progress at his own rate, completing as many problems as possible within the class period. If forced to be away from school, he may return to pick up where he left off. The gifted child will advance rapidly, but can be kept from getting too far ahead either by being excused from arithmetic for a time or by being given special sets of problems which take him into some of the interesting by-paths of mathematics.

The device makes it possible to present carefully designed material in which one problem can depend upon the answer to the preceding and where, therefore, the most efficient progress to an eventually complex repertoire can be made. Provision has been made for recording the commonest mistakes so that the tapes can be modified as experience dictates. Additional steps can be inserted where pupils tend to have trouble, and ultimately the material will reach a point at which the answers of the average child will almost always be right.

If the material itself proves not to be sufficiently reinforcing, other reinforcers in the possession of the teacher or school may be made contingent upon the operation of the device or upon progress through a series of problems. Supplemental reinforcement would not sacrifice the advantages gained from immediate reinforcement and from the possibility of constructing an optimal series of steps which approach the complex repertoire of mathematical behavior most efficiently.

A similar device in which the sliders carry the letters of the alphabet has been designed to teach spelling. In addition to the advantages which can be gained from precise reinforcement and careful programming, the device will teach reading at the same time. It can also be used to establish the large and important repertoire of verbal relationships encountered in logic and science. In short, it can teach verbal thinking. As to content instruction, the device can be operated as a multiple-choice self-rater.

Some objections to the use of such devices in the classroom can easily be foreseen. The cry will be raised that the child is being treated as a mere animal and that an essentially human intellectual achievement is being analyzed in unduly mechanistic terms. Mathematical behavior is usually regarded, not as a repertoire of responses involving numbers and numerical operations, but as evidences of mathematical ability or the exercise of the power of reason. It is true that the techniques which are emerging from the experimental study of learning are not designed to "develop the mind" or to further some vague "understanding" of mathematical relationships. They are designed, on the contrary, to establish the very behaviors which are taken to be the evidences of such mental states or processes. This is only a special case of the general change which is under way in the interpretation of human affairs. An advancing science continues to offer more and more convincing alternatives to traditional formulations. The behavior in terms of which human thinking must eventually be defined is worth treating in its own right as the substantial goal of education.

Of course the teacher has a more important function than to say right or wrong. The changes proposed would free her for the effective exercise of that function. Marking a set of papers in arithmetic—"Yes, nine and six *are* fifteen; no, nine and seven *are not* eighteen"—is beneath the dignity of any intelligent individual. There is more important work to be done —in which the teacher's relations to the pupil cannot be duplicated by a mechanical device. Instrumental help would merely improve these relations. One might say that the main trouble with education in the lower grades today is that the child is obviously not competent and *knows it* and that the teacher is unable to do anything about it and *knows that too*. If the advances which have recently been made in our control of behavior can give the child a genuine competence in reading, writing, spelling, and arithmetic, then the teacher may begin to function, not in lieu of a cheap machine, but through intellectual, cultural, and emotional contacts of that distinctive sort which testify to her status as a human being.

Another possible objection is that mechanized instruction will mean technological unemployment. We need not worry about this until there are enough teachers to go around and until the hours and energy demanded of the teacher are comparable to those in other fields of employment. Mechanical devices will eliminate the more tiresome labors of the teacher but they will not necessarily shorten the time during which she remains in contact with the pupil.

A more practical objection: Can we afford to mechanize our schools? The answer is clearly yes. The device I have just described could be produced as cheaply as a small radio or phonograph. There would need to be far fewer devices than pupils, for they could be used in rotation. But even if we suppose that the instrument eventually found to be most effective would cost several hundred dollars and that large numbers of them would be required, our economy should be able to stand the strain. Once we have accepted the possibility and the necessity of mechanical help in the classroom, the economic problem can easily be surmounted. There is no reason why the school room should be any less mechanized than, for example, the kitchen. A country which annually produces millions of refrigerators, dish-washers, automatic washing-machines, automatic clothes-driers, and automatic garbage disposers can certainly afford the equipment necessary to educate its citizens to high standards of competence in the most effective way.

69 | GROUP INTERVIEWING IN A CAMP FOR DISTURBED BOYS

WILLIAM C. MORSE AND DAVID WINEMAN

One of the functions of leadership is to maintain harmony within the group. This article describes how one discussion leader achieved this. Although the boys described are delinquents and their language is flashier than usual, the group processes demonstrated are the same as those in the home, at school, or at work: the individual who is being hurt by another person may try to hurt someone smaller than he; when attacked, the individual defends himself; and no group member "squeals" on another who is accused by an outsider.

When a camp plays host for the summer to ninety disturbed boys the staff must be fully aware of the potential volatility of this group. . . .

. . . . .

The problems that appear may range from periodic minor conflicts to sustained and painful disruptions which threaten to disintegrate the group. Since the staff aim

Excerpts reprinted from *Journal of Social Issues,* XIII, No. 1 (1957), 23–31, by permission of the authors and publisher.

is to maintain the group as an intact and relatively peaceful social unit, and since many of the individual personality difficulties appear most sharply when confronted with the challenges of group living, much time is spent in emergency interview sessions with the cabin groups. We have found that these interviews have been most effectively conducted by a staff member who embodies both administrative and therapeutic responsibility.

Naturally each group session runs its own course over a period of forty-five minutes to two hours and great flexibility must be used in working each one through. . . .

. . . . .

Let us turn to a sample of a group interview at the Fresh Air Camp. Although in dialogue form, this is not a transcript of an interview. It is a post-situational recall of the essential material. It is very much condensed, since the particular interview ran about one and one-half hours, but many of the expressions are verbatim and we feel the style itself contains few, if any, distortions. The group represented in this interview were senior boys between the ages of twelve and fourteen. The following member by member thumbnail sketch may serve to identify them sufficiently to clarify the dialogue.

Tony, leader of the group—a slick, manipulative delinquent—detention home background—has a well-oiled, pleasant manner with adults except in moments of sudden negative rapport—can exert positive effect on the group when motivated to do so.

Rusty, overtly aggressive—a bully—distrustful—Tony's lieutenant—highly dependent upon him—at rare times betrays an almost infantile need for adult attention and affection which is usually under very expert concealment.

Jim, sole Negro in the group—detention home background—dangerously violent during outburst of rage—sadistic—once, before camp, beat a younger boy so badly with a lead pipe that he had to be hospitalized. In the cabin he is teased and scapegoated by Tony and Rusty; he in turn vents his fury on weaker members of the group.

"Ears," so called by the group because of the large size of the members referred to—ironically enough he has developed an ear infection, carrying around huge wads of cotton which he has stuffed in them—a compulsive stealer—dependent

and insecure—he tries to avoid aggressive situations—scapegoated by Tony and Rusty when they are not attacking Jim.

Howie, a reserved, truculent boy—plays the role of an isolate in the group—jealous of Rusty's lieutenancy to, and intimacy with, Tony.

Chuck, an infantile, inept kid—the group stooge. Two other quiet boys who, together with Chuck and Ears, form a more subdued group in the cabin. As a group they are frequently scapegoated by Tony, Rusty, and Jim.

From these descriptions the reader can make an accurate guess about the nature of the problem facing this group. By the second week in camp the group is becoming progressively more disturbed because of Tony's corrupt leadership. Neighboring cabins are disturbed by the depredations of Tony and Rusty; these two, however, finagle events so that their innocent cabinmates are the ones subjected to reprisal by the enraged victim. Due to progressive needling from Tony and Rusty, Jim has had severe blowups in which he recklessly tries to maim less powerful group members, such as Ears, with whatever weapon is at hand. As the group disturbance gains momentum the staff is alert for the appearance of a fresh incident which might serve as a basis for a group interview.

It should be emphasized that waiting for a typical episode which the group interview will seek to exploit is a deliberate strategy. It is not enough simply to know the general tenor and shape of group action in a cabin. The utmost concreteness and temporal immediacy is necessary or else the alibi experts in the group will quickly seize the opportunity to accuse you of being a fussy autocrat who wants only to bore them with discussion. If you say, "Yesterday there was some trouble," this is not enough. "Well what the hell are you talking about that for? Christ, that's over. Let's get outa this goddam joint," will inevitably greet you. And even the most miserably scapegoated and protection-hungry member of the group will be swayed by this lure and chime in, echoing, "Yeh, let's get out of here," turning his energies toward gaining acceptance from his tormentor by joining in the attack on the adult.

In this case an incident soon made its appearance. Before supper, between the time they come out of swimming and the actual serving of the meal (about 45 minutes), Jim has had one of his sadistic temper outbursts against Ears, cutting him by hurling a chunk of plaster at him. We learn from the counselor that during most of the day Tony and Rusty have been needling Jim. A contagious wave of unrest and impulsivity has spread even to the quiet youngsters in the group. Tony and Rusty are riding high on the crest of this choppy sea, finding it amenable to both their tastes and talents.

An interview is held in the evening after supper, the injury to Ears having been reported to the main lodge. The interview proceeds as follows:

DISCUSSION LEADER: I called you guys together so we could talk over some of the things that are happening in the cabin. Today, for instance, there has been a lot of wild stuff and Ears [1] got hurt.

TONY [immediately assuming the role as group spokesman]: Yeh, Ears here got hurt, didn't you, Ears?

EARS [excitedly]. I'm sitting on my bunk reading a comic book and this boy [pointing to Jim] starts foolin' around.

TONY: That's right.

JIM [heatedly]: Yeh, goddamit, them two bastards are always fussing around with me [indicating, of course, Tony and Rusty].

DISCUSSION LEADER: What do you mean, Jim, fooling around with you? What do they do?

---

[1] The discussion leader never refers to the camper as "Ears" although it is printed here for purposes of easy identification.

JIM: Rusty started with me when we were in the boat—shoving me and grabbing my line and trying to throw my bait away. I ain't gonna take that, so I shoved back and then he beat the hell outa me. Boy, if they get my temper up I'll grind them so full of holes that they'll look like they was put through a sawmill.

DISCUSSION LEADER: How about it, Rusty?

RUSTY: I don't have to say a goddamn thing.

DISCUSSION LEADER: Look, you guys have got almost three more weeks out here at camp. The way things are going now, I don't think you can live with each other that long without working out some of the things that are bothering you.

Let us take our first brief recess from the interview at this point. The discussion leader is stressing as vividly as possible an elemental piece of social reality. In their present state of tension this has yet to penetrate the group's awareness. The keynote for the meeting is set: to survive together for the next three weeks we have to get down to the business of working out our problems. Let's return to our meeting and observe the impact of this on Rusty's defiant, clam-up mechanism.

RUSTY: Well, that S.O.B. [pointing to Jim] doesn't have to insult me.

DISCUSSION LEADER: How does he insult you?

RUSTY [smiling in embarrassment]: He keeps calling me "stale-crusty."

JIM [in great indignation]: Oh, you bastard, how 'bout when Tony calls you that? I don't see you smacking him around and he even tells other guys to do it.

DISCUSSION LEADER: How about that, Rusty?

RUSTY: I can let whoever I want to call me that. I don't have to take it from Jim though.

DISCUSSION LEADER: I don't mean that part of it. I agree with that. But how about the other thing that Jim said, that about Tony egging on the other guys to call you stale-crusty and then you turning around and pounding them for it?

TONY: I suppose you're gonna tell us what we can say or not! Did you ever hear of freedom of speech?

Here we see Tony suddenly taking up the defense. For, trained as he is in the logic of group behavior, as befits a good delinquent leader, he sees the interviewer's last statement for what it is—a beginning attack on his manipulation of the group power structure.

DISCUSSION LEADER: I'm only asking Rusty how he squares it with himself to pound other guys for what *you* seem to put them up to.

This is a feint by the discussion leader which has a double strategic purpose. It alludes to Tony's petty Machiavellianism while it confronts Rusty with something of a value issue: is it right to vent on other guys a fury which is really inspired by Tony? But Tony, not Rusty, carries on the counter-attack with a swift change in tactics.

TONY [*with menacing facial leers and yet, with a hint of childlike indignation*]. Listen—I have moods. When I was in the detention home I talked to the psychiatrist about them but I don't have to talk to you about them, see. And when I have moods I do what I want, see!

Here we are beginning to obtain a picture of Tony's rationale. He is a sick guy —certified as such by no less an authority than the psychiatrist at the detention home. And he maneuvers himself away from guilt about his acts as nimbly as he maneuvers the group into doing what he wishes. He fights fire with fire. In this case the admission of sickness is turned against the clinical invaders. When he has moods

he can do what he wants. And now, let us watch Rusty, who having been cued in by Tony, springs alertly into the breech.

RUSTY: Goddamit! He has moods and I have a brother who pounds hell outa me at home and I'm not gonna take anything from anybody out here. And I told it all to a visiting teacher at my school, whatever that bag's name is, and I don't have to talk about it out here and I'm not.

JIM [*with a fine sarcastic fury*]: Oh, sure. HE [*pointing to Tony*] has moods and HE [*designating Rusty*] has a brother who beats hell out of him so he turns around and beats hell outa me and around and around we go and where does that leave me?

Now we have one of the fascinating spectacles of the group interview. Here are these three tough, anti-verbal, case-work-hardened youngsters one after another spitting out vital case history information. They don't want to talk, least of all about themselves, but even when they use their case histories to defeat our clinical effort, as Tony and Rusty are doing, they bring a valuable piece of grist to our clinical mill. They confront us with the spectacle of their case histories clashing with one another. The scene they draw for themselves (better than a trained therapist could) can now be turned into a tool for surgery on their group pathology. Let's return to Jim, who, having so acidly etched out for us his plight in the pincer of Tony's moods and Rusty's brother hatred, waits sardonically for the discussion leader to reply.

DISCUSSION LEADER: O.K. Jim, you're a good psychiatrist when it comes to Tony and Rusty, let's see what you can do about yourself. Whom do you turn around and pound?

JIM [*who knows his Fifth Amendment as well as the next one*]: I don't have to talk a damn word.

DISCUSSION LEADER: Yes, Jim, but how did the trouble start with Ears today?

EARS: Yeh, ask him, ask him. All I'm doing is reading my comic and this guy Jim starts climbing up on my bunk and yanking at my feet and yelling, "Hey Ears!" And when I say please get off and he don't, I push him and then he blows his top and starts heaving around and I get hit.

DISCUSSION LEADER: Isn't that part of the answer of where you're left, Jim? You turn around and pound Ears.

JIM [angrily]: Well, I'm not gonna take it from those bastards.

With this resistive remark Jim shows that he has understood our interpretive maneuver designed to clarify the chain of aggression between Tony, Rusty, himself, and Ears. What we will have to try to show him is that just as he shouldn't take it from them, he has a certain moral blindness in taking it out on Ears. This will be, perhaps, the topic of some of the post group-interview case work sessions we will have.

The interview continues:

DISCUSSION LEADER: How about the stale-crusty crack?

HOWIE: Aw, hell, Tony started that this morning.

DISCUSSION LEADER: How about it, Tony?

TONY [refuses to comment]: The other group members look at Tony and remain silent.

DISCUSSION LEADER: All the guys here seem to want to stay in good with you, Tony. They won't say anything.

TONY [jeeringly]: Because they're my friends, that's why.

DISCUSSION LEADER: Well, Tony, I think that's swell, but it also seems like it's part of the trouble too. Let me tell you how it looks to me from what you have have been saying. The guys like you; they want you to like them. O.K., then

you have moods. Why you have them I don't know. But when you have them, for some reason you seem to get kind of mean. You have learned how to make guys fight with each other to stay in good with you. I guess when you have these mean moods you want them to do that.

TONY: Who do you think you are, a psychiatrist or something? Hey, let's call him psycho, guys.

The interpretation threatens Tony. No leader wants his own psychology to be clearly understood by his submissive following. So what he does is to try to defame the discussion leader. For who is more to be feared and despised by the acting-out delinquent than a psychiatrist? Tony's subtle yet clear challenge to the group is: "Going to believe what he says —this imitation psycho?" It is now clearly the time to anoint Tony's wound and to take the pressure off while we simultaneously summarize the group problem as this part of the group interview has highlighted it:

DISCUSSION LEADER: Look, Tony—this is not pleasant. I don't blame you for being a little sore. But let's be reasonable. It seems that you have a problem that we are going to have to work out if the guys in the cabin, including you, are going to have a decent time in camp. And you're not the only one with a problem either. Rusty here has a brother that pounds him so he is ramming around looking for a fight. Jim has a bad temper and he'd knock somebody silly if he wasn't stopped when he blows his top. Each guy is handing it out to another guy who either doesn't like to fight or who can't fight so well. Certainly you three guys—Tony, Rusty, and Jim—are going to have to work on that. Can anybody tell me why Ears has to take it from Jim, or Jim from

Rusty, or Rusty be teased into fighting by Tony? [*no group comment*]

DISCUSSION LEADER: My suggestion would be to talk it over with your counselor and also with some of the special people we have out here to help with your problems [*here the casework staff, whom they all know, are specified*]. Anytime you want to get together again as a group I'll be glad to talk to you.

We have tried to illustrate, through a synopsis of one type of group session at the Fresh Air Camp, the role of the group interview in the clinical management of the kind of boys who comprise a significant percentage of our clientele. Children with different pathologies of course react much differently than this group did. Some are quiet, some anxious and guilty. Some of the older boys seem to develop a fascination for the "round table" and ask for sessions on their own. There are times too when skilled adult leadership is needed to manage the intensity of emotional outbursts during the sessions. Seen in terms of the total clinical design of the camp, the group interview emerges as a valuable tool in coping with the problems these youngsters bring with them to the camp setting. It is seen as serving a variety of functions and as utilizing various processes that are specific to the group psychological scene. These processes serve to concretize individual pathologies which may become sources of conflict for the group. While it is a valuable tool, the group interview is still only one of many strategies that must be woven closely together for the most efficient clinical action against the pathology in these children. The most important aids to group interviewing are the followup by individual casework and the counselor handling of these issues when they arise again. The group interview seems to pave the way for an easy entré to these problems on future occasions, and the campers seem willing to use material from these meetings as a starting point for further discussion.

It should be recalled that each group session, and series of sessions with the same cabin, has its own characteristics. With the eight-year olds it is difficult to produce any problem-solving pattern while with the ten- and eleven-year olds there is discernible movement, during the session, from savage attack to workable solution. We are currently studying tape recordings of these group sessions to gain a fuller understanding of the shifting dynamics of the group in this situation. A particularly interesting phenomenon we have observed is the shift in content in the interviews following the discussion leader's understanding acceptance of guilt-producing behavior on the part of the boys. Hostility and tension seem to melt, and the campers reveal real empathy when, out of concern over the meaning of their own behavior, they discuss individual and group needs and problems. More needs to be known about how these defenses are penetrated and of the subsequent effect of such sessions on the group life.

70 | TEACHER—ANNE SULLIVAN MACY

HELEN KELLER

Helen Keller's teacher, in helping the deaf, dumb, and blind child to make contact with the world, also found her own way back to society. What enabled this institutionalized orphan girl, herself plagued by poverty, isolation, prejudice, and half-blindness, to find the patience, kindness, strength, and persistence to provide both Helen's salvation and her own? Here Miss Keller describes this twofold miracle.

I

A daughter of Irish immigrants, at that time the most despised social group in the Northeast, Annie Sullivan was born in squalid poverty on April 4, 1866, in Feeding Hills, Massachusetts, and as far back as she could remember she had had trouble with her eyes. They still bothered her. Her mother died when she was eight years old, leaving two other children. Her father abandoned all three two years later and Annie never learned what became of him. Her younger sister Mary was placed with relatives and Annie and her seven-year-old brother Jimmie were sent to the State Infirmary, the almshouse, at Tewksbury, Annie because she was difficult to manage and too blind to be useful, Jimmie because he was becoming helplessly lame with a tubercular hip.

They entered the almshouse in February 1876 and Jimmie died in May. Annie stayed four years. No one outside was interested in her and she had no friends but her fellow paupers. It was one of them who told her that there were special schools for the blind and as time went on—she lost track of time in Tewksbury—her desire for an education grew. To escape from the pit of degradation and disease in which she lived seemed impossible until the stench from the almshouse rose so high that the State Board of Charities ordered an investigation. The investigators did not discover her. The inmates knew the name of the chairman and when the committee members arrived she flung herself towards them, unable to distinguish one from another, and cried out, "Mr. Sanborn, Mr. Sanborn, I want to go to school!"

She reached the Perkins Institution in October 1880 and there, at the age of fourteen, began her education by learning to read with her fingers. The school had no facilities for taking care of its pupils during vacations and when summer came she was put out to work in a rooming house in Boston. Through one of the lodgers she found her way to the Massachusetts Eye and Ear Infirmary and in August Dr. Bradford performed an operation on her left eye. The next August he attended to the right eye and when the operations were over Annie could see well enough to read in the ordinary way for limited periods of time, but not well enough to warrant transfer to a school for the seeing. She remained at Perkins for six years, graduating in 1886 as valedictorian of her class. The school had done what it could. The rest was up to her.

She recognized her handicaps—her meager years of education, her lack of contact with the amenities of gracious living, and, above all, her uncertain, precarious sight—but she had hoped for something more exciting than looking after a deaf-blind child. Captain Keller's offer was the best she had. After she had accepted it she spent some months reading Dr. Howe's reports on Laura Bridgman, a painful task because of her eyes. She already knew the manual alphabet. Like her schoolmates, she had learned it so as to talk with Laura, who was still cloistered at the Perkins Institution because she had never been able to adapt herself to any other kind of life. And yet Laura was the mark to aim at. No other deaf-blind person had come near the peak upon which she stood.

Red-eyed from another operation on her eyes and from crying with homesickness, Annie Sullivan arrived in Tuscumbia on March 3, 1887, a date that Helen has always cherished as her "soul's birthday." She began at once spelling into Helen's hand, suiting the word to the action, the action to the word, and the child responded by imitating the finger motions like a bright, inquisitive animal. It took a month to reach the human mind. On April 5, a date not second to March 3 in importance, the Phantom Helen made contact with reality. While Annie Sullivan pumped water over her hand it came to the child in a flash that water, wherever it was found, was water, and that the finger motions she had just felt on her palm meant water and nothing else. In that thrilling moment she found the key to her kingdom. Everything had a name and she had a way to learn the names. She formed a question by pointing to Annie Sullivan. "Teacher," Annie replied.

From that date Helen's progress was so rapid that educators soon became aware that a great teacher was at work, greater even than Dr. Howe. At the age of ten Helen announced that she was going to learn to talk with her mouth like other people instead of with her fingers like a deaf person, and when, after eleven lessons in oral speech she was able to say, however haltingly, "I-am-not-dumb-now," there seemed no limit to what she might achieve. But a fragmentation had occurred in public opinion. One segment pushed the teacher aside and called Helen a miracle. Another gave the whole credit to the teacher and called Helen an automaton. . . .

That hurt—it still hurts. But there were a few, notable among them Dr. Bell, who understood that it was the combination of gifted, intuitive teacher and eager, intelligent pupil that was producing the astonishing results. Helen and Teacher kept to their course, never apart, and Helen went on to Radcliffe College, entering in 1900 when she was twenty years old and coming out four years later with a *cum laude* degree won in open competition with girls who could see and hear. But even this

was not enough. As long as Annie Sullivan lived, and she died in 1936, a question remained as to how much of what was called Helen Keller was in reality Annie Sullivan. The answer is not simple. During the creative years neither could have done without the other.

. . . . .

II

It was a bright, clear spark from Teacher's soul that beat back the sooty flames of thwarted desire and temper in little Helen's no-world. That spark was the word "water." Compassion in the old sense does not describe the springs of Teacher's motives. Her disbelief in nature as an unfailing friend of humanity lay back of her efforts to liberate Helen—"Phantom" I prefer to call the little being governed only by animal impulses, and not often those of a docile beast. Teacher's fight against her own blindness began in her childhood, and the partial restoration of her sight while she was in school at Perkins Institution for the Blind in Boston had not ended her struggle to maintain her ascendancy over nature. That struggle lasted as long as her earth-life.

Secretly or openly she always resented what seemed to her the purposeless evils that had marred her sight and laid waste the health, sanity, and happiness of millions throughout the world. How ruthless then was her assault upon the blindness, deafness, and muteness that bound her little pupil in triple dungeon of thwarted instincts. Boldly she resolved to put herself in the place of nature and topple it from its aimless supremacy over Helen by substituting love and inventive thought for the unconscious cruelty of the child's fate.

This is a period in Teacher's life which distresses me to remember. Naturally I wish that after the intoxicating tide of delight that swept over her when the operations made it possible for her to read with her eyes, she might have found a child responsive to her sympathetic touch. But, alas! Phantom had no sense of "natural" bonds with humanity. All the sweetness of childhood created by friendly voices and the light of smiling faces was dormant in her. She did not understand obedience or appreciate kindness. I remember her as plump, strong, reckless, and unafraid. She refused to be led, and had to be carried by force upstairs when she received her first lesson. Another time her table manners required correction. Phantom was in the habit of picking food out of her own plate and the plates of others with her fingers. Annie Sullivan would not put up with such behavior, and a fight followed during which the family left the room. Phantom acted like a demon, kicking, screaming, pinching her would-be deliverer and almost throwing her out of her chair, but Annie succeeded in compelling her to eat with a spoon and keep her hands out of the plate. Then Phantom threw her napkin on the floor, and after an hour's battle Annie made her pick it up and fold it. One morning Phantom would not sit down to learn words which meant nothing to her, and kicked over the table. When Annie put the table back in its place and insisted on continuing the lesson, Phantom's fist flew like lightning and knocked out two of Annie's teeth.

A sorrier situation never confronted a young woman on fire with a noble purpose. Phantom's parents were apt to interfere whenever attempts were made to discipline her. For this reason Annie won their consent to get her away to a quiet place, and, at their suggestion, took the child to a vine-covered annex near the homestead, Ivy Green. The furniture was changed so that Phantom would not recognize it—my smell memory too is different—and it was agreed that the family would come to them every day, without letting Helen know of their visits. From Teacher's later testimony I know that the two were, so to speak, caged in the annex,

and I marvel that Annie dared to stay alone with such a menace to her personal safety.

Already I have referred to several fights between Annie and Phantom, not because I have any coherent or detailed remembrance of them, but because they indicate the grueling nature of the work Teacher had undertaken. In *The Story of My Life*, which I wrote with the carelessness of a happy, positive young girl, I failed to stress sufficiently the obstacles and hardships which confronted Teacher—and there are other defects in the book which my mature sense of her sacrifice will not permit to go uncorrected.

In my memory of the annex I am conscious of a Phantom lost in what seemed to her new surroundings. I perceive sudden jerks, pulls, and blows not dealt by Annie but by Phantom herself trying to escape restraining arms. How like a wild colt she was, plunging and kicking! Certainly it was a sturdy Phantom who belabored her supposed enemy. There comes back to me a scuffle round and round an object that my touch recollections represent as a bed, and a firm gesture of Annie to make her lie down or get up and dress.

Phantom had no sense of time, and it was years before she learned of the many exhausting hours which Annie spent trying to bring her under control without breaking her spirit. Even that was only partly accomplished when the two went home. Then Phantom grew angry over Annie's repeated attempts to impress upon her the difference between "water" and "mug." Tactually I recall quick footsteps in the room, a hand—my mother's—seizing Phantom and dragging her away for a sound spanking. After that Phantom began to improve, but still she lacked the normal child's love of praise. She was not aware that she had been punished because she did not distinguish between right and wrong. Her body was growing, but her mind was chained in darkness as the spirit of fire within the flint. But at last, on April

5, 1880, almost exactly a month after her arrival in Tuscumbia, Annie reached Phantom's consciousness with the word "water." This happened at the well-house. Phantom had a mug in her hand and while she held it under the spout Annie pumped water into it and as it gushed over the hand that held the mug she kept spelling w-a-t-e-r into the other hand. Suddenly Phantom understood the meaning of the word, and her mind began to flutter tiny wings of flame. Caught up in the first joy she had felt since her illness, she reached out eagerly to Annie's ever-ready hand, begging for new words to identify whatever objects she touched. Spark after spark of meaning flew through her mind until her heart was warmed and affection was born. From the well-house there walked two enraptured beings calling each other "Helen" and "Teacher." Surely such moments of delight contain a fuller life than an eternity of darkness.

71 | THE ACCURACY OF TEACHERS' JUDGMENTS CONCERNING THE SOCIOMETRIC STATUS OF SIXTH-GRADE PUPILS

NORMAN E. GRONLUND

This synopsis of a much longer article describes a way of measuring a teacher's empathy or sensitivity to the feelings of pupils by determining the accuracy with which he predicts how children will select one another. It also shows that complex and thorough work may be reported efficiently and precisely.

This study is an attempt to determine the accuracy of teachers' judgments concerning the degree to which sixth-grade pupils are accepted by their classmates, and the relationship of certain variables to the accuracy of these judgments. The acceptance of sixth-grade pupils by their classmates was determined by a sociometric test and referred to as the pupils' sociometric status.

The method of investigating the problem consisted of the following procedures: A sociometric test administered to the pupils in forty sixth-grade classes requested each pupil to choose the five classmates with whom he would most prefer to work, the five classmates near whom he would most prefer to sit. In addition, each pupil was requested to respond to eight questions concerning the freedom he had in carrying out routine class activities.

Each teacher, in the same forty classes, made judgments concerning the sociometric status of her pupils on the criteria of work companion, play companion, and seating companion. Each teacher also indicated which three boys and three girls she most preferred and which three boys and three girls she least preferred as pupils in her class. Information concerning the teacher's training and experience were obtained for each teacher.

The . . . data were analyzed with standard statistical procedures and found to be consistent with the following conclusions:

Reprinted from *Sociometry Monographs*, No. 25 (1951), p. 66, by permission of the author.

1. There is a difference between teachers in the accuracy of their judgments of the sociometric status of sixth-grade pupils in the classroom. Correlation coefficients representing the average accuracy of each teacher's judgments ranged from .268 to .838, with a mean of .595.

2. There is *no* difference in the accuracy of teachers' judgments of the sociometric status of boys and girls.

3. There is a difference in the accuracy of teachers' judgments of the sociometric status of pupils among the criteria of work companion, play companion, and seating companion.

4. There is *no* relationship between the average accuracy of the teachers' judgments of the sociometric status of pupils and each of the following variables: age of teacher, years of teaching experience, length of time in present position, semester hours of college training, recency of college training, semester hours in education courses, semester hours in psychology courses, size of class, marital status of teacher, and length of time the teacher had been in contact with the class.

5. There is a relationship between taking a course in Child Development and more accurate judgments of the sociometric status of pupils.

6. There is a tendency for teachers to over-judge the sociometric status of pupils they most prefer, and to under-judge the sociometric status of pupils they least prefer.

7. There is a negative relationship between the degree to which a teacher's judgments are biased in the direction of her preferences and the accuracy of her judgments of sociometric status.

8. There is *no* relationship between the freedom pupils have in class and the accuracy of teachers' judgments of sociometric status.

72 | THE DISCOVERY AND ENCOURAGEMENT OF EXCEPTIONAL TALENT

LEWIS M. TERMAN

After studying intelligence for over fifty years, Terman summarized in an address delivered in 1954 his research on children of high talent. Exploding the myths that genius is akin to insanity and that talented children soon "burn themselves out," his studies revealed that superior children are healthier, better adjusted than average, and continue to be superior through adulthood.

I have often been asked how I happened to become interested in mental tests and gifted children. My first introduction to the scientific problems posed by intellec-

Excerpts reprinted from *American Psychologist*, IX (1954), 221–30, by permission of T. E. Terman, Executor of the Estate of Lewis M. Terman, and of the American Psychological Association.

tual differences occurred well over a half-century ago when I was a senior in psychology at Indiana University and was asked to prepare two reports for a seminar, one on mental deficiency and one on genius. Up to that time, despite the fact that I had graduated from a normal college as a Bachelor of Pedagogy and had taught school for five years, I had never so much as heard of a mental test. The reading for those two reports opened up a new world to me, the world of Galton, Binet, and their contemporaries. The following year my MA thesis on leadership among children (Terman, 1904) was based in part on tests used by Binet in his studies of suggestibility.

Then I entered Clark University, where I spent considerable time during the first year in reading on mental tests and precocious children. Child prodigies, I soon learned, were at that time in bad repute because of the prevailing belief that they were usually psychotic or otherwise abnormal and almost sure to burn themselves out quickly or to develop postadolescent stupidity. "Early ripe, early rot" was a slogan frequently encountered. By the time I reached my last graduate year, I decided to find out for myself how precocious children differ from the mentally backward, and accordingly chose as my doctoral dissertation an experimental study of the intellectual processes of fourteen boys, seven of them picked as the brightest and seven as the dullest in a large city school (Terman, 1906). These subjects I put through a great variety of intelligence tests, some of them borrowed from Binet and others, many of them new. The tests were given individually and required a total of 40 or 50 hours for each subject. The experiment contributed little or nothing to science, but it contributed a lot to my future thinking. Besides "selling" me completely on the value of mental tests as a research method, it offered an ideal escape from the kinds of laboratory work which I disliked and in which I was more than ordinarily inept. (Edward Thorndike confessed to me once that *his* lack of mechanical skill was partly responsible for turning *him* to mental tests and to the kinds of experiments on learning that required no apparatus.)

However, it was not until I got to Stanford in 1910 that I was able to pick up with mental tests where I had left off at Clark University. By that time Binet's 1905 and 1908 scales had been published, and the first thing I undertook at Stanford was a tentative revision of his 1908 scale. This, after further revisions, was published in 1916. The standardization of the scale was based on tests of a thousand children whose IQ's ranged from 60 to 145. The contrast in intellectual performance between the dullest and the brightest of a given age so intensified my earlier interest in the gifted that I decided to launch an ambitious study of such children at the earliest opportunity.

My dream was realized in the spring of 1921 when I obtained a generous grant from the Commonwealth Fund of New York City for the purpose of locating a thousand subjects of IQ 140 or higher. More than that number were selected by Stanford-Binet tests from the kindergarten through the eighth grade, and a group mental test given in 95 high schools provided nearly 400 additional subjects. The latter, plus those I had located before 1921, brought the number close to 1,500. The average IQ was approximately 150, and 80 were 170 or higher (Terman *et al.*, 1925).

The twofold purpose of the project was, first of all, to find what traits characterize children of high IQ, and secondly, to follow them for as many years as possible to see what kind of adults they might become. This meant that it was necessary to select a group representative of high-testing children in general. With the help of four field assistants, we canvassed a school population of nearly a quarter-million in the urban and semi-urban areas of California. Two careful checks on the methods used showed that not more than 10 or 12 per cent of the children who could have qualified for the group in the schools canvassed were missed. A sample of close to 90 per cent insured that whatever traits were typical of these children would be typical of high-testing children in any comparable school population.

Time does not permit me to describe the physical measurements, medical examinations, achievement tests, character and interest tests, or the trait ratings and other supplementary information obtained from parents and teachers. Nor can I here describe the comparative data we obtained for control groups of unselected children. The more important results, however, can be stated briefly: children of IQ 140 or higher are, in general, appreciably superior to unselected children in physique, health, and social adjustment; markedly superior in moral attitudes as measured either by character tests or by trait ratings; and vastly superior in their mastery of school subjects as shown by a three-hour battery of achievement tests. In fact, the typical child of the group had mastered the school subjects to a point about two grades beyond the one in which he was enrolled, some of them three or four grades beyond. Moreover, his ability as evidenced by achievement in the different school subjects is so general as to refute completely the traditional belief that gifted children are usually one-sided. I take some pride in the fact that not one of the major conclusions we drew in the early 1920's regarding the traits that are typical of gifted children has been overthrown in the three decades since then.

Results of thirty years' follow-up of these subjects by field studies in 1927–28, 1939–40, and 1951–52, and by mail follow-up at other dates, show that the incidence of mortality, ill health, insanity, and alcoholism is in each case below that for the generality of corresponding age, that the great majority are still well adjusted socially, and that the delinquency rate is but a fraction of what it is in the general population. Two forms of our difficult Concept Mastery Test, devised especially to reach into the stratosphere of adult intelligence, have been administered to all members of the group who could be visited by the field assistants, including some 950 tested in 1939–40 and more than 1,000 in 1951–52. On both tests they scored on the average about as far above the generality of adults as they had scored above the generality of children when we selected them. Moreover, as Dr. Bayley and Mrs. Oden have shown, in the twelve-year interval between the two tests, 90 per cent increased their intellectual stature as measured by this test. "Early ripe, early rot" simply does not hold for these subjects. So far, no one has developed post-adolescent stupidity!

As for schooling, close to 90 per cent entered college and 70 per cent graduated. Of those graduating, 30 per cent were awarded honors and about two-thirds remained for graduate work. The educational record would have been still better but for the fact that a majority reached college age during the great depression. In their undergraduate years 40 per cent of the men and 20 per cent of the women earned half or more of their college expenses, and the total of undergraduate and graduate expenses earned amounted to $670,000, not counting stipends from scholarships and fellowships, which amounted to $350,000.

The cooperation of the subjects is indicated by the fact that we have been able to keep track of more than 98 per cent of the original group, thanks to the rapport fostered by the incomparable field and office assistants I have had from the beginning of the study to the present. I dislike to think how differently things could have gone with helpers even a little less competent.

The achievement of the group to mid-life is best illustrated by the case histories of the 800 men, since only a minority of the women have gone out for professional careers (Terman, 1954). By 1950, when the men had an average age of 40 years, they had published 67 books (including 46 in the fields of science, arts, and the humanities, and 21 books of fiction). They had published more than 1,400 scientific, technical, and professional articles; over 200 short stories, novelettes, and plays; and 236 miscellaneous articles on a great variety of subjects. They had also authored more than 150 patents. The figures on publications do not include the hundreds of publications by journalists that classify as news stories, editorials, or newspaper columns; nor do they include the hundreds if not thousands of radio and TV scripts.

The 800 men include 78 who have taken a PhD degree or its equivalent, 48 with a medical degree, 85 with a law degree, 74 who are teaching or have taught in a four-year college or university, 51 who have done basic research in the physical sciences or engineering, and 104 who are engineers but have done only applied research or none. Of the scientists, 47 are listed in the 1949 edition of *American Men of Science*. Nearly all of these numbers are from 10 to 20 or 30 times as large as would be found for 800 men of corresponding age picked at random in the general population, and are sufficient answer to those who belittle the significance of IQ differences.

The follow-up of these gifted subjects has proved beyond question that tests of "general intelligence," given as early as six, eight, or ten years, tell a great deal about the ability to achieve either presently or 30 years hence. Such tests do not, however, enable us to predict what direction the achievement will take, and least of all do they tell us what personality factors or what accidents of fortune will affect the fruition of exceptional ability. Granting that both interest patterns and special aptitudes play important roles in the making of a gifted scientist, mathematician, mechanic, artist, poet, or musical composer, I am convinced that to achieve greatly in almost any field, the special talents have to be backed up by a lot of Spearman's g, by which is meant the kind of general intelligence that requires ability to form

many sharply defined concepts, to manipulate them, and to perceive subtle relationships between them; in other words, the ability to engage in abstract thinking.

The study by Catharine Cox (1926) of the childhood traits of historical geniuses gives additional evidence regarding the role of general intelligence in exceptional achievement. That study was part of our original plan to investigate superior ability by two methods of approach: (a) by identifying and following living gifted subjects from childhood onward; and (b) by proceeding in the opposite direction and tracing the mature genius back to his childhood promise. With a second grant from the Commonwealth Fund, the latter approach got under way only a year later than the former and resulted in the magnum opus by Cox entitled *The Early Mental Traits of Three Hundred Geniuses* (1926). Her subjects represented an unbiased selection from the top 510 in Cattell's objectively compiled list of the 1,000 most eminent men of history. Cox and two able assistants then scanned some 3,000 biographies in search of information that would throw light on the early mental development of these subjects. The information thus obtained filled more than 6,000 typed pages. Next, three psychologists familiar with mental age norms read the documentary evidence on all the subjects and estimated for each the IQ that presumably would be necessary to account for the intellectual behavior recorded for given chronological ages. Average of the three IQ estimates was used as the index of intelligence. In fact two IQ's were estimated for each subject, one based on the evidence to age 17, and the other on evidence to the mid-twenties. The recorded evidence on development to age 17 varied from very little to an amount that yielded about as valid an IQ as a good intelligence test would give. Examples of the latter are Goethe, John Stuart Mill, and Francis Galton. It was the documentary information on Galton, which I summarized and published in 1917 (Terman, 1917), that decided me to prepare plans for the kind of study that was carried out by Cox. The average of estimated IQ's for her 300 geniuses was 155, with many going as high as 175 and several as high as 200. Estimates below 120 occurred only when there was little biographical evidence about the early years.

It is easy to scoff at these post-mortem IQ's, but as one of the three psychologists who examined the evidence and made the IQ ratings, I think the author's main conclusion is fully warranted; namely, that "the genius who achieves highest eminence is one whom intelligence tests would have identified as gifted in childhood."

Special attention was given the geniuses who had sometime or other been labeled as backward in childhood, and in every one of these cases the facts clearly contradicted the legend. One of them was Oliver Goldsmith, of whom his childhood teacher is said to have said "Never was so dull a boy." The fact is that little Oliver was writing clever verse at 7 years and at 8 was reading Ovid and Horace. Another was Sir Walter Scott, who at 7 not only read widely in poetry but was using correctly in his written prose such words as "melancholy" and "exotic." Other alleged childhood dullards included a number who disliked the usual diet of Latin and Greek but had a natural talent for science. Among these were the celebrated German chemist Justus von Liebig, the great English anatomist John Hunter, and the naturalist Alexander von Humboldt, whose name is scattered so widely over the maps of the world.

In the cases just cited one notes a tendency for the direction of later achievement to be foreshadowed by the interests and preoccupations of childhood. I have tried to determine how frequently this was true of the 100 subjects in Cox's group whose childhood was best documented. Very marked foreshadowing was noted in the

case of more than half of the group, none at all in less than a fourth. Macaulay, for example, began his career as historian at the age of 6 with what he called a "Compendium of Universal History," filling a quire of paper before he lost interest in the project. Ben Franklin before the age of 17 had displayed nearly all the traits that characterized him in middle life: scientific curiosity, religious heterodoxy, wit and buffoonery, political and business shrewdness, and ability to write. At 11 Pascal was so interested in mathematics that his father thought it best to deprive him of books on this subject until he had first mastered Latin and Greek. Pascal secretly proceeded to construct a geometry of his own and covered the ground as far as the 32nd proposition of Euclid. His father then relented. At 14 Leibnitz was writing on logic and philosophy and composing what he called "An Alphabet of Human Thought." He relates that at this age he took a walk one afternoon to consider whether he should accept the "doctrine of substantial forms."

Similar foreshadowing is disclosed by the case histories of my gifted subjects. A recent study of the scientists and nonscientists among our 800 gifted men (Terman, 1954) showed many highly significant differences between the early interests and social attitudes of those who became physical scientists and those who majored in the social sciences, law, or the humanities. Those in medical or biological sciences usually rated on such variables somewhere between the physical scientists and the nonscientists.

What I especially want to emphasize, however, is that both the evidence on early mental development of historical geniuses and that obtained by follow-up of gifted subjects selected in childhood by mental tests point to the conclusion that capacity to achieve far beyond the average can be detected early in life by a well-constructed ability test that is heavily weighted with the g factor. It remains to be seen how much the prediction of future achievement can be made more specific as to field by getting, in addition, measures of ability factors that are largely independent of *g*. It would seem that a 20-year follow-up of the thousands of school children who have been given Thurstone's test of seven "primary mental abilities" would help to provide the answer. At present the factor analysts don't agree on how many "primary" mental abilities there are, nor exactly on what they are. The experts in this field are divided into two schools. The British school, represented by Thomson, Vernon, and Burt, usually stop with the identification of at most three or four group factors in addition to *g*, while some representing the American school feed the scores of 40 or 50 kinds of tests into a hopper and manage to extract from them what they believe to be a dozen or fifteen separate factors. Members of the British school are as a rule very skeptical about the realities underlying the minor group factors. There are also American psychologists, highly skilled in psychometrics, who share this skepticism. It is to be hoped that further research will give us more information than we now have about the predictive value of the group factors. Until such information is available, the scores on group factors can contribute little to vocational guidance beyond what a good test of general intelligence will provide.

I have always stressed the importance of *early* discovery of exceptional abilities. Its importance is now highlighted by the facts Harvey Lehman (1953) has disclosed in his monumental studies of the relation between age and creative achievement. The striking thing about his age curves is how early in life the period of maximum creativity is reached. In nearly all fields of science, the best work is done between ages 25 and 35, and rarely later than 40. The peak productivity for works of lesser merit is usually reached 5 to 20 years later; this is true in some twenty fields of science, in philosophy, in most kinds of

musical composition, in art, and in literature of many varieties. The lesson for us from Lehman's statistics is that the youth of high achievement potential should be well trained for his life work before too many of his most creative years have been passed.

This raises the issue of educational acceleration for the gifted. It seems that the schools are more opposed to acceleration now than they were thirty years ago. The lockstep seems to have become more and more the fashion, notwithstanding the fact that practically everyone who has investigated the subject is against it. Of my gifted group, 29 per cent managed to graduate from high school before the age of 16½ years (62 of these before 15½), but I doubt if so many would be allowed to do so now. The other 71 per cent graduated between 16½ and 18½. We have compared the accelerated with the nonaccelerated on numerous case-history variables. The two groups differed very little in childhood IQ, their health records are equally good, and as adults they are equally well adjusted socially. More of the accelerates graduated from college, and on the average nearly a year and a half earlier than the nonaccelerates; they averaged high in college grades and more often remained for graduate work. Moreover, the accelerates on the average married .7 of a year earlier, have a trifle lower divorce rate, and score just a little higher on a test of marital happiness (Terman and Oden, 1947). So far as college records of accelerates and nonaccelerates are concerned, our data closely parallel those obtained by the late Noel Keys (1938) at the University of California and those by Pressey (1949) and his associates at Ohio State University.

The Ford Fund for the Advancement of Education (1953) has awarded annually since 1951 some 400 college scholarships to gifted students who are not over 16½ years old, are a year or even two years short of high school graduation, but show good evidence of ability to do college work. Three quarters of them are between 15½ and 16½ at the time of college entrance. A dozen colleges and universities accept these students and are keeping close track of their success. A summary of their records for the first year shows that they not only get higher grades than their classmates, who average about two years older, but that they are also equally well adjusted socially and participate in as many extracurricular activities. The main problem the boys have is in finding girls to date who are not too old for them! Some of them started a campaign to remedy the situation by urging that more of these scholarships be awarded to girls.

The facts I have given do not mean that all gifted children should be rushed through school just as rapidly as possible. If that were done, a majority with IQ of 140 could graduate from high school before the age of 15. I do believe, however, that such children should be promoted rapidly enough to permit college entrance by the age of 17 at latest, and that a majority would be better off to enter at 16. The exceptionally bright student who is kept with his age group finds little to challenge his intelligence and all too often develops habits of laziness that later wreck his college career. I could give you some choice examples of this in my gifted group. In the case of a college student who is preparing for a profession in science, medicine, law, or any field of advanced scholarship, graduation at 20 instead of the usual 22 means two years added to his professional career; or the two years saved could be used for additional training beyond the doctorate, if that were deemed preferable.

Learned and Wood (1938) have shown by objective achievement tests in some 40 Pennsylvania colleges how little correlation there is between the student's knowledge and the number of months or years of his college attendance. They found some beginning sophomores who had ac-

quired more knowledge than some seniors near their graduation. They found similarly low correlations between the number of course units a student had in a given field and the amount he knew in that field. Some with only one year of Latin had learned more than others with three years. And, believe it or not, they even found boys just graduating from high school who had more knowledge of science than some college seniors who had majored in science and were about to begin teaching science in high schools! The sensible thing to do, it seems, would be to quit crediting the individual high school or the individual college and begin crediting the individual student. That, essentially, is what the Ford Fund scholarships are intended to encourage.

Instruments that permit the identification of gifted subjects are available in great variety and at nearly all levels from the primary grades to the graduate schools in universities.

. . . . .

I have discussed only tests of intelligence and of school achievement. There is time to mention only a few of the many kinds of personality tests that have been developed during the last thirty-five years: personality inventories, projective techniques by the dozen, attitude scales by the hundred, interest tests, tests of psychotic and predelinquent tendencies, tests of leadership, marital aptitude, masculinity-femininity, et cetera. The current output of research on personality tests probably equals or exceeds that on intelligence and achievement tests, and is even more exciting.

Along with the increasing use of tests, and perhaps largely as a result of it, there is a growing interest, both here and abroad, in improving educational methods for the gifted. Acceleration of a year or two or three, however desirable, is but a fraction of what is needed to keep the gifted child or youth working at his intellectual best. The method most often advocated is curriculum enrichment for the gifted without segregating them from the ordinary class. Under ideal conditions enrichment can accomplish much, but in these days of crowded schools, when so many teachers are overworked, underpaid, and inadequately trained, curriculum enrichment for a few gifted in a large mixed class cannot begin to solve the problem. The best survey of thought and action in this field of education is the book entitled *The Gifted Child*, written by many authors and published in 1951 (Witty). In planning for and sponsoring this book, The American Association for Gifted Children has rendered a great service to education.

But however efficient our tests may be in discovering exceptional talents, and whatever the schools may do to foster those discovered, it is the prevailing *Zeitgeist* that will decide, by the rewards it gives or withholds, what talents will come to flower. In Western Europe of the Middle Ages, the favored talents were those that served the Church by providing its priests, the architects of its cathedrals, and the painters of religious themes. A few centuries later the same countries had a renaissance that included science and literature as well as the arts. Although presumably there are as many potential composers of great music as there ever were, and as many potentially great artists as in the days of Leonardo da Vinci and Michaelangelo, I am reliably informed that in this country today it is almost impossible for a composer of *serious* music to earn his living except by teaching, and that the situation is much the same, though somewhat less critical, with respect to artists.

The talents most favored by the current *Zeitgeist* are those that can contribute to science and technology. If intelligence and achievement tests don't discover the potential scientist, there is a good chance that the annual Science Talent Search will, though not until the high school years.

Since Westinghouse inaugurated in 1942 this annual search for the high school seniors most likely to become creative scientists, nearly 4,000 boys and girls have been picked for honors by Science Service out of the many thousands who have competed. As a result, "Science Clubs of America" now number 15,000 with a third of a million members—a twentyfold increase in a dozen years (Davis, 1953). As our need for more and better scientists is real and urgent, one can rejoice at what the talent search and the science clubs are accomplishing. One may regret, however, that the spirit of the times is not equally favorable to the discovery and encouragement of potential poets, prose writers, artists, statesmen, and social leaders.

But in addition to the over-all climates that reflect the *Zeitgeist*, there are localized climates that favor or hinder the encouragement of given talents in particular colleges and universities. I have in mind especially recent investigations of the differences among colleges in the later achievement of their graduates. One by Knapp and Goodrich (1952) dealt with the undergraduate origin of 18,000 scientists who got the bachelor's degree between 1924 and 1934 and were listed in the 1944 edition of *American Men of Science*. The list of 18,000 was composed chiefly of men who had taken a PhD degree, but included a few without a PhD who were starred scientists. The IBM cards of these men were then sorted according to the college from which they obtained the bachelor's degree, and an index of productivity was computed for each college in terms of the proportion of its male graduates who were in the list of 18,000. Some of the results were surprising, not to say sensational. The institutions that were most productive of future scientists between 1924 and 1934 were not the great universities, but the small liberal arts colleges. Reed College topped the list with an index of 132 per thousand male graduates. The California Institute of Technology was second with an index of 70. Kalamazoo College was third with 66, Earlham fourth with 57, and Oberlin fifth with 56. Only a half-dozen of the great universities were in the top fifty with a productivity index of 25 or more.

· · · · ·

The causes of these differences are not entirely clear. Scores on aptitude tests show that the intelligence of students in a given institution is by no means the sole factor, though it is an important one. Other important factors are the quality of the school's intellectual climate, the proportion of able and inspiring teachers on its faculty, and the amount of conscious effort that is made not only to discover but also to motivate the most highly gifted. The influence of motivation can hardly be exaggerated.

In this address I have twice alluded to the fact that achievement in school is influenced by many things other than the sum total of intellectual abilities. The same is true of success in life. In closing I will tell you briefly about an attempt we made a dozen years ago to identify some of the nonintellectual factors that have influenced life success among the men in my gifted group. Three judges, working independently, examined the records (to 1940) of the 730 men who were then 25 years or older, and rated each on life success. The criterion of "success" was the extent to which a subject had made use of his superior intellectual ability, little weight being given to earned income. The 150 men rated highest for success and the 150 rated lowest were then compared on some 200 items of information obtained from childhood onward (Terman and Oden, 1947). How did the two groups differ?

During the elementary school years, the A's and C's (as we call them) were almost equally successful. The average grades were about the same, and average scores on achievement tests were only a trifle higher for the A's. Early in high school the groups began to draw apart in scholarship, and by the end of high school the slump of the C's was quite marked. The slump could not be blamed on extracurricular activities, for these were almost twice as common among the A's. Nor was much of it due to difference in intelligence. Although the A's tested on the average a little higher than the C's both in 1922 and 1940, the average score made by the C's in 1940 was high enough to permit brilliant college work, in fact was equaled by only 15 per cent of our highly selected Stanford students. Of the A's, 97 per cent entered college and 90 per cent graduated; of the C's, 68 per cent entered but only 37 per cent graduated. Of those who graduated, 52 per cent of the A's but only 14 per cent of the C's graduated with honors. The A's were also more accelerated in school; on the average they were six months younger on completing the eighth grade, 10 months younger at high school graduation, and 15 months younger at graduation from college.

The differences between the educational histories of the A's and C's reflect to some degree the differences in their family backgrounds. Half of the A fathers but only 15 per cent of the C fathers were college graduates, and twice as many of A siblings as of C siblings graduated. The estimated number of books in the A homes was nearly 50 per cent greater than in the C homes. As of 1928, when the average age of the subjects was about 16 years, more than twice as many of the C parents as of A parents had been divorced.

Interesting differences between the groups were found in the childhood data on emotional stability, social adjustments, and various traits of personality. Of the 25 traits on which each child was rated by parent and teacher in 1922 (18 years before the A and C groups were made up), the only trait on which the C's averaged as high as the A's was general health.

The superiority of the A's was especially marked in four volitional traits: prudence, self-confidence, perseverance, and desire to excel. The A's also rated significantly higher in 1922 on leadership, popularity, and sensitiveness to approval or disapproval. By 1940 the difference between the groups in social adjustment and all-round mental stability had greatly increased and showed itself in many ways. By that time four-fifths of the A's had married, but only two-thirds of the C's, and the divorce rate for those who had married was twice as high for the C's as for the A's. Moreover, the A's made better marriages; their wives on the average came from better homes, were better educated, and scored higher on intelligence tests.

But the most spectacular differences between the two groups came from three sets of ratings, made in 1940, on a dozen personality traits. Each man rated himself on all the traits, was rated on them by his wife if he had a wife, and by a parent if a parent was still living. Although the three sets of ratings were made independently, they agreed unanimously on the four traits in which the A and C groups differed most widely. These were "persistence in the accomplishment of ends," "integration toward goals, as contrasted with drifting," "self-confidence," and "freedom from inferiority feelings." For each trait three critical ratios were computed showing, respectively, the reliability of the A–C differences in average of self-ratings, ratings by wives, and ratings by parents. The average of the three critical ratios was 5.5 for perseverance, 5.6 for integration toward goals, 3.7 for self-confidence, and 3.1 for freedom from inferiority feelings. These closely parallel the traits that Cox (1926) found to be especially characteristic of the 100 leading geniuses in her group whom she rated on many aspects of personality; their three outstanding traits she defined as "persistence of motive and effort," "confidence in their abilities," and "strength or force of character."

There was one trait on which only the parents of our A and C men were asked to rate them; that trait was designated "common sense." As judged by parents, the A's are again reliably superior, the A–C difference in average rating having a critical ratio of 3.9. We are still wondering what self-ratings by the subjects and ratings of them by their wives on common sense would have shown if we had been impudent enough to ask for them!

Everything considered, there is nothing in which our A and C groups present a greater contrast than in drive to achieve and in all-round mental and social adjustment. Our data do not support the theory of Lange-Eichbaum (1932) that great achievement usually stems from emotional tensions that border on the abnormal. In our gifted group, success is associated with stability rather than instability, with absence rather than with presence of disturbing conflicts—in short with well-balanced temperament and with freedom from excessive frustrations. The Lange-Eichbaum theory may explain a Hitler, but hardly a Churchill; the junior senator from Wisconsin, possibly, but not a Jefferson or a Washington.

At any rate, we have seen that intellect and achievement are far from perfectly correlated. To identify the internal and external factors that help or hinder the fruition of exceptional talent, and to measure the extent of their influences, are surely among the major problems of our time. These problems are not new; their existence has been recognized by countless men from Plato to Francis Galton. What is new is the general awareness of them caused by the manpower shortage of scientists, engineers, moral leaders, statesmen, scholars, and teachers that the country must have if it is to survive in a threatened world. These problems are now being investigated on a scale never before approached, and by a new generation of workers in several related fields. Within a couple of decades vastly more should be known than we know today about our resources of potential genius, the environmental circumstances that favor its expression, the emotional compulsions that give it dynamic quality, and the personality distortions that can make it dangerous.

REFERENCES

1. COX, CATHARINE C. *The early mental traits of three hundred geniuses.* Vol. II of *Genetic studies of genius*, Terman, L. M. (Ed.) Stanford: Stanford Univer. Press, 1926.

2. DAVIS, W. Communicating science. *J. Atomic Scientists*, 1953, 337–340.

3. KEYS, N. The underage student in high school and college. *Univer. Calif. Publ. Educ.*, 1938, 7, 145–272.

4. KNAPP, R. H., & GOODRICH, H. B. *Origins of American scientists.* Chicago: Univer. of Chicago Press, 1952.

5. KNAPP, R. H., & GREENBAUM, J. J. *The younger American scholar: his collegiate origins.* Chicago: Univer. of Chicago Press, 1953.

6. LANGE-EICHBAUM, W. *The problem of genius.* New York: Macmillan, 1932.

7. LEARNED, W. S., & WOOD, B. D. The student and his knowledge. *Carnegie Found. Adv. Teaching Bull.*, 1938, No. 29.

8. LEHMAN, H. C. *Age and achievement.* Princeton: Princeton Univer. Press, 1953.

9. PRESSEY, S. L. *Educational acceleration: appraisals and basic problems.* Columbus: Ohio State Univer. Press, 1949.

10. TERMAN, L. M. A preliminary study in the psychology and pedagogy of leadership. *Pedag. Sem.*, 1904, 11, 413–451.

11. TERMAN, L. M. Genius and stupidity: a study of some of the intellectual processes of seven "bright" and seven "dull" boys. *Pedag. Sem.*, 1906, 13, 307–373.

12. TERMAN, L. M. The intelligence quotient of Francis Galton in childhood. *Amer. J. Psychol.*, 1917, 28, 209–215.

13. TERMAN, L. M. (Ed.), et al. *Mental and physical traits of a thousand gifted children.* Vol. I of *Genetic studies of genius*, Terman, L. M. (Ed.) Stanford: Stanford Univer. Press, 1925.

14. TERMAN, L. M., & ODEN, M. H. *The gifted child grows up.* Vol. IV of *Genetic studies of genius*, Terman, L. M. (Ed.) Stanford: Stanford Univer. Press, 1947.

15. TERMAN, L. M. Scientists and nonscientists in a group of 800 gifted men. *Psychol. Monogr.*, 1954, 68, in press.

16. WITTY, P. (Ed.) *The gifted child.* Boston: Heath, 1951.

17. *Bridging the gap between school and college.* New York: The Fund for the Advancement of Education, 1953.

73 | SOME CHARACTERISTICS OF VERY SUPERIOR CHILDREN

W. DRAYTON LEWIS

The findings discussed here concur, in general, with those reported in selection 72, although, unlike Terman, Lewis contends that individuals with very high IQs—over 145—tend to be maladjusted, and he finds all socio-economic levels represented in his superior group.

Popular opinion has long held the very superior individual to be some kind of freak, a very different and queer person who is likely to come to no good end,

Reprinted from the *Journal of Genetic Psychology*, LXII (1943), 301–9, by permission of the author and The Journal Press.

who can probably only look to a rather futile future at best. Psychologists have shown this popular belief to be erroneous, as they have done with so many popular ideas, but they have raised the question whether or not it is possible that very superior children may be too bright for their own good. The late Leta Hollingworth was quoted in the press on several occasions as having stated that the most desirable level of intelligence probably lies between IQ's 125 and 145, that if one could choose his child's level of ability he should choose within this range since the best adjustment, educational, personal, and social, appears to be made by children whose ability falls within this range and since those who possess intelligence quotients above the level may be so bright, may be so superior, and thus different from the children with whom they must associate in school and on the playground, that adjustment may be very difficult in the ordinary school and social situation.

Dr. Hollingworth also expressed the belief in various articles that the adjustment of superior children becomes increasingly difficult as the IQ's rise above 150. This study is concerned with very superior children and endeavors to throw some light upon the educational and personality adjustments of children of varying degrees of superiority with the hope of determining, in some measure, whether or not adjustments do become increasingly difficult as the IQ rises above 145 or 150.

Coördinated Studies in Education, Incorporated, was able to collect a large amount of data on some 45,000 elementary school children in grades four to eight, inclusive. These children were found in 455 schools and 310 communities in 36 states. The children included in this survey were given the Kuhlmann-Anderson Test and these test results were made the basis of selection for the subjects included in this study. Two methods of selection were used. For some phases of this study all those who obtained an IQ rating of 145 or more were selected and they are compared with those whose IQ ratings were between 125 and 144 in order to determine whether those of the latter group were making superior adjustments to those of the most superior group at the

time the tests were given. The second method of selection used was to choose the 10 with the highest intelligence quotients in each grade since the intelligence quotients did not run as high in some grades as in others, indicating, perhaps, that the Kuhlmann-Anderson Tests are not of equal difficulty at all grade levels.

The writer feels that he is justified in stating that the children included in these two groups possess very superior ability since each child represents approximately one in a thousand in ability as measured by the Kuhlmann-Anderson Test. The purpose of this study is to investigate the home backgrounds and the personal and educational adjustments of these very superior children within the limits of the data available.

The methods of selection used in setting up the groups of superior children which have been publicized the most extensively in the literature have been such that some have expressed the opinion, which many have accepted almost without question, that superior children come from quite superior socio-economic levels. A socio-economic rating scale was set up for the purpose of investigating the origins of the very superior children included in this study. The socio-economic rating scale used takes account of the father's occupation, the presence in the home of a telephone, auto, radio, regular servant, and newspaper, and the room-per-person ratio. This scale gives a possible range of ratings from 0 to 18. The teachers also gave the home an economic rating of inferior, average, or superior—inferior to represent the lowest quarter and superior to represent the top quarter of the community economically.

The homes from which these very superior children come, that is, the children with IQ ratings of 145 and over, obtained ratings from 2 to 15, with a median rating of 8. The teachers were unable to give a rating relative to the economic status of many of the homes but 38 of the homes were rated. Seven were rated inferior, 27 average, and only four superior. This means that only four of the homes from which these very superior children came were judged to be on a par with the upper fourth of the community economically, whereas seven were rated as falling in the lower fourth economically, with approximately 70 per cent representing the middle half of the community economically. This means that some of the children come from homes where poverty is present, some from homes which are characterized by abundance, while the majority come from a wide range of middle class homes.

The highly significant finding, though, is that these very superior children can be expected in practically any type of home, as far as socioeconomic rating is concerned. It is true that they tend to come from homes which have average ratings slightly higher than the average of the total population surveyed, but this fact can easily be over-emphasized and misinterpreted. It must be recognized that averages may be very misleading and that one gets an incorrect picture of the origins of these very superior children if emphasis is placed upon the average. The important finding is that these children can be expected in all kinds of homes, that the distribution of very superior ability is such that it might be termed a highly democratic distribution.

It is interesting to note that the median socio-economic rating for the group of superior children whose intelligence quotients range from 125 to 144 is slightly higher than that of the very superior group, 8.5 as compared with 8.0. Throughout this study the number of subjects, 930 for the 125 to 144 group and 50 for the very superior group, is too small to give statistically reliable results. For this reason, the writer does not believe that one is justified in interpreting the above results as indicating that the very superior group comes from homes which are in-

ferior to those of the 125 to 144 group, but it does seem evident that they do not come from superior homes. The superiority of the homes of both of these groups is not very great when compared with the median rating for the entire population surveyed, which is 6.61.

The occupations of the fathers of the [very superior children] were listed. This listing, which is given in Table 1, emphasizes the fact that very superior ability may be expected in all types of homes.

One child was in an orphanage, and no information was available relative to the father, and the father of another child was an inmate of a state mental hospital.

A survey of the interests of this group of very superior children, as revealed by participation in the extra-curricular activities of the school and by their hobbies, gives no evidence of abnormality of interests for the group as a whole. They have, as a group, more extensive interests than average children and their interests in music and reading are very definitely superior to those of the total population surveyed. Three out of every five of these very superior children are designated as being interested in music, which is far greater than the interest of any other group in music. Equally significant is the fact that they have quite normal interests in all types of sports and games. The most significant finding here, we believe, is that the interests of this group of very superior children are quite normal in every sense of the term.

Most of the [very superior] children included in this study were given the *BPC Personal Inventory* and the scores obtained indicate that, as a group, their adjustment, as measured by this Inventory, is superior to that of any other group of children included in this survey [population of survey was approximately 45,000 children]. Their median score was 23.6, as compared with 27.8 for the group whose intelligence quotients lie between 125 and 144, 28.5 for the entire upper

TABLE 1.	
Professional group—5	**Skilled labor—16**
High school principal	Farmer—6
Captain—United States Army	Barber
Doctor	Printer
Minister	Mechanic—3
Designer	Mason
	Mail carrier
Business and managerial group—18	Plumber
Merchant—2	Sign painter
Salesman—5	Sergeant in army
Fruit broker	
Grocer—2	**Semi-skilled and unskilled labor—12**
Pharmacist	Road work—2
Jeweler	Mill hand—2
Security exchange commission	Miner
Aviator	Logger—2
Clerk	Truck driver
Insurance	Common laborer—2
Postmaster	Factory worker—2
Assistant superintendent of railroad	

10 per cent of this population, and 35 for an unselected group. This would appear to indicate that this very superior group has achieved a type of emotional stability, as revealed by this Inventory, which is quite superior to that of the other groups.

The entire population included in this study was rated on the basis of a list of 70 personality traits. It was suggested to those doing the rating that they pick out not less than five or more than 12 traits which they deemed to be most characteristic of each child to be rated. These personality ratings indicate that, on the whole, these very superior children have achieved personalities which are far superior to those of average children, or even to those of the upper 10 per cent. The data appear to justify a statement to the effect that very superior children, at least those included in this study, have superior personalities.

The characteristic which appears to differentiate this very superior group most definitely is *adventuresome*. One in three of these children is rated as being adventuresome whereas only one in 6.5 of the upper 10 per cent, and one in 10 of the total population surveyed are so characterized. Other personality characteristics which the teachers who did the rating believed to be particularly characteristic of this group are ambitious, dependable, energetic, friendly, happy, honest, investigative, leader, likes jokes, original, polite, and tidy.

Most individuals who have given any thought to the matter will concede that the very superior child, as judged by intelligence tests, is the most promising material which comes to the schools. It is important, therefore, to note any information, available in the data at hand, relative to the adjustment of the very superior children to the school situation which they must face. It would appear, offhand, that any teacher should recognize as possessing exceptional ability a child who rates one in a thousand on an intelligence test. It certainly is not to be expected that any of these would be rated as dull or mentally sluggish. Neither of these expectations is realized, if we are to judge by the ratings made by the teachers.

Only one boy in five and two girls in five are characterized as being *precocious* or *mentally quick*. It must be recalled that these children rate as one in a thousand on tested mental ability. When children of such unusual ability do not stand out in the ordinary classroom one would appear to be justified in assuming that the school is failing to challenge the child of exceptional ability. It is to be noted that this is even more the case with the boys than with the girls. It is equally significant to note that two of this group have been designated as *dull* or *mentally sluggish* by their teachers. While this is not a large percentage, it is hardly to be expected that teachers would so designate such brilliant children. The fact that a higher percentage of the group whose intelligence quotients are above 144 are so designated than of those with intelligence quotients between 125 and 144 might be interpreted as indicating some greater maladjustment relative to the school situation for the very superior group, but the subjects are too few to justify anything more than a hazardous guess since it may be wholly a chance distribution. There is nothing in these characterizations, however, to indicate that the schools are doing much for these very exceptional children.

There is some evidence that those with the highest intelligence quotients are somewhat more maladjusted than those who are slightly below them in intelligence. Of the 10 children who attained intelligence quotients of 160 or more, seven appear to be somewhat maladjusted as far as personality traits or educational achievement are concerned. On the basis of personailty traits which are assigned to them by their teachers, six of the 10 appear to be suffering from personality maladjustments. That is, they are listed by their teachers as possessing several traits which mental hygienists rate as undesirable. The traits referred to here are "goody-goody," cute, destructive, domineering, day-dreaming, cruel, immature, nervous, over-sensitive about self, over-critical of others, too easily frightened, stubborn, inattentive in class, slovenly, suggestible, quarrelsome, lack of interest in work, pouting, unhappy, moody, or depressed, and self-conscious. If only one of these traits was ascribed to a child it was not considered to be particularly significant. The child was only considered maladjusted when the teacher believed that several of these traits were characteristic of the child. The Personal Inventory only indicated maladjustment in about a third of these cases and it should be noted that whenever the Inventory indicated maladjustment the teachers' ratings also indicated maladjustment. This would appear to indicate that the Inventory is not sensitive enough to detect maladjustment in all cases. A seventh of the 10 children mentioned above appears to have had a well-adjusted personality but was quite retarded educationally. That is, the educational age achieved on a battery achievement test fell below the mental age as indicated by the intelligence test. Twelve children obtained intelligence quotients between 150 and 160, and there is evidence of maladjustment in the case of only two of these.

Few of these very superior children who are maladjusted give evidence of aggressive behavior. Rather, they are characterized by behavior of the withdrawing or egocentric type. The characteristics most frequently attributed to them, as noted above, are day-dreaming, nervous, moody, depressed, unhappy, over-sensitive about self, over-critical of others, suggestible, inattentive in class, lazy, self-conscious.

Unfavorable living conditions appear to react very powerfully, and even disastrously, upon these very superior children. Ten of the 50 were shown as having come from homes of poverty. All except one of the 10 appear to show the effects of this type of background and that one is well-adjusted both personally and educationally. . . .

Those with intelligence quotients above 145 show more educational maladjustment than those with intelligence quotients from 125 to 144. Sixty-four and five-tenths per cent of the former have educational ages which are below their mental ages whereas only 52.5 per cent of the latter have educational ages below their mental ages.

Decile scores were available for each grade of the total population on reading, geography, arithmetic problems, and language usage, the scores having been obtained from the *Unit Scales of Attainment Battery* which was administered to all of the children. In order to determine how these very superior children were achieving relative to the entire population surveyed, their scores were scattered in the various deciles in which they fell. No consideration is given here to the fact that these children, if working up to ability, should obtain scores which would fall in the extreme upper ranges of the highest decile since they are one in a thousand in ability. Rather they are treated as if they were one in 10 in ability.

It is striking, indeed, that so many of these very able children are doing so little in the way of achievement. As usual, they are doing better in reading than in other subjects, which again emphasizes that reading is more closely dependent upon intelligence than the other school subjects. It would appear to be a severe indictment of our present set up in the elementary school that less than half of these exceedingly able students, if we are to trust our measure of intelligence and achievement, are obtaining achievement scores which fall in the top decile and it is even more severe indictment that so many of them are so low in achievement that they earn scores which fall in the lowest five deciles. The comparisons shown in Table 2 indicate that the highest group, those with *IQ*'s of 145 or more, are achieving very little more than those with quotients from 125–144, in spite of their superior ability. It is evident from Table 2 that as large a percentage, except for reading, of the latter group obtain scores falling within the two highest deciles as there are of the former group.

The latter part of this study has stressed the maladjustments of the very superior group. Too much emphasis can be placed on this aspect of the study and there is a danger that the reader will conclude that these children represent a badly adjusted group. The writer believes, after a careful study of all cases, that the only conclusion which can be arrived at is that, as a group, they are by no means as badly adjusted as some previous studies might lead us to believe. Many, in fact the majority, have made excellent adjustments. The data at

TABLE 2. A COMPARISON OF THE PERCENTAGES OF CHILDREN WITH *IQ*'s ABOVE 144 AND THOSE WITH *IQ*'s FROM 125 TO 144 WHOSE SCORES ON DESIGNATED ACHIEVEMENT TESTS FELL IN VARIOUS DECILES AS SHOWN	TENTH DECILES		NINTH AND TENTH DECILES		LOWEST FIVE DECILES	
	IQ		*IQ*		*IQ*	
	125–144	145 Up	125–144	145 Up	125–144	145 Up
Reading	40.2	46.7	56.2	63.9	14.5	9.6
Geography	32.9	42.0	49.6	51.7	15.6	19.3
Arithmetic problem	33.8	42.8	52.4	52.3	17.2	22.3
Language usage	34.5	35.0	50.2	49.2	19.7	19.0

hand indicate, we believe, that the majority are very normal children making normal adjustments and there is no evidence here that abnormality or queerness is the typical characteristic. There is maladjustment to be sure, but it does appear to be evident that their very superior ability has enabled them to adjust, in the majority of cases, to an educational system which we know neglects them. When maladjustment is present, especially in the very superior group, it indicates great social waste, and there is maladjustment. This maladjustment appears to be slightly more prevalent in the very superior group as might well be anticipated. All of this calls for a readjustment of our elementary educational program in order to serve more adequately the most promising material which comes to our schools.

74 | REACHING REJECTED YOUTH

RALPH DAVID FERTIG

This description of a street worker's prevention of delinquencies forces the editors to conclude that if Chicago had 200 such trained workers, and New York, 400, delinquency would be dealt a death blow in these cities. This is not a large number, considering that Chicago's 10,000 police and New York's more than 26,000 have failed to slow down the tragic increase in juvenile crime in those cities.

Hyde Park had become concerned about its hostile youth. Some young people did not "fit" into the *nice* church and community center programs. Most of them loitered threateningly on a street corner to which little bands drifted—or were pushed. In time a street corner would become the chief bond of these rejected youths; it would be their holding in the community and—their fort. Fear led to further confusion and rejection by the community, and this to further development of the street clubs in isolation from society and social values.

In 1955 the Welfare Council of Metropolitan Chicago, under a grant from the Wieboldt Foundation, set up the Hyde Park Youth Project. This agency was to test and demonstrate a bringing-together of various social work techniques and community forces for a neighborhood-centered attack on juvenile delinquency.

Revised from the article in *Teleclass Study Guide in Child Psychology*, 1958, by permission of the author and the Chicago Board of Education.

In partnership with the Hyde Park Neighborhood Club, a local settlement house, Youth Project staff helped stimulate a public recognition of delinquency as a problem of the total community.

As part of this broad approach to a community and all of its young people, a worker was sent out to the street corners to meet with some of the clusters of antisocial youth. This Street Club Worker, identified as a Group worker from the Neighborhood Club, met with the staffs of both agencies. He would meet with the youth on the streets, come to know them, help them find new channels for expression which would reduce or obviate anti-social behavior. In finding new opportunities and channels for his young clients, he would draw on every fibre and resource in the community before he was through. The help began as he met the youths where they were. This study follows some of his work.

The boys on the corners were 13 through 20 years of age; 90% of those past

16 had left school; less than 40% of them lived with their natural parents, over half lived in buildings slated for demolition for civic redevelopment. They were of American-Negro, Irish, Mexican, German, Scandinavian, Asiatic, Southern Mountain (white), Eastern European, and Italian backgrounds, in that order of frequency.

Many of these boys had common roots in their co-membership in a onetime "protective alliance." This alliance was in existence at the time the worker first established contact. It was formed by fifty-five teenaged American boys. This group included some Mexicans and Indians but excluded Negroes. These youths, whose delinquent tendencies may have had diverse origins, were provided with a focus for uniting themselves partly by the community's ambivalent reactions to the in-migration of Negroes. The movement of Negroes into the community so stimulated a conflict in the values of the dominant culture, that aggression directed against Negroes did not appear to be seriously disapproved of for the teen-agers in the groups which were encountered in the street club program. Community groups verbalized acceptance and brotherhood for the Negro newcomers, and local organizations passed resolutions supporting this point of view. However, the reactions of a substantial proportion of the adult community was the traditional pattern of whites moving out and raising the general level of rental to the newcomers moving in.

The boys interpreted these apparent inconsistencies as tacit approval by the adult community for resistance to and aggression against the Negroes who were moving in. However, the boys had to unite themselves outside of existing community agencies and institutions because they couldn't hope for approval of their aggressive behavior despite the opposition that was apparent to them. Antagonism toward the Negro newcomers was thus the chief focus of the alliance when the worker first encountered the boys considered here. An early job, then, was helping to set up a "peace club" which arbitrated disputes between white and Negro teenagers.

SPLITTING BY AGE GROUPS

Representatives from the rival, racially based street club met with the worker and the Director of the Neighborhood Club in the Neighborhood Club building. Over the course of several months, aggression between the two racial groups was diminished. The worker encouraged the group to split into two smaller groups, the "big guys" and the "little guys." The behavior of the "big guys" in social situations was directed, goal-oriented and reserved. In social situations the behaviors of the "little guys" was diffused, dis-oriented and conspicuous. The "big guys" formed the Cobras, and their twenty-four members were served both in the building-centered program of the Neighborhood Club and outside of it. They now spoke of being "free" from identification with the more irresponsible "little guys" whose loud-mouthed and ostentatious activities helped focus police and community concern on them all. Furthermore, it was the "little guys" who started a disturbance and then came running to the "big guys" to help them "finish" the job.

On the other hand, the twenty-two "little guys" spoke of being happily relieved of the bullying "bigger guys." And now that they could not implicate the older fellows so easily, they tended to turn more to one another for other kinds of satisfactions within their own group, one which they called the Serpents.

FORMING AN AUTO-MECHANICS CLUB

As the Redevelopment moved many of the teenagers out of the area, some came to rely heavily upon means of transportation to retain their social lives. This, combined with the interest American adolescents have come to express in cars, suggested the formation of an auto-mechanics club. Seven of the Cobras, who had become proficient at socialized forms of organization combined with five of the working boys who, in the course of their semi-skilled means of employment, had picked up some knowledge of mechanics. At the worker's suggestion, five of the boys in lower status clubs were involved; these boys were especially responsive to the opportunity of moving up into this kind of association, and were willing to work hard. Still a fourth clique of four boys joined the group from among those in the Serpents who had not been involved in the building program at the Neighborhood Club; the young men were especially articulate and had helped talk around the idea of an auto-mechanics club for a long time before it got formed. When the group actually got underway, the verbal abilities of these boys was put to use in a public relations program with the neighbors on the block in which the garage was located.

Out of their own organization, the 21 members raised money for garage rent and tools, fashioned a constitution and came to demand conformity to written group agreements. The specialized, functional cliques of "organizers," "mechanics," "workers," and "talkers" eventually gave way to a more integrated, comprehensive organization. Responsibility and safe driving practices were militantly demanded by the group, and by the fall of 1956, 4 months after the group was founded, 6 of the members were dropped from the organization. Of these 6, three were picked up in the less demanding group of Serpents who moved into the agency; 2 were helped in personalized plans; and one joined the Jr. Raiders.

THE RAIDERS

Until quite recently, there was a well known gang in the community with an almost 30 year tradition. Passed on from father to son, this organization remained isolated from the middle class intellectual dominant culture and often preyed upon it. This gang was known as the Raiders.

When some of those from the Serpents who did not move into the Neighborhood Club building cast about for identification with a street corner tradition, they picked up on the defunct Raiders and called themselves the Jr. Raiders. Altogether 19 boys gathered on the corner which had been dominated by their namesakes, though it had been abandoned to an almost all-Negro populace. They bought jackets with the name "Raiders" printed on them, and enjoyed the identities with which they were associated. Overnight, this device stimulated community concern and fear. Attracting attention to their control of this vital corner, the boys blocked the sidewalk, shouted vulgar language, and engaged in a great deal of conspicuous horseplay. Leaders of the group went a few steps further and burglarized stores and taverns.

THE ROLES OF THE STREET WORKER

These, then, are some of the groups with which the street club worker was engaged. The intent of his engagement was to present to each of these groups a person who, through his connection with a neighborhood agency, can represent the community's interest in the boys and concern for helping them find solutions for their needs. He shows his own sincere acceptance of them and at the same time communicates to them through his actions, the standards of mature behavior that he hopes they may take as a model for their own. This process of identification is mediated through the liking and respect that the boys develop for him, in response to the same attitude on his part towards them. As he gains their confidence and trust he is in a position to know ahead of time about crisis situations and to take preventive or, through his presence, protective action, while supporting the new and incompletely developed standards. Some examples of techniques used are provided below.

Shortly after first contact with the Cobras, the worker was still feeling his way in relationships with the boys and was less judgmental than he was to be at a later, more securely accepted stage. His responses to modify anti-social behavior were largely in terms of *appealing to the self interest* of the group or individual. The "Peace Club" was formed with this appeal, and the worker, in an encounter with a youth not a member of a street group, had this experience:

Encountered Ned Beaverman[1] in front of the hot dog stand and asked him how things were. He told me how his brother had been beaten up last night out on the West Side. Ned was going out there tonight to see his "girlfriend," but he was prepared, he affirmed, patting the chest of his black leather jacket. "What've you got there?" I asked. Ned showed me a lead pipe; "They ain't gonna' get me without a fight!" You know what will happen to you if you're found with that on you," worker admonished Ned who had been in trouble with the police before. "Yeah, but I'll get a black eye or a bloody nose if I don't have this on me." "Which is worse," I asked, "a black eye or 6 months in 'Parental'?" "The six months," growled Ned, as he passed the lead pipe to the worker.

After a relationship of greater acceptance the worker tended to be more personally judgmental. Some months later, Lefty Leoni was discovered with a piece of rubber hose which suggested an attempt at siphoning gas from cars.

"That's a screwy damn thing . . . to do," worker asserted. "I know you talk big and tough but I always had you figured for a pretty straight guy, underneath it all," Lefty was embarrassed; he told of all the times he had felt temptation hot on his back but had kicked it off. "Cris', all the times I wanted to

---

steal hub caps and it would've been so easy but I never once did it!" Lefty spoke of his economic needs; worker pointed out hazards of stealing as so much greater than those of gasoline poverty. This led to a discussion of money earning and Lefty's need for a job. Worker explained he couldn't recommend anyone for a job who could so easily go astray. Lefty asked for another chance to prove himself, but he needed a job in order to stay out of trouble. Worker reflected on how Lefty would have to avoid getting into trouble on the job, indicated we'd see how things went for the next week.

The inadequacy of this approach alone was discovered at an early point. Boys whose acting out behavior was part of a deep-seated emotional difficulty had little concern for consequences. There was, for example, Guy Nelson, 17, who lives with his mother and two brothers, and mother's boy friend in a building slated for demolition. Guy's father is a chronic alcoholic, lives with another woman in a nearby tenement flat; mother and father have never formalized their separation by divorce and father occasionally returns to his wife. Neither parent accepts much responsibility for the children; father provides no support. Guy suffers from bad eyesight and chronic headaches. He has quite a police record.

"You want to know how screwy I was? Last night I walked out on my back porch, I was going to jump. The headache drove me nuts! Went out in my shorts, too."

Worker reassured Guy that the headaches could be cured. Guy wouldn't let the Neighborhood Club subsidize the clinical costs which would be involved, because the Club was keeping him out for a month as disciplinary action because of his drunken behavior at last Friday night's dance. He had scaled the roof of the building and perched there, threatening to jump before a grand audience that poured out from the gym and disrupted the dance. "I can't let the Club pay for curing my headaches, because I'm going to break into their dances!"

Why did Guy climb up onto the roof? "I like it up there; that's why I like steeplejack

work. I like being up high, on top of everybody, where nobody can tell me what to do.
Even if they came up after me, they couldn't
get me down—they wouldn't push me down.
Not even the cops would get me cause they
wouldn't shoot at me as long as I was up
there. Man, it's nice up there!"

He returned to suicide. "About 8 months
ago, tried to hang myself—don't tell anybody
—used an old raggedy suede belt and the
damned thing broke. I've thought of it plenty
of times. Nothing to do or think about at
home, with my headaches killing me."

In another encounter with Guy, the
worker had this experience:

Guy "tested" me by letting me know of a
burglary he was going to pull in the company
of Robert West and Jr. Sorillo (both of these
latter are now in detention—the first at St.
Charles and the second at Pontiac for subsequent acts). Guy told the others they could
"trust" this worker even though this worker
tried to talk the three out of this on the basis
of it not being smart, the harshness of the
consequences could far exceed the possible
joy of the act. But the three boys went on,
with the worker standing 10 feet or so away
and tossed a rock through the window of a
laundry around the corner from Hot Dog
Haven; then, very much scared, the boys took
rapid flight down 55th Street, urging the
worker to come on along fast with them,
before anyone got caught. Their fear had
fortunately preceded their taking anything,
but just to make sure this local laundry would
not be robbed blind by the morning, I called
in a complaint to the police station, stating
an old man had just broken into the laundry
—he was probably drunk, I told the law over
the phone. Then a few minutes later, as I
crouched in an alley-way with the boys in
back of the infamous "Dorchester building,"
we heard the squad cars tear down to the
laundry and the fellows allowed as maybe
they hadn't been too wise, after all.

This somewhat-less-than-honest handling of the incident appears, in retrospect, to have been unwise; it could not
but help to advance confusion around
values. This was least helpful to Guy who
so needed a consistent set of standards.

Much later, when the worker was out of
town and Guy got into some more trouble, he related it to the worker's absence,
saying,

"If you'd'a been around, this never
would've happened, but I got to feeling that
way and there was nobody else I could go to."

It was clear that Guy needed much
more help, and efforts were made to reach
him through his medical needs toward
eventual involvement in case work services. The trouble reported above, however,
intervened, and he is now incarcerated.

When group anti-social acts are anticipated, it would be most common for the
worker to move in with *suggestions of
socially acceptable alternatives*. For example, an incident with some Cobras:

After they began necking I moved down
to the corner on the steps of Frank's Movers
caddy-cornered from Walgreen's. Here, were
Eddie————, Ted Kinally, and another guy.
The three fellows spent a great deal of time
suggesting to one another what he would do
with each I'll chick who hovered into view on
any of the four corners. And they delighted
in shouting out abusive suggestions to those
too old, ugly, or harmless looking to resist
remarks concerning their cars or persons. After
picking up this drift, I was even further convinced that the one area of interest which
would involve these kids is an objective discussion of sex and dating problems. These
fellows want to, but just cannot relate in any
personal or real terms. And they lack great
knowledge in the procedures by which one
gains entry to such relating.

This led to a discussion program and
social events which did "involve" these
otherwise lethargic youth and which led
into making the Cobras a co-ed group at
the Neighbor Club.

. . . According to Claude there was going
to be a fight against the Puerto Rican kids.
The story I was able to put together went
like this: Al Blinski had been walking down
55th St. with his girl-friend, Lila Lopez (of
Filipine origin), when three Puerto Rican
fellows marched out from the hot dog stand

and grabbed Lila. Al threw the offending fellow off and threatened to fight him. This fellow along with his two friends ran down the street to Blackstone a block and a half east, saying that they would form their gang and be back to take care of Al. These fellows claimed that the Puerto Ricans, even now, were organizing themselves two blocks east on Blackstone and further down the block from me a group was huddling at the corner of Blackstone and 55th.

The police came by and asked the mob to disperse. This gave me a chance to walk the two blocks to Blackstone where I encountered a group of 8 or 9 Puerto Rican fellows. I addressed the group partly in English, partly in Spanish, and they formed themselves in a semi-circle about me. I told them that I was a worker from the Hyde Park Neighborhood Club, mentioned its location, and said that I hoped that these fellows would be coming to the Neighborhood Club in the Fall at which time we will reopen once again in night time programs. I said that I understood, however, that some of the fellows from the Neighborhood Club planned to fight "you fellows" tonight and that I didn't think it was very smart to fight with our neighbors, that we all have to live in the same neighborhood, together, and certainly we ought to be able to be friends.

These Puerto Rican fellows agreed that they wanted to be friends but proceeded to explain what their interpretation was of the incident between Al Blinski and Lila Lopez, and three of their group. They claimed as they left Hot Dog Haven one of their group approached Lila for some matches. Al did not understand what he was saying and Al suddenly jumped on him from behind and shouted at them, they thought, because they are from Puerto Rico and they were not going to take this sort of persecution lying down. So they were going to run off and form their gang and properly put those persons who persecute Puerto Ricans in their place. They explained that they don't want to start a fight and they do not have many numbers in this neighborhood, but they could call friends from other neighborhoods who would get down here in a hurry to join them in any fight. Among those who represented this point of view worker spotted Luis Villareal. I asked him whether I had seen him at the Neighbor-

hood Club. He said yes, and we went on to discuss some of the prejudices against the Puerto Ricans. I said that I agreed with them that there are some prejudices that other kids have that have to be gotten rid of, but the way we are going to get rid of these prejudices is by working together as friends and not fighting one another. They agreed to this and said if the other fellows wanted to have peace and call the fight off they would be willing to have peace and call the fight off. I asked if they would be willing to send two representatives to a truce meeting and they said they would. I asked them to wait for me while I returned to where the Cobras and the Copperheads were re-forming their ranks across 55th Street from Hot Dog Haven. I asked for two representatives from this conglomeration of kids for the purpose of talking things over with the other gang of Puerto Ricans. Lefty stepped forth and named Flash Berry to join him as representatives to the truce meeting. Lefty asked for Luis by name suggesting that he and one other fellow come from the Puerto Rican group. Lefty knows Luis well, being a next door neighbor to him, in the Dorchester building. Lefty and Flash headed toward Dorchester, the street which lay half way between the vantage points of each of the gangs. I ran ahead and then asked Luis and one other fellow to come forth. Luis willingly took position as spokesman for the group and was joined by Tony, last name unknown. Tony, Luis, Lefty, Flash and I met on the corner of Dorchester and 55th while gangs hovered awaiting our actions or decisions a block in either direction. Luis started it off saying, "We don't want to start any fights." Lefty held his hand out agreeing, saying, "We don't want to start a fight either, but if you guys are ready for one——." Luis went on to say, "Well we don't want to start it. If you're ready for one we'll fight you, but we don't want to start this one." There was a good deal of repetition of this point back and forth. Lefty agreed strongly that we have to live in the same neighborhood together, there is no point our fighting each other every night which is what we have to do if we were to get this thing started tonight.

At worker's suggestion hands were shaken all around and the delegates returned to their respective gangs. I could see Luis and Tony returning to their fellow Puerto Rican friends joyously and being greeted joyously. There were, however, mixed reactions from the Cobras. The fellows were somewhat quiet, saying, "Yea, I guess its a good thing as long as we are going to be living in the same neighborhood with those guys." The girls, however, notably Lea, Bootie, Joyce Anderson, and Minda Mayer were quite angry, and disappointed in the fact that there was no fight. They egged the fellows on suggesting that they were yellow, that they were cowards because they weren't willing to take on the Puerto Ricans.

These *mediating* techniques have specific application to inter-group conflicts; however the worker often must help mediate between the social standards for which he stands and the behavior of individuals who reject these standards. One way of doing this is by *example setting*. Without verbally imposing demands for the more desirable behavior, the worker communicates what he considers desirable by doing it . . . :

Went to Hot Dog Haven for a quick bite and encountered Harry who vilified worker's name as thoroughly as this worker has ever been cursed at. Basis for the swelling hostility was the worker's use of Liza's car for the Neighborhood Club. He suggested that it had all been a plot against him because he drives her car and ranted on about worker's nose, ears, etc., daring worker to take a punch at him. In the brief interludes in-between either Lem Wilcox or Alan O'Hanahan would slide up alongside worker who was seated on steps adjacent to Hot Dog Haven and reassure him that Harry was no good and worker was o.k. Alan asked "Why doesn't Harry like you," and worker explained about the loan of the car. Then Alan asked, "Do you dislike Harry?" to which worker said no, "Harry was o.k., he's just angry now but he'll get over it." Alan communicated that he very definitely disliked Harry and thought him no good. Worker reiterated some of Harry's sterling qualities. Then it came time for the meeting with the Copperheads and worker walked off slowly leaving a sputtering and signifying Harry.

On the following day:

Harry was present along with Alan O'Hana-

han. Harry was sounding guilty for his behavior the night before and said in tone which made it clear he admired worker's reaction, "I tried to get you to fight me last night" and . . . he was glad there had been no fight.

. . . . .

Another technique is the *support and encouragement of tendencies toward socially acceptable behavior*. Doing this, the worker encourages those with the most socialized standards to take positions of leadership in the group. In one instance, the girl-friends of the Cobras were challenged and, egged on by the boys, a fight loomed. With the worker's support, Joan Anderson stepped forth and asserted that there was no basis for a fight. The girls concluded with a grumbling cold-war truce, but an immediate follow-up would be necessary to avoid further complications. The worker helped Joan formalize some leadership by having her bring the other girls together to set forth a new kind of club structure at the Neighborhood Club. The crafts teacher they met showed them jewelry making and started them toward the development of a group more independent of the boys and more socialized in its direction.

Shortly after the formation of the Serpents, misconduct by some of its members caused the entire group to be denied entry to a Friday night dance. The group responded by ejecting Junior, one of the more irresponsible members. As they were preparing to attend the next dance, Junior sought another chance; his story is told in the following diary excerpt:

Before the dance (which was scheduled for 8:00) many of the boys drifted into Hot Dog Haven, the Club, or waited on the street. Junior appeared in the Club building at 7:00 and I took him aside to explain what the group had decided last night: that he was no longer a member of the Serpents and hence could not, according to Club rules, be a member of the larger Club (having no other involvement) and could not be admitted to the dance. Junior was upset, at first denied the possibility of this decision, then asked me to overlook it. I interpreted to him that whatever decision the group would make, I would have to stick by and enforce.

He urged me then to not "see" him at the dance, to not look his way so that I wouldn't have to enforce the ruling. When he finally realized that this was impossible and that only the group as a whole could decide on this, he explained that the group had made a mistake. He claimed that they must have kicked him out because they thought he had put the egg in "Mr. Peeper's" (Joe's, a staff member) pocket; also he said he had been charged with putting an open match book in Joe's back pocket and lighting it. He insisted that he hadn't been the one to do it, saying he didn't want to squeal on the real culprit before, but he'll get that guy to admit it before the meeting. Also, he would tell Mr. Peepers. Now couldn't he come to the dance? Well, I explained, that would still be up to the group. "Then could the group decide tonight?" if he could get the guys together either at the Club or at Hot Dog Haven. I explained to him they could—if they so chose—let him come back temporarily until the next Thursday meeting at which they would have to make the final decision on his membership. So he dashed over to Hot Dog Haven to try to round up a sizeable group of the members. Junior got the group together and we met in the lobby of the Club. The group was made to understand how this decision could only be temporary if, and this was a matter of indifference, they chose to make any decision at all. They voted Junior in temporarily.

Wherever possible, we have tried to *work with the family* in helping the boy make a more sociable adjustment. When indicated, referral was made to the case work—and often into the treatment units of the Hyde Park Youth Project. However in many instances, the street club worker could adequately stimulate existing strengths of the family members to aid the child themselves. The following diary excerpt tells of an approach to parents whose son was in difficulty with the police. The father is a professor. The oc-

casion was a party for the Kenwood Car Club.

The party took place at the Nye home. Shortly after it had begun the question of drinks came up. Richard assured the group that his parents wouldn't mind if they sent out for liquor. The pressure was on him since the group had been allowed to drink at the homes of two of the Adult Advisory Board members. The worker insisted that they must first have the expressed approval of the host—Richard's parents. Richard stuck to his story that his parents would approve it, and offered to go upstairs with the worker to ask them. Mr. Nye said, "No, I'd rather they did not have any drinking. Richard has been to a few parties where drinks were served and I've been disturbed about it." Worker accepted and supported this position, turned to leave with Richard. On the way down the stairs, worker asked Richard if he had a few decks of cards. He did. "Then get them" worker asserted and we re-entered the living room with cards in hand. "What'll it be?" asked worker shuffling like mad. About half the guys started emptying their pockets to announce their support for poker. Worker moved them into the dining room, set up the poker game, and returned to the living room to set up another poker game for chips—no money. Ray Nester was uncomfortable in either game so worker put him in charge of refreshments. After a short while Mr. Nye came downstairs and tried to busy himself with emptying ashtrays. Worker approached him, tried to interpret further what his position was on the drinking question. Pappa appeared somewhat unhappy, announced that earlier this day Richard had received his school grades and he had flunked all of his courses this semester. "I think its all due to that lousy car he's been spending all of his time on!" "Well, Mr. Nye, if it hadn't been the car, just what do you suppose it would have been?" worker asked Mr. Nye, suggesting a new concept on the role of the car. "You mean you think it was just a symptom of something— his working on the car?" "I don't know Mr. Nye, but I do think that Richard is a sensitive kid who finds it necessary to act out things that are disturbing him. Working on cars *could* serve that function." "That's interesting" mused the professor who was well acquainted, intellectually, with these concepts, but had apparently never considered them in the light of his bringing up his own sons. Then he asked worker, "What do you think is wrong?" "That boy just won't do his school work. I've tried to talk with him and I've told him again and again that he's got to be reliable. He just won't listen to me, and he won't accept his responsibilities."

"Maybe" worker suggested, "you've been talking past Richard, not with him. He surely must feel a pretty unhappy relationship with his father; how more effectively could he reject you than to flunk in school, how could he more clearly bring shame upon himself than to fail where his home places greatest stress, in intellectual achievement?"

"Why would he want to do that? No, that boy is just plain unreliable, he just won't listen to me and he won't accept his responsibilities." "Take those automobile accidents, now. I tried to reason with him after that but he just wouldn't react." Mr. Nye spoke of two accidents just previous to Richard's joining the Car Club. "Maybe that's where the problem lies, Mr. Nye" suggested the worker, "maybe you were concerned with what to Richard was entirely the wrong thing. Did you ever try talking with Richard about what was on his mind at the time of the accident, what had occurred before it which he may associate with the whole mess that followed?" "You know, these kids tie up sudden crisis events like an accident with a lot of other things in their lives, and maybe you could help him untie the knot by helping him get at that underneath thing which may have led him into the accident, which may be forcing Richard into a lot of acting-out behavior, including his failure at school. You say Richard doesn't react to your talking with him, but Richard is a kid with a pretty overwhelming super-ego. He doesn't show it in the outward signs of shame, but he turns his guilt inward and has accidents, and flunks. . . ."

"Oh, I don't see why he just can't have an accident. All he did was push the shift into second instead of reverse; that was perfectly simple" said the professor. "Mr. Nye, how many thousands of times do you suppose Richard has made the same movement of the shift? No, you won't grant 'accidents' in your Laboratory, and I don't think I'll permit them

to explain anything in mine," the worker asserted. "You may have something there, especially since there were *two* accidents right close to one another," Mr. Nye began to give in. Then recognizing that he was getting uncomfortably close to real life, he tried to dismiss the subject by saying, "Maybe he's just on the wrong track, he'll probably outgrow this behavior." "You've got yourself a sensitive, creative kid who's striking out against structures that are too tight for him." Worker pressed the point, "You're going to have to help him grow out of this behavior and in the right kind of direction." "What can I do?" Mr. Nye asked the worker. "Get in there and play with him" suggested the worker. "But I don't know how" said Mr. Nye. And then he reflected, "I can see what you mean; maybe that's at the root of this trouble."

"C'mon with me" worker then led the way and proceeded to show Mr. Nye how to play with his son. The game was poker, the no-money table. Worker turned to Richard saying "We've got an old codger here who wants to learn how to play poker. Think you can teach him?" Richard allowed as to how he could. From then on it was a continuous kidding.

As a figure more in touch with social agencies and processes, the street club worker is often called upon to *help in environmental problems.* We spent many weeks in setting up an odd jobs service with local agencies. Many clients and their families were counseled on their rights as tenants. Still others have been helped to find new quarters as their old apartments were vacated for demolition and redevelopment. We helped ten boys to receive hospital or medical services; another thirteen were aided in scholastic adjustments through conferences with teachers. Still others were given help on studies. Many boys were given support in their court appearances, all kinds of support: from cutting one lad's hair on the Sunday night before his appearance, to helping the court develop plans for the boy and/or family. In a number of cases, the case work unit of the Hyde Park Youth Project was given supervision of street club members in plans worked out with the court authorities.

The use and the effectiveness of each of these techniques depended heavily upon the kind of relationship that existed between the worker and the group. This relationship is based in part upon the worker's liking of the boys, but he must also show that he understands them and their problems for what they are. Though he likes the kids, this does not mean that he always likes or is willing to take part in all of their behavior. He never would conceal his identification with a welfare agency. He helps the boy who has committed a crime reach an adjustment with society, but he never suggests that committing the crime was unimportant or was excusable.

PART SIX
ADOLESCENCE

Adolescence is a period of rapid physical change affecting both the child's glands and bones and society's expectations regarding his behavior. It is a time for looking forward—to new purposes in life, to an occupation, to marriage, to independence from parents, and to a sense of self-identity.

In the selections in this part, Feiffer's cartoons and Updike's short story both describe the humor and tragedy that accompany "growing-up"—a process that may extend over a part of the life-span. Kinsey and Jones discuss important physiological developments and some of their social and cultural consequences. Komarovsky analyzes family techniques in our society by which independence is inculcated in sons and dependence in daughters, providing meaning and significance for the term "sex role." Excerpts from the life of Mahatma Gandhi show how the family in other cultures may select bride and groom. Whiting, Terman, and Allen discuss physiological, sociological, and psychological influences in choosing a career and a mate. Erikson's thoughtful analysis gives new meaning to the concept of self-identity.

75 | HOLD ME!

JULES FEIFFER

Some of our most perceptive observers of behavior are the artists, cartoonists, and comedians who mirror human beings as they struggle to deal with their inner conflicts. Here, Feiffer poignantly illustrates the ambivalent feelings that may accompany an adolescent's striving for independence.

TRY TO SEE IT MY WAY. I AM NEARLY TWENTY AND IF I WAS EVER GOING TO MAKE THE BREAK NOW WAS THE TIME TO DO IT. IMAGINE, HALF MY GIRL FRIENDS WERE ALREADY SEPARATED FROM THEIR HUSBANDS AND HERE I WAS STILL LIVING AT HOME!

SO I TOLD MY PARENTS I WAS MOVING OUT.

YOU CAN'T **IMAGINE** THE YELLING AND SCREAMING. MY FATHER SAID- "YOU'RE BREAKING YOUR MOTHER'S HEART!" MY MOTHER SAID- "WHAT WAS MY CRIME? WHAT WAS MY **TERRIBLE** CRIME?"

AND BEFORE I KNEW IT WE WERE IN THE MIDDLE OF A BIG ARGUMENT AND I TOLD THEM THEY BOTH NEEDED ANALYSIS AND THEY TOLD ME I HAD A FILTHY MOUTH AND SUDDENLY I WAS OUT ON THE STREET WITH MY RAINCOAT, MY SUITCASE AND MY TENNIS RACKET BUT I HAD NO PLACE TO **MOVE!**

SO I LOOKED AROUND DOWNTOWN AND EVERYTHING WAS TOO EXPEN- SIVE AND EVENING CAME AND ALL MY GIRL FRIENDS HAD RECONCILED WITH THEIR HUSBANDS SO THERE WAS ABSOLUTELY **NO** PLACE I COULD SPEND THE NIGHT.

WELL, **FRANKLY**, WHAT ON EARTH COULD I **DO**? I WAITED TILL IT WAS **WAY** PAST MY PARENTS BED- TIME- THEN I **SNEAKED** BACK INTO THE HOUSE AND SET THE ALARM IN MY BEDROOM FOR SIX THE NEXT MORNING.

THEN I SLEPT ON TOP OF THE BED SO I WOULDN'T WRINKLE ANY SHEETS, SNEAKED SOME BREAKFAST IN THE MORNING AND GOT OUT BEFORE ANY- ONE WAS UP.

I'VE BEEN LIVING THAT WAY FOR TWO MONTHS NOW.

EVERY NIGHT AFTER MIDNIGHT I SNEAK INTO MY BEDROOM, SLEEP ON TOP OF THE BED TILL SIX THE NEXT MORNING, HAVE BREAKFAST AND SNEAK OUT.

AND EVERY DAY I CALL UP MY PARENTS FROM THE DOWNSTAIRS DRUGSTORE AND THEY YELL AND CRY AT ME TO COME BACK. BUT, OF COURSE, I ALWAYS TELL THEM NO.

I'LL **NEVER** GIVE UP MY INDEPENDENCE.

76 | ACE IN THE HOLE

JOHN UPDIKE

Many realities are better sensed and more effectively conveyed by the artists and novelists of an age than by social scientists. Updike, in the following "vignette," creates what may be a contemporary version of "Everyman." The hero, less than heroic, is caught in the web of life, as is each of us, and is using whatever resources he can scrape together to cope with his peculiar needs.

No sooner did his car touch the boulevard heading home than Ace flicked on the

radio. He needed the radio, especially today. In the seconds before the tubes warmed up, he said aloud, doing it just to hear a human voice, "Jesus. She'll pop her lid." His voice, though familiar, irked him; it sounded thin and scratchy, as if the bones in his head were picking up static. In a deeper register Ace added, "She'll murder me." Then the radio came on, warm and strong, so he stopped worrying. The Five Kings were doing "Blueberry Hill"; to hear them made Ace feel so sure inside that from the pack pinched between the car roof and the sun shield he plucked a cigarette, hung it on his lower lip, snapped a match across the rusty place on the dash, held the flame in the instinctive spot near the tip of his nose, dragged, and blew out the match, all in time to the music. He rolled down the window and snapped the match so it spun end-over-end into the gutter. "Two points," he said, and cocked the cigarette toward the roof of the car, sucked power-fully, and exhaled two plumes through his nostrils. He was beginning to feel like himself, Ace Anderson, for the first time that whole day, a bad day. He beat time on the accelerator. The car jerked crazily. "On Blueberry Hill," he sang, "my heart stood still. The wind in the wil-low tree" —he braked for a red light—"played love's suh-*weet* melodee—"

"Go, Dad, bust your lungs!" a kid's voice blared. The kid was riding in a '52 Pontiac that had pulled up beside Ace at the light. The profile of the driver, another kid, was dark over his shoulder.

Ace looked over at him and smiled slowly, just letting one side of his mouth lift a little. "Shove it," he said, good-naturedly, across the little gap of years that separated them. He knew how they felt, young and mean and shy.

But the kid, who looked Greek, lifted his thick upper lip and spat out the win-dow. The spit gleaned on the asphalt like a half-dollar.

"Now isn't that pretty?" Ace said, keep-ing one eye on the light. "You miserable wop. You are *mis*erable." While the kid was trying to think of some smart come-back, the light changed. Ace dug out so hard he smelled burned rubber. In his rear-view mirror he saw the Pontiac lurch forward a few yards, then stop dead, right in the middle of the intersection.

The idea of them stalling their fat tin Pontiac kept him in a good humor all the way home. He decided to stop at his mother's place and pick up the baby, in-stead of waiting for Evey to do it. His mother must have seen him drive up. She came out on the porch holding a plastic spoon and smelling of cake.

"You're out early," she told him.

"Friedman fired me," Ace told her.

"Good for you," his mother said. "I al-ways said he never treated you right." She brought a cigarette out of her apron pocket and tucked it deep into one corner of her mouth, the way she did when some-thing pleased her.

Ace lighted it for her. "Friedman was O.K. personally," he said. "He just wanted too much for his money. I didn't mind working Saturdays, but until eleven, twelve Friday nights was too much. Everybody has a right to some leisure."

"Well, I don't dare think what Evey will say, but I, for one, thank dear God you had the brains to get out of it. I always said that job had no future to it—no fu-ture of any kind, Freddy."

"I guess," Ace admitted. "But I wanted to keep at it, for the family's sake."

"Now, I know I shouldn't be saying this, but any time Evey—this is just between us—any time Evey thinks she can do better, there's room for you *and* Bonnie right in your father's house." She pinched her lips together. He could almost hear the old lady think, *There, I've said it.*

"Look, Mom, Evey tries awfully hard, and anyway you know she can't work that way. Not that *that*—I mean, she's a realist, too . . ." He let the rest of the thought fade as he watched a kid across the street dribbling a basketball around a telephone pole that had a backboard and net nailed on it.

"Evey's a wonderful girl of her own

kind. But I've always said, and your father agrees, Roman Catholics ought to marry among themselves. Now I know I've said it before, but when they get out in the greater world—"

"*No*, Mom."

She frowned, smoothed herself, and said, "Your name was in the paper today."

Ace chose to let that go by. He kept watching the kid with the basketball. It was funny how, though the whole point was to get the ball up into the air, kids grabbed it by the sides and squeezed. Kids just didn't think.

"Did you hear?" his mother asked.

"Sure, but so what?" Ace said. His mother's lower lip was coming at him, so he changed the subject. "I guess I'll take Bonnie."

His mother went into the house and brought back his daughter, wrapped in a blue blanket. The baby looked dopey. "She fussed all day," his mother complained. "I said to your father, 'Bonnie is a dear little girl, but without a doubt she's her mother's daughter.' You were the best-natured boy."

"Well I *had* everything," Ace said with an impatience that made his mother blink. He nicely dropped his cigarette into a brown flowerpot on the edge of the porch and took his daughter into his arms. She was getting heavier, solid. When he reached the end of the cement walk, his mother was still on the porch, waving to him. He was so close he could see the fat around her elbow jiggle, and he only lived a half block up the street, yet here she was, waving to him as if he was going to Japan.

At the door of his car, it seemed stupid to him to drive the measly half block home. His old coach, Bob Behn, used to say never to ride where you could walk. Cars were the death of legs. Ace left the ignition keys in his pocket and ran along the pavement with Bonnie laughing and bouncing at his chest. He slammed the door of his landlady's house open and shut, pounded up the two flights of stairs, and was panting so hard when he reached the door of his apartment that it took him a couple of seconds to fit the key into the lock.

The run must have tuned Bonnie up. As soon as he lowered her into the crib, she began to shout and wave her arms. He didn't want to play with her. He tossed some blocks and a rattle into the crib and walked into the bathroom, where he turned on the hot water and began to comb his hair. Holding the comb under the faucet before every stroke, he combed his hair forward. It was so long, one strand curled under his nose and touched his lips. He whipped the whole mass back with a single pull. He tucked in the tufts around his ears, and ran the comb straight back on both sides of his head. With his fingers he felt for the little ridge at the back where the two sides met. It was there, as it should have been. Finally, he mussed the hair in front enough for one little lock to droop over his forehead, like Alan Ladd. It made the temple seem lower than it was. Every day, his hairline looked higher. He had observed all around him how blond men went bald first. He remembered reading somewhere, though, that baldness shows virility.

On his way to the kitchen he flipped the left-hand knob of the television. Bonnie was always quieter with the set on. Ace didn't see how she could understand much of it, but it seemed to mean something to her. He found a can of beer in the refrigerator behind some brownish lettuce and those hot dogs Evey never got around to cooking. She'd be home any time. The clock said 5:12. She'd pop her lid.

Ace didn't see what he could do but try and reason with her. "Evey," he'd say, "you ought to thank God I got out of it. It had no future to it at all." He hoped she wouldn't get too mad, because when she was mad he wondered if he should have married her, and doubting that made him feel crowded. It was bad enough, his mother always crowding him. He punched the two triangles in the top of the beer can, the little triangle first, and then the big one, the one he drank from. He hoped Evey wouldn't say anything that couldn't be forgotten. What women didn't seem to realize was that there were things you knew but shouldn't say.

He felt sorry he had called the kid in the car a wop.

Ace balanced the beer on a corner where two rails of the crib met and looked under the chairs for the morning paper. He had trouble finding his name, because it was at the bottom of a column on an inside sports page, in a small article about the county basketball statistics:

"Dusty" Tremwick, Grosvenor Park's sure-fingered center, copped the individual scoring honors with a season's grand (and we do mean grand) total of 376 points. This is within eighteen points of the all-time record of 394 racked up in the 1949–1950 season by Olinger High's Fred Anderson.

Ace angrily sailed the paper into an armchair. Now it was Fred Anderson; it used to be Ace. He hated being called Fred, especially in print, but then the sportswriters were all office boys anyway, Behn used to say.

"Do not just ask for shoe polish," a man on television said, "but ask for *Emu Shoe Gloss*, the *only* polish that absolutely *guarantees* to make your shoes look shinier than new." Ace turned the sound off, so that the man moved his mouth like a fish blowing bubbles. Right away, Bonnie howled, so Ace turned it up loud enough to drown her out and went into the kitchen, without knowing what he wanted there. He wasn't hungry; his stomach was tight. It used to be like that when he walked to the gymnasium alone in the dark before a game and could see the people from town, kids and parents, crowding in at the lighted doors. But once he was inside, the locker room would be bright and hot, and the other guys would be there, laughing it up and towel-slapping, and the tight feeling would leave. Now there were whole days when it didn't leave.

A key scratched at the door lock. Ace decided to stay in the kitchen. Let *her* find *him*. Her heels clicked on the floor for a step or two; then the television set went off. Bonnie began to cry. "Shut up, honey," Evey said. There was a silence.

"I'm home," Ace called.

"No kidding. I thought Bonnie got the beer by herself."

Ace laughed. She was in a sarcastic mood, thinking she was Lauren Bacall. That was all right, just so she kept funny. Still smiling, Ace eased into the living room and got hit with, "What are *you* smirking about? Another question: What's the idea running up the street with Bonnie like she was a football?"

"You saw that?"

"Your mother told me."

"You saw her?"

"Of course I saw her. I dropped by to pick up Bonnie. What the hell do you think?—I read her tiny mind?"

"Take it easy," Ace said, wondering if Mom had told her about Friedman.

"Take it easy? Don't coach *me*. Another question: Why's the car out in front of her place? You give the car to her?"

"Look, I parked it there to pick up Bonnie, and I thought I'd leave it there."

"Why?"

"Whaddeya mean, why? I just did. I just thought I'd walk. It's not that far, you know."

"No, I don't know. If you'd be on your feet all day a block would look like one hell of a long way."

"Okay. I'm sorry."

She hung up her coat and stepped out of her shoes and walked around the room picking up things. She stuck the newspaper in the wastebasket.

Ace said, "My name was in the paper today."

"They spell it right?" She shoved the paper deep into the basket with her foot. There was no doubt; she knew about Friedman.

"They called me Fred."

"Isn't that your name? What *is* your name anyway? Hero J. Great?"

There wasn't any answer, so Ace didn't try any. He sat down on the sofa, lighted a cigarette, and waited.

Evey picked up Bonnie. "Poor thing stinks. What does your mother do, scrub out the toilet with her?"

"Can't you take it easy? I know you're tired."

"You should. I'm always tired."

Evey and Bonnie went into the bathroom; when they came out, Bonnie was clean and Evey was calm. Evey sat down in an easy chair beside Ace and rested her stocking feet on his knees. "Hit me," she said, twiddling her fingers for the cigarette.

The baby crawled up to her chair and tried to stand, to see what he gave her. Leaning over close to Bonnie's nose, Evey grinned, smoke leaking through her teeth, and said, "Only for grownups, honey."

"Eve," Ace began, "there was no future in that job. Working all Saturday, and then Friday nights on top of it."

"I know. Your mother told *me* all that, too. All I want from you is what happened."

She was going to take it like a sport, then. He tried to remember how it *did* happen. "It wasn't my fault," he said. "Friedman told me to back this '51 Chevvy into the line that faces Church Street. He just bought it from an old guy this morning who said it only had thirteen thousand on it. So in I jump and start her up. There was a knock in the engine like a machine gun. I almost told Friedman he's bought

a squirrel, but you know I cut that smart stuff out ever since Palotta laid me off."

"You told me that story. What happens in this one?"

"Look, Eve. I *am* telling ya. Do you want me to go out to a movie or something?"

"Suit yourself."

"So I jump in the Chevvy and snap it back in line, and there was a kind of scrape and thump. I get out and look and Friedman's running over, his arms going like *this*"—Ace whirled his own arms and laughed—"and here was the whole back fender of a '49 Merc mashed in. Just looked like somebody took a planer and shaved off the bulge, you know, there at the back." He tried to show her with his hands. "The Chevvy, though, didn't have a dent. It even gained some paint. But *Friedman*, to *hear* him—Boy, they can rave when their pocketbook's hit. He said"—Ace laughed again—"never mind."

Evey said, "You're proud of yourself."

"No, listen. I'm not happy about it. But there wasn't a thing I could *do*. It wasn't my driving at all. I looked over on the other side, and there was just two or three inches between the Chevvy and a Buick. *Nobody* could have gotten into that hole. Even if it had hair on it." He thought this was pretty good.

She didn't. "You could have looked."

"There just wasn't the *space*. Friedman said stick it in; I stuck it in."

"But you could have looked and moved the other cars to make more room."

"I guess that would have been the smart thing."

"I guess, too. Now what?"

"What do you mean?"

"I mean now what? Are you going to give up? Go back to the Army? Your mother? Be a basketball pro? What?"

"You know I'm not tall enough. Anybody under six-six they don't want."

"Is that so? Six-six? Well, please listen to this, Mr. Six-Foot-Five-and-a-Half: I'm

fed up. I'm ready as Christ to let you run."
She stabbed her cigarette into an ashtray
on the arm of the chair so hard the ashtray jumped to the floor. Evey flushed and
shut up.

What Ace hated most in their arguments was these silences after Evey had
said something so ugly she wanted to take
it back. "Better ask the priest first," he
murmured.

She sat right up. "If there's one thing
I don't want to hear about from you it's
priests. You let the priests to me. You
don't know a damn thing about it. Not a
damn thing."

"Hey, look at Bonnie," he said, trying to
make a fresh start with his tone.

Evey didn't hear him. "If you think,"
she went on, "if for one rotten moment
you think, Mr. Fred, that the be-all and
end-all of my life is you and your hot-
shot stunts—"

"Look, Mother," Ace pleaded, pointing at Bonnie. The baby had picked up
the ashtray and put it on her head for a
hat and was waiting for praise.

Evey glanced down sharply at the child.
"Cute," she said. "Cute as her daddy."

The ashtray slid from Bonnie's head and
she patted where it had been and looked
around puzzled.

"Yeah, but watch," Ace said. "Watch
her hands. They're really terrific hands."

"You're nuts," Evey said.

"No, honest. Bonnie's great. She's a natural. Get the rattle for her. Never mind,
I'll get it." In two steps, Ace was at Bonnie's crib, picking the rattle out of the
mess of blocks and plastic rings and bean-
bags. He extended the rattle toward his
daughter, shaking it delicately. Made
wary by this burst of attention, Bonnie
reached with both hands; like two separate

animals they approached from opposite
sides and touched the smooth rattle
simultaneously. A smile bubbled up on
her face. Ace tugged weakly. She held on,
and then tugged back. "She's a natural,"
Ace said, "and it won't do her any good
because she's a girl. Baby, we got to have
a boy."

"I'm not your baby," Evey said, closing
her eyes.

Saying "Baby" over and over again, Ace
backed up to the radio and, without turning around, switched on the volume knob.
In the moment before the tubes warmed
up, Evey had time to say, "Wise up,
Freddy. What shall we do?"

The radio came in on something slow:
dinner music. Ace picked Bonnie up and
set her in the crib. "Shall we dance?" he
asked his wife, bowing.

"I want to talk."

"Baby. It's the cocktail hour."

"This is getting us no place," she said,
rising from her chair, though.

"Fred Junior. I can see him now," he
said, seeing nothing.

"We will have no Juniors."

In her crib, Bonnie whimpered at the
sight of her mother being seized. Ace fitted
his hand into the natural place on Evey's
back and she shuffled stiffly into his lead.
When, with a sudden injection of saxo-
phones, the tempo quickened, he spun
her out carefully, keeping the beat with
his shoulders. Her hair brushed his lips
as she minced in, then swung away, to the
end of his arm; he could feel her toes dig
into the carpet. He flipped his own hair
back from his eyes. The music ate through
his skin and mixed with the nerves and
small veins; he seemed to be great again,
and all the other kids were around them,
in a ring, clapping time.

77 | THE ADOLESCENCE OF MAHATMA GANDHI

LOUIS FISCHER

Here a remarkable man describes his adolescence with astonishing frankness. Particularly interesting is the constant juxtaposition in Gandhi's personality of a strong sense of duty, morality, personal integrity, and denial of bodily wants with a natural lustiness, adventurousness, and interest in the forbidden. His relationship with his wife, whom he married when he was thirteen, is at the same time childish and mature.

In talking of his awkwardness on his wedding night and of his immoral activities "behind the barn" as a youth, Gandhi effectively denies the myth of the hero—"I am the great man, with only superior concerns"—and honestly affirms his inherent sense of brotherhood and humility—"I am like other common men in my awkwardness, my inconsiderateness, and my bungling."

THE BEGINNINGS OF AN EXTRAORDINARY MAN

Gandhi belonged to the Vaisya caste. In the old Hindu social scale, the Vaisyas stood third, far below the Brahmans who were the number one caste, and the Kshatriyas, or rulers and soldiers, who ranked second. The Vaisyas, in fact, were only a notch above the Sudras, the working class. Originally, they devoted themselves to trade and agriculture.

The Gandhis belonged to the Modh Bania subdivision of their caste. Bania is a synonym in India for a sharp, shrewd businessman. Far back, the Gandhi family were retail grocers: "Gandhi" means grocer. But the professional barriers between castes began to crumble generations ago, and Gandhi's grandfather Uttamchand served as prime minister to the princeling of Porbandar, a tiny state in the Kathiawar peninsula, western India, about halfway between the mouth of the Indus and the city of Bombay. Uttam-

chand handed the office down to his son Karamchand who passed it to his brother Tulsidas. The job had almost become the family's private property.

Karamchand was the father of Mohandas Karamchand Gandhi, the Mahatma.

The Gandhis apparently got into trouble often. Political intrigues forced grandfather Uttamchand out of the prime ministership of Porbandar and into exile in the nearby little state of Junagadh. There he once saluted the ruling Nawab with his left hand. Asked for an explanation, he said, "The right hand is already pledged to Porbandar." Mohandas was proud of such loyalty; "My grandfather," he wrote, "must have been a man of principle."

Gandhi's father likewise quit his position as prime minister to Rana Saheb Vikmatji, the ruler of Porbandar, and took the same office in Rajkot, another miniature Kathiawar principality 120 miles to the northwest. Once, the British Political Agent spoke disparagingly of Thakor Saheb Bawajiraj, Rajkot's native ruler. Karamchand sprang to the defense of his chief. The Agent ordered Karamchand to apologize. Karamchand refused and was forthwith arrested. But Gandhi's father

Reprinted from *The Life of Mahatma Gandhi* (New York: Harper & Brothers, 1950), pp. 12–23, 29, 35–37, by permission of the publisher. Copyright, 1950, by Louis Fischer.

stood his ground and was released after several hours. Subsequently he became prime minister of Wankaner.

In the 1872 census, Porbandar state had a population of 72,077, Rajkot 36,770 and Wankaner 28,750. Their rulers behaved like petty autocrats to their subjects and quaking sycophants before the British.

Karamchand Gandhi "had no education save that of experience," his son, Mohandas, wrote; he was likewise "innocent" of history and geography; "but he was incorruptible and had earned a reputation for strict impartiality in his family as well as outside." He "was a lover of his clan, truthful, brave and generous, but short-tempered. To a certain extent he might have been even given to carnal pleasures. For he married for the fourth time when he was over forty." The other three wives had died.

Mohandas Karamchand Gandhi was the fourth and last child of his father's fourth and last marriage. He was born at Porbandar on October 2, 1869. That year the Suez Canal was opened, Thomas A. Edison patented his first invention, France celebrated the hundredth anniversary of the birth of Napoleon Bonaparte, and Charles W. Eliot became president of Harvard University. Karl Marx had just published *Capital*, Bismarck was about to launch the Franco-Prussian War, and Victoria ruled over England and India.

Mohandas was born in the dark, right-hand corner of a room, 11 feet by 19½ feet and 10 feet high, in a three-story humble house on the border of town. The house is still standing.

The little town of Porbander, or Porbundar, rises straight out of the Arabian Sea and "becomes a vision of glory at sunrise and sunset when the slanting rays beat upon it, turning its turrets and pinnacles into gold," wrote Charles Freer Andrews, a British disciple of the Mahatma. It and Rajkot and Wankaner were quite remote, at the time of Gandhi's youth, from the European and Western influences which

had invaded less isolated parts of India. Its landmarks were its temples.

Gandhi's home life was cultured and the family, by Indian standards, was well-to-do. There were books in the house; they dealt chiefly with religion and mythology. Mohandas played tunes on a concertina purchased especially for him. Karamchand wore a gold necklace and a brother of Mohandas had a heavy, solid gold armlet. Karamchand once owned a house in Porbandar, a second in Rajkot, and a third in Kutiana. But in his last three years of illness he lived modestly on a pension from the Rajkot prince. He left little property.

Gandhi's elder brother Laxmidas practiced law in Rajkot and later became a treasury official in the Porbander government. He spent money freely and married his daughters with a pomp worthy of petty Indian royalty. He owned two houses in Rajkot. Karsandas, the other brother, served as sub-inspector of police in Porbandar and ultimately of the princeling's harem. His income was small.

Both brothers died while Mohandas K. Gandhi was still alive. A sister, Raliatbehn, four years his senior, survived him. She remained resident in Rajkot.

Mohania, as the family affectionately called Mohandas, received the special treatment often accorded a youngest child. A nurse named Rambha was hired for him and he formed an attachment to her which continued into mature life. His warmest affection went to his mother Putlibai. He sometimes feared his father, but he loved his mother and always remembered her "saintliness" and her "deeply religious" nature. She never ate a meal without prayer, and attended temple services daily. Long facts did not dismay her, and arduous vows, voluntarily made, were steadfastly performed. In the annual Chaturmas, a kind of Lent lasting through the four-month rainy season, she habitually lived on a single meal a day, and, one year, she observed, in addition, a complete fast on alternate days. Another Chaturmas, she vowed not to eat unless the sun appeared. Mohandas and his sister and brothers would watch for the sun, and when it showed through the clouds they would rush into the house and announce to Putlibai that now she could eat. But her vow required her to see the sun herself and so she would go outdoors and by then the sun was hidden again. "That does not matter," she would cheerfully comfort her children. "God does not want me to eat today."

As a boy, Mohandas amused himself with rubber balloons and revolving tops. He played tennis and cricket and also "gilli danda," a game, encountered in so many widely separated countries, which consists in striking a short, sharpened wooden peg with a long stick: "peggy" or "pussy" some call it.

Gandhi started school in Porbandar. He encountered more difficulty mastering the multiplication table than in learning naughty names for the teacher. "My intellect must have been sluggish, and my memory raw," the adult Mahatma charges against the child of six. In Rajkot, whither the family moved a year later, he was again a "mediocre student," but punctual. His sister recalls that rather than be late he would eat the food of the previous day if breakfast was not ready. He preferred walking to going to school by carriage. He was timid: "my books and lessons were my sole companions." At the end of the school day, he ran home. He could not bear to talk to anybody; "I was even afraid lest anyone should poke fun at me." When he grew older, however, he found some congenial mates and played in the streets. He also played by the sea.

In his first year at the Alfred High School in Rajkot, when Mohandas was twelve, a British educational inspector named Mr. Giles came to examine the pupils. They were asked to spell five English words. Gandhi misspelled "kettle." Walking up and down the aisles, the reg-

ular teacher saw the mistake and motioned Mohandas to copy from his neighbor's slate. Mohandas refused. Later the teacher chided him for this "stupidity" which spoiled the record of the class; everybody else had written all the words correctly.

The incident, however, did not diminish Gandhi's respect for his teacher. "I was by nature blind to the faults of elders. . . . I had learned to carry out the orders of elders, not to scan their actions." But obedience did not include cheating with teacher's permission.

Perhaps the refusal to cheat was a form of self-assertion or rebellion. In any case, compliance at school did not preclude revolt outside it. At the age of twelve, Gandhi began to smoke. And he stole from elders in the house to finance the transgression. His partner in the adventure was a young relative. Sometimes both were penniless; then they made cigarettes from the porous stalks of a wild plant. This interest in botany led to the discovery that the seeds of a jungle weed named dhatura were poisonous. Off they went to the jungle on the successful quest. Tired of life under parental supervision, they joined in a suicide pact. They would die, appropriately, in the temple of God.

Having made their obeisances, Mohandas and pal sought out a lonely corner for the final act. But maybe death would be long in coming, and meanwhile they might suffer pain. Maybe it was better to live in slavery. To salvage a vestige of self-respect they each swallowed two or three seeds.

Presently, serious matters claimed the juvenile's attention.

Mohandas K. Gandhi married when he was a high school sophomore—age thirteen. He had been engaged three times, of course without his knowledge. Betrothals were compacts between parents, and the children rarely learned about them. Gandhi happened to hear that two girls to whom he had been engaged—probably as a toddler—had died. "I have a faint recollection," he reports, "that the third bethrothal took place in my seventh year," but he was not informed. He was told six years later, a short time before the wedding. The bride was Kasturbai, the daughter of a Porbandar merchant named Kokuldas Nakanji. The marriage lasted sixty-two years.

Writing about the wedding more than forty years later, Gandhi remembered all the details of the ceremony, as well as the trip to Porbandar where it took place. "And oh! that first night," he added. "Two innocent children all unwittingly hurled themselves into the ocean of life." Kasturbai, too, was thirteen. "My brother's wife had thoroughly coached me about my behavior on the first night. I do not know who had coached my wife." Both were nervous and "the coaching could not carry me far," Gandhi wrote. "But no coaching is really necessary in such matters. The impressions of the former birth are potent enough to make all coaching superfluous." Presumably, they remembered their experiences in an earlier incarnation.

The newlyweds, Gandhi confesses, were "married children" and behaved accordingly. He was jealous and "therefore she could not go anywhere without my permission" for "I took no time in assuming the authority of a husband." So when the thirteen-year-old wife wanted to go out to play she had to ask the thirteen-year-old Mohandas; he would often say no. "The restraint was virtually a sort of imprisonment. And Kasturbai was not the girl to brook any such thing. She made it a point to go out whenever and whereever she liked." The little husband got "more and more cross"; sometimes they did not speak to each other for days.

He loved Kasturbai. His "passion was entirely centered on one woman" and he wanted it reciprocated, but the woman was a child. Sitting in the high school classroom he daydreamed about her. "I used to keep her awake till late at night with my idle talk."

"The cruel custom of child marriage," as Gandhi subsequently castigated it, would have been impossible but for the ancient Indian institution of the joint family: parents and their children and their sons' wives and children, sometimes thirty or more persons altogether, lived under one roof; newly wed adolescents therefore had no worry about a home, furniture, or board. Later, British law, seconding Indian reformers, raised the minimum marriage age. In its time the evil was mitigated by enforced separations for as much as six months per year when the bride went to live with her parents. The first five years of Gandhi's marriage—from thirteen to eighteen—included only three years of common life.

The "shackles of lust" tormented Gandhi. They gave him a feeling of guilt. The feeling grew when sex seemed to clash with the keen sense of duty which developed in him at an early age. One instance of such a conflict impressed itself indelibly. When Mohandas was sixteen his father Karamchand became bedridden with a fistula. Gandhi helped his mother and an old servant tend the patient; he dressed the wound and mixed the medicines and administered them. He also massaged his father's legs every night until the sufferer fell asleep or asked his son to go to bed. "I loved to do this service," Gandhi recalls.

Kasturbai had become pregnant at fiftten and she was now in an advanced stage. Nevertheless, "every night whilst my hands were busy massaging my father's legs," Gandhi states in his autobiography, "my mind was hovering about [my wife's] bedroom—and that too at a time when religion, medical science, and common sense alike forbade sexual intercourse."

One evening, between ten and eleven, Gandhi's uncle relieved him at massaging Karamchand. Gandhi went quickly to his wife's bedroom and woke her. A few minutes later the servant knocked at the door and urgently summoned Gandhi. He jumped out of bed, but when he reached the sickroom his father was dead. "If passion had not blinded me," Gandhi ruminated forty years later, "I should have been spared the torture of separation from my father during his last moments. I should have been massaging him, and he would have died in my arms. But now it was my uncle who had had this privilege."

The "shame of my carnal desire at the critical moment of my father's death . . . is a blot I have never been able to efface or forget," Gandhi wrote when he was near sixty. Moreover, Kasturbai's baby died three days after birth, and Mohandas blamed the death on intercourse late in pregnancy. This doubled his sense of guilt.

Kasturbai was illiterate. Her husband had every intention of teaching her, but she disliked studies and he preferred lovemaking. Private tutors also got nowhere with her. Yet Gandhi took the blame upon himself and felt that if his affection "had been absolutely untainted with lust, she would be a learned lady today." She never learned to read or write anything but elementary Gujarati, her native language.

Gandhi himself lost a year at high school through getting married. Modestly he asserts he "was not regarded as a dunce." Every year he brought home a report on study progress and character; it was never bad. He even won some prizes but that, he says, was only because there were few competitors.

When Mohandas merited a teacher's rebuke it pained him and he sometimes cried. Once he was beaten at school. The punishment hurt less than being considered worthy of it; "I wept piteously."

Gandhi neglected penmanship and thought it unimportant. Geometry was taught in English, which was then a new language for him, and he had difficulty in following. But "when I reached the thirteenth proposition of Euclid the utter simplicity of the subject was suddenly revealed to me. A subject which only required a pure and simple use of one's reasoning powers could not be difficult. Ever since that time geometry has been both easy and interesting for me." He likewise had trouble with Sanskrit, but after the teacher, Mr. Krishnashanker, reminded him that it was the language of Hinduism's sacred scriptures, the future Mahatma persevered and succeeded.

In the upper grades, gymnastics and cricket were compulsory. Gandhi disliked both. He was shy, and he thought physical exercises did not belong in education. But he had read that long walks in the open air were good for the health, and he formed the habit. "These walks gave me a fairly hardy constitution."

Mohandas envied the bigger, stronger boys. He was frail compared to his older brother and especially compared to a Moslem friend named Sheik Mehtab who could run great distances with incredible speed. Sheik Mehtab was spectacular in the broad and high jumps as well. These exploits dazzled Gandhi.

Gandhi regarded himself a coward. "I used to be haunted," he asserts, "by the fear of thieves, ghosts, and serpents. I did not dare to stir out of doors at night." He could not sleep without a light in his room; his wife had more courage than he and did not fear serpents or ghosts or darkness. "I felt ashamed of myself."

Sheik Mehtab played on this sentiment. He boasted that he could hold live snakes in his hand, feared no burglars, and did not believe in ghosts. Whence all this prowess and bravery? He ate meat. Gandhi ate no meat; it was forbidden by his religion.

The boys at school used to recite a poem which went:

> Behold the mighty Englishman,
> He rules the Indian small,
> Because being a meat-eater
> He is five cubits tall.

If all Indians ate meat they could expel

the British and make India free. Besides, argued Sheik Mehtab, boys who ate meat did not get boils; many of their teachers and some of the most prominent citizens of Rajkot ate meat secretly, and drank wine, too.

Day in, day out, Sheik Mehtab propagandized Mohandas, whose older brother had already succumbed. Finally, Mohandas yielded.

At the appointed hour the tempter and his victim met in a secluded spot on the river bank. Sheik Mehtab brought cooked goat's meat and bread. Gandhi rarely touched baker's bread (the substitute was chappatis, an unleavened dough cushion filled with air), and he had never even seen meat. The family was strictly vegetarian and so, in fact, were almost all the inhabitants of the Gujurat district in Kathiawar. But firm in the resolve to make himself an effective liberator of his country, Gandhi bit into the meat. It was tough as leather. He chewed and chewed and then swallowed. He became sick immediately.

That night he had a nightmare: a live goat was bleating in his stomach. However, "meat-eating was a duty," and, in the midst of the terrible dream, therefore, he decided to continue the experiment.

It continued for a whole year. Irregularly throughout that long period he met Sheik Mehtab at secret rendezvous to partake of meat dishes, now tastier than the first, and bread. Where Sheik got the money for these feasts Gandhi never knew.

The sin of consuming and liking meat was compounded by the sin of lying. In the end he could not stand the dishonesty and, though still convinced that meat-eating was "essential" for patriotic reasons, he vowed to abjure it until his parents' death enabled him to be a carnivore openly.

By now Gandhi developed an urge to reform Sheik Mehtab. This prolonged the relationship. But the naïve and younger Gandhi was no match for the shrewd, moneyed wastrel who offered revolt and adventure. Sheik also knew how to arrange things. Once he led Gandhi to the entrance of a brothel. The institution had been told and paid in advance. Gandhi went in. "I was almost struck blind and dumb in this den of vice. I sat near the woman on her bed, but I was tongue-tied. She naturally lost patience with me, and showed me the door, with abuses and insults." Providence, he explains, interceded and saved him despite himself.

About that time—Mohandas must have been fifteen—he pilfered a bit of gold from his older brother. This produced a moral crisis. He had gnawing pangs of conscience and resolved never to steal again. But he needed the cleansing effect of a confession: he would tell his father. He made a full, written statement of the crime, asked for due penalty, promised never to steal again, and, with emphasis, begged his father not to punish himself for his son's dereliction.

Karamchand sat up in his sickbed to read the letter. Tears filled his eyes and fell to his cheeks. Then he tore up the paper and lay down. Mohandas sat near him and wept.

Gandhi never forgot that silent scene. Sincere repentance and confession induced by love, rather than fear, won him his father's "sublime forgiveness" and affection.

Lest he give pain to his father, and especially his mother, Mohandas did not tell them that he absented himself from temple. He did not like the "glitter and pomp" of the Hindu temples. Religion to him meant irksome restrictions like vegetarianism which intensified his youthful protest against society and authority. And he had no "living faith in God." Who made the world; who directed it, he asked. Elders could not answer, and the sacred books were so unsatisfactory on such matters that he inclined "somewhat towards atheism." He even began to believe that it was quite moral, indeed a duty, to kill serpents and bugs.

Gandhi's anti-religious sentiments quickened his interest in religion, and he listened attentively to his father's frequent discussions with Moslem and Parsi friends on the differences between their faiths and Hinduism. He also learned much about the Jain religion. Jain monks often visited the house and went out of their way to accept food from the non-Jain Gandhis.

When Karamchand died, 1885, Mohandas's mother Putlibai took advice on family matters from a Jain monk named Becharji Swami, originally a Hindu of the Modh Bania sub-caste. Jain influence was strong in the Gujarat region. And Jainism prohibits the killing of any living creature, even insects. Jain priests wear white masks over their mouths lest they breathe in, and thus kill, an insect. They are not supposed to walk out at night lest they unwittingly step on a worm.

Gandhi was always a great absorber. Jainism, as well as Buddhism, perceptibly colored Gandhi's thoughts and shaped his works. Both were attempts to reform the Hindu religion, India's dominant faith; both originated in the sixth century B.C. in northeastern India, in what is now the province of Bihar.

The Jain monk, Becharji Swami, helped Gandhi go to England. After graduating from high school, Gandhi enrolled in Samaldas College, in Bhavnagar, a town on the inland side of the Kathiawar peninsula. But he found the studies difficult and the atmosphere distasteful. A friend of the family suggested that if Mohandas was to succeed his father as prime minister he had better hurry and become a lawyer; the quickest way was to take a three-year course in England. Gandhi was most eager to go. But he was afraid of law; could he pass the examinations? Might it not be preferable to study medicine? He was interested in medicine. Mohandas's brother objected that their father was opposed to the dissection of dead bodies and intended Mohandas for the bar. A Brahman friend of the family did not take the same dark view of the medical profession; but could a doctor become prime minister?

Mother Putlibai disliked parting with her last-born. "What will uncle say? He is the head of the family, now that father is no more." And where will the money come from?

Mohandas had set his heart on England. He developed energy and unwonted courage. He hired a bullock cart for the five-day journey to Porbandar where his uncle lived. To save a day, he left the cart and rode on a camel; it was his first camel ride.

Uncle was not encouraging; European-trained lawyers forsook Indian tradition; cigars were never out of their mouth; they ate everything; they dressed "as shamelessly as Englishmen." But he would not stand in the way. If Putlibai agreed he would, too.

So Mohandas was back where he had started. His mother sent him to uncle and uncle passed to mother. Meanwhile, Gandhi tried to get a scholarship from the Porbandar government. Mr. Lely, the British administrator of the state, rebuffed him curtly without even letting him present his case.

Mohandas returned to Rajkot. Pawn his wife's jewels? They were valued at two to three thousand rupees. Finally, his brother promised to supply the funds, but there remained his mother's doubts about young men's morals in England. Here Becharji Swami, the Jain monk, came to the rescue. He administered an oath to Mohandas who then solemnly took three vows: not to touch wine, women, or meat. Therewith, Putlibai consented.

Joyfully, in June, 1888, Gandhi left for Bombay with his brother, who carried the money. That did not end his tribulations. People said the Arabian Sea was too rough during the summer monsoon season; one ship had sunk in a gale. Departure was delayed. Meanwhile, the Modh Banias of Bombay heard about the projected trip. They convened a meeting of the clan and summoned Mohandas to attend. No Modh Bania had ever been to England, the elders argued; their religion forbade voyages abroad because Hinduism could not be practiced there.

Gandhi told them he would go nevertheless. At this, the headman ostracized Mohandas. "This boy shall be treated as an outcaste from today," the elder declared.

Undaunted, Gandhi bought a steamer ticket, a necktie, a short jacket, and enough food, chiefly sweets and fruit, for the three weeks to Southampton. On September 4th, he sailed. He was not yet eighteen. Several months earlier, Kasturbai had borne him a male child, and they called it Harilal. Now the trip to England gave Gandhi "a long and healthy separation" from his wife.

GANDHI AND THE GITA

Gandhi first read the *Gita* in Sir Edwin Arnold's translation while he was a second-year law student in London. He admits it was shameful not to have read it until the age of twenty, for the *Gita* is as sacred to Hinduism as the *Koran* is to Islam, the Old Testament to Judaism, and the New Testament to Christianity.

Subsequently, however, Gandhi read the original Sanskrit of the *Gita* and many translations. In fact, he himself translated the *Gita* from Sanskrit, which he did not know very well, into Gujarati and annotated it with comments.

. . . . .

Soon after reading the *Gita*, and especially in South Africa, Gandhi began his strivings to become a Karma yogi. Later, defining a Karma yogi, Gandhi wrote, "He will have no relish for sensual pleasures and will keep himself occupied with such activity as ennobles the soul. That is the path of action. Karma yoga is the yoga [means] which will deliver the self [soul] from the bondage of the body, and in it there is no room for self-indulgence."

Krishna puts it in a nutshell couplet:

For me, O Partha, there is naught to do in the three worlds, nothing worth gaining that I have not gained; yet I am ever in action.

In a notable comment of the *Gita*, Gandhi further elucidates the ideal man or the perfect Karma yogi: "He is a devotee who is jealous of none, who is a fount of mercy, who is without egotism, who is selfless, who treats alike cold and heat, happiness and misery, who is ever forgiving, who is always contented, whose resolutions are firm, who has dedicated mind and soul to God, who causes no dread, who is not afraid of others, who is free from exultation, sorrow and fear, who is pure, who is versed in action yet remains unaffected by it, who renounces all fruit, good or bad, who treats friend and foe alike, who is untouched by respect or disrespect, who is not puffed up by praise, who does not go under when people speak ill of him, who loves silence and solitude, who has a disciplined reason. Such devotion is inconsistent with the existence at the same time of strong attachments."

The *Gita* defines detachment precisely:

Freedom from pride and pretentiousness; non-violence, forgiveness, uprightness, service of the Master, purity, steadfastness, self-restraint. Aversion from sense-objects, absence of conceit, realization of the painfulness and evil of birth, death, age and disease.
Absence of attachment, refusal to be wrapped up in one's children, wife, home and family, even-mindedness whether good or evil befall. . . .

By practicing these virtues, the yogi will achieve "union with the Supreme" or Brahman, "disunion from all union with pain" and "an impartial eye, seeing Atman in all beings and all beings in Atman."

Gandhi summarized it in one word: "Desirelessness."

Desirelessness in its manifold aspects became Gandhi's goal and it created innumerable problems for his wife and children, his followers, and himself. Krishna declares,

But there is a unique reward. The great yogis, the Mahatmas or Great souls having come to Me, reach the highest perfection; they come not again to birth, unlasting and abode of misery.

Thus the yogi's highest recompense is to become so firmly united with God that he need never again return to the status of migrating mortal man. Several times during his life Gandhi expressed the hope not to be born anew.

. . . . .

There are devout Hindus, and mystic Hindus, who sit and meditate and fast and go naked and live in Himalayan caves. But Gandhi aimed to be ever active, ever useful, and ever needless. This was the realization he craved. Like everybody else, Gandhi had attachments. He sought to slough them off.

Hindu detachment includes but also transcends unselfishness; it connotes the religious goal of auto-disembodiment or non-violent self-effacement whereby the devotee discards his physical being and becomes one with God. This is not death; it is Nirvana. The attainment of Nirvana is a mystic process which eludes most Western minds and is difficult of achievement even by Hindus who assume, however, that mortals like Buddha and some modern mystics have accomplished the transformation. Gandhi did not accomplish it.

Gandhi did, however, achieve the status of yogi. . . .

The *Gita* concentrates attention on the purpose of life. In the West a person may ponder the purpose of life after he has achieved maturity and material success. A Hindu, if moved by the *Gita*, ponders the purpose of life when he is still on its threshold. Gandhi was very much moved by the spirit of the *Gita*.

78 | PRE-ADOLESCENTS—WHAT MAKES THEM TICK?

FRITZ REDL

The wild antics of some preadolescents are reported in this amusing article. Two possible explanations of such behavior are offered, along with some suggestions as to how parents can manage to live through this period of their children's metamorphosis.

The period of pre-adolescence is a stretch of no-man's land in child study work. By pre-adolescence I mean the phase when the nicest children begin to behave in a most awful way. This definition cannot

Reprinted from *Child Study*, XXI (1944), 44-48, 58–59, by permission of the author and the Child Study Association of America.

exactly be called scientific, but those who have to live with children of that age will immediately recognize whom I am talking about. This also happens to be the age about which we know least. Most of our books are written either about Children or about Adolescents. The phase I am talking about lies somewhere between the two—crudely speaking, between about nine and thirteen, in terms of chronological age, or between the fifth and eighth grade in terms of school classification.

It is surprising that we know so little about this age, but there certainly is no doubt that it is one of the most baffling phases of all. Most referrals to child guidance clinics occur around this age, and if you look for volunteers to work on programs in recreation or child care, you will make this peculiar discovery: you will have no trouble finding people who just love to bathe little babies until they smell good and shine. You will have a little more, but not too much, trouble finding people who are just waiting for a chance to "understand" adolescents who "have problems" and long for a shoulder on which to cry. But the pre-adolescent youngster offers neither of these satisfactions. You won't find many people who will be very happy working with him.

Are they children? No. Of course, they still look like young children. Practically no visible change has as yet taken place in their sex development. The voice is about as shrill and penetrating as it ever was, the personal picture which they represent as still highly reminiscent of a child —of about the worst child you have met, however, definitely not of the child they themselves were just a short time ago.

Are they adolescent? No. While filled with a collector's curiosity for odd elements of information about human sex life at its worst, they are not as yet really maturing sexually. While they occasionally like to brag about precocity in their sex attitude, "the boy" or "the girl" of the other sex is still something they really don't know what to do with if left alone with it for any length of time. While impertinent in their wish to penetrate the secrets of adult life, they have no concepts about the future, little worry about what is going to happen to them, nothing they would like to "talk over with you."

The reason why we know so little about this phase of development is simple but significant: it is a phase which is especially disappointing for the adult, and especially so for the adult who loves youth and is interested in it. These youngsters are hard to live with even where there is the most ideal child-parent relationship. They are not as much fun to love as when they were younger, for they don't seem to appreciate what they get at all. And they certainly aren't much to brag about, academically or otherwise. You can't play the "friendly helper" toward them either—they think you are plain dumb if you try it; nor can you play the role of the proud shaper of youthful wax—they stick to your fingers like putty and things become messier and messier the more you try to "shape" that age. Nor can you play the role of the proud and sacerdotal warden of the values of society to be pointed out to eager youth. They think you are plain funny in that role.

So the parent is at a loss and ready for a desperate escape into either of two bad mistakes—defeatism or tough-guy-stubbornness. The teacher shrugs her shoulders and blames most of this pre-adolescent spook on the teacher the youngster had before her, or on lack of parental cooperation, and hopes that somehow or other these children will "snap out of it." Even the psychiatrist, otherwise so triumphantly cynical about other people's trouble with children, is in a fix. For with these children you can't use "play techniques" any longer. They giggle themselves to death about the mere idea of sitting in one room with an adult and playing a table game while that adult desperately pretends that this is all there is to it. And one can't use the usual "interview technique" either. They find it funny that they should talk about themselves and their life, that they should consider as a "problem" what has "just happened," that they should try and remember how they felt about things, and that they are constantly expected to have "worries" or "fears"—two emotions which they are most skillful at hiding from their own self-perception, even if they do occur. Most of these youngsters seriously think the adult himself is crazy if he introduces such talk, and they naïvely enjoy the troubles they make, rather than those they have, and would much rather bear the consequences of their troubles than talk about them, even though those consequences include frustration or a beating or two.

Research, too, with very few exceptions, has skipped this period. If you study adolescence, you certainly can have graphs and charts on the rate at which the growth of pubic hair increases, the timing between that and the change of voice, and the irrelevance of both in terms of psychosexual development. Unfortunately, at the age we are talking about little of all this seems to take place. No drastic body changes occur, and whatever may happen within the glands is certainly not dramatic enough to explain the undoubtedly dramatic behavior of that phase. For a while some Yale biologists tried to discover an increase in hormone production around the age of eight, long before there is any visible sex maturation. However, they had trouble in making their research results useful for practical purposes. It took them weeks for one specimen of urine to be boiled in the right way as to show up the existence or non-existence of these hormones, and in the meantime Johnny would probably have been kicked out of five more schools anyway. In short, research has discreetly left this phase alone, and has retired from it, as it always does from things which are either too hard to demonstrate by statistical methods, or too hot to talk about after they have been discovered.

Thus, the practitioner—the parent, the teacher, counsellor or group worker—is left to his own devices. Fortunately, most of the things which are characteristic symptoms of this phase are known to us all.

PRE-ADOLESCENT BEHAVIOR— BAD AND IMPROPER

Here are some of the most frequent complaints adults raise in connection with their attempts to handle pre-adolescents: Outwardly, the most striking thing about them is their extreme physical restlessness. They can hardly stand still, running is more natural to them than walking, the word sitting is a euphemism if applied to what they do with a table and a chair. Their hands seem to need constant occupational therapy—they will turn up the edges of any book they handle, will have to manipulate pencils, any objects near them, or any one of the dozen-odd things they carry in their pockets, or even parts of their own body, whether it be nose and ears, scratching their hair, or parts of the anatomy usually taboo in terms of infantile upbringing. The return to other infantile habits is surprisingly intensive in many areas: even otherwise well-drilled and very housebroken youngsters may again show symptoms like bed-wetting, soiling, nail-biting, or its substitutes, like skin-chewing, finger-drumming, etc. Funny gestures and antics seem to turn up overnight with little or no reason—such things as facial tics, odd gestures and jerky movements, long-outgrown speech disorders, and the like.

In other areas these youngsters do not return to exactly the same habits of their infancy, but they go back to typical problem areas of younger childhood and start again where they had left off. Thus their search for the facts of life which had temporarily subsided under the impact of partial parental explanations will be resumed with vehemence, and with the impudence and insistence of a news correspondent rather than with the credulity of an obedient young child. It is the oddity, the wild fantastic story and the gory detail which fascinate them more than parental attempts at well-organized explanations of propagation, which they find rather boring.

Their old interpretation of the difference of sexes is revived, too. Girls seem obviously inferior to boys, who again interpret the difference in sex as that of a minus versus plus rather than of a difference in anatomical function. Thus girls are no good unless they are nearly like boys; and where the direct pride in masculine sexuality is subdued, indirect bragging about the size and strength of the biceps takes its place and becomes and sets the evaluation of anybody's worth. The girls go through somewhat the same phase, accept the interpretation of the boys all too eagerly and often wander through a period of frantic imitation of boyish behavior and negation of their female role. What sex manipulation does occur at this age usually happens in terms of experimentation and is on a highly organic level and very different from the masturbation of later adolescent years.

The fantasy life of youngsters of this age is something to look into, too. Wild day-dreams of the comic strip type of adventure, on the one hand, long stages of staring into empty space with nothing going on in their conscious mind on the other, are the two poles between which their fantasy life moves rapidly back and forth. Often manipulative play with a piece of string or the appearance of listening to the radio cover long stretches of quickly changing flights of ideas, and youngsters who reply "nothing," when you ask them what they were thinking about, do not necessarily lie. This description really fits the content as far as it could possibly be stated in any acceptable logical order and grammatical form.

The most peculiar phenomena, though, are found in the area of adult-child relationships. Even youngsters who obviously love their parents and have reason to do

so, will develop stretches of surprising irritability, distrust, and suspicion. Easily offended and constantly ready with accusations that adults don't understand them and treat them wrongly, they are yet very reckless and inconsiderate of other people's feelings and are quite surprised if people get hurt because of the way they behave. The concept of gratitude seems to be something stricken from the inventory of their emotions. The worst meal at the neighbors', at which they weren't even welcome, may be described more glowingly in its glory than the best-planned feast that you arranged for their birthday. The silliest antics, the most irrelevant possessions or skills of neighbors will be admired 'way beyond any well-rooted qualities and superior achievements of father and mother.

Daily life with Junior becomes a chain of little irritations about little things. The fight against the demands of obeying the rules of time and space is staged as vehemently as if the children were one or two years old again. Keeping appointed meal times, coming home, going to bed at a prearranged hour, starting work, stopping play when promised—all these demands seem to be as hard to get across and as badly resented, no matter how reasonable the parents try to be about them, as if they were the cruel and senseless torments of tyranny.

Lack of submission to parent-accepted manners becomes another source of conflict. If these youngsters would listen as attentively to what Webster has to say as they do the language of the worst ragamuffin on the street corner, their grades in English would be tops. Dressing properly, washing, keeping clean are demands which meet with obvious indignation or distrust. In a way, they seem to have lost all sense of shame and decency. Previously clean-minded youngsters will not mind telling the dirtiest jokes if they can get hold of them, and the most charming angels of last year can spend an hour giggling over the acrobatics which a youngster performs with his stomach gas and consider it the greatest joke.

And yet, while unashamed in so many ways, there are other areas of life where they become more sensitive rather than more crude: the idea of being undressed or bathed by their own parent may all of a sudden release vehement feelings of shame hitherto unknown to their elders, and the open display of affection before others makes them blush as though they had committed a crime. The idea of being called a sissy by somebody one's own age is the top of shamefulness and nearly intolerably because of the pain it involves.

One of the most interesting attitude changes during this period is that in boy-girl relationships. The boy has not only theoretical contempt for the girl but he has no place for her socially. Social parties which adults push so often because they find the clumsiness of their youngsters so cute, and because it is so safe to have boys and girls together at that age, such social dances are a pain in the neck to youngsters, who would obviously much rather have a good free-for-all or chase each other all over the place. The girls have little place in their lives for the same-age boys either. It is true that with them the transition through this pre-adolescent period usually is shorter than with the boys. But for a time their actual need for boy company is nil. The picture is different, though, if you watch the children within their own sex gangs. Then, all of a sudden, in talks under safe seclusion with their buddies, the boys or girls will display a trumped-up interest in the other sex, will brag about their sexual knowledge or precocity or about their success in dating. All this bragging, however, though it is about sex, is on an entirely unerotic level; the partner of the other sex only figures in it as the fish in the fisherman's story. The opposite sex, like the fish, serves only an indirect means for self-glorification.

WHAT MAKES THEM TICK?

The explanation of this peculiar phenomenon of human growth must, I think, move along two lines. One is of an *individualistic* nature, the second is a chapter in *group psychology.*

Explanation No. I: During pre-adolescence the well-knit pattern of a child's personality is broken up or loosened, so that adolescent changes can be built into it and so that it can be modified into the personality of an adult

Thus, the purpose of this developmental phase is not *improvement* but *disorganization;* not a permanent disorganization, of course, but a disorganization for future growth. This disorganization must occur, or else the higher organization cannot be achieved. In short, a child dōes not become an adult by becoming bigger and better. Simple "improvement" of a child's personality into that of an adult would only produce an over-sized child, an infantile adult. "Growing" into an adult means leaving behind, or destroying some of what the child has been, and becoming something else in many ways.

The real growth occurs during adolescence: pre-adolescence is the period of preliminary loosening up of the personality pattern in order that the change may take place. It is comparable to soaking the beans before you cook them. If this explanation is true, then we can understand the following manifestations:

1. During this "breaking-up-of-child-personality" period, old, *long-forgotten or repressed* impulses of earlier childhood will come afloat again, for awhile, before they are discarded for good. This would explain all that we have described about the return to infantile habits, silly antics, irritating behavior, recurring naughty habits, etc.

2. During this period of the breaking up of an established pattern, we also find that *already developed standards and values* lose their power and become ineffectual. Therefore the surprising lack of self-control, the

high degree of disorganization, the great trouble those youngsters have in keeping themselves in shape and continuing to live up to at least some of the expectations they had no difficulty living up to a short time ago. The individual conscience of the child seems to lose its power, and even the force of his intelligence and insight into his own impulses is obviously weakened. This would explain all we have said about their unreliability, the lowering of these standards of behavior, the disappearance of some of the barriers of shame and disgust they had established and their surprising immunity to guilt feelings in many areas of life.

3. During a period of loosening up of personality texture, we would expect that the whole individual will be full of conflict, and that the *natural accompaniments* of conflict will appear again, namely, *anxieties and fears*, on the one hand, and *compulsive mechanisms of symbolic reassurance*, on the other. This is why so many of these youngsters really show fears or compulsive tics which otherwise only neurotic children would show. Yet this behavior is perfectly normal and will be only temporary. This would explain the frequent occurrence of fantastic fears in the dark, of ghosts and burglars, and it would also explain the intensity with which some of these youngsters cling to protective mechanisms, like the possession of a flashlight or gun as a symbol of protection, or the display of nervous tics and peculiar antics which usually include magic tricks to fool destiny and assure protection from danger or guilt.

For a long time I thought that all this about finishes the picture of pre-adolescent development, until a closer observation of the group life of pre-adolescents showed me that such a theory leaves much unexplained. It seems to me that there is still another explanation for a host of pre-adolescent symptoms.

Explanation No. II: During pre-adolescence it is normal for youngsters to drop their identification with adult society and establish a strong identification with a group of their peers

This part of pre-adolescent development is of a group psychological nature, and is as important to the child's later functioning as a citizen in society as the first principle is for his personal mental and emotional health. This group phenomenon is surprisingly universal and explains much of the trouble we adults have with children of pre-adolescent age. To be sure that I am rightly understood, I want to emphasize that what happens during this age goes way beyond the personal relationship between Johnny and his father. Johnny's father now becomes for him more than his father: he becomes, all of a sudden, a representative of the value system of adult society versus the child, at least in certain moments of his life. The same is true the other way around. Johnny becomes more to his father than his child: at certain moments he isn't Johnny any more but the typical representative of Youth versus Adult. A great many of the "educational" things adults do to children, as well as many of the rebellious acts of children toward adults, are not meant toward the other fellow at all; they are meant toward the general group of "Adults" or "Youth" which this other person represents. To disentangle personal involvement from this group psychological meaning of behavior is perhaps the most vital and so far least attempted problem of education in adolescence.

If this explanation is true, then it seems to me that the following phenomena of pre-adolescent behavior will be well understood:

1. In no other age do youngsters show such a deep need for *clique and gang formation* among themselves as in this one. From the adult angle this is usually met with much suspicion. Of course, it is true that youngsters will tend to choose their companions from among those who are rejected, rather than approved of, by their parents. Perhaps we can understand why the more unacceptable a youngster is on the basis of our adult behavior code, the more highly acceptable he will be in the society of his own peers. The clique formation of youngsters among them-

selves usually has some form of definitely "gang" character: that means it is more thoroughly enjoyed by being somewhat "subversive" in terms of adult standards. Remember how youngsters often are magically fascinated by certain types of ring-leaders, even though this ring-leadership may involve rather harmless though irritating activities— such as smoking, special clothes, late hours, gang language, etc.

From the angle of the adult and his anxieties, much of this seems highly objectionable. From the angle of the youngster and his normal development, most of it is highly important. For it is vital that he satisfy the wish for identification with his pals even though or just because such identification is sometimes frowned upon by the powers that be. The courage to stick to his pal against you, no matter how much he loves you and otherwise admires your advice is an important step forward in the youngster's social growth.

2. In all groups something like an *unspoken behavior code* develops, and it is this unwritten code on which the difference between "good" and "bad" depends. Up to now the youngster has lived within the psychological confines of the adult's own value system. Good and bad were defined entirely on the basis of adult tastes. Now he enters the magical ring of peer-codes. And the code of his friends differs essentially from that of adult society. In some items the two are diametrically opposed. In terms of the adult code, for instance, it is good if children bring home high grades, take pride in being much better than the neighbor's children, in being better liked by the teacher, and more submissive to the whims of the teaching adult than are other people's children. In terms of peer-standards things are directly reversed. Studying too much exposes you to the suspicion of being a sissy, aggressive pride against other children in suspiciously close to teacher-pet roles, and obedience to the adult in power often comes close to being a fifth columnist in terms of "the gang."

Some of the typically adult-fashioned values are clearly rejected by peer standards; others are potentially compatible at times, while conflicting at other times; some of them can be shared in common. Thus, a not too delinquent "gang" to which your youngster is proud to belong may be characterized by the following code-range: it is all right in this gang to study and work reasonably well in school. It is essential, though, that you dare to smoke, lie, even against your own father, if it means the protection of a pal in your gang, that you bear the brunt of scenes at home if really important gang activities are in question. At the same time this gang would not want you to steal, would be horrified if your sex activity went beyond the telling of dirty stories, and would oust you tacitly because they would think you too sophisticated for them. The actual group of pre-adolescents moves between hundreds of different shades of such gang-codes, and the degree to which we adults have omitted opening our eyes to this vital phase of child development is astounding.

3. The change from *adult-code* to *peer-code* is not an easy process for a youngster but full of conflict and often painful. For, while he would like to be admired by his pals on a peer-code basis, he still loves his parents personally and hates to see them misunderstand him or have them get unhappy about what he does. And, while he would love to please his family and be again accepted by them and have them proud of him, he simply couldn't face being called a sissy or be suspected of being a coward or a teacher's pet by his friends. In most of those cases where we find a serious conflict between the two sets of standards, we will find the phenomenon of *social hysteria*. This applies to youngsters who so overdo their loyalty to either one of the two behavior standards that they then have to go far beyond a reasonable limit. Thus, you find youngsters so scared of being thought bad by their parents that they don't dare to mix happily with children of their own age; and you find others so keen to achieve peer status with friends of their own age that they begin to reject parental advice, every finer feeling of loyalty to the home, and accept all and any lure of gang prestige even if it involves delinquent and criminal activity. It is obvious that a clear analysis by the adult and the avoidance of counter-hysteria can do much to improve things.

HOW TO SURVIVE LIFE WITH JUNIOR

If any of the above is true, then it should have an enormous impact on education. For then most of this pre-adolescent spook isn't merely a problem of things that shouldn't happen and ought to be squelched, but of things that should happen, but need to be regulated and channelized. Of course, you can't possibly just let Junior be as pre-adolescent as he would like without going crazy yourself, and you definitely shouldn't think of self-defense only and thus squelch the emotional and social development of your offspring. How to do both—survive and also channelize normal but tough growth periods without damage to later development—is too long a story to complete in a short article. But here are a few general hints:

1. Avoid Counter-Hysterics

It seems to me that ninety per cent of the more serious problems between children and parents or teachers on which I have ever been consulted could have been easily avoided. They were not inherent in the actual problems of growth. They were produced by the hysterical way in which the adults reacted to them. Most growth problems—even the more serious ones—can be outgrown eventually, though this may be a painful process—provided the adults don't use them as a springboard for this own over-emotional reactions. This does not mean that I advocate that you give up and let everything take its course. I do suggest you study the situation and decide where to allow things and where to interfere. The problem is: whichever you decide to do—the *way* you do it should be realistic, free from hysteric over-emotionalism. With this policy in mind you can enjoy all the fun of having problems with your child without producing a problem child.

2. Don't Fight Windmills

Let's not forget that pre-adolescents are much more expert in handling us than we ever can be in handling them. Their skill in sizing us up and using our emotions and weaknesses for their own ends has reached a peak at this age. It took them eight to ten years to learn, but they have learned by thorough observation. While we were worrying about them, they were not worried about us, and they had ample time and leisure to study psychology. This means that if they now go out on the venture of proving to themselves how emancipated they are, they will choose exactly the trick which will irritate us most. They will develop pre-adolescent symptoms in accordance with their understanding of our psychology. Thus, some of them will smoke, curse, talk about sex, or stay out late. Some will stop being interested in their grades, get kicked out of school, or threaten to become the type of person who will never be acceptable in good society. Others again will develop vocational interests which we look down on, will choose the company we dread, talk language which makes us jump, or may even run away at intervals.

But whatever surface behavior they display—don't fall for it. Don't fight the behavior. Interpret the cause of it first, then judge how much and in what way you should interfere. Thus, Johnny's smoking may really mean he is sore that his father never takes him to a football match, or it may mean he thinks you don't appreciate how adult he already is, or it may mean he has become dependent on his class-clown. Mary's insistence upon late hours may mean she doesn't know how to control herself, or it may mean she is sore because her school pals think you are social snobs who live a life different from theirs, or it may mean she is so scared that her sex ignorance will be discovered that she has to run around with a crowd more sophisticated about staying up late, so as to hide her lack of sophistication in another respect.

In any case, all these things are not so hard to figure out. Instead of getting excited and disapproving of the strange behavior, just open your eyes for a while and keep them open without blinking.

3. Provide a Frame of Life Adequate for Growth

No matter how much you dislike it, every pre-adolescent youngster needs the chance to have some of his wild behavior come out in some place or other. It will make a lot of difference whether or not he has a frame of life adequate for such growth. For example: Johnny needs the experience of running up against some kind of adventurous situation where he can prove he is a regular guy and not just mother's boy. Cut him off from all life situations containing elements of unpredictability and he may have to go stealing from the grocery store to prove his point. Give him a free and experimental camp setting to be adventurous in and he will be happily pre-adolescent without getting himself or anybody else in trouble. All youngsters need some place where pre-adolescent traits can be exercised and even tolerated. It is your duty to plan for such places in their life as skillfully as you select their school or vocational opportunities.

4. Watch Out for Pre-adolescent Corns

Most people don't mind their toes being stepped on occasionally. But if there is a corn there, that is a different matter. Well, all pre-adolescents have certain corns, places where they are hypersensitive. Avoid these as much as possible. One of the most important to avoid is harking back to their early childhood years. The one thing they don't want to be reminded of is of themselves as small children, yourself as the mother or father of the younger child. If you punish—don't repeat ways you used when they were little. If you praise—don't use arguments that would please a three-year-old but make a thirteen-year-old red with shame or fury. Whether you promise or reward, threaten or blackmail, appeal to their sense, morals, or anything else, always avoid doing it in the same way you used to do when they were little.

I have seen many pre-adolescents reject what their parents wanted, not because they felt that it was unreasonable or unjustified, but on account of the way in which the parents put the issue. There is something like a developmental level of parental control as well as developmental levels of child behavior. The two have to be matched or there will be fireworks.

5. If in Doubt, Make a Diagnostic Check-up

Not all the behavior forms we described above are always merely "pre-adolescent." Some of them are more than that. After all, there are such things as juvenile delinquents and psycho-neurotics, and we shouldn't pretend that everything is bound to come out in the wash.

Usually you can get a good hunch about dangerous areas if you check on these points: How deep is the pre-adolescent trait a youngster shows? If it is too vehement and impulsive, too unapproachable by even the most reasonable techniques, then the chances are that Johnny's antics are symptoms not only of growth but also of something being wrong somewhere and needing repair. Often this may be the case: Five of Johnny's antics are just pre-adolescent, pure and simple, and should not be interfered with too much. However, these five are tied up with five others which are definitely serious, hang-overs from old, never really solved problems, results of wrong handling, wrong environmental situations, or other causes. It will do no good to brush off the whole matter by calling it pre-adolescent. In that case the first five items need your protection and the other five need a repair job done. Whenever you are very much in doubt, it is wise to consult expert help for the checkup—just as you would in order to decide whether a heart murmur is due to too fast growth or to an organic disturbance.

79 | SEXUAL BEHAVIOR IN THE HUMAN FEMALE

ALFRED C. KINSEY *et al.*

Sexual relations before marriage are not sanctioned in our society.
Since young people mature sexually in their early teens, and since most
people marry in their early twenties, adolescents usually have
no socially acceptable outlets for their strong sexual urges for a period of
approximately ten years. Few societies in the world are as sexually
repressive as our own.

Kinsey deals with some of the sexual outlets which young people
discover for themselves. His comments raise a number of questions
which should be investigated further: Have laws, punishment,
and police action been effective in controlling sexual activity? What
are the problems here?

SEXUAL PROBLEMS OF UNMARRIED YOUTH

As . . . [an] instance of the everyday need for a wider general understanding of human sexual behavior, there are the sexual problems of unmarried individuals in our social organization, and particularly of unmarried youth. The problems are products of the fact that the human female and male become biologically adults some years before our social custom and the statute law recognize them as such, and of the fact that our culture has increasingly insisted that sexual functions should be confined to persons who are legally recognized as adults, and particularly to married adults.

This failure to recognize the mature capacities of teen-age youth is relatively recent. Prior to the last century or so, it was well understood that they were the ones who had the maximum sexual capacity, and the great romances of literature turned around the love affairs of teen-age boys and girls. Achilles' intrigue with Deidamia, by whom a son

was born, had occurred some time before he was fifteen. Acis had just passed sixteen at the time of his love affair with Galatea. Chione was reputed to have had "a thousand suitors when she reached the marriageable age of fourteen." Narcissus had reached his sixteenth year when "many youths and many maidens sought his love." Helen was twelve years old when Paris carried her off from Sparta. In one of the greatest of pastoral romances, Daphnis was fifteen and Chloe was thirteen. Heloise was eighteen when she fell in love with Abelard. Tristram was nineteen when he first met Isolde. Juliet was less than fourteen when Romeo made love to her. All of these youth, the great lovers of history, would be looked upon as immature adolescents and identified as juvenile delinquents if they were living today. It is the increasing inability of older persons to understand the sexual capacities of youth which is responsible for the opinion that there is a rise in juvenile delinquency, for there are few changes in the sexual behavior of the youth themselves.

There is an increasing opinion that these youth should ignore their sexual responses and should abstain from sexual activities prior to marriage—which means,

Excerpts reprinted from *Sexual Behavior in the Human Female* (W. B. Saunders Co., 1953), pp. 13–21, 101–26, by permission of the publisher and the Institute for Sex Research, Inc.

for the average male and female in this country today, until they are somewhere between twenty-one and twenty-three years of age. But neither the law nor the custom can change the age of onset of adolescence, nor the development of the sexual capacities of teen-age youths. Consequently they continue to be aroused sexually, and to respond to the point of orgasm. There is no evidence that it is possible for any male who is adolescent, and not physically incapacitated, to get along without some kind of regular outlet until old age finally reduces his responsiveness and his capacity to function sexually. While there are many females who appear to get along without such an outlet during their teens, the chances that a female can adjust sexually after marriage seem to be materially improved if she has experienced orgasm at an earlier age. . . .

In actuality, the teen-age and twenty-year-old males respond more frequently than most older males; their responses are, on the whole, more intense than those of older males; and, in spite of their difficulty in finding socio-sexual outlets, they reach orgasm more frequently than most older males. Among unmarried males the frequency of orgasm is at a maximum somewhere between the ages of sixteen and eighteen. Similarly, among married males there is no age group in which sexual activity is, on an average, more frequent than it is among the males in their late teens and early twenties.

The attempt to ignore and suppress the physiologic needs of the sexually most capable segment of the population has led to more complications than most persons are willing to recognize. This is why so many of our American youth, both females and males, depend upon masturbation instead of coitus as a pre-marital outlet. Restraints on pre-marital heterosexual contacts appear to be primary factors in the development of homosexual activities among both females and males. . . . The considerable development of pre-marital petting, which many foreigners consider one of the unique aspects of the sexual pattern in this country, is similarly an outgrowth of this restraint on pre-marital coitus. . . . The law specifies the right of the married adult to have regular intercourse, but it makes no provision whatsoever for the approximately 40 per cent of the population which is sexually mature but unmarried. Many youths and older unmarried females and males are seriously disturbed because the only sources of sexual outlet available to them are either legally or socially disapproved.

Most unmarried males, and not a few of the unmarried females, would like to know how to resolve this conflict between their physiologic capacities and the legal and social codes. They would like to know whether masturbation will harm them physically or interfere with their subsequent responses to a marital partner; they would like to know whether they should or should not engage in petting; and, apart from the moral issues that may be involved, they would like to know what pre-marital petting experience may actually do to their marital adjustments. Should they or should they not have coitus before marriage? What effect will this sort of experience have on their subsequent marital adjustments? In any type of sexual activity, what things are normal and what things are abnormal? What has been the experience of other youth faced with these same problems? On all of these matters most youth are ready to consider the social and moral values, but they would also like to know what correlations the scientific data show between pre-marital and marital experience.

In an attempt to answer some of these questions, we have tried to discover the incidences and frequencies of non-marital activities among American females and males, and have attempted to discover what correlations there may be between pre-marital patterns of behavior and subsequent sexual adjustments in marriage. . . .

SEXUAL EDUCATION OF CHILDREN

Within the last thirty years, parents in increasing number have come to realize the importance of the early education of their children on matters of sex. But what things children should be taught, who should teach them, at what age they should be taught, and how the teaching should be conducted, are matters about which there has been much theory but few data on which to base any program of sex education. For some years we have, therefore, obtained information from our subjects in regard to the ages at which they acquired their first knowledge of various aspects of sex, the sources of their first knowledge, and the ages at which they first became involved in each type of sexual activity. In addition to obtaining this record from each adult, we have engaged in a more detailed study of younger children and particularly of children between two and five years of age. The study needs to be carried further before we are ready to report in detail, but some things already seem clear.

It is apparent that considerable factual knowledge about most sexual phenomena is acquired by most children before they become adolescent, but there is a considerable number who acquire their first information in their youngest years, as soon as they are able to talk. Although some persons insist that the sex education of the child should be undertaken only by the child's parents or religious mentors, not more than a few per cent—perhaps not more than 5 per cent—of all the subjects in the present study recalled that they had received anything more than the most incidental sort of information from either of those sources. Most of the children had acquired their earliest information from other children. Whether it is more desirable, in terms of the ultimate effects upon their lives, that such information should come first from more experienced adults, or whether it is better that children should learn about sex from other children, is a question which we are not yet able to answer. At this stage in our study we are quite certain that no one has any sufficient information to evaluate objectively the relative merits of these diverse sources of sexual education.

It is apparent, however, that if parents or other adults are to be the sources of the child's first information on sex, they must give that information by the time the child is ten or twelve, and in many instances at some earlier age. Otherwise the child, whatever the parents may wish, will have previously acquired the information from its companions.

Our studies indicate, moreover, that the way in which a child reacts to the sexual information which it receives, and to the overt sexual activity in which it may become involved in later years, may depend upon attitudes which it develops while it is very young. Early attitudes in respect to nudity, to anatomic differences between the sexes, to the reproductive function, to verbal references to sex, to the qualities and prerequisites which our culture traditionally considers characteristic of females or males, and to still other aspects of sex are developed at very early ages. Emotional reactions on some of these matters have been discernible in some of the two-year-olds with which we have worked, and the three-year-old children have had pronounced reactions on most of these matters. When the child becomes older these early attitudes may influence its reactions to sexual manifestations in its own body, its capacity to meet sexual situations without serious disturbance, its acceptance or non-acceptance of socio-sexual contacts, and, as an adult, his or her capacity to adjust sexually in marriage. Because early training may be so significant, most parents would like to have information on the most effective methods of introducing the child to the realities of sex.

Most parents would like to know more about the significance of pre-adolescent sex play, about the sexual activities in which children actually engage, about the possibilities of their children becoming sexually involved with adults, and what effect such involvements may have upon a child's subsequent sexual adjustments. Most parents would like to know whether the sexual responses of a child are similar, physiologically, to those of an adult. They would like to know whether there are differences between the sexual problems of adolescent boys and those of adolescent girls; and if there are differences, they would like to know on what they depend. The data in the present volume will answer some of these questions.

In this study, we have had the excellent cooperation of a great many parents because they are concerned with the training of their children, and because they realize how few data there are on which to establish a sound program of sex education.

SOCIAL CONTROL
OF SEXUAL BEHAVIOR

Most societies have recognized the necessity of protecting their members from those who impose sexual relationships on others by the use of force, and our own culture extends the same sort of restriction to those who use such intimidation as an adult may exercise over a child, or such undue influence as a so-

cial superior may exercise over an underling. In its encouragement of marriage society tries to provide a socially acceptable source of sexual outlet, and it considers that sexual activities which interfere with marriages and homes, and sexual activities which lead to the begetting of children outside of marriage, are socially undesirable. The social organization also tries to control persons who make nuisances of themselves, as the exhibitionist and voyeur may do, by departing from the generally approved custom. In addition our culture considers that social interests are involved when an individual departs from the Judeo-Christian sex codes by engaging in such sexual activities as masturbation, mouth-genital contacts, homosexual contacts, animal contacts, and other types of behavior which do not satisfy the procreative function of sex.

The Incidence of Sex Offenses

Within the last decade, there has been a growing concern in this country over an apparent increase in the number of persons who engage in sexual activities which are contrary to our law and custom. Reports in the press and the information which is officially released often suggest that the number of sex offenders is steadily increasing.

Unfortunately, however, there has been no good measure of the actual extent of the problem that is involved. The conclusion that the incidences of sex offense have increased is based primarily upon an increase in the number of arrests on sex charges, but it is not substantiated by our information on the incidences of various types of sexual activity among older and younger generations in the population as a whole. Statements concerning increasing incidences usually do not allow for the considerable increase in the total population of the country, the more complete reporting of sex crimes by the press and by the agencies which contribute to the official statistics, and the fact that the newer sex laws make felonies of some acts which were never penalized or which were treated as minor misdemeanors until a few years ago. Moreover, there has been no adequate recognition of the fact that fluctuations in the number of arrests may represent nothing more than fluctuations in the activities of law enforcement officers.

Preliminary analyses of our data indicate that only a minute fraction of one per cent of the persons who are involved in sexual behavior which is contrary to the law are ever apprehended, prosecuted, or convicted, and that there are many other factors besides the behavior of the apprehended individual which are responsible for the prosecution of the particular persons who are brought to court. The prodding of some reform group, a newspaper-generated hysteria over some local sex crime, a vice drive which is put on by the local authorities to distract attention from defects in their administration of the city government, or the addition to the law-enforcement group of a sadistic officer who is disturbed over his own sexual problems, may result in a doubling—a hundred per cent increase—in the number of arrests on sex charges, even though there may have been no change in the actual behavior of the community, and even though the illicit sex acts that are apprehended and prosecuted may still represent no more than a fantastically minute part of the illicit activity which takes place every day in the community.

The Sex Offender

A primary fault in most studies of sex offenders is the fact that they are confined to the study of sex offenders. Just as the laboratory scientist needs a control group to interpret what he finds in his experimental animals, so we need to understand the sexual behavior of persons who have never been involved with the law.

Psychologists, psychiatrists, sociologists, and criminologists have given us some understanding of the personalities of criminals, including some sex offenders, but the studies have rarely compared convicted individuals with persons involved in similar behavior in the population at large. It does not suffice to find that sex offenders were breast fed, or bottle fed, without knowing how many other persons who were similarly fed did not become sex offenders. It does not suffice to discover that sex offenders come from disrupted homes without learning why so many other persons who come from similarly disrupted homes do not end up as sex offenders. It does not suffice to find that the homosexual offenders preferred their mothers to their fathers, when a survey of non-offenders shows that most children, for perfectly obvious reasons, are more closely associated with their mothers. We need to know why certain individuals, rather than all of those who engage in similar behavior, become involved with the law. We need to learn more about the circumstances of the particular activities which led to their apprehension, and about the way they were handled by the arresting police officer, the prosecutor, the court-attached psychiatrist, the judge, and the local press.

In the course of this present study we have secured the histories of some thirteen hundred persons who have been convicted and sentenced to penal institutions as sex offenders, but these histories would be difficult to interpret if we had not gathered the histories of more than fourteen thousand persons who have never been involved with the law.

We have been in a peculiarly favorable position to secure data from persons serving time in penal institutions as sex offenders. We have been able to guarantee the confidence of the record as no law enforcement officer, no clinician connected with the courts, and no institutional officer could guarantee. From coast to coast, the grapevine has spread the word that we have not violated the confidences which we have recorded in our histories, and that we have always refused to work in any institution in which the administration has not agreed to uphold our right to preserve such confidences. In addition to the information which we have secured directly from the prisoners, we have had access to the institutional files on each inmate, and in many instances we have had access to the court records, the probation records, and the records from the departments of public welfare or other agencies which had had contact with these cases.

Throughout our research, whether with persons who have been convicted as sex offenders or with our subjects in the population at large, we have tried to make it apparent that we wanted to understand their activities as they understood them. Consequently we have not found sex offenders prone to deny their guilt, or to rationalize their behavior. In actuality, most of them have given us a record of activity that far exceeded anything that had been brought out in the legal proceedings or in the records of the penal institution.

Effective Sex Law

Out of this study of sex offenders, and of the sexual behavior of females and males who have never been involved with the law, should come data which may some day be used by legislators in the development of a body of sex law that may provide society with more adequate protection against the more serious types of sex offenders. While we shall need to continue this part of our study before we are ready to summarize the data which we have been gathering, our present information seems to make it clear that the current sex laws are unenforced and are unenforceable because they are too completely out of accord with the realities of human behavior, and because they attempt too much in the way of social control. Such a high proportion of the females and males in our population is involved in sexual activities which are prohibited by the law of most of the states of the union, that it is inconceivable that the present laws could be administered in any fashion that even remotely approached systematic and complete enforcement. . . . . The consequently capricious enforcement which these laws now receive offers an opportunity for maladministration, for police and political graft, and for blackmail which is regularly imposed both by underworld groups and by the police themselves.

The Protection of the Individual

Many people, perhaps fortunately, have no conception that their everyday sexual activities may, in actuality, be contrary to the law. On the other hand, many other persons live in constant fear that certain of their sexual activities, even though they are typical of those which occur in the histories of most females and males, may be discovered and lead to social or possibly legal difficulties. In its attempt to protect itself from serious sex offenders, society has threatened the security of most of its members who are old enough to perform sexually. The efficiency of many individuals and their integration into the social organization is, thereby, seriously impaired. While this is especially true of persons with histories of extra-marital coitus, with homosexual histories, and with histories of animal contacts on the farm, it is also true of some persons who have pre-marital coitus, of many of those who engage in mouth-genital contacts, and even of some of those who engage in pre-marital petting. Because of the social taboos there are many individuals who, even in this generation, are disturbed over their masturbatory histories.

In many instances the law, in the course of punishing the offender, does more damage to more persons than was ever done by the individual in his illicit sexual activity. The histories which we have accumulated contain many such instances. The intoxicated male who accidentally exposes his genitalia before a child, may receive a prison sentence which leave his family destitute for some period of years, breaks up his marriage, and leaves three or four children wards of the state and without the sort of guidance which the parents might well have supplied. The older, unmarried women who prosecute the male whom they find swimming nude, may ruin his business or professional career, bring his marriage to divorce, and do such damage to his children as the observation of his nudity could never have done to the women who prosecuted him. The child who has been raised in fear of all strangers and all physical manifestations of affection, may ruin the lives of the married couple who had lived as useful and honorable citizens through half or more of a century, by giving her parents and the police a distorted version of the old man's attempt to bestow grandfatherly affection upon her.

The male who is convicted because he has made homosexual advances to other males, may be penalized by being sent to an institution where anywhere from half to three-quarters of the inmates are regularly having homosexual activity within the institution. The laws penalizing homosexual approaches as well as homosexual activities, and which offer the possibility in some states of an individual being incarcerated for life because he "shows homosexual tendencies," have developed a breed of teenage law-breakers who first seek satisfaction in sexual contacts with these males, and then blackmail and assault and murder, if necessary, and escape legal punishment on the specious plea that they were protecting themselves from "indecent sexual advances." Still more serious is the utilization of the same sort of blackmail and physical assault by the police in many of our larger cities. The pre-adolescent boy who is convicted of some offense may be sent to a juvenile institution where he turns adolescent and reaches the peak of his sexual capacity in a community which is exclusively male, and where he can find no socio-sexual outlet except with other males. If kept in such an institution until he reaches his middle teens, he may find it difficult to make social and socio-sexual adjustments with girls when he gets out of the institution, and may continue his homosexual activities for the rest of his life. Then he may be penalized for being what society has made him.

Somehow, in an age which calls itself scientific and Christian, we should be able to discover more intelligent ways of protecting social interests without doing such irreparable damage to so many individuals and to the total social organization to which they belong.

We began our research, as we have said, for the sake of increasing knowledge in an area in which knowledge was limited. We have continued the research through these years, in part because we have come to understand that the total social organization, and many individuals in it, may benefit by an increase in our understanding of human sexual behavior.

. . . . .

PRE-ADOLESCENT SEXUAL RESPONSE AND ORGASM

At least some newborn mammals, including some human infants, both female and male, are capable of being stimulated by and responding to tactile stimulation in a way which is sexual in the strictest sense of the term. We now understand that this capacity to respond depends upon the existence of end organs of touch in the body surfaces, nerves connecting these organs with the spinal cord and brain, nerves which extend from the cord to various muscles in the body, and the autonomic nervous system through which still other parts of the body are brought into action. . . . All of these structures are present at birth, and the record supplied by the recall of the adult females and males who have contributed to the present study, and direct observations made by a number of qualified observers, indicate that some children are quite capable of responding in a way which may show all of the essential physiologic changes which characterize the sexual responses of an adult.

Among both young children and adults, there appear to be differences in the capacity to be aroused sexually. Some individuals respond quickly and frequently to a wide variety of physical and psychologic stimuli. Others respond more slowly and infrequently. Even in a single individual the levels of response may vary from time to time as his general health, nutritional state, fatigue, and still other circumstances may affect his physiologic capacities. Levels of response may also depend on the age of the individual. Although all individuals may be born with the necessary anatomy and capacity to respond to tactile stimulation, the capacity to respond in a way which is specifically sexual seems to increase as the child develops physically, and in many children it does not appear until near the time of adolescence. In some females it may not appear until some years after the onset of adolescence. We do not understand all of the factors which are involved, but some of

the capacity to respond sexually seems to depend on certain hormones which develop in the body of the growing boy and girl. . . .

Whether the late appearance of sexual responsiveness in some individuals means that they were actually not capable of responding at an earlier age, or whether it means that they had not previously been subjected to sexual stimuli which were sufficient to bring response, is a matter which it has not yet been possible to determine. It is possible that some younger children are not at all capable of responding sexually, or at least incapable of responding to the sorts of stimuli which would arouse an adult, but of this we are not certain. It is certain, however, that there are children, both female and male, who are quite capable of true sexual response.

Accumulative Incidence of Pre-adolescent Response

What seem to be sexual responses have been observed in infants immediately at birth, and specifically sexual responses, involving the full display of physiologic changes which are typical of the responses of an adult, have been observed in both female and male infants as young as four months of age, and in infants and pre-adolescent children of every older age.

About one per cent of the older females who have contributed histories to the present study recalled that they were making specifically sexual responses to physical stimuli, and in some instances to psychologic stimuli, when they were as young as three years of age. . . . This, however, must represent only a portion of the children who were responding at that age, for many children would not recognize the sexual nature of their early responses.

About 4 per cent of the females in our sample thought they were responding sexually by five years of age. Nearly 16 per cent recalled such responses by ten years of age. All told, some 27 per cent recalled that they had been aroused erotically—sexually—at some time before the age of adolescence which, for the average female, occurs sometime between her twelfth and thirteenth birthdays. . . . However, the number of pre-adolescent girls who are ever aroused sexually must be much higher than this record indicates.

Comparisons of the records contributed by subjects who had terminated their schooling at the grade school, high school, college, and graduate school levels, indicate that pre-adolescent erotic responses may have occurred in a higher percentage of the groups which subsequently obtained the most extensive schooling . . . ; but this may simply reflect a greater capacity of the better educated females to recall their experience.

· · · · ·

Accumulative Incidence of Pre-adolescent Orgasm

About 14 per cent of all the females in our sample—nearly half of those who had been erotically aroused before adolescence—recalled that they had reached orgasm either in masturbation or in their sexual contacts with other children or older person (*i.e.*, in their *socio-sexual* contacts) prior to adolescence. It is not all impossible that a still higher percentage had actually had such experience without recognizing its nature.

On the basis of the adult recall and the observations which we have just recorded, we can report 4 cases of females under one year of age coming to orgasm, and a total of 23 cases of small girls three years of age or younger reaching orgasm. The incidences, based on our total female sample, show some 0.3 per cent (16 individuals) who recalled that they had reached orgasm by three years

of age, 2 per cent by five years, 4 per cent by seven years, 9 per cent by eleven years, and 14 per cent by thirteen years of age. . . . Thus, there had been a slow but steady increase in the number of girls in the sample who had reached orgasm prior to adolescence. In the case of the male, the percentages of those who had reached orgasm also rose steadily through the early pre-adolescent years, but they began to rise more abruptly in the later pre-adolescent years.

Sources of Early Arousal and Orgasm

One per cent of the females in our sample recalled that they were masturbating (in the strict sense of the term) by three years of age, and 13 per cent recalled masturbation by ten years of age. . . . The record does not show what percentage of the early masturbation had brought sexual arousal, but it does show 0.3 per cent of the females in the total sample masturbating to the point of orgasm by three years of age, and 8 per cent by ten years of age. . . .

Psychologic reactions or physical contacts with other girls were, in a few instances, the sources of sexual arousal at three years of age. About 3 per cent had been aroused by other girls by eleven years of age, and 6 per cent by thirteen years of age.

Reaction to or contacts with boys had brought similar arousal in a fraction of one per cent at three years of age, but in about 7 per cent of the sample by eleven, and in 12 per cent of the sample by thirteen years of age. . . .

Out of the 659 females in the sample who had experienced orgasm before they were adolescent, 86 per cent had had their first experience in masturbation, some 7 per cent had discovered it in sexual contacts with other girls, 2 per cent in petting, and 1 per cent in coitus with boys or older males. Interestingly enough, 2 per cent had had their first orgasm in physical contacts with dogs or cats. Some 2 per cent had first reached orgasm under other circumstances, including the climbing of a rope.

Orgasm had been discovered in self-masturbation more often by the girls than by the boys. In earlier pre-adolescence, the boy's first orgasms are frequently the product of physical and emotional situations which bring spontaneous sexual reactions; and although there is a great deal of incidental manipulation of genitalia among younger boys, it rarely brings orgasm. Among the adolescent boys in our sample, masturbation appears to have accounted for only 68 per cent of the first orgasms. . . .

. . . . .

The child's initial attempts at self-masturbation had been inspired in some instances by the observation of other children who were engaged in such activity, or through the more deliberate instruction given by some older child or adult. These were quite commonly the first sources of information for most of the males in the sample; but in the great majority of instances females learn to masturbate, both in pre-adolescent and later years, by discovering the possibilities of such activity entirely on their own. . . .

PRE-ADOLESCENT HETEROSEXUAL PLAY

Although 30 per cent of the females in the sample recalled pre-adolescent heterosexual play, and 33 per cent recalled pre-adolescent homosexual play, only 48 per cent recalled any sort of socio-sexual play before adolescence. This means that 15 per cent had had sex play only with boys, 18 per cent had had it only with girls, and another 15 per cent had had it with both boys and girls.

Accumulative Incidence of Heterosexual Play

Our data on the incidence and frequency of sex play among pre-adolescent children are drawn in part from the studies we have made of children of very young ages, but they depend largely upon the recall of the adults who have contributed to the present study. It has been apparent, however, that the adults have recalled only a portion of their pre-adolescent experience, for even children forget a high proportion of their experience within a matter of weeks or months. This is due sometimes to the incidental nature of the sex play, and in some instances to the fact that the child was emotionally disturbed by the experience and blocked psychologically in recalling a taboo activity. But even though the child may not be able to recall its experience, it is possible that it has acquired information and attitudes which will affect its subsequent patterns of behavior. While the records show that 48 per cent of the adult females in the sample had recalled some sort of pre-adolescent sex play . . . , we are inclined to believe, for the above reasons, that a much higher percentage must have had sexual contacts as young children.

About equal numbers of the females recalled contacts with girls and with boys. There is no evidence that their interest in their own sex (the homosexual interest) had developed either before or after their interest in the opposite sex (the heterosexual interest). Freudian hypotheses of psychosexual development proceeding, as a rule, from narcissistic (masturbatory) interests and activities to interests in other individuals whose bodies are similar (the homosexual interests), and finally to interests in individuals who are physically different (the heterosexual interests), are not substantiated by the pre-adolescent or adolescent histories of either the females or the males in the sample.

Because of the restrictions which parents and our total social organization place upon the free intermingling of even small children of the opposite sex, it is not surprising to find that 52 per cent of the females in the sample had had more girls than boys as childhood companions, and that another 33 per cent had had boys and girls in about equal numbers as childhood companions. Only about 15 per cent had had more boys than girls as companions. This lesser significance of boys as the pre-adolescent companions of girls makes it all the more notable that the pre-adolescent sexual activities of the females in the sample were had with boys about as often as with girls. This had undoubtedly depended upon the fact that small boys are usually more aggressive than girls in their physical activities, and even at that age boys are more likely to initiate the sexual activities.

One per cent of the adult females in the sample recalled childhood sex play with boys when they were as young as three, but 8 per cent recalled such play by five, and 18 per cent by seven years of age. . . . All told, some 30 per cent recalled some play with boys before they turned adolescent. The figures differed for the various educational levels represented in the sample: among those females who had never gone beyond high school, some 24 per cent recalled sex play with boys, but 30 per cent of those who had gone on into college, and 36 per cent of those who had gone still further into graduate school, recalled such pre-adolescent play.

The data indicate that the percentage of children engaging in any kind of pre-adolescent sex play had increased in the course of three of the decades represented in the sample. In comparison with the females born before 1900, some 10 per cent more of those born between 1910 and 1919 recalled pre-adolescent sex play. . . .

. . . . .

Techniques of Heterosexual Play

Genital exhibition had occurred in 99 per cent of the pre-adolescent sex play. . . . In perhaps 40 per cent of the histories that was all that was involved.

Anatomic differences are of considerable interest to most children. Their curiosity is whetted by the fact that they have in many instances been forbidden to expose their own nude bodies and have not had the opportunity to see the nude bodies of other children. Their curiosity is especially stimulated by the fact that they have been cautioned not to expose their own genitalia, or to look at the genitalia of other children. The genital explorations often amount to nothing more than comparisons of anatomy, in much the same way that children compare their hands, their noses or mouths, their hair, their clothing, or any of their other possessions. As we have noted in regard to the boy, it is probable that a good deal of the emotional content which such play may have for the small girls is not sexual as often as it is a reaction to the mysterious, to the forbidden, and to the socially dangerous performance.

On the other hand, we have the histories of females who were raised in homes that accepted nudity within the family circle, or who attended nursery schools or summer camps or engaged in other group activities where boys and girls of young, pre-adolescent ages used common toilets and freely bathed and played together without clothing. In such groups the children were still interested in examining the bodies of the other children, although they soon came to accept the nudity as commonplace and did not react as emotionally as they would have if nudity were the unusual thing.

. . . . .

. . . In a goodly number of instances, these had amounted to nothing more than incidental touching. The heterosexual contacts had been specifically masturbatory in only a small number of cases. There had been mouth-genital contacts among only 2 per cent of the girls, and insertions of various objects (chiefly fingers) into the female vagina in only 3 per cent of the cases.

There had been some sort of coitus in 17 per cent of the cases for which any heterosexual play was reported, but it has been difficult to determine how much of the "coitus" of pre-adolescence involves the actual union of genitalia. In all instances recorded in the sample, there had been some apposition of the genitalia of the two children; and since erections frequently occur among even very young boys, pentrations may have been and certainly were effected in some of the pre-adolescent activity. However, the small size of the male genitalia at that age had usually limited the depth of penetration, and much of the childhold "coitus" had amounted to nothing more than genital apposition.

On the other hand, we have 29 cases of females who had had coitus as preadolescents with older boys or adult males with whom there had been complete genital union.

PRE-ADOLESCENT CONTACTS
WITH ADULT MALES

There is a growing concern in our culture over the sexual contacts that pre-adolescent children sometimes have with adults. Most persons feel that all such contacts are undesirable because of the immediate disturbance they may cause the child, and because of the conditioning and possibly traumatic effects which they may have on the child's socio-sexual development and subsequent sexual adjustments in marriage. Press reports might lead one to conclude that an appreciable percentage of all children are subjected, and frequently subjected, to sexual approaches by adult males, and that physical injury is a frequent consequence of such contacts. But most of the published data are based on cases which come to the attention of physicians, the police, and other social agencies, and there has hitherto . . . been no opportunity to know what proportion of all children is ever involved.[1]

Incidence and Frequency
of Contacts with Adults

We have data from 4441 of our female subjects which allow us to determine the incidence of pre-adolescent sexual contacts with adult males, and the frequency of such contacts. For the sake of the present calculations we have defined an adult male as one who has turned adolescent and who is at least fifteen years of age; and, in order to eliminate experiences that amount to nothing more than adolescent sex play, we have considered only those cases in which the male was at least five years older than the female, while the female was still pre-adolescent. On this basis, we find that some 24 per cent (1075) of the females in the sample had been approached while they were pre-adolescent by adult males who appeared to be making sexual advances, or who had made sexual contacts with the child. Three-fourths of the females (76 per cent) had not recognized any such approach.

---

[1] The following indicate the nature of the . . . concern over adult sexual approaches to children: Hoover, J. Edgar, "How Safe is Your Daughter?" *American Magazine*, July, 1947:32 ("depraved human beings, more savage than beasts, are permitted to roam America almost at will"). Wittels, "What Can We Do About Sex Crimes?" *Saturday Evening Post*, Dec. 11, 1948:31 ("at least tens of thousands of them [sex killers] are loose in the country today"). Frankfurter, Justice Felix, dissenting in Maryland v. Baltimore Radio Show, 1950:338 U.S. 912.

AGES OF FEMALES HAVING ADULT CONTACTS	Age	Percent of Active Sample	Percent of Total Sample	Age	Percent of Active Sample	Percent of Total Sample
	4	5	1	9	16	4
	5	8	2	10	26	6
	6	9	2	11	24	6
	7	13	3	12	25	7
	8	17	4	13	19	6
	CASES				1039	4407

Approaches had occurred most frequently in poorer city communities where the population was densely crowded in tenement districts; and while many of the subjects covered by the present volume were raised in such communities, we would have found higher incidences of pre-adolescent contacts with adults if we had had more cases from lower educational groups, or if we had included the data which we have on females who had served penal sentences, and on Negro females. These latter groups, however, were excluded from the calculations in the present volume for reasons which we have already explained.

The frequencies of the pre-adolescent contacts with adults were actually low. Some 80 per cent of the females who were ever involved seem to have had only a lone experience in all of their pre-adolescent years. Another 12 per cent reported two such experiences, and 3 per cent reported something between three and six childhood experiences. On the other hand, 5 per cent of those who had been involved reported nine or more experiences during pre-adolescence. Repetition had most frequently occurred when the children were having their contacts with relatives who lived in the same household. In many instances, the experiences were repeated because the children had become interested in the sexual activity and had more or less actively sought repetitions of their experience.

Among the females who had been approached by adult males when they were pre-adolescent children, the ages at which they were approached were distributed as shown in the table above.

Adult Partners

The adult males who had approached these pre-adolescent children were identified as follows:

Adult Partners	Percent of Active Sample
Strangers	52
Friends and acquaintances	32
Uncles	9
Fathers	4
Brothers	3
Grandfathers	2
Other relatives	5
CASES REPORTING	609

Some 85 per cent of the subjects reported that only a single male had approached them when they were children. Some 13 per cent reported that two different males had made such approaches, 1 per cent reported three males, and another 1 per cent reported four or more males making such approaches.

Nature of Contacts with Adults

The early experiences which the 1075 females in the sample had had with adult males had involved the following types of approaches and contacts (numbers given are per cent): approach only, 9;

exhibition, male genitalia, 52; exhibition, female genitalia, 1; fondling, no genital contact, 31; manipulation of female genitalia, 22; manipulation of male genitalia, 5; coitus, 3; other, 2.

. . . . .

Significance of Adult Contacts

There are as yet insufficient data, either in our own or in other studies, for reaching general conclusions on the significance of sexual contacts between children and adults. The females in the sample who had had pre-adolescent contacts with adults had been variously interested, curious, pleased, embarrassed, frightened, terrified, or disturbed with feelings of guilt. The adult contacts are a source of pleasure to some children, and sometimes may arouse the child erotically (5 per cent) and bring it to orgasm (1 per cent). The contacts had often involved considerable affection, and some of the older females in the sample felt that their pre-adolescent experience had contributed favorably to their later sociosexual development.

On the other hand, some 80 per cent of the children had been emotionally upset or frightened by their contacts with adults. A small portion had been seriously disturbed; but in most instances the reported fright was nearer the level that children will show when they see insects, spiders, or other objects against which they have been adversely conditioned. If a child were not culturally conditioned, it is doubtful if it would be disturbed by sexual approaches of the sort which had usually been involved in these histories. It is difficult to understand why a child, except for its cultural conditioning, should be disturbed at having its genitalia touched, or disturbed at seeing the genitalia of other persons, or disturbed at even more specific sexual contacts. When children are constantly warned by parents and teachers against contacts with adults, and when they receive no explanation of the exact nature of the forbidden contacts, they are ready to become hysterical as soon as any older person approaches, or stops and speaks to them in the street, or fondles them, or proposes to do something for them, even though the adult may have had no sexual objective in mind. Some of the more experienced students of juvenile problems have come to believe that the emotional reactions of the parents, police officers, and other adults who discover that the child has had such a contact, may disturb the child more seriously than the sexual contacts themselves. The current hysteria over sex offenders may very well have serious effects on the ability of many of these children to work out sexual adjustments some years later in their marriages.

There are, of course, instances of adults who have done physical damage to children with whom they have attempted sexual contacts, and we have the histories of a few males who had been responsible for such damage. But these cases are in the minority, and the public should learn to distinguish such serious contacts from other adult contacts which are not likely to do the child any appreciable harm if the child's parents do not become disturbed. The exceedingly small number of cases in which physical harm is ever done the child is to be measured by the fact that among the 4441 females on whom we have data, we have only one clear-cut case of serious injury done to the child, and a very few instances of vaginal bleeding which, however, did not appear to do any appreciable damage.

ADOLESCENT DEVELOPMENT

Physical Development

Shortly after the end of the first decade, the female begins to develop physically at a faster rate than she had before, and acquires pubic hair, hair under the arms, more mature breasts, and a body form more nearly like that of an adult. During this period of development, she menstruates for the first time. It is during this period that her ovaries mature and, for the first time, begin to release eggs which are capable of being fertilized and developing into new individuals.

This period in which there is an increased rate of physical growth and the final development of reproductive function is the period which has come to be known as adolescence. Various physical developments are involved in this adolescent growth, and they do not all begin or reach their conclusion simultaneously. Consequently, there is no single point at which adolescence may be said to begin, or any point at which it may be said to stop, but from the onset of the first adolescent development to the completion of all adolescent development, the time involved for the average (median) female is something between three and four years.

Corresponding adolescent developments in the male usually do not begin until a year or two after adolescence has begun in the female, and they usually take four years or more to reach their conclusion. In consequence, as far as physical development is concerned, the girl begins to "mature" at an earlier age, and reaches complete maturity before the average boy.

Exact studies of adolescent development should, of course, be based upon the direct examination and measurement of developing children, and our own data, based upon the recall of adults, cannot be as certain; but the average ages at each stage of development, calculated from our records, agree quite closely with those from the observational studies.

. . . . .

It has been customary, both in general thinking and in technical studies, to consider that adolescence in the female begins at the time of first menstruation (barring any unusual disturbance of normal menstrual development). This is an error, and for several reasons an unfortunate error; for considerable physical growth which should be recognized as adolescent usually precedes the occurrence of the first menstruation. Most of the females in our sample reported the appearance of pubic hair as the first of the adolescent developments. Some of the females reported pubic hair development at ages as young as 8, but others did not recall that pubic hair had developed until the age of 18. . . . For the median female in the sample, the hair had begun developing by 12.3 years of age.

Almost simultaneously with the appearance of pubic hair, breast development became noticeable. The observational studies show that the very first signs of breast development may actually precede the appearance of the pubic hair. Among the females in our sample there were some who recalled such development by the age of 8, and some who did not recall breast development until the age of 25. . . . The median age of breast development was 12.4 years for the females in the sample.

Only a few of the adult females in the sample were able to recall the age at which a marked increase in the rate of growth had first begun. It is difficult to notice the onset of a process which is as continuous as this increase in rate of growth during adolescence. A much larger number of the females in the sample thought they could recall the ages at which they had completed their development in height. These ages ranged from 9 to 25 years, but for the median female growth seemed to have been completed by 15.8 years of age. . . .

The age of first menstruation had ranged from 9 to 25 years in the

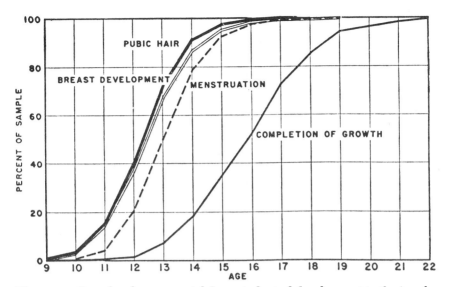

Figure 1. *Cumulated percents: Adolescent physical development in the female.*

sample. . . . For the median female it had been 13.0 years. For the median female, there had been a lapse of 8.4 months between the onset of pubic hair and breast development, and the first menstruation. The first menstruation is such a specific event and, in many instances, such a dramatic event in the girl's history, that its appearance is recalled more often than any other adolescent development. It is, therefore, quite natural that since the time of ancient Jewish law, menstruation should have been taken as the best single sign of sexual maturity in the female. Unfortunately, menstruation is a phenomenon which is affected by a larger number of factors, chiefly hormonal, than most of the other biological developments at adolescence. In a few instances it may begin before there are any other adolescent developments. Not infrequently, however, it may be delayed for a considerable period of time, and in some instances for several years, after all of the other adolescent developments have been completed. It is customary today for parents to seek medical aid when first menstruation does not appear by

the time the other adolescent developments are well under way; but among many of the older women in our histories, menstruation would have been a poor indicator of adolescent development.

It is popularly believed that the appearance of menstruation is an indication that a girl has become "sexually mature" enough to conceive and reproduce. On the basis of recent studies, it becomes clear, however, that the initial release of mature eggs from the ovaries is not always correlated with menstruation. There are known cases of fertile eggs and pregnancy occurring before menstruation had ever begun; and there is a considerable body of data indicating that the average female releases mature eggs only sporadically, if at all, during the first few years after she has begun to menstruate. This is the period of so-called adolescent sterility. It is probable that the sterility is not complete, and more probable that eggs are occasionally released in that period; but regular ovulation in each menstrual cycle probably does not begin in the average female until she is sixteen to

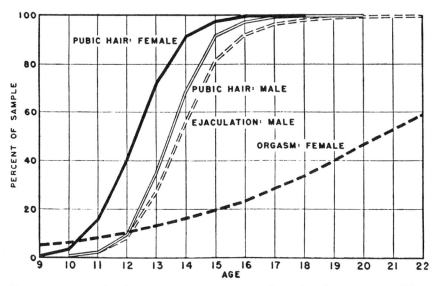

Figure 2. Cumulated percents, comparing female and male: Onset of adolescence and sexual response. Taking appearance of pubic hair as first adolescent development, and orgasm or ejaculation as specific evidence of erotic response.

eighteen years of age. Precise studies on this point are still to be made.

Psychosexual Development in Adolescence

While these physical changes at adolescence are a fundamental part of the process by which the female becomes mature enough to reproduce, they seem to have little relation to the development of sexual responsiveness in the female. The steady increase in the accumulative incidence of erotic arousal and response to orgasm which we have seen in the pre-adolescent data continues into adolescence and for some years beyond. There is a slight but no marked upsurge in the incidence and frequency of arousal and orgasm during adolescence, but they do not reach their maximum development until the middle twenties or even thirties. . . .

In the case of the male, there is a sudden upsurge in sexual activity which may begin a year or more before adolescence, and usually reaches its peak within a year or two after the onset of

adolescence. . . . From that point the male's sexual responses and overt activity begin to drop and continue to drop steadily into old age. . . . These striking differences between female and male psychosexual development may depend upon basic hormonal differences between the sexes. . . .

Because of the earlier appearance of adolescence in the female, and because of her more rapid physical development in that period, the opinion is generally held that the girl matures sexually more rapidly than the boy. Mature reproductive cells may appear in the average female before they appear in the average male, but the capacity to reproduce is not synonymous with the capacity to be aroused erotically and to respond to the point of orgasm. The irregular release of mature eggs from the ovaries during the years of adolescent sterility makes it uncertain whether the capacity for reproduction develops earlier in one sex than in the other, and in regard to sexual responsiveness the female matures much later than the male. . . .

We have found that the human female is born with the nervous equipment on which sexual responses depend, but we have found that only a portion of the females respond before the onset of adolescence. The acquirement of any full capacity for response depends upon the sort of sexual experience that the female has in pre-adolescence, adolescence, and the later years, and on the variety of social factors which may condition her psychologically. . . .

80 | FUNCTIONAL ANALYSIS OF SEX ROLES

MIRRA KOMAROVSKY

"A son is a son till he gets him a wife,/But a daughter's a daughter for all of her life." It is often difficult to establish a truth from folklore, because for every proverb there is another which contradicts it. Here is one proverb, however, which has been confirmed by social research.

The concept of social roles with special reference to sex and age roles has been the subject of increasing sociological interest. But the problem of sex roles in various segments of our society requires further systematic empirical study. This paper attempts to outline what is believed to constitute a fruitful theoretical orientation for such research and to illustrate the application of this theoretical approach in a pilot study, involving twenty intensive case histories of middle class urban married women, in the summer of 1949. The study was focused on the "problem" aspects of sex roles, and while the discussion will be thus delimited, the theoretical approach it advocates appears equally applicable to other aspects of this general subject.

That there exists a great deal of strain in women's roles among the urban middle classes is generally recognized but the description and analysis of this phenomenon remain to be developed. The mere diversity of roles that women must play at different ages or in different relations need not in itself create a problem. Many societies show such diversity without causing either social conflict or personal disorganization. Indeed in any society, age, sex, class, occupation, race, and ethnic background involve the individual in a variety of socially sanctioned patterns of interaction *vis-à-vis* different categories of persons. Why, then, to put the question most generally, do sex roles today present such an arena of social and mental conflict?

Probably the most influential and systematically developed answer to this question today is the one found in psychiatric literature. This answer centers upon two explanatory models. The orthodox analysts say with Freud: "Anatomy is her fate." They see women's problem in terms of the psychological dynamics arising out of some biologically determined sexual characteristic, i.e., penis envy or masochism. The individual life history is then taken as determining whether the development of this characteristic will follow normal or neurotic patterns. The other explanatory model takes more account of cultural factors.

Reprinted from *American Sociological Review,* XV, 4 (August, 1950), 508–16, by permission of the author and the American Sociological Society.

But, again, the root of the problem is seen in the clash between the biologically determined feminine impulses, on the one hand, and the social roles, on the other, which today, it is alleged, are peculiarly at variance with the biologically set needs of the feminine psyche.

In contrast to the psychiatric, the theoretical approach of this paper is sociological. It seeks to interpret social and mental conflict and the institutional malfunctioning which constitute the social problem in question, in terms of interrelation of elements within and between relevant social and cultural systems. It accepts the general premise that our culture is full of contradictions and inconsistencies with regard to women's roles, that new social goals have emerged without the parallel development of social machinery for their attainment, that norms persist which are no longer functionally appropriate to the social situations to which they apply, that the same social situations are subject to the jurisdiction of conflicting social codes, that behavior patterns useful at some stage become dysfunctional at another, and so on.

AN APPLICATION
OF FUNCTIONAL ANALYSIS

It is well known that the family of procreation occupies a dominant position in our kinship system. This is evidenced in a large variety of ways. Typically, the family of procreation is residentially segregated from the family of orientation of either spouse which, of course, is not the case in the joint or stem family systems. The ties to ancestors which obtain in a clan society and the ties to siblings maintained in the consanguine family type are much weaker in our society. Furthermore, all social norms, from those expressed in the legal code to those expressed in the "advice to the lovelorn" column, reiterate the theme

that the primary loyalty is to one's spouse and children as against parents or siblings. The legal expression of this theme is found in our inheritance and support laws. If a man dies intestate it is generally true that his wife and children get *all* his property. It is only in the absence of direct descendants that parents or collateral relatives share the inheritance with his widow. While statutes are fairly common requiring a son to contribute to the support of an indigent parent, his responsibility is more limited than it is toward his wife and children. These laws are deeply rooted in the mores. As an example, undergraduates have been observed by the writer to be shocked to learn that these cultural norms are far from being universal and that among the Arapaho, to take one instance, a dead man's brother has superior claim to his property even if the widow and his children are left destitute.

In fact, the priority of the marriage relationship over the parental family in our culture has in recent years found expression even in certain intellectual fields of inquiry. As the result of the diffusion of the psychiatric point of view, close ties to a parent are under suspicion as the "silver cord" and, conversely, the emancipation from the family of orientation is viewed as the touchstone of emotional maturity. These presuppositions often find their most explicit and unquestioned expression in textbooks. Thus, for example, a popular textbook on marriage states: "If there is a bona-fide in-law problem the young couple need first of all to be certain of their perspective. The success of their marriage should be put above everything else, even above attachment to parents. Husband and wife must come first. Otherwise the individual exhibits immaturity." Another textbook affirms: "Close attachments to members of the family, whether parents or siblings, accentuate the normal difficulties involved in achieving the response role expected in marriage." Again, ". . . there is a call for a new attitude, a subordinating of and to some extent an aloofness from the home of one's childhood." "Do not live with or in the neighborhood of your relatives and in-laws, and do not allow them to live with you."

Some recent research such as Morgan's and Dinkel's again testify to the extent to which the dominance of the family of procreation is rooted in our mores. Though these mores show some ethnic, religious and other variations, all available evidence points to the primacy of the family of procreation as the dominant American cultural pattern.

But although this pattern of the primacy of the family of procreation *vis-à-vis* the family of orientation has been abundantly recognized, it has not been systematically related to the wide range of its functional and dysfunctional consequences. From within this range we may mark out the problem of sociopsychological continuities and discontinuities in the kinship structure. More particularly, we wish to consider to what extent the training in the parental family makes for subsequent adjustment to the well-nigh exclusive loyalty to spouse and children. We are raising two specific problems. Which particular elements of role training in the parental family can be discerned to have by-products which affect later adjustment of the members in their own families of procreation? Which of the two sexes is enabled to make the shift from the parental family to marriage with the minimum of psychological hazards?

DIFFERENTIAL TRAINING OF THE SEXES IN THE PARENTAL FAMILY

Illuminating material bearing upon differential training of boys and girls in the parental family was collected by the writer in the form of 73 biographical documents prepared by women under-graduates. The documents reveal that despite increasing similarity in the upbringing of the sexes among middle-class families, some sex differences relevant to our problem still persist. The girls who had brothers testified that in various ways the parents *tended to speed up, most often unwittingly, but also deliberately, the emancipation of the boy from the family, while they retarded it in the case of his sister.*

Judging from these documents, there are three different mechanisms through which this is achieved. Interesting as these are in themselves, our main problem is to consider presently their further consequences for the operation of the kinship system. Among these mechanisms is, first of all, the pattern of providing sons with *earlier and more frequent opportunities for independent action.* The boys are freer to play away from home grounds, to return later, and to pick their own activities, movies and books. They are ordinarily allowed the first independent steps earlier than their sisters, such as the first walk to school without an adult, the first unaccompanied movie or baseball game, and later in life, the train trip or the job away from home.

A student writes:

It was thought to be a part of my brother's education to be sent away to school. I was expected to go to a local college so that I could live at home. When my brother got his first job he got a room so that he would not have to commute too far. My sister, at 22, turned down several offers of jobs at a high salary and took a much less desirable one only because she could live at home. She continues to be as much under parental control as she was when in college. Frankly, if anything should happen to my parents, I would be at a complete loss while I know that my brothers could carry on alone very well.

The second mechanism through which the emancipation of sons is speeded up involves a *higher degree of privacy in personal affairs* allowed the boys. One girl writes:

My mother is very hurt if I don't let her read the letters I receive. After a telephone call she expects me to tell her who called and what was said. My brother could say "a friend" and she would not feel insulted.

And again:

My brother is 15, 3 years younger than I am. When he goes out after supper mother calls out: "Where are you going, Jimmy?" "Oh, out." Could I get away with this? Not on your life. I would have to tell in detail where to, with whom, and if I am half an hour late mother sits on the edge of the living-room sofa watching the door.

States another student:

I have a brother of 23, and a sister of 22, and a younger brother who is 16. My sister and I had a much more sheltered life than my brothers. My brothers come and go as they please. Even my younger brother feels that his current girl friend is his personal affair. No one knows who she is. But the family wants voluminous files on every boy my sister and I want to date. It is not easy for us to get the complete genealogy of a boy we want to go out with.

Thirdly, the *daughters* of the family *are held to a more exacting code of filial and kinship obligations.* When the grandmother needs somebody to do an errand for her, or Aunt Jane who doesn't hear well needs help, the girl is more likely to be called upon. The pressure to attend and observe birthdays, anniversaries, and other family festivals is apparently greater upon her than upon the boy.

These patterns of differential training of the sexes in the parental family are generally recognized to be functionally oriented to their respective adult roles. The role of the provider, on the one hand, and of the homemaker on the other, call for different attitudes and skills. Competitiveness, independence, dominance, aggressiveness, are all traits felt to be needed by the future head of the family. Although the girl can train for her adult role and rehearse it within the home, the boy prepares for *his* outside the home, by taking a "paper route" or a summer job away from home. Again, the greater sheltering of the girl may be functionally appropriate in the light of greater risks incurred by her in the case of sexual behavior and also in marriage since, for the woman, marriage is not only a choice of a mate but also of a station in life.

The parents at times explicitly recognize this functional character of their training. One girl, for example, reports that both her parents were more indulgent to her. With a little pleading she could usually get what she wanted. Her brother, on the other hand, was expected to earn money for his little luxuries because "boys need that kind of training." In a couple of cases the girls testified that their brothers were expected to work their way through college, while the girls were supported. A student writes:

My brother is two years younger than I am. When we started going to school my father would always say as he saw us off in the morning, "Now, Buddy, you are the man and you must take good care of your sister." It amused me because it was I who always had to take care of him.

Another student recollects that when her brother refused to help her with her "math" on the ground that no one was allowed to help *him*, her mother replied: "Well, she is a girl, and it isn't as important for her to know 'math' and to learn how to get along without help."

More often, however, the proximate ground for enforcing the proper roles is expressed in terms of what constitutes manly or unmanly behavior or just "the right thing to do." The degree to which the recognition of functional implications is explicit is in itself an important problem bearing upon social change.

But if the differential upbringing of the sexes thus constitutes a preparation for their adult roles, it also has unintended consequences. This role training or, more specifically, the greater sheltering of the girl, has, as unintended by-products, further consequences for kinship roles which are not perceived. And it is to this that we now address ourselves. We are now prepared to advance a hypothesis that the greater sheltering of the girl has what Merton terms a "latent dysfunction" for the woman and for marriage in general. More specifically, we suggest that the major unintended consequence of this greater sheltering of the girl is to create in her such ties to the family of orientation that she is handicapped in making the psycho-social shift to the family of procreation which our culture demands. Our problem is not merely to demonstrate the fact of discontinuities in role training so perceptively discerned in other spheres by Benedict and others. These discontinuities must be related to their structural contexts. We shall show how tendencies created within one social structure react back upon the operation of another structure within the same kinship system without the intention or, indeed, the awareness of the participants.

The hypothesis just set forth requires us to examine the actual mechanisms through which these postulated consequences follow. Essentially it is assumed that to the extent that the woman remains more "infantile," less able to make her own decisions, more dependent upon one or both parents for initiating or channeling behavior and attitudes, more closely attached to them so as to find it

difficult to part from them or to face their disapproval in case of any conflict between her family and spouse, or shows any other indices of lack of emotional emancipation—to that extent she may find it more difficult than the man to conform to the cultural norm of primary loyalty to the family she establishes later, the family of procreation. It is possible, of course, that the only effect of the greater sheltering is to create in women a generalized dependency which will then be transferred to the husband and which will enable her all the more readily to accept the role of wife in a family which still has many patriarchal features. In contrast to this, we shall explore the hypothesis that this dependency is specific; it is a dependency upon and attachment to the family of orientation.

For the purposes of testing, this hypothesis may be restated in two steps: first, the alleged greater attachment of the girl to her family of orientation and, second, the resulting difficulties for marriage.

Turning to family studies in the search for data bearing crucially upon this hypothesis, we find the data to be scanty indeed. The comparative absence of materials suggests that the hypothesis requiring this material was not at hand. With regard to the first step, the greater attachment to and dependence of the woman upon her family of orientation, the evidence, though scanty, is consistent and confirming.

SEX DIFFERENCES IN ATTACHMENT TO AND DEPENDENCE UPON THE FAMILY OF ORIENTATION

In a recent study, Winch discovers a contrast between the sexes with respect to attachment and submissiveness to parents. Among the 435 college males included in the study, age correlated negatively with love for both parents and submissiveness to them, whereas among the 502 college women neither of these correlations is significant. The author puts forth and is inclined to support the hypothesis that, at least while in college, women do not become emancipated from their families to the same degree or in the same manner as men do.

Another set of data, . . . from the same study, of 936 college men and women also tends to support our hypothesis. It suggests that the college women are somewhat more attached to parents, less likely to make decisions contrary to the wishes of the parents, more frequently experience homesickness than is the case with the male undergraduates. No sex differences were found in feelings that parents have attempted to dominate their lives.

Another confirming datum concerning undergraduates is found in a study of some 1500 students at the University of Minnesota. The author observes: "In two widely separated surveys of the total group, the frequency and type of family problems were found to be related to several other descriptive factors: girls, for example, had family problems more often than boys, especially such problems as 'difficulty in achieving independence.' "

The relative attachment to parents on the part of older men and women is revealed by Burgess and Cottrell. The authors studied a sample of 526 couples, the majority of whom had been married from two to four years. Two tables record the extent of attachment to parents derived from the statements made by the respondents themselves. Four degrees of attachment were distinguished: little or none, moderate, a good deal, and very close. The tables show that a slightly greater proportion of wives than of husbands characterized their own attachment to parents as "very close." The

difference is greater in attitudes towards the father than towards the mother (to whom both sexes were, incidentally, more attached).

	Husbands (526 cases)	Wives (526 cases)
Attachment to Father		
Very close	21%	30%
Attachment to Mother		
Very close	35%	42%

Terman's findings are on the whole similar. The figures are as follows:

	Husbands (734 cases)	Wives (721 cases)
Attachment to Father		
Greatest	16.7%	20.1%
Attachment to Mother		
Greatest	28.9%	35.1%

To sum up, when asked to characterize their own attachment to parents, somewhat more women than men give the response, "Very close." The size of the difference is small but the pattern is consistent. The sex difference is greater with regard to the father.

These studies were cited because they are almost the only ones available. It should be noted that they all depend upon the direct testimony of respondents. Except when the verbally expressed attitude is precisely what is wanted, all such studies raise the question of the relation of the verbal index to the phenomenon it allegedly represents. Failures of memory, of honesty, of self-knowledge often stand between the verbal index and the phenomenon studied. The next datum bearing upon our hypothesis has the advantage of having been derived from the study of behavior rather than from verbal attitudes alone though it would have been given added meaning had it also included the latter.

The Women's Bureau (Bulletin No. 138) made a study of two communities widely different in employment offered to women: City of Cleveland and the State of Utah. The report concludes:

In families with unmarried sons and daughters, daughters supply more of the family supporting income than sons supply, though earning less than their brothers earn (p. 13). In Cleveland twice the proportion of boys as of girls contributed nothing to the family support. With working sons and daughters under 21 years, about a third of the girls compared with a fourth of the boys turn over *all* their earnings to their families.

It would be important to determine whether such a pattern of greater contribution of single daughters to family support is generally true. For if it is, it would have bearing upon a more general problem. It would represent a standardized pattern of behavior *which is not directly called for by social norms, but is a by-product of social roles.* In other words, it would mean that differential training of boys and girls in anticipation of adult sex roles has had, as an unintended by-product, a closer identification of the girl with her family and her greater responsibility for family support. Tracing this by-product brings out anew how interrelations of institutional patterns operate to produce other ramified patterns which are below the threshold of recognition.

So much for the first step of our hypothesis: the lesser emancipation of the daughter in the middle class kinship structure from the family of orientation. In so far as it is valid, we may expect that the transition from the role of the daughter to that of the spouse will be more difficult for her than for the son. She might find it more difficult, as was suggested earlier, to face parental disapproval in case of conflict between parents and spouse and, in general, to sever ties to her parents and to attain the degree of maturity demanded of a wife in our culture.

WOMAN'S LESSER EMANCIPATION FROM HER FAMILY OF ORIENTATION AS A FACTOR IN MARITAL DISCORD

That marriage difficulties arise as a result of the attachment of the wife to her family was amply illustrated in the pilot study conducted by the writer. In some cases the problem took the form of a mental conflict over the claims of parents and husband. For example, one woman said:

When I was single, I always helped my family. Now I have just heard that my father isn't well and should have a week's vacation. If only I had some money of my own I wouldn't hesitate a minute to send him a check. As it is, even if my husband would agree to give me the money, have I the right to ask him to deny himself the new radio for the sake of my family?

In other cases, the relation of the wife to her family caused marital conflict. The overt conflicts were sometimes about the excessive (in the husband's view) concern of the wife over her younger siblings. One husband accused his wife of neglecting their children in her preoccupation with the problems of her adolescent brother and sister whom, he maintained, she "babied too much." She telephoned them daily, waiting, however, for the husband to leave for work because the telephone conversations irritated him. The relation of the wife to her mother was the focal point of marriage conflict in still other cases. The husband objected to the frequent visits of the wife to her mother, the mother-in-law's excessive help with the housework ("You are shirking your duties as a wife"), the wife's dependence upon her mother for opinions, the mother-in-law's interference, and so on.

If our hypothesis is valid, we should find that such in-law problems in marriage more frequently involve the wife's parents than the husband's parents.

Given this theoretical expectation we

examined the body of relevant opinion and data contained in some twenty texts and other books on the family. Of those examined, the bulk were written by sociologists, a few by psychiatrists and psychologists. As far as the sociologists were concerned, the field is virtually barren of data bearing crucially upon our hypothesis. The reason is simple—the problem was never posed. Several writers suggested that the mother-in-law constitutes a greater hazard to marriage than the father-in-law *but they do not raise the question of the side from which the in-law problem is more likely to arise.*

This gap reveals vividly the decisive role of theory in empirical studies. Evidently the sociologists were concerned with the explicit and acknowledged cultural norms which assert the structural symmetry of our bilateral family with identical relations to both families of orientation on the part of the spouses. Deviations from the norm of symmetry, then, tend to be interpreted in terms of individual pathologies. It was the failure to perceive that deviations from the norm of symmetry may themselves be induced by other workings of the kinship structure and not merely by individual abnormality that resulted in the observed gap. Indeed, the illustrations used in books were inadvertently misleading. While the text implied a symmetrical relation to the two sets of in-laws as the norm, the illustrations of deviance cited more frequently a "mother's boy." Illustrations frequently come from clinical sources which are selective. Furthermore, in-law trouble which is due to the husband's dependence upon his parents, although rarer, may be more acute and, therefore, more obvious.

The psychiatrists, represented by Hamilton and Dreikurs, have passing references to the problem which are contrary to our hypothesis, but with no supporting data. Dreikurs asserts that the husband's family is more disturbing in

marriage. Hamilton considers that the male "mother love victim" is the greater threat to marriage because "fathers seldom get a chance to absorb their daughters' emotions so much that they never love any other man."

It may be suggested that whatever the merits of the case, a certain theoretical bias has predisposed the psychoanalyst to this position. The psychoanalysts have been absorbed in the childhood drama of emotional development. The Oedipus complex has been more prominent in the orthodox theory than the Electra complex. In speculating about the in-law problem, the fixation of the son upon the mother would naturally loom important. The writers have not explored the possibility that the cultural definitions of sex roles may have differential consequences for the adjustment at issue.

An indirect but confirming bit of evidence comes from Burgess and Cottrell. The authors cite a result for which they offer no explanation. They find that "closeness of attachment . . . in the association of parents and son show a consistent though small positive relation to marital adjustment." No such consistent pattern appears in the association between parents and daughter, although "no" attachment to the father and "little" or "no" attachment to the mother appear to work against a high marital adjustment score. In terms of our hypothesis, it is possible that *more* women than men who checked "a good deal of attachment" represented cases of "over-attachment" with its inimical influence upon marriage happiness.

Terman studied the same relationship. He cites the mean happiness scores of husbands and wives according to the degree of parent-child attachment and also correlations of happiness scores with parent-child attachment. In contrast to Burgess and Cottrell he finds a positive correlation between attachment and happiness for *both* men and women. He does not state in the text what appears in the figures, however, that the correlation is lower for women. Again it is possible that the favorable features in good relations with parents are counterbalanced in the case of women by the too close a tie which is sometimes hidden in the response "very close attachment."

If future research is to bear crucially upon the hypothesis that the "overattachment" of the wife to her family of orientation creates marriage conflict as evidenced by "in-law" trouble, it must be so designed as to disentangle various contradictory tendencies. It is possible, for example, that such marriage conflict is much more frequent among women whereas among men, though rarer, it may be experienced more acutely. Excessive ties to parents would be even more dysfunctional for the male role of the family head than for the housewife. Our culture is less permissive towards unusually close son-parent ties. Consequently, the "silver cord" may be more socially visible and better reported even if (and because?) it is a rare occurrence as compared with the daughter-mother ties.

Another refinement suggests itself. The role of in-laws as sources of tension may vary with the stages of the family cycle.

We have hitherto stressed the attitudes of the spouses towards their parents as the source of in-law trouble. But the parents contribute their share. And here it is possible that during engagement and perhaps even in the first year of marriage it is the husband's family which creates more trouble for the young couple. As a rule, the girl's family may be more favorably disposed to marriage because a reasonably early marriage is more advantageous to the woman. Furthermore, the very attachment of the girl to her family means, as the folklore has it, that "when your son marries, you lose a son, when your daughter marries, you gain one," or, "your son is your son till he takes him a wife, your daughter is your daughter all her life." Again, the greater control exercised over the choice of mates by the girl's family may mean that the prospective son-in-law is more acceptable than the prospective daughter-in-law . . . But whereas in the engagement period the husband's family may figure more prominently in in-law conflicts, it is assumed, in the light of this paper, that as the marriage continues, the basic dependence of the woman upon her family tends to make her parents the principal actors in the in-law drama.

81 | THE FUNCTION OF MALE INITIATION CEREMONIES AT PUBERTY

JOHN W. M. WHITING, RICHARD KLUCKHOHN, AND ALBERT ANTHONY

Describing the manner in which teenagers are initiated into adulthood in various cultures, this remarkable study indicates the influence of the general values in each culture on its attitude toward children. Strangely enough, it suggests that a society's behavior toward its adolescents is precisely the reverse of that toward its infants. If it indulges one, it is strict toward the other.

Contemporary American society seems to fit into the category of cultures which deprive infants and indulge teenagers. Individual parents may feel that they are deciding for themselves how they will treat their children, but when cultures are compared around the world, it appears that parents in each culture tend to treat their children just as most of the other parents in that culture treat theirs.

Our society gives little formal recognition of the physiological and social changes a boy undergoes at puberty. He may be teased a little when his voice changes or when he shaves for the first time. Changes in his social status from childhood to adulthood are marked by a number of minor events rather than by any single dramatic ceremonial observance. Graduation from grammar school and subsequently from high school are steps to adulthood, but neither can be considered as a *rite de passage.* Nor may the accomplishment of having obtained a driver's license, which for many boys is the most important indication of having grown up, be classed as one. Legally the twenty-first birthday is the time at which a boy becomes a man; but, except for a somewhat more elaborate birthday party this occasion is not ceremonially marked and, therefore, cannot be thought of as a *rite de passage.* Neither physiologically, socially, nor legally is there a clear demarcation between boyhood and manhood in our society.

Such a gradual transition from boyhood to manhood is by no means universal. Among the Thonga, a tribe in South Africa, every boy must go through a very elaborate ceremony in order to become a man. When a boy is somewhere between ten and 16 years of age, he is sent by his parents to a "circumcision school" which is held every four or five years. Here in company with his

age-mates he undergoes severe hazing by the adult males of the society. The initiation begins when each boy runs the gauntlet between two rows of men who beat him with clubs. At the end of this experience he is stripped of his clothes and his hair is cut. He is next met by a man covered with lion manes and is seated upon a stone facing this "lion man." Someone then strikes him from behind and when he turns his head to see who has struck him, his foreskin is seized and in two movements cut off by the "lion man." Afterwards he is secluded for three months in the "yards of mysteries," where he can be seen only by the initiated. It is especially taboo for a woman to approach these boys during their seclusion, and if a woman should glance at the leaves with which the circumcised covers his wound and which form his only clothing, she must be killed.

During the course of his initiation, the boy undergoes six major trials: beatings, exposure to cold, thirst, eating of unsavory foods, punishment, and the threat of death. On the slightest pretext he may be severely beaten by one of the newly initiated men who is assigned to the task by the older men of the tribe. He sleeps without covering and suffers bitterly from the winter cold. He is forbidden to drink a drop of water during the whole three months. Meals are often made nauseating by the half-digested grass from the stomach of an antelope which is poured over his food. If he is caught breaking any important rule governing the ceremony, he is severely punished. For example, in one these punishments, sticks are placed between the fingers of the offender, then a strong man closes his hand around that of the novice practically crushing his fingers. He is frightened into submission by being told that in former times boys who had tried to escape or who revealed the secrets to women or to the uninitated were hanged and their bodies burnt to ashes.

Although the Thonga are extreme in the severity of this sort of initiation, many other societies have rites which have one or more of the main features of the Thonga ceremony. Of a sample of 55 societies chosen for this study, 18 have one or more of the four salient features of the Thonga ceremony, e.g., painful hazing by adult males, genital operations, seclusion from women, and tests of endurance and manliness, the remaining 37 societies either have no ceremony at all or one which does not have any of the above features.

HYPOTHESIS

It is the purpose of this paper to develop a set of hypotheses concerning the function of male initiation rites which accounts for the presence of these rites in some societies and the absence of them in others. The theory that we have chosen to test has been suggested by previous explanations for the rites, particularly those of psychoanalytic origin. These explanations were modified to fit the problem of this research in two respects. First, certain of the concepts and hypotheses were restated or redefined so as to be coherent with the growing general behavioral theory of personality development, and second, they were restated in such a way as to be amenable to cross-cultural test, i.e., cultural indices were specified for each variable.

We assume that boys tend to be initiated at puberty in those societies in which they are particularly hostile toward their fathers and dependent upon

their mothers. The hazing of the candidates, as well as the genital operations, suggests that one function of the rites is to prevent open and violent revolt against parental authority at a time when physical maturity would make such revolt dangerous and socially disruptive. Isolation from women and tests of manliness suggest that another function of the rites is to break an excessively strong dependence upon the mother and to ensure identification with adult males and acceptance of the male role.

It is to be noted here that the educational and disciplinary functions of the initiation are not limited in time to the actual period of initiation. The boy knows all during childhood and latency about the initiation which he will face at puberty. While he is overtly not supposed to know any of the secrets of the rite, he actually knows almost everything that will happen to him. He is both afraid of what he knows will happen and also envious of the kudos and added status which his older friends have acquired through having successfully gone through this rite. Thus, through the boy's whole life the initiation ceremony serves as a conditioner of his behavior and his attitudes towards male authority, while at the same time emphasizing the advantages of becoming a member of the male group through initiation.

We assume that a long and exclusive relationship between mother and son provides the conditions which should lead to an exceptionally strong dependence upon the mother. Also, we assume that if the father terminates this relationship and replaces his son, there should be strong envy and hostility engendered in the boy which, although held in check during childhood, may dangerously manifest itself with the onset of puberty, unless measures are taken to prevent it.

As we indicated above, the hypothesis is derived from psychoanalytic theory. However, it should be noted that there are some modifications which may be important. First, no assumption is being made that the envy is exclusively sexual in character. We are making the more general assumption that if the mother for a prolonged period devotes herself to the satisfaction of all the child's needs—including hunger, warmth, safety, freedom from pain, as well as sex—he will become strongly dependent upon her. In accordance with this we believe rivalry may be based upon a competition for the fulfillment of any of these needs. Second, we do not propose, as most psychoanalysts do, that Oedipal rivalry is a universal, but rather we claim it is a variable which may be strong or weak depending upon specific relationships between father, mother, and son. Thus, we assume father-son rivalry may range from a value of zero to such high intensities that the whole society may be required to adjust to it.

An illustration of cultural conditions which should intensify the dependency of a boy on his mother and rivalry with his father is found in the following case. *Kwoma Dependency.* The Kwoma, a tribe living about 200 miles up the Sepik River in New Guinea, have initiation rites similar to those of the Thonga. Examination of the differences in the relationship of a mother to her infant during the first years of his life reveals some strong contrasts between the Kwoma and our own society. While in our society an infant sleeps in his own crib and the mother shares her bed with the father, the Kwoma infant sleeps cuddled in his mother's arms until he is old enough to be weaned, which is generally when he is two or three years old. The father, in the meantime, sleeps apart on his own bark slab bed. Furthermore during this period, the Kwoma mother abstains from sexual intercourse with her husband in order to avoid having to care for two dependent children at the same

time. Since the Kwoma are polygynous and discreet extramarital philandering is permitted, this taboo is not too hard on the husband. In addition, it is possible that the mother obtains some substitute sexual gratification from nursing and caring for her infant. If this be the case, it is not unlikely that she should show more warmth and affection toward her infant than if she were obtaining sexual gratification from her husband. Whether or not the custom can be attributed to this sex taboo, the Kwoma mother, while her co-wife does the housework, not only sleeps with her infant all night but holds it in her lap all day without apparent frustration. Such a close relationship between a mother and child in our society would seem not only unbearably difficult to the mother, but also somewhat improper.

When the Kwoma child is weaned, a number of drastic things happen all at once. He is suddenly moved from his mother's bed to one of his own. His father resumes sexual relations with his mother. Although the couple wait until their children are asleep, the intercourse takes place in the same room. Thus, the child may truly become aware of his replacement. He is now told that he can no longer have his mother's milk because some supernatural being needs it. This is vividly communicated to him by his mother when she puts a slug on her breasts and daubs the blood-colored sap of the breadfruit tree over her nipples. Finally he is no longer permitted to sit on his mother's lap. She resumes her work and goes to the garden to weed or to the swamp to gather sago flour leaving him behind for the first time in his life. That these events are traumatic to the child is not surprising. He varies between sadness and anger, weeping and violent temper tantrums.

It is our hypothesis that it is this series of events that makes it necessary, when the boy reaches adolescence, for the society to have an initiation rite of the type we have already described. It is necessary to put a final stop to (1) his wish to return to his mother's arms and lap, (2) to prevent an open revolt against his father who has displaced him from his mother's bed, and (3) to ensure identification with the adult males of the society. In other words, Kwoma infancy so magnifies the conditions which should produce Oedipus rivalry that the special cultural adjustment of ceremonial hazing, isolation from women, and symbolic castration, etc., must be made to resolve it.

If our analysis of the psychodynamics in Kwoma society is correct, societies with initiation rites should have similar child-rearing practices, whereas societies lacking the rite should also lack the exclusive mother-son sleeping arrangements and *post-partum* sexual taboo of the Kwoma.

TESTING THE HYPOTHESIS

To test this hypothesis a sample of 56 societies was selected. First, the ethnographic material on more than 150 societies was checked to determine whether or not there was an adequate description of our variables, e.g., sleeping arrangements, *post-partum* sex taboo, and initiation rites at puberty. Only half of the societies reviewed fulfilled these conditions. Although we had initially endeavored to select our cases so as to have maximum distribution throughout the world, we found that some areas were represented by several societies, while others were not represented by any. To correct for any bias that might result from this sample, we made a further search of the ethnographic literature in order to fill in the gaps, and we thereby added several societies from areas previously not represented. Finally, to maximize diversity and to minimize duplication through selec-

tion of closely related societies, whenever there were two or more societies from any one culture area which had the same values on all our variables, we chose only one of them. Using these criteria, our final sample consisted of 56 societies representing 45 of the 60 culture areas designated by Murdock.

The societies comprising our final sample range in size and type from small, simple, tribal groups to segments of large, complex civilizations such as the United States or Japan. In the latter case, our information has been drawn from ethnographic reports on a single delineated community.

When this sample had finally been chosen, the material relevant to our variables was first abstracted, and then judgments were made for each society as to the nature of the transition from boyhood to manhood, the sleeping arrangements, and the duration of the *post-partum* sex taboo. To prevent contamination, the judgments on each variable were made at different times and the name of the society disguised by a code. All judgments were made by at least two persons and in every case where there was a disagreement (less than 15 percent of the cases for any given variable), the data were checked by one of the authors, whose judgment was accepted as final. Our findings with respect to initiation rites have been tabulated in Table 1 below.

We discovered that only five societies out of the total number had sleeping arrangements similar to our own, that is, where the father and mother share a bed and the baby sleeps alone. In only three societies did the mother, the father, and the baby each have his or her own bed. In the remaining 48, the baby slept with his mother until he was at least a year old and generally until he was weaned. In 24 of the latter, however, the father also shared the bed, the baby generally sleeping between the mother and father. The remaining 24 societies had sleeping arrangements like the Kwoma in which the mother and child sleep in one bed and the father in another. Often the father's bed was not even in the same house. He either slept in a men's club house or in the hut of one of his other wives leaving mother and infant not only alone in the same bed but alone in the sleeping room.

Similarly, the societies of our sample were split on the rules regulating the resumption of sexual intercourse following parturition. Twenty-nine, like our own, have a brief taboo of a few weeks to permit the mother to recover from her delivery. In the remaining 27, the mother

did not resume sexual intercourse for a least nine months after the birth of her child, and in one instance, the Cheyenne, the ideal period adhered to was reported as ten years. The duration of the taboo generally corresponded to the nursing period and in many cases was reinforced by the belief that sexual intercourse curdles or sours the mother's milk, thus making it harmful for the infant. In other societies, like the Kwoma, the taboo is explicitly for the purpose of ensuring a desired interval between children where adequate means of contraception are lacking. In these societies the taboo is terminated when the infant reaches some maturational stage, e.g.,

TABLE 1.

THE RELATIONSHIP BETWEEN EXCLUSIVE MOTHER-SON
SLEEPING ARRANGEMENTS AND A POST-PARTUM SEX TABOO*
AND THE OCCURRENCE OF INITIATION CEREMONIES AT PUBERTY

CUSTOMS IN INFANCY		CUSTOMS AT ADOLESCENT INITIATION CEREMONIES	
Exclusive Mother-Son Sleeping Arrangements	*Post-partum Sex-Taboo*	*Absent*	*Present*
Long	Long		Azande hgs †
			Camayura hs
			Chagga hgs
			Cheyenne ht
			Chiricahua ht
			Dahomeans hgs
			Fijians gs
			Jivaro ht
		Ganda	Kwoma hgs
		Khalapur (Rajput)	Lesu gs
		Nyakyusa	Nuer hs
		Tepoztlan	Samoans g
		Trobrianders	Thonga hgs
		Yapese	Tiv hgs
	Short	Ashanti	
		Malaita	Cagaba ht
		Siriono	
Short	Long	Araucanians	Kwakiutl s
		Pilaga	Ojibwa t
		Pondo	Ooldea hgs
		Tallensi	
	Short	Alorese	Hopi hs
		Balinese	Timbira hst

TABLE 1 (*cont.*)

CUSTOMS IN INFANCY		CUSTOMS AT ADOLESCENT INITIATION CEREMONIES	
Exclusive Mother-Son Sleeping Arrangements	*Post-partum Sex-Taboo*	*Absent*	*Present*
		Druz	
		Egyptians (Silwa)	
		Eskimos (Copper)	
		French	
		Igorot (Bontoc)	
		Japanese (Suye Mura)	
		Koryak (Maritime)	
		Lakher	
		Lamba	
		Lapps	
		Lepcha	
		Maori	
		Mixtecans	
		Navaho	
		Ontong Javanese	
		Papago	
		Serbs	
		Tanala (Menabe)	
		Trukese	
		United States (Homestead)	
		Yagua	

* Both of a year or more duration.
† The letters following the tribal designations in the right-hand column indicate the nature of the ceremony—h = painful hazing, g = genital operations, s = seclusion from women, and t = tests of manliness.

"until the child can crawl," "until the child can walk," or "until he can take care of himself." For the 27 societies that have this taboo, more than a few weeks long, the average duration is slightly more than two years.

RESULTS AT THE CULTURAL LEVEL

Our hypothesis may now be restated in cultural terms as follows: *Societies which have sleeping arrangements in which the mother and baby share the same bed for at least a year to the exclusion of the father and societies which have a taboo restricting the mother's sexual behavior for at least a year after childbirth will be more likely to have a ceremony of transition from boyhood to manhood than those societies where these condi-* *tions do not occur (or occur for briefer periods).* For the purposes of this hypothesis, transition ceremonies include only those ceremonies characterized by at least one of the following events: painful hazing of the initiates, isolation from females, tests of manliness, and genital operations.

The test of this hypothesis is presented in Table 1. It will be observed from this table that of the 20 societies where both antecedent variables are present, 14 have initiation ceremonies and only six do not. Where both antecedent variables are absent only two of the 25 societies have the ceremonies. Thus, over 80 per cent of the 45 pure cases correspond with the prediction. Though our hypothesis was not designed for predicting the mixed cases, that is, where only one of the antecedent variables is present, it seems that they tended not to have the transition ceremonies.

Although the eight cases which are exceptional to our theory, the six in the upper left-hand column and the two in the lower right-hand column may be simply misclassified through error of measurement, re-examination uncovers some other unanticipated factor which may account for their placement. This analysis turns out to be enlightening.

Reviewing, first the six cases in the upper left-hand column, that is, the societies which have both exclusive mother-son sleeping arrangements and a *post-partum* sex taboo but no initiation, we found that four of them (Khalapur, Trobrianders, Nyakusa, and Yapese) have an adjustment at adolescence which may serve as a psychological substitute for the initiation ceremony. The boys at this time leave the parental home and move to a men's house or a boys' village where they live until they are married. Malinowski observed this type of adjustment amongst the Trobrianders in 1927. He wrote:

> But the most important change, and the one which interests us most is the partial break-up of the family at the time when the adolescent boys and girls cease to be permanent inmates of the parental home . . . a special institution . . . special houses inhabited by groups of adolescent boys and girls. A boy as he reaches puberty will join such a house. . . . Thus the parent home is drained completely of its adolescent males, though until the boy's marriage he will always come back for food, and will also continue to work for his household to some extent. . . .
> At this stage, however, when the adolescent has to learn his duties, to be instructed in traditions and to study his magic, his arts and crafts, his interest in his mother's brother, who is his teacher and tutor, is greatest and their relations are at their best.

This account suggests that this change

of residence serves the same functions that we have posited for initiation ceremonies, for example, by establishing male authority, breaking the bond with the mother, and ensuring acceptance of the male role. It is important for our hypothesis, also, that there are only two other societies in our sample where such a change of residence occurs. One of these is the Malaita which has one but not both of our antecedent variables; the other is the Ashanti where the boy may move to the village of his mother's brother at or before puberty, but this is not mandatory and only half the boys do so. Thus, if we were to revise our hypothesis such that a change of residence was considered to be equivalent to initiation, the four societies mentioned should be moved over to the right-hand column and the exceptional cases would be reduced from eight to four.

Some comment should be made on the two remaining cases in the upper left-hand column. The Ganda are reported to have an interesting method of child rearing which may or may not be relevant to our theory. For the first three years of his life, a Ganda child sleeps exclusively with his mother and she is subject to a sexual taboo. At this point the boy is reported to be weaned and transferred to the household of his father's brother by whom he is brought up from then on. It might be assumed that this event would obviate the need for later ceremonial initiation into manhood. Since several other societies that do have initiation also have a change of residence at weaning, however, this simple explanation cannot be accepted and the Ganda must remain an unexplained exception. Finally Lewis reports for the Tepoztlan that there was some disagreement among his informants as to the length of the taboo and exclusive sleeping arrangements. Since again there were other equally equivocal cases, we shall have to accept the verdict of our judges and let this case also remain an exception.

A reconsideration of the two exceptions in the lower right-hand column, the Hopi and the Timbira, which have the type of initiation into manhood required by our theory but have neither exclusive sleeping arrangements nor a prolonged *post-partum* sex taboo, also turns out to be fruitful. In neither of these societies does the father have authority over the children. This is vested in the mother's brother who lives in another household. That these societies should have an initiation rite, again, does not seem to contradict our general theory, even though it does contradict our specific hypothesis. From clinical studies in our own society it is clear that even with the lack of exclusive sleeping arrangements and a minimal *post-partum* sex taboo, an appreciable degree of dependence upon the mother and rivalry with the father is generated. The cases here suggest that, although these motives are not strong enough to require ceremonial initiation into manhood if the father is present in the household and has authority over the child, this may be required if he lacks such authority.

But what of the cases which have but one of the antecedent variables? Taking into account the societies with exclusive sleeping arrangements but no *post-partum* sex taboo, our theory predicts that these conditions should produce dependency and rivalry. However, since the mother is receiving sexual satisfaction from her husband, she has less need to obtain substitute gratification from nurturing her infant, so that the dependency she produces in her child would be less intense and the need for initiation should be attenuated. Three of the four cases with exclusive sleeping arrangements but no taboo appear to fulfill these conditions. As we have reported above, the Ashanti and the Malaita practice a change of residence which, it could be argued, is somewhat less drastic than initiation. In any case this is permissive and not required for the Ashanti. When the Cagaba boy reaches adolescence, he is given instruction in sexual intercourse by a priest and then sent to practise these instructions with a widow who lives with him temporarily in a specially built small hut. The boy is not allowed to leave this hunt until he succeeds in having sexual intercourse with her. This trial is reported to be terrifying to the boy and it is often several days before he does succeed. This type of initiation, however, does not seem to compare with other societies which like the Thonga have a full-fledged ceremony. The Siriono, on the other hand, do not have any ceremonial recognition of the shift from boyhood to manhood and they must be regarded as an exception to our theory.

The final group of cases to consider are those that have a long *post-partum* sex taboo but not exclusive mother-son sleeping arrangements. For these, our theory would also predict an attenuated need for initiation ceremonies. Although the mothers of this group are presumed to gain substitute sexual gratification from being especially nurturant and loving toward their infants, they have less opportunity to do so than with those of societies where there are also exclusive sleeping arrangements.

As in the previous group of societies the ceremonies are, except for the Ooldea which will be discussed below, mild. The Kwakiutl have a ceremony which consists of a potlach given by the father for the son. There the boys undergo no hazing or genital operations but are secluded and expected to perform a dance. For the Ojibwa, the boy is expected to obtain a guardian spirit in a vision before he reaches maturity. Thus, generally when he is 11 or 12 years old, he goes alone into the forest where he stays often for several days without food, water, and generally without sleep until he either has a vision or returns home to recuperate before trying again. Again neither hazing or genital operations are involved.

The Ooldea, a tribe situated in southwestern Australia do, however, have a full-fledged initiation rite with hazing, isolation, and a very painful genital operation. This apparently runs counter to our assumption that the rites should be mild if only one determinant is present.

Radcliffe-Brown, however, reports that in many Australian tribes

. . . the discipline of very young children is left to the mother and the other women of the horde. A father does not punish and may not even scold his infant children, but if they misbehave he will scold the mother and perhaps give her a blow with a stick. He regards the mother as responsible for misbehavior by very young children. When they are a little older, the father undertakes the education of the boys but leaves the education of the girls to the mother and the women of the horde. But the father behaves affectionately and is very little of a disciplinarian. Discipline for a boy begins when he approaches puberty and is exercised by the men of the horde. The big change comes with the initiation ceremonies when, in some tribes, the father, by a ceremonial (symbolic) action, hands over his son to the men who will carry out the initiation rites. During the initiation period of several years the boy is subjected to rigid and frequently painful discipline by men other than his father.

If the Ooldea be one of those Australian tribes described above, they fall, along with the Trobrianders, Hopi, and Timbira, into the class of societies where the function of initiation is to make up for the lack of discipline exercised by a father over the boy during childhood.

A study of those societies without exclusive sleeping arrangements and with a long *post-partum* sex taboo which do not have the rites is interesting. In the first place both the Pondo and the Araucanians are reported to have had

initiation ceremonies in the recent past, indicating that they are perhaps near the threshold of needing them. The Tallensi also are interesting. An observer notes that the Tallensi should have invented the Oedipus-conflict theory since they are quite open and conscious of the strong rivalry and hostility between father and son, a conflict which remains strong and dangerous, guarded only by ritualized forms of etiquette, until the father dies and the son takes his place. Furthermore, family fissions are reported to occur frequently and the oldest son often leaves the family to establish a new lineage of his own.

Thus, the presence of a *post-partum* sex taboo alone seems to produce tension, which these societies commonly seek to resolve through initiation ceremonies. Societies in this group which do not have ceremonies either had them recently or show evidence of unresolved tension.

SUMMARY

The cross-cultural evidence indicates that:

1. A close relationship is established between mother and son during infancy as a consequence of either (a) their sleeping together for at least a year to the exclusion of the father or (b) the mother being prohibited from sexual intercourse for at least a year after the birth of her child or (c) both of these together have measurable consequences which are manifested in cultural adjustments at adolescence.

2. The cultural adjustments to the presence of the above factors are made when the boy approaches or reaches sexual maturity. These adjustments are either (a) a ceremony of initiation into manhood involving at least one and generally several of the following factors; painful *hazing* by the adult males of the society, tests of endurance and manliness, seclusion from women, and genital

TABLE 2.

THE RELATIONSHIP OF INFANCY FACTORS
TO CULTURAL ADJUSTMENTS AT ADOLESCENCE

| CUSTOMS IN INFANCY AND CHILDHOOD | | | CULTURAL ADJUSTMENT AT ADOLESCENCE | | |
Authority of Father over Son	Exclusive Mother-Son Sleeping Arrangement	Post-partum Sex Taboo	None	Change of Residence	Initiation Ceremony
Present	Long	Long	2	3	14
		Short	1	2	1
	Short	Long	4	0	2
		Short	23	0	0
Absent			0	1	3

operations, or (b) a change of residence which involves separation of the boy from his mother and sisters and may also include some formal means for establishing male authority such as receiving instructions from and being required to be respectful to the mother's brother or the members of the men's house.

3. If both the factors specified in (1) are present, the consequences at adolescence tend to be more elaborate and severe than if only one is present.

4. The cultural adjustments specified in (2) also occur in societies where the father does not have the right to discipline his son, whether or not the conditions specified in (1) are present.

The evidence for these statements are summarized in Table 2.

THE SOCIOPSYCHOLOGICAL IMPLICATIONS

So much for the manifest results at the cultural level. But what is the most reasonable sociopsychological interpretation of these relationships? What are the psychodynamics involved? We are not concerned with the bizarre rites of the Thonga or the peculiar life of a Kwoma infant, for their own sakes, but rather in discovering some general truth about human nature. We, therefore, wish to state what we believe to be the underlying processes that are involved. These are processes that we have not directly observed and which must be accepted or rejected on the grounds of their plausibility or, more important, on the basis of further research implied by our theory.

We believe that six sociopsychological assumptions are supported by our findings:

1. The more exclusive the relationship between a son and his mother during the first years of his life, the greater will be his emotional dependence upon her.

2. The more intensely a mother nurtures (loves) an infant during the early years of his life, the more emotionally dependent he will be upon her.

3. The greater the emotional dependence of a child upon a mother, the more hostile and envious he will be toward anyone whom he perceives as replacing him in her affection.[1]

4. If a child develops a strong emotional dependence upon his mother dur-

[1] If, however, the mother herself is perceived by the child as the one responsible for terminating the early intense relationship, this should lead the boy to both envy her and identify with her. This should produce conflict with respect to his sex role identity, which initiation rites would serve to resolve.

ing infancy, and hostility toward and envy of his father in early childhood at the time of weaning and the onset of independence training, these feelings (although latent during childhood) will manifest themselves when he reaches physiological maturity in (a) open rivalry with his father and (b) incestuous approaches to his mother, unless measures are taken to prevent such manifestations.

5. Painful hazing, enforced isolation from women, trials of endurance or manliness, genital operations, and change of residence are effective means for preventing the dangerous manifestation of rivalry and incest.

6. Even a moderate or weak amount of emotional dependence upon the mother and rivalry with the father will be dangerous at adolescence if the father has no right to (or does not in fact) exercise authority over his son during childhood.

If these sociopsychological hypotheses are true, they have some interesting implications for individual differences in our own society.[2] It has long been known that there is an association between certain types of juvenile delinquency and broken homes. We would predict that

the probability of a boy becoming delinquent in such instances would be highest where the separation of the mother and father occurred during the early infancy of the boy and where she remarried when he was two or three years old.

We would further predict that insofar as there has been an increase in juvenile delinquency in our society, it probably has been accompanied by an increase in the exclusiveness of mother-child relationships and/or a decrease in the authority of the father. It is not unreasonable that industrialization and urbanization have done just this, but, of course, this matter should be investigated before such an interpretation is accepted.

Finally, if further research shows that juvenile delinquency in our society is in part a function of the early childhood factors that have been described in this paper, then it can be countered either by decreasing the exclusiveness of the early mother-child relationship, increasing the authority of the father during childhood, or instituting a formal means of coping with adolescent boys functionally equivalent to those described in this paper. Change of residence would seem more compatible with the values of our society than an initiation ceremony. The Civilian Conservation Corps camps of the 1930's were an experiment which should provide useful data in this regard. The present institution of selective service would perhaps serve this purpose were the boys to be drafted at an earlier age and exposed to the authority of responsible adult males.

---

[2] In a study of infant training William Sewell reports that "the children who slept with their mothers during infancy made significantly poorer showings on the self-adjustment, personal freedom, and family relations components of the California Test of Personality and suffered more sleep disturbances than did those who slept alone." W. H. Sewell, "Infant Training and the Personality of the Child," *Am. J. Sociol.*, 1953, LVIII, 157.

82 | THE LATER CAREERS OF BOYS WHO WERE EARLY- OR LATE-MATURING

MARY COVER JONES

Physical changes in adolescence have tremendous social and psychological significance for the individual. For example, a boy who matures early gains social status among his' peers and elders, and his own self-esteem is probably enhanced as well.

Mary Cover Jones compared a group of early- and late-maturing boys to reveal the superior social-emotional adjustment of the early-maturers. Here she traces the boys into manhood and discovers that the advantages of the early-maturers, elaborated in more successful careers, have been maintained into adult life.

Similar studies of girls show the reverse to be true: early maturation is a handicap.

A previous study (6) compared two groups of boys who had been classified as physically accelerated or retarded, in terms of skeletal age. These groups represented approximately the 20 per cent at each extreme of a normal public school sample. The comparison showed differences in physical growth, sexual maturing, and in a number of psychological measures, and led to the conclusion that ". . . those who are physically accelerated are usually accepted and treated by adults and other children as more mature. They appear to have relatively little need to strive for status. From their ranks come the outstanding student body leaders in senior high school. In contrast, the physically retarded boys exhibit many forms of relatively immature behavior: this may be in part because others tend to treat them as the little boys they appear to be. Furthermore, a fair proportion of these give evidence of needing to counteract their physical disadvantages in some way—usually by greater activity and

striving for attention, although in some cases by withdrawal."

It is clear that early- or late-maturing may have a considerable bearing upon the social life and personal adjustment of some individuals during the middle years of their adolescence. Perhaps of greater importance, however, is the inquiry as to longer-term effects or relationships in adult life, and on this point no evidence has previously been offered.

The subjects who participated in the original study are now in their early thirties. Contacts have been maintained with many of the group during the intervening years; in a systematic follow-up study beginning in 1954 current data have been obtained for 20 of the early- and late-maturing boys, out of an original sample of 32.

Reprinted from *Child Development*, XXVIII, 1 (March, 1957), 113–28, by permission of the author and the Society for Research in Child Development.

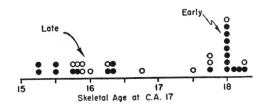

Figure 1. Skeletal ages at 17 years, of the late- and early-maturing.

ADOLESCENT DIFFERENCES

Figures 1, 2, 3, 4, and 5 present data from the adolescent period for the original groups, and for the subsamples available in the present study. Figure 1 shows the distribution of skeletal ages (at around chronological age 17) for the early- and late-maturing. Each circle represents an individual case: the black circles those included in the follow-up and the open circles those who have dropped out. It can be seen that the new selection has not substantially altered the maturity differential of the two groups.

Figures 2 and 3 present cumulative records for height and weight in terms of standard scores at ages 12 to 17. Standard scores (in which 50 is taken as the mean and 10 as the SD) are indicated on the left vertical axis, and per-

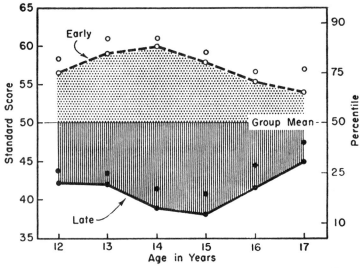

Figure 2.   Height comparisons for two contrasting groups of boys.

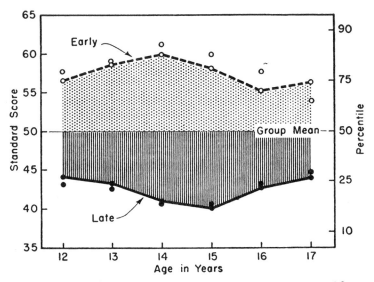

Figure 3.   Weight comparisons for two contrasting groups of boys.

centiles on the right. In these and the following figures, the points on connecting lines represent averages for the follow-up group, consisting of 11 early- and 9 late-maturing individuals. The adjacent points denote averages for the original 16 early- and 16 late-maturing.

The early-maturing tend to fall at the 75 percentile or above, and the late-maturing at the 25 percentile or below, with differences which are at a maximum at around 14 years, when the early-maturing are on the average approximately 8 inches taller and 34 pounds heavier.

In these physical measures the adolescent data for the follow-up sample are similar to those of the original sample, and this is also shown in Figure 4, based on a measure of static dynamometer strength (right grip).

Other physical comparisons included Greulich's (5) 5-point standards of maturity (rated by physicians from pubic hair and external genitalia) and Bayley's ratings of androgeny (1). On the Greulich scale the late-maturing boys at age 14 averaged only 2.0, well below the norm; while the early-maturing averaged 4.5, or close to the scale maximum. In the androgeny asessments, the early-maturing were nearly all in the "masculine" or "hyper-masculine" zone, while approximately half of the late-maturing were classified as "asexual," "bisexual," "hypo-bisexual," or physically "disharmonious." In these as in other respects the follow-up samples yielded distributions ,similar to those of the original study.

With such marked adolescent differences in size, strength, masculine conformation, and associated athletic abilities, we might also predict, in our culture, average differences in reputational status and in some aspects of self-acceptance. In the original study comparisons were presented, at an average age of 16, for a series of ratings made in "free play" situations. The early-maturing were judged to be more attractive in physique and as showing more attention to grooming. They tended to be more relaxed, more matter-of-fact and less affected in their behavior. Differences were significant at the .05 level for each of these traits; for a number of other characteristics, such as interest in the opposite sex, and "good-naturedness," quite consistent differences were ob-

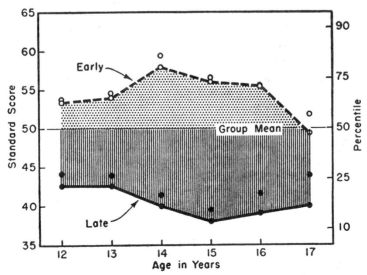

Figure 4. Strength comparisons: *Right grip of boys.*

tained over nine semesters of observation. The late-maturing were significantly more expressive, but their small-boy eagerness was also associated with greater tenseness and more affected attention-seeking mannerisms.

. . . The early-maturing are centered close to the average in this characteristic [physical attractiveness and expressive behavior] while the late-maturing are judged to be more juvenile and less poised in their expressiveness, especially in the middle years of adolescence. Similar results were found for such characteristics as "animated," "talkative," and "uninhibited."

On behavior items suggesting a large component of self-acceptance (being relaxed, unaffected and matter-of-fact) the early-maturing were rated higher at the end of the study, with the late-maturing becoming increasingly "tense" and "affected" in the high school years. Figure 5 illustrates this for the characteristic which we have called "matter-of-fact." Both groups fluctuate around the average in this trait until age 16 when they separate noticeably, the early-maturing falling on the favorable or well-adjusted side, and the late-maturing on the attention-seeking or showoff side of the scale. Similar wide separation at

ages 16 and 17 has been found for the trait "unaffected-affected" and for "relaxed-tense." In these, as in other relevant psychological measures, the follow-up groups had adolescent records similar to those of the original study; the loss of cases has not substantially changed the selection.

ADULT DIFFERENCES

We may now consider the adult characteristics of the early- and late-maturing, as observed at an average age of 33 years. As was predicted at age 17, the differences in gross size tend to disappear. The early-maturing average only half an inch taller, at 5 feet 10 inches; and 7 pounds heavier, at 172 pounds. These differences are not significant. In body build, the prediction is that the early-maturing would be more mesomorphic. The tendency is in this direction, but the differences are not significant. The chief thing to note is the wide range of physiques within each group (both in adolescence and in adulthood) and the marked consistency over the years. A slight change is apparent in the direction of greater mesomorphy in eight of the nine late-maturing and they now present a somewhat more developed and sturdy appearance.

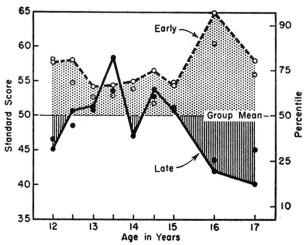

Figure 5. Comparative ratings of "matter-of-factness" of boys.

Some differences would be expected in constitutional indices of masculinity. Among the late-maturing, the majority of the original study and of those included in the follow-up were rated as having a deficiency in masculine development, at age 17. At age 33, however, Sheldon ratings of gynandromorphy (7) in the two groups showed considerable overlap and only a small and nonsignificant difference in favor of the early-maturing.

Personality differences in adult life have been examined with reference to a number of criteria. Two sources of data to be considered here are Gough's California Psychological Inventory and the Edwards Personal Preference Schedule. The first of these, the C.P.I., attempts to appraise aspects of character and temperament which are significant for social living and interpersonal behavior and which are related to personal maturity and creative achievement. Eighteen scales are available which describe individuals in terms of social responsibility, tolerance, flexibility, academic motivation, self-control and the like (3).

Most of the above scales did not show significant differences between the groups. One outstanding exception is the scale entitled "good impression," (interest in, and capacity for, creating a "good impression" on others) (4). Differences here favored the early-maturing with a significance at the .006 level.

Some of the interpretative phrases associated with high scores on this scale include: "is turned to for advice and reassurance; fatherly; is concerned with making a good impression; is persistent in working toward his goal." High scorers on this "Gi" scale are also designated as responsible, cooperative, enterprising, sociable and warm.

In our groups the early-maturing tend in addition to obtain higher scores on the C.P.I. scales for socialization, dominance, self-control and responsibility. Although none of these shows differences at a significance level better than .07, it is true that the early-maturing have high average scores and present a consistently favorable personality picture with regard to these important social variables.

The phrases and adjectives associated with high scores on these five scales (good impression, socialization, dominance, self-control, and responsibility) remind us strikingly of the social behavior and personal traits attributed, by their peers and by adults, to the early-maturing boys in adolescence. For the total group of 43 boys thus far included in the follow-up, a correlation of .50 (significant at the .01 level) was found between the "good impression" score on the C.P.I., and their level of sketetal maturity 18 years earlier. The corresponding Pearson r for the socialization score at age 33, and sketetal maturity at age 15, was .40, significant at the .01 level. For these correlations skeletal quotients were computed (skeletal age over chronological age), to make allowance for slight differences in the age at which the skeletal X-rays were obtained.

One other scale yields an interesting difference, significant at the .05 level. This is the scale for what has been termed "flexibility." Those who score high on this scale are described by Gough as tending to be rebellious, touchy, impulsive, self-indulgent, assertive, and also insightful. Low scorers are described as deliberate, methodical, and industrious, rigid, mannerly, overly-controlling of impulses, compliant. In these terms, the late-maturers tend to be more "flexible" than the early-maturers.

We might hazard the guess that some of the little boy behavior—the impulsiveness, playfulness and also the "touchiness" repeatedly noted in late-maturing adolescents is mirrored in the description of high scorers on this scale. We might speculate further that in the course of having to adapt to difficult status problems, the late-maturers have gained some insights and are indeed more flexible, while the early-maturing, capitalizing on their ability to make a good impression, may have clung to their earlier success pattern to the extent of becoming somewhat rigid or over-controlled.

The Edwards Personal Preference test shows relatively few significant differences between the two groups. This is a self-report device which measures 15 variables named from Murray's list of needs (2).

On the Edwards test, two of the scales are discriminating for our groups

at the 4 and 5 per cent levels respectively. The early-maturing group scores high on the *dominance* scale: "to be a leader, persuade, argue for a point of view," while the late-maturing score high in *succorance*: "to seek encouragement, to be helped by others, to have a fuss made over one when hurt." For the total group of 40 who took the Edwards test at around age 33, skeletal maturing at age 17 correlated .40 with dominance, and —.48 with succorance (both significant at the .01 level). Table 1 summarizes the statistical findings for the follow-up comparisons.

To those of us who have known these young men for over 20 years, some of

TABLE 1.
SUMMARY OF
STATISTICAL FINDINGS
FOR THE FOLLOW-UP
COMPARISONS

Physical Measures: Means

	EARLY		LATE	
	Age 14	*Age 33*	*Age 14*	*Age 33*
Height	5 ft. 8 in.	5 ft. 10 in.	5 ft.	5 ft. 9½ in.
Weight	126.9 lb.	172 lb.	93.2 lb.	165 lb.
Endomorphy*	2.6	3.1	3.1	3.3
Mesomorphy*	4.5	4.6	3.9	4.3
Ectomorphy*	3.4	3.4	3.7	3.7

Psychological Scales

	MEANS		Signif. of		Signif.
	Early	*Late*	*Difference* †	*r* ‡	*Level*
California Psychological Inventory					
Good Impression	25.6	15.7	.006	.50	<.01
Flexibility	9.7	13.8	.05	—.23	
Delinquency §	13.9	20.3	.07	—.40	<.01
Impulsivity	17.1	23.4	.13	—.31	<.05
Dominance	31.7	27.4	.17	.26	
Responsibility	32.9	30.0	.19	.35	<.05
Edwards Personal Preference Schedule					
Dominance	19.4	12.6	.04	.40	<.01
Succorance	7.1	12.4	.05	—.48	<.01

* Rating on 7-point scale; 7 is high.
† Significance level, Wilcoxon Rank Test.
‡ Pearson product-moment correlation with skeletal age/chronological age, at 15 years.
§ A low score indicates "socialization."

the most interesting questions remain to be answered. What have been their successes and failures in achieving occupational and personal goals? All are married, and in each group the present number of children averages 2.3. Socioeconomic ratings, based on homes and neighborhoods, show no differences for the two groups. There are no significant differences in average educational level, although a slightly higher proportion of the later-maturing have college degrees and the only college teacher is in this group.

There is some indication that more of the early-maturing have attained vocational goals which are satisfying and status-conferring. Among this group five are in professional careers; four are executives; one is a skilled mechanic and one in a clerical position. Of the executives, three are in positions of somewhat impressive status.

Among the late-maturing, four are in professions, two are still university students, two are salesmen, and one is a carpenter. None has attained an important managerial position and several, by their own account and the nature of their work, seem somewhat precariously unsettled.

. . . . .

SUMMARY AND CONCLUSION

Boys who had been classified as physically accelerated or retarded in terms of skeletal age during adolescence were compared as young adults at age 33, to determine the long-term effects of rate of maturing upon personality.

Although some cases were lost from the original sample, the data for the follow-up group as reconstituted showed no substantial alteration in the adolescent differentials of the early- and late-maturing.

For the original sample and for the subsample available in the present study, analysis of ratings by adults and classmates indicated that the early-maturing boys were significantly more attractive in physique, more relaxed, poised and matter-of-fact. Consistent differences in other characteristics, such as interest in the opposite sex and "good-naturedness," were obtained over nine semesters of observation. Late-maturing boys were described as more expressive, active, talkative, eager, attention-getting.

The physical differences noted for these boys at adolescence have tended to disappear in adulthood. Personality characteristics as appraised by the California Psychological Inventory and the Edwards Personal Preference Schedule have shown a number of significant differences on the various scales for which the tests are scored (e.g., higher scores for the early-maturing on measures of "good impression" and "socialization"). Where such differences were found, they tended to describe the young adults much as they had been described in adolescence.

No differences were found between the early- and late-maturing in present marital status, family size or educational level. A few of the early-maturing have made exceptionally rapid progress as junior executives and a few of the late-maturing are still somewhat unsettled, vocationally.

The foregoing presentation of data and the case summaries remind us again of the conclusions to the original study which stressed individual differences within each group, resulting from the complex interplay of factors. During the adolescent period late-maturing is a handicap for many boys and can rarely be found to offer special advantages. Early-maturing carries both advantages and disadvantages. In our culture it frequently gives competitive status, but sometimes also involves handicaps in the necessity for rapid readjustments and in requiring the adolescent to meet adult expectations which are more appropriate to size and appearance than to other aspects of maturing. The adolescent handicaps and advantages associated with late- or early-maturing appear to carry over into adulthood to some extent, and perhaps to a greater extent in psychological than in physical characteristics.

REFERENCES

1. BAYLEY, NANCY, & BAYER, LEONA M. The assessment of somatic androgyny. *Amer. J. phys. Anthrop.*, 1946, 4, 433–462.

2. EDWARDS, A. L. *Edwards Personal Preference Schedule.* New York: Psychological Corporation, 1954.

3. GOUGH, H. G. *The California Psychological Inventory.* Stanford: Consulting Psychologists' Press, Copyright, 1951.

4. GOUGH, H. G. On making a good impression. *J. educ. Res.*, 1952, 46, 33–42.

5. GREULICH, W. W., *et al.* Somatic and endocrine studies of puberal and adolescent boys. *Monogr. Soc. Res. Child Develpm.*, 1942, 7, No. 3.

6. JONES, MARY C., & BAYLEY, NANCY. Physical maturing among boys as related to behavior. *J. educ. Psychol.*, 1950, 41, 129–148.

7. SHELDON, W. H., STEVENS, S. S., & TUCKER, W. B. *The varieties of human physique.* New York: Harper, 1940.

83 | CHILDHOOD BACKGROUND OF SUCCESS IN A PROFESSION

PHILIP J. ALLEN

Where is the self-made man, the one who pulls himself up by his bootstraps by personal qualities alone, in true Horatio Alger style? The more evidence we have from social science, the more the image fades. The following study presents some statistical and sociological data about the person who succeeds in one profession, the Methodist ministry. He is from a large city; he attended a large school; he is an only child of a mother and father who were only children. His father and mother are well educated and happily married. If one matches the pattern, his chances are good in any profession.

The general run of vertical mobility studies seem to constitute an attempt to delineate occupational movement along a vertical axis between two or more male generations. However valuable some of these studies may be, they do not seem to throw much light upon vertical movement within a given occupation group.

Reprinted from the article in the *American Sociological Review*, XX, 2 (April, 1955), 186–90, by permission of the author and the American Sociological Society.

Does anyone know what makes for success within any occupation?

. . . . .

Several investigators have attempted to relate background factors to *general* achievement. What seem to be needed are studies of *specific* achievement within specific occupations, relating such achievement to background factors in the life history. If a large enough number of independent variables among background factors could be discovered associated with success within a given occupation, vocational counseling could be done with greater confidence.

The difficulties confronting an investigator of success, or upward mobility, within an occupation are numerous. Some of these are related to the construction of an accurate and valid scale for measuring status as well as vertical movement within a given occupation. The present investigator utilized what seems to be a fruitful method for studying vertical mobility within a profession.

The profession studied is the Methodist ministry, and the measurement of status within the professional group is, with qualifications, annual salary. This occupational group was selected because it seems to possess certain desirable features: (1) its status system seems to be reflected in annual salary, (2) the salary is available in annual publications, and (3) upward mobility within this profession seems greatly determined by publicly demonstrated and evaluated performance in a field of clearly defined values to be achieved.

Upward mobility is a consequence of successful face-to-face social interaction with laymen and fellow ministers. One's salary is commensurate with his desirability as pastor and preacher, a desirability based upon his reputation and observed performance. In such performance, whether from the pulpit or in small group interaction, there is something revealed, not merely in the nature of professional skills which can be learned by the average person through formal education and years of professional experience, but particularly in the nature of crucial factors related to personality structure which, although known, cannot be readily learned, factors possibly explained through childhood social interaction. One's testing is continuous and status must be continuously validated by current performance.

A minister's social skills, repeatedly demonstrated, become a favorite topic of conversation among church members. His unusual·accomplishments, as well as his unfortunate blunders, very rapidly are passed around the church community by the few who were there to the many, via grape-vine. This gossip has the effect of raising or lowering the minister's prestige, influencing subsequent attendance at church services by members as well as by non-members who are potential members or who, at any rate, currently contribute to the church. Status is continuously validated through social interaction, and there is no escape from the process.

The social selection of those who move upward in this profession requires of them an insight into the nature of human motivation, social organization, sources of social power, as well as channels through which such power flows. It requires not only the knowledge but, what is equally important, an ability to utilize it, applying it strategically at appropriate times in social interaction. This, it seems, is crucial for upward mobility. Many appear to have the knowledge of and insight into factors indicated above. But relatively few seem able to use such knowledge and insight to achieve deliberately sought results.

SELECTION OF SAMPLE

The sample was drawn from a sub-universe within a universe of over 20,000 Methodist ministers. The sub-universe comprised only those who had been in the active ministry between 20 and 26 years. It had been found in an earlier pilot study that the highest status attainable within the Methodist clergy, that of bishop, takes on an average of 20 to 26 years to reach. On the other hand, some downward mobility, except in the case of bishops, tends to occur during the last decade or so of professional life.

Since present salary was to be used as the present status differentiating measure, the sample was selected from those who had been in the profession from 20 to 26 years. Only white subjects were included in the sample, in order to avoid an important variable. All 44 white bishops were arbitrarily included. In all, the original sample included 608 persons.

METHOD

After 17 case histories were secured through interviews with a cross-sectional sample and with 3 bishops, a detailed questionnaire was constructed, calling for data on the life history, particularly on childhood background. Together with a personally typed letter, this questionnaire was sent to all 608 in the "gross" sample. Adding deaths of subjects in the sample of questionnaires returned by the post office, stamped "Address Unknown," a total of 60 had to be discarded from the original sample of 608, leaving 548. Of these, 332 returned questionnaires, including 24 bishops. Only 316 of those returned were usable.

The 316 subjects represented in the usable returned questionnaires were ranked according to salary, with qualifications. Each subject was first ranked with his own geographic area, the Annual Conference area, of which there are 106. Of these, 93 are white Annual Conference areas, of which 77 are represented in the sample.

In the ranking of subjects, a salary frequency distribution was first made for each Annual Conference area, and each subject was ranked within his own area on salary, a percentile rank score being calculated for him. Then, all 316 subjects were ranked with each other, the order of rank being determined by the numerical value of the rank score of each. This, it is believed, neutralized the regional variation in annual salary. Bish-

ops were arbitrarily assigned the topmost rank.

In the analysis, the sample was stratified into quarters of 79 each, and comparisons were made of the upper with the lower parts of the distribution. Chi-square was used to test for difference. Only those differences between the more successful and less successful subjects which could have occurred by chance less than 5 times out of 100 are being presented here.

FINDINGS

No special effort is here made to relate the findings to each other. They are being merely listed in the following tables, where Q_1 and Q_4 represent the highest ranking and lowest-ranking quartiles, respectively. Table 1 lists those correlates of success which could have occurred by chance less than one time out of 100. Table 2 lists those with a probability between .01 and .05.

DISCUSSION

A number of the above correlates suggest relatively stable culturally defined patterns of social interaction involving familiar roles, child-father, child-mother, older sibling-younger sibling, social-class role, school role, community role, and the like. . . . No detailed analysis of roles, social, cultural, or situational, is being attempted here. What is being suggested is that roles provide ready-made molds for channeling and gratifying impulse, as well as for habitual patterning of responses. Indeed, culture seems to be internalized largely through assumption of roles in group living, or through covert internal rehearsal of observed roles in anticipation of enacting them overtly sometime in the future. Through role-playing one internalizes basic responses which seem to persist

TABLE 1.	Correlate	Direction of Association
CORRELATES OF SUCCESS OF METHODIST MINISTERS WITH A LEVEL OF SIGNIFICANCE BELOW .01	Size of community of residence, age 6–12	Q_1 resided in largest communities and Q_4 in smallest
	Size of school subject attended, age 6–12	Q_1 attended the largest and Q_4 the smallest
	Age when subject started high school	Q_1 started earliest and Q_4 latest
	Age when subject felt himself accepted as equal by mother	Q_1 felt accepted at earliest age and Q_4 at latest
	Age when subject *first* got idea of entering ministry	Q_1 got idea at earliest age and Q_4 latest
	How favorably mother of subject viewed ministers during subject's childhood	Q_1 mothers viewed ministers most favorably and mothers of Q_4 least favorably
	How often subject's mother's counsel was sought by friends and neighbors	Counsel of Q_1 mothers was sought most often and that of Q_4 mothers least often
	Number of children in subject's childhood family	Q_1 had smallest and Q_4 largest
	Subject's major field in college: Social Sciences	Q_1 had largest number and Q_4 smallest
	Philosophy	Q_1 had largest number and Q_4 smallest
	Religion	Q_1 had smallest number and Q_4 largest

tenaciously into adulthood and which seem to be related to success within this profession under analysis.

Although the correlates listed here focus largely upon the external situation, it is realized that roles have both objective and subjective components. . . .

. . . . .

. . . The roles which seem to leave the deepest imprint are those which, of the many tried, have been found satisfying or necessary to the social interaction in which one must participate, particularly those roles with which one has become most deeply ego-involved. These roles may have emerged from trial-and-error or they may have been adopted by way of one's identification with an admired other. Roles adopted may be found already tailored and may be put on as a ready-made suit or they may be personally tailored by one for his own individual use. In any case, once adopted, roles provide a mold for the deposit of

current experience, on the one hand, and a ready vehicle for entering the parade, or drama, of social interaction, on the other.

CONCLUSIONS

Among the correlates of success in the professional listed above, about a half-dozen or so may be found to comprise independent variables around which others are clustered. For example, size of community of residence may represent an independent variable around which are clustered such factors as size of school, intercommunity residential mobility and, possibly, number of children parents had. On the other hand, this latter factor of number of children may also be related to what appears to be another independent variable, occupation of father. Clearly, some statistical device should be applied to the above correlates, such as multiple correlation, in an effort to interrelate what appear

TABLE 2.	Correlate	Direction of Association
CORRELATES		
OF SUCCESS OF	Size of community of residence of subject:	
METHODIST	age 0–5	Largest for Q_1 and smallest for Q_4
MINISTERS	age 13–college	Largest for Q_1 and smallest for Q_4
WITH A LEVEL	Size of school attended, aged 13 to	Largest for Q_1 and smallest for Q_4
OF SIGNIFI-	college age	
CANCE	Age when subject started school (except bishops)	Q_1 earliest and Q_4 latest
BETWEEN		
.01 AND .05	Number of times subject moved from one community to another before high school graduation	Q_1 greatest number and Q_4 smallest
	Subject's sibling position: Only child	Q_1 greatest number and Q_4 smallest
	Mother's sibling position: Only child	Q_1 greatest number and Q_4 had *none*
	Father's sibling position: Only child	Q_1 greatest number and Q_4 had *none*
	Older or oldest	Q_1 greatest number and Q_4 smallest
	Younger or youngest	Q_4 greatest number and Q_1 smallest
	Age-interval between subject and next older sibling, in months	Interval between Q_1 and sibling was greatest, and interval between Q_4 and sibling was smallest
	Number of children subject's mother ever had	Q_4 had greatest number and Q_1 smallest
	father ever had.*	Q_4 had greatest number and Q_1 smallest
	Occupation of subject's father:	
	Professional	Q_1 had greatest number and Q_4 smallest
	Proprietors, Managers and Officials	Q_1 had greatest number and Q_4 smallest
	Farmers (including owners and laborers)	Q_4 had greatest number and Q_1 smallest
	Years of education for:	
	father	Q_1 had greatest number and Q_4 smallest
	mother	Q_1 had greatest number and Q_4 smallest
	subject	Q_1 had greatest number and Q_4 smallest
	Age when subject felt himself accepted as equal by father (except bishops)	Q_1 at lowest age and Q_4 at highest
	How happily married father was	Q_1 most happily and Q_4 least

* Some remarried parents had children with two or more mates, hence the necessity for indicating separately the number of children for each parent.

to be the more important variables. But the task of designing this project, of selecting the sample, of constructing the questionnaire, of securing the cooperation of respondents and, finally, of isolating the above correlates was so enormous that it was decided to postpone further analysis. Meanwhile, it was believed desirable to publish results so far, in the interest of suggesting to other potential investigators in this field what seems to be a fruitful methodological procedure for studying upward mobility within a single vocational group.

The present investigator believes that, after a large enough number of independent variables have been isolated for a given occupation, it may be possible to construct an aptitude test for that occupation, of sufficient validity and reliability to permit vocational counselors to advise high school and college students.

84 | THE EVIL EYE: FEAR OF SUCCESS

MORRIS L. HAIMOWITZ AND

NATALIE READER HAIMOWITZ

There has been much discussion of the fear of failure, but very little of the fear of success. The general prevalence of failure throughout the world may, however, indicate that more people fear success than fear failure. This study describes how children and adults unconsciously strive to avoid the terrifying consequences of success.

The evil eye is the fear that calamity will fall in the hour of success and rejoicing, that afflictions will harass the fortunate and prosperous. Among the Italians it is called *jettatura*; among the Jews, *nehurrah*. Among American Indians and prerevolutionary New Englanders, the evil eye (the power to afflict) was attributed to witches. Those accused of being witches were usually poor, miserable, elderly, crippled—persons with less than their neighbors. The evil eye is obviously the envious eye. It appears among people everywhere from time immemorial that the poor envy the rich, the lame envy the strong, the ugly envy the beautiful, and those who are blessed with desirable attributes or possessions expect to be envied. For the rich empathize with the poor, hating themselves as they are hated, and cursing the poor for this vicarious misery.

SOME EXAMPLES OF THE EVIL EYE AMONG PRELITERATES[1]

When Sumner wrote his study of *Folkways* in 1906 he described the evil eye among primitive people. In Bornu, for example, when a horse is sold, if it is a fine one, it is delivered by night, for fear of the evil eyes (covetous and envious eyes) of bystanders (one of whom might lose his self-control and steal it?). In the Sudan food is usually covered with a conical straw cover to prevent the evil eye (of hungry people who might admire and long for it?). Customs of eating and drinking in private belong here (in many societies children and parents must not see each other eating). At Katanga, Central Africa, only the initiated may watch the smelting of copper, for fear of the evil eye, which would spoil the process (or lay bare the secrets of the trade). The cloistering and veiling of women was intended to

Revised from the article in *Teleclass Study Guide in Child Psychology*, 1958, pp. 84-91, by permission of the Chicago Board of Education.

[1] William Graham Sumner, *Folkways* (Ginn & Co., 1906), pp. 515–19.

protect them, especially if they were beautiful, from the covetous eye. The admiration they would attract would be fatal (or would steal them away). The notion of the evil eye led to covering some parts of the body and so to notions of decency. Shells, fig leaves, strips of leather, clothing, etc. catch attention to divert the evil eye from the organs which are valued.

PROTECTIONS AGAINST THE EVIL EYE

Certain customs seem to be an attempt of the successful to hide their success, or protect themselves from the retaliation it provokes. Sumner observed this in many groups. In the East Indies the phallus, or the symbol of it, is a charm against the evil eye. Roman boys wore such a symbol. In India they used teeth or claws or obscene symbols or strings of shells. Whatever dangles and flutters attracts attention to itself away from the thing to be protected. Mohammed believed in the evil eye. Children, horses and asses were disfigured amongst Moslems to protect them from the risk they would suffer if beautiful. Homer's heroes were taught as a life policy to avert envy; self-disparagement was an approved pose. Soldiers of Rome followed the chariot of the triumphant general and shouted derisive and sarcastic verses while the populace showered him with small stones and garbage. (As we shower a bride with rice or an old shoe.) Modern Egyptians leave their children ragged and dirty especially when out of doors for fear of admiration and envy. Boys are greatly envied. They are kept long in the harem and dressed in girls' clothes for the same protection. In Cairo as part of the marriage ritual fancy chandeliers are hung before the bridegroom's house. If a crowd gathers to look at it, a jar is broken to distract attention from it, lest an envious eye should cause it to fall. In China, children are often given ugly names: "dog," "hog," "flea." In Southern Europe one does not permit

his children to be praised or caressed. If someone does admire a child, he should then spit on it three times or say "What an ugly child." If someone asks "How are you feeling" one says "Knock on wood, I'm fine." The knocking on wood diverts the evil eye. When a young girl first menstruates her mother may slap her or spit on her.[2]

The fear of success, the need to hide or to deny assets, or in some instances the need to fail, is, an expression of the evil eye syndrome. It is difficult to find any society, in any period of history, where this phenomena has been absent. It is the purpose of this article to explore the ways in which the evil eye, which is an ancient heritage, actively influences us today. Let us look at our own tradition.

THE EVIL EYE IN OUR OWN TRADITION (OR SECRET FORCES FOR THE PREVENTION OF SUCCESS)

The Holy Bible eloquently describes the Fall as the consequence of success. Adam and Eve discovered and ate the sweet fruit of the tree of knowledge. How were they rewarded for this example of initiative, curiosity, exploration, (and disobedience)? Their eyes were opened so they could see, learn, and be ashamed.

Unto the woman, God said, I will greatly multiply thy sorrow and thy conception; in sorrow thou shalt bring forth children . . . and unto Adam, He said, cursed is the ground for thy sake; in sorrow shalt thou eat of it all the days of thy life. In the sweat of thy face shalt thou eat, till thou return unto the ground; for dust thou art and unto dust shalt thou return.

The moral? If you discover something new, if you taste the good fruit of the tree of knowledge, or the sweet taste of freedom or success, you may be punished. If you violate the norms, if you disobey the rules, you will suffer severely. Be safe.

---

[2] *Ibid.*

Conform. A similar theme is repeated in the story of Eve's children. Cain, a poor farmer, was envious of his successful brother Abel, and killed him. The moral? If you do too well, your brother may kill you.

In recent literature the evil eye has been rediscovered, renamed (Riesman's "other directed" man, Whyte's "organization man"), and erroneously regarded as a modern phenomenon.

Many persons own jewelry they never wear, or if they don't own the gems, want them but do not buy them. Some women, after buying a fur coat, fear to wear it lest it become soiled or torn or stolen, at least that's what they say. But if they are questioned somewhat more closely it often turns out they fear the envious glances of their sisters without fur coats, just as they themselves had been envious previously.

Some feel that if they only could have a baby they would be happy. Having a baby would mean success to them. Once pregnant however, they develop fears: perhaps the baby will be a monster, have two heads, be born ugly, have scars, be defective.

Some men can never wear their best pants or the tie they really like, or their new coat or hat or can't use their new watch or fountain pen. Or they can't use their new broom or hammer or even a new nail. They may have new ones, but would rather use the old, until the new ones get rusty. Sometimes this is "thrift," sometimes it is the "Secret Society" we are describing—that part of our customs which says one must not boast, one must not show off one's success. To many this means one must not have success.

What often passes for modesty or humility, benevolence or altruism, or even miserliness may have the same underlying feeling: if I do well or show that I am doing well or take what I want, others who want as much as I will hate me (as I used to hate those who had what I wanted).

A blind man reported that he had had the opportunity to have his sight restored by a cornea replacement, but that he preferred not to have the operation. The reason he gave is interesting. He might have said he feared the operation, or that it cost too much, but he didn't. He said "They could use that cornea for other blind people who are not as well off as I. I have a business selling Christmas cards; I have a lovely wife. We have been married fourteen years and are getting along fine. Give the sight to a man who needs it worse, or who is younger than I." It is noteworthy that he compared himself not with seeing persons but with other blind persons, persons younger or weaker than himself, persons who might envy his vision.

The humble kinds of success may also be fraught with anxiety. To the obese, a successful self is not so heavy. The obese person who wants to reduce sometimes suffers from fantasies of dying of starvation, of looking like a skeleton, of becoming ill, nauseous or weak if he should reduce to a normal weight. Although it is well known that food may be a source of gratification when interpersonal gratifications are disappointing, and that people may feel hungry when they are disappointed in not receiving something for which they long (love, approval, consideration), it is suggested here that an important aspect of the body weight is the value placed upon it.

Similarly with the underweight. His humble goal in life is to gain a few pounds and be like others. He diets and exercises too, and eats a lot of butter and milk and becomes panicky after he has gained a few pounds, catches a cold, has nightmares, or feels nervous and places the cause for his distress on the butter or other special foods. "A doctor told me to eat yellow corn meal with butter to help me gain weight. It is not expensive and I like it. But when I have gained a couple of pounds I catch a bad cold, lose my appetite and go back to where I was before I started gaining."

Success has many meanings:—it may mean winning a tennis match, or getting married, or going swimming, or painting a picture or changing a tire or building a home or having a child or getting a job or gaining weight or making a million or having a birthday party. Specific fantasies of success are thus highly idiosyncratic, specific for each individual. The fears and penalties associated with achieving success, however, appear to be an age-old phenomena which few entirely escape.

Success may also mean, "I am my brother's keeper." If one is successful, one must take care of those less successful, which may be something of a burden. At family reunions there is talk of the successes and failures of relatives. If everyone has been healthy and prosperous, the meeting is pleasurable. If, however, one has not been successful, or has been ill, the success of his brothers irritates him, even as his failure casts a shadow on the gathering. If his ill fortune continues, others will have to take care of him. It is only when such responsibility is felt strongly that people adopt extreme behavior to avoid helping the unfortunate. A common example of this is the miser who has lots of money but pretends to be poor. Similarly, persons who are strongly tempted to help a beggar and feel enormous guilt when they pass him by, nourish the fantasy that this beggar may really be a wealthy man whose Cadillac brings him to the corner each day and picks him up in the evening. This idea appeared in one of the adventures of Sherlock Holmes. We have found it in many clients who feel pursued by the evil eye. The non-giver is thus exonerated. Many men who achieve, who acquire, have freed themselves partially as compared with their brothers who have been more timid, but they pay a certain price for their success in their inner psychological state. They are haunted by guilt,

shame, or fear of coming face to face with their unwillingness to share.

One of the ideals of our society is the rugged individualist. He is productive, creative; he uses initiative, he gets ahead, he is aggressive, fights for the things he feels are right regardless of where the crowd is heading. Although such vigor is ideal, most people experience considerable ambivalence about achieving it; there is both desire for it and fearful avoidance of it.

Below is an account of an experiment conducted to study some of the forces described above, as they operate in people at a less conscious level.

THE ASSOCIATIONS OF 100 STUDENTS TO SYMBOLS OF SUCCESS

Problem

It is well known that many people function at a level much lower than their potential, and it is often difficult for them to increase their ability up to their potential.

Hypothesis

Success is associated with anxiety. One reason some persons are not fully productive is their anxiety regarding success.

Method of Testing the Hypothesis

ASSUMPTIONS | 1. In our society, certain words and phrases such as *promotion, new car, graduation, best in class,* and *a lovely marriage* would symbolize success to college students.

2. Other words and phrases such as *open air, wood, crayon, billboard, here and now,* would not symbolize success to college students.

3. Students asked to associate to the words above will write down whatever comes to mind.

4. If more words and phrases suggesting anxiety or blocking behaviors occur with the success words than with the non-success words, our hypothesis is supported.

PROCEDURE | One hundred college freshmen were read the following instructions:

This is an exercise to show how different words bring forth different associations or responses. I am going to write some words on the blackboard and ask that you write down on a sheet of paper whatever comes to your mind. You will have 20 seconds for each. Write down as many words or phrases as you can think of, and write down every one that comes to your mind. If you don't think of any word or phrase, don't write down anything. For example: if I say "green," what does it make you think of? (red, grass, park, sky, blue, dress, etc.) Don't say anything out loud. It will disturb the others. Here is the first word. You have 20 seconds. Copy the word first: (Write on blackboard "open air." Twenty seconds later, "billboard," and so on with this list: promotion, wood, new car, crayon, graduation, here and now, best in class, a lovely marriage.)

Since each of the 100 students associated to ten expressions, there were a total of 1,000 sets of associations. Since most students associated more than once to each expression, the total number of associations came to approximately 3,000.

The 3,000 associations were read and those judged to be symbolic of anxiety, displeasure, or negation were tabulated. It is assumed that crossing out or misspelling simple words, or blocking (inability to associate to a word) may also symbolize, connote, reveal or be an expression of some inner anxiety. Approximately 300 or 10 per cent of the expressions were judged to express anxiety.

Table 1 lists the stimulus words and the number of persons responding with unpleasant, blocking, or crossed-out and misspelled words in response to each. Thus three students gave one or more unpleasant associations to the stimulus word "open air"; nine students gave one or more unpleasant associations to the stimulus word "promotion". (See Table 2.) The totals 20 and 67 do not indicate the number of different students because some students had anxiety expressions for several words. The average number of students expressing anxiety for the non-success words was four; the average number of students expressing anxiety for the success words was thirteen—three times as many. If we compare blocking, we find thirteen blocking responses to the success words compared to only two for non-success words. And if we compare crossed out and misspelled words, we find

TABLE 1. THE NUMBER OF PERSONS RESPONDING WITH ANXIETY TO NON-SUCCESS AND TO SUCCESS WORDS	STIMULUS WORD	ANXIETY ASSOCIATIONS		
	NON-SUCCESS	Unpleasant	Blocking	Crossed-out Misspelled	Total
	1. open air	3	0	0	3
	2. billboard	6	0	0	6
	4. wood	4	0	0	4
	6. crayon	3	0	0	3
	8. here and now	4	2	0	6
	Totals	20	2	0	22
	SUCCESS				
	3. promotion	9	1	1	11
	5. new car	18	3	0	21
	7. graduation	9	0	3	12
	9. best in class	14	7	3	24
	10. a lovely marriage	17	2	4	23
	Totals	67	13	11	91

TABLE 2. A LIST OF THE STIMULUS WORDS IN THE ORDER PRESENTED WITH THE WORDS OR PHRASES JUDGED TO BE UNPLEASANT OR NEGATIVE, OR SYMBOLIC OF ANXIETY. (COMMA SEPARATES RESPONSES OF DIFFERENT SUBJECTS, HYPHEN SEPARATES RESPONSES OF THE SAME SUBJECTS)		
	Open air:	air raid, lust, fall - hurt
	Billboard:	pain in the neck - waste of wood, train wreck, sloppy - gaudy, nuisance, hard sleep - tension, obnoxious
	Promotion:	big shot, longer hours to work, test, grey hair, con-man, fight, flunk ⌐ sad, me - never - damm (sic), top floor - mess
	Wood:	floods, knife, knife, boo
	New car:	big payments but nice, increased budget, monthly payments (4), show-off, expensive, scratches, traffic ticket, too much chrome, too-big, too expensive, accident, accident, junk, unhappiness, unemployment-recession
	Crayon:	problems, kids-wall-scolding, defacing property
	Graduation:	sadness, never, look for job, me - bottom, mistakes, phoney, bad grades, work, joy and tears
	Here and now:	boring class, anxiety, tired, fight
	Best in class:	stupid bum, teacher's pet, apple polisher, exam, time for nothing but study - no friends - showoff, hard work, brown noser, con-man, no one, wrong emphasis, odd ball - non-socialistic, me - no - I want, worst (2)
	A lovely marriage:	far, far away, selfish, divorce, quick divorce, struggle, unlikely, one of few, never, hard to find, arguments - children - difficulty - mother-in-law, no mother-in-law, is over, - too bad, - good, - too short, stopped, no fights, nuts - no such thing, sorrow, worry - tired - impossible - people are not grown up.

eleven to zero. (Only misspelling of one-syllable words was included.)

CONCLUSION | The hypothesis is supported. Approximately thirteen per cent of our sample of 100 students associated to success words with anxiety, while only four per cent associated to non-success words with anxiety.

DISCUSSION

Having experimentally demonstrated the ambivalence about success, let us proceed to examine some of the manifestations of ambivalence in more complex situations. The cost to our society of this ambivalence is inestimable in terms of dollars, human creativity, and maximum use of individual capacities. Take, for example, the following incidents.

A soldier told us this experience:

During the war we were stationed on an island in the Pacific. The only lumber available was in the army lumberyard. The army was burning tons of scrap lumber every week. Occasionally natives would ask for a piece of lumber, or request that the scrap lumber be set aside and given or sold to the natives. The Commanding General would not hear of this. "We must burn the lumber," he said, "Otherwise if we let people come in and get some, they might stumble over it, hurt themselves and sue us."

A commuter reported:

A bus was held up for several minutes while cars slipped and spun in the snow in front of it. While waiting for a car to dislodge itself, several passengers of the bus, very impatient at being late for work, went to the driver of the bus and said we want to go out and help that car. We'll be right back. The driver said, "If you go out, I'll have to charge you another fare." "That's crazy," the passenger said. "That man is holding up the bus and traffic for blocks while his wheels are spinning in the snow and we could push him out in just a minute." The driver said "If I let you out of the bus to push that car, and if you slipped and broke a leg, I'd get sued."

A student told us he wanted to use some tools in the school workshop:

Students were not permitted to use the huge workshop, "Because," the engineer seriously related, "a student once cut off his finger." Today the workshop stands idle most of the time, used only by the engineers.

A beautiful swimming pool in a public school is closed most of the time because "Once someone drowned in the pool."

We find such conflicts often heightened in specific crisis situations in which the individual, confronted with a problem to be solved, or an opportunity to be grasped, either initiates effective activity in response to it, or retires passively to "safe," "well-tested" ground.

In these four examples there were strong psychological factors preventing the individual decision-maker from extending himself, from "going out on a limb," or from showing initiative by improvising better solutions to problems. What are these factors? Are we all equally bound by them? Are there some factors in our life experience which intensify fear of success, intensify inhibition, and are there other factors that reduce it?

The common element to these apparently diverse phenomena, wearing clothing to distract attention from the genitals, knocking on wood when admitting success, fear of abandoning "usual" inadequate procedures of problem solving to explore new, untested ones, appears to be the expectation of loss ("bad luck"). The expectation of loss or punishment is accompanied by rationalizations to justify the feelings. The reasons given in the four examples above are good reasons (some-times bad reasons) but they are not the primary reasons. The fear apparently originates unconsciously from childhood experiences and is reinforced during adult life.

CHILDHOOD ORIGINS OF THE EVIL EYE: SOME HYPOTHESES

We may understand the evil eye as originating in the early life experience of each individual. For some, the significant early experiences are so severe that the fear of success, the need to conform, establishes rigid limits of living. Any temptation to compete, to strive, to create, to own, brings with it such severe anxiety that the individual withdraws within the area of the safe status quo. A conflict appears when, as part of general mobility, those individuals who are fearful of success must achieve in order to conform to a group in which everybody else is achieving, graduating, getting married, having a baby, buying a car, a home, getting a better job or giving a superior performance on whatever job he has. In such circumstances the individual must achieve just to conform, a situation which requires him to surpass others in order to be inconspicuous in his intimate social group, and one which may arouse continuous anxiety.

What are some of these significant early experiences which influence later freedom? First is the universal experience of envy. Everyone has wanted what someone else owned. This is often first experienced in the Oedipus Complex and in sibling rivalry. One child in the family gets admiration or new clothing, and the other children may get none. When a less-favored child envies, he wishes to harm or to destroy his more fortunate brother (as with Cain and Abel, Jacob and Esau, and with Joseph and his brothers). Apparently, then, a most significant factor in later life is the extent to which envy is aroused in the early family life. If we have envied greatly and hated intensely, throughout our lives we are alerted to these feelings, in ourselves and in others (or imagine them). Similarly, if we have been greatly envied and hated by other members of the family, the discomfort of this experience makes us highly ambivalent about being in this special position again. It may be that where children feel loved and appreciated, and where no child is continually favored, envy is reduced. Children who feel loved can tolerate the experience of another child's getting some needed clothing or food or attention without intense hatred. Conversely, where a child seriously doubts parental affection, "buying one for everybody" brings little comfort for him, for he suspects that "his brother's is better, or bigger or in some way more desirable," and his envy (really envy of parental love) is aroused anyway.

A second feature is the extent to which parents can tolerate strength and adequacy in their children. Many parents are able to be protective and tender when their children are docile and weak and helpless; but when the children begin to show signs of strength or skill, the parents may become anxious. When parents feel inadequate, and unable to compete with their contemporaries, they may be driven to compete with their children. Such parents being, at least for a while, stronger, older, more skillful, defeat the child, whose early attempts to develop strength and initiative thus result in pain and punishment, as well as with the subtle threat of the loss of parental love and the loss of the necessities of life. It follows then that feelings of adequacy on the part of parents, in comparison with their contemporaries, is one factor in their tolerance of initiative, skillfulness and aggressiveness in their children.

A young man we know was thinking about making a fireplace screen. He planned to cut the screen, pound, twist and polish the wrought iron. He thought not only of how beautiful his handiwork would be, but also of the danger. He might hurt himself. "I keep thinking of the saw blade slipping and cutting off a hand and the pliers slipping and nipping a finger." Such fears were associated with his father, who he scorned as being a weak braggart, but whose strength and power he also envied. A constant fantasy was that his father envied him. As a child, each time he was successful in some task his father would compete, to prove that the father was better. On the chinning bar the boy chinned three times. He ran proudly to tell his father. That's nothing, the father chided, and to prove it he went to the bar and chinned *six* times. One day, when he hit a home run while playing baseball, he ran to tell his father, who replied, "That's not bad, but when I was your age I was hitting *two* home runs." The son felt the father was weak in having to prove his superiority, because he was not successful with men his own age. But the father was also strong in that each time, he was able to better his son. This strength the son envied and hated. His fear was that if he bettered his father, the father would then envy him as he previously had envied and hated his father. The fact that his father had been dead for years made little difference until the young man understood why he feared being cut, and in psychotherapy worked through his Oedipal problem.

There are several factors related to unexpected, unavoidable tragedies. As a child grows, and becomes aggressive, death or illness of a sibling or parent may constitute a severe shock to the child, leading him to the conclusion that it was his aggressiveness that caused the damage. Children are not logical in their cause-and-effect reasoning, and they cannot realistically assess their own strength. When early beginnings of assertiveness occur simultaneously with painful losses, the child may associate these and feel one to be the consequence of the other, making him forever fearful of his own initiative. Similarly, a child may regard the birth of younger children as parental retaliation for assertiveness. Very often, in a family where parents feel burdened by several young children, any show of strength or adequacy (ability to walk, dress oneself, carry a package) is met with the strain of parental expectation that the new achievement is to be repeated "from now on." The more adequate the child reveals himself to be, the more is expected of him. He not only gives up the pleasure of parental doting and assistance, but is expected to take on additional duties in the care of younger children. He may regard this as punishment for accomplishment. "You're a big boy now. You have to walk. The baby rides in the buggy." So who wants to be big? One may expect loss of support when one demonstrates strength.

A boy reports:

I was translating Latin. The teacher had called on me and I knew the lesson well. But suddenly I felt everyone was watching me; they usually did not know the lesson. If I knew the lesson and no one else did, the kids would make fun of me. Suddenly I was stumbling. I pretended to labor over every word. The teacher said something sharp and my turn was over. I felt a little relieved that it was over, and a little ashamed at my failure.

Older girls say they must not finish college. "If I finish college I can't get a husband because boys don't like girls with too much education; so I'm quitting this semester, before I graduate."

A similar argument is used by fathers who tell their sons: "Why should you stay in school and learn all that malarky. I never went to school and look at me." A father in trouble with the truant officer because he kept his son out of school recently told us, "I don't see why he has to go to school. That boy can already read and write." The father could not read or write. And in a few minutes, we found out all the boy could write was his name. He told us, "School ain't for me. You won't have no friends if you go to school."

Some people fear such common acts as asking for a job, asking for a date, asking for a loan, seeking information on the highway, information on how to operate a machine in a factory. For some people to ask for help means to put himself in an inferior position, in a vulnerable position. It is an acknowledgement of weakness. Or is it a fear of being punished for being aggressive, for getting ahead?

"My brother is a year younger than I. We attended the same grammar school. He had some of the same teachers that I had the year before. He was not as obedient as I had been. He made poorer marks. All through school his teachers would say, 'Why can't you behave like your sister?' There was always a little bitterness in the way he felt towards me which disturbed me a great deal. Because of this we went to different high schools."

"I and several of my friends were in a contest for homecoming queen. As the day for selection approached, tension among us rose. Nobody would talk to anyone else. And after I was elected queen, my best friend wouldn't talk to me anymore." Her best friend was the lady-in-waiting to her majesty.

Many students will not run for office because they fear the crowd won't like them if they win, and they will hate themselves if they lose.

One boy we were counseling who got many gold stars in spelling suddenly could not spell any more. After some rambling he told us "Someone stole my gold stars, so I got the idea the other kids didn't like me for having too many gold stars so I missed words the rest of the year."

85 | IDENTITY VERSUS SELF-DIFFUSION

ERIK H. ERIKSON

Adolescent behavior is frequently dictated by the individual's desire to develop a sense of identity. He strives to know what he is and what he is not; he sees himself as others see him and yet wishes to be himself openly and undefensively. Erikson analyzes several aspects of this search for personal "integrity."

With the establishment of a good relationship to the world of skills and to those who teach and share the new skills, childhood proper comes to an end. Youth begins. But in puberty and adolescence all sameness and continuities relied on earlier are questioned again because of a rapidity of body growth which equals that of early childhood and because of the entirely new addition of physical genital maturity. The growing and developing youths, faced with this physiological revolution within them, are now primarily concerned with attempts at consolidating their social roles. They are sometimes morbidly, often curiously, preoccupied with what they appear to be in the eyes of others as compared with what they feel they are and with the question of how to connect the earlier cultivated roles and skills with the ideal prototypes of the day. In their search for a new sense of continuity and sameness, some adolescents have to refight many of the crises of earlier years, and they are ever ready to install lasting idols and ideals as guardians of a final identity.

The integration now taking place in the form of an ego identity is more than the sum of the childhood identifications. It is the inner capital accrued from all the experiences of each successive stage, when

successful identifications led to a successful alignment of the individual's *basic drives* with his *endowment* and his *opportunities*. In psychoanalysis we ascribe such successful alignments to "ego synthesis"; this writer has tried to demonstrate that the ego values accrued in childhood culminate in what he has called a sense of ego identity. The sense of ego identity, then, is the accrued confidence that one's ability to maintain inner sameness and continuity (one's ego in the psychological sense) is matched by the sameness and continuity of one's meaning for others.

. . . . .

In general it is primarily the inability to settle on an occupational identity which disturbs young people. To keep themselves together they temporarily overidentify, to the point of apparent complete loss of identity, with the heroes of cliques and crowds. On the other hand, they become remarkably clannish, intolerant, and cruel in their exclusion of others who are "different," in skin color or cultural background, in tastes and gifts, and often in entirely petty aspects of dress and gesture arbitrarily selected as *the* signs of an in-grouper or out-grouper. It is important to understand (which does not mean condone or participate in) such intolerance as the necessary *defense against a sense of self-diffusion*, which is unavoidable at a time of life when the body changes its proportions radically, when genital maturity floods body and imagination with

Reprinted from "Growth and Crises" in *Symposium on the Healthy Personality*, edited by Milton J. Senn (Josiah Macy Jr. Foundation, 1950), pp. 134–43, by permission of the author and publisher.

all manner of drives, when intimacy with the other sex approaches and is, on occasion, forced on the youngster, and when life lies before one with a variety of conflicting possibilities and choices. Adolescents help one another temporarily through such discomfort by forming cliques and by stereotyping themselves and their ideals.

It is important to understand this because it makes clear the appeal which simple totalitarian doctrines have on the minds of the youth of such countries and classes as have lost or are losing their group identities (feudal, agrarian, national, and so forth) in these times of world-wide industrialization. The dynamic quality of the tempestuous adolescence lived through in patriarchial and agrarian countries (countries which face the most radical changes in political structure and in economy) explains the fact that their youths find convincing and satisfactory identities in the simple totalitarian doctrines of race, class, or nation. Even though we may be forced to win wars against their leaders, we still are faced with the job of winning the peace with these grim youths by convincingly demonstrating to them (by living it) a democratic identity which can be strong and yet tolerant, judicious and still determined.

But it is equally important to understand this in order to treat the intolerances of our adolescents at home with understanding and guidance rather than with verbal stereotypes or prohibitions. It is difficult to be tolerant if deep down you are not quite sure that you are a man (or a woman), that you will ever grow together again and be attractive, that you will be able to master your drives, that you really know who you are, that you know what you want to be, that you know what you look like to others, and that you will know how to make the right decisions without, once for all, committing yourself to the wrong friend, girl, or career.

Religions help the integration of such identity with "confirmations" of a clearly defined way of life. In many countries, nationalism supports a sense of identity. In primitive tribes puberty rites help to standardize the new identity, often with horrifying impressive rituals.

. . . . .

Here childhood and youth come to an end; life, so the saying goes, begins: by which we mean work or study for a specified career, sociability with the other sex, and in time, marriage and a family of one's own. But it is only after a reasonable sense of identity has been established that real *intimacy* with the other sex (or, for that matter, with any other person or even with oneself) is possible. Sexual intimacy is only part of what I have in mind, for it is obvious that sexual intimacies do not always wait for the ability to develop a true and mutual psychological intimacy with another person. What I have in mind is that late-adolescent need for a kind of fusion with the essence of other people. The youth who is not sure of his identity shies away from interpersonal intimacy; but the surer he becomes of himself, the more he seeks it in the forms of friendship, combat, leadership, love, and inspiration. There is a kind of adolescent attachment between boy and girl which is often mistaken either for sexual attraction or for love. Except where the mores demand heterosexual behavior, such attachment is often devoted to an attempt at arriving at a definition of one's identity by talking things over endlessly, by confessing what one feels like and what the other seems like, and by discussing plans, wishes, and expectations. Where a youth does not accomplish such intimate relation with others—and, I would add, with his own inner resources—in late adolescence or early adulthood, he may either isolate himself and find, at best, highly stereotyped and formal interpersonal relations (formal in the sense of lacking in spontaneity, warmth, and real exchange of fellowship), or he must seek them in repeated attempts and repeated failures. Unfortunately, many young people marry under such circumstances, hoping to find themselves in finding one another; but alas, the early obligation to act in a defined way, as mates and as parents, disturbs them in the completion of this work on themselves. Obviously, a change of mate is rarely the answer, but rather some wisely guided insight into the fact that the condition of a true twoness is that one must first become oneself.

. . . . .

The problem of genitality is intimately related to the seventh criterion of mental health, which concerns parenthood. Sexual mates who find, or on the way to finding, true genitality in their relations will soon wish (if, indeed, developments wait for the express wish) to combine their energies in the care of common offspring. This wish I have termed the desire for generativity, because it concerns the establishment (by way of genitality and genes) of the next generation. No other fashionable term, such as creativity or productivity, seems to me to convey the necessary idea. Generativity is primarily the interest in establishing and guiding the next generation, although there are people who, from misfortune or because of special and genuine gifts in other directions, do not apply this drive to offspring but to other formal creativity, which may absorb their kind of parental responsibility. The principal thing is to realize that this is a stage of the growth of the healthy personality and that where such enrichment fails altogether, regression from generativity to an obsessive need for pseudointimacy takes place, often with a pervading sense of stagnation and interpersonal impoverishment. Individuals who do not develop generativity often begin to indulge themselves as if they were their own one and only child. The

mere fact of having or even wanting children does not, of course, involve generativity; in fact the majority of young parents seen in child-guidance work suffer, it seems, from the inability to develop this stage. The reasons are often to be found in early childhood impressions; in faulty identifications with parents; in excessive self-love based on a too strenuously self-made personality; and finally (and here we return to the beginnings) in the lack of some faith, some "belief in the species," which would make a child a welcome trust of the community.

Only he who in some way has taken care of things and people and has adapted himself to the triumphs and disappointments adherent to being, by necessity, the originator of others and the generator of things and ideas—only he may gradually grow the fruit of the seven stages. I know no better word for it than integrity. Lacking a clear definition, I shall point to a few attributes of this state of mind. It is the acceptance of one's one and only life cycle and of the people who have become significant to it as something that has to be and that, by necessity, permitted of no substitutions. It thus means a new, a different love of one's parents, free of the wish that they should have been different, and an acceptance of the fact that one's life is one's own responsibility. It is a sense of comradeship with men and women of distant times and of different pursuits, who have created orders and objects and sayings conveying human dignity and love. Although aware of the relativity of all the various life styles which have given meaning to human striving, the possessor of integrity is ready to defend the dignity of his own life style against all physical and economic threats. For he knows that an individual life is the accidental coincidence of but one life cycle with but one segment of history; and that for him all human integrity stands or falls with the one style of integrity of which he partakes.

86 | REALITY THERAPY

WILLIAM GLASSER, M.D.

In his Foreword to the volume from which the following selection is taken, research psychologist O. Hobart Mowrer says, "This is an extraordinarily significant book. Readers themselves will discover that it is courageous, unconventional, and challenging. . . . For more than a decade now, it has been evident that something is seriously amiss in contemporary psychiatry and clinical psychology. Under the sway of Freudian psychoanalysis, these disciplines have not validated themselves either diagnostically or therapeutically." Dr. Glasser, convinced of the frequent ineffectiveness of such disciplines, has developed a different therapeutic approach, one in which morality and self-discipline play an important part. Reality therapy is one of the most significant recent developments in the fields of psychiatry and juvenile delinqency and control.

THE BASIC CONCEPTS OF REALITY THERAPY

What Is Wrong with Those Who Need Psychiatric Treatment?

What is it that psychiatrists attempt to treat? What is wrong with the man in a mental hospital who claims he is Jesus, with the boy in and out of reform schools who has stolen thirty-eight cars, the woman who has continual crippling migraine headaches, the child who refuses to learn in school and disrupts the class with temper outbursts, the man who must lose a promotion because he is afraid to fly, and the bus driver who suddenly goes berserk and drives his bus load of people fifty miles from its destination in a careening danger-filled ride?

Do these widely different behaviors indicate different psychiatric problems requiring a variety of explanations, or are they manifestations of one underlying difficulty? We believe that, regardless of how he expresses his problem, everyone who needs psychiatric treatment suffers from

one basic inadequacy: he is unable to fulfill his essential needs. The severity of the symptom reflects the degree to which the individual is unable to fulfill his needs. No one can explain exactly why one person expresses his problem with a stomach ulcer while another fears to enter an elevator; but whatever the symptom, it disappears when the person's needs are successfully fulfilled.

. . . . .

In their unsuccessful effort to fulfill their needs, no matter what behavior they choose, all patients have a common characteristic: *they all deny the reality of the world around them.* Some break the law, denying the rules of society; some claim their neighbors are plotting against them, denying the improbability of such behavior. Some are afraid of crowded places, close quarters, airplanes, or elevators, yet they freely admit the irrationality of their fears. Millions drink to blot out the inadequacy they feel but that need not exist if they could learn to be different; and far too many people choose suicide rather than face the reality that they could solve their problems by more responsible behavior. . . .

A therapy that leads all patients toward reality, toward grappling successfully with the tangible and intangible aspects of the real world, might accurately be called a therapy toward reality, or simply *Reality Therapy*.

As mentioned above, it is not enough to help a patient face reality; he must also learn to fulfill his needs. Previously when he attempted to fulfill his needs in the real world, he was unsuccessful. He began to deny the real world and to try to fulfill his needs as if some aspects of the world did not exist or in defiance of their existence. A psychotic patient who lives in a world of his own and a delinquent boy who repeatedly breaks the law are common examples of these two conditions. Even a man with a stomach ulcer who seems to be facing reality in every way is upon investigation often found to be attempting more than he can cope with, and his ulcer is his body's reaction to the excess stress. Therefore, to do Reality Therapy the therapist must not only be able to help the patient accept the real world, but he must then further help him fulfill his needs in the real world so that he will have no inclination in the future to deny its existence.

How Do We Fulfill Our Needs?

Before discussing the basic needs themselves, we must clarify the process through which they are fulfilled. Briefly, *we must be involved with other people*, one at the very minimum, but hopefully many more than one. At all times in our lives we must have at least one person who cares about us and whom we care for ourselves. If we do not have this essential person, we will not be able to fulfill our basic needs. . . .

. . . . .

. . . Psychiatry must be concerned with two basic psychological needs: *the need to love and be loved and the need to feel that we are worthwhile to ourselves and*

to others. Helping patients fulfill these two needs is the basis of Reality Therapy.

. . . . .

Responsibility

Responsibility, a concept basic to Reality Therapy, is here defined as the ability to fulfill one's needs, and to do so *in a way that does not deprive others of the ability to fulfill their needs.* To illustrate, a responsible person can give and receive love. If a girl, for example, falls in love with a responsible man, we would expect him either to return her love or to let her know in a considerate way that he appreciates her affection but that he does not share her feelings. If he takes advantage of her love to gain some material or sexual end, we would not consider him responsible.

A responsible person also does that which gives him a feeling of self-worth and a feeling that he is worthwhile to others. He is motivated to strive and perhaps endure privation to attain self-worth. When a responsible man says that he will perform a job for us, he will try to accomplish what was asked, both for us and so that he may gain a measure of self-worth for himself. An irresponsible person may or may not do what he says depending upon how he feels, the effort he has to make, and what is in it for him. He gains neither our respect nor his own, and in time he will suffer or cause others to suffer.

. . . We are not, however, directly concerned with those who have learned to lead responsible lives. *Our concern is with those who have not learned, or who have lost the ability—those who fill our mental hospitals and prisons, our psychiatric clinics and offices.*

Throughout the remainder of this [selection], *these people are described as irresponsible.* Their behavior is their effort, inadequate and unrealistic as it may be, to fulfill their needs.

The Teaching of Responsibility

The teaching of responsibility is the most important task of all higher animals, man most certainly included. Except for man this task is performed primarily under the pressure of instinct—instinct related directly to the continuation of the species. . . .

. . . . .

. . . The younger we are exposed to love and discipline the easier and the better we will learn responsibility. That it can be taught *only* to the young is not true—responsibility can be learned at any age. . . .

. . . Through discipline tempered with love, parents must teach their children to behave better. The child learns thereby that the parents care.

Children want to become responsible, but they won't accept discipline and learn better ways unless they feel the parents care enough to show them actively the responsible way to behave.

For example, the other night our five-year-old son was asked if he wanted to use the large bathtub, which was full, to splash and play. In his own inimitable way he said no, probably because he recognized that allowing him in the big tub was easier for us than filling his smaller tub. He wanted to assert his independence of our wishes, a very common but trying five-year-old characteristic. Asked again, he repeated his refusal, whereupon his ten-year-old sister flew out of her room, shedding her clothes, and popped into the big tub, a real treat for her. Immediately the five-year-old started to scream that he really wanted to bathe in it himself. I had to pick up fifty pounds of tantrum and place him in his own tub where he continued to wail his protests.

When he realized that his complaints were doing no good he became quiet and I went in to talk to him. I said, "Let me give you some good advice. Do you know what advice is?" He did, so I told him, "Never say no when you mean yes," and I explained this a little more with several examples from previous behavior. Later I heard him telling his grandmother, "Dad gave me some good advice," and repeating what I said with great understanding. . . .

. . . *Parents who are willing to suffer the pain of the child's intense anger by firmly holding him to the responsible course are teaching him a lesson that will help him all his life.* Parents who do not do so are setting the pattern for future irresponsibility which prevents the child from fulfilling the need to feel worthwhile.

In essence, we gain self-respect through discipline and closeness to others through love. Discipline must always have within it the element of love. "I care enough about you to force you to act in a better way, in a way you will learn through experience to know, and I already know, is the right way." Similarly, love must always have an element of discipline. "I love you because you are a worthwhile person, because I respect you and feel you respect me as well as yourself."

. . . . .

Therapy is a special kind of teaching or training which attempts to accomplish in a relatively short, intense period what should have been established during normal growing up. The more irresponsible the person, the more he has to learn about acceptable realistic behavior in order to fulfill his needs. However, the drug addict, the chronic alcoholic, and the severely psychotic are examples of deeply irresponsible people with whom it is difficult to gain sufficient involvement so that they can learn or relearn better ways to fulfill their needs.

Easy or difficult as its application may be in any particular case, the specialized learning situation which we call Reality Therapy is made up of three separate but intimately interwoven procedures. First, there is the involvement; the therapist must become so involved with the patient that the patient can begin to face reality and see how his behavior is unrealistic. Second, the therapist must reject the behavior which is unrealistic but still accept the patient and maintain his involvement with him. Last, and necessary in varying degrees depending upon the patient, the therapist must teach the patient better ways to fulfill his needs within the confines of reality.

Usually the most difficult phase of therapy is the first, the gaining of the involvement that the patient so desperately needs but which he has been unsuccessful in attaining or maintaining up to the time he comes for treatment. Unless the requisite involvement exists between the necessarily responsible therapist and the irresponsible patient, there can be no therapy. The guiding principles of Reality Therapy are directed toward achieving the proper involvement, a completely honest, human relationship in which the patient, for perhaps the first time in his life, realizes that someone cares enough about him not only to accept him but to help him fulfill his needs in the real world.

· · · · ·

The ability of the therapist to get involved is the major skill of doing Reality Therapy, but it is most difficult to describe. How does one put into words the building of a strong emotional relationship quickly between two relative strangers? . . .

· · · · ·

The therapist must be a very responsible person—tough, interested, human, and sensitive. He must be able to fulfill his own needs and must be willing to discuss some of his own struggles so that the patient can see that acting responsibly is possible though sometimes difficult. Neither aloof, superior, nor sacrosanct, he must never imply that what he does, what he stands for, or what he values is unimportant. He must have the strength to become involved, to have his values tested by the patient, and to withstand intense criticism by the person he is trying to help. Every fault and defect may be picked apart by the patient. Willing to admit that, like the patient, he is far from perfect, the therapist must nevertheless show that a person can act responsibly even if it takes great effort.

The therapist must always be strong, never expedient. He must withstand the patient's requests for sympathy, for an excess of sedatives, for justification of his actions no matter how the patient pleads or threatens. Never condoning an irresponsible action on the patient's part, he must be willing to watch the patient suffer if that helps him toward responsibility. Therefore, to practice Reality Therapy takes strength, not only the strength for the therapist to lead a responsible life himself, but also the added strength both to stand up steadily to patients who wish him to accede to their irresponsibility, and to continue to point out reality to them no matter how hard they struggle against it.

· · · · ·

The therapist must have knowledge and understanding about the person who is isolated or different because he cannot properly fulfill his needs. The therapist must accept him as he is at first. An important distinguishing trait of a good psychotherapist is his ability to accept patients uncritically and understand their behavior. He must never be frightened or rebuffed by the patient's behavior no matter how aberrant it is. . . .

· · · · ·

When Annie Sullivan arrived in Alabama after an arduous trip from Boston, she was horrified to see how badly her pupil, Helen Keller, behaved, with little effort on the part of anyone to correct her animal-like actions. Rather than take the family attitude of feeling sorry for Helen because she was blind and deaf, Annie felt anguish because Helen, with her handicap, was accepted as capable of nothing. Annie's initial attempts to get involved failed because Helen would always run to her doting parents to gain her irresponsible ends.

Certainly Helen was accepted for what she was; the problem was that no one had understood the need for taking the next step—to continue to accept her but to reject her irresponsible behavior. Annie recognized that unless they could become so deeply involved that Helen would be completely dependent upon Annie alone, there could be no change.

Against much family disapproval, Annie persuaded Captain Keller to allow her to keep Helen alone for two weeks in a small house on the farm. During those two weeks, through love and discipline, Helen began to understand that there was more to living than the life she had known. Annie's will, her strength, her love, and her keen perception that Helen must be taught to fulfill her basic needs, achieved the miracle of Helen Keller.

. . . . .

Developing a therapeutic involvement may take anywhere from one interview to several months, depending upon the skill of the therapist, his control over the patient, and the resistance of the patient. Once it occurs, the therapist begins to insist that the patient face the reality of his behavior. He is no longer allowed to evade recognizing what he is doing or his responsibility for it. When the therapist takes this step—and he should start as soon as involvement begins—the relationship deepens because now someone cares enough about the patient to make him face a truth that he has spent his life trying to avoid: *he is responsible for his behavior.* Now, continually confronted with reality by the therapist, he is not

allowed to excuse or condone any of his behavior. No reason is acceptable to the therapist for any irresponsible behavior. He confronts the patient with his behavior and asks him to decide whether or not he is taking the responsible course. The patient thus finds a man who cares enough about him to reject behavior which will not help him to fulfill his needs.

In Reality Therapy we are much more concerned with behavior than with attitudes. . . .

. . . . .

The way Reality Therapy differs from conventional therapy on each of the six points to be discussed contributes to the major difference in involvement. The six points may be considered briefly from the standpoint of involvement.

1. Because we do not accept the concept of mental illness, the patient cannot become involved with us as a mentally ill person who has no responsibility for his behavior.

2. Working in the present and toward the future, we do not get involved with the patient's history because we can neither change what happened to him nor accept the fact that he is limited by his past.

3. We relate to patients as ourselves, not as transference figures.

4. We do not look for unconscious conflicts or the reasons for them. A patient cannot become involved with us by excusing his behavior on the basis of unconscious motivations.

5. We emphasize the morality of behavior. We face the issue of right and wrong which we believe solidifies the involvement, in contrast to conventional psychiatrists who do not make the distinction between right and wrong, feeling it would be detrimental to attaining the transference relationship they seek.

6. We teach patients better ways to fulfill their needs. The proper involvement will not be maintained unless the patient

is helped to find more satisfactory patterns of behavior. Conventional therapists do not feel that teaching better behavior is a part of therapy.

. . . . .

Under the heading of "mentally ill" are numerous diagnoses such as schizophrenic, neurotic, depressed, sociopathic, and psychosomatic, all describing some kind of irresponsible behavior. From Chapter 1 we have learned that all these various terms only describe the best the patient has been able to manage in his effort to fulfill his needs. The psychotic patient who believes he is Jesus Christ seems very different from a man with a stomach ulcer, but we should not be fooled by appearances. Like the blind men's descriptions of the elephant, each variety of irresponsible behavior seems much different from all others. Irresponsibility, however, is as basic to the various kinds of behavior as the elephant is basic to the trunk, tail, or legs, and it is the irresponsibility, the whole elephant, which must be treated.

Unfortunately for taxpayers as well as patients, almost all teaching of psychiatry, psychology, and social work follows traditional thinking that considers the diagnosis of mental illness to be essential to successful treatment. . . .

. . . . .

Without denying that the patient had an unsatisfactory past, we find that to look for what went wrong does not help him. What good comes from discovering that you are afraid to assert yourself because you had a domineering father? Both patient and therapist can be aware of this historical occurrence, they can discuss it in all of its ramifications for years, but the knowledge will not help the patient assert himself now. In fact, in our experience the more he knows why he cannot assert himself, the less inclined he will be to do so because he now understands that self-assertion is psychologically painful.

Most patients will then lean on the psychiatrist, saying, "Now that I know why I can't assert myself, what will make me lose the fear?" . . .

For Reality Therapy it makes little difference what relationship the patient had with his father. We want to know what is going on now in all aspects of his life. . . . We don't have to know the detailed history of his previous failures or his life during those times. The details of his life now, of his present failures, are the material we need.

. . . . .

We are looking for neither conformity nor mediocrity in the guise of normal behavior. The most responsible men, such as Lincoln or Schweitzer, are those farthest from the norm. Our job is not to lessen the pain of irresponsible actions, but to increase the patient's strength so that he can bear the necessary pain of a full life as well as enjoy the rewards of a deeply responsible existence.

. . . . .

In Reality Therapy we do not search for the insights so vital to conventional psychiatry. Instead we take every opportunity to teach patients better ways to fulfill their needs. We spend much time painstakingly examining the patient's daily activity and suggesting better ways for him to behave. We answer the many questions that patients ask and suggest ways to solve problems and approach people. . . .

. . . . .

THE TREATMENT OF SERIOUSLY
DELINQUENT ADOLESCENT GIRLS

The Ventura School for Girls

In 1962, on a beautiful level site near Ventura, in the Santa Clara Valley, the state of California opened a new institution for the treatment of older adolescent girls. The previous institution . . . was outdated and inadequate to house the increasing number of fourteen to twenty-one-year-old girls who were being committed for offenses ranging from incorrigibility to first-degree murder. The low, rambling, one-story red brick buildings, surrounded by a high fence and secure against escape, house approximately four hundred girls from all over California. . . . A girl committed by the county to the state for transfer to the Ventura School has usually had several years of supervision by county probation services without success. Many have had psychotherapy as a condition of probation; all have been in juvenile halls, some for many months. Profiting little from this treatment, they have continued to break the law. Finally sent to the Ventura School, the last stop before adult prison, they are confined, in most cases, for six to eight months for rehabilitation.

For the most part these girls are very sophisticated, at least in their own milieu. They enter the school often poorly motivated to change toward leading a more responsible life. Usually they have failed in public school through poor attendance and effort; many are poor readers, and few have held any regular job. They are characterized by their lack of deep feeling for themselves or anyone else and by their common history of usually taking to be what they thought the easy, irresponsible course when any choice was presented. Most have multiple self-inflicted tattoos on their arms, legs, and even their faces, a pathetic effort to gain attention from their peers. Initially resentful at being locked up in the security of our institution, few admit that strict custody is probably what they most need.

The job of the school is difficult. Our goal is to take every girl, no matter how antagonistic she may be, and within six to eight months rehabilitate her so that, with the guidance of a parole officer, she will be able to stay out of further serious

trouble in the community. Naturally, we do not succeed with everyone, but we do with about 80 per cent of the girls. Operating essentially with an indeterminate commitment, we have permission to keep the seriously irresponsible girls longer if we feel it is necessary; only a few, however, are kept over one year. Although girls who commit serious crimes such as murder, assault with a deadly weapon, or armed robbery are held at the school for one year, these commitments can be reduced if they show signs of earlier rehabilitation. According to our present superintendent, who used to supervise a parole office, 90 per cent of the girls who violate their parole are returned to the institution. Considering that on a recent count out of a total of 370 girls only 43 were returnees, we feel that our program is generally successful.

. . . . .

The school program consists of three main parts:

1. *The Custody Program* is administered by warm and skillful counselors who use the principles of Reality Therapy. The girl's knowledge that she is in an institution from which she cannot escape is basic to the program. With the guidance of the staff, she is forced to take the responsibility for her behavior in a total situation where responsibility is continually stressed.

2. *The Treatment Program* is administered by a group of competent psychologists, social workers, and a consulting psychiatrist. The treatment personnel not only work with the girls directly, but they continually work with the custody staff to help them treat the girls according to the principles of Reality Therapy.

3. *The School Program* consists of both academic and vocational courses taught by qualified teachers. All girls have a full daily schedule taking either an academic or a vocational course, or sometimes both. Those who enter the Ventura School with

sufficient credits and who stay long enough and complete enough work to graduate receive a regular graduation certificate which does not indicate that it comes from a correctional institution.

Vocational training is given in power sewing; cosmetology; cooking; laundry operation as well as in the specific jobs of waitress, dental assistant, and nurses' aide. Business courses, clerical practice, and business machine operation are also a part of an expanding business program closely attached to the academic classes. The full recreational program includes competitive sports, swimming, and roller skating. Cottage activities include parties, arts and crafts, and housekeeping. Cleanliness and preparation for the tasks that women fulfill are emphasized throughout the program.

All three parts of the program—custody, treatment, and school—work smoothly together so that during her stay the girl experiences a total treatment program in which everyone is interested in her progress. Now she is not allowed to indulge in the irresponsible behavior that she has shown elsewhere. One part of the program is never considered more important than another. For example, no one arrives at the school specifically for psychiatric treatment to the detriment of the rest of the program. Everything we do makes up a treatment program in which the girl is asked from beginning to end to take increasing responsibility. We try to the best of our ability never to allow a girl to leave the school who has not gained in responsibility or who, within our power to predict, cannot live satisfactorily in the community. Naturally we make mistakes, but we have long since stopped releasing girls into the community because we cannot help them or because they do not seem to adjust to the institution. Unless a girl has gained by her stay in the institution, she is not discharged to parole.

. . . . .

Institutional Philosophy

The philosophy which underlies all treatment at the Ventura School is that mental illness does not exist.

We accept no excuses for irresponsible acts. Students are held responsible for their behavior and cannot escape responsibility on the plea of being emotionally upset, mistreated by mother, neglected by father, or discriminated against by society. Most girls soon learn that the Ventura School is different from any place they have been before. The difference is our caring enough to keep them until they are responsible enough to leave. When they tell us how unfortunate they have been, we accept this uncritically; but from the beginning, in a warm and firm manner, we tell them that while they are here they are responsible for what they do, regardless of how miserable, inconsistent, or unloving the past may have been.

The students learn immediately that we are not interested in their history beyond one important fact: they have broken the law or they would not be in the school. Finding out how bad the past was does not help unless the person can learn better and more responsible ways to behave now and in the future. The girls must learn what responsibility is and act reasonably upon that knowledge. We are interested in what they can do now that will help them live better in the future, such as how they can get along better with their parents, rather than dwelling upon how their parents have treated them in the past.

. . . . .

In the program we have developed, the student gets a definite school schedule a week after her arrival and is permanently assigned to a cottage. At Ventura status is gained by cooperating with the program, not by defying it. A high standard of performance is expected in the various work and vocational programs, and if the student is in psychiatric treatment, even better behavior is required. Psychiatric treatment is not considered anything more than a part of the program suited to certain girls; it never relieves them of any responsibility. Throughout her stay at the school, each girl is continually evaluated by the staff and she is informed of our evaluation both in person and in writing. We expect her to act better, look better, talk better, and to maintain the school's high standards.

We have discovered that unless we have high standards, the students conclude that we are "phony" and don't really care for them. However, once they are aware of the high standards we maintain by enforcing strict, consistent rules, they realize, perhaps for the first time in their lives, that real care is implied by discipline. We reward them when they accept responsibility and explain that they are not yet ready to go further in the program when they do not accept responsibility. In the latter case, the only major punishment is exclusion from the regular program. The girls are locked in a special cottage, with an in-cottage program which excludes them from the regular school and from their own cottage. When they show enough responsibility, they are allowed to leave this cottage and return to the school program. Confinement is not held against them, although of course they lose time from the regular program. Only by strictly enforcing understandable rules can we teach the girls that we mean what we say, and that they must take the responsibility for their behavior.

Our school program, therefore, must be attractive enough so that exclusion from it is indeed painful. In addition, it is up to the institution to work toward developing an increasingly better program—one that is more interesting, more effective, and more mature. The students must feel that we are never satisfied with the status quo, but that we are continually trying to provide them with every opportunity to

better themselves and to find some happiness when they do so. Unlike punishment, removal from the program is a positive measure, a motivation for the girls to work hard to return to a program in which they learn that responsibility is not an abstract word but a vital experience.

The Girls

A school for older delinquent girls is thought to be a prisonlike institution housing droves of antagonistic, hard-boiled, tough-talking, sex-starved girls who are intensely resistant to reforming their ways. Those who work there are imagined to be tough, wisecracking, hostile, and cleverly suspicious of everything the girls do, especially of any good behavior. These common movie, TV, or popular magazine stereotypes are actually completely false. Ventura may house the most delinquent adolescent girls in California, but a visitor to the school is hard pressed to recognize them as such. He sees a group of girls, laughing, talking, and moving freely around the school with seemingly little supervision or restraint. They appear little different from a group of girls in a high school in a middle-class neighborhood except that they are a little plumper (institution food is high in calories) and not too well dressed (girls artificially separated from boys tend to let their dress go, as much as we encourage them not to).

. . . . .

Out of the almost four hundred girls at Ventura, there are usually one or two kept in the discipline cottage because their behavior is too disruptive to allow them to mix with the other girls. They may stay months in this cottage while they are worked with intensively to help them learn control. The remaining ten to fifteen girls in the discipline cottage are not long-term, serious problems, but they have broken various rules. They will stay from two days to two weeks in close custody in a program in which they can demonstrate through their attitude and cooperation that they are ready to go back to their regular cottage on campus. . . .

. . . . .

SHARON | Sharon was a beautiful, very intelligent sixteen-year-old girl who had entered college, having graduated from high school early because she had gone to school in custody the year around for the past two and one-half years. She was sent to Ventura for running away from home, failing to report to her probation officer, living illegally with a man, and taking occasional narcotic pills. She was also suspected of homosexuality, prostitution, and petty theft. It was not these offenses that made her such a difficult case, however; it was her refusal to allow anyone to get really close to her.

Because she had already graduated from high school, she was assigned to work rather than to classes at school. Although she worked efficiently as a student secretary in the school office, we began to hear complaints that she was using her position to manipulate girls and, in subtle ways, even staff. She influenced girls to ask for certain classes in which they could be with their friends, promised to intercede with the principal on behalf of the girls, generally acted the big shot, and got girls to do her favors for what she supposedly was doing for them.

During this time I had been seeing her informally at her cottage after lunch. My routine at that time was to eat in her cottage and spend time after lunch talking to the girls, who are free to relax for about forty-five minutes. Although we became friendly in a superficial way, I was still very much the outsider trying to reach her. She responded by toying with my attempts to get close, pretending to be nice, yet underneath laughing at me and what I represented of the Ventura program. She often said, "I'll do whatever you want me to do here, and I will not be back," intimating she would be too smart to be caught again. My response, and this became an old refrain, was, "It doesn't look as if you will be leaving here for a long time; you're not ready." When she asked why I answered this way, I replied, "You will have to figure that out. I really can't tell you, but I will tell you when you are ready to leave."

Believing that I was just making conversation, she enjoyed what she thought was a game until she was passed over when the time came for referral to parole. She was told, "Dr. Glasser did not think you were ready." At our next after-lunch talk she asked, "Did you really hold me up?" She could not believe it. When I answered, "Yes," she did not get angry. Smiling, she said, "That's okay, I like it here; I'll stay." Her whole aim was to make me feel foolish in my attempt to affect her in any way.

We continued to talk as before, mostly about books. Because I had read many of the books she was reading, we were able to have some genuine discussions, but she did little more than acknowledge by her friendly attitude that she enjoyed our talks. Resentment, however, was building inside her, especially as our conversations indicated I was not disturbed by her lack of progress. While she continued to be nice to everyone, she stepped up her campaign to divide the people in the school office and cause trouble, both to get revenge against us and also in the hope we would get tired of her and throw her out. Working very hard, she gained great favor with the academic school principal, who used her as his private secretary. Because she was so intelligent and efficient, he was not immediately aware that she was using her position to lord it over the other students and to snub the regular office staff. Eventually her behavior caused a disturbance in the school office and, because I knew her better than anyone, I was asked to see her.

In my office for the first time, Sharon blandly asked me what all the fuss was about, knowing full well that the school office was in a turmoil because of her. When I confronted her with the facts, she denied everything. Disregarding her denial, I told her that finally we had something to work on. Rather than removing her from the office, I would point out the behavior that we considered wrong, and if she wanted to help herself, she could correct it. Knowing that it would take time for her to improve her behavior, I told her that from now on she had to see me regularly. She said she would not. I told her that she was in serious trouble because of the commotion she had created in the school office, and if she refused to see me to help her change, I would place her in the discipline unit. She looked right at me and said, "You would, wouldn't you?" I replied, "I won't have to. You'll come, won't you?" She said, "I'll think it over." Giving her until Monday (this was Thursday), I told her if she did not come then I would see her next in the discipline unit. She left in a mild huff, but on Monday she came to my office.

It might appear that threatening Sharon would be the worst way to start therapy, because our relationship, tenuous as it was, would be weakened rather than strengthened. Actually she had been looking for someone who was genuinely interested in her and who was tough enough to mean what he said. At the same time she could feel the pain it caused me to have to threaten her. Had the threat been made with any feeling on my part of "now I was going to show her," she probably would still be in discipline, but she understood me correctly even as she did in the interview when she first arrived. What happened here illustrates the crux of therapy. Patients want you to correct their irresponsible behavior, but they want it to be done in the genuine spirit of helping them, not to satisfy yourself by winning a power struggle. This is the caring that leads to involvement. Unless Sharon could feel that I was truly interested in

helping her, she would never let down her guard.

When she came to therapy on Monday she did not refer to the past Thursday except to say that she was going to stop causing trouble in the office. At the end of our interview she asked when I was going to recommend her for referral. I told her, "As soon as possible," which means about three months in our program during which time she could demonstrate her sincerity. Answering this question affirmatively so soon after her change of attitude was critical in Sharon's case. She was asking me to trust her change of attitude and I did. She was ready to show us but she needed this trust to start. It takes experience to recognize this point and even with experience we make mistakes, but we did not with Sharon. Because the timing is a necessary part of keeping faith, the indeterminate commitment we have at Ventura is a great advantage. Correctional institutions which have rigid sentence structures are severely handicapped in their rehabilitation efforts.

Now our conversation shifted to her biggest problem, how she was going to live with her mother. As can be seen by the second paragraph of her letter, we succeeded in solving the problem. When she treated her mother well, her mother responded by treating her better. Many of our girls do this and later remark, as did Sharon, "Mother is so changed." Her parole officer, whose recent visit to Ventura was a year after Sharon left the school, could not say enough good things about her. Telling us that she will miss Sharon when she leaves parole, which will be soon, she cannot understand why I was concerned about her. "She is such a pleasure to have in my case load," were her words.

LINDA | Finally, I would like to introduce some letters written by Linda, a girl with whom I worked intensively, but who gave us no trouble at the school despite her stormy course in previous institutions. We became involved following our first impromptu lunch table conversation in the same cottage that Sharon later came to. Her first words, stated with mock seriousness, were: "Dr. Glasser, I'm here because I'm a very emotionally disturbed girl." I answered on the same note, "I can't understand that. Our girls aren't here because they are emotionally disturbed, only because they violated the law. If your only trouble is being emotionally disturbed, I will make it my business to get you out of here because we don't understand anything about complicated psychiatric problems like that." Then I asked her whether, besides being emotionally disturbed, she happened to do anything that broke the law. She replied, "I started a riot and slugged a counselor." This was at a previous school. I said, "Well, now I understand why you are here." I then shifted my emphasis and asked her with point-blank seriousness, "Are you going to do that at Ventura?" Probably my direct, honest question reached her because she immediately answered, "No, I don't think so, I like it here."

· · · · ·

HOSPITAL TREATMENT
OF PSYCHOTIC PATIENTS

The application of Reality Therapy to the treatment of long-term hospitalized psychotic patients is examined here. The hospital is the Veterans Administration Neuropsychiatric Hospital in West Los Angeles, the building is 206, and the physician in charge is Dr. G. L. Harrington.

Building 206, composed of four wards totaling 210 patients, has been in existence for almost twenty years at the V.A. hospital. Until recently, when Dr. Harrington introduced the concepts of Reality Therapy, it housed the most chronic, stable, psychotic patients in the hospital. It had the traditional mental hospital approach in which the patients were accepted as

mentally ill and were given good standard care. Any active treatment, however, was oriented toward helping them maintain themselves at as high a level as possible *within the hospital*. No dramatic change in their condition was expected and the average discharge rate was about two patients a year. The patients' problems were categorized into the standard, meaningless, hospital diagnoses: paranoid schizophrenia, catatonic schizophrenia, hebephrenic schizophrenia, and the old wastebasket diagnosis of chronic, undifferentiated schizophrenia. Labeled with these anti-therapeutic terms, the patients did about what was expected of them. They hallucinated a little, suffered from a few delusions, but mostly they sat around in the relatively plush V.A. mental hospital. . . .

The Program of Building 206

Prior to 1962, Building 206 was known as the chronic or "crock" ward. All patients had received therapy of various kinds without success and had been sent to Building 206 for custodial care. The building was an open ward with off-building privileges but few off-building responsibilities. Because it was so easy to live in the hospital, there was little incentive to change. Tender, loving care was the order of the day. Off-building privileges, passes into town, passes home for weekends, Thanksgiving, Christmas, and the Fourth of July were considered to be every patient's dream. All patients' requests and demands were fulfilled whenever possible, a marked difference from any world they would have to live in if they left.

· · · · ·

Dr. Harrington instituted the Reality Therapy program when he took over Building 206. Rather than concentrating on making the patient happy, the program stressed carefully graded increments of responsibility so that the patient could slowly work his way back to reality. The building was divided into a fifty-man closed ward, a fifty-man semi-open ward, and a one hundred-man open ward. All personnel, including clerk-typist, clothing-room clerk, aides, nurses, social worker, and psychologist, were given responsibilities of reporting behavior concerning the patients' readiness for movement either in the direction of greater or lesser responsibility. During a regular building meeting attended by both staff and patients, patient problems were discussed, ward assignments were made (usually along the progression from closed to semi-open to open ward status), and individual patient programs were established. The results of all meetings were typed and placed on the patients' bulletin boards.

. . . . .

As it was in the Ventura School for Girls, the first and perhaps most important step in applying Reality Therapy in Building 206 was to convince each staff member that, because it is a total program he is just as important to the success of the program as is the ward psychiatrist. Dr. Harrington carefully taught and retaught each staff member to forget the concept of schizophrenia and mental illness, and to consider the patients as people who are behaving this way because that is the best they have been able to do up to now. He instructed them, however, not to respond to the abnormal behavior and thinking, but to treat each patient as if he is capable of not being crazy now; in this ward he does not have to be.

. . . . .

. . . The patients sensed from the total ward attitude that something new was happening, that someone really cared, and that they were involved in a very different hospital experience than any they had had before. In the locked ward, patients who were violent or destructive were put in a belt and cuffs because crazy behavior is not tolerated. Hyperactive patients were

given sedation. The aides and nurses worked toward becoming involved with the patients and then asked them to give up their crazy symptoms.

The involvement now becomes critical. The men selected for the closed ward were those least involved with others and most isolated from reality. Here the aides and nurses engage in a continual therapeutic effort to involve the patient first with them and then with the minimum closed ward program. In a totally accepting, protected atmosphere, the ward staff use patience, humor, and persistence to force themselves into the patient's life. Attaining the initial involvement takes anywhere from a few weeks to as long as six months, but sooner or later the effort by the ward staff begins to show. The patient responds either by increasing his symptoms or by decreasing them and thus changing to more reasonable behavior. In either case his response shows that the first part of therapy, the initial involvement, has been accomplished.

Now the attitude can be changed toward continued acceptance of the patient but rejection of the symptoms. For the first time in years the patients genuinely respond to human efforts. Those who show an increase in symptoms are trying to avoid involvement, but this behavior indicates that they are already beginning to be involved. In addition they may be testing the intent and persistence of the ward staff, for many therapists had tried in the past to get them involved, but they had not devoted enough time or effort, nor had they worked in the proper closed ward atmosphere. Little attention is paid to an increase in symptoms or to withdrawal, and these patients soon change their response and begin to give up their symptoms.

The final step on the closed ward is to help the patients begin to function; that is to eat, bathe, shave, brush their teeth, change clothes, and take needed medicine.

Even in cuffs they are expected to take some responsibility for their personal care, awkward as it might be. Available but not required of patients are television, ward games, and a weekly trip to the canteen accompanied by an aide. When they can perform the minimum functions, the patients no longer need cuffs and sedation. When they are able to act sensibly most of the time they are ready for step two.

Recommendations for a patient to move to the semi-open ward are made by the staff at the building meeting, although Dr. Harrington makes all the decisions and the patients know this. He becomes a vital part of their world, and it is his training and judgment that the patients, as well as the staff, learn to depend on. They trust him not to move them until they are ready, yet they strive for progress because they can and do understand that the Reality Therapy program is the start of a new life for them. *It is the whole ward attitude, where everyone is involved, but where mental illness is not accepted, that brings the understanding home to them.*

Between two and six months are usually needed to prepare patients for the semi-open ward where they are told that they must stay in the ward although it is not locked. Here they are expected to attend a group meeting run by aides in which their responsibility within the ward program is discussed. Adding at least an hour of ward detail to their closed ward duties, they are slowly but surely given increased responsibility and told that they now have an opportunity to make progress.

By taking steadily increasing responsibility, they begin to gain self-respect and self-worth. Now they are easier for the staff to like and thus they are more likely to fulfill their need for love. They start to feel better and to look and act like men, not like permanent mental hospital residents. . . .

In contrast to therapy on the closed ward, which is essentially continuous, therapy now becomes more structured. An important part of the new program is a daily meeting of a therapy group led by an aide trained in Reality Therapy in which the patients discuss their progress in detail. Here they experience the good feeling that results from expressing themselves in a group. . . .

Because it has been discovered that the patient is usually ready to move downstairs to a completely open ward in about ninety days, this time limit is made a condition of the group on the semi-open ward. Downstairs the patient enters another time-limited group led by either a social worker or a psychologist specially trained in Reality Therapy, who actively prepares groups of patients for the next step, the move out of the hospital. Setting time limits of ninety days motivates the patients to work harder toward the goal of leaving. If they do not succeed in ninety days, they are moved back; but well over 90 per cent do succeed. Dr. Harrington believes that those who succeed should increase to almost 100 per cent as everyone learns more about applying the principles of Reality Therapy.

Patients who cannot manage the rapid movement are moved backwards, even to the locked ward. Such regression is neither failure nor admission that the craziness was too well established, but rather a sign that the ward doctor had erred in his judgment. The patient in his characteristic way communicates his feeling by acting crazy or irresponsible. But whether or not regression occurs, movement generally continues forward.

. . . . .

When a patient is finally moved out to his family, a foster home, an apartment (or, if he is old and feeble, to the old soldiers' home), he is instructed not to look for work. In the beginning, after ten or twenty years in the hospital, it is enough just to leave. Work comes later. To expect too much too soon from men who have been separated so long from the real world will produce a return of irresponsible behavior. Timing and judgment are critical; but if the patient is not yet ready, he can retrace as many steps as necessary—just as a girl who can't succeed on parole returns to the school as a part of a continuing program which in the end will produce permanently increased responsibility.

Building 206 sets a standard for proper treatment of chronic mental patients. Its program takes less money and less time than do traditional methods, but it does demand a high degree of skill and training for the staff. Vital to the program on Building 206 but difficult to describe are the detailed plans and the intricate personal relationships which help each man to move over critical hurdles. . . .

. . . . .

[For excellent reading on current methods of individual and group therapies, see Eric Berne, *Principles of Group Treatment* (New York: Oxford University Press, 1966); Bernard L. Greene, *The Psychotherapies of Marital Disharmony* (New York: The Free Press of Glencoe, 1965); Ivan Boszormenyi-Nagy and James L. Framo, *Intensive Family Therapy* (New York: Harper and Row, 1965); and Jerome L. Schulman, *et al., The Therapeutic Dialogue* (Springfield, Ill.: Charles C Thomas, 1964). Eds.]

CORRELATION OF THIS BOOK
WITH REPRESENTATIVE TEXTS

Bossard and Boll
THE SOCIOLOGY OF
CHILD DEVELOPMENT, 3D ED.
Harper, 1960

Text chapters	Related selections
1	1, 3, 4, 36
2	16, 81
3	2, 11, 12, 13
4	5
5	12, 69
6	14, 15
7	46, 47
8	8
9	77
10	46, 84
11	21, 22
12	16, 17
13	9, 10, 22
14	75, 76
15	70
16	80, 81
17	19, 25, 26, 27, 28
18	2, 3, 9, 12, 81
19	62, 83, 84
20	2, 6, 24, 37, 38, 43, 51, 53, 66
21-23	23, 43, 44, 45, 46, 47, 48, 49, 50, 51, 52
24	18, 19, 20, 31, 32, 33
25	12, 17, 45, 46, 77
26	60, 63, 64, 65
27	35, 40, 41, 44, 45, 55, 56, 74, 77, 78, 79, 81, 82
28	39, 42, 57, 58, 60, 61, 62, 63, 64, 65, 67, 68, 70, 71, 72, 73
29-30	2, 3, 11, 12, 13, 14, 15, 16, 81
31-32	1, 86

Breckenridge & Vincent
CHILD DEVELOPMENT, 5TH ED.
Saunders, 1965

Text chapters	Related selections
1	18, 19, 20, 21, 30
2	22, 23, 24
3	36, 37, 38, 39, 43, 44, 45, 46, 66
4	8, 29, 53
5	5, 6, 7, 25, 26, 27, 28, 46, 47, 69
6	8, 9, 10, 11, 12, 13, 14, 15, 16, 81
7	18, 23
8	60, 61, 62, 63, 64, 65
9	31, 32, 33, 40, 41, 42
10	6, 7
11	70, 75, 76
12	8, Part 2 (Intro.), 34, 35, 36, 39, 43, 44, 45, 46, 47, 48, 55, 56, 57, 65
13	1, 2, 3, 4, 22, 25, 35, 37, 44, 45, 64, 69, 74
14	17, 34, 36, 77, 79, 85
15	78, 86

Crow & Crow
CHILD DEVELOPMENT
AND ADJUSTMENT
Macmillan, 1962

Text chapters	Related selections
1	1, 2, 3, 4, 8
2	24, 30
3	14, 19, 20, 21
4	18, 23
5	18
6	70
7	57, 58, 68
8	31, 32, 33, 72, 73
9	6, 7, 35, 37, 38
10	23, 25, 26, 27, 28, 37, 44, 45, 46, 47, 48, 49, 50, 51, 66
11	40, 41, 42, 46, 47, 71
12	1, 22, 79, 80, 81, 83, 84
13	48, 51, 52, 67, 68
14	Part 2 (Intro), 34, 54, 60, 63
15	36, 76, 77, 78, 79, 80, 81, 82
16	5, 40, 44, 45, 46, 85, 86
17	1, 2, 3, 4, 54
18	55, 56, 57, 58, 60, 64, 69
19	25, 26, 44, 47, 59, 62
20	61, 63, 70, 71, 72, 73

Horrocks
PSYCHOLOGY OF
ADOLESCENCE, 2D ED.
Houghton Mifflin, 1962

Text chapters	Related selections
1	8, 75, 76
2	5, 40, 41, 48
3	11, 12, 13, 14, 15, 16. 62
4	9, 10, 34
5	22, 35, 40, 41, 46, 52, 71
6	27, 28, 43, 46, 74, 77, 79, 80, 81, 82, 84
7	55
8	25, 26, 36, 44, 45, 46
9	54, 55, 56, 58, 59, 60, 64, 65, 66, 69, 86
10	79, 80, 81, 84
11	82
12	
13	22
14	31, 32, 33, 34, 58, 67, 68, 70, 72, 73
15	1, 2, 3, 4
16	8, 78, 84, 85, 86
17	77
18	
19	1, 2, 3, 4, 55
20	83, 84

Hurlock
CHILD DEVELOPMENT, 4TH ED.
McGraw-Hill, 1964

Text chapters	Related selections
1	
2	18, 19, 20
3	
4	21, 22, 24, 53
5	23
6	70
7	25, 26, 27, 28, 48, 49, 50, 51, 66
8	5, 6, 7, 8, 9, 10, 11, 12, 13, 14, 15, 16
9	40, 41, 42, 43, 44, 45, 46, 47, 71, 82, 83, 84
10	34, 35, 36, 37, 38, 60, 64, 65, 85
11	30, 31, 32, 33, 54, 55, 56, 57, 58, 72, 73
12	1, 2, 3, 4, 17, 39, 44, 45, 46, 47, 55, 74, 77
13	55, 56, 57, 61, 63, 79
14	10, 11, 12, 13, 14, 15, 16, 25, 26, 27, 28, 46, 59
15	54, 55, 56, 67, 68, 69, 85, 86

Jersild
CHILD PSYCHOLOGY, 5TH ED.
Prentice-Hall, 1960

Text chapters	Related selections
1	30, 56
2	18, 21, 24
3	19, 20
4	25, 26, 27, 28, 29, 36, 45
5	18, 24
6	Part 2; 34, 56, 85
7	25, 26, 37, 43, 44, 46, 47
8	5, 11, 12, 13, 14, 15, 16, 36
9	22, 40, 41, 42, 70, 84
10	44, 48, 71, 74, 78, 79
11	6, 7, 23, 27, 35, 36, 37, 79
12	43, 48, 49, 50, 51, 52, 66, 75, 76
13	45, 78
14	31, 32, 33, 39
15	37, 38, 55, 56, 58, 60
16	61, 62, 67, 68, 69, 70
17	63, 64, 65, 72, 73
18	1, 2, 3, 4, 12, 16, 34, 36, 40, 41, 42, 74, 77, 84
19	6, 8, 9, 10, 14, 37
20	1, 55, 56, 57, 58, 59, 61, 63, 64, 65

Jersild
PSYCHOLOGY OF
ADOLESCENCE, 2D ED.
Macmillan, 1963

Text parts	Related selections
1	*34, 56, 75, 76, 77, 78, 85*
2	*19, 20, 21, 79, 80, 81, 82*
3	*5, 6, 7, 8, 31, 32, 33, 35, 37, 38, 39, 43, 58, 72, 73*
4	*22, 23, 25, 26, 27, 28, 29, 43, 44, 45, 48, 49, 50, 51*
5	*9, 10, 11, 12, 13, 14, 15, 16, 36, 40, 41, 42, 44, 45, 56, 57, 69, 74*
6	*1, 2, 3, 4, 39, 55, 58, 61, 62, 63, 64, 65, 67, 68, 70, 71*
7	*54, 59, 84, 86*

Mussen, Conger, and Kagan
CHILD DEVELOPMENT
AND PERSONALITY, 2D ED.
Harper and Row, 1963

Text chapters	Related selections
1	*1, 2, 3, 4, 5, 30*
2-3	*18, 19, 20, 24*
4	*21, 22, 23, 24*
5	*31, 32, 33, 34, 66, 67, 68*
6	*25, 26, 27, 28, 29, 52*
7	*36, 37, 38, 66*
8	*64, 65, 67*
9	*46, 49, 50, 53, 54, 79, 80, 81, 84*
10	*35, 37, 38, 43, 44, 45, 47, 51, 60, 65, 74*
11	*39, 40, 41, 42, 48*
12	*40, 57, 58, 61, 62, 63, 67, 69, 70, 71, 82*
13	*9, 10, 11, 12, 13, 14, 15, 16, 17, 77, 78, 80, 81*
14	*83, 85*
15	*44, 45, 46, 47, 72, 73, 74, 75, 76, 86*

Johnson & Medinnus
CHILD PSYCHOLOGY
Wiley, 1965

Text chapters	Related selections
1	*21, 22, 27, 28, 30, 51, 52, 64, 65, 66*
2	*19, 24*
3	*20, 25, 26, 29, 82*
4	*9, 10, 18, 25, 26, 31, 32, 33, 39, 50, 53, 68, 70, 72, 73, 74*
5	*58*
6	*6, 7*
7	*1, 2, 3, 4, 11, 12, 13, 14, 15, 36, 52, 67, 81*
8	*5, 7, 8, 10, 19, 34, 36, 44, 48, 59, 62, 73*
9	*19, 21, 25, 26, 27, 28, 29, 36, 52, 53, 66*
10	*16, 17, 25, 26, 27, 46, 47, 48, 56, 59, 73, 84*
11	*8, 28, 34, 35, 40, 41, 42, 45, 69, 73*
12	*7, 33, 34, 39, 50, 57, 58, 61, 63, 65, 68, 71, 72*
13	*55, 60, 70, 74, 75, 76, 77, 78, 80*
14	*7, 18, 22, 24, 30, 32, 33*
15	*73, 79, 82, 83, 85*
16	*23, 35, 37, 38, 44, 45, 47, 48, 49, 51, 53, 58, 62, 63, 64, 69, 70, 74, 84*

McCandless
CHILDREN AND
ADOLESCENTS
Holt, Rinehart &
Winston, 1961

Text chapters	Related selections
1	*1, 2, 3, 4, 12, 13, 14, 15, 16, 18, 19, 20, 21, 25, 26, 29, 31*
2	*27, 28, 36, 39, 40, 41, 50, 51, 58, 64, 65, 66, 81*
3	*17, 21, 22, 24, 25, 26, 27, 45, 47, 52, 53*
4	*18, 34, 57, 65, 66, 67*
5	*34, 43, 48, 50, 51, 53, 58, 64, 65, 66, 70, 76, 77*
6	*17, 44, 45, 46, 56, 59, 60, 65, 71, 75, 80, 83, 85*
7	*6, 7, 18, 19, 20, 31, 32, 33, 72, 73*
8	*19, 24, 25, 26, 36, 51, 72, 73*
9	*18, 19, 20, 23, 27*
10	*5, 8, 9, 10, 39, 48, 55, 59, 69, 75, 77, 78, 79, 80, 83, 85, 86*
11	*9, 10, 48*
12	*5, 36*
13	*34, 39, 50, 51, 57, 58, 61, 63, 65, 68, 70, 74, 76, 84*
14	*1, 5, 36, 39, 62, 63, 69, 71, 74*

Rogers
THE PSYCHOLOGY
OF ADOLESCENCE
Appleton-Century-Crofts,
1962

Text chapters	Related selections
1	20, 69, 74, 75, 76, 77, 78, 81
2	74, 85
3	82
4	5, 75, 76, 77, 78
5	7, 8, 17, 33, 34, 57, 61, 63, 70, 71, 72, 73, 74
6	1, 2, 3, 4, 5, 6, 44, 45, 46, 55, 56, 69
7	27, 28, 76, 79, 80, 81, 82
8	5, 12, 13, 15, 16, 35, 36, 44, 81
9	34, 37, 40, 41, 42, 44, 45, 62, 69, 82, 85
10	48, 80
11	39, 61, 67, 68, 71, 82
12	6, 9, 10, 11, 12, 14, 17, 36, 44
13	67, 70, 76, 80, 82, 83, 84, 85
14	9, 10, 12, 34, 35, 44, 45, 59, 74, 86
15	5, 8, 18, 20, 36, 56, 75, 76, 77, 84

Thompson
CHILD PSYCHOLOGY, 2D ED.
Houghton Mifflin, 1962

Text chapters	Related selections
1	1, 58
2	5, 17, 24, 27, 29, 30, 40, 43, 49, 51, 52, 64, 65, 66, 71, 77
3	18, 19, 21
4	24, 25, 26, 27, 29
5	31, 32, 33, 34, 53, 66, 68
6	6, 7, 39, 50, 57, 65, 70, 72, 73, 83
7	18, 19, 20
8	23, 24, 25, 26, 27, 28, 37, 43, 47, 48, 49, 50, 51, 53, 60
9	18, 31, 32, 39
10	18, 37, 38, 58, 70
11	5, 6, 7, 18, 19, 24, 50, 61, 68, 72, 73, 83
12	1, 8, 9, 10, 16, 28, 37, 39, 40, 41, 42, 66, 79, 80
13	1, 5, 6, 7, 35, 44, 45, 55
14	5, 8, 25, 26, 34, 36, 37, 38, 43, 48, 51, 57, 58, 64, 65, 66, 74
15	5, 19, 21, 27, 29, 35, 56, 59, 83, 84, 86
16	2, 3, 4, 11, 12, 13, 14, 15, 17, 36, 40, 41, 42, 44, 52, 62, 63, 67, 69, 71, 76, 77, 81, 82

Watson
PSYCHOLOGY OF THE
CHILD, 2D ED.
Wiley, 1965

Text chapters	Related selections
1	2, 3
2	8, 30
3	18
4	1, 4, 5, 6, 11, 12, 13, 14, 15, 16, 17
5	31, 32, 33, 36, 37, 38, 39, 43
6	19, 21
7	20, 24
8	25, 26, 43, 46, 47
9	16, 27, 28, 32, 36, 51
10	45, 48, 49, 58, 59
11	18, 19, 20, 21, 23, 24, 29, 30, 31, 32, 33, 50, 64, 65
12	1, 5, 6, 7, 9, 10, 17, 19, 25, 26, 27, 34, 35, 36, 44, 46, 47, 48, 51, 52, 56, 57, 59, 62, 65, 83, 86
13	1, 2, 3, 4, 5, 6, 7, 8, 9, 10, 21, 24, 25, 26, 34, 36, 37, 38, 47, 48, 49, 56, 60, 61, 64, 65, 85
14	27, 28, 30, 36, 37, 45, 48, 58, 59, 75, 76, 77, 78, 79, 80, 81, 82, 84, 85, 86
15	20, 31, 32, 33
16	17, 22, 28, 34, 36, 44, 45, 48, 83, 84, 85
17	22, 35, 37, 40, 41, 42, 44, 45, 54, 57, 62, 63, 73, 74, 78, 82, 84, 85
18	20, 78, 79, 81, 82

INDEX

abilities:
of interpersonal relations, 55–70
measurement of, 580–81, 587
abnormal fixation, 447–49
abnormalities:
from birth process, 124–25, 132–33, 139–40
prenatal, 132, 136–39
Abraham, 13
Abramyan, L. A., 291, 299
Absalom, 82–86
absolute threshold, 256–58
acceptance:
of child by parent, 332, 481
in play therapy, 522–25
in reality therapy, 692–93, 701
of self, 44–45, 667, 668
in street gang social work, 594–95
in therapist's attitude, 482, 484, 486, 487
achievement:
academic pressure for, 498, 537–38
and aspiration level, 536–38
in children's books, 348–51, 353
for conformity, 683
of gifted persons, 578–81, 584–85, 591
and intelligence, 578–81, 584–85, 591
and maturation rate, 665, 671
maximum, and age, 581
occupational, 672–77
training for, 102–108 passim
achievement tests:
of gifted children, 578, 582, 584, 591
of mobile children, 531–32
activity:
in children's books, 348–53
level of, and discipline, 29–30, 33
in social contact, 308
and stress, 194–95
see also motor activity
Adams, John Quincy, 5–6
adaptation:
and abnormal fixation, 448
behavioral individuality in, 198, 201
to dark, 257
diseases of, 176–77
sensory, 257, 274
to stress, 170–95
adaptation level, 274–75
adaptation syndrome, general, 176–80, 188–93

adjustment:
and children's books, 351–53
of gifted persons, 46–47, 578, 584–85, 586–92
of institution-reared adults, 210–11
to marriage, 647, 649
and maturation rates, 665–72
measurement of, 46, 588–92
and mental health, 79
and normality, 72–76, 77–79
adolescence, 603–703
delinquency in, 394, 396–403, 566–71, 592–601, 644, 694–700
of Gandhi, 611–19
interpersonal competence in, 60, 61, 62
maturation during, 144–45, 148, 641–45, 665–72
puberty rites in, 653–63, 687
and self-identity, 391, 686–88
sexual problems of, 61, 628–29, 634, 644–45
therapy in, 566–71, 694–700
adrenal glands, 130, 170–94 passim
adult-child relations:
in family of orientation, 512–13
sexual contacts in, 631, 634, 639–41
see also parent-child relations
adultery, 14, 16–17
adults:
as characters in children's books, 348, 355–56
and children's humor, 336–40
in French culture, 93–95
interpersonal competence for, 60–62
play activity by, 302, 303
affection:
ambivalence in, 508–509
as a basic need, 115–17, 220, 690, 702
and dependency, 329–30
deprivation of, 115–17, 146, 205–19, 425
development of, 219–30
and dietary needs of infants, 115–16, 236
in discipline, 21, 332–33, 691, 697
and empathic capacity, 64
and frustration, 449
and liberal children, 438
in monkeys, study of, 219–30
in mother-infant relations, 656, 663
parental, 21, 60–61, 115–17,

affection (cont.)
214–20, 332–33, 417–21, 425–26
and prejudiced children, 437
as a social value, 12
and toilet training, 327
withdrawal of, 329–33
affectionless characters, 207–209, 214, 218
affiliation, in children's books, 348–55 passim
age:
and affectional response, in monkeys, 228–29
for childbearing, 139
and creative achievement, 581
critical, in deprivation, 231, 232
critical, for imprinting, 116, 150–161 passim
and discipline standards, 25
and group pressure, 370–74
and maternal separation, 208–10, 218–19
in pecking order, 163, 164
in toilet training, 327, 328
aggression:
in American culture, 332
in children's humor, 335, 338–39
in children's books, 348–55
in experimental group atmosphere, 362–63, 365–66
fear of, 684–85
French restraint on, 91, 92
and frustration, 31, 449, 450, 539, 544–46, 549–51
of Helen Keller, 574
and maternal rejection, 234
in overprotected children, 426–27
and parental discipline, 21, 22, 25, 30–32
of parent to child, 216–17, 507
toward parents, 325, 329, 330, 338–39
and pecking order, 163–65
of prejudiced children, 431–33, 438
in primitive societies, 655–57, 661–64
punishment of, 329–30, 333, 351
in reading disability, 504–505, 508–11
and self-concept, 394–95
by street gangs, 593
in therapy, 450, 515, 522–26
Ainsworth, Mary D., 117, 119

Date Due